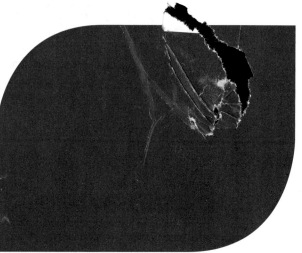

Thalia Dorwick

**Ana M.
Pérez-Gironés**
WESLEYAN UNIVERSITY

Anne Becher
UNIVERSITY OF
COLORADO, BOULDER

Puntos
de partida

Mc
Graw
Hill

PUNTOS DE PARTIDA, 2024 RELEASE

Published by McGraw Hill LLC, 1325 Avenue of the Americas, New York, NY 10019. Copyright
©2024 by McGraw Hill LLC. All rights reserved. Printed in the United States of America. Previous
editions ©2021, 2017, and 2012. No part of this publication may be reproduced or distributed in any
form or by any means, or stored in a database or retrieval system, without the prior written consent
of McGraw Hill LLC, including, but not limited to, in any network or other electronic storage or
transmission, or broadcast for distance learning.

Some ancillaries, including electronic and print components, may not be available to customers
outside the United States.

This book is printed on acid-free paper.

1 2 3 4 5 6 7 8 9 LWI 29 28 27 26 25 24

ISBN 978-1-266-41130-4 (bound)
MHID 1-266-41130-5 (bound)

ISBN 978-1-264-60612-2 (loose-leaf)
MHID 1-264-60612-5 (loose-leaf)

ISBN 978-1-264-62968-8 (annotated instructor edition)
MHID 1-264-62968-0 (annotated instructor edition)

Senior Portfolio Manager: Sadie Ray
Senior Product Development Manager: Dawn Groundwater
Product Developer: Tasha Lewis Bisante
Marketing Manager: Moisés Rimeris
Content Project Managers: Sandy Wille; Vanessa McClune
Senior Manufacturing Project Manager: Laura Fuller
Senior Designer: Beth Blech
Lead Content Licensing Specialist: Carrie Burger
Cover Image: McGraw Hill
Compositor: Aptara®, Inc.

All credits appearing on page or at the end of the book are considered to be an extension of the
copyright page.

Library of Congress Cataloging-in-Publication Data

Names: Dorwick, Thalia, 1944- author. | Pérez-Gironés, Ana María,
   author. | Becher, Anne, author.
Title: Puntos de partida / Thalia Dorwick, Ana M. Pérez Gironés, Wesleyan
   University, Anne Becher, University of Colorado, Boulder.
Description: 2024 release edition. | New York, NY : McGraw Hill, 2024. |
   Previous edition: 2021.
Identifiers: LCCN 2023024454 (print) | LCCN 2023024455 (ebook) | ISBN
   9781266411304 (hardcover) | ISBN 1266411305 (hardcover) | ISBN
   9781264606122 (loose-leaf) | ISBN 1264606125 (loose-leaf) | ISBN
   9781264629688 (hardcover ; instructor's edition) | ISBN 1264629680
   (hardcover ; instructor's edition) | ISBN 9781265443375 (ebook) | ISBN
   9781264607600 (ebook other)
Subjects: LCSH: Spanish language—Textbooks for foreign speakers—English.
   | LCGFT: Textbooks.
Classification: LCC PC4129.E5 P86 2024 (print) | LCC PC4129.E5 (ebook) |
   DDC 460.71—dc23/eng/20230814
LC record available at https://lccn.loc.gov/2023024454
LC ebook record available at https://lccn.loc.gov/2023024455

The Internet addresses listed in the text were accurate at the time of publication. The inclusion of a
website does not indicate an endorsement by the authors or McGraw Hill LLC, and McGraw Hill
LLC does not guarantee the accuracy of the information presented at these sites.

mheducation.com/highered

Puntos de partida has what you need.

In any language-learning setting, students require numerous and various opportunities to read, write, hear, and speak. *Puntos de partida* sets the standard for Spanish-language teaching with its concise grammar explanations, practical vocabulary, integration of cultures, and abundant resources. An innovative program that has been continuously refined for today's classroom, *Puntos* delivers proven pedagogy with clear and effective presentations, activities from form-focused to task-based, comprehensive teaching materials, and powerfully adaptive digital tools.

Puntos builds on the holistic 5Cs approach promoted by ACTFL, and offers a wealth of resources for every instructor and every learner. Your students are unique. *Puntos* has what they need.

Proven Approach

Puntos de partida has been the starting point for over a million beginning students of Spanish. Its winning combination is digital innovation plus a proven approach.

Here is how *Puntos* sets the standard for Introductory Spanish programs:

Comprehensive scope and sequence

In *Puntos*, the hallmark approach to vocabulary and grammar focuses on the acquisition of vocabulary during the early stages of language learning (**Capítulo 1: Ante todo**) and then at the start of each chapter throughout the text. Grammar is introduced in thorough explanations, with careful attention given to skill development rather than grammatical knowledge alone.

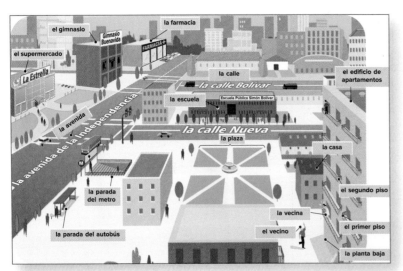

To this end, the overall organization carefully progresses from formulaic expressions to vocabulary and grammar relevant to daily life and personal interests (studies, family, home, leisure activities), goes on to prepare students for survival situations (ordering a meal, traveling), and finally branches out to broader themes (current events, social and environmental issues). This forward progress is reinforced by a cyclical structure where vocabulary, grammar, and language functions are continuously reviewed and recycled.

Students come to class ready

Our students tell us that, thanks to the clear, concise grammar explanations and recaps in *Puntos*, they are able to grasp new concepts more readily and feel better prepared. They love the conversational language, practical examples, and the organization of complex explanations into manageable chunks which are accompanied by engaging videos. By making grammar concepts more approachable outside of class, *Puntos* helps raise students' confidence, and creates constant opportunities for active communication in the target language in your classroom. And with *Puntos* you can have a flipped classroom!

Attention to the World-Readiness Standards

Puntos is informed by the World-Readiness Standards that guide most language instructors and language teachers' associations in North America. The five C's, the five goal areas that frame second-language pedagogy (Communication, Cultures, Connection, Comparison, and Communities) are evident in many features of the text:

- Everyday topics that are relevant in this country as well as in the global community

- A careful sequencing of activities that move students from controlled to free-form tasks, including **Proyectos** that prepare students to function in a Spanish-speaking environment

- A rich array of reading and audiovisual texts that bring a sense of immersion to language learning and make cultural products and perspectives salient to beginning learners, so that they can connect to new communities and compare them with their own

Cultural content that connects to students' worlds

Puntos goes beyond merely introducing students to the vast and diverse Spanish-speaking world. Cultural information appears at various points in every chapter, even tied to vocabulary and grammar activities. The **Algo sobre...** feature closes with a question that makes students reflect on practices and perspectives that may coincide with or differ with their own. And the **Salu2** video segments make the Spanish-speaking world come to life.

Hlphoto/Shutterstock

Comprehensive *Teaching Resources*

Puntos de partida was designed to provide novice and experienced instructors alike with the tools needed to enter the classroom (be it face-to-face or online) well-prepared to engage students in learning. As a comprehensive program, *Puntos* offers a wide array of resources and supporting materials to function as a flexible framework that can be tailored to individual teaching situations and goals. Whether you're using the program for your face-to-face, hybrid, or online class, the wealth of resources sets up both instructors and students for success.

Instructor's annotations every step of the way

Instructors can find teaching suggestions for each and every grammar presentation and practice activity in the text, with point-by-point guidance on presenting the material in class, in addition to a wealth of helpful facts and resources, variations on and supplements to the existing material, and suggestions for follow-up and extension. Taking into account that Introductory Spanish classrooms typically contain a mix of true beginners, false beginners, and heritage learners, *Puntos* offers a designated space for expanded suggestions for heritage speakers that makes it even easier to meet the needs of students with varying levels of language proficiency.

The Heritage Learner Support Modules referenced in the instructor's annotations are designed to help heritage learners avoid some common pitfalls. The modules are assignable on Connect and available in PowerPoint format, and may be accessed by going to the Library tab on Connect and navigating to "Instructor resources."

> **HERITAGE SPEAKERS**
>
> En muchos países latinoamericanos y en España, *adiós* y *hasta luego* son saludos muy comunes que usan dos personas que se encuentran pero no se detienen a hablar. En estas circunstancias, *adiós* y *hasta luego* son realmente un saludo, no una despedida.

Workbook / Laboratory Manual

The Workbook / Laboratory Manual that accompanies *Puntos* provides additional written, listening, and speaking practice with each chapter's vocabulary and grammar. The Manual also features more cultural information, as well as focused and free-form writing activities and reading practice.

Flexible testing program

A key part of the instructor resources available with *Puntos* is the comprehensive testing program, available in both print and digital formats. Whether you use the testing program as a model to customize your own tests, or you want to quickly and easily assign existing exams or poolable questions, the testing program offers multiple versions for each chapter from which instructors can draw.

Updated supplemental activities manual

The 2024 release can be accompanied by the updated *Supplementary Materials to Accompany* Puntos de partida, by Sharon Foerster. The supplementary materials are an updated teacher's guide to *Puntos* and consist of worksheets, short pronunciation practice activities, listening exercises, grammar worksheets, integrative communication-building activities, comprehensive chapter reviews, and language games.

Grammar tutorial videos

Short and engaging, the grammar tutorial videos, which are conveniently available in the eBook, are hosted by a friendly cast of characters, who provide clear explanations in English with examples of Spanish grammatical concepts.

Engaging and Immersive
Digital Tools

Connect is the most powerful and flexible course management system available. Rooted in research on effective student learning practices, the platform integrates adaptive learning tools with dynamic, engaging language-practice activities. The result is better student learning of the Spanish language.

A personalized and adaptive learning and teaching experience

No two students learn a language the same way or at the same rate. Students enter the Introductory Spanish course with a wide range of knowledge and experience, from true beginners to heritage learners.

McGraw Hill's Adaptive Learning Assignments provide each student with a personalized and adaptive learning experience based on individual needs. As the student works through a series of probes around the vocabulary and grammar presented in each chapter, our adaptive technology identifies what the student knows and doesn't know, and continuously tailors the subsequent probes to focus on those areas where the student needs the most help. Each student learns and masters core vocabulary and grammar at his or her own pace and comes to class better prepared to communicate in the target language.

And just as no two students learn a language the same way, no two Spanish courses are taught the same way. Connect provides the instructor with both the ability and flexibility to pull from the robust set of content available in the platform and craft a unique learning path based on the goals of the course. Be it in a face-to-face, hybrid, or fully online course, Connect can adapt to you and to your students to create the ideal learning environment.

Student-centered

Students learn best when they are involved and interested in the material being taught. In the text itself, a majority of the activities require personalized responses and ask students to perform real world tasks. Then, *Practice Spanish: Study Abroad*, the market's first 3-D immersive language game designed exclusively by McGraw Hill, brings the language to the students in a fun, engaging, and immersive gaming experience. Students "study abroad" virtually in Colombia where they will create their very own avatar, live with a host family, make new friends, and navigate a variety of real-world scenarios using their quickly developing Spanish-language skills. Students earn points and rewards for successfully accomplishing these tasks, and instructors have the ability to assign specific tasks, monitor student achievement, and incorporate the game into the classroom experience. Your Learning Technology Representative can provide more information.

ReadAnywhere app

Our ReadAnywhere app lets students access important course materials on their mobile device, both online and offline. ReadAnywhere includes the same functionality as the eBook offered in Connect, with auto-sync across both platforms. Visit mheducation.com/ReadAnywhere to learn more.

Communication tools

The 2024 release of *Puntos* offers two communication tools so students can easily interact in the target language with their classmates and instructors online.

Recordable Video Chat powered by GoReact, is a chat tool available on Connect that allows students to practice live, synchronous communication. Up to nine students can participate in a recorded conversation and instructors can provide personalized and on-the-spot feedback. Instructors can choose from a wide variety of pre-built activities or create their own.

Voice Board, also powered by GoReact, is our asynchronous voice tool that gives students the chance to post video, audio, or text comments related to the topic, as well as respond to their classmates' posts.

Robust data

Instructors and students alike want to know how students are performing in the course and where they can improve. The powerful reporting tools in Connect highlight actionable data to both instructors and students so steps can be taken by both groups to ensure student success.

The first and only analytics tool of its kind, Connect Insight is a series of visual data displays—each framed by an intuitive question—to provide instructors at-a-glance information regarding how your class is doing. Connect Insight provides analysis on five key insights, available at a moment's notice from your Connect course.

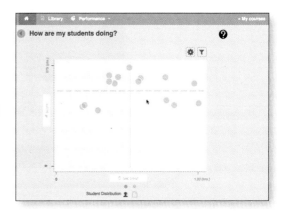

The Adaptive Learning Assignments provide powerful reports to view student progress by module and detail with completion breakdown, along with class performance data, frequency of missed questions, and a view into the most challenging learning objectives. Metacognitive reports allow instructors to view statistics on how knowledgeable their students are about their own comprehension and learning. What's more, LearnSmart provides students their own progress reports so they can take full responsibility for their own learning.

Practice Spanish:
Study Abroad

Practice Spanish: Study Abroad is a 3-D language game designed for college and university students looking to make the Spanish language come to life in an engaging, motivating, and immersive environment.

Practice Spanish: Study Abroad

Attend a fictional study abroad program in Colombia and live with a host family, make friends, and experience life in a Spanish-speaking environment.

Choose and customize an avatar and interact with non-player game characters in a variety of real-life quests to earn points and rewards.

Fun, adaptive mini-games are also available to practice the target vocabulary and grammar.

WHAT'S NEW AND IMPROVED

Functional design and increased accessibility

- Visually fresh: Many new photos, realia, and updated drawings.
- Improved layout of activities in the electronic version.
- Colorblind-friendly text: All red text used as a call-out is also underlined.
- Language-tagged eBook: Our eBook is coded to allow screen readers to flip seamlessly from Spanish to English pronunciations, as appropriate.

Integrated culture

- Culturally-based activities: Grammar and vocabulary exercises center on cultural context.
- **Textos de todos los días** is a new recurring feature that asks students to deal with texts that native speakers of Spanish use in their daily lives. From writing an email to communicate with a classmate to reading GPS directions, *Puntos* provides students with culturally immersive tasks, bringing them closer to the Spanish-speaking world. There is one **Texto...**, with appropriate scaffolding, at a relevant point in every chapter (usually in the **Vocabulario: Preparación** section).
- **Mundo hispano:** This section's content has been updated and made more visually appealing, with more photos and comprehension questions that support students' reading experience and help them connect to the information.

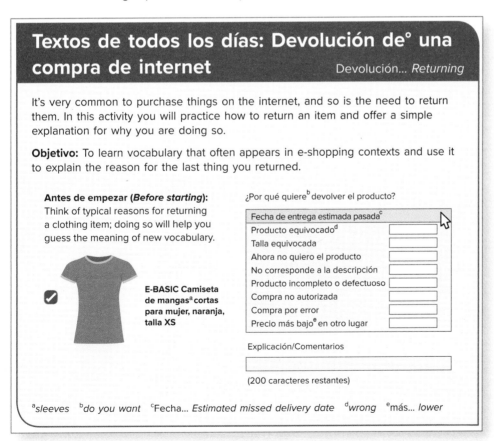

Textos de todos los días: Devolución de° una compra de internet

Devolución... *Returning*

It's very common to purchase things on the internet, and so is the need to return them. In this activity you will practice how to return an item and offer a simple explanation for why you are doing so.

Objetivo: To learn vocabulary that often appears in e-shopping contexts and use it to explain the reason for the last thing you returned.

Antes de empezar (*Before starting*):
Think of typical reasons for returning a clothing item; doing so will help you guess the meaning of new vocabulary.

E-BASIC Camiseta de mangas° cortas para mujer, naranja, talla XS

¿Por qué quiere° devolver el producto?

Fecha de entrega estimada pasada°	
Producto equivocado°	
Talla equivocada	
Ahora no quiero el producto	
No corresponde a la descripción	
Producto incompleto o defectuoso	
Compra no autorizada	
Compra por error	
Precio más bajo° en otro lugar	

Explicación/Comentarios

(200 caracteres restantes)

°sleeves °do you want °Fecha... *Estimated missed delivery date* °wrong °más... *lower*

Opportunities for practicing real-world communication

- **Mundo hispano (*The Hispanic World*):** This section of each chapter has three parts that delve deeper into each chapter's country of focus and other countries in **Enfoque cultural. Lectura** showcases authentic materials from the Spanish-speaking world, including literature. **Textos orales** presents authentic listening tasks.

- **Portafolio:** This section of each chapter has five parts. **Entrevista** presents questions to be answered with personal information. **Escritura** provides an opportunity to write essays and do other real-world writing tasks in Spanish. **En la comunidad** inspires ideas for interviewing a Spanish speaker from the community. **Producción audiovisual** provides suggestions for filming interviews in Spanish with classmates and other people. Finally, **Más ideas para el portafolio** suggests ideas for creating a portfolio to showcase what can be done in Spanish.

- **En acción:** Brief communication tasks tied to the chapter themes and topics of the readings encourage student production in the target language.

- **Proyectos:** Engaging communication tasks guide students to accomplish culturally significant goals in Spanish.

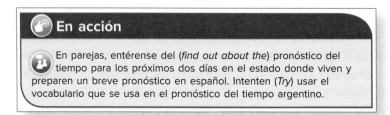

En acción

En parejas, entérense del (*find out about the*) pronóstico del tiempo para los próximos dos días en el estado donde viven y preparen un breve pronóstico en español. Intenten (*Try*) usar el vocabulario que se usa en el pronóstico del tiempo argentino.

ABOUT THE AUTHORS

Thalia Dorwick retired as McGraw Hill's Editor-in-Chief for Humanities, Social Sciences, and Languages. For many years she was also in charge of McGraw Hill's World Languages college list in Spanish, French, Italian, German, Japanese, and Russian. She has taught at Allegheny College, California State University (Sacramento), and Case Western Reserve University, where she received her Ph.D. in Spanish in 1973. She was recognized as an Outstanding Foreign Language Teacher by the California Foreign Language Teachers Association in 1978. Dr. Dorwick is the coauthor of several textbooks and the author of several articles on language teaching issues. She was a frequent guest speaker on topics related to language learning, and she was also an invited speaker at the *II Congreso Internacional de la Lengua Española*, in Valladolid, Spain, in October 2001. In retirement, she consulted for McGraw Hill, especially in the area of world languages, which is of personal interest to her. She was a Vice President of the Board of Trustees of Case Western Reserve University and a past President of the Board of Directors of Berkeley Repertory Theatre.

Ana María Pérez-Gironés a native of Seville, Spain, is an Adjunct Professor of Spanish at Wesleyan University, Middletown, Connecticut. She received a *Licenciatura en Filología Anglogermánica* from the Universidad de Sevilla, and an M.A. in General Linguistics from Cornell University. At Wesleyan, she teaches and coordinates Spanish language courses at all levels, including Spanish for heritage speakers. She has also served as resident director of the Vassar-Wesleyan Program in Madrid. She has published a variety of pedagogical material, including *Más, Español Intermedio* (McGraw Hill), and the series *En una palabra* (Georgetown University Press).

Anne Becher received her M.A. in Hispanic Linguistics in 1992 from the University of Colorado Boulder, and now coordinates first-year Spanish courses and teaches pedagogy and methods courses for the Department of Spanish and Portuguese there. She has taught beginning through advanced levels of Spanish since 1996, including several years teaching Modified Spanish classes for students with difficulty learning languages. She presents frequently at the Colorado Congress of Foreign Language Teachers (CCFLT) and other conferences on language teaching, and serves on the board of the Colorado chapter of American Association of Teachers of Spanish and Portuguese. Recently she won teaching excellence awards from CCFLT and the Southwest Conference on Language Teaching (SWCOLT). She co-edited the bilingual literary journal *La selva subterránea* from 1987–1996.

ACKNOWLEDGMENTS

We would like to thank the many friends and colleagues who served on boards of advisors or as consultants, completed reviews or surveys, and attended symposia or focus groups. Their feedback was indispensable in creating the *Puntos* program. The appearance of their names in the following lists does not necessarily constitute their endorsement of the program or its methodology.

Reviewers

Jorge Alas
Monroe Community College

Javier Alvarez
Eastern Kentucky University

Maria Barker
Sam Houston State University

Wanda Baumgartel
Snead State Community College

Lina L Callahan
Fullerton College

Amber Carey
Pensacola State College

Gabriela Carrion
Regis College

Esther Castro
San Diego State University

Rosa Maria Chism
Penn State Abington

Mara Colomer-Flores
Merced College

Kit Decker
Piedmont Virginia Community College

Irene Fernandez
North Shore Community College

Jose Juan Gómez-Becerra
Eastern Kentucky University

Carla Greszler-Gomez
Northwest Vista College

Amarilis Hidalgo de Jesus
Bloomsburg University

René Ibarra
Campbell University

Gioia Kerlin
Rogers State University

Luisa Kou
University of Hawaii at Manoa

Stephanie Krueger
Lone Star College CyFair

Jeremy Larochelle
University of Mary Washington

Kathleen Leonard
University of Nevada, Reno

Edward Linggi
Fullerton College

Monica Malamud
Cañada College

Ornella Mazzuca
Dutchess Community College

Julio Medina
Sam Houston State University

Wendy Mendez-Hasselman
Palm Beach State College

Rosalinda Nericcio
San Diego State University

Ann Ortiz
Campbell University

Ana Perez-Manrique
Worcester State University

Lori Rake
Harford Community College

Alexandra Rodriguez
Texas A&M University

Claudia Sahagun
Broward College

David Sánchez Jiménez
NYC College of Technology, CUNY

Steven Sheppard
University of North Texas

Louis Silvers
Monroe Community College

Natalie Sobalvarro
Merced College

Craig Stokes
Dutchess Community College

Maria Z Tovar
University of North Texas

Tamara Townsend
Wheaton College

Bernardo Vallejo
Houston Community College

Christina Wolff
Johnson County Community College

Gloria Yampey-Jorg
Houston Community College

Additional Thanks

The authors wish to thank the following friends and professional colleagues. Their feedback, support, and contributions are greatly appreciated.

- The colleagues of Ana Pérez-Gironés at Wesleyan University, for their support and for answering many dialectal questions; special thanks to Louise Neary, for all of her constructive feedback

- Anne Becher's colleagues—graduate students, lecturers, faculty, and administrators—at the University of Colorado, Boulder

- A. Ray Elliott, for his excellent work on the Heritage Speaker and end-of-chapter Suggestions in the Annotated Instructor's Edition, over many editions

- Laura Chastain, for her meticulous work on the language and linguistic accuracy of the manuscript, over many editions

- Margaryta Bondarenko, of McGraw Hill, a wonderful collaborator whose work and careful guidance on this edition is greatly appreciated

- Tasha Lewis Bisante, who admirably performed the much appreciated task of picking up this project mid-stream

- Avi Kotzer, from whose eagle eye the authors of this edition have learned much

¡Con todo nuestro cariño y nuestra gratitud!

Finally, the authors would like to thank their families and close personal friends for all of their love, support, and patience throughout the creation of this edition.

Contributors

Soraya Alem, Norma Andrada, Margaryta Bondarenko, Nicole Casnettie, Laura Chastain, Kevin Donnelly, A. Raymond Elliott, Eileen Fancher, Sharon Foerster, Allison Hawco, Ana Vanesa Hidalgo Del Rosario, Juliana Jiménez, Jae Johnson, Constance Kihyet, Avi Kotzer, Christopher LaFond, Gabriella Licata, Paul Listen, Misha Maclaird, Celia Meana, Ron Nelms, Pennie Nichols, Claudia Quesito, María Sabló-Yates, Artis Trice, Nina Tunac Basey

Product Team

Editorial and Marketing: Sadie Ray, Joshua Pongan, Tasha Lewis Bisante, Tim Vertovec, Eric Weber, Moisés Rimeris, Dawn Groundwater, Amy Reed, Jamie Laferrera

Art, Design, and Production: Vanessa McClune, Beth Blech, Carrie Burger, Sandy Wille, Danielle Clement

Media Partners: Aptara, Eastern Sky Studios, Editec Soluciones Editoriales, Hurix, Klic Video Productions, Inc., KnowledgeWorks Global Ltd., Straive, Latinallure Voiceover, LearningMate, Lumina Datamatics

CONTENTS

| Capítulo | VOCABULARY & PRONUNCIATION | GRAMMAR |

1 Ante todo 2

Mark Lewis/Photographer's Choice/Getty Images

Primera parte
Saludos y expresiones de cortesía 4
Nota comunicativa
Más expresiones de cortesía 6
Pronunciación
Las vocales: **a, e, i, o, u** 7
El alfabeto español 8
Nota comunicativa
Los cognados 9
Segunda parte
Nota comunicativa
Cómo expresar la hora 18

Primera parte
¿Cómo es usted? (Part 1) 10
Segunda parte
Los números del 0 al 30; *Hay* 14
Nota comunicativa El género (*gender*) y los números 14
Los gustos y preferencias (Part 1) 16
¿Qué hora es? 18

2 En la universidad 28

Simon Jarratt/Fuse/Getty Images

Los Estados Unidos de América

En el salón de clase 30
Las materias 32
Nota comunicativa
Más palabras interrogativas 34
Pronunciación
Diphthongs and Linking 36

1 Naming People, Places, Things, and Ideas (Part 1) • Singular Nouns: Gender and Articles 37
2 Naming People, Places, Things, and Ideas (Part 2) • Nouns and Articles: Plural Forms 40
3 Expressing Actions • Subject Pronouns (Part 1) • Present Tense of *-ar* Verbs; Negation 43
Nota comunicativa Cómo expresar las partes del día 48
Nota comunicativa El verbo *estar* 49
4 Getting Information (Part 1) • Asking Yes/No Questions 50

TEXTS AND PROJECTS

En acción 13
En acción 22

Textos de todos los días Hoja de información 35
Proyecto Perfil académico de la clase 55
En acción 56
Lectura Un anuncio de Inglés USA 57
Proyecto ¿Y en su universidad? 58
Textos orales Un anuncio para los cursos de verano
 de una universidad 59
En acción 59
Portafolio 60
Escritura Un ensayo sobre este semestre/trimestre 60

CULTURE AND VIDEO

Video Salu2 «Salu2 desde Los
 Ángeles» 21
Primera parte
 Nota cultural Los saludos
 en el mundo hispano 5
 Mundo hispano
 ¡Aquí se habla español! 12
Segunda parte
 Algo sobre...
 los números 14
 Mundo hispano
 La geografía del mundo hispanohablante 23

Rido/Shutterstock

Nota cultural El sistema universitario en los países
hispanohablantes 32
Algo sobre...
 la universidad 31
 el nombre América 50
 los murales y el arte urbano 53
 el español en las universidades de los
 Estados Unidos 54
Todo junto Lengua y cultura: Dos
 universidades fabulosas... y diferentes 54
Video Salu2 «¡Qué bacán!» Online
 Appendix
Mundo hispano
 Enfoque cultural: La universidad
 En los Estados Unidos 56
 En otros países hispanos 56

LUCY NICHOLSON/Alamy
Stock Photo

	VOCABULARY & PRONUNCIATION	GRAMMAR

3 La familia *64*

UpperCut Images/Alamy Stock Photo

México

¿Quiénes forman la familia? 66

¿Cuánto es? Los números del 31 al 100 68

Nota comunicativa
Cómo expresar la edad: *tener... años* 69

¿Cómo es? Los adjetivos descriptivos 71

Pronunciación
Stress and Written Accent Marks (Part 1) 72

5 Describing • Adjectives: Gender, Number, and Position 73

Nota comunicativa Otras nacionalidades 77

6 Expressing *to be* • Present Tense of *ser;* Summary of Uses (Part 2) 79

Nota comunicativa Cómo dar explicaciones: *¿Por qué?, porque* y *para + infinitivo* 83

7 Expressing Possession • Unstressed Possessive Adjectives (Part 1) 84

8 Expressing Actions • Present Tense of *-er* and *-ir* Verbs; Subject Pronouns (Part 2) 88

Nota comunicativa Cómo expresar la frecuencia de las acciones 92

---

4 De compras *102*

Danny Lehman/Getty Images

Guatemala   **Honduras**

¿Qué ropa llevan? 104

Nota comunicativa
Preguntas coletillas 106

Los colores: ¿De qué color es? 107

Los números a partir del 100 110

Pronunciación
Stress and Written Accent Marks (Part 2) 112

9 Pointing Out People and Things • Demonstrative Adjectives (Part 2) and Pronouns 114

10 Expressing Actions and States • *Tener, venir, poder, preferir, querer;* Some Idioms with *tener* 118

Nota comunicativa *Mucho* y *poco* 121

11 Expressing Destination and Future Actions • *Ir;* The Contraction *al; Ir + a + infinitive* 123

---

5 En casa *134*

Jon Arnold Images Ltd/Alamy Stock Photo

El Salvador   **Nicaragua**

¿Cómo es su hogar? ¿Qué muebles tiene? 136

¿Qué día es hoy? 138

Nota comunicativa
Cómo expresar *on* con los días de la semana 139

¿Cuándo? • Las preposiciones (Part 1) 140

12 Expressing Actions • *Hacer, oír, poner, salir, traer, ver* 142

13 Expressing Actions • Present Tense of Stem-changing Verbs (Part 2) 148

14 Expressing *-self/-selves* • Reflexive Pronouns (Part 1) 153

Nota comunicativa Cómo expresar una secuencia de acciones 156

TEXTS AND PROJECTS

Textos de todos los días El certificado
de nacimiento 70

Proyecto Las familias de las personas de la clase 94

En acción 95

Lectura Infografía: La familia en México 96

Proyecto La demografía de las familias de la clase 97

Textos orales La familia de Lucía Jiménez Flores 97

En acción 97

Portafolio 98

Escritura Un ensayo sobre la familia 98

CULTURE AND VIDEO

Nota cultural El sistema hispano de apellidos 68

Algo sobre...

los estados mexicanos 69

una gran ciudad mexicana 75

las culturas indígenas mexicanas 78

una pintora mexicana 83

la comida de México 90

Todo junto Lengua y cultura: Las
familias 93

Video Salu2 «Padres
modernos» Online Appendix

Mundo hispano

Enfoque cultural: La familia
En México 95
En otros países hispanos 95

Keith Dannemiller/Alamy
Stock Photo

Textos de todos los días Devolución de una compra
de internet 109

Proyecto Encuesta sobre las preferencias de la clase con
relación a la moda y los estilos 126

En acción 127

Lectura Algo más que ropa 128

Proyecto Preferencias de la clase con respecto
a la ropa 129

Textos orales Dos amigas hacen planes para ir
de compras 129

En acción 129

Portafolio 130

Escritura Un ensayo sobre los estilos en el campus 130

Nota cultural Las tallas de ropa y zapatos 109

Algo sobre...

un artista guatemalteco 107

el Popol Vuh 113

la civilización maya: Tikal y Copán 121

las compras en Guatemala y Honduras 125

Todo junto Lengua y cultura: Pero,
¿no se puede regatear? 125

Video Salu2 «¡Moda, moda,
moda!» Online Appendix

Mundo hispano

**Enfoque cultural: La ropa y los
mercados**
En Guatemala y Honduras 127
En otros países hispanos 127

Erwin Guillermo/Artwork
courtesy of La Antigua
Galería de Arte Antigua
Guatemala

Textos de todos los días Correo electrónico a una
persona de la clase 152

Proyecto Hogar dulce hogar 160

En acción 161

Lectura La sicología de los colores en la decoración
interior 162

Proyecto Decoración de un espacio interior 163

Textos orales Enrique y Víctor necesitan muebles 163

En acción 163

Portafolio 164

Escritura Un ensayo sobre una semana típica de los
estudiantes universitarios 164

Nota cultural Las casas en el mundo hispano 138

Algo sobre...

la costa centroamericana 141

los lagos de Nicaragua 146

los volcanes de El Salvador y Nicaragua 147

las casas tradicionales centroamericanas 158

Todo junto Lengua y cultura: ¿Dónde viven los
hispanohablantes? 159

Video Salu2 «Vivir con la
familia» Online Appendix

Mundo hispano

Enfoque cultural: La vivienda
En El Salvador y Nicaragua 161
En otros países hispanos 161

Nancy Hoyt Belcher/
Alamy Stock Photo

VOCABULARY & PRONUNCIATION

GRAMMAR

6 Las estaciones y el tiempo *168*

Paul Souders/The Image Bank/Getty Images

Costa Rica

¿Qué tiempo hace hoy? 170

Nota comunicativa
Otras expresiones con *tener* 171

Los meses y las estaciones del año 173

¿Dónde está? Las preposiciones (Part 2) 175

15 *¿Qué están haciendo?* • Present Progressive: **Estar + -ndo** 177

Nota comunicativa El gerundio con otros verbos 181

16 *¿Ser o estar?* • Summary of the Uses of **ser** and **estar** 182

Nota comunicativa El uso de adjetivos + *por* 185

17 Describing • Comparisons 189

---

7 ¡A comer! *204*

The Visual Explorer/ Shutterstock

Panamá

La comida y las comidas 206

Nota comunicativa
Más vocabulario para hablar de la comida 207

¿Qué sabe usted y a quién conoce? 210

18 Expressing *what* or *who(m)* • Direct Objects: The Personal **a**; Direct Object Pronouns 213

Nota comunicativa Cómo expresar una acción muy reciente: *acabar + de + infinitivo* 218

19 Expressing Negation • Indefinite and Negative Words 219

20 Influencing Others • Commands (Part 1): Formal Commands 223

---

8 De viaje *236*

GiuseppeCrimeni/Shutterstock

La República Dominicana

De viaje 238

De vacaciones 240

Nota comunicativa Otro uso de la palabra *se:* para expresar acciones impersonales 242

21 Expressing *to whom* or *for whom* • Indirect Object Pronouns; **Dar** and **decir** 244

22 Expressing Likes and Dislikes • **Gustar** (Part 2) 250

Nota comunicativa Otras maneras de expresar los gustos y preferencias 253

23 Talking About the Past (Part 1) • Preterite of Regular Verbs and of **dar, hacer, ir,** and **ser** 255

TEXTS AND PROJECTS

Textos de todos los días Un mensaje sobre el tiempo 172

Proyecto Expresiones comparativas 196

En acción 197

Lectura Prepara a tu familia para la temporada de lluvias 198

Proyecto Comparación de infografías 199

Textos orales El pronóstico del tiempo en la Argentina 199

En acción 199

Portafolio 200

Escritura Un ensayo sobre preferencias climáticas 200

Textos de todos los días Mensaje de texto para encontrarse para cenar 223

Proyecto ¿Cómo come esta clase? 228

En acción 229

Lectura Una receta 230

Proyecto Una receta 231

Textos orales En un restaurante 231

En acción 231

Portafolio 232

Escritura Las opciones de comida en esta universidad 232

Textos de todos los días Comunicación sobre la llegada a un apartamento 249

Proyecto Turismo en la República Dominicana 262

En acción 263

Lectura *I love* viajes 264

Proyecto Una solicitud para una beca de un viaje educativo 265

Textos orales Las actividades de Arturo y David 265

En acción 265

Portafolio 266

Escritura Un ensayo sobre el verano pasado 266

CULTURE AND VIDEO

Nota cultural El clima en el mundo hispano 174

Algo sobre...
los valores de los costarricenses 179
¡Pura vida! 185
San José y Buenos Aires 189

Todo junto Lengua y cultura: Dos hemisferios 195

Video Salu2 «En la Mitad del Mundo» Online Appendix

Mundo hispano

Enfoque cultural: La diversidad climática
En Costa Rica 197
En otros países hispanos 197

Jesse Kraft/123RF

Nota cultural La comida del mundo hispano 209

Algo sobre...
Rubén Blades 210
el canal de Panamá, un símbolo nacional 212
la ciudad de Panamá 217
los emberás 222

Todo junto Lengua y cultura: La cocina panameña 227

Video Salu2 «¡De viaje!» Online Appendix

Mundo hispano

Enfoque cultural: La comida
En Panamá 229
En otros países hispanos 229

Gonzalo Azumendi/Getty Images

Nota cultural Tipos de turismo en el mundo hispano 241

Algo sobre...
el colmado dominicano 243
el casabe 248
el merengue 254
las hermanas Mirabal 260

Todo junto Lengua y cultura: Mi abuela dominicana 261

Video Salu2 «¡Qué rico!» Online Appendix

Mundo hispano

Enfoque cultural: El turismo
En la República Dominicana 263
En otros países hispanos 263

Martin Corr/Shutterstock

VOCABULARY & PRONUNCIATION	GRAMMAR

9 Los días festivos 270

Evelyn Paley/Alamy Stock Photo

Cuba

Una fiesta de cumpleaños para Javier 272

Las emociones 276

Nota comunicativa
Cómo enfatizar: *-ísimo* 277

24 Talking About the Past (Part 2) • Irregular Preterites 279

25 Talking About the Past (Part 3) • Preterite of Stem-changing Verbs 283

26 Avoiding Repetition • Expressing Direct and Indirect Object Pronouns Together 287

---

10 El tiempo libre 298

Alfred Wekelo/Shutterstock

Puerto Rico

¿Practica usted algún deporte? 300

Las tareas domésticas 303

Nota comunicativa
Cómo expresar la obligación 305

27 Talking About the Past (Part 4) • Descriptions and Habitual Actions in the Past: Imperfect of Regular and Irregular Verbs 306

Nota comunicativa El progresivo en el pasado 309

28 Getting Information (Part 2) • Summary of Interrogative Words 312

29 Expressing Extremes • Superlatives 315

Nota comunicativa Los diminutivos 317

---

11 La salud 326

ZUMA Press Inc/Alamy Stock Photo

Venezuela

La salud y el bienestar 328

Una cita en el consultorio 330

Nota comunicativa
Cómo expresar una cualidad general: *lo + adjetivo* 332

30 Talking About the Past (Part 5) • Using the Preterite and the Imperfect 333

Nota comunicativa Algunas palabras y expresiones asociadas con el pretérito y el imperfecto 336

31 Recognizing *que, quien(es), lo que* • Relative Pronouns 341

32 Expressing *each other* (Part 2) • Reciprocal Actions with Reflexive Pronouns 344

Textos de todos los días Una tarjeta de
felicitación 278

Proyecto El Día de... 291

En acción 292

Lectura Una declaración de propósitos 293

Proyecto Cumplir un propósito para el Año Nuevo 294

Textos orales El mensaje telefónico de Pilar 294

En acción 294

Portafolio 295

Escritura Un ensayo sobre una celebración
memorable 295

Nota cultural Los días festivos importantes del mundo
hispano 275

Algo sobre...
las parrandas cubanas 273
José Martí 285
la palma 286
el son cubano 289

Todo junto Lengua y cultura: La Virgen de Guadalupe,
quince siglos (*centuries*) de historia 290

Video Salu2 «De fiesta en
fiesta» Online Appendix

Mundo hispano

    **Enfoque cultural: Los días
festivos**
        En Cuba 292
        En otros países hispanos 292

Lucy.Brown/Shutterstock

Textos de todos los días Anuncio de un evento en
una red social 314

Proyecto Reacciones y actitudes de la adolescencia 319

En acción 320

Lectura Volver a conectar 321

Proyecto Una encuesta sobre «la dependencia
electrónica» 322

Textos orales Unos compañeros hablan de
«un desastre» 322

En acción 322

Portafolio 323

Escritura Un ensayo sobre los pasatiempos y
diversiones 323

Nota cultural Los deportes más populares del mundo
hispano 302

Algo sobre...
el Viejo San Juan 304
el coquí 305
Borinquen 311
la bomba y la plena 318

Todo junto Lengua y cultura: Un poco de la historia de
Puerto Rico 318

Video Salu2 «Deportes que mueven
masas» Online Appendix

Mundo hispano

    Enfoque cultural: El tiempo libre
        En Puerto Rico 320
        En otros países hispanos 320

Textos de todos los días Telemedicina 340

Proyecto Un anuncio de prevención contra una
enfermedad común 348

En acción 349

Lectura «Prescripción», de Daisy Zamora 350

Proyecto Una cura infalible 350

Textos orales Campaña de vacunación contra la gripe 351

En acción 351

Portafolio 352

Escritura La historia de una enfermedad 352

Nota cultural El cuidado médico en el mundo hispano 331

Algo sobre...
la harina de maíz blanco 332
Simón Bolívar 338
la emigración venezolana de años recientes 341
el lago de Maracaibo 346

Todo junto Lengua y cultura: La
leyenda del lago de Maracaibo 346

Video Salu2 «Remedios para
todos» Online Appendix

Mundo hispano

    **Enfoque cultural: El cuidado de
la salud**
        En Venezuela 349
        En otros países hispanos 349

Niday Picture Library/
Alamy Stock Photo

VOCABULARY & PRONUNCIATION

GRAMMAR

12 ¡Conectad@s! *356*

Radius/SuperStock

Colombia

¿Dónde vive usted? 358

La tecnología 361

33 Influencing Others (Part 2) • **Tú** (Informal) Commands 364

Nota comunicativa Verbos derivados de *poner, tener* y *venir* 367

34 Expressing Subjective Actions or States • Present Subjunctive (Part 1): An Introduction 369

35 Expressing Desires and Requests • Use of the Subjunctive (Part 2): Influence 375

13 El arte y la cultura *388*

Bernai Velarde

El Ecuador **Bolivia**

Las artes 390

Nota comunicativa
Más sobre los gustos y preferencias 392

Los ordinales 394

36 Expressing Feelings • Use of the Subjunctive (Part 3): Emotion 395

Nota comunicativa Cómo expresar los deseos con *ojalá* 398

37 Expressing Uncertainty • Use of the Subjunctive (Part 4): Doubt and Denial 400

Nota comunicativa Verbos que requieren preposiciones 403

38 Expressing Influence, Emotion, Doubt, and Denial • The Subjunctive (Part 5): A Summary 404

TEXTS AND PROJECTS

Textos de todos los días Alquiler de vivienda 360

Proyecto Cómo mejorar la contaminación acústica 380

En acción 381

Lectura «Cuadrados y ángulos», de Alfonsina Storni 382

Proyecto Un poema sobre un lugar 383

Textos orales Un doctor habla de un proyecto tecnológico 383

En acción 383

Portafolio 384

Escritura La educación universitaria: ¿presencial o a distancia? 384

CULTURE AND VIDEO

Nota cultural El español y la tecnología 363

Algo sobre...
    la ciudad de Medellín 359
    la cumbia 368
    el café 374
    Gabriel García Márquez 377

Todo junto Lengua y cultura: La ciudad de Cartagena, Colombia 379

Video Salu2 «¡No sin mi celular!» Online Appendix

Mundo hispano

    Enfoque cultural: Espacios urbanos
        En Colombia 381
        En otros países hispanos 381

Chester Voyage/Alamy Stock Photo

Textos de todos los días Un poema 408

Proyecto Presentación oral sobre una obra de arte 410

En acción 411

Lectura «Sale caro ser poeta», de Gloria Fuertes 412

Proyecto Sale caro el trabajo artístico 413

Textos orales Una reseña de la película *La vida de Susana Jiménez* 413

En acción 413

Portafolio 414

Escritura Un ensayo sobre la expresión artística en las escuelas 414

Nota cultural La arquitectura en el mundo hispano 393

Algo sobre...
    Oswaldo Guayasamín 393
    la Amazonia y los Andes 399
    la diversidad étnica y lingüística en el Ecuador y Bolivia 403
    las islas Galápagos 404
    el Lago Titicaca 408

Todo junto Lengua y cultura: En un museo, contemplando una obra de Fernando Botero 408

Video Salu2 «Arte angelino» Online Appendix

Mundo hispano

    Enfoque cultural: Las artes
        En el Ecuador y Bolivia 411
        En otros países hispanos 411

Age fotostock/Alamy Stock Photo

VOCABULARY & PRONUNCIATION

GRAMMAR

---

14 Las presiones de la vida *418*

Stephane Roussel/Alamy Stock Photo

El Perú

Las presiones de la vida académica 420

¡Qué mala suerte! 423

Nota comunicativa
Más sobre los adverbios: *adjetivo + -mente* 425

39 Telling How Long and Expressing *Ago* • **Hace... que:** Another Use of **hacer** 427

40 Expressing Unplanned or Unexpected Events • Another Use of **se** 430

41 *¿Por o para?* • A Summary of Their Uses 434

---

15 La naturaleza y el medio ambiente *448*

Paul Stead/Alamy Stock Photo

La Argentina   **El Uruguay**

¿Dónde prefiere usted vivir? 450

¿Sabe usted manejar? 454

Nota comunicativa
Frases para indicar cómo llegar a un lugar 456

42 *Más descripciones* • Past Participle Used as an Adjective 458

43 *¿Qué has hecho?* • Perfect Forms: Present Perfect Indicative and Present Perfect Subjunctive 462

Nota comunicativa El pluscuamperfecto: *había + participio pasado* 466

---

16 La vida social y afectiva *476*

Nora Pelaez/Visual Ideas/Getty Images

El Paraguay

Las relaciones sentimentales 478

Nota comunicativa
El uso del infinitivo como sustantivo 480

Las etapas de la vida 481

44 *¿Hay alguien que... ? ¿Hay un lugar donde... ?* • The Subjunctive (Part 6): The Subjunctive After Nonexistent and Indefinite Antecedents 482

45 *Lo hago para que tú...* • The Subjunctive (Part 7): The Subjunctive After Conjunctions of Purpose and Contingency 487

Nota comunicativa *¿Para qué? / para (que)...* and *¿por qué? / porque...* 490

TEXTS AND PROJECTS

Textos de todos los días Correos electrónicos para pedir una extensión o pedir disculpas 439

Proyecto Encuesta sobre la vida universitaria 440

En acción 441

Lectura «Ciencias naturales», de Washington Cucurto 442

Proyecto La biofilia, un antídoto al estrés de ser humano 443

Textos orales La depresión entre los adolescentes 443

En acción 443

Portafolio 444

Escritura Un ensayo sobre las presiones de la vida estudiantil 444

CULTURE AND VIDEO

Nota cultural Megalópolis estresantes... y pueblitos relajantes 424

Algo sobre...
la marinera 426
la herencia indígena peruana 429
el cajón 433
Mario Vargas Llosa 438

Todo junto Lengua y cultura: De turismo por el Perú 439

Video Salu2 «¡Ay, qué estrés!» Online Appendix

Mundo hispano

Enfoque cultural: Preocupaciones y motivos de ansiedad
En el Perú 441
En otros países hispanos 441

Xinhua/Alamy Stock Photo

Textos de todos los días Direcciones en el GPS 457

Proyecto Viñetas 468

En acción 469

Lectura «Azul Cielo», de Laura Busom Fuertes 470

Proyecto Fijarse en el camino 471

Textos orales Una campaña para Greenpeace en la radio 471

En acción 471

Portafolio 472

Escritura Un ensayo sobre los efectos del cambio climático 472

Nota cultural Programas medioambientales 451

Algo sobre...
el Río de la Plata 452
la Pampa 453
el mate 460
el tango 465

Todo junto Lengua y cultura: El Parque Nacional Los Glaciares 467

Video Salu2 «EcoSalu2» Online Appendix

Mundo hispano

Enfoque cultural: Diversidad y recursos naturales
En la Argentina y el Uruguay 469
En otros países hispanos 469

Buena Vista Images/The Image Bank/Getty Images

Textos de todos los días Anuncio para compartir un apartamento o casa 486

Proyecto Frases famosas 492

En acción 493

Lectura «Amor cibernauta», de Diego Muñoz Valenzuela 494

Proyecto Mensajes de cibernautas en un sitio de citas 495

Textos orales Un anuncio para Naranjas, un sitio web para encontrar pareja 495

En acción 496

Portafolio 497

Escritura Consejos sentimentales 497

Nota cultural Expresiones familiares de cariño 479

Algo sobre...
el Gran Chaco 481
la represa de Itaipú 486
el té paraguayo 489
la cultura guaraní 491

Todo junto Lengua y cultura: ¿Cómo se divierten los jóvenes hispanos? 491

Video Salu2 «Cosas del amor» Online Appendix

Mundo hispano

Enfoque cultural: Relaciones románticas
En el Paraguay 493
En otros países hispanos 493

roberto hunger/Alamy Stock Photo

	VOCABULARY & PRONUNCIATION	GRAMMAR

17 ¿Trabajar para vivir o vivir para trabajar? *500*

John Warburton-Lee Photography/Alamy Stock Photo

Chile

Las profesiones y ocupaciones 502
El mundo laboral 504
Una cuestión de dinero 505
Nota comunicativa
Más pronombres posesivos 507

46 Talking About the Future • Future Verb Forms 509
Nota comunicativa Cómo expresar probabilidad con el futuro 513
47 Expressing Future or Pending Actions • The Subjunctive (Part 8): The Subjunctive and Indicative After Conjunctions of Time 515

18 La actualidad *528*

Pablo Blazquez Dominguez/ Getty Images

España

Las noticias 530
El gobierno y la responsabilidad cívica 532

48 *Queríamos que todo el mundo votara* • The Subjunctive (Part 9): The Past Subjunctive 536
Nota comunicativa Cómo expresar deseos imposibles 542
49 Expressing What You Would Do • Conditional Verb Forms 543
Nota comunicativa Cláusulas con *si* 546

Lectura cultural final
El español en el resto del mundo 558
• Guinea Ecuatorial 558
• Las Islas Filipinas 559
• El Canadá 559

TEXTS AND PROJECTS

Textos de todos los días Un curriculum (vitae) 508

Proyecto Mucho más que un título 520

En acción 521

Lectura «La oportunidad de Salomón Bobadilla», de Tito Matamala 522

Proyecto La recreación de una obra de arte 523

Textos orales Mundo laboral 523

En acción 523

Portafolio 524

Escritura Un trabajo ideal 524

CULTURE AND VIDEO

Nota cultural Nuevas tendencias del español para evitar el sexismo lingüístico 503

Algo sobre...
 «Gracias a la vida» 511
 los Andes 512
 la Isla de Pascua 514
 el pueblo mapuche 518

Todo junto Lengua y cultura: Trabajos para estudiantes universitarios 519

Video Salu2 «Los hispanos que admiramos» Online Appendix

Mundo hispano

 Enfoque cultural: El mundo laboral
 En Chile 521
 En otros países hispanos 521

Martin Bernetti/AFP/ Getty Images

Textos de todos los días Secciones de un periódico 535

Proyecto Una encuesta sobre decisiones personales 550

En acción 551

Lectura Constitución española, Capítulo segundo. Derechos y libertades 552

Proyecto Una comparación entre los derechos y libertades de dos constituciones 553

Textos orales Una breve historia de España 554

En acción 554

Portafolio 555

Escritura Un ensayo sobre la mayoría de edad 555

Nota cultural El panorama social y político en el mundo hispano 533

Algo sobre...
 la diversidad lingüística de España 534
 el flamenco 542
 las tapas 545
 Don Quijote de la Mancha 548

Todo junto Lengua y cultura: Maneras de practicar el español fuera de clase 549

Video Salu2 «¡Noticias!» Online Appendix

Mundo hispano

 Enfoque cultural: Sociedad, historia y economía
 En España 551
 En todo el mundo hispano 551

Pixtal/age fotostock

Appendices

1. Glossary of Grammatical Terms A-1
2. Using Adjectives as Nouns A-6
3. More About Stressed Possessives A-7
4. Additional Perfect Forms (Indicative and Subjunctive) A-8
5. Verbs A-9

Vocabulary

Spanish-English Vocabulary V-1
English-Spanish Vocabulary V-38

Index I-1
Mandatos y frases comunes en el salón de clase MF-1
Selected Verb Forms SVF-1
Maps

An Invitation to Puntos de partida

Puntos de partida means *points of departure* in Spanish. This program will be your point of departure for learning Spanish and for learning about Hispanic cultures. With *Puntos de partida*, you will get ready to communicate with Spanish speakers in this country and in other parts of the Spanish-speaking world. To speak a language means much more than just learning its grammar and vocabulary. To know a language is to know the people who speak it. For this reason, *Puntos de partida* will provide you with cultural information to help you understand and appreciate the traditions and values of Spanish-speaking people all over the world. Get ready for the adventure of learning Spanish!

1

Ante todo°

Ante... *First of all*

En este capítulo°

En... *In this chapter*

VOCABULARY

Greetings and courtesy   4
Describing yourself   10
Numbers 0–30   14
Likes and dislikes   16
Telling time   18

COUNTRIES OF FOCUS: THE SPANISH-SPEAKING WORLD

Zócalo (*Main Plaza*),
Ciudad de México,
México

Plaza de España,
Barcelona, España

Mark Lewis/Photographer's Choice/Getty Images

T.Tstudio/Shutterstock

EL MUNDO HISPANOHABLANTE°

El... *The Spanish-speaking world*

- Más de[a] 500 (quinientos) millones de personas hablan español.
- El español es la lengua oficial de 20 (veinte) naciones y de Puerto Rico.

[a]Más... *More than*

🔊 ENTREVISTA°   *Interview*

These questions related to the chapter theme are answered here by a native speaker. You will be able to ask and answer them yourself with personal information in the **Entrevista** activity in the **Portafolio** section at the end of the chapter (beginning in **Capítulo 2**).

Alejandra Hernández Soto contesta las preguntas.[a]

— **¡Hola! ¿Cómo está usted?**[b]

— ¡Hola! Estoy[c] muy bien. ¿Y usted?[d]

— **¿Cómo se llama?**[e]

— Me llamo Alejandra Hernández Soto.

— **¿De dónde es?**[f]

— Soy de[g] Guanajuato, México.

— **¿Cómo es usted?**[h]

— ¿Cómo soy?[i] Optimista, responsable, sentimental y muy independiente. ¿Y cómo es usted?

[a]contesta... *answers the questions* [b]¡Hola!... *Hello! How are you?* [c]*I am* [d]¿Y... *And (how are) you?* [e]¿Cómo... *What's your name?* [f]¿De... *Where are you from?* [g]Soy... *I'm from* [h]¿Cómo... *What are you like?* [i]¿Cómo... *What am I like?*

Saludos° y expresiones de cortesía

You can hear the pronunciation of theme vocabulary words and phrases in the eBook.

Greetings

Here are some words, phrases, and expressions for meeting and greeting others in Spanish. Can you tell the difference between those that are formal and those that are more informal or familiar (as on a first-name basis)?

Situaciones formales

1.
ELISA VELASCO: Buenas tardes, señor Gómez.
MARTÍN GÓMEZ: Muy buenas, señora Velasco. ¿Cómo está?
ELISA VELASCO: Bien, gracias. ¿Y usted?
MARTÍN GÓMEZ: Muy bien, gracias. Hasta luego.
ELISA VELASCO: Adiós.

2.
LUPE: Buenos días, profesor.
JUAN PÉREZ: Buenos días. ¿Cómo se llama usted, señorita?
LUPE: Me llamo Lupe Carrasco.
JUAN PÉREZ: Mucho gusto, Lupe.
LUPE: Igualmente.

Situaciones informales

3.
JOSÉ: ¡Hola, Carmen!
CARMEN: ¿Qué tal, José? ¿Cómo estás?
JOSÉ: Muy bien. ¿Y tú?
CARMEN: Regular. Nos vemos mañana, ¿eh?
JOSÉ: Bien. Hasta mañana.

4.
MATEO: Hola. Me llamo Mateo. ¿Y tú? ¿Cómo te llamas?
CAMILA: Me llamo Camila. Mucho gusto.
MATEO: Encantado, Camila. Y, ¿de dónde eres?
CAMILA: Soy de Venezuela. ¿Y tú?
MATEO: Yo soy de México.

> Translations of short dialogues like the ones on this page will usually be at the foot of the page, but you should try to read them without the translations first!

---

1. *EV: Good afternoon, Mr. Gómez. MG: Afternoon, Mrs. Velasco. How are you? EV: Fine, thank you. And you? MG: Very well, thanks. See you later. EV: Bye.*

2. *L: Good morning, professor. JP: Good morning. What's your name, miss? L: My name is Lupe Carrasco. JP: Nice to meet you, Lupe. L: Likewise.*

3. *J: Hi, Carmen! C: How's it going, José? How are you? J: Very well. And you? C: OK. See you tomorrow, OK? J: Fine. Until tomorrow.*

4. *M: Hello. My name is Mateo. And you? What's your name? C: My name is Camila. Nice to meet you. M: Nice to meet you, Camila. And where are you from? C: I'm from Venezuela. And you? M: I'm from Mexico.*

Note the use of **red** and **<u>underlined</u>** text to highlight aspects of Spanish that you should pay special attention to.

	Formal		Informal	
Títulos	**señor (Sr.)**	Mr.		
	señora (Sra.)	Mrs., ma'am		
	señorita (Srta.)	Miss		
	profesor (*for a man*)			
	profesora (*for a woman*)			
Saludos	**buenos días**	good morning	**hola**	hi
	buenas tardes	good afternoon/ evening		
	buenas noches	good evening/night		
	(muy) buenas	good day (*any time*)		
Preguntas (*Questions*)	**¿Cómo está?**	How are you?	**¿Cómo estás?** **¿Qué tal?**	How are you?
	¿Y usted?	And you?	**¿Y tú?**	And you?
	—**¿Cómo se llama (usted)?** —**Me llamo...** "What's your name?" "My name is ... "		—**¿Cómo te llamas (tú)?** —**Me llamo...** "What's your name?" "My name is ... "	
	—**¿De dónde es (usted)?** —**(Yo) Soy de...** "Where are you from?" "I'm from ... "		—**¿De dónde eres (tú)?** —**(Yo) Soy de...** "Where are you from?" "I'm from ... "	

¡OJO! means *Watch out!* or *Pay attention!* in Spanish.

¡OJO!

There is no Spanish equivalent for *Ms.;* use **Sra.** or **Srta.,** as appropriate.

¡OJO!

Note the accent marks on Spanish words that ask questions.

¡OJO!

Pay attention to the word endings and other words associated with **tú** and **usted.**

Nota cultural: Los saludos en el mundo° hispano

world

Rido/Shutterstock

¿Qué pasa, hombre? (*What's up, man?*)

Hispanics all over the world hug and kiss when they are greeting each other a lot more frequently than do non-Hispanics in this country. Younger people especially greet in this way, even when they have just met. Two men will typically hug or pat each other on the back, and if they are family, they will sometimes give a kiss on the cheek and embrace, as do women.

 How do you greet your friends? Your relatives?

Así se dice (*That's how it's said*) introduces optional vocabulary from the Spanish-speaking world.

Así se dice

The following greetings express *What's up?*, *What's happening?*, or *How's it going?*

¿Qué hay? ¿Qué pasa? ¿Qué hubo? ¿Qué onda? (*Mexico*)

—**Encantad<u>o</u>.** (*for a man*)
—**Encantad<u>a</u>.** (*for a woman*) ⎫ "Nice to meet you."
—**Mucho gusto.** ⎭

—**Igualmente.** "Likewise."

Gracias. Thanks. Thank you.

Muchas gracias. Thank you very much.

De nada. / No hay de qué. You're welcome.

You will use these expressions in **Comunicación.**

Por favor. Please. (*also used to get someone's attention*)

Perdón. Pardon me. Excuse me. (*to ask forgiveness or to get someone's attention*)

(Con) Permiso. Pardon me. Excuse me. (*to request permission to pass by or through a group of people*)

Comunicación

A. Expresiones de cortesía. How many different ways can you respond to the following greetings and phrases?

1. Buenas tardes.
2. Adiós.
3. ¿Qué tal?
4. Hola.
5. ¿Cómo está?
6. Buenas noches.

7. Muchas gracias.
8. Hasta mañana.
9. ¿Cómo se llama usted?
10. Mucho gusto.
11. ¿De dónde eres?
12. Buenos días.

B. Situaciones. If the following people met or passed each other at the times given, what might they say to each other? Role-play the situations with a classmate.

1. Mr. Santana and Miss Pérez, at 5:00 P.M.
2. Mrs. Ortega and Pablo, at 10:00 A.M.
3. Professor María Hernández and Olivia, at 11:00 P.M.
4. you and a classmate, just before your Spanish class

C. Situaciones. What would you say in Spanish in the following situations?

1. Your classmate passes you a handout from the professor.
2. You want to pass through a group of students outside of your classroom.
3. You just dropped your drink on a friend's book.
4. Your professor thanks you for opening the door for her.
5. You need your professor's attention.

D. Más (*More*) situaciones. Are the people in this drawing saying **por favor, con permiso,** or **perdón? ¡OJO!** More than one response is possible for some items.

E. Entrevista (*Interview*)

Paso (*Step*) 1. Turn to a person sitting next to you and do the following.

- Greet them appropriately, that is, with informal forms.
- Ask how they are.
- Find out their name.
- Ask where they are from.
- Conclude the exchange.

Paso 2. Now have a similar conversation with your instructor, using the appropriate formal or familiar forms, according to your instructor's request.

Pronunciación: Las vocales:° *a, e, i, o, u*

vowels

There is a very close relationship between the way Spanish is written and the way it is pronounced. This makes it relatively easy to learn the basics of Spanish spelling and pronunciation.

Many Spanish sounds, however, do not have an exact equivalent in English, so you can't always trust English to be your guide to Spanish pronunciation. Even words that are spelled the same in both languages are usually pronounced quite differently.

English vowels can have many different pronunciations or may be silent. Spanish vowels are almost always pronounced, and they are almost always pronounced in the same way. They are always short and tense. They are never drawn out with a *u* or *i* glide as in English: **lo** ≠ *low;* **de** ≠ *day.*

> **a:** pronounced like the *a* in *father,* but short and tense
> **e:** pronounced like the *e* in *they,* but without the *i* glide
> **i:** pronounced like the *i* in *machine,* but short and tense
> **o:** pronounced like the *o* in *home,* but without the *u* glide
> **u:** pronounced like the *u* in *rule,* but short and tense

> **¡OJO!**
>
> In English, most unstressed vowels are pronounced like an *uh* sound or schwa: c**a**nal, wait**e**d, at**o**m. This sound does not exist in Spanish.

> **¡OJO!**
>
> The word **y** (*and*) is pronounced like the letter **i**, as is the letter **y** at the end of a word: **¡ay!**

Práctica

A. Palabras. (*Words.*) Repeat the following words after your instructor.

1. hasta	tal	nada	mañana	natural	normal	fascinante
2. me	qué	Pérez	Elena	rebelde	excelente	elegante
3. sí	señorita	permiso	terrible	imposible	tímido	Ibiza
4. yo	con	como	noches	profesor	señor	generoso
5. gusto	usted	tú	mucho	Perú	Lupe	Úrsula

B. Nombres. Here is a list of the most popular names for babies (female and male) in **México** in 2021 (**dos mil veintiuno**).

Los nombres de bebé preferidos por los mexicanos en 2021	
Niña	**Niño**
Valentina	Santiago
Regina	Mateo
Victoria	Leonardo
Romina	Emiliano
Camila	Matías
Sofía	Liam
Renata	Sebastián
Natalia	Alejandro
Luciana	Emilio
Isabella	Daniel

Source: Hispana Global

(Continúa).

Photodisc/Getty Images

Paso 1. Can you find the Spanish word for *boy*? for *girl*? for the phrase *preferred by Hispanics*?

Paso 2. Working in pairs, try to give the English version of some of these names. Say the Spanish names aloud and, as you do, focus on the different pronunciation and spelling as compared to English. **¡OJO!** Two names in the list, Isabella and Liam, are not Spanish, but they have become fashionable recently in the Spanish-speaking world.

Paso 3. In pairs, make a list of other Hispanic first names you know and say them out loud, trying to pronounce them in Spanish.

¡OJO!

- The **ll** and **rr** combinations occur frequently in Spanish, but they are not separate letters.
- The only other consonants that are ever doubled are **c** and **n**, but they don't have a special sound.

El alfabeto español

The Spanish *alphabet* (**el alfabeto** or **el abecedario**) is slightly different from the English alphabet.

- It has 27 letters (not 26).
- The extra letter is **ñ**.
- The letters **k** and **w** appear only in words borrowed from other languages.

Letters	Names of Letters	Examples			Pronunciation
a	a	A̱na	América̱	mañana̱	
b	be	Benito	Bolivia	colom̱biano	
c	ce	Carlos	Cecilia	cómo	c + a / o / u = like English *k*; c + e/i = like English *s* (in Spain, a *th* sound)
d	de	Dolores	Dinamarca	dónde	
e	e	Eduardo	Ecuador	eres	
f	efe	Felipe	Francia	favor	
g	ge	Gerardo	Guatemala	gracias	g + e/i = like hard English *h*; g + a / o / u and **gue/gui** = like English *g* in *got*
h	hache	Héctor	Hortensia	alcohol	always silent; in **ch** combination = like English *cheese*
i	i	Ignacio	Ibiza	igualmente	
j	jota	Julia	San José	ojo	like hard English *h*; similar to g + e/i
k	ca (ka)	Karina	Kabul	kétchup	like English *k*
l	ele	Luis	Lima	luego	like English *l*; when doubled (**ll**), like *y* in English *yes*
m	eme	Manuel	Mallorca	me llamo	
n	ene	Nadia	Nicaragua	nada	
ñ	eñe	Íñigo	España	señora	close to *ny* in English *canyon*
o	o	Octavio	Orinoco	buenos	
p	pe	Paula	Perú	perdón	
q	cu	Enrique	Quito	que	like English *ke* and *ki*; appears only in the combinations **que** and **qui**
r	erre	Rosa	Caracas	burro	like *tt* in English *butter*; trilled at beginning of a word or as **rr**
s	ese	Salvador	San Juan	soy	
t	te	Teresa	Turquía	estás	
u	u	Úrsula	Uruguay	tú	
v	uve	Víctor	Valdivia	nos vemos	like Spanish **b**
w	doble uve	Willie	Washington	kiwi	like English *w*
x	equis	Xavier	Luxemburgo	extremo	like English *x*; at beginning of a word and in **México, mexicano, x** = Spanish **j**
y	ye	Yolanda	Nueva York	y	like *y* in English *yes*
z	zeta	Zoila	Zaragoza	zona	like English *s* (in Spain, a *th* sound); never like English *z*

Práctica

A. Pronunciación. Match the Spanish letters with their equivalent pronunciation and pronounce the example words.

EXAMPLES/SPELLING

1. _____ mucho: **ch**
2. _____ Geraldo: **ge** (also: **gi**); Jiménez: **j**
3. _____ hola: **h**
4. _____ gusto: **gu** (also: **ga, go**)
5. _____ me llamo: **ll**
6. _____ señor: **ñ**
7. _____ profesora: **r**
8. _____ Ramón: **r** (to start a word); burro: **rr**
9. _____ nos vemos: **v**

PRONUNCIATION

a. like the *g* in English *garden*
b. similar to *tt* of *butter* when pronounced very quickly
c. like *ch* in English *cheese*
d. like Spanish **b**
e. similar to a "strong" English *h*
f. like *y* in English *yes*
g. a trilled sound, several Spanish **r**'s in a row
h. like the *ny* sound in *canyon*
i. never pronounced

B. ¿Cómo se escribe... ? (*How do you write ... ?*)

Paso 1. Pronounce these United States place names in Spanish. Then spell the names aloud in Spanish. All of them are of Hispanic origin: **Toledo, Los Ángeles, Montana, Colorado, El Paso, Florida, Las Vegas, Amarillo, San Francisco.**

Paso 2. Spell your own name aloud in Spanish, and listen as your classmates spell their names. Try to remember as many of their names as you can.

MODELO: Me llamo María: **M** (eme) **a** (a) **r** (erre) **í** (i con acento) **a** (a).

Nota comunicativa: Los cognados

As you study Spanish, note that many Spanish and English words are similar or identical in form and meaning. These related words are called *cognates* (**los cognados**). It's useful to begin recognizing and using cognates immediately; they will help you enrich your Spanish vocabulary and develop language proficiency more quickly. Here are some examples.

TO DESCRIBE PEOPLE			TO NAME PLACES AND THINGS		
cruel	inteligente	realista	alcohol	estudiante	parque
elegante	interesante	responsable	bar	examen	teatro
idealista	optimista	sentimental	café	hotel	teléfono
importante	paciente	terrible	clase	museo	televisión
independiente	pesimista	tolerante	diccionario	oficina	universidad

You will practice this vocabulary throughout this chapter.

El Teatro Juárez, Guanajuato, México

¿Cómo es usted?° (Part 1) ¿Cómo... *What are you like?*

Ángela Suárez del Pino

Ismael Figueroa García

—¿Quién **es usted** y cómo **es**?
—**Soy** Ángela Suárez del Pino. **Soy** optimista y tolerante.

—¿Quién **eres tú**?
—Me llamo Ismael Figueroa García y **soy** estudiante de universidad.
—Ismael, ¿cómo **eres**?
—**Soy** inteligente, romántico y responsable.

> *a verb / un verbo* = a word that describes an action or a state of being

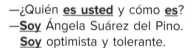
Remember to watch for the words in **red** and **underlined**. Check the translation at the bottom of the page only if you need to.

> **¡OJO!**
>
> In Spanish, subject pronouns are not always used because the verb form often indicates the person. See how this works in the dialogues on this page.

Use the following verb forms to describe yourself or another person.

Subject Pronouns / **Pronombres personales***	**ser (to be):† Formas singulares**	
yo	**soy**	I am
tú	**eres**	you (*familiar*) are
usted	**es**	you (*formal*) are
él	**es**	he is
ella	**es**	she is

> Notice that *Puntos de partida* will address you as **usted**, so that you become familiar with the formal forms. In partner/pair activities, however, the model will always encourage you to use **tú** with your classmates, which is what young people in the Spanish-speaking world typically do.

Comunicación

A. ¿Cómo es usted?

Paso 1. Indique todas (*all*) las palabras apropiadas (*appropriate words*).

(Yo) Soy...

- ☐ diligente
- ☐ idealista
- ☐ impaciente
- ☐ extravagante
- ☐ elegante

- ☐ pesimista
- ☐ materialista
- ☐ normal
- ☐ profesor
- ☐ importante

- ☐ independiente
- ☐ estudiante
- ☐ diferente
- ☐ profesora
- ☐ ¿ ?

"Who are you and what are you like?" "I'm Ángela Suárez del Pino. I'm optimistic and tolerant."

"Who are you?" "My name is Ismael Figueroa García, and I'm a university (college) student." "Ismael, what are you like?" "I'm intelligent, romantic, and responsible."

*You will learn more about subject pronouns in **Gramática 3** (Cap. 2) and **Gramática 8** (Cap. 3).*

†*You will learn more about **ser** in **Gramática 6** (Cap. 3).*

Paso 2. With a classmate, use the adjectives and nouns in **Paso 1** to ask each other what you are like and who you are.

MODELO: diligente ➜
           ESTUDIANTE 1: ¿Eres diligente?
           ESTUDIANTE 2: Sí, soy diligente. / No, no soy diligente.

Paso 3. Now ask your instructor about their personality traits.

MODELO: Profesor(a), ¿es usted diligente?

B. ¿Quién es... ?

Paso 1. With a classmate, take turns asking and answering questions about the following celebrities. If an adjective doesn't fit any of them in your opinion, you can say **Nadie es...** (*No one is ... *)

MODELO: **1.** arrogante ➜
           ESTUDIANTE 1: ¿Quién es arrogante?
           ESTUDIANTE 2: Enrique Iglesias es arrogante.

Personas

Camila Cabello

Leo Messi

Sonia Sotomayor

¿ ?

1. arrogante	**5.** impresionante	**9.** fascinante
2. independiente	**6.** interesante	**10.** intelectual
3. paciente	**7.** elegante	
4. materialista	**8.** terrible	

Paso 2. Now describe the people in negative terms, using **no** in front of the verb.

MODELO: Enrique Iglesias **no** es arrogante.

C. Una encuesta (*A poll*)

Paso 1. Use cognates from **Nota comunicativa** (page 9) and others you have heard or seen to describe the following people and things.

MODELO: **1.** Jennifer López ➜ Jennifer López es **independiente.**

1. Jennifer López
2. este país (*this country*)
3. _____ (un programa de televisión)
4. _____ (una persona famosa)

Paso 2. Now poll three classmates about the same four items. Write their answers in the chart.

MODELO: To ask: **ESTUDIANTE 1:** En tu opinión, ¿cómo es Jennifer López?
         To answer: **ESTUDIANTE 2:** Es independiente.

Estudiantes (nombre)	Jennifer López	este país	____ (programa de televisión)	____ (persona famosa)

¡Aquí se habla español! If you sometimes have the feeling that Spanish is everywhere, that's because it's true, and it may become even more so during your lifetime. Here are some interesting facts.

- Spanish is spoken as a first or second language by almost 550 million people worldwide, and nearly 500 million of them are native speakers. This makes Spanish the fourth most widely spoken language in the world. (English is the most widely spoken.) Some Spanish speakers also speak another language, like **náhuatl** in Mexico, **mapuche** in Chile, or **catalán** in Spain.

- Spanish is an official language of 20 countries.

- More than 60 million people in the United States speak Spanish as a first or second language (excluding the more than 3 million people who live in **Puerto Rico**). This makes the United States the second largest Spanish-speaking country in the world, preceded only by **México** (**Colombia** is third).

- Spanish is the official language (along with English) of **Puerto Rico**, a commonwealth (**un estado libre asociado**) of the United States.

- Spanish is present in Equatorial Guinea (where it is an official language), in the Philippines as a heritage from the not-so-distant past when the islands were colonies of Spain, and in Canada.

- Spanish is second only to English in terms of the number of people studying it worldwide.

Knowing a second language has many personal and professional advantages. If you live in a country like the United States, there is no need to explain to you why it's a good thing to study Spanish. The language and its cultures are part of the country's historical and cultural past. And, from an economic standpoint, Spanish speakers provide a huge market of consumers of all kinds of goods and services, including the entertainment industry and the world of art.

Spanish is also a great asset for traveling for business or pleasure, within this country or abroad. Like all languages spoken by a large number of people, modern Spanish varies from region to region. The Spanish of Madrid is different from that spoken in Mexico City, Buenos Aires, or Los Angeles. Although these differences are most noticeable in pronunciation ("accent"), they are also found in vocabulary and special expressions used in different areas of the world. But most vocabulary items are common to the many varieties of Spanish, and the grammar is the same throughout the Spanish-speaking world.

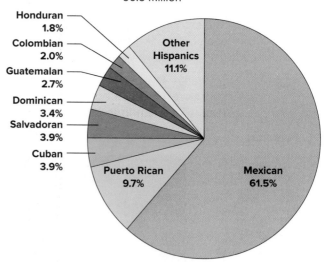

Comparing Origins of U.S. Hispanic Population
Total Hispanic Population
Pew Research Center, 2019 Estimate
60.6 Million

- Honduran 1.8%
- Colombian 2.0%
- Guatemalan 2.7%
- Dominican 3.4%
- Salvadoran 3.9%
- Cuban 3.9%
- Puerto Rican 9.7%
- Mexican 61.5%
- Other Hispanics 11.1%

La Misión Basílica San Diego de Alcalá, cerca de (*near*) San Diego, California

America/Alamy Stock Photo

Knowing Spanish also opens the door to a fascinating culture. Actually, *cultures,* plural, would be more accurate. Spanish was the language of one of the most impressive intersections of culture and civilization the world has ever known, when a small group of Spaniards landed on an island in the Caribbean over 500 years ago. No two of the Spanish-speaking American countries that arose from that fusion of European and indigenous cultures (including those of enslaved Africans) are alike. They offer a rich and diverse cultural panorama, one that you will learn about in every chapter of *Puntos de partida.*

So ... welcome to the Spanish-speaking world! Actually, you know, you're already in it.

Comprensión

¿Cierto o falso? (*True or false?*)

1. There are more than 500 million Spanish speakers in the world.
2. There are more than 60 million Spanish speakers in the United States.
3. Only indigenous and European cultures contributed to the culture of Spanish-speaking countries in the Americas.
4. Speakers of one variety of Spanish usually cannot understand what speakers of another variety of Spanish say.
5. The Spaniards brought Spanish to the Americas about 300 years ago.

En acción

In the collage of flags, identify the flags of at least three Spanish-speaking countries. You can find them on the chapter-opening pages of Chapters 2–18 of *Puntos de partida*.

Los números del 0 al 30; *Hay*

Algo sobre... (*Something about ...*) offers cultural information, usually about the chapter's country of focus.

Algo sobre los números

In Spanish-speaking countries, hand-written numbers may look a little different from the way they do in the United States.

Julio López Saguar/Getty Images

Do you notice any differences in the way the numbers are written in these photos and the way you write them?

Wavebreakmedia/Shutterstock

En un salón de clase

Hay una profesora.
Hay cuatro estudiantes.

Los números del 0 al 30

0 cero		
1 uno	11 once	21 veintiuno
2 dos	12 doce	22 veintidós
3 tres	13 trece	23 veintitrés
4 cuatro	14 catorce	24 veinticuatro
5 cinco	15 quince	25 veinticinco
6 seis	16 dieciséis	26 veintiséis
7 siete	17 diecisiete	27 veintisiete
8 ocho	18 dieciocho	28 veintiocho
9 nueve	19 diecinueve	29 veintinueve
10 diez	20 veint**e**	30 treint**a**

a noun / **un sustantivo** = a word that denotes a person, place, thing, or idea

¡OJO!

uno, dos,... veinti**uno**, veintidós,...
but
un señor, veinti**ún** señores
una señora, veinti**una** señoras

Nota comunicativa: El género (*gender*) y los números

The number *one* has several forms in Spanish. **Uno** is the form used in counting. The forms **un** and **una** are used before *nouns* (**los sustantivos**). How will you know which one to use? It depends on the *gender* (**el género**) of the noun.

All Spanish nouns are either masculine or feminine. For example, the noun **señor** is masculine (*m.*) in gender, and the noun **señora** is feminine (*f.*). (As you will learn, even nouns that are not sex-linked have gender.) Here is how *one* is expressed with these nouns: **un señor, una señora.** The number **veintiuno** has similar forms before nouns: **veintiún señores, veintiuna señoras.** Just get used to using **un** and **una** with nouns now. You'll learn more about gender and number in **Capítulo 2.**

Hay

The word **hay** expresses both *there is* and *there are* in Spanish. It can be made negative (**no hay**) and can also be used to ask a question: **¿Hay... ?** (*Is there ... ? Are there ... ?*)

Hay un teatro en esta universidad, pero **no hay** un museo.

There's a theater at this university, but there isn't a museum.

—¿Cuántos estudiantes **hay** en la clase?
—(**Hay**) Treinta.

*"How many students **are there** in the class?"*
*"(**There are**) Thirty."*

Práctica y comunicación

A. **Una canción infantil. (*A children's song*.)** This is a popular song for children from all over the Spanish-speaking world. Complete it with the missing numbers. It's basic math!

Dos y dos son _____, cuatro y dos son _____,
seis y dos son _____, y ocho _____,
y ocho _____, y _____ treinta y dos...

B. **Los números.** Practique los números, según (*according to*) el modelo. **¡OJO!** *f.* = femenino; *m.* = masculino.

MODELO: 1 señor → Hay **un** señor.

1. 4 señoras	**6.** 1 idea (*f.*)	**11.** 28 naciones
2. 12 pianos	**7.** 21 ideas (*f.*)	**12.** 5 guitarras
3. 1 café (*m.*)	**8.** 11 personas	**13.** 1 león (*m.*)
4. 21 cafés (*m.*)	**9.** 15 estudiantes	**14.** 30 señores
5. 14 días	**10.** 13 teléfonos	**15.** 20 oficinas

C. **Problemas de matemáticas.** Express the following simple mathematical equations in Spanish. Note: + (**y**), − (**menos**), = (**son**).

MODELOS: $2 + 2 = 4$ → Dos y dos son cuatro.
$4 - 2 = 2$ → Cuatro menos dos son dos.

1. $2 + 4 = 6$	**8.** $15 - 2 = 13$	**15.** $8 - 7 = 1$
2. $8 + 17 = 25$	**9.** $9 - 9 = 0$	**16.** $13 - 9 = 4$
3. $11 + 1 = 12$	**10.** $13 - 8 = 5$	**17.** $2 + 3 + 10 = 15$
4. $3 + 18 = 21$	**11.** $14 + 12 = 26$	**18.** $28 - 6 = 22$
5. $9 + 6 = 15$	**12.** $23 - 13 = 10$	**19.** $30 - 17 = 13$
6. $5 + 4 = 9$	**13.** $1 + 4 = 5$	**20.** $28 - 5 = 23$
7. $1 + 13 = 14$	**14.** $1 + 3 - 1 = 3$	**21.** $19 - 7 = 12$

D. **Intercambios. (*Exchanges*.)** With a classmate, ask and answer the following questions.

1. ¿Cuántos (*How many*) estudiantes hay en la clase de español? ¿Cuántos estudiantes hay en clase hoy (*today*)? ¿Hay tres profesores o un profesor / una profesora?

2. ¿Cuántos días hay en una semana (*week*)? ¿Hay seis? **(No, no hay...)** ¿Cuántos días hay en un fin de semana (*weekend*)? ¿Cuántos días hay en febrero? ¿en junio? ¿Cuántos meses hay en un año (*year*)?

3. En esta (*this*) universidad, ¿hay una cafetería? **(Sí, hay... / No, no hay...)** ¿un teatro? ¿un laboratorio de lenguas (*languages*)? ¿un bar? ¿una clínica? ¿un hospital? ¿un museo? ¿muchos (*many*) estudiantes? ¿muchos profesores?

Los gustos° y preferencias (Part 1)*

Los... *Likes*

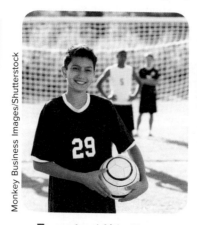

—¿**Te gusta** el fútbol?
—Sí, ¡**me gusta** mucho!

—Y **a usted**, señor, ¿**le gusta** el fútbol también?
—No, **no me gusta** mucho el fútbol, pero sí **me gusta** el fútbol americano.

Use these patterns with the verb **gustar** to express likes and dislikes.

Me gusta _____.	I like _____.
No **me** gusta _____.	I don't like _____.
(No) **Te** gusta _____. (*familiar*)	
(No) **Le** gusta _____. (*formal*)	You (don't) like _____.

In the following activities you will use **el** to mean *the* with masculine nouns and **la** with feminine nouns. Don't try to memorize which words are masculine or feminine at this time. You will also use Spanish verbs in the infinitive form, which always ends in **-r**. Here are some examples: **estudiar** = *to study*, **comer** = *to eat*. You will be able to guess the meaning of other infinitives from context (the surrounding words).

Práctica y comunicación

A. ¿Yo, tú o usted? Indicate which pronoun you associate with each question or statement.

1. ¿Te gusta la pizza?
2. ¿Le gusta la Coca-Cola?
3. Me gusta mucho el chocolate.

B. Versión bilingüe. Match the ideas.

1. _____ —¿Te gusta esquiar?
   —No, no me gusta.
2. _____ —¿Le gusta esquiar?
   —Sí, me gusta.
3. _____ —Me gusta esquiar.
   —¿Sí? A mí no me gusta.

a. "Do you (*formal*) like to ski?" "Yes, I like to."
b. "I like to ski." "Yeah? I don't like to."
c. "Do you (*familiar*) like to ski?" "No, I don't like to."

"Do you like soccer?" "Yes, I like it a lot!" "And (what about) you, sir, do you also like soccer?" "No, I don't like soccer that much, but I do like football."

*You will learn more about **gustar** in Gram. 22 (Cap. 8).

C. Los gustos y preferencias

Paso 1. Make a list of six things you like and six things you don't like, following the model. You may choose items from the **Vocabulario útil** box.

MODELO: **1.** Me gusta **la clase de español.** No me gusta **la clase de matemáticas.**

> **Vocabulario útil** (*Useful vocabulary*) is not active; that is, you don't need to focus on learning it. But it will help you do this activity.

Vocabulario útil

el actor _____, la actriz _____
el café, el té, la limonada, la Coca-Cola
el/la cantante (*singer*) _____
el cine (*movies*), el teatro, la ópera, el arte abstracto, el fútbol
la música moderna, la música clásica, *el hip hop*, la música *country*
la pizza, la pasta, la comida (*food*) mexicana, la comida de la cafetería
_____ (**programa de televisión**)
_____ (**ciudad** [*city*])

¡OJO!

The word **cantante** is used for both men *and* women.

1. Me gusta _____. No me gusta _____.
2. _____
3. _____
4. _____
5. _____
6. _____

Paso 2. Now ask a classmate if they share your likes and dislikes.

MODELO: **ESTUDIANTE 1:** ¿Te gusta la clase de español?
ESTUDIANTE 2: Sí, me gusta (la clase de español). (No me gusta [la clase de español].)
ESTUDIANTE 1: ¿Y la clase de matemáticas?
ESTUDIANTE 2: Sí, también me gusta (la clase de matemáticas). (No me gusta [la clase de matemáticas].)

D. Más (*More*) gustos y preferencias

Paso 1. Here are some useful verbs and nouns to talk about what you like. For each item, combine an infinitive (shaded) with a noun to form a sentence that is true for you. The verb **estudiar** is an easily recognizable cognate. Use context to guess the meaning of verbs that are not cognates.

MODELO: Me gusta _____. → Me gusta **estudiar inglés.**

1.	beber	café / chocolate / limonada / té
2.	comer	enchiladas / ensalada / hamburguesas / pasta / pizza
3.	estudiar	español / historia / inglés / matemáticas
4.	hablar	con mis amigos (*with my friends*) / por teléfono (*on the phone*)
5.	jugar	al basquetbol / al béisbol / al fútbol / al fútbol americano
6.	tocar	la guitarra / el piano / el violín

Paso 2. Ask a classmate about their likes, using your own preferences as a guide.

MODELO: ¿Te gusta **comer enchiladas**?

Paso 3. Now ask your professor if they like certain things. **¡OJO!** Remember to address your professor in a formal manner if that is their preference.

MODELO: ¿Le gusta **jugar al tenis**?

¿Qué hora es?

Es la una.

Son las dos.

Son las cinco.

¿Qué hora es? is used to ask *What time is it?* In telling time, one says **Es la una** but **Son las dos** (**las tres, las cuatro,** and so on).

Es la una y $\left\{\begin{array}{l}\underline{\text{cuarto.}} \\ \underline{\text{quince.}}\end{array}\right.$

Son las dos y $\left\{\begin{array}{l}\underline{\text{media.}} \\ \underline{\text{treinta.}}\end{array}\right.$

Son las cinco **y diez.**

Son las ocho **y veinticinco.**

Note that from the hour to the half-hour, Spanish, like English, expresses time by adding minutes or a portion of an hour to the hour.

Son las dos **menos** $\left\{\begin{array}{l}\underline{\text{cuarto.}} \\ \underline{\text{quince.}}\end{array}\right.$

Son las ocho **menos diez.**

Son las once **menos veinte.**

From the half-hour to the hour, Spanish usually expresses time by subtracting minutes or a part of an hour from the *next* hour.

¡OJO!

Es la… / Son las… = to tell time
A la… / A las… = to tell *at* what time something happens or an event takes place

Nota comunicativa: Cómo expresar la hora

de la mañana.	A.M., in the morning
de la tarde	P.M., in the afternoon (and early evening)
de la noche	P.M., in the evening
en punto	exactly, on the dot, sharp
¿a qué hora… ?	(at) what time … ?
a la una (las dos,…)	at 1:00 (2:00, …)
Son las cuatro **de la tarde en punto.**	*It's exactly 4:00 P.M.*
—**¿A qué hora** es la clase de español?	*"What time is Spanish class (at)?"*
—Es **a las** once **de la mañana.**	*"It's at 11:00 A.M."*

You will practice these phrases in **Práctica y comunicación.**

Práctica y comunicación

A. ¡Atención! Listen as your instructor says a time of day. Find the clock face that corresponds to the time you heard and say its number in Spanish.

1.

2.

3.

4.

5.

6.

7.

8.

B. ¿Qué hora es?

Paso 1. Express the following times in full sentences in Spanish.

1. 1:00
2. 6:00
3. 11:00
4. 1:30 P.M.
5. 3:15 A.M.
6. 7:45 P.M.
7. 4:15 A.M.
8. 11:45 exactly
9. 9:10 on the dot
10. 9:50 sharp

Paso 2. With a classmate, take turns inventing times in Spanish. One student invents a time and the other writes it down in numbers.

MODELO: **ESTUDIANTE 1 SAYS:** Son las nueve y media de la mañana.
ESTUDIANTE 2 WRITES: 9:30 AM

C. Situaciones en la calle (*street*). Complete los diálogos con un compañero / una compañera.

Diálogo 1: Por la mañana, en la calle

SR. ROLDÁN: Buenos días, Sra. Valdés. ¿Cómo _____?
SRA. VALDÉS: Muy bien. ¿_____, Sr. Roldán?
SR. ROLDÁN: _____. Perdón, ¿qué hora _____?
SRA. VALDÉS: _____ las _____ (*10:30*), señor.
SR. ROLDÁN: _____ gracias, señora.

Diálogo 2: Por la tarde

SILVIA: ¡Hola!, muy _____, Julio. ¿Cómo _____?
JULIO: Bien, ¿y _____? ¡Huy!, perdón, ¿qué hora _____?
SILVIA: _____ las _____.
JULIO: ¡Ay! La clase de historia es a las _____ y diez. Me voy corriendo.[a] ¡Hasta luego!
SILVIA: Oye,[b] ¿nos vemos el sábado[c] en la fiesta?
JULIO: ¡Sí, sí!

[a]Me... *I have to run.* [b]*Hey* [c]*Saturday*

D. Intercambios (*Exchanges*)

Paso 1. Read and practice pronouncing the words in **Vocabulario útil**.

Vocabulario útil

¿cuándo?	when?
los días de la semana*	the days of the week
el lunes	on Monday
el martes	on Tuesday
el miércoles	on Wednesday
el jueves	on Thursday
el viernes	on Friday
el sábado	on Saturday
el domingo	on Sunday

Paso 2. With a partner, take turns asking and answering questions about when the following events or activities take place, according to the schedule. Can you guess the meaning of the new words in the schedule?

Esta (*This*) semana

L	M	X	J	V	S	D
español: 9 A.M.		*español:* 9 A.M.		*español:* 9 A.M.	*excursión:* 8:45 A.M.	
física: 11:50 A.M.	*historia:* 11:50 A.M.	*física:* 11:50 A.M.	*historia:* 11:50 A.M.	*física:* 11:50 A.M.		*tenis:* 10 A.M.
	laboratorio: 3:10 P.M.		*laboratorio:* 3:10 P.M.			*concierto:* 7:30 P.M.
					fiesta: 10 P.M.	

MODELO: **1.** la clase de español ➜
> ESTUDIANTE 1: ¿Cuándo es la clase de español?
> ESTUDIANTE 2: El lunes, el miércoles y el viernes a las nueve de la mañana.

1. la clase de español
2. la clase de física
3. la clase de historia
4. la sesión de laboratorio
5. la excursión
6. la fiesta
7. el partido (*game*) de tenis
8. el concierto

Paso 3. Now ask when your partner likes to perform the following activities on a given day.

MODELO: **1.** cenar (*to have dinner*) ➜
> ESTUDIANTE 1: ¿Cuándo te gusta cenar **el sábado**?
> ESTUDIANTE 2: El sábado me gusta cenar **a las seis y media.**

1. cenar
2. estudiar español
3. mirar (*to watch*) la televisión
4. ir al (*to go to the*) gimnasio
5. ir al cine
6. ir a una fiesta

---

*You will learn more about the days of the week in Spanish in **Capítulo 5.**

SALU2

Antes de mirar°

Antes... *Before watching*

What is a morning news and talk television show usually like? Check all of the phrases that apply.

- ☐ un poco (*a little*) cómico
- ☐ un poco serio
- ☐ informativo
- ☐ muy dramático
- ☐ para (*for*) una audiencia diversa
- ☐ solo para las personas mayores (*only for older people*)

Este° programa

This

This is the introductory program of a new morning show, based in Los Angeles, California.

> Reading part of the script before watching each segment of *Salu2* will help you understand more of the show.

Fragmento del guion°

del... *of the script*

VÍCTOR: Muchas gracias, Laura. La presencia del español en la ciudad de Los Ángeles es impresionante, ¿no crees,ᵃ Ana?

ANA: Absolutamente. Y personas de todo tipo hablan español, no soloᵇ los hispanos. Bueno, es hora de decirᶜ adiós por hoy. Espero que les haya gustado nuestro primer programa.ᵈ Nos vemos muy pronto.ᵉ

VÍCTOR: Desde el estudio de *Salu2* en la ciudad de Los Ángeles, California, les mandamosᶠ saludos a todos los telespectadores y esperamos verlos en nuestro próximo programa.ᵍ ¡Hasta entonces!ʰ

ᵃ¿no... *don't you think* ᵇno... *not only* ᶜBueno... *Well, it's time to say* ᵈEspero... *I hope you liked our first program.* ᵉmuy... *very soon*
ᶠles... *we send* ᵍesperamos... *we hope to see you at our next program* ʰ¡Hasta... *Until then!*

> The words and phrases in **Vocabulario del programa** (given in the order in which they appear in the show) will help you understand more when you watch this episode.

Vocabulario del° programa

of the

hoy les presentamos	today we're introducing ... to all of you
un nombre	a name
antiguo	former
la ciudad	the city
el país	the country, nation
el tema	the topic, subject
dentro y fuera de	within and outside of
vamos a hablar/escuchar	we're going to talk/listen to
cuarenta y ocho	forty-eight
les saludo	I'm greeting all of you
la playa	the beach
disculpa	pardon me
¿de dónde vienes?	**¿de dónde eres?**
(yo) vengo de	**(yo) soy de**
¿cuántos años tienes?	how old are you?

Estrategia

You will not understand every word in *Salu2*. In fact we never catch everything in any program even in our native language. But you will be able to get the gist of the show by catching some key words and phrases that you *do* know and by using context, both in the program as well as in the text and images in this section.

If you scan **Después de mirar** *before* watching the show, you will understand more of what is in the program.

Después de mirar°

Después... *After watching*

A. ¿Está claro? ¿Cierto o falso? Corrija (*Correct*) las oraciones (*sentences*) falsas, según (*according to*) el video.

	CIERTO	FALSO
1. *Salu2* es un programa matinal (*morning*) de televisión.	☐	☐
2. Es un programa informativo para un público hispanohablante diverso.	☐	☐
3. El estudio está en San Francisco.	☐	☐
4. Hay tres presentadores (*anchors*) y una reportera.	☐	☐
5. Pocas (*Few*) personas hablan español en Los Ángeles.	☐	☐

Laura Sánchez Tejada es reportera. Es de México pero hoy está en California.

B. ¿Quién lo dice? (*Who says it?*) Indique el presentador: **A** = Ana o **V** = Víctor.

1. «...el Pueblo de Nuestra Señora la Reina de los Ángeles de Porciúncula.»

_____

2. «...el nombre de Los Ángeles es un nombre español... » _____

3. «Y vamos a escuchar a personas hispanohablantes de varios países... »

_____

4. «...vamos a escuchar a miembros de la comunidad hispana de Los Ángeles.» _____

5. «...es evidente que muchas personas no hispanas sí hablan español.»

_____

6. «Y hoy vamos a escuchar los saludos de algunos angelinos... » _____

C. Un poco más. (*A little more.*) Match each person with their place of origin.

ORIGEN

a. Chicago   **b.** Los Ángeles   **c.** México   **d.** Puerto Rico   **e.** no se sabe (*not known*)

PERSONAS

1. ___ Ricardo

4. ___ **Michelle y Amy**

2. ___ Wally

5. ___ **Miriam y Verónica**

3. ___ Jennifer

6. ___ **Rubí**

En acción

Filme los saludos de dos o tres personas en español.

¡OJO!

Starting in **Capítulo 2,** two segments of *Salu2* are presented in the **Video: Salu2** section, found at the end of the eBook.

D. Y ahora, ustedes. (*And now it's your turn.*) Practique su (*your*) pronunciación y su talento como presentador(a). Haga el papel (*Play the role*) de Laura y complete el fragmento con su propia (*your own*) información.

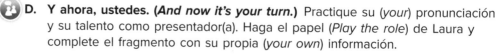

Buenos días a todos. ¿Cómo están ustedes? Yo estoy muy bien. Me llamo _____ y soy **el reportero / la reportera** del programa *Salu2*. Les saludo desde° _____, en el estado de _____.

°Les... *I'm speaking to you (lit. I'm greeting you from)*

Antes de leer°

Antes... *Before reading*

This reading consists of a series of photos and captions. In it, you will learn the names of important geographical features in the Spanish-speaking world. Before you read each photo caption, study the image and identify what is in it. This will help you understand the key words in the caption, which are underlined. These words are often cognates; if not, they are guessable in the context provided by the photo.

As you read, you will probably "get" a lot of information from the captions without actually knowing or understanding all of the words. This happens even when you read in your native language.

Finally, it's a good idea to read the captions more than once. Start by reading them all through quickly, without looking up any words, then start back at the beginning again. You will be surprised by how much more you will understand the second time around.

La geografía del mundo hispanohablante°

mundo... *Spanish-speaking world*

La diversidad del mundo hispano es fabulosa. Lea[a] el texto, mire[b] las fotos ¡y consulte los mapas en la página 13 y al final del libro[c]!

Boyd Hendrikse/Shutterstock

1.

El **volcán** Chimborazo (en el Ecuador), en la **cordillera** de Los Andes. Los Andes forman la cordillera más larga[d] del mundo (ocho mil quinientos[e] kilómetros), y se extienden por[f] siete naciones de Sudamérica.

Al Rod/Pixtal/Age fotostock

2.

Una **playa** en la **península** de Samaná, República Dominicana. En el **mar** Caribe hay tres **islas** de habla española. El mundo hispano también tiene[g] **costas** en el **océano** Atlántico y en el Pacífico.

[a]*Read* [b]*look at* [c]*al... at the end of the book* [d]*más... longest* [e]*ocho... 8,500* [f]*se... they pass through* [g]*has*

(Continúa).

3.

Una selva[h] en México. Hay selvas también en otros países[i] de Centroamérica y Sudamérica.

4.

El **desierto** de Atacama, Chile. Es el más árido[j] del mundo. También hay zonas desérticas en otros países hispanos de Norteamérica a Sudamérica: México, el Perú, Bolivia, la Argentina, Colombia. Y también en España.

5.

El **glaciar** Perito Moreno, en la Patagonia argentina. Chile y la Argentina tienen[k] territorio en la Patagonia y en el continente de la Antártida.

6.

Madrid, la capital de España, en Europa. Es una **ciudad** de gran[l] importancia histórica y cultural. En Latinoamérica también hay muchas ciudades grandes,[m] como la Ciudad de México, Buenos Aires, Santiago,...

[h]*jungle* [i]*naciones* [j]*más... driest* [k]*have* [l]*great* [m]*large*

Comprensión

A. ¿Qué significa? (*What does it mean?*)

Paso 1. In pairs, decide on the meaning of the Spanish words for geographical features that are underlined in the reading.

Paso 2. With your partner, give examples of these geographical features in the United States (or other part of the world) and in the Spanish-speaking world.

1. un volcán
2. una cordillera
3. una playa
4. una península

5. un mar
6. un océano
7. un desierto

B. Los nombres de las regiones del mundo. ¿Cómo se dice *(How do you say it)* en español?

1. Latin America
2. Central America
3. North America

4. South America
5. Europe
6. Antarctica

EN RESUMEN En este capítulo°

En... *In this chapter*

AFTER STUDYING THIS CHAPTER I CAN ...

☐ meet and greet others appropriately in Spanish (4–6)

☐ pronounce words in Spanish and say the alphabet (7–8)

☐ recognize the meaning of many Spanish cognates (9)

☐ describe myself and others (10)

☐ say the numbers 0–30 and use **hay** (14–15)

☐ talk about some of my likes and dislikes (16)

☐ tell time (18)

☐ recognize/describe at least 2–3 facts about the Spanish-speaking world

Vocabulario

This is the active vocabulary for **Capítulo 1.** Be sure that you know all the words, including the meaning of the group titles, before beginning **Capítulo 2.**

Saludos y expresiones de cortesía

Buenos días. Buenas tardes. Buenas noches. Buenas. Muy buenas

**Hola. ¿Qué tal?
¿Cómo estás? ¿Cómo está?**

**Bien. Muy bien. Regular.
¿Y tú? ¿Y usted?**

Adiós. Hasta luego. Hasta mañana. Nos vemos.

(Continúa).

¿Cómo te llamas? ¿Cómo se llama usted?
Me llamo _____ .

¿De dónde eres (tú)? ¿De dónde es (usted)?
(Yo) Soy de _____ .

señor (Sr.), señora (Sra.), señorita (Srta.)
profesor, profesora

Gracias. Muchas gracias.
De nada. No hay de qué.
Por favor. Perdón. (Con) Permiso.

Mucho gusto. Igualmente. Encantado/a.

el saludo   greeting

¿Cómo es usted?

> All forms of infinitives in **red** and **underlined** can be found in Appendix 5.

ser: soy, eres, es

¿Cómo es usted?   What are you like?

Los gustos y preferencias

¿Te gusta _____ ? ¿(A usted) Le gusta _____ ?
(Sí,) Me gusta _____ . (No,) No me gusta _____ .

los gustos   likes

Los números del 0 al 30

cero
uno   once   veintiuno
dos   doce   veintidós
tres   trece   veintitrés
cuatro   catorce   veinticuatro
cinco   quince   veinticinco
seis   dieciséis   veintiséis
siete   diecisiete   veintisiete
ocho   dieciocho   veintiocho
nueve   diecinueve   veintinueve
diez   veinte   treinta

¿Qué hora es?

es la... , son las...
y/menos cuarto (quince)
y media (treinta)

en punto
de la mañana (tarde, noche)
¿a qué hora... ?, a la(s)...

¿Qué hora es?   What time is it?

Las palabras interrogativas

¿cómo?   how?; what?
¿dónde?   where?
¿qué?   what?
¿quién?   who?

la palabra   word

Palabras adicionales

sí/no	yes/no
hay	there is/are
no hay	there is not / are not
¿hay?	is there / are there?
hoy/mañana	today/tomorrow
y/o	and/or
a	to; at (*with time*)
de	of; from; in (*with time*)
en	in; on; at
muy	very
pero	but
también	also

Vocabulario personal

Use this space or a vocabulary notebook to write down other words and phrases you learn in this chapter.

Rodrigo Torres/Glow Images

An Introduction to the Rest of

Puntos de partida

Each chapter of the rest of this textbook has a chapter theme and follows a consistent organization. In addition, every chapter focuses on one or more countries of the Spanish-speaking world.

- **The opening pages of the chapter:** Here you will begin to learn about each chapter's theme and geographical focus. In **Entrevista,** a Spanish speaker will provide a model of things you will be able to say after studying the vocabulary and grammar in the chapter, which are previewed in **En este capítulo.**
- **Vocabulario: Preparación:** This section presents vocabulary related to each chapter's theme. It often has an activity called **Textos de todos los días** that will help you do real-world writing tasks in Spanish. (Sometimes the **Textos** activity is found in the **Gramática** section.)
- **Pronunciación:** Found in **Capítulos 2–4,** this section presents important aspects of Spanish pronunciation and orthography (spelling).
- **Gramática:** This section presents grammar points in context and offers many opportunities for you to practice Spanish, alone and with a partner or group. In a subsection of **Gramática** called **Todo junto** (*All together*), you will practice all of the grammar points from the chapter plus review important grammar topics from previous chapters.
- **Mundo hispano (*The Hispanic World*):** This section of each chapter has three parts. You will learn more about the chapter's countries of focus and other countries (**Enfoque cultural**) and also read authentic materials from the Spanish-speaking world (**Lectura**), including literature. In **Textos orales,** you will practice authentic listening tasks.
- **Portafolio:** This section of each chapter has five parts. In **Entrevista** you will have the chance to answer the questions from the beginning of each chapter with personal information. In **Escritura,** you will write essays and do other real-world writing tasks in Spanish. In **En la comunidad,** you will find ideas for interviewing a Spanish speaker from your community. **Producción audiovisual** provides suggestions for filming interviews in Spanish with classmates and other people. Finally, in **Más ideas para el portafolio,** you will find some ideas for creating a portfolio to showcase what you can do in Spanish.
- **En resumen: En este capítulo:** This section shows you vocabulary and grammar you need to know from each chapter.

2

En la universidad

En este capítulo°

En... *In this chapter*

VOCABULARY

Campus vocabulary   30

Academic subjects   32

GRAMMAR

Singular and plural nouns, plus articles   37, 40

Verbs ending in **-ar**   43

Asking simple questions   50

COUNTRY OF FOCUS: THE UNITED STATES OF AMERICA

En un salón de clase universitario

Simon Jarratt/Fuse/Getty Images

LOS ESTADOS UNIDOS DE AMÉRICA

332,2 (trescientos treinta y dos coma dos) millones de habitantes

- En los Estados Unidos hay más de 60,5 (sesenta coma cinco) millones de personas de origen hispano.
- Es el quinto país del mundo más grande por[a] número de hispanohablantes.
- Hay muchos estados y ciudades con nombres[b] en español.

[a]quinto... *fifth largest country in the world in* [b]muchos... *many states and cities with names*

ENTREVISTA°

Interview

These questions related to the chapter theme are answered here by a native speaker. You will be able to ask and answer them yourself with personal information in the **Entrevista** activity in the **Portafolio** section at the end of the chapter.

Alejandra Hernández Soto contesta las preguntas.

– **¿En qué universidad estudia usted[a]?**

– Estudio Relaciones Internacionales en la UNAM, la Universidad Nacional Autónoma de México.

– **¿Qué materias[b] estudia este[c] semestre/trimestre?**

– Este semestre tomo[d] seis clases: estadística, historia, geografía, economía, sistemas políticos, teorías de las relaciones internacionales. ¡Ah! Y también estudio inglés.

– **¿Cuál[e] es su[f] clase favorita?**

– ¿Mi materia favorita este semestre? No sé.[g] ¡Me gusta todo[h]!

[a]estudia... *are you studying* [b]*subjects* [c]*this* [d]*I'm taking* [e]*Which* [f]*your*
[g]No... *I don't know.* [h]*everything*

You can hear the pronunciation of theme vocabulary words and phrases in the eBook.

En el salón de clase

el pizarrón (blanco)

la profesora

el mapa

el profesor

la ventana

la puerta

la estudiante

Rosa

el libro de texto

la silla

el libro

el estudiante

la mesa

la mochila

el cuaderno

la botella (de agua)

el lápiz

Paco

el papel   Javier

el teléfono celular

el bolígrafo

Nina

el escritorio

la computadora portátil

¿Dónde? Lugares en la universidad

la **biblioteca**	the library
la **cafetería**	the cafeteria
el **cuarto**	the room
el **edificio**	the building
la **librería**	the bookstore
la **oficina**	the office
la **residencia**	the dormitory
el **salón de clase**	the classroom

¿Quién? Personas

el **bibliotecario**	the (male) librarian
la **bibliotecaria**	the (female) librarian
el **compañero (de clase)**	the (male) classmate
la **compañera (de clase)**	the (female) classmate

el **compañero de cuarto**	the (male) roommate
la **compañera de cuarto**	the (female) roommate
el **consejero**	the (male) advisor
la **consejera**	the (female) advisor
el **hombre**	the man
la **mujer**	the woman
el **secretario**	the (male) secretary
la **secretaria**	the (female) secretary

¿Qué? Objetos

la **calculadora**	calculator
la **computadora (portátil)**	(laptop) computer
el **diccionario**	dictionary
el **dinero**	money
el **pizarrón (blanco)**	(white) board
el **teléfono (celular)**	(cellular) telephone

Comunicación

A. Identificaciones. ¿Es hombre o mujer?

MODELO: ¿El profesor? → Es hombre.

1. ¿La consejera?
2. ¿La estudiante?
3. ¿El secretario?
4. ¿El estudiante?
5. ¿La bibliotecaria?
6. ¿El compañero de cuarto?

B. ¿Dónde están (are they)? Tell where these people are in the drawings and identify the numbered people and things.

MODELO: El dibujo (drawing) 1: **Están** en el salón de clase.
1 → la profesora, 2 → la estudiante,...

1.

2.

3.

Nota cultural: El sistema universitario en los países°
hispanohablantes

naciones

El sistema universitario en los países hispanohablantes es muy diferente del sistema de los Estados Unidos. Los estudiantes entran[a] en la universidad directamente en un programa de estudios: sociología, medicina, historia... No existe el concepto de **especialización** o **concentración** (*major*) o **concentración menor o secundaria** (*minor*).

En los países latinoamericanos el título[b] *BA* o *BS* se llama **la licenciatura** (en España se llama **el grado**). Los estudios universitarios para obtener[c] la licenciatura duran[d] de tres a seis años,[e] aunque[f] cuatro años es la norma.

 ¿Cuál[g] es su concentración?

[a]*enter* [b]*degree* [c]*para... for earning*
[d]*last* [e]*years* [f]*although* [g]*What*

Roberaten/123RF

La Universidad de Salamanca, la más antigua (*oldest*) de España

Las materias°

Las... *Subject areas*

The names for most of these subject areas are cognates. See if you can recognize their meaning without looking at the English equivalent. You should learn in particular the names of subject areas that are of interest to you.

la administración de empresas	business administration
las comunicaciones	communications
la economía	economics
el español	Spanish
la filosofía	philosophy
la literatura	literature
las matemáticas	mathematics
la sociología	sociology
las ciencias	sciences
naturales	natural
políticas	political
sociales	social
las humanidades	humanities
las lenguas (extranjeras)	(foreign) languages

la computación

el arte

la química

la física   Rosa   Javier

la sicología

English 101

el inglés

la historia

Así se dice

la administración de empresas = los negocios (*U.S.*)
la computación = la informática (*Spain*)
el español = el castellano (*Spain, Latin America*)

Comunicación

A. Asociaciones. ¿Qué materia(s) asocia usted con (*with*) las siguientes (*following*) personas y cosas (*things*)?

1. la zoología, la botánica, la química
2. Sigmund Freud, Carl Jung, B.F. Skinner
3. CNN, NBC, ESPN
4. la ética, la moral, la esencia de la realidad
5. Shakespeare, Sandra Cisneros, Isabel Allende
6. Frida Kahlo, Pablo Picasso, Salvador Dalí
7. Apple, Microsoft, Google
8. la Guerra (*War*) de la Independencia, la presidencia de Barack Obama, el Imperio Romano

B. ¿Qué estudia usted? Create sentences about your academic interests by using one word or phrase from each column. Can you guess the meaning of the phrases in the left-hand box? If you need help, they are translated at the bottom of the page.*

MODELOS: Deseo estudiar **español y antropología.**
Necesito estudiar **matemáticas.**

1. (No) Estudio_____.	español, francés (*French*), inglés
2. (No) Deseo estudiar_____.	arte, filosofía, literatura, música
3. (No) Necesito estudiar_____.	ciencias políticas, historia
4. (No) Me gusta estudiar_____.	antropología, sicología, sociología
+	biología, física, química
	computación, matemáticas
	¿ ?

¡OJO!

The word **no** before the verb or verb phrase makes the sentence negative.

Vocabulario útil

la contabilidad	accounting
la ingeniería	engineering
el mercadeo	marketing
el periodismo	journalism

These **Repaso** boxes will help you review content you already know on which new material is based.

♻ Repaso° *Review*

In **Capítulo 1**, you used a number of interrogative words to get information: **¿cómo?, ¿dónde?, ¿qué?,** and **¿quién?** Tell what those words mean in these questions. Then answer the questions.

1. ¿Cómo estás?
2. ¿Cómo es usted?
3. ¿De dónde eres?
4. ¿Qué hora es?
5. ¿Quién es la profesora / el profesor?

As you listen to your instructor say questions with those words, you will notice that, in Spanish, the voice falls at the end of questions that begin with interrogative words.

¿Qué hora es?   ¿Cómo es usted?

You will learn more about asking questions in the **Nota comunicativa** on the next page and in **Gramática 4** in this chapter.

an interrogative word / **una palabra interrogativa** = a word used to ask a question about specific information (*who?, where?,* and so on)

---

*1. *I'm studying (I'm not studying)* **2.** *I want to study (I don't want to study)* **3.** *I need to study (I don't need to study)* **4.** *I like to study (I don't like to study)*

Nota comunicativa: Más° palabras interrogativas

More

What? can be expressed with two different words in Spanish.

- **¿Qué?** = asks for a definition or explanation

  ¿Qué es un hospital?   **¿Qué** es esto (*this*)?

- **¿Cuál?** = used for other contexts

  ¿Cuál es la capital de Colombia?   **¿Cuál** es tu materia favorita?

You will learn more about using these words in **Gramática 28 (Cap.10).**

Here are more interrogative words. Guess their meaning from the context in which they appear.

1. —**¿Cuándo** es la clase?
   —Es mañana, a las nueve.
2. —**¿Cuánto** cuesta (*costs*) el cuaderno?
   —Dos dólares.

3. —**¿Cuántos** estudiantes hay en la clase?
   —Hay quince.
4. —**¿Cuántas** naciones hay en Centroamérica?
   —Hay siete.

Remember to drop your voice at the end of a question that begins with a Spanish interrogative word, the opposite of what happens in English, where the voice usually rises. This feature of Spanish may cause you to "hear" a Spanish question as a statement. Compare these questions.

| ¿Qué es un tren? | What's a train? |
| ¿Cuándo es el programa? | When is the program? |

You will use many interrogative words in **Comunicación C** and **D.**

C. **Preguntas y respuestas. (*Questions and answers.*)** Choose the appropriate interrogative words to create meaningful questions, then answer the questions.

cómo   cuál   cuándo   cuántos   dónde   qué   quién

Esta (*This*) universidad

1. ¿_____ se llama esta universidad?
2. ¿_____ está? ¿en (Georgia, Ohio...)?
3. ¿_____ es el presidente / la presidenta?
4. ¿_____ estudiantes hay aproximadamente?

   (mil = 1000, dos mil, tres mil...)

Esta (*This*) clase

5. ¿_____ es el profesor / la profesora? ¿interesante? ¿optimista?
6. ¿ A _____ hora es la clase?
7. ¿_____ está el salón de clase?
8. ¿_____ es la clase? ¿los (*on*) martes y los jueves?
9. ¿_____ estudiantes hay en la clase?

¿Dónde le gusta estudiar a usted?

Lifesize/Yellow Dog Productions/ Getty Images

D. **Intercambios (*Exchanges*)**

Paso 1. Answer the following questions. Pay attention to the words and endings in bold; you have seen most of them before and should be able to guess what they mean.

1. —¿Qué **estudias** este (*this*) semestre/trimestre?
   —**Estudio** _____.
2. —¿Cuál es **tu** (*your*) materia favorita?
   —**Mi** materia favorita es el/la _____.
3. —¿Quién es **tu** profesor(a) en la clase de español?
   —Es el profesor / la profesora _____.
4. —¿Cuántas horas **estudias** al día (*per day*)?
   —**Estudio** _____ horas al día.

> **Estrategia**
>
> Use **el** or **la** with a title when talking about a person, as in item 3.
> **el** profesor Arana
> **la** señora Castellano
> **el** doctor Brook

5. —¿Dónde estud**ias**?

   —**Estudi<u>o</u>** en _____ (la residencia,
   la biblioteca, mi cuarto, mi apartamento, la cafetería...).

6. —¿**Te gusta** estudiar por (*in*) la mañana, por la tarde o por la noche (*at night*)?

   —**Me gusta** estudiar por _____.

Paso 2. Now practice the exchanges in **Paso 1** with a classmate. Use **¿Y tú?**
to ask about your partner.

MODELO: **ESTUDIANTE 1:** ¿Qué **estud<u>ias</u>** este semestre/trimestre?
   ESTUDIANTE 2: **Estudi<u>o</u>** matemáticas, historia, literatura y español. ¿Y tú?
   ESTUDIANTE 3: **Y<u>o</u> estudi<u>o</u>** español, biología, física y arte.

Textos de todos los días°: Hoja de información   todos... *everyday*

At the beginning of a college course, students usually fill out an information sheet. In this activity, you are going to fill out that kind of questionnaire, although this one is probably a bit shorter and easier.

Objetivo: To learn words and categories that often appear in questionnaires, especially academic ones.

Antes de empezar (*Before starting*): Keep in mind the typical things instructors want to know about you and your classmates at the beginning of a semester/quarter. Doing so will help you anticipate and guess the meaning of new words.

Hoja de información - Español Elemental

CURSO

Código del curso (Ej.: SPAN101): _____ Sección: _____

Curso académico: 202___ - 202___

Semestre/Trimestre: __otoño   __invierno   __primavera   __verano[a]

Nombre del profesor / de la profesora: _____

Edificio y salón de clase: _____

Hora de la sección: _____

ESTUDIANTE

Nombre completo: _____

Nombre en clase: _____

Identificación de género: __ hombre __ mujer __ no binario __ prefiero no decirlo

Correo[b] electrónico:

Domicilio[c] durante el curso: _____ en el campus _____ fuera del[d] campus

Soy estudiante del año: __primero (1°)   __segundo (2°)   __tercero (3°)   __cuarto (4°)

Otros cursos que tomas este semestre/trimestre: _____

Nombre de tu consejero académico / consejera académica: _____

Concentración académica (declarada o de interés[e]): _____

---

[a]otoño... *fall winter spring summer*   [b]*Mail*   [c]*Address*   [d]fuera... *off*   [e]declarada... *declared or intended*

PRONUNCIACIÓN

Diphthongs and Linking

 Repaso

Review what you already know about the pronunciation of Spanish vowels by saying the following names and nicknames aloud.

1. Ana **2.** Pepe **3.** Pili **4.** Momo **5.** Lulú

---

a diphthong / **un diptongo** = a combination of two vowel sounds in one syllable

Two successive weak vowels (**i, u**) or a combination of a strong vowel (**a, e, o**) and a weak vowel (**i, u**) are pronounced as a single syllable in Spanish, forming a *diphthong* (**un diptongo**): **Lu**is, s**ie**te, c**ua**derno.

When words are combined to form phrases, clauses, and sentences, they are linked together in pronunciation. In spoken Spanish, it is often difficult to hear the word boundaries—that is, where one word ends and another begins.

Práctica

A. Vocales. Más práctica con las vocales.

1. hablar	regular	reservar	compañera
2. trece	clase	papel	general
3. pizarrón	oficina	bolígrafo	libro
4. hombre	profesor	dólares	los
5. universidad	gusto	lugar	mujer

B. Diptongos. Practique las siguientes (*following*) palabras.

1. historia	secretaria	gracias	estudiante	materia
2. bien	Oviedo	siete	ciencias	diez
3. secretario	biblioteca	adiós	diccionario	Antonio
4. cuaderno	Eduardo	el Ecuador	Guatemala	Managua
5. bueno	nueve	luego	pueblo	Venezuela

C. Frases y oraciones (*sentences*). Practice saying each phrase or sentence as if it were one long word, pronounced without a pause.

1. el papel y el lápiz
2. la profesora y la estudiante
3. las ciencias y las matemáticas
4. la historia y la sicología
5. la secretaria y el profesor
6. el inglés y el español
7. la clase en la biblioteca
8. el libro en la librería
9. Es la una y media.
10. Hay siete estudiantes en la oficina.
11. No estoy muy bien.
12. No hay consejero aquí (*here*).

GRAMÁTICA

As you know, in English and in Spanish, a noun is the name of a person, place, thing, or idea. You have been using nouns since the beginning of *Puntos de partida*. Remember that **el** and **la** mean *the* before nouns. If you can change the Spanish words for *the* to *one* in the following phrases, you already know some of the material in **Gramática 1.**

1. el libro   2. la mesa   3. el profesor   4. la estudiante

1 Naming People, Places, Things, and Ideas (Part 1) • Singular Nouns: Gender and Articles*

Gramática en acción: La lista de la profesora Lifante para el primer día de clase

> Note the use of text in <u>red</u> and <u>underlined</u> in **Gramática en acción** to indicate examples of the grammar point of focus.

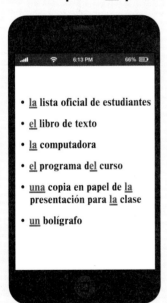

- la lista oficial de estudiantes
- el libro de texto
- la computadora
- el programa del curso
- una copia en papel de la presentación para la clase
- un bolígrafo

Comprensión

Según (*According to*) la lista, ¿es posible o no?

	SÍ	NO
1. **La** materia de **la** profesora Lifante es **el** Español Elemental.	☐	☐
2. **La** lista está en **el** teléfono celular.	☐	☐
3. Hay **una** presentación de PowerPoint en clase hoy.	☐	☐
4. Hay **un** libro de texto obligatorio.	☐	☐

Fstop123/Getty Images

La profesora Lifante

You use nouns to name people, places, things, and ideas. In Spanish, all *nouns* (**los sustantivos**) have either masculine or feminine *gender* (**el género**). This is a purely grammatical feature; it does not mean that Spanish speakers perceive things or ideas as having male or female attributes.

Professor Lifante's list for the first day of class ■ *the official list of students* ■ *the textbook* ■ *the computer* ■ *the course syllabus* ■ *a paper copy of the class presentation* ■ *a pen*

*The grammar sections of **Puntos de partida** are numbered consecutively throughout the book. If you need to review a particular grammar point, the index will refer you to its page number.*

Since the gender of all nouns must be memorized, it is best to learn the definite article along with the noun; that is, learn **el lápiz** rather than just **lápiz**. The definite article is given with nouns in vocabulary lists in this book.

an article / **un artículo** = a determiner that sets off a noun

a definite article / **un artículo definido** = an article that indicates a specific noun (*the*)

an indefinite article / **un artículo indefinido** = an article that indicates an unspecified noun (*a, an*)

Nouns / **Los sustantivos**

	Masculine / **Masculino**		Feminine / **Femenino**	
Definite Articles / **Los artículos definidos**	<u>el</u> hombre <u>el</u> lib<u>ro</u>	the man the book	<u>la</u> mujer <u>la</u> mes<u>a</u>	the woman the table
Indefinite Articles / **Los artículos indefinidos**	<u>un</u> hombre <u>un</u> lib<u>ro</u>	a man a book	<u>una</u> mujer <u>una</u> mes<u>a</u>	a woman a table

Gender / **El género**

Note the two-column format of grammar explanations. Explanations are on the left, examples are on the right, and text in <u>red</u> and <u>underlined</u> will help you see what's important.

1. Masculine Nouns
Nouns that refer to male beings and most other nouns that end in **-o** are *masculine* (**masculino**) in gender.

Sustantivos masculinos
<u>hombre</u>, lib<u>ro</u>

2. Feminine Nouns
Nouns that refer to female beings and most other nouns that end in **-a, -ción, -sión, -xión, -tad,** and **-dad** are *feminine* (**femenino**) in gender.

Sustantivos femeninos
<u>mujer</u>, mes<u>a</u>, sill<u>a</u>   na<u>ción</u>, mi<u>sión</u>, cone<u>xión</u>   liber<u>tad</u>, universi<u>dad</u>

3. Other Endings
Nouns that have other endings and that do not refer to either male or female beings may be masculine or feminine. The gender of these words must be memorized.

el lápi<u>z</u>, el pape<u>l</u>, el saló<u>n</u> de clas<u>e</u>, la clas<u>e</u>, la noch<u>e</u>, la tard<u>e</u>

4. Spelling Changes
Many nouns that refer to people indicate gender ...
• by changing the last vowel
OR
• by adding **-a** to the last consonant of the masculine form to make it feminine

el compañer<u>o</u> → la compañer<u>a</u>
el bibliotecari<u>o</u> → la bibliotecari<u>a</u>

un profeso<u>r</u> → una profeso<u>ra</u>

5. Some Nouns that Refer to People
Many other nouns that refer to people have a single form for both masculine and feminine genders. Gender is made clear by context or by an article.

However, a few such nouns that end in **-e** also have a feminine form that ends in **-a.**

Masculino	Femenino
<u>el</u> estudiante	<u>la</u> estudiante
<u>el</u> dentista	<u>la</u> dentista
<u>el</u> presidente	<u>la</u> presidenta
<u>el</u> cliente	<u>la</u> clienta
<u>el</u> dependiente (*clerk*)	<u>la</u> dependienta

¡OJO!

Common exceptions to the normal rules of gender are the words **el día** and **el mapa**, which are masculine in gender. Many words ending in **-ma** are also masculine: **el problema, el programa, el sistema,** and so on.

Articles / Los artículos

1. Definite Articles

In English, there is only one *definite article* (**el artículo definido**): *the*.

In Spanish, there are two definite articles for singular nouns, one masculine (**el**) and one feminine (**la**).

Artículo definido: *the*		
m. sing.	→	**el**
f. sing.	→	**la**

2. Indefinite Articles

In English, the singular *indefinite article* (**el artículo indefinido**) is *a* or *an*.

In Spanish, the indefinite article, like the definite article, must agree with the gender of the noun: **un** for masculine nouns, **una** for feminine nouns.

Un and **una** can mean *one* or *a/an*, depending on context.

Artículo indefinido: *a, an*		
m. sing.	→	**un**
f. sing.	→	**una**

¡OJO!

The word **hay** is followed by indefinite articles only, singular or plural: **Hay una computadora / unas computadoras en la mesa.** You will learn about plural articles in **Gramática 2**.

One of the first two activities in **Práctica y comunicación** will always include a brief **Autoprueba** (*Self-test*). Take it to see if you understand the basics of the grammar point. The answers are at the bottom of the page.

Gender Summary

MASCULINO	FEMENINO
el, un	**la, una**
-o	-a
	-ción, -sión, -xión
	-dad, -tad

Práctica y comunicación

A. **Autoprueba.** Escoja (*Choose*) el artículo definido apropiado.

1. _____ (el / la) libro
2. _____ (el / la) mujer
3. _____ (el / la) oficina
4. _____ (el / la) escritorio
5. _____ (el / la) libertad
6. _____ (el / la) acción

B. Los artículos

Paso 1. Dé (*Give*) el artículo definido apropiado (**el, la**).

1. edificio
2. biblioteca
3. bolígrafo
4. mochila
5. hombre
6. diccionario
7. universidad
8. estudiante
9. señora
10. nación
11. bibliotecario
12. calculadora

Paso 2. Ahora (*Now*) dé el artículo indefinido apropiado (**un, una**).

1. día
2. mañana
3. problema
4. lápiz
5. clase
6. dentista
7. condición
8. programa

C. Escenas de la universidad

Paso 1. Haga una oración (*Form a sentence*) con las palabras indicadas.

MODELO: estudiante / librería → **Hay un** estudiante **en la** librería.

1. consejero / oficina
2. profesora / salón de clase
3. lápiz / mesa
4. cuaderno / escritorio
5. libro / mochila
6. bolígrafo / silla
7. palabra / papel
8. oficina / residencia
9. compañero / biblioteca
10. diccionario / librería

Paso 2. Now create new sentences by changing one of the words in each item in **Paso 1.** Try to come up with as many variations as possible.

MODELOS: Hay un estudiante en **la residencia.** Hay **una profesora** en la librería.

D. Definiciones. En parejas (*pairs*), definan las siguientes (*following*) palabras en español como (*as*) **edificio, materia, objeto** o **persona,** según (*according to*) el modelo.

> MODELO: biblioteca → **ESTUDIANTE 1:** ¿Qué es una biblioteca?
> **ESTUDIANTE 2:** Es **un edificio.**

1. cliente
2. bolígrafo
3. residencia

4. dependienta
5. hotel (*m.*)
6. computadora

7. computación
8. inglés
9. ¿ ?

 E. Nuestra (*Our*) universidad. En parejas (*pairs*), hagan oraciones (*form sentences*) sobre su (*about your*) universidad.

> MODELOS: **1.** mi consejero/a → El profesor Márquez es mi consejero.
> cafetería → Hay una cafetería. Se llama (*It's called*)
> Foster Hall. (No hay una cafetería.)

1. mi consejero/a
2. mi profesor(a) de _____ (materia)
3. residencia

4. biblioteca principal
5. cafetería
6. edificio de clases

Estrategia

Remember to use the article **el** or **la** to refer to someone who has a title: **el profesor Márquez.**

2 Naming People, Places, Things, and Ideas (Part 2) • Nouns and Articles: Plural Forms

Gramática en acción: Un anuncio

You don't have to understand all of the words in this ad (**anuncio**) to get its general meaning. What is it an ad for?

ᵃen... *abroad*

Comprensión

1. How many nouns (including proper nouns) can you find in the ad? Can you guess the meaning of most of them?
2. Some of the nouns in the ad are plural. Can you tell how to make nouns plural in Spanish?
3. Look for the Spanish equivalent of these words: *adults, preparation, program, courses.*
4. The word **idioma** is a false cognate; it never means *idiom.* What do you think it means?

	Singular	Plural	
Nouns Ending in a Vowel / **Los sustantivos que terminan en una vocal**	**el** libro **la** mesa **un** libro **una** mesa	**los** libros **las** mesas **unos** libros **unas** mesas	the books the tables some books some tables
Nouns Ending in a Consonant / **Los sustantivos que terminan en una consonante**	**la** universidad **un** papel **un** lápiz	**las** universidades **unos** papeles **unos** lápices	the universities some papers some pencils

Sustantivos plurales
vowel + **-s**
consonant + **-es**
-z ➔ **-ces**

1. Plural Endings

Spanish nouns that end in a vowel form plurals by adding **-s.** Nouns that end in a consonant add **-es.** Nouns that end in the consonant **-z** change the **-z** to **-c** before adding **-es: lápiz ➔ lápices.**

Artículos plurales
el ➔ **los**   **un** ➔ **unos**
la ➔ **las**   **una** ➔ **unas**

2. Plural of Articles

The definite and indefinite articles also have plural forms:

el ➔ los, la ➔ las, un ➔ unos, una ➔ unas.

Unos and **unas** mean *some, several,* or *a few.*

3. Groups of People

In Spanish, the masculine plural form of a noun is used to refer to a group that includes both males and females.

los amigos = *the friends* (all male or both male and female)
las amigas = *the friends* (only female)
unos extranjeros = *some foreigners* (all male or both male and female)
unas extranjeras = *some foreign women*

Práctica y comunicación

Plural Forms Summary

el ➔ los un ➔ unos
la ➔ las una ➔ unas
vowel + **-s**
consonant + **-es**
-z ➔ -ces

A. **Autoprueba.** Empareje (*Match*) los sustantivos con los artículos apropiados.

1. libros
2. hombre
3. librería
4. profesoras

   a. el
   b. las
   c. unos
   d. una

B. **Los artículos de un texto.** Lea (*Read*) **Algo sobre el nombre América** (al final de **Gramática 3**) e (*and*) indique los artículos. ¿Son femeninos o masculinos, definidos (**el, la…**) o indefinidos (**un…**), plurales o singulares?

MODELO: la = femenino, definido, singular

C. **Cambios (*Changes*)**

Paso 1. Singular ➔ plural.

1. la mesa
2. el papel
3. el amigo
4. la oficina
5. un cuaderno
6. un lápiz
7. una universidad
8. un bolígrafo
9. un teléfono

Paso 2. Plural ➔ singular.

1. los profesores
2. las computadoras
3. las bibliotecarias
4. los estudiantes
5. unos hombres
6. unas tardes
7. unas residencias
8. unas sillas
9. unos escritorios

Prác. A: Answers 1. c 2. a 3. d 4. b

Vocabulario útil

el experimento
el laboratorio

D. Identificaciones. Nombre (*Name*) las personas, los objetos y los lugares.

MODELOS: Hay _____ en _____. → Hay **unos estudiantes** en **el salón de clase.**

Hay **una profesora** en **el laboratorio.**

1.

2.

E. ¡Ojo alerta!*

Paso 1. ¿Cuáles son las semejanzas (*similarities*) y las diferencias entre (*between*) los dos salones de clase? Hay por lo menos (*at least*) seis diferencias.

En el dibujo A, hay _____.
En el dibujo B, hay solo (*only*) _____.
En el escritorio del dibujo A, hay _____.
En el escritorio del dibujo B, (no) hay _____.

A.

B.

Paso 2. Ahora indique qué hay en su propio (*your own*) salón de clase.

MODELO: En mi salón de clase hay _____. En mi escritorio hay _____.

In Spanish, activities like this one are often called **¡Ojo alerta!** = *Eagle Eye!*

These sentences contain Spanish verbs that you have already used. Pick them out.

1. Soy estudiante en la Universidad de _____.
2. Este (*This*) semestre/trimestre, estudio español.
3. En el futuro, deseo estudiar francés.

If you selected **estudiar** in addition to three other words, you did very well! You will learn more about Spanish verbs and how they are used in **Gramática 3**.

3 Expressing Actions • Subject Pronouns (Part 1) • Present Tense of -ar Verbs; Negation

Gramática en acción: ¿Una escena típica?

Manu **habla** enfrente de la clase porque hoy es su presentación. Pero... ¡varias personas **no escuchan**!

- Laila **manda** un mensaje de texto.
- Kevin y Lisa **trabajan** en otras materias.
- Teresa **mira** por la ventana.
- ¿Y **usted**? ¿También **desea estar** en otro lugar?

Comprensión

En la escena...

1. ¿Cuántos estudiantes **hablan**?
2. ¿Cuántas personas **escuchan** la presentación?
3. ¿Quién **manda** un mensaje de texto?
4. ¿Quién **estudia** chino?

Subject Pronouns / **Los pronombres personales**

Singular		Plural	
yo	I	**nosotros / nosotras**	we
tú	you (*familiar*)	**vosotros / vosotras**	you (*familiar, Spain*)
usted (Ud.)*	you (*formal*)	**ustedes (Uds.)***	you (*formal*)
él	he	**ellos**	they (*m., m. + f.*)
ella	she	**ellas**	they (*f.*)

> *a subject* / **un sujeto** = the person or thing that performs the action in a sentence
>
> *a pronoun* / **un pronombre** = a word that takes the place of a noun or represents a person

---

A typical scene? *Manu is talking in front of the class because today is his presentation. But ... several people are not listening!* ■ *Laila is sending a text message.* ■ *Kevin and Lisa are working on other subjects.* ■ *Teresa is looking out the window.* ■ *And you? Do you want to be somewhere else too?*

Usted** *and* **ustedes** *are frequently abbreviated in writing as* **Ud.** *or* **Vd., and* **Uds.** *or* **Vds.***, respectively.*

1. Subject Pronouns and Gender

The person that performs the action in a sentence is expressed by *subject pronouns* (**los pronombres personales**).

In Spanish, the equivalents of *he* and *she* and all plural subject pronouns have masculine and feminine forms. The masculine plural form is used to refer to a group of males as well as to a group of males and females.

Manuel	→ **él**	*he*
Sara	→ **ella**	*she*
Manuel + Juan	→ **ellos**	*they*
Manuel + Sara	→ **ellos**	*they*
María + Sara	→ **ellas**	*they*

¡OJO!

As in English-speaking countries, Spanish speakers are creating multiple ways of expressing non-binary gender identities.

2. Pronouns for *you*

Spanish has different words for *you*. In general,

- **tú** is used with a friend or a family member.
- **usted** is used with people with whom the speaker has a more formal or distant relationship.

The situations in which **tú** and **usted** are used also vary among different countries and regions.

tú	→	friend, family member
usted	→	formal or distant relationship

¡OJO!

- Unless your professor says otherwise, use **usted**.
- In the text, direction lines address you as **usted**, so that you become familiar with those forms. Models for interactions with classmates use **tú**.

3. Plural of *you*

In Latin American Spanish, the plural for both **usted** and **tú** is **ustedes**.

In Spain, however, **vosotros/vosotras** is exclusively the plural of **tú**, while **ustedes** is exclusively used as the plural of **usted**.

Latinoamérica

tú		
usted	→	**ustedes**

España

tú	→	**vosotros/vosotras**
usted	→	**ustedes**

4. Omitting Subject Pronouns

Subject pronouns are not used as frequently in Spanish as they are in English, and they are very often omitted. You will learn more about the uses of Spanish subject pronouns in **Gramática 8 (Cap. 3)**.

Present Tense of **-ar** Verbs / **El tiempo presente de los verbos -ar**

1. Infinitives

As you know, the *infinitive* (**el infinitivo**) of a verb indicates the action or state of being, with no reference to who or what performs the action or when it is done (present, past, or future).

Infinitives in English are indicated by *to: to* speak, *to* eat, *to* live.

In Spanish, all infinitives end in **-ar, -er,** or **-ir**.

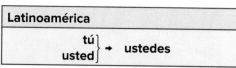

-ar:	**hablar**	to speak
-er:	**comer**	to eat
-ir:	**vivir**	to live

an infinitive / **un infinitivo** = a verb form that indicates action or state of being without reference to person, tense, or number

a tense / **un tiempo** = the quality of a verb form that indicates time: present, past, or future

2. Conjugating Verbs

To *conjugate* (**conjugar**) a verb means to give the various forms of the verb with their corresponding subjects: *I speak, you speak, she speaks,* and so on.

All regular Spanish verbs are conjugated by adding *personal endings* (**las terminaciones personales**) that reflect the subject doing the action. These are added to the *stem* (**la raíz**), which is the infinitive minus the infinitive ending.

Infinitive / **Infinitivo**		Stem / **Raíz**
habl<u>ar</u>	→	habl-
com<u>er</u>	→	com-
viv<u>ir</u>	→	viv-

3. Present Tense Endings

The personal endings that are added to the stem of all regular **-ar** verbs to form the *present tense* (**el presente**) are given here. The chart below shows those same endings attached to the stem of the infinitive **hablar** (**habl-**).

Las terminaciones *-ar* del tiempo presente
-o, -as, -a, -amos, -áis, -an

habl<u>ar</u> (*to speak; to talk*): habl-					
Singular			**Plural**		
(yo)	habl**o**	I speak	**(nosotros)** **(nosotras)**	habl<u>amos</u>	we speak
(tú)	habl<u>as</u>	you speak	**(vosotros)** **(vosotras)**	habl<u>áis</u>	you speak
(usted) **(él)** **(ella)**	habl<u>a</u>	you speak he speaks she speaks	**(ustedes)** **(ellos)** **(ellas)**	habl<u>an</u>	you speak they (*m., m. + f.*) speak they (*f.*) speak

4. Important *-ar* Verbs

Here are some **-ar** verbs used in this chapter.

Los verbos *-ar*	
bailar	to dance
buscar	to look for
cantar	to sing
comprar	to buy
desear	to want
enseñar	to teach
escuchar	to listen (to)
estudiar	to study
hablar	to speak; to talk
hablar por teléfono	to talk on the phone
mandar un mensaje (de texto)	to (send a) text
necesitar	to need
pagar	to pay (for)
practicar	to practice
regresar	to return (*to a place*)
tocar	to play (*a musical instrument*)
tomar	to take; to drink
trabajar	to work

¡OJO!

Note that in Spanish the meaning of the English word *for* is included in the verbs **buscar** (*to look for*) and **pagar** (*to pay for*); *to* is included in **escuchar** (*to listen to*).

5. Conjugated Verb + *Infinitive*

As in English, when two Spanish verbs are used in a row and there is no change of subject, the second verb is usually in the infinitive form.

Necesito mand<u>ar</u> *I need to send a*
un mensaje de texto. *text (message).*

Me gusta bail<u>ar</u>. *I like to dance.*

6. Tense

In both English and Spanish, conjugated verb forms also indicate the *time* or *tense* (**el tiempo**) of the action: *I speak* (present), *I spoke* (past).

Some English equivalents of the present tense forms of Spanish verbs are shown at the right.

hablo	I speak	Simple present tense
	I am speaking	Present progressive (indicates an action in progress)
	I will speak	Near future action

¡OJO!

The exact English equivalent of a Spanish verb form depends on the context in which the verb appears. In the following sentence, the word **mañana** indicates a future action, so **hablo** means *I will speak:* **Hablo con Juan mañana.**

Negation / **La negación**

In Spanish the word **no** is placed before the conjugated verb to make a negative sentence.

*subject + **no** + verb*

El estudiante **<u>no</u> habla** español. *The student doesn't speak Spanish.*

No, **<u>no</u> necesito** dinero. *No, I don't need money.*

Summary of *-ar* Verb Endings

(yo) -o	(nosotros/as) -amos
(tú) -as	(vosotros/as) -áis
(usted, él/ella) -a	(ustedes, ellos/as) -an

Práctica y comunicación

A. Asociaciones. ¿Qué verbos asocia usted con las siguientes (*following*) ideas? Dé (*Give*) infinitivos.

MODELO: la música → escuchar, tocar, bailar,...

1. español
2. mucho (*a lot of*) dinero
3. en la librería
4. en el salón de clase
5. un coche (*car*)
6. a la residencia
7. Coca-Cola o café (*coffee*)
8. la música

B. Mi compañero/a y yo

Paso 1. Autoprueba. Complete los verbos con las terminaciones apropiadas.

1. pagar: (yo) pag_____
2. tocar: (tú) toc_____
3. hablar: (ella) habl_____
4. comprar: (nosotros) compr_____
5. escuchar: (usted) escuch_____
6. trabajar: (ellos) trabaj_____

Paso 2. ¿Sí o no? Complete las oraciones de forma personal con la forma **yo** de los verbos. Use **no** delante del (*in front of the*) verbo si es necesario.

MODELO: **1.** Necesit___ un coche. → Necesit**o** un coche. (**No** necesit**o** un coche.)

1. Necesit___ un coche.
2. Trabaj___ en la biblioteca de la universidad.
3. Cant___ en un coro (*choir*).
4. Tom___ una clase de ciencias sociales este (*this*) semestre/trimestre.
5. Bail___ salsa en las fiestas.
6. Habl___ inglés como (*as a*) lengua nativa.
7. Mand___ muchos mensajes todos los días (*every day*).
8. Toc___ un instrumento musical.

Paso 3. En parejas (*pairs*), hagan y contesten preguntas (*ask and answer questions*) basadas en el **Paso 2.**

MODELO: **1.** Necesito un coche. → ESTUDIANTE 1: ¿**Necesitas** un coche?

ESTUDIANTE 2: Sí, **necesito** un coche. (No, **no necesito** un coche.)

Prác. A: Answers, Paso 1. 1. pago 2. tocas 3. habla 4. compramos 5. escucha 6. trabajan

46 ■ cuarenta y seis

Capítulo 2 En la universidad

C. Una o más personas

Paso 1. Cambie por (*Change to*) un sujeto plural.

MODELOS: Él no desea tomar café. → **Ellos** no **desean** tomar café.
Yo no deseo tomar café. → **Nosotros** no **deseamos** tomar café.

1. Ella no desea estudiar francés.
2. Usted baila muy bien el tango.
3. ¿Mandas mensajes con frecuencia?
4. Escucho la radio con frecuencia.

Paso 2. Ahora cambie por un sujeto singular. En los números 2 y 4 hay más de una opción.

1. Ellas no buscan el dinero.
2. Los estudiantes no necesitan seis clases.
3. Pagamos mucho dinero de matrícula (*tuition*).
4. ¿Compran ustedes muchos libros?

D. La fiesta de Marcos

Paso 1. Complete el párrafo con las formas apropiadas de los verbos entre paréntesis.

Esta noche[a] hay una fiesta en casa de Marcos.[b] Marcos es de Guatemala y su compañero de apartamento, Julio, es de Honduras. Hay quince amigos en la fiesta. Una persona _____ (tocar)[1] la guitarra y las otras personas _____ (cantar)[2] o _____ (escuchar).[3] ¡Yo solo _____ (desear)[4] bailar!

Marta _____ (hablar)[5] con Nati mucho tiempo.[c] Pero Nati _____ (desear)[6] bailar con Miguel, el estudiante mexicano, porque[d] él _____ (bailar)[7] muy bien. Eduardo, Marcos y yo _____ (bailar)[8] en grupo.

A las once de la noche Julio _____ (buscar)[9] pizza para todos.[e] Pero todos _____ (pagar).[10]

¡La fiesta es fantástica! _____ (*Yo:* Practicar)[11] español toda la noche[f] porque todos los amigos de Marcos _____ (hablar)[12] español. ¡Eduardo y yo _____ (regresar)[13] a casa[g] a las dos de la mañana!

Una foto en una fiesta

Wassily-architect/Shutterstock

[a]Esta... *Tonight* [b]en... *at Marco's place (lit., house)* [c]mucho... *for a long time* [d]*because* [e]para... *for everyone* [f]toda... *all night* [g]a... *home*

Paso 2. Comprensión. Indique si las siguientes (*following*) oraciones son **ciertas, falsas** o **no se sabe** (*not known*).

	CIERTO	FALSO	NO SE SABE
1. La persona que (*who*) habla es hispanohablante.	☐	☐	☐
2. Nati baila muy bien.	☐	☐	☐
3. Marcos y Julio compran la pizza.	☐	☐	☐
4. Todos tocan la guitarra y bailan.	☐	☐	☐
5. Marta habla mucho (*a lot*) en la fiesta.	☐	☐	☐

E. Oraciones lógicas. Form eight complete logical sentences by using one word or phrase from each column. Many combinations are possible. Use the correct form of the verbs and make any sentences negative.

MODELO: (Yo) No estudio francés.

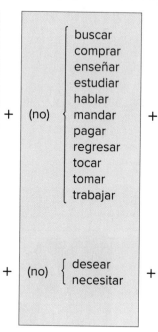

yo
tú (un[a] estudiante)
nosotros (los miembros de esta clase)
los estudiantes de aquí (*here*)
el extranjero
un secretario
una profesora de español
una dependienta

¡OJO!

Remember that the verb form that follows **desear** or **necesitar** is the infinitive, just as in English.

+ (no)
buscar
comprar
enseñar
estudiar
hablar
mandar
pagar
regresar
tocar
tomar
trabajar

+

la guitarra, el piano, el violín
el edificio de ciencias
en la cafetería, en la universidad, en casa (*at home*)
en una oficina, en una librería
a casa muy tarde (*very late*)/temprano (*early*)
a la biblioteca a las dos
muchos/pocos (*many/few*) mensajes
francés, alemán (*German*), italiano, inglés
bien el español
los libros de texto, la matrícula
libros y cuadernos en la librería

+ (no)
desear
necesitar

+

tomar una clase de computación
hablar bien el español
estudiar más
comprar una calculadora, una mochila
pagar la matrícula en septiembre

¡OJO!

Remember that **de la mañana (tarde, noche)** are used when a specific hour of the day is mentioned. Also, remember to use **a la una / a las dos (tres...)** to express a specific time of day.

Generalmente estudio en casa **por** la mañana. Hoy estudio con Javier en la biblioteca **a las** diez **de** la mañana.

Nota comunicativa: Cómo expresar las partes del día

You can use the preposition **por** to mean *in* or *during* when expressing the part of the day in which something happens.

Estudio **por** la mañana y trabajo **por** la tarde. **Por** la noche, estoy en casa.

I study in the morning and I work in the afternoon. At night I'm at home.

You will practice these phrases in **Práctica F.**

F. Intercambios (*Exchanges*)

Paso 1. Use los siguientes verbos y frases para crear (*create*) cinco preguntas (*questions*) interesantes.

MODELO: ¿**Cantas** bien?

1. cantar o bailar
2. estudiar o trabajar
3. necesitar
4. tomar
5. tomar

+

bien/mal (*poorly*), mucho/poco (*a little*)
muchas/pocas (*few*) horas, todos los días
dinero, libros, una computadora, pagar la matrícula
_____ (número de clases) / café o té por la mañana
clases por la mañana / por la tarde / por la noche

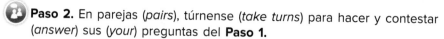 **Paso 2.** En parejas (*pairs*), túrnense (*take turns*) para hacer y contestar (*answer*) sus (*your*) preguntas del **Paso 1.**

MODELO: **ESTUDIANTE 1**: ¿Cantas bien?
ESTUDIANTE 2: Sí, **canto** bien. (No, **canto** mal.)

Nota comunicativa: El verbo *estar*

> Remember that all forms of infinitives in **red** and **underlined** can be found in Appendix 5.

Estar is a Spanish **-ar** verb that means *to be*. You have already used forms of it to ask how others are feeling or to tell where things are located. Here is the complete present tense conjugation of **estar.** Note that the **yo** form is irregular. The other forms take regular **-ar** endings, and some have an accent to maintain the stress pattern.

(yo)	est<u>oy</u>	I am	(nosotros/as)	estamos	we are
(tú)	est<u>ás</u>	you are	(vosotros/as)	estáis	you are
(usted)	est<u>á</u>	you are	(ustedes)	est<u>á</u>n	you are
(él/ella)	est<u>á</u>	he/she is	(ellos/ellas)	est<u>á</u>n	they are

You will learn the uses of the verb **estar,** along with those of **ser** (a second Spanish verb that means *to be*) gradually, over the next several chapters. Review what you already know by answering these questions.

1. ¿Cómo está usted en este momento (*right now*)?
2. ¿Cómo están sus (*your*) compañeros? (**Mis** compañeros...)
3. ¿Dónde está usted en este momento?

You will use **estar** in **Práctica G.**

G. ¿Dónde están? Tell where these people are and what they are doing.

> MODELO: **FOTO 1:** La Srta. Martínez _____. →
> La Srta. Martínez **está en una oficina. Trabaja por la tarde. Necesita...**

Vocabulario útil

buscar información	**tomar apuntes**
hablar por teléfono	to take notes
mandar un mensaje	**usar una computadora**
preparar la lección	
pronunciar las palabras	

¡OJO!

Remember to use the definite article with titles when you are talking *about* a person: **el señor Santana, la profesora Aguilar,** and so on.

Fabio Cardoso/Tetra images/Getty Images

Digital Vision/Getty Images

1. La Srta. Martínez _____.
   Trabaja por _____.
   Necesita _____.

2. Estas (*These*) personas _____.
   El profesor _____.
   Una estudiante _____.
   Muchos (*Many*) estudiantes _____.

Algo sobre° el nombre América

Algo... *Something about*

En los países[a] hispanohablantes América es un continente que incluye[b] Norteamérica, Centroamérica y Sudamérica. Por eso,[c] el término **americano/a** define a las personas y cosas de todo el continente, no solo de los Estados Unidos. La palabra **estadounidense** es específica para los Estados Unidos.

Para abreviar el nombre de los Estados Unidos hay varias formas comunes (según[d] los países): E.U., EU, E.U.A, EE.UU., EEUU. *USA* no es una abreviatura del español.

¿Cuántos continentes hay en este[e] hemisferio, según se enseña[f] en los Estados Unidos?

[a]naciones   [b]que... *that includes*   [c]Por... *That's why*   [d]*according to*   [e]*this*   [f]según... *as is taught*

4 Getting Information (Part 1) • Asking Yes/No Questions

Gramática en acción: La matriculación

Digital Vision/Getty Images

PENÉLOPE: ... y ahora necesito una clase más por la mañana. **¿Hay espacio** en la clase de Sociología 2?

JAVIER: A ver... No, no hay.

PENÉLOPE: **¿Hay una clase** de historia o de matemáticas?

JAVIER: Solo por la noche. **¿Deseas tomar** una clase por la noche?

PENÉLOPE: ¡Ay, chico, es imposible! Trabajo por la noche.

JAVIER: Pues... ¿qué tal la clase de Literatura Hispana en los Estados Unidos?

PENÉLOPE: ¡Perfecto! ¡Me gusta mucho la literatura! ¿Cuándo es la clase?

Comprensión

1. **¿Necesita Penélope** dos clases más?
2. **¿Hay espacio** en Sociología 2?
3. ¿Cuál es el problema con los cursos de historia y matemáticas?
4. ¿Qué curso recomienda Javier por fin?

You have been asking questions since the beginning of *Puntos de partida*, and you learned more about asking questions in **Nota comunicativa** (page 34). This section will help you review all that you know about this topic as well as learn another way to ask questions in Spanish.

Registration PENÉLOPE: ... *and now I need one more class in the morning. Is there room in Sociology 2?* JAVIER: *Let's see ... No, there isn't (room).* PENÉLOPE: *Is there a history or a math class?* JAVIER: *Only at night. Do you want to take a night class?* PENÉLOPE: *Oh boy, that's impossible! I work at night.* JAVIER: *Well ... what about the class about Hispanic Literature in the United States?* PENÉLOPE: *Perfect! I love literature! When is the class?*

Types of Questions / **Tipos de preguntas**

There are two kinds of *questions* (**las preguntas**) in English and in Spanish.

1. *Information questions* ask for information, for facts. They typically begin with *interrogative words* (**las palabras interrogativas**). You have already learned a number of them.

> **Preguntas informativas**
>
> —¿**Qué** lengua habla usted?
> —Hablo español.

2. *Yes/No questions* can be answered by a simple **sí** or **no**.

> **Preguntas informativas**
>
> —¿Habla usted francés?
> —No.

¡OJO!

Remember that intonation drops at the end of an information question in Spanish, whereas it rises in English.

Forming Yes/No Questions / **La formación de preguntas sí/no**

There are two ways to form this kind of question.

1. *Rising intonation:* The simplest way is to make your voice rise at the end of a statement. Doing so makes the statement into a question.

> **STATEMENT:** Usted trabaja aquí todos los días.
> *You work here every day.*
>
> **QUESTION:** ¿Usted trabaja aquí todos los días?
> *Do you work here every day?*

2. *Inversion:* Another way to form yes/no questions is to invert (transpose) the order of the subject and verb, in addition to making your voice rise at the end of the question. You can also put the subject all the way at the end of the question.

> **STATEMENT:** **Usted** trabaja aquí todos los días.
>
> **QUESTION:** ¿Trabaja **usted** aquí todos los días?
>
> **STATEMENT:** **María** toca el piano.
>
> **QUESTION:** ¿Toca el piano **María**?

Subjects in Questions and Answers / **Los sujetos en las preguntas y respuestas**

1. When a question is asked about a third person or persons (**Tomás, ella, ellos, los amigos,**...), the subject and the verb of the question and answer *are the same*. However, the subject is usually not repeated in the answer. In fact, the subject may not even appear in the question if it is clear to whom the question refers to.

> **SUBJECT:** **Tomás**
> **VERB:** **toca**
>
> ¿**Toca** el piano Tomás? ⎤
> ¿**Toca** Tomás el piano? ⎬ →
> ¿Tomás **toca** el piano? ⎦
>
> Sí, **toca** el piano muy bien.
>
> *Does Tom play the piano?* →
> *Yes, he plays the piano very well.*
>
> ¿**Toca** más instrumentos? →
> Sí, **toca** la trompeta también. /
> No, no **toca** más instrumentos.
>
> *Does he play more instruments?* →
> *Yes, he also plays the trumpet. / No, he doesn't play any more instruments.*

(Continúa).

¡OJO!

Notice that the subjects (**Tomás, Ángela y Carlos**) are not expressed in the answers, and no subject pronouns (**él, ellos**) are needed in the Spanish answers because in this context **toca** = *he plays* and **toman** = *they are taking*.

SUBJECTS: **Ángela y Carlos**
VERB: **toman**

¿**Toman** cálculo Ángela y Carlos? ⎫
¿**Toman** Ángela y Carlos cálculo? ⎬ →
¿Ángela y Carlos **toman** cálculo?

Sí, **toman** cálculo y álgebra.

Are Angela and Carlos taking calculus? →
Yes, they're taking calculus and algebra.

---

2. When asking a question directly *to* a person with whom you are speaking, the subject and verb *are different* in the question and answer.

¡OJO!

¿tú? → yo
¿Cant**as**? → Cant**o**.
¿ustedes? → nosotros/as
¿Dese**an**? → Dese**amos**.

QUESTION SUBJECT: **tú**	¿**Cantas** bien? → *Do you sing well?* →
ANSWER SUBJECT: **yo**	Sí, **canto** bien. *Yes, I do (sing well).*
QUESTION SUBJECT: **ustedes**	¿**Desean** ustedes trabajar más? → *Do you want to continue working?* →
ANSWER SUBJECT: **nosotros**	No, **deseamos** regresar a casa. *No, we want to go home.*

Práctica y comunicación

Summary of Question Formation

- with interrogative words
- with intonation
- by inverting the subject and verb

A. Preguntas

Paso 1. Autoprueba. ¿Cómo se dice (*How do you say it*) en inglés?

1. ¿Habla usted inglés?
2. ¿Necesitan ustedes otra clase?
3. ¿Tomas biología?
4. ¿Trabajo mañana?

Paso 2. Ahora exprese las siguientes oraciones como preguntas. **¡OJO!** Hay dos o tres formas.

MODELO: Alicia toca el violín. → ¿**Toca Alicia** el violín? ¿**Toca** el violín **Alicia**? ¿**Alicia toca** el violín?

1. Susana toca la guitarra.
2. Los estudiantes compran muchos libros.
3. Ustedes miran el teléfono en clase.
4. Diego manda mensajes en clase.
5. Ustedes toman cinco clases este semestre/trimestre.

Paso 3. Ahora, en parejas, usen las oraciones del **Paso 2** para hacer y contestar preguntas. **¡OJO!** No es necesario usar los pronombres **tú** y **yo** en la pregunta o en la respuesta (*answer*).

MODELO: tocar la guitarra →
ESTUDIANTE 1: ¿**Tocas** la guitarra?
ESTUDIANTE 2: Sí, **toco** la guitarra. (No, no **toco** la guitarra.)

Prác. A: Answers, Paso 1. 1. Do you speak English? *2.* Do you (pl.) need another class? *3.* Are you taking (a) biology (class)? *4.* Do (Will) I work tomorrow?

B. Una conversación inventada. Imagine that you have just met Diego and Irene, new students on campus. You asked them some questions and they gave you the following answers. What were the questions that you asked?

MODELO: Sí, estudiamos antropología. → **¿Estudian** antropología?

1. Sí, tomamos una clase de español.
2. Sí, estudiamos en la biblioteca con frecuencia.
3. No, no tocamos el piano.
4. No, no deseamos trabajar más horas.
5. No, no hablamos francés, pero hablamos italiano un poco.
6. ¡Sí, estamos muy bien en esta (*this*) universidad!

C. Preguntas sobre un texto

Paso 1. Lea **Algo sobre los murales y el arte urbano** y tome nota de las ideas más importantes o interesantes.

 Paso 2. En parejas (*pairs*), creen (*create*) tres preguntas informativas (con palabras interrogativas) y tres preguntas **sí/no** sobre el texto.

 Paso 3. Ahora cambien de pareja (*change partners*). Hagan sus preguntas (*Ask your questions*) y contesten (*answer*) las preguntas de la otra persona.

D. Intercambios: Sus (*Your*) actividades

Paso 1. Use the following cues as a guide to form questions that you will ask a classmate. You may ask other questions as well. Write the questions on a sheet of paper. **¡OJO!** Use the **tú** form of the verbs.

MODELO: escuchar música por la mañana →
 ¿Escuchas música por la mañana?

1. estudiar en la biblioteca todos los días
2. practicar español con un amigo o amiga
3. tomar mucho / un poco de (*a little bit of*) café por la mañana
4. bailar mucho en las fiestas
5. cantar en la ducha (*shower*)
6. regresar a casa muy tarde los fines de semana (*on the weekends*)
7. comprar los libros en la librería de la universidad
8. mandar muchos (*many*) mensajes
9. trabajar los fines de semana
10. usar (*to use*) un diccionario bilingüe online

 Paso 2. Now use the questions to get information from your partner. Jot down their answers for use in **Paso 3.**

MODELO: **ESTUDIANTE 1:** ¿Escuchas música por la mañana?
 ESTUDIANTE 2: Sí, (No, no) **escucho** música por la mañana.

Paso 3. With the information you gathered in **Paso 2,** report your partner's answers to the class. (You will use the **él/ella** form of the verbs when reporting.)

MODELO: Jenny no **escucha** música por la mañana.

Algo sobre° los murales y el arte urbano Algo... *Something about*

LUCY NICHOLSON/Alamy Stock Photo

El mural *Resurrection of the Green Planet,* del artista chicano Ernesto de la Loza, en *East Los Angeles*

La tradición muralista mexicana está muy presente en las comunidades latinas de los Estados Unidos, especialmente en California y los estados del Suroeste.[a] Presenta motivos indigenistas,[b] históricos y sociales. Ahora hay ejemplos del arte urbano en los grandes[c] museos, desde[d] grafitis hasta[e] murales.

¿Hay murales interesantes en su[f] universidad o en su ciudad?[g] ¿Dónde están?

[a]*Southwest* [b]*motivos... indigenous (native) themes or elements* [c]*great* [d]*from* [e]*to* [f]*your* [g]*city*

✿ Todo junto

El español es muy importante en los Estados Unidos porque hay millones de hispanohablantes de diferentes orígenes nacionales y culturales. Por eso[a] el español es una lengua de gran interés nacional y hay clases de español en todas las universidades de los Estados Unidos. Además,[b] en muchas universidades hay una concentración de español y programas de estudios hispanos o latinos.

🖼 **¿Cuántos cursos de español hay (aproximadamente[c]) en su[d] universidad cada[e] semestre/trimestre? ¿Hay una concentración de español? ¿y una concentración menor?**

[a]Por... *For that reason* [b]*In addition* [c]*approximately* [d]*your* [e]*every*

Un profesor de español en clase

A. Lengua y cultura: Dos universidades fabulosas... y diferentes

Paso 1. Completar. Complete the following description of two well-known universities. Give the correct form of the verbs in parentheses, as suggested by context. When the subject pronoun is in *italics,* don't use it in the sentence. When two possibilities are given in parentheses, select the correct word.

¿Cómo es la universidad perfecta? Hay muchas[a] opciones. Aquí _____ (hay / es)[1] dos ejemplos de _____ (universidad / universidades)[2] muy famosas en los Estados Unidos.

La Colección Latinoamericana Benson, una colección muy completa de libros, documentos, revistas (*magazines*) y periódicos (*newspapers*) relacionados con (*related to*) Latinoamérica

El primer[b] ejemplo es _____ (el / la)[3] Universidad de Texas, en Austin. ¡Es _____ (un / una)[4] universidad muy grande[c]! Hay muchos grupos sociales para estudiantes hispanos y una _____ (librería / biblioteca)[5] con una colección latinoamericana fantástica, _____ (el / la)[6] Colección Latinoamericana Benson. Algunas[d] materias populares en la UT son: administración de empresas, ingeniería, humanidades y comunicaciones. Muchos estudiantes _____ (tomar)[7] cursos en _____ (el / la)[8] Instituto de Estudios Latinoamericanos y en _____ (el / la)[9] Centro para Estudios Mexicoamericanos.

Stanford, en _____ (el / la)[10] estado de California, es una universidad más pequeña.[e] Tiene[f] una residencia para estudiantes de español, la Casa Zapata. Allí,[g] _____ (los / las)[11] estudiantes _____ (practicar)[12] español y _____ (participar)[13] en celebraciones hispanas. Las materias más populares en Stanford son[h]: biología, economía, inglés y ciencias políticas. _____ (El / La)[14] problema en Stanford es que los estudiantes _____ (pagar)[15] mucho por[i] la matrícula.

¿Prefiere usted la UT o Stanford? ¿ _____ (*Usted:* Desear)[16] _____ (estudia / estudiar)[17] en California o en Texas?

---

[a]*many* [b]*first* [c]*big* [d]*Some* [e]*más... smaller* [f]*It has* [g]*There* [h]*are* [i]*for*

Paso 2. Comprensión. Las siguientes oraciones son falsas. Corríjalas. (*Correct them.*)

1. En la Universidad de Texas hay solo un grupo social para estudiantes hispanos.
2. En el Instituto de Estudios Latinoamericanos hay pocos (*few*) estudiantes.
3. La Universidad de Stanford está en Texas.
4. La Casa Zapata es una biblioteca importante.

Paso 3. En acción

Ahora complete la siguiente información sobre su (*about your*) universidad.

Mi universidad _____ (estar) en el estado de _____ .

En mi universidad...

1. **muchos / pocos** (*many/few*) estudiantes _____ (tomar) clases de español.
2. **hay / no hay** un centro o **un / una** programa de estudios latinoamericanos.
3. **hay / no hay** organizaciones de estudiantes latinos
4. las materias más populares son: _____ .
5. los estudiantes _____ (pagar) **mucho / poco** dinero.

B. Proyecto: Perfil° académico de la clase   *Profile*

Working in groups, create a profile of the academic preferences of your class by polling your classmates about how many and which classes they are taking and when. When you analyze the results, you will determine which are the most popular subjects among the classmates you interviewed and at what times.

Paso 1. Preparación. In your group, prepare one question for each member of the group. You will use these questions in **Paso 2** to interview some classmates. Some questions can elicit yes/no answers, while other questions will use interrogative words such as **¿cuándo... ?, ¿a qué hora... ?,** and so on.

Paso 2. Encuesta. (*Poll.*) Each member of your group should poll as many classmates as possible using their particular question. Before you start polling, create a table on which to record the answers. And don't forget to ask for and record the names of the classmates you poll.

MODELO: ¿Cuántas clases tomas por la mañana (tarde, noche)?

nombre / número de clases	por la mañana	por la tarde	por la noche

Estrategias

- Use the question **¿Cuántas clases tomas?** to find out how many classes someone is taking.
- Use the question **¿Cómo se dice _____ en español?** when you need help with a new word.

Paso 3. Análisis de datos (*data*). Gather the information from your group's polling, and prepare 4 to 5 statements to share with the rest of the class. Here are some examples of statements. You can use them or create your own.

1. En nuestra (*Our*) encuesta hay información de _____ (número) estudiantes.
2. _____ (número) estudiantes de la clase toman _____ (número) clases.
3. Las tres materias más (*most*) / menos (*least*) populares son _____ .
4. Muchos/Pocos (*Many/Few*) estudiantes toman clases por la mañana / tarde / noche.

Video: Salu2 «¡Qué bacán!°»   *¡Qué... How great!*

You can watch two segments of this chapter's video in the **Video: Salu2** section, found at the end of the eBook.

Estudiantes estadounidenses con una familia peruana

MUNDO° HISPANO *World*

Enfoque cultural: La universidad

Antes de leer°   Antes... *Before reading*

¿Hay muchos estudiantes de origen hispano en su (*your*) universidad? ¿Hay organizaciones para ellos? ¿Es usted miembro de una organización estudiantil?

En los Estados Unidos

La Casa Latina Student Center, Portland Sate University, Portland, Oregón

En la actualidad[a] hay muchos estudiantes latinos en las universidades de los Estados Unidos.

    La experiencia universitaria típica en los Estados Unidos incluye[b] la participación en organizaciones de estudiantes con diversos intereses. Por eso,[c] las universidades estadounidenses tienen[d] una variada representación de organizaciones latinas.

• Algunas[e] son para todos los hispanos de la universidad, como **Latinos Unidos.**

• Otras son para un grupo específico, como **Fuerza Quisqueyana** (estudiantes dominicanos) o **(La) Raza** (estudiantes mexicanoamericanos o chicanos).

Las organizaciones latinas coordinan eventos sociales y académicos: bailes de gala[f] con música hispana, conferencias de escritores[g] hispanohablantes, servicios sociales, etcétera. Con frecuencia, también hay una Casa Latina, donde miembros de la organización viven juntos.[h]

[a]*En... Currently*   [b]*includes*   [c]*Por... For this reason*   [d]*have*   [e]*Some (organizations)*   [f]*bailes... formal dances*   [g]*writers*   [h]*viven... live together*

Comprensión ¿Qué actividades organizan los grupos hispanos de las universidades?

En otros países° hispanos   naciones

Estas son[a] las universidades más antiguas[b] en el mundo hispanohablante.

La biblioteca de la Universidad Nacional Autónoma de México (UNAM), Ciudad de México

En España

• la Universidad de Salamanca, Salamanca (1218 = mil doscientos dieciocho)

En Latinoamérica

• la Universidad Nacional Mayor de San Marcos, Lima, Perú (1551 = mil quinientos cincuenta y uno)

• la Universidad Nacional Autónoma de México (UNAM), la Ciudad de México, México (1551 = mil quinientos cincuenta y uno)

• la Universidad Nacional de Córdoba, Argentina (1621 = mil seiscientos veintiuno)

• la Universidad San Francisco Xavier de Chuquisaca, Sucre, Bolivia (1624 = mil seiscientos veinticuatro)

• la Universidad de San Carlos de Guatemala, Antigua, Guatemala (1676 = mil seiscientos setenta y seis)

[a]*Estas... These are*   [b]*más... oldest*

Comprensión ¿En qué países hispanos hay una universidad muy antigua?

En acción

Haga (*Make*) una lista de organizaciones para los estudiantes latinos de su (*your*) universidad. ¿Son (*Are they*) para una comunidad hispana específica, como la comunidad dominicana o la chicana?

Lectura°

Reading

Antes de leer°

Antes... *Before reading*

What is a good way for an adult to learn another language? On the job (**el trabajo**), with friends who speak the language, in school (**una escuela**)? Can you think of other ways? Explain your answer. In a school, how many other learners would there ideally be in each class? How many days per week would the class meet? How many hours per day?

Un anuncio° de Inglés USA

Un... *An ad*

Vocabulario para leer

los altos ejecutivos	high executives
las empresas	companies
incluido/a	included

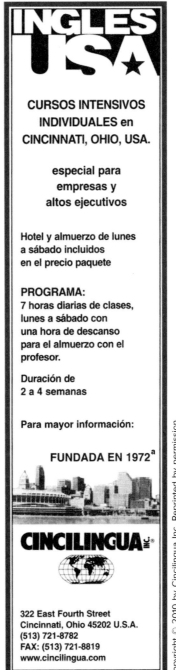

INGLÉS USA ★

CURSOS INTENSIVOS INDIVIDUALES en CINCINNATI, OHIO, USA.

especial para
empresas y
altos ejecutivos

Hotel y almuerzo de lunes
a sábado incluidos
en el precio paquete

PROGRAMA:
7 horas diarias de clases,
lunes a sábado con
una hora de descanso
para el almuerzo con el
profesor.

Duración de
2 a 4 semanas

Para mayor información:

FUNDADA EN 1972[a]

CINCILINGUA INC.®

322 East Fourth Street
Cincinnati, Ohio 45202 U.S.A.
(513) 721-8782
FAX: (513) 721-8819
www.cincilingua.com

[a]mil novecientos setenta y dos

Comprensión

A. Traducciones. (*Translations.*) Empareje (*Match*) las frases en español del anuncio con sus equivalentes en inglés.

1. _____ especial
2. _____ diarias
3. _____ una hora de descanso
4. _____ el almuerzo
5. _____ semanas
6. _____ mayor

a. *more*
b. *an hour-long break*
c. *special*
d. *lunch*
e. *daily*
f. *weeks*

B. En el anuncio. Busque (*Look for*) la siguiente información en el anuncio.

1. ¿Cómo se llama la escuela?
2. ¿Dónde está la escuela?
3. ¿Cuántos estudiantes hay en una clase?
4. ¿Qué tipo de estudiantes hay en la escuela?
5. ¿Cuántas horas de clase hay al (*per*) día?

⚙ Proyecto: ¿Y en su° universidad?   *your*

Create a similar advertisement for the Spanish program at your college or university.

Paso 1. Answer the following questions to gather information about your Spanish program. You may need to ask your instructor some questions.

1. ¿Cuántos niveles (*levels*) de cursos de español hay?
2. Cómo máximo, ¿cuántos estudiantes hay por sección en los cursos para principiantes (*for beginners*)?
3. ¿Son las clases para principiantes presenciales (*face-to-face*)? ¿virtuales? ¿semipresenciales?
4. ¿Son las clases por la mañana, por la tarde o por la noche?
5. ¿Cuántos días por semana (*days a week*) hay clases? ¿Cuántos créditos vale (*is worth*) cada (*each*) curso?
6. ¿Hay actividades extracurriculares relacionadas con el (*related to*) español en el campus? (Por ejemplo: cine [*movies*], teatro, horas de conversación...)
7. ¿Hay otras oportunidades para los estudiantes de español? (Por ejemplo: estudiar en países [*countries*] hispanohablantes, participar en actividades para voluntarios,...)

Paso 2. Now that you have some information about your institution's Spanish program, create an advertisement for it, similar to the ad for **Cincilingua.**

🔊 Textos orales

Un anuncio° para los cursos de verano° de una universidad

ad / summer

Antes de escuchar°

Antes... *Before listening*

What kind of information do you expect to hear in an ad for a summer course?

Vocabulario para escuchar	
anuncia	announces
el verano	summer
mayo	May
la semana	week
junio	June
agosto	August

Comprensión

A. Información básica. Indique las respuestas (*answers*) apropiadas.

1. El período de matrícula es en...

   ____ mayo   ____ junio   ____ julio   ____ agosto

2. Hay cursos de...

   ____ 2 semanas   ____ 4 semanas   ____ 8 semanas   ____ 10 semanas

3. Con seguridad (*For sure*) hay cursos de... según (*according to*) el anuncio.

   ____ sociología   ____ arte   ____ matemáticas   ____ literatura

4. Por internet se ofrecen (*are offered*) cursos de...

   ____ alemán   ____ filosofía   ____ italiano   ____ portugués

B. Más información. Según (*According to*) el anuncio, ¿cuál es el nombre de la residencia? ¿la dirección (*address*) de la página web? ¿el teléfono de contacto?

👆 En acción

Create a short Facebook ad about your university. Here is a basic model to which you can add ideas based on **Comprensión A.**

> MODELO: ¿Desea estudiar con estudiantes fantásticos? La Universidad de _____ es perfecta. Hay un extenso catálogo que incluye (*that includes*)... Visitar la página web...

🎤 Entrevista

Use de (*as a*) modelo las preguntas y respuestas (*answers*) de la sección **Entrevista** al principio (*at the beginning*) de este capítulo para hablar de sus propios estudios universitarios (*your own university studies*).

💻 Escritura°

Writing

Un ensayo sobre este° semestre/trimestre

ensayo... *essay
about this*

¿Qué estudia usted? ¿Trabaja? ¿Es su horario (*schedule*) este semestre/trimestre muy diferente del (*from the*) horario de sus (*your*) compañeros de clase? ¿O es similar?

Un grupo de estudiantes en la biblioteca

Andersen Ross/Getty Images

👥 Antes de escribir°

Antes... *Before writing*

Primero (*First*), complete la columna de la izquierda (*left-hand column*) con información personal. Luego entreviste (*Then interview*) a un compañero / una compañera y complete la columna de la derecha.

Yo	Mi compañero/a
Mi especialización[a] **es / puede ser**[b]:	Su[c] especialización **es / puede ser:**
Clases que[d] tomo este semestre/trimestre:	Clases que toma este semestre/trimestre:
Mi clase favorita es:	Su clase favorita es:
No trabajo. / Trabajo en...	**No trabaja. / Trabaja** en...
(No) Me gusta este semestre/trimestre.	(No) Le gusta[e] este semestre/trimestre.

[a]*major* [b]*puede... might be* [c]*His/Her* [d]*that* [e]*Le... He/She likes*

A escribir°

A... *Let's write*

Ahora combine la información para escribir (*to write*) un ensayo. Hay más ayuda (*help*) en Connect.

En la comunidad

As you know, all Spanish-speaking countries use the word **universidad** to refer to colleges or universities, big or small, public or private. But there is a lot of variation in the words that Spanish speakers use for *elementary school*, *middle school*, and *high school*. There is also variation in how the following words and phrases are expressed: (*academic*) *grade* (and the symbols used to give grades), *to pass*, *to fail*.

Preguntas posibles

- Ask someone who was raised in a Hispanic country what language is used in their country to express different levels of schooling and the grading system.
- Ask the person to describe their educational experience in the country of origin.
- If relevant, ask for a comparison with the educational system in this country.

> ### Para escribir bien
>
> Here are some words and phrases that can be useful in your essay.
>
> - Words to qualify your actions (adverbs): **mucho/poco, bien/mal, solo**
> - Time expressions (adverbs): **con frecuencia, el fin de semana, por la mañana (tarde, noche), todos los días**
> - Words to connect ideas: **pero, también, y/o**

Producción audiovisual

Con las preguntas de la **Entrevista** como modelo, filme una o dos entrevistas con compañeros de clase sobre (*about*) las materias que estudian y su (*their*) especialización universitaria.

Más ideas para el portafolio

- Make a list of reasons why you are studying Spanish. No reason is too silly or too small!
- Make a list of things you'd like to be able to do eventually with your Spanish. Let your imagination run wild!
- If you have been playing Practice Spanish: Study Abroad, in Quest 1 you saw the importance of the **plaza.** Where can **plazas** generally be found? How do people use them within their communities?

Sugerencia: You are now ready to play Quest 1 in **Practice Spanish: Study Abroad.**

AFTER STUDYING THIS CHAPTER I CAN ...

☐ name people, places, and things in the classroom and the university (30–31)

☐ name academic subject areas (32)

☐ recognize nouns and articles as masculine or feminine, singular or plural (37–39, 40–41)

☐ talk about actions with **-ar** verbs and subject pronouns (43–46)

☐ ask questions with interrogatives and yes/no questions with proper intonation (34, 50–52)

☐ recognize/describe at least 2–3 aspects of the Hispanic population of the United States.

Gramática en breve

1. Singular nouns: Gender and Articles

Noun Endings

Masculine	**-o**
Feminine:	**-a, -ción, -sión, -xión, -dad, -tad**
Masculine or feminine:	**-e, other consonants**

2. Nouns and Articles: Plural Forms

Plural Endings

-o → -os

-a → -as

-e → -es

z → -ces

consonant +-es

Definite Articles		**Indefinite Articles**	
Masculine el → los		un → unos	
Feminine la → las		una → unas	

3. Subject Pronouns; Present Tense of -ar Verbs; Negation

Subject Pronouns

yo, tú, usted, él, ella, nosotros/as, vosotros/as, ustedes, ellos/as

Regular -ar Verb Endings

-o, -as, -a, -amos, -áis, -an

4. Asking Yes/No Questions

- Rising intonation
- Inversion of word order:
- **subject** + verb → verb + **subject**

Vocabulario

¡OJO!

- Infinitives shown in **red** and **underlined** in **Vocabulario** lists are conjugated in all tenses and moods in Appendix 5.
- Be sure that you know the meaning of the group headings in addition to the meaning of the words in each group.
- If you are not sure of the meaning of a word, you can look it up in the end-of-book Spanish-English Vocabulary.

Los verbos

bailar	to dance
buscar	to look for
cantar	to sing
comprar	to buy
desear	to want
enseñar	to teach
escuchar	to listen (to)
estar (estoy, estás,...)	to be
estudiar	to study
hablar	to speak; to talk
hablar por teléfono	to talk on the phone
mandar un mensaje (de texto)	to (send a) text
necesitar	to need
pagar	to pay (for)
practicar	to practice
regresar	to return (to a place)
regresar a casa	to go home
tocar	to play (a musical instrument)
tomar	to take; to drink
trabajar	to work

Las personas

el/la amigo/a	friend
el/la bibliotecario/a	librarian
el/la cliente/a	client
el/la compañero/a (de clase)	classmate
el/la compañero/a de cuarto	roommate
el/la consejero/a	advisor
el/la dependiente/a	clerk
el/la estudiante	student
el/la extranjero/a	foreigner
el hombre	man
la mujer	woman
el/la secretario/a	secretary
Repaso: el/la profesor(a)	

Repaso (*Review*) indicates vocabulary listed as active in this chapter that you learned in previous chapters.

Los lugares

la biblioteca	library
el cuarto	room
el edificio	building
la fiesta	party
la librería	bookstore
la residencia	dormitory
el salón de clase	classroom
la universidad	university
el lugar	place

Cognados: el apartamento, la cafetería, la oficina

> Cognado(s) lists vocabulary you should be able to recognize because the words are close cognates of English.

Los objetos

la botella (de agua)	bottle (of water)
el bolígrafo	pen
la calculadora	calculator
la computadora (portátil)	(laptop) computer
el cuaderno	notebook
el diccionario	dictionary
el dinero	money
el escritorio	desk
el lápiz (pl. lápices)	pencil
el libro (de texto)	(text) book
el mapa	map
la mesa	table
la mochila	backpack
el papel	paper
el pizarrón (blanco)	(white) board
la puerta	door
la silla	chair
el teléfono (celular)	(cell) phone
la ventana	window

Las materias

la administración de empresas	business administration
la ciencia	science
la computación	computer science
la física	physics
la química	chemistry
la sicología	psychology
la materia	subject area

Cognados: el arte, las ciencias (naturales / políticas / sociales), las comunicaciones, la economía, la filosofía, la historia, las humanidades, la literatura, las matemáticas, la sociología

Las lenguas (extranjeras)

el alemán	German
el español	Spanish
el francés	French
el inglés	English
el italiano	Italian
la lengua (extranjera)	(foreign) language

En resumen

Otros sustantivos

el café	coffee
la clase	class (of students); class, course (academic)
el día	day
la matrícula	tuition
la oración	sentence (gram.)

Las palabras interrogativas

¿cuál?	what?; which?
¿cuándo?	when?
¿cuánto?	how much?
¿cuántos/as?	how many?

Repaso: ¿cómo?, ¿(de) dónde?, ¿qué?, ¿quién?

¿Cuándo?

ahora	now
con frecuencia	frequently
el fin de semana	weekend
por la mañana/tarde	in the morning/afternoon
por la noche	at night, in the evening
tarde/temprano	late/early
todos los días	every day

Los pronombres personales

yo	I
tú	you (fam. sing.)
usted	you (form, sing.)
él	he
ella	she
nosotros/as	we
vosotros/as	you (fam., plural)
ustedes	you (form., plural)
ellos/as	they

Palabras adicionales

aquí	here
con	with
en casa	at home
mal	poorly
más	more
mucho (adverb)	much; a lot
poco (adverb)	(a) little
un poco (de)	a little bit (of)
solo	only

Repaso: no

> ## Vocabulario personal
>
> Use this space or a vocabulary notebook to write down other words and phrases you learn in this chapter.

3

La familia

En este° capítulo

this

VOCABULARY
Words for family members   66
Numbers 31–100   68
Adjectives   71

GRAMMAR
Using adjectives   73
The verb **ser**   79
Expressing ownership   84
Verbs ending in **-er** and **-ir**   88

COUNTRY OF FOCUS: MEXICO

Una familia mexicana en una celebración especial

UpperCut Images/Alamy Stock Photo

MÉXICO

130 (ciento treinta) millones de habitantes

- El nombre oficial de México es Estados Unidos Mexicanos. Hay 31 estados mexicanos.

- Es el primer país del mundo más grande por[a] número de hispanohablantes.

- Un 61,5% (sesenta y uno coma cinco por ciento) de los hispanos de los Estados Unidos de América son de origen mexicano.

[a]el... *the number one country in the world by*

ENTREVISTA

These questions related to the chapter theme are answered here by a native speaker. You will be able to ask and answer them yourself with personal information in the **Entrevista** activity in the **Portafolio** section at the end of the chapter.

Alejandra Hernández Soto contesta las preguntas.

– **¿Cómo es su[a] familia, grande[b] o pequeña[c]?**

– Mi familia más cercana[d] es pequeña porque[e] soy hija única.[f]

– **¿Cuántas personas hay en su familia extendida?**

– Mi familia extendida es muy grande: tengo seis tías[g] y tíos y doce primos.[h]

– **¿Cómo se llama su padre[i]/madre?**

– Mi padre se llama Juan y mi madre se llama Susana. Yo me llamo como mi abuela[j] materna.

– **¿Le gusta celebrar su cumpleaños[k] con sus amigos? ¿con su familia?**

– Me gusta celebrar mi cumpleaños con mis padres[l] y también con mis amigos pero ¡por separado!

[a]*your* [b]*big* [c]*small* [d]más... *closest, nuclear* [e]*because* [f]hija... *an only child* [g]*aunts* [h]*cousins* [i]*father* [j]*grandmother* [k]*birthday* [l]*parents*

VOCABULARIO: PREPARACIÓN

You can hear the pronunciation of theme vocabulary words and phrases in the eBook.

¿Quiénes forman la familia?

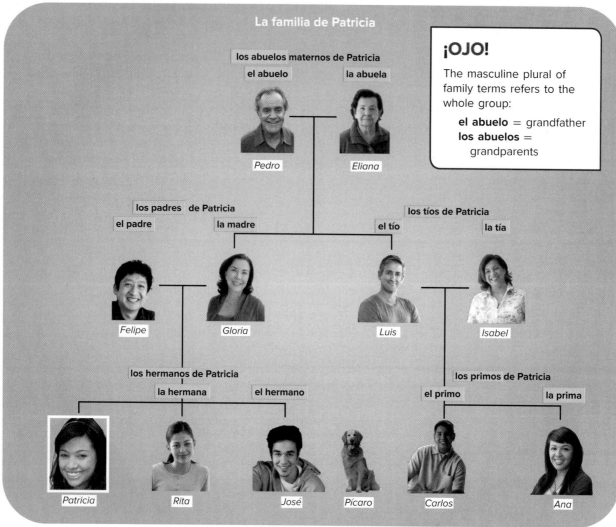

La familia de Patricia

los abuelos maternos de Patricia
el abuelo — *Pedro*
la abuela — *Eliana*

¡OJO!

The masculine plural of family terms refers to the whole group:

el abuelo = grandfather
los abuelos = grandparents

los padres de Patricia
el padre — *Felipe*
la madre — *Gloria*

los tíos de Patricia
el tío — *Luis*
la tía — *Isabel*

los hermanos de Patricia
la hermana — *Patricia* / *Rita*
el hermano — *José*
Pícaro

los primos de Patricia
el primo — *Carlos*
la prima — *Ana*

(Pedro) Jack Hollingsworth/Getty Images; (Eliana) Pablo Hidalgo/123RF; (Felipe) Marcos Castillo/Shutterstock; (Gloria) Sam Edwards/Caia Image/Glow Images; (Luis) Monkey Business Images/Shutterstock; (Isabel) John Henley/Blend Images/Getty Images; (Patricia) Glow Images/SuperStock; (Rita) PNC/Digital Vision/Getty Images; (José) Rob Melnychuk/Brand X Pictures/Getty Images; (Pícaro) G.K. & Vikki Hart/Getty Images; (Carlos) Ryan McVay/Getty Images; (Ana) Hill Street Studios/Blend Images LLC

la madre (mamá)	mother (mom)
el padre (papá)	father (dad)
los padres	parents
la hija	daughter
el hijo	son
los hijos	children
la esposa / la mujer	wife
el esposo / el marido	husband
la pareja	partner; significant other; couple
la nieta	granddaughter
el nieto	grandson
el/la pariente	relative

la sobrina	niece
el sobrino	nephew

Cómo expresar *to have*

Remember that the conjugation of infinitives in <u>**red**</u> and <u>underlined</u> is given in Appendix 5.

<u>tener</u>	to have
tengo	I have
tienes	you (*fam.*) have
tiene	you (*form.*) have, he/she/it has

Las mascotas°

Las... *Pets*

el gato	cat
el pájaro	bird
el perro	dog

Más parientes

Learn as many of the following terms for additional family relationships as you need to describe your own family as completely as possible. Write the terms you learn in **Vocabulario personal** on the **En resumen** page at the end of the chapter.

el padrastro / la madrastra	stepfather / stepmother
el hijastro / la hijastra	stepson / stepdaughter
el hermanastro / la hermanastra	stepbrother / stepsister
el medio hermano / la media hermana	half-brother / half-sister
el suegro / la suegra	father-in-law / mother-in-law
el yerno / la nuera	son-in-law / daughter-in-law
el cuñado / la cuñada	brother-in-law / sister-in-law
<u>ser</u> adoptado/a	to be adopted
…(ya) murió	… has (already) died

Así se dice

The terms **mamá/mami** and **papá/papi** are used to speak *to* one's parents.

Many Spanish speakers use the terms **abuelito/tata** and **abuelita/nana** to speak *to* their grandparents.

Here is vocabulary for referring to non-traditional families:

- **una familia reconstituida** (family whose parents were previously married and have other children with previous spouses)
- **una unión civil**
- **una pareja de hecho** (non-married couple with formalized status)
- **un matrimonio entre personas del mismo** (*same*) **sexo**

Comunicación

A. La familia de Patricia. Mire (*Look at*) el árbol (*tree*) genealógico de Patricia en la página de **Vocabulario: Preparación.** Indique si las siguientes oraciones son ciertas o falsas. Corrija (*Correct*) las oraciones falsas.

	CIERTO	FALSO
1. José es el hermano de Ana.	☐	☐
2. Eliana es la abuela de Patricia.	☐	☐
3. Ana es la sobrina de Felipe y Gloria.	☐	☐
4. Patricia y José son (*are*) primos.	☐	☐
5. Gloria es la tía de José.	☐	☐
6. Carlos es el sobrino de Isabel.	☐	☐
7. Pedro es el padre de Luis y Gloria.	☐	☐
8. Isabel y Gloria son las esposas de Luis y Felipe, respectivamente.	☐	☐

B. ¿Quién es?

Paso 1. Complete las siguientes oraciones lógicamente.

1. La madre de mi (*my*) padre es mi _____.
2. El hijo de mi tío es mi _____.
3. La hermana de mi padre es mi _____.
4. El esposo (marido) de mi abuela es mi _____.

Paso 2. Ahora defina la relación de estas (*these*) personas, según (*according to*) el modelo de las oraciones del **Paso 1.**

MODELOS: El _____ de mi _____ es mi _____.
La _____ de mi _____ es mi _____.

1. prima   **2.** sobrino   **3.** tío   **4.** abuelo

C. Intercambios. Find out as much as you can about the family of a classmate, using the following dialogue as a guide.

MODELO: **E1:** ¿Cuántos hermanos tienes?
E2: Tengo dos hermanos. Además,[a] tengo una hermanastra.
E1: ¿Cómo se llaman tus hermanos?
E2: Se llaman Dixon y Lisa.
E1: ¿Y cuántos primos tienes?
E2: ¡Uf! Tengo un montón.[b] Más de[c] veinte.
E1: ¿Tienes una mascota?
E2: Sí, tengo un perro. Se llama Bear.

[a]*In addition* [b]*bunch* [c]*Más… More than*

From this point on in the text, **ESTUDIANTE 1** *and* **ESTUDIANTE 2** *will be abbreviated as* **E1** *and* **E2,** *respectively.*

¡OJO!

¿cuánt<u>o</u>s? (*with male relatives*)
¿cuánt<u>a</u>s? (*with female relatives*)

CREDENCIAL PARA VOTAR

Nombre
QUINTANA
FLORES
CATALINA

EDAD 21
SEXO M

Domicilio
C. LUNA 60
COL. MORELOS 06100
CUAJIMALPA DE MORELOS, D.F.

ESTADO 09   MUNICIPIO 004   SECCION 0747
LOCALIDAD 005   EMISIÓN 2008   VIGENCIA 2018

FIRMA

(logo): Yuiyui/Alamy Stock Photo
(photo): Maria Markevich/
Shutterstock

En este documento de identidad nacional, de México, están el nombre y los dos apellidos de la persona: primero, los apellidos y después (*next*), el nombre.

Nota cultural: El sistema hispano de apellidos°

last names

En los países hispanos las personas llevan sistemáticamente dos apellidos oficiales. Típicamente, el primer[a] apellido es el del[b] padre y el segundo,[c] el de la madre.

PADRE	MADRE
Antonio **Lázaro** Ochoa	Marina **Aguirre** Salmero

HIJOS
Marta **Lázaro Aguirre**
Jacobo **Lázaro Aguirre**

 Según el sistema hispano, ¿cómo se llamaría usted?[d]

[a]*first* [b]*el... that of the* [c]*second* [d]*¿cómo... what would your name be?*

¿Cuánto es? Los números del 31 al 100

Continúe las secuencias:

- treinta y uno, treinta y dos...
- ochenta y cuatro, ochenta y cinco...

31	treinta y uno	40	cuarenta
32	treinta y dos	50	cincuenta
33	treinta y tres	60	sesenta
34	treinta y cuatro	70	setenta
35	treinta y cinco	80	ochenta
36	treinta y seis	90	noventa
37	treinta y siete	100	cien
38	treinta y ocho		
39	treinta y nueve		

setenta y ocho años
cincuenta y cinco años
treinta y nueve años
cuarenta y cinco años
cuarenta y siete años
ochenta y cinco años

«El abuelito Pedro tiene 85 años y la abuelita Eliana tiene 78 años».

(Eliana) Pablo Hidalgo/123RF; (Felipe) Marcos Castillo/Shutterstock; (Isabel) John Henley/Blend Images/Getty Images; (Luis) Monkey Business Images/ Shutterstock; (Gloria) Sam Edwards/Caia Image/Glow Images; (Pedro) Jack Hollingsworth/Getty Images; (Patricia) Glow Images/SuperStock;

- Beginning with 31, Spanish numbers are *not* written as one word. **Treinta y uno, cuarenta y dos, sesenta y tres,** and so on, must be three separate words.
- **Cien** is used before nouns and in counting.

cien casas	a (one) hundred houses
noventa y ocho, noventa y nueve, cien	ninety-eight, ninety-nine, one hundred

- When **uno** is part of a compound number (**treinta y uno, cuarenta y uno,** and so on), it becomes **un** before a masculine noun and **una** before a feminine noun.

setenta y un hombres   **cincuenta y una mesas**

Comunicación

A. Más problemas de matemáticas. Recuerde (*Remember*): + **y,** − **menos,** = **son.**

1. 30 + 50 = 80
2. 45 + 45 = 90
3. 68 − 28 = 40
4. 77 + 23 = 100
5. 100 − 40 = 60
6. 55 + 15 = 70

B. Bingo

Paso 1. Mire el cartón (*card*) de bingo mexicano. Observe el patrón (*pattern*) de organización de los números y cree su propio (*create your own*) cartón con números de su elección (*of your choice*).

12	32	56		74	88
7	27		59	61	90
	18	34	44	68	77

Paso 2. Ahora, en parejas, lean sus números. ¿Hay repetición de números?

C. Estados y naciones

Paso 1. Lea **Algo sobre los estados (*states*) mexicanos** y tome nota del número de estados.

Paso 2. Ahora, en parejas, contesten las siguientes preguntas sin (*without*) buscar la información en internet. ¿Qué pareja de la clase tiene más respuestas correctas?

1. ¿Cuántos estados hay en los Estados Unidos?
2. ¿Cuántas naciones hispanohablantes hay en Centroamérica?
3. ¿Cuántas naciones hispanohablantes hay en Sudamérica? ¿Y en Europa?

Nota comunicativa: Cómo expresar la edad:° tener... años

age

In Spanish, age is expressed with the phrase **tener... años** (literally, *to have ... years*).

> NORA: ¿Cuántos **años tienes**, abuela?
> ABUELA: Setenta y ocho. ¿Y cuántos **años tienes** tú?
> NORA: Yo **tengo** ocho.

You will practice telling how old people are in **Comunicación D.**

Sam Edwards/Glow Images

D. Hablemos (*Let's talk*) de la edad (*age*)

Paso 1. Complete las siguientes oraciones.

1. Yo tengo _____ años.
2. La persona mayor (*oldest*) de mi familia es mi _____. Tiene _____ años.
3. La persona más joven (*youngest*) de mi familia es mi _____. Tiene _____ años.
4. En mi opinión, una persona es vieja (*old*) cuando tiene _____ años.
5. La edad ideal para casarse (*for getting married*) es a los _____ años.
6. La edad ideal para tener hijos es a los _____ años.

Paso 2. Ahora haga preguntas basadas en las oraciones del **Paso 1** y haga (*conduct*) una encuesta (*poll*) entre (*among*) un mínimo de seis compañeros de clase.

Estrategia

En el **Paso 2**, cambie (*change*) la palabra **mi** para formar las preguntas, según el modelo:

mi → tu

MODELO: **2.** E1: ¿Quién es la persona mayor de **tu** familia? ¿Cuántos años tiene?
E1: Es **mi** abuela. Tiene noventa y siete años.

Paso 3. Finalmente, presente sus (*your*) resultados a la clase.

Algo sobre los estados° mexicanos

states

El escudo (símbolo) de los Estados Unidos Mexicanos es un águila sobre un nopal.

Yuiyui/Alamy Stock Photo

México tiene 32 entidades federativas: 31 estados y 1 distrito federal, que[a] es la capital, la Ciudad de México. Los mexicanos la llamaban[b] el D.F. (Distrito Federal).

¿Cuántos estados hay en los Estados Unidos? La capital, Washington D.C., ¿es un estado?

[a]*which*   [b]*la... used to call it (i.e., the capital)*

Textos de todos los días: El certificado de nacimiento°

El... *Birth certificate*

To get a passport or a national identification card in any country, people need to show a birth certificate. In this activity you will fill out a form based on the Mexican birth certificate.

Objetivo: To learn words and categories that often appear in forms, especially those related to a person's identification.

Antes de empezar (*Before starting*): Read the **Nota cultural** on p. 68. Also, to help you anticipate and guess the meaning of new words, think about the information that usually appears in a birth certificate.

Folio de impresión
00000000

Certificado

Entidad

Estados Unidos Mexicanos
Acta de Nacimiento

Municipio

Oficialía	Fecha[a]	Libro	Acta

Datos de la Persona Registrada

Nombre(s)	Primer Apellido	Segundo Apellido

__Femenino __Masculino
Sexo · Fecha de Nacimiento[b] · Lugar de nacimiento

Datos de Filiación[b] de la Persona Registrada

Nombre(s)	Primer Apellido	Segundo Apellido	Nacionalidad

Nombre(s)	Primer Apellido	Segundo Apellido	Nacionalidad

Anotaciones	Certificación

(logo): Yuiyui/Alamy Stock Photo

[a]*Date* [b]*birth*

¿Cómo es? Los adjetivos descriptivos

Otros adjetivos

guapo	handsome, good-looking (*people*)
bonito	pretty (*people and things*)
feo	ugly
grande	large, big
pequeño	small
simpático	nice, likable (*people*)
antipático	unpleasant, unlikable (*people*)
corto	short (*in length*)
largo	long
bueno	good
malo	bad
listo	smart; clever
tonto	silly, foolish
trabajador	hardworking
perezoso	lazy
rico	rich
pobre	poor
delgado	thin, slender
gordo	fat

¡OJO!

You will learn how to describe feminine and plural nouns in **Gramática 5**.

Comunicación

 A. Descripciones

Paso 1. En parejas, describan estas (*these*) imágenes opuestas (*opposite*).

MODELO: **1.** Un _____ es _____ y el otro es _____ .

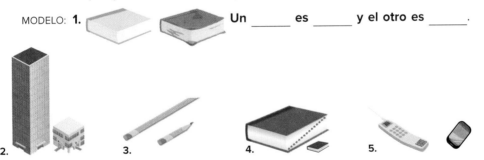

Paso 2. Ahora describan las siguientes (*following*) palabras.

MODELO: fumar (*to smoke*) → Fumar es malo. No es bueno.

1. bailar
2. Neil deGrasse Tyson
3. Dwayne Johnson
4. estudiar toda la noche (*all night*)
5. el edificio Empire State
6. el monstruo de Frankenstein
7. un átomo
8. Santa Claus

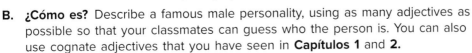 **B. ¿Cómo es?** Describe a famous male personality, using as many adjectives as possible so that your classmates can guess who the person is. You can also use cognate adjectives that you have seen in **Capítulos 1** and **2**.

MODELO: Es un hombre importante; controla una compañía de *software* muy importante. Es muy trabajador y muy rico. → Bill Gates

Some Spanish words have *written accent marks* over one of the vowels. That mark is called **el acento (ortográfico).** It means that the syllable containing the accented vowel is stressed when the word is pronounced, as in the word **bolígrafo (bo-LÍ-gra-fo),** for example.

Although all Spanish words of more than one syllable have a stressed vowel, most words do not have a written accent mark. Most words have the spoken stress exactly where native speakers of Spanish would predict it. These two simple rules tell you which syllable is stressed when there is no written accent on the word.

¡OJO!

You will learn about words that have a written accent mark in **Capítulo 4.**

> **1. Las palabras llanas** = words ending in a vowel, **-n,** or **-s**

Las palabras llanas have the word stress on the *next-to-last syllable* (**la penúltima sílaba**). When they end in a vowel, **-n,** or **-s,** they don't need a written accent mark. This is the largest group of Spanish words; it includes most nouns and adjectives as well as their plurals, most verb forms, and so on. Here are some examples.

me-sa   me-xi-**ca**-no   e-**xa**-men   **gra**-cias   **e**-res

> **2. Las palabras agudas** = words ending in a consonant other than **-n** or **-s**

Las palabras agudas have the word stress on the *last syllable* (**la última sílaba**). When they end in consonants other than **-n** or **-s** (typically **-d, -l,** and **-r**), they don't need a written accent mark. This group includes all infinitives and many common words that end in **-dad, -or,** and **-al.** Here are some examples.

us-**ted**   es-pa-**ñol**   pro-fe-**sor**   es-**tar**   doc-**tor**

Práctica

Estrategia

llana (ends in a vowel, **-n,** or **-s**) = stress on the second-to-last syllable

aguda (ends in a consonant other than **-n** or **-s**) = stress on the last syllable

A. Tipos de palabras: ¿Llanas o agudas? None of these words needs a written accent mark. Categorize each one as **llana** or **aguda,** then pronounce the word.

1. can-tan
2. ar-te
3. cla-se
4. mu-jer

5. me-sa
6. es-pa-ñol
7. a-mi-gos
8. us-ted

9. se-ñor
10. na-tu-ral
11. com-pu-ta-do-ra
12. bai-las

B. Vocales. Indicate the stressed vowel in the following words.

1. mo-chi-la
2. me-nos
3. re-gu-lar

4. i-gual-men-te
5. E-cua-dor
6. e-le-gan-te

7. li-be-ral
8. hu-ma-ni-dad

GRAMÁTICA

5 Describing • Adjectives: Gender, Number, and Position

Gramática en acción: Un poema sencill<u>o</u>

Amig<u>o</u>
Fiel
Amable
Simpátic<u>o</u>
¡Lo admiro!

Amig<u>a</u>
Fiel
Amable
Simpátic<u>a</u>
¡La admiro!

Comprensión

Which of the following adjectives can be used to describe Mario? And Marta?

fiel   amable   simpátic<u>a</u>   simpátic<u>o</u>

Adjectives (**Los adjetivos**) are words used to talk about nouns or pronouns. Adjectives may describe or tell how many of something there are around you.

> *large* desk   *few* desks
>
> *tall* woman   *several* women

You have been using adjectives to describe people since **Capítulo 1.** In this section, you will learn more about describing the people and things around you. As you read, remember that all nouns (people, animals, places, things, ideas) are either masculine or feminine in Spanish.

> *an adjective* / **un adjetivo** = a word used to describe a noun or a pronoun

Adjectives with *ser* / Los adjetivos con *ser*

In Spanish, forms of **ser** are used with adjectives that describe basic, inherent qualities or characteristics of the nouns or pronouns they modify. **Ser** establishes the "norm," that is, what is considered basic reality: *snow is cold, water is wet.*

La casa **es grande.**
The house is big.

Mi hermana **es trabajadora.**
My sister is hardworking.

¡Eres muy amable!
You are very kind!

A simple poem *Friend Loyal Kind Nice I admire him/her!*

Gramática

Forms of Adjectives / **Las formas de los adjetivos**

Spanish adjectives "agree" with the noun or pronoun they modify. This agreement is shown in two ways:

> *agreement* / **la concordancia** = when one word "agrees," or must be coordinated, with an aspect of another (for example, *he + speaks* but *you + speak*)

- gender agreement (masculine or feminine): **una amiga alta**
- number agreement (singular or plural): **los amigos ricos**

For this reason, Spanish adjectives have more than one form.

1. Adjectives with Four Forms

Adjectives that end in **-o** (**alto**) and **-dor** (**trabajador**) have four forms, showing gender and number.

Adjetivos con 4 formas	Masculino	Femenino
Singular	amigo alto amigo trabajador	amiga alta amiga trabajadora
Plural	amigos altos amigos trabajadores	amigas altas amigas trabajadoras

2. Adjectives with Two Forms

Adjectives that end in **-e** (**amable**), many consonants (**fiel**), and **-ista** (**idealista**) have only two forms, singular and plural. The plural of adjectives is formed in the same way as that of nouns, by adding **-s** or **-es**.

Adjetivos con 2 formas	Masculino	Femenino
Singular	amigo amable amigo fiel amigo idealista	amiga amable amiga fiel amiga idealista
Plural	amigos amables amigos fieles amigos idealistas	amigas amables amigas fieles amigas idealistas

> **¡OJO!**
>
> When the adjective **joven** is made plural, an accent mark is added to retain the original word stress: **joven → jóvenes**.

3. Nationality Adjectives

Many adjectives of nationality have four forms.

> **¡OJO!**
>
> Nationality adjectives ending in **-e** generally have only two forms: **estadounidense(s)** (from the United States), **canadiense(s).**

Adjetivos con 4 formas	Masculino	Femenino
Singular	el doctor mexicano español	la doctora mexicana española
Plural	los doctores mexicanos españoles	las doctoras mexicanas españolas

4. Names of Languages

The names of many languages—which are masculine in gender—are the same as the masculine singular form of the corresponding adjective of nationality.

Lengua	Adjetivo
el inglés	inglés, inglesa, ingleses, inglesas
el francés	francés, francesa, franceses, francesas
el italiano	italiano, italiana, italianos, italianas
el alemán	alemán, alemana, alemanes, alemanas

> **¡OJO!**
>
> Note that in Spanish the names of languages and adjectives of nationality are not capitalized, but the names of countries are: **el español, española,** but **España.**

> **¡OJO!**
>
> When the last syllable of an adjective has a written accent mark (**inglés, alemán**), the accent is dropped in the feminine and plural forms, as shown in the box above.

Position of Adjectives / **La posición de los adjetivos**

As you have probably noticed, adjectives do not always precede the noun in Spanish as they do in English. Note the following rules for adjective placement.

1. Adjectives of <u>Quantity</u>

Like numbers, adjectives of quantity *precede* the noun, as do the interrogatives **¿cuánto/a?** and **¿cuántos/as?**

> **¡OJO!**
>
> **Otro/a** is an adjective of quantity. By itself it means *another* or *other*. The indefinite article is never used with **otro/a.**

¿Cuántas sillas hay?
How many chairs are there?

Hay **muchas sillas** y también **dos escritorios.**
There are many chairs and also two desks.

¿Cuánto dinero necesitas?
How much money do you need?

Busco **otro coche.**
I'm looking for another car.

2. Descriptive Adjectives (Adjectives of <u>Quality</u>)

Adjectives that describe the qualities of a noun and distinguish it from others generally *follow* the noun. Adjectives of nationality are included in this category.

un **perro <u>listo</u>**
un **dependiente <u>trabajador</u>**
una **mujer <u>delgada</u>** y **<u>morena</u>**
un **profesor <u>español</u>**

3. *Bueno* and *malo*

The adjectives **bueno** and **malo** may *precede or follow* the noun they modify. When they precede a masculine singular noun, they shorten to **buen** and **mal,** respectively.

un **<u>buen</u> perro** / un **perro <u>bueno</u>**
una **<u>buena</u> perra** / una **perra <u>buena</u>**

un **<u>mal</u> día** / un **día <u>malo</u>**
una **<u>mala</u> noche** / una **noche <u>mala</u>**

4. *Grande*

The adjective **grande** may also *precede or follow* the noun.
- When it precedes a singular noun—masculine or feminine— it shortens to **gran** and means *great* or *impressive.*
- When it follows the noun, it means *large* or *big.*

Nueva York es una **<u>gran</u> ciudad.**
New York is a great (impressive) city.

Nueva York es una **ciudad <u>grande</u>.**
New York is a large city.

Forms of *this/these* / **Formas de *este/estos*** (Part 1)

1. *This/These*

The adjective *this/these* has four forms in Spanish. Learn to recognize them when you see them.

You will learn all forms of this type of adjective (*this, that, these, those*) in **Gramática 9 (Cap. 4).**

est<u>e</u> hijo	this son
est<u>a</u> hija	this daughter
est<u>os</u> hijos	these sons
est<u>as</u> hijas	these daughters

2. *Esto*

You have already seen the neuter demonstrative **esto.** It refers to something that is as yet unidentified.

¿Qué es **<u>esto</u>**?
What is this?

Algo sobre una gran ciudad mexicana

Más de[a] 22 millones de personas viven en el área metropolitana de la Ciudad de México. Su[b] abreviatura es CDMX. Es una ciudad fascinante por su historia, su belleza[c] y su variedad de atracciones: más de 160 museos, 30 salas de conciertos y varios parques.

 ¿Cuántos habitantes hay en su[d] ciudad?
(En mi ciudad...)

[a]*Más... More than* [b]*Its* [c]*beauty* [d]*your*

Carlos S. Pereyra/Pixtal/ Age fotostock

Ciudad de México

Adjective Agreement Summary

SINGULAR ENDINGS	PLURAL ENDINGS
-o, -a	-os, -as
-e	-es
-[consonant]	-[consonant] + -es
-dor, -dora	-dores, -doras

Práctica y comunicación

A. La familia

Paso 1. Autoprueba. Complete los adjetivos con la forma apropiada.

1. La madre es alt_____ y trabajador_____.
2. El padre es baj_____ y amabl_____.
3. Los abuelos son viej_____ y simpátic_____.
4. Las hijas son pequeñ_____ y adorabl_____.
5. Hay much_____ parientes en la familia.
6. La familia tiene buen_____ amigos.

Paso 2. Ahora complete las siguientes oraciones según la familia de usted.

1. Mi **padre / hermano / tío** es _____ y _____.
2. Mi **madre / hermana / tía** es _____ y _____.
3. Mis abuelos son (*are*) _____ y _____. (Mi abuelo es _____. Mi abuela es _____).
4. _____ (nombre) y _____ (nombre) son buen _____ **amigos / amigas** de mi familia.

 Paso 3. Ahora, en parejas, túrnense para hacer y contestar (*take turns asking and answering*) preguntas sobre su (*about your*) familia. Usen las oraciones del **Paso 2** como modelo.

MODELO: **E1:** Mis abuelos son mexicanos y simpáticos. ¿Y tus abuelos?
E2: Mis abuelos son estadounidenses y viejos.

B. Descripciones

Paso 1. Haga oraciones con los siguientes adjetivos para describirse (*describe yourself*). **¡OJO!** Use la forma apropiada del adjetivo.

(No) Soy...

1. alto
2. trabajadora
3. estadounidense
4. rico
5. rubia
6. fiel
7. simpático
8. europeo
9. delgado
10. hispana (latina)
11. dedicado
12. social
13. estudiosa
14. listo
15. hijo único / hija única

Paso 2. Ahora haga oraciones para describir a una persona muy importante en su vida (*your life*), como su madre, padrastro, pareja, mejor amigo/a (*best friend*), etcétera.

MODELOS: **Mi** mejor amiga es moren**a**, simpátic**a** y pobre.
Mi esposo es alt**o**, trabaja**dor** y muy dedicad**o**.

C. La familia de Carlos. Estos son los parientes de Carlos. Complete las oraciones con los adjetivos apropiados según la forma de los adjetivos.

1. **El tío Felipe** es _____. (trabajador / alto / joven / gran / amable)
2. **Los abuelos** son _____. (rubio / antipático / inteligentes / viejos / religiosos / sinceras)
3. **Mi tía Gloria,** la madre de Patricia, es _____. (rubio / elegante / sentimental / buenas / hispanas / simpática)
4. **Mis primos** son _____. (trabajadores / morenos / lógica / bajas / mala)

Estrategia

- Use **mi** to express *my* with one relative, **mis** for more than one: *mi* **hermano**, *mis* **hermanos**.
- Use **tu** to express *your* with one relative, **tus** for more than one.

Carlos, un estudiante mexicano

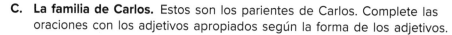

Prác. A, Paso 1: **Answers: 1.** *alta, trabajadora* **2.** *bajo, amable* **3.** *viejos, simpáticos* **4.** *pequeñas* **5.** *muchos* **6.** *buenos*

D. ¡Dolores es igual! Cambie (*Exchange*) **Diego** por **Dolores.**

Diego es un buen estudiante. Es listo y trabajador y estudia mucho. Es estadounidense de origen mexicano, y por eso[a] habla español. Desea ser profesor de antropología. Diego es moreno, guapo y atlético. Le gustan las fiestas grandes y tiene buenos amigos en la universidad. Tiene parientes estadounidenses y mexicanos. Diego tiene 20 años.

[a]por... *for that reason*

Nota comunicativa: Otras nacionalidades

You learned some nationality adjectives on page 74. Here are some more. Most of them are not active. If you don't find the adjective(s) you need to describe yourself and your family, ask your instructor. Write the adjectives you need in **Vocabulario personal** on the **En resumen** page.

Norteamérica, Centroamérica y el Caribe:	canadiense, costarricense, cubano/a, dominicano/a, guatemalteco/a, hondureño/a, mexicano/a, nicaragüense, panameño/a, salvadoreño/a
Sudamérica:	argentino/a, boliviano/a, brasileño/a, chileno/a, colombiano/a, ecuatoriano/a, paraguayo/a, peruano/a, uruguayo/a, venezolano/a
Europa y Asia:	chino/a, coreano/a, indio/a, iraní (*pl.* iraníes), iraquí (*pl.* iraquíes), israelí (*pl.* israelíes), japonés/japonesa, pakistaní (*pl.* pakistaníes), palestino/a, ruso/a, tailandés/tailandesa, vietnamita
África:	egipcio/a, ghanés/ghanesa, nigeriano/a, sudafricano/a
Australia:	australiano/a, fiyiano/a, neozelandés/neozelandesa

You will use many of these adjectives in **Práctica E.**

E. Países (*Countries*) y nacionalidades del mundo (*world*)

Paso 1. Diga (*Tell*) la nacionalidad de las siguientes personas.

1. Monique es de Francia; es _____ .
2. Piero y Andri son (*are*) del Uruguay; son (*they are*) _____ .
3. Indira y su (*her*) hermana son de la India; son _____ .
4. Ronaldo y Ronaldinho son del Brasil; son _____ .
5. Saji es un hombre del Japón; es _____ .
6. La familia Musharraf es de Pakistán; son _____ .
7. Paul es de Inglaterra; es _____ .
8. Samuel y su (*his*) hermana son de Guatemala; son _____ .
9. Sonia es de la Argentina; es _____ .
10. Ramón y José son de Colombia; son _____ .
11. Jimena es de Costa Rica; es _____ .
12. Bill y Susan son de los Estados Unidos; son _____ .

Paso 2. En parejas, hagan oraciones con las nacionalidades hispanas, según el modelo. Busquen (*Look for*) los nombres de las naciones hispanas en el mapa de la página 13.

MODELO: **E1:** ¿Una mujer de Costa Rica?
E2: Es **costarricense.** ¿Y un hombre?
E1: Es **costarricense.** ¿Una mujer de El Salvador?
E2: Es...

¡OJO!

Remember that adjectives of nationality and the names of languages don't start with a capital letter in Spanish.

Sor Juana Inés de la Cruz, 1651 – 1695 (mil seiscientos cincuenta y uno hasta mil seiscientos noventa y cinco)

F. Una mujer sorprendente (surprising)

Paso 1. Complete con las terminaciones apropiadas la siguiente descripción de una mujer muy especial.

Sor[a] Juana Inés de la Cruz es una mujer religios____[1] mexican____[2] del siglo[b] XVII. Es una gran____[3] poeta y una mujer muy inteligent____[4] y muy ilustrad____[c5] para su[d] época. Es muy famos____[6] internacionalmente. Escribió[e] much____[7] poemas important____[8] de la literatura hispan____[9].

[a]Sister   [b]century   [c]ilustrado/a = educated   [d]para... for her   [e]She wrote

Paso 2. Comprensión. ¿Cierto o falso? Corrija las oraciones falsas.

	CIERTO	FALSO
1. Sor Juana es de Nicaragua.	☐	☐
2. Escribió poemas en español.	☐	☐
3. Es famosa solamente en México.	☐	☐

G. Asociaciones. En grupos, hablen (talk) de las personas o cosas (things) que (that) asocian con las siguientes frases.

MODELO: una buena serie →
   E1: Creo que (I believe that) **Stranger Things** es una buena serie.
   E2: Estoy de acuerdo.

1. un buen / mal restaurante
2. una buena / mala serie
3. una gran mujer / un gran hombre
4. un buen libro / una buena aplicación para el celular

Estrategia

Use **Estoy de acuerdo** to express agreement and **No estoy de acuerdo** to express disagreement.

H. Descripciones. En parejas, describan a su (your) familia, haciendo (forming) oraciones completas con estas palabras, con cualquier (any) otro adjetivo que conozcan (that you may know) y con los adjetivos de nacionalidad. **¡OJO!** Cuidado (Be careful) con la forma de los adjetivos.

MODELO: Mi familia no es grande. Es pequeña. Mi padre tiene 50 años.
   Es pakistaní de nacimiento (by birth).

| mi familia
mi padre/madre
mi esposo/esposa
mi ¿ ? (otro pariente)
mi perro/gato | + | (no) es

tiene...
años | + | agresivo
amable
animado (lively)
antipático
bueno
cariñoso (affectionate)
comprensivo (understanding)
difícil (difficult) | famoso
grande
(im)paciente
importante
inteligente
interesante
malo
nuevo | pequeño
sensible (sensitive)
sentimental
serio
simpático
tolerante
travieso (mischievous)
viejo |

Algo sobre las culturas indígenas mexicanas

En México hay numerosos centros arqueológicos, muy famosos y visitados, como Teotihuacán y Chichen Itzá. Pero la historia indígena de México está viva[a]: hay más de[b] 60 pueblos indígenas en territorio mexicano, con su propia[c] lengua y cultura. Los más numerosos son los nahuas, mayas, zapotecas y mixtecas.

¿Cuáles son los pueblos indígenas en el estado donde está su universidad? ¿Hay centros arqueológicos en su estado?

[a]alive   [b]más... more than   [c]su... their own

Mujeres mixtecas con sus hijos

Repaso

Before beginning **Gramática 6**, review the forms and uses of **ser** that you know already by answering these questions.

1. ¿Es usted estudiante o profesor(a)?
2. ¿Cómo es usted? ¿Es una persona sentimental? ¿inteligente? ¿paciente? ¿elegante?
3. ¿Qué hora es? ¿A qué hora es la clase de español?
4. ¿Qué es un hospital? ¿Es una persona? ¿un objeto? ¿un edificio?

6 Expressing *to be* • Present Tense of ser; Summary of Uses (Part 2)

Gramática en acción: Presentaciones

Lea lo que dice Francisco y luego complete su descripción de su esposa.

—Hola. Me llamo Francisco Durán Ferrer, pero todos me llaman Pancho.
- **Soy** profesor de la universidad.
- **Soy** alto y moreno.
- **Soy** de Guanajuato, México.

—¿Y Lola Benítez Velasco, mi esposa?
- **Es** _____ (profesión).
- **Es** _____ y _____ (descripción).
- **Es** de _____ (origen).

Vocabulario útil

guapa, pesimista, muy inteligente
Jalisco (un estado de México)
médica en el Hospital Central, profesora también

ser (*to be*)			
(yo)	soy	(nosotros/as)	somos
(tú)	eres	(vosotros/as)	sois
(usted)		(ustedes)	
(él)	es	(ellos)	son
(ella)		(ellas)	

As you know, two Spanish verbs mean *to be:* **ser** and **estar.** They are not interchangeable; the meaning the speaker wants to convey determines their use. Here, you will review the uses of **ser** that you already know and learn some new ones. Remember to use **estar** to express location and to ask how someone is feeling. You will learn more about **estar** in **Gramática 15–16 (Cap. 6).**

Some basic uses of **ser** are presented on the following pages. You have used or seen all of them already in this and previous chapters.

Introductions Read what Francisco says and then complete his description of his wife. Hello. My name is Francisco Durán Ferrer, but everyone calls me Pancho. ■ I'm a university professor. ■ I'm tall and brunet. ■ I'm from Guanajuato, Mexico. And Lola Benítez Velasco, my wife? ■ She's _____. ■ She's _____ and _____. ■ She's from _____.

Gramática

Identification / La identificación

To *identify* people (including their profession) and things

> **¡OJO!**
>
> Note that the indefinite article is not used after **ser** before unmodified (undescribed) nouns of profession: **Carmen es profesora.** *but* **Carmen es una buena profesora.**

> **¡OJO!**
>
> Note the use of **e** instead of **y** when the next word starts with the sound **i-**. Also note the use of **u** instead of **o** when the next word starts with the sound **o-**.

Soy estudiante.
I'm a student.

Esto **es** un libro.
This is a book.

—¿Quiénes **son**?
—**Son** Camila e Ismael.
"Who are they?"
"They're Camila and Ismael."

—¿**Es** Mateo u Omar?
—Es Omar.
"Is he Mateo or Omar?"
"He's Omar?"

Description / La descripción

To *describe* people and things

You practiced this use of **ser** in **Gramática 5** in this chapter.

Soy sentimental.
I'm sentimental (a sentimental person).

El coche **es** muy viejo.
The car is very old.

Origin / El origen

With **de**, to express *origin*

Somos de Chile, pero nuestros padres **son de** la Argentina. ¿**De** dónde **es** usted?
We're from Chile, but our parents are from Argentina. Where are you from?

Generalizations / Las generalizaciones

To express *generalizations* (with **es** + *adjective*)

> **¡OJO!**
>
> Note that **es** + *adjective* is followed by an infinitive in this context, just like in English.

Es necesario estudiar. Por eso no **es posible** mirar la tele(visión) todos los días.
It's necessary to study. For that reason (That's why) it's not possible to watch television every day.

Here are two basic functions of **ser** that you have not yet practiced.

Possession / Las posesiones

With **de,** to express *possession*, to whom something belongs.

> **¡OJO!**
>
> Note that there is no **'s** in Spanish.

—Este **es** el perro **de** Carla. ¿**De** quién **son** las gatas?
—**Son** las gatas **de** Jorge.
"This is Carla's dog. Whose are those cats?"
"They're Jorge's cats."

The masculine singular article **el** contracts with **de** to form **del.** (No other article contracts with **de**.)

Use **¿de quién es... ?** to ask to whom something belongs.

> **¡OJO!**
>
> The subject pronoun **él** never contracts with **de**: **Es la casa de él.**

Esta **es** la casa **del** abuelo.
Esta **es** la casa **de la** abuela.

—¿**De quién es** esta casa?
—**Es del** abuelo.
"Whose house is this?"
"It's grandfather's."

Destination / **El destino**

With **para,** to tell for whom or what something *is intended*

¿Romeo y Julieta? **Es para** la clase de inglés.
Romeo and Juliet? It's for English class.

¿**Para** quién **son** los regalos? ¿**Para** mi nieto?
Who are the presents for? For my grandson?

Práctica y comunicación

A. Así es mi familia. (*That's what my family is like.*)

> **Paso 1. Autoprueba.** Complete las frases con las formas apropiadas del verbo **ser.**
>
> **1.** yo _____
> **2.** tú _____
> **3.** usted _____
> **4.** Pedro _____
>
> **5.** tú y yo _____
> **6.** Pedro y Alicia _____
> **7.** usted y sus (*your*) amigos _____
> **8.** tú y tus amigos _____

Paso 2. Complete las siguientes oraciones con formas del verbo **ser** y el adjetivo o frase apropiados.

1. Yo _____ miembro de una familia _____ (grande/pequeña).
2. Mi familia _____ de origen (*m.*) _____ (adjetivo de nacionalidad).
3. Mi familia más cercana (*closest*) y yo _____ de _____ (estado o país).
4. Otros parientes de mi familia _____ de _____ (estado o país).
5. Mi _____ (abuelo paterno/materno / abuela paterna/materna) _____ de _____ (estado o país).
6. En mi familia, (no) _____ normal _____ (celebrar fiestas familiares / bailar en las fiestas familiares / estar en contacto con frecuencia...).

Paso 3. Ahora use formas del verbo **ser** y las ideas del **Paso 2** para entrevistar (*interview*) a un compañero o una compañera.

1. ¿_____ miembro de una familia grande o pequeña?
2. ¿De qué nacionalidad _____ tu (*your*) familia? (**Mi** familia...)
3. ¿De qué estado o país _____ tu familia y tú? (Somos de...)
4. ¿De dónde _____ otros de tus parientes? (Otros de **mis** parientes...)
5. ¿De dónde _____ tu abuelo paterno/materno / tu abuela paterna/materna?
6. En tu familia, ¿_____ normal _____ (celebrar los cumpleaños [*birthdays*] / comer pizza / ...)?

B. Nacionalidades

Paso 1. ¿De dónde son, según los nombres, apellidos y ciudades?

MODELO: João Gonçalves, Lisboa → João Gonçalves **es de** Portugal.

1. John Doe, Nueva York
2. Karl Lotze, Berlín
3. Graziana Lazzarino, Roma
4. Malee Saetang, Bangkok

5. María Gómez, San Salvador
6. Claudette Moreau, París
7. Timothy Windsor, Londres
8. Hai Wang, Beijing

Paso 2. Ahora, dé su (*your*) información personal: ¿De dónde es usted? ¿De este estado / una metrópoli / un área rural? ¿Es de otro país?

Summary of Uses of *ser*

- to identify
- to describe
- to express origin
- to express generalizations
- to express possession
- to express whom or what something is intended for

Naciones

Alemania
China
El Salvador
los Estados Unidos
Francia
Inglaterra
Italia
Portugal
Tailandia

Prác. A, Paso 1: Answers: 1. soy 2. eres 3. es 4. es 5. somos 6. son 7. son 8. sois/son

C. Personas extranjeras

Paso 1. ¿Quiénes son, de dónde son y dónde trabajan ahora?

MODELO: **Teresa**: actriz / de Madrid / en Cleveland →
Teresa **es** actriz. **Es** de Madrid. **Ahora trabaja** en Cleveland.

1. **Carlos Miguel:** médico / de Cuba / en Milwaukee
2. **Pilar:** profesora / de Barcelona / en Miami
3. **Mariela:** dependienta / de Buenos Aires / en Nueva York
4. **Juan:** dentista* / de Lima / en Los Ángeles

Paso 2. Ahora hable sobre (*talk about*) un amigo o pariente, según el modelo del **Paso 1.** También puede (*you can*) usar el verbo **estudiar.**

D. ¿De quién es? Las siguientes cosas (*things*), ¿son de la rica actriz Jennifer Sánchez o de Martín Osborne, el estudiante pobre? En parejas, hagan y contesten preguntas. Las respuestas pueden (*can*) variar.

MODELO: la mochila →
E1: ¿De quién es la mochila?
E2: Es la mochila **del** estudiante. (La mochila es **del** estudiante).

1. la casa grande
2. la computadora
3. la limusina
4. los libros de texto
5. el Óscar

6. los exámenes
7. los exesposos
8. el teléfono celular
9. los mensajes

E. ¡Somos buenos amigos!

Paso 1. Complete el párrafo con las formas correctas de **ser** o con **hay.**

Me llamo Antonia y _____¹ de Chicago. (Yo) _____² estudiante de ingeniería en la Universidad de Illinois. En mis clases _____³ estudiantes de todas partesᵃ y muchos de ellos _____⁴ hispanos. Mi familia _____⁵ de origen mexicano y aunque nunca he vividoᵇ en México, hablo bastante bienᶜ el español. Me gusta hablar español con mi amigo Javier. Javier _____⁶ de Costa Rica y estudia ingeniería también. Javier y yo _____⁷ los asistentes del profesor Thomas; por eso pasamos mucho tiempo juntos.ᵈ Javier _____⁸ muy guapo y simpático, pero nosotros solo _____⁹ buenos amigos. Javier _____¹⁰ el novioᵉ de mi mejorᶠ amiga.

ᵃplaces ᵇaunque... *although I have never lived* ᶜbastante... *rather well* ᵈpasamos... *we spend a lot of time together* ᵉboyfriend ᶠbest

Paso 2. Comprensión. ¿Cierto o falso? Corrija las oraciones falsas.

	CIERTO	FALSO
1. Javier es costarricense.	☐	☐
2. Antonia es de México.	☐	☐
3. Antonia y Javier son novios.	☐	☐

---

*A number of professions end in **-ista** in both masculine and feminine forms. The article indicates gender: **el/la dentista, el/la artista**, and so on.*

F. Frida Kahlo

Paso 1. Complete las oraciones para hablar de Kahlo.

Frida Kahlo fue (*was*) …

1. _____
   (profesión).
2. _____
   (país).
3. _____
   (adjetivo).
4. _____
   (relación familiar).

Paso 2. Ahora use el modelo del **Paso 1** para hablar de una persona de su (*your*) familia.

Algo sobre una pintora mexicana

Frida Kahlo es una pintora mexicana muy famosa. Fue[a] la esposa del famoso muralista mexicano Diego Rivera. Los dos vivieron[b] por un tiempo en los Estados Unidos, en Nueva York y San Francisco.

En sus obras,[c] Frida se enfoca en sí misma.[d] Sus obras son autorretratos que incluyen elementos de la cultura mexicana.

 ¿Hay pintoras famosas en los Estados Unidos?

[a]*She was*   [b]*lived*   [c]*sus… her works*
[d]*se… looks inward at herself*

© 2022 Banco de México Diego Rivera Frida Kahlo Museums Trust, Mexico, D.F./ Artists Rights Society (ARS), New York

Autorretrato (*Self-portrait*) con monos (*monkeys*)

Digital image: Archivart/Alamy Stock Photo

Nota comunicativa: Cómo dar° explicaciones: *¿Por qué?, porque y para + infinitivo*

to give

¿por qué? = why
porque = because

—**¿Por qué** trabajas tanto?
—**¡Porque** necesito el dinero!

"Why do you work so much?"
"Because I need the money!"

para + *inf.* = in order to (*do something*)

—¿Por qué necesitamos otro paquete de canales de televisión?
—Pues… **para** mirar los partidos de fútbol…

"Why do we need another package of TV channels?"
"Well … (in order) to watch the soccer games …"

¡OJO!

Note: **porque** (one word, no accent) versus the interrogative **¿por qué?** (two words, accent on **qué**), meaning *why?*

You will practice using these words in **Práctica G.**

G. El regalo ideal

Paso 1. Look at Diego's list of gifts and what his family members like. With a partner, decide who receives each gift and why. A sample item is done for you.

MODELO: la camiseta (*t-shirt*) de la selección (*team*) nacional de México →
   E1: **¿Para quién** es la camiseta de la selección nacional de México?
   E2: **Es para** la prima.
   E1: **¿Por qué?**
   E2: **Porque** le gusta (*she likes*) el fútbol.

LOS REGALOS DE DIEGO

1. _____ una calculadora grande
2. _____ unas entradas (*tickets*) para un concierto
3. _____ un teléfono celular
4. _____ la última (*latest*) novela de Isabel Allende
5. _____ un balón (*ball*) oficial de la Copa del Mundo
6. _____ dinero

LOS MIEMBROS DE LA FAMILIA DE DIEGO

a. el primo: Desea estudiar en el extranjero (*abroad*).
b. el padre: Le gusta mucho el fútbol.
c. los abuelos: Les gusta mucho la música clásica.
d. el hermano: Estudia ingeniería y toma clases de matemáticas.
e. la hermana pequeña: Tiene 11 años y no tiene teléfono propio (*of her own*).
f. la madre: Le gusta mucho leer (*to read*).

Vocabulario útil

los audífonos	earphones
el coche	car
la ropa	clothing

Paso 2. With a partner, exchange ideas about good gifts for members of your family and also about good gifts for you.

MODELO: Para mi mamá, deseo comprar ropa, porque ella necesita ropa nueva. Yo necesito ropa nueva también.

H. ¿Qué opina usted? Exprese opiniones originales, afirmativas o negativas, con estas palabras como base.

MODELO: En mi opinión, **es importante hablar español en la clase de español.**

(no) es importante	
(no) es muy práctico	
(no) es necesario	
(no) es absurdo	
(no) es fascinante	
(no) es una molestia	+
(bother, pain)	
(no) es posible	

mirar series en la portátil
hablar español en la clase
tener muchas mascotas
llegar (*to arrive*) a clase puntualmente
tomar café en el salón de clase
hablar con los animales / las plantas
tomar mucho café
trabajar dieciocho horas al día
tener muchos hermanos
ser amable con todos los miembros de la familia
estar mucho tiempo (*a lot of time*) con la familia

 Repaso

You have already learned one way to express possession in Spanish: **de** + *noun*. Express these ideas in Spanish.

1. Juan's house
2. Jorge and Estela's grandfather
3. the man's niece
4. the student's book

You will learn another way to express possession in **Gramática 7.**

7 Expressing Possession • Unstressed Possessive Adjectives (Part 1)*

Gramática en acción: Invitación y posesión

Santiago y Sam
Juanita
los señores Gil

A. «¡Pasen, por favor! **Nuestra** casa es **su** casa».

Joaquín

B. «¡No son **tus** juguetes! ¡Son **mis** juguetes!».

Comprensión

En el dibujo A:
1. ¿De quién es la casa?
2. ¿Quiénes visitan la casa?

En el dibujo B:
3. ¿De quién son los juguetes?
4. ¿Quién desea jugar (*to play*) con los juguetes?

Invitation and Ownership A. "Come in, please! Our house is your house." *B.* "They're not your toys! They're my toys!"

*Another kind of possessive is called the stressed possessive adjective. It can be used as a noun. You will learn more about using stressed possessive adjectives in **Capítulo 17.**

Possessive adjectives (**Los adjetivos posesivos**) are words that tell *to whom* or *to what* something belongs: *my, her, their* ... You have already seen and used several possessive adjectives in Spanish. Here is the complete set.

Los adjetivos posesivos					
my	**mi** hijo/hija **mis** hijos/hijas	our	**nuestro** hijo **nuestros** hijos	**nuestra** hija **nuestras** hijas	
your (*fam.*)	**tu** hijo/hija **tus** hijos/hijas	your (*fam.*)	**vuestro** hijo **vuestros** hijos	**vuestra** hija **vuestras** hijas	
your (*form.*), his, her, its	**su** hijo/hija **sus** hijos/hijas	your (*form.*), their	**su** **sus**	hijo / hija hijos / hijas	

a possessive adjective / **un adjetivo posesivo =** an adjective that expresses who owns or has something

¡OJO!

The possessive adjective **tu** has no accent, but the subject pronoun **tú** does.

1. Agreement with Person or Thing Possessed

In Spanish, the ending of a possessive adjective agrees in form with the person or thing owned, not with the owner or possessor. Note that these possessive adjectives are placed before the noun.

The possessive adjectives **mi(s), tu(s),** and **su(s)** show agreement in number only (as seen in the chart above and to the right). **Nuestro/a/os/as** and **vuestro/a/os/as,** like all adjectives that end in **-o,** show agreement in both number and gender.

Es { mi / tu / su } herman**o**. Son { mi**s** / tu**s** / su**s** } herman**os**.

Es { nuestra / vuestra / su } famili**a**. Son { nuestra**s** / vuestra**s** / su**s** } famili**as**.

2. *Su(s)*

As you have seen, the word **su(s)** has several equivalents in English: *your* (sing.), *his, her, its, your* (pl.), and *their.* Usually its meaning is clear in context. When the meaning is not clear, the construction **de** + *pronoun* is used to indicate possession.

su hijo = **el** hijo de { usted, ustedes / él/ella / ellos/ellas }

sus hijos = **los** hijos de { usted, ustedes / él/ella / ellos/ellas }

3. *Su(s)* versus *vuestro/a/os/as*

The forms **vuestro/a/os/as** are the possessives that correspond to the subject pronoun **vosotros.** They are used only in Spain.

Latinoamérica
ustedes → su, sus

España
vosotros/as → vuestro/a/os/as ustedes → su, sus

Summary of Possessive Adjectives

mi(s)	nuestro/a(s)
tu(s)	vuestro/a(s)
su(s)	su(s)

A. Las posesiones

Paso 1. Autoprueba. Complete la tabla con los posesivos apropiados. **¡OJO!** Preste atención a (*Pay attention to*) las personas y los sustantivos. ¿Son masculinos o femeninos? ¿singulares o plurales? Siga (*Follow*) el modelo del número 1.

Personas	Adjetivos posesivos	Sustantivos
1. yo	mi	compañero de clase
2. nosotros/as = mi compañero/a y yo		computadoras
3. usted		mesa
4. las otras personas de la clase		escritorios
5. tú		teléfono celular
6. Luisa		profesoras

Paso 2. Ahora indique los sustantivos posibles para cada (*each*) adjetivo posesivo según su forma.

1. **su:** problema primos dinero tías escritorios familia
2. **tus:** perro idea hijos profesoras abuelo examen
3. **mi:** ventana médicos cuarto coche abuela gatos
4. **sus:** animales oficina nietas padre hermana abuelo
5. **nuestras:** guitarra libros materias lápiz sobrinas tía
6. **nuestros:** gustos consejero parientes puertas clases residencia

Paso 3. Ahora, en parejas, indiquen tres sustantivos para cada uno de los siguientes adjetivos posesivos.

MODELO: tu → **computadora, tía, perro**

Adjetivos posesivos (personas)	Tres sustantivos
1. mis	
2. su (de los estudiantes de la clase)	
3. sus (del profesor / de la profesora)	
4. nuestras (de nosotros dos)	

B. ¿Cuáles son sus hijos? Empareje (*Match*) las fotos de padres e hijos.

LOS PADRES

LOS HIJOS

1. 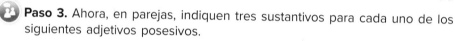 Su hija es _____.

a. David

2. Sus hijos son _____.

b. Sara

3. Sus hijas son _____.

c. Maribel y Julia

4. Su hijo es _____.

d. Joaquín y Rosa

Prác. A, Paso 1: Answers: 2. nuestras 3. su 4. sus 5. tu 6. sus

C. David y su familia

David

Paso 1. Describa a la familia de David.

MODELO: familia / pequeño →
  Su familia **es** pequeñ**a.**

1. hijo / alto
2. perro / feo
3. hija / pequeño
4. padre / simpático
5. esposa / amable

Paso 2. Ahora imagine que usted es David y modifique (*change*) las respuestas (*answers*).

MODELO: familia / pequeño →
  Mi familia es pequeñ**a.**

Paso 3. Ahora imagine que usted es la esposa de David. Hable por (*Speak for*) usted y por su esposo. Modifique solo las respuestas del 1 al 3.

MODELO: familia / pequeño →
  Nuestra familia es pequeñ**a.**

> ### Estrategia
>
> You must provide a possessive adjective for the noun, then a verb, as in the model. Then be sure that the adjective agrees with the noun!

D. ¿Sí o no?
Are the following things or people in your classroom right now? In these items, **su(s)** = *your* (**de usted**).

MODELOS: ¿su libro? → Sí, **mi** libro está en mi mochila. (No, **mi** libro está en casa).
  ¿los amigos de ustedes? → No, **nuestros** amigos no están en el salón de clase. Están en la cafetería.

1. ¿su computadora portátil?
2. ¿los libros de ustedes?
3. ¿el profesor / la profesora de ustedes?
4. ¿la computadora del profesor / de la profesora de ustedes?
5. ¿los teléfonos celulares de ustedes?
6. ¿su silla?
7. ¿sus padres? / ¿su esposo/a?
8. ¿la mochila de otro estudiante?
9. ¿su dinero? (la cartera = *wallet*)

> ### Estrategia
>
> Remember to use forms of **estar** to express location.

E. Intercambios

Paso 1. With a partner, take turns asking and answering questions about your families. Talk about what family members are like, their ages, some things they do, and so on. Use the model as a guide. Take notes on what your partner says.

MODELO: tu abuela →
  E1: Mi abuela es alta. ¿Y tu abuela? ¿Es alta?
  E2: Bueno, no. Mi abuela es baja.
  E1: ¿Cuántos años tiene?...

1. tu familia en general
2. tus padres
3. tus abuelos
4. tus hermanos/hijos
5. tu esposo/a / compañero/a de cuarto/casa

Paso 2. Tell the class one thing that you and your partner have in common.

MODELO: Nuestras abuelas tienen 75 años.

> ### ♻ Repaso
>
> The personal endings used with **-ar** verbs share some characteristics with those of **-er** and **-ir** verbs, which you will learn in **Gramática 8.** Review the present tense endings of **-ar** verbs by telling which subject pronoun(s) you associate with each of these endings.
>
> 1. -amos 2. -as
> 3. -an 4. -o 5. -a
> 6. -áis

8 Expressing Actions • Present Tense of -er and -ir Verbs; Subject Pronouns (Part 2)

Gramática en acción: Un estudiante típico

- Se llama Samuel Flores Toledo.
- Estudia en la UNAM (Universidad Nacional Autónoma de México).
- **Vive** con su familia en la Ciudad de México.
- **Come** pizza y tacos con frecuencia.
- **Bebe** café por la mañana.
- **Recibe** muchos e-mails de sus primos del Canadá.
- **Lee** y **escribe** mucho para su especialización.
- **Aprende** inglés porque desea visitar a su familia en Ontario.

Klic Video Productions/McGraw Hill

Samuel Flores Toledo

¿Y usted?

Complete las oraciones con formas verbales que terminan en **-o** (= **yo**) y con información personal.

1. Yo (no) viv**o** con mi familia.
2. (No) Com_____ muchos tacos.
3. Recib_____ muchos e-mails de_____.
4. Le_____ y escrib_____ mucho para mi clase de _____.
5. Aprend_____ español en esta clase.

In **Capítulo 2** you learned a number of verbs whose infinitive ends in **-ar.** Remember that in Spanish verbs have three types of infinitive endings: **-ar, -er,** and **-ir.** These endings are very important in Spanish, because they determine the verb conjugation, that is, the endings for the different persons of the conjugation. In this section you will learn about verbs whose infinitive ends in **-er** or **-ir.**

Present Tense of -er/-ir Verbs / El tiempo presente de los verbos -er/-ir

1. Present Tense Endings
The present tense of **-er** and **-ir** verbs is formed by adding personal endings to the stem of the verb (the infinitive minus its **-er/-ir** ending). The personal endings for **-er** and **-ir** verbs are the same except for the first and second person plural.

Las terminaciones -er/-ir del tiempo presente			
-er		**-ir**	
-o	-**e**mos	-o	-**í**mos
-es	-**é**is	-es	-**í**s
-e	-en	-e	-en

¡OJO!

Only the endings for **nosotros** and **vosotros** are different for **-er** and **-ir** verbs.

com**er** (*to eat*)				viv**ir** (*to live*)			
(yo)	com**o**	(nosotros/as)	com**emos**	(yo)	viv**o**	(nosotros/as)	viv**ímos**
(tú)	com**es**	(vosotros/as)	com**éis**	(tú)	viv**es**	(vosotros/as)	viv**ís**
(usted)		(ustedes)		(usted)		(ustedes)	
(él)	com**e**	(ellos)	com**en**	(él)	viv**e**	(ellos)	viv**en**
(ella)		(ellas)		(ella)		(ellas)	

A typical student ■ *His name is Samuel Flores Toledo.* ■ *He studies at UNAM (the National Autonomous University of Mexico).* ■ *He lives with his family in Mexico City.* ■ *He frequently eats pizza and tacos.* ■ *He drinks coffee in the morning.* ■ *He gets a lot of e-mails from his cousins in Canada.* ■ *He reads and writes a lot for his major.* ■ *He's learning English because he wants to visit his family in Ontario.*

2. Important -er/-ir Verbs

These are the frequently used **-er** and **-ir** verbs you will find in this chapter.

leer

escribir

-er verbs		-ir verbs	
aprender	to learn	**abrir**	to open
aprender + **a** + *inf.*	to learn how to (*do something*)	**asistir (a)**	to attend, go to (*a class, a function*)
beber	to drink	**escribir**	to write
comer	to eat	**recibir**	to receive
comprender	to understand	**vivir**	to live
creer (en)	to think; to believe (in)		
deber + *inf.*	should, must, ought to (*do something*)		
leer	to read		
vender	to sell		

- **Deber,** like **desear** and **necesitar,** is followed by an infinitive.

- **Aprender** + **a** + *infinitive* means *to learn how to* (*do something*).

Debes leer tus e-mails todos los días.
You should read your e-mails on a daily basis.

Muchos niños **aprenden a hablar** español con sus abuelos.
Many children learn to speak Spanish with their grandparents.

3. English Equivalents of the Present Tense

Remember that the Spanish present tense has a number of present tense equivalents in English. It can also be used to express future meaning.

como = *I eat, I am eating, I will eat*

Uses of Subject Pronouns / Los usos de los pronombres personales

In English, a verb must have an expressed subject (a noun or pronoun): *the train* arrives, *she* says. In Spanish, however, as you have probably noticed, an expressed subject is not required. Verbs are accompanied by a subject pronoun only for clarification, emphasis, or contrast.

- *Clarification:* When the context does not make the subject clear, the subject pronoun is expressed. This happens most frequently with third person singular and plural verb forms.

- *Emphasis:* Subject pronouns are used in Spanish to emphasize the subject when in English you would stress it with your voice.

- *Contrast:* Contrast is a special case of emphasis. Subject pronouns are used to contrast the actions of two individuals or groups.

Unclear: Escribe cartas. Nunca **escribe** cartas. →
Ella escribe cartas. **Él** nunca escribe cartas.
She writes letters. He never writes letters.

—¿Quién debe pagar?   *"Who should pay?"*
—¡**Tú** debes pagar!   *"**You** should pay!"*

Ellos leen mucho; **nosotros** leemos poco.
__They__ read a lot; __we__ read little.

¡OJO!

Avoid using subject pronouns in Spanish when they are not necessary. The overuse of subject pronouns sounds overbearing to native speakers of Spanish.

Unnecessary: Yo soy de Tampa. Yo soy estudiante universitario. Yo vivo con mi familia.
Natural: (Yo) Soy de Tampa. Soy estudiante universitario. Vivo con mi familia.

Práctica y comunicación

A. Asociaciones. Empareje (*Match*) las ideas y cosas (*things*) con el verbo más lógico. Luego (*Then*) dé otras ideas para cada (*each*) verbo.

MODELO: **1.** abrir → e: abrir **una puerta** También: abrir **una ventana...**

VERBOS

1. abrir
2. aprender
3. asistir a
4. beber
5. comer
6. deber
7. escribir
8. leer
9. vivir

IDEAS Y COSAS

a. una revista (*magazine*)
b. una composición
c. un té
d. las materias
e. una puerta
f. un concierto
g. tortillas y tamales
h. estudiar más
i. en un apartamento
j. la tarea (*homework*)

Algo sobre la comida° de México

food

El maíz[a] es el producto esencial en la comida de los mexicanos y otros pueblos[b] americanos desde[c] 1500 a. e. c. (mil quinientos antes de la era común). Es la base para las tortillas y los tamales. El tamal consiste en masa[d] de maíz con otros ingredientes, envuelta[e] y cocida[f] en hojas[g] de maíz (u hojas de otras plantas, como el plátano[h]).

 En su opinión, ¿qué ingredientes son esenciales en la comida de su país de origen?

[a]*corn*   [b]*peoples*   [c]*since*   [d]*dough*   [e]*wrapped*   [f]*steamed*   [g]*leaves*   [h]*plantain*

Un delicioso tamal mexicano

Sergio Salvador/Getty Images

B. En la clase de español

Paso 1. Autoprueba. Dé la forma apropiada de los infinitivos.

1. yo: comer _____, vivir _____
2. tú: aprender _____, escribir _____
3. él: creer _____, abrir _____
4. nosotros: leer _____, asistir _____
5. ustedes: comprender _____, recibir _____

Paso 2. Ahora use las siguientes ideas para expresar acciones que usted hace (*do*) o no hace en la clase de español.

MODELO: comer en clase → **Como** en clase. (No **como** en clase.)

1. escribir respuestas en un cuaderno
2. aprender palabras nuevas
3. asistir a clase todos los días
4. beber café o té en clase
5. comprender las instrucciones para las actividades
6. abrir la portátil en clase
7. leer mis mensajes de texto
8. comer

Paso 3. Ahora, en parejas, túrnense para hacer y contestar preguntas basadas en el **Paso 2.** Luego (*Then*), digan (*tell*) a la clase algo (*something*) que ustedes tienen en común.

MODELO: **1.** escribir respuestas en un cuaderno →
E1: ¿Escribes respuestas en un cuaderno?
E2: No, no escribo respuestas en un cuaderno.
E2: Yo tampoco. (*Me neither.*) (Yo sí).
EN COMÚN: Nosotros/as dos (no) escribimos respuestas en un libro de texto.

Prác. B, Paso 1: Answers: 1. como, vivo 2. aprendes, escribes 3. cree, abre 4. leemos, asistimos 5. comprenden, reciben

C. Diego habla de su padre. Complete el siguiente párrafo con la forma correcta de los verbos entre paréntesis.

Mi padre _____ (vender)[1] coches y trabaja mucho. Mis hermanos y yo _____ (aprender)[2] mucho de papá. Según mi padre, los jóvenes _____ (deber)[3] _____ (asistir)[4] a clase todos los días, porque es su obligación. Papá también _____ (creer)[5] que no es necesario mirar la televisión por la noche. Es más interesante _____ (leer)[6] el periódico,[a] una revista o un buen libro. Por eso _____ (*nosotros:* leer)[7] o _____ (escribir)[8] por la noche y no miramos la televisión. Yo admiro a mi papá y _____ (creer)[9] que él _____ (comprender)[10] la importancia de la educación.

[a]*newspaper*

Comprensión. ¿Cierto o falso? Corrija las oraciones falsas.

	CIERTO	FALSO
1. Diego y sus hermanos venden coches.	☐	☐
2. Diego mira mucho la televisión.	☐	☐
3. El padre de Diego lee mucho.	☐	☐

D. Este domingo, tamalada

Paso 1. Una tamalada consiste en hacer (*making*) y comer tamales. Hay familias que hacen una tamalada en ocasiones especiales.

Complete las siguientes oraciones con la forma apropiada de un verbo de **Vocabulario útil.** El número 2 entre paréntesis indica que usted debe usar el verbo dos veces (*twice*) en las oraciones.

Charlie Neuman/U-T San Diego/ZUMA Wire/Alamy Stock Photo

Una escena típica de una tamalada

¡OJO!

Hay verbos de todos tipos en la lista: **-ar, -er, -ir,** irregular.

Vocabulario útil

aprender, asistir, beber, celebrar, comprender, creer, deber, leer (2), **mirar, preparar, ser** (2), **vivir**

1. Hoy todos nosotros _____[1] el cumpleaños (*birthday*) de mi abuela y hay una tamalada.
2. Toda la familia _____[2] a la tamalada en nuestra casa.
3. Mis padres y mis tíos _____[3] los tamales, con la ayuda (*help*) de las mujeres de la familia.
4. Después de comer (*After eating*), los adultos _____[4] café.
5. Muchos _____[5] la tele y mi padre _____[6] el periódico.
6. Yo _____[7] un libro a los niños pequeños. Mi prima Lucy _____[8] descansar (*rest*) porque solo tiene 2 años.
7. Mi primo Rudy, que (*who*) _____[9] en Oklahoma, no _____[10] todo porque su español no _____[11] perfecto. Pero _____[12] rápido.
8. Yo _____[13] que todos mis tíos _____[14] cocineros (*cooks*) excelentes.

Paso 2. Comprensión. Complete las oraciones con información del **Paso 1.**

1. _____ es un ejemplo de una fiesta familiar.
2. Esta familia celebra _____ de la abuela.
3. _____ preparan los tamales; _____ ayudan (*help*).
4. Después de comer, unos _____ y _____.
5. La persona que narra la historia (*story*) _____.
6. Rudy no _____ bien el español.

Nota comunicativa: Cómo expresar la frecuencia de las acciones

AT THE BEGINNING OR END OF A SENTENCE

a veces	sometimes, at times
con frecuencia	frequently
siempre	always
todos los días	every day
una vez a la semana	once a week

AT THE BEGINNING OF A SENTENCE

casi nunca	almost never
nunca	never

Hablo con mis amigos **todos los días.** Hablo con mis padres **una vez a la semana. Casi nunca** hablo con mis abuelos. Y **nunca** hablo con mis tíos que viven en Italia.

You will use these expressions in **Práctica E.**

Estrategia

- Use **nunca** and **casi nunca** at the beginning of the sentence instead of **no.**
- Don't use **yo** in front of the verbs.
- Adjust the possessive adjectives, as needed.

E. ¿Con qué frecuencia?

Paso 1. Indique con oraciones completas la frecuencia con que usted hace (*do*) las siguientes actividades.

EXPRESIONES DE FRECUENCIA:

todos los días   con frecuencia   a veces   casi nunca   nunca

MODELO: **1.** recibir un e-mail de **sus** padres/abuelos ➜
Todos los días recibo e-mails de **mis** abuelos. / **Nunca recibo** un e-mail de **mis** abuelos.

1. recibir un e-mail de sus padres/abuelos
2. escribir en su Facebook
3. usar la computadora en una clase
4. comer pizza
5. leer revistas
6. beber café
7. comprar cosas por (*things on the*) internet
8. vender sus libros al final del semestre/trimestre

Paso 2. Ahora compare sus oraciones con las (*those*) de dos compañeros/compañeras. Luego (*Then*), digan (*tell*) a la clase algo (*something*) que ustedes tienen en común.

MODELO: **1.** recibir un e-mail de **sus** padres/abuelos ➜
EN COMÚN: Todos los días los/las tres recibimos un e-mail de **nuestros** abuelos. (Nunca recibimos un e-mail de **nuestros** abuelos).

F. Intercambios. Use las siguientes frases para entrevistar (*interview*) a un compañero o una compañera. Use expresiones de frecuencia cuando sea (*it is*) apropiado. Luego (*Then*) digan (*tell*) a la clase algo (*something*) que ustedes tienen en común.

MODELO: leer + novelas de terror
➜ Carmen, ¿lees novelas de terror a veces?
EN COMÚN: Los/Las dos leemos novelas de terror a veces. (Nunca leemos novelas de terror).

| (nombre de estudiante), (tú) tus padres/hijos tus abuelos tu mejor (*best*) amigo/a | + | abrir beber comprender escribir leer recibir vender vivir ¿ ? | + | mucho/poco la situación / los problemas de los estudiantes Coca-Cola/café antes de (*before*) la clase tu ropa (*clothing*), un auto viejo la puerta a (*for*) las mujeres / los hombres novelas de ciencia ficción / de terror el periódico / una revista todos los días muchas/pocas cartas, novelas, revistas muchos/pocos ejercicios, libros, regalos en una casa / un apartamento / una residencia en otra ciudad / en otro estado/país en un cuaderno / con un bolígrafo/lápiz |
| | + | deber | + | mirar mucho/poco la televisión llegar a casa tarde/temprano |

G. **Una fiesta.** There is a Spanish saying, **«Una fiesta se hace** (*is made*) **con tres personas: una canta, otra baila y la otra toca.»** In pairs, use this saying as a model to tell what the following things are "made of."

MODELO: una clase → Una clase **se hace con** un profesor o una profesora. Esta persona enseña la clase. Además hay unos estudiantes. Desean aprender la materia y estudian mucho. Leen su libro de texto y escriben informes (*papers*). También hay un salón de clase, un pizarrón...

¿Cómo se hace... ?

1. una clase de español
2. una fiesta en esta universidad
3. una universidad
4. una familia

Estrategia

Use ...
- all of the **-ar/-er/-ir** verbs that you know
- the irregular verbs <u>**ser**</u> and <u>**estar**</u>
- forms of <u>**tener:**</u> **tengo, tienes, tiene**
- the verb form **hay**

Todo junto

A. Lengua y cultura: Las familias

Paso 1. Completar. Complete the following paragraphs about families. Give the correct form of the words in parentheses, as suggested by context.

¿Existe la familia hispana típica? La idea de que las familias hispanas son muy _____ (grande)[1] es un estereotipo del pasado,[a] especialmente en las _____ (grande)[2] ciudades. Ahora, la norma _____ (ser)[3] una familia con uno o dos hijos. Es difícil[b] tener _____ (mucho)[4] hijos cuando las madres y los padres _____ (trabajar)[5] fuera de la casa,[c] y cuando los abuelos o tías no _____ (vivir)[6] en casa para cuidar a[d] los niños.

A pesar de[e] la reducción en el número de hijos, los hispanos _____ (creer)[7] que la familia es su institución _____ (principal).[8] Muchos hispanos mantienen[f] relaciones con parientes que _____ (estar)[9] en otro país y muchos les mandan[g] dinero y regalos para ayudarlos.[h] En las reuniones _____ (familiar)[10] también es frecuente incluir a parientes de _____ (vario)[11] generaciones.

En su opinión, ¿hay _____ (mucho)[12] diferencias entre su familia y las familias hispanas que conoce[i]?

[a]*past* [b]*difficult* [c]fuera... *outside the home* [d]cuidar... *care for* [e]A... *In spite of* [f]*keep up, maintain* [g]les... *send them* [h]*help them* [i]*you know*

Una familia mexicana que celebra un día especial

Paso 2. Comprensión. ¿Cierto o falso? Corrija las oraciones falsas.

	CIERTO	FALSO
1. Todas las familias hispanas son grandes.	☐	☐
2. Por lo general (*Generally*), las familias urbanas son pequeñas.	☐	☐
3. Para los hispanos, la familia es una institución social fundamental.	☐	☐

Paso 3. En acción

Ahora, en parejas, contesten la pregunta del final del **Paso 1.** Deben escribir 3 o 4 oraciones para expresar su opinión. Usen las oraciones de **Lengua y cultura** como modelo y hagan los cambios (*changes*) necesarios. **¡OJO!** No es necesario usar todo el texto original.

MODELOS: En **nuestra** opinión (no) hay muchas diferencias entre **nuestras** familias y las familias hispanas.
No estamos de acuerdo. Yo creo que... pero mi compañera cree...
En la familia típica estadounidense/mexicana, hay...

Vocabulario útil

juntos/as	together
mismo/a	same
unido/a	close
para ti/usted	for you, in your case
la tradición	

Un abuelo hispano con su hijo y su nieto

B. Proyecto: Las familias de las personas de la clase

Working in groups, create a profile of the types of families your classmates have and/or their ideas about family.

Paso 1. Preparación. In groups, think of characteristics or actions that are relevant to family life. Make a list of one or two ideas for each member of your group. Ideas to consider: if parents live together, proximity to or interaction with grandparents, actions family members do together, the presence of another language or traditions, and so on.

MODELOS: Los abuelos (no) viven en la misma ciudad.
(No) Es importante comer juntos todos los días.

Now use those ideas to create questions to poll your classmates. Use different polling options. For example: **cierto o falso,** open-ended questions (like **¿Cuántos/as... ?**), or a series of options (asking about frequency with **todos los días, con frecuencia,...**) You can also ask for opinions using **creer + que... ¡OJO!** Don't forget to use the appropriate possessive adjectives.

MODELOS: Los abuelos (no) viven en la misma ciudad. →

¿Viven **tus** abuelos en la misma ciudad?
¿Cierto o falso para ti? **Mis** abuelos viven en la misma ciudad.

Es importante comer juntos todos los días. →

¿Crees que es importante comer juntos todos los días?

Paso 2. Encuesta. (Poll.) Each member of your group should poll as many classmates as possible using their particular question(s). Before you start polling, create a table on which to record the answers. And don't forget to ask for and record the names of the classmates you poll.

Nombre	Los abuelos viven en la misma ciudad. Sí No	Cree que es importante comer juntos todos los días. Sí No

Video: Salu2 «Padres modernos»

You can watch two segments of this chapter's video in the **Video: Salu2** section, found at the end of the eBook.

Una familia californiana de origen mexicano

Paso 3: Análisis de datos (data). Gather the information from your group's polling, and prepare 4 or 5 statements to share with the rest of the class. Here are some examples of statements. You can use them or create your own.

1. En nuestra encuesta / Para esta pregunta hay información de _____ (número) estudiantes.
2. Los abuelos de _____ (número) estudiantes viven en la misma ciudad.
3. _____ (número) estudiantes creen que es importante comer juntos todos los días. _____ creen que no es importante.

Enfoque cultural:
La familia

Antes de leer

¿Es normal para los jóvenes estadounidenses vivir con su familia cuando tienen 20 años o más? Si usted vive con su familia, ¿le gusta? ¿Le gusta vivir cerca de (*close to*) su familia?

En México

Ozgur Coskun/Alamy Stock Photo

Un padre con su hija adulta

Por tradición,[a] las familias en México son muy unidas.[b] Esto tiene ventajas[c] para los niños y adolescentes: tienen el apoyo[d] de sus padres, hermanos y parientes cercanos.[e] Pero hay personas que creen que esta unión familiar presenta problemas. Cuando los jóvenes viven con sus padres hasta que[f] son adultos, pueden perder[g] parte de su identidad individual. Muchos jóvenes viven con su familia hasta que contraen matrimonio.[h] Y si no contraen matrimonio, siempre viven en casa de sus padres.

Aquí hay unas cifras para pensar.[i]

- El 89% (por ciento) de los hogares[j] mexicanos son de tipo familiar, es decir,[k] entre[l] las personas que los forman[m] existe una relación familiar.
- El 17% de los hogares familiares son monoparentales. Las mujeres son responsables de su familia[n] en la inmensa mayoría[ñ] de los hogares monoparentales.
- El número promedio[o] por hogar familiar es de casi cuatro personas.

[a]Por... *Traditionally* [b]*close-knit* [c]*advantages* [d]*support* [e]*close* [f]hasta... *until* [g]pueden... *they can lose* [h]hasta... *until they marry* [i]cifras... *numbers to think about* [j]*homes* [k]es... *that is* [l]*among* [m]los... *make them up* [n]responsables... *the heads of the household* [ñ]la... *the great majority* [o]*average*

Comprensión ¿Cuál es una característica de las familias mexicanas? ¿Es normal para las personas jóvenes vivir independiente de sus familias en México antes (*before*) del matrimonio?

En otros países hispanos

Mike Kemp/Tetra Images/Alamy Stock Photo

Una familia numerosa española

- **En todo el mundo hispanohablante** Es impresionante cómo los hispanos de todos los países coinciden en cuanto a[a] la importancia de la familia. También es típico en todo el mundo hispano que los hijos se independicen[b] tarde.

- **En España** Las familias numerosas (con tres o más hijos) reciben ayuda[c] económica estatal[d] en muchos contextos: tienen descuentos en los transportes, en los museos, en la universidad, etcétera. Es una manera de ayudar[e] a las familias con muchos hijos. Además, es importante incentivar familias con más hijos porque España es un país con una tasa de natalidad[f] muy baja (1,21 hijos por[g] mujer en 2019).

[a]en... *with regard to* [b]se... *become independent* [c]*help* [d]*from the state* [e]*helping* [f]tasa... *birth rate* [g]*per*

Comprensión ¿Qué tipo de familias recibe ayuda especial del estado en España? ¿Por qué?

👆 En acción

Investigue (*Research*) cuál es el índice de natalidad de su país. ¿Es alto o bajo en comparación con el (*that*) de otros países?

Vocabulario para leer

anterior	previous
creciente	growing
mayor	older
menos	less, fewer
mismo/a	same
solo/a	single; alone
varios/as	various
cuidar (a)	to care for

Lectura

Antes de leer

¿Tiene usted idea de cuántas personas viven en los hogares *(households)* de los Estados Unidos y el Canadá? Seleccione el número correcto para cada *(each)* espacio: **9, 25, 28.**

- El _____% (por ciento) de la población vive sola *(alone)*.
- El _____% de los hogares consiste en *(consists of)* parejas con hijos.
- El _____% de los hogares son monoparentales.

Infografía: La familia en México

En México las familias están evolucionando.[a] Este tipo de evolución es representativo de la institución de la familia por todo el mundo.[b]

Roles diversificados

Madres y padres trabajan fuera de la casa[c] y también cuidan a sus hijos.

Microfamilias

Hogares que consisten en una sola persona, una tendencia creciente[d] en todo el mundo.

Amigos y mascotas

La estructura familiar incluye más que[e] parientes.

Datos clave[f]

- El 89% de los mexicanos viven en familia (padres e hijo[s]).
- El 1% de las familias mexicanas son homoparentales, y el 53% de estas familias tienen hijo(s).
- En el 57% de los hogares hay mascotas, y el 85% de las mascotas son perros.

Más allá de[g] la familia nuclear tradicional: Otros tipos de hogares comunes

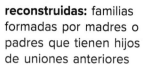

monoparentales: solo la madre o el padre con sus hijos

reconstruidas: familias formadas por madres o padres que tienen hijos de uniones anteriores

homoparentales: los padres son personas del mismo sexo

sin[h] hijos: parejas jóvenes, por lo general

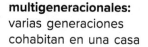

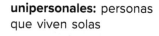

mayores de 60 años: si tienen hijos, no están en el hogar familiar

multigeneracionales: varias generaciones cohabitan en una casa

unipersonales: personas que viven solas

---

[a]están... *are evolving* [b]por... *worldwide* [c]fuera... *outside of the home* [d]*growing* [e]más... *more than* [f]Datos... *Key facts*
[g]Más... *Beyond* [h]*without*

Comprensión

A. ¿Cierto o falso? Según la infografía, ¿son ciertas o falsas las siguientes oraciones?

	CIERTO	FALSO
1. Todos los mexicanos viven en una familia de dos padres e hijo(s).	☐	☐
2. No son muy comunes las familias en las que *(which)* las madres y los padres trabajan y cuidan a sus hijos.	☐	☐
3. Las mascotas no son importantes para los mexicanos.	☐	☐
4. Las parejas sin hijos son ancianas *(elderly)* por lo general.	☐	☐

Capítulo 3 La familia

B. Clasificación. Mire los siete tipos de familias de la infografía. ¿De qué tipo es cada (*each*) una de las siguientes familias?

1. Matías tiene dos hijos y está divorciado. Sofía tiene una hija y está divorciada. Ahora Matías y Sofía viven juntos (*together*) con sus tres hijos.
2. Juan Carlos y Alonso tienen un hijo de 12 años.
3. Diego y Camila son ancianos. Sus hijos viven en otro estado.
4. Ana y Martín tienen tres hijos pequeños de 3, 5 y 7 años. Viven con los padres de Martín.
5. Lucía vive sola con su perro Atila.
6. Samuel está divorciado; vive con sus dos hijas, Elena y Emilia.

Proyecto: La demografía de las familias de la clase

Paso 1. ¿Cómo son las familias de sus compañeros de clase? Mire la infografía y determine la información que desea recoger (*to gather*) de sus compañeros de clase. Después prepare unas preguntas específicas.

Paso 2. Use las preguntas del **Paso 1** para entrevistar a varias personas de su clase.

Paso 3. En grupos, organicen la información demográfica de su clase de manera visual, con gráficos y tablas o en una infografía.

Textos orales

La familia de Lucía Jiménez Flores

Antes de escuchar

¿Cómo es su familia? ¿Tiene usted hermanos casados (*married*)? ¿Tiene buenas relaciones con sus cuñados (*brothers- and sisters-in-law*)? ¿Tiene padrinos (*godparents*) o es padrino o madrina de un niño?

Vocabulario para escuchar	
la escuela	school
la cuñada	sister-in-law
travieso/a	troublemaker
las mellizas	twins
juntos/as	together

Comprensión

A. El árbol genealógico de la familia. Complete el árbol genealógico con los nombres de los miembros de la familia.

B. ¿Quién es quién? Complete las oraciones.

1. La cuñada de Lucía se llama _____.
2. El cuñado de José se llama _____.
3. Lucía tiene tres _____.
4. La abuela de Camila tiene _____ años.
5. El nombre del padre de Lucía es _____.
6. La familia de Lucía es de _____ (ciudad).
7. En México, Lucía tiene muchos _____.

En acción

Complete las siguientes ideas sobre usted y su familia.

1. La mayor parte de mi familia vive en (el área de) _____.
2. Muchas personas de mi familia son _____ y _____ (adjetivos).
3. Creo que mi familia es / no es muy unida (*close-knit*).
4. En mi familia existe / no existe la tradición de madrinas y padrinos (*godparents*).

Fabrice Lerouge/SuperStock

Erik Isakson/Blend Images/ Getty Images

¿Una familia típica?

🎤 Entrevista

Use de (*as a*) modelo las preguntas y respuestas (*answers*) de la sección **Entrevista** al principio (*at the beginning*) de este capítulo para hablar de sus propios estudios universitarios (*own university studies*).

💻 Escritura

Un ensayo sobre° la familia

ensayo... *essay about*

¿Cómo son las familias estadounidenses? ¿Hay una familia estereotípica? ¿Qué une (*unites*) a los miembros de una familia?

👥 Antes de escribir

Decida un enfoque (*focus*) para su ensayo. Luego (*Then*) use las siguientes preguntas y otras más para entrevistar (*interview*) a varios miembros de la clase. Las respuestas pueden (*can*) ser útiles para documentar las diferentes estructuras familiares y usar como ejemplos en su ensayo. Repase (*Review*) el vocabulario de **Más parientes** (pág. 67).

- ¿Viven tus padres en el mismo domicilio (*same residence*)?
- ¿Cuántos hermanos tienes?
- ¿Tienes padrastro / madrastra / hermanastro/a(s) / hijastro/a(s) / medio/a(s) hermano/a(s) / ... ?
- ¿Viven tus abuelos cerca (*nearby*)?
- ¿Cuál es el país de origen de tu familia?
- _____ (una pregunta propia [*of your own*])

Estrategia

As you learn Spanish, you will often need to look up words in the dictionary. Here are a few suggestions for using the dictionary efficiently.

- Pay attention to the gender of nouns (nouns are typically marked with *m.* for masculine or *f.* for feminine.)
- Don't settle for the first translation given; words in all languages can have more than one meaning. The extra seconds spent looking at all of the translations can be very informative!
- Notice if the word has an accent mark.
- Take full advantage of the audio capabilities of online dictionaries and listen to the pronunciation of the words you look up.
- Using an online dictionary is not the same as using an online translator. The translator may give you an accurate final product, but using it prevents you from the exploration and mistakes that are necessary for language learning.

A escribir

Ahora use sus opiniones y las respuestas de sus compañeros para escribir un ensayo sobre (*about*) la familia moderna. Hay más ayuda (*help*) en Connect.

Para escribir bien

Here are some words and phrases that can be useful in your essay.

- Words to describe and quantify nouns (adjectives): **grande/pequeña, muchas/pocas,...**
- Expressions that indicate frequency (adverbs): **a veces, (casi) nunca, (casi) siempre, con frecuencia,...**
- Words to connect ideas: **pero, también, y (e), o (u)**

En la comunidad

Entreviste a (*Interview*) una persona hispana sobre (*about*) su familia.

Preguntas posibles

- ¿Tiene esta persona una familia grande o pequeña? ¿Cuáles son los miembros de la familia?
- ¿Cuál es el país de origen de los abuelos de la persona? ¿Viven solos (*alone*) o con un pariente?
- ¿Los parientes se reúnen (*get together*) con frecuencia? ¿En qué ocasiones?

Producción audiovisual

Con las preguntas de la **Entrevista** como modelo, filme una o dos entrevistas con personas que hablan de sus familias.

Más ideas para el portafolio

- Busque (*Look for*) una fotografía de su familia y seleccione un adjetivo especial para cada (*each*) persona de la foto.
- Escriba un breve poema sobre (*about*) una persona de su familia que es muy especial para usted. Use el modelo de la página 73.
- Dé tres palabras favoritas de este capítulo para usted. ¿Por qué son interesantes para usted? ¿Con qué las asocia usted (*do you associate them*)?
- Si ha estado jugando (*you have been playing*) Practice Spanish: Study Abroad, en Quest 2, usted conoció (*met*) a un fantasma (*ghost*) que se llama la Mancarita. Dibuje (*Draw*) a la Mancarita y luego escriba cuatro oraciones que la describen (*that describe her*).

Sugerencia: You are now ready to play Quest 2 in **Practice Spanish: Study Abroad.**

EN RESUMEN En este capítulo

AFTER STUDYING THIS CHAPTER I CAN ...

☐ name family members (66–67)

☐ count from 31 to 100 (68)

☐ describe people, places, things, and ideas using adjectives and the verb **ser** (71, 73–75)

☐ also use **ser** to express identification, origin, generalizations, possession, and destination (79–81)

☐ use possessive adjectives to distinguish what's mine and what belongs to others (84–85)

☐ talk about more actions with **-er** and **-ir** verbs (88–89)

☐ avoid subject pronouns but use them to clarify or emphasize the subject (89)

☐ recognize/describe at least 2–3 aspects of Mexican cultures

Gramática en breve

5. Adjectives: Gender, Number, and Position

Adjective Endings

Singular	Plural
-o	**-os**
-a	**-as**
-e	**-es**
-[consonant]	-[consonant] + **-es**

6. Present Tense of *ser*; Summary of Uses

ser: soy, eres, es, somos, sois, son

Uses of **ser:** identification, description, origin, generalizations, possession, destination

de + el → del

7. Unstressed Possessive Adjectives

yo → mi(s)   nosotros/as → nuestro/a(s)

tú → tu(s)   vosotros/as → vuestro/a(s)

usted, → su(s)   ustedes, → su(s)

(él, ella)   (ellos, ellas)

8. Present Tense of *-er* and *-ir* Verbs; Subject Pronouns

Regular -er Verb Endings

-o, -es, -e, -emos, -éis, -en

Regular -ir Verb Endings

-o, -es, -e, -imos, -ís, -en

When to use subject pronouns: for clarification, emphasis, and contrast

Vocabulario

Los verbos

¡OJO!

Remember that all forms of infinitives shown in <u>**red**</u> and <u>**underlined**</u> in **Vocabulario** lists are conjugated in all tenses and moods in Appendix 5.

abrir	to open
aprender	to learn
aprender a + *inf.*	to learn how to (*do something*)
asistir (a)	to attend, go to (a *class, a function*)
beber	to drink
comer	to eat
comprender	to understand
<u>**creer**</u> **(en)**	to think; to believe (in)
deber + *inf.*	should, must, ought to (*do something*)
escribir	to write
leer	to read
llegar	to arrive
mirar	to look at; to watch
mirar la tele(visión)	to watch television
recibir	to receive
<u>**ser**</u>	to be
vender	to sell
vivir	to live

La familia y los parientes

el/la abuelo/a	grandfather/grandmother
los abuelos	grandparents
el/la esposo/a	husband/wife
el/la hermano/a	brother/sister
los hermanos	siblings
el/la hijo/a	son/daughter
los hijos	children
la madre (mamá)	mother (mom)
el marido	husband
la mujer	wife
el/la nieto/a	grandson/granddaughter
el/la niño/a	small child; boy/girl
el padre (papá)	father (dad)
los padres	parents
la pareja	partner; significant other; couple
el/la primo/a	cousin
los primos	cousins
el/la sobrino/a	nephew/niece
el/la tío/a	uncle/aunt
los tíos	aunts and uncles
el/la pariente	relative

Las mascotas

el gato	cat
el pájaro	bird
el perro	dog
la mascota	pet

Otros sustantivos

la carta	letter
la casa	house, home
la ciudad	city
el coche	car
el estado	state
el/la médico/a	(medical) doctor
el mundo	world
el país	country
el periódico	newspaper
el regalo	present, gift
la revista	magazine
la tarea	homework

Los adjetivos

alto/a	tall
amable	kind; nice
antipático/a	unpleasant, unlikable (*people*)
bajo/a	short (*in height*)
bonito/a	pretty (*people and things*)
buen, bueno/a	good
corto/a	short (*in length*)
delgado/a	thin, slender
este/a	this
estos/as	these
feo/a	ugly
fiel	loyal
gordo/a	fat
gran, grande	large, big; great
guapo/a	handsome, good-looking (*people*)
joven	young
largo/a	long
listo/a	smart; clever
mal, malo/a	bad
moreno/a	brunet(te)
mucho/a	a lot (of)
muchos/as	many
nuevo/a	new
otro/a	other, another
pequeño/a	small
perezoso/a	lazy
pobre	poor
rico/a	rich
rubio/a	blond(e)
simpático/a	nice, likable (*people*)
todo/a	all; every
tonto/a	silly, foolish
trabajador(a)	hardworking
viejo/a	old

Cognados: hispano/a, inteligente, necesario/a, posible

Los adjetivos de nacionalidad

alemán/alemana	German
español(a)	Spanish
estadounidense	U.S.
inglés/inglesa	English
mexicano/a	Mexican

Los adjetivos posesivos

mi(s)	my
tu(s)	your (*fam. sing.*)
nuestro/a(s)	our
vuestro/a(s)	your (*fam. pl., Sp.*)
su(s)	his, hers, its; your (*form. sing.*); their; your (*form. pl.*)

Los números del 31 al 100

treinta, cuarenta, cincuenta, sesenta, setenta, ochenta, noventa, cien

¿Con qué frecuencia... ?

a veces	sometimes, at times
casi	almost
casi nunca	almost never
nunca	never
siempre	always
una vez a la semana	once a week
¿con qué frecuencia... ?	how often ... ?

Repaso: con frecuencia, todos los días

Palabras adicionales

además	besides
¿de quién?	whose?
del (de + el)	of the, from the
e	and (*before words beginning with the sound* i-)
estar de acuerdo / no estar de acuerdo	to agree / to disagree
esto	this (*neuter*)
para	(intended) *for*
para + *inf.*	in order to (*do something*)
por eso	for that reason
¿por qué?	why?
porque	because
que	that, which; who
según	according to
tener... años (tengo, tienes, tiene)	to be ... years old
u	or (*before words beginning with the sound* o-)

Repaso: ¿de dónde es usted?

Vocabulario personal

Use this space or a vocabulary notebook to write down other words and phrases you learn in this chapter.

4

De compras°

De... *Shopping*

En este capítulo

VOCABULARY
Clothing and colors   104, 107
Numbers from 100 on   110

GRAMMAR
Using words like *this* and *that*   114
Expressing actions and states with additional verbs   118
Expressing destination and future actions with the verb **ir**   123

COUNTRIES OF FOCUS: **GUATEMALA AND HONDURAS**

En un mercado (*market*),
en Tecpán, Guatemala

Danny Lehman/Getty Images

GUATEMALA

18 millones de habitantes

- Guatemala es el centro de la civilización maya. También hay población maya en Honduras, México, El Salvador y Belice.

HONDURAS

10 millones de habitantes

- Honduras tiene una población afroindígena[a] muy grande: los garífunas. Viven en la costa del golfo de Honduras, incluyendo Guatemala, Belice y Nicaragua.

[a]*native African*

🔊 ENTREVISTA

These questions related to the chapter theme are answered here by a native speaker. You will be able to ask and answer them yourself with personal information in the **Entrevista** activity in the **Portafolio** section at the end of the chapter.

Alejandra Hernández Soto contesta las preguntas.

– **¿Qué tipo de ropa[a] le gusta llevar[b] con más frecuencia, ropa formal o informal?**

– Me gusta todo tipo de ropa. Para ir[c] a la universidad todos los días, llevo ropa cómoda:[d] *jeans*, camisetas[e] y suéteres grandes, zapatos bajos o deportivos.[f] Pero me gusta la ropa elegante para ocasiones especiales.

– **¿Prefiere usar ropa de muchos colores o prefiere la ropa de colores muy básicos, como el blanco y el negro[g]?**

– Me gusta mucho combinar el negro con el blanco y colores vivos,[h] como el rojo[i] y el turquesa.

– **¿Le gusta ir de compras[j] o prefiere comprar por[k] internet? Cuando va[l] de compras, ¿va a centros comerciales o a pequeñas tiendas[m] locales?**

– Prefiero ir de compras. Con frecuencia voy[n] a un centro comercial. Pero a veces, voy a tiendas pequeñas en el centro que tienen cosas[ñ] un poco diferentes. ¡Nunca compro por internet!

[a]*clothing* [b]*to wear* [c]*Para... To go* [d]*comfortable* [e]*T-shirts* [f]*zapatos... low or sporty shoes* [g]*el... white and black* [h]*strong, vibrant* [i]*red* [j]*ir... to go shopping* [k]*on the* [l]*you go* [m]*shops* [n]*I go* [ñ]*things*

Fabrice Lerouge/SuperStock

VOCABULARIO: PREPARACIÓN

You can hear the pronunciation
of theme vocabulary words
and phrases in the eBook.

¿Qué ropa llevan?°

¿Qué... *What clothing are they wearing?*

la camiseta
la blusa
la falda
los pantalones cortos
el bolso
las sandalias

la corbata
el reloj
el cinturón
la chaqueta
los pantalones
los zapatos
los zapatos

la camisa
la chaqueta
el traje
los pantalones
los tenis

Halay Alex/Shutterstock
Dima Babushkin/Shutterstock
Minerva Studio/Shutterstock
Peopleimages/Getty Images

1.   2.   3.   4.

Más ropa° y complementos°   *clothing / accessories*

el abrigo	coat
los aretes	earrings
las botas	boots
los calcetines	socks
la cartera	wallet; handbag
las chanclas	flip-flops
las gafas de sol	sunglasses
la gorra	baseball cap
el impermeable	raincoat
los *jeans*	blue jeans, jeans
las medias	stockings
la ropa interior	underwear
el suéter	sweater
el sombrero	hat
la sudadera	sweatshirt
el traje de baño	bathing suit
el vestido	dress

Para hablar de ropa y compras°   *shopping*

la ganga	bargain
el precio	price
las rebajas	sales, reductions
barato/a	inexpensive
caro/a	expensive
cómodo/a	comfortable

¿Cuánto cuesta(n)?	How much does it (do they) cost?
comprar (por internet)	to buy online
llevar	to wear; to carry; to take
usar	to wear; to use
vender	to sell
venden de todo	they sell (have) everything

Lugares para comprar

el almacén	department store
el centro	downtown
el centro comercial	shopping mall
el mercado	market(place)
la plaza	(city) square; plaza
la tienda	shop, store

¿Cómo es? ¿De qué material es?

<u>estar</u> de (última) moda*	to be the (latest) trend
<u>ser</u> de† (cuadros, lunares, rayas)	to be (plaid, polka-dot, striped)
<u>ser</u> de (algodón, cuero, lana, oro, plata, seda)	to be made of (cotton, leather, wool, gold, silver, silk)

---

*Estar de última moda *literally means* to be the latest fashion, to be trendy. *Note the meaning of* última/a: latest; last.
†*Note another use of* ser + de: *to tell what material something is made of.*

Así se dice

el almacén = los grandes almacenes (*Spain*)
el bolso = la bolsa (*Mexico*)
la camiseta = la polera (*Argentina*), la
  playera (*Mexico*), el polo (*Peru*)
la cartera = la billetera (*Argentina, El
  Salvador*); *coin purse* = el monedero

la falda = la pollera (*Argentina, Uruguay*)
los *jeans* = los mahones (*Puerto Rico,
  Dominican Republic*), los vaqueros (*Spain*)
el suéter = el jersey (*Spain*), el pulóver
  (*Argentina*)

To talk about sales, you can say **hay rebajas** or say that something **está de/en rebaja**
or **está en liquidación/venta.**

Comunicación

A. La ropa

Paso 1. ¿Qué ropa llevan estas personas?

Javi_indy/Shutterstock

1.

Vocabulario útil

la chica	girl
el chico	guy
el hombre	
la mujer	

DRB Images/Getty Images

2.

Roman Samborskyi/Shutterstock

3.

Ljupco Smokovski/Shutterstock

4.

Paso 2. De estas personas, ¿quién trabaja hoy? ¿Quién probablemente no
trabaja en este momento? ¿Quién va a (*is going to*) una fiesta?

B. Descripciones. Complete las siguientes oraciones lógicamente con palabras de **¿Qué ropa llevan?**

1. Un _____ es una tienda grande, con muchos departamentos.
2. El _____ es la cantidad de dinero que pagamos cuando compramos una cosa (*thing*).
3. En el _____ venden de todo: ropa, complementos, zapatos, electrónica, etcétera. Con frecuencia, también hay opciones de cosas caras o _____.

4. Hay grandes _____ en las tiendas al final de la temporada (*season*).
5. ¿Comprar por internet es más caro o más _____ que comprar en una tienda?
6. En las ciudades hispanohablantes es común tener un _____ de todo tipo de cosas.
7. Muchos aretes son de oro o de _____.
8. Muchos zapatos elegantes son de _____ (material).

C. El estilo personal. Complete las siguientes oraciones lógicamente para hablar de sus preferencias con relación a la ropa.

1. Para ir a la universidad, llevo _____.
2. Para ir a las fiestas con los amigos, llevo _____.
3. Para pasar un día en la playa (*beach*), me gusta llevar _____.
4. Para estar en casa todo el día, me gusta llevar _____.
5. Nunca uso _____.
6. No puedo vivir sin (*I can't live without*) _____ y _____.

Nota comunicativa: Preguntas coletillas°

tag

Tag phrases can change statements into questions.

Aquí venden de todo, {	**¿no?**	*They sell everything here, right?*
	¿verdad?	*(don't they?)*
No necesito impermeable hoy, **¿verdad?**		*I don't need a raincoat today, do I?*

¿Verdad? is found after affirmative or negative statements; **¿no?** is usually found after affirmative statements only.

¡OJO!

The inverted question mark comes immediately before the tag question, not at the beginning of the statement.

You will practice using tag phrases in **Comunicación D**.

 D. Intercambios. En parejas, usen las coletillas **¿no?** y **¿verdad?** para intercambiar (*exchange*) información de sus hábitos y preferencias sobre (*about*) las compras.

MODELO: **1.** Hay un buen centro comercial cerca de (*close to*) tu casa. →
    E1: Hay un buen centro comercial cerca de tu casa, ¿no? (¿verdad?)
    E2: Sí, hay un centro comercial muy grande a cinco millas (*five miles away*) de mi casa. (No, no hay un buen centro comercial cerca de mi casa).

1. Hay un buen centro comercial cerca de tu casa.
2. Te gusta la ropa deportiva (*sports*) más que (*more than*) la ropa elegante.
3. Tienes muchos zapatos.
4. Te gusta llevar ropa de moda.
5. No compras en las tiendas de ropa usada (*used*).
6. Compras muchas cosas (*things*) por internet.
7. No hay muchos mercados en esta ciudad.

Los colores: ¿De qué color es?

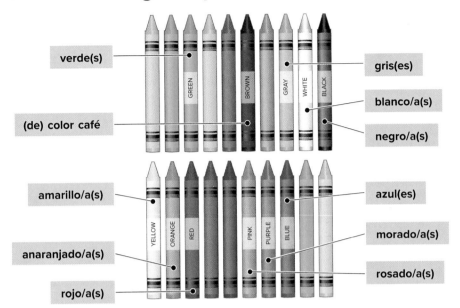

verde(s)

(de) color café

gris(es)

blanco/a(s)

negro/a(s)

amarillo/a(s)

anaranjado/a(s)

rojo/a(s)

azul(es)

morado/a(s)

rosado/a(s)

- Because of their ending, some adjectives of color (**azul**, **gris**, and **verde**) have only two forms, singular and plural.

  la camisa gris   el traje gris   las camisetas gris**es**

- The expression **(de) color café** is invariable; that is, it does not show gender or number agreement. Sometimes **de** is not used.

  el sombrero (de) color café   las gorras (de) color café

- Another way to express colors is to just say **de color (rojo, verde...).**
- When the colors are used as nouns, they are always masculine, and are preceded by an article:

  Me gusta **el** rojo.   **El** azul y **el** verde son mis colores favoritos.
  I like (the color) red.   (The color) Blue and (the color) green are my favorite colors.

Comunicación

A. Un cuadro colorido (*colorful painting*). Hay muchos colores en este cuadro de Edwin Guillermo. ¿Cuáles son?

Erwin Guillermo/Artwork courtesy of La Antigua Galería de Arte Antigua Guatemala

El cortejo (*Courting*), de Erwin Guillermo

Algo sobre un artista guatemalteco

Erwin Guillermo (1951– [mil novecientos cincuenta y uno]) vive y trabaja en la Ciudad de Guatemala. Su estilo es representativo del arte contemporáneo guatemalteco: es muy expresivo y simbólico. Con frecuencia, como se ve[a] en este cuadro,[b] las figuras de Guillermo tienen una forma estilizada y sensual, con muchos colores.

 ¿Le gusta el estilo del cuadro de Guillermo? ¿Qué pintor(a) le gusta mucho a usted?

[a]*se... is seen*   [b]*painting*

B. Asociaciones. ¿Qué asocia usted con los siguientes colores?

1. gris
2. verde
3. blanco y negro
4. amarillo
5. rojo
6. azul

C. ¡Ojo alerta! ¿Escaparates (Window displays) idénticos? These window displays are almost alike ... but not quite! Can you find at least nine differences between them?

MODELO: En el dibujo A hay _____, pero en el dibujo B hay _____.

A.

B.

D. ¿De qué color es?

Paso 1. Describa el color de la ropa y de las cosas (things) de sus compañeros.

MODELOS: El bolígrafo de Anita es amarillo. Un libro de Anita es... azul.

Paso 2. Ahora describa la ropa que lleva una persona de la clase sin decir (without saying) su nombre. Sus compañeros tienen que (have to) identificar a la persona de la descripción.

MODELO: E1: Lleva botas negras, una camiseta blanca y jeans.
E2: Es Anne.

E. Un artículo representativo

Paso 1. En parejas o grupos, diseñen (design) un artículo de uso personal que las personas universitarias llevan con frecuencia, mejor (even better) si es representativo de toda la universidad o de un grupo específico. Deben especificar el color o colores básicos y también incluir una imagen y/o un texto de logo.

su imagen y texto aquí

Paso 2. Ahora expliquen su diseño a la clase.

MODELO: Nuestra camiseta es de color _____ y tiene uno(a) / unos/as _____ porque...

Nota cultural: Las tallas° de ropa y zapatos

sizes

En todos los países donde se habla español es común encontrar[a] que las tallas de la ropa son idénticas a las de[b] los Estados Unidos (XS, S, M, L y XL). Pero si la ropa es fabricada en un país latinoamericano, es posible que las tallas estén[c] en español:

CH = chico (sinónimo de pequeño)   M = mediano

G = grande   EG = extra grande

Las tallas más específicas expresadas en números son diferentes de las de los Estados Unidos y pueden variar[d] de país a país. Además, es importante recordar[e] que en los países hispanos se usa[f] el sistema métrico decimal, y no el sistema estadounidense:

1 pulgada[g] = 2.54 centímetros   1 yarda = .91 metro
                                    (91 centímetros)

Por otro lado,[h] los números de los zapatos son diferentes en muchos países hispanohablantes. En general, los números más comunes[i] para las mujeres son del 35 al 40, y para los hombres del 39 al 44.

Las personas que venden en las tiendas pueden[j] preguntar: **¿Qué talla necesita(s)?** No hay problema si usted no lo sabe[k]: ellas saben[l] convertir y calcular tallas.

¿Cuál es su talla de zapatos en este país?

GUÍA DE TALLAS CALZADO[a] MUJER						
TALLAS	5	6	7	8	9	10
EQUIVALENTE	36	37	38	39	40	41
CM	22	23	24	25	26	27

GUÍA DE TALLAS CALZADO HOMBRE							
TALLAS	5	6	7	8	9	10	11
EQUIVALENTE	38	39	40	41	42	43	44
CM	23	24	25	26	27	28	29

[a]*SHOES*

[a]*to find*   [b]*las... those of*   [c]*will be*   [d]*pueden... they can vary*   [e]*to remember*   [f]*se... is used*   [g]*inch*   [h]*Por... On the other hand*   [i]*más... most frequent*   [j]*may*   [k]*no... don't know*   [l]*know how*

Textos de todos los días: Devolución de° una compra de internet

Devolución... Returning

It's very common to purchase things on the internet, and so is the need to return them. In this activity you will practice how to return an item and offer a simple explanation for why you are doing so.

Objetivo: To learn vocabulary that often appears in e-shopping contexts and use it to explain the reason for the last thing you returned.

Antes de empezar (*Before starting*):
Think of typical reasons for returning a clothing item; doing so will help you guess the meaning of new vocabulary.

E-BASIC Camiseta de mangas[a] cortas para mujer, naranja, talla XS

¿Por qué quiere[b] devolver el producto?

Fecha de entrega estimada pasada[c]
Producto equivocado[d]
Talla equivocada
Ahora no quiero el producto
No corresponde a la descripción
Producto incompleto o defectuoso
Compra no autorizada
Compra por error
Precio más bajo[e] en otro lugar

Explicación/Comentarios

(200 caracteres restantes)

[a]*sleeves*   [b]*do you want*   [c]*Fecha... Estimated missed delivery date*   [d]*wrong*   [e]*más... lower*

Los números a partir del 100°

a... *from 100 on*

Continúe las secuencias:
- noventa y nueve, cien, ciento uno...
- mil, dos mil...
- un millón, dos millones...

100	cien, ciento	**700**	setecientos/as
101	ciento uno/una	**800**	ochocientos/as
200	doscientos/as	**900**	novecientos/as
300	trescientos/as	**1.000**	mil
400	cuatrocientos/as	**2.000**	dos mil
500	quinientos/as	**1.000.000**	un millón
600	seiscientos/as	**2.000.000**	dos millones

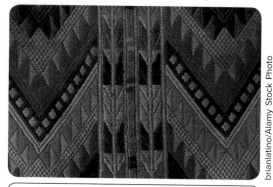

brianlatino/Alamy Stock Photo

Este huipil guatemalteco hecho a mano (*handmade*) cuesta 750 (setecientos cincuenta) quetzales.

- **Cien** is used in counting: **...noventa y nueve, cien.** It is also used to refer to exactly one hundred of something: **cien** dólares.
- **Ciento** is used in combination with numbers from 1 to 99 to express the numbers 101 to 199: cien, **ciento** uno, **ciento** dos...
- **Cien** is used before numbers greater than 100: **cien mil, cien millones.**
- When counting, the masculine form of words containing **cientos** is used: **doscientos uno, doscientos dos...**
- When the numbers 200 to 900 modify a noun, they must agree in gender: **doscient<u>os</u> veintiún dólares, quinient<u>as</u> ocho sillas.**
- **Mil** means *one thousand* or *a thousand*. It does not have a plural form in counting, but **millón** does. When followed directly by a noun, **millón (dos millones,** and so on) must be followed by **de.**

mil gracias
3.000 habitantes　　　　　**tres mil habitantes**
14.000.000 <u>de</u> habitantes　　**catorce millones <u>de</u> habitantes**

- Years are expressed like regular numbers in Spanish, and they are written without any separation, just as in English.

1899　**mil ochocientos noventa y nueve**
2008　**dos mil ocho**

¡OJO!

In many parts of the Spanish-speaking world, a period (**punto**) is used where a comma (**coma**) is used in English and vice versa.

$1.500　　$1.000.000
$10,45　　65,9%

Comunicación

A. La población de varios países. ¿Cuánto sabe usted (*do you know*) del mundo hispano? Practique los números grandes emparejando (*matching*) los países con su población (estimaciones de 2023). ¡No debe mirar las respuestas correctas antes de (*before*) contestar!

1. 129.000.000
2. 50.800.000
3. 45.200.000
4. 17.900.000
5. 9.900.000
6. 3.500.000

a. la Argentina
b. Colombia
c. Guatemala
d. Honduras
e. México
f. el Uruguay

B. ¿Cuánto cuestan?

Paso 1. Empareje de manera lógica las cantidades con las cosas (*things*) de la lista y exprese los precios. **¡OJO! el dólar → los dólares.**

CANTIDADES

1. $100
2. $150
3. $225
4. $330
5. $2.500
6. $75.000
7. $2.600.000
8. $15.800.000

COSAS

a. un coche de lujo (*luxury*)
b. un anillo (*ring*) de diamantes
c. un edificio de apartamentos
d. un bolso de una diseñadora (*designer*) famosa
e. unos aretes de oro
f. un apartamento en San Francisco
g. unos tenis de moda
h. unos boletos (*tickets*) para un concierto

Paso 2. Ahora, en parejas, una persona piensa en (*will think of*) un precio aproximado para las siguientes cosas (*things*). La otra persona debe adivinar (*guess*) el precio. Usen **más** y **menos** (*less*) según el modelo.

MODELO: unos *jeans* de moda muy caros →
     E1: $250. E2: No, menos.
     E1: $175. E2: No, más.
     E1: $200. E2: ¡Correcto!

1. un Tesla
2. la matrícula de esta universidad
3. un libro de texto de biología
4. un iPhone de última generación
5. un viejo coche usado (*used*)
6. una cena (*dinner*) en un restaurante elegante

C. Precios en otras divisas (*currency*)

Paso 1. ¿Cuánto cuestan estas cosas (*things*) de encuentra24 (un sitio web como eBay)? **¡OJO! Q = el quetzal / los quetzales**, la divisa de Guatemala.

Vestido largo; nuevo
Q250

Tarzhanova/Shutterstock

Pantalones Boss
Q6 100

Cesare Andrea Ferrari/Shutterstock

Camiseta de fútbol; como nueva
Q175

Karammiri/Getty Images

Zapatos de mujer, talla 37; casi nuevos
Q350

Ken Karp/McGraw Hill

Paso 2. Ahora, en parejas, calculen los precios del **Paso 1** en las divisas de otros países. Las siguientes correspondencias son aproximadas.

1 quetzal = 3 lempiras hondureños
8 quetzales = 1 dólar estadounidense
8 quetzales = 1 euro

D. Fechas (*Dates*) importantes. Exprese las siguientes fechas en español.

1. este año, el año pasado y el próximo (*next*) año
2. el año de su nacimiento (*birth*)
3. 1821, el año de la independencia de Guatemala y Honduras (de España)
4. 1776, el año de la independencia de los Estados Unidos (de Inglaterra)

PRONUNCIACIÓN

Stress and Written Accent Marks (Part 2)

In the **Pronunciación** section of **Capítulo 3,** you learned that most Spanish words do not need a written accent mark because their pronunciation is completely predictable. Review the two basic rules of Spanish word stress in words that do not have a written accent mark by looking at the examples and completing the rules. The stressed syllable is underlined.

- Examples: l<u>i</u>bro, <u>me</u>sa, ex<u>a</u>men, im<u>a</u>gen, <u>e</u>res, gr<u>a</u>cias

  A word that ends in a _____, _____, or _____ is stressed on the next-to-last syllable.

- Examples: bail<u>ar</u>, ust<u>ed</u>, pap<u>el</u>, est<u>oy</u>

  A word that ends in _____ is stressed on the last syllable.

In Spanish, the written accent mark is used in the following situations.

1. A written accent mark is needed when a word does not follow the two basic rules reviewed in **Repaso.**

    Look at the words in this group.

ta-bú	a-le-mán	in-glés
ca-fé	na-ción	es-tás

    The preceding words end in a vowel, **-n,** or **-s,** so one would predict that they would be stressed on the *next-to-last syllable* (**la penúltima sílaba**). But the written accent mark shows that they are in fact accented on the *last syllable* (**la última sílaba**).

    Now look at the words in this group.

    lá-piz   dó-lar   ál-bum   á-gil   dó-cil

    The preceding words end in a consonant (other than **-n** or **-s**), so one would predict that they would be stressed on the last syllable. But the written accent mark shows that they are in fact accented on the next-to-last syllable.

2. All words that are stressed on the *third-to-last syllable* (**la antepenúltima sílaba**) must have a written accent mark, regardless of which letter they end in. These are called **palabras esdrújulas.**

    bo-lí-gra-fo   ma-trí-cu-la   ma-te-má-ti-cas

3. When two consecutive vowels do not form a diphthong (see **Pronunciación, Cap. 2**), the weak vowel (**i, u**) that receives the spoken stress will have a written accent mark. This pattern is very frequent in words that end in **-ía.**

Ma-rí-a	po-li-cí-a	as-tro-no-mí-a
dí-a	bio-lo-gí-a	

4. Accent marks are also added to preserve the original stress of a word when the word is changed in some way, for example, when it becomes plural. Here are some examples:

    joven → j<u>ó</u>venes   examen → ex<u>á</u>menes

    You will learn about other situations in which accents are added for this reason in upcoming chapters.

¡OJO!

Contrast the pronunciation of the words in **Point 3** with the following words in which the vowels **i** and **a** *do* form a diphthong: **Patr<u>i</u>cia, Fr<u>a</u>ncia, inf<u>a</u>ncia, dist<u>a</u>ncia.**

¡OJO!

As you know, the accent mark is sometimes dropped when a word is made plural.

pantal<u>ó</u>n → pantal<u>o</u>nes
franc<u>é</u>s → franc<u>e</u>ses
naci<u>ó</u>n → naci<u>o</u>nes

5. Some one-syllable words have accents to distinguish them from other words that are pronounced the same but have different meanings. This type of accent does not follow the general rules of accentuation; it is called the *diacritic accent* (**el acento diacrítico**). Here are some of the most common examples.

él (*he*) / el (*the*)   tú (*you*) / tu (*your*)
sí (*yes*) / si (*if*)   mí (*me*) / mi (*my*)

6. Interrogative and exclamatory words have a written accent on the stressed vowel. For example:

¿quién?   ¿dónde?   ¡Qué ganga! (*What a bargain!*)

Práctica

A. Sílabas. The following words have been separated into syllables for you. Read them aloud, paying careful attention to where the spoken stress should fall. Don't worry about the meaning of words you haven't heard before. The rules you have learned will help you pronounce them correctly.

1. a-quí	pa-pá	a-diós	bus-qué
2. prác-ti-co	mur-cié-la-go	te-lé-fo-no	ar-chi-pié-la-go
3. Ji-mé-nez	Ro-drí-guez	Pé-rez	Gó-mez
4. si-co-lo-gí-a	so-cio-lo-gí-a	sa-bi-du-rí-a	e-ner-gí-a
5. his-to-ria	te-ra-pia	Pre-to-ria	me-mo-ria

B. Reglas. *(Rules.)* Indicate the stressed vowel of each word in the following list. Explain your answer by referring to the following rules:

1. written accent
2. ends in a consonant other than **-n** or **-s**
3. end in a vowel, **-n,** or **-s**

1. exámenes	**5.** actitud	**9.** están	**13.** plástico
2. lápiz	**6.** acciones	**10.** hombre	**14.** María
3. necesitar	**7.** dólares	**11.** peso	**15.** Rodríguez
4. perezoso	**8.** francés	**12.** mujer	**16.** Patricia

C. En el texto. Lea **Algo sobre el Popol Vuh** y explique por qué necesitan acento o no cuatro palabras de su elección (*of your choice*).

Algo sobre el Popol Vuh

El *Popol Vuh* es el libro sagrado[a] del pueblo maya, la población originaria de Guatemala y Honduras. El libro fue escrito[b] en el siglo[c] XVI (dieciséis). Es la historia de la creación del mundo, según las creencias[d] de los mayas.

¿Cuál es un libro o un texto muy importante en su cultura?

[a]*sacred*   [b]*fue... was written*
[c]*century*   [d]*beliefs*

Ilustración de Diego de Rivera, basada en la creación de la humanidad según el *Popol Vuh*

GRAMÁTICA

9 Pointing Out People and Things • Demonstrative Adjectives (Part 2) and Pronouns

Gramática en acción: Suéteres a buenos precios

el vendedor

Jorge Susana

Susana busca un suéter con su amigo Jorge.

SUSANA: ¿Cuánto cuesta **este** suéter?

VENDEDOR: Bueno, **ese** que usted tiene en la mano cuesta 800 quetzales. **Este** aquí cuesta 700 quetzales.

SUSANA: ¡Qué caros!

VENDEDOR: Es que todos son de pura lana. Mire **aquellos** suéteres de rayas sobre **aquella** mesa. Solo cuestan 300 quetzales. Son acrílicos.

SUSANA: Muchas gracias.

Comprensión

¿Quién habla, Susana, su amigo Jorge o el vendedor?

1. «**Estos** suéteres de rayas son bonitos. Y solo cuestan 300 quetzales».
2. «Los suéteres en **aquella** mesa no son de pura lana».
3. «Compro **este** suéter. Me gusta la ropa de lana».
4. «**Estos** suéteres acrílicos son más baratos que **aquellos** de lana».

Demonstrative Adjectives / Los adjetivos demostrativos

Singular		Plural			Adverbs / Los adverbios
this { **este** abrigo	**esta** gorra	these { **estos** abrigos	**estas** gorras		**aquí** = here
that { **ese** abrigo	**esa** gorra	those { **esos** abrigos	**esas** gorras		**allí** = there
aquel abrigo	**aquella** gorra	**aquellos** abrigos	**aquellas** gorras		**allá** = way over there

¡OJO!

Note that the final **-e** in the singular forms **este** and **ese** changes to an **-o-** in the plural: **estos, esos.**

a demonstrative adjective / **un adjetivo demostrativo** = an adjective used to indicate a particular person, place, thing, or idea

---

Sweaters at good prices *Susana is looking for a sweater with her friend Jorge.* SUSANA: *How much is this sweater?* SALESMAN: *Well, that one that you have in your hand costs 800 quetzales. This one here costs 700 quetzales.* SUSANA: *(They're) So expensive!* SALESMAN: *It's because they're all made of pure wool. Take a look at those striped sweaters on that table (over there). They only cost 300 quetzales. They're acrylic.* SUSANA: *Thanks a lot.*

1. Agreement

Demonstrative adjectives are used to indicate a specific noun or nouns. In Spanish, **los adjetivos demostrativos** precede the nouns they modify. They also agree in number and gender with the nouns.

2. Using este and *ese*

Forms of **este** (*this, these*) and **ese** (*that, those*) are used just like *this/these* and *that/those* in English.

- When two people are speaking, forms of **este** are used to refer to nouns that are close to the speaker in space or time.
- Forms of **ese** refer to nouns that are close to the person spoken *to*.
- When the noun is distant from both speakers, forms of **ese** are used.

3. Using ese and *aquel*

There are two ways to say *that/those* in Spanish.

- Forms of **ese** refer to nouns that are not close to the speaker(s) (point 2).
- Forms of **aquel** refer to nouns that are even farther away from the speaker(s).

In the chart on the previous page, the *adverbs* (**los adverbios**) **aquí, allí,** and **allá** are associated with the forms of **este, ese,** and **aquel,** respectively. However, it is not obligatory to use these words with the demonstrative adjectives.

an adverb / **un adverbio** = a word (such as *very* and *quickly*) that modifies a verb, adjective, or another adverb

Este niño es mi hijo. **Ese** joven allí es mi otro hijo. Y **aquel** señor allá es mi esposo.
This boy is my son. That young man there is my other son. And that man way over there is my husband.

Demonstrative Pronouns / **Los pronombres demostrativos**

1. Demonstrative Pronouns

In English, the *demonstrative pronouns* are usually the demonstrative adjective + the word *one(s)*, as in the examples. In Spanish, **los pronombres demostrativos** are the same as demonstrative adjectives, except that the noun is not used and there is no direct equivalent for English *one(s)*.

—¿Te gusta **aquella** casa allá?
—¿Cuál?
—**Aquella,** la de las ventanas grandes.
—Sí, me gusta mucho. Mucho más que **esta...**

*"Do you like **that** house way over there?"*
"Which one?"
***"That one,** the one with the big windows."*
*"Yes, I like it a lot. A lot more than **this one** ..."*

2. Agreement

In Spanish, demonstrative pronouns agree in gender and number with the noun they are replacing.

ese libro, en la mesa → **ese** en la mesa
aquellos señores, en el café → **aquellos** en el café

3. Neuter Demonstrative Pronouns

Use the neuter demonstrative pronouns **esto, eso,** and **aquello** to refer to as yet unidentified objects or to a whole idea, concept, or situation.

¿Qué es **esto**?
What is this?

Eso es todo.
That's it. / That's all.

¡**Aquello** es terrible!
That's terrible!

¡OJO!

Esto es una mochila. (to identify in general)
This is a backpack.
Esta es mi mochila. (to identify one out of a group)
This (one) is my backpack.

Summary of
Demonstratives

near	este/a, estos/as, esto
far	ese/a, esos/as, eso
farther	aquel(la), aquellos/as, aquello

Práctica y comunicación

A. Una cuestión de perspectiva

Paso 1. Autoprueba. Empareje (*Match*) las palabras con su significado apropiado en inglés.

1. estas
2. aquellos
3. ese
4. esas
5. este

a. *that*
b. *those* (*over there*)
c. *these*
d. *this*
e. *those*

Paso 2. Autoprueba. Ahora empareje los siguientes demostrativos con los objetos apropiados, según la perspectiva de la mujer.

1. esta _____
2. estas _____
3. este _____
4. aquel _____
5. aquellos _____
6. esos _____

 Paso 3. Ahora, en parejas, usen los siguientes demostrativos para identificar los objetos de la clase o del lugar donde usted está.

1. estos _____ y esta _____
2. ese _____ y esas _____
3. aquel _____ y aquellos _____

B. Cambios (*Changes*)

Paso 1. Cambie (*Change*) las formas de **este** por **ese** y añada (*add*) **también,** según el modelo.

MODELO: Este abrigo es muy grande. →
Ese abrigo **también** es muy grande.

1. Esta falda es muy corta.
2. Este reloj es muy caro.

3. Este bolso es muy bonito.
4. Esta corbata es muy fea.

Paso 2. Ahora cambie **este** por **aquel** y añada **allá** también.

MODELO: Este abrigo es muy grande. →
Aquel abrigo **allá también** es muy grande.

Paso 3. Finalmente, cambie las oraciones del singular al plural.

MODELO: Este abrigo es muy grande. →
Est**os** abrigo**s son** muy grande**s.**

C. Reacciones. Empareje (*Match*) cada (*each*) situación de la columna A con un comentario de la columna B.

A	B
1. _____ Aquí hay un regalo para usted.	**a.** ¡Eso es un desastre!
2. _____ Ocurre un accidente de coche.	**b.** ¡Eso es magnífico!
3. _____ No hay clases mañana.	**c.** ¿Qué es esto?
4. _____ La matrícula cuesta más este semestre/ trimestre.	**d.** ¡Eso es terrible!
5. _____ Usted saca (*get*) A en su examen de español.	

D. En una tienda

Paso 1. Complete el siguiente diálogo con los demostrativos apropiados. Asuma (*Take*) el punto de vista (*point of view*) del vendedor y el cliente.

VENDEDOR: ¿Qué suéter le gusta? ¿_____¹ rojo que está aquí?

CLIENTE: No, el rojo no.

VENDEDOR: ¿_____² suéter amarillo?

CLIENTE: No, tampocoᵃ el amarillo. ¡Me gusta _____³ anaranjado de allá!

ᵃNo... *No, not (the yellow one) either*

Paso 2. Ahora indique el demostrativo apropiado para los pantalones de cada maniquí, según la perspectiva de los dos hombres.

1. _____ pantalones negros
2. _____ pantalones azules
3. _____ pantalones color kaki

E. En la habitación (*bedroom*) de Ernesto. Working with a partner, imagine that you are the person depicted in the drawing, who is looking into Ernesto's bedroom. Some objects and items of clothing are close to you, some are a bit farther away, and some are at the other end of the room. Describe them as accurately as you can, using the appropriate demonstrative adjectives and all of the vocabulary you have learned so far.

MODELOS: _____ gato es blanco y
_____ gato es negro.
_____ libro es verde.

F. En el salón de clase

Paso 1. En parejas, usen demostrativos para identificar cinco pares (*pairs*) de personas o cosas en el salón de clase.

MODELO: Esta joven es rubia. Aquella joven cerca de la puerta es morena.

Paso 2. Ahora compartan (*share*) sus oraciones con el resto de la clase. Sus compañeros deben adivinar (*guess*) a qué personas u objetos se refieren ustedes.

Gramática

You began using the singular forms of the verb **tener** in **Capítulo 3**. Review them by completing the following verb forms.

1. tú t__nes **2.** yo te__o **3.** Julio t__ne

You will learn about similar patterns in **Gramática 10**.

10 Expressing Actions and States • *Tener, venir, poder, preferir, querer;* Some Idioms with **tener**

Gramática en acción: Un mensaje telefónico

Fabrice Lerouge/SuperStock

Hola, Jorge. Soy Jaqui. Esta tarde **tengo** que comprar un regalo para Miguel y no **quiero** ir sola. **¿Vienes** conmigo? **Podemos** encontrarnos en ese centro comercial que está cerca de tu casa. O si **prefieres**, **puedo** pasar por ti antes. ¡Llámame!

Comprensión

Ahora vuelva a contar (*retell*) el mensaje de Jaqui. Estas formas verbales son como **tiene**.

1. Jaqui **tien**_____ que comprar un regalo.
2. **Quier**_____ ir de compras con Jorge.
3. **Pued**_____ encontrarse con Jorge en el centro comercial.
4. O si Jorge **prefier**_____, Jaqui **pued**_____ pasar por la casa de él.

Tener, venir, poder, preferir, querer

> Remember that infinitives in **red** and **underlined** are conjugated in their entirety in Appendix 5.

tener (*to have*)		venir (*to come*)		poder (*to be able, can*)		preferir (*to prefer*)		querer (*to want*)	
tengo	tenemos	vengo	venimos	puedo	podemos	prefiero	preferimos	quiero	queremos
tienes	tenéis	vienes	venís	puedes	podéis	prefieres	preferís	quieres	queréis
tiene	tienen	viene	vienen	puede	pueden	prefiere	prefieren	quiere	quieren

The five verbs shown here share a number of characteristics.

- The **yo** forms of **tener** and **venir** are irregular.
- In other forms of **tener** and **venir**, and in **preferir** and **querer**, when the stem vowel **e** is stressed, it becomes **ie**.
- Similarly, the stem vowel **o** in **poder** becomes **ue** when stressed.

tener: yo **tengo**, tú **tienes** (e → ie)...
venir: yo **vengo**, tú **vienes** (e → ie)...
preferir, **querer:** (e → ie)
poder: (o → ue)

> In vocabulary lists, these changes are shown like this in parentheses after the infinitive: **poder** (**puedo**).

¡OJO!

The **nosotros** and **vosotros** forms of these verbs do not have changes in the stem vowel because it is not stressed.

A phone message *Hello, Jorge. It's Jaqui. This afternoon I have to buy a gift for Miguel, and I don't want to go alone. Will you come with me? We can meet at that shopping center that's near your house. Or if you prefer, I can come by for you ahead of time. Call me!*

- Like **deber, desear,** and **necesitar,** the verbs **poder, preferir,** and **querer** can be followed by an infinitive.

Verbs like these are called *stem-changing verbs.* You will learn more verbs of this type in **Gramática 13 (Cap. 5).**

> **¡OJO!**
>
> You will learn to use the verb **hacer** (*to do or to make*) in **Gramática 12 (Cap. 5).** Learn to recognize it in questions and direction lines.

¿Puedes <u>correr</u> muy rápido?
Can you run very fast?

¿Qué quieres/prefieres <u>hacer</u> hoy?
What do you want/prefer to do today?

Prefiero <u>no ir</u> a la biblioteca el sábado por la noche.
I prefer not to go to the library Saturday night.

Some Idioms with **tener** / Algunos modismos con *tener*

1. Conditions or States

Many ideas expressed in English with the verb *to be* are expressed in Spanish with *idioms* (**los modismos**) that use **tener.**

Idioms are often different from one language to another. For example, in English, *to pull Mary's leg* usually means *to tease her,* not *to grab her leg and pull it.* In Spanish, *to pull Mary's leg* is **tomarle el pelo a Mary** (lit., *to take hold of Mary's hair*).

You already know one **tener** idiom: **tener... años.** Here are some more **tener** idioms. They all describe a condition or state. Based on the drawings, can you guess what these idioms mean?

> *an idiom* / **un modismo =** an expression whose meaning cannot be inferred from the literal meaning of the words that form it

tener sueño

tener prisa

tener razón

no **tener** razón

tener miedo (de + *noun / infinitive*)

Note that **de** (in **tener miedo de**) can be followed by an infinitive or a noun.

Tengo miedo <u>de estar</u> solo aquí. ¡Tengo miedo <u>de la oscuridad</u>!
I'm afraid of being alone here. I'm afraid of the dark!

2. *Tener* Idioms + *infinitive*

Other **tener** idioms include the following:

> **¡OJO!**
>
> Note that the English equivalent of the infinitive in expressions with **tener ganas** is expressed with *-ing,* not with the infinitive as in Spanish.

tener ganas de + *infinitive* = to feel like (*doing something*)

tener que + *infinitive* = to have to (*do something*)

Tengo ganas de comer.
I feel like eating.

¿No <u>tiene</u> usted <u>que leer</u> este capítulo?
Don't you have to read this chapter?

tener: ten<u>g</u>o, ti<u>e</u>nes...
venir: ven<u>g</u>o, vi<u>e</u>nes...
poder: p<u>ue</u>do...
preferir: pref<u>ie</u>ro...
querer: qu<u>ie</u>ro...

Práctica y comunicación

A. Esta semana

Paso 1. Autoprueba. Dé (*Give*) la forma verbal apropiada para cada sujeto.

1. poder: yo, tú, nosotras
2. preferir: yo, nosotros, Len y Sara
3. querer: yo, usted, Natalia y yo
4. tener: yo, tú, nosotros
5. venir: yo, Javi, tú y yo

Paso 2. Ahora conjugue el verbo para completar las siguientes oraciones sobre sus obligaciones y preferencias para esta semana. Dé un detalle (*detail*) específico en cada caso: por qué, el día de la semana, etcétera. Use **no** para crear oraciones negativas.

MODELO: **1.** (tener) que _____. **Tengo** que estudiar mucho porque tengo un examen de química el viernes. / No **tengo** que estudiar mucho porque no tengo exámenes.

Esta semana (yo)...

1. (tener) que _____.
2. (tener) ganas de _____.
3. (poder) _____.
4. (querer) _____.
5. (preferir) _____.

Paso 3. Finalmente, en parejas, usen sus oraciones del **Paso 2** como base para hacer y contestar preguntas. Luego (*Then*) digan (*tell*) a la clase algo (*something*) que ustedes tienen en común.

MODELO: **1.** Tengo que estudiar mucho porque tengo un examen de química el viernes. →

E1: ¿**Tienes** que estudiar mucho? ¿Por qué?

E2: Sí, **tengo** que estudiar mucho porque tengo un examen de química el martes. ¿Y tú?

B. ¿Qué tienen?

Paso 1. Empareje las situaciones con los comentarios apropiados.

SITUACIONES

1. _____ El niño es muy pequeño.
2. _____ En esa casa, hay un perro muy grande.
3. _____ Son las tres de la mañana.
4. _____ «Dos y dos son... seis».
5. _____ «Buenos Aires es la capital de la Argentina».
6. _____ Tenemos que estar en el centro a las tres y ya son (*it's already*) las tres menos cuarto.
7. _____ Mañana estos estudiantes tienen un examen.

COMENTARIOS

a. Tengo mucho sueño.
b. Tengo miedo de ese perro.
c. Tiene solo dos años.
d. Tienes razón.
e. Por eso tienen que estudiar esta noche.
f. No tienes razón.
g. Por eso tenemos mucha prisa.

Paso 2. Ahora en parejas, túrnense para hacer y contestar preguntas basadas en las siguientes ideas.

MODELO: **1.** tener sueño →

E1: ¿**Tienes** sueño ahora?

E2: Sí. ¡Siempre **tengo** sueño!

1. tener sueño ahora
2. tener que hacer (*do*) hoy
3. tener ganas de hacer ahora
4. tener prisa generalmente antes de (*before*) la clase de español
5. tener miedo de los verbos en español / las arañas (*spiders*)...
6. tener razón cuando habla con su madre/padre

Prác. A, Paso 1: Answers: 1. puedo, puedes, podemos 2. prefiero, preferimos, prefieren 3. quiero, quiere, queremos 4. tengo, tienes, tenemos 5. vengo, viene, venimos

Nota comunicativa: *Mucho y poco*

In this chapter, you learned that words like **aquí, allí,** and **allá** are *adverbs* (**los adverbios**), words that modify a verb (*run **quickly***), an adjective (***very** smart*), or another adverb (***very** quickly*). One very common Spanish adverb that you have used frequently is **muy** (*very*).

In the first chapters of *Puntos de partida*, you have used the words **mucho** and **poco** as both adjectives and adverbs. In English and in Spanish, adverbs are invariable in form. Spanish adjectives, however, agree in gender and number with the words they modify, as you know.

ADVERBIOS:	mucho	Rosa estudia **mucho**.	*Rosa studies a lot.*
	poco	Julio come **poco**.	*Julio doesn't eat much.*
ADJETIVOS:	mucho/a(s)	Rosa tiene **mucha** ropa.	*Rosa has a lot of clothes.*
		Tiene **muchos** zapatos.	*She has a lot of shoes.*
	poco/a(s)	Julio come **poca** pasta.	*Julio doesn't eat much pasta.*
		Come **pocos** postres.	*He eats few desserts.*

You will use these words in **Práctica C, D,** and **E.**

C. En mi armario (*closet*)

Paso 1. Haga rápidamente una lista aproximada de su ropa y complementos. Escriba (*Write*) **muchos, muchas, pocos, pocas** o **no tengo,** según sea (*is*) apropiado.

	MUCHOS/AS	POCOS/AS	NO TENGO
camisas / blusas			
camisetas			
pantalones cortos / largos			
faldas / vestidos			
chaquetas			
zapatos (de todo tipo)			
botas / chanclas / sandalias			
complementos			
¿ ?			

 Paso 2. Ahora, en parejas, túrnense para hacer y contestar preguntas sobre cuánta ropa tienen y de qué tipo.

MODELO: E1: ¿Tienes muchas camisas?
E2: No, no tengo muchas camisas. Solo tengo dos o tres. ¿Y tú?
E1: Yo tengo más de seis.

 Paso 3. Para terminar, hagan una evaluación mutua de su vestuario (*wardrobe*). ¿Qué es obvio que prefieren llevar o no llevar? ¿Tienen su propio (*own*) estilo? ¿Qué tienen en exceso? ¿Qué tienen que comprar?

Algo sobre la civilización maya: Tikal y Copán

La civilización maya ocupa un vasto territorio en México, Guatemala, Honduras, El Salvador y Belice. Hoy en estos países existen millones de personas mayas que forman diversos grupos lingüísticos.

Dos importantes centros arqueológicos mayas son Tikal en Guatemala y Copán en Honduras. Son lugares muy visitados y estudiados para aprender sobre la vida[a] y la historia de los antiguos[b] mayas, que eran[c] una civilización muy avanzada y expertos en astronomía, entre[d] otras cosas.

George Bailey/iStockphoto/Getty Images

El Templo del Gran Jaguar, en Tikal

¿Le gusta visitar sitios históricos en sus vacaciones? ¿O prefiere las ciudades modernas?

[a]*life* [b]*ancient* [c]*were* [d]*among*

Vocabulario útil

demasiados/as	too many
deportivo/a	sporty
más/menos	more/less
de + *number*	than

D. Circunstancias personales

Paso 1. In pairs, use the following list to predict your partner's answers.

MODELO: tener muchos / pocos libros en su cuarto ➜
Mi compañero tiene muchos libros en su cuarto.

1. tener que estudiar _____ (mucho / poco) este semestre/trimestre
2. querer tomar _____ (muchas / pocas) clases de ciencias en la universidad
3. venir _____ (en coche / en autobús / a pie [*on foot*]) a la universidad todos los días
4. preferir estudiar en _____ (la biblioteca / casa / la residencia)
5. tener _____ (muchas / pocas) cosas con el logotipo (*logo*) de la universidad
6. poder correr (*run*) una milla en _____ (menos / más) de (*than*) cinco minutos
7. tener muchas ganas de _____ (estudiar / mirar una serie) esta noche
8. tener _____ (mucha / poca) ropa
9. preferir el _____ (verde / rojo / amarillo)

Paso 2. Now, using tag questions (**preguntas coletillas**), ask your partner questions to find out if you guessed correctly in **Paso 1.**

MODELO: E1: Tienes muchos libros en tu cuarto, ¿verdad?
E2: Sí, tengo muchos libros en mi cuarto. (No, tengo pocos libros).

 E. Intercambios. En parejas, túrnense para entrevistarse (*take turns interviewing each other*) sobre los siguientes temas (*topics*). Deben añadir (*add*) una pregunta original para cada (*each*) verbo.

VERBO INICIAL	OPCIONES
preferir	¿los gatos o los perros? ¿mirar una película (*movie*) en casa o en el cine (*movie theater*)? ¿la ropa elegante o la ropa cómoda? ¿ ?
tener	¿mucho dinero o muchas deudas (*debts*)? ¿una familia grande o pequeña? ¿sueño en clase con frecuencia? ¿ ?
venir	¿a clase muy tarde o temprano? ¿de una familia anglosajona, hispana o de otro origen? ¿a clase todos los días? ¿ ?
(¿qué?) querer	¿comprar esta semana? ¿comprar en el futuro? ¿mirar en la tele esta noche? ¿ ?
poder	¿hablar una lengua extranjera? ¿vivir sin (*without*) dinero? ¿escribir poemas? ¿ ?

F. ¿Deseos u obligaciones? En parejas, usen **tener ganas de** + *infinitivo* y **tener que** + *infinitivo* para entrevistarse sobre su semana.

MODELOS: ¿Qué tienes ganas de comer hoy?
¿Qué tienes que hacer esta noche?

ACCIONES POSIBLES

aprender el vocabulario sobre la ropa
bailar salsa/reguetón
dormir to sleep

hablar con _____ (una persona)
mirar _____ (una serie o una película [*movie*])
trabajar

Vocabulario útil

esta noche
este fin de semana
este _____ (día de la semana)

11 Expressing Destination and Future Actions • *Ir;* The Contraction al; *Ir + a + infinitive*

Gramática en acción: ¿Adónde vas?

El Mercado Central, Ciudad de Guatemala

Lucy.Brown/Shutterstock

Rosa y Casandra son compañeras de casa.

CASANDRA:	¿Adónde **vas**?
ROSA:	**Voy al** Mercado Central.
CASANDRA:	¿Qué **vas a comprar** allá?
ROSA:	**Voy a comprar** unos regalos para mi familia en Nueva Jersey.
CASANDRA:	**¿Vas a viajar** a los Estados Unidos pronto?
ROSA:	Sí, en quince días. ¿Por qué no vienes conmigo **al** Mercado?
CASANDRA:	¡Sí! **Vamos.**

Comprensión

¿Cierto o falso? Corrija las oraciones falsas.

	CIERTO	FALSO
1. Rosa **va a estudiar.**	☐	☐
2. Rosa **va a comprar** regalos.	☐	☐
3. Casandra **va** a los Estados Unidos.	☐	☐

The Verb **ir** / **El verbo** *ir*

ir *(to go)*			
(yo)	**voy**	(nosotros/as)	**vamos**
(tú)	**vas**	(vosotros/as)	**vais**
(usted, él, ella)	**va**	(ustedes, ellos/as)	**van**

The irregular Spanish verb **ir** expresses *to go.*

Rosa **va** al centro.
Rosa is going downtown.
¿Adónde **vas** tú?
Where are you going?

The first person plural of **ir, vamos** (*we go, are going, do go*), is also used to express *let's go.*

Vamos a clase ahora mismo.
Let's go to class right now.

The Contraction **al** / **La contracción** *al*

As you can see in the preceding examples, the verb **ir** is often used with the preposition **a** to indicate where someone is going (to).

When **a** is followed by **el,** it contracts to **al,** just as **de + el → del** (Capítulo 3). **Al** and **del** are the only *contractions* (**las contracciones**) in Spanish.

a + el → al

Voy **al** centro comercial.
I'm going to the mall.

Vamos a la tienda.
We're going to the store.

¡OJO!

The preposition **a** *does not* contract with any article other than **el.**

Note that **a** does not contract with the pronoun **él.**

• **el** (article) = the → no accent mark
• **él** (pronoun) = he → with accent mark

Where are you going? Rosa and Casandra are housemates. CASANDRA: Where are you going? ROSA: I'm going to the Central Market. CASANDRA: What are you going to buy there? ROSA: I'm going to buy some presents for my family in New Jersey. CASANDRA: Are you going to travel to the United States soon? ROSA: Yes, in two weeks. Why don't you come to the Market with me? CASANDRA: Yes! Let's go.

Gramática

ciento veintitrés ■ **123**

Using **ir** to Talk About the Future / **El uso de *ir* para hablar del futuro**

You can use the verb **ir** + **a** + *infinitive* to talk about the future in Spanish.

Van a venir a la fiesta esta noche.
They're coming to the party tonight.
Voy a comer en un restaurante en el centro.
I'm going to eat at a downtown restaurant.

¡OJO!

The **ir** + **a** + *infinitive* structure is like **aprender** + **a** + *infinitive*, which you learned in **Gramática 8 (Cap. 3).**

This use of the preposition **a** is different from the use of **a** to indicate where someone is going. Compare these two sentences.

Voy al centro para comer.
I'm going downtown to eat.

Voy a ir al centro para comer.
I'm going to go downtown to eat.

Práctica y comunicación

<table>
<tr><td>

Summary of *ir*

voy, vas...

<u>ir</u> + a + infinitivo

</td></tr>
</table>

A. Mañana

Paso 1. Autoprueba. Complete las siguientes frases con formas del verbo **ir.**

1. tú _____
2. Manuela y yo _____
3. yo _____
4. Manu y usted _____
5. usted _____
6. Manuel y Bruno _____

Paso 2. Ahora use las siguientes frases para expresar lo que (*what*) usted va a hacer o no hacer mañana.

MODELO: estudiar → Mañana **no voy a** estudiar.

1. ir de compras (*to go shopping*)
2. comer en la cafetería de la universidad
3. estudiar en la biblioteca
4. escribir e-mails
5. venir a la clase de español
6. poder hacer toda mi tarea
7. bailar en una discoteca

Paso 3. Ahora use las frases del **Paso 2** para entrevistar (*interview*) a un compañero o una compañera.

MODELO: estudiar → ¿**Vas a** estudiar mañana?

B. ¿Adónde van de compras? Haga oraciones completas, usando (*using*) **ir.** ¡OJO! a + el → al.

MODELO: Marta / el centro → Marta **va al** centro.

1. tú y yo / la *boutique* Regalitos
2. Francisco / el almacén Goya
3. Juan y Raúl / el centro comercial
4. (tú) / el Mercado Central
5. usted / la tienda Gómez
6. yo / ¿ ?

C. ¿Adónde va usted si... ? ¿Cuántas oraciones puede hacer?

| (No) Me gusta | + | leer / hacer tarea.
ir de compras.
buscar gangas y cosas usadas.
estudiar fuera (*away from*) casa / la residencia.
cantar / bailar.
ver series / películas (*movies*). | + | Por eso (no) voy a / al / a la / a los _____. |

<table>
<tr><td>

Vocabulario útil

el cine movie theater
el mercadillo flea market

</td></tr>
</table>

Prác. A, Paso 1: Answers: 1. vas **2.** vamos **3.** voy **4.** van **5.** va **6.** van

D. Intercambios

Paso 1. En parejas, túrnense para hacer y contestar preguntas sobre sus planes para el fin de semana. Aquí hay unas actividades posibles. Traten de obtener (*Try to get*) mucha información. **¡OJO! ¿adónde?** = *where to?*

MODELO: **1.** ir de compras → ¿**Vas a ir** de compras **este fin de semana**? ¿**Adónde** vas a ir? ¿**Por qué** vas a ese centro comercial? ¿**Qué** vas a comprar?

1. ir de compras
2. leer una novela
3. asistir a un evento en la universidad
4. estudiar para un examen
5. ir a casa de _____
6. escribir un ensayo (*essay*)
7. mirar tu serie favorita

Paso 2. Ahora elijan (*choose*) una actividad para hacer juntos/as (*do together*). Inviten al resto de la clase a participar con **vamos a.**

MODELO: Jordan y yo vamos a asistir el sábado al concierto de música clásica en el campus. ¡Vamos a ir al concierto toda la clase!

Algo sobre las compras en Guatemala y Honduras

Igual que[a] en los Estados Unidos, en el mundo hispano abundan[b] los centros comerciales. De hecho,[c] en algunos[d] países, como en Guatemala y Honduras, se llaman «malls». Algunos centros comerciales están en el centro de la ciudad y otros en las afueras.[e] En las tiendas de los centros comerciales los precios son siempre fijos.[f]

¿Hay grandes centros comerciales en el centro de su ciudad? ¿O están en las afueras?

[a]Igual... *Just as* [b]*there are many* [c]De... *In fact* [d]*some* [e]en... *in the outskirts* [f]*fixed*

City Mall, San Pedro Sula, Honduras. Es probablemente el centro comercial más grande y moderno de todo el país.

©Miami In Focus, Inc.

Todo junto

A. Lengua y cultura: Pero, ¿no se puede regatear (*can't one bargain*)?

Paso 1. Completar. Complete the following paragraphs about shopping. Give the correct form of the words in parentheses, as suggested by context. When two possibilities are given in parentheses, select the correct word.

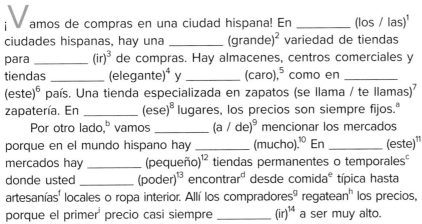

Tienda de sombreros en el mercado de San Francisco el Alto, Guatemala

Sharpshooters/VWPics/Alamy Stock Photo

¡Vamos de compras en una ciudad hispana! En _____ (los / las)[1] ciudades hispanas, hay una _____ (grande)[2] variedad de tiendas para _____ (ir)[3] de compras. Hay almacenes, centros comerciales y tiendas _____ (elegante)[4] y _____ (caro),[5] como en _____ (este)[6] país. Una tienda especializada en zapatos (se llama / te llamas)[7] zapatería. En _____ (ese)[8] lugares, los precios son siempre fijos.[a]

Por otro lado,[b] vamos _____ (a / de)[9] mencionar los mercados porque en el mundo hispano hay _____ (mucho).[10] En _____ (este)[11] mercados hay _____ (pequeño)[12] tiendas permanentes o temporales[c] donde usted _____ (poder)[13] encontrar[d] desde comida[e] típica hasta artesanías[f] locales o ropa interior. Allí los compradores[g] regatean[h] los precios, porque el primer[i] precio casi siempre _____ (ir)[14] a ser muy alto.

[a]*fixed* [b]Por... *On the other hand* [c]*temporary* [d]*find* [e]desde... *everything from food*
[f]*arts and crafts* [g]*shoppers, buyers* [h]*negotiate, bargain* [i]*first*

(Continúa).

Paso 2. Comprensión. Complete las oraciones.

1. En las ciudades hispanas hay tiendas,
   _____, _____ y _____.
2. Una tienda de zapatos se llama una _____.
3. Si a usted le gusta practicar español y regatear, debe ir a _____.

 Paso 3. En acción

 En parejas, hagan una lista de los tres lugares de compras más interesantes o buenos en la ciudad donde está su universidad. Luego comparen su lista con las (*those*) de otras parejas. ¿Hay coincidencias?

 B. Proyecto: Encuesta° sobre las preferencias de la clase con relación a la moda y los estilos *Survey*

Working in groups, create a profile of the fashion preferences of your class.

Paso 1. Preparación In groups, think of style and fashion trends; they may be current or not. Express them as phrases, as in the model. Create one to two phrases for each member of your group.

> MODELO: llevar un arete en la nariz

Now turn those phrases into questions to poll your classmates. Consider your polling options: **cierto o falso,** open-ended questions, or a series of options.

> MODELOS: llevar un arete en la nariz →
> ¿Llevas un arete en la nariz? / ¿Quieres llevar un arete en la nariz?
> ¿Cierto o falso para ti? Te gusta llevar aretes en la nariz.
> ¿Cuál es tu opinión sobre la idea de llevar aretes en la nariz?
> Es bonito / absurdo / irrelevante.

Paso 2. Encuesta. Working individually, poll as many of your classmates as possible using the questions you created. Before you start polling, create a table on which to record the answers. Remember to ask for and record the names of the classmates you poll.

Paso 3. Análisis de datos. Gather the information from your group's polling, and prepare 4 to 5 statements to share with the rest of the class. Here are some examples of statements. You can use them or create your own.

1. _____ (número) personas tienen un arete en la nariz, _____ (número) quieren tener un arete en la nariz y _____ (número) no quieren.

2. _____ (número) estudiantes piensan (*think*) que tener un arete en la nariz es bonito, _____ (número) piensan que es absurdo y _____ (número) piensan que es irrelevante.

Vocabulario útil

el brazo	arm
el labio	lip
la lengua	tongue
nadie	no one
la nariz	nose
la oreja	ear
el *piercing*	piercing
los pantalones muy bajos (*low*) / muy estrechos (*tight*)	
el tatuaje	tattoo

Charlie Bonallack/Alamy Stock Photo

¿Le gustan los tatuajes?

Video: Salu2 «¡Moda°, moda, moda!» *Fashion*

You can watch two segments of this chapter's video in the **Video: Salu2** section, found at the end of the eBook.

Klic Video Productions/ McGraw Hill

Javier Claudio es dueño (*owner*) de la tienda Icónica, que se especializa en diseños (*designs*) de camisetas.

Enfoque cultural: La ropa y los mercados

> ### Antes de leer
> ¿Hay mercados en su ciudad o en la zona donde usted vive? ¿Qué se vende (*is sold*) allí: productos locales, artesanías (*arts and crafts*), ropa y zapatos... ?

En Guatemala y Honduras

Un huipil maya: un tipo de blusa tradicional

En Guatemala y Honduras hay mercados donde se puede comprar artículos de artesanía a buen precio. Son famosos los mercados guatemaltecos de las ciudades de Guatemala, Antigua, Chichicastenango y Quetzaltenango. En estos mercados existe la costumbre[a] del «regateo»: el comprador[b] de un artículo debe negociar el precio con el vendedor.[c] Los vendedores invitan a los compradores a regatear y con frecuencia se escucha decir[d]: «...pero tiene rebaja, ofrezca un precio[e]».

En Guatemala, los tejidos[f] de tradición maya son especialmente populares entre los turistas por su colorido y belleza.[g] En Honduras, además de[h] artesanías, los turistas también compran café, ron,[i] vainilla y puros.[j]

[a]*custom* [b]*buyer, customer* [c]*seller* [d]*se... one hears people say* [e]*pero... but a discount is possible, make an offer* [f]*weavings* [g]*por... for their colors and beauty* [h]*además... besides* [i]*rum* [j]*cigars*

Comprensión ¿Qué es el regateo? ¿Qué cosas compran los turistas en estos países?

En otros países hispanos

Unos huaraches

Un poncho

Una guayabera

- **En Latinoamérica** La ropa tradicional en los países hispanohablantes es muy diversa, porque hay regiones y climas muy diferentes. Algunas prendas[a] son ahora conocidas[b] por todo el mundo:
  - la guayabera, una camisa de hombres de mangas[c] largas o cortas (el Caribe)
  - los huaraches, un tipo de sandalias (México)
  - el poncho, una prenda de abrigo[d] (los Andes)
- **En los países andinos** En estos países hay una lana excelente que viene de los camélidos[e] de la región: la llama, la vicuña, la alpaca y el guanaco. La lana de estos animales es de excelente calidad y se utiliza para hacer[f] prendas de abrigo, como suéteres, gorros y ponchos.

[a]*Algunas... Some clothing* [b]*well-known* [c]*sleeves* [d]*de... warm (for cold weather)* [e]*camel-like animals* [f]*making*

Comprensión ¿Qué prendas de ropa de origen latinoamericano ahora tienen un mercado internacional? ¿Qué animales andinos tienen una lana excelente?

 ### En acción

Haga una lista de los productos más típicos de la zona donde usted vive. ¿Son productos agrícolas (*agricultural*), artesanales o industriales? ¿Qué productos u objetos compran los turistas cuando visitan la zona? Use el diccionario si no sabe (*you don't know*) las palabras.

Lectura

Antes de leer

Conteste las siguientes preguntas.

1. ¿Qué significa para usted la frase «ropa activa»? ¿Cuándo y dónde es buena idea usar «ropa activa»? ¿Tiene usted ropa de este tipo?
2. Para usted, ¿son importantes estas características en la ropa? ¿Por qué?
   - Repeler los mosquitos.
   - Proveer (*Provide*) protección solar.
   - Ser impermeable.
   - Neutralizar malos olores (*odors*).

Vocabulario para leer

la calle	street	**medioambiental**	environmental
la colina	hill	**nevado/a**	snowy
la prenda	la ropa		
el sol	sun	**auxiliar**	to help
		ayudar	to help
		proporcionar	to offer

Algo[a] más que ropa
por Gregori Dolz

➡ Desde[b] las calles de Manhattan a las colinas nevadas de Aspen, Exofficio proporciona a sus clientes algo más que ropa activa. Parte de sus beneficios ayudan a causas medioambientales como la Conservation Alliance o World Concern, que auxilian a comunidades necesitadas[c] de todo el mundo. Además, sus prendas proporcionan protección contra los insectos, contra el sol y el agua, contra los olores corporales[d] y muchas otras inconveniencias.

» www.exofficio.com

[a]*Something* [b]*From* [c]*needy* [d]*olores... bodily odors*

Comprensión

A. Un resumen del artículo. Las tres oraciones del artículo «Algo más que ropa» describen tres de las características de la compañía Exofficio y de la ropa que vende. Empareje (*Match*) las tres oraciones del artículo con los siguientes resúmenes.

_____ **a.** La compañía dona (*donates*) parte de sus ganancias (*earnings*) a organizaciones conservacionistas y humanitarias.

_____ **b.** La ropa de Exofficio protege (*protects*) contra diversos inconvenientes.

_____ **c.** La ropa de Exofficio es adecuada para muchos lugares diferentes.

B. Usted y Exofficio. Indique la importancia que tienen para usted las siguientes características de Exofficio y la ropa que produce. Luego (*Then*) explique sus respuestas.

	MUY IMPORTANTE	IMPORTANTE	POCO IMPORTANTE	NADA (*NOT*) IMPORTANTE
1. La compañía dona parte de sus ganancias a varias causas.	☐	☐	☐	☐
2. Es ropa protectora.	☐	☐	☐	☐
3. Es «ropa activa» que uno puede usar en muchas situaciones.	☐	☐	☐	☐

⚙ Proyecto: Preferencias de la clase con respecto a la ropa

Paso 1. Haga una lista de tres de las características que usted prefiere en la ropa. Incluya al menos (*Include at least*) un aspecto diferente de los que aparecen (*from those that appear*) en el anuncio de Exofficio. Use el modelo y un diccionario si es necesario.

> MODELO: Para mí, la ropa debe ser elegante.

Paso 2. Ahora, en grupos, hagan una lista completa de las características que prefieren las personas de su grupo en su ropa.

Paso 3. Comenten las características preferidas por (*by*) los miembros del grupo o de toda la clase. Usen la escala (*scale*) de opinión de **Comprensión B** para evaluar cada (*each*) preferencia. ¿Cuáles son las características más (*most*) importantes? ¿Y las menos (*least*) importantes? ¿Hay tendencias generales?

🔊 Textos orales

Dos amigas hacen planes para ir de compras

Antes de escuchar

¿Espera usted (*Do you wait for*) las rebajas para ir de compras? ¿Para comprar qué tipo de cosas (*things*) busca usted rebajas? ¿ropa? ¿objetos electrónicos?

Comprensión

A. ¿Cierto o falso? Las siguientes oraciones son falsas. Corríjalas. (*Correct them.*)

1. Las rebajas empiezan hoy.
2. Cristina tiene clases mañana por la mañana.
3. Lidia no tiene clases mañana.
4. Cristina y Lidia van a encontrarse (*meet up*) en la universidad.
5. Lidia no tiene hermanos.

B. Intercambios. Invente la parte que falta (*is missing*), usando expresiones del diálogo.

1. — _____
   —Hola, soy yo.

2. — _____
   —Muy bien. ¿Y tú?

3. — _____
   —Perfecto. En Zara, a las 7.

Vocabulario para escuchar

¿Qué onda?	What's up? (*Mexico*)
conmigo	with me
empiezan	they start
¡Qué padre!	Great! (*Mexico*)

✋ En acción

En parejas, creen (*create*) un pequeño diálogo similar a la conversación de Lidia y Cristina para hacer planes para ir de compras a un centro comercial o a las tiendas locales.

🎤 Entrevista

Fabrice Lerouge/SuperStock

Use de modelo las preguntas y respuestas (*answers*) de la sección **Entrevista** al principio (*at the beginning*) de este capítulo para hablar de su ropa favorita y su propio estilo de vestir.

💻 Escritura

Un ensayo sobre los estilos en el campus

¿Cree usted que hay un estilo de ropa que llevan los estudiantes universitarios en general o hay más de (*more than*) un estilo? En su opinión, ¿se ven (*are seen*) en este campus las tendencias de la moda (*fashion*) que predominan en el resto del país?

👥 Antes de escribir

Hongqi Zhang/Alamy Stock Photo

Blue Jean Images/Alamy Stock Photo

En parejas, hagan una lista del estilo o los estilos de moda típicos en su universidad. Para cada (*each*) estilo, hagan una lista de la ropa más característica del estilo, con una descripción básica (por ejemplo: pantalones elásticos muy estrechos [*tight*]...). La siguiente tabla va a ayudarlos (*help you*) a organizar sus ideas. ¡Deben incluir el estilo de los profesores también! Pónganle (*Give*) un nombre a cada estilo si no lo tiene todavía (*yet*). ¡Sean (*Be*) originales!

	El más (*most*) popular	El segundo (*2nd*) más popular	El tercero (*3rd*) más popular
Nombre del estilo			
Personas (estudiantes, profesores, personal administrativo...)			
Descripción de la ropa			

A escribir

Ahora use sus ideas para escribir un ensayo sobre la moda en su universidad. Incluya unas oraciones sobre su propio estilo. Hay más ayuda (*help*) en Connect.

Para escribir bien

Here are some words and phrases that can be useful in your essay.

- Words to quantify nouns (adjectives) and actions (adverbs): **mucho/poco**
- Expressions that indicate frequency (adverbs): **a veces, (casi) nunca, (casi) siempre, con frecuencia,...**
- Words to indicate to a place (adverbs): **aquí/allí/allá**
- Words to connect ideas: **además, o (u), pero, por eso, también, y (e)**

❖ En la comunidad

Entreviste a una persona hispana de su universidad o ciudad para informarse de (*find out about*) sus preferencias con respecto a las compras y la moda.

Preguntas posibles

- ¿Cuáles son las tiendas favoritas de esta persona para comprar ropa?
- ¿Hay mercados en su país de origen? ¿Qué venden en los mercados? ¿Se puede regatear (*bargain*) allí?
- En su opinión, ¿dónde hay más preocupación por la ropa, en este país o en su país de origen?

▣ Producción audiovisual

Con las preguntas de la **Entrevista** como modelo, filme una o dos entrevistas con personas que hablan de su estilo de vestir y de sus tiendas de ropa favoritas.

Más ideas para el portafolio

- Busque (*Find*) una fotografía reciente de usted llevando (*wearing*) ropa bonita o interesante en una ocasión especial y descríbala (*describe it*).
- Busque la página web de su tienda o marca favorita y determine si tiene una página en español. Si la tiene (*If it has one*), incluya (*include*) unos detalles de la página.
- Si ha estado jugando (*you have been playing*) Practice Spanish: Study Abroad, en Quest 2 usted pasó su primer día (*spent your first day*) en el Instituto de Lenguas y tuvo que aprender (*had to learn*) información sobre sus clases y el campus. Ahora cree (*create*) un folleto (*brochure*) para estudiantes nuevos sobre la universidad a la que (*that*) asiste usted. Incluya (*Include*) detalles sobre las clases y las actividades que ofrece (*that it offers*).

Sugerencia: You are now ready to play Quest 2 in **Practice Spanish: Study Abroad.**

EN RESUMEN En este capítulo

AFTER STUDYING THIS CHAPTER I CAN ...

☐ name items of clothing and use color adjectives (104–105, 107)

☐ talk about shopping (104–105)

☐ count beyond 100 and express years (110)

☐ use demonstratives to describe people and things at different distances (114–115)

☐ talk about more actions with a different kind of **-er** and **-ir** verbs (118–119)

☐ use very frequent expressions with **tener** (119)

☐ talk about where I'm going and what I'm going to do in the near future, using the verb **ir** (123–124)

☐ recognize/describe at least 2–3 aspects of Guatemalan and Honduran cultures

Gramática en breve

9. Demonstrative Adjectives and Pronouns

this → these	that/those	that/those (over there)
est<u>e</u> → est<u>os</u>	es<u>e</u> → es<u>os</u>	aquel → aquel<u>los</u>
est<u>a</u> → est<u>as</u>	es<u>a</u> → es<u>as</u>	aquell<u>a</u> → aquell<u>as</u>
neuter: **esto**	neuter: **eso**	neuter: **aquello**

10. *Tener, venir, poder, preferir, querer*; Some Idioms with *tener*

<u>tener</u>: tengo, t<u>ie</u>nes, t<u>ie</u>ne, tenemos, tenéis, t<u>ie</u>nen

<u>venir</u>: vengo, v<u>ie</u>nes, v<u>ie</u>ne, venimos, venís, v<u>ie</u>nen

<u>poder</u>: p<u>ue</u>do, p<u>ue</u>des, p<u>ue</u>de, podemos, podéis, p<u>ue</u>den

<u>preferir</u>: pref<u>ie</u>ro, pref<u>ie</u>res, pref<u>ie</u>re, preferimos, preferís, pref<u>ie</u>ren

<u>querer</u>: qu<u>ie</u>ro, qu<u>ie</u>res, qu<u>ie</u>re, queremos, queréis, qu<u>ie</u>ren

Idioms with <u>tener</u>:

<u>tener</u> **miedo de / prisa / razón / sueño / no** <u>tener</u> **razón**

<u>tener</u> **ganas de** + *inf.* **/ que** + *inf.*

11. *Ir*; The Contraction al; *Ir* + *a* + *inf.*

<u>ir</u>: voy, vas, va, vamos, vais, van

a + el → <u>al</u>

Vocabulario

Remember that changes like **e → ie** and **o → ue** will be shown like this in vocabulary lists.

Los verbos

<u>ir</u> (voy, vas,...)	to go
ir a + *inf.*	to be going to (*do something*)
poder (p<u>ue</u>do)	to be able, can
prefer<u>i</u>r (pref<u>ie</u>ro)	to prefer
<u>querer</u> (qu<u>ie</u>ro)	to want
tener (tengo, t<u>ie</u>nes,...)	to have
<u>venir</u> (vengo, v<u>ie</u>nes,...)	to come

La ropa

llevar	to wear; to carry; to take
usar	to wear; to use
el abrigo	coat
los aretes	earrings
la blusa	blouse
el bolso	purse
las botas	boots
los calcetines	socks
la camisa	shirt
la camiseta	T-shirt
la cartera	wallet; handbag
las chanclas	flip-flops
la chaqueta	jacket (*for a woman or a man*)
el cinturón	belt
el complemento	accessory
la corbata	tie
la falda	skirt
las gafas de sol	sunglasses
la gorra	baseball cap
el impermeable	raincoat
las medias	stockings
los pantalones	pants
los pantalones cortos	shorts
el reloj	watch
la ropa interior	underwear
las sandalias	sandals
el sombrero	hat
la sudadera	sweatshirt
el traje	suit
el traje de baño	swimsuit
el vestido	dress
los zapatos	shoes
la ropa	clothing

Cognados: los *jeans*, el suéter, los tenis

De compras

comprar por internet	to buy online
estar de (última) moda	to be the (latest) trend
ir (voy, vas...) de compras	to go shopping

Repaso: comprar, vender

la ganga	bargain
el precio	price
las rebajas	sales, reductions
¿cuánto cuesta(n)?	how much does it (do they) cost?
de todo	everything

Los materiales

de...	
cuadros	plaid
lunares (*m.*)	polka-dot
rayas	striped
es de...	it is made of ...
algodón (*m.*)	cotton
cuero	leather
lana	wool
oro	gold
plata	silver
seda	silk

Los lugares

el almacén	department store
el centro	downtown
el centro comercial	shopping mall
el mercado	market(place)
la tienda	shop, store

Cognado: la plaza

Los colores

amarillo/a	yellow
anaranjado/a	orange
azul	blue
blanco/a	white
(de) color café	brown
gris	gray
morado/a	purple
negro/a	black
rojo/a	red
rosado/a	pink
verde	green

Otros sustantivos

el/la chico/a	guy/girl
el examen	exam, test

Cognado: el dólar

Los adjetivos

barato/a	inexpensive
caro/a	expensive
cómodo/a	comfortable
poco/a	little, few
propio/a	own, one's own
último/a	latest; last

Repaso: mucho/a

Los números a partir del 100

ciento, ciento uno/una, ciento dos... ciento noventa y nueve, doscientos/as, trescientos/as, cuatrocientos/as, quinientos/as, seiscientos/as, setecientos/as, ochocientos/as, novecientos/as, mil, un millón (de)

Repaso: cien

Las formas demostrativas

aquel, aquella, aquellos/as	that, those ([way] over there)
aquello (*neuter*)	that ([way] over there)
ese/a, esos/as	that, those
eso (*neuter*)	that

Repaso: este/a, esto (*neuter*), estos/as

Palabras adicionales

¿adónde?	where (to)?
al (a + el)	to the
allá	(way) over there
allí	there
si	if
sobre	about
tener...	
ganas de + *inf.*	to feel like (*doing something*)
miedo (de)	to be afraid (of)
prisa	to be in a hurry
que + *inf.*	to have to (*do something*)
razón	to be right
sueño	to be sleepy
no tener razón	to be wrong
vamos	let's go
¿verdad?, ¿no?	right, don't they (you, and so on)?

Repaso: aquí, mucho (*adv.*), poco (*adv.*), tener... años

Vocabulario personal

Use this space or a vocabulary notebook to write down other words and phrases you learn in this chapter.

5

En casa

En este capítulo

VOCABULARY
Parts of a house and furniture   136
Days of the week   138
Words like *before* and *after*   140

GRAMMAR
Expressing actions with additional verbs   142
Other verbs like **poder, querer,** and **preferir**   148
Verbs that are used reflexively (*self/selves*)   153

COUNTRIES OF FOCUS: EL SALVADOR AND NICARAGUA

Casas de muchos colores en una calle (*street*) del centro de Granada, Nicaragua

EL SALVADOR

6,4 (coma cuatro)
millones de habitantes

- El Salvador es el país más
  pequeño de Centroamérica,
  pero tiene la densidad de
  población más alta.

NICARAGUA

6,5 (coma cinco)
millones de habitantes

- Nicaragua tiene diecisiete
  volcanes y dos lagos
  inmensos.

 ENTREVISTA

These questions related to the chapter theme are answered here by a
native speaker. You will be able to ask and answer them yourself with
personal information in the **Entrevista** activity in the **Portafolio**
section at the end of the chapter.

Manuel Gil del Valle contesta las preguntas.

— **¿Dónde vive usted? ¿En qué parte de la ciudad? ¿en el centro, en la
zona universitaria o en una zona residencial? ¿Vive en una residencia,
en una casa o en un apartamento?**

— Vivo en Managua, en un apartamento en una zona residencial que está
a 5 kilómetros del centro de la ciudad.

— **¿Cómo es su habitación[a], grande o pequeña? ¿Tiene un cuarto de
baño[b] propio?**

— Es un apartamento muy cómodo, con tres habitaciones y dos baños. Mi
mujer y yo tenemos la habitación de matrimonio,[c] que es muy amplia y
luminosa y tiene su propio baño. La habitación de mis hijas también está
muy bien, pero no tiene cuarto de baño propio. La otra habitación es más
pequeña y funciona como un estudio.

— **¿Cómo se siente usted[d] cuando está en casa?**

— Me gusta mucho estar en casa. Allí me siento bien porque puedo
descansar y relajarme.[e] Pero sobre todo[f] porque en mi casa estoy con mi
mujer y mis hijas, que son lo más importante en mi vida.[g]

[a]*bedroom* [b]*cuarto... bathroom* [c]*habitación... master bedroom (lit., of the marriage)*
[d]*se... do you feel* [e]*descansar... rest and relax* [f]*Pero... But above all* [g]*lo... the most important
thing in my life*

You can hear the pronunciation of theme vocabulary words and phrases in the eBook.

¿Cómo es su hogar°? ¿Qué muebles° tiene?* *home / furniture*

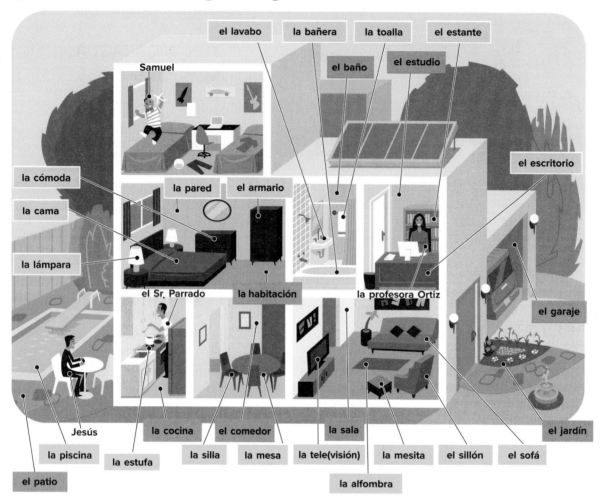

el lavabo · la bañera · la toalla · el estante · el baño · el estudio · el estante · Samuel · la cómoda · la pared · el armario · el escritorio · la cama · la lámpara · el Sr. Parrado · la habitación · la profesora Ortiz · el garaje · Jesús · la piscina · la estufa · la cocina · el comedor · la silla · la mesa · la tele(visión) · la sala · la mesita · el sillón · el sofá · la alfombra · el jardín · el patio

Así se dice

el armario = el ropero
la bañera = la tina
el estudio = el despacho (*Sp.*)
el lavabo = la pileta (*L.A.*)

la piscina = la alberca (*Mex.*), la pileta (*Arg.*)
la sala = el *living*
la televisión = el televisor

There is great variation in the ways in which Spanish speakers refer to the bedroom. Besides **la habitación,** it is called **el cuarto** and **el dormitorio** in several countries, **la pieza** by Argentines, and **la recámara** by Mexicans.

---

*This is the first group of words you will learn for talking about where you live and the things found in your room, house, or apartment. You will learn additional vocabulary for those topics in *Capítulos 10* and *12.*

Comunicación

A. ¿Dónde? ¿En qué cuarto o parte de la casa hace usted estas actividades?

¡OJO! se + *verb* = *one (does something).*

1. Es donde se trabaja en la computadora.
2. Es donde se come con toda la familia.
3. Allí se guarda (*one keeps*) el coche.
4. Allí se nada (*one swims*).
5. Allí se duerme (*one sleeps*).
6. Es donde se prepara la comida (*food*).

B. Asociaciones

Paso 1. En parejas, hagan una lista de los muebles o partes de la casa que ustedes asocian con las siguientes actividades.

1. estudiar para un examen
2. dormir la siesta (*to take a nap*) por la tarde
3. pasar (*to spend*) una noche en casa con la familia
4. celebrar con una comida (*meal*) especial
5. lavar (*to wash*) el perro
6. hablar de temas (*topics*) serios con los amigos (padres, esposo/a, hijos)

Paso 2. Ahora comparen sus respuestas con las (*those*) del resto de la clase. ¿Tienen todos las mismas costumbres (*same customs*)?

C. ¿Qué necesita? ¿Qué muebles u objetos se necesitan lógicamente en estas situaciones?

1. No puedo leer bien porque hay poca luz (*light*). Necesito _____.
2. Para hacer la tarea en casa necesito _____.
3. Para mi ropa interior necesito _____.
4. Para todos mis libros necesito _____.
5. Después de bañarme (*After bathing*) necesito _____.

> **Vocabulario útil**
>
> **la bicicleta**
> **las cortinas**
> **la planta**

D. Esta casa

Paso 1. En parejas, identifiquen las partes de esta casa y lo que (*what*) hay en cada (*each*) una. Mencionen los colores también.

MODELO: E1: El número 1 corresponde al **garaje.**
E2: ¿Qué hay en el garaje?
E1: Hay **un coche verde** y...

Paso 2. Ahora amplíen (*enlarge*) el plano de esta casa para incorporar dos partes más. Deben pensar (*think*) en la utilidad (*purpose*) que tienen esas partes y poner (*put in*) los muebles apropiados. Luego (*Then*) prepárense para describir sus cambios.

Paso 3. Describan al resto de la clase las nuevas partes de la casa sin (*without*) leer.

MODELO: Las nuevas partes de nuestra casa son... En el/la _____ hay...

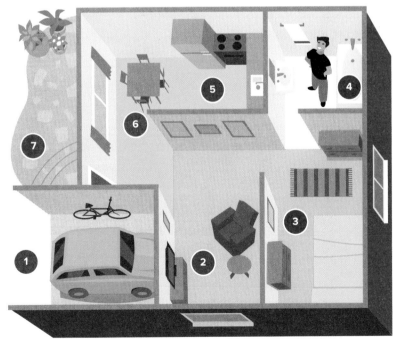

Nota cultural: Las casas en el mundo hispano

El hogar significa *home,* literalmente. Sin embargo,[a] la palabra **casa** se usa de manera genérica en español con el significado de **hogar,** como en estas expresiones comunes:

ir/regresar a casa	to go/return home
estar en casa	to be at home
Estás en tu casa.	Welcome. (*Lit.,* You're in your home.)

Hay una gran variedad de tipos de casas en el mundo hispano y no se puede decir que haya[b] «una casa típica». Las construcciones dependen del[c] uso, de la zona (rural o urbana), del clima y de las tradiciones históricas y culturales. Y, por supuesto,[d] del factor económico.

John Mitchell/Alamy Stock Photo

El Museo Casa Natal (*Birthplace*) de Rubén Darío, en Ciudad Darío, Nicaragua

En las ciudades, la mayoría de las personas no vive en casas sino[e] en apartamentos. Otras palabras para apartamento son **piso** (España) y **departamento** (México, Argentina).

En su ciudad, ¿es más común vivir en un apartamento o en una casa? En su estado o país, ¿hay un estilo de casas predominante o tradicional?

[a]Sin... *However*   [b]decir... *say that there is*   [c]*on the*   [d]por... *of course*   [e]*but rather*

¿Qué día es hoy?

¡OJO!

To express *on* with days of the week, use **el** (for singular) or **los** (to generalize), as appropriate. The word **en** is not used with days of the week in Spanish. See **Nota comunicativa,** later in this section.

lunes

1. Javier asiste a clase el lunes a las ocho.

martes

2. Javier mira la televisión el martes.

miércoles

3. Javier va al gimnasio el miércoles.

jueves

4. Javier trabaja cuatro horas el jueves.

viernes

5. El viernes va al mercado con unos amigos.

el fin de semana (sábado y domingo)

6. El fin de semana juega al basquetbol con sus amigos.

¿Por qué no hay otro día entre el domingo y el lunes?

¡Necesito descansar[a] del fin de semana!

[a]to rest

Hoy es viernes (domingo,...).	Today is Friday (Sunday, ...).
Mañana es sábado (lunes,...).	Tomorrow is Saturday (Monday, ...).
Ayer <u>fue</u> martes (miércoles,...).	Yesterday was Tuesday (Wednesday, ...).
el fin de semana	the weekend
pasado mañana	the day after tomorrow
anteayer	the day before yesterday
el próximo jueves (viernes,...) el jueves (viernes,...) que viene }	next Thursday (Friday, ...)
la próxima semana la semana que viene }	next week

- In Spanish-speaking countries, the week usually starts with **el lunes.**
- The days of the week are not capitalized in Spanish.
- The words **sábado** and **domingo** have plural forms: **los sábado<u>s</u>, los domingo<u>s</u>.** The rest of the days do not change in the plural: **el lunes/los lunes.** See the examples in **Nota comunicativa.**

Nota comunicativa: Cómo expresar *on* con los días de la semana

The definite article (singular or plural) is used to express *on* with the days of the week in Spanish.

> **el** + *day* = on (Monday, Tuesday ...)
> Esta semana, tengo que ir al mercado **el** lunes.
> *This week, I have to go to the market **on** Monday.*

> **los** + *day* (plural form, if any) = on (Mondays, Tuesdays ...)
> Por lo general voy al mercado **los** viernes o **los** sábados.
> *I generally go to the market **on** Fridays or **on** Saturdays.*

You will use **el** and **los** with days of the week in **Comunicación A** and **B**.

Comunicación

A. La semana

Paso 1. Complete las oraciones.

1. Hoy es _____. Mañana es _____.
2. Ayer fue _____ y anteayer fue _____.
3. Si hoy es sábado, mañana es _____. Ayer fue _____.
4. Si ayer fue domingo, hoy es _____ y mañana es _____.
5. Hay clase de español los _____, _____ y _____.
6. No tengo clases los _____ ni (*nor*) los _____.
7. Mi próximo examen de _____ es este _____.
8. Trabajo los _____ por la mañana/tarde/noche.
9. Los _____ por la tarde nunca estudio en la biblioteca.
10. Casi todos los _____ salgo (*I go out*) con mis amigos.

Paso 2. En parejas, intercambien (*exchange*) la información de los números 6–10. Luego digan (*tell*) a la clase las actividades que tienen en común.

B. Mi semana. Primero (*First*), indique lo que usted va a hacer **el** (lunes...) que viene. Luego indique una actividad típica de todos **los** (lunes...). Siga los modelos.

MODELOS: **El lunes** tengo que ir al gimnasio. (Voy a ir al gimnasio **el lunes**).
Por lo general (Generalmente) voy al gimnasio **los lunes.**

lunes
martes
miércoles
jueves
viernes
sábado
domingo

+

ir a + *place*
ir a + *inf.*

deber
desear
necesitar
poder
preferir
tener ganas de
tener que

+

el bar
la biblioteca
el centro
el cine (*movies*)
el gimnasio
el museo
el parque
¿ ?

descansar (*to rest*) en cama hasta
    muy tarde
jugar (*to play*) al (tenis, golf, voleibol,
    basquetbol)
¿ ?

¿Cuándo? • Las preposiciones (Part 1)*

1. Antes de la fiesta, Rosa prepara la ensalada.

2. Durante la fiesta, Rosa baila y baila hasta el final.

3. Después de la fiesta, Rosa limpia la sala.

a preposition / **una preposición** = a word or phrase that specifies the relationship of one word to another

Prepositions link words or phrases to other words or phrases. The prepositions are indicated in the following sentences. Can you tell what words or phrases are linked by them?

1. The book is **on** the table.
2. The homework is **for** tomorrow.
3. Los sábados siempre descanso **hasta** muy tarde.
4. Voy a mirar la tele **después de** comer.

You have already used many common Spanish prepositions, including: **a, con, de, en, hasta** (as in **hasta mañana**), **para, por** (*in, during*, as in **por la mañana**), and **sobre.**

You will learn prepositions that express spatial relationships (close to, on top of, ...) in the **Vocabulario: Preparación** *section of* **Capítulo 6**.

In English, prepositions are often followed by the *-ing* form of a verb. However, in Spanish, the infinitive is the only verb form that can follow a preposition. You learned this with the expressions **para** + *inf.* and **ir a** + *inf.*

¿Adónde vas **después de** <u>estudiar</u>?	Where are you going after studying (after you study)?
Tengo ganas de comer **antes de** <u>ir</u> a la biblioteca esta noche.	I feel like eating before going / (before I go) to the library tonight.

Comunicación

A. ¿Cuándo?

Paso 1. Complete las siguientes oraciones lógicamente. Puede usar sustantivos, infinitivos, días de la semana, etcétera.

1. Por lo general, prefiero estudiar _____ (antes de / después de) las nueve de la noche.
2. Siempre tengo mucho sueño durante la clase de _____.
3. Voy a la clase de español _____ (antes de / después de) la clase de _____.
4. El/Los _____ (día o días), estoy en la universidad / en clase hasta _____ (hora).
5. No puedo ir a fiestas durante la semana. Voy el/los _____ (día o días).
6. Tengo que estudiar en esta universidad hasta el año _____.
7. Antes de / Después de mi primera (*first*) clase los _____ (día), voy a _____.

Paso 2. Ahora entreviste (*interview*) a una persona de la clase, usando (*using*) las oraciones del **Paso 1.**

MODELOS: **1.** ¿Prefieres estudiar antes de las nueve de la noche?
¿Prefieres estudiar antes o después de las nueve de la noche?
¿Cuándo prefieres estudiar, antes o después de las nueve de la noche?

B. Intercambios. En parejas, túrnense para entrevistarse. Hagan sus preguntas, usando una palabra o frases de cada columna.

estudiar hablar por teléfono leer trabajar ¿ ?	+	antes de después de durante hasta	+	tu serie favorita (de televisión) las clases las conferencias (*lectures*) de _____ los viernes por la noche, los domingos por la mañana... estudiar, mirar la tele... las tres de la mañana, medianoche (*midnight*), muy tarde... ¿ ?

Algo sobre la costa centroamericana

Los países centroamericanos tienen costa en los océanos Pacífico y Atlántico (el mar Caribe), excepto El Salvador, que solo tiene costa en el Pacífico. El Salvador es un poco más pequeño que el estado de Massachusetts. Así que, aunque[a] solo tiene costa en el Pacífico, ¡el mar nunca está muy lejos[b] para ir a bañarse[c]!

¿Tiene su estado (o país) costa marítima? ¿En qué océano o mar?

[a]Así... *So although* [b]*far* [c]*swimming*

Playa la Paz, El Salvador, un lugar ideal para bañarse y surfear

Nicholas Gill/Alamy Stock Photo

GRAMÁTICA

12 Expressing Actions • *Hacer, oír, poner, salir, traer, ver*

Gramática en acción: ¿Qué <u>hace</u> Rigo?

1. Siempre **traigo** mi portátil a clase.

2. No **oigo** bien. Por eso **hago** muchas preguntas en clase.

3. Siempre **pongo** los subtítulos cuando veo la tele.

4. Los viernes **salgo** con mi grupo de teatro después de ensayar.

Comprensión

1. ¿Qué **trae** Rigo al salón de clase?
2. ¿Por qué **hace** muchas preguntas en clase? ¿**Ve** bien? ¿**Oye** bien?
3. ¿Qué hace cuando **ve** la tele?
4. ¿Con quién **sale** los viernes?

hacer (to do; to make)		oír (to hear)		poner (to put; to place)		salir (to leave [a place]; to go out)		traer (to bring)		ver (to see)	
hago	hacemos	oigo	oímos	pongo	ponemos	salgo	salimos	traigo	traemos	veo	vemos
haces	hacéis	oyes	oís	pones	ponéis	sales	salís	traes	traéis	ves	veis
hace	hacen	oye	oyen	pone	ponen	sale	salen	trae	traen	ve	ven

What does Rigo do? **1.** *I always bring my laptop to class.* **2.** *I don't hear well. That's why I ask a lot of questions in class.* **3.** *I always put the subtitles on when I watch TV.* **4.** *On Fridays I go out with my theater group after rehearsing.*

1. hacer = *to do; to make*

Pero, Julio, ¿qué **haces**?
But, Julio, what are you doing?

Siempre **hago** la tarea en la cafetería.
I always do my homework in the cafeteria.

Alicia **hace** unos tamales deliciosos.
Alicia makes delicious tamales.

Hacer is used in a number of common idioms.

> **hacer un viaje**
> **hacer una pregunta**

Quieren **hacer un viaje** al Perú.
They want to take a trip to Peru.

Los niños siempre **hacen muchas preguntas.**
Children always ask a lot of questions.

Irene **hace** ejercicio todos los días.
Irene exercises every day.

Hacer is also used to express *to do* with academic and physical exercises.

En la clase de matemáticas **hacemos** muchos **ejercicios** y problemas.
In math class, we do a lot of exercises and problems.

---

2. oír = *to hear*
The command forms of **oír** are used to attract someone's attention in the same way that English uses *Listen up!* or *Hey!*

> **oye** (tú)   **oiga** (usted)   **oigan** (ustedes)

> **¡OJO!**
>
> **oír** = to hear   **escuchar** = to listen (to)
> Some native speakers of Spanish use **oír** to mean *to listen to* things like music or the news. But **escuchar** can never mean *to hear*.

No **oigo** bien a la profesora.
I can't hear the professor well.

Oye, Juan, ¿vas a la fiesta?
Hey, Juan, are you going to the party?

¡Oigan! ¡Silencio, por favor!
Listen up! Silence, please!

Oímos/Escuchamos música en clase.
We listen to music in class.

No **oigo** bien por el ruido.
I can't hear well because of the noise.

---

3. poner = *to put; to place*
Many Spanish speakers use **poner** with appliances to express *to turn on*.

Voy a **poner** la televisión.
I'm going to turn on the TV.

Rigo **pone** el despertador para las 8 de la mañana.
Rigo sets the alarm clock for 8 am.

Siempre **pongo** leche y mucho azúcar en el café.
I always put milk and a lot of sugar in my coffee.

---

4. salir = *to leave* (a place); *to go out*
Note in the examples at the right how different prepositions are used with it to express different meanings.

> **salir de** + *place*
> **salir con** + *person*
> **salir para** + *destination*

Here's another useful expression: **salir bien/mal,** which means *to turn/come out well/poorly; to do well/poorly.*

Salgo con el hermano de Cecilia.
I'm going out with / dating Cecilia's brother.

Salimos para la sierra pasado mañana.
We're leaving for the mountains the day after tomorrow.

Todo va a **salir** bien.
Everything is going to turn out OK (well).

No quiero **salir** mal en esta clase.
I don't want to do poorly in this class.

Salen de clase ahora.
They're leaving class now.

---

5. traer = *to bring*

> **¡OJO!**
>
> **Traer** and **llevar** are somewhat related in meaning, but they are actually antonyms, like *bring* and *take* in English. **Traer** expresses *to bring* as in *to have* something *with* or *on* one. It also expresses *to bring* something *to* the person who is speaking. **Llevar** means *to take* someone or something *to* a place.
>
> Este año voy a **llevar** a mi familia a Nicaragua.
> *This year I'm going to take my family to Nicaragua.*

¡Por favor! ¿Me **traes** una toalla?
Please! Can you bring me a towel?

¿Por qué no me **traes** una de las sillas del comedor?
Why don't you bring me one of the chairs from the dining room?

Lo siento, pero no **traigo** dinero.
Sorry, but I have no money on me/didn't bring any money.

6. ver = *to see*

Ver can also mean *to watch* as in watching television or a movie, which is also expressed with the verb **mirar.**

> **¡OJO!**
>
> **Mirar** never expresses *to see* (except with movies and television). It only means *to watch, look at.*

Los niños **ven/miran** una película.
The kids are watching a movie.

No **veo** bien sin mis lentes.
I don't see well without my glasses.

Práctica y comunicación

A. Mi rutina

Verb Summary

hacer ⎫
oír ⎪
poner ⎬ -go
salir ⎪
traer ⎭

oír   o**y**es, o**y**e(n), oímos
ver   v**e**o, ves...

Paso 1. Autoprueba. Dé la forma indicada para cada verbo.

1. hacer: yo
2. oír: Rigo y Sam
3. poner: yo
4. salir: yo
5. traer: yo
6. ver: yo

Paso 2. Ahora complete las siguientes oraciones lógicamente usando los verbos del **Paso 1** solo una vez. Añada (*Add*) una expresión de tiempo a cada oración y la palabra **no,** si es necesario.

Expresiones de tiempo

Before or after the verb: **los lunes/martes... , los fines de semana, (casi) todos los días, a veces...**

Before the verb: **(casi) siempre, (casi) nunca**

1. _____ ejercicio en el gimnasio _____ .
2. _____ a mis amigos los _____ por la _____ .
3. _____ de casa antes de las _____ de la mañana.
4. _____ mi libro de texto a la clase de español _____ .
5. _____ las noticias (*news*) por la tele _____ .
6. _____ la ropa en la cómoda y el armario _____ .

Prác. A, Paso 1: Answers: 1. hago 2. oyen 3. pongo 4. salgo 5. traigo 6. veo

Paso 3. Ahora, en parejas, túrnense para hacer y contestar preguntas basadas en las oraciones del **Paso 2.** Luego digan (*tell*) a la clase algo (*something*) que ustedes tienen en común o que hacen de manera muy diferente o peculiar.

MODELO: **1.** Hago ejercicio en el gimnasio casi todos días. →
¿Con qué frecuencia haces ejercicio en el gimnasio? (¿Haces ejercicio en el gimnasio todos los días?) →
Hannah y yo casi nunca hacemos ejercicio en el gimnasio.

B. Lógicamente

Paso 1. Complete las siguientes oraciones con la forma apropiada de **hacer, oír, poner, salir, traer** o **ver.** Use **no** cuando es necesario para que (*so that*) las oraciones sean (*will be*) apropiadas para usted.

MODELO: Los estudiantes de esta clase _____ mucha tarea. →
Los estudiantes de esta clase **hacemos/hacen** mucha tarea.

1. (Yo) _____ la tele por la noche.
2. Los sábados por la noche siempre (tú) _____ solo/a (*alone*) / con tus amigos.
3. (Nosotros) _____ el libro de texto de español a clase.
4. Muchas personas no _____ ejercicio.
5. Muchas personas _____ la radio cuando van en el auto.
6. Yo _____ azúcar (*sugar*) en mi café.
7. Tengo un amigo que va a _____ un viaje a Nicaragua en diciembre.
8. En general, (yo) _____ bien en los exámenes.
9. Me gusta _____ películas extranjeras.

Paso 2. Use las respuestas del **Paso 1** para hacerle preguntas a otra persona de la clase. ¿Tienen muchas coincidencias?

MODELO: Los estudiantes de esta clase **hacemos** mucha tarea. →
¿Crees que los estudiantes de esta clase hacemos mucha tarea?

C. Los nuevos verbos

Paso 1. Lea (*Read*) el siguiente afiche, que ilustra una expresión idiomática.

LOS TRES MONOS SABIOS

NO OÍR, NO VER, NO HABLAR

Jan Stromme/Alamy Stock Photo

<table>
<tr><td colspan="2">Vocabulario útil</td></tr>
<tr><td>el afiche</td><td>poster</td></tr>
<tr><td>sabio/a</td><td>wise</td></tr>
</table>

1. ¿Qué dicen los monos sabios en inglés?
2. ¿Qué diría (*would say*) cada mono en español hablando (*speaking*) en primera persona?
3. ¿Dónde sería (*would it be*) apropiado poner un afiche como este?

Paso 2. Los nuevos verbos se usan en más expresiones idiomáticas. Pero el significado (*meaning*) de los modismos no es siempre transparente. ¿Puede usted emparejar cada expresión con su significado?

EXPRESIONES

1. _____ poner en duda
2. _____ poner un límite
3. _____ salir en las noticias
4. _____ hacer el papel (*role*) de
5. _____ ver para creer

SIGNIFICADOS

a. ¡tener sus 15 minutos de fama!
b. pensar que una información no es cierta
c. necesitar la observación personal para aceptar que una cosa (*something*) es verdad
d. decidir hasta dónde puede llegar una situación
e. actuar en una película o una obra de teatro (*play*)

Algo sobre los lagos de Nicaragua

En Nicaragua hay dos lagos inmensos: el lago de Nicaragua y el lago de Managua. Los dos están unidos por el río[a] Tipitapa. El lago de Nicaragua es el lago más grande[b] de Centroamérica y el segundo[c] más grande de Latinoamérica, después del lago Titicaca en Bolivia. En el lago de Nicaragua hay volcanes e islas.

 ¿Cómo se llama el lago más grande de este país? ¿y el río más grande?

[a]*river* [b]*más... biggest* [c]*second*

Paul Taylor/Getty Images

El lago de Nicaragua, con el volcán Maderas al fondo (*in the background*)

 D. Consecuencias lógicas. En parejas, indiquen acciones lógicas o consecuencias relacionadas con cada situación. No se limiten a usar los verbos de esta sección del libro. ¡Usen su imaginación!

Vocabulario útil

gritar «¡silencio!» to shout "silence!"
hacer una cita to make an appointment
los vecinos neighbors

1. Me gusta nadar (*to swim*) en los lagos. Por eso...
2. Todos los días usamos este libro en la clase de español. Por eso...
3. Mis hijos / compañeros de cuarto hacen mucho ruido en la sala. Por eso...
4. La televisión no funciona. Por eso...
5. Hay mucho ruido en el salón de clase. Por eso...
6. Estoy en la biblioteca y ¡no puedo estudiar más! Por eso...
7. Queremos bailar y necesitamos música. Por eso...
8. No comprendo la lección. Por eso...
9. Me gusta hacer ecoturismo y hablar español. Por eso...

 E. Intercambios

Paso 1. En parejas, hagan y contesten las siguientes preguntas.

EN CASA

1. ¿Qué pones en el armario? ¿y en la cómoda? ¿en el cajón (*drawer*) del escritorio?
2. ¿Pones la televisión con frecuencia cuando estás en casa? ¿Qué programa(s) ves todos los días? ¿Qué programa o serie muy popular no ves nunca? (**Nunca veo...**)
3. ¿Pones el radio con frecuencia? ¿Prefieres oír las noticias por radio o por internet? ¿Cuál es la estación de radio que más escuchas? ¿Por qué te gusta tanto?

4. ¿Qué haces los _____ (día) por la noche? ¿Cuándo sales con los amigos? ¿Adónde van cuando salen? ¿Sales solo/a a veces?

5. ¿Te gusta hacer ejercicio? ¿Haces ejercicios aeróbicos? ¿Dónde haces ejercicio?

PARA LAS CLASES

6. Generalmente, ¿qué traes en tu mochila o bolsa por lo general?

7. ¿A qué hora sales para las clases los lunes? ¿A qué hora sales de clase los viernes?

8. ¿Cuándo haces la tarea? ¿Por la mañana? ¿Dónde haces la tarea? ¿En casa? ¿Haces la tarea mientras (*while*) ves una serie? ¿mientras oyes música?

9. ¿Siempre sales bien en los exámenes? ¿En qué clase no sales bien? ¿Qué haces si sales mal en un examen?

Paso 2. Ahora digan (*tell*) a la clase dos o tres cosas (*things*) que ustedes tienen en común.

MODELO: Jim y yo nunca ponemos la ropa en el armario. Hacemos ejercicio todos los días: Jim hace ejercicios aeróbicos y yo voy al gimnasio. Los dos vemos el programa _____ los lunes por la noche; es nuestro programa favorito.

Algo sobre los volcanes de El Salvador y Nicaragua

Los volcanes son una imagen representativa en estos dos países, que están dentro del llamadoª Arcoᵇ Volcánico Centroamericano. En Nicaragua solamente,ᶜ hay diecinueve volcanes. Por eso, los escudos de las banderasᵈ nicaragüense y salvadoreña muestranᵉ una cordilleraᶠ con cinco volcanes.

¿Hay volcanes en este país? ¿Son volcanes activos?

ªdentro... *inside the so-called* ᵇ*Rim, Arch* ᶜ*En... In Nicaragua alone* ᵈescudos... *shields on the flags* ᵉ*show* ᶠ*mountain range*

Galyna Andrushko/Shutterstock

El volcán Izalco, también llamado (*called*) «el Faro (*Lighthouse*) del Pacífico», todo un símbolo salvadoreño

♻ Repaso

The change in the stem vowels of **preferir, querer,** and **poder** was presented in **Gramática 10.** Review the forms of **preferir, querer,** and **poder** now.

poder: o → __

p__do	podemos
p__des	podéis
p__de	p__den

preferir: e → __

pref__ro	preferimos
pref__res	preferís
pref__re	pref__ren

querer: e → __

qu__ro	queremos
qu__res	queréis
qu__re	qu__ren

If you could complete those verb forms correctly, you already know most of the important information in **Gramática 13.**

13 Expressing Actions • Present Tense of Stem-changing Verbs (Part 2)

Gramática en acción: ¿Una fiesta exitosa?

Es la noche del sábado y todos están en una fiesta en casa de Ernesto.

- Aurora **duerme** en el sofá.
- Samuel **juega** a las cartas... a solas.
- Ernesto **sirve** las bebidas. Kevin **pide** una Coca-Cola.
- Noemí sale y **vuelve** con más amigas.
- ¿Es una fiesta exitosa? ¿Qué **piensa** usted? ¿Por qué?

¿Y usted? ¿Qué hace en las fiestas?

1. ¿**Duerme** usted en el sofá?
2. ¿**Juega** a las cartas?
3. ¿**Sirve** las bebidas?
4. ¿**Pide** Coca-Cola?
5. ¿Sale y **vuelve** con más amigos?

e → ie: <u>pensar</u> (to think)		o → ue: <u>volver</u> (to return)		e → i: <u>pedir</u> (to ask for; to order)	
p**ie**nso	pensamos	v**ue**lvo	volvemos	p**i**do	pedimos
p**ie**nsas	pensáis	v**ue**lves	volvéis	p**i**des	pedís
p**ie**nsa	p**ie**nsan	v**ue**lve	v**ue**lven	p**i**de	p**i**den

> **¡OJO!**
>
> Remember that the Spanish present tense has a number of present tense equivalents in English. It can also be used to express future meaning.
>
> **pienso** = I think, am thinking, will think
>
> **vuelvo** = I return, am returning, will return
>
> **pido** = I ask, am asking, will ask

1. Stem-changing Verbs

You have already used three *stem-changing verbs* (**los verbos que cambian el radical**): <u>poder</u>, **preferir**, and <u>querer</u>. And you also know two other verbs that are similar (<u>tener</u> and <u>venir</u>), but whose first person singular forms are irregular.

2. Stem Vowel Changes

There are three groups of stem-changing verbs. You already know about the first two.

- verbs like **preferir** and **querer**, in which the stem vowel **e** becomes **ie** in stressed syllables
- verbs like **poder**, in which the stem vowel **o** becomes **ue** in stressed syllables

Here is the third group.

- verbs in which the stem vowel **e** becomes **i**

The stem-changing pattern of all three groups is shown at the right. The stem vowels are stressed (and so they change) in all present tense forms except **nosotros/as** and **vosotros/as**. All three groups follow this regular pattern, which looks like a boot.

> **¡OJO!**
>
> **Nosotros/as** and **vosotros/as** forms *do not* have a stem vowel change.

Las vocales que cambian el radical		
e → <u>ie</u>	-ie-	-e-
	-ie-	-e-
	-ie-	-ie-
o → <u>ue</u>	-ue-	-o-
	-ue-	-o-
	-ue-	-ue-
e → <u>i</u>	-i-	-e-
	-i-	-e-
	-i-	-i-

A successful party? It's Saturday night and everybody is at a party at Ernesto's house. ■ Aurora is sleeping on the couch. ■ Samuel is playing cards ... alone. ■ Ernesto is serving beverages. Kevin asks for a Coke. ■ Noemí leaves and comes back with more girl friends. ■ Is it a successful party? What do you think? Why?

3. Important Stem-changing Verbs

Some stem-changing verbs practiced in this chapter include the following.

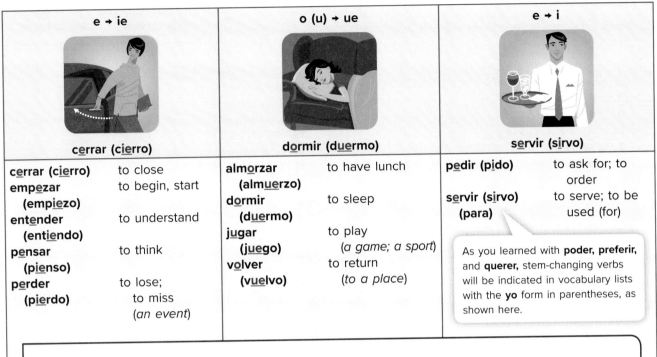

e → ie	o (u) → ue	e → i
cerrar (cierro)	dormir (duermo)	servir (sirvo)

e → ie		o (u) → ue		e → i	
cerrar (cierro)	to close	almorzar (almuerzo)	to have lunch	pedir (pido)	to ask for; to order
empezar (empiezo)	to begin, start	dormir (duermo)	to sleep	servir (sirvo) (para)	to serve; to be used (for)
entender (entiendo)	to understand	jugar (juego)	to play (a game; a sport)		
pensar (pienso)	to think	volver (vuelvo)	to return (to a place)		
perder (pierdo)	to lose; to miss (an event)				

> As you learned with **poder, preferir,** and **querer,** stem-changing verbs will be indicated in vocabulary lists with the **yo** form in parentheses, as shown here.

¡OJO!

Jugar is the only **u → ue** stem-changing verb in Spanish. **Jugar** is usually followed by **al** when used with the name of a sport: **Juego al tenis.** Some Spanish speakers, however, omit the **al.** Games expressed in the plural use **a los** or **a las** after **jugar: Juego a las cartas.**

---

4. Verb + *a* + Infinitive

Like **aprender** and **ir,** the stem-changing verbs **empezar** and **volver** are followed by **a** before an infinitive.

The meaning of **empezar** does not change in this structure, but **volver a** + *infinitive* expresses *to do (something) again.*

Ustedes **empiezan a hablar** muy bien el español.
You're starting to speak Spanish very well.

¿Cuándo **vuelves a jugar** al tenis?
When are you going to play tennis again?

---

5. Uses of *pensar*

Like other verbs you already know (**desear, necesitar, deber,...**), **pensar** can be followed directly by an infinitive. In that case, it expresses *to intend, plan.*

The phrase **pensar en** can be used to express *to think about.*

Pensar de indicates one's opinion about someone or something. The answer to a question with **pensar de** usually starts with **Pienso que...**

¿Cuándo piensas almorzar?
When do you plan to eat lunch?

—¿En qué piensas?
—Pienso en las cosas que tengo que hacer el domingo.
"What are you thinking about?"
"I'm thinking about the things I have to do on Sunday."

—¿Qué piensas de esa situación?
—¡Pienso que es un desastre!
"What do you think about that situation?"
"I think (that) it's a real mess!"

—¿Qué piensas del nuevo apartamento de Cristina?
—Pienso que es elegante... pero ¡muy caro!
"What do you think of/about Cristina's new apartment?"
"I think (that) it's fancy ... but very expensive!"

Práctica y comunicación

A. Asociaciones

Paso 1. Dé por lo menos un infinitivo que asocia con las siguientes ideas y cosas.

1. una bebida
2. una lección (*lesson*)
3. a casa
4. una cama
5. una hamburguesa
6. el tenis
7. una opinión
8. una puerta
9. las llaves (*keys*)
10. la cocina
11. una siesta
12. un favor
13. las cartas
14. una palabra o frase
15. la música

Paso 2. Explique para qué sirven las siguientes cosas.

MODELO: las cartas → **Sirven para** jugar.

1. las llaves
2. una almohada (*pillow*)
3. una bandeja (*tray*)
4. un menú
5. un diccionario
6. el cerebro (*brain*)

B. La vida (*Life*) en la universidad

Paso 1. Autoprueba. Dé la forma de cada verbo para **yo** y para **nosotros**.

1. almorzar
2. entender
3. pedir
4. perder
5. dormir
6. jugar
7. pensar
8. volver

Paso 2. Ahora complete las siguientes oraciones lógicamente usando los verbos del **Paso 1** solo una vez. Añada (*Add*) una expresión de tiempo y la palabra **no** delante del (*in front of the*) verbo, si es necesario.

Expresiones de tiempo

los lunes/martes... , los fines de semana, (casi) siempre, (casi) nunca, (casi) todos los días, a veces, constantemente (*constantly*)...

MODELO: **1.** _____ la siesta _____. → **Duermo** la siesta **casi todos los días.** / No **duermo** la siesta **casi nunca.**

1. _____ la siesta _____.
2. _____ en la cafetería _____.
3. _____ pizza para almorzar _____.
4. _____ a las cartas con mi familia _____.
5. _____ en mis notas (*grades*) _____.
6. _____ mi carnet de identificación de la universidad _____.
7. _____ a casa de mis padres / de mi familia _____.
8. _____ muchas cosas en mi clase de _____ (materia).

Paso 3. Ahora, en parejas, túrnense para hacer y contestar preguntas basadas en las oraciones del **Paso 2**. Luego digan (*tell*) a la clase algo (*something*) que ustedes tienen en común o que hacen de manera muy diferente o peculiar.

MODELOS: **1.** Duermo la siesta casi todos días. →
¿Con qué frecuencia duermes la siesta? (¿Duermes la siesta todos los días?) →
Jacob y yo dormimos la siesta casi todos los días.

Prác. B, Paso 1: Answers: 1. almuerzo, almorzamos **2.** entiendo, entendemos **3.** pido, pedimos **4.** pierdo, perdemos **5.** duermo, dormimos **6.** juego, jugamos **7.** pienso, pensamos **8.** vuelvo, volvemos

C. Una tarde típica en casa. ¿Cuáles son las actividades de todos? Haga oraciones completas, usando una palabra o frase de cada columna.

(yo) mi padre/madre mi esposo/a los niños mi amigo/a _____ y yo el perro/gato mi compañero/a (de cuarto)	+	(no)	almorzar dormir empezar a entender jugar a/al pedir pensar pensar en perder preferir volver volver a ¿ ?	+	descansar, dormir solo/a en un sillón / en la cocina toda la tarde / la siesta su pelota (*ball*), sus llaves, su mochila tarde/temprano a casa en el patio / en la piscina / afuera (*outside*) golf (tenis, voleibol...), las cartas las películas viejas/recientes mis notas, mis clases, los exámenes la lección, la oración hablar bien el español ver una película con frecuencia ¿ ?

D. La semana que viene

Paso 1. ¿Qué va a hacer usted la semana que viene? Organice la próxima semana en la siguiente agenda. Escriba frases con el infinitivo, por ejemplo: **jugar un videojuego.** Incluya actividades que tiene que hacer, pero también algunas (*some*) que tiene ganas de hacer.

	por la mañana	**por la tarde**	**por la noche**
lunes			
martes			
miércoles			
jueves			
viernes			
sábado			
domingo			

 Paso 2. En parejas, hablen de su horario (*schedule*) para esta semana, basándose (*based on*) en la agenda del **Paso 1.** Luego digan (*tell*) algunas (*some*) respuestas interesantes a la clase.

MODELO: ver la televisión →
E1: ¿Qué **piensas** hacer el domingo por la tarde?
E2: **Pienso** ver la televisión. Y tú, ¿qué haces el domingo?
E1: El domingo **juego** al tenis con mi amigo Alex.

Estrategia

e → ie
o → ue
e → i

 E. Intercambios. En parejas, túrnense para hacer y contestar preguntas sobre los siguientes temas con las frases sugeridas (*suggested*).

MODELOS: **1.** almorzar (¿dónde? ¿con quién? ¿a qué hora?) →
Por lo general, ¿dónde **almuerzas** de lunes a viernes?
¿Con quién **vas a almorzar** hoy?
¿A qué hora **piensas almorzar** el domingo?

1. almorzar (¿dónde? ¿con quién? ¿a qué hora?)
2. perder (¿qué? ¿dónde? ¿con frecuencia? ¿siempre?)
3. dormir (¿cuántas horas? ¿mucho o poco? ¿siestas frecuentes o infrecuentes? ¿largas o cortas?)
4. jugar (¿juegos de mesa [*board games*]? ¿cuáles? ¿con quién? ¿dónde?)

Estrategia

generalizations: present tense
future: **ir** + **a** + *inf.*
definite plans: **pensar** + *inf.*

Textos de todos los días: Correo electrónico (e-*mail*) a una persona de la clase

You probably often need to make arrangements to collaborate with other people at school or work. In this activity you will practice how to write a short e-mail to a classmate in order to meet to work on an assignment.

Objetivo: To learn basic vocabulary for writing an e-mail to a classmate, introducing yourself and signing off, plus setting the time to meet.

Antes de empezar: Think about what you typically write in these kinds of messages in your native language. Then focus on the essential information. Although your Spanish is still limited, you know how to identify yourself, and express the days and times when you are free. Also decide if you want to meet in person or electronically.

Vocabulario útil

Hola   an informal greeting for a message to a classmate

Saludos   a closing, appropriate in most formal and informal situations when you are not close friends with the person(s) addressed in a message of any kind

---

Enviar	De:	
	Para:	
	Asunto:	¿Cuándo podemos encontrarnos[a]?

¡Hola!

Soy _____, tu pareja para la actividad de la clase _____.
Tenemos que encontrarnos para hacer la tarea.
Yo puedo _____ (días y horas).
Prefiero reunirnos[b] en persona / en Zoom porque _____.
¿Y tú?
Espero[c] tu respuesta pronto.
Saludos,
(Firma[d]: tu nombre y otros detalles que te identifican[e])

---

[a]*meet*   [b]*to meet*   [c]*I hope to get*   [d]*Signature*   [e]*te... identify you*

♻ Repaso

In **Capítulo 1,** you learned how to ask what someone's name is and express your own name by using phrases with the verb **llamar.** Show what you remember by completing the following phrases.

1. (yo) ____ llamo

2. (tú) ____ llamas

3. usted ____ llama

The words with which you completed those phrases are part of a pronoun system that you will learn about in **Gramática 14.**

14 Expressing -self/-selves • Reflexive Pronouns (Part 1)*

Gramática en acción: La rutina diaria de Andrés

La rutina de Andrés empieza a las siete y media.

1. Me despierto a las siete y media y **me levanto** enseguida.

2. Primero, **me ducho**.

3. Luego **me cepillo** los dientes.

4. Me peino.

5. Me pongo la bata.

6. Voy al cuarto a **vestirme**.

7. Por fin, salgo para la universidad. No tomo nada antes de salir porque, por lo general, ¡tengo prisa!

¿Y usted? ¿Cómo es su rutina diaria?

1. Yo **me levanto** a las _____.
2. **Me ducho** por la mañana / noche.
3. **Me visto** en el baño / mi cuarto.
4. **Me peino** antes de / después de **vestirme**.
5. Antes de salir para las clases, tomo / no tomo el desayuno (*breakfast*).

Andrés's daily routine *Andrés's routine begins at seven-thirty.* **1.** *I wake up at seven-thirty and I get up right away.* **2.** *First, I take a shower.* **3.** *Then I brush my teeth.* **4.** *I comb my hair.* **5.** *I put on my robe.* **6.** *I go to my room to get dressed.* **7.** *Finally, I leave for the university. I don't eat or drink anything before leaving because I'm generally in a hurry!*

*You will learn how to use reflexive pronouns to express each other in **Gramática 32 (Cap. 11)**.

Gramática

Verbs Used Reflexively / **Los verbos que se usan con pronombres reflexivos**

bañarse (*to take a bath, bathe*)					
Singular			**Plural**		
(yo)	me baño	I take a bath	(nosotros)	nos bañamos	we take a bath
(tú)	te bañas	you take a bath	(vosotros)	os bañáis	you take a bath
(usted)		you take a bath	(ustedes)		you take a bath
(él)	se baña	he takes a bath	(ellos)	se bañan	they take a bath
(ella)		she takes a bath	(ellas)		they take a bath

1. Reflexive Pronouns

In Spanish, some verbs are used reflexively. This means that they are used with reflexive pronouns that indicate that the subject is doing something *to* or *for itself.* The reflexive pronouns that correspond to the subject accompany the verb and must come before it. The pronoun **-se** at the end of an infinitive indicates that the verb is used reflexively: **bañarse** (to take a bath; to bathe oneself).

> ### ¡OJO!
> Verbs used reflexively often do not have an exact parallel in the English translation, and there is not always a reflexive pronoun in the translation.

Los pronombres reflexivos		
yo	me	myself
tú	te	yourself (*fam., sing.*)
usted/ él/ella	se	yourself (*form. sing.*); himself, herself, itself
nosotros/as	nos	ourselves
vosotros/as	os	yourselves (*fam. pl. Sp.*)
ustedes/ ellos/as	se	yourselves (*form. pl.*); themselves

me baño = I take a bath (bathe myself)
me ducho = I shower (take a shower)

2. Important Verbs Used Reflexively

Many English verbs that describe parts of one's daily routine—to get up, to take a bath, and so on—are expressed in Spanish with a reflexive construction. Here are some that are frequently used.

> ### ¡OJO!
> Notice that some of these reflexive verbs also have stem changes: **e → ie, o → ue, e → i.**

despertarse (me despierto)	ducharse	afeitarse	vestirse (me visto)	sentarse (me siento)

> Note the **-se** on the end of these infinitives. This is how reflexive verbs will be shown in vocabulary lists.

acostarse (me acuesto)	to go to bed	levantarse	to get up (out of bed); to stand up
afeitarse	to shave	llamarse	to be called
bañarse	to take a bath, bathe	maquillarse	to put on makeup
cepillarse los dientes	to brush one's teeth	peinarse	to do (brush/comb) one's hair
despertarse (me despierto)	to wake up	ponerse (me pongo) + *clothing*	to put on (*an article of clothing*)
divertirse (me divierto)	to have a good time, enjoy oneself	quitarse + *clothing*	to take off (*an article of clothing*)
dormirse (me duermo)	to fall asleep	sentarse (me siento)	to sit down
ducharse	to take a shower	vestirse (me visto)	to get dressed

¡OJO!

After **ponerse** and **quitarse,** the definite article, not the possessive as in English, is used with articles of clothing.

Me siento y **me quito** <u>los</u> zapatos. Luego **me quito** <u>los</u> pantalones y <u>la</u> camisa y **me pongo** <u>la</u> pijama.
I sit down and take off my shoes. Then I take off my pants and shirt and put on my pajamas.

3. Placement of Reflexive Pronouns

- Reflexive pronouns are placed before a conjugated verb.
- In a negative sentence, the reflexive pronoun is placed between **no** and the conjugated verb.
- When a conjugated verb is followed by an infinitive that is used reflexively, the reflexive pronoun may either precede the conjugated verb or be attached to the infinitive.
- Remember that the infinitive form follows prepositions in Spanish. The reflexive pronouns are attached at the end of the infinitive: **antes de acostar<u>se</u>, después de duchar<u>me</u>.**

¡OJO!

The reflexive pronoun must be repeated with each verb in a series of verbs.

<u>Me</u> **levanto** temprano todos los días.
I get up early every day.

Matías **no** <u>se</u> **levanta** temprano los domingos.
Matías doesn't get up early on Sundays.

Pienso **acostar<u>me</u>** temprano esta noche.
<u>Me</u> pienso **acostar** temprano esta noche.
I plan to go to bed early tonight.

<u>Me</u> **cepillo** los dientes y <u>me</u> **peino** antes de **vestir<u>me</u>.**
I brush my teeth and do my hair before dressing (before I get dressed).

Mi esposo <u>se</u> **baña,** yo <u>me</u> **ducho** y los dos <u>nos</u> **peinamos** antes de las seis.
My husband takes a bath, I shower, and the two of us do our hair before six o'clock.

4. Nonreflexive Use of Verbs

All of these verbs can also be used nonreflexively, often with a different meaning. Here are some examples.

dormir = to sleep	**dormirse** = to fall asleep
poner = to put, place	**ponerse** = to put on

Camila duerme.

No quiere dormir<u>se</u>.

Antonio <u>se</u> **pone** un suéter.

Su mamá **pone** la ropa en la lavadora.

Práctica y comunicación

Reflexive Pronoun Summary

yo →	<u>me</u>
tú →	<u>te</u>
usted, él, ella →	<u>se</u>
nosotros/as →	<u>nos</u>
vosotros/as →	<u>os</u>
ustedes, ellos, ellas →	<u>se</u>

A. Asociaciones. ¿Cuántas palabras puede usted asociar con los siguientes infinitivos? Piense (*Think*) en grupos de palabras que usted ya conoce (*you already know*): los cuartos de una casa, los muebles, la ropa, otros verbos, los adverbios, etcétera.

1. llamarse
2. levantarse
3. bañarse
4. sentarse
5. ponerse
6. despertarse
7. divertirse
8. acostarse

B. Su rutina diaria

Paso 1. Autoprueba. Empareje los pronombres reflexivos con los verbos apropiados.

PRONOMBRES
1. me _____
2. te _____
3. se _____
4. nos _____

VERBOS
a. acuesta
b. baño
c. ponemos

d. duermen
e. despierta
f. vistes

Paso 2. Escoja (*Choose*) el verbo apropiado para completar las siguientes oraciones. Luego use verbos en la primera persona singular (**yo**) para describir su propia rutina. No repita los verbos.

VERBOS: acostarse, despertarse, divertirse, ducharse, levantarse, ponerse

1. _____ a la(s) _____ (hora) con la ayuda (*help*) del reloj despertador (*alarm clock*).
2. ¡Siempre/Nunca _____ inmediatamente cuando escucho el despertador!
3. _____ después de levantarme por la mañana / antes de acostarme por la noche.
4. _____ después de la(s) _____ (hora) los días de entresemana (*weekdays*).
5. _____ con mis amigos / mi familia los fines de semana.
6. Generalmente, para ir a clase (no) _____ ropa deportiva (*sports*) y tenis.

Paso 3. Ahora, en parejas, túrnense para hacer y contestar preguntas basadas en las oraciones del **Paso 2.** Luego digan (*tell*) a la clase algo (*something*) que ustedes tienen en común o que hacen de manera muy diferente o peculiar.

MODELO: **1.** Me despierto a las siete con la ayuda del reloj despertador. →
¿Te despiertas a las siete con la ayuda del reloj despertador? →
Sam y yo nos despertamos con la ayuda del reloj despertador. Pero yo me despierto a las siete y Sam no se despierta hasta las diez.

C. La oración correcta. Elija (*Choose*) la mejor oración para cada dibujo.

1.

a. La mamá baña a los niños.

b. Los niños se bañan.

2.

a. Un joven despierta a otro.

b. Los dos jóvenes se despiertan.

3.

a. El papá sienta a su hijo a la mesa.

b. El papá se sienta a la mesa.

4.

a. Elena se viste para el frío.

b. Elena viste a su perro para el frío.

Nota comunicativa: Cómo expresar una secuencia de acciones

The following adverbs and expressions will help you indicate the sequence of actions or events.

primero	first	**enseguida**	immediately	**por fin**	finally
luego, después	then, later, next	**finalmente**	finally		

Primero, me ducho y me visto. **Luego,** tomo un café y leo el periódico. **Después,** me cepillo los dientes. **Finalmente,** salgo para el trabajo.

First, I shower and get dressed. Then I drink a cup of coffee and read the paper. Afterwards, I brush my teeth. Finally, I leave for work.

You will use these words and phrases in **Práctica D** and **E.**

D. El día de Ángela

Paso 1. Ángela es dependienta en una tienda de ropa para jóvenes en El Paso. ¿Cómo es un día normal de trabajo para ella? Complete la narración con los verbos apropiados, según los dibujos. **¡OJO!** Algunos (*Some*) verbos se usan más de una vez (*more than once*).

1.

Verbos: **comer, levantarse, vestirse**

Me despierto a las nueve de la mañana y _____ enseguida. (Yo) _____ rápidamente y salgo de casa sin _____. Llego a la tienda a las diez menos diez de la mañana con mis compañeras de trabajo.

2.

Verbos: **empezar, ser**

Primero (yo) _____ mi trabajo, ordenando[a] la ropa. La ropa de la tienda _____ muy bonita.

3.

Verbos: **almorzar, dormir, pedir, sentarse, volver**

(Yo) _____ a las doce y media con mi amiga Susie, que trabaja en una zapatería. Generalmente podemos _____ en la pizzería San Marcos y casi siempre _____ pizza. Luego, (yo) _____ a la tienda y _____ a trabajar. Nunca _____ la siesta.

4.

Verbos: **cerrar, acostarse, pensar, ponerse, quitarse, volver**

Por fin, la supervisora _____ la tienda a las seis en punto. Luego yo _____ a casa. _____ la ropa de trabajo[b] y _____ un vestido y zapatos elegantes. _____ salir a bailar con unos amigos... ¡y no pienso ir a _____ hasta muy, muy tarde!

[a]*putting in order*   [b]*ropa... work clothes*

Paso 2. Ahora vuelva a completar la narración usando **Ángela** como sujeto en vez de **yo.**

E. Un día ideal

Paso 1. ¿Cuál es su día favorito de la semana? ¿Qué hace ese día? Describa su día ideal completando las siguientes oraciones.

1. Me levanto antes/después de la(s) _____ (hora).
2. Después de levantarme, (yo) _____ y _____. (verbos)
3. Luego, _____ y _____ (verbos).
4. Me acuesto a las(s) _____, después de _____. (verbo)

Paso 2. En parejas, comparen sus días y digan a la clase una acción que tienen en común y otra diferente.

MODELO: Leni y yo preferimos el sábado y nos levantamos después de las 11 de la mañana. Pero después de levantarse Leni va al gimnasio y yo como un *brunch*.

F. Intercambios: Su rutina

Paso 1. Prepare cinco preguntas para entrevistar a una persona de la clase. Sus preguntas deben incluir un verbo de la rutina diaria y una expresión de tiempo.

EXPRESIONES DE TIEMPO

los lunes (martes...) / los días entre semana (*weekdays*) / los fines de semana / todos los días

tarde / temprano

antes de / después de

MODELOS: ¿A qué hora te acuestas los días entre semana?
¿Te maquillas todos los días?

Paso 2. En parejas, túrnense para entrevistarse con sus preguntas del **Paso 1.** Después digan a la clase algo interesante o peculiar de su compañero/a.

MODELO: Sebastián se acuesta todas las noches con su perro y sus dos gatos. ¡Y su cama es pequeña!

Todo junto

Algo sobre las casas tradicionales centroamericanas

En Centroamérica y en otras regiones latinoamericanas hay casas de bajareque, un tipo de construcción tradicional de origen indígena.[a] Se usan materiales locales y económicos: paredes sostenidas por palos[b] y rellenas de barro y cañas.[c] Las casas de bajareque son generalmente modestas,[d] pero también son construcciones ecológicas y sismorresistentes,[e] una característica importante para una región de alta actividad sísmica como es Centroamérica.

En los Estados Unidos, ¿es la construcción de las casas típicas del norte diferente de la (*that*) de las casas del sur?

[a]*native (before the arrival of Columbus)*   [b]*sostenidas... held up by sticks or logs*   [c]*rellenas... filled with mud and reeds*
[d]*humble*   [e]*resistant to earthquakes*

Una casa de bajareque, en Nicaragua

BrazilPhotos/Alamy Stock Photo

A. Lengua y cultura: ¿Dónde viven los hispanohablantes?

Paso 1. Completar. Complete the following paragraphs about different types of living arrangements in the Spanish-speaking world. Give the correct form of the words in parentheses, as suggested by context. When two possibilities are given in parentheses, select the correct one.

Como es de imaginar, en los países hispanohablantes hay una gran variedad de viviendas.[a] _____ (Este)[1] variaciones corresponden a diferencias socioeconómicas y también tienen relación con el urbanismo[b] y el clima.

Las _____ (grande)[2] ciudades _____ (tener)[3] muchos edificios de apartamentos que _____ (poder)[4] acomodar la _____ (alto)[5] densidad de población (el 80 por ciento de los latinoamericanos vive en zonas urbanas). Sin embargo,[c] los gobiernos[d] _____ (entender)[6] la necesidad de tener ciudades más _____ (verde)[7] y habitables para todas las personas. Cada día hay más preocupación (e / y)[8] interés por tener más parques, _____ (jardín)[9], carriles[e] para bicicletas, excelentes sistemas de transporte, etcétera.

En contraste, las casas predominan en las áreas _____ (rural)[10] y en las zonas residenciales fuera de[f] una ciudad. Por cierto,[g] la palabra *suburbio* es un falso cognado en español: significa una zona fuera de la ciudad, pero no un _____ (bueno)[11] lugar para vivir.

También se pueden encontrar[h] muchas casas en los centros históricos de las ciudades, donde (a / en)[12] veces hay viviendas en muy _____ (malo)[13] estado habitadas por[i] personas de bajos recursos[j] cerca de[k] _____ (precioso)[14] casas antiguas que _____ (costar)[15] mucho dinero.

La ciudad de San Salvador, capital de El Salvador

[a]*housing* [b]*urban development* [c]*Sin... However* [d]*governments* [e]*lanes* [f]*fuera... outside of* [g]*Por... By the way* [h]*se... one can find* [i]*habitadas... inhabited by* [j]*bajos... low income* [k]*cerca... close to*

Paso 2. Comprensión. ¿Cierto o falso? Corrija las oraciones falsas.

	CIERTO	FALSO
1. El clima afecta los tipos de vivienda.	☐	☐
2. En Latinoamérica hay una gran población rural.	☐	☐
3. En los centros históricos todas las casas están en un estado excelente.	☐	☐
4. Las ciudades latinoamericanas tienen interés en tener viviendas habitables para todas las personas.	☐	☐

👆 Paso 3. En acción

Conteste las siguientes preguntas con información y ejemplos específicos. Prepare la información para presentarla (*present it*) a la clase de manera concisa y eficiente.

1. ¿Hay una gran densidad de población en su estado? ¿Tiene muchas grandes ciudades o muchas personas que viven en zonas rurales? ¿Cuáles son las ciudades más grandes (*biggest*)?

2. ¿Qué tipos de viviendas hay en su ciudad? ¿Qué es más común: vivir en un gran edificio de apartamentos o en casas unifamiliares (*single family*)? ¿vivir en el centro (histórico) o en una zona residencial fuera de la ciudad?

EN ESTA CASA...

somos humanos

cometemos errores

decimos lo siento[a]

damos segundas oportunidades[b]

nos divertimos

NOS RESPETAMOS

NOS AMAMOS[c]

¡NUESTRO HOGAR!

[a]decimos... *we say I'm sorry*   [b]damos... *we give second chances*   [c]nos... *we love each other*

B. Proyecto: Hogar dulce° hogar

sweet

¿Cómo son los hogares de los miembros de la clase? ¿Cuáles son las preferencias de la clase en cuanto a (*as far as*) las actividades típicas en casa?

Paso 1. Preparación. En grupos, piensen en ideas (1 o 2 por miembro del grupo) relacionadas con el hogar para encuestar (*poll*) al resto de la clase. Pueden hacer preguntas sobre cómo es su casa, si hacen ciertas actividades o dónde las hacen (*you do them*), si hay muebles u otras cosas que desean para mejorar (*improve*) su hogar, etcétera.

MODELOS: tener sótano (*basement*)
quitarse los zapatos para entrar en la casa

Ahora preparen las preguntas para hacer la encuesta. Consideren varias opciones: cierto o falso, preguntas directas o una serie de opciones.

MODELOS: tener sótano → ¿Hay sótano en tu casa?
¿Cierto o falso para ti? Hay sótano en mi casa o edificio.
¿Cuál es tu opinión de los sótanos? Son necesarios / poco útiles (*not very useful*) / irrelevantes.

Paso 2. Encuesta. Cada miembro de su grupo debe hacerles su pregunta / sus preguntas a varias personas de la clase. Antes de empezar a preguntar, deben tener un plan para apuntar (*write down*) las respuestas.

Paso 3. Análisis de datos. Analicen la información y preparen varias oraciones para presentar los datos al resto de la clase.

MODELOS:

_____ (número) personas de la clase viven en una casa o en un edificio con sótano.

_____ (número) estudiantes desean tener una casa con sótano.

_____ (número) estudiantes creen que los sótanos son poco útiles.

Video: Salu2 «Vivir con la familia»

You can watch two segments of this chapter's video in the **Video: Salu2** section, found at the end of the eBook.

Lorena Campos Verduzco quiere alquilar (*to rent*) un cuarto en su casa a un estudiante extranjero.

Enfoque cultural:
La vivienda°

La... *Housing*

En El Salvador y Nicaragua

Casas de colores en León, Nicaragua

En otros países hispanos

Una frase de bienvenida (*welcome*)

Como en todo el mundo, la vivienda en El Salvador y Nicaragua puede variar mucho. Hay lujosas[a] mansiones para las personas ricas y casas muy pobres y humildes[b] con un solo cuarto para toda una familia. En las ciudades principales hay edificios de apartamentos, como en cualquier[c] otro país.

En las ciudades de León y Granada, en Nicaragua, hay hermosas[d] casas de la época colonial. Estas casas cuentan con[e] muchos cuartos y tienen techos de tejas,[f] un jardín en medio de la casa y un patio trasero.[g]

[a]*luxurious*   [b]*humble, simple*   [c]*any*   [d]*beautiful*   [e]*cuentan... tienen*   [f]*techos... tiled roofs*   [g]*out back*

Comprensión ¿De qué manera es similar la situación de la vivienda en Nicaragua y El Salvador a la de (*to that*) del resto del mundo?

En todo el mundo hispanohablante Los hispanos en general tienen un concepto muy generoso de la hospitalidad en su hogar y les gusta ofrecer algo[a] de comer y beber a sus invitados.[b] Otra característica es que la hospitalidad en los hogares hispanos es más formal que en los Estados Unidos, una formalidad que los hispanos comprenden bien. Por ejemplo, es una falta[c] de respeto abrir el refrigerador en la casa de un amigo sin su permiso, aun si[d] se trata de[e] la casa de un amigo íntimo.

[a]*les... they like to offer something*   [b]*guests (in their home)*   [c]*lack*   [d]*aun... even if*   [e]*se... it involves*

Comprensión En general, ¿cómo es la hospitalidad de los hispanos?

🖐 En acción

Haga una lista de acciones que son comunes cuando tenemos personas invitadas en casa, y una lista de acciones que las personas invitadas no deben hacer.

Lectura

Antes de leer

¿Le gustan los colores de su casa? ¿Cuáles son los colores de las paredes exteriores de su propia casa o edificio? ¿De qué color o colores son las paredes interiores? ¿Son todas las paredes del mismo (*same*) color o hay toques de color (*color accents*) en diferentes cuartos?

Vocabulario para leer	
la bienvenida	welcome
la calidez	warmth
la confianza	confidence
el estado de ánimo	mood
la frialdad	coolness
la luz	light
la relajación	relaxation
elegir	to choose

La sicología de los colores en la decoración interior

Los colores que tenemos en nuestro hogar nos afectan.[a] Cada color estimula diferentes asociaciones y estados de ánimo. Por eso debemos estar conscientes a la hora de elegir los colores para los diferentes espacios de nuestra casa.

Colores: Sus efectos sicológicos

verde — estabilidad, calma, armonía, naturaleza

amarillo — felicidad, positividad, discreción, juventud[b]

anaranjado — energía, movimiento, sensación de bienvenida, vivacidad

rojo — pasión, alerta, prestigio, trascendencia

morado — creatividad, romance, inspiración, intimidad

azul — responsabilidad, paz, relajación, equilibrio

café — calidez, seguridad, confianza, orden

negro — poder,[c] elegancia, modernidad, frialdad

blanco — pureza,[d] virtud, simplicidad, luz

[a]nos... *affect us*   [b]*youth*   [c]*power*   [d]*purity*

Comprensión

A. ¿Qué color deben usar? Use la información en la tabla de colores para decidir de qué color pintar (*paint*) los hogares de las siguientes personas. Explique las razones de cada decisión.

MODELO: Amalia trabaja duro (*hard*) todo el día y cuando regresa a casa necesita descansar. → Debe pintar su sala de color **azul** porque **tiene el efecto de paz y relajación.**

1. Ricardo trabaja en el estudio de su apartamento. Su trabajo es repetitivo; por eso se distrae fácilmente (*he gets distracted easily*).
2. Marta está sola en casa todo el día con sus tres hijos pequeños, que (*who*) son muy activos.
3. Arturo es inversionista (*investor*) y hace cenas (*dinners*) elegantes en su apartamento para clientes importantes.
4. Gloria es sicóloga y recibe clientes en casa. Muchos de ellos sufren de depresión y ansiedad.
5. Marcos tiene un pequeño gimnasio en su garaje, donde enseña clases de pilates a personas mayores (*older*).

B. Colores complementarios. Es común pintar un cuarto de dos o tres colores: un color de base y otro(s) de acento. Piense en uno de sus propios espacios y describa una buena combinación de colores para ese lugar. Explique sus razones para seleccionar esos colores.

 Proyecto: Decoración de un espacio interior

Imagine que usted es experto/a en decoración de interiores.

Paso 1. Imagine que usted tiene un cliente / una clienta que es dueño/a (*owner*) de un negocio. ¿Cómo es su cliente/clienta? ¿Qué servicios ofrece (*offers*) en su negocio? ¿Cómo es el espacio donde trabaja? ¿Qué tipo de ambiente (*environment*) necesita en su espacio?

Paso 2. Ahora, en grupos, escriban recomendaciones para decorar el espacio de su cliente/a. Incluyan colores de acento en las paredes y la decoración.

Paso 3. Finalmente, hagan una breve presentación a la clase sobre su diseño (*design*). ¿Qué grupo tiene los diseños más creativos (*most creative*)? ¿más atractivos? ¿más prácticos?

Textos orales

Enrique y Víctor necesitan muebles

Antes de escuchar

¿Qué es más usual entre los estudiantes universitarios: alquilar (*to rent*) un apartamento amueblado o uno sin amueblar (*furnished or unfurnished*)? ¿Tiene usted muchos muebles propios donde usted vive? En su cuarto, casa o apartamento, ¿qué cosas son de usted?

Comprensión

A. ¿Qué necesitan? Enrique y Víctor acaban de alquilar (*have just rented*) un apartamento que tiene muy pocos muebles, pero no importa porque ellos tienen varias cosas. Dibuje (*Draw*) o escriba en el plano del apartamento el nombre de los muebles y cosas que ellos ya tienen para cada cuarto.

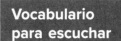 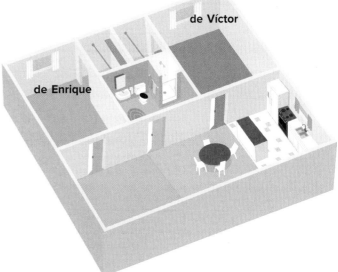

de Víctor

de Enrique

B. Más detalles. Conteste las siguientes preguntas.

1. ¿Qué cosas tienen que comprar Víctor y Enrique para sus habitaciones?
2. ¿Qué parte de la casa no mencionan en la conversación?
3. ¿Qué muebles no necesitan comprar para la sala comedor?
4. ¿Cuántos televisores tienen entre los dos?

 En acción

En parejas, imaginen que tienen que compartir (*share*) un pequeño apartamento el próximo semestre/trimestre. ¿Qué cosas tienen? ¿Qué muebles pueden compartir? ¿Qué necesitan?

Entrevista

Use de modelo las preguntas y respuestas (*answers*) de la sección **Entrevista** al principio (*at the beginning*) de este capítulo para hablar de su casa y su habitación.

Escritura

Un ensayo sobre una semana típica de los estudiantes universitarios

¿Cree usted que los estudiantes universitarios en general tienen una manera típica de vivir? Y, en particular, ¿los estudiantes de su universidad? ¿Por qué?

Antes de escribir

Un joven que estudia mucho

En una hoja de papel aparte, complete una tabla como la siguiente con información sobre 5 o 6 actividades que usted hace de lunes a viernes y durante el fin de semana en una semana típica. Luego entreviste (*interview*) a dos compañeros de clase sobre sus actividades y complete la tabla con su respectiva información.

	de lunes a viernes	fines de semana
usted		
estudiante A		
estudiante B		

A escribir

Ahora use la información para escribir un ensayo sobre la semana típica de los estudiantes de su universidad, si cree que es posible hablar de una semana típica. Hay más ayuda (*help*) en Connect.

Para escribir bien

Here are some words and phrases that can be useful in your essay.

- Prepositions: **antes de, después de, durante, hasta, sin, sobre...**
- Expressions that indicate days and frequency: **el/los lunes/martes... , el fin de semana, todas las semanas, todos los días, por lo general...**
- Words that organize and connect ideas: **además, primero, después/luego, finalmente, por eso...**

⚙️ En la comunidad

Entreviste a (*Interview*) una persona hispana de su universidad o ciudad sobre las viviendas (*housing*) de su país de origen.

Preguntas posibles

- ¿En qué tipo de vivienda vive la mayoría de las personas en su país de origen?
- ¿Hay un tipo o estilo de casa «típico»? ¿Cómo es?
- ¿Dónde vive su familia?

◉ Producción audiovisual

Con las preguntas de la **Entrevista** como modelo, filme una o dos entrevistas con estudiantes de su universidad que hablan del lugar donde viven mientras (*while*) asisten a la universidad.

Más ideas para el portafolio

- Incluya (*Include*) una foto de su cuarto o habitación y descríbalo (*describe it*).
- Describa con muchos detalles la casa de sus sueños (*dreams*).
- Describa un día ideal para usted. ¿Qué día de la semana es, dónde está usted y qué hace durante todo el día?
- Si ha estado jugando (*you have been playing*) Practice Spanish: Study Abroad, en Quest 3 usted almorzó (*you had lunch*) en la casa de su familia colombiana. ¿Cómo es la casa? Dibuje el plano (*Draw the floorplan*) de la casa de su familia colombiana, incluyendo (*including*) todos los cuartos que usted recuerde (*remember*). Luego, nombre (*name*) dos actividades que se hacen (*are done*) en cada cuarto.

Sugerencia: You are now ready to play Quest 3 in **Practice Spanish: Study Abroad.**

AFTER STUDYING THIS CHAPTER I CAN ...

☐ name the parts of a house or apartment and furniture (136)

☐ use the names of the days of the week as well as other time expressions (138–139)

☐ use some words and expressions that put actions in sequence (140–141, 156)

☐ use important irregular and stem-changing verbs (142–144, 148–150)

☐ talk about my daily routine and other actions that require reflexive pronouns (153–155)

☐ recognize/describe at least 2–3 aspects of Salvadoran and Nicaraguan cultures

Gramática en breve

12. Present Tense of *hacer, oír, poner, salir, traer, ver*

hacer: **hago, haces, hace, hacemos, hacéis, hacen**

oír: **oigo, oyes, oye, oímos, oís, oyen**

poner: **pongo, pones, pone, ponemos, ponéis, ponen**

salir: **salgo, sales, sale, salimos, salís, salen**

traer: **traigo, traes, trae, traemos, traéis, traen**

ver: **veo, ves, ve, vemos, veis, ven**

13. Present Tense of Stem-changing Verbs

Stem-changing Patterns

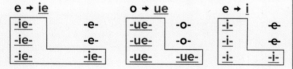

e → ie		o → ue		e → i	
-ie-	-e-	-ue-	-o-	-i-	-e-
-ie-	-e-	-ue-	-o-	-i-	-e-
-ie-	-ie-	-ue-	-ue-	-i-	-i-

14. Reflexive Pronouns

yo → me	nosotros/as → nos
tú → te	vosotros/as → os
usted/él/ella → se	ustedes/ellos/ellas → se

Vocabulario

Los verbos

almorzar (almuerzo)	to have lunch
cerrar (cierro)	to close
descansar	to rest

dormir (duermo)	to sleep
dormir la siesta	to take a nap
empezar (empiezo)	to begin, start
empezar a + *inf.*	to begin to (*do something*)
entender (entiendo)	to understand
hacer	to do; to make
hacer ejercicio	to exercise
hacer un viaje	to take a trip
hacer una pregunta	to ask a question
jugar (juego) (a; al)	to play (*a game; a sport*)
oír (oigo, oyes,...)	to hear; to listen to (*music, the radio*)
pedir (pido)	to ask for; to order
pensar (pienso) (en)	to think (about)
pensar de/que	to think of/that, have an opinion about
pensar + *inf.*	to intend, plan to (*do something*)
perder (pierdo)	to lose; to miss (*an event*)
poner (pongo)	to put; to place; to turn on (*an appliance*)
salir (salgo) (de)	to leave (*a place*); to go out
salir bien/mal	to turn/come out well/poorly; to do well/poorly
salir con	to go out with, date
salir para	to leave for (*a place*)
servir (sirvo)	to serve
servir para	to be used for
traer (traigo)	to bring
ver (veo)	to see; to watch (*a program, movie*)
volver (vuelvo)	to return (*to a place*)
volver a + *inf.*	to (*do something*) again

Los verbos que se usan con pronombres reflexivos

acostarse (me acuesto)	to go to bed
afeitarse	to shave
bañarse	to take a bath, bathe
cepillarse los dientes	to brush one's teeth
despertarse (me despierto)	to wake up
divertirse (me divierto)	to have a good time, enjoy oneself
dormirse (me duermo)	to fall asleep
ducharse	to take a shower
levantarse	to get up (out of bed); to stand up
llamarse	to be called
maquillarse	to put on makeup
peinarse	to do (brush/comb) one's hair

ponerse (me pongo) + clothing	to put on (an article of clothing)
quitarse + clothing	to take off (an article of clothing)
sentarse (me siento)	to sit down
vestirse (me visto)	to get dressed

Los cuartos y otras partes de una casa

el baño	bathroom
la cocina	kitchen
el comedor	dining room
el estudio	office (in a home)
la habitación	bedroom
el hogar	home
el jardín	garden
la pared	wall
el patio	patio; yard
la piscina	swimming pool
la sala	living room

Cognado: el garaje

Repaso: la casa, el cuarto

Los muebles y otras cosas de una casa

la alfombra	rug
el armario	armoire, free-standing closet
la bañera	bathtub
la cama	bed
la cómoda	bureau; dresser
el estante	bookcase
la estufa	stove
la lámpara	lamp
el lavabo	(bathroom) sink
la mesita	end table
el sillón	armchair
la toalla	towel
el mueble	piece of furniture

Cognado: el sofá

Repaso: el escritorio, la mesa, la silla, la tele(visión)

Otros sustantivos

la bebida	drink
el cine	movies; movie theater
la cosa	thing
el diente	tooth
el ejercicio	exercise
la llave	key
la nota	grade
las noticias	news
la película	movie
la pregunta	question
el ruido	noise

| la rutina | routine |
| el viaje | trip |

Los adjetivos

cada inv.*	each, every
diario/a	daily
primero/a†	first
próximo/a	next
siguiente	following
solo/a	alone

Las preposiciones

antes de	before
después de	after
durante	during
sin	without

Repaso: a, con, de, en, hasta, para, por (in, during), sobre

¿Qué día es hoy?

los días de la semana:
    lunes, martes, miércoles, jueves, viernes, sábado, domingo

anteayer	the day before yesterday
ayer fue (miércoles...)	yesterday was (Wednesday ...)
el lunes (martes...)	on Monday (Tuesday ...)
los lunes (los martes...)	on Mondays (Tuesdays ...)
pasado mañana	the day after tomorrow
el próximo (martes...)	next (Tuesday ...)
la próxima semana	next week
la semana (el lunes...) que viene	next week (Monday ...)

Repaso: el día, el fin de semana, hoy, mañana

Palabras adicionales

después adv.	then, later, next
enseguida	immediately
finalmente	finally
lo que	what, that which
luego	then, later, next
por fin	finally
por lo general	generally
primero adv.	first

Vocabulario personal

Use this space or a vocabulary notebook to write down other words and phrases you learn in this chapter.

---

*The abbreviation inv. means invariable, unchanging (in form). The adjective cada is used with masculine and feminine nouns (cada libro, cada mesa), and since its meaning (each) is singular, it is never used with plural nouns.

†The adjective primero shortens to primer before masculine singular nouns: el primer libro, but la primera clase.

En resumen

6

Las estaciones y el tiempo°

Las... *Seasons and the weather*

En este capítulo

VOCABULARY
Weather   170
Months of the year and seasons   173
Words like *close to* and *far from*   175

GRAMMAR
Talking about what's happening   177
Using **ser** and **estar**   182
Making comparisons   189

COUNTRY OF FOCUS: COSTA RICA

Una catarata (*waterfall*) del río Celeste, en el Parque Nacional Volcán Tenorio, Costa Rica

Paul Souders/The Image Bank/Getty Images

COSTA RICA

5 millones de habitantes

- La Constitución de Costa Rica prohíbe la organización de fuerzas armadas.[a]

- El ecoturismo es fundamental para la economía de Costa Rica y para preservar sus bosques[b] y selvas,[c] que cubren[d] un 30% (por ciento) de su territorio.

[a]fuerzas... *armed forces* [b]*forests* [c]*jungles* [d]*cover*

🔊 ENTREVISTA

These questions related to the chapter theme are answered here by a native speaker. You will be able to ask and answer them yourself with personal information in the **Entrevista** activity in the **Portafolio** section at the end of the chapter.

Manuel Gil del Valle contesta las preguntas.

– ¿Cómo es el clima de su país?

– El clima de Managua es poco variado. Solo hay dos estaciones, una lluviosa[a] y otra seca.[b] La temperatura diaria varía poco: alrededor de[c] 30 grados de máxima y 21 de mínima. Es decir,[d] hace calor[e] todo el año.

– ¿Qué le gusta hacer cuando el tiempo[f] es bueno?

– Bueno,[g] no hago nada[h] en especial, porque no hay una estación de calor y otra de frío.[i]

– ¿Cuál es su estación[j] favorita?

– Prefiero la estación seca. Es que[k] puede llover[l] mucho durante la estación lluviosa y no me gusta estar mojado.[m]

[a]una... *a rainy one* [b]otra... *a dry one* [c]alrededor... *around* [d]Es... *That is* [e]hace... *it's hot* [f]*weather* [g]*Well* [h]no... *I don't do anything* [i]*cold* [j]*season* [k]Es... *That's because* [l]*rain* [m]*wet*

Purestock/Getty Images

VOCABULARIO: PREPARACIÓN

You can hear the pronunciation of theme vocabulary words and phrases in the eBook.

¿Qué tiempo hace hoy?°

¿Qué... What's the weather like today?

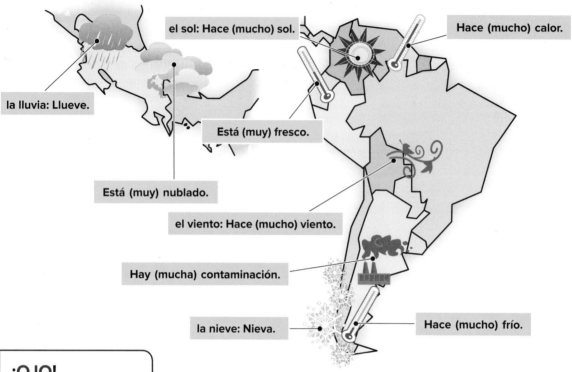

el sol: Hace (mucho) sol.

Hace (mucho) calor.

la lluvia: Llueve.

Está (muy) fresco.

Está (muy) nublado.

el viento: Hace (mucho) viento.

Hay (mucha) contaminación.

la nieve: Nieva.

Hace (mucho) frío.

¡OJO!

el tiempo = *weather* and *time* in general, but: *What time is it?* = **¿Qué hora es?**

¡OJO!

There is no Spanish equivalent for the English subject *it* in these weather expressions. The verb alone (**hace, está, hay**) is sufficient.

- Many weather conditions are expressed with **hace** (**hacer**) in Spanish.

  Hace (muy) buen/mal tiempo.   It's (very) good/bad weather. It's (very) nice/bad out.

  Hace (mucho) calor/frío/sol/viento.   It's (very) hot/cold/sunny/windy.

- The words **calor** (*heat*), **frío** (*cold*), **sol** (*sun*), and **viento** (*wind*) are all nouns, which is why the adjective **mucho** is used with them, and not an adverb (as in English, which uses *very*).

- *To rain* and *to snow* are expressed with stem-changing verbs. Only the third person singular is used.

  ll<u>o</u>ver: ll<u>ue</u>ve   to rain: it's raining   **n<u>e</u>var: n<u>ie</u>va**   to snow: it's snowing

- There are also weather expressions with the verbs **está** and **hay**.

  Está (muy) fresco.   It's (very) cool.

  Está (muy) nublado.   It's (very) cloudy.

  Hay (mucha) contaminación.   There's (a lot of) pollution.

Así se dice

Here are some other weather expressions that you might hear.

Está nublado. = Está nubloso.
Nieva. = Está nevoso.
Llueve. = Está lluvioso.
Hace sol. = Está soleado.

Comunicación

A. El tiempo y la ropa. Diga qué tiempo hace, según la ropa de cada persona.

MODELO: Todos llevan traje de baño y chanclas. →
Hace calor. (Hace buen tiempo.)

1. María lleva pantalones cortos y camiseta.
2. Juan lleva suéter, pero no lleva chaqueta.
3. Roberto lleva sudadera y chaqueta.
4. Ramón lleva impermeable y botas y también tiene paraguas (*umbrella*).
5. Todos llevan abrigo, botas y sombrero.

B. El clima en el mundo

Paso 1. ¿Qué clima o condición metereológica asocia usted con las siguientes ciudades?

1. Seattle, Washington
2. Los Ángeles, California
3. San José, Costa Rica
4. Buffalo, Nueva York
5. Waikiki, Hawái
6. Chicago, Illinois

Paso 2. ¿Qué clima o condición asocia usted con los siguientes lugares?

1. un desierto
2. una playa (*beach*)
3. una montaña muy, muy alta
4. una ciudad grande
5. la Antártida
6. una zona tropical
7. una zona templada (*temperate*)
8. Londres

C. El tiempo y las actividades.
Haga oraciones completas, indicando una actividad apropiada para cada situación. Es necesario conjugar los verbos a la derecha (*right*).

MODELO: Cuando hace buen tiempo, almuerzo afuera (*outside*) / muchos estudiantes almuerzan afuera.

cuando hace buen/mal tiempo
cuando hace (mucho)
  calor/frío
cuando hay mucha
  contaminación
cuando llueve
cuando nieva
	+ (no) **+**	jugar al basquetbol/voleibol con mis amigos
		almorzar afuera / en el parque
		divertirse en el parque / en la playa con mis
		  amigos
		salir de casa
		volver a casa
		trabajar o estudiar
		quedarse (*to stay*) en casa

Nota comunicativa: Otras expresiones con *tener*

In addition to those you have already learned, some other conditions are expressed in Spanish with **tener** idioms—not with *to be,* as in English.

tener (mucho) calor   to be/feel (very) warm, hot
tener (mucho) frío   to be/feel (very) cold

These expressions are used to describe people or animals only. *To be comfortable*—neither hot nor cold—is expressed with **estar bien.**

You will use these expressions in **Comunicación D.**

D. ¿Tienen frío o calor? ¿Están bien? En parejas, describan el tiempo que hace en cada dibujo. También deben indicar cómo están las personas. Si ustedes creen que no tienen ni (*neither*) frío ni (*or*) calor, pueden decir (*say*): «**Está(n) bien**».

1.

2.

3.

4.

5.

6.

Textos de todos los días: Un mensaje sobre el tiempo

En conversaciones diarias con personas conocidas o desconocidas (*known or unknown*), es muy común hacer referencia al tiempo: para hacer planes, para decidir qué ropa ponerse o simplemente para hacer un comentario social. En esta actividad va a practicar cómo hablar del tiempo escribiendo (*by writing*) un mensaje de texto a una persona amiga o de su familia.

Objetivo: Escribir un mensaje de texto hablando del tiempo que hace (las condiciones meteorológicas) y cómo se siente usted (*you feel*).

Antes de empezar: Piense (*Think*) en las siguientes preguntas: Cuando usted y otras personas hablan del tiempo, ¿qué mencionan? ¿la temperatura? ¿Hacen comentarios que expresan su reacción personal? ¿Hablan de actividades que piensan hacer?

¡OJO!

En los países hispanos las temperaturas se expresan en grados Celsius:

32° F = 0° C
34° F = 1° C
100° F = 37.8° C

Vocabulario útil

¡Me encanta!	I love it!
¡No me gusta (para) nada!	I don't like it at all!
¡Me muero de... !	I'm dying of ... !
calor/frío	heat/cold
la humedad	humidity
¡Qué calor/frío!	It's so hot/cold!
¡Qué rico!	It's so nice out!
¡Qué asco!	It's so disgusting out!

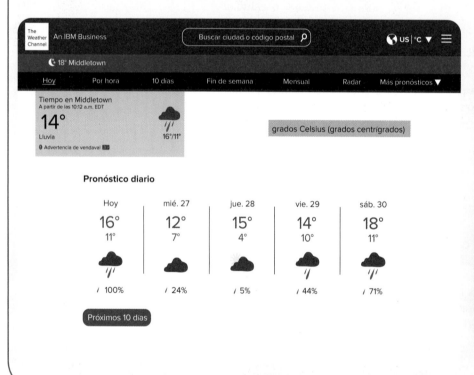

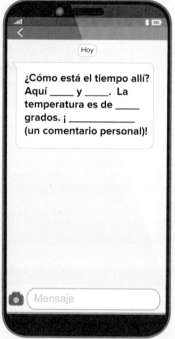

¿**Cómo está el tiempo allí?**
Aquí _____ y _____. La
temperatura es de _____
grados. ¡ _____
(un comentario personal)!

Los meses y las estaciones° del año

seasons

Las cuatro estaciones en el hemisferio norte

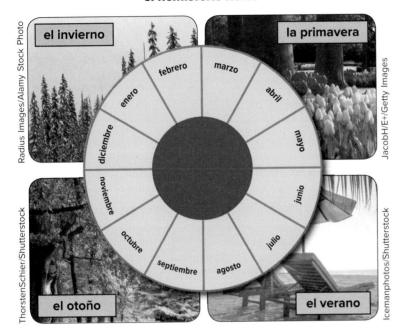

el invierno

la primavera

el otoño

el verano

¿Cuál es la fecha de hoy?	What's today's date?
¿Qué fecha es hoy?	
(Hoy) Es el primero de abril.	(Today is) It's the first of April.
(Hoy) Es el cinco de febrero.	(Today is) It's the fifth of February.

- The ordinal number **primero (1°)** is used to express the first day of the month. Cardinal numbers (**dos, tres,** and so on) are used for other days.
- The definite article **el** is used before the date. However, when the day of the week is expressed, **el** is omitted: **Hoy es jueves, 3 de octubre.**
- As you know, **mil** is used to express the year (**el año**) after 999.

1950 mil novecientos cincuenta   2025 dos mil veinticinco

Así se dice

Other ways to ask what day it is include:

¿Qué día es hoy?
¿A cuántos estamos?

In the last sentence, **cuántos** is masculine because it refers to **días** (*m.*).

Comunicación

A. ¿Cuántos días hay en cada mes? Piense en el poema que se usa en inglés para recordar (*remember*) el número de días en cada mes: *Thirty days ...* Aquí está el poema en español. Para completarlo (*complete it*), usted tiene que hacer rimar los dos primeros versos (*lines*).

Treinta días tiene _____,
Con abril, _____ y _____.
De veintiocho solo hay uno,
Y los demás,[a] treinta y uno.

———————————
[a]los... *the rest*

B. Las fechas

Paso 1. Exprese estas fechas en español. ¿En qué estación caen (*do they fall*)?

MODELO: February 15 → Es **el** quince **de** febrero. Cae (*It falls*) en invierno.

1. March 7
2. August 24
3. December 1
4. June 5
5. September 19, 1997
6. May 30, 1842
7. January 31, 1660
8. July 4, 1776

¡OJO!

Remember: **el... de** = *on the ... of*

Paso 2. ¿Cuándo se celebran (día y mes)?*

Se celebra...

1. el Día del Año Nuevo
2. el Día de los Enamorados (de San Valentín)
3. la Navidad (*Christmas*)
4. el Día de los Inocentes (*Fools*), en los Estados Unidos
5. su cumpleaños (*birthday*)
6. el cumpleaños de su pareja, novio/a (*boyfriend/girlfriend*), esposo/a, mejor (*best*) amigo/a,...

Nota cultural: El clima en el mundo hispano

El mundo hispanohablante es inmenso. Se extiende en las Américas desde los Estados Unidos hasta la Argentina. Por eso, el clima de los países hispanohablantes es muy variado.

- No todos los países tienen cuatro estaciones. Costa Rica y otros países centroamericanos y sudamericanos solo tienen dos: una estación seca[a] y otra húmeda, con mucha lluvia. Esto es normal en los países de la zona tropical.
- El Niño, un fenómeno meteorológico, afecta directamente a varios países hispanos. Está caracterizado por temperaturas más calientes de lo normal[b] en la zona ecuatorial del océano Pacífico. El fenómeno se llama El Niño porque se presenta típicamente alrededor de[c] Navidad, época en que nace el Niño Jesús[d] (para los cristianos).

La costa del Perú, donde se descubrió (*was discovered*) el fenómeno de El Niño en el siglo (*century*) XIX

S. Buonamici/DEA/Getty Images

 ¿Cómo es el clima de su estado o país? ¿Están las estaciones bien diferenciadas?

[a]*dry* [b]*más... warmer than normal* [c]*alrededor... around* [d]*nace... the Baby Jesus is born*

Los signos del horóscopo

Aries	Libra
Tauro	Escorpión
Géminis	Sagitario
Cáncer	Capricornio
Leo	Acuario
Virgo	Piscis

 ## C. Intercambios

Paso 1. En parejas, túrnense para entrevistarse sobre los siguientes temas. Deben obtener detalles interesantes y personales de su compañero/a.

MODELO: **1.** la fecha de su cumpleaños →
¿Cuál es la fecha de tu cumpleaños? ¿Qué tiempo hace, generalmente, ese día? ¿Cómo celebras tu cumpleaños?

1. la fecha de su cumpleaños
2. su signo del horóscopo
3. su estación favorita
4. una estación que no le gusta

Paso 2. Digan a la clase lo que ustedes tienen en común.

MODELO: Nosotras tenemos el cumpleaños en abril. La fecha de María es el 16 y mi fecha es el 18. Nuestro signo es Aries. Las dos (*Both of us*) preferimos la primavera. ¿Por qué? Porque nuestro cumpleaños es en primavera y es una estación muy bonita.

---

*Remember that the word **se** before a verb changes the verb's meaning slightly. ¿Cuándo se celebran? = *When are they celebrated?* You will see this construction throughout **Puntos de partida**. You will learn about this usage in **Capítulo 8**.

¿Dónde está? Las preposiciones (Part 2)

cerca de	close to
lejos de	far from
debajo de	below
encima de	on top of
al lado de	alongside of
entre	between; among
delante de	in front of
detrás de	behind
a la derecha/ izquierda de	to the right/ left of
al norte/ sur/este/ oeste de	to the north/ south/east/ west of

Nueva York está **al norte de** Miami. México está **al sur de** los Estados Unidos.

la maestra

Pablito

Los estudiantes están **delante de** la maestra.

Luis

Carmen

Teresa

Teresa está **entre** Carmen y Pablito.

El libro está **encima de** la mesa.

La mochila está **debajo de** la mesa.

Pablito está **a la derecha de** Teresa.

- In Spanish, the *pronoun objects of prepositions* (**los pronombres preposicionales**) are identical in form to the subject pronouns, except for **mí** and **ti**.

Julio está delante de <u>mí</u>.	Julio is in front of me.
María está detrás de <u>ti</u>.	María is behind you.
Me siento a la izquierda de <u>ella</u>.	I sit on her left.

- The pronouns **mí** and **ti** combine with the preposition **con** to form **conmigo** (*with me*) and **contigo** (*with you*), respectively.

—¿Vienes <u>conmigo</u>?	"Are you coming with me?"
—Sí, voy <u>contigo</u>.	"Yes, I'll go with you."

> **¡OJO!**
>
> As in English, possessives are often used instead of the article to express location.
>
> María está a **mi** izquierda.
> Luis se sienta a **tu** derecha.

> **¡OJO!**
>
> Note that **mí** has a written accent, but **ti** does not. This diacritical accent (**Capítulo 4**) distinguishes the object of a preposition (**mí**) from the possessive adjective (**mi**).

Comunicación

A. En el salón de clase

Paso 1. Describa a las personas o cosas de su clase en relación con usted. Siga el modelo. Use **nadie** (*no one*) cuando sea (*it's*) necesario.

MODELO: **1.** está cerca de la puerta. → **Jaime** está cerca de la puerta.

Una persona o una cosa que...

1. está cerca/lejos de la puerta.
2. está detrás de la mesa del profesor / de la profesora.
3. está delante del pizarrón.
4. se sienta a su izquierda/ derecha.
5. habla con usted en la clase.
6. hoy trabaja con usted.

Vocabulario: Preparación

Paso 2. En parejas, túrnense para describir la posición de una persona o de un objeto en el salón de clase para que su compañero/a lo adivine (*guess it*).

MODELO: Es una persona. Hoy está a la derecha de Paul, pero muchas veces se sienta al lado de la puerta. ¿Quién es?

B. ¿De qué país se habla?

Paso 1. Escuche la descripción de un país de Latinoamérica que da (*gives*) su profesor(a). ¿Cuál es ese país?

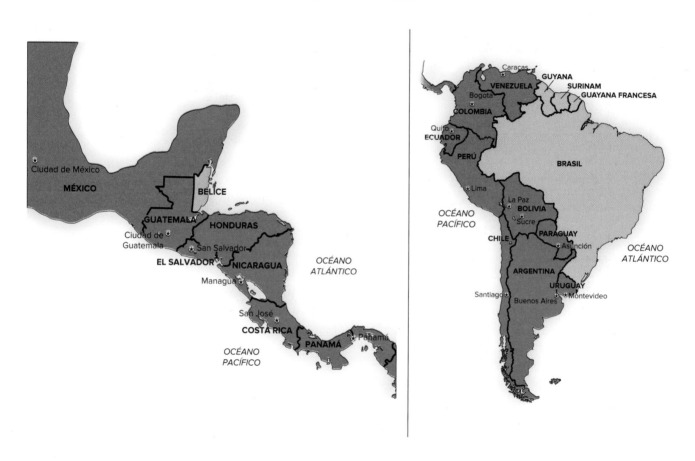

Paso 2. Ahora describa un país de Latinoamérica. Sus compañeros de clase van a decir cuál es. Siga (*Follow*) el modelo, usando todas las frases que sean (*are*) apropiadas.

MODELO: Este país está al norte/sur/este/oeste de _____. También está cerca de _____. Pero está lejos de _____. Está entre _____ y _____. Su capital es _____. ¿Cómo se llama?

C. Intercambios. En parejas, túrnense para entrevistarse. Deben averiguar (*find out*) información sobre la ubicación (*location*) de las ciudades y los estados o países de donde son ustedes, y sobre su clima.

MODELO: E1: ¿De dónde eres?
E2: Soy de Tylertown.
E1: ¿Dónde está Tylertown?
E2: Está en el estado de _____, al oeste de _____.
E1: ¿Cómo es el clima?

15 ¿Qué están haciendo? • Present Progressive: Estar + -ndo

Gramática en acción: ¿Qué <u>está haciendo</u> Elisa esta tarde?

Janis Christie/Getty Images

Elisa es periodista. Por eso escribe y habla mucho por teléfono en su trabajo. Pero ahora mismo no **está trabajando**. **Está descansando** en casa. **Está escuchando** música, **leyendo** una novela y **tomando** un café.

¿Y usted?

En el salón de clase, ¿quién está haciendo las siguientes cosas en este momento? **¡OJO!**
nadie = *nobody*.

1. _____ **está hablando** por teléfono.
2. _____ **está leyendo** un periódico.
3. _____ **está tomando** un café.
4. _____ **está mandando** mensajes.
5. _____ **está escuchando** música.

The Progressive / El progresivo

estoy		I am
estás		you (*fam.*) are
está	**tom**<u>ando</u>	he, she, it, you (*form.*) are
estamos	**com**<u>iendo</u>	we are
estáis	**abr**<u>iendo</u>	you (*pl. fam.*) are
están		they, you (*pl. form.*) are

drinking
eating
opening

Uses of the Progressive / Los usos del progresivo

1. The Progressive
Spanish and English form the *progressive* (**el progresivo**) in similar ways, as you can see in the preceding chart, but the use of the progressive is not the same in both languages.

> *the progressive* / **el progresivo** = a verb form that expresses continuing or developing action

---

What's Elisa doing this afternoon? Elisa is a journalist. That's why she writes and talks a lot on the phone at work. But she's not working right now. She's resting at home. She's listening to music, reading a novel, and having a cup of coffee.

2. Uses of the Progressive

As shown in the example sentences, English uses the present progressive to tell:

- what is happening *right now* **(1)**
- what is happening *over a period of time* **(2)**
- what is *going to* happen **(3)**

In Spanish, the present progressive is used only:

- to express an action that is happening *right now* **(1)**. This is the primary use of the present progressive in Spanish.
- to express an action that is happening *over a period of time* **(2)**. This can also be expressed in Spanish with the simple present tense.

1. *Ramón **is eating** right now.*
   Ramón **está comiendo** ahora mismo.
2. *Adelaida **is studying** chemistry this semester.*
   Adelaida **está estudiando** química este semestre.
   Adelaida **estudia** química este semestre.
3. *We**'re buying** the house tomorrow.*
   Compramos (Vamos a comprar) la casa mañana.

> ### ¡OJO!
> The Spanish present progressive is *never* used to express an action that is *going to* happen. For that, Spanish uses the simple present tense or **ir a** + *infinitive* **(3)**.

Forming the Present Progressive / La formación del presente progresivo

1. Spanish Present Progressive

The Spanish *present progressive* (**el presente progresivo**) is formed with **estar** plus the *present participle* (**el gerundio**).

The present participle is formed by adding **-ando** to the stem of **-ar** verbs and **-iendo** to the stem of **-er** and **-ir** verbs.

The present participle never varies; it always ends in **-o.**

> *a present participle / **un gerundio** = the verb form that ends in -ing in English*

estar + *present participle*	
to**mar → to**mando	taking; drinking
compren**der → compren**diendo	understanding
ab**rir → ab**riendo	opening

> ### ¡OJO!
> Unaccented **i** between two vowels becomes the letter **y.**

leer: le + iendo → leyendo
oír: o + iendo → oyendo

---

2. Present Participle of *-ir* Stem-changing Verbs

-Ir stem-changing verbs also have a stem change in the present participle.

- The stem vowel **e** changes to **i.**
- The stem vowel **o** changes to **u.**

As you can see, sometimes that change is the same as in the present tense (as in **pedir**) and sometimes it is different (as in **preferir** and **dormir**).

The verbs you have learned so far that show this second change are: **divertirse, dormir(se), pedir, preferir, servir,** and **vestirse.**

preferir (prefiero) (i)	**→ prefiriendo**
pedir (pido) (i)	**→ pidiendo**
dormir (duermo) (u)	**→ durmiendo**

Note that (**duermo**) shows you the present tense stem change for **dormir: o → ue.** The (**u**) shows you the change in the present participle of **dormir: o → u (durmiendo).**

In vocabulary lists from this point on in *Puntos de partida*, this second stem change will be shown in parentheses after the first person singular form of the verb.

---

3. Position of Reflexive Pronouns

Reflexive pronouns can be attached to a present participle or precede the conjugated form of **estar.** Note the accent that is added to the present participle when pronouns are attached.

Pablo **se está** bañando. Pablo **está bañándose.**	*Pablo is taking a bath.*
Estoy empezando a vestir**me.** **Me estoy** empezando a vestir.	*I'm starting to get dressed.*

Práctica y comunicación

A. Un sábado típico

Paso 1. Autoprueba. Complete el gerundio de los siguientes verbos con una de las siguientes terminaciones.

a. -ando   **b. -iendo**   **c. -yendo**

1. acost_____   **6.** pid_____
2. bañ_____   **7.** prefir_____
3. durm_____   **8.** divirt_____
4. hac_____   **9.** cre_____
5. le_____   **10.** empez_____

Paso 2. Ahora piense en su rutina de un sábado típico. Indique dos acciones que es posible que usted esté (*might be*) haciendo a las siguientes horas. Hay una lista de **Frases útiles,** pero usted puede modificarlas (*modify them*) o añadir otras.

MODELO: **1.** a las ocho de la mañana →
A las ocho de la mañana estoy durmiendo o duchándome.

1. a las 8 de la mañana
2. a las 10:30 de la mañana
3. al mediodía (*noon*)
4. a las 4 de la tarde
5. a las 9 de la noche
6. a la medianoche (*midnight*)

Frases útiles

almorzar	**levantarse**
despertarse	**oír** música
dormir (la siesta)	**pedir** una pizza
ducharse	**ver** una película
estudiar	
hacer ejercicio	**volver** a casa

Paso 3. Ahora, en parejas, túrnense para determinar si hacen las mismas (*same*) cosas a la misma hora.

MODELO: **E1:** A las ocho de la mañana los sábados, ¿estás durmiendo?
E2: No, a esa hora estoy trabajando.

B. Hoy, en casa de Lola.
Hoy no es un día como todos los días para la familia de Lola, porque su tío de Costa Rica está de visita. Complete las siguientes oraciones para expresar lo que está pasando (*happening*).

MODELO: Casi siempre, Lola almuerza con su hija. Hoy Lola…
(**almorzar** con su tío en un restaurante) →
Hoy Lola **está almorzando** con su tío en un restaurante.

1. Generalmente, Lola pasa la mañana en la universidad. Hoy Lola… (**pasar** el día con su tío Ricardo)
2. Casi siempre, Lola toma un café en la cafetería después de sus clases. Hoy Lola y su tío… (**tomar** un café en casa)
3. De lunes a viernes, Marta, la hija de Lola, va a la escuela (*school*) por la tarde. Pero esta tarde ella… (**jugar** con Ricardo)
4. Generalmente, la familia cena (*has dinner*) a las nueve. Esta noche todos… (**cenar** a las diez)

Summary of Present Progressive

estar + -ando
      -iendo
      -yendo

Algo sobre los valores° de los costarricenses   *values*

Martin Siepmann/Imagebroker/Alamy Stock Photo

El Parque Nacional Rincón de la Vieja, parte de la importante industria ecoturística de Costa Rica

Dos cualidades caracterizan el país de Costa Rica. Una es la paz.[a] Esta nación no tiene fuerzas armadas[b] desde 1948. Hay una expresión que ilustra este sentimiento nacional: «Donde haya[c] un costarricense, habrá[d] paz». La segunda[e] característica es la importancia que la ecología tiene para el país. Costa Rica no solo preserva su biodiversidad; también la explota[f] con el turismo ecológico.

¿Qué cualidades caracterizan este país? ¿Es la paz un valor estadounidense?

[a]*peace*   [b]*fuerzas… armed forces*
[c]*Donde… Wherever there is*
[d]*there will be*   [e]*second*
[f]*la… she develops it*

C. En casa con la familia Duarte

Paso 1. Describa lo que pasa en cada dibujo, explicando quién está haciendo la acción —el padre, la madre, la hija, los gemelos (*twins*), el perro— y a qué hora. Use los verbos de la lista u otros verbos, si desea. Puede hacer más de (*than*) una oración para cada dibujo, si quiere. **¡OJO!** Hay verbos reflexivos en las listas.

MODELO: salir de la ducha (*shower*) → El padre **está saliendo** de la ducha a las seis de la mañana.

Por la mañana: A las seis de la mañana

Acciones

<u>dormir</u> todavía still
leer el periódico
levantarse
<u>salir</u> de la ducha
tomar un café

1.
2.
3.
4.

Más tarde: A las ocho de la mañana

Acciones

desayunar
leer sus e-mails
<u>pensar</u> en el examen
   que tiene hoy
<u>salir</u> para la universidad
trabajar en la oficina
vestirse

5.
6.
7.
8.

Por la tarde: A las seis y media de la tarde

Acciones

<u>hacer</u> la tarea
jugar
leer un libro de texto
preparar la cena dinner
quitarse la ropa

9.
10.
11.
12.

Paso 2. Ahora explique qué hacen usted y otros miembros de su familia o sus compañeros de cuarto/casa a la misma hora que ve en los dibujos.

Nota comunicativa: El gerundio con otros verbos

As in English, the Spanish *present participle* (**el gerundio**) can be used with verbs other than **estar**. The following verbs are commonly followed by the present participle.

> Remember that the letter in parentheses indicates the change in the present participle of the verb, which in this case would be **siguiendo** and **divirtiendo.**

- **pasar tiempo** + *present participle* — to spend time (doing something)
  ¿**Pasas** mucho tiempo **haciendo** la tarea? — *Do you spend a lot of time doing homework?*

- **seguir (sigo) (i) / continuar*** **(continúo)** + *present participle* — to continue (doing something)
  Sigue lloviendo mucho. — *It continues to rain / raining a lot.*

- **divertirse (me divierto) (i)** + *present participle* — to enjoy (doing something)
  ¿Te **diviertes** mucho **bailando** salsa? — *Do you have a good time dancing salsa?*

You will use these verbs in **Práctica D** and **E.**

D. Acciones continuadas

Paso 1. Conteste las siguientes preguntas.

1. **Los fines de semana:** ¿Cómo se divierte usted? ¿Cuánto tiempo pasa haciendo la tarea o trabajando? ¿En qué otras actividades pasa mucho o poco tiempo? **(Paso mucho/poco tiempo +** *gerundio.***)**
2. **Antes y ahora:** ¿Qué actividades que ya hacía (*you already did*) en la escuela secundaria continúa haciendo en la universidad? ¿Sigue practicando algún deporte o saliendo con las mismas personas?

Paso 2. Ahora en parejas, compartan sus respuestas. ¿Qué tienen en común y en qué son muy diferentes?

MODELO: **E1:** Paso los fines de semana durmiendo. Pero durante el semestre también paso mucho tiempo haciendo la tarea.
E2: Yo también paso mucho tiempo haciendo la tarea y trabajando, porque trabajo en un restaurante los sábados.

E. ¿Qué están haciendo?

Imagine lo que están haciendo las siguientes personas ahora mismo. También puede decir (*say*) si pasan tiempo o se divierten haciendo esas acciones. Use una palabra o frase de cada columna y la forma progresiva.

(yo) mi mejor (*best*) amigo/a mi madre/padre mis padres/abuelos mi profesor/profesora de español / de ¿? ¿ ?	+	estar pasar (mucho) tiempo divertirse seguir/continuar	+	descansar mirar la tele preparar sus clases hacer la tarea mandar mensajes jugar a los videojuegos leer las redes sociales (*social media*) ¿ ?

Vocabulario útil

ducharse por la mañana/noche...
escribir ensayos aburridos (*boring*)
jugar un deporte (al fútbol, al béisbol...) o a videojuegos
levantarse/acostarse temprano/tarde
perder el tiempo (*to waste time*) mirando el celular
tener estrés por los estudios / el trabajo
tocar un instrumento (la guitarra, el piano,...)

---

*Note the present tense forms of **continuar,** which have an accent on the **u** when it is stressed (like the boot pattern of stem-changing verbs): **continúo, continúas, continúa, continuamos, continuáis, continúan.**

You have been using forms of **ser** and **estar** since **Capítulo 1.** The following section will help you consolidate everything you know so far about these two verbs, both of which express *to be* in Spanish. You will learn a bit more about using them as well.

Before you begin **Gramática 16,** think in particular about the following questions: **¿Cómo está usted? ¿Cómo es usted?** What do these questions tell you about the difference between **ser** and **estar**?

16 ¿*Ser o estar?* • Summary of the Uses of ser and estar

Gramática en acción: Una conversación a larga distancia

Aquí hay un lado de la conversación entre una esposa que **está** en un viaje de negocios y su esposo, que **está** en casa. Habla el esposo.

«Aló. [...] ¿Cómo **estás**, querida? [...] ¿Dónde **estás** ahora? [...] ¿Qué hora **es** allí? [...] ¡Huy!, **es** muy tarde. Y el hotel, ¿cómo **es**? [...] Oye, ¿qué **estás** haciendo ahora? [...] Ay, lo siento. **Estás** muy ocupada. ¿Con quién tienes cita mañana? [...] ¿Quién **es** el dueño de la compañía? [...] Ah, él **es** de Costa Rica, ¿verdad? [...] Bueno, ¿qué tiempo hace allí? [...] Muy bien. Hasta luego, ¿eh? [...] Adiós».

Comprensión

Complete las oraciones con **es** o **está.**

1. El esposo _____ en casa.
2. La esposa _____ una mujer de negocios.
3. La esposa _____ en un viaje de negocios.
4. No sabemos (*We don't know*) cómo _____ el hotel.
5. _____ muy tarde donde _____ la esposa.
6. La esposa _____ trabajando ahora.
7. El dueño de la compañía _____ de Costa Rica.

A long-distance conversation Here is one side of a conversation between a wife who is on a business trip and her husband, who is at home. The husband is speaking. "Hello ... How are you, dear? ... Where are you now? ... What time is it there? ... Wow, it's very late. And how's the hotel? ... Hey, what are you doing now? ... Gosh, I'm sorry. You're very busy. Whom do you have an appointment with tomorrow? ... Who's the owner of the company? ... Ah, he's from Costa Rica, isn't he? ... Well, what's the weather like there? ... Great. See you later, OK? ... Good-bye."

Summary of the Uses of ser / Resumen de los usos de ser

• To *identify* people (including their profession) and things	Ella **es doctora.** Tikal **es una ciudad maya.**
• To express *nationality;* with **de** to express *origin*	**Son cubanos.** **Son de** La Habana.
• With **de** to tell of what *material* something is made	Este bolígrafo **es de plástico.**
• With **de** to express *possession*	**Es de** Carlota.
• With **para** to tell *for whom something is intended*	El regalo **es para** Sara.
• To tell *time* and give the *date*	**Son las once.** **Es la una y media.** Hoy **es martes,** tres de octubre.
• With *adjectives* that describe *basic, inherent characteristics*	Ramona **es inteligente.**
• To form many *generalizations* or *impersonal expressions* (only **es**)	**Es necesario** llegar temprano. **Es importante** estudiar.

Summary of the Uses of estar / Resumen de los usos de estar

• To tell *location*	El libro **está en la mesa.**
• To describe *health* and *condition* with adverbs	**Estoy** muy **bien,** gracias. Las respuestas **están mal.**
• With *adjectives* that describe *conditions*	**Estoy** muy **ocupada.**
• In a number of *fixed expressions*	**(No) Estoy de acuerdo.** **Está bien.** (*It's fine, OK.*)
• With *present participles* to form the *present progressive*	**Estoy estudiando** ahora mismo.

Ser and estar with Adjectives / *Ser* y *estar* con adjetivos

1. *Ser* = Fundamental Characteristics
Ser is used with adjectives that describe the *fundamental qualities* (**las características fundamentales**) of a person, place, or thing.

Esa mesa **es** muy **baja.**
That table is very short.

Sus calcetines **son morados.**
His socks are purple.

Este sillón **es cómodo.**
This armchair is comfortable.

Sus padres **son cariñosos.**
Their parents are affectionate people.

2. *Estar* = Conditions
Estar is used with adjectives to express *conditions* (**las condiciones**) or observations that are true at a given moment but that do not describe inherent qualities of the noun. The adverbs **bien** and **mal** are often used in this context. The following adjectives are generally used with **estar.**

(Continúa).

Temporary Conditions / **Las condiciones temporales**					
abierto/a	open	**desordenado/a**	messy	**ocupado/a**	busy
aburrido/a	bored	**enfermo/a**	sick	**ordenado/a**	neat
alegre	happy	**furioso/a**	furious, angry	**preocupado/a**	worried
cansado/a	tired	**limpio/a**	clean	**seguro/a**	sure, certain
cerrado/a	closed	**loco/a**	crazy	**sucio/a**	dirty
congelado/a	frozen; very cold	**molesto/a**	annoyed	**triste**	sad
contento/a	content, happy	**nervioso/a**	nervous		

3. ***Ser* or *estar*?**

Many adjectives can be used with either **ser** or **estar,** depending on what the speaker intends to communicate. In general, when *to be* implies *looks, feels,* or *appears,* **estar** is used. Compare the use of **ser** and **estar** in the sample sentences.

Daniel **es** guapo.
Daniel is handsome. (He is a handsome person.)

Daniel **está** muy guapo esta noche.
Daniel looks very nice (handsome) tonight.

Amalia **es** muy simpática, pero hoy **está** muy seria.
Amalia is very nice, but she's very serious today.

Summary of *ser* and *estar*

ser = inherent qualities
identification
nationality, origin
material
possession
for whom
time, date,
generalizations
estar = conditions
location
fixed
expressions
present
   progressive

Práctica y comunicación

A. ***¿Soy o estoy?***

Paso 1. Autoprueba. ¿Ser o **estar**? ¿Cuál es el verbo apropiado para cada caso?

_____ **1.** to describe a health condition
_____ **2.** to tell time
_____ **3.** to describe inherent characteristics
_____ **4.** to tell where a thing or person is located
_____ **5.** to tell someone's profession
_____ **6.** to say to whom something belongs
_____ **7.** to tell where someone is from
_____ **8.** to describe a temporary condition
_____ **9.** to make a generalization
_____ **10.** to tell what something is intended for

Paso 2. Ahora complete las siguientes oraciones con **estoy** o **soy.** También identifique la razón para usar cada verbo, usando los números de las explicaciones del **Paso 1.**

RAZÓN DEL **Paso 1**

a. _____ bien. _____
b. _____ simpático/a. _____
c. _____ contento/a de tomar español este semestre/trimestre. _____
d. _____ estudiante universitario/a. _____
e. _____ de _____ (ciudad, estado o país). _____

Paso 3. Ahora, en parejas, túrnense para hacer y contestar preguntas basadas en el **Paso 2.** Luego digan a la clase algo (*something*) que ustedes tienen en común.

MODELO: **a.** Estoy bien. →
    E1: ¿Cómo estás?
    E2: Estoy muy bien. ¿Y tú?
    EN COMÚN: Los dos estamos bien hoy.

Prác. A Paso 1: Answers: 1. estar **2.** ser **3.** ser **4.** estar **5.** ser **6.** ser **7.** ser **8.** estar **9.** ser (es) **10.** ser

B. Un regalo estupendo. Use **es** o **está** para describir la computadora que los padres de su compañero/a de cuarto acaban de comprarle (*just bought for him/her*).

La computadora...

1. _____ en la mesa del comedor.
2. _____ un regalo de cumpleaños.
3. _____ para mi compañero/a de cuarto.
4. _____ de la tienda Computec.
5. _____ en una caja (*box*) verde.

6. _____ de los padres de mi compañero/a.
7. _____ un regalo muy caro, pero estupendo.
8. _____ de metal y plástico gris.
9. _____ una IBM último modelo.
10. _____ muy fácil (*easy*) de usar.

Nota comunicativa: El uso de adjetivos + *por*

Por often expresses *because of* or *about* (as in *due to*), especially with adjectives such as **contento/a, furioso/a, nervioso/a,** and **preocupado/a.**

> Amalia está preocupada **por** los exámenes finales.
> *Amalia is worried about her final exams.*

You will use **por** in this way in **Práctica C** and **D.**

C. ¿Quiénes son? En parejas, inventen detalles para describir a las personas de la foto, haciendo oraciones con **ser** o **estar.**

1. ¿quiénes?
2. ¿de qué país?
3. simpáticos/antipáticos / ¿ ?
4. en este momento, contentos/ tristes / ¿ ?
5. molestos/cansados por el viaje / ¿ ?
6. aquí por un mes / una semana / ¿ ?
7. ¿ ?

nuestros primos de San José
Gabriela   Julio

Paul Burns/Getty Images

Algo sobre ¡Pura vida°!

life

Cada país hispanohablante tiene expresiones típicas y ¡Pura vida! es la más típica de Costa Rica. Los costarricenses usan esta frase para expresar que algo[a] es bueno, y también para decir[b] «hola» y «adiós». Como muchas expresiones, la traducción[c] literal no tiene mucho sentido[d] y no es aplicable en otra lengua.

Otra cosa típica del país: los costarricenses usan el pronombre **vos** en lugar de[e] **tú.** El uso de **vos** no es exclusivo de Costa Rica, sino que[f] es prevalente en la Argentina, el Uruguay, el Paraguay y en Centroamérica, excepto en Panamá.

—¿Cómo estás vos?
—¡Pura vida!

¿Qué expresión es típica de la región donde usted vive?

[a]*something* [b]*say* [c]*translation* [d]*no... doesn't make much sense*
[e]*en... instead of* [f]*sino... but*

Niki Harry/Getty Images

Gramática

D. Costa Rica como destino turístico

Paso 1. Complete el siguiente texto promocional sobre Costa Rica con la forma apropiada de **ser, estar** o **hay**, según el contexto.

Costa Rica, ¡pura vida!

¿(*Tú:* _____)[1] de una gran ciudad? ¿(*Tú:* _____)[2] una persona aventurera? ¿(_____)[3] la naturaleza[a] una gran atracción en tu vida[b]? ¿(_____)[4] preocupado/a por los cambios[c] en el clima global? Entonces,[d] Costa Rica (_____)[5] el país para ti. Imagina: (_____)[6] en un lugar cerca del mar[e] en donde (_____)[7] increíbles especies de animales y plantas: iguanas, caimanes, orquídeas, heliconias...

(*Nosotros:* _____)[8] los expertos en turismo natural en Costa Rica. Todos nuestros guías[f] (_____)[9] costarricenses de nacimiento[g] y (*ellos:* _____)[10] contentos de conocer[h] a personas de todo el mundo y hacer nuevos amigos. Por sus conocimientos,[i] por su gran paciencia y por su español, (*ellos:* _____)[11] como profesores... pero sus clases (_____)[12] mucho más interesantes que las clases académicas... ¡y menos difíciles!

No (_____)[13] necesario viajar[j] a Costa Rica en una estación específica. (_____)[14] bueno viajar a Costa Rica en cualquier[k] mes del año. ¡Ven![l] ¡Costa Rica (_____)[15] esperándote[m]!

[a]*nature* [b]*life* [c]*changes* [d]*Then* [e]*sea, ocean* [f]*guides* [g]*de... by birth* [h]*de... to meet* [i]*knowledge* [j]*to travel* [k]*any* [l]*Come (to visit)!* [m]*waiting for you*

Paso 2. Comprensión. ¿Cierto o falso? Corrija las oraciones falsas.

	CIERTO	FALSO
1. En Costa Rica, la naturaleza tiene mucha importancia para el turismo.	☐	☐
2. El turista no va a ver animales exóticos allí.	☐	☐
3. El turista puede aprender español allí.	☐	☐
4. No todas las estaciones son apropiadas para el turismo.	☐	☐

E. Una conversación entre esposos

Paso 1. En parejas, organicen el diálogo entre el esposo de **Gramática en acción** (**Columna A**) y su esposa (**Columna B**), que está en un viaje de negocios. Primero, emparejen los elementos de las dos columnas. El esposo empieza el diálogo, contestando el teléfono.

A: Habla el esposo

1. _____ Aló.
2. _____ Bien. ¿Cómo estás tú, querida?
3. _____ ¿Dónde estás ahora?
4. _____ ¿Qué hora es allí?
5. _____ ¡Huy!, es muy tarde. Y el hotel, ¿cómo es?
6. _____ Oye, ¿qué estás haciendo ahora?
7. _____ Ay, lo siento. Estás muy ocupada. ¿Con quién tienes cita mañana?
8. _____ ¿Quién es el dueño de la compañía?
9. _____ Ah, él es de Costa Rica, ¿verdad?
10. _____ Bueno, ¿qué tiempo hace allí?
11. _____ Muy bien. Hasta luego, ¿eh?

B: Habla la esposa

a. _____ muy moderno y _____ muy limpio.
b. Sí, pero ahora _____ trabajando en Nueva York.
c. _____ las once de la noche.
d. Hola, querido. ¿Qué tal?
e. El señor Cortina.
f. _____ leyendo unos informes (*reports*) para la reunión de mañana. _____ que leer uno más todavía.
g. Sí. Hasta mañana.
h. _____ en el hotel, en Nueva York.
i. _____ un poco cansada por el viaje y _____ sueño.
j. _____ fresco y nublado.
k. Con un señor de Computec.

Paso 2. Ahora completen las oraciones de la señora con la forma correcta de **estar, hacer, ser** o **tener.** Luego practiquen la conversación completa.

Una heliconia

F. Una tarde terrible

Paso 1. Hoy es un día desastroso para la familia Castañeda. Usted va a describir lo que está pasando en su casa en el **Paso 2**. Para prepararse, repase (*review*) primero unos adjetivos, cambiando (*exchanging*) las palabras subrayadas (*underlined*) por antónimos en las siguientes oraciones.

1. No hace <u>buen</u> tiempo; hace _____ tiempo.
2. El bebé no está <u>bien</u>; está _____.
3. El gato no está <u>limpio</u>; está _____.
4. El esposo no está <u>tranquilo</u>; está _____ por el bebé.
5. El garaje no está <u>cerrado</u>; está _____.
6. Los niños no están <u>tranquilos</u>; están _____, porque tienen miedo.
7. La esposa no está <u>contenta</u>; está _____ por el tiempo.
8. El grifo (*faucet*) del baño no está <u>cerrado</u>; está _____.

Paso 2. Ahora use los adjetivos del **Paso 1** y otros que usted conozca (*you know*) para expresar lo que **están haciendo** todos los miembros de la familia en este momento. Póngales (*Give*) nombres a todos y exprese su **estado de ánimo** (*their feelings*) o sus deseos. ¡Use su imaginación! Si puede, diga también **lo que usualmente hacen** estas personas a esta hora.

Estrategia

lo que están haciendo = <u>**el presente progresivo**</u>

el estado de ánimo = **el presente simple**

lo que usualmente hacen = **el presente simple**

Vocabulario útil

la cena	dinner	**cocinar**	to cook
los truenos y relámpagos	thunder and lightning	<u>**conducir**</u> (condu<u>zc</u>o)*	to drive
		ladrar	to bark
cenar	to have dinner	**llorar**	to cry

---

*Only the first person singular of the verb **conducir** is irregular, as noted. The other forms of the present tense are regular: **conduces, conduce...**

G. Compañeras ideales

Paso 1. Conteste las preguntas para describir el siguiente dibujo de un cuarto de dos estudiantes. Use su imaginación e invente todos los detalles posibles.

Vocabulario útil

el acuario	
el afiche	poster
el cajón	drawer
el corazón	heart
la cortina	curtain
las luces	lights
el tatuaje	

1. ¿Cómo es cada una de las jóvenes?
2. ¿Qué estudian?
3. ¿Qué están haciendo en este momento?
4. ¿Cómo es el cuarto? ¿Qué hay? ¿Cómo está?

 Paso 2. Ahora, en parejas, hablen de sus cuartos. Preguntas posibles: ¿Cómo son? ¿Cómo están? ¿Qué hay en ellos? ¿Dónde están? ¿Comparten (*Do you share*) su cuarto? Etcétera. Hablen también de las características que prefieren en las personas que comparten su cuarto o casa. Idealmente, ¿cómo deben ser esas personas?

H. Intercambios. ¿Cómo están ustedes en estas situaciones? En parejas, túrnense para hacer y contestar preguntas, según el modelo. También pueden usar expresiones con **tener.**

MODELO: **1.** cuando / tener mucha tarea ➜
    E1: ¿Cómo estás cuando **tienes** mucha tarea?
    E2: Estoy cansado y estresado, como ahora. ¿Y tú?
    E3: Yo también.

Vocabulario útil

agobiado/a	overwhelmed
deprimido/a	depressed
desahogado/a	relieved
estresado/a	

1. cuando / tener mucha tarea / una tarea fácil/difícil
2. cuando / no tener trabajo (*work*) académico
3. cuando / sacar (*to get*) A/D en un examen
4. en verano/invierno
5. cuando llueve/nieva
6. los lunes por la mañana / los domingos por la tarde / los...
7. después de una fiesta / un examen
8. durante la clase de _____
9. ¿ ?

Gramática en acción: Buenos Aires y San José

El centro de Buenos Aires, Argentina

El centro de San José, Costa Rica

David Forman/Image Source

Mtcurado/Getty Images

- Buenos Aires es **más** grande **que** San José.
- Tiene **más** edificios altos **que** San José.
- Generalmente, en Buenos Aires no hace **tanto** calor **como** en San José.

Pero...
- San José es **menos** antigua **que** Buenos Aires.
- No tiene **tantos** habitantes **como** Buenos Aires.
- Sin embargo, los costarricenses son **tan** simpáticos **como** los argentinos.

¿Y usted?

1. Mi ciudad/pueblo...
   - (no) es **tan grande** como Chicago.
   - es **más/menos** cosmopolita **que** San Francisco.
2. Me gusta _____ (nombre de mi ciudad/pueblo)...
   - **más que** _____ (nombre de otra ciudad).
   - **menos que** _____ (nombre de otra ciudad).
   - **tanto como** _____ (nombre de otra ciudad).

Algo sobre San José y Buenos Aires

San José
- Fundada en 1738 y capital de Costa Rica desde 1823
- Población: 342.000 habitantes
- Clima: 2 estaciones; 23° C (grados Celsius) promedio[a] todo el año

Buenos Aires
- Fundada en 1580 y capital de la Argentina desde 1853
- Población: 3.000.000 de habitantes
- Clima: 4 estaciones; 30° C de máximas temperaturas (de diciembre a febrero) y 8° C de mínimas (de junio a agosto)

 La ciudad donde usted vive, ¿es una ciudad capital? ¿Cuántos habitantes tiene, aproximadamente? ¿Cuántas estaciones hay?

[a]*average*

In English *comparisons* (**las comparaciones**) are formed in a variety of ways. Equal comparisons are expressed with the word *as*. Unequal comparisons are expressed with the adverbs *more* or *less,* or by adding *-er* to the end of the adjective.

as cold as
as many as

more intelligent,
less important
taller, smarter

a comparative / **un comparativo** = a form of or structure with nouns, adjectives, and adverbs used to compare nouns, qualities, or actions

Buenos Aires and San José ■ *Buenos Aires is bigger than San José.* ■ *It has more tall buildings than San José.* ■ *It is not as hot in Buenos Aires as it is in San José, generally. But ...* ■ *San José is newer (lit., less ancient) than Buenos Aires.* ■ *It doesn't have as many inhabitants as Buenos Aires.* ■ *Nevertheless, Costa Ricans are as nice as Argentines.*

Comparatives / **Los comparativos**			
Inequality / **La desigualdad**		Equality / **La igualdad**	
más... que more ... than **más que** more than	**menos... que** less ... than **menos que** less than	**tan... como** **tanto/a/os/as... como** **tanto como**	as ... as as much/many ... as as much as

Inequality / **La desigualdad: más/menos... que, más/menos que**

1. Comparing Adjectives, Adverbs, and Verbs

Para describir
más/menos + *adjective* + **que**
more/less + *adjective*} + *than*   *adjective* + *-er*

Juan es **más** alto **que** Elena.
Juan is taller than Elena.

Elena es **menos** alta **que** Juan.
Elena is shorter than Juan.

Para describir cómo se hace una acción
más/menos + *adverb* + **que**
more/less + *adverb*} + *than*   *adverb* + *-er*

Juan corre **más** rápido **que** Elena.
Juan runs faster (more quickly) than Elena.

Elena corre **menos** rápido **que** Juan.
Elena runs slower (less quickly) than Juan.

¡OJO!

Look at the examples under the drawings and notice the use of **yo**, (never **mí**) to complete the comparison.

Para expresar la frecuencia o intensidad de una acción
verb + **más/menos que**
verb + *more/less than*

Juan **corre más que** Elena.
Juan runs more than Elena.

Elena **corre menos que** Juan.
Elena runs less than Juan.

2. Comparing Nouns

Para comparar la cantidad
más/menos + *noun* + **que**
more/less (fewer) + *noun* + *than*

Rigoberto tiene **más** coches **que** Carmen.
Rigoberto has more cars than Carmen.

Carmen tiene **menos** coches **que** Rigoberto.
Carmen has fewer cars than Rigoberto.

3. *More/Fewer than* + *number*

¡OJO!

The preposition **de** is used instead of **que** when the comparison is followed by a number.

Para expresar una cantidad
más/menos de + *number* + *noun*
more/fewer than + *number* + *noun*

Juan tiene **más de dos** lápices.
Juan has more than two pencils.

Elena tiene **menos de dos** lápices.
Elena has fewer than two pencils.

Equality / **La igualdad: tan... como, tanto como, tanto/a/os/as... como**

1. Comparing Adjectives, Adverbs, and Verbs

Ernesto

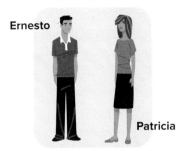

Patricia

Patricia habla: «Ernesto es **tan** alto y **tan** delgado **como** <u>yo</u>».

Ernesto
Patricia

MARTES

JUEVES

SÁBADO

Ernesto habla: «Patricia juega **tan** agresivamente **como** <u>yo</u>. También juega **tanto como** <u>yo</u>».

Para describir
tan + *adjective* + **como**
as + adjective + as

Patricia es **tan** alta **como** Ernesto. También es **tan** delgada **como** él.

Patricia is as tall as Ernesto (is). She's also as thin as him.

Para describir cómo se hace una acción
tan + *adverb* + **como**
as + adverb + as

Ernesto juega al tenis **tan** bien **como** Patricia. También juega **tan** agresivamente **como** ella.

Ernesto plays tennis as well as Patricia (does). He also plays as aggressively as her.

Para expresar la frecuencia o intensidad de una acción
verb + **tanto como**
verb + as much as

Patricia **juega** al tenis **tanto como** Ernesto. También **gana** **tanto como** él.

Patricia plays tennis as much as Ernesto. She also wins as much (often) as him.

2. Comparing Nouns

Ernesto   Patricia

¡OJO!

Like all adjectives, **tanto** must agree in gender and number with the noun it modifies: **tanto** diner<u>o</u>, **tanta** pris<u>a</u>, **tant<u>os</u>** abrig<u>os</u>, **tant<u>as</u>** herman<u>as</u>.

Para comparar la cantidad
tanto/a/os/as + *noun* + **como**
as much/many + noun + as

Ernesto tiene **tantos** trofeos **como** Patricia. También tiene **tantas** raquetas de tenis **como** ella.

Ernesto has as many trophies as Patricia. He also has as many tennis rackets as her.

Patricia y Ernesto tienen **tantas** hermanas **como** hermanos.

Patricia and Ernesto each have as many sisters as (they have) brothers.

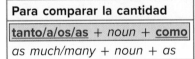
Ernesto

Patricia

Patricia habla: «Ernesto tiene **tantos** hermanos **como** <u>yo</u>».

Irregular Forms / **Las formas irregulares**

- **bueno/a/os/as** *adj.* → **mejor, mejores (que)**

  Estos coches son **buenos,** pero esos son **mejores** (que estos).
  These cars are good, but those are better (than these).

- **bien** *adv.* → **mejor (que)**

  Yo hablo español **bien,** pero mi amigo Dennis lo habla **mejor** (que yo).
  I speak Spanish well, but my friend Dennis speaks it better (than I [do]).

- **malo/a/os/as** *adj.* → **peor, peores (que)**

  La nueva película de este director es **mala,** pero la primera es **peor.**
  This director's new movie is bad, but his first one is worse.

- **mal** *adv.* → **peor (que)**

  La profesora canta **mal,** pero yo canto **peor** (que ella).
  The professor sings badly, but I sing worse (than she does).

- **viejo/a/os/as** → **mayor, mayores (que)**

  La abuela es **viejita,** pero el abuelo es **mayor** (que ella).
  Grandmother is old, but grandfather is older than her.

- **joven, jóvenes** → **menor, menores (que)**

  Delia es **joven,** pero su esposo es **menor** (que ella).
  Delia is young, but her husband is younger than her.

Comparison Summary

| más... que
más que/de | menos... que
menos que/de | tan... como
tant**o/a/os/as**... como
tant**o** como |

Práctica y comunicación

A. Comparaciones

> **Paso 1. Autoprueba.** Complete las frases con la palabra comparativa apropiada.
>
> **a.** como   **b.** que
>
> **1.** más _____   **3.** peor _____   **5.** menos _____
> **2.** tantos _____   **4.** tan _____   **6.** tanta _____

Paso 2. Ahora compárese *(compare yourself)* con su mejor amigo/a, haciendo oraciones con los siguientes verbos y las formas comparativas del **Paso 1** u otras.

MODELO: **1.** tener años → Tengo **tantos años como** mi mejor amiga. (Soy [un año] **mayor/menor que** mi mejor amiga).

1. tener años   **4.** tener dinero   **6.** tener pasión por
2. tomar cursos   **5.** ser inteligente   (el baile/el fútbol/
3. bailar   los estudios...)

Paso 3. Ahora, en parejas, usen las oraciones del **Paso 2** para entrevistarse. Luego digan a la clase algo *(something)* que tienen en común.

MODELO: E1: Tengo tantos años como mi mejor amiga. ¿Y tú?
          E2: Sí, tengo tantos años como mi mejor amiga. (No, soy [un año] mayor que mi mejor amiga).
          EN COMÚN: Las dos tenemos tantos años como nuestras mejores amigas. (Las dos no tenemos tantos años como nuestras mejores amigas).

Prác. A, Paso 1: Answers: 1. b 2. a 3. b 4. a 5. b 6. a

B. Alfredo y Gloria

Alfredo
San José, Costa Rica
Profesor universitario
Casado. (*Married.*) Vive en
una casa cerca del campus.
Dos hijos

Gloria
Punta Arenas, Chile
Estudiante universitaria
Vive en una casa en el centro
con ocho compañeros.
No tiene hijos.

Paso 1. ¿Quién probablemente tiene más de las siguientes cosas y cualidades y quién tiene menos? **¡OJO!** Los dos son similares en los números 4, 5 y 6.

1. botas de invierno
2. camisas de manga (*sleeves*) corta
3. chanclas
4. inteligencia
5. parientes
6. camisetas

Paso 2. ¿Quién probablemente hace más o hace menos? **¡OJO!** Los dos son similares en los números 4, 5 y 6.

1. ganar (*to earn*) dinero
2. salir con sus amigos
3. dormir
4. levantarse temprano
5. hacer ejercicio
6. trabajar

Paso 3. Use los comparativos irregulares para hablar de Alfredo y Gloria.

1. Es obvio que Alfredo tiene más años: es _____ _____ Gloria.
2. Los padres de Alfredo tienen más de 65 años. Probablemente, los padres de Gloria son _____ _____ los padres de Alfredo.
3. Gloria toma clases de danza. Así que (*So*), Gloria baila _____ _____ Alfredo.

C. Opiniones

Paso 1. Complete las siguientes declaraciones para expresar su opinión.

MODELO: las películas / las series: ser / interesante ➔
Las películas **son más** interesantes **que** las series. (**tan... como**)

1. el fútbol / el fútbol americano: ser / aburrido
2. la clase de historia / la clase de español: ser / interesante
3. en esta universidad, las artes / los deportes (*sports*): ser / importante
4. el español / el inglés: ser / difícil
5. mis amigos / mis padres: divertirme con
6. los niños / los adultos: dormir
7. los profesores / los estudiantes: trabajar
8. en primavera / en otoño: llover

 Paso 2. Ahora, en parejas, comparen sus respuestas y expliquen sus opiniones. Luego digan a la clase una idea que los dos comparten (*share*).

D. Más opiniones

Paso 1. Compare las siguientes personas y cosas para expresar su opinión sobre ellas. Puede añadir (*add*) más palabras si quiere.

MODELO: el basquetbol y el golf: interesante, rápido, fácil de aprender ➔
El basquetbol es **menos** interesante **que** el golf.

1. Meryl Streep y Millie Bobby Brown: joven, bonito, tener premios Óscar
2. Usted y sus padres (hijos): joven, conservador, tener experiencia, desordenado
3. un Prius y un Tesla: grande, barato, gastar (*to use*) gasolina, elegante
4. los perros y los gatos: independiente, inteligente, cariñoso, activo
5. Nevada y Delaware: grande, tener habitantes, petróleo, estar lejos de California

(*Continúa*).

Paso 2. En parejas, comparen sus opiniones. Traten de (*Try to*) explicar sus razones. Luego digan a la clase algo (*something*) que tienen en común.

> MODELO: el basquetbol y el golf: interesante, rápido →
> > **E1:** El basquetbol es **menos** interesante **que** el golf.
> > **E2:** No estoy de acuerdo. El basquetbol es **más** interesante **que** el golf porque es **más** rápido.

E. Comparaciones. Complete las siguientes oraciones según su experiencia personal.

1. En mi familia, yo soy mayor que _____ y menor que _____.
2. En esta clase, _____ estudia(n) tanto como yo.
3. En esta universidad, los estudiantes _____ más que _____.
4. _____ es más guapo que Bad Bunny.
5. _____ es más guapa que Shakira.
6. _____ tiene tanto talento como Bruno Mars.

F. La familia de Lucía y Miguel

el abuelo Jaime   Lucía   Miguel   la abuela Lucía   Amalia

Sami   Sancho

Jack Hollingsworth/Getty Images

Lucía con su esposo, sus padres y sus hijos

Paso 1. En parejas, miren la foto e identifiquen a los miembros de la familia de Lucía. Piensen en la edad (*age*) de cada persona.

> MODELO: Sancho es mayor que sus hermanos.

Paso 2. Comparen a cada miembro de la familia con otra persona.

> MODELO: Amalia es menor que Sancho pero es más alta que él.

Paso 3. Ahora comparen a los miembros de su propia familia. Haga por lo menos cinco declaraciones.

> MODELOS: **E1:** Mi hermana Mary es mayor que yo, pero yo soy más alto que ella.
> > **E2:** Mi abuela es mayor que mi abuelo, pero ella es más activa que él.

G. La rutina diaria... en invierno y en verano

Paso 1. ¿Es diferente nuestra rutina diaria en cada estación? Complete las siguientes oraciones sobre su rutina.

Vocabulario útil

el gimnasio
el parque

	EN INVIERNO	EN VERANO
1. Me levanto a _____ (hora).	_____	_____
2. Almuerzo en _____.	_____	_____
3. Me divierto con mis amigos / mi familia en _____.	_____	_____
4. Estudio _____ horas todos los días.	_____	_____
5. Estoy / Me quedo en _____ (lugar) por la noche.	_____	_____
6. Me acuesto a _____ (hora).	_____	_____

Paso 2. En parejas, comparen sus actividades de invierno con las (*those*) de verano.

> MODELOS: **E1:** En invierno, ¿te levantas más temprano que en verano?
> > **E2:** No, en invierno, me levanto tan temprano como en verano. (No, en invierno, me levanto a la misma hora que en verano).

Paso 3. Ahora digan a la clase una o dos cosas que ustedes tienen en común.

> MODELO: Nosotros nos levantamos más tarde en verano que en invierno. En verano no hay clases y, por lo general, nos acostamos más tarde.

⚙ Todo junto

A. Lengua y cultura: Dos hemisferios

Paso 1. Completar. Complete the following paragraphs with the correct forms of the words in parentheses, as suggested by context. When two possibilities are given in parentheses, select the correct word.

Las estaciones del año varían[a] entre el hemisferio norte y sur. Cuando (ser / estar)[1] invierno en este país, por ejemplo, (ser / estar)[2] verano en la Argentina, en Bolivia, en Chile... Cuando yo _____ (salir)[3] para la universidad en enero, con frecuencia tengo que _____ (llevar)[4] abrigo y botas. En (los / las)[5] países del hemisferio sur, un estudiante _____ (poder)[6] asistir (a / de)[7] un concierto en febrero llevando solo pantalones _____ (corto),[8] camiseta y sandalias.

En _____ (mucho)[9] estados de (este / esto)[10] país, (antes de / durante)[11] las vacaciones de diciembre, casi siempre _____ (hacer)[12] frío y a veces _____ (nevar).[13] En _____ (grande)[14] parte de Sudamérica, al otro lado del ecuador, hace calor y (muy / mucho)[15] sol durante (ese / eso)[16] mes. A veces en los periódicos hay fotos de personas que _____ (tomar)[17] el sol y nadan[b] en las playas sudamericanas en enero.

[a]*vary* [b]*swim*

Es diciembre en Buenos Aires. ¿Qué tiempo hace?

Meunierd/Shutterstock

Paso 2. Comprensión. ¿Probable o improbable?

	PROBABLE	IMPROBABLE
1. Los estudiantes argentinos van a la playa en julio.	☐	☐
2. Muchas personas sudamericanas hacen viajes de vacaciones en enero.	☐	☐
3. En Santiago (Chile) hace frío en diciembre.	☐	☐

Paso 3. En acción

En parejas, lean el anuncio (*ad*) del inicio del año escolar (*school*) en el Perú. Luego contesten las preguntas y escriban un párrafo comparando el año escolar en los dos países.

1. ¿En qué mes cae (*occurs*) el inicio del año escolar en los Estados Unidos? ¿En qué estación cae?
2. ¿En qué mes empieza en el Perú? ¿En qué estación cae?
3. ¿Por qué empiezan las clases en meses diferentes en los dos países?
4. ¿Cuándo son las vacaciones de verano en los Estados Unidos?
5. ¿Cuándo creen ustedes que empiezan las vacaciones de verano en el Perú?

Buen inicio del año escolar

10 de marzo

(left): Paul Bradbury/Age fotostock; (center): GlowImages/
Getty Images; (right): Jamie Grill/JGI/Blend Images LLC

⚙️ B. Proyecto: Expresiones comparativas

Robert Giusic/Corbis/Getty Images

Unos pinos altos

👥 ¿Conocen (*Are you familiar with*) las expresiones *fast as lightning* o *slow as molasses*? En español también hay expresiones descriptivas que incluyen comparaciones. En este proyecto van a aprender algunas (*some*) y van a crear (*create*) sus propias expresiones.

Paso 1. Preparación. En grupos, lean las siguientes comparaciones que son aplicables a personas y cosas. Intenten (*Try to*) explicar lo que significan. ¿Creen que son positivas, negativas o neutras? ¿Tienen equivalentes en inglés? ¿Hay algún (*any*) símbolo en particular muy positivo?

1. ser más alto/a que un pino (*pine tree*)
2. ser delgado/a como un espagueti
3. ser más bueno/a que el pan (*bread*)
4. ser más largo/a que una semana sin carne (*meat*)
5. estar más claro que el agua
6. ser más viejo/a que Matusalén (un personaje [*character*] de la Biblia)

Vocabulario útil

ser divertido/a to be fun
ser pesado/a to be overbearing or boring

Holly Hildreth/McGraw Hill

Un vaso de agua

Paso 2. Creación. Ahora, en grupos, creen (*create*) varias comparaciones similares a las (*those*) del **Paso 1** para describir personas, cosas o situaciones. Pueden usar como base expresiones e ideas comunes en su cultura o pueden inventarlas (*invent them*). Luego, den un ejemplo concreto del uso de cada expresión en su entorno (*environment*) universitario. Consideren bien los siguientes factores.

- la estructura de las comparaciones en español
- el uso de los verbos (**ser** / **estar** + adjetivos, expresiones con **tener** + sustantivo...)

MODELO: Comparación: más lento (*slow*) que la melaza (*molasses*)
Ejemplo concreto: Podemos decir que una persona trabaja más lento que la melaza.

Paso 3: Competición. Escuchen las comparaciones de los otros grupos. ¿Cuáles son las expresiones más interesantes y divertidas de todas? ¿Cuál es el grupo más creativo?

Video: Salu2 «En la Mitad del Mundo°» Mitad... *Middle of the World*

You can watch two segments of this chapter's video in the **Video: Salu2** section, found at the end of the eBook.

Klic Video Productions/McGraw Hill

Un maestro tejedor (*master weaver*) ecuatoriano

Enfoque cultural: La diversidad climática

Antes de leer

¿Es muy variado el clima en el país donde usted vive? ¿Cómo es el clima de su estado o región? ¿Varía mucho durante el año?

En Costa Rica

La catarata (*falls*) del río Celeste

Iglesia (*Church*) cerca de San Pedro de Atacama, Chile

En otros países hispanos

- **En Chile** Al norte de este país se encuentra[a] el desierto de Atacama, que es el más seco[b] del mundo.

- **En España** La diversidad climática y geográfica de este país europeo es espectacular para su tamaño.[c] La zona más caliente de Europa (el área de Córdoba y Sevilla) coexiste con una de las cordilleras[d] más altas del continente (la Sierra Nevada). Hasta hay[e] una zona desértica (en Almería).

[a]*se... is found* [b]*mas... driest* [c]*size* [d]*mountain ranges* [e]*Hasta... There's even*

Comprensión ¿Dónde está el desierto de Atacama? ¿Por qué es interesante la geografía española?

Se puede decir[a] que el clima de Costa Rica es tropical. Esto significa que propiamente[b] no tiene una estación de invierno. Lo que sí tiene son dos temporadas:[c] una seca[d] y otra lluviosa.[e] En la mayor parte del país, esta última[f] ocurre entre mayo y noviembre. En las zonas más lluviosas del país, las lluvias son muy abundantes y llegan a ocasionar muchas inundaciones.[g]

Sin embargo, el clima de Costa Rica es muy diverso. Esto llama mucho la atención de los turistas, ya que[h] en pocas horas se puede pasar de un clima lluvioso en las montañas a uno caluroso[i] en la playa.

[a]*say* [b]*really* [c]*seasons* [d]*dry* [e]*rainy* [f]*esta... the latter* [g]*llegan... they cause a lot of floods* [h]*ya... since* [i]*uno... a warm one (i.e., warm climate)*

Comprensión ¿Qué tipo de clima tiene Costa Rica? ¿Cuándo son sus meses secos?

Lectura

Antes de leer

Esta infografía explica cómo prepararse para un fenómeno climático extremo que puede causar un desastre (*disaster*) natural. ¿Cuáles son los fenómenos climáticos extremos más comunes donde usted vive? ¿Cómo se prepara usted para ellos?

 En acción

Usted ya tiene mucha información sobre la geografía y el clima del mundo hispanohablante. Seleccione un país que usted considera ideal para vivir y hablar español. Describa su clima y geografía en unas oraciones y luego escriba una lista de razones para vivir allí.

Prepara a tu familia para la temporada de lluvias

Mi plan familiar en TEMPORADA DE LLUVIAS

La lluvia hace posible la vida,[a] pero puede ser peligrosa también si es demasiado[b] intensa o llueve durante mucho tiempo causando deslaves[c] e inundaciones.[d] Crea un plan familiar para estas emergencias.

1 Planifica

- Prepara tu hogar para fuertes lluvias.
- Crea un plan de evacuación y practica con toda la familia.

2 Prepara la lista

- Haz[e] una lista de cosas necesarias para llevar en caso de evacuación: agua, comida de larga duración, medicinas, documentos, celulares y cargadores, linternas y pilas.

3 Actúa

Si el Servicio de Protección Civil anuncia que tienen que salir...

- conserva la calma
- prepara la bolsa de emergencia
- sigue[f] las instrucciones de Protección Civil

[a]*life* [b]*too* [c]*landslides* [d]*floods* [e]*Make* [f]*follow*

Comprensión

A. Acciones. Indique cuándo se debe (*one should*) hacer las siguientes acciones: antes de la posibilidad de inundación o deslave (**antes**), si hay alerta para los próximos días (**alerta**) o en caso de anuncio de Protección Civil (**anuncio**).

	ANTES	ALERTA	ANUNCIO
1. Mantener la serenidad	☐	☐	☐
2. Pensar en los artículos necesarios en caso de emergencia	☐	☐	☐
3. Decidir la ruta que van a tomar en caso de evacuación	☐	☐	☐
4. Escuchar la radio o la tele para saber si hay anuncio de evacuación	☐	☐	☐
5. Poner las cosas del kit de emergencia en la bolsa	☐	☐	☐
6. Calmar a las personas nerviosas por la evacuación	☐	☐	☐

B. Razones lógicas. Empareje las acciones de la columna A con las razones de la columna B.

A

1. _____ Si preparas tu hogar para fuertes lluvias,
2. _____ Si preparas y practicas un plan de evacuación,
3. _____ Si haces una lista de lo que vas a necesitar para una evacuación,
4. _____ Si conservas la calma,
5. _____ Si sigues las instrucciones de Protección Civil,

B

a. no vas a olvidar (*forget*) artículos importantes.
b. vas a pensar más claramente durante la evacuación.
c. menos agua va a entrar en tu casa.
d. la situación va a ser menos peligrosa para ti y toda la comunidad.
e. no vas a sentir demasiada (*experience too much*) confusión en el momento de salir de la casa.

⚙ Proyecto: Comparación de infografías

Es común usar infografías para educar y alertar a la población porque son textos simples y visuales.

Paso 1. Elija (*Choose*) un fenómeno climático extremo para su investigación (*research*): vientos intensos, huracanes...

Paso 2. Haga una investigación por internet para encontrar infografías sobre el fenómeno climático: una en español de un país hispanohablante y otra de este país.

Paso 3. Estudie las infografías y prepare una breve lista de diferencias y semejanzas (*similarities*) entre ellas. ¿Hay sorpresas?

🔊 Textos orales

El pronóstico° del tiempo en la Argentina

forecast

Antes de escuchar

¿Mira usted el pronóstico del tiempo todos los días? ¿Le gustan los pronósticos con muchos detalles o solo quiere saber (*know*) la información básica, como la temperatura máxima y mínima y si va a hacer sol o va a llover?

Vocabulario para escuchar

despejado	clear, no clouds	**el granizo**	hail
los grados	degrees	**la borrasca**	storm
se espera(n)	is/are expected	**la bajada**	dip, lowering
soleado	sunny	**bajo**	below
la franja	coastal area		

BOLIVIA · PARAGUAY · JUJUY · Salta · BRASIL · CHILE · ARGENTINA · Córdoba · URUGUAY · Mendoza · Buenos Aires · PAMPA · San Carlos de Bariloche · Río Gallegos

Comprensión

A. Temperaturas y condiciones atmosféricas. Complete los espacios en blanco (*blanks*) en el mapa con las temperaturas máximas y mínimas y las condiciones atmosféricas que se mencionan: granizo, lluvia, nieve, sol.

B. El pronóstico en general. Conteste las siguientes preguntas.

1. ¿Qué tiempo va a hacer el domingo en la mayoría de las regiones argentinas?
2. ¿Qué estación es hoy en la Argentina?

👉 En acción

👥 En parejas, entérese del (*find out about the*) pronóstico del tiempo para los próximos dos días en el estado donde viven y preparen un breve pronóstico en español. Intenten (*Try*) usar el vocabulario que se usa en el pronóstico del tiempo argentino.

PORTAFOLIO

Purestock/Getty Images

Entrevista

Use de modelo las preguntas y respuestas de la sección **Entrevista** al principio (*at the beginning*) de este capítulo para hablar del clima donde usted vive y de su estación del año favorita y lo que le gusta hacer en esa estación.

Escritura

Un ensayo sobre preferencias climáticas

En este ensayo, va a escribir sobre sus preferencias con respecto al tiempo y las preferencias de sus compañeros. ¿Cuál es su estación favorita? ¿Con qué la asocia (*do you associate it*)? ¿Cuál es la estación del año que menos le gusta? ¿Por qué? ¿Cree que hay una estación más o menos popular, en general? ¿Puede justificar su opinión?

Antes de escribir

Elena Zajchikova/Shutterstock

Las cuatro estaciones del año

Entreviste a dos personas de la clase sobre la estación del año que más les gusta (*they like the most*) y la que (*that which*) menos les gusta. También debe preguntarles por qué. Complete la tabla con la información respectiva.

nombre	estación preferida	estación que menos le gusta	¿por qué?
yo			
compañero/a 1			
compañero/a 2			

A escribir

Ahora use sus opiniones y las respuestas de sus compañeros para escribir su ensayo. Hay más ayuda (*help*) en Connect.

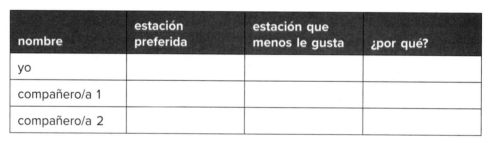

Para escribir bien

Recuerde (*Remember*) y considere las siguientes opciones para su ensayo.

- Conectores: **además, por eso, sin embargo...**
- Comparaciones:
  más/menos... que, tan/tant(o/a/os/as)... como...
- Otras palabras útiles: **afuera, ahora mismo, todavía...**

🔆 En la comunidad

Entreviste (*Interview*) a una persona hispana de su universidad o ciudad sobre el clima de su país de origen y los horarios (*schedules*) de clases durante el año.

Preguntas posibles

- ¿Hay en su país cuatro estaciones o solo dos?
- ¿Coinciden con las estaciones del lugar donde usted vive ahora?
- ¿Cómo es el clima en cada estación?
- ¿En qué mes empiezan las clases en las escuelas? ¿Y en qué mes terminan?

🎬 Producción audiovisual

Mire (*Look at*) el pronóstico del tiempo de su ciudad para los próximos tres días y filme su propio informe meteorológico. Puede tener un tono serio o cómico.

Más ideas para el portafolio

- Incluya (*Include*) una imagen del mapa del tiempo de una ciudad donde usted desea vivir. Explique por qué le gusta (o no le gusta) el tiempo de esta ciudad.
- Dé tres palabras que usted asocia con el clima del estado donde vive y tres palabras que asocia con el clima del estado o país donde le gustaría (*you would like*) vivir en el futuro. Incluya una foto que represente el clima de su estado o el clima del país de su futuro.
- Si ha estado jugando (*you have been playing*) Practice Spanish: Study Abroad, en Quest 4 usted participó (*participated*) en una telenovela (*soap opera*) sobre una compañía que se especializa en la moda. Busque información en internet sobre dos personas hispanas famosas en la industria de la moda y escriba por lo menos seis oraciones que los comparen (*compare them*). Incluya una foto de cada una y escriba dos o tres oraciones sobre la ropa que llevan en la foto.

Sugerencia: You are now ready to play Quest 4 in **Practice Spanish: Study Abroad.**

AFTER STUDYING THIS CHAPTER I CAN ...

- ☐ talk about the weather (170)
- ☐ talk about months and seasons of the year and express dates (173)
- ☐ use prepositions and cardinal points to locate people, places, and things (175)
- ☐ use the present progressive to express what I'm doing right now (177–178)
- ☐ use the verbs **ser** and **estar** correctly, especially with adjectives (182–184)
- ☐ compare people, places, things, and actions (189–192)
- ☐ recognize/describe at least 2–3 aspects of Costa Rican cultures

Gramática en breve

15. Present Progressive estar + -ndo
-ar → -ando
-er/-ir → -iendo

unaccented -i- → -y- (le**y**endo)

-ir stem-changing Verbs: e → i (p**i**diendo)
o → u (d**u**rmiendo)

16. Summary of the Uses of *ser* **and** *estar*

ser	estar
inherent qualities, characteristics	mental, physical, health conditions
identification (including profession)	location
nationality, origin	present progressive
material	fixed expressions
possession	
for whom intended	
time and date	
generalizations	

Idioms with tener (expressing *to be*)
tener (mucho) calor, (mucho) frío

17. Comparisons

Comparisons of Inequality	Comparisons of Equality
más/menos... que	**tan... como**
más/menos que	**tanto/a/os/as... como**
más/menos de + *número*	
mayor/menor que	
mejor/peor que	

Vocabulario

Los verbos

celebrar	to celebrate
continuar (continúo)	to continue
pasar	to happen
pasar tiempo	to spend time
quedarse	to stay, remain (*in a place*)
seguir (sigo) (i)	to continue
Repaso: divertirse (me divierto) (i)	

Remember that the parenthetical letter gives you the stem change for the present participle.

¿Qué tiempo hace?

el clima	climate
está...	it's ...
(muy) fresco	(very) cool
(muy) nublado	(very) cloudy, overcast
hace...	it's ...
(muy) buen/mal tiempo	(very) good/bad weather, (very) nice/bad out
(mucho) calor	(very) hot
(mucho) frío	(very) cold
(mucho) sol	(very) sunny
(mucho) viento	(very) windy
hay (mucha) contaminación	there's (lots of) pollution
llover: llueve	to rain: it rains, it's raining
la lluvia	rain
nevar: nieva	to snow: it snows, it's snowing
la nieve	snow
el tiempo	weather; time
¿qué tiempo hace?	what's the weather like?

Los meses del año

¿Cuál es la fecha de hoy? / ¿Qué fecha es hoy?	What's today's date?
el primero de	the first of (*month*)

enero	abril	**julio**	**octubre**
febrero	mayo	**agosto**	**noviembre**
marzo	junio	**septiembre**	**diciembre**

el año	year
la fecha	date (*calendar*)
el mes	month

Las estaciones del año

la primavera	spring
el verano	summer

el otoño	fall, autumn
el invierno	winter
la estación	season

Los lugares

la capital	capital city
la playa	beach

Otros sustantivos

el cumpleaños	birthday
la medianoche	midnight
el mediodía	noon
el/la novio/a	boyfriend/girlfriend
la respuesta	answer

Los adjetivos

abierto/a	open
aburrido/a	bored
alegre	happy
cansado/a	tired
cariñoso/a	affectionate
cerrado/a	closed
congelado/a	frozen; very cold
contento/a	content, happy
desordenado/a	messy
difícil	hard, difficult
enfermo/a	sick
fácil	easy
furioso/a	furious, angry
limpio/a	clean
loco/a	crazy
mismo/a	same
molesto/a	annoyed
nervioso/a	nervous
ocupado/a	busy
ordenado/a	neat
preocupado/a	worried
querido/a	dear
seguro/a	sure, certain
sucio/a	dirty
triste	sad

Las comparaciones

más/menos de + number	more/fewer than + number
más/menos que	more/less than
más/menos... que	more/less (-er) ... than
tan... como	as ... as
tanto como	as much as
tanto/a/os/as... como	as much/many ... as

mayor(es) (que)	older (than)
mejor(es) (que)	better (than); best
menor(es) (que)	younger (than)
peor(es) (que)	worse (than)

Las preposiciones

a la derecha de	to the right of
a la izquierda de	to the left of
al lado de	alongside of
cerca de	close to
debajo de	below
delante de	in front of
detrás de	behind
encima de	on top of
entre	between; among
lejos de	far from

Los puntos cardinales

el norte, el sur, el este, el oeste

Palabras adicionales

afuera (adv.)	outdoors
ahora mismo	right now
conmigo	with me
contigo	with you (fam.)
está bien	it's fine, OK
esta noche	tonight
estar bien	to be comfortable (temperature)
mí (obj. of prep.)	me
por	because of; about
sin embargo	nevertheless
tener (mucho) calor	to be (very) warm, hot
tener (mucho) frío	to be (very) cold
ti (obj. of prep.)	you (fam.)
todavía	still

Repaso: estar de acuerdo

Vocabulario personal

Use this space or a vocabulary notebook to write down other words and phrases you learn in this chapter.

7

¡A comer!°

¡A... *Let's eat!*

En este capítulo

VOCABULARY
Foods and meals   206
Two verbs that express *to know*   210

GRAMMAR
Using direct objects (*what* or *who*[*m*]) after a verb   213
Words like *some*, *none*, and *no one*   219
Telling someone to do something   223

COUNTRY OF FOCUS: PANAMA

Un puesto (*stand*) de fruta y vegetales en Panamá

The Visual Explorer/Shutterstock

PANAMÁ

4,2 (coma dos) millones de habitantes

- Vasco Núñez de Balboa fue[a] el primer europeo que vio[b] el océano Pacífico en 1514, desde una colina[c] de Panamá. Este descubrimiento[d] cambió[e] la comprensión[f] de la geografía de nuestro planeta.

- El arroz con pollo[g] es uno de los platos[h] panameños más típicos. Es también típico el sancocho, un tipo de sopa que muestra[i] la influencia de varias culturas: la indígena, la hispana, la africana y la afroantillana.[j]

[a]*was* [b]*saw* [c]*hill* [d]*discovery* [e]*changed* [f]*understanding* [g]*arroz... chicken with rice* [h]*dishes* [i]*shows* [j]*Afro-Caribbean*

 ## ENTREVISTA

These questions related to the chapter theme are answered here by a native speaker. You will be able to ask and answer them yourself with personal information in the **Entrevista** activity in the **Portafolio** section at the end of the chapter.

Manuel Gil del Valle contesta las preguntas.

– ¿Cuál es su comida[a] favorita?

– Eso es difícil de contestar porque me gusta comer bien y me gusta casi todo. Pero si tengo que elegir un plato[b], elijo la paella de mariscos.[c]

– ¿Cuáles son algunos[d] de los platos típicos de su país?

– Los «nacatamales» son muy populares. Son tamales muy grandes, rellenos de carne, verduras, arroz, ciruelas[e] y otros ingredientes más. Una bebida típicamente nicaragüense es el pinolillo, una especie de horchata hecha de harina de maíz.[f] Pero en Nicaragua también son populares las comidas originarias de otros países, como la española, italiana, mexicana, china, etcétera.

– ¿Dónde y a qué hora almuerza y cena[g] usted, por lo general?

– Trabajo en el centro de Managua. Así que,[h] por lo general, almuerzo en uno de los muchos restaurantes pequeños que hay en el centro. La hora siempre depende del trabajo, pero con frecuencia almuerzo al mediodía. ¿Y la cena? Casi siempre cenamos en casa con toda la familia, a eso de[i] las ocho. Mi esposa es una cocinera[j] estupenda.

[a]*food* [b]*dish* [c]*paella... seafood paella* [d]*some* [e]*rellenos... stuffed with meat, vegetables, rice, plums* [f]*hecha... made with corn flour* [g]*have dinner* [h]*Así... So* [i]*a... around* [j]*cook*

VOCABULARIO: PREPARACIÓN

You can hear the pronunciation of theme vocabulary words and phrases in the eBook.

La comida y las comidas°

La... *Food and meals*

el desayuno

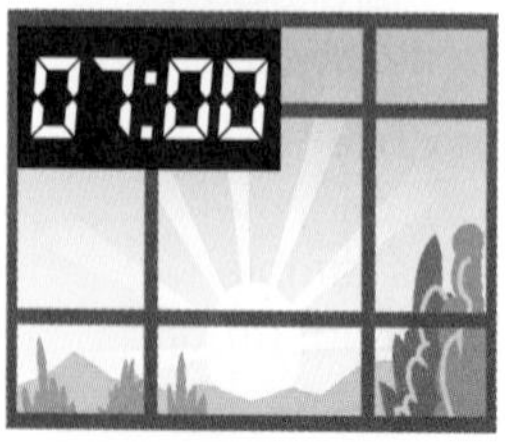

07:00

desayunar

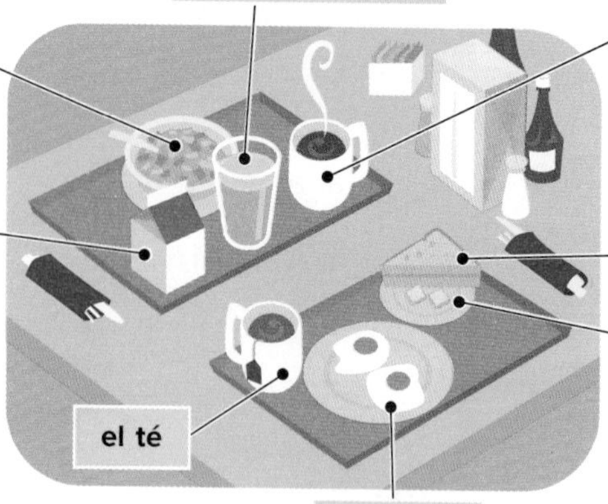

el jugo (de fruta)
el cereal
el café
la leche
el pan tostado
la mantequilla
el té
el huevo

el almuerzo

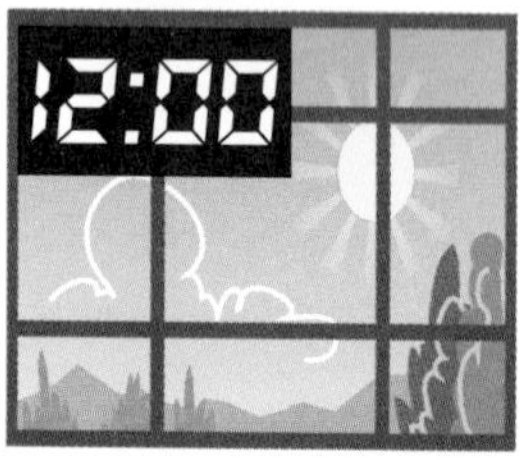

12:00

almorzar (almuerzo)

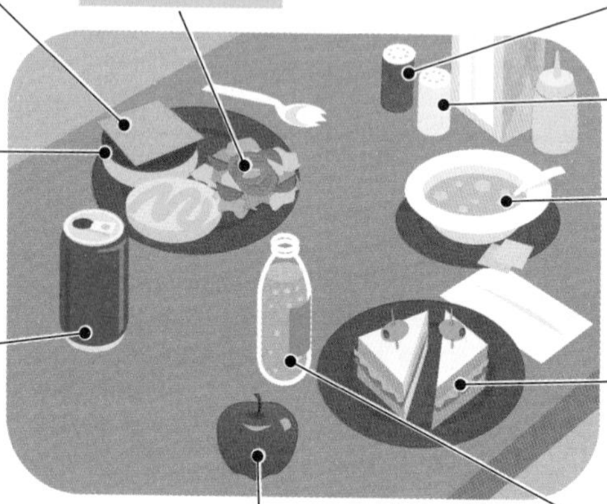

el queso
la ensalada
la pimienta
la sal
la hamburguesa
la sopa
el refresco
el sándwich
la manzana
el agua (mineral)

la cena

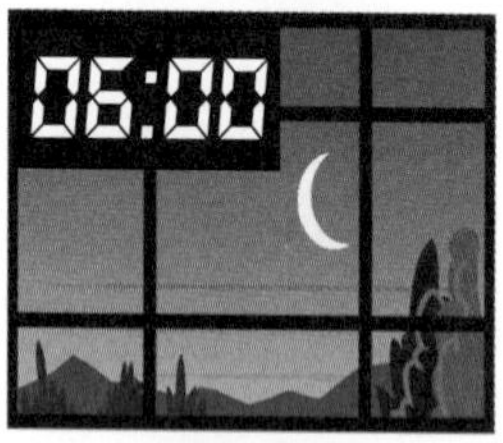

06:00

cenar

la papa
el bistec
el vino blanco
el vino tinto
el pan
el pastel
los espárragos
el pescado
el pollo (asado)
el arroz
la cerveza

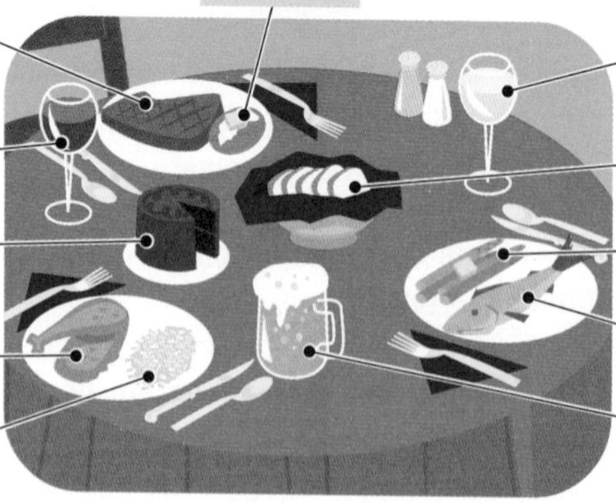

¡OJO!

The noun **agua** is feminine, but it is used with masculine articles in the singular and feminine adjectives: **el agua fría**. This occurs with feminine nouns that begin with a stressed **a-**. Other examples**: el águila** (*eagle*), **el alma** (*soul*).

Otras frutas

la **banana**	banana
la **naranja**	orange

Otras verduras

el **aguacate**	avocado
las **arvejas**	green peas
la **cebolla**	onion
los **champiñones**	mushrooms
los **frijoles**	beans
los **garbanzos**	chickpeas
la **lechuga**	lettuce
el **pepino**	cucumber
el **tomate**	tomato
la **zanahoria**	carrot

Otras carnes

la **barbacoa**	barbeque
la **chuleta (de cerdo)**	(pork) chop
el **jamón**	ham
el **pavo**	turkey
la **salchicha**	sausage; hot dog

Otros pescados y mariscos

el **atún**	tuna
los **camarones**	shrimp
la **langosta**	lobster
el **salmón**	salmon

Otros postres

los **dulces**	sweets; candy
el **flan**	(baked) custard
la **galleta**	cookie
el **helado**	ice cream

Otras comidas

el **aceite (de oliva)**	(olive) oil
el **azúcar**	sugar
la **salsa**	salsa
el **yogur**	yogurt

Los verbos

alm<u>o</u>rzar (alm<u>ue</u>rzo)	to have (eat) lunch
cenar	to have (eat) dinner, supper
cocinar	to cook
desayunar	to have (eat) breakfast

Así se dice

There is great variety in the words used to refer to foods in the Spanish-speaking world. The following are only a few of the most common ones.

las arvejas = los guisantes (*Sp.*)	la papa = la patata (*Sp.*)
los camarones = las gambas (*Sp.*)	el refresco = la gaseosa, la soda
el jugo = el zumo (*Sp.*)	(**¡OJO!** = *soda water* in some areas)

There are **supermercados** everywhere. But there are many words for food stores, depending on the country: **la tienda de alimentos** o **comestibles, la bodega** (the Caribbean, U.S.), **la pulpería** (C.A., S.A.), and **la trucha** (C.A.), and so on.

Nota comunicativa: Más vocabulario para hablar de la comida

¡Buen provecho!	Bon appetit!
t<u>e</u>ner (mucha) hambre	to be (very) hungry
t<u>e</u>ner (mucha) sed	to be (very) thirsty
mer<u>e</u>ndar (mer<u>ie</u>ndo)	to snack
la **merienda**	snack
la **cocina**	cuisine
los **comestibles**	groceries, foodstuff
el **plato**	plate; dish (*food prepared in a particular way*); course
el **plato principal**	main course
caliente	hot (*in temperature, not taste*)
frito/a	fried
picante	hot, spicy
rico/a	tasty, savory; rich (*in calories*)

La merienda (typically a late afternoon snack) is a traditional custom in those countries where the dinner hour is quite late, such as Spain, for example, where people may have dinner at 10:00 or 11:00 P.M. or even later. **La merienda** tides people over until the late evening meal.

You will use these words and phrases in **Comunicación A** and **B.**

Comunicación

A. Menús

Paso 1. Empareje cada comida con su descripción.

DESCRIPCIONES

1. _____ una sopa fría, langosta, espárragos, ensalada de lechuga y tomate, vino blanco y, para terminar, un pastel

2. _____ jugo de fruta, huevos con jamón, pan tostado y café

3. _____ un vaso (*glass*) de leche y unas galletas

4. _____ pollo asado, arroz, arvejas, agua mineral y, para terminar, una manzana

5. _____ una hamburguesa con papas fritas, un refresco y un helado

COMIDAS

a. un menú ligero (*light*)
b. una comida rápida
c. una cena elegante
d. un desayuno estilo estadounidense
e. una merienda

Paso 2. Ahora, en parejas, túrnense para describir su menú favorito para cada una de las comidas de un día, incluyendo la merienda (*afternoon snack*). Puede ser para un día normal o para un día especial.

B. Definiciones

Paso 1. Empareje cada adivinanza con lo que significa.

A

1. _____ Rojo y anaranjado por fuera[a], amarillo por dentro[b] y con un corazón[c] en el centro.

a.

Anna Kucherova/ 123RF

2. _____ Delgada y larga, lleva pelo[d] verde y es anaranjada. ¿Qué es?

b. el durazno

Maks Narodenko/ Shutterstock

3. _____ Con tomate y con lechuga, en la ensalada puedo estar; puedo ser un poco picante[e] y te puedo hacer llorar.[f]

c.

Andrjuss/ Shutterstock

4. _____ Soy verde, amarilla o roja. Voy con tu almuerzo o en dulces y tortas[g], pero no voy en la sopa.

d.

Valentina Razumova/Shutterstock

[a]por... *outside*   [b]por... *inside*   [c]*heart*   [d]*hair*   [e]*sharp*   [f]te... *I can make you cry*
[g]*pies*

Paso 2. Ahora, en parejas, inventen una o dos adivinanzas sobre las comidas para que el resto de la clase adivine (*for the rest of the class to guess*). ¡No necesitan rima, pero sí creatividad!

Nota cultural: La comida del mundo hispano

No se puede hablar de una sola comida hispana, porque en el mundo hispanohablante hay una gran variedad culinaria.

- La comida cambia de país a país, dependiendo de los productos locales y de influencias nativas y externas. Sin embargo, sí hay productos de origen americano que se utilizan[a] en prácticamente todas las cocinas latinoamericanas: el maíz, las papas, los frijoles, los tomates y los aguacates.
- El arroz es también fundamental, pero es de origen asiático. Fue introducido en las Américas por[b] los españoles.

Una de las influencias básicas en la cocina de todos los países latinoamericanos es la cocina española. Se combina con la tradición culinaria indígena de cada región y, en algunos[c] países, también con la tradición culinaria africana, gracias a la influencia de las personas esclavizadas[d] que fueron traídas[e] a América.

Nicholas Gill/Alamy Stock Photo

El maíz, uno de los ingredientes básicos de casi todos los países latinoamericanos

¿Cuáles son los ingredientes básicos de la cocina de su familia o su país?

[a]se... *are used* [b]*by* [c]*some* [d]personas... *enslaved people* [e]fueron... *were brought*

 C. Consejos (*Advice*) a la hora de comer. ¿Qué puede comer o beber su compañero/a en las siguientes situaciones? Dé consejos, según el modelo.

MODELO: **1.** Tengo mucha/poca hambre (sed). →
    E1: Tengo mucha hambre.
    E2: Puedes comer un bistec con papas fritas.

1. Tengo mucha/poca hambre (sed).
2. Tengo hambre a las cuatro de la mañana, después de una fiesta.
3. Estoy a dieta.
4. Estoy de vacaciones en Maine (Texas, California, la Florida,...).
5. Es hora de merendar. Estoy en casa (la universidad).
6. Soy vegano/a.

D. Las preferencias gastronómicas

Paso 1. Complete las siguientes oraciones para describir lo que usted come y no come.
1. Por la mañana siempre como _____.
2. En el desayuno me gusta comer _____.
3. Para cenar, prefiero comer _____.
4. Nunca como _____ y nunca bebo _____.
5. No me gusta comer _____, pero lo/la como (*I eat it*) en casa de mis padres/hijos/abuelos.

Paso 2. Haga una lista de los tres tipos de cocinas que usted prefiere.

 Paso 3. Entre todos, comparen las listas. ¿Cuáles son los platos, lugares para comer y cocinas favoritos de la clase? ¿Cuáles son los ingredientes más necesarios para cocinar sus platos favoritos?

¿Qué sabe usted y a quién conoce?° ¿Qué... *What do you know and who do you know?*

As you know, two Spanish verbs express *to be:* **ser** and **estar.** They are not interchangeable, and their use depends on the meaning the speaker wishes to express. Similarly, two Spanish verbs express *to know:* **saber** and **conocer.** Note their uses in the drawings and text below.

saber
- un número de teléfono
- un nombre (Juan, María)
- que el cálculo es difícil
- tocar el piano
- una dirección (Avenida Juárez, 47)
- la letra (palabras) de una canción

conocer
- <u>a</u> una persona
- una ciudad o un país
- una cosa o una situación

<u>saber</u> = to know (*facts, information*)

+ *inf.* = to know how to (*do something*)

<u>sé</u>	sabemos
sabes	sabéis
sabe	saben

cono<u>c</u>er = to know (*a person*)

to meet (*a person*)

to be acquainted, familiar with (*a place or thing*)

cono<u>zc</u>o	conocemos
conoces	conocéis
conoce	conocen

¡OJO!

Note the **a** before the phrase **una persona,** and before **quién** in the title of this section (¿**a** **quién conoce?**). You will learn about this **a** in **Gramática 18** in this chapter. For now, always use it when you see it in the text.

Algo sobre Rubén Blades

El panameño Rubén Blades (1948–) es uno de los cantautores[a] de salsa más conocidos[b] en todo el mundo. Su álbum *Siembra*[c] se considera uno de los más importantes de la historia salsera. Además de[d] músico, Blades es actor, abogado[e] y político.

 ¿Tiene usted un cantautor favorito? ¿Quién es?

[a]*singer-songwriters* [b]*más... best known, most famous* [c]*Planting time* [d]*Además... Besides being a* [e]*lawyer*

Rubén Blades, en un concierto en Miami

John Parra/Getty Images

Comunicación

A. ¿Cuánto sabe usted de Panamá?

Paso 1. ¿Cierto o falso? Complete las oraciones con la forma **yo** del verbo **saber** o **conocer.** Luego diga si las oraciones son ciertas o falsas para usted.

		CIERTO	FALSO
1.	_____ Panamá.	☐	☐
2.	_____ dónde está Panamá.	☐	☐
3.	_____ el nombre de la capital de Panamá.	☐	☐
4.	_____ a una persona panameña famosa.	☐	☐
5.	_____ quién es Rubén Blades.	☐	☐
6.	_____ la música de Blades.	☐	☐
7.	_____ la letra de una canción de Blades.	☐	☐
8.	_____ bailar salsa.	☐	☐
9.	_____ un restaurante panameño.	☐	☐

Paso 2. Ahora, en parejas, túrnense para hacer y contestar preguntas basadas en las oraciones del **Paso 1.**

MODELO: **1. E1:** ¿Conoces Panamá?
        E2: No, no conozco Panamá. ¿Y tú?
        E1: Yo sí. / Yo tampoco. (*Me neither.*)

B. Los usos de *saber* y *conocer*

Paso 1. Llene (*Fill in*) los espacios en blanco con la forma apropiada de **saber.**

—¿(Tú) _____¹ si hay un restaurante panameño cerca de aquí?

—¡Cómo no!ᵃ Hay uno en la calleᵇ Park. El chef, Felipe, _____² hacer unos platos muy originales.

—¿(Tú) _____³ a qué hora abren los sábados?

—(Yo) No _____⁴ exactamente. ¡Pero _____⁵ que tiene una página web!

ᵃ¡Cómo... *Of course!* ᵇ*street*

Paso 2. Ahora llene los espacios en blanco con la forma apropiada de **conocer.** Luego dé su equivalente en inglés.

—¿(Tú) _____¹ ese restaurante panameño que está en la calle Park?

—Sí, y también (yo) _____² al chef, Felipe.

—¿Ah sí? Yo loᵃ quiero _____³. Es muy famoso.

ᵃ*him*

C. ¿Dónde cenamos?

Paso 1. Lola y Manolo quieren salir a cenar. Complete su diálogo con las formas apropiadas de **saber** o **conocer.**

LOLA: ¿(Tú) _____¹ adónde quieres ir a cenar?

MANOLO: No _____².¿Y tú?

LOLA: No, pero hay un restaurante nuevo en la calleᵃ Betis. Creo que se llama Guadalquivir. ¿_____³ el restaurante?

MANOLO: No, pero (yo) _____⁴ que tiene mucha fama. Es el restaurante favorito de Pepa. Ella _____⁵ al dueño.ᵇ

LOLA: ¿(Tú) _____⁶ qué tipo de comida tienen?

MANOLO: Creo que española. Tenemos que llamarᶜ a Pepa porque quiere venir con nosotros. ¿(Tú) _____⁷ su teléfono?

LOLA: Sí, está en mi celular.

(*Continúa.*)

ᵃ*street* ᵇ*owner* ᶜ*call*

Vocabulario: Preparación

Paso 2. Comprensión. Conteste las siguientes preguntas.

1. ¿Saben Lola y Manolo dónde quieren cenar?
2. ¿Conocen el nuevo restaurante?
3. ¿Saben qué tipo de comida se sirve allí?
4. ¿Saben el número de teléfono de Pepa?
5. ¿Conocen al dueño del restaurante?

D. Encuesta (*Poll*) sobre los talentos especiales de la clase

Paso 1. Haga una lista de dos cosas interesantes que usted sabe hacer bien. Use infinitivos, según el modelo.

MODELO: tocar el acordeón, hacer paella, esquiar

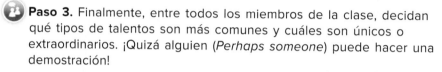 **Paso 2.** Ahora haga una encuesta entre las personas de clase para ver si los talentos de usted son únicos o comunes en su clase.

MODELO: tocar el acordeón → ¿**Sabes** tocar el acordeón?

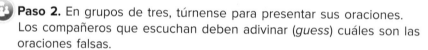 **Paso 3.** Finalmente, entre todos los miembros de la clase, decidan qué tipos de talentos son más comunes y cuáles son únicos o extraordinarios. ¡Quizá alguien (*Perhaps someone*) puede hacer una demostración!

E. ¿Sabe usted mentir (*to lie*) bien?

Paso 1. Escriba dos oraciones con **saber** sobre algunas (*some*) cosas que sabe hacer y dos oraciones sobre personas interesantes que conoce. Algunas oraciones deben ser falsas. **¡OJO!** No olvide (*Don't forget*) usar la **a** con **conocer**.

Paso 2. En grupos de tres, túrnense para presentar sus oraciones. Los compañeros que escuchan deben adivinar (*guess*) cuáles son las oraciones falsas.

Este joven sabe tocar el acordeón.

¡OJO!

conocer a (una persona)

Conozco **a** Rubén Blades.

Vocabulario útil

la mentira   lie, falsehood

Algo sobre el canal de Panamá, un símbolo nacional

Es una de las obras[a] de ingeniería más importantes del mundo por su impacto en el transporte mundial. Une el mar Caribe con el océano Pacífico. Fue inaugurado[b] en 1914. Antes de su existencia, los barcos tenían que dar la vuelta por el estrecho de Magallanes.[c] La ruta del canal fue descubierta[d] en 1514 por el explorador español Vasco Núñez de Balboa. Desde entonces[e] los españoles tuvieron[f] la idea de construir un canal. Pero su construcción no se hizo[g] realidad hasta principios del siglo XX.[h] Recientemente, el canal se ha ampliado.[i]

El canal de Panamá: 48 millas de canales y esclusas (*locks*)

Nombre dos obras de ingeniería muy importantes en los Estados Unidos. ¿Por qué son importantes?

[a]*works* [b]*Fue... It was opened* [c]*tenían... had to go around the Strait of Magellan* [d]*discovered* [e]*Desde... Since then* [f]*had* [g]*no... didn't become* [h]*principios... the beginning of the 20th century* [i]*se... has been enlarged*

18 Expressing *what* or *who(m)* • Direct Objects; The Personal a; Direct Object Pronouns

Gramática en acción: La pirámide alimenticia

Dulces

Carnes rojas

ALGUNAS VECES[a] AL MES
Pollo   Legumbres[b]

Huevos

Pescado

ALGUNAS VECES A LA SEMANA
Leche   Aceite   Queso   Yogures

Verduras   Papas

Frutas

Pan   Cereales   Pasta   Arroz

TODOS LOS DÍAS

[a]Algunas... *Several times*   [b]*Legumes*

¿Y usted?

Indique cuáles de estas declaraciones expresan lo que usted hace.

1. el pollo
- **Lo** como todos los días. Por eso tengo que comprar**lo** con frecuencia.
- **Lo** como de vez en cuando (*once in a while*). Por eso no **lo** compro a menudo (*often*).
- Nunca **lo** como. No necesito comprar**lo**.

2. la fruta
- **La** como todos los días. Por eso tengo que comprar**la** con frecuencia.
- **La** como de vez en cuando. Por eso no **la** compro a menudo.
- Nunca **la** como. No necesito comprar**la**.

3. los refrescos
- **Los** bebo todos los días. Por eso tengo que comprar**los** con frecuencia.
- **Los** bebo de vez en cuando. Por eso no **los** compro a menudo.
- Nunca **los** bebo. No necesito comprar**los**.

4. las bananas
- **Las** como todos los días. Por eso tengo que comprar**las** con frecuencia.
- **Las** como de vez en cuando. Por eso no **las** compro a menudo.
- Nunca **las** como. No necesito comprar**las**.

Direct Objects / **Los complementos directos**

In English and in Spanish, the *direct object* (**el complemento directo**) of a sentence answers the question *what?* or *who(m)?* in relation to the subject and verb.

> *the direct object* / **el complemento directo** = the noun or pronoun that receives the action of the verb

SUBJECT (S)	VERB (V)	DIRECT OBJECT (DO)
Ana	is preparing	**dinner.**
They	can't hear	**the waiter.**

What is Ana preparing? → **dinner**
Who(m) can't they hear? → **the waiter**

Indicate the subjects, verbs, and direct objects in the following sentences.

1. *I don't see Betty and Mary here.*
2. *We don't have any money.*
3. No veo a Betty y María aquí.
4. No tenemos dinero.
5. Julio va a poner la sopa en la mesa.
6. ¿Necesitas el libro y un bolígrafo?

The Personal **a** / **La *a* personal**

In Spanish, the word **a** immediately precedes the direct object of a sentence when the direct object refers to a specific person or persons. This **a**, called the *personal a* (**la *a* personal**), has no equivalent in English.

Vamos a visitar **a nuestros abuelos.**
We're going to visit our grandparents.
but
Vamos a visitar **la casa de nuestros abuelos.**
We're going to visit our grandparents' house.

Necesitan **a sus padres.**
They need their parents.
but
Necesitan **el coche de sus padres.**
They need their parents' car.

The personal **a** is not used when the direct object is a nonspecific person or an unknown person.

Conozco **a un buen chef.**
I know a great chef.
but
Necesito **un buen chef para una fiesta.**
I need a great chef for a party.

Pets (but not all animals) are treated like people and take the personal **a.**

¿Ves **a Bear,** mi perro?
Do you see Bear, my dog?
but
¿Ves **el perro** allí?
Do you see the dog over there?

¡OJO!

The personal **a** is used before the interrogative words **¿quién?** and **¿quiénes?** when they function as direct objects.

¿A quién llamas? **¿al** camarero?
Who(m) are you calling? The waiter?

¡OJO!

The English verbs *to listen **to** / look **at** / look **for** / wait **for*** require prepositional phrases (a *preposition* + *noun* or *pronoun*). However, the Spanish equivalents of those verbs (**escuchar, mirar, buscar,** and **esperar**) are not followed by prepositions. They *are* followed by the personal **a** before a specific person or pet. Compare these pairs of sentences.

Miro el menú. *I'm looking at the menu.*
Miro **al** niño. *I'm looking at the boy.*

Espero el autobús. *I'm waiting for the bus.*
Espero **al** niño. *I'm waiting for the boy.*

¡OJO!

Don't confuse the personal **a** with other uses of the word **a** that you have learned so far.

- **a** = the preposition *to*
- **a** = used after some verbs before an infinitive

Voy **a** la universidad.
En esta clase **aprendemos a** hablar español.
Vamos a salir mañana.

Direct Object Pronouns / **Los pronombres del complemento directo**

me	me	**nos**	us
te	you (*fam. sing.*)	**os**	you (*fam. pl.*)
lo	you (*form. sing.*), him, it (*m.*)	**los**	you (*form. pl.*), them (*m., m. + f.*)
la	you (*form. sing.*), her, it (*f.*)	**las**	you (*form. pl.*), them (*f.*)

1. Direct Object Pronouns

Like direct object nouns, *direct object pronouns* (**los pronombres del complemento directo**) are the first recipient of the action of the verb.

If the direct object noun were repeated in the English answer, it would sound very repetitive: *"Where are the carrots?" "Do you need the carrots right now?"* Direct object pronouns avoid that kind of unnecessary repetition: *"Do you need **them** right now?"*

—Necesito **una receta** para hacer empanadas.
—¿**La** necesitas ahora mismo?
*"I need **a recipe** for making empanadas."*
*"Do you need **it** right now?"*

2. Placement of Direct Object Pronouns with Conjugated Verbs and *no*

In Spanish, direct object pronouns are placed:

- before a conjugated verb
- after the word **no** when it appears

—¿Quién **te** llama más por teléfono?
—Mi madre **me** llama más.
"Who calls you the most?"
"My mother calls me the most."

—¿Conoces a **Diego**?
—No, no **lo** conozco.
"Do you know Diego?"
"No, I don't know him."

3. With Infinitives or Present Participles

The pronouns either precede the conjugated verb or follow (and are attached to it) when the conjugated verb is followed by:

- the infinitive
- the present participle

Las tengo que leer.
Tengo que leer**las**. } *I have to read them.*

Lo estoy comiendo.
Estoy comiéndo**lo**. } *I am eating it.*

¡OJO!

When the pronoun is added to the end of a present participle, an accent mark is added to retain the original stress: **mirando → mirándolo.**

4. Multiple Meanings of *lo/la/los/las*

Note that the direct object pronouns **lo/la/los/las** have different meanings depending on the context. In the following sentences, it is impossible to know what **lo** and **las** mean.

No **lo** veo.

lo = { el pan (*it*)
al niño (*him*)
a usted (*you [form., sing., masc.]*)

Las oigo bien.

Las = { las guitarras (*them*)
a las niñas (*them*)
a ustedes (*you [form., pl., fem.]*)

5. The Pronoun *lo*

The direct object pronoun **lo** can also refer to actions, situations, or ideas in general. When used in this way, **lo** expresses English *it* or *that.*

Lo comprende muy bien.
He understands it (that) very well.

No **lo** creo.
I don't believe it (that).

Lo sé.
I know (it).

Summary of Direct Object Pronouns

yo →	**me**
tú →	**te**
usted, él →	**lo**
usted, ella →	**la**
nosotros/as →	**nos**
vosotros/as →	**os**
ustedes, ellos →	**los**
ustedes, ellas →	**las**

A. ¿Los conoce? ¿Los necesita?

Paso 1. Autoprueba. Haga oraciones completas con **(No) Conozco...** y **(No) Necesito...** Use la **a** personal y la contracción **al** cuando sea (*whenever it is*) necesario.

(No) Conozco...

1. el presidente / la presidenta del país en persona.
2. la ciudad de Nueva York.
3. el estado de Montana.
4. el profesor / la profesora _____ (apellido).
5. los padres de mi compañero/a de cuarto.

(No) Necesito...

6. el libro de texto en esta clase.
7. más clases para graduarme.
8. mi familia.
9. mis buenos amigos.
10. mi perro/gato.

Paso 2. Ahora vuelva a expresar las oraciones del **Paso 1** con el pronombre del complemento directo apropiado.

MODELO: **1.** Conozco al presidente del país en persona. → **Lo** conozco.

Paso 3. Ahora, en parejas, túrnense para hacer preguntas usando las oraciones del **Paso 1** y contestarlas usando pronombres como en el **Paso 2.**

MODELO: **4.** Conozco al profesor... →
E1: ¿Conoces al profesor Rodríguez?
E2: Sí, **lo** conozco. (No, no **lo** conozco). ¿Y tú?

B. Correspondencias. Empareje los pronombres del complemento directo con las personas. A veces hay más de una correspondencia posible.

PRONOMBRES

1. _____ los
2. _____ la
3. _____ te
4. _____ lo
5. _____ las
6. _____ nos

PERSONAS

a. Ana
b. tú
c. Pedro y Carolina
d. María y yo
e. Jorge
f. Elena y Rosa
g. ustedes
h. usted

C. ¿Qué comen las personas vegetarianas? Aquí hay una lista de diferentes comidas. ¿Cree usted que las come una persona vegetariana? Conteste según los modelos.

MODELOS: el bistec → No **lo** come.
la banana → **La** come.

1. las papas
2. el arroz
3. las chuletas de cerdo
4. las zanahorias
5. las manzanas
6. los camarones
7. los champiñones
8. los frijoles
9. la ensalada

D. La cena de Lola y Manolo

Paso 1. La siguiente descripción de la cena de Lola y Manolo es muy repetitiva. Combine las oraciones, según el modelo.

MODELO: El camarero (*waiter*) trae un menú. Lola lee **el menú.** →
El camarero trae un menú y Lola **lo** lee.

1. El camarero trae una botella de vino tinto. Pone **la botella** en la mesa.
2. Lola quiere la especialidad de la casa. Va a pedir **la especialidad de la casa.**
3. Manolo prefiere el pescado fresco (*fresh*). Pide **el pescado fresco.**
4. Lola quiere una ensalada también. Por eso pide **una ensalada.**
5. El camarero trae la comida. Sirve **la comida.**
6. «¿La cuenta (*bill*)? El dueño está preparando **la cuenta** para ustedes».
7. Manolo quiere pagar con tarjeta (*card*) de crédito. Pero no tiene **su tarjeta.**
8. Por fin, Lola toma la cuenta. Paga **la cuenta.**

Prác. A, Paso 1: Answers: 1. al / a la 2. ø 3. ø 4. al / a la 5. a los 6. ø 7. ø 8. ø 9. a 10. a

Paso 2. Las siguientes oraciones describen la cena de Lola y Manolo. Diga en español a qué se refieren los pronombres indicados. Luego diga quién hace cada acción.

1. **Lo** pide.
2. **La** sirve.
3. No **la** tiene.
4. **La** paga.

E. **Minidiálogos**

Paso 1. Complete los siguientes minidiálogos con los pronombres del complemento directo que faltan (*are missing*).

1. —¿(Me/Te) _____ quieres (*do you love*)?
   —¡(Me/Te) _____ quiero muchísimo!
2. —Voy a Panamá y tengo un boleto (*ticket*) de avión extra. ¿(Me/Te) _____ acompañas?
   —¡Claro que (me/te) _____ acompaño! ¿Cuándo nos vamos?
3. —Buenas noches, señor. ¿(Lo/Te) _____ atienden ya? (*Is someone already helping you?*)
   —No, todavía no, gracias.
   —Perdón. Entonces (*Then*) voy a atender(lo/te)_____ yo.
4. —¡Mi hija nunca (la/me) _____ llama por teléfono!
   —¡Tu hija solo tiene 19 años! Seguro que (la/te) _____ llama si necesita dinero.
5. —¿Cuándo van a visitarlos a ustedes sus primos panameños?
   —(Los/Nos) _____ van a visitar este verano.
6. —Buenos días, señora. ¿En qué (la/te) _____ puedo ayudar (*help*)?
   —Buenos días. Busco una blusa negra de mi talla (*size*).
7. —¡Qué perro tan bonito (*What a beautiful dog*) tienes!
   —Si quieres, puedes tocar(la/lo)_____ (*to touch*).

Paso 2. Ahora, en parejas, indiquen el tipo de relaciones que tienen las personas de cada minidiálogo.

MODELO: **1.** Puede ser una pareja con una relación romántica o...

Paso 3. Comparen sus respuestas al **Paso 2** con las (*those*) de los otros estudiantes de la clase. ¿Están todos de acuerdo?

F. **¿Acciones reflexivas o no?**

Paso 1. Mire cada dibujo y complete cada oración con la mejor opción.

1. El papá _____
   a. la baña.
   b. se baña.
2. La niña _____
   a. la peina.
   b. se peina.
3. A su nuevo perro, el niño _____
   a. lo llama Max.
   b. se llama Max.

Paso 2. Ahora conteste las siguientes preguntas personales. Ponga (*Pay*) atención a los pronombres.

1. ¿Cómo se llama su mejor amigo/a? ¿Cómo lo/la llama usted algunas veces (*sometimes*)?
2. ¿A qué hora se despierta usted los días de clase? ¿Lo/La despierta el reloj despertador o puede despertarse sin la alarma?
3. ¿Tiene usted perro? ¿Con qué frecuencia lo baña y lo cepilla?

Nota comunicativa: Cómo expresar una acción muy reciente: *acabar + de + infinitivo*

To talk about what you have *just* done, use the phrase **acabar + de +** *infinitive*. The verb **acabar** literally means *to finish*.

Acabo de almorzar con Beto.   *I just had lunch with Beto.*

Acabas de celebrar tu cumpleaños,   *You just celebrated your birthday,*
¿verdad?   *didn't you?*

Note that the infinitive follows the preposition **de**.

You will practice talking about what you have *just* done in **Práctica G.**

 G. **¡Acabo de hacerlo!** En parejas, túrnense para practicar cómo se expresan las acciones que uno acaba de hacer. Sigan el modelo.

MODELO: **E1:** ¿Por qué no haces la ensalada? →
E2: Acabo de hacer**la.** (**La** acabo de hacer).

1. ¿Por qué no preparas las chuletas para la fiesta?
2. ¿Vas a comprar la fruta hoy?
3. ¿Por qué no pagas los cafés?
4. ¿Vas a cocinar la comida para la cena?
5. ¿Quieres ayudarme?
6. ¿Por qué no me invitas a cenar?

H. ¡Ayuda! (*Help!*)

Paso 1. Todos necesitamos ayuda alguna vez (*at some point*), ¿no? ¿Quién lo/la ayuda a usted en los siguientes casos?

MODELO: con el coche → **Mi padre me** ayuda con el coche.

1. con las cuentas (*bills*)
2. con la tarea
3. con la matrícula
4. con el horario de clases
5. con el español
6. pagar las deudas (*debts*)
7. estudiar para los exámenes
8. resolver los problemas personales

 Paso 2. Ahora, en parejas, túrnense para hacer y contestar preguntas basadas en el **Paso 1.**

MODELO: con el coche →
E1: ¿Quién **te** ayuda con el coche?
E2: Generalmente, **mis padres me** ayudan un poco. A veces también **me** ayudan **mis abuelos.**

I. Intercambios. En parejas, túrnense para hacer y contestar preguntas sobre los alimentos (*foods*) que consumen y con qué frecuencia. Expliquen por qué tienen esos hábitos. Luego digan a la clase algo (*something*) que tienen en común.

MODELO: **1. E1:** ¿Comes pan sin gluten?
E2: No, no **lo** como porque no soy celíaco.

1. pan sin gluten
2. refrescos sin azúcar
3. productos bajos en sodio
4. frutas y verduras orgánicas
5. pescados y mariscos
6. hamburguesas
7. bebidas alcohólicas
8. café
9. productos lácteos (*milk*)
10. comidas congeladas (*frozen*)

Vocabulario útil

ayudar + a + *inf.* to help to (*do something*)

Estrategia

Use the word **nadie** before the object pronoun and verb to express that *no one* does something. For example, in item 1: **Nadie me ayuda con las cuentas.**

Vocabulario útil

la cafeína
las calorías
el colesterol
la grasa fat

estar a dieta
ser alérgico/a a
ser bueno/a para la salud (*health*)
ser celíaco/a

me pone(n) nervioso/a it/they make me nervous
me sienta(n) mal it/they don't agree with me
lo/la/los/las detesto

You have been using a few words that express indefinite and negative qualities since the first chapter of this text. Review what you already know about the content of **Gramática 19** by giving the English equivalent of the following words.

1. siempre _____ **2.** nunca _____ **3.** también _____

19 Expressing Negation • Indefinite and Negative Words

Gramática en acción: ¿Un refrigerador típico?

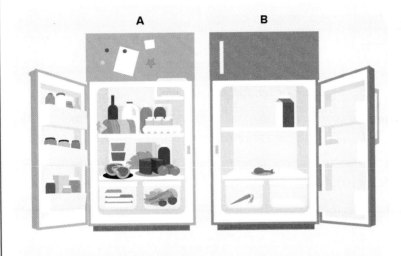

A   B

Empareje las siguientes respuestas con el refrigerador A o el B.

1. ¿Hay **algo** bueno de comer en este refrigerador?
_____ Sí, hay **algo**.
_____ No, **no** hay **nada**.

2. ¿Hay fruta y pan?
_____ Sí, hay fruta y pan.
_____ No, **no** hay fruta. **Tampoco** hay pan.

3. ¿Hay chuletas de cerdo?
_____ No, **no** hay **ninguna** chuleta.
_____ Sí, hay **algunas** chuletas.

4. En esta casa, ¿**alguien** compra comida con frecuencia?
_____ No, **nadie** la compra.
_____ Sí, **alguien** la compra.

¿Y usted?

¿Cuál de los dos refrigeradores se parece (*resembles*) más al refrigerador de su casa o apartamento? ¿Cuál se parece más al típico refrigerador de los estudiantes? ¿de una familia con hijos? ¿de jóvenes profesionales?

Indefinite and Negative Words / Las palabras indefinidas y negativas

Los adverbios indefinidos y negativos		
siempre	always	**Siempre** estudio en casa. Estudio en casa **siempre**.
nunca, jamás	never	**Nunca/Jamás** estudio en la biblioteca. **No** estudio **nunca/jamás** en la biblioteca.
también	also	Yo **también** sé preparar una paella. Yo sé preparar una paella **también**.
tampoco	neither, not either	**Tampoco** sé preparar una paella. Yo **no** sé preparar una paella **tampoco**.

A typical refrigerator? **1.** *Is there something good to eat in this refrigerator? Yes, there is something. No, there is nothing.* **2.** *Is there (some) fruit and bread? Yes, there is (some) fruit and bread. No, there is no fruit. There isn't any bread either.* **3.** *Are there pork chops? No, there aren't any chops. (Lit., No, there is no chop.) Yes, there are some chops.* **4.** *In this house, does anyone buy food frequently? No, no one buys it. Yes, someone buys it.*

Los sustantivos indefinidos y negativos		
alguien **nadie**	someone, anyone no one, nobody, not anybody	En esta clase **alguien** habla chino. En esta clase **nadie** habla chino. En esta clase **no** habla chino **nadie**. Conozco **a** **alguien** en esa fiesta. **No** conozco **a** **nadie** en esa fiesta.
algo **nada**	something, anything nothing, not anything	Sé **algo** de la cocina panameña. **No** sé **nada** de la cocina panameña.

¡OJO!

The personal **a** is used with **alguien** and **nadie** when they function as direct objects, as in the examples.

Pronunciation Hint: Pronounce the **d** in **nada** and **nadie** as a fricative, that is, like the *th* sound in *the*: [**na-ḍa**], [**na-ḍie**].

Los adjetivos indefinidos y negativos		
algún, alguna, algunos/as **ningún, ninguna**	some, any no, not any	**algún** tomate, **algunas** chuletas **ningún** tomate, **ninguna** chuleta

¡OJO!

Note how **alguno** and **ninguno** shorten (**algún**, **ningún**) before masculine singular nouns. You've seen something similar with **uno (→ un), bueno (→ buen), grande (→ gran),** and **primero (→ primer).**

algún / **ningún** problema
alguna / **ninguna** cosa
algunos problemas
algunas cosas

The Double Negative / **La doble negación**

A double negative is avoided in English but is often necessary in Spanish.

- When the negative word comes *before* the conjugated verb, that is all that is needed.
- When the negative word comes *after* the conjugated verb, another negative word—usually **no**—must be placed before the verb.

negative word + verb
no + *verb + negative word*

¿**Nadie** estudia?
¿**No** estudia **nadie**? } *Isn't anyone studying?*

Nunca estás en clase.
No estás en clase **nunca**. } *You're never in class.*

Tampoco quieren cenar aquí.
No quieren cenar aquí **tampoco**. } *They don't want to have dinner here either.*

The Adjectives **algún** and **ningún** / Los adjetivos *algún* y *ningún*

The indefinite words **algún/alguna/algunos/algunas** and the negative **ningún/ninguna** are adjectives. That's why they must agree with the noun they modify.

The singular negative forms **ningún/ninguno** and **ninguna** indicate that there is none of something. The only exception occurs with nouns that are always plural, like **las gafas** or **los pantalones: ningunas gafas, ningunos pantalones.**

¡OJO!

When a masculine noun is not expressed, the words **alguno** and **ninguno** (rather than **algún** and **ningún**) are used.

—¿Hay **algunos** mensajes para mí hoy?
—No, no hay **ningún** mensaje para usted.
"Are there any messages for me today?"
"No, there are no messages for you today."
   (*"There is not a single message for you today."*)

—¿Ves a **algunas** de tus amigas aquí?
—No, no veo a **ninguna**.
"Do you see any of your friends here?"
"No, I don't see any (of them)."

—¿Hay **algún** problema?
—No, **ninguno**.
"Is there a problem?"
"No, none."

algo	nada	siempre	nunca, jamás
alguien	nadie	también	tampoco
algún/alguna/os/as	ningún, ninguna		

Práctica y comunicación

A. Cosas esenciales

Paso 1. Autoprueba. Dé la palabra negativa correspondiente.

1. siempre   **2.** también   **3.** algo   **4.** alguien   **5.** alguna

Paso 2. Complete las siguientes oraciones para que sean (*so that they are*) verdaderas para usted. Siga (*Follow*) las indicaciones en paréntesis.

1. Siempre tengo _____ (algo) en mi cuarto y también tengo _____ (algo más).
2. (Yo) Nunca _____ (una acción) temprano por la mañana. Tampoco me gusta _____ (otra acción en infinitivo).
3. Algo que siempre hay en mi refrigerador es _____. Algo que nunca hay es _____.
4. Para mí, no hay nada tan importante como mi(s) _____ (algo).
5. En este momento, nadie es tan importante en mi vida (*life*) como mi(s) _____ (alguien).

Paso 3. Ahora, en parejas, comparen sus oraciones del **Paso 2** y digan a la clase algo que tienen en común.

MODELO: Para nosotros/as dos, no hay nada tan importante como nuestras familias.

B. ¿Qué pasa esta noche en esta casa?

Paso 1. Complete las siguientes oraciones con la palabra indefinida o negativa apropiada según el dibujo.

Estrategia

Remember that **ninguno** is always used in the singular and that it shortens to **ningún** before a masculine, singular noun.

1. Hay _____ cantando en el baño.
2. Hay _____ niños jugando en su habitación.
3. Hay _____ en la mesa del comedor.
4. Hay _____ comida en la barbacoa.
5. Hay _____ personas en la sala.
6. No hay _____ en la cocina.
7. No hay _____ plato en la mesa del comedor.

Paso 2. Ahora haga otras oraciones ciertas, pero contrarias a las (*those*) del **Paso 1**.

MODELO: **1. No** hay **nadie** cantando en **el jardín.**

C. ¡Nadie come allí! Exprese las oraciones de manera negativa, usando la doble negación.

MODELO: Hay alguien en el restaurante. ➙ **No** hay **nadie** en el restaurante.

1. Hay algo interesante en el menú.
2. Tienen algunos platos típicos.
3. El profesor cena allí también.
4. Mis amigos siempre almuerzan allí.
5. Preparan algo especial para grupos.
6. Siempre hacen platos nuevos.
7. Y también sirven paella, mi plato favorito.

Prác. A, Paso 1: Answers: 1. *nunca* 2. *tampoco* 3. *nada* 4. *nadie* 5. *ninguna*

Gramática   doscientos veintiuno ■ **221**

D. Extremos

Paso 1. Modifique las siguientes declaraciones para hacerlas negativas.

MODELO: Hay muchas personas antipáticas en mi familia. →
No hay **ninguna persona** antipática (**No** hay **nadie** antipático) en mi familia.

1. Tengo muchos planes interesantes para este fin de semana.
2. Todas mis clases este semestre/trimestre son maravillosas (*wonderful*).
3. Me gusta toda la comida de la cafetería.
4. Hay muchas noticias (*news*) buenas últimamente (*lately*).
5. Siempre estudio en la biblioteca.
6. Todos los estudiantes de esta universidad son internacionales.

Paso 2. Ahora modifique las oraciones del **Paso 1** para que expresen (*so that they express*) su opinión.

MODELOS: Hay muchas personas antipáticas en mi familia. →
No hay ninguna persona antipática en mi familia.
En mi familia hay algunas personas antipáticas, pero muy pocas.

 Paso 3. Ahora, en parejas, túrnense para hacer y contestar preguntas basadas en las oraciones del **Paso 2.**

MODELO: En mi familia hay algunas personas antipáticas, pero muy pocas. →
E1: En tu familia ¿hay alguna persona antipática (alguien antipático)?
E2: Sí, mi tío Gerry es muy antipático. (No, no hay nadie antipático).

 E. Intercambios

Paso 1. En parejas, túrnense para entrevistarse sobre los siguientes temas. Deben obtener detalles interesantes y personales de su compañero/a.

MODELO: E1: ¿Tienes alguna buena excusa para no ir al gimnasio esta semana?
E2: No, no tengo ninguna buena excusa esta semana. (Sí, tengo una buena excusa. ¡No tengo tiempo!)

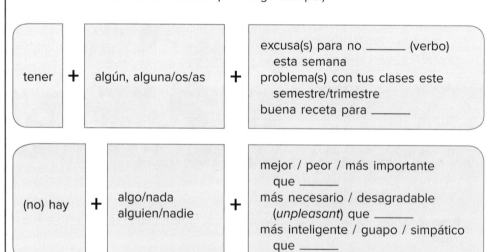

| tener | **+** | algún, alguna/os/as | **+** | excusa(s) para no _____ (verbo) esta semana problema(s) con tus clases este semestre/trimestre buena receta para _____ |

| (no) hay | **+** | algo/nada alguien/nadie | **+** | mejor / peor / más importante que _____ más necesario / desagradable (*unpleasant*) que _____ más inteligente / guapo / simpático que _____ |

Paso 2. Ahora digan a la clase una respuesta interesante o peculiar.

MODELOS: Algo interesante de Jim es que tiene una excusa muy buena para no hacer la tarea esta noche. Va a...
Algo interesante de Aurora es que, en su opinión, no hay nada más desagradable que la arrogancia.

Algo sobre los emberás

Lissa Harrison

Unas casas típicas de los emberás

Los emberás son un pueblo amerindio del este de Panamá y también de la región noroeste de Colombia y del Ecuador. Tradicionalmente viven en la selva,[a] junto a ríos,[b] en zonas donde llueve todo el año. Por eso sus casas están en alto.[c] Están cubiertas[d] de hojas[e] de palma.

¿Hay algún pueblo indígena en su estado? ¿Qué sabe de ellos?

[a]*jungle* [b]junto... *next to rivers* [c]en... *raised up* [d]*covered* [e]*leaves*

Textos de todos los días: Mensaje de texto para encontrarse° para cenar

meeting

Seguro que (*Of course*) usted escribe mensajes todos los días por muchas razones. En esta actividad va a practicar cómo escribir un mensaje para hacer planes.

Objetivo: Escribir un mensaje de texto (SMS o WhatsApp, o algo similar) para hacer planes con alguien para cenar.

Antes de empezar

- Considere cómo son sus mensajes de este tipo en su lengua nativa. ¿Tienen oraciones muy largas? Si el tema del mensaje es complicado, ¿hay solo un mensaje o más de uno?
- Es posible cambiar la lengua de uso en el celular. Si pone el español como la lengua de su celular, el autocorrector puede ayudar con la corrección del mensaje.
- El saludo más corto y frecuente es **Hola** u **¡Hola!**. Como en inglés, con frecuencia no se usan palabras para cerrar el mensaje, pero sí un emoji.
- Mire el intercambio (*Look at the exchange*) de mensajes en la imagen para tener más ideas.
- El texto de su(s) mensaje(s) debe mencionar la hora, lugar o tipo de comida que usted prefiere y también solicitar las opciones y preferencias de la otra persona. También puede sugerir (*suggest*) invitar a alguien más.

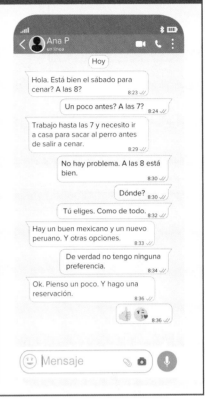

> **Hoy**
>
> Hola. Está bien el sábado para cenar? A las 8? 8:23
>
> Un poco antes? A las 7? 8:24
>
> Trabajo hasta las 7 y necesito ir a casa para sacar al perro antes de salir a cenar. 8:29
>
> No hay problema. A las 8 está bien. 8:30
>
> Dónde? 8:30
>
> Tú eliges. Como de todo. 8:32
>
> Hay un buen mexicano y un nuevo peruano. Y otras opciones. 8:33
>
> De verdad no tengo ninguna preferencia. 8:34
>
> Ok. Pienso un poco. Y hago una reservación. 8:36
>
> 👍 8:36
>
> 😊 Mensaje 🔗 📷 🎤

Vocabulario útil

el<u>e</u>gir (el<u>ij</u>o) (<u>i</u>)	to choose
<u>hacer</u> una reservación	
<u>ser</u>	
celíaco/a	
vegano/a	
vegetariano/a	

🔄 Repaso

Review what you already know about irregular first person present tense forms by giving the **yo** form of the following infinitives. You will need to know this information in **Gramática 20.**

1. salir _____
2. tener _____
3. conocer _____
4. pedir _____
5. hacer _____
6. dormir _____
7. perder _____
8. traer _____

20 Influencing Others • Commands (Part 1): Formal Commands

Gramática en acción: Receta para guacamole

El guacamole

Ingredientes

1 aguacate
1 diente de ajo,[a] prensado[b]
1 tomate
jugo de un limón[c]
sal
un poco de cilantro fresco

Cómo se prepara

Corte el aguacate y el tomate en trozos[d] pequeños. Añada el jugo del limón, el ajo, el cilantro y la sal a su gusto. Mezcle bien todos los ingredientes y sírvalo con tortillas de maíz[e] fritas.

[a]diente... *clove of garlic*   [b]*crushed*   [c]*lime*   [d]*pieces*   [e]*corn*

En español, los mandatos se usan con frecuencia en las recetas. Los siguientes verbos se usan en forma de mandato en esta receta. ¿Puede encontrarlos?

añadir	to add
cortar	to cut
mezclar	to mix
s<u>e</u>rvir (s<u>i</u>rvo) (<u>i</u>)	

¿Y usted?

¿Le gusta el guacamole? ¿Lo pide o lo hace con frecuencia? ¿Con qué lo come?

Formal Command Forms / **Los mandatos formales (usted, ustedes)**

In *Puntos de partida* you have seen formal commands in the direction lines of activities since the beginning of the text: **haga, complete, conteste,** and so on.

Commands (imperatives) are verb forms used to tell someone to do something. In Spanish, *formal commands* (**los mandatos formales**) are used with people whom you address as **usted** or **ustedes**.* Here are some of the basic forms.

	hablar	comer	escribir	<u>volver</u>	<u>poner</u>
usted	habl<u>e</u>	com<u>a</u>	escrib<u>a</u>	vuelv<u>a</u>	pong<u>a</u>
ustedes	habl<u>en</u>	com<u>an</u>	escrib<u>an</u>	vuelv<u>an</u>	pong<u>an</u>
	speak	*eat*	*write*	*come back*	*put, place*

1. Regular Verbs

Most formal command forms can be derived from the **yo** form of the present tense.

Note that the "opposite" vowel is used:
-ar → <u>e</u>
-er/-ir → <u>a</u>

-ar: -o → -e, -en		-er/-ir: -o → -a, -an	
habl<u>o</u> →	habl<u>e</u>	com<u>o</u> →	com<u>a</u>
	habl<u>en</u>		com<u>an</u>
		escrib<u>o</u> →	escrib<u>a</u>
			escrib<u>an</u>

2. Stem-changing Verbs

Formal commands for stem-changing verbs show the stem change, since the stem vowel is stressed. Base the command on the **yo** form to get the stem change right.

p<u>e</u>nsar (p<u>ie</u>nso) → p<u>ie</u>nse, p<u>ie</u>nsen
v<u>o</u>lver (v<u>ue</u>lvo) → v<u>ue</u>lva, v<u>ue</u>lvan
p<u>e</u>dir (p<u>i</u>do) → p<u>i</u>da, p<u>i</u>dan

3. Verbs Ending in *-car, -gar, -zar*

These verbs have a spelling change to preserve the **-c-, -g-,** and **-z-** sounds of the infinitives.

c → qu   bus<u>c</u>ar: bus<u>que</u>, bus<u>quen</u>
g → gu   pa<u>g</u>ar: pa<u>gue</u>, pa<u>guen</u>
z → c   empe<u>z</u>ar: empie<u>ce</u>, empie<u>cen</u>

¡OJO!

From this chapter on, these three spelling changes for verbs in formal commands will be indicated in parentheses in vocabulary lists. If these three verbs were active in this chapter, they would be listed in the end-of-chapter vocabulary list as follows: **bus<u>c</u>ar (<u>qu</u>), pa<u>g</u>ar (<u>gu</u>), empe<u>z</u>ar (empie<u>z</u>o) (<u>c</u>).**

---

4. Verbs with Irregular Present Tense *yo* Forms

Verbs that have an irregular **yo** form in the present tense will keep the irregularity in the **usted/ustedes** commands.

conocer: **cono<u>z</u>co**   → cono<u>z</u>ca, cono<u>z</u>can
decir[†] (*to say, tell*): **di<u>g</u>o** → di<u>g</u>a, di<u>g</u>an
hacer: **ha<u>g</u>o**   → ha<u>g</u>a, ha<u>g</u>an
oír: **oi<u>g</u>o**   → oi<u>g</u>a, oi<u>g</u>an
salir: **sal<u>g</u>o**   → sal<u>g</u>a, sal<u>g</u>an
tener: **ten<u>g</u>o**   → ten<u>g</u>a, ten<u>g</u>an
traer: **trai<u>g</u>o**   → trai<u>g</u>a, trai<u>g</u>an
venir: **ven<u>g</u>o**   → ven<u>g</u>a, ven<u>g</u>an
ver: **v<u>e</u>o**   → v<u>e</u>a, v<u>e</u>an

5. Irregular Formal Commands*

Five verbs have irregular **usted/ustedes** command forms that are not based on the **yo** form of the present tense.

dar[†] (*to give*) → <u>dé</u>, *but* **den**
estar   → <u>esté</u>, <u>estén</u>
ir   → <u>vaya</u>, <u>vayan</u>
saber   → <u>sepa</u>, <u>sepan</u>
ser   → <u>sea</u>, <u>sean</u>

You will learn how to form informal (tú**) commands in **Gramática 36 (Cap. 13).**

[†]**Decir** and **dar** are used primarily with indirect objects. Both of these verbs and indirect object pronouns will be formally introduced in **Gramática 21 (Cap. 8).**

Position of Pronouns / **El lugar de los pronombres**

1. Pronouns with Affirmative Commands

Direct object pronouns and reflexive pronouns must *follow* affirmative commands and are attached to them. In order to maintain the original stress of the verb form, an accent mark is added to the stressed vowel if the original command has two or more syllables.

mandato afirmativo: 1 palabra	
mandato + pronombre	
Pídalo usted.	*Order it.*
Siéntense, por favor.	*Sit down, please.*

2. Pronouns with Negative Commands

Direct object and reflexive pronouns must *precede* the verb form in negative commands.

mandato negativo: 3 palabras	
no + *mandato + pronombre*	
No **lo** pida usted.	*Don't order it.*
No **se** levanten, por favor.	*Don't get up.*

¡OJO!

Now that you know how to form formal commands, be sure to use them carefully when speaking to native speakers of Spanish. Commands are strong forms in any language. It is wise to soften formal commands with **por favor** and by using a polite tone, just as you would in English. Example: **Abra la puerta, por favor.**

Práctica y comunicación

A. Mandatos de esta clase

Paso 1. Autoprueba. Dé el mandato formal de **usted** para cada infinitivo.

1. hablar
2. escribir
3. llegar
4. aprender
5. cerrar
6. dormir
7. leer
8. hacer
9. empezar
10. buscar

> **Summary of Formal Commands**
>
> -ar → **-e**(n)
> -er/-ir → **-a**(n)
>
> **Affirmative:** *command +* pronoun (**1** word)
> **Negative: no** + *pronoun + command* (**3** words)

Paso 2. Cambie las siguientes frases en mandatos lógicos y típicos de una clase de español. **¡OJO!** Pueden ser afirmativos o negativos.

MODELO: abrir los libros en la página x →
Abr**an** los libros en la página x.

1. cerrar los libros
2. traer la tarea mañana
3. sentarse en círculo
4. dormirse
5. leer el texto
6. hacer preguntas
7. hablar en inglés
8. repetir (*like* pedir) más alto (*louder*)

Paso 3. En parejas, indiquen cuáles de los mandatos del **Paso 2** se oyen en su clase de español. Luego añadan (*add*) otros tres mandatos típicos de su clase.

B. El mundo al revés (*The world upside down*)

Paso 1. Hoy, los estudiantes son los «jefes» (*bosses*)... pero ¡solo por un día! Cambie las siguientes acciones en mandatos «lógicos» para todos sus profesores, no solo para su profesor(a) de español. Haga mandatos afirmativos y negativos.

1. llegar a tiempo
2. venir a la universidad
3. pedir la tarea
4. volver a casa
5. poner música de _____
6. pensar en _____
7. traer _____ (¿comida?) a clase
8. sentarse en _____
9. hacer _____
10. dar _____ a los estudiantes
(*Continúa*).

> **Vocabulario útil**
>
> el examen
> la nota
> la prueba   quiz

Prác. A, Paso 1: Answers: 1. hable 2. escriba 3. llegue 4. aprenda 5. cierre 6. duerma 7. lea 8. haga 9. empiece 10. busque

Paso 2. ¿Qué otros mandatos pueden dar a sus profesores hoy? En parejas, inventen tres mandatos para ellos.

C. Los problemas del Sr. Casiano

Paso 1. El Sr. Casiano no se siente (*feel*) bien. Lea la descripción que él da de las cosas que hace.

Trabajo[1] muchísimas horas —¡me gusta trabajar! **Soy**[2] impaciente y **doy**[3] mi opinión muy directamente. Por eso **tengo**[4] muchos conflictos con otras personas. **Soy**[5] un poco impulsivo y **hago**[6] demasiadas compras por internet. **Almuerzo**[7] y **ceno**[8] fuerte,[a] pero **desayuno**[9] solo café. Por la noche, **me acuesto**[10] tarde porque **salgo**[11] con amigos a beber cerveza. Es verdad que no **duermo**[12] mucho.

[a]*a lot*

Paso 2. Comprensión. ¿Cierto o falso?

	CIERTO	FALSO
1. El Sr. Casiano es una persona muy simpática.	☐	☐
2. Tiene algunos hábitos malos.	☐	☐
3. Por la noche, siempre está en casa.	☐	☐

Paso 3. ¿Qué *no* debe hacer el Sr. Casiano? Aconséjelo (*Advise him*) y dígale (*tell him*) lo que no debe hacer. Use los verbos en **negrilla** o cualquier (*any*) otro.

MODELOS: **1. Trabajo → Sr. Casiano, no trabaje** tanto.
2. Soy → No sea tan impaciente.

D. Estrategias para una dieta mejor. ¿Qué debe o no debe comer y beber una persona que quiere comer de manera más sana (*in a healthier way*)?

MODELOS: ensalada → E1: ¿Ensalada?   postres → E1: ¿Postres?
                    E2: Cóma**la**.   E2: No **los** coma.

1. bebidas alcohólicas
2. verduras
3. pan
4. dulces
5. leche entera (*whole*)
6. hamburguesas con queso
7. frutas frescas
8. refrescos dietéticos

E. ¡Qué desastre! Imagine los mandatos que esta madre va a darles a sus hijos adolescentes. ¿Le resultan (*Do they sound*) familiares a usted estos mandatos?

MODELO: **no acostarse** muy tarde →
            ¡**No se acuesten** muy tarde!

1. **levantarse** más temprano
2. **bañarse** todos los días
3. **quitarse** esa ropa sucia
4. **ponerse** ropa limpia
5. **no divertirse** todas las noches con los amigos
6. **ir** más a la biblioteca y **estudiar** más
7. ¿ ?

F. Consejos sobre los buenos modales (*good manners*) en la mesa

Paso 1. Use las siguientes ideas para dar consejos en forma de mandatos formales sobre cómo se debe comer en una ocasión formal. **¡OJO!** Algunos consejos son normas en los países hispanos y *no* coinciden con las normas que se practican en este país. ¿Puede decir cuáles son las normas específicamente hispanas?

1. **poner** las dos manos en la mesa
2. no **poner** los codos (*elbows*) en la mesa
3. para cortar, **agarrar** (*to hold*) el tenedor con la mano izquierda y el cuchillo con la derecha
4. **cortar** solo el pedazo (*piece*) de comida que puede poner en la boca
5. no **cambiar** (*to change*) de mano el tenedor para llevar la comida a la boca
6. no **eructar** (*to burp*) en público

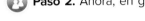 **Paso 2.** Ahora, en grupos, inventen por lo menos (*at least*) cuatro consejos más.

> ## Vocabulario útil
>
> | | |
> |---|---|
> | la cuchara | spoon |
> | el cuchillo | knife |
> | la mano | hand |
> | la servilleta | napkin |
> | el tenedor | fork |
> | masticar (**qu**) | to chew |
> | servirse (me sirvo) (i) a uno mismo | to help one's self |
> | con la boca llena | with one's mouth full |
> | despacio | slowly |

⊛ Todo junto

A. Lengua y cultura: La cocina panameña

Paso 1. Completar. Complete the following paragraphs with the correct form of the words in parentheses, as suggested by context. When two possibilities are given in parentheses, select the correct word. **¡OJO!** As you conjugate the verbs in this activity, note that you will make formal commands with some infinitives.

¿Creen ustedes que la comida panameña es similar a la[a] de México y que los tacos y las tortillas (ser / estar)[1] parte de la comida típica de los panameños? Si creen eso, entonces[b] no (*ustedes:* saber / conocer)[2] (algo / nada)[3] de la comida de _____ (este)[4] nación. _____ (*Ustedes:* Seguir)[5] _____ (leer),[6] porque van a aprender mucho.

El ceviche, un típico plato panameño

La influencia _____ (extranjero)[7] en la comida de la cosmopolita ciudad de Panamá es muy visible. Hay _____ (mucho)[8] restaurantes que _____ (servir)[9] comida italiana, china, _____ (francés),[10] etcétera.

Sin embargo, los panameños no _____ (perder)[11] su identidad nacional, y frecuentemente _____ (preferir)[12] la comida tradicional. En la cocina panameña hay muchos platos de mariscos y pescados, entre ellos el ceviche. Las personas vegetarianas no _____ (tener)[13] problema (también / tampoco)[14] porque hay una variedad de platos con arroz y verduras. Para los panameños el plato nacional es el arroz con pollo. Si va a la ciudad de Panamá, _____ (*usted:* pedirlo).[15] Le va a gustar.

[a]*a... to that* [b]*then*

Paso 2. Comprensión. Conteste las siguientes preguntas.

1. ¿Cómo se sabe que la ciudad de Panamá es cosmopolita?
2. ¿Cuál es el plato que representa mejor la cocina panameña?
3. ¿Qué ingredientes son comunes en la comida de Panamá?

(Continúa).

Paso 3. En acción

En parejas, den consejos a turistas extranjeros sobre dónde pueden encontrar las siguientes comidas, que son típicas de algunas partes de los Estados Unidos. Den sus recomendaciones en forma de mandatos. Luego comparen sus recomendaciones con las (*those*) del resto de la clase para ver si todos están de acuerdo.

MODELO: la mejor sopa de almejas (*clams*) → Vayan a los estados del noreste, a la región de Nueva Inglaterra. Pidan la sopa que se llama *clam chowder*. Tiene almejas y con frecuencia tiene leche.

1. la mejor barbacoa
2. los mejores mariscos
3. la mejor comida china
4. la mejor comida hispana
5. el mejor queso
6. la mejor langosta

B. Proyecto: ¿Cómo come esta clase?

Para este proyecto van a documentar los hábitos relacionados con la comida de las personas de la clase.

Paso 1. Preparación. En grupos, piensen en ideas (1–2 por miembro del grupo) relacionadas con los hábitos de comer para encuestar al resto de la clase: qué comen, dónde, con quién, con qué frecuencia, qué hacen mientras (*while*) comen, etcétera. Hay algunas ideas en el **Manifiesto de la comida.** Para hacer las preguntas, consideren varias opciones, como se muestran (*are shown*) en los modelos.

MANIFIESTO DE LA COMIDA

AGRADECE LOS ALIMENTOS QUE **COME SÓLO CUANDO** VAS A RECIBIR NO TODOS LOS TIENEN **TENGAS HAMBRE** COMIENZA CON UNA **COME DESPACIO Y** ENSALADA CONSCIENTEMENTE LLENA SOLO EL 80% **COME CON** Y DEJA EL 20% DEL **UNA BUENA** ESTÓMAGO VACÍO **COMPAÑÍA** NO HABLES TEMAS APAGA EL CELULAR QUE TE ALTEREN TODOS MERECEMOS UNA COMIDA TRANQUILA **COME** SI COMES SOLO SENTADO NO TRATES DE DISTRAERTE **MIENTRAS COMES** DEJA DE COMER CUANDO YA NO SIENTAS HAMBRE **COME COMIDA... NO PRODUCTOS**

©Valeria Lozano. Grupo Hábitos, 2015. Reprinted by permission.

MODELOS: comer verduras → ¿Con qué frecuencia comes verduras? En todas las comidas. En algunas comidas. Casi nunca.

tener una dieta sana → Evalúa tu dieta del 1 al 5: 1 significa mala y 5 significa excelente.

actividades durante la comida → Indica dos de las acciones que haces con más frecuencia mientras comes: hablar con otra persona, ver algún programa en una pantalla (*screen*), leer, concentrarte en la comida.

Paso 2. Encuesta. Ahora háganles sus preguntas a varias personas de la clase (¡o a todas!). Recuerden (*Remember*) preparar un método para apuntar (*noting down*) las respuestas.

Paso 3. Análisis de datos. Analicen las respuestas y preparen una serie de oraciones para presentar los datos al resto de la clase.

MODELOS: Un total de _____ (número) de _____ (número) personas encuestadas prefiere...

Más del 50% (por ciento) de los encuestados...

¡OJO!

You have just learned formal commands. But you may want to use informal commands in this activity. Two of them are shown in the models (**Evalúa, Indica**), and several others appear in **Manifiesto de la comida.**

Video: Salu2 «¡De viaje!»

You can watch two segments of this chapter's video in the **Video: Salu2** section, found at the end of the eBook.

Klic Video Productions/ McGraw Hill

Un puesto (*stand*) de tacos en México

Enfoque cultural: La comida

> ## Antes de leer
> ¿Cuáles son algunos de los platos típicos de su país? ¿Hay alguna comida típica de su ciudad o estado?

En Panamá

El arroz con pollo al estilo panameño es uno de los platos más típicos de Panamá. Otro plato típico es el sancocho, una sopa que también es parte de la cocina de otros países caribeños y que lleva algún tipo de carne, verduras y legumbres.[a] Y es necesario mencionar también las frituras, es decir,[b] la comida frita. Hay gran variedad de frituras: la yuca frita, las carimañolas (unas bolas de masa[c] de yuca con carne dentro[d]), los patacones (rebanadas[e] de plátano frito), las empanadas[f] al estilo panameño, etcétera.

De beber, se debe probar[g] las chichas, que son refrescos naturales de frutas panameñas, como el coco, la guanábana y el maracuyá.[h]

Charoen Krung Photography/Shutterstock

Deliciosa chicha de maracuyá

[a]beans   [b]es... that is   [c]bolas... balls of dough   [d]inside   [e]slices
[f]see **En otros países hispanos**   [g]try   [h]coco... coconut, soursop, and passion fruit

Comprensión ¿Qué es el sancocho? ¿Y las frituras panameñas?

 En acción

Haga dos listas: una de los cinco platos más tradicionales de los Estados Unidos, y la otra de los cinco productos más representativos de este país. Si no sabe el nombre de alguno, use un diccionario. Prepárese para justificar su selección.

En otros países hispanos

Hlphoto/Shutterstock

Unas empanadas de carne

- **En todo el mundo hispanohablante** Las empanadas son probablemente la constante culinaria más notable de todos los países hispanohablantes. Consisten en una masa de pan[a] rellena[b] de algo dulce o salado.[c] Pueden ser pequeñas e individuales o grandes para ser compartidas.[d] Las empanadas son de procedencia española... y los españoles las heredaron[e] de los árabes. ¡Una larga y deliciosa tradición!

- **En los Estados Unidos** La comida latina es omnipresente en los Estados Unidos hoy día. La cocina mexicana es muy popular, como también lo es su variante *Tex-Mex,* genuinamente estadounidense. Pero también se puede encontrar la comida de casi todas las otras cocinas hispanas: las pupusas[f] salvadoreñas, la tortilla[g] española (con papas y cebollas), el arroz con gandules[h] puertorriqueño, el dulce de leche[i] (una comida panhispánica), etcétera.

[a]masa... bread dough   [b]filled   [c]salty   [d]shared   [e]inherited   [f]corn masa stuffed with cheese, refried beans, or meat, then fried like a tortilla   [g]omelet   [h]pigeon peas   [i]dulce... caramelized milk

Comprensión ¿Qué comida es muy típica del mundo hispano? ¿Qué cocina genuinamente estadounidense es de origen hispano?

la cacerola	pot
las espinacas	spinach
la fuente	serving dish
el horno	oven
el maíz	corn
la sartén	pan
cal<u>e</u>ntar	
(cal<u>ie</u>nto)	to warm
h<u>e</u>rvir	
(h<u>ie</u>rvo) (i)	to boil
licuar (lic<u>ú</u>o)	to blend

Lectura

Antes de leer

Piense en la lasaña, un plato italiano tradicional. ¿Cuáles de estos ingredientes contiene una lasaña típica? ¿pollo, aceite de oliva, papas, pimienta, pasta, tomates, sal, champiñones, tortillas, frijoles, agua, salchicha, lechuga, queso?

Una receta

Lasaña de tortillas Para 6 porciones

D and S Food Photography/Alamy Stock Photo

INGREDIENTES

18 tortillas de maíz en cuadrados[a]
480 gramos de queso ricotta
60 gramos de espinacas
60 gramos de cebolla picada[b]
60 gramos de tomates en dados[c]
2 cucharadas[d] de mantequilla
Sal y pimienta

Salsa de tomate
4 tomates
1/2 cebolla
1 diente de ajo[e]
2 cucharadas de mantequilla
100 gramos de puré de tomate
100 mililitros de agua
Sal, pimienta y orégano al gusto[f]

PREPARACIÓN

Salsa de tomate
1. Corte los tomates y la cebolla y póngalos a hervir en una cacerola con el agua, el puré de tomate, el ajo y el orégano. Licúelo todo.
2. Vuelva a calentarlo con la mantequilla y sazone con sal y pimienta.

Lasaña
1. Lave las espinacas y póngalas a hervir en un poco de agua; después, escúrralas y saltéelas[g] en una sartén con la mantequilla, sal y pimienta.
2. En una fuente, ponga la mitad de la salsa de tomate en el fondo[h] y encima[i] coloque las tortillas, el queso, las espinacas, el tomate y la cebolla en capas[j] hasta formar dos capas de todo. Después, cúbralo[k] con el resto de la salsa de tomate.
3. Ponga la lasaña al horno 30 o 40 minutos a 180 grados Celsius.

[a]squares [b]chopped [c]cubes [d]tablespoons [e]diente... *clove of garlic* [f]al... *to taste* [g]escúrralas... *drain them (the spinach leaves) and sauté them* [h]bottom [i]on top [j]layers [k]cover it

Comprensión

A. Los mandatos de la receta. Todos los verbos para preparar esta receta son mandatos formales. Empareje los siguientes mandatos con su traducción en inglés, según el contexto de la receta.

MANDATOS
1. _____ corte
2. _____ sazone
3. _____ lave
4. _____ coloque
5. _____ meta

TRADUCCIONES
a. *put (into)*
b. *wash*
c. *place, arrange*
d. *cut*
e. *season*

B. Paso por (by) paso. Ponga en orden cronológico (de 1 a 4) los siguientes pasos para preparar la lasaña, según la receta.

_____ Cocinar la lasaña en el horno.
_____ Hervir las espinacas y luego cocinarlas en una sartén.
_____ Preparar la salsa de tomate.
_____ Poner en una fuente, en capas, todos los ingredientes preparados para formar la lasaña.

Proyecto: Una receta

Paso 1. Piense en un plato que usted considera delicioso. Puede ser un plato tradicional de su familia y/o de su cultura. ¿Por qué le gusta?

Paso 2. Escriba la receta para este plato. Incluya la lista de los ingredientes con las cantidades específicas y los pasos para su preparación. También escriba una breve introducción para explicar en qué ocasiones y con qué otras comidas es costumbre (*it's customary*) servirlo.

Paso 3. ¡Comparta (*Share*) su receta con sus compañeros de clase!

Textos orales

En un restaurante

Antes de escuchar

¿Sale con frecuencia a comer en restaurantes? ¿Tiene algún restaurante favorito? ¿En qué se especializa?

Los señores Robles en el restaurante

Vocabulario para escuchar			
la carta	menu	**mixto/a**	mixed (with **paella** = having both meat and seafood)
los entrantes	starters, first courses		
el segundo plato	main course	**cómo no**	of course

Comprensión

A. **¿Qué desean?** Los señores Robles cenan esta noche en un restaurante elegante. ¿Qué piden?

1. El Sr. Robles:

   Entrante _____ Segundo plato _____

2. La Sra. Robles:

   Entrante _____ Segundo plato _____

3. De beber:

   _____

B. **Más detalles.** Conteste las siguientes preguntas.

1. ¿Qué platos tienen fama en este restaurante?
2. ¿Cuándo van a pedir el postre los Sres. Robles?

En acción

Escriba un párrafo para una página web sobre restaurantes, dando su opinión sobre un restaurante en particular. Además de dar (*Besides giving*) el nombre del restaurante, explique en qué tipo de comida se especializa, cuáles son sus platos favoritos (con algunos detalles) y por qué usted lo recomienda... ¡o no lo recomienda!

Purestock/Getty Images

🎤 Entrevista

Use de modelo las preguntas y respuestas de la sección **Entrevista** al principio (*at the beginning*) de este capítulo para hablar de la comida de su país y de sus preferencias culinarias.

💻 Escritura

Las opciones de comida en esta universidad

Usted va a escribir un ensayo sobre cómo y dónde comen los estudiantes en su universidad y si, en general, hay satisfacción con las opciones para comer en el campus.

¿Come usted con frecuencia en la cafetería universitaria?

Fuse/Corbis/Getty Images

👥 Antes de escribir

En parejas, compartan (*share*) sus ideas sobre las opciones que se ofrecen en su campus para comer. La conversación los/las ayudará (*will help you*) a clarificar sus propias ideas y determinar un enfoque para su ensayo.

- ¿Ofrecen las cafeterías y otros restaurantes una buena variedad de comidas? Ejemplos: platos vegetarianos, comida baja en calorías.
- ¿Hay buenos planes de comida?
- ¿Cuáles son los platos que más piden los estudiantes?
- En general, ¿está rica la comida? ¿Es cara o barata?
- ¿Hay alguna cafetería mejor que otra?
- ¿Creen que hay bastante satisfacción entre los estudiantes con respecto a las opciones que se ofrecen? Justifiquen sus respuestas.

A escribir

Ahora use sus opiniones y las (*those*) de su compañero/a (recuerde citarlo/la [*remember to quote him or her*]) para escribir su ensayo. Escoja (*Choose*) un enfoque desde el principio (*from the beginning*) para organizar bien su texto. Hay más ayuda en Connect.

Para escribir bien

Considere estas opciones para su ensayo:

- Conectores: **además, por eso, por un lado** (*on the one hand*), **por otro lado** (*on the other hand*), **sin embargo**
- Comparaciones
- Las palabras indefinidas y negativas
- Las expresiones con **tener**

✿ En la comunidad

Entreviste a una persona hispana de su universidad o ciudad sobre la cocina y la comida de su país.

Preguntas posibles

- ¿Cuáles son los ingredientes más importantes?
- ¿Puede encontrar estos ingredientes en los supermercados de aquí?
- ¿Cuál es la comida principal del día? ¿Comen un desayuno fuerte (*heavy*)?
- ¿Cuáles son algunos de los platos típicos?
- ¿Hay muchos restaurantes especializados en la comida de su país en este estado? ¿Cuál es su favorito?

◎ Producción audiovisual

Filme un programa culinario en el que (*which*) presente al menos (*at least*) dos platos o ingredientes tradicionales de una cocina nacional o regional.

Más ideas para el portafolio

- Incluya una lista de sus comidas y bebidas favoritas. Incluya los lugares (restaurantes, la casa de alguien) donde las come o las bebe porque son mejores.
- Incluya una receta familiar favorita.
- Entreviste a un(a) hispanohablante sobre los platos más tradicionales de su cultura y pídale (*ask him/her for*) una receta fácil.
- Si ha estado jugando (*you have been playing*) Practice Spanish: Study Abroad, en Quest 4 usted participó (*participated*) en una telenovela (*soap opera*) sobre una compañía que se especializa en (*specializes in*) la moda. En grupos, escriban una escena (*scene*) de una telenovela que tenga lugar (*takes place*) en un restaurante. Usen vocabulario de este capítulo ¡y sean creativos! Después, ustedes pueden interpretar (*act out*) su escena para la clase.

Sugerencia: You are now ready to play Quest 4 in **Practice Spanish: Study Abroad.**

AFTER STUDYING THIS CHAPTER I CAN ...

☐ talk about food and the meals of the day (206–207)

☐ use the verbs **saber** and **conocer** to express *to know* (210)

☐ use direct object pronouns to avoid repetition in conversation (213–215)

☐ use negative and indefinite words (219–220)

☐ give and understand formal commands (223–225)

☐ recognize/describe at least 2–3 aspects of Panamanian cultures

Gramática en breve

18. Direct Object Pronouns

me, te, lo/la, nos, os, los/las

19. Indefinite and Negative Words

algo	nada
alguien	nadie
algún (alguna/os/as)	ningún (ninguna)
siempre	nunca, jamás
también	tampoco

<u>no</u> + verb + negative word
negative word + verb

20. Formal Commands

-ar → -<u>e</u>(n)
-er/-ir → -<u>a</u>(n)

Affirmative: command + pronoun (**1** word)
Negative: no + pronoun + command (**3** words)

Vocabulario

Los verbos

acabar de + *inf.*	to have just (*done something*)
ayudar	to help
ayudar a + *inf.*	to help to (*do something*)
cono<u>c</u>er (cono<u>zc</u>o)	to know (*a person*); to be acquainted, familiar with (*a place or thing*); to meet (*a person*)
contestar	to answer
esperar	to wait (for); to expect

invitar	to invite
llamar	to call
<u>saber</u> (<u>sé</u>)	to know (*facts, information*)
saber + *inf.*	to know how to (*do something*)

La comida

cenar	to have/eat dinner, supper
cocinar	to cook
desayunar	to have/eat breakfast
mer<u>e</u>ndar (mer<u>ie</u>ndo)	to snack
preparar	to prepare

Repaso: alm<u>o</u>rzar (alm<u>ue</u>rzo) (<u>c</u>)

el aceite (de oliva)	(olive) oil
el aguacate	avocado
el arroz	rice
las arvejas	green peas
el atún	tuna
el azúcar	sugar
el bistec	steak
los camarones	shrimp
la carne	meat
la cebolla	onion
los champiñones	mushrooms
la chuleta (de cerdo)	(pork) chop
los dulces	sweets; candy
los espárragos	asparagus
el flan	(baked) custard
los frijoles	beans
la galleta	cookie
los garbanzos	chickpeas
el helado	ice cream
el huevo	egg
el jamón	ham
la langosta	lobster
la lechuga	lettuce
la mantequilla	butter
la manzana	apple
los mariscos	shellfish
la naranja	orange
el pan	bread
el pan tostado	toast
la papa (frita)	(French fried) potato
el pastel	cake; pie
el pavo	turkey
el pepino	cucumber
el pescado	fish
la pimienta	pepper
el pollo (asado)	(roast) chicken

> Remember that this letter (<u>c</u>) indicates the spelling change that happens in the formal commands of verbs that end in **-car, -gar,** or **-zar.**

el postre	dessert
el queso	cheese
la sal	salt
la salsa	salsa; sauce
la salchicha	sausage; hot dog
la sopa	soup
las verduras	vegetables
la zanahoria	carrot
la comida	food

Cognados: la banana, la barbacoa, el cereal, la ensalada, la fruta, la hamburguesa, el salmón, el sándwich, el tomate, el yogur

Las bebidas

el agua (*but f.*) (mineral)	(mineral) water
la cerveza	beer
el jugo (de fruta)	(fruit) juice
la leche	milk
el refresco	soft drink
el vino (blanco, tinto)	(white, red) wine

Cognado: el té

Repaso: la bebida, el café

Las comidas

el almuerzo	lunch
la cena	dinner, supper
el desayuno	breakfast
la merienda	snack
la comida	meal

En un restaurante

el/la camarero/a	waiter/waitress
la cuenta	check; bill
el plato	plate; dish (*food prepared in a particular way*); course
el plato principal	main course

Cognado: el menú

Otros sustantivos

la ayuda	help
la canción	song
la cocina	cuisine
los comestibles	groceries, foodstuff
el consejo	(piece of) advice
la dirección	address
el/la dueño/a	owner

la letra	lyrics (*of a song*)
el mandato	command
el nombre	name
la receta	recipe
la tarjeta de crédito	credit card

Los adjetivos

asado/a	roast(ed), grilled
caliente	hot (*in temperature, not taste*)
fresco/a	fresh
frito/a	fried
ligero/a	light, not heavy
picante	hot, spicy
rico/a	tasty, savory; rich (*in calories*)
tostado/a	toasted

Las palabras indefinidas y negativas

algo	something, anything
alguien	someone, anyone
algún (alguna/os/as)	some, any
jamás	never
nada	nothing, not anything
nadie	no one, nobody, not anybody
ningún (ninguna)	no, not any
tampoco	neither, not either

Repaso: nunca, siempre, también

Palabras adicionales

¡Buen provecho!	Bon appetit!
<u>estar</u> a dieta	to be on a diet
<u>tener</u> (mucha) hambre	to be (very) hungry
<u>tener</u> (mucha) sed	to be (very) thirsty

Vocabulario personal

Use this space or a vocabulary notebook to write down other words and phrases you learn in this chapter.

8

De viaje°

De... *On a trip, Traveling*

En este capítulo

VOCABULARY

Traveling   238

Vacations   240

GRAMMAR

Indirect object pronouns (*to whom* or *for whom* after a verb)   244

Using the verb **gustar**   250

One way to talk about the past   255

COUNTRY OF FOCUS: THE DOMINICAN REPUBLIC

Un café en Santo Domingo, República Dominicana

LA REPÚBLICA DOMINICANA

11,2 (coma dos) millones de habitantes

- La República Dominicana comparte[a] la isla de La Española (*Hispaniola,* en inglés) con el país de Haití.

- La ciudad de Santo Domingo, capital del país, fue fundada[b] por el hermano de Cristóbal Colón en 1496. Y es la primera ciudad fundada por los europeos en América.

[a]*shares* [b]*founded*

ENTREVISTA

These questions related to the chapter theme are answered here by a native speaker. You will be able to ask and answer them yourself with personal information in the **Entrevista** activity in the **Portafolio** section at the end of the chapter.

Cecilia Figueroa Martín contesta las preguntas.

— **¿Dónde le gusta pasar las vacaciones? ¿en la playa? ¿en las montañas? ¿visitando una ciudad o un país que usted no conoce?**

— Prefiero ir de viaje a otros países y también visitar a mis parientes en los Estados Unidos. Como[a] soy de Puerto Rico y tengo el mar[b] y el calor todo el tiempo, me gusta irme de vacaciones a lugares con un clima diferente. ¡Me encanta[c] ver la nieve!

— **¿Qué le gusta hacer cuando está en la playa? ¿nadar[d]? ¿tomar el sol[e]? ¿surfear u otros deportes[f]?**

— Cuando voy a la playa, me gusta nadar y estar en la arena[g] leyendo.

— **¿Qué es lo peor[h] de hacer un viaje, hacer la maleta,[i] el viaje mismo[j] o volver a casa?**

— Para mí, lo peor de un viaje es tener que trasladarse.[k] Odio[l] especialmente los viajes en avión.[m] Pero si el viaje es muy divertido,[n] ¡odio volver!

[a]*Since* [b]*ocean* [c]*¡Me... I love* [d]*swim* [e]*tomar... sunbathe* [f]*sports* [g]*sand* [h]*lo... the worst part* [i]*hacer... packing* [j]*el... the trip itself* [k]*travel* [l]*I hate* [m]*en... by plane* [n]*muy... a lot of fun*

You can hear the pronunciation of theme vocabulary words and phrases in the eBook.

De viaje°

De... *On a trip, Traveling*

Los medios de transporte

la cabina	cabin (*on a plane*)
el crucero	cruise (ship)
la estación	station
de autobuses	bus station
de trenes	train station
el puerto	port
la sala de espera	waiting room
la sala de fumar /	smoking area
de fumadores	
el vuelo	flight
ir en...	to go/travel by ...
autobús	bus
avión	plane
barco	boat, ship
tren	train

El viaje

el asiento	seat
el billete (*Sp.*) /	ticket
el boleto (*L.A.*)	
de ida	one-way ticket
de ida y vuelta	round-trip ticket
electrónico	e-ticket
la demora	delay
el destino	destination
la llegada	arrival
el pasaje	fare, price (*of a transportation ticket*)
el pasaporte	passport
el pasillo	aisle
la puerta de embarque	boarding gate
la salida	departure
la tarjeta de embarque	boarding pass
la ventanilla	small window (*on a plane*)

anunciar	to announce	<u>ir</u> al extranjero	to go abroad

bajarse (de)	to get down (from); to get off (of) (*a vehicle*)	pasar por
		  la aduana
			to go/pass through
			  customs

<u>estar</u> atrasado/a	to be late	el control de seguridad	security (check)
facturar el equipaje	to check baggage	quejarse (de)	to complain (about)
guardar (un puesto)	to save (a place [*in line*])	<u>salir</u>/lle<u>g</u>ar (<u>gu</u>) a tiempo	to depart/arrive on time
<u>hacer</u> cola	to stand in line	subir (a)	to go up; to get on
<u>hacer</u> escala/parada	to make a stop		(*a vehicle*)

<u>hacer</u> la(s)
  maleta(s)
	to pack one's
	  suitcase(s)
		viajar	to travel

<u>hacer</u> un viaje	to take a trip	v<u>o</u>lar (v<u>ue</u>lo) en avión	to fly; to go by plane

Comunicación

A. **Hablando de medios de transporte.** ¿Con qué medio de transporte relaciona usted las siguientes personas y cosas? Hay más de una respuesta posible en algunos casos.

1. un crucero
2. un(a) asistente de vuelo
3. un puerto
4. una estación
5. una cabina
6. una agencia de viajes
7. un asiento
8. un(a) piloto
9. un capitán / una capitana
10. la llegada

B. **Un viaje al extranjero**

Paso 1. Use los números del 1 al 9 para organizar un viaje de manera lógica.

a. _____ subir al avión cuando se anuncia el vuelo
b. _____ pasar por el control de seguridad
c. _____ hacer cola para obtener la tarjeta de embarque y facturar el equipaje
d. _____ pedir un taxi y llegar al aeropuerto
e. _____ oír el anuncio de la salida del vuelo
f. _____ hacer la maleta y poner el pasaporte en el bolso
g. _____ esperar en la puerta de embarque mandando mensajes
h. _____ sentarse en el asiento junto a la ventanilla
i. _____ llegar al aeropuerto de destino y pasar por el control de inmigración y la aduana

Paso 2. Ahora narre la secuencia en primera persona (**yo**).

C. **En el aeropuerto.** En parejas, nombren o describan las cosas y acciones representadas en este dibujo.

Así se dice

Travel and transportation words are expressed in a variety of ways in different parts of the Spanish-speaking world, but there is rarely any confusion about meaning among native speakers.

el autobús = el camión
  (*Mex.*), el bus (*C.A.*),
  la guagua (*Cuba, P.R.*),
  el colectivo (*Arg.*)

la maleta = la valija
  (*Arg.*), la petaca (*Mex.*)

el billete / el boleto = el
  tiquete (*Mex, C.A.*)

D. Definiciones

Paso 1. Dé las palabras definidas.

1. Es necesario pasar por este control al llegar a otro país.
2. Es la cosa que se compra antes de hacer un viaje.
3. Es el antónimo de **subir a.**
4. Se va allí cuando se hace un viaje en avión.
5. Se va allí cuando se hace un viaje en tren.
6. Es la persona que nos ayuda durante un vuelo.

 Paso 2. Ahora prepare dos definiciones para leer a toda la clase. Sus compañeros van a dar (*give*) la palabra que usted define.

De vacaciones°

De... *On vacation*

el *camping*	campground
el mar	sea
el océano	ocean
estar de vacaciones	to be on vacation
ir(se) de vacaciones a...	to (go on) vacation to/in ...
pasar las vacaciones en...	to spend one's vacation in ...
salir de vacaciones	to leave on vacation
tomar unas vacaciones	to take a vacation

Así se dice

la camioneta = la ranchera, la rubia, el coche rural, el coche familiar, el monovolumen (*Sp.*)
el *camping* = el campamento
hacer *camping* = acampar
sacar fotos = tomar fotos
la tienda de campaña = la tienda de acampar, la carpa, la casa de campaña

Comunicación

A. ¿Qué hace usted?

Paso 1. Diga si las siguientes declaraciones son ciertas o falsas para usted. Corrija las declaraciones falsas.

MODELO: **1.** Cuando voy a la playa, siempre tomo el sol. →
Cuando voy a la playa, tomo el sol algunas veces. En realidad, no me gusta mucho la playa.

1. Cuando voy a la playa, siempre tomo el sol.
2. Es fácil ir a playas bonitas desde (*from*) aquí.
3. Me gusta nadar en el mar.
4. Prefiero irme de vacaciones a las montañas.
5. Tengo mucha experiencia haciendo *camping*.
6. Cuando estoy en un viaje de vacaciones, saco muchas fotos y las subo (*I upload them*) a Facebook o Instagram.
7. Durante un viaje, me gusta mandar algunas tarjetas postales.

Paso 2. En parejas, túrnense para hacer y contestar preguntas basadas en las oraciones del **Paso 1.**

Vocabulario útil

| en realidad | actually |
| la verdad es que | the truth is (that) |

Nota cultural: Tipos de turismo en el mundo hispano

En el mundo hispano hay ciudades y lugares impresionantes que visitar y playas maravillosas[a] donde pasar las vacaciones. Pero hay también una gran variedad de lugares de destino para las personas que desean disfrutar de[b] unas vacaciones excepcionales.

- **El ecoturismo**
Consiste en visitar lugares poco explotados por los seres[c] humanos y hacerlo de una manera ecológicamente responsable. La selva costarricense y la selva amazónica (en el Ecuador y el Perú) son destinos populares, así como[d] la Patagonia (en la Argentina y Chile) y las Islas Galápagos. En el Perú está la opción del Camino[e] Inca, la ruta a pie[f] más famosa de América. Es un camino que va desde Cusco a Machu Picchu entre increíbles vistas de los Andes. Y en España está el Camino de Santiago. Es un camino de peregrinación[g] de origen religioso, pero ahora muchas personas lo hacen porque es una actividad física y social que permite conocer a nuevas personas y ver bellos paisajes.[h]

- **El agroturismo**
Este tipo de vacaciones implica pasar las vacaciones en un lugar rural. Los turistas pueden quedarse[i] en casas renovadas que ofrecen la experiencia de hacer trabajo agrícola y excursiones educativas. En la isla chilena de Chiloé, por ejemplo, hay ofertas agroturísticas interesantes.

El Camino de Santiago, España

Gregorioa/Shutterstock

- **El aventurismo**
Es para aquellos[j] que buscan aventuras emocionantes y físicas. Se puede esquiar en los Andes o en las montañas españolas, hacer ciclismo de montaña, navegar en rápidos, etcétera.

¿Practica usted alguno de estos tipos de turismo? ¿Dónde lo hace?

[a]*wonderful* [b]*disfrutar... to enjoy* [c]*beings* [d]*así... as are* [e]*Trail*
[f]*ruta... walking trail* [g]*pilgrimage* [h]*bellos... beautiful scenery*
[i]*be lodged* [j]*those (people)*

B. Intercambios

Paso 1. Complete los siguientes párrafos sobre sus vacaciones típicas y sus vacaciones más memorables.

Mis vacaciones típicas
Voy a _____¹ en _____² (medio de transporte) en el mes de _____.³
Voy con _____⁴ (personas) y esto es lo que hago: _____.⁵

Mis vacaciones más memorables
Fuiᵃ a _____⁶ en _____⁷ en el mes de _____.⁸ Fui con _____.⁹ Hiceᵇ
las siguientes actividades: _____¹⁰ (infinitivos).

ᵃI went   ᵇI did

Paso 2. Ahora, en parejas, túrnense para hacer y contestar preguntas basadas en las ideas del **Paso 1.** Obtengan (*Get*) mucha información de su compañero/a.

MODELOS: ¿Adónde vas para tus vacaciones, generalmente? ¿Prefieres algún lugar en especial? ¿Vas allí todos los años? ¿Por qué vas allí? Y para tus vacaciones más memorables, ¿a qué lugar fuiste (*did you go*)?

Nota comunicativa: Otro uso de la palabra *se*: para expresar acciones impersonales

If there are native Spanish speakers living in your area, you probably have seen signs like the one in the photo: **Se habla español.** The word **se** in front of the verb (rather than a specific subject, like **Juan** or **ellos**) changes the English equivalent of the verb. In English, **se habla español** can mean: *Spanish is spoken here. We/They speak Spanish here. People speak Spanish here.* You have already seen this use of **se** in direction lines and readings in *Puntos de partida.*

Here are some additional examples of this use of **se** to talk about things that "people," rather than specific individuals, do.

Richard Thornton/Shutterstock

Se va al aeropuerto para tomar un vuelo.

One goes / People go / You go to the airport to catch a flight.

Se aprende mucho viajando.

One learns / People learn / You learn a lot by traveling.

Be alert to this use of **se** in *Puntos de partida* as well as in real-life Spanish; it is very frequent and you need to understand it. You will practice it in **Comunicación C** and **D.** You will also see (and hear) plural verbs with **se,** but you will not practice using them in this text.

C. ¿Dónde se hace esto? Indique el lugar (o los lugares) donde se hacen las siguientes actividades.

MODELO: Se come. → Se come en un restaurante, en casa, en la cafetería...

1. Se factura el equipaje y se anuncia el vuelo.
2. Se hace la maleta.
3. Se compra un boleto.
4. Se espera el avión.
5. Se pide una bebida.
6. Se mira una película.
7. Se nada y se toma el sol.
8. Se habla francés.
9. Se habla portugués.
10. Se viaja en barco.

D. Los viajes y la vida (*life*)

Paso 1. Elija (*Choose*) una experiencia o etapa (*phase*) importante o interesante en la vida de una persona y descríbala con dos o tres oraciones impersonales. Siga el modelo de esta descripción de los viajes.

Vocabulario útil

Experiencias y etapas de la vida

la adolescencia
la comida de la cafetería
la compra de...
la maternidad
la paternidad
la primera cita · first date
el trabajo · work

Acciones

evitar · to avoid
experimentar · to experience
planear · to plan
rec**o**rdar (rec**ue**rdo) · to remember
s**o**ñar (s**ue**ño) · to dream
sufrir · to suffer, endure

Un viaje se vive tres veces: cuando se sueña,ᵃ cuando se vive y cuando se recuerdaᵇ

ᵃse... *it is dreamed*   ᵇse... *it is remembered*

 Paso 2. Ahora, en parejas, compartan (*share*) sus ideas y traten de añadir (*try to add*) una oración más a las oraciones que escribió (*wrote*) su compañero/a.

Algo sobre el colmado dominicano

En todo el mundo hispanohablante hay tiendas en los barriosᵃ donde se venden comestibles, bebidas y las cosas que en este país se compran en los supermercados. En la República Dominicana, estas tiendas se llaman «colmados». Un colmado es un punto de encuentroᵇ para la genteᶜ del barrio. A veces es como un bar-discoteca, donde se baila merengue y bachataᵈ y otros tipos de música.

Un colmado dominicano

 ¿Existe en el lugar donde usted vive alguna tienda similar a los colmados? ¿Qué se hace allí?

ᵃ*neighborhoods*   ᵇpunto... *meeting place*   ᶜ*people*   ᵈ*dance music (typically Dominican but danced in all Spanish-speaking countries)*

In Gramática 18 (Cap. 7), **Repaso**

In Gramática 18 (Cap. 7), you learned how to use direct object pronouns to avoid repetition. Can you identify the direct object pronouns in the following exchange? To what or to whom do these pronouns refer?

ROBERTO: ¿Tienes los boletos?

ANA: No, no los tengo, pero mi agente de viajes ya los tiene listos (*ready*).

ROBERTO: Si quieres, te acompaño a la agencia.

ANA: Encantada. Casi nunca te veo.

21 Expressing *to whom* or *for whom* • Indirect Object Pronouns; **Dar** and **decir**

Gramática en acción: En el aeropuerto

En el mostrador

—**¿Me** puede dar un asiento de ventanilla, por favor?

—Lo siento, pero ya no hay. Pero sí puedo asignar**le** un asiento de pasillo.

En el control de seguridad

—**¿Le** enseño la tarjeta de embarque?

—No es necesario, señorita.

—**¿Le** enseño el pasaporte?

—Tampoco es necesario.

Comprensión

¿Dónde se oye, en el mostrador o en el control de seguridad?

1. «¿Puede enseñar**me** (*show me*) lo que hay en su bolso?»
2. «No **me** gusta sentarme en el asiento de en medio (*middle*)».
3. «En un momento **le** doy la nueva tarjeta de embarque».
4. «**¿Me** enseña el pasaporte, por favor?»

Indirect Object Pronouns / **Los pronombres del complemento indirecto**

the indirect object / **el complemento indirecto** = the noun or pronoun that indicates *to whom* or *for whom* an action is performed

me	to/for me	**nos**	to/for us
te	to/for you (*fam. sing.*)	**os**	to/for you (*fam. pl.*)
le	to/for you (*form. sing.*), him, her, it	**les**	to/for you (*form. pl.*), them

¡OJO!

Note that indirect object pronouns have the same form as direct object pronouns, except in the third person: **le, les.**

At the airport At the counter: *"Could you please give me a window seat?" "I'm sorry, but there aren't any more (available). But I **can** give you an aisle seat."* **At the security check:** *"Do I show you my boarding pass?" "That's not necessary, miss." "Do I show you my passport?" "That isn't necessary either."*

1. Indirect Objects

Indirect object nouns and pronouns are the person affected by the action of the verb. They usually answer the question *to whom?* or *for whom?* in relation to the verb. The word *to* is frequently omitted in English.

	INDIRECT	DIRECT	
Ana is making	**them**	dinner.	
I'll give	**her**	the gift	tomorrow.
For whom is Ana making dinner? → **(for) them**			
To whom am I giving the gift? → **(to) her**			

Indicate the indirect objects in the following sentences.

1. *He'll give me the car tomorrow.*
2. *Please tell me the answer now.*
3. Me va a dar el coche mañana.
4. Dígame la respuesta ahora, por favor.
5. El profesor nos va a hacer algunas preguntas.
6. ¿No me compras una revista ahora?

2. Placement of Indirect Object Pronouns

Like direct object pronouns, *indirect object pronouns* (**los pronombres del complemento indirecto**) precede the conjugated verb.

When the conjugated verb is followed by an infinitive or a present participle, the pronouns either precede the conjugated verb *or* follow (and are attached to):

- the infinitive
- the present participle

Remember to add an accent mark to the present participle when you attach a pronoun to it.

No, no **te** presto el coche.
No, I won't lend you the car.

Voy a **guardarte** el asiento.
Te voy a guardar el asiento.
I'll save your seat for you.

Le estoy escribiendo un e-mail a Marisol.
Estoy **escribiéndole** un e-mail a Marisol.
I'm writing Marisol an email.

3. Placement of Indirect Object Pronouns with Commands

As with direct object pronouns, indirect object pronouns:

- are attached to the affirmative command form.
- precede the negative command form.

Remember to add an accent to most affirmative commands when you attach a pronoun.

Sírvanos un café, por favor.
Serve us some coffee, please.

No me dé su número de teléfono ahora.
Don't give me your phone number now.

4. Redundancy of the Indirect Object

Even when a sentence has a third person indirect object *noun*, it usually also has a third person indirect object *pronoun*. The noun object is preceded by **a,** which expresses *to* or *for*. This redundancy may sound repetitive to you, but it is what happens in Spanish most of the time.

Vamos a **mandarle** un mensaje **a Juan.**
Let's send Juan a message.
(Lit., *Let's send **him** a message **to Juan.**)*

¿**Les** guardo los asientos **a los niños?**
Shall I save the seats for the kids?
(Lit., *Shall I **them** save the seats **for the kids?**)*

5. Multiple Meanings of *le(s)*

Le and **les** can have several different meanings. When context does not make the meaning clear, the meaning is clarified with a prepositional phrase: **a** + *pronoun object of a preposition*. This redundancy is appropriate in Spanish.

Voy a **mandarle** un telegrama. = meaning of **le** unclear unless specified
Voy a **mandarle** un telegrama **a usted** / ...**a él** / ...**a ella.**
I'm going to send you/him/her a telegram.

¡OJO!

Object of prepositions = subject pronouns, except for **mí** and **ti.**

6. Clarification or Emphasis of Indirect Object Pronouns

To clarify or emphasize the indirect object pronouns **me, te, nos,** and **os,** a phrase with **a** + *object pronoun* is also used. English accomplishes this by tone of voice, but Spanish does it with redundancy.

¿Usted **me** habla **a mí?**
*Are you talking to **me?***

Pedro **te** dio el pasaporte **a ti,** no **a mí.**
*Pedro gave **you** the passport, not (to) **me.***

7. Verbs Often Used with Indirect Objects

Here are some verbs frequently used with indirect objects. You already know the meaning of the ones marked with *.

c<u>o</u>ntar (c<u>ue</u>nto)	to tell; to narrate	*p<u>e</u>dir (p<u>i</u>do) (i)	to ask for
entre<u>g</u>ar (<u>gu</u>)	to hand in	preguntar	to ask (*a question*)
*escribir	to write	prestar	to lend
expli<u>c</u>ar (<u>qu</u>)	to explain	prometer	to promise
*hablar	to speak	recom<u>e</u>ndar (recom<u>ie</u>ndo)	to recommend
*mandar	to send	regalar	to give (*as a gift*)
m<u>o</u>strar (m<u>ue</u>stro)	to show	*s<u>e</u>rvir (s<u>i</u>rvo) (i)	to serve
ofr<u>e</u>cer (ofr<u>ez</u>co)	to offer		

Dar and *decir*

dar (*to give*)		decir (*to say; to tell*)	
doy	damos	digo	decimos
das	dais	dices	decís
da	dan	dice	dicen
dando		diciendo	

Juan **dice** que tiene muchos gastos (*expenses*) en la universidad. Por eso Juan les **dice** a sus padres que necesita dinero.

Sus padres le **dan** un cheque.

1. *dar*

Dar means *to give*. It is almost always used with indirect object pronouns.

> **¡OJO!**
>
> Another Spanish verb expresses *to give* as a gift: **regalar.**

Los profesores **nos dan** mucha tarea en todas las clases.
Professors give us a lot of homework in all my classes.

Mis abuelos **me regalan** dinero para mi cumpleaños.
My grandparents give me money for my birthday.

2. *decir*

Decir means *to say* or *to tell*. When **decir** means *to tell*, it is almost always used with indirect object pronouns, like **dar.**

> **¡OJO!**
>
> Other verbs related to speaking are used to express different meanings.
>
> hablar   to speak
> c<u>o</u>ntar (c<u>ue</u>nto)   to tell; to narrate

Mi profesor **dice** que la historia es fascinante.
My professor says that history is fascinating.

Y **nos dice** que tenemos mucho que aprender de la historia.
And he tells us that we have a lot to learn from history.

El profesor **habla** varias lenguas.
The professor speaks several languages.

A veces **nos cuenta** algunas de sus experiencias en Latinoamérica.
At times he tells us (about) some of his experiences in Latin America.

3. Formal Commands of *dar* and *decir*

As you know, **dar** and **decir** also have irregular formal command forms. There is a written accent on **dé** to distinguish it from the preposition **de.**

Mandatos formales
dar → d<u>é</u>, den
decir → diga, digan

Práctica y comunicación

A. Asociaciones. ¿Qué verbos asocia usted con los siguientes objetos y situaciones?

1. un coche, el dinero
2. la comida en un restaurante
3. las fotos
4. hacer algo por (for) alguien
5. la gramática, un profesor

6. la tarea, un informe (report, paper)
7. algo para un cumpleaños
8. un restaurante, una película, un libro
9. flores (flowers), un e-mail
10. un secreto, un chiste (joke)

B. Partes de una oración. Identifique las partes subrayadas (underlined) de las siguientes oraciones. Pueden ser sujetos (s), complementos directos (cd) o complementos indirectos (ci). **¡OJO!** No todas las oraciones tienen complemento directo e indirecto.

MODELO: <u>Mi madre</u> <u>nos</u> regala <u>boletos de avión</u> para los viajes familiares. →
Mi madre = s, nos = ci, boletos de avión = cd

1. <u>Mi hermana</u> <u>me</u> regala <u>un suéter</u> cada año para Navidad.
2. Escribo <u>poemas de amor</u> en español.
3. <u>Les</u> mando <u>unos e-mails</u> <u>a mis estudiantes</u>.
4. ¿Quién está mandándo<u>te</u> <u>mensajes</u>?
5. ¿<u>Me</u> enseñas <u>una foto de tu perro</u>?

C. Dar y recibir

Paso 1. Autoprueba. Complete las siguientes oraciones con el pronombre del complemento indirecto apropiado de la lista: **me, te, le, nos, les.**

1. _____ presto el coche a ti, Carolina, no a tu hermano.
2. Los señores Gómez _____ mandan saludos a su amigo dominicano.
3. No _____ dé más galletas a los niños, por favor.
4. ¿ _____ pasas el pan, por favor? Está muy lejos de mí.
5. Profesora, no podemos terminar el examen si no _____ da más tiempo.
6. El tío Juan siempre _____ dice a mis hermanos y a mí que la ciudad de Santo Domingo es muy bonita.

Paso 2. Complete las siguientes declaraciones sobre su vida (life) con el pronombre del complemento indirecto apropiado. Si la oración no es cierta para usted, hágala negativa usando **no** u otras palabras negativas.

1. Todos los años _____ doy/mando una tarjeta de cumpleaños a mi mejor amigo/a.
2. Todos los años mi mejor amigo/a _____ da/manda una tarjeta de cumpleaños.
3. Todos los días _____ escribo un mensaje a mis padres o a mis abuelos.
4. Todos los días mis madre / mis padres o mis abuelos (mis hijos) _____ mandan un mensaje.
5. Mis profesores y profesoras _____ cuentan chistes y anécdotas en clase con frecuencia.
6. Con frecuencia, _____ cuento chistes y anécdotas en las clases.
7. Mi(s) abuelo(s) _____ regala(n) dinero para mi cumpleaños o para un día especial.
8. _____ regalo dinero a mis abuelos/hijos con frecuencia.

Paso 3. Ahora, en parejas, túrnense para hacer y contestar preguntas, usando las oraciones del **Paso 2.** Luego díganle al resto de la clase algo que ustedes tienen en común. **¡OJO!** Hagan los cambios necesarios, según el modelo.

MODELO: **1.** Todos los años _____ doy una tarjeta de cumpleaños a mi mejor amigo/a. →
E1: ¿Todos los años **le das** una tarjeta de cumpleaños a **tu** mejor amiga?
E2: No, nunca **le doy** una tarjeta de cumpleaños a **mi** mejor amiga. ¿Y tú?
E1: Yo tampoco. →
Nosotros nunca **les damos** una tarjeta de cumpleaños a **nuestras** mejores amigas.

Summary of Indirect Object Pronouns

a mí → **me**
a nosotros/as → **nos**

a ti → **te**
a vosotros/as → **os**

a usted, él, ella → **le**
a ustedes, ellos, ellas → **les**

D. De vuelta (*Returning*) a la República Dominicana

Paso 1. Unos amigos dominicanos necesitan ayuda para arreglar (*arrange*) su vuelta (*return*) a casa. Explíqueles cómo usted los puede ayudar.

MODELO: imprimir (*to print*) el boleto electrónico → **Les** imprimo el boleto electrónico.

1. llamar un taxi
2. bajar (*to carry down*) las maletas de su habitación
3. guardar (*to keep an eye on*) el equipaje

4. guardar un puesto en la cola
5. comprar una revista
6. por fin dar un abrazo (*hug*)

Paso 2. Ahora describa las acciones, pero desde el punto de vista (*point of view*) de sus amigos.

MODELO: imprimir el boleto electrónico → **Nos** imprimes el boleto electrónico.

E. ¿Qué hacen estas personas? Complete las siguientes oraciones lógicamente con un verbo y un pronombre del complemento indirecto.

MODELO: El vicepresidente _____ consejos al presidente. →
El vicepresidente **le ofrece** consejos al presidente.

1. Romeo _____ flores a Julieta.
2. Snoopy _____ besos (*kisses*) a Lucy... ¡Y a ella no le gusta!
3. Eva _____ una manzana a Adán.
4. Los psicólogos _____ consejos a la gente (*people*) que los necesita.
5. Los bancos _____ dinero a las personas que quieren comprar una casa.
6. Los asistentes de vuelo _____ bebidas a los pasajeros.
7. Yo siempre _____ la verdad a todos.

F. En un restaurante. Explíquele al pequeño Benjamín, que tiene solo 4 años, lo que se hace en un restaurante. Llene los espacios en blanco con pronombres del complemento indirecto.

Primero el camarero _____[1] ofrece una mesa desocupada.[a] Luego tú _____[2] pides el menú al camarero. También _____[3] haces preguntas sobre los platos y las especialidades de la casa y _____[4] dices lo que quieres comer. El camarero _____[5] trae la comida. Por fin tu papá _____[6] pide la cuenta al camarero. Si tú quieres pagar, _____[7] pides dinero a tu papá y _____[8] das el dinero al camarero.

[a]*vacant*

G. ¿Quién te hace eso? En parejas, túrnense para hacerse y contestar preguntas sobre qué personas en su vida hacen las siguientes acciones. Usen la palabra **nadie** si es necesario. Traten de (*Try to*) continuar la conversación dando o pidiendo detalles.

MODELO: hacer buenos regalos →
E1: **¿Quién te** hace buenos regalos?
E2: Mis padres siempre me hacen buenos regalos. (¡Nadie me hace buenos regalos!)
E1: **¿Qué te** regalan, por ejemplo?
E2: Bueno, me regalan dinero, ropa, cosas para mi apartamento...

1. hacer regalos buenos y caros / feos o inútiles
2. decir la verdad /mentiras (*lies*)
3. contar los secretos propios (*of his/her own*) / de otras personas
4. hacer favores / recomendaciones / la cena
5. dar recomendaciones sobre cómo vivir
6. prometer cosas que luego no hace

Vocabulario útil

<u>dar</u>
<u>decir</u>
ofre<u>c</u>er (ofre<u>zc</u>o)
prestar
regalar
s<u>e</u>rvir (s<u>i</u>rvo) (<u>i</u>)

Algo sobre el casabe

Alea Image/iStock/Getty Images

El casabe, un producto que representa la cultura de la República Dominicana

El casabe es una especie de tortilla que se hace con la yuca.[a] Es un producto básico de alimentación[b] de los dominicanos. Como comida, el casabe es una tradición que viene de los taínos, los indígenas de la isla de La Española (hoy día, Haití y la República Dominicana).

 En su cultura, ¿qué alimento se puede comparar con el casabe?

[a]*manioc, cassava root* [b]*diet, what people eat*

Textos de todos los días: Comunicación sobre la llegada a un apartamento

A veces las horas de entrada y salida de un hotel o de un apartamento de alquiler (*rental*) no coinciden con las necesidades de un viaje. En ese caso, se puede preguntarle a la persona indicada en el hotel o en el apartamento si hay flexibilidad con las horas.

Objetivo: Escribir un correo electrónico pidiendo un cambio en la hora de entrada o salida de un apartamento de alquiler. En la página web se dice que la hora de entrada es a las 3 de la tarde y la (*that*) de salida a las 11 de la mañana.

Antes de empezar

- Primero, invente una situación: un viaje a un lugar determinado con una hora de llegada o salida específica y una razón para solicitar (*request*) una hora diferente. ¡Se puede volar con la imaginación, pero sea convincente!
- Considere cuáles son las ideas esenciales que usted quiere comunicarle a la persona indicada.

Vocabulario útil

Saludos: ¡Hola! Buenos días. Buenas tardes/noches.
Cierre (*Closing*): **Le doy/damos las gracias por su consideración de antemano** (*in advance*).

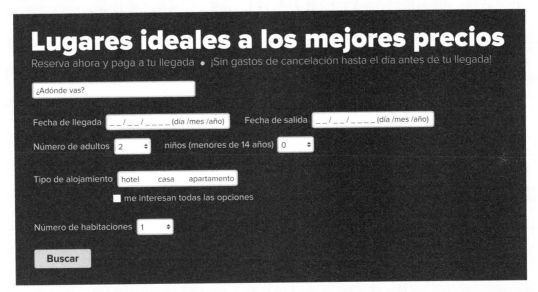

Lugares ideales a los mejores precios

Reserva ahora y paga a tu llegada • ¡Sin gastos de cancelación hasta el día antes de tu llegada!

¿Adónde vas?

Fecha de llegada _ _ / _ _ / _ _ _ _ (día /mes /año)   Fecha de salida _ _ / _ _ / _ _ _ _ (día /mes /año)

Número de adultos 2 ▲▼   niños (menores de 14 años) 0 ▲▼

Tipo de alojamiento   hotel   casa   apartamento

☐ me interesan todas las opciones

Número de habitaciones 1 ▲▼

Buscar

Contactar al anfitrión/anfitriona[a]

[blank text box]

[a]*host*

🌳 Repaso

In **Capítulo 1** you started to use forms of **gustar** to express your likes and dislikes. Review what you know by answering the following questions. Then, changing their form as needed, interview your instructor.

1. ¿Te gusta el café (el vino, el té...)?
2. ¿Te gusta jugar al béisbol (al golf, al voleibol, al...)?
3. ¿Te gusta viajar en avión (fumar, viajar en tren...)?
4. ¿Qué te gusta más, estudiar o ir a fiestas (trabajar o descansar, cocinar o comer)?

22 Expressing Likes and Dislikes • *Gustar* (Part 2)

Gramática en acción: Vacaciones en la República Dominicana

En la República Dominicana se puede hacer de todo en las vacaciones.

- **A** algunas personas **les gusta** relajarse en la playa.
- **A** otras personas **les gustan** las vacaciones que les permiten hacer actividades deportivas (*sporting*).
- **A** algunos turistas **les gustan** los museos y los monumentos históricos.
- **A** mucha gente **le gusta** hacer de todo un poco.

¿Y a usted?

¿Qué **le gusta** hacer en sus vacaciones? ¿**Le gusta** ir a un sitio donde hace buen tiempo? ¿**Le gustan** las actividades deportivas o las culturales (*cultural ones*)?

Courtesy of Dominican Republic Tourism Board

Using **gustar** / Los usos de *gustar*

Spanish	English Phrasing	Literal Equivalent
Me gusta la playa.	*I like the beach.*	The beach is pleasing to me.
No le gustan esos cursos.	*You* (form.) / *He / She doesn't like those courses.*	Those courses are not pleasing to you (*form.*) / him / her.
Nos gusta esquiar.	*We like to ski.*	Skiing is pleasing to us.

You have been using the verb **gustar** since the beginning of *Puntos de partida* to express likes and dislikes. However, **gustar** does not literally mean *to like*, but rather *to be pleasing*.

Me gusta viajar.
Traveling is pleasing to me. (I like to travel.)

Me gustan los viajes de aventura.
Adventure trips are pleasing to me. (I like adventure trips.)

---

1. *Gustar* + **Indirect Object Pronouns**
   Gustar is always used with an indirect object pronoun: something is pleasing *to* someone. The verb agrees with the subject of the sentence = the thing that is pleasing. In the first two examples, **gusta** is used with the singular noun **asiento, gustan** with the plural **asientos.**

   (**no**) *indirect object pronoun* + **gusta(n)** + *subject*

   Me gust**a** **este asiento** de pasillo.
   This aisle seat is pleasing to me. (I like this aisle seat.)

   No **me** gust**an** **los asientos** de ventanilla.
   Window seats are not pleasing to me. (I don't like window seats.)

   Me gust**a** mucho **volar** en avión.
   Flying is really pleasing to me. (I really like to fly.)

   Me gust**a** **nadar** y **tomar** el sol.
   I like to swim and sunbathe.

¡OJO!

An infinitive is a singular subject in Spanish. **Gusta** is used even if there are two or more infinitive subjects.

---

2. Redundancy of Indirect Object

When the person pleased is a noun or a proper name, the indirect object pronoun is still used. This redundancy (repetition) is the same concept you learned with **le** and **les** in **Gramática 21**.

> **a** + *noun* + **(no) le / les gusta(n)** + *subject*
> **(no) le / les gusta(n)** + *subject* + **a** + *noun*

¡OJO!

Remember: The indirect object pronoun *must* be used with **gustar** even when the prepositional phrase **a** + *noun* or *pronoun* is used.

Al niño no **le** gustan los aviones.
No **le** gustan los aviones **al niño.**
The child doesn't like airplanes.

A Raquel y a Arturo les gusta viajar juntos.
Les gusta viajar juntos **a Raquel y Arturo.**
Raquel and Arturo like to travel together.

3. Clarification or Emphasis

A phrase with **a** + *pronoun* is often used for clarification or emphasis. The prepositional phrase can appear before the indirect object pronoun or after the verb.

¡OJO!

Remember that subject pronouns (**usted, él, ella...**) are used as the object of prepositions, except for **mí** (accent) and **ti** (no accent). (Exceptions: **conmigo, contigo.**)

CLARIFICATION

¿**Le** gusta **a usted** viajar? ¿**A usted** le gusta viajar?
Do you like to travel?

¿**Le** gusta **a él** viajar? ¿**A él** le gusta viajar?
Does he like to travel?

EMPHASIS

A mí me gusta viajar en avión, pero **a mi esposo** le gusta viajar en coche. Y **a ti,** ¿en qué **te** gusta viajar?
I like to travel by plane, but my husband likes to travel by car. How do you like to travel?

4. *Gustar* + determiner + noun

When the thing liked is a noun, it is always preceded by a determiner of some kind: an article, an adjective of quantity (like **muchos**), a possessive, or a demonstrative.

¡OJO!

In English, the definite article is omitted with the verb *like*. In Spanish, the definite article is *never* omitted with **gustar** unless another determiner is used.

Me gusta **el** chocolate. Me gustan **los** dulces.
I like chocolate. I like sweets.

Me gustan **muchas** canciones de Shakira.
I like many of Shakira's songs.

Me gustan **tus** sugerencias, pero no me gusta **ese** tipo de vacaciones.
I like your suggestions, but I don't like that type of vacation.

Would Like / Wouldn't Like = **Gustaría**

To express what you *would* or *would not* like to do, use **gustaría** + *infinitive* with the appropriate indirect objects.

A mí me **gustaría viajar** a Colombia.
I would like to travel to Colombia.

No nos **gustaría hacer** camping este verano.
We would not like to go camping this summer.

Práctica y comunicación

A. Los gustos y preferencias para las vacaciones

Paso 1. Autoprueba. Complete las siguientes oraciones con **-a** or **-an.**

1. Me gust_____ nadar. Por eso me gust_____ las playas caribeñas.
2. A mi familia y a mí nos gust_____ esquiar. Por eso nos gust_____ las vacaciones de invierno.
3. A mi mejor amigo le gust_____ el sol. Por eso siempre le gust_____ la República Dominicana para las vacaciones.
4. ¿A ti te gust_____ las vacaciones activas o relajantes (*relaxing*)?

> **Summary of the Uses of *gustar***
>
> **me (te...) gusta +**
> singular noun or infinitive(s)
> **me (te...) gustan +**
> plural noun

(Continúa).

Prác. A, Paso 1: Answers: 1. gusta, gustan 2. gusta, gustan 3. gusta, gusta 4. gustan

Paso 2. Haga oraciones para indicar sus gustos sobre las siguientes cosas.

MODELOS: viajar → (No) Me **gusta** viajar.
los aviones → (No) Me **gustan** los aviones.

1. nadar
2. los viajes con mi familia
3. los vuelos
4. el calor
5. el invierno
6. las playas caribeñas
7. los aeropuertos
8. viajar en coche

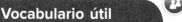

Paso 3. Ahora, en parejas, túrnense para entrevistarse sobre las ideas del **Paso 2.** Luego díganle al resto de la clase algo que ustedes tienen en común.

MODELO: E1: A mí me gusta viajar. ¿Y a ti?
E2: A mí también. →
A nosotros nos gusta viajar.

B. Vacaciones y viajes. Complete las oraciones con el pronombre del complemento indirecto apropiado y la forma apropiada del verbo **gustar.**

1. A la profesora / Al profesor _____ _____ viajar en primera clase... ¡pero nunca puede!
2. A mí _____ _____ los viajes a otros países y a todos mis amigos _____ _____ también.
3. A ti no _____ _____ el mar y a tu amiga no _____ _____ tampoco.
4. ¡A todos los estudiantes de esta clase _____ _____ las vacaciones! ¡Y también _____ _____ viajar!

C. ¿Cómo van a organizar las vacaciones los Soto?

Paso 1. Los Soto tienen gustos muy diversos. Explique el gusto de cada persona con oraciones completas. Luego nombre una actividad que probablemente le gusta hacer en las vacaciones.

MODELO: **1.** la madre: las novelas de Julia Álvarez →
A la madre **le gustan** las novelas de Julia Álvarez. **Seguro que** (*For sure*) **le gusta** leer en la playa.

1. la madre: las novelas de Julia Álvarez
2. el padre: los deportes (*sports*) acuáticos
3. los abuelos: el arte
4. Lucas: la naturaleza (*nature*)
5. Elena, la hija adolescente: la música pop
6. los mellizos (*twins*) de 11 años: jugar en la piscina

Paso 2. Ahora, en parejas, nombren un lugar al que (*to which*) a cada una de esas personas les gustaría ir para las vacaciones.

MODELO: A la madre le **gustaría** ir a una playa tranquila.

Paso 3. Finalmente, escojan un destino en el que (*which*) todos los miembros de la familia puedan (*can*) hacer algo que les gusta.

D. ¿Conoce bien a... ?

Paso 1. ¿Cree usted que conoce bien a su profesor(a) de español? Haga oraciones completas para decir si a él/ella le gustan o no las siguientes cosas.

MODELO: **1.** la música clásica →
(No) Le gusta la música clásica.

1. la música clásica
2. bailar salsa
3. los niños pequeños
4. las canciones de los años 80
5. viajar
6. los destinos exóticos
7. el arte surrealista
8. ¿ ?

Vocabulario útil

A mí también. So do I.
A mí tampoco. I don't either. / Neither do I.
Pues a mí, sí. Well, I do.
Pues a mí, no. Well, I don't.

Vocabulario útil

surfear

la discoteca
el hotel
el museo
el parque nacional

Paso 2. Ahora entreviste a su profesor(a) para saber si le gustan las cosas del **Paso 1** o no.

MODELOS: **1.** ¿A usted le gusta la música clásica?

A usted le gusta la música clásica, ¿verdad?

Paso 3. Ahora entreviste a un compañero o una compañera sobre las mismas cosas.

MODELO: **1.** E1: ¿Te gusta la música clásica?

E2: Sí. ¿Y a ti?

E. Perfiles (*Profiles*) personales

Paso 1. En parejas, inventen un perfil más o menos realista para cada una de las personas de los dibujos: quiénes son, dónde están, por qué están allí y, finalmente, tres de las cosas y actividades que les gustan.

1.

2.

3.

Vocabulario útil	
el arte	
el *rap* / el *hip hop*	
<u>hacer</u> senderismo	to hike

Paso 2. Ahora, digan con cuál de los personajes (*characters*) que inventaron (*you invented*) en el **Paso 1** se identifican más y expliquen por qué.

MODELO: Me identifico más con la persona del dibujo _____ porque...

Nota comunicativa: Otras maneras de expresar los gustos y preferencias

Here are some ways to express intense likes and dislikes. Note that most of these verbs are used like **gustar.**

> Verbs that are used like **gustar** will be noted in vocabulary lists with the parenthetical note (like **gustar**).

INTENSE LIKES

- **gustar mucho/muchísimo**

  ¿El té? Me gusta **muchísimo.**   *Tea? I like it a lot.*

- **encantar** (used like **gustar**)

  Me encantan las películas extranjeras.   *I love foreign films.*

  Me encanta estar con mi familia.   *I love being with my family.*

INTENSE DISLIKES

- **no gustar (para) nada** (with **gustar**)

  No me gusta **(para) nada** la comida japonesa.   *I don't like Japanese food at all.*

- **odiar** (conjugated like a regular **-ar** verb)

  Unlike **encantar,** which is used like **gustar, odiar** is conjugated like regular **-ar** verbs. It is a transitive verb, that is, a verb that can take a direct object.

  Odio los champiñones.   *I hate mushrooms.*

  Mi madre **odia** viajar sola.   *My mother hates traveling alone.*

Use as many of these verbs and expressions as you can in **Práctica F.**

F. Intercambios. En parejas, túrnense para describir lo que les gusta y lo que odian cuando están en las siguientes situaciones. Inventen los detalles necesarios.

MODELO: **1.** en la playa → Cuando estoy en la playa, me encanta nadar en el mar, pero no me gusta el sol ni me gusta la arena (*sand*). Por eso odio pasar todo el día en la playa. Prefiero nadar en una piscina.

1. en la playa
2. cuando voy de *camping*
3. en un autobús/tren
4. en un vuelo
5. en un viaje de muchas horas en auto
6. en casa con mi familia
7. cuando salgo con mis amigos y amigas
8. en un centro comercial
9. en una discoteca
10. ¿ ?

Algo sobre el merengue

El merengue es un tipo de música dominicana que se conoce y se baila en todo el mundo hispano. Empezó a tocarse[a] con instrumentos de cuerda,[b] pero se incorporó[c] el acordeón (de influencia europea), el güiro[d] (de origen taíno) y la tambora[e] (de origen africano). Hoy se incluyen el piano y los instrumentos de viento.

 ¿Conoce usted el merengue? ¿Lo sabe bailar?

[a]Empezó... *It was first played*
[b]*string* [c]*se... were added*
[d]*percussion instrument made of the gourd of the calabash tree*
[e]*bass drum*

Jon McLean/Alamy Stock Photo

Un grupo de merengueros dominicanos

 Repaso

You have already learned one of the irregular past tense verb forms that is presented in **Gramática 23**. Review it now by telling what day yesterday was: **Ayer...**

Talking About the Past (Part 1) • Preterite of Regular Verbs and of **dar, hacer, ir,** and **ser**

Gramática en acción: Un viaje a la República Dominicana

Elisa Velasco es reportera. Hace poco, **fue** a la República Dominicana para escribir un artículo sobre la isla de La Española. Elisa nos cuenta su experiencia.

- «**Hice** el viaje en avión.
- El vuelo **fue** largo porque el avión **hizo** escala en Miami.
- **Pasé** una semana entera en la Isla.
- **Visité** muchos sitios de interés turístico e histórico.
- **Comí** mucha comida típica del Caribe.
- **Tomé** el sol, **nadé** en el mar y **escribí** muchas tarjetas postales.
- ¡Lo **pasé** muy bien!»

Comprensión

¿Cierto o falso? Corrija las oraciones falsas.

		CIERTO	FALSO
1.	Elisa **fue** a la República Dominicana para pasar sus vacaciones.	☐	☐
2.	El avión **hizo** escala en los Estados Unidos.	☐	☐
3.	Elisa no **visitó** ningún lugar importante de la Isla.	☐	☐
4.	No lo **pasó** bien en la playa.	☐	☐

So far, you have almost always spoken in the present tense. In this section, you will use forms of the preterite, one of the past tenses in Spanish.

To talk about the past in Spanish, there are two simple tenses: the preterite and the imperfect. In this chapter, you will learn the regular forms of the preterite and those of four irregular verbs: **dar, hacer, ir,** and **ser.** Then in Capítulos 9, 10, and 11, you will learn more about both tenses.

> **a simple tense / un tiempo simple** = *I ate, she ran, we talked* (in contrast to *I have eaten, she has run, we have talked,* which are not simple tense verbs)

Preterite: Regular Verbs / **El pretérito: Los verbos regulares**

-ar Verbs	
hablar	
hablé	I spoke (did speak)
hablaste	you spoke
habló	you/he/she spoke
hablamos	we spoke
hablasteis	you spoke
hablaron	you/they spoke

-er/-ir Verbs			
comer		**vivir**	
comí	I ate (did eat)	**viví**	I lived (did live)
comiste	you ate	**viviste**	you lived
comió	you/he/she ate	**vivió**	you/he/she lived
comimos	we ate	**vivimos**	we lived
comisteis	you ate	**vivisteis**	you lived
comieron	you/they ate	**vivieron**	you/they lived

A trip to the Dominican Republic *Elisa Velasco is a reporter. A little while ago, she went to the Dominican Republic to write an article about the island of Hispaniola. Elisa tells us about her experience.* ■ *"I made the trip by plane.* ■ *The flight was long because the plane made a stop in Miami.* ■ *I spent a whole week on the Island.* ■ *I visited a lot of interesting tourist and historical sites.* ■ *I ate a lot of typical Caribbean food.* ■ *I sunbathed, swam in the ocean, and wrote a lot of postcards.* ■ *I had a really good time!"*

1. Uses of the Preterite

As you saw in the chart on the previous page, the *preterite* (**el pretérito**) has several English equivalents.

The preterite is used to report finished, completed actions or states of being in the past. If the action or state of being is viewed as completed—no matter how long it lasted or took to complete—it will be expressed with the preterite. Look at the examples: In the first one, a two-month period is specified in the sentence; that period is over. In the second example, no time span is specified, but the action is clearly over since it took place *last summer*.

hablé = I spoke, I did speak

Pasé dos meses en el Caribe el año pasado.
I spent two months in the Caribbean last year.

El verano pasado **hicimos** camping en Puerto Rico.
Last summer we went camping in Puerto Rico.

2. *Nosotros* forms

Note that the **nosotros** forms of regular preterites for **-ar** and **-ir** verbs are the same as the present tense forms. Context usually helps determine meaning. If the translation were not available, what words would tell you that the first **hablamos** means *we spoke* and the second one *we'll speak*?

Ayer **hablamos** del viaje con nuestros amigos. Hoy, más tarde, **hablamos** con el agente de viajes a las dos de la tarde.
Yesterday we spoke about the trip with our friends. Today, later on, we'll speak with the travel agent at 2:00 P.M.

3. Accent Marks

Note the accent marks on the first and third person singular of the preterite tense. These accent marks are not used in the conjugation of **ver: vi, vio.**

bailé, bailó
bebí, bebió
asistí, asistió

but

vi, vio

4. Verbs ending in *-car*, *-gar*, and *-zar*

These kinds of verbs show a spelling change in the first person singular (**yo**) of the preterite. This is the same change you have already learned to make in formal commands, **Gramática 20 (Cap. 7).**

-car → qu buscar	busqué	buscamos
	buscaste	buscasteis
	buscó	buscaron
-gar → gu pagar	pagué	pagamos
	pagaste	pagasteis
	pagó	pagaron
-zar → c empezar	empecé	empezamos
	empezaste	empezasteis
	empezó	empezaron

5. Unstressed *-i-*

An unstressed **-i-** between two vowels becomes **-y-**. Also, note the accent on the **í** in the **tú, nosotros,** and **vosotros** forms.

creer		leer	
creí	creímos	leí	leímos
creíste	creísteis	leíste	leísteis
creyó	creyeron	leyó	leyeron

6. *-ar* and *-er* Stem-changing Verbs

Stem-changing verbs that end in **-ar** and **-er** do not show the stem change in the preterite. However, the preterite of **-ir** stem-changing verbs is not regular. You will learn the preterite of those verbs in **Gramática 25 (Cap. 9).**

despertar (despierto): desperté, despertaste,...

volver (vuelvo): volví, volviste,...

Irregular Forms / **Las formas irregulares**

1. *Dar*

The preterite endings for **dar** are the same as those used for regular **-er/-ir** verbs, except that the accent marks are dropped.

dar	
d**i**	d**imos**
d**iste**	d**isteis**
d**io**	d**ieron**

2. Hacer

All forms of **hacer** are irregular in the preterite, especially the third person singular, **hizo,** which is spelled with a **z** rather than a **c** to keep the [s] sound of the infinitive.

hacer	
h**ice**	h**icimos**
h**iciste**	h**icisteis**
h**izo**	h**icieron**

2. *Ir* and *ser*

These verbs have identical forms in the preterite. Context will make the meaning clear. For example, in the first sentence to the right, the word **a** is a clue that **Fui** means *I went*, since forms of the verb **ir** are often followed by **a.** In the second sentence, **Fui** is followed directly by a noun; forms of **ir**/*to go* are never *directly* followed by a noun, so **fui** must mean *I was*.

ir/ser	
f**ui**	f**uimos**
f**uiste**	f**uisteis**
f**ue**	f**ueron**

Fui a la playa el verano pasado.
I went to the beach last summer.

Fui agente de viajes.
I was a travel agent.

Práctica y comunicación

A. Una tarjeta postal. Durante su viaje, Elisa, la reportera de **Gramática en acción,** le mandó una tarjeta postal a su abuela, que vive en una residencia de personas mayores. A ella le gusta recibir cartas por correo (*snail mail*). Ponga las siguientes oraciones en el orden en que Elisa las escribió (del 1 al 8).

a. ___ Y terminé en el Parque Independencia.

b. ___ Ahora estoy cenando un mangú delicioso en la Calle de las Damas.

c. ___ Hoy empecé el día visitando la catedral.

d. ___ Te escribo desde Santo Domingo, la ciudad donde tú viviste de niña. ¡Me encanta!

e. ___ Después fui al Alcázar de Colón.

f. ___ Te quiere, Eli

g. ___ Mañana salgo para Samaná para ver las ballenas.

h. ___ Querida abuela:

B. El verano pasado

Paso 1. Autoprueba. Dé la forma apropiada del pretérito para cada sujeto.

1. tú: comprar, ir, acostarse, beber, hacer, llegar
2. usted: comprender, empezar, creer, afeitarse, dar, volar
3. nosotros: hacer, ser, ir, pagar, leer, subir
4. ellas: asistir, volver, terminar, despertarse, salir, viajar

Summary of Preterite Endings

-ar: **-é, -aste, -ó, -amos, -asteis –aron**
-er/-ir: **-í, -iste, -ió, -imos, -isteis, -ieron**
dar: **di...** hacer: **hice...** ir/ser: **fui...**

Una ballena (*whale*) en aguas de la península de Samaná

Kit Korzun/Shutterstock

---

*Prác. B, Paso 1: **Answers: 1.** compraste, fuiste, te acostaste, bebiste, hiciste, llegaste **2.** comprendió, empezó, creyó, se afeitó, dio, voló **3.** hicimos, fuimos, fuimos, pagamos, leímos, subimos **4.** asistieron, volvieron, terminaron, se despertaron, salieron, viajaron*

Gramática

doscientos cincuenta y siete ■ **257**

Paso 2. Complete las siguientes oraciones sobre el verano pasado con las terminaciones apropiadas de la primera persona singular (**yo**). Si es necesario, use **no** para hacer oraciones que son ciertas para usted.

El verano pasado...

1. tom_____ clases en la universidad.
2. asist_____ a un concierto en otra ciudad.
3. trabaj_____ mucho y gan_____ mucho dinero. (**ganar** = to earn)
4. hi_____ *camping* con unos amigos.
5. viv_____ todo el tiempo con mi familia.
6. me qued_____ trabajando y estudiando en la universidad.
7. fu_____ a la playa.
8. me levant_____ tarde casi todos los días.

Paso 3. Ahora, en parejas, túrnense para entrevistarse sobre las ideas del **Paso 2.** Luego díganle a la clase dos cosas que ustedes tienen en común.

MODELO: **1. tomé** clases en la universidad. ➜
     E1: El verano pasado, ¿**tomaste** alguna clase en la universidad?
     E2: No, ¿y tú?
     E1: Yo tampoco. ➜
     Nosotros no **tomamos** ninguna clase el verano pasado.

C. El viernes pasado por la tarde

Paso 1. Narre la secuencia de las acciones que hizo Julio el viernes pasado por la tarde. **¡OJO! Julio** es el sujeto de muchas oraciones, pero no de todas. A veces el sujeto es **ellos** (Julio y su amigo Roberto).

El viernes por la tarde, Julio...

1. **volver** a casa después de trabajar todo el día

2. **llamar** a su amigo Roberto y los dos: **decidir** ir al cine juntos

3. **ducharse** y **afeitarse**

4. **salir** de casa rápidamente e **ir** al cine en autobús

5. los dos: **hacer** cola para comprar las entradas (*tickets*) y luego **comprar** palomitas (*popcorn*)

6. **entrar** en la sala y **sentarse**

7. **ver** la película pero no **gustarles** para nada

8. **ir** a un restaurante a cenar y **quedarse** conversando hasta muy tarde

Paso 2. Comprensión. ¿Cierto, falso o no lo dice?

	CIERTO	FALSO	NO LO DICE
1. El amigo de Julio se llama Roberto.	☐	☐	☐
2. Son compañeros de clase.	☐	☐	☐
3. A los dos amigos les interesa el cine.	☐	☐	☐
4. Vieron una película extranjera.	☐	☐	☐
5. Odiaron la película.	☐	☐	☐
6. Cenaron después de la película.	☐	☐	☐
7. Julio regresó a casa en autobús.	☐	☐	☐

Paso 3. Ahora, en parejas, y sin mirar las imágenes, vuelvan a contar la secuencia de acciones de Julio. ¿Pueden recordarlo todo? Usen palabras de **Estrategia.**

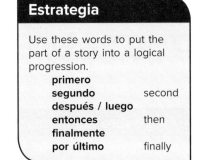

<table>
<tr><td colspan="2">Estrategia</td></tr>
<tr><td colspan="2">Use these words to put the part of a story into a logical progression.</td></tr>
<tr><td>primero</td><td></td></tr>
<tr><td>segundo</td><td>second</td></tr>
<tr><td>después / luego</td><td></td></tr>
<tr><td>entonces</td><td>then</td></tr>
<tr><td>finalmente</td><td></td></tr>
<tr><td>por último</td><td>finally</td></tr>
</table>

D. Un semestre en la República Dominicana

Paso 1. Cuente la siguiente historia, usando el pretérito de los verbos.

MODELO: *yo*: viajar a la República Dominicana el año pasado →
   Viajé a la República Dominicana el año pasado.

1. *yo:* pasar todo el semestre en Santo Domingo
2. mis padres: pagarme el vuelo
3. *yo:* trabajar para ganar el dinero para los otros gastos (*expenses*)
4. *yo:* vivir con una familia dominicana
5. *yo:* aprender mucho sobre la la cultura dominicana
6. mis amigos: escribirme con frecuencia
7. *yo:* comprarles recuerdos (*souvenirs*) a todos
8. *yo:* volver a casa a fines de junio

Paso 2. Ahora, piense en las cosas que posiblemente hacen los turistas en la República Dominicana y añada dos acciones más a la lista de lo que hizo la persona que narra su experiencia en el **Paso 1.**

E. El día de ayer de dos compañeras

Paso 1. Teresa y Liliana son compañeras de apartamento en la universidad. Haga oraciones completas según el modelo para describir su día.

MODELO: 7:30 **levantarse** → **Se levantó a** las siete y media.

TERESA

1. 8:00 **ducharse** y **desayunar**
2. 9:00 **salir** de casa / **ir** a la universidad
3. 10:00 **estudiar** toda la mañana
4. 12:00 **almorzar** con unos compañeros de la universidad
5. 1:00 **hacer** experimentos en el laboratorio de química
6. 3:15 **volver** a casa

LILIANA

7. 9:45 **despertarse,** pero no **levantarse** pronto
8. 10:30 **desayunar** y **empezar** a hacer la tarea de matemáticas
9. 12:30 **terminarla** y **ver** la tele
10. 2:00 **empezar** a hacer un pastel para el cumpleaños de Miriam
11. 2:30 **mandar** unos e-mails.
12. 4:30 **terminar** el pastel / **decorarlo**

TERESA Y LILIANA

13. 5:00 **ir** al gimnasio cerca de su apartamento / allí **hacer** ejercicio por una hora
14. 6:30 **volver** a casa / **ducharse** y **hablar** de la fiesta de Miriam
15. 9:30 **ir** a casa de Miriam / **cantarle** «Cumpleaños feliz» / **darle** su regalo y **comer** el pastel

¿Quién es, Teresa o Liliana? ¿Cómo lo sabe?

Paso 2. Ahora, use las acciones del **Paso 1** para describir su propio día de ayer. Incluya en su lista por lo menos diez acciones y algunas palabras de secuencia: **primero, después, luego, por la tarde/noche, finalmente.**

Paso 3. Ahora, en parejas, túrnense para describir sus días respectivos. ¿En qué coincidieron y en qué fueron muy diferentes?

Vocabulario útil

<u>dar</u> una presentación
<u>hacer</u> mucha tarea
leer un artículo
<u>tener</u> una reunión   to have a meeting

Algo sobre las hermanas Mirabal

H.S. Photos/Alamy Stock Photo

Un billete (*bill*) de 200 pesos dominicanos con fotos de las hermanas Mirabal

Patria (1924–1960), Minerva (1926–1960) y María Teresa (1935–1960) Mirabal, conocidas[a] como las Mariposas,[b] son heroínas dominicanas que lucharon[c] contra la terrible dictadura[d] de Rafael Trujillo. Las tres fueron brutalmente asesinadas por orden del dictador. La hermana sobreviviente,[e] Dedé, dedicó el resto de su vida a preservar la memoria de sus hermanas. Ahora hay una provincia dominicana con el nombre de Hermanas Mirabal. Las Mariposas también aparecen[f] en los billetes de 200 pesos dominicanos.

La Asamblea General de las Naciones Unidas designó el día de la muerte[g] de las Mirabal como el Día Internacional de la Eliminación de la Violencia contra la Mujer.

 ¿Cuáles son algunos de los héroes y heroínas nacionales más importantes de su país? ¿Por qué son importantes?

[a]*known* [b]*Butterflies* [c]*fought* [d]*dictatorship* [e]*surviving*
[f]*appear* [g]*death*

F. **La última vez (*The last time*)**

Paso 1. Conteste las siguientes preguntas. Añada más detalles si puede.

MODELO: **1.** La última vez que usted hizo un viaje, ¿le mandó una tarjeta a alguien? →
Sí, **les** mandé una tarjeta a mis bisabuelos (*great grandparents*). / No, no **le** mandé ninguna tarjeta a nadie.

La última vez que usted...

1. hizo un viaje, ¿le mandó una tarjeta a alguien?
2. tomó el autobús/metro, ¿le ofreció su asiento a alguien?
3. vio a su profesor(a) de español en público, ¿le habló en español?
4. comió en un restaurante, ¿le pagó la cena a alguien?
5. entró en un edificio, ¿le abrió la puerta a otra persona?
6. voló en avión, ¿le pidió algo a uno de los asistentes de vuelo?
7. le regaló algo a alguien, ¿le gustó el regalo a la persona?
8. le prometió a alguien hacer algo, ¿lo hizo?

Paso 2. Ahora, en parejas, túrnense para hacer y contestar preguntas basadas en las oraciones del **Paso 1.** Después, díganle al resto de la clase una o dos cosas interesantes de su compañero/a.

G. **Intercambios**

Paso 1. En parejas, túrnense para entrevistarse sobre su último viaje. Deben obtener información relacionada con las siguientes preguntas.

1. ¿cuándo?
2. ¿adónde?
3. ¿en qué medio de transporte?
4. ¿cuántos días?
5. ¿con quién?

Paso 2. Ahora cuéntenles a todas las personas de la clase los detalles esenciales del viaje de su compañero/a.

MODELO: Susie fue a Puerto Rico el verano pasado. Hizo el viaje en avión. Se quedó en Puerto Rico una semana. Viajó con su novio y su familia.

⊛ Todo junto

A. Lengua y cultura: Mi abuela dominicana

Paso 1. Completar. Complete the following paragraphs with the correct form of the words in parentheses, as suggested by context. When two possibilities are given in parentheses, select the correct word. **¡OJO!** The verbs in the paragraphs will be present tense or preterite; the context will indicate which tense to use.

Mix Tape/Shutterstock

Ayer llegó de visita mi abuela Manuela. Ella vive en Santo Domingo, con mi tía Zaira, la (hermana / sobrina)¹ de mi mamá. _____ (*Nosotros*: Ir)² a recibir(la / le)³ al aeropuerto y nos _____ (*ella*: dar)⁴ un abrazoᵃ muy fuerte. (Mi / Mí)⁵ abuela va (a / de)⁶ pasar dos meses con nosotros en Connecticut, y luego _____ (ir)⁷ a quedarse un mes con el tío Julián en Nueva York. Así es la vidaᵇ de muchas abuelas con hijos en otro país.

A mi abuela (le / se)⁸ gustaría tener a todos sus hijos y (nietos / sobrinos)⁹ en Santo Domingo y siempre _____ (ser / estar)¹⁰ muy triste cuando _____ (volver)¹¹ a la República Dominicana. A ella (le / la)¹² gusta mucho la vida en los Estados Unidos. _____ (*Ella*: Decir)¹³ que aquí se vive muy bien y que las casas son muy buenas. (El / La)¹⁴ problema es que no le (gustan / gustarían)¹⁵ los inviernos de (este / esto)¹⁶ país.

Mi familia tiene muchos (parientes / padres)¹⁷ en Santo Domingo y (les / los)¹⁸ mandamos regalos con mi abuela. A mis padres (le / les)¹⁹ gusta muchísimo ir de vacaciones a la República Dominicana para visitarlos y visitar los lugares de su juventud.ᶜ Mis padres _____ (vivir)²⁰ allí hasta que _____ (salir)²¹ para estudiar en los Estados Unidos.

> La abuela sacando un selfi

ᵃ*hug* ᵇAsí... *Such is the life* ᶜ*youth*

Paso 2. Comprensión. Conteste las siguientes preguntas.

1. ¿Quién habla en la narración? ¿Se sabe si es hombre o mujer?
2. ¿Dónde vive la tía Zaira?
3. ¿Qué le gusta de la vida en los Estados Unidos a la abuela?
4. ¿Qué no le gusta?
5. ¿Cuándo emigraron a los Estados Unidos los padres del narrador / de la narradora?

🤟 Paso 3. En acción

👥 Casi todos los estadounidenses son descendientes de inmigrantes; muchos son inmigrantes recientes. En parejas, túrnense para aprender algo de un pariente o un amigo / una amiga de su compañero/a que llegó a este país como inmigrante. Usen las siguientes preguntas.

1. ¿Quién es el pariente o amigo/a? ¿Dónde nació (*was he/she born*)?
2. ¿Cuándo llegó a los Estados Unidos?
3. ¿Vino (*Did he/she come*) solo/a? ¿A quién(es) dejó (*did he/she leave behind*) en su país de origen?
4. Si ese pariente o amigo/a vive todavía, ¿visita a veces su país de origen? Si ya murió (*he/she is already deceased*), ¿volvió a visitar su país de origen antes de morir (*dying*)? ¿Cuántas veces fue?

Gramática

B. Proyecto: Turismo en la República Dominicana

OCÉANO ATLÁNTICO

San Felipe de Puerto Plata
San Francisco de Macorís
Península de Samaná
HAITÍ
Concepción de la Vega
Parque Nacional Los Haitises
REPÚBLICA DOMINICANA
San Pedro de Macorís
Punta Cana
Santo Domingo
La Romana

Mar Caribe

Para este proyecto, van a preparar un guion (*script*) para un video sobre el turismo en la República Dominicana que muestre (*shows*) la variedad de lo que les ofrece a los turistas este país. El video debe narrar lo que hicieron unos turistas en un viaje reciente, desde su punto de vista (*point of view*).

Paso 1. Preparación. En parejas o grupos, preparen los siguientes aspectos del proyecto.

Aspecto 1: Inventar el perfil (*profile*) de unos de los turistas de la siguiente lista.

- la familia Ortiz, de la Ciudad de Nueva York, con raíces (*roots*) dominicanas
- Jordan y Jay, una pareja en su luna de miel (*honeymoon*)
- cuatro amigas que estudian español en la universidad

Aspecto 2: Investigar lugares dominicanos interesantes por diferentes razones para los turistas. Usen la siguiente tabla, pero pueden añadir (*add*) más categorías si quieren. Piensen en unas vacaciones de una semana.

Lugar(es)	Cómo llegar	Qué ver / Qué hacer	Dónde comer

Paso 2. Desarrollo. (*Development.*) Ahora desarrollen el guion, narrándolo en el pretérito desde el punto de vista de los personajes que eligieron (*you chose*).

Paso 3. Competición. Enseñen (*Show*) su guion a la clase. Pueden hacer su presentación con fotos de los lugares que visitaron sus turistas ficticios. ¿Qué grupo tiene el mejor plan? ¿Por qué es tan bueno su plan?

Estrategia

You have not yet learned the irregular preterite forms of a few frequently used verbs. Here are their first person forms.

estar: estuve, estuvimos
poner: puse, pusimos
tener: tuve, tuvimos
venir: vine, vinimos

Video: Salu2 «¡Qué rico!°»

¡Qué... *How delicious!*

You can watch two segments of this chapter's video in the **Video: Salu2** section, found at the end of the eBook.

Klic Video Productions/ McGraw Hill

Un arcoíris (*rainbow*) en las cataratas (*falls*) del Iguazú.

Enfoque cultural: El turismo

> ### Antes de leer
> ¿Es el turismo un sector económico muy importante en su ciudad o estado?

En la República Dominicana

E2dan/Shutterstock

La zona colonial de Santo Domingo

El turismo es el sector económico más importante de la República Dominicana. Es un país que ofrece lugares de interés para cualquier[a] visitante: bosques,[b] parques nacionales, ríos, lagos, playas, ciudades y zonas rurales. Uno de los destinos turísticos más populares es Punta Cana, al este del país. Allí se puede disfrutar de[c] un clima tropical y de bellas[d] playas de arena[e] blanca y fina. Santo Domingo, la capital del país, tiene una hermosa[f] zona colonial con museos, casas antiguas y otros monumentos históricos. En 1990, esta zona fue reconocida[g] como Patrimonio Cultural de la Humanidad[h] por la UNESCO.

[a]*any* [b]*forests* [c]*disfrutar... enjoy* [d]*beautiful* [e]*sand* [f]*beautiful* [g]*recognized* [h]*Patrimonio... World Cultural Heritage site*

Comprensión ¿Cuáles son dos de los lugares turísticos importantes en la República Dominicana?

En otros países hispanos

- **En todo el mundo hispanohablante** En muchos países hispanos, y no solo en los países tropicales, hay playas maravillosas.[a] El Uruguay, la Argentina y Chile tienen costas fabulosas sin estar en el trópico.

[a]*wonderful*

- **En España** La industria del turismo es un importante motor[b] de la economía española. En 2021, España fue el sexto[c] país más visitado del mundo. El primero fueron los Estados Unidos.
- **En los Estados Unidos** Gran parte del actual[d] territorio estadounidense fue antes parte de España y de México. Así que[e] se puede visitar lugares históricos en Florida, Texas, California, etcétera, para aprender sobre la historia del mundo hispano... ¡sin salir de este país!

[b]*engine* [c]*sixth* [d]*present-day* [e]*Así... So*

Jessi Walker/McGraw Hill

La misión de San José, San Antonio, Texas

Comprensión ¿Qué país hispanohablante es uno de los lugares de destino más populares entre los turistas del mundo? ¿En qué lugares estadounidenses podemos visitar lugares históricos de origen hispano?

> **En acción**
>
> Elija un estado o una ciudad estadounidense con raíces (*roots*) hispanas y entérese de (*find out about*) su historia. ¿Por cuánto tiempo fue un territorio dominado por hispanohablantes? ¿Qué lugares se debe visitar para saber su historia antes de formar parte de los Estados Unidos?

Lectura

Antes de leer

¿Le interesa a usted el aventurismo? (Vea la **Nota cultural** en la página 241). ¿Por qué? En su opinión, ¿cómo son las personas que practican este estilo de viajar?

I love viajes

Norte de África en 4x4[a]
Explora el Marruecos[b] más desconocido y aventúrate[c] en 4x4 entre las dunas del Sahara. Descubre oasis perdidos[d] en lo más profundo[e] del desierto y disfruta de una flora que no esperarías[f] encontrar en estas latitudes. ¡Pon rumbo a[g] la aventura!

Tierra del Fuego
Lugar de belleza única con sus nevados picos, montañas, bosques y maravillosos lagos. Ushuaia es la ciudad más al sur del mundo. Tierra del Fuego es una isla de belleza extrema que une el Pacífico y el Atlántico. Parajes vírgenes[h] por explorar.

Safari por África
El espectacular parque natural del delta del Okavango (Botsuana) es una gran concentración de animales salvajes. Visita las cataratas Victoria (en Zimbabue) donde observarás[i] la cortina de agua más caudalosa del mundo. ¡Refréscate![l]

[a]*four-wheel drive (cuatro por cuatro)* [b]*Morocco* [c]*venture out* [d]*lost* [e]*lo... the deepest part* [f]*no... you wouldn't expect*
[g]*¡Pon... Get ready for* [h]*virgin* [i]*vas a observar* [l]*Cool off!*

Comprensión

Vocabulario para leer

la belleza	beauty
el bosque	forest
la catarata	waterfall
la cortina	curtain
el paraje	place, expanse
el pico	peak
caudaloso/a	fast-flowing
desconocido/a	unknown
nevado/a	snowy
disfrutar de	to enjoy
unir	to connect

A. ¡Sea agente de viajes! ¿Adónde deben ir de viaje las siguientes personas? Dé una recomendación lógica para cada caso, explicando por qué hace esa sugerencia. Use **Le recomiendo...** o **Les recomiendo...** , según el caso.

MODELO: **El profesor Legrán:** «Tengo todo el verano para viajar. Quiero escaparme del calor de Nuevo México en el verano y visitar lugares remotos». → Le recomiendo Tierra del Fuego, porque allí no hace calor y está en el extremo sur de Sudamérica. Hay montañas, lagos y bosques allí. También hay una ciudad interesante.

1. **Los Sres. Ávila:** «Queremos viajar a un lugar cálido (*warm*) y seco (*dry*) durante el invierno».
2. **El Sr. Sorkin:** «Me gusta observar los animales y verlos en su espacio natural».
3. **Alejandra:** «Conozco Norteamérica, Europa y África. Para mis próximas vacaciones, quiero visitar un continente totalmente nuevo para mí».
4. **Jorge y Jimena:** «Somos especialistas en la flora tropical. Pero para estas vacaciones queremos algo diferente».

 B. Preferencias personales. En parejas, hagan y contesten las siguientes preguntas sobre los destinos turísticos.

1. De los tres destinos que sugiere (*suggests*) la lectura, ¿cuál es el más atractivo para ti? ¿Por qué? ¿Cuál es la mejor estación del año para visitar ese lugar? ¿Por qué?
2. ¿Hay algún lugar de los tres destinos que no te gustaría visitar? ¿Por qué?
3. ¿Qué otros lugares conoces o puedes nombrar donde se pueda (*one can*) hacer el mismo tipo de turismo de los destinos mencionados en los anuncios?

Proyecto: Una solicitud para una beca° de un viaje educativo solicitud... *application for a scholarship*

 Para este proyecto, van a planear un viaje educativo a una ciudad hispanohablante y solicitar una beca de la universidad para el viaje.

Paso 1. En grupos, elijan la ciudad hispana que quieren visitar. Después, hagan una investigación en internet para identificar: varios destinos de interés (museos, monumentos, parques y otros sitios naturales, etcétera), otras actividades culturales en la ciudad y un hotel donde quedarse (*in which to stay*).

Paso 2. Escriban la solicitud, especificando:

- una breve explicación de por qué quieren viajar a ciudad que seleccionaron
- un itinerario de 7 días con los destinos de interés y descripciones concisas de las actividades que piensan hacer en cada lugar
- un presupuesto (*budget*) aproximado, pero realista, por cada participante, incluyendo los costos del vuelo, del hotel y de la comida

Paso 3. Ahora, van a cambiar de papel (*change roles*). Imaginen que forman parte del comité que evalúa las solicitudes. ¿A qué solicitudes deben darse las becas? ¡Los fondos son limitados!

Textos orales

Las actividades de Arturo y David

Antes de escuchar

Por lo general, ¿qué hace usted en su tiempo libre (*free time*)? ¿Qué actividades le gusta hacer cuando va a la playa? ¿Y cuando va al centro de su ciudad?

Vocabulario para escuchar	
apagado/a	turned off
¡No me digas que... !	Don't tell me that ... !
¿De veras?	Really?
corriendo	running (in a hurry)

David habla por teléfono.

Westend61/Getty Images

Comprensión

A. ¿Qué pasó ayer? Conteste las siguientes preguntas según la conversación telefónica para decir lo que hicieron ayer unos amigos dominicanos.
   1. ¿Qué hicieron David y Paula?
   2. ¿Qué hicieron Arturo y Cristina?
   3. ¿Cuál de los cuatros amigos hizo la actividad más relajada (*relaxing*)?

B. ¿Qué va a pasar hoy? ¿Cierto o falso? Corrija las oraciones falsas.

	CIERTO	FALSO
1. Arturo y Cristina no quieren salir con David y Paula.	☐	☐
2. Hace viento hoy.	☐	☐
3. Van a la playa en coche.	☐	☐
4. No van a llevar nada de comer.	☐	☐

En acción

Haga una lista de las actividades que usted hizo el fin de semana pasado. ¿Hizo algo como lo que hicieron Arturo y David?

Mundo hispano

doscientos sesenta y cinco ■ **265**

PORTAFOLIO

Iborgephoto123/Shutterstock

🎙 Entrevista

Use de modelo las preguntas y respuestas (*answers*) de la sección **Entrevista** al principio (*at the beginning*) de este capítulo para hablar de sus vacaciones favoritas.

⌨ Escritura

Un ensayo sobre el verano pasado

¿Qué hizo usted el verano pasado? ¿Fue un buen verano? Para este proyecto, va a escribir un ensayo descriptivo sobre el último verano.

Nopphon_1987/Shutterstock

Un joven en una tienda de campaña

Shannon Fagan/Image Source

Una joven que trabaja en un café

Gorodenkoff/Shutterstock

Un joven jugando a videojuegos

Dragon Images/Shutterstock

Una joven de viaje

Para escribir bien

Considere estas opciones para su ensayo:

- Conectores de secuencia: **primero, después, luego, entonces...**
- Otros conectores: **por eso, sin embargo, además, por un lado** (*on the one hand*), **por otro lado** (*on the other hand*)
- Expresiones para hablar de los gustos: **muchísimo, (para) nada**

👥 Antes de escribir

Para ayudarlos a pensar en su ensayo, en parejas, hablen de lo que hicieron el verano pasado. Den muchos detalles de sus actividades y pídanle a su pareja de conversación que haga lo mismo (*the same thing*). Use algunas de las siguientes palabras interrogativas.

¿cuándo?

¿con quién?

¿dónde?

¿por cuánto tiempo?

¿por qué?

¿te divertiste?

Para terminar, pídale a su pareja que conteste (*ask your partner to answer*) la siguiente pregunta: ¿Qué fue lo que más/menos te gustó del verano?

A escribir

Con su propia información, escriba un ensayo individual sobre cómo pasaron el verano. Hay más ayuda en Connect.

En la comunidad

Entreviste a una persona hispana de su universidad o ciudad sobre sus últimas vacaciones y los lugares más populares de su país para ir de vacaciones.

Preguntas posibles

- ¿Cuándo fue de vacaciones a su país la última vez? ¿Con quién fue? ¿Cuánto tiempo pasó allá? ¿Se quedó en casa de su familia o en un hotel? ¿Con cuánta frecuencia va de vacaciones a su país?
- ¿Cuáles son los lugares de vacaciones más famosos de su país? ¿Los visitan solo los turistas extranjeros o los nacionales también? ¿Cuál es su lugar favorito? ¿Por qué?

Producción audiovisual

Haga un fotomontaje con voz en off (*voiceover*) sobre un destino turístico. Puede ser un destino que usted ya conoce o uno que le gustaría visitar.

Más ideas para el portafolio

- Haga una lista de seis palabras que usted asocia con la palabra **vacaciones.**
- Incluya una imagen de unas vacaciones memorables, explicando qué hizo durante ese tiempo.
- Ponga la foto de un lugar que le gustaría conocer y diga qué cosas se ven y se hacen allí típicamente.
- Si ha estado jugando (*you have been playing*) Practice Spanish: Study Abroad, en Quest 5 usted fue a un mercado al aire libre en Colombia y tuvo que regatear (*had to haggle*). En parejas, conversen sobre la costumbre de regatear. ¿Dónde se hace típicamente? ¿Es aceptable regatear en el país donde ustedes viven? ¿En qué situaciones es aceptable regatear (o incluso esperado [*even expected*])? Luego, hagan una lista de instrucciones para una persona que quiera aprender a regatear.

Sugerencia: You are now ready to play Quest 5 in **Practice Spanish: Study Abroad.**

AFTER STUDYING THIS CHAPTER I CAN ...

☐ talk about travel, transportation, and vacations (238–240)

☐ understand and use pronouns to explain *to* or *for whom* an action is done (244–246)

☐ use **gustar** and other verbs to talk about likes and dislikes in more detail (250–251)

☐ talk about actions in the past with many types of verbs (255–257)

☐ recognize/describe at least 2–3 aspects of Dominican culture

Gramática en breve

21. Indirect Object Pronouns; *Dar* and *decir*

me, te, le, nos, os, les

dar: d**o**y, das, da, damos, dais, dan

decir: d**i**go, d**i**ces, d**i**ce, decimos, decís, d**i**cen

22. *Gustar*

(no) *indirect object pronoun* + **gusta** + *singular subject*

(no) *indirect object pronoun* + **gustan** + *plural subject*

Would like: **gustaría**

23. Preterite of Regular Verbs and of *dar, hacer, ir,* and *ser*

-ar Verbs: -é, -aste, -ó, -amos, -asteis, -aron

-er/-ir Verbs: -í, -iste, -ió, -imos, -steis, -ieron

dar: d**i** d**iste**, d**io**, d**imos**, d**isteis**, d**ieron**

hacer: h**ice**, h**iciste**, h**izo**, h**icimos**, h**icisteis**, h**icieron**

ir/ser: **fui**, **fuiste**, **fue**, **fuimos**, **fuisteis**, **fueron**

Vocabulario

Los verbos

c**o**ntar (c**ue**nto)	to tell; to narrate
dar (d**o**y)	to give
decir (d**i**go) (**i**)	to say; to tell
encantar (*like* **gustar**)	to like very much; to love
entre**g**ar (**gu**)	to hand in
expli**c**ar (**qu**)	to explain

gustar	to be pleasing
m**o**strar (m**ue**stro)	to show
odiar	to hate
ofre**c**er (ofre**zc**o)	to offer
preguntar	to ask (*a question*)
prestar	to lend
prometer	to promise
recom**e**ndar (recom**ie**ndo)	to recommend
regalar	to give (*as a gift*)

Repaso: escribir, hablar, mandar, pe**dir (p**i**do) (i), s**e**rvir (s**i**rvo) (i)**

De viaje

la aduana	customs (*at a border*)
el aeropuerto	airport
el asiento	seat
el/la asistente de vuelo	flight attendant
el autobús	bus
el avión	airplane
el barco	boat, ship
el billete (*Sp.*) / el boleto (*L.A.*)	ticket
de ida	one-way ticket
de ida y vuelta	round-trip ticket
electrónico	e-ticket
la cola	line (*of people*)
el control de seguridad	security (check)
el crucero	cruise (ship)
la demora	delay
el destino	destination
el equipaje	baggage, luggage
la escala	stop
la estación	station
de autobuses	bus station
de trenes	train station
la llegada	arrival
la maleta	suitcase
el/la maletero/a	porter
el medio de transporte	means of transportation
el mostrador	counter
la parada	stop
el pasaje	fare, price (*of a transportation ticket*)
el/la pasajero/a	passenger
el pasillo	aisle
la puerta de embarque	boarding gate
el puerto	port
el puesto	place (*in line*)
la sala de espera	waiting room

la sala de fumar / de fumadores	smoking area	el *camping*	campground
la salida	departure	la foto(grafía)	photo(graph)
la tarjeta de embarque	boarding pass	el mar	sea
la ventanilla	small window (*on a plane*)	la montaña	mountain
el vuelo	flight	el océano	ocean
		la tarjeta (postal)	(post)card
de viaje	on a trip, traveling	la tienda (de campaña)	tent

Cognados: el/la agente, la cabina, el pasaporte, el/la piloto, el tren

Repaso: el viaje

anunciar	to announce
bajarse (de)	to get down (from); to get off (of) (*a vehicle*)
facturar el equipaje	to check baggage
fumar	to smoke
guardar (un puesto)	to save (a place [*in line*])
<u>hacer</u> cola	to stand in line
<u>hacer</u> escala/parada	to make a stop
<u>hacer</u> la(s) maleta(s)	to pack one's suitcase(s)
<u>ir</u> al extranjero	to go abroad
<u>ir</u> en...	to go/travel by ...
autobús	bus
avión	plane
barco	boat, ship
tren	train
pasar por	to go/pass through
la aduana	customs
el control de seguridad	security (check)
quejarse (de)	to complain (about)
subir (a)	to go up; to get on (*a vehicle*)
viajar	to travel
v<u>o</u>lar (v<u>ue</u>lo) en avión	to fly; to go by plane

Repaso: <u>hacer</u> un viaje, <u>ir</u>, llegar, <u>salir</u>

De vacaciones

el bloqueador solar	sunscreen
la camioneta	(mini)van

de vacaciones — on vacation

Repaso: la playa, el sol

<u>estar</u> de vacaciones	to be on vacation
<u>hacer</u> *camping*	to go camping
<u>ir</u>(se) de vacaciones a...	to go on vacation to/in ...
nadar	to swim
pasar las vacaciones en...	to spend one's vacation in ...
sa<u>c</u>ar (<u>qu</u>) fotos / fotografías	to take photos
<u>salir</u> de vacaciones	to leave on vacation
tomar el sol	to sunbathe
tomar unas vacaciones	to take a vacation

Repaso: <u>estar</u>, <u>hacer</u>, <u>salir</u>, tomar

Otros sustantivos

el chiste	joke
la flor	flower
la gente	people
la historia	story

Los adjetivos

atrasado/a (*with* <u>estar</u>)	late
juntos/as	together

Palabras adicionales

a tiempo	on time
entonces	then; in that case
me gustaría (mucho)...	I would (really) like ...
muchísimo	an awful lot
(para) nada	at all
por	through; for

Vocabulario personal

Use this space or a vocabulary notebook to write down other words and phrases you learn in this chapter.

9

Los días festivos° Los... *Holidays*

En este capítulo

VOCABULARY
Celebrations and holidays   272
Talking about feelings and emotions   276

GRAMMAR
The preterite of more types of verbs   279, 283
Using direct and indirect object pronouns in the same sentence   287

COUNTRY OF FOCUS: CUBA

El Carnaval de Santiago de Cuba, que se celebra en julio, con música, bailes y desfiles (*parades*)

CUBA

11,3 (coma tres) millones de habitantes

- La isla de Cuba está a solo 150 kilómetros (90 millas) de la costa sur de Florida.
- Cuba es un destino turístico importante para europeos y canadienses.
- Es un país con una tradición musical impresionante y que también se destaca[a] en el béisbol y en la danza.

[a]se... *excels*

 ## ENTREVISTA

These questions related to the chapter theme are answered here by a native speaker. You will be able to ask and answer them yourself with personal information in the **Entrevista** activity in the **Portafolio** section at the end of the chapter.

Cecilia Figueroa Martín contesta las preguntas.

— **¿Cuáles son las celebraciones más importantes de su país?**

— En Puerto Rico celebramos las fiestas de los Estados Unidos: el Día de los Presidentes, el Cuatro de Julio, el Día de Gracias, la Navidad. Y luego hay las fiestas patronales[a] de cada ciudad.

— **¿Qué días celebran más usted y su familia? ¿Cómo los celebran ustedes?**

— Para nosotros la Navidad es un día muy importante de reunión familiar. Aunque,[b] en realidad,[c] nosotros festejamos[d] en Nochebuena.[e] La familia se reúne,[f] vienen amigos, comemos, bebemos, cantamos, bailamos...

— **¿Tuvo usted[g] una fiesta en su último cumpleaños? ¿Quién se la dio[h]?**

— ¡Sí! Mi marido me hizo una fiesta muy grande para mi cumpleaños. Invitó a toda la familia y a nuestros amigos. ¡Estuvimos[i] de fiesta hasta las cuatro de la mañana!

[a]fiestas... *holidays of the patron saints* [b]*Although* [c]en... *actually* [d]nosotros... *we celebrate* [e]*Christmas Eve* [f]se... *gets together* [g]¿Tuvo... *Did you have* [h]se... *gave it for you* [i]*We were*

VOCABULARIO: PREPARACIÓN

You can hear the pronunciation of theme vocabulary words and phrases in the eBook.

Una fiesta de cumpleaños para Javier

¡FELICITACIONES!

el anfitrión

Sí, la fiesta es en casa de Javier.

la anfitriona

bailar

Jorge

Melisa

Carmen

Pedro

los regalos

Javier

las tarjetas

los refrescos

20 años

Javier

el champán

las botanas / las tapas

el pastel de cumpleaños

las velas

Para comer y beber

las botanas (*Mex.*) / las tapas	appetizers

Otros sustantivos

el anfitrión / la anfitriona	host (*of an event*)
el cumpleaños	birthday
el día festivo	holiday
el invitado / la invitada	guest

Los verbos

celebrar	to celebrate
comer/beber (demasiado)	to eat/drink (too much)
cumplir años	to have a birthday
darle una fiesta (a alguien)	to give (someone) a party; to have a party (for someone)
divertirse (me divierto) (i)	to have a good time, enjoy oneself
faltar (a)	to be absent (from); to not attend
gastar	to spend (*money*)

hacerle una fiesta (a alguien)	to give (someone) a party; to have a party (for someone)
invitar	to invite
pasarlo bien/mal	to have a good/bad time
regalar	to give (*as a gift*)
reunirse (me reúno) con	to get together (with)
ser + en + *place*	to take place in/at (*a place*)
¿Dónde es la fiesta?	Where is the party (at)?

¡OJO!

Note the accent that occurs on **-u-** in forms of **reunirse** when the weak vowel **-u-** is stressed: **me reúno, te reúnes, se reúne, nos reunimos, os reunís, se reúnen.** This pattern is like that of stem-changing verbs (that is, the stem vowel changes when it is stressed.)

Palabras adicionales

¡Felicitaciones!	Congratulations!
gracias por + *noun/inf.*	thanks for + *noun/verb* (*-ing*)
Gracias por la invitación / invitarme.	Thanks for the invitation / inviting me.

¡OJO!

This is a list of holidays in the U.S. Only the highlighted items are active vocabulary, and they coincide with widespread important days in the Hispanic world. Learn the Spanish names of the holidays that you need to talk about your traditions, and write them down in your **Vocabulario personal** list.

el Día de los Reyes Magos	Day of the Magi (Three Kings) (Jan. 6)
el Día de San Patricio	St. Patrick's Day
la Pascua	Easter
la Pascua judía	Passover
el Cinco de Mayo	Cinco de Mayo
el Cuatro de Julio	July 4th
el Día de los Pueblos Indígenas	Columbus Day (Oct. 12)
el Día de los Muertos	Day of the Dead (Nov. 2)
el Día de (Acción de) Gracias	Thanksgiving Day
la Janucá	Hanukkah
la Nochebuena	Christmas Eve
la Navidad	Christmas
la Nochevieja	New Year's Eve
la quinceañera	young woman's fifteenth birthday party

Note that **el 12 de octubre** receives different names in different countries (**el día de las Comunidades Indígenas, el Día de la Raza,...**). It corresponds to what is Indigenous People's Day in this country (traditionally Columbus Day).

Algo sobre las parrandas cubanas

Una parranda en Remedios, Cuba

Las parrandas son grandes fiestas navideñas[a] típicas de los pueblos y ciudades de una región de la Cuba central. Las más famosas son las[b] de Remedios. La costumbre de las parrandas data del siglo XVIII.[c] Cada barrio[d] de una ciudad monta[e] una parranda y hay una competición entre los barrios para ver cuál es la mejor.[f] Estas fiestas incluyen fuegos artificiales y disfraces,[g] como las fiestas de carnaval.

 ¿En qué fiestas de su país hay fuegos artificiales? ¿y disfraces?

[a]*Christmas* [b]*those* [c]*data... dates back to the 18th century* [d]*neighborhood* [e]*throws, organizes* [f]*la... the best one (parranda)* [g]*fuegos... fireworks and costumes*

Así se dice

la quinceañera = la fiesta de quince años
el pastel = la torta, la tarta, el queque (*L.A.*)
la Pascua = la Pascua Florida
el Día de los Muertos = el Día de los Difuntos
la Navidad = las Pascuas

The figure of **Santa Claus** is a familiar one in Hispanic countries. That is what he is called in Mexico and Puerto Rico. In other parts of the Spanish-speaking world, he is more often called **el Papá Noel** or **San Nicolás.**

Comunicación

A. Una fiesta para Javier.

Paso 1. Conteste las siguientes preguntas sobre el dibujo de la fiesta de Javier.

1. ¿Qué tipo de fiesta es? ¿Dónde es la fiesta?
2. ¿Quiénes son los anfitriones de la fiesta? ¿Quién es el invitado de honor?
3. ¿Qué hay de comer y de beber? ¿Qué hacen los invitados?
4. ¿Qué le dan los invitados a Javier, además de regalos?
5. ¿Quién falta a la fiesta? ¿Quién lo invita por teléfono?
6. ¿Qué le van a decir todos a Javier cuando corte (*he cuts*) el pastel?
7. ¿Qué cree usted que Javier les va a decir a Carmen y Pedro después de la fiesta?

Paso 2. Ahora, en parejas, miren las fotos y describan lo que está pasando y lo que están haciendo estas personas. ¿Qué se dice en cada ocasión?

1.

2.

B. Asociaciones. ¿Qué palabras asocia usted con las siguientes ideas? Dé por lo menos (*at least*) dos palabras asociadas con cada idea.

1. un cumpleaños
2. una fiesta
3. los fuegos artificiales (*fireworks*)

4. un árbol (*tree*)
5. los regalos
6. una comida grande

En este Día de Gracias, ¡gracias por comer solo verduras!

C. Definiciones

Paso 1. Dé las palabras definidas.

1. Algo de comer o beber que se sirve en las fiestas.
2. El día en que, por tradición, algunas personas visitan los cementerios.
3. La fiesta de una muchacha (*girl*) que cumple 15 años.
4. Lo que uno le dice a un amigo que celebra algo.
5. Una fiesta de los judíos (*Jewish people*) que dura 8 días.

Paso 2. Ahora, en parejas, creen (*create*) por lo menos dos definiciones como las del **Paso 1.** La clase va a adivinar (*guess*) la palabra definida.

Vocabulario útil	
el fin	end
el nacimiento	birth

Nota cultural: Los días festivos importantes del mundo hispano

Algunas fiestas se celebran en casi todos los países hispanos.

- **La Nochebuena**
  La noche antes del día de Navidad hay una cena especial en prácticamente todos los hogares de tradición cristiana. Muchas personas asisten a una misa[a] a medianoche. En varios países, esa noche el Niño Jesús o el Niño Dios les trae regalos a los niños.

- **La Nochevieja**
  La noche antes del día de Año Nuevo es una ocasión para grandes celebraciones, tanto en familia como en lugares públicos. En España y otros países algunos siguen la tradición de comer una uva[b] por cada una de las doce campanadas[c] de medianoche.

- **El Día de los Reyes Magos**
  En muchos países esta fiesta se celebra el 6 de enero. Esa mañana los niños y niñas hispanohablantes se despiertan y encuentran los regalos que les dejaron[d] los Reyes Magos. Estos Reyes son tres y vienen en camello.

- **El Día de la Independencia**
  Muchos países latinoamericanos celebran el día de la declaración de su independencia de España. Por ejemplo, Cuba celebra su independencia el 10 de octubre; México, el 16 de septiembre; Bolivia, el 6 de agosto; el Paraguay, el 15 de mayo; El Salvador, el 15 de septiembre.

Unos bailarines (*dancers*) durante las celebraciones del Día de los Reyes Magos, en La Habana, Cuba

- **La quinceañera**
  En muchos países latinoamericanos y en este país, esta fiesta celebra la llegada de las niñas a los 15 años, es decir, su transición de niña a mujer. La familia y los amigos de la joven le dan una gran fiesta, en la que[e] ella se viste de largo.[f] A veces se celebra una misa especial, pero siempre hay una cena y una fiesta con música para bailar.

 ¿Cuáles de estas fiestas se celebran en su familia? Si no se celebra ninguna de ellas, ¿cuáles son las fiestas familiares más importantes para usted?

[a]*mass* [b]*grape* [c]*bell strokes* [d]*left* [e]*la... which* [f]*se... dresses up (in a gown)*

 D. Hablando de fiestas

Paso 1. ¿Cuáles de estas fiestas le gustan a usted? ¿Cuáles no le gustan? Explique por qué. Compare sus respuestas con las (*those*) de sus compañeros de clase.

MODELO: el Cuatro de Julio → Me gusta mucho el Cuatro de Julio porque vemos fuegos artificiales (*fireworks*) en el parque y...

1. el Cuatro de Julio
2. el Día de (Acción de) Gracias
3. la Nochevieja
4. la Navidad

Vocabulario útil	
el árbol	tree
el barrio	neighborhood
la corona	wreath
el desfile	parade
el globo	balloon

(Continúa).

Paso 2. Ahora, en parejas, túrnense para describir su día festivo o celebración favorita, dando detalles sobre:

- dónde se celebra y las personas que participan
- los preparativos que ustedes u otras personas hacen
- las comidas o bebidas para la celebración
- cómo se visten para la ocasión

Paso 3. Ahora, en parejas, compartan (*share*) con el resto de la clase las preferencias o tradiciones que tienen en común.

Las emociones

¡OJO!

The verbs **reír** and **sonreír** are **e → i** stem-changing verbs. However, an accent is required on *all* present tense forms of these verbs (as well as on the infinitives) to show the breaking of diphthongs **io, ie, ei** by stressing the weak vowel **i**: **(son)río, (son)ríes, (son)ríe, (son)reímos, (son)reís, (son)ríen.** No accent mark is needed on the present participle, in which the **i** is not stressed: **(son)riendo.**

llorar

discutir con (alguien) por/sobre (algo)

enojarse con (alguien) por (algo)

ponerse rojo/a

Para expresar *to become / get* **y** *to feel*

estar/ sentirse (me siento) (i) + *adj./adv.*	to be / to feel + *adj./adv.*
ponerse + *adj./adv.*	to become/get + *adj./adv.*

Me pongo triste cuando escucho malas noticias y luego **estoy triste** todo el día.
I get sad when I hear bad news, and then I'm sad all day long.

Cuando **me pongo enfermo/a, me siento muy mal.**
When I get sick, I feel awful.

Los adjetivos

enojado/a	angry; upset
feliz (*pl.* **felices**)	happy
tranquilo/a	calm

Repaso: alegre, contento/a, furioso/a, nervioso/a, triste

Otros verbos

olvidar	to forget
portarse bien/mal	to (mis)behave
quejarse de	to complain about
recordar (recuerdo)	to remember
reírse (me río) (i) (de)	to laugh (about)
sonreír (sonrío) (i)	to smile

Comunicación

A. Asociaciones

Paso 1. ¿Con qué verbos asocia usted las siguientes cosas y situaciones? Use verbos de **Las emociones** o cualquier (*any*) otro.

1. ver un bebé
2. una situación injusta
3. un número de teléfono nuevo
4. algo memorable que pasó
5. un chiste muy bueno
6. un perro muy joven
7. un desacuerdo (*disagreement*) con un amigo
8. estar equivocado/a (*wrong*) en público / delante de una clase

Paso 2. Ahora, en parejas, digan las palabras o frases que ustedes asocian con los siguientes verbos o frases.

1. recordar
2. sonreír
3. ponerse nervioso/a
4. discutir con alguien

Nota comunicativa: Cómo enfatizar: -ísimo

To emphasize the quality described by an adjective or an adverb in English, you can put *very very* or *really really* before the word: *I tried very very hard. I really really like it.* This is expressed in Spanish by adding **-ísimo** to an adverb and **-ísimo/a(os/as)** to an adjective. You already know one adverb formed like this: **muchísimo.**

> Mi madre se emocionó **muchísimo** porque las tarjetas y los regalos eran **lindísimos.**
> *My mother got very very emotional because the cards and gifts were super nice.*

- If the word ends in a consonant, **-ísimo** is added to the singular form and any accents on the original word are dropped: **difícil → dificilísimo.**

  Estas tapas son **dificilísimas** de preparar.
  These appetizers are very, very hard to prepare.

- If the word ends in a vowel, that vowel is dropped before adding **-ísimo** and any accents on the original word are also dropped.

  tarde → tardísimo   **rápida → rapidísima**

- There are spelling changes when the final consonant is a **c, g,** or **z.** This is the same spelling change you have learned to make in the formal command and preterite forms of verbs that end in **-car, -gar,** and **-zar.**

  rico → riquísimo   **largas → larguísimas**   **feliz → felicísimo**

You can use adjectives and adverbs formed in this way in **Comunicación B** and **C.**

B. Reacciones. ¿Cómo se pone o se siente usted en estas situaciones? Use los adjetivos y verbos que usted sabe y también algunas formas enfáticas (**-ísimo**). ¿Cuántas emociones puede usted describir?

MODELO: Llueve todo el día. → Me pongo / Me siento **triste/tristísima.**

1. No funciona el wifi de su residencia/casa.
2. Es Navidad. Alguien le hace un regalo carísimo.
3. Usted quiere bañarse. No hay agua caliente.
4. Usted está solo/a en casa una noche y oye un ruido.
5. En una película romántica que usted está viendo, muere (*dies*) el protagonista.
6. Usted tiene un examen importantísimo pero no estudió nada.
7. Usted cuenta un chiste pero nadie se ríe.
8. Usted acaba de terminar un examen difícil. Cree que lo hizo muy mal.

C. ¿Cuándo... ?

Paso 1. En parejas, completen las siguientes oraciones con un lugar y una acción o situación, según su experiencia. Sigan el modelo.

MODELO: **1.** Me quejo cuando... (acción o situación) →
　　　　E1: Me quejo cuando estoy en el aeropuerto y tengo que hacer cola... ¡y la cola es larguísima!
　　　　E2: Y yo me quejo cuando tengo que esperar muchísimo en el supermercado para pagar.

(Continúa).

Vocabulario útil

avergonzado/a
　embarrassed
de buen/mal humor
contento/a
feliz/triste
furioso/a
impaciente
nervioso/a
preocupado/a

---

1. Me quejo en... cuando...
2. Me río muchísimo en... cuando...
3. Sonrío en... cuando...
4. Lloro en... cuando...
5. Mis padres se enojan en... cuando... (Mis hijos... Mi esposo/a... Mi novio/a...)
6. Los niños se portan bien/ malísimo en... cuando...
7. Las mascotas se portan bien/ mal en... cuando...
8. Me pongo rojo/a en... cuando...

Paso 2. Ahora comparen sus respuestas con las (*those*) del resto de la clase. ¿En qué son similares o diferentes las respuestas de todos?

Textos de todos los días: Una tarjeta de felicitación

En ciertos días festivos y celebraciones importantes, es típico mandar tarjetas de felicitación. En esta actividad usted va a escribir una.

Objetivo: Escribir una tarjeta de felicitación para una ocasión especial: Navidad u otra fiesta religiosa importante, un cumpleaños, el Día de la Madre, etcétera.

Antes de empezar

- Piense en los mensajes típicos de este tipo de textos. Con frecuencia son cortos y hay una fórmula que se repite con frecuencia. Pero también es común añadir una o dos oraciones más personales.
- Elija una ocasión y una persona destinataria (*recipient*).

Vocabulario útil

querido/a
desear + pronombre de complemento indirecto: **Te / Le / Les deseo...**
　　una feliz Navidad/Janucá/graduación...
　　un feliz cumpleaños / un próspero Año Nuevo
　　unas felices fiestas
en compañía de...　　　　together with ...
y que cumplas muchos más　　and may you have many more (birthdays)

Para cerrar
　　Abrazos　　　　　　　Hugs
　　Un fuerte abrazo　　　A big hug
　　Con todo mi cariño　　With all my affection

GRAMÁTICA

♻ **Repaso**

You already know the irregular preterite stem and endings for **hacer.** All verbs presented in **Gramática 24** have irregular stems used with those same preterite endings as **hacer.** Review those endings by completing these forms.

1. yo: hic____   **2.** nosotros: hic____   **3.** usted: hiz____   **4.** ellos: hic____

24 Talking About the Past (Part 2) • Irregular Preterites

Gramática en acción: ¿Qué pasó en la fiesta de fin de año en casa de Sofía y Paco?

Mire con atención los verbos en rojo. Son formas del pretérito. Dé el infinitivo y luego conteste las preguntas.

1. ¿Quién **estuvo** hablando por teléfono?
2. ¿Quién **dio** la fiesta?
3. ¿Quién no **pudo** ir a la fiesta?
4. ¿Quién **puso** su copa sobre la televisión?
5. ¿Quién **hizo** mucho ruido?
6. ¿Quién no **quiso** beber más?
7. ¿Quién probablemente **tuvo** que irse temprano?

¿Y usted?

1. ¿**Estuvo** usted alguna vez en una fiesta de fin de año como esta? (**Estuve...**)
2. ¿**Tuvo** que irse temprano de la fiesta? (**Tuve...**) ¿O se quedó hasta medianoche?
3. ¿Recuerda qué ropa **se puso** para la fiesta? (**Me puse...**)

Irregular Forms / **Las formas irregulares**

1. Additional Irregular Forms

You have already learned the irregular preterite forms of **hacer.** The verbs to the right are also irregular in the preterite, like **hacer.**

- Their stem (shown in red and underlined) is irregular.
- They use the same preterite endings as **hacer.**

Only the first and third person singular endings are irregular (they have no accent marks). The verb **estar** is conjugated for you. The other verbs listed are conjugated like **estar.**

estar	
estuv**e**	estuv**imos**
estuv**iste**	estuv**isteis**
estuv**o**	estuv**ieron**

¡OJO!

There are no accents on **-e** and **-o.**

		Las terminaciones irregulares	
estar:	estuv-		
poder:	pud-	**-e**	**-imos**
poner:	pus-	**-iste**	**-isteis**
querer:	quis-	**-o**	**-ieron**
saber:	sup-		
tener:	tuv-		
venir:	vin-		

(Continúa).

2. Preterite of *decir* and *traer*

The irregular preterite stems of these two verbs end in **-j-**. They use the same endings as the verbs on the previous page, except that the **-i-** of the third person plural is omitted: **dijeron, trajeron.**

decir: <u>dij-</u> traer: <u>traj-</u>	-e, -iste, -o, -imos, -isteis, <u>-eron</u>

3. Preterite of *hay*: *hubo*

Hay (*There is/are*) comes from the infinitive **haber.** Its preterite form is **hubo** = *there was/were.*

<u>Hubo</u> un accidente ayer en el centro.
There was an accident yesterday downtown.

<u>Hubo</u> muchas fiestas de Navidad el año pasado.
There were a lot of Christmas parties last year.

Changes in Meaning / **Cambios de significado**

The following Spanish verbs have an English equivalent in the preterite tense that is different from that of the infinitive.

Infinitive	Present Tense	Preterite Meaning
saber =	to know (*facts, information*) Ya lo **sé.** *I already know it.*	<u>to find out, learn</u> Lo <u>**supe**</u> ayer. *I found it out (learned it) yesterday.*
conocer =	to know, be familiar with (*people, places*) Ya la **conozco.** *I already know her.*	<u>to meet (**for the first time**)</u> La **conocí** ayer. *I met her yesterday.*
querer =	to want **Quiero** hacerlo hoy. *I want to do it today.*	<u>to try</u> **Quise** hacerlo ayer. *I tried to do it yesterday.*
no querer =	not to want **No quiero** hacerlo hoy. *I don't want to do it today.*	<u>to refuse</u> **No quise** hacerlo anteayer. *I refused to do it the day before yesterday.*

Práctica y comunicación

A. La última Nochevieja

Paso 1. Autoprueba. Dé la forma indicada del pretérito.

1. yo: saber
2. ellos: tener
3. tú: venir
4. él: poner
5. nosotros: querer
6. usted: poder
7. ellos: decir
8. haber

> **Summary of Irregular Preterites**
>
> Endings: -e, -iste, -o, -imos, -isteis, -ieron
> Irregular stems: dij-, estuv-, hic-, pud-, pus-, quis-, sup-, traj-, tuv-, vin-

Paso 2. Ahora diga lo que usted hizo o no hizo el último día del año pasado. Haga oraciones completas con la forma apropiada del pretérito.

MODELO: **1.** (no) querer hacer algo / nada especial ese día →
Quise hacer **algo** especial ese día. / **No quise** hacer **nada** especial ese día.

El último día del año pasado, (yo)...

1. (no) querer hacer algo / nada especial ese día
2. (no) dar una fiesta en mi casa/apartamento
3. (no) estar con unos buenos amigos
4. (no) tener que hacer algo/nada de comida

Prác. A, Paso 1: Answers: 1. supe **2.** tuvieron **3.** viniste **4.** puso **5.** quisimos **6.** pudo **7.** dijeron **8.** hubo

280 ■ doscientos ochenta

Capítulo 9 Los días festivos

5. conocer a alguien / no conocer a nadie interesante

6. (no) decirle ¡Feliz Año Nuevo! a alguien/nadie

7. (no) poder quedarme despierto/a (*awake*) hasta la medianoche

8. (no) ponerse ropa elegante esa noche

Paso 3. Ahora, en parejas, túrnense para hacer y contestar preguntas basadas en las oraciones del **Paso 2.** Luego díganle a la clase lo que tienen en común.

MODELO: **1. E1:** ¿**Quisiste** hacer algo especial ese día?
E2: No, no **quise** hacer nada especial. ¿Y tú?
E1: Yo tampoco. ➜
Ninguno de nosotros **quiso** hacer nada especial ese día.

B. En una fiesta. ¿Cómo se dice en inglés?

1. Conocí al primo cubano de una amiga.

2. Quise abrir una botella de champán.

3. Supe algo interesante sobre los anfitriones.

4. No quise bailar. ¡La música era (*was*) malísima!

C. Una Nochebuena en Santiago de Cuba

Paso 1. Complete la siguiente narración sobre la celebración de la Nochebuena de una familia cubana de la ciudad de Santiago, al sur de la isla de Cuba. Habla Manuel, el padre de la familia. Use el pretérito de los verbos.

Estrategia

Not all of the verbs in this story are irregular in the preterite. As you conjugate each infinitive, first ask yourself if its preterite is regular or irregular.

El año pasado mi esposa y yo celebramos la Nochebuena en casa con toda la familia. _____ (Estar)[1] con nosotros mi primo Andrés, de la Florida, quien _____ (quedarse)[2] con nosotros toda la semana.

_____ (Venir)[3] mis padres, mis suegros,[a] hermanos y cuñados[b] con sus hijos. También _____ (*nosotros*: invitar)[4] a nuestros vecinos[c] de toda la vida,[d] los Benjumea. Pero ellos no _____ (poder)[5] asistir porque _____ (irse)[6] a La Habana para estar con su hija, que _____ (tener)[7] un niño en noviembre.

Mi esposa _____ (preparar)[8] lechón asado, arroz y frijoles negros, yuca y tostones.[e] ¡Todo _____ (estar)[9] riquísimo! Mi cuñado _____ (traer)[10] turrón[f] español y cava.[g] A las 10:30, mi hermana _____ (decir)[11] que era[h] hora de ir a la Misa del Gallo[i] y _____ (llevar)[12] a los abuelos a la iglesia.[j] Los demás[k] no _____ (querer)[13] ir y seguimos armando bochinche[l] hasta que _____ (volver)[14] los otros. Todo _____ (ir)[15] bien chévere.[m] Como regalo de Navidad, mi primo Andrés me _____ (dar)[16] un álbum con fotos y cartas de mis parientes en la Florida y Nueva Jersey. Yo _____ (ponerse)[17] tan emocionado[n] que _____ (llorar).[18]

El lechón (*suckling pig*) con arroz y frijoles negros y plátanos maduros (*fried sweet plantains*)

[a]*in-laws* [b]*brothers- and sisters-in-law* [c]*neighbors* [d]*de... long-time (lit., of one's whole life)*
[e]*fried plantains* [f]*almond Christmas candy* [g]*Spanish sparkling wine* [h]*it was* [i]*Misa... Midnight Mass* [j]*church* [k]*Los... The others* [l]*armando... partying* [m]*great* [n]*touched, emotional*

Paso 2. Comprensión

1. ¿Qué tuvo de especial la Nochebuena del año pasado para Manuel?

2. ¿Por qué no pudieron asistir los Benjumea?

3. ¿Quiénes fueron a la Misa del Gallo?

4. ¿Qué comieron y bebieron todos?

(Continúa).

Paso 3. Ahora complete las siguientes oraciones basadas en lo que pasó en la celebración de la pasada Navidad, Pascua judía u otra fiesta de importancia para su familia. Conjugue los verbos en el pretérito, añadiendo el sujeto y otra información apropiada.

MODELO: **1. celebrar** _____ (fiesta) en _____ (lugar) →
   Mi familia **celebró** la Nochebuena en casa de mis abuelos.

1. **celebrar** _____ (fiesta) en _____ (lugar)
2. **querer** asistir / (no) **poder**
3. **ir** _____ (servicio religioso) **antes/después** de cenar
4. **comer** _____ (platos) y **beber** _____ (bebidas)
5. **ponerse** muy emocionado/a porque _____
6. **dar**le un regalo a _____ (persona)

D. Eventos famosos. Describan ustedes algunos eventos famosos, usando el pretérito de los verbos y una palabra o frase de cada columna. Su profesor(a) los puede ayudar con los datos (*information*) que no saben.

la Unión Soviética los estadounidenses Adán y Eva George Washington los europeos Romeo la princesa Diana	conocer estar poner saber traer	en Valley Forge con sus soldados a un hombre en la luna (*moon*) en 1969 un satélite en el espacio por primera vez en 1957 el significado (*meaning*) de un árbol especial a Nelson Mandela en Sudáfrica el caballo (*horse*) al Nuevo Mundo a Julieta en Verona

E. Intercambios

Paso 1. Haga preguntas en el pretérito con los siguientes verbos. En el **Paso 2,** usted va a usar las preguntas para entrevistar a una persona de la clase.

MODELO: **1. conocer** → ¿Cuándo **conociste** a tu mejor amigo/a?

1. conocer
2. saber
3. estar
4. tener
5. hacer
6. dar

Paso 2. En parejas, túrnense para hacer y contestar sus preguntas. Luego díganle a la clase algo que los/las dos tienen en común.

MODELO: **1. conocer** → Los dos **conocimos** a nuestros mejores amigos en la escuela secundaria.

F. La última fiesta

Paso 1. Haga una lista de todos los detalles (*details*) que usted recuerda de la última fiesta a la que (*which*) fue. Puede ser una fiesta que usted organizó o que otra persona dio. Use los siguientes verbos: **conocer, dar, estar, invitar, organizar, poder, saber, ser, venir.**

MODELO: Di una fiesta para el cumpleaños de mi mejor amigo.
   Mi amigo Clark y yo organizamos la fiesta...

Paso 2. Ahora entreviste a una persona de la clase sobre la última fiesta a la que (*to which*) fue o que dio. Haga preguntas con las palabras interrogativas y el pretérito.

Palabras interrogativas: ¿cuándo?, ¿dónde?, ¿quién?, ¿con quién?, ¿qué?, ¿por qué?

MODELOS: **¿Quién dio** la fiesta?
   ¿Qué hubo de comer y beber?

Paso 3. Luego díganle a la clase dos detalles interesantes sobre las últimas fiestas a las que (*to which*) ustedes fueron o que ustedes organizaron.

Repaso

You learned in **Gramática 15 (Cap. 6)** to make a change in the **-ndo** form of **-ir** stem-changing verbs. That same change occurs in some forms of the preterite of that type of verb. Review the change in the present participle by completing the following forms.

1. pedir: p____diendo   **2.** dormir: d____rmiendo

You will learn about this change in the preterite in **Grámatica 25.**

25 Talking About the Past (Part 3) • Preterite of Stem-changing Verbs

Gramática en acción: Una fiesta de quinceañera

Escoja las respuestas más lógicas para describir la fiesta de quinceañera de Lupe Carrasco. Al leer (*As you read*), mire con atención los verbos en rojo. Son formas del pretérito. ¿Puede usted dar el infinitivo de esos verbos?

1. Para su fiesta, Lupe **se vistió** con...
   ☐ un vestido amarillo muy elegante.
   ☐ una camiseta y *jeans*.
2. Mientras Lupe cortaba[a] el pastel de cumpleaños, la madre de ella...
   ☐ **empezó** a llorar.
   ☐ **se rio** mucho.
3. Lupe **pidió** un deseo[b] al cortar[c] el pastel. Ella...
   ☐ les dijo a todos qué fue lo que **pidió.**
   ☐ **prefirió** guardarlo en secreto.
4. En la fiesta **sirvieron...**
   ☐ champán y refrescos.
   ☐ solo té y café.
5. Todos los invitados...
   ☐ **se divirtieron** mucho.
   ☐ se quejaron.
6. A las tres de la mañana, el último invitado
   ☐ **se despidió.**[d]
   ☐ **sonrió.**

Una celebración de quinceañera

Hill Street Studios/Blend Images LLC

[a]Mientras... *While Lupe was cutting*   [b]*wish*   [c]al... *as she cut*   [d]se... *said good-bye*

¿Y usted?

1. ¿Recuerda usted qué hizo cuando cumplió 15 años?
2. ¿Qué regalos **pidió**? (**Pedí...**)
3. ¿Qué **sirvieron** en la fiesta? (**Sirvieron...**)
4. ¿Se **divirtió**? (**Me divertí...**)
5. ¿Cómo se **sintió** ese día? (**Me sentí...**)

1. Preterite of -ar and -er Stem-changing Verbs

In **Gramática 23 (Cap. 8)** you learned that **-ar** and **-er** stem-changing verbs have no stem change in the preterite (or in the present participle).

El pretérito de los verbos en *-ar/-er*			
rec<u>o</u>rdar (rec<u>ue</u>rdo)		**p<u>e</u>rder (p<u>ie</u>rdo)**	
rec<u>o</u>rdé	rec<u>o</u>rdamos	p<u>e</u>rdí	p<u>e</u>rdimos
rec<u>o</u>rdaste	rec<u>o</u>rdasteis	p<u>e</u>rdiste	p<u>e</u>rdisteis
rec<u>o</u>rdó	rec<u>o</u>rdaron	p<u>e</u>rdió	p<u>e</u>rdieron
	rec<u>o</u>rdando		p<u>e</u>rdiendo

2. Preterite of -ir Stem-changing Verbs

-Ir stem-changing verbs *do* have a stem change in the preterite.

- The change occurs only in the third person singular and plural forms.
- The stem vowels **e** and **o** change to **i** and **u**, respectively. This is the same change that occurs in the present participle of **-ir** stem-changing verbs.

El pretérito de los verbos en *-ir*			
e → i		o → u	
pedir (pido) (i)		dormir (duermo) (u)	
pedí	pedimos	dormí	dormimos
pediste	pedisteis	dormiste	dormisteis
pidió	pidieron	durmió	durmieron
pidiendo		durmiendo	

¡OJO!

Remember that this change is indicated in parentheses after the infinitive in vocabulary lists: **pedir (pido) (i), dormir (duermo) (u).** Now you know that it indicates two different changes: (1) in the present participle, and (2) in the third person singular and plural of the preterite.

3. Important -ir Stem-changing Verbs

You already know or have seen many of these verbs. New ones are indicated with *.

*conseguir (consigo) (i)	to get; to obtain; to succeed	sonreír (sonrío) (i)	to smile
conseguir + *inf.*	in (*doing something*)	*sugerir (sugiero) (i)	to suggest
*despedirse (me despido) (i) (de)	to say good-bye (to)	vestirse (me visto) (i)	to get dressed
divertirse (me divierto) (i)	to have a good time		
dormir (duermo) (u)	to sleep;		
dormirse	to fall asleep		
*morirse (me muero) (u)	to die		
pedir (pido) (i)	to ask for; to order		
preferir (prefiero) (i)	to prefer		
reírse (me río) (i) (de)	to laugh (at)		
seguir (sigo) (i)	to continue; to follow		
sentirse (me siento) (i)	to feel		
servir (sirvo) (i)	to serve		

¡OJO!

The verbs **reírse** and **sonreír** are **e → i** stem-changing verbs, but they drop the **e** completely in the third persons of the preterite and in the present participle.

(me reí, te reíste)   (nos reímos, os reísteis)
    se **río**   se **rieron** → **riendo**

(sonreí, sonreíste)   (sonreímos, sonreísteis)
    sonrió   sonrieron → sonriendo

Práctica y comunicación

A. ¿Quién lo hizo?

Paso 1. Autoprueba. Complete las siguientes formas del pretérito.

1. nos divert____mos
2. se d____rmieron
3. tú s____rviste
4. se v____stió
5. yo sug____rí
6. ustedes p____dieron

Summary of the Preterite of Stem-changing Verbs

-ar / -er = no change
-ir = change in the third persons singular and plural
    e → i
    o → u

Paso 2. Ahora indique quiénes de sus compañeros de clase hicieron las siguientes acciones la semana pasada (*last week*). Use verbos en el pretérito. Si nadie lo hizo, simplemente diga **Nadie...** Si más de una persona lo hizo, use el verbo en plural.

MODELO: **1.** _____ vestirse con ropa elegante/extravagante para venir a clase
    → Tom **se vistió** con ropa elegante para venir a clase.

1. _____ vestirse con ropa elegante/extravagante para venir a clase
2. _____ dormirse en clase
3. _____ pedirle al profesor / a la profesora más tarea
4. _____ sentirse bien/mal con el resultado de un examen

Prác. A, Paso 1: Answers: 1. nos divertimos 2. se durmieron 3. tú serviste 4. se vistió 5. yo sugerí 6. ustedes pidieron

5. _____ divertirse muchísimo en un concierto

6. _____ reírse a carcajadas (*out loud*)

7. _____ sugerir tener la clase afuera

8. _____ no recordar traer la tarea a clase

9. _____ despedirse en español de sus amigos de la clase

10. _____ morirse de vergüenza (*embarrassment*) por algo

 Paso 3. Ahora, en parejas, comparen sus respuestas del **Paso 2.** Luego díganle a la clase una o dos de las respuestas que tienen en común. Mencionen el día, si lo recuerdan.

MODELO: **1.** Pensamos que Tom **se vistió** con ropa **elegante** para venir a clase **el miércoles de la semana pasada.**

B. José Martí

Paso 1. Complete la siguiente narración con formas del pretérito para saber más sobre José Martí.

José Martí _____ (servir)[1] por la causa de la independencia cubana toda su vida.[a] Siempre _____ (pedir)[2] la libertad de Cuba, de España, y se opuso a la esclavitud.[b] Nació[c] en 1853 en Cuba, hijo de españoles.

_____ (Estudiar)[3] en España, donde _____ (recibir)[4] el título de abogado[d] en 1874. Pero no _____ (poder)[5] ejercer[e] esta profesión en Cuba. Luego _____ (vivir)[6] en México, Guatemala y los Estados Unidos.

En 1876 _____ (conocer)[7] a la mujer que luego _____ (ser)[8] su esposa, María, y se casaron.[f] _____ (*Ellos:* Tener)[9] un hijo, pero el matrimonio se separó y Martí _____ (perder)[10] contacto con su hijo.

En 1895 _____ (decidir)[11] empezar una guerra[g] de independencia en Cuba. _____ (Morirse)[12] luchando[h] en su querida[i] isla.

Algunos de sus versos son especialmente famosos en todo el mundo gracias a la canción «Guantanamera».

[a]*life* [b]*se... he opposed slavery* [c]*He was born* [d]*título... law degree* [e]*practice* [f]*se... they got married* [g]*war* [h]*fighting* [i]*beloved*

Paso 2. Ahora, haga cinco preguntas usando verbos en el pretérito que se puedan contestar (*can be answered*) con información del texto.

MODELO: ¿Cuántos años vivió Martí?

C. Las historias que todos conocemos

Paso 1. Empareje los personajes (*characters*) de la columna de la izquierda con las acciones de la columna de la derecha para crear oraciones en el pretérito basadas en unos cuentos o historias muy famosos. ¿Puede adivinar (*guess*) quiénes son Caperucita Roja, la Cenicienta y Blancanieves?

PERSONAJES

1. Caperucita Roja, el lobo (*wolf*)

2. la Cenicienta, el Príncipe, las hermanastras

3. Blancanieves, los siete enanos (*dwarfs*)

4. Romeo, Julieta

ACCIONES

a. conocer a una mujer misteriosa en un baile

b. divertirse bailando con un joven muy guapo

c. dormirse después de comer una manzana

d. morirse por el amor de su novia

e. perderse en el bosque (*forest*)

f. perder un zapato muy bonito

g. encontrar (*to find*) un zapato de cristal (*glass*)

h. sentirse preocupados por su amiga

i. vestirse de (*as a*) abuela

j. no conseguir ponerse el zapato de cristal

k. hablar con un joven guapo desde su balcón

(Continúa).

Algo sobre José Martí

José Martí, llamado el Apóstol de la independencia cubana

José Martí (1853-1895) fue un escritor[a] y periodista[b] cubano considerado un héroe nacional por su lucha[c] por la independencia y por la libertad de su país. Fue uno de los grandes intelectuales hispanohablantes del siglo XIX.[d]

 ¿Hay algún héroe político o social que usted admire mucho? ¿Por qué lo/la admira?

[a]*writer* [b]*journalist* [c]*fight* [d]*siglo... 19th century*

Carl DeAbreu/Alamy Stock Photo

Paso 2. Ahora, en parejas, inventen dos acciones más en el pretérito para cada historia, pero sin incluir el nombre del personaje. La clase va a adivinar a qué personaje, cuento o historia se refieren sus oraciones.

MODELO: Una mujer **quiso** ponerse el zapato de cristal, pero no **pudo.** →
la hermanastra de la Cenicienta

D. Una entrevista indiscreta

Paso 1. Lea las siguientes preguntas y escriba una respuesta para cada una. **¡OJO!** Tres de sus respuestas deben ser falsas.

1. ¿A qué hora te dormiste anoche?
2. ¿Perdiste mucho dinero alguna vez?
3. ¿Con qué programa o serie de televisión te divertiste mucho en los días o meses pasados... pero te avergüenzas de (*you're ashamed*) admitirlo?
4. ¿Seguiste haciendo algo después de que tu padre/madre (compañero/a, esposo/a) te dijo que no lo hicieras (*not to do it*)?
5. ¿Pediste una bebida alcohólica antes de tener 21 años?
6. ¿Qué cosa o tarea no conseguiste terminar el mes pasado?

Paso 2. En parejas, usen las preguntas del **Paso 1** para entrevistarse. Traten de (*Try to*) adivinar las respuestas falsas de su compañero/a.

Paso 3. Ahora presenten a la clase una de las respuestas interesantes de su compañero/a. La clase va a adivinar si la respuesta es cierta o falsa.

MODELO: **E1:** Julie, ¿a qué hora te dormiste anoche?
E2: Me dormí a las tres de la mañana.
E1: (*a la clase*): Julie se durmió a las tres de la mañana anoche.
CLASE: No es cierto.
E1: Tienen razón. No es cierto. Me dormí a las once.

Algo sobre la palma

La palma real[a] (también llamada palmera en otros países) es un ícono nacional que se encuentra por toda la isla. Forma parte del escudo[b] nacional como símbolo del espíritu cubano: siempre alto y orgulloso.[c] José Martí la menciona en sus famosos versos:[d]

> Yo soy un hombre sincero
> De donde crece[e] la palma,
> Y antes de morirme quiero
> Echar[f] mis versos del alma.[g]

 ¿Cuáles son dos o tres cosas que usted considera más simbólicas de este país? Pueden ser un animal, una planta, una canción, un objeto...

[a]*royal* [b]*coat of arms* [c]*proud* [d]*lines (of a poem)* [e]*grows* [f]*Release* [g]*soul*

Unas palmas reales en La Habana, Cuba

In **Gramática 18 (Cap. 7)** you learned about direct object nouns and pronouns. In **Gramática 21 (Cap. 8)**, you learned about indirect object nouns and pronouns. Review both types of object pronouns by identifying the indicated pronouns in the following sentences.

	DIRECT OBJECT	INDIRECT OBJECT
1. El profesor **les** dio la tarea.	☐	☐
2. El profesor **la** asignó para hacer en casa.	☐	☐
3. La profesora **me** vio.	☐	☐
4. La profesora **me** dio la tarea.	☐	☐

26 Avoiding Repetition • Expressing Direct and Indirect Object Pronouns Together

Gramática en acción: La fiesta de Anita

Berta **Anita**

❶

Berta le hizo un pastel a Anita y **se lo** dio en la fiesta.

Anita **Berta**

❷

Anita le prestó unos aretes a Berta.

Anita **Berta**

❸

Berta le sacó una foto a Anita y **se la** mostró.

Comprensión

¿Quién lo dijo? ¿De qué habla?
1. «**Me lo** hizo para mi cumpleaños».
2. «**Me los** prestó para la fiesta».
3. «**Se la** mostré en el celular».

¿Y usted?

Describa los siguientes detalles de su último cumpleaños.
1. ¿Un pastel? ¿Alguien **se lo** hizo? (**Alguien/ Nadie me...**)
2. ¿Unas fotos? ¿Alguien **se las** sacó?
3. ¿Algo de vestir? ¿Alguien **se lo** prestó?

complemento indirecto	complemento directo
me	lo / la / los / las
te	lo / la / los / las
(le →) <u>se</u>	lo / la / los / las

complemento indirecto	complemento directo
nos	lo / la / los / las
os	lo / la / los / las
(les) → <u>se</u>	lo / la / los / las

(Continúa).

Order of Pronouns / **La secuencia de los pronombres**

1. Both Object Pronouns in the Same Sentence

When both an indirect and a direct object pronoun appear in the same sentence, the indirect object pronoun comes first, followed by the direct object pronoun. (This is the opposite of English.) You can remember the order of the Spanish pronouns by thinking of **ID = (1)** **I**ndirect **(2)** **D**irect.

¿El almuerzo? **Te lo** sirvo ahora mismo.
Lunch? I'll serve it to you right now.

¿El trofeo? No **nos lo** dieron.
The trophy? They didn't give it to us.

2. Position of Double Object Pronouns

The placement of double object pronouns in relation to the verb is the same as for single object pronouns. The pronouns come:

- before a conjugated verb
- after an infinitive or present participle

or

- before the conjugated verb that precedes them

- before a negative command
- after an affirmative command

¿El libro? Manu **me lo dio.**

¿La bicicleta? Mis padres **acaban de regalármela.** /
  Me la acaban de regalar mis padres.

¿Las fotos? **Te las estoy mandando** ahora mismo. / **Estoy mandándotelas** ahora mismo.

¿La comida? **No me la traiga** ahora.

¿Las bebidas? **Tráigamelas,** por favor.

Using **se** instead of **le** or **les** / **El uso de *se* en vez de *le* o *les***

1. Use of *se*

When both the indirect and the direct object pronouns begin with the letter **l**, the indirect object pronoun *always* changes to **se.**

This change from **le/les** to **se** happens when the indirect object refers to **usted/ustedes** or to a third person singular or plural (**él, ella, ellos, ellas**), the equivalents of English *(I'll give) it/them to you/him/her/them.*

Four pronoun combinations with **se** instead of **le/les** are possible: **se lo, se la, se los, se las.** In these combinations:

- <u>se</u> = indirect object pronoun (**le** or **les**)
- **lo/la/los/las** = direct object pronouns (no change)

(1) indirect (2) direct

Les dimos <u>el coche</u> (a ustedes). *We gave you the car.*
↓ (les lo)
Se lo dimos.   *We gave it to you.*

Le escribí <u>la carta</u> ayer (a ella). *I wrote her the letter yesterday.*
↓ (le la)
Se la escribí ayer.   *I wrote it to her yesterday.*

Le regaló <u>esos zapatos</u> (a él). *He gave him those shoes.*
↓ (le los)
Se los regaló.   *He gave them to him.*

Les mandamos a todos <u>las invitaciones</u>. (les las) *We sent all of them the invitations.*
Se las mandamos.   *We sent them to them.*

2. Clarifying *se*

Since **se** can stand for **le** (*to/for you* [sing.], *him, her*) or **les** (*to/for you* [pl.], *them*), it is often necessary to clarify its meaning by using **a** plus the prepositional pronoun.

You learned to clarify the indirect object pronouns **le** and **les** in this way in **Capítulo 8.** This is exactly the same thing, since **se** represents **le** and **les.**

¿La carta de recomendación? Voy a escribír**sela.** (meaning of **se** unclear unless specified)

¿La carta de recomendación? Voy a escribír**sela a** <u>usted</u> / **a** <u>ustedes</u>.
  a <u>él</u> / **a** <u>ellos</u>.
  a <u>ella</u> / **a** <u>ellas</u>.

Práctica y comunicación

A. Oraciones «familiares»

Paso 1. Autoprueba. Complete las siguientes oraciones con los pronombres apropiados del complemento directo e indirecto: **se lo, se la, se los, se las.**

1. Le dieron el libro. ➜ _____ _____ dieron.
2. Les sirvieron la ensalada. ➜ _____ _____ sirvieron.
3. Le di las direcciones. ➜ _____ _____ di.
4. Les trajo los boletos. ➜ _____ _____ trajo.

> **Summary of Indirect and Direct Object Pronouns**
>
> | INDIRECT | DIRECT |
> |---|---|
> | me/te/nos/os | |
> | | + lo/la/los/las |
> | le(s) ➜ <u>se</u> | |

Prác. A, Paso 1: Answers: 1. Se lo 2. Se la 3. Se las 4. Se los

Paso 2. Complete las oraciones con información personal. Las oraciones en la columna A se refieren a las acciones que usted hace por otros = usted es el sujeto de la oración. Las oraciones en la columna B se refieren a lo que otras personas hacen por usted = esas personas son el sujeto.

	COLUMNA A	COLUMNA B
1. «¡Te quiero!»:	Se lo digo a ____.	Me lo dice ____.
2. «¡Te lo dije!»:	Se lo digo a ____.	Me lo dice ____.
3. Regalos:	Se los doy a ____.	Me los dan ____.
4. Favores:	Se los hago a ____.	Me los hacen ____.

 Paso 3. Ahora, en parejas, túrnense para preguntarse sobre las acciones del **Paso 2.**

MODELO: **1.** «¡Te quiero!» ➜
      E1: ¿Le dices «¡Te quiero!» a alguien?
      E2: Sí, se lo digo a mi madre. ¿Y tú?
      E1: Yo también se lo digo a mi madre. / Yo no se lo digo a nadie.

B. En la mesa. Siga el modelo para pedir durante una comida cosas que están en la mesa. **¡OJO!** Preste atención al uso del tiempo presente para pedir algo de manera informal. Este tipo de oración es de uso muy frecuente.

MODELO: ensalada ➜ ¿Hay más **ensalada**? ¿Me **la** pasas, por favor?

1. pan	**3.** tomates	**5.** vino
2. tortillas	**4.** fruta	**6.** jamón

C. En el aeropuerto. Cambie los sustantivos por pronombres para evitar (*avoid*) la repetición.

MODELO: ¿La maleta? Van a prestarme **la maleta** mañana. ➜
      Van a prestá**mela** (**Me la** van a prestar) mañana.

1. ¿La hora de la salida? Acaban de decirnos **la hora de la salida.**
2. ¿El horario (*schedule*)? Sí, léame **el horario,** por favor.
3. ¿Los boletos? No, no tiene que darle **los boletos** aquí.
4. ¿El equipaje? ¡Claro que le guardo **el equipaje**!
5. ¿Los boletos? Ya te compré **los boletos.**
6. ¿El puesto? No te preocupes. Te puedo guardar **el puesto.**

Algo sobre el son cubano

El son es un género musical cubano que dio lugar[a] al mambo, a la rumba y a la salsa, entre otros bailes. También está presente en el jazz latino.

El son se originó en el este de Cuba a finales del siglo XIX[b] con elementos musicales africanos y españoles. A principios[c] del siglo XX llegó a La Habana y de allí salió al mundo. Los grupos soneros originales tocaban[d] con un tres cubano (una guitarra con tres pares de cuerdas[e]), bongós y maracas. Después empezaron a usar la guitarra, el contrabajo[f] y la trompeta.

En su opinión ¿cuál es el género musical de su país que más influencia tiene en el mundo? ¿Qué sabe de esa música?

[a]dio... *gave rise, created* [b]siglo... *19th century*
[c]A... *At the beginning* [d]*played* [e]*strings* [f]*string bass*

Celia Cruz (1925–2003), la gran cantante cubana que llevó el son por todo el mundo

ZUMA Press, Inc./Alamy Stock Photo

(Continúa).

D. Minidiálogos

Paso 1. Complete las respuestas usando los pronombres necesarios.

1. —¿Me vas a dar dinero? —¡No! No _____.
2. —¿Por qué no me dices la verdad? —¡Yo siempre _____!
3. —¿Podemos hacerle una fiesta a Paula por su cumpleaños?
   —¡Por supuesto (*Of course*) que _____!
4. —¿Les doy (*Shall I give*) una buena nota final a todos ustedes?
   —Por favor, ¡_____!

Paso 2. Ahora, en parejas, inventen un contexto para cada minidiálogo. ¿Quiénes son las personas? ¿Dónde están? ¿Cuál es el tono: serio, en broma (*joking*), enojado... ?

E. Regalos

Carta a los Reyes Magos
Entrega tu carta al Cartero Real[a]

[a]Cartero... *Royal Mail Deliverer*

Paso 1. Conteste las preguntas usando los pronombres del complemento directo e indirecto necesarios en vez de las palabras subrayadas.

1. Según sus tradiciones, ¿los Reyes Magos les traen los regalos a los niños en la madrugada (*night/early morning*) del día 6 de enero?
2. En su tradición, ¿hay un personaje (*character*) que les trae regalos a los niños? ¿Cuándo se los trae?
3. ¿Les da usted regalos a personas de su familia en algún día especial? ¿Y a sus amigos/as? ¿Cuándo se los da?
4. Por lo general, ¿quién le da a usted los mejores regalos?

Paso 2. Ahora, haga una lista de los tres mejores regalos que le han hecho a usted (*you've received*) en su vida (*life*). Piense en los siguientes detalles en cada caso: ¿Quién se lo regaló? ¿Cuándo y por qué se lo dio?

Paso 3. Finalmente, en parejas, túrnense para hablar de los regalos más especiales de su vida. Recuerden usar pronombres para evitar la repetición.

⚙ Todo junto

A. Lengua y cultura: La Virgen de Guadalupe, quince siglos (*centuries*) de historia

Paso 1. Completar. Complete the following paragraphs with the correct form of the words in parentheses, as suggested by context. When two possibilities are given in parentheses, select the correct word. Use the present tense or the preterite of the infinitives, according to context.

E̶n todos los países hispanohablantes, hay festividades religiosas que son días de fiesta nacionales. Por ejemplo, el día de Navidad se _____ (celebrar)[1] en todo el mundo hispano. Otra celebración religiosa que también (es / está)[2] una fiesta nacional en _____ (mucho)[3] países es el 12 de diciembre. Es el día de la fiesta de la Virgen de Guadalupe, una imagen venerada[a] por todo el mundo católico, especialmente en México.

　　La historia de la Virgen de Guadalupe _____ (venir)[4] a México desde[b] España. En el siglo VI,[c] el papa[d] Gregorio tenía[e] una estatua de la Virgen y (se lo / se la)[5] regaló al obispo[f] de Sevilla. Pero luego la estatua _____ (desaparecer)[6] durante los siglos en que los árabes ocuparon la Península. Después de la expulsión de los árabes, un pastor[g] cristiano (le / la)[7] _____ (encontrar)[8] cerca de la ciudad de Guadalupe. Por eso la estatua _____ (tomar)[9] el nombre de la Virgen de Guadalupe.

Beren Patterson/Alamy Stock Photo

La tilma (*shawl*) de Juan Diego en la Basílica de Santa María de Guadalupe, en la Ciudad de México

[a]imagen... *image venerated, adored* [b]*from* [c]el... *the sixth century* [d]*Pope (head of the Catholic Church)* [e]*had* [f]*Bishop* [g]*shepherd*

En lo que hoy es México, en el siglo XVI, un campesino[h] indígena, Juan Diego, se convirtió[i] al cristianismo. Un día _____ (*él*: ver)[10] a la Virgen en un lugar llamado Tepeyac. Por un milagro,[j] la Virgen _____ (dejar[k])[11] su imagen impresa[l] en la tilma de Juan Diego. Esta imagen _____ (recibir)[12] el nombre de Virgen de Guadalupe porque Tepeyac (es / está)[13] cerca del pueblo mexicano de Guadalupe.

La tilma de Juan Diego, con la imagen de la Virgen, todavía se puede _____ (ver)[14] en la Basílica[m] de Santa María de Guadalupe, en la Ciudad de México.

[h]*peasant*   [i]*se... converted*   [j]*miracle*   [k]*to leave*   [l]*imprinted*   [m]*large church*

Paso 2. Comprensión. ¿Cierto o falso? Corrija las oraciones falsas.

	CIERTO	FALSO
1. La Virgen de Guadalupe española es una estatua.	☐	☐
2. El papa Gregorio vio a la Virgen en Tepeyac.	☐	☐
3. El campesino Juan Diego era (*was*) de origen español.	☐	☐
4. La tilma de Juan Diego ya no (*no longer*) existe.	☐	☐

Paso 3. En acción

En parejas, vuelvan a contar la historia de la Virgen de Guadalupe. Primero, hagan una lista de los hechos importantes en la historia, usando infinitivos. Ejemplo: **venir de España.** Luego, cuenten la historia.

B. Proyecto: El Día de...

Para este proyecto van a inventar un día de fiesta nuevo para celebrar algo que no se celebra todavía o no se celebra lo suficiente. Sean creativos: puede ser sobre algo serio o divertido, relacionado con (*related to*) su universidad, su localidad, este país o algo global.

Paso 1. Idea. En grupos, elijan un motivo de celebración y un día para celebrarlo. Justifiquen sus elecciones.

Paso 2. Desarrollo. (*Development.*) Ahora desarrollen esa celebración e inventen un mensaje (*slogan*). Piensen en los siguientes detalles.

- La celebración: ¿Qué se puede hacer para celebrar ese día? ¿Con quién se celebra? ¿Dónde?
- Publicidad y mensaje: Creen (*Create*) un mensaje para animar (*urge*) a la gente a celebrar ese día con entusiasmo. Para esto, consideren modelos como el (*that*) de la imagen para el Día de la Madre y de otros días festivos que ustedes conocen (el Día del Padre, el Día de [Acción de] Gracias, etcétera).

Paso 3. Competición. Toda la clase va a hacer de comité para seleccionar los dos días festivos nuevos del calendario.

Día de la Madre
¿Quiere decirle a su mamá «gracias, te quiero»?
¡Dígaselo con flores!

Video: Salu2 «De fiesta en fiesta»

You can watch two segments of this chapter's video in the **Video: Salu2** section, found at the end of the eBook.

Klic Video Productions/ McGraw Hill

La Fiesta Broadway, una celebración que conmemora una victoria mexicana

MUNDO HISPANO

Enfoque cultural: Los días festivos

Antes de leer

¿Hubo en este país alguna época de intolerancia política o religiosa?

En Cuba

Estatua de Carlos Manuel de Céspedes, en la Plaza de Armas en La Habana

En Cuba se conmemoran dos días muy importantes. El primero es el 10 de octubre, que se conoce como el Día de la Independencia Nacional. En este día de 1868, el patriota cubano Carlos Manuel de Céspedes declaró libres a todos los esclavos.[a] También llamó a todos los cubanos a liberarse del dominio[b] colonial de España. Esto marca el inicio[c] de la primera guerra[d] de independencia de Cuba.

   El otro día festivo de mucha importancia para los cubanos es la Navidad. Como resultado del cambio[e] político de 1959 y durante muchos años bajo el régimen de Fidel Castro, no se les permitió a los cubanos celebrar la Navidad de manera oficial. Todo cambió[f] con la visita a Cuba del papa[g] Juan Pablo II (segundo) en el año 1998. Desde[h] entonces los cubanos pueden asistir a la iglesia y celebrar este día tan importante con su familia y amigos.

[a]*enslaved people* [b]*control* [c]*beginning* [d]*war* [e]*change (that is, the regime of Fidel Castro)* [f]*changed* [g]*Pope (Head of the Catholic Church)* [h]*Since*

Comprensión ¿Cuáles son los días festivos más importantes de Cuba? ¿Desde cuándo se permite celebrar la Navidad sin restricciones otra vez en Cuba?

En otros países hispanos

Alfombra de aserrín (*saw dust*) de colores para una procesión de Semana Santa en Antigua, Guatemala

En todo el mundo hispanohablante Estas festividades se celebran en todas partes.

- **La Semana Santa** Así[a] se llama a la semana que va desde el Domingo de Ramos[b] hasta el Domingo de Pascua. En muchas ciudades hay procesiones[c] para conmemorar la pasión, muerte[d] y resurrección de Jesús. Tiene lugar[e] entre marzo y abril.

- **El Carnaval** Esta fiesta ocurre entre febrero y marzo, justo antes de la Cuaresma,[f] que son los cuarenta días antes de Semana Santa. El Carnaval más famoso del mundo es el[g] de Río de Janeiro (Brasil), pero hay Carnavales hispanos que también son famosos por la exuberancia de su música, bailes y colorido, como los Carnavales de Cádiz (España), Barranquilla (Colombia) y Santiago de Cuba (Cuba).

[a]*That's how* [b]*el... Palm Sunday* [c]*street processions* [d]*la... passion (that is, suffering), death* [e]*Tiene... It takes place* [f]*Lent (period from Ash Wednesday to Good Friday)* [g]*that*

Comprensión ¿Cuándo se celebra la Semana Santa? ¿Cuándo se celebra el Carnaval?

 En acción

En parejas, decidan cuáles son en su ciudad o estado las tres celebraciones en las que (*which*) una persona de otro país debería (*should*) tener la oportunidad de participar. Expliquen si son ocasiones para celebrar en público o con una familia local.

Lectura

Antes de leer

Es muy común hacerse algunos propósitos (*resolutions*) cuando un año empieza. ¿Se los hace usted generalmente? Haga una lista de cuatro propósitos que usted hizo en años pasados o quiso hacer. Use infinitivos en su lista. ¿Pudo cumplirlos todos?

Una declaración de propósitos

Vocabulario para leer

la basura	trash
la membresía	membership
la muestra	exhibition
sano/a	healthy
comprometerse a	to commit to
cumplir	to meet an expectation/promise

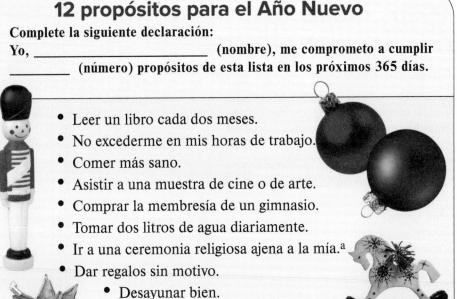

12 propósitos para el Año Nuevo

Complete la siguiente declaración:

Yo, _____ (nombre), me comprometo a cumplir _____ (número) propósitos de esta lista en los próximos 365 días.

- Leer un libro cada dos meses.
- No excederme en mis horas de trabajo.
- Comer más sano.
- Asistir a una muestra de cine o de arte.
- Comprar la membresía de un gimnasio.
- Tomar dos litros de agua diariamente.
- Ir a una ceremonia religiosa ajena a la mía.[a]
- Dar regalos sin motivo.
- Desayunar bien.
- Ir a votar.
- Ir de excursión a un lugar remoto.
- Separar la basura en orgánica e inorgánica.

(Soldier): Ingram Publishing/SuperStock; (Star): Ingram Publishing; (Red): Comstock/Getty Images; (Blue): magicoven/Shutterstock; (Pony): Ekaterina V. Ryabikina/Shutterstock

[a]ajena... *different from mine*

Comprensión

A. Tipos de propósitos. Clasifique los propósitos de esta lectura según las tres categorías a continuación (*following*), dando su justificación. (Algunos se pueden poner en más de un grupo).

1. Los (*Those*) que pueden mejorar la salud (*health*) física
2. Los que pueden mejorar la salud mental o espiritual
3. Los que pueden mejorar las relaciones con otras personas y con el medio ambiente (*environment*)

B. Actitudes hacia el cambio. ¿Se identifica usted con una (o más) de estas actitudes? Explique.

1. Es imposible cambiar (*to change*) los hábitos. Somos como somos y no podemos cambiar.
2. Siempre podemos tener una vida (*life*) mejor y debemos hacer lo posible para conseguirla (*attain it*).
3. Es difícil cambiar nuestros hábitos, pero es posible hacerlo con un propósito firme y mucho apoyo (*support*) de la familia y los amigos.

Proyecto: Cumplir un propósito para el Año Nuevo

Paso 1. Elija (*Choose*) un propósito de la lista de la lectura u otro diferente que usted se compromete (*commit*) a cumplir para el Año Nuevo (o antes).

Paso 2. Escriba un plan que usted puede seguir para cumplir su propósito. Incluya por lo menos tres de las cosas que debe hacer y el tipo de ayuda que va a necesitar de sus amigos, parejas o parientes.

Paso 3. Comparta (*Share*) su plan con sus compañeros de clase para saber cómo reaccionan y oír sus sugerencias.

Textos orales

El mensaje telefónico de Pilar

Antes de escuchar

¿Qué actividades generalmente se hacen en una boda (*wedding*)? Haga una lista de todas las actividades que pueda imaginar. Consulte el **Vocabulario para escuchar** al hacer (*while making*) su lista.

Vocabulario para escuchar

¡Qué lástima!	What a shame!	**tirar**	to throw, toss
los novios	bride and groom	**lo sintió mucho**	was very sorry
cortar	to cut	**el recuerdo**	souvenir, party favor
ensuciarse la cara	to dirty each other's faces		

Comprensión

A. ¿Quién hizo qué? Indique quién hizo qué, emparejando las acciones con las personas que las hicieron. Hay más de una opción en algunos casos.

ACCIONES
_____ **1.** bailar
_____ **2.** cortar el pastel y tirarlo
_____ **3.** llorar
_____ **4.** mandar un recuerdo
_____ **5.** tocar salsa
_____ **6.** no ir a la boda

PERSONAS
a. Estela
b. un conjunto (*group*) musical
c. Pilar
d. la mamá de Estela
e. los novios
f. la amiga de Pilar y de Estela

B. Más información. ¿Qué más se sabe o deduce usted del mensaje?

1. La amiga de Pilar, ¿es amiga de Estela también?
2. ¿Cómo se llama el novio?
3. ¿Por qué no fue la amiga de Pilar a la boda?
4. ¿Por qué cree Pilar que su amiga no contesta su llamada (*call*)?
5. ¿Cuál es la profesión de la amiga de Pilar?

En acción

Describa algo curioso o diferente que ocurrió en una celebración reciente. ¿Qué y cómo ocurrió? ¿Dónde? ¿Cuándo? ¿Quién lo hizo? ¿A quién o a quiénes afectó?

PORTAFOLIO

🎤 Entrevista

Use de modelo las preguntas y respuestas de la sección **Entrevista** al principio de este capítulo para hablar de los días festivos que usted celebra.

💻 Escritura

Un ensayo sobre una celebración memorable

¿Cuál es la celebración más memorable de su vida (*life*)? ¿un baile de fin de curso (*prom night*)? ¿una boda (*wedding*)? ¿un cumpleaños? ¿una fiesta de Nochevieja? ¿el bautizo (*baptism*) de una hija o un hijo? ¿Qué es memorable de esa celebración?

👥 Antes de escribir

En parejas, hagan una lista de los aspectos que su ensayo debe incluir. Pueden hacer la lista con preguntas: **¿qué?, ¿quién(es)?,** etcétera. No olviden mencionar lo que más les gustó de sus respectivas celebraciones.

A escribir

Use las ideas de **Antes de escribir** para escribir su ensayo. Debe expresar sus sentimientos o los (*those*) de otras personas que estuvieron o no estuvieron en la celebración. Hay más ayuda en Connect.

🌐 En la comunidad

Entreviste a una persona hispana de su universidad o ciudad sobre las celebraciones tradicionales de su país y de su familia.

Preguntas posibles

- ¿Cuáles son los días festivos más importantes de su país? ¿Son celebraciones de origen civil o religioso? ¿Se celebran en familia? ¿También hay eventos en la ciudad?

- ¿Cuáles son las celebraciones más importantes en su familia? ¿Y sus favoritas?

- ¿Cuál fue la última fiesta que usted celebró en su país? ¿Cómo y con quién la celebró?

> **Para escribir bien**
>
> Considere estas opciones para su ensayo:
>
> - Palabras que describen nombres (adjetivos) y acciones (adverbios): **demasiado, por lo menos**
>
> - La terminación de adjetivos que significa "very": **-ísimo/a**
>
> - Conectores de secuencia: **para empezar/terminar, primero, después, luego, finalmente**
>
> - Otros conectores: **además, sin embargo, por eso**

◯ Producción audiovisual

Filme una entrevista con una persona hispana no estadounidense en su universidad o su comunidad. Hágale preguntas sobre un día festivo muy especial que se celebra en su ciudad o país, pero que no se celebra en los Estados Unidos.

Sugerencia: You are now ready to play Quest 6 in **Practice Spanish: Study Abroad.**

Más ideas para el portafolio

- Escriba una o dos oraciones sobre unos momentos emocionantes de su vida (*life*): cuándo se puso más feliz (rojo/a, triste...), cuándo lloró más desconsoladamente (*nonstop*) o se rio con más ganas (*most uproariously*), etcétera.
- Escriba unas oraciones sobre una fiesta de un país hispanohablante a la que (*which*) usted quiere asistir algún día.
- Si ha estado jugando (*you have been playing*) Practice Spanish: Study Abroad, en Quest 6 usted pasó tiempo en el museo del pueblo. Si hay una galería de arte en su ciudad o en el campus de su universidad haga un afiche (*poster*) o un folleto (*brochure*) con información sobre la galería para la comunidad hispanohablante.

EN RESUMEN En este capítulo

AFTER STUDYING THIS CHAPTER I CAN ...

- ☐ talk about holidays (272–273)
- ☐ express more feelings and emotions (276)
- ☐ use more types of verbs in the preterite (279–280, 283–284)
- ☐ understand double object pronouns and use them to avoid repetition 287–288
- ☐ recognize/describe at least 2–3 aspects of Cuban cultures

Gramática en breve

24. Irregular Preterites

Irregular Preterite Endings

estuv-			dij-	-e	-imos
pud-				-iste	-isteis
pus-	-e	-imos	traj-	-o	-eron
quis-	-iste	-isteis			
sup-	-o	-ieron			
tuv-					
vin-					

hay: **haber → hubo** (*there was/were*)

25. Preterite of Stem-changing Verbs

Preterite Stem-changing Patterns
-ar/-er = no change
-ir   = change in the third person singular and plural

e → **i**

o → **u**

26. Direct and Indirect Object Pronouns Together

Indirect	Direct
me/te/nos/os	
	lo/la/los/las
le(s) → **se**	

Vocabulario

Los verbos

adivinar	to guess
conseguir (*like* **seguir**)	to get; to obtain
conseguir +*inf.*	to succeed in (*doing something*)
despedirse (*like* **pedir**) (de)	to say good-bye (to)
enc**o**ntrar (enc**ue**ntro)	to find

morirse (me muero) (u)　　to die
sugerir (sugiero) (i)　　to suggest

Repaso: divertirse (me divierto) (i), dormir(se) ([me]
　　duermo) (u), pedir (pido) (i), preferir (prefiero) (i),
　　seguir (sigo) (i), servir (sirvo) (i), vestirse (me visto) (i)

Los días festivos y las fiestas

el anfitrión, la anfitriona	host (*of an event*)
las botanas (*Mex.*)	appetizers
el champán	champagne
el/la invitado/a	guest
el pastel de cumpleaños	birthday cake
las tapas	appetizers
la vela	candle
el día festivo	holiday

Repaso: el cumpleaños, la fiesta, el pastel, el refresco,
　　el regalo, la tarjeta

cumplir años	to have a birthday
darle una fiesta (a alguien)	to give (someone) a party; to have a party (for someone)
faltar (a)	to be absent (from); to not attend
gastar	to spend (*money*)
hacerle una fiesta (a alguien)	to give (someone) a party; to have a party (for someone)
pasarlo bien/mal	to have a good/bad time
reunirse (me reúno) (con)	to get together (with)
ser en + *place*	to take place in/at (*a place*)

Repaso: bailar, beber, celebrar, comer, divertirse
　　(me divierto) (i), invitar, regalar

Las emociones

discutir con (alguien) por/sobre (algo)	to argue with (someone) about (something)
enojarse con (alguien) por (algo)	to get angry with (someone) about (something)
llorar	to cry
olvidar	to forget (about)
ponerse + *adj./adv.*	to become/get + *adj./adv.*
ponerse rojo/a	to blush
portarse bien/mal	to (mis)behave
recordar (recuerdo)	to remember
reírse (me río) (i) (de)	to laugh (about)
sentirse (me siento) (i) + *adj./adv.*	to feel + *adj./adv.*
sonreír (sonrío) (i)	to smile

Repaso: estar, quejarse (de)

Otros sustantivos

el árbol	tree
el detalle	detail
el fin de año	end of the year

Los adjetivos

avergonzado/a	embarrassed
enojado/a	angry; upset
feliz (*pl.* felices)	happy
festivo/a	festive, celebratory
tranquilo/a	calm
-ísimo/a	very very

Repaso: alegre, contento/a, furioso/a, nervioso/a, triste

Algunos días festivos

el Día de (Acción de) Gracias	Thanksgiving Day
el Día de los Pueblos Indígenas	Columbus Day (Oct. 12)
el Día de los Reyes Magos	Day of the Magi (Three Kings) (Jan. 6)
la Navidad	Christmas
la Nochebuena	Christmas Eve
la Nochevieja	New Year's Eve
la Pascua	Easter
la quinceañera	young woman's fifteenth birthday party

Palabras adicionales

demasiado (*adv.*)	too; too much
¡Felicitaciones!	Congratulations!
gracias por + *noun/inf.*	thanks for + *noun/verb* (*-ing*)
-ísimo (*adv.*)	very very
por lo menos	at least
ya	already

Repaso: muchísimo

Vocabulario personal

Use this space or a vocabulary notebook to write down other words and phrases you learn in this chapter.

10

El tiempo libre°

El... *Free time*

En este capítulo

VOCABULARY

Leisure time activities   300
Household tasks   303

GRAMMAR

Another way to talk about the past   306
Review of interrogative words   312
How to express *the most, least ...*   315

COUNTRY OF FOCUS: **PUERTO RICO**

Alfred Wekelo/Shutterstock

Un grupo de bomba en San Juan, Puerto Rico

OCÉANO
ATLÁNTICO

REPÚBLICA
DOMINICANA

PUERTO
RICO

San Juan

Ponce

Mar Caribe

0   100   200 Millas
├────┬────┬────┬────┤
0   100   200 Kilómetros

PUERTO RICO

3,3 (coma tres) millones de habitantes

- Puerto Rico es un Estado Libre Asociado a los Estados Unidos. Esto significa que Puerto Rico no es independiente, pero sí tiene autonomía interna. Las personas nacidas[a] en Puerto Rico tienen ciudadanía[b] estadounidense.

- El pueblo[c] puertorriqueño siente mucho orgullo[d] de su herencia[e] indígena, africana e hispana.

[a]*born* [b]*citizenship* [c]*people* [d]*pride* [e]*heritage*

🔊 ENTREVISTA

These questions related to the chapter theme are answered here by a native speaker. You will be able to ask and answer them yourself with personal information in the **Entrevista** activity in the **Portafolio** section at the end of the chapter.

Cecilia Figueroa Martín contesta las preguntas.

– **¿Qué le gusta a usted hacer en su tiempo libre? ¿Prefiere las actividades al aire libre[a]? ¿O prefiere las actividades sedentarias?**

– En mi tiempo libre, además de[b] descansar, me gusta hacer cosas con mi familia y con mis amigos. Algunas de las actividades que me gustan son sedentarias, como leer, ver películas, jugar al dominó y a las cartas. Pero también juego al tenis y me encanta nadar en el mar.

– **¿Es el baile una de sus diversiones preferidas? ¿Qué tipo de música le gusta más para bailar?**

– ¡Claro que sí![c] Ahora no bailo tanto como cuando era[d] joven, pero me encanta bailar siempre que[e] puedo. Cualquier[f] tipo de música: pop, rock, salsa, merengue... lo que sea.[g]

– **¿Tiene que pasar a veces parte de su tiempo libre haciendo quehaceres domésticos[h]?**

– ¡Quién no! Tengo dos niños chicos.[i] Pero, en mi opinión, hacer los quehaceres domésticos no es parte del tiempo libre. ¡Es otro trabajo[j]!

[a]*al... outdoor* [b]*además... besides* [c]*¡Claro... Of course!* [d]*I was* [e]*siempre... whenever* [f]*Any* [g]*lo... whatever* [h]*quehaceres... household chores* [i]*niños... small, young kids* [j]*job*

You can hear the pronunciation
of theme vocabulary words
and phrases in the eBook.

¿Practica usted algún deporte°?

sport

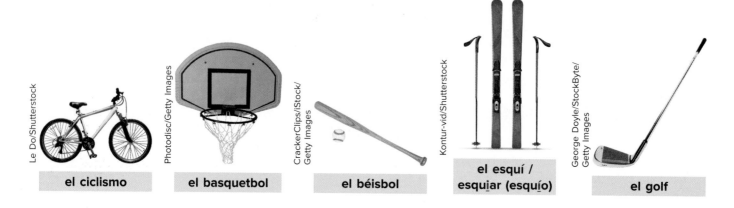

el ciclismo	el basquetbol	el béisbol	el esquí / esquiar (esquío)	el golf

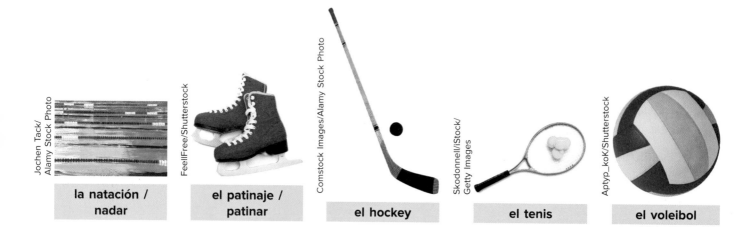

la natación / nadar	el patinaje / patinar	el hockey	el tenis	el voleibol

Más actividades deportivas°   *sports-related*

<u>andar</u>* en bicicleta	to ride a bike
caminar	to walk
correr	to run; to jog
<u>dar</u> una caminata	to hike
<u>hacer</u> (el) yoga	to do yoga
<u>jugar</u> (<u>juego</u>) (<u>gu</u>) al...	to play (*a sport*)
fútbol	soccer
fútbol americano	football
montar a caballo	to ride a horse
surfear	to surf

*The preterite forms of <u>andar</u> are irregular: <u>anduve</u>, <u>anduviste</u>, <u>anduvo</u>, <u>anduvimos</u>, <u>anduvisteis</u>, <u>anduvieron</u>.

Un partido°   *game, match*

el/la atleta	athlete
el equipo	team
el jugador / la jugadora	player
el entrenador / la entrenadora	coach
la pelota	ball
entrenar(se)	to practice; to train
ganar	to win
p<u>e</u>rder (p<u>ie</u>rdo)	to lose
practi<u>c</u>ar (<u>qu</u>)	to practice; to participate (*in a sport*)

¿Qué hace usted en su tiempo libre?

la afición	hobby
la diversión	fun activity
el pasatiempo	pastime
aburrirse	to get bored
<u>dar</u> un paseo	to take a walk
<u>hacer</u>...	
camping	to go camping
planes (*m.*) para + *inf.*	to make plans to (*do something*)
un pícnic	to have a picnic
<u>ir</u>...	to go ...
a un bar / a un club	to a bar / to a club
a un concierto	to a concert
a un museo	to a museum
a una discoteca	to a disco
al cine	to the movies
al teatro	to the theater
ju<u>g</u>ar (j<u>ue</u>go) (<u>gu</u>)...	to play ...
a las cartas	cards
a los videojuegos	video games
al ajedrez	chess
<u>ser</u>...	to be ...
aburrido/a	boring
aficionado/a (a)	a fan (of)
divertido/a	fun
al aire libre	outdoors, in the open air

Comunicación

A. El tiempo libre

Paso 1. ¿Cierto o falso? Corrija las oraciones falsas, según su opinión.

Así se dice

andar en bicicleta = montar/pasear en bicicleta
surfear = hacer *surf* (*P.R.*)
el voleibol = el vólibol, el volibol

	CIERTO	FALSO
1. Es más aburrido ver un partido en la tele que en el estadio.	☐	☐
2. Me aburro más con mi familia que con mis amigos.	☐	☐
3. Me encantan las actividades culturales, como ir a un museo.	☐	☐
4. Odio el béisbol tanto como el fútbol.	☐	☐
5. Tengo más tiempo libre este semestre/trimestre que el anterior (*the last one*).	☐	☐
6. Jugar al ajedrez es más aburrido que jugar a las cartas.	☐	☐
7. No me gustan las actividades al aire libre.	☐	☐

Paso 2. ¿Cuáles son sus tres actividades favoritas? ¿Y cuáles son las tres que no le gustan o que odia?

MODELOS: Me gusta / Me encanta... → Me gusta ir a museos. / Me encanta la natación.
No me gusta / Odio... → No me gusta ir a museos. / Odio el béisbol.

Paso 3. En parejas, comparen sus listas. ¿Qué preferencias comparten (*do you share*)? Si sus listas no tienen nada en común, hablen de otras actividades para encontrar algo en común.

B. Definiciones sobre los deportes

Paso 1. Dé la palabra para cada definición.

MODELO: entrar en un lugar para ver una película → ir al cine

1. un grupo de jugadores
2. salir bien en una competencia; salir mal
3. practicar un deporte intensamente
4. el deporte más popular en las escuelas secundarias de este país
5. un deporte que se practica en una piscina

(Continúa).

Paso 2. Ahora defina las siguientes palabras, según el modelo del **Paso 1.**

1. un jugador
2. un partido
3. aburrirse

4. el ciclismo
5. la pelota
6. esquiar

Nota cultural: Los deportes más populares del mundo hispano

Dos deportes predominan en el panorama deportivo del mundo hispano: el fútbol y el béisbol.

- **El fútbol** Sin duda este es el rey[a] de los deportes en el mundo hispano, como en el resto del mundo. Ningún evento deportivo se compara en seguimiento[b] a la Copa Mundial de Fútbol, en la cual[c] compiten regularmente muchas naciones hispanohablantes. En todos los países hispanos, el fútbol se juega en cualquier calle,[d] plaza o espacio abierto y hay innumerables ligas[e] de todo tipo.

- **El béisbol** Un deporte inmensamente popular en los países de la costa caribeña es el béisbol. En las grandes ligas estadounidenses hay muchos jugadores de primer orden[f] con apellidos hispanos. Muchos de estos «peloteros[g]», como se les llama[h] en muchos países, vienen de las ligas de sus respectivos países de origen, como la República Dominicana, Venezuela y México.

- **El basquetbol, el tenis y el ciclismo** Estos deportes también tienen gran seguimiento en el mundo hispano. El basquetbol está creciendo[i] en cuanto al[j]

El equipo nacional de béisbol puertorriqueño, que celebra una victoria

número de espectadores y tiene dos grandes potencias[k] hispanas: España y la Argentina. Estos países tienen varios jugadores en la NBA.

 ¿Qué deportistas hispanos puede usted nombrar?

[a]*king* [b]*following* [c]*la... which* [d]*cualquier... any street* [e]*leagues* [f]*de... first-class* [g]*ballplayers* [h]*se... they are called* [i]*growing* [j]*en... as far as the* [k]*superpowers*

C. Actividades del año pasado

Paso 1. Indique todas las actividades en que usted participó o que hizo por lo menos una vez el año pasado.

1. Fui a un concierto. ☐
2. Di una caminata por el bosque (*forest*). ☐
3. Hice *camping*. ☐
4. Jugué a un juego de mesa (las cartas, el ajedrez, *Life*...) ☐
5. Hice yoga. ☐
6. Anduve en bicicleta. ☐
7. Corrí. ☐
8. Nadé. ☐
9. Entrené con un equipo. ☐
10. Gané/Perdí un partido / una competición. ☐

Paso 2. En parejas, comparen sus respuestas y compartan (*share*) con la clase dos de las actividades que hicieron y dos de las (*those*) que no hicieron. También deben dar unos detalles interesantes.

MODELO: Mati y yo nos entrenamos con un equipo. Yo me entrené con el equipo de natación de la universidad y Mati se entrenó con el equipo de tenis. Perdimos muchos partidos. Pero no nos aburrimos. No hicimos *camping*.

Las tareas domésticas°

Las... *Household chores*

Limpiar (la casa)°

Limpiar... *To clean (house)*

barrer el piso

pasar la aspiradora

planchar la ropa

hacer la cama

sacar (qu) la basura

lavar los platos

poner la mesa

quitar la mesa

Algunos aparatos domésticos

la aspiradora	vacuum cleaner	**la lavadora**	washing machine
la cafetera	coffee maker	**el lavaplatos**	dishwasher
el congelador	freezer	**el refrigerador**	refrigerator
la estufa	stove	**la secadora**	clothes dryer
el horno de microondas	microwave oven	**la tostadora**	toaster

Comunicación

> ### Así se dice
>
> el congelador = la nevera
> la estufa = la cocina
> hacer la cama = tender la cama
> lavar los platos = fregar los platos
> el refrigerador = el frigorífico, la heladera,
> la nevera, la refrigeradora

A. Las tareas domésticas. ¿En qué cuarto o parte de la casa se hacen las siguientes actividades? Hay más de una respuesta en muchos casos.

1. Se hace la cama en _____.
2. Se saca la basura de _____ y se pone en _____.
3. Uno se baña en _____, pero baña al perro en _____.
4. Se barre el piso del / de la _____.
5. Se pasa la aspiradora en _____.
6. Se lava y se seca la ropa en _____.
7. La ropa se plancha en _____.
8. Se usa la cafetera en _____.

B. Aparatos electrodomésticos y productos

Paso 1. ¿Para qué se usa cada uno de estos aparatos electrodomésticos? ¿Para qué sirven?

MODELO: el congelador → El congelador sirve para poner la comida muy fría y preservarla mucho tiempo.

> ### Vocabulario útil
>
> **calentar (caliento)**   to heat up
> **lavar**
> **limpiar**
> **tostar**

1. una aspiradora
2. una cafetera
3. un lavaplatos
4. una lavadora
5. una tostadora
6. la estufa
7. el horno de microondas
8. la secadora

(Continúa).

Vocabulario útil

se usa para...
sirve para...

el fregadero   sink

Paso 2. ¿Conoce estas marcas (*brand names*)? ¿Para qué se usa cada producto?

MODELO: Mr. Coffee → Mr. Coffee sirve para hacer el café.

1. Windex
2. a Glad bag
3. Lysol
4. Tide
5. Cascade
6. Palmolive

 C. ¿Cómo pasa usted su tiempo?

Paso 1. Complete la tabla con el tiempo medio (*average*) que usted pasa diariamente haciendo las actividades indicadas.

Actividad	Media[a] de tiempo diario (aproximada)
Estudios	
Vida[b] social con los amigos (en persona o a distancia)	
Vida familiar	
Tareas domésticas	
Deportes	
Ver medios de comunicación[c]	
Leer por placer	
Otras actividades	

[a]*Average* [b]*Life* [c]*medios... media*

 Paso 2. Ahora, en parejas, hagan comparaciones sobre el tiempo que ustedes pasan haciendo las actividades de cada categoría. Díganle a la clase algo que tienen en común.

Algo sobre el Viejo San Juan

El Castillo (*Castle*) de San Felipe del Morro, que protegía (*used to protect*) el puerto de la bahía de San Juan, Puerto Rico

San Juan es una de las primeras ciudades fundadas por los españoles en América y su primer puerto importante. El Viejo San Juan es el nombre que se da al centro histórico de la capital de Puerto Rico. Sus calles adoquinadas,[a] edificios coloniales, fuertes majestuosos[b] (San Felipe del Morro y San Cristóbal) además de excelentes restaurantes, hacen de la ciudad de San Juan un lugar maravilloso[c] para visitar.

 ¿Qué le gustaría hacer a usted en una visita a San Juan?

[a]*calles... cobblestone streets* [b]*fuertes... majestic forts* [c]*wonderful*

Nota comunicativa: Cómo expresar la obligación

You already know several ways to express the obligation to do something.

Tengo que ⎫		I have to ⎫	
Necesito ⎬	barrer el piso.	I need to ⎬	sweep the floor.
Debo ⎭		I should, must ⎭	

Of the three, **deber** + *infinitive* expresses the strongest sense of obligation (like a moral obligation), and **tener que** expresses the greatest sense of urgency or immediacy. **Tener que** is the most frequently used for everyday commitments.

The concept *to be someone's turn or responsibility* (to do something) is expressed in Spanish with the verb **to<u>c</u>ar (<u>qu</u>)** plus an indirect object.

—**¿A quién <u>le</u> toca** lavar los platos esta noche?
"Whose turn is it to wash the dishes tonight?"

—**A mí. Pero <u>a ti te</u> toca** sacar la basura.
"Mine. But it's your turn to take out the garbage."

You will use these expressions in **Comunicación D** and **E**.

D. **Las tareas domésticas de esta semana**

Paso 1. Use los verbos de la **Nota comunicativa** para decir cuáles son las tareas domésticas que usted tiene que hacer esta semana, y diga cuándo necesita hacerlas. También indique una tarea que no le toca hacer esta semana.

MODELO: **Tengo que** hacer la cama todos los días y **necesito / tengo que** sacar la basura el viernes. Pero **no me toca** planchar porque nunca **tengo que** planchar mi ropa.

Paso 2. Ahora, en parejas, hablen de sus hábitos domésticos. ¿Con qué frecuencia hacen ciertas tareas? ¿Quién se preocupa más por la limpieza y la organización de su cuarto u hogar?

MODELOS: **E1:** ¿Yo hago la cama todos los días. ¿Y tú?
E2: Yo también. Y lavo la ropa una vez a la semana. ¿Y tú?

E. **Las obligaciones.** En parejas, hablen de sus obligaciones frecuentes o regulares. Incluyan sus obligaciones de todo tipo: tareas domésticas, ayudar a miembros de la familia, voluntariado (*volunteering*), etcétera. Expliquen también cuáles son las cosas que les gusta o no les molesta (*don't bother you*) hacer y las que (*those that*) sí les molesta.

Algo sobre el coquí

Los coquíes son ranas[a] de varias especies de un género[b] nativo de Puerto Rico. Son muy pequeños (alrededor de una pulgada[c]) y viven en los árboles.[d] Su nombre es una versión onomatopéyica del sonido[e] que algunas especies de coquíes machos[f] hacen cuando cantan desde la caída del sol[g] hasta el amanecer.[h] La canción del coquí se puede oír por toda la isla y por eso esta ranita es uno de los grandes símbolos puertorriqueños. Desgraciadamente, los coquíes están en peligro[i] de extinción.

¿Qué animales son considerados símbolos de su estado o país? ¿Por qué lo representan?

[a]*frogs* [b]*genus* [c]*alrededor... about an inch* [d]*trees* [e]*sound* [f]*male* [g]*caída... sunset* [h]*dawn* [i]*danger*

Un coquí puertorriqueño

Geordie Torr/Alamy Stock Photo

GRAMÁTICA

Repaso

In **Capítulos 8** and **9**, you learned the forms and some uses of the preterite. Before you learn the other simple past tense (in **Gramática 27**), you might want to review the forms of the preterite in those chapters. The verbs in the following sentences are in the preterite. Can you identify any words in the sentences that emphasize the completed nature of the actions expressed by the verbs?

1. Esta mañana me levanté a las seis.
2. Ayer fui al cine con un amigo.
3. La semana pasada saqué la basura todos los días.

27 Talking About the Past (Part 4) • Descriptions and Habitual Actions in the Past: Imperfect of Regular and Irregular Verbs

Gramática en acción: Los indígenas taínos

- Los taínos **eran** los habitantes originales de las Antillas Mayores, que son las islas de Jamaica, Puerto Rico, Cuba y La Española (que incluye los países de la República Dominicana y Haití).
- Estos indígenas **vivían** allí cuando llegaron los españoles en el siglo XV.
- El pueblo taíno **era** pacífico y generoso.
- **Tenían** una sociedad matrilineal.
- **Llamaban** «cacique» a su jefe y «Borinquen» a su isla.
- Las palabras *hamaca, huracán, canoa, tabaco* y *barbacoa* **eran** parte de la lengua que **hablaban**.

Comprensión

1. ¿De cuántas islas están formadas las Antillas Mayores?
2. ¿Cómo **era** el pueblo taíno?

¿Y usted?

1. ¿Qué significan en inglés las últimas palabras del párrafo?
2. ¿Conoce algunos de los pueblos que **vivían** en lo que hoy son los Estados Unidos cuando llegaron los europeos?

The Taíno Indians ■ *The Taínos were the original inhabitants of the Greater Antilles, which are the islands of Jamaica, Puerto Rico, Cuba, and Hispaniola (which includes the countries of the Dominican Republic and Haiti).* ■ *These natives were living there when the Spanish arrived in the 15th century.* ■ *The Taíno people were peaceful and generous.* ■ *They had a matrilineal society.* ■ *They called their leader "cacique" and their island "Borinquen."* ■ *The words* hamaca, huracán, canoa, tabaco, *and* barbacoa *were part of the language they spoke.*

You have already used the *preterite* (**el pretérito**) to express events in the past. The *imperfect* (**el imperfecto**) is the second simple past tense in Spanish. The preterite is used when you view actions or states of being as begun or completed in the past. The imperfect is used when you view past actions or states of being as habitual or as "in progress." It is also used for describing the past, especially for giving background details.

Forms of the Imperfect / Las formas del imperfecto

hablar		comer		vivir	
hablaba	hablábamos	comía	comíamos	vivía	vivíamos
hablabas	hablabais	comías	comíais	vivías	vivíais
hablaba	hablaban	comía	comían	vivía	vivían

Pronunciation Hints

- The **b** between vowels, such as in the imperfect ending **-aba,** is pronounced as a *soft* [b] sound.
- In **-er/-ir** imperfect forms, it is important not to pronounce the ending **-ía** as a diphthong, but to pronounce the **i** and the **a** in separate syllables. The accent mark over the **í** helps remind you of this.

> **¡OJO!**
>
> Note that the first and third person singular forms are identical for **-ar, -er,** and **-ir** verbs. When context does not make meaning clear, subject pronouns are used.
>
> Los sábados **yo** **jugaba** al tenis y **él** **paseaba** en bicicleta.
> *On Saturdays I used to play tennis and he used to ride his bike.*

Los verbos en *-ar*		Los verbos en *-er/-ir*	
-aba	-ábamos	-ía	-íamos
-abas	-abais	-ías	-íais
-aba	-aban	-ía	-ían

1. English Equivalents

As you can see in the box, the imperfect has several English equivalents. Most of them indicate that the action was still in progress (*was/were -ing*) or that it was habitual (*used to, would*).

The word *would* is also an English equivalent of the imperfect. But keep in mind that *would* expresses two different things in English: a repeated action in the past and a hypothetical situation. The Spanish imperfect is used only in the first case. (Hypothetical situations are expressed with other tenses in Spanish. You have learned to use **gustaría** to express *I would like*. You will learn more about this in **Capítulo 18**.)

> **yo** **hablaba** = *I spoke, I was speaking, I used to speak, I would speak*
> **comíamos** = *we ate, we were eating, we used to eat, we would eat*
> **él** **vivía** = *he lived, he was living, he used to live, he would live*

> **¡OJO!**
>
> The simple English equivalents in the box (*I spoke, we ate, he lived*) can correspond to either the preterite or the imperfect, but they usually correspond to the preterite. You'll learn more about this in **Capítulo 11**.

> **¡OJO!**
>
> *would* = repeated action → imperfect

Comíamos allí todos los domingos.
We would eat there every Sunday.

¡Cuando era joven, **jugaba** al fútbol todo el día en el verano!
When I was young, I would play soccer all day long in the summer!

BUT

Me **gustaría** dar un paseo hoy.
I would like to take a walk today.

2. Stem-changing Verbs and *hay*

Stem-changing verbs do not show a change in the imperfect.

The imperfect of **hay** is **había.** It means *there was, there were,* or *there used to be,* and its form never changes.

> almorzar (almuerzo) → almorzaba, almorzabas,...
> perder (pierdo) → perdía, perdías,...
> pedir (pido) (i) → pedía, pedías,...

Había muchos estudiantes en el salón de clase.
There were a lot of students in the class.

3. Irregular Imperfect Forms

Only three verbs are irregular in the imperfect: __ir__, __ser__, and __ver__.

ir		ser		ver	
iba	íbamos	era	éramos	ve<u>í</u>a	ve<u>í</u>amos
ibas	ibais	eras	erais	ve<u>í</u>as	ve<u>í</u>ais
iba	iban	era	eran	ve<u>í</u>a	ve<u>í</u>an

Uses of the Imperfect / **Los usos del imperfecto**

If you know when to use the imperfect, it will be easy to understand when the preterite is used. When talking about the past, the preterite *is* used when the imperfect *isn't*. That's an oversimplification, but at the same time it's a general rule of thumb that will help you out at first.

The imperfect has the following uses. Notice that the first three have clear English equivalents. Also, pay attention to the words that indicate time and frequency.

---

1. To describe *repeated habitual actions* in the past

> used to ⎫
> ⎬ +verb
> would ⎭

De niños, **siempre jugábamos** en el parque todas las tardes.
As children, we always played (used to play, would play) in the park in the afternoon.

Todos los domingos, teníamos un partido de liga.
Every Sunday we had (used to have, would have) a league game.

---

2. To describe an *action that was in progress* (when something else happened)

> was/were + -ing

Ramón **pedía** la cena (cuando Cristina **llamó**).
Ramón was ordering dinner (when Cristina called).

Los taínos **vivían** en Puerto Rico (cuando **llegó** Colón).
The Taíno Indians were living in Puerto Rico (when Columbus arrived).

---

3. To describe two *simultaneous past actions in progress*, with **mientras**

> was/were + -ing

Tú **leías mientras** Juan **escribía** la carta.
You were reading while Juan was writing the letter.

Mientras yo **veía** la tele, los niños **jugaban** a las cartas.
While I was watching TV, the kids were playing cards.

---

4. To describe ongoing *physical, mental,* or *emotional states* in the past

Estaban muy **distraídos.**
They were very distracted.

Él la **quería** muchísimo.
He loved her a lot.

Hacía calor, pero Luis **tenía** frío.
It was hot (out) but Luis was cold.

---

5. To tell *time* in the past and to express *age* with **tener**

> **¡OJO!**
>
> Just as in the present, the singular form of the verb __ser__ is used with one o'clock, the plural form from two o'clock on.

Era la una. / **Eran** las dos.
It was one o'clock. / It was two o'clock.

Tenía 18 años.
She / He was 18 years old.

> ### Summary of the Uses of the Imperfect
>
> used to, would
> was/were + -ing
> simultaneous actions (**mientras**)
> physical, mental, and emotional states
> time
> age

Práctica y comunicación

A. Cuando yo tenía 16 años...

> **Paso 1. Autoprueba.** Dé la forma apropiada del imperfecto para cada verbo.
>
> **1.** hablar: yo _____   **3.** comer: nosotros _____   **5.** tener: tú _____
> **2.** ser: ustedes _____   **4.** ir: Pedro _____

Paso 2. Haga oraciones basadas en las siguientes frases, usando el imperfecto para hablar de su vida a los 16 años. Si alguna oración no es cierta para usted, use **No...** .

1. ser muy estudioso/a
2. lavar mi ropa
3. tener que _____ (tarea doméstica)
4. ir a la escuela secundaria en autobús
5. sacarse muchos selfis
6. tocar un instrumento en la orquesta de la escuela
7. estar en el equipo de _____
8. perder muchas competiciones / muchos partidos de _____

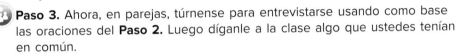 **Paso 3.** Ahora, en parejas, túrnense para entrevistarse usando como base las oraciones del **Paso 2.** Luego díganle a la clase algo que ustedes tenían en común.

MODELO: **1. E1:** Cuando tenías 16 años, ¿eras muy estudioso?
    E2: No, no era nada estudioso. ¿Y tú?
    E1: Yo sí.

B. La vida a los 7 años

Paso 1. Haga oraciones sobre la vida de Tina Acevedo, que vivía en Puerto Rico cuando tenía 7 años. Use el imperfecto de los verbos.

1. Tina: **vivir** en Bayamón, Puerto Rico
2. asistir a una escuela católica
3. hablar español todo el tiempo
4. aprender inglés en la escuela
5. dibujar (*to draw*) mucho en clase
6. jugar con sus compañeros en el parque
7. ir a casa de sus abuelos después de la escuela
8. ver sus programas favoritos en la tele
9. sus padres: **llegar** por ella a las 7:30
10. sus padres: **llevarla** a casa

Paso 2. Ahora haga oraciones similares a las oraciones del **Paso 1** pero con información de su propia vida a los 7 años.

MODELOS: **1.** Tina: **vivir** en Bayamón, Puerto Rico. →
    Yo **vivía** en St. Louis, Missouri.

Nota comunicativa: El progresivo en el pasado

Just like the present progressive, the *past progressive* (**el imperfecto progresivo**) emphasizes that an action was happening at that very moment. The past progressive is formed with the imperfect of **estar** plus the present participle (**-ndo**) of another verb.

Cuando mi tío llamó, **estábamos cenando.**
When my uncle called, we were having dinner.

El sábado a las 10 de la noche, ¿**estabas estudiando**?
Saturday night at 10, were you studying?

You will use the past progressive in **Práctica C.**

Prác. A, Paso 1: Answers: 1. hablaba 2. eran 3. comíamos 4. iba 5. tenías

Vocabulario útil

el bebé	
el timbre	doorbell
gritar	to shout
ladrar	to bark
pelear	to fight
sonar	to ring;
(suena)	to sound

C. Trabajos (*Jobs*) de adolescentes

Paso 1. Muchos adolescentes trabajan de niñeros (*babysitters*), un trabajo que puede ser pesado (*annoying*) o difícil. ¿Qué estaba pasando cuando esta niñera perdió por fin la paciencia? Describa todas las acciones que pueda (*you can*), usando **estaba(n)** + *present participle* (**-ndo**).

MODELO: El bebé **estaba llorando.**

Vocabulario útil

caerse	to fall down
(cayendo)	
cuidar	to take care of
sacar (qu)	to take something out

1900

HOY

Paso 2. De adolescentes, ¿tenían ustedes un trabajo? ¿Tenían que cuidar a sus hermanos menores o a otros niños? En parejas, túrnense para hablar de sus experiencias de trabajo cuando tenían 15, 16 o 17 años. Háganse preguntas para obtener mucha información.

MODELO: **E1:** Cuando yo tenía 15 años, cuidaba a mi hermano menor.
E2: ¿Lo cuidabas todos los días? ¿Cuánto te pagaban tus padres? ¿Se portaba bien tu hermano o era mucho trabajo?

D. Los tiempos cambian (*change*). Las siguientes oraciones describen aspectos de la vida de hoy. En parejas, comparen estos aspectos con el estilo de vida alrededor del (*around the*) año 1900. Luego, describan dos cambios más.

MODELO: **E1:** Ahora la gente se comunica electrónicamente. →
E2: Alrededor del año 1900, la gente **se comunicaba por carta.**

1. Ahora muchísimas mujeres trabajan fuera de (*outside of the*) casa.
2. Hoy día la gente lee libros en formato electrónico.
3. Ahora la gente puede escuchar música en casa todo el tiempo.
4. Hoy día las mujeres se ponen pantalones.
5. Ahora hay hombres enfermeros (*nurses*) y maestros (*grade school teachers*).
6. Hoy, tenemos más máquinas y por eso hacemos menos trabajo físicamente.
7. Hoy día las familias son más pequeñas.
8. Ahora muchas parejas viven juntas sin estar casadas (*married*).

E. Descripción de un momento en el pasado

Paso 1. Conteste las siguientes preguntas, pensando en el mediodía de ayer.

1. ¿Qué tiempo hacía?
2. ¿Dónde estaba usted?
3. ¿Qué estaba haciendo?
4. ¿Qué ropa llevaba?
5. ¿Con quién estaba?
6. ¿Cómo se sentía usted? ¿Por qué?

Paso 2. Ahora, en parejas, comparen lo que ustedes estaban haciendo ayer al mediodía. ¿Quién estaba teniendo el día más productivo? ¿Quién se sentía mejor en ese momento y por qué?

F. Este semestre/trimestre

Paso 1. En parejas, comparen el semestre/trimestre pasado con el presente (*the current one*), hablando de los siguientes temas.

1. hacer ejercicio o deportes
2. la primera clase del día
3. la última clase de la semana
4. las actividades extracurriculares
5. su cuarto / residencia / apartamento / casa
6. sus hábitos de estudio y/o de comer

Paso 2. Ahora díganle al resto de la clase algo que ustedes tenían en común el semestre/trimestre pasado y algo que tienen en común este semestre/trimestre.

Algo sobre Borinquen

Borinquen es el nombre que los taínos, los habitantes originales de Puerto Rico, le daban a su isla. El pueblo taíno se extinguió[a] en el siglo XVI, como consecuencia de la colonización. Pero los puertorriqueños están muy orgullosos[b] de su origen taíno. Los términos[c] **boricua** y **borinqueño/a** se usan con frecuencia para referirse a las personas, instituciones y tradiciones de la Isla. De hecho,[d] el himno oficial[e] puertorriqueño se llama «La borinqueña».

 ¿Sabe usted quiénes eran los habitantes originales de su estado? ¿Está presente su herencia en el folclore de su estado?

[a]se... *died out* [b]*proud* [c]*terms* [d]De... *In fact* [e]himno... *national anthem*

©Sherwood Donahue

Un recuerdo (*souvenir*) de Puerto Rico

♻ Repaso

You have been using interrogative words since the beginning of *Puntos de partida*, so not much will be new for you in **Gramática 28**. Review what you already know by telling which interrogative word or phrase you associate with the following phrases.

1. un lugar
2. la hora
3. una persona
4. la manera de hacer algo
5. una selección

6. la razón (*reason*) por algo
7. el lugar de origen de una persona
8. un destino
9. una cantidad
10. ser el dueño de algo

28 Getting Information (Part 2) • Summary of Interrogative Words

Gramática en acción: Un restaurante de Connecticut

El Boricua
RESTAURANTE · CLUB DE BAILE

32 GARVEY ST., NEW HAVEN, CT

Gran espacio para banquetes y celebraciones

Especialidad en comida puertorriqueña

Venga y deléitese con nuestros sabrosos platos
ABIERTO TODOS LOS DÍAS DE LAS 11:30 A.M. A LAS 2:00 A.M.

VIERNES, 6 DE OCTUBRE

· LOS GRANDES SALSEROS DE CONNECTICUT ·
ORQUESTA INTENSIDAD

1. ¿**Cómo** se llama el restaurante?
2. ¿En **qué** ciudad de Connecticut está?
3. ¿En **qué** tipo de cocina se especializa el restaurante?
4. ¿**Qué** grupo toca el viernes, 6 de octubre?
5. ¿**Cuál** es la dirección del restaurante?

¿Y usted?

¿**Cuántas** preguntas más puede usted hacer sobre este restaurante, por (*based on*) lo que dice el anuncio?

Here are all of the interrogatives that you have learned so far. The only new information in this section is about using ¿**qué**? and ¿**cuáles**?, both of which express *what*? or *which*? in Spanish.

¡OJO!

Remember that interrogative words always have an accent mark in Spanish, and that questions have two question marks: ¿ ?

¿**Cómo**?	How?	¿**Dónde**?	Where?
¿**Cuándo**?	When?	¿**De dónde**?	From where?
¿**A qué hora**?	At what time?	¿**Adónde**?	Where (to)?
¿**Qué**?	What? Which?	¿**Cuánto/a**?	How much?
¿**Cuál(es)**?	What? Which one(s)?	¿**Cuántos/as**?	How many?
¿**Por qué**?	Why?	¿**Quién(es)**?	Who?
		¿**De quién(es)**?	Whose?

Uses of ¿qué? and ¿cuál? / Los usos de ¿qué? y ¿cuál?

1. ¿Qué? + es/son = Definition/Explanation
Use ¿Qué es/son... ? to ask for a definition or for the explanation of what something is.

¿**Qué es** esto?
What is this?

¿**Qué son** las Antillas?
What are the West Indies?

---

2. ¿Qué? + verb = Information
Use ¿Qué... ? with any verb to ask for information.

¿**Qué** quieres comer?
What do you want to eat?

¿**Qué** hacen ustedes por la mañana?
What do you do in the morning?

---

3. ¿Qué? + noun = Choice
Use a question with ¿qué? + a noun to ask the listener to specify a preference or make a choice.

¿**Qué deporte** prefieres?
What (Which) sport do you prefer?

¿**Qué playa** te gusta más?
What (Which) beach do you like most?

Capítulo 10 El tiempo libre

4. ¿Cuál(es)? + verb = Choice

Use **¿cuál(es)?** + a *verb* to express *what* when it means *which one*, that is, when it calls for a choice. Sometimes a phrase like **de los dos (tres...)** makes the choice more obvious.

¡OJO!

¿Qué?, not **¿cuál?**, is followed by a noun. Compare these sentences:

¿Qué <u>libro</u> quieres? = *which book?*
¿Cuál (es el libro que) **<u>quieres?</u>** = *which one?*
¿Cuál de los dos <u>quieres?</u> = *which one of the two?*

<u>¿Cuál</u> prefieres?
Which one do you prefer?

<u>¿Cuál</u> es la cafetería más grande?
What (Which [one]) is the biggest cafeteria?

<u>¿Cuál</u> <u>de los dos coches</u> vas a comprar?
Which of the two cars are you going to buy?

5. ¿Cuál(es)? + ser = Information

¿Cuál(es) + ser? means *What is/are ... ?* related to specific information.

<u>¿Cuál es</u> el número de teléfono y la dirección del restaurante?
What's the phone number and address of the restaurant?

<u>¿Cuales son</u> los equipos que juegan hoy?
What are the teams that are playing today?

Práctica y comunicación

A. Preguntas personales

Paso 1. Autoprueba. Empareje las palabras interrogativas con la información que piden.

1. ¿Cuándo?
2. ¿Dónde?
3. ¿Qué?
4. ¿Cuánto?
5. ¿Cuál?

a. un lugar
b. una selección
c. un número o una cantidad
d. una definición
e. la hora
f. información

> **Summary of *¿qué?* Versus *¿cuál?***
>
> **¿qué?** + **es/son** = definition/explanation
>   + *verb* = information
>   + *noun* = choice
> **¿cuál(es)?** + *verb* = choice
> **¿cuál(es)?** + **ser** = information

Paso 2. Complete las siguientes preguntas con **qué** o **cuál(es)** y contéstelas.

1. ¿Tiene usted un segundo nombre (*middle name*)? ¿_____ es? ¿_____ son sus dos apellidos, según el sistema hispano de apellidos?
2. ¿_____ es su número de teléfono?
3. ¿_____ es su dirección postal? ¿_____ es su e-mail?
4. ¿_____ son las materias que usted toma este semestre/trimestre? ¿_____ es su favorita?
5. ¿_____ clase le gusta menos?
6. ¿_____ de las redes (*networks*) sociales mira usted más?
7. ¿_____ tarea doméstica odia más?
8. ¿_____ es un equipo? ¿_____ es su equipo de fútbol americano favorito?

Paso 3. Ahora, en parejas, túrnense para hacer y contestar las preguntas del **Paso 2.** Luego díganle a la clase algo que ustedes tienen en común.

Prác. A, Paso 1: Answers: 1. e 2. a 3. d, f 4. c 5. b

B. **Intercambios**

Paso 1. En parejas, túrnense para entrevistarse sobre los siguientes temas. Empiecen las preguntas con **¿Qué... ?** or **¿Cuál(es)... ?** Hablen de sus preferencias actuales (*current*) o de sus preferencias de niño/a (usando el imperfecto).

MODELOS: estaciones del año ➜
        ¿Qué estación del año **prefieres**? (¿**Qué** estación del año **preferías** de niño/a?)
        ¿Cuál es / Cuál era tu estación del año favorita?

1. estilo de música
2. pasatiempos o deportes
3. programas de televisión
4. materias este semestre/trimestre
5. colores
6. tipos de comida

Paso 2. Ahora, díganle a la clase una cosa que tienen en común y otra en la que (*which*) no están de acuerdo.

Textos de todos los días: Anuncio de un evento en una red° social

network

Varias redes sociales sirven constantemente para anunciar eventos. Eso es lo que usted va a practicar en esta actividad.

Objetivo: Poner la información de un evento en una de sus redes sociales habituales (Facebook, Instagram, Twitter, etcétera).

Antes de empezar

- Elija el evento que quiere crear o anunciar (organizar un partido deportivo entre amigos, una sesión de entrenamiento (*entertainment*) o de estudio, un concierto especial,...).
- Elija una red social.
- Organice toda la información que debe aparecer en su anuncio usando palabras interrogativas para no olvidar ningún detalle importante (¿qué?, ¿quién[es]?,...).

Sábado 9 de septiembre, de 2 a 4 de la tarde

MERIENDA CON ESTUDIANTES INTERNACIONALES

¡Ven[a] a conocer a los estudiantes de todo el mundo que están en nuestra universidad! Son más de 150, de 30 países diferentes.

★ ¡Sí voy!   ❓ Quizás[b]   🔖 No me interesa

📍 En el Patio de las Banderas (frente al Centro de Estudios Globales)

🥤 **Qué traer:** tu propia bebida

🍽 ¡La universidad pone la comida!

[a]*Come*   [b]*Maybe*

You learned how to make comparisons in **Gramática 17 (Cap. 6)**. Before you start **Gramática 29**, review what you remember about comparisons by completing the following comparative phrases with the appropriate word.

1. más dinero _____ tú
2. tan simpáticos _____ ellos
3. _____ hermanas como...

4. menos libros _____ Cecilia
5. correr _____ como usted
6. tener un hermano _____

29 Expressing Extremes • Superlatives

Gramática en acción: Los puertorriqueños <u>más famosos</u>

¿Está usted de acuerdo? Corrija las declaraciones falsas, según su opinión.

	CIERTO	FALSO
1. Jennifer López es <u>la</u> cantante puertorriqueña <u>**más conocida del**</u> mundo.	☐	☐
2. Benicio del Toro es <u>el</u> actor puertorriqueño <u>**más famoso del**</u> mundo.	☐	☐
3. Roberto Clemente, de origen puertorriqueño, es <u>**el mejor**</u> beisbolista hispano <u>de</u> todos los tiempos.	☐	☐

¿Y usted?

Complete las siguientes declaraciones para expresar su opinión.

1. <u>**El**</u> cantante hispano / <u>**La**</u> cantante hispana <u>**más popular del**</u> momento es _____.
2. <u>**La mejor**</u> película reciente es _____.
3. <u>**El mejor**</u> restaurante local es _____.

Comparatives / **Los comparativos**	Superlatives / **Los superlativos**
Julio es **más** alto **que** Juanito.	Julio es <u>**el**</u> niño **más** alto <u>**de**</u> la clase. (Julio es <u>**el más**</u> alto <u>**de**</u> la clase.*)
El fútbol es **más** popular **que** el golf.	El fútbol es <u>**el**</u> deporte **más** popular <u>**del**</u> mundo. (El fútbol es <u>**el más**</u> popular <u>**del**</u> mundo.*)
La comida italiana es **buena,** pero la comida mexicana es **mejor**.	La comida mexicana es <u>**la mejor**</u> comida <u>**de**</u> todas las comidas del mundo. (La comida mexicana es <u>**la mejor de**</u> todas las comidas del mundo.*)

The most famous Puerto Ricans *Do you agree? Correct the false statements, according to your opinion.* **1.** *Jennifer Lopez is the best known Puerto Rican singer in the world.* **2.** *Benicio del Toro is the most famous Puerto Rican actor in the world.* **3.** *Roberto Clemente, of Puerto Rican descent, is the best Hispanic baseball player of all time.*

*Notice how adjectives can be used as nouns: **el niño más alto** (the tallest child) → **el más alto** (the tallest one), and so on. You can learn more about using adjectives in this way in Appendix 2, Using Adjectives as Nouns.*

the superlative / **el superlativo** = an adjective or adverb that expresses an extreme

Superlatives / **Los superlativos**

1. Forming the Superlative
To express the *most / best / least / worst,* and so on, the comparative forms are used with the definite article.

> **¡OJO!**
> *in/of* = **de**

el / la / los / las + *noun* + **más** / **menos** + *adjective* + **de**

el
la
los
las
} + *noun* + **mas/menos** } + *adjective* + **de**

El basquetbol es **el deporte más** competitivo **del** mundo.
Basketball is the most competitive sport in the world.

El golf es **el deporte menos** peligroso **de** todos.
Golf is the least dangerous sport of all.

2. Irregular Superlatives
Mejor and **peor** generally precede the noun.

el / la / los / las + **mejor(es) / peor(es)** + *noun* (+ **de**)

el
la
los
las
} + **mejor(es) / peor(es)** } + *noun* (+ **de**)

La verdad es que es **el peor** jugador **del** equipo.
The truth is that he's the worst player on the team.

Son **las mejores** lavadoras.
They're the best washing machines.

Note that **mejor** and **peor** are often used with possessives instead of the articles.

Ana es **mi mejor** amiga.
Ana is my best friend.

Mayor and **menor** are often used without the noun.

Lorenzo es **el mayor de** los hermanos y Leticia es **la menor.**
Lorenzo is the oldest of the siblings and Leticia is the youngest.

Práctica y comunicación

A. Opiniones personales

Paso 1. Autoprueba. Ordene las palabras para hacer oraciones con sentido (*meaningful*) que expresan ideas superlativas.

1. **Es...** ciudad / más / el / grande / la / parque / de
2. **Son...** familia / los / listos / de / niños / la / más
3. **Visité...** del / los / mundo / museos / mejores
4. **Vi...** peor / año / película / la / del

Summary of Superlatives

el / la / los / las + *noun* + **más** / **menos** + *adjective* + **de**

el / la / los / las + {
mejor(es) / peor(es)
mayor(es) / menor(es)
} + *noun* + **de**

Paso 2. Use las siguientes ideas para dar su opinión sobre lo que es «más» en cada categoría.

MODELO: una estación del año (frío) → **La** estación **más fría del** año es el invierno.

1. un día festivo del año (divertido)
2. una materia de este semestre/ trimestre (difícil)
3. una persona de la familia (vieja)
4. una persona de la familia (joven)
5. un mes del año (bueno)
6. un día de la semana (malo)
7. un amigo / una amiga (bueno/a)

Paso 3. Ahora, en parejas, usen las ideas del **Paso 2** para entrevistarse. Luego, díganle a la clase algo que tienen en común.

> MODELO: **7. E1:** ¿Cómo se llama tu mejor amigo o amiga?
> **E2:** Mi mejor amigo es Jacobo. ¿Y tu mejor amigo?
> **E1:** (Es) Luis.

B. Superlativos

Paso 1. Modifique las siguientes oraciones para hacer una forma superlativa.

> MODELO: Es una persona muy **alta. (de nuestra clase)** →
> Es **la** persona **más alta de nuestra clase.**

1. Es una clase muy **interesante/aburrida. (todas mis clases)**
2. Es una persona muy **inteligente/amable. (todos mis amigos)**
3. Son ciudades muy **grandes. (los Estados Unidos)**
4. Es un estado muy **pequeño. (el país)**
5. Es un perro muy **pequeño/grande. (el mundo)**
6. Es una residencia muy **ruidosa** (*noisy*). **(la universidad)**
7. Es una montaña muy **alta. (el mundo)**

Paso 2. Ahora repita cada oración con información verdadera.

> MODELO: **Carla** es la estudiante más alta de la clase.

C. Intercambios. En parejas, túrnense para expresar sus opiniones sobre las siguientes ideas. Luego compartan (*share*) sus opiniones con la clase.

> MODELO: **el peor/mejor** restaurante de la ciudad →
> **E1:** Yo creo que _____ es **el peor** restaurante **de** la ciudad.
> **E2:** En mi opinión, **el peor** restaurante **de** la ciudad es _____.
> → No estamos de acuerdo. Yo creo que _____ es **el peor** restaurante **de** la ciudad. Mi compañero/a cree que **el peor** es _____.

1. el **peor/mejor** restaurante de la ciudad
2. un libro **interesantísimo/aburridísimo**
3. un plato **riquísimo/malísimo**
4. un programa de televisión **interesantísimo/pesadísimo**
5. un lugar **tranquilísimo / animadísimo / peligrosísimo** (*very dangerous*)
6. la canción más **bonita/fea** del año
7. la **mejor/peor** película del año

> **Estrategia**
>
> Emphatic forms formed with **-ísimo/a** cannot be used in a superlative construction. You can use **-ísimo/a** adjectives in this activity, but only as shown in some of the activity's items.

Nota comunicativa: Los diminutivos

In Spanish, it is very common to add a suffix to nouns and adjectives to express littleness or affection. The most common diminutive ending is **-ito/a.**

- If the word ends in a consonant, **-ito/a** is added to the singular form (and any accent on the word is dropped): **papel → papelito, fácil → facilito.**
- If the word ends in a vowel, the final vowel is dropped before adding **-ito/a** (and any accent on the word is

dropped): **guapo → guapito, libro → librito (libros → libritos), rápido → rapidito.**
- Spelling changes occur when the final consonant is **c, g,** or **z: poco → poquito, amiga → amiguita, pedazos** (*chunks*) **→ pedacitos.**

You will use diminutives in **Práctica D.**

 D. ¿Diminutivos para usted? Los diminutivos se usan para hablar de algo con afecto y ternura (*tenderness*). ¿Usarían ustedes (*Would you use*) un diminutivo para hablar de las siguientes personas y cosas? Expliquen sus respuestas.

> MODELO: **1.** ¿su cuarto? →
> **E1:** Sí, mi **cuartito,** porque es muy pequeño / es un lugar especial.
> **E2:** No, no quiero llamarlo **cuartito,** porque no es pequeño / no me gusta.

1. ¿su cuarto?
1. ¿su libro de español?
3. ¿su hermano/a (sobrino/a) menor?
4. ¿su gorra favorita?
5. ¿su abuelo/a?
6. ¿su perro/a?

Algo sobre la bomba y la plena

Helen H. Richardson
Denver Post/Getty Images

Un grupo puertorriqueño con sus congas

La bomba y la plena son dos géneros musicales de Puerto Rico que son productos del sincretismo[a] musical típico del Caribe. La bomba está marcada por la herencia[b] africana, mientras que la plena muestra la influencia de la tradición española. La bomba es un diálogo entre los bailarines y los tambores.[c] La plena incluye instrumentos como el cuatro (una evolución de la guitarra española) y la pandereta.[d]

¿Cuál es el origen de un género musical típico de los Estados Unidos? ¿Qué instrumentos se usan en esa música?

[a]*blending* [b]*heritage* [c]*drums* [d]*tambourine*

Todo junto

A. Lengua y cultura: Un poco de la historia de Puerto Rico

Paso 1. Completar. Complete the following passage with the correct form of the words in parentheses, as suggested by context. When two possibilities are given in parentheses, select the correct word. **¡OJO!** Give the preterite form of the verbs marked *P* and the imperfect of those marked *I*.

EJ Rojas/Alamy Stock Photo

Estatua de una mujer taína, en Cataño, Puerto Rico

En la isla de Puerto Rico, como en todas las Antillas Mayores, _____ (*I:* vivir)[1] los indígenas taínos. Cristóbal Colón _____ (*P:* llegar)[2] a la isla en 1493, en su segunda[a] expedición al Nuevo Mundo. (Se / Le)[3] dice que el jefe[b] de los taínos, que _____ (*I:* tener)[4] el título de cacique, _____ (*P:* recibir)[5] a Colón con un collar[c] de oro. (Por / Para)[6] eso Colón pensó que _____ (*I:* haber)[7] mucho oro en la isla, pero no tenía (razón / prisa).[8] De todas formas,[d] los españoles explotaron la isla intensamente. En poco tiempo, la población taína prácticamente _____ (*P:* desaparecer[e])[9] debido a[f] tres factores: (el / la)[10] explotación física causada por labores intensas,[g] las rebeliones de los nativos y las enfermedades[h] que los españoles _____ (*P:* llevar)[11] consigo,[i] que _____ (*I:* ser)[12] nuevas para los taínos. La población africana, que los los españoles llevaron esclavizadas[j] al Caribe, _____ (*P:* empezar)[13] a llegar en el siglo XVI.

En el siglo XIX, por toda Latinoamérica, _____ (*P:* haber)[14] guerras[k] contra España para obtener la independencia. Pero Puerto Rico no _____ (*P:* poder)[15] independizarse. En 1898, los Estados Unidos _____ (*P:* ganar)[16] una guerra contra España, y Puerto Rico se convirtió en[l] territorio estadounidense. En inglés, la guerra _____ (*P:* recibir)[17] el nombre de «*the Spanish-American War*» (la Guerra hispanoamericana).

En 1917 los puertorriqueños _____ (*P:* ser)[18] declarados ciudadanos[m] _____ (estadounidense)[19] y, desde 1953, su país es un Estado Libre Asociado a los Estados Unidos de América. Esto significa que no es independiente.

[a]*second* [b]*chief* [c]*necklace* [d]*De... In any case* [e]*to disappear* [f]*debido... due to* [g]*labores... hard labor* [h]*illnesses* [i]*with them* [j]*enslaved* [k]*wars* [l]*se... became a* [m]*citizens*

Paso 2. Comprensión. Conteste las siguientes preguntas.

1. ¿De qué grupo de islas forma parte Puerto Rico?
2. ¿Quiénes eran los habitantes originales de Puerto Rico?
3. ¿Cuándo llegaron los españoles a Puerto Rico por primera vez?
4. Después del siglo XVI, ¿qué otros grupos raciales había en la isla?
5. ¿Desde cuándo es Puerto Rico territorio de los Estados Unidos?
6. ¿Cuál es la situación política actual de Puerto Rico?

 Paso 3. En acción

 Ahora, en parejas, den información histórica sobre su estado (o país) comparable a la información sobre Puerto Rico. Aquí hay unas sugerencias.

1. qué pueblo(s) vivía(n) en su estado (país) originalmente
2. qué otros pueblos llegaron más tarde y cuándo
3. si hubo guerra(s) con otro país y cuándo
4. si obtuvo (*obtained*) su independencia de otro país y cuándo
5. cuándo se convirtió en estado de la Unión estadounidense

B. Proyecto: Reacciones y actitudes de la adolescencia

 Hay muchos estereotipos que se asocian con la adolescencia. Ustedes van a hacer una encuesta (*poll*) para ver si esos estereotipos son de verdad (*really*) muy comunes.

Paso 1. Preparación. En parejas o grupos, hagan una lista de cinco de las reacciones o actitudes que generalmente se asocian con los jóvenes entre los 14 y 18 años.

Paso 2. Encuesta. (*Survey.*) Ahora, usen las ideas del **Paso 1** para hacerles preguntas a varias personas de la clase sobre sus hábitos o actitudes cuando eran adolescentes. Recuerden establecer un formato para preguntar (sí/no, escala de posibilidades, etcétera) y un método para apuntar (*noting down*) las respuestas.

> MODELO: discutir con los padres/hermanos →
> ¿Discutías mucho con tus padres?
> 1 = nunca o casi nunca; 5 = todo el tiempo

Paso 3. Análisis de datos. Según los resultados de su encuesta, ¿son válidos los estereotipos que ustedes eligieron (*chose*)? Preparen un breve informe (*report*) para la clase que incluya (*includes*) la lista de preguntas, el número de personas encuestadas (*polled*) por cada pregunta y un resumen (*summary*) de las respuestas.

cambios · independencia · imagen · grupos · celular · niñez · adolescencia · actitud · juventud · familia · rebeldía · acné · amigos · selfies

Vocabulario útil

discutir con los padres/hermanos
encerrarse (me encierro) *(to shut oneself up)* **en su cuarto**
preocuparse *(to worry)* **mucho por la imagen que se proyecta**
sacar(se) *selfies* **con frecuencia**
sentirse (me siento) (i) cohibido/a por *(self-conscious about)*
tener acné

Video: Salu2 «Deportes que mueven masas»

You can watch two segments of this chapter's video in the **Video: Salu2** section, found at the end of the eBook.

Klic Video Productions/McGraw Hill

Una porra (*fan club*) camina al campo (*field*) de fútbol de su equipo.

MUNDO HISPANO

Enfoque cultural: El tiempo libre

Antes de leer

¿Hay playas muy frecuentadas por la gente cerca de su ciudad o estado? En la zona donde usted vive, ¿cuáles son los lugares que más visita la gente en el tiempo libre?

En Puerto Rico

Una bonita playa de Vieques

A la gente de Puerto Rico le gusta pasar el tiempo junto al[a] mar. Es lógico: Puerto Rico y sus islas más pequeñas, como Vieques y Culebra, están rodeadas de[b] deliciosas aguas cálidas[c] y hermosas[d] playas. Muchas son de arena[e] fina y mar tranquilo, ideales para relajarse y nadar. Otras, especialmente en el norte, son excelentes para surfear. Y otras (al este y al sur) ofrecen el espectáculo natural de la bioluminiscencia: unos microorganismos llamados dinoflagelados iluminan el agua del mar por la noche.

Aunque[f] en Puerto Rico hace buen tiempo todo el año, es en los meses de verano (de mayo a septiembre) cuando los puertorriqueños van más a la playa. Amigos y familia, música, comida, una hamaca entre dos palmas... ¿Qué más se puede pedir?

[a]junto... *next to the* [b]rodeadas... *surrounded by* [c]*warm*
[d]*beautiful* [e]*sand* [f]*Although*

Comprensión ¿Cuál es una de las grandes diversiones de la gente de Puerto Rico y cuándo la practican? ¿Qué es la bioluminiscencia?

En otros países hispanos

Un juego de dominó

- **En todo el mundo hispanohablante** Jugar al dominó y hacer la sobremesa son pasatiempos muy populares en muchos países hispanos. El dominó es un juego muy fácil de aprender, pero el juego se complica muchísimo —y también se hace más interesante— jugando en parejas. La sobremesa es el tiempo que se pasa charlando[a] en la mesa después de la comida. No es nada extraño[b] que un grupo de parientes o amigos hispanos pase dos o tres horas sentados[c] a la mesa, primero comiendo, luego tomando café y charlando, hasta unir el almuerzo con la merienda.
- **En la Argentina** En este país sudamericano hay gran afición por el deporte del polo. La Argentina domina ese deporte en el panorama mundial.

[a]*chatting* [b]*strange* [c]*seated*

Comprensión ¿Cuál es un juego de mesa muy popular en el mundo hispano? ¿Qué es la sobremesa?

👉 En acción

Haga una lista de los pasatiempos familiares que usted considera típicos de su país y otra lista de los pasatiempos más comunes de su familia.

Lectura

Antes de leer

Piense en cómo usted usa su teléfono celular. ¿Cuáles son los aspectos positivos y negativos de su uso?

Vocabulario para leer

el dispositivo	device	**la señal**	sign
el entrenamiento	training		
el interlocutor /	conversation partner	**aportar**	to contribute
la interlocutora			
		apagado/a	turned off
la llamada	(phone) call	**saludable**	healthy
la pantalla	screen	**sano/a**	healthy

Volver a conectar

Aunque[a] las tabletas, los *smartphones* y otros dispositivos están pensados y diseñados[b] para servirnos, los estudios realizados[c] hasta ahora constatan[d] nuestra «dependencia electrónica». Sin embargo, desconectar es posible. El psicólogo Fernando Azor nos aporta algunas sugerencias:

PRIORIZAR Hay que atender[e] primero a aquellos que se dirigen a[f] nosotros en persona; después las llamadas; después los mensajes instantáneos y, por último, los correos electrónicos.

RESPONDER MÁS TARDE No responder de inmediato es un buen entrenamiento para combatir la ansiedad. Ni nosotros estamos obligados a contestar al instante,[g] ni ellos pueden sentirse cuestionados[h] porque no se les escriba en el acto.[i]

ABSTENERSE[j] Ser capaz[k] de pasar un fin de semana o un día entero con el teléfono apagado es una señal de

sana independencia. Si este período es demasiado largo, hay que tratar de desconectar todas las redes[l] (si no, al menos[m] el wifi) en determinados momentos del día, por ejemplo durante la noche.

CONFIGURAR Configure su dispositivo para que los nuevos correos o mensajes instantáneos solo lleguen cuando usted actualice[n] manualmente. Evitará así[ñ] las constantes miradas a la pantalla en busca de notificaciones.

HUMANIZAR La tecnología crea una ilusoria sensación de intimidad y contacto. Por ello[o] es aconsejable,[p] al

menos una vez a la semana, «desvirtualizar» nuestras relaciones y quedar con[q] ese interlocutor para tomar un café o dar un paseo real.

SELECCIONAR A menudo[r] mantenemos relaciones virtuales que, en realidad, no aportan nada a nuestra vida,[s] o que incluso nos restan[t] energía y tiempo. Por ello, es muy saludable ser un poco más darwinistas* con nuestra agenda de contactos, y no dudar a la hora de dejar de[u] ser «amigo» de aquellas personas a las que, en el fondo, no nos une nada.[v]

[a]*Although* [b]*pensados... imagined and designed* [c]*completed* [d]*show* [e]*pay attention* [f]*se... address* [g]*al... immediately* [h]*let down*
[i]*en... immediately* [j]*ABSTAIN* [k]*capable* [l]*hay... it's necessary to try to disconnect the networks* [m]*al... at least* [n]*refresh, update*
[ñ]*Evitará... That way you will avoid* [o]*Por... Por eso* [p]*advisable* [q]*quedar... to meet, to make a date with* [r]*A... Con frecuencia* [s]*life*
[t]*incluso... even take away from us* [u]*no... not hesitate when it comes to stopping* [v]*a... who, in the final analysis, we have no ties with*

Comprensión

A. Ideas principales. ¿Cuál de las siguientes oraciones resume mejor la lectura? Señale (*Point out*) evidencia en el texto para la respuesta que seleccione.

1. Los teléfonos celulares son dispositivos esenciales para la vida moderna y no se puede vivir sin ellos.
2. La dependencia de los teléfonos celulares y otros dispositivos es un problema, pero es posible controlarla.
3. Es mejor vivir sin teléfonos celulares y otros dispositivos.

B. Aplicación personal. De las seis sugerencias que ofrece la lectura, ¿cuáles implementa usted ahora? ¿Cuáles quiere implementar? ¿Cuáles no son ni (*neither*) apropiadas ni (*nor*) aceptables para usted? Explique sus respuestas.

---

*Darwinistas *refers to Charles Darwin, the nineteenth-century theorist of biological evolution. In this context, the term refers to an action that will lead to self-preservation.*

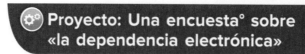

Proyecto: Una encuesta° sobre «la dependencia electrónica»

survey

En este proyecto, va a realizar una encuesta para determinar si usted y el resto de la clase sufren de «la dependencia electrónica».

Paso 1. Escriba varias preguntas para la encuesta, basadas (*based*) en las sugerencias de la lectura **Volver a conectar.**

MODELO: ¿Te sientes obligado/a a contestar mensajes de texto de inmediato?

Paso 2. En grupos, evalúen las preguntas de todas las personas y seleccionen las mejores para la encuesta. También decidan cómo van a implementarlas. ¿Van a contestar las preguntas individualmente o van a entrevistar a sus compañeros de clase? ¿Van a hacer una encuesta oral o electrónica? Cuando tengan (*you have*) la lista de preguntas finalizada, hagan la encuesta.

Paso 3. Analicen las respuestas y compartan los resultados con toda la clase. ¿Hay tendencias y/o problemas frecuentes en su clase? ¿Creen ustedes que sufren de «la dependencia electrónica»?

Textos orales

Unos compañeros hablan de «un desastre»

Antes de escuchar

¿Qué tareas hace usted para mantener limpio su apartamento o habitación? ¿Cuál de las tareas hace con más frecuencia? ¿Cuál le molesta más hacer?

Vocabulario para escuchar

verdadero/a	real
no te preocupes	don't worry
arreglar	to tidy up
no discutamos	let's not argue
yo me encargo de	I'll take care of
¡muévete!	move it!, get a move on!

Comprensión

A. ¿Quién lo va a hacer? Empareje cada tarea con la persona que la va a hacer.

TAREAS

1. _____ limpiar la cocina
2. _____ limpiar el baño
3. _____ pasar la aspiradora
4. _____ sacar la basura

PERSONAS

a. Jorge
b. Gilda
c. Ana

B. Otros detalles. Conteste las siguientes preguntas según el diálogo.

1. ¿Por qué es urgente limpiar el apartamento?
2. ¿Quién está dispuesto (*willing*) a ayudar?
3. ¿Quién no tiene muchas ganas de ayudar?

 En acción

Haga un horario (*schedule*) para este fin de semana empezando por el viernes por la tarde. Incluya (*Include*) pasatiempos, tareas académicas y tareas domésticas. ¡Seguro que hay por lo menos (*Surely there must be at least*) una cosa que usted tiene que hacer en su cuarto o en su casa/apartamento!

PORTAFOLIO

🎤 Entrevista

Use de modelo las preguntas y respuestas (*answers*) de la sección **Entrevista** al principio (*at the beginning*) de este capítulo para hablar de su tiempo libre y de sus pasatiempos favoritos.

Iborgephoto123/Shutterstock

💻 Escritura

Un ensayo sobre los pasatiempos y diversiones

¿Cuáles son las actividades típicas de los estudiantes de su universidad? ¿Y qué hacía usted cuando era más joven? ¿Era similar a lo que hace ahora? Usted va a escribir un ensayo sobre estas ideas.

👥 Antes de escribir

En parejas, piensen en las actividades típicas de la gente de su edad (*age group*) y en concreto de los estudiantes de su universidad. La tabla sugiere (*suggests*) algunas categorías, pero ustedes las pueden ampliar o modificar.

Personas adultas		En la adolescencia	
actividades de tiempo libre	obligaciones	actividades de tiempo libre	obligaciones

A escribir

Ahora use la información de **Antes de escribir** para escribir un ensayo comparativo. ¿Es usted una persona representativa de su generación y de su universidad? Cuando usted era más joven, ¿hacía las mismas cosas? Hay más ayuda en Connect.

> **Para escribir bien**
>
> Considere estas opciones para su ensayo:
>
> - Expresiones para marcar momentos de la vida: **de niño/a, de adolescente, en la actualidad, entonces, mientras, durante los años universitarios**
> - Conectores de ideas: **pero, también, además, sin embargo, en contraste (con)**
> - El uso del **imperfecto** para hablar de las actividades que hacía regularmente en el pasado

🔗 En la comunidad

Entreviste a una persona hispana de su universidad o ciudad sobre lo que hace en su tiempo libre.

Preguntas posibles

- ¿Practica algún deporte? ¿Es su deporte favorito uno de los deportes más populares de su cultura?
- ¿Cuáles son sus pasatiempos favoritos? ¿Cuáles eran sus pasatiempos favoritos cuando era niño/a?
- ¿Hace muchas tareas domésticas? ¿Cuáles son? ¿Cuáles son las tareas que más odia? ¿Qué tareas domésticas tenía que hacer cuando tenía 12 o 13 años?

📹 Producción audiovisual

Filme una entrevista con un(a) atleta hispanohablante de su universidad. Si no encuentra ninguno/a, entreviste a un(a) atleta anglohablante (*English-speaking*) y use su voz en off (*voiceover*) para traducir al español las ideas principales de lo que dice el/la atleta.

Hola Images/Getty Images

En el Bosque (*Forest*) Nacional el Yunque, en Puerto Rico

Portafolio

Sugerencia: You are now ready to play Quest 7 in **Practice Spanish: Study Abroad.**

Más ideas para el portafolio

- Si usted juega en un equipo o hace un deporte a nivel competitivo, incluya una foto suya (*of yourself*) haciendo ese deporte. Describa su posición en el equipo y otros detalles importantes (*ranking*, nombre del entrenador / de la entrenadora, etcétera). Si no practica ningún deporte, describa el tipo de ejercicio físico que hace, incluyendo una foto si es posible. Y si no hace ningún tipo de ejercicio físico, explique cómo pasa su tiempo libre.
- Incluya dos imágenes de lugares favoritos o especiales que usted relaciona con el tiempo libre y los pasatiempos de su infancia o adolescencia. Explique por qué iba allí, y qué hacía, con quiénes, etcétera.
- Si ha estado jugando (*you have been playing*) Practice Spanish: Study Abroad, en Quest 7 usted supo que su amigo David está leyendo *El ingenioso hidalgo don Quijote de la Mancha*, de Miguel de Cervantes Saavedra, en su tiempo libre. Busque información sobre la trama (*plot*), el autor, el contexto histórico, los personajes (*characters*), etcétera, de esta novela. ¿Por qué cree usted que esta novela es tan famosa? ¿Ve paralelos entre los personajes de *Don Quijote* y los personajes del juego? Escriba un informe (*report*) y entrégueselo a su profesor(a) o presente sus ideas en clase.

EN RESUMEN En este capítulo

AFTER STUDYING THIS CHAPTER I CAN ...

- ☐ talk about sports and other pastimes (300)
- ☐ talk about household chores (303–304)
- ☐ use the imperfect to describe past actions (306–308)
- ☐ use interrogatives more effectively, especially **¿qué?** and **¿cuál(es)?** (312–313)
- ☐ use superlatives to describe "the most" in a category (315–316)
- ☐ recognize/describe at least 2–3 aspects of Puerto Rican cultures

Gramática en breve

26. The Imperfect

Regular -ar Endings
-aba, -abas, -aba, -ábamos, -abais, -aban

Regular -er/-ir Endings
-ía, -ías, -ía, -íamos, -íais, -ían

Verbs Irregular in the Imperfect
ir: iba, ibas, iba, íbamos, ibais, iban
ser: era, eras, era, éramos, erais, eran
ver: veía, veías, veía, veíamos, veíais, veían

27. Superlatives

el / la / los / las + *noun* + **más/menos** + *adjective* + **de**

el / la / los / las + **mejor(es)/peor(es)** + *noun* + **de**

28. Interrogative Words

¿qué? } = definition, explanation
= identification: + *noun* = *what/which* ... ?
¿cuál(es)? = choice: + *verb* = *what/which (one)* ... ?

Vocabulario

Los verbos

pelear	to fight
sonar (suena)	to ring; to sound
tocarle (qu) a uno (like **gustar**)	to be someone's turn

Repaso: deber, necesitar, tener que

Un partido

el/la atleta	athlete
el equipo	team
el jugador / la jugadora	player
el entrenador / la entrenadora	coach
la pelota	ball

entrenar(se)	to practice; to train
ganar	to win
el partido	game, match

Repaso: perder (ie), practicar (qu)

El tiempo libre

la afición	hobby
la diversión	fun activity
el pasatiempo	pastime
aburrirse	to get bored
dar un paseo	to take a walk
hacer...	
planes (m.) para + inf.	to make plans to (do something)
un pícnic	to have a picnic
ir...	to go ...
a un concierto	to a concert
a un museo	to a museum
a una discoteca	to a disco
al teatro	to the theater
jugar (juego) (gu)...	to play ...
a las cartas	cards
a los videojuegos	video games
al ajedrez	chess
ser...	to be ...
aburrido/a	boring
aficionado/a (a)	a fan (of)
divertido/a	fun
libre	free

Repaso: hacer camping, ir al cine / a un bar / a un club, jugar (juego) (gu)

Los deportes

andar en bicicleta	to ride a bicycle
caminar	to walk
correr	to run; to jog
dar una caminata	to hike
esquiar (esquío)	to ski
hacer (el) yoga	to do yoga
montar a caballo	to ride a horse
patinar	to skate
surfear	to surf

Repaso: jugar (juego) (gu) al + sport, nadar, perder (pierdo), practicar (qu)

el ciclismo	bicycling
el fútbol	soccer
el fútbol americano	football
la natación	swimming
el patinaje	skating
el deporte	sport

Cognados: el basquetbol, el béisbol, el esquí, el golf, el hockey, el tenis, el voleibol

Las tareas domésticas

barrer el piso	to sweep the floor
hacer la cama	to make the bed
lavar	to wash
limpiar (la casa)	to clean (house)
pasar la aspiradora	to vacuum
planchar	to iron
poner la mesa	to set the table
quitar la mesa	to clear the table
sacar (qu) la basura	to take out the trash
la tarea doméstica	household chore

Repaso: la cama, la casa, hacer, la mesa, los platos, poner, la ropa

Algunos aparatos domésticos

la aspiradora	vacuum cleaner
la cafetera	coffee maker
el congelador	freezer
el horno de microondas	microwave oven
la lavadora	washing machine
el lavaplatos	dishwasher
el refrigerador	refrigerator
la secadora	clothes dryer
la tostadora	toaster
el aparato doméstico	home appliance

Repaso: la estufa

Otros sustantivos

la escuela	school
el/la niñero/a	babysitter
el siglo	century
el trabajo	work; job

Los adjetivos

deportivo/a	sports-related, sports (adj.); sports-loving
doméstico/a	domestic, related to the home
libre	free, unoccupied
pesado/a	boring

Palabras adicionales

al aire libre	outdoors, in the open air
de adolescente	as an adolescent
de niño/a	as a child
en la actualidad	currently, right now
-ito/a	diminutive suffix
mientras	while

Repaso: ¿a qué hora?, ¿adónde?, ¿cómo?, ¿cuál(es)?, ¿cuándo?, ¿cuánto/a?, ¿cuántos/as?, ¿de dónde?, ¿de quién(es)?, ¿dónde?, ¿por qué?, ¿qué?, ¿quién(es)?

Vocabulario personal

Use this space or a vocabulary notebook to write down other words and phrases you learn in this chapter.

La salud°

La... *Health*

En este capítulo

VOCABULARY

Talking about health and wellness   328

Common illnesses and going to doctors   330

GRAMMAR

Talking about the past with two tenses   333

Connecting ideas   341

Expressing *each other*   344

COUNTRY OF FOCUS: VENEZUELA

En un consultorio médico (*doctor's office*), en Venezuela

ZUMA Press Inc/Alamy Stock Photo

Mar Caribe

Golfo de Venezuela

Caracas

Maracaibo

Lago de Maracaibo

VENEZUELA

Río Orinoco

COLOMBIA

Río Orinoco

GUYANA

TRINIDAD Y TOBAGO

BRASIL

0   150   300 Millas
0   150   300 Kilómetros

VENEZUELA

29 millones de habitantes

- Venezuela es un país muy rico en petróleo.[a] Petróleos de Venezuela Sociedad Anónima[b] (PDVSA) es una de las empresas (compañías) petroleras más grandes del mundo. Es una corporación del estado que controla la exploración, producción y venta[c] de todo el petróleo del país.

- La Fundación del Estado para el Sistema Nacional de las Orquestas Juveniles e Infantiles de Venezuela (FESNOJIV) es una iniciativa que fomenta la instrucción musical «como instrumento de organización social y desarrollo[d] comunitario».

[a]*oil*   [b]Sociedad... *Incorporated*   [c]*sale*
[d]*development*

ENTREVISTA

These questions related to the chapter theme are answered here by a native speaker. You will be able to ask and answer them yourself with personal information in the **Entrevista** activity in the **Portafolio** section at the end of the chapter.

Cecilia Figueroa Martín contesta las preguntas.

— **¿Cómo es su salud[a] en general? ¿Lleva usted una vida sana[b]?**

— Creo que mi salud es excelente, afortunadamente. ¡Toco madera![c] La verdad es que llevo una vida sana por lo general. Como bien, no bebo mucho, no fumo nada...

— **¿Hace usted ejercicio con frecuencia? ¿Hizo usted ejercicio ayer?**

— Sí, trato de[d] hacer ejercicio por lo menos tres o cuatro días a la semana: voy al gimnasio o corro tres o cuatro millas. Ayer corrí.

— **¿Cuándo fue la última vez que usted fue al médico? ¿Fue por algo grave o fue una visita rutinaria?**

— La última vez que fui al médico fue el mes pasado, para mi chequeo anual.

[a]*health*   [b]*healthy*   [c]¡Toco... *Knock on wood!*   [d]trato... *I try to*

VOCABULARIO: PREPARACIÓN

You can hear the pronunciation of theme vocabulary words and phrases in the eBook.

La salud y el bienestar°

La... *Health and well-being*

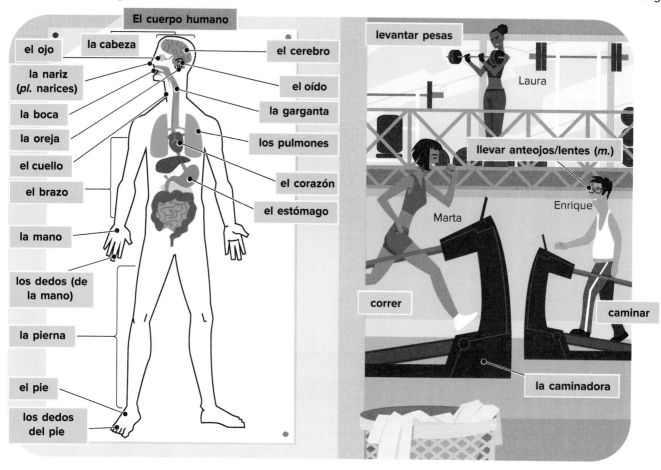

El cuerpo humano

el ojo · la cabeza · el cerebro · la nariz (*pl.* narices) · el oído · la boca · la garganta · la oreja · los pulmones · el cuello · el brazo · el corazón · el estómago · la mano · los dedos (de la mano) · la pierna · el pie · los dedos del pie

levantar pesas — Laura
llevar anteojos/lentes (*m.*) — Enrique
Marta
correr — caminar — la caminadora

El cuerpo humano

la cabeza	head
el oído	inner ear

¿Cómo se cuida usted?° — se... *do you take care of yourself*

cuidarse	to take care of oneself
dejar de + *inf.*	to stop (*doing something*)
dormir (duermo) (u) lo suficiente	to get enough sleep
hacer ejercicio	to exercise; to get exercise

hacer...	to do ...
ejercicios aeróbicos	aerobics
pilates / zumba	Pilates / Zumba
llevar lentes (m.) de contacto	to wear contact lenses
llevar una vida sana/tranquila	to lead a healthy/calm life
practicar (qu) deportes	to practice, sports
respirar	to breathe
sano/a	healthy

¡OJO!

El oído refers to the *inner ear,* while **la oreja** means the *outer ear.*

El cuello means *neck,* while **la garganta** means *throat.*

The gender of **la mano** is irregular.

Así se dice

los anteojos, los lentes = las gafas (*Sp.*)
los lentes de contacto = las lentes de contacto (*Sp.*), las lentillas (*Sp.*)
la caminadora = la cinta de andar (*Sp.*), la cinta de correr, la cinta rodante, la trotadora (*P.R.*)

Comunicación

A. Asociaciones

Paso 1. ¿Qué partes del cuerpo humano asocia usted con las siguientes palabras? **¡OJO!** A veces hay más de una respuesta posible.

1. llevar aretes
2. comer
3. cantar
4. llorar
5. pensar
6. llevar anillos
7. amar (*to love*)
8. fumar
9. escuchar música
10. oler (*to smell*) un perfume
11. nadar
12. boxear

 Paso 2. En parejas, hagan una lista de todos los verbos que pueden asociar lógicamente con las siguientes partes de cuerpo.

1. los ojos
2. los dedos
3. la boca
4. el oído
5. el estómago
6. los pulmones

B. Hablando de la salud. ¿Qué significan para usted las siguientes oraciones?

MODELOS: Se debe comer comidas sanas. →
Eso quiere decir (*means*) que es necesario comer muchas verduras, que...
También significa que no debemos comer muchos dulces o...

1. Se debe dormir lo suficiente todas las noches.
2. Hay que hacer ejercicio.
3. Es necesario llevar una vida tranquila.
4. En general, uno debe cuidarse mucho.
5. Es importante llevar una vida sana.

> ### Vocabulario útil
>
> **Eso quiere decir...**
> **Esto significa que...**
> **También...**

C. ¿Una vida sana?

Paso 1. Indique las cosas que usted hace para llevar una vida sana y cuidar de su salud.

	SÍ	NO
1. comer comidas sanas en general	☐	☐
2. no comer demasiados (*too many*) dulces	☐	☐
3. comer muchas frutas y verduras	☐	☐
4. hacer ejercicio moderado diariamente	☐	☐
5. beber agua suficiente todos los días	☐	☐
6. dormir siete u ocho horas todos los días	☐	☐
7. tomar demasiadas bebidas alcohólicas	☐	☐
8. no beber mucho café o té	☐	☐
9. no fumar	☐	☐

Paso 2. Ahora, en parejas, entrevístense sobre los hábitos del **Paso 1** e indiquen si hay algún hábito que desean dejar (*to break*) o adquirir (*to acquire*).

MODELO: E1: Yo como comidas sanas, pero como muchos dulces. ¿Y tú?
E2: Yo también. Comer muchos dulces es un hábito que quiero dejar. →
Nosotros comemos muchos dulces y es un hábito que queremos dejar.

D. Expresiones idiomáticas con partes del cuerpo.
Como en inglés, en español hay muchas expresiones que hacen referencia a partes del cuerpo humano. Empareje cada expresión con su significado.

1. ___ tener un corazón de oro
2. ___ no tener ni pies ni cabeza
3. ___ costar un ojo de la cara
4. ___ hablar por los codos (*elbows*)
5. ___ un gato comer(le) la lengua (*tongue*)
6. ___ levantarse con el pie izquierdo

a. tener mala suerte
b. ser muy caro
c. hablar mucho
d. no hablar nada
e. ser una situación o explicación ilógica
f. ser muy buena persona

Hablar por los codos

Una cita en el consultorio°

Una... *An appointment at the doctor's office*

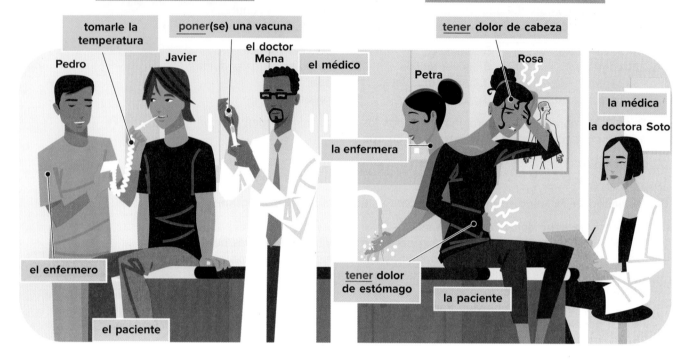

Una visita rutinaria

- **tomarle la temperatura**
- Pedro
- **poner(se) una vacuna**
- Javier
- **el doctor Mena**
- **el médico**
- **la enfermera**
- **el enfermero**
- **el paciente**

Una visita por enfermedad

- **tener dolor de cabeza**
- Rosa
- Petra
- **la médica**
- **la doctora Soto**
- **tener dolor de estómago**
- **la paciente**

el antibiótico	antibiotic	**estar...**	to be ...
la cita	appointment; date	enfermo/a	sick
el dolor (de)	pain, ache (in)	mareado/a	dizzy; nauseated
el diente / la muela	tooth / molar	resfriado/a	congested, stuffed up
la enfermedad	illness	sano/a	healthy
el enfermero / la enfermera	nurse	**guardar cama**	to stay in bed
el farmacéutico / la farmacéutica	pharmacist	**molestar**	to bother
		poner(se)...	to get
		una inyección	an injection
la fiebre	fever	una vacuna (de)	a vaccine (against)
la gripe	flu	**resfriarse (me resfrío)**	to get/catch a cold
el jarabe	(cough) syrup	**sacar (qu) la lengua**	to stick out one's tongue
la medicina	medicine	**sentirse (me siento) (i)...**	to feel ...
el médico / la médica	doctor, physician	bien / mal	well / sick
la pastilla	pill	enfermo/a	sick
la receta	prescription	**tener...**	to have ...
el resfriado	cold (*illness*)	el/la COVID-19	COVID-19
la tos	cough	(el) dolor de cabeza / estómago / muela	a headache / a stomachache / a toothache
el tratamiento	treatment		
		(la) fiebre / (la) tos / un resfriado	a fever / cough / cold

Cognados: el/la dentista, la visita

doler (duele)	to hurt, ache	(la) gripe	the flu
enfermarse	to get sick	**toser**	to cough

¡OJO!

Use the term **el médico / la médica** to talk *about* doctors in general and **el/la dentista** for the dentist. However, when you use the doctor or dentist's name, you should use the definite article plus the title: **el doctor Gómez, la dentista Velázquez**. To speak directly *to* him or her, just use the title **doctor(a)**.

¡OJO!

Doler and **molestar** are used like **gustar**:

> Me duele **la** cabeza.
> Me molestan **los** ojos.

Comunicación

A. Estudio de palabras. Complete las siguientes oraciones con una palabra derivada de la palabra en **rojo y subrayada**.

1. Si me **resfrío**, tengo _____.
2. La **respiración** ocurre cuando alguien _____.
3. Si me _____, estoy **enfermo/a**. Un(a) _____ me toma la temperatura.
4. Cuando alguien **tose**, es porque tiene _____.
5. Si me **duele** el estómago, tengo _____ de estómago.

B. Enfermedades comunes

Paso 1. ¿Con qué enfermedad se relacionan las siguientes situaciones, con la gripe, con el resfriado común o con un virus gastrointestinal?

1. tener tos
2. tener fiebre
3. tener dolor de garganta
4. ponerse una vacuna
5. tomar antibióticos

6. ir al médico
7. tener vómitos y diarrea
8. tener dolor de estómago
9. tomar pastillas
10. guardar cama

 Paso 2. En parejas, hablen de la última vez que ustedes sufrieron (*you had*) una enfermedad común. ¿Cuándo fue? ¿Cómo se sentían? ¿Fueron al médico?

Nota cultural: El cuidado° médico en el mundo hispano *care*

En el mundo hispano el cuidado médico puede ser muy variado. Depende principalmente del[a] nivel económico del país y después (como ocurre en este país) del nivel económico del individuo. Pero en todos los países hispanos hay excelente personal médico en todo tipo de especialidades, con buena preparación en las universidades de su país o en el extranjero. Aquí hay unos aspectos interesantes del cuidado de la salud en el mundo hispanohablante.

- **Las farmacias** En los países hispanos con frecuencia se va a la farmacia para consultar sobre una medicina o un remedio para una enfermedad leve.[b] Por supuesto,[c] las farmacéuticas y los farmacéuticos recomiendan ir a la consulta médica en caso de duda.[d]

- **Los remedios tradicionales o alternativos** Homeópatas, naturópatas, sanadores,[e] tiendas de botánica[f]... Hay una importante tradición, de gran diversidad en el mundo hispanohablante, de consultar a personas que tienen conocimiento[g] de los remedios naturales o de curaciones basadas en la fe,[h] especialmente para las molestias y enfermedades leves más frecuentes.

A diferencia de las farmacias en este país, en las farmacias de muchos países hispanos no se venden muchos productos para la higiene personal ni comestibles.

 ¿A quién consulta usted cuando está enfermo/a?

[a]*on the*   [b]*mild*   [c]*Por... Of course*   [d]*en... in case of doubt*   [e]*healers*   [f]*herbs*   [g]*knowledge*   [h]*faith*

C. Hablando de la salud

Paso 1. Complete las oraciones lógicamente para describir la situación de las personas de las fotos.

1. Irene está
   _____ ahora.
   _____ muy
   sana y siempre
   _____ bien.
   Todos los días
   _____. Nunca
   le duele _____
   y nunca tiene
   _____.

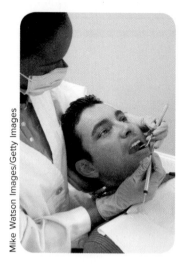

2. Martín está con su
   _____. Ayer tuvo que
   hacer una _____
   urgente porque le dolía
   mucho una _____.

 Paso 2. ¿Y ustedes? En parejas, hablen de cómo se sienten últimamente (*lately*). ¿Les duele alguna parte del cuerpo? ¿Toman pastillas u otras medicinas para el dolor? ¿Se ponen la vacuna de la gripe regularmente?

Algo sobre la harina[a] de maíz blanco

Una arepa

La harina de maíz blanco es el ingrediente básico para hacer dos platos típicos venezolanos: las arepas y las hallacas. Las arepas son similares al pan de pita y se pueden comer como sándwiches. Las hallacas son parecidas[b] a los tamales; son una comida tradicional de la Navidad y la Nochevieja.

 ¿Hay algo similar a las arepas o a las hallacas en la cocina de su familia?

[a]*flour*   [b]*similar*

Nota comunicativa: Cómo expresar una cualidad general: *lo + adjetivo*

To describe the general qualities or characteristics of something, use **lo** with the masculine singular form of an adjective.

lo bueno/malo   **lo más importante**   **lo mejor/peor**   **lo menos interesante**

This structure has a number of English equivalents, especially in colloquial speech.

lo bueno = the good thing / part / news, what's good

lo más importante = the most important thing / part / news, what's most important

You will use expressions of this type in **Comunicación D.**

D. Visitas de salud. En parejas, usen algunos de los siguientes adjetivos para describir una visita al médico / a la médica o al / a la dentista, según el modelo.

MODELO: **peor → Lo peor** de ir a mi dentista es tener que esperar antes de mi cita.

1. malo / bueno   2. peor / mejor   3. más importante

E. Refranes hispanos. Empareje una frase de la columna A con otra de la columna B para formar algunos refranes muy comunes en el mundo hispano. En algunos casos lo/la puede ayudar la rima. Luego explique lo que significan los refranes. ¿Cuál es el equivalente en inglés?

COLUMNA A	COLUMNA B
1. ___ La salud no se compra:	a. engorda (*fattens*).
2. ___ Músculos de Sansón	b. no tiene precio (*it is priceless*).
3. ___ Si quieres vivir sano,	c. y cerebro de mosquito.
4. ___ Para enfermedad de años,	d. no hay medicina.
5. ___ Ojos que no ven,	e. acuéstate y levántate temprano.
6. ___ Lo que no mata (*doesn't kill*),	f. corazón que no siente.

GRAMÁTICA

♻ Repaso

Since **Capítulo 8** you have been using first the preterite and then the imperfect in appropriate contexts. Indicate which tense you use to do each of the following.

	PRETERITE	IMPERFECT
1. to tell what you did yesterday	☐	☐
2. to tell what you used to do when you were in grade school	☐	☐
3. to describe background details, like physical or mental states	☐	☐
4. to tell about a completed action	☐	☐
5. to talk about the way things used to be	☐	☐
6. to describe an action that was in progress	☐	☐

If you understand these uses of the preterite and the imperfect, the summary of their uses in **Gramática 30** will be very easy for you.

30 Talking About the Past (Part 5) • Using the Preterite and the Imperfect

Gramática en acción: En el consultorio de la Dra. Méndez

Rick Brady/McGraw Hill

DRA. MÉNDEZ: ¿Cuándo **empezó** a sentirse mal su hijo?

MADRE: Ayer por la tarde. **Estaba** resfriado, **tosía** mucho y **se quejaba** de que le **dolían** el cuerpo y la cabeza.

DRA. MÉNDEZ: ¿Y le **notó** algo de fiebre?

MADRE: Sí. Por la noche le **tomé** la temperatura y **tenía** treinta y nueve grados.*

DRA. MÉNDEZ: A ver... Abre la boca, por favor.

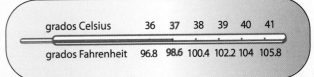

grados Celsius	36	37	38	39	40	41
grados Fahrenheit	96.8	98.6	100.4	102.2	104	105.8

¿Y usted?

1. ¿Cómo **se sentía** usted ayer por la noche?
2. ¿A qué hora **se acostó**?

You have already learned and used the preterite (**Capítulos 8** and **9**) and imperfect tenses (**Capítulo 10**). In this chapter you will begin to use them together to talk about the past.

Keep the following points in mind.

1. The preterite and the imperfect are both past tenses.
2. They are both used to talk about the same point in the past.

In Dr. Méndez's office DR. MÉNDEZ: *When did your son begin to feel ill?* MOTHER: *Yesterday afternoon. He was stuffed up, he was coughing a lot, and he was complaining that his body and head were hurting.* DR. MÉNDEZ: *And did you notice any fever?* MOTHER: *Yes. At night I took his temperature, and it was thirty-nine degrees.* DR. MÉNDEZ: *Let's see ... Open your mouth, please.*

*Normal body temperature is 37°C (98.6°F).

(Continúa).

Gramática

They *differ* in the point of view (aspect) about the past that they each convey. This is the same as with English usage. When you decide to say *I ran, I used to run,* or *I was going to run,* you are making a decision about the aspect of the past action that you want to communicate.

Here is a summary of the main uses of the two tenses. You will learn about them on the next pages.

Pretérito	Imperfecto
• beginning/end of an action	• habitual/repeated action
• completed action	• ongoing action
• series of completed actions	• background information
• the action on the "stage"	• the setting for the action

Note: I, II, III = completed actions in the past, one, two, three or more
~~~~~ = ongoing or repeated actions in the past, background detail

Note: The examples in points 1–4 form a continuing story: **la historia de una competición de natación.**

Differences between the Preterite and the Imperfect / Las diferencias entre el pretérito y el imperfecto

1. Beginning/End vs. Habitual

Use the **preterite** to tell about the beginning or the end of a past action. II

El sábado pasado, el campeonato estatal de natación **empezó** a las siete de la mañana y **terminó** al mediodía.
Last Saturday the state swimming championship started at seven A.M. and ended at noon.

Use the **imperfect** to talk about the habitual nature of an action (something you always did). ~~~~

El año pasado **había** competiciones **todos los sábados. Cada semana competíamos** con una escuela diferente.
Last year there were meets every Saturday. Every week we would compete with a different school.

2. Completed vs. Ongoing

Use the **preterite** to express an action that is viewed as **completed**. II

El campeonato estatal **duró** cinco horas y fue muy emocionante. Nuestro equipo **ganó** varias competiciones.
The state championship lasted five hours and it was very exciting. Our team won various competitions.

Use the **imperfect** to tell about **simultaneous events** (with **mientras** = *while*).
~~~~ mientras ~~~~
Mientras ~~~~, ~~~~

Mientras los estudiantes **nadaban,** yo **estaba** nerviosa. ¡Soy la entrenadora!
While the students were swimming, I was nervous. I'm the coach!

Use the **imperfect** and the **preterite** in the same sentence to tell what **was happening** when another action **took place**. I ~~~~

Cuando nos **llamaron** para darnos el trofeo, yo **estaba** llorando de felicidad.
When they called us to give us the trophy, I was crying with happiness.

3. Series of Completed Actions vs. Background Details

Use the **preterite** to express a ||series of completed actions||. ||

Use the **imperfect** to give |background| details of many kinds: time, location, weather, mood, age, physical and mental characteristics.

Durante el campeonato, mis estudiantes **nadaron** muy bien y lo **dieron** todo.
During the championship, my students swam well and gave it their all.

La competición **era** muy temprano por la mañana y **hacía** frío, pero mis estudiantes **estaban** preparadas física y mentalmente.
The competition was very early in the morning and it was cold, but my students were prepared physically and mentally.

4. Action vs. the Setting

The **preterite** and **imperfect** are also used together in the presentation of an event.

- The **imperfect** sets the |stage|, describes the |conditions| that caused the action, or emphasizes the |continuing nature| of a particular action.

- The **preterite** narrates the actions. ||||

El campeonato estatal **fue** el 10 de enero. **Era** un día de sol, pero **era** invierno y **hacía** mucho frío. **Salimos** de la escuela en bus a las cinco de la mañana para llegar a tiempo al centro deportivo. **Llegamos** pronto y **tuvimos** una reunión de equipo antes de calentar.
The state championship was on January 10th. It was a sunny day, but it was winter and it was very cold. We left the school by bus at five in the morning to arrive on time at the sports center. We arrived early and we had a team meeting before warming up.

Changes in Meaning / Los cambios de significado

Remember that, when used in the **preterite**, **saber, conocer,** and **(no) querer** have English equivalents different from that of their infinitives. (See **Gramática 24 [Cap. 9]**) In the **imperfect**, the English equivalents of these verbs do not differ from the infinitive meanings.

—¿Ya **sabías** que se murió el abuelo de Miguel?
—Sí, lo **supe** el mes pasado.
*"**Did** you already **know** that Miguel's grandfather passed away?"*
*"Yes, I **found out** (**learned**) about it last month."*

—Anoche **conocí** a Roberto.
—¿Anoche? Yo pensaba que ya lo **conocías.**
*"Last night I **met** Roberto."*
*"Last night? I thought you already **knew** him."*

—¿No **querías** hablar con el profesor ayer?
—Sí, **quise** llamarlo, pero no estaba en su oficina.
*"Didn't you **want** to talk to the professor yesterday?"*
*"Yes, I **tried** to call him but he wasn't in his office."*

Práctica y comunicación

A. En la escuela secundaria

Paso 1. Autoprueba. ¿Se usa el pretérito (P) o el imperfecto (I)?

1. _____ para dar detalles de fondo (*background details*) y descripciones como el tiempo y la hora
2. _____ para hablar de acciones habituales
3. _____ para narrar acciones completadas
4. _____ para hablar de una acción en progreso
5. _____ para narrar una secuencia de acciones
6. _____ para decir lo que pasaba cuando otra acción ocurrió
7. _____ para describir condiciones y estados físicos o afectivos

> **Preterite** vs. **Imperfect** Summary
>
> beginning/middle vs. habitual/repeated
> completed vs. ongoing
> actions vs. background
> action vs. setting

Prác. A, Paso 1: Answers: 1. I | 2. I | 3. P | 4. I | 5. P | 6. I | 7. I

Paso 2. ¿Cómo era su salud cuando usted estaba en la secundaria? ¿Tuvo algún problema de salud específico? Complete las siguientes oraciones con la forma apropiada del imperfecto o el pretérito. Use **no** cuando sea (*it's*) necesario. **¡OJO!** Si la situación ocurría regularmente o con frecuencia, use el **imperfecto**; si ocurrió solo una o dos veces, use el **pretérito**.

Cuando estaba en la secundaria...

1. _____ (resfriarse) con frecuencia
2. _____ (tener) alergias
3. _____ (tener) una operación
4. _____ (ir) al dentista con regularidad

5. _____ (tener) COVID / mononucleosis
6. _____ (hacer) mucho ejercicio
7. _____ (sufrir) (*to have*) un accidente de coche
8. _____ (gustarme) quedarme en casa y no ir a la escuela

Paso 3. Ahora, en parejas, túrnense para hacer y contestar preguntas basadas en las oraciones del **Paso 2**. Luego díganle a la clase algo que tienen en común.

MODELO: **1.** E1: Cuando estabas en la secundaria, ¿te resfriabas con frecuencia?
E2: No, no me resfriaba con frecuencia. ¿Y tú?
E1: Yo tampoco.

B. **En el consultorio.** Estos son algunos de los pacientes que el Dr. Sánchez vio ayer en el consultorio. Describa los síntomas de cada paciente. Luego empareje cada caso con lo que hizo el Dr. Sánchez y complete las oraciones.

LOS SÍNTOMAS (IMPERFECTO)

1. Un paciente: **tener** fiebre y dolor de cabeza
2. Una paciente: **tener** tos y dolor de garganta
3. A un niño: **doler** el pie
4. Una señora: **sentirse** muy mal en general
5. Un adolescente: solo **necesitar** el chequeo anual

POR ESO, EL DR. SÁNCHEZ... (PRETÉRITO)

a. _____ **pedirle** un análisis de sangre.
b. _____ **hacerle** sacar la lengua.
c. _____ **tomarle** la temperatura y **hacerle** un test de COVID.
d. _____ **decirle** que estaba muy bien.
e. _____ **pedirle** una radiografía (*X-ray*).

Nota comunicativa: Algunas palabras y expresiones asociadas con el pretérito y el imperfecto

Certain words and expressions are frequently associated with the preterite, others with the imperfect. Only the words that are translated are new.

Some words often associated with the **preterite** are:

ayer, anteayer, anoche (*last night*)	**de repente** (*suddenly*)
una vez, dos veces (*twice*)...	**enseguida**
el año pasado (*last*), **el lunes pasado**...	

Some words often associated with the **imperfect** are:

todos los días, todos los lunes...	**mientras**
siempre, frecuentemente (*frequently*)	**de niño/a, de adolescente**

As you continue to practice using the preterite and imperfect, these expressions can help you determine which tense to use. These words do not *automatically* cue either tense, however. The most important consideration is the meaning that you want to express.

Ayer <u>cenamos</u> temprano.	*Yesterday we had dinner early.*
Ayer <u>cenábamos</u> cuando Juan llamó.	*Yesterday we were having dinner when Juan called.*
<u>Jugaba</u> al fútbol **de niño**.	*He played soccer as a child.*
<u>Empezó</u> a jugar al fútbol **de niño**.	*He began to play soccer as a child.*

You will see these words and expressions in activities in the rest of this section and throughout the rest of *Puntos de partida*.

C. La última vez que...

Paso 1. Complete las siguientes oraciones con detalles personales verdaderos. Luego añada otros detalles.

La última vez que alguien me llamó por teléfono...

1. La última vez que alguien me llamó por teléfono fue _____ (ayer, anoche, esta mañana,...).
2. Cuando sonó el teléfono yo estaba _____ (estudiando, durmiendo,...) y estaba _____ (solo/a, con un amigo / una amiga, con...).
3. La persona que me llamó era _____ y hablamos por _____ (tiempo).
4. Cuando colgué (*I hung up*) el teléfono, me sentía _____ (contento/a, preocupado/a,...) y quería _____.

La última vez que me reí a carcajadas (*I laughed out loud*)...

1. La última vez que me reí a carcajadas fue _____.
2. Estaba en... y estaba _____ (acción).
3. Me reí tanto (*so much*) porque _____.
4. Después de reírme tanto, _____ (me sentí bien, me dolía el estómago,...).

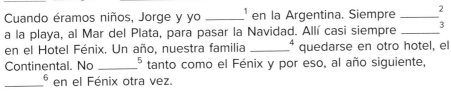

Paso 2. Ahora, en parejas, compartan (*share*) sus oraciones. Escojan (*Choose*) las respuestas más interesantes y compártanlas con la clase.

D. Pequeñas historias

Paso 1. Complete el siguiente párrafo con una de las palabras o frases de la lista. Antes de empezar, mire la foto que acompaña el párrafo para tener una idea general del tema de la historia.

íbamos, **nos gustó**, **nos quedábamos**, **nos quedamos**, **decidió**, **vivíamos**

Cuando éramos niños, Jorge y yo _____[1] en la Argentina. Siempre _____[2] a la playa, al Mar del Plata, para pasar la Navidad. Allí casi siempre _____[3] en el Hotel Fénix. Un año, nuestra familia _____[4] quedarse en otro hotel, el Continental. No _____[5] tanto como el Fénix y por eso, al año siguiente, _____[6] en el Fénix otra vez.

Paso 2. Ahora, para completar la siguiente historia, debe escoger (*choose*) entre el pretérito y el imperfecto en cada caso. Antes de empezar, mire el dibujo que acompaña el párrafo.

Eran las once de la noche y yo (**estaba** / **estuve**)[1] leyendo un libro, cuando de repente se (**apagaban** / **apagaron**[a])[2] todas las luces[b] de la casa. (**Ponía** / **Puse**)[3] el libro en el suelo[c] y luego (**usaba** / **usé**)[4] mi celular para tener algo de luz. La verdad es que (**tenía** / **tuve**)[5] mucho miedo. Por eso, (**salía** / **salí**)[6] a la calle.[d] Entonces (**podía** / **pude**)[7] ver que (**había** / **hubo**)[8] un apagón por todo el barrio.[e] La luz (**volvía** / **volvió**)[9] media hora después.

[a]apagar = *to go out*   [b]*lights*   [c]*floor*   [d]*street*   [e]un... *a power outage in the whole neighborhood*

E. Rubén y Soledad

Paso 1. Complete el párrafo con la forma apropiada de los infinitivos, en el pretérito o en el imperfecto.

Rubén estaba estudiando cuando Soledad entró en el cuarto. Ella le _____ (preguntar)[1] a Rubén si _____ (querer)[2] ir al cine. Rubén le _____ (decir)[3] que sí porque _____ (sentirse)[4] un poco aburrido de estudiar. Los dos _____ (salir)[5] enseguida para el cine. _____ (Ver)[6] una película cómica y _____ (reírse)[7] mucho. Luego, como _____ (hacer)[8] frío, _____ (entrar)[9] en su café favorito, El Gato Negro, y _____ (tomar)[10] churros y chocolate. _____ (Ser)[11] las dos de la mañana cuando por fin _____ (regresar)[12] a casa. Soledad _____ (acostarse)[13] enseguida porque _____ (estar)[14] cansada, pero Rubén _____ (empezar)[15] a estudiar otra vez.

Una merienda típicamente española: churros (*fried dough rolled in sugar*) y chocolate

Paso 2. Comprensión. Ahora conteste las siguientes preguntas, según el párrafo.

1. ¿Qué hacía Rubén cuando Soledad entró?
2. ¿Qué le preguntó Soledad a Rubén?
   (**Le preguntó si...**)
3. ¿Por qué le contestó Rubén que sí?
4. ¿Les gustó la película? ¿Cómo se sabe?
5. ¿Por qué tomaron churros y chocolate después de salir del cine?
6. ¿Qué hora era cuando regresaron a casa?
7. ¿Qué hicieron cuando llegaron a casa?

Estrategia

Una pregunta *no* se contesta siempre con el mismo tiempo verbal de la pregunta. Por ejemplo, si es necesario explicar por qué ocurrió algo (pretérito), se usa el imperfecto.

F. La historia afectiva de Simón Bolívar

Paso 1. Complete los siguientes párrafos con la forma apropiada de los infinitivos, en el pretérito o el imperfecto.

Simón Bolívar (1783–1830) fue el gran héroe de la independencia sudamericana. Bolívar no _____ (tener)[1] una vida personal muy afortunada. _____ (Ser)[2] hijo de una familia aristocrática española. _____ (Tener)[3] tres hermanos mayores. Sus padres _____ (morirse)[4] cuando Bolívar _____ (ser)[5] muy pequeño y por eso _____ (vivir)[6] varios años con otros parientes.

En 1798, cuando _____ (tener)[7] 15 años, _____ (irse)[8] a estudiar a Madrid. Allí _____ (conocer)[9] a María Teresa, con quien _____ (casarse[a])[10] en 1802. Bolívar _____ (regresar)[11] a Venezuela con su joven esposa. Pero María Teresa _____ (morir)[12] ocho meses después, víctima de la fiebre amarilla. Bolívar _____ (empezar)[13] su carrera[b] como líder nacional viajando por Europa para poder soportar[c] la muerte[d] de María Teresa. Nunca _____ (volver)[14] a casarse.

[a]*to marry* [b]*career* [c]*to deal with* [d]*death*

Paso 2. Comprensión. Conteste las siguientes preguntas.

1. En la familia de Bolívar, ¿era él hermano mayor o el menor (*the younger one*)?
2. ¿Cuántos años tenía Bolívar cuando se casó con María Teresa?
3. ¿De qué murió María Teresa?
4. ¿Por qué empezó a viajar Bolívar?

G. Una enfermedad durante la Navidad

Paso 1. Haga oraciones completas con la forma apropiada de los infinitivos, en el pretérito o el imperfecto.

1. Cuando yo _____ (ser) niño, _____ (pensar) que lo mejor de estar enfermo _____ (ser) pasar el día en casa.
2. Lo peor _____ (ser) que yo _____ (resfriarse) con frecuencia durante las vacaciones.
3. Una vez _____ (*yo*: ponerse) muy enfermo durante la Navidad.
4. Mi madre _____ (llamar) al médico porque yo _____ (tener) una fiebre muy alta.
5. El Dr. Matamoros _____ (venir) a casa enseguida y _____ (ponerme) una inyección de antibióticos porque yo _____ (tener) una infección de garganta.
6. Desgraciadamente (*Unfortunately*), mis padres _____ (tener) que darme un baño de agua fría para bajarme la fiebre, y eso no _____ (gustarme) para nada.

Algo sobre Simón Bolívar

Simón Bolívar (1783–1830), el Libertador

Simón Bolívar fue un general y político venezolano que es conocido[a] en Latinoamérica como el Libertador. Fue la figura principal en el movimiento por la independencia de España de varios países latinoamericanos (Venezuela, Colombia, Panamá, el Perú, Bolivia y el Ecuador). Desde 1819 hasta 1830 fue presidente de la Gran Colombia, una unión de naciones hispanohablantes que se estableció después de ganar su independencia de España. La Gran Colombia duró[b] solo hasta 1831.

 ¿Quién es el gran héroe de la independencia de los Estados Unidos? ¿Qué cargos[c] tuvo?

[a]*known* [b]*lasted* [c]*positions*

7. Tengo que decir que no _____ (ser) la mejor Navidad de mi vida.

8. Mis primos _____ (venir) a casa, pero yo _____ (estar) demasiado enfermo para jugar.

9. ¡Pero esa Navidad mis abuelos _____ (regalarme) mi primera PlayStation!

Paso 2. Ahora, en parejas, hablen de la última vez que no se sintieron bien. No olviden usar los verbos en la forma de **tú** para entrevistarse y en la forma de **yo** para contestar.

MODELO: **1.** **E1:** ¿Cuándo te enfermaste la última vez?
E2: Me enfermé el mes pasado. ¿Y tú?

1. ¿Cuándo se enfermaron la última vez?
2. ¿Fue algo serio? ¿Qué síntomas tenían?
3. ¿Fueron al médico? ¿Pudieron ir a clase o al trabajo?
4. ¿Qué hicieron para cuidarse? ¿Alguien los cuidó?
5. ¿Tomaron alguna medicina?

H. Una historia famosa

Paso 1. En la siguiente historia, los verbos se dan en el presente. Póngalos en el pretérito para narrar la historia en el pasado.

La niña _____ (abre)[1] la puerta y _____ (entra)[2] en la casa. _____ (Ve)[3] tres sillas. _____ (Se sienta)[4] en la primera silla, luego en la segunda,[a] pero no le _____ (gusta)[5] ninguna. Por eso _____ (se sienta)[6] en la tercera.[b] _____ (Ve)[7] tres platos de comida en la mesa y _____ (decide)[8] comer el más pequeño. Luego, _____ (va)[9] a la habitación para descansar un poco. Después de probar[c] las camas grandes, _____ (se acuesta)[10] en la cama más pequeña y _____ (se queda)[11] dormida.[d]

[a]second [b]third [c]trying [d]asleep

Paso 2. ¿Reconoce usted la historia? Es el cuento de Ricitos de Oro (lit., *Little Golden Curls*) y los tres osos (*bears*). Pero el cuento es un poco aburrido tal como está escrito (*as it is written*) en el **Paso 1.** Mejórelo (*Improve it*) con palabras de **Vocabulario útil** y dando detalles y descripciones (usando el imperfecto). También debe terminar el cuento: ¿Qué pasó al final?

MODELO: Había una vez una niña que **se llamaba** Ricitos de Oro. Un día la niña **fue...**

I. Un evento increíble: Cuando conocí a...

Paso 1. Imagine que usted conoció recientemente a su persona famosa favorita. Conteste las siguientes preguntas de su amigo/a, que siente mucha curiosidad y envidia (*envy*). Puede cambiar el orden de las preguntas de su amigo/a para adaptar el diálogo a sus necesidades. ¡Use su creatividad y diviértase!

—¿Qué? ¿En serio conociste a _____?
—¿Dónde estabas?
—¿Qué hora era?
—¿Con quién estabas? ¿Y con quién estaba él/ella?
—¿Qué estaban haciendo?
—¿Cómo se conocieron? ¿Alguien los presentó (*introduced*)?
—¡No me digas! ¿Qué te dijo? Y tú, ¿qué le dijiste?
—¿Y entonces qué pasó?

> **Vocabulario útil**
>
> **Había una vez... +** *imp.* Once upon a time there was ...
> **Un día... +** *pret.*
>
> **el bosque** forest
> **la casita** little house
>
> **huir** to flee*

> **Vocabulario útil**
>
> **¿En serio?** Seriously?
> **¡No me digas!** Really! (*lit. Don't tell me!*)
> **¡Es increíble!** It's incredible/amazing!

---

*Present tense forms of **huir** have a **y** (*rather than an* **i**) *in the stem-changing pattern:* **huyo, huyes**... **Y** *is also used in the preterite third person singular and plural forms* (*like* **leer**): **huyó, huyeron**. *The present participle is* **huyendo.**

(Continúa).

Paso 2. Ahora, en parejas, túrnense para representar sus diálogos. ¿Quién tiene la historia más increíble?

J. Una visita extraña

Paso 1. En parejas, usen las siguientes ideas para inventar una ocasión extraordinaria: el día que vieron un ovni (objeto volante no identificado [*UFO*]). Recuerden que el color del verbo indica qué tiempo deben usar: verde = el imperfecto y rojo = el pretérito.

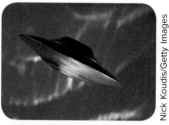
Nick Koudis/Getty Images

Un ovni (objeto volante no identificado)

Vocabulario útil

el casco	helmet
la luz	light
(*pl.* **luces**)	
la nave	space
espacial	craft
el traje	space
espacial	suit
quedarse	to stay
salir huyendo	to flee
saludar	to greet

- el trasfondo (*background*) y la situación
  ser (fecha o estación del año, tiempo del día)
  ser/hacer (tiempo atmosférico)
  estar (qué personas en su grupo / el lugar)

- el principio del contacto
  aterrizar (*to land*) una nave espacial
  abrirse la puerta
  salir los extraterrestres

- descripción de los extraterrestres
  ser (color, tamaño [*size*], número de ojos...)
  llevar (ropa o complementos)

- más acciones y el final
  decir/hacer (los extraterrestres, ustedes)

Paso 2. Compartan su historia con el resto de la clase. ¿Cuál es la historia mejor narrada (*narrated*)? ¿Y la más fantástica o divertida?

Textos de todos los días: Telemedicina

Hoy día es frecuente que muchas personas tengan una telecita con un médico o médica (por teléfono o videollamada). En esta actividad usted va a hacer una telecita.

Objetivo: Mandar un mensaje electrónico para hacer una cita de telemedicina, explicando por qué necesita la cita. Esto requiere una explicación breve de sus síntomas.

Antes de empezar: Piense en el tipo de información que normalmente es necesario proporcionar (*to provide*) para obtener una cita médica.

TELECONSULTA

Para pedir una cita es necesario introducir todos los datos.[a]
Nombre(s)

Apellido(s)

¿Está asegurada/o[b] con nosotros?   ☐ Sí   ☐ No
Número de asegurado/a

Teléfono de contacto

¿Cómo desea la cita?   ☐ Por teléfono   ☐ Por videollamada
¿Cómo desea recibir la hora de su cita?

☐ Por correo electrónico   ☐ Por mensaje telefónico
Describa brevemente cuáles son sus síntomas, incluyendo cuándo comenzó a sentirlos.

Enviar

Recibirá[c] la hora de su cita en menos de dos horas.

[a]*information*   [b]*insured*   [c]*You will receive*

Algo sobre la emigración venezolana de años recientes

Desde principios de este milenio, se calcula que más de siete millones de venezolanos han abandonado[a] su país, debido a[b] la gravísima crisis política y económica que sufre Venezuela desde entonces. Este éxodo se considera la crisis migratoria más grave de la historia de Latinoamérica. Colombia y el Perú, seguidos del[c] Ecuador, los Estados Unidos, Chile y España, son los países que han recibido[d] un mayor número de personas de Venezuela.

 ¿Hay una comunidad de origen venezolano o de algún país hispanohablante donde usted vive?

[a]han... *have left*   [b]debido... *due to*   [c]seguidos... *followed by*   [d]han... *have received*

Un hombre con la bandera venezolana protesta contra la situación del país.

Ruben Alfonzo/Shutterstock

Repaso

Que is one of the most frequently used words in the Spanish language, and it has several meanings. Review what you already know about **que** by expressing the following sentences in English.

1. ¿Qué estudias?
2. Tengo que hacer la tarea.
3. No entiendo lo que usted me dice.
4. Creo que la fórmula es correcta.

In **Gramática 31,** you will learn more about **que** and other related terms that you have been using for a while: **quien** and **lo que.**

---

31 Recognizing **que, quien(es), lo que** • Relative Pronouns

Gramática en acción: Personal médico hispanohablante: Siempre contigo

> La Organización de Clínicas Hispanohablantes ¡Te cuidamos en tu lengua!
>
> *Tu personal médico hispanohablante son personas...*
>
> - con **quienes** puedes hablar de TODAS tus cuestiones de salud.
> - **que** pueden explicarte TODO **lo que** necesitas saber y comprender.
> - **que** tienen consultorios y personal **que** están CERCA de ti.
> - **que** ofrecen TELECONSULTAS.
> - **que** hablan ESPAÑOL.

¿Y usted?

Complete las oraciones con el nombre de una persona que usted conoce. Incluya la relación que tiene con usted, por ejemplo: **mi madre.**

1. Una persona **que** tiene mi total confianza es _____.
2. Una persona con **quien** hablo si necesito ayuda, no importa en qué situación, es _____.
3. Una persona **que** sabe todo—o casi todo—**lo que** pasa en mi vida es _____.

Spanish-speaking medical personnel: Always with you. The Organization of Spanish-speaking Clinics We take care of you in your language! Your Spanish-speaking medical personnel are people ■ *with whom you can speak about ALL of your health-related questions.* ■ *who can explain to you EVERYTHING that you need to know and understand.* ■ *who have offices and personnel that are CLOSE to you.* ■ *who offer TELEVISITS.* ■ *who speak SPANISH.*

Gramática   trescientos cuarenta y uno ■ **341**

Relative Pronouns / **Los pronombres relativos**

a relative pronoun / **un pronombre relativo** = a pronoun that refers back to a noun or phrase already mentioned

Relative pronouns (**Los pronombres relativos**) are words that connect ideas within one sentence. Most frequently they refer back to a noun or an idea that has already been mentioned. In both English and Spanish, these words make communication more efficient and fluid because they help to avoid unnecessary repetition by linking ideas. Notice how this happens in these sentences.

Conozco a una **médica**. Es de Venezuela. → Conozco a una médica **que** es de Venezuela.

*I know a **doctor**. She is from Venezuela.* → *I know a doctor **who** is from Venezuela.*

The Spanish language has several relative pronouns. You will learn only three of them in this section.

1. Relative Pronouns

There are four principal *relative pronouns* in English: *that, which, who,* and *whom.* They are usually expressed in Spanish by the relative pronouns in the chart, all of which you already know.

Los pronombres relativos	
que = refers to things and people	*that, which, who*
quien(es) = refers only to people	*who(m)*
lo que = refers to a situation	*what, that which*

2. *que* = *that, which, who*

Que is by far the most frequently used relative pronoun in Spanish. It refers to people and things.

¡OJO!

Que cannot be used after a preposition to refer to people. See Point 3.

Tuve **una cita** con mi médico **que** duró una hora.
*I had an appointment with my doctor **that** lasted an hour.*

Es **un buen médico que** tiene mucha experiencia.
*He's a good doctor **who** has a lot of experience.*

3. *quien, quienes* = *who(m)*

Quien and **quienes** can refer only to people. They are almost always used after a preposition.

La mujer **con quien** hablaba es mi médica.
*The woman **with whom** I was speaking is my doctor. (The woman I was speaking with is my doctor.)*

Las enfermeras **a quienes** les dimos las flores cuidaron a mi padre.
*The nurses **to whom** we gave the flowers took care of my dad. (The nurses we gave the flowers to took care of my dad.)*

4. *lo que* = *what, that which, the thing that*

Lo que always refers to a whole situation or idea. It can refer to something that has been mentioned before or to something that will be referred to later in the sentence. It frequently starts sentences.

¡OJO!

If you can substitute *that which* for *what* in a sentence, use **lo que**, not **que**.

No entiendo **lo que** dijo.
*I don't understand **what (that which)** he said.*

Lo que necesito es **estudiar más.**
What (The thing that) I need is to study more.

5. Relative Pronouns versus Interrogatives

Que and **quien(es)** sound like **¿qué?** and **¿quién(es)?**, but they are not the same.

- **Que** and **quien(es)** link words within a sentence.
- **¿Qué?** and **¿quién(es)?** ask questions (and they have an accent mark to distinguish them from the relative pronouns).

—**¿Qué** es eso?
—Es una cosa **que** sirve para ver mejor.
"**What** is this?"
"It's something **that** helps you see better."

—**¿Quién** es ese señor?
—Es el profesor con **quien** tengo la clase de psicología.
"**Who** is that man?"
"He's the professor **with whom** I take Psychology."

Práctica y comunicación

A. ¿Que, quien(es) o lo que?

Paso 1. Autoprueba. Complete las oraciones con el pronombre relativo apropiado. **¡OJO!** Uno de los pronombres se puede usar en dos oraciones.

lo que   que   quien   quienes

1. ¿Ves el teléfono _____ está en la mesa de Tino?
2. Tino es un enfermero _____ habla español.
3. Tino es el enfermero con _____ hablé ayer.
4. Tino y Luis son los profesionales a _____ consulté.
5. _____ Tino me dijo me ayudó mucho.

> **Summary of Relative Pronouns**
>
> **que** = that, which, who
> **quien(es)** = preposition + whom
> **lo que** = what, that which, the thing that

Paso 2. Empareje los elementos de las dos columnas. **¡OJO!** Puede repetir las personas de la Columna B.

COLUMNA A

1. _____ Es lo que me dijo mi madre antes de salir para la universidad.
2. _____ Es la persona en quien yo más confío.
3. _____ Es lo que más me importa en la vida.
4. _____ Es la persona que más me apoya (supports).
5. _____ Es lo que necesito hacer para graduarme.

COLUMNA B

a. «Come bien y duerme lo suficiente».
b. mi mejor amigo/a
c. mi familia
d. mi madre/padre
e. sacar notas aceptables

Paso 3. Ahora, en parejas, túrnense para hacer y contestar preguntas usando las ideas de la Columna A en el **Paso 2.**

MODELO: **4.** E1: ¿Quién es la persona **que** más te apoya?
E2: (Es) Mi madre. ¿Y a ti?
E1: (Es) Mi mejor amiga.

B. El estrés, la condición humana. Lea la siguiente tira cómica y complete las oraciones.

[a]cansancio... fatigue, restlessness, worry, nervousness, (emotional) imbalance, and anxiety   [b]as of yet

1. Lo que quiere el padre de Libertad es _____.
2. Lo que su padre tiene es _____.
3. Según el médico, lo que tiene su padre es _____.

Prác. A, Paso 1: Answers: 1. que 2. que 3. quien 4. quienes 5. Lo que

C. En la preadolescencia

Paso 1. Complete las siguientes oraciones con detalles de su vida personal.

Cuando yo tenía doce o trece años...

1. lo que más me divertía/molestaba era _____.
2. el personaje (*character*) que más me gustaba era _____.
3. la persona / las personas que yo más quería (*loved*) era(n) _____.

Paso 2. Ahora, en parejas, comparen sus respuestas.

♻ Repaso

Before learning how to express reciprocal actions in **Gramática 32,** review the reflexive pronouns in **Gramática 14 (Cap. 5),** and then provide the correct reflexive pronouns for the following sentences.

1. _____ levanté a las ocho y media.
2. Laura _____ puso el vestido.
3. Mis amigos y yo _____ sentamos en un café.
4. ¿Prefieres duchar_____ o bañar_____?

---

32 Expressing *each other* (Part 2) • Reciprocal Actions with Reflexive Pronouns

Gramática en acción: La amistad

Hola Images/Getty Images

Los buenos amigos...

- **se conocen** bien.
- **se respetan.**
- **se quieren.**
- **se recuerdan** siempre.

En las culturas hispanas, cuando las buenas amigas **se encuentran, se besan** en la mejilla.

¿Y usted?

Cuando usted y sus amigos **se encuentran,** ¿cómo **se saludan** (*do you greet each other*)? **¿Se dan** la mano? ¿**Se besan?**

Reciprocal Actions / Las acciones recíprocas

1. Reciprocal Actions

Reciprocal actions (**Las acciones recíprocas**) are actions that involve two or more people doing something *to* or *for* each other. They are usually expressed in English with *each other* or *one another.* In Spanish, reciprocal actions are expressed with pronouns that are identical to the plural reflexive pronouns.

nos = each other (**nosotros/as**)
os = each other (**vosotros/as**)
se = each other (**ustedes, ellos/as**)

Nos queremos.	*We love each other.*
¿Os ayudáis?	*Do you help one another?*
Se miran con ternura.	*They're looking at each other tenderly.*

Friendship Good friends ... ■ *know each other well.* ■ *respect each other.* ■ *are fond of each other.* ■ *always remember each other. In Hispanic cultures, when close women friends meet, they kiss each other on the cheek.*

2. Verbs Frequently Used to Express Reciprocal Actions

Verbs frequently used in this way include those at right, but any verb to whose meaning the phrase *each other* can be added may express a reciprocal action: **hablarse, mirarse, pelearse,** and so on.

Most of these verbs are new. The verbs **darse, encontrarse,** and **quererse** are new to you with their reciprocal meaning.

abra<u>z</u>arse (<u>c</u>)	to embrace
besarse	to kiss each other
<u>d</u>arse la mano	to shake hands
enc<u>o</u>ntrarse	to meet (*someone*
(se enc<u>ue</u>ntran)	*somewhere*)
<u>q</u>uer<u>e</u>rse	to love each other; to be fond of each other
saludarse	to greet each other

¡OJO!

Sometimes a preposition is added in English to express the meaning of these verbs: **hablarse** = *to talk **to** each other*, **mirarse** = *to look **at** each other*, **pelearse** = *to fight **with** each other*. But no preposition is needed in Spanish.

Práctica y comunicación

A. Los buenos amigos

> ### Reciprocal Action Summary
>
> **nos, os, se** + verb = each other, one another

Paso 1. Autoprueba. Dé el pronombre apropiado para expresar acciones recíprocas.

1. _____ miramos
2. _____ pelearon
3. _____ conocen
4. _____ llamaban
5. _____ saludamos

Paso 2. ¿Qué hace usted con sus buenos amigos? Conteste usando **nos** (el pronombre recíproco). Si una oración no es cierta para usted, use **no**.

MODELO: abrazar cuando ver → **Nos abrazamos** cuando **nos vemos.**

1. _____ (ver) con frecuencia
2. _____ (conocer) bien
3. _____ (respetar) mucho
4. _____ (ayudar) cuando necesitamos ayuda
5. _____ (mandar) muchos mensajes
6. _____ (hablar) por teléfono con frecuencia
7. _____ (decir) la verdad siempre, lo bueno y lo malo
8. ¿ ?

Paso 3. Ahora, en parejas, túrnense para hacer y contestar preguntas basadas en el **Paso 2.** Luego, díganle a la clase algo que tienen en común.

MODELO: E1: ¿Tus amigos y tú **se abrazan** cuando **se ven**?
E2: Sí, con frecuencia **nos abrazamos** cuando **nos vemos** después de un tiempo. ¿Y ustedes?
E1: Nosotros también **nos abrazamos.**

B. ¿Qué pasa entre ellos? Describa las siguientes relaciones familiares o sociales, haciendo oraciones completas con una palabra o frase de cada columna.

MODELO: Los buenos amigos **se conocen** bien.

los buenos amigos los parientes los esposos los padres y los niños los amigos que no viven en la misma ciudad los profesores y los estudiantes los compañeros de cuarto/casa	+ (no) +	visitarse con frecuencia quererse, respetarse, necesitarse, conocerse bien ayudarse mutuamente (en las tareas domésticas, cuando tienen problemas económicos o problemas personales) verse (todos los días, con frecuencia) llamarse por teléfono, escribirse mirarse (con cariño [*affection*]) saludarse, darse la mano quejarse sinceramente, escucharse

Prác. A, Paso 1: Answers: 1. nos 2. se 3. se 4. se 5. nos

C. Intercambios

Paso 1. Haga una pregunta en el presente con cada una de las siguientes frases. En el **Paso 2,** va a usar esas preguntas para entrevistar a alguien de la clase sobre sus relaciones con su pareja, sus amigos, sus padres y sus parientes.

MODELOS: **6.** besarse → ¿Tu pareja y tú se besan en público?

1. verse
2. escribirse
3. mantenerse en contacto
4. llamarse por teléfono
5. abrazarse
6. besarse
7. saludarse dándose la mano
8. pelearse

Paso 2. Ahora, en parejas, túrnense para hacerse las preguntas del **Paso 1.** Luego, díganle a la clase lo que tienen en común.

Todo junto

Algo sobre el lago de Maracaibo

Paolo Costa/Shutterstock

El lago de Maracaibo, el más grande de toda Latinoamérica

El lago de Maracaibo ocupa el puesto[a] 19 entre los lagos más grandes del mundo. En la actualidad, conecta con el golfo de Venezuela en el norte, que lo hace una bahía semicerrada salobre.[b] Pero está documentado que fue originalmente un lago cerrado, uno de los más antiguos de la Tierra. Numerosos ríos[c] vierten[d] sus aguas en el lago de Maracaibo.

¿Cuál es el lago más grande de su estado? ¿Y del país?

[a]*spot* [b]*bahía... semi-closed brackish bay* [c]*rivers* [d]*empty*

A. Lengua y cultura: La leyenda del lago de Maracaibo

Paso 1. Completar. Complete the following legend with the correct form of the word in parentheses, as suggested by context. The verbs will be in the preterite or imperfect. When two possibilities are given in parentheses, select the correct word.

Había una vez[a] un cacique[b] indígena que se llamaba Zapara. Este[c] tenía una hija, Maruma, que _____ (ser)[1] muy bonita. Al padre y a la hija (se / les)[2] _____ (gustar)[3] pasar tiempo juntos y caminar por el bosque.[d]

Un día Zapara _____ (comprender)[4] que su hija ya _____ (ser)[5] una mujer y (se / le)[6] _____ (decir)[7]: «Debes escoger[e] esposo. Pero (su / tu)[8] esposo debe ser guerrero,[f] como todos los hombres de nuestra familia».

Un día, Maruma _____ (salir)[9] sola a cazar[g] en el bosque. Iba a dispararle a un ciervo[h] pero un joven lo _____ (matar[i])[10] antes. Primero Maruma _____ (ponerse)[11] muy enojada, pero el joven, (que / quienes)[12] _____ (ser[13]) guapo y simpático, dijo: «El ciervo es para (tú / ti).[14] Solo quiero conocerte. Me llamo Tamaré». A partir de ese día[j] los _____ (joven)[15] _____ (hacerse[k])[16] amigos. Pronto se enamoraron.[l]

Desgraciadamente, Tamaré no _____ (ser)[17] un buen guerrero. Por eso el padre de Maruma _____ (enojarse)[18] muchísimo con la elección de esposo de su hija. Entonces _____ (haber)[19] grandes desastres naturales que cubrieron[m] de agua sus tierras. Esta _____ (ser)[20] la creación del lago de Maracaibo y Zapara se convirtió en una de sus pequeñas islas.

[a]Había... *Once upon a time there was* [b]*chief* [c]*He* [d]*forest* [e]*choose* [f]*a warrior* [g]*hunt* [h]Iba... *She was going to shoot a deer* [i]*to kill* [j]A... *From that day on* [k]*to become* [l]se... *they fell in love* [m]*covered*

Paso 2. Comprensión. Conteste las siguientes preguntas.

1. ¿Quién era Zapara?
2. ¿De quién se enamoró (*fell in love*) Maruma?
3. ¿Por qué se enojó Zapara?
4. ¿Cómo se formó el lago de Maracaibo?

 Paso 3. En acción

 Ahora, en parejas, cuenten una versión sencilla (*simple*) de una leyenda de su país. Si no saben una leyenda, pueden contar un cuento (*story*) tradicional.

Estrategia

Aquí hay varias sugerencias (*suggestions*) para contar la leyenda.

- Para empezar la historia (*story*): Había una vez... + **imperfecto** (Use más de un verbo para describir a los protagonistas o el lugar donde estaban).
- Para empezar con la acción: Un día / Una noche... + **pretérito**
- Para continuar con la secuencia de acciones: Entonces / Después / Luego... + **pretérito**
- Para terminar: Finalmente / Afortunadamente / Desgraciadamente... + **pretérito**

B. Proyecto: Un anuncio° de prevención contra una enfermedad común

announcement

En grupos, van a trabajar juntos para crear y grabar (*create and record*) un anuncio informativo audiovisual sobre una enfermedad común y cómo prevenirla. Imaginen que están haciendo el anuncio para la población hispanohablante en general.

Paso 1. Preparación. Primero, elijan una enfermedad o condición física común. Busquen en internet un artículo o documento de algún país hispanohablante sobre una campaña de prevención de esa enfermedad o condición. Ese texto va a ser útil para aprender el vocabulario necesario.

Paso 2. Organización. Identifiquen la información más importante que deben darles a sus oyentes (*listeners*) y preparen el texto. Consideren:

- de qué forma van a dar la información (Recuerden que es un anuncio para la población en general, por eso no deben usar palabras muy difíciles y especializadas).
- las formas de los mandatos para dar instrucciones
- qué tipo de imágenes van a usar
- la pronunciación de las palabras nuevas

Paso 3. Creación. Finalmente, graben su anuncio y preséntenlo a la clase.

Video: Salu2 «Remedios para todos»

You can watch two segments of this chapter's video in the **Video: Salu2** section, found at the end of the eBook.

Klic Video Productions/McGraw Hill

Una botánica (*herb store*) en Puerto Rico

Enfoque cultural: El cuidado de la salud

Antes de leer

¿Tiene usted seguro (*insurance*) médico? ¿Lo tiene a través de (*through*) la universidad, de su trabajo o del trabajo de sus padres?

En Venezuela

Caracas, Venezuela

Desde el cambio[a] de milenio Venezuela sufre una grave crisis política y económica. La situación empeoró[b] en 2013, cuando hubo un cambio de presidente y un descenso[c] en la producción de petróleo, la fuente de ingresos[d] más importante del país. Esta situación ha provocado una emigración venezolana de más de siete millones de personas y se considera la segunda crisis migratoria internacional más grave en tiempos recientes, solo después de la[e] de Siria.

Uno de los sectores más afectados por la crisis es el[f] de la salud, que es, en general, muy deficiente. Existía un sistema público de salud que cubría[g] a la gente que no podía pagar un seguro médico privado.

Había consultorios médicos, clínicas y hospitales que proveían de[h] todo tipo de servicios relacionados con la salud a las personas que los necesitaban. Pero en la actualidad el país no tiene recursos[i] suficientes para mantener[j] los hospitales y clínicas. Y, desgraciadamente, pocos venezolanos tienen dinero suficiente para pagar los tratamientos que necesitan.

[a]Desde... *Since the change*   [b]*became worse*   [c]*decline*   [d]fuente... *source of income*   [e]*that*   [f]*that*   [g]*covered*   [h]proveían... *provided*   [i]*resources*   [j]*maintain*

Comprensión ¿Cuál es la situación de Venezuela en la actualidad? ¿Qué consecuencias tiene esta situación?

En otros países hispanos

Señal para un centro de salud español

- **En Latinoamérica** Es muy diversa la manera en que cada país provee de asistencia sanitaria[a] a sus habitantes: a través de[b] un sistema exclusivamente gubernamental[c] o por medio de[d] una combinación de sistemas públicos y privados. El acceso al cuidado médico también varía mucho de país a país. Hay países como la Argentina, Cuba y Costa Rica que proporcionan[e] acceso a todas las personas. Desgraciadamente, en otros países hay un considerable número de personas que no tienen acceso fácil a médicos y medicinas.

- **En España** España tiene un sistema nacional de seguridad social y médico para todos los ciudadanos.[f] Este sistema, con otros factores, contribuye a que los españoles tengan una de las esperanzas de vida[g] más largas del mundo.

[a]*health*   [b]a... *via*   [c]*government-run*   [d]por... *through*   [e]*provide*   [f]*citizens*   [g]esperanzas... *life expectancies*

Comprensión ¿Es similar en los países hispanohablantes el acceso a la asistencia médica? ¿Qué país tiene un sistema nacional para toda la población?

En acción

Haga una lista de seis tipos de profesionales relacionadas a la medicina (no debe usar médico/a, enfermero/a o dentista). Puede buscar en internet o preguntarle a una persona hispanohablante. ¿Hay muchos cognados?

<table>
<tr><td colspan="2">Vocabulario para leer</td></tr>
</table>

la infusión de hierbas	herbal tea
la jaqueca	migraine
curarse	to be cured
dejar	to leave

Lectura

Antes de leer

Las relaciones sentimentales pueden ser complicadas y a veces difíciles. ¿Puede usted pensar en algunos consejos o sugerencias para darle a una persona que está en una relación sentimental que le está causando mucho estrés *(stress)*?

«Prescripción», de Daisy Zamora

Ni acupuntura,
ni infusión de hierbas,
ni antidepresivos,
ni inyecciones —señora—
la jaqueca se cura solamente
dejando a su marido.

Comprensión

A. Un problema de salud. Identifique lo siguiente en el poema.

1. un problema de salud
2. cuatro tratamientos posibles
3. una cura

B. Un problema del corazón. Imagine la situación, entre la señora y su marido, implícita en este poema.

1. En su opinión, ¿son apropiados para curar una jaqueca los tratamientos mencionados en los primeros cuatro versos *(lines)* del poema? Explique.
2. ¿Está usted de acuerdo con la cura que se sugiere en este poema? ¿Hay situaciones donde la única solución apropiada es dejar a la pareja?
3. ¿Cuál es el tono del poema? ¿Es dramático, humorístico, irónico... ? ¿Por qué piensa usted así *(so)*?

⚙ Proyecto: Una cura infalible

Ahora usted va a escribir su propio poema describiendo tratamientos posibles e infalibles para curar algún problema de salud.

Paso 1. Identifique un problema de salud física o mental muy común.

Paso 2. Luego piense en dos o tres tratamientos inútiles *(useless)* y una solución más efectiva para el problema que ha identificado *(you have identified)*.

Paso 3. Ahora escriba un poema para una persona que sufre este problema, siguiendo el mismo formato de «Prescripción».

🔊 Textos orales

Campaña de vacunación contra la gripe

Antes de escuchar

¿Qué precauciones toma usted para no enfermarse? ¿Tuvo usted algún resfriado el año pasado? ¿alguna gripe? ¿Fue al médico con frecuencia durante el último año?

Vocabulario para escuchar

vacunarse	to get a shot	**de alto riesgo**	high-risk
la muerte	death	**embarazadas**	pregnant
contraer (*like* <u>traer</u>)	to get; to contract (*an illness*)	**peligroso/a**	dangerous

---

Comprensión

A. La gripe. Conteste las siguientes preguntas sobre esta enfermedad, según la información en el anuncio.

1. ¿Aproximadamente cuántas personas van al hospital cada año en los Estados Unidos a causa de la gripe?
2. ¿Cuántas personas mueren anualmente en los Estados Unidos a causa de la gripe, aproximadamente?
3. ¿Hay solo un tipo de virus de gripe?

B. La vacuna. Conteste las siguientes preguntas sobre la campaña de vacunación.

1. ¿Quiénes deben vacunarse contra la gripe?
2. ¿Quiénes se consideran personas de alto riesgo?
3. ¿Quiénes no pueden recibir la vacuna?

👆 En acción

👥 Haga una encuesta entre las personas de la clase para ver quién ya se vacunó contra la gripe y si se vacuna todos los años. ¿Cree que el porcentaje de personas vacunadas en la clase es alto, normal o bajo en comparación con el (*that*) del resto del país?

Iborgephoto123/Shutterstock

🎤 Entrevista

Use de modelo las preguntas y respuestas de la sección **Entrevista** al principio de este capítulo para hablar del tipo de vida que usted lleva y de su salud en general.

💻 Escritura

La historia de una enfermedad

Usted ya ha hablado (*You've already talked*) en este capítulo de sus enfermedades. Ahora va a escribir un ensayo sobre una enfermedad que sufrió una persona de la clase.

Tenía fiebre y tuvo que guardar cama.

Eldar Nurkovic/123RF

👥 Antes de escribir

En parejas, entrevístense sobre una enfermedad que sufrieron. Piensen en la información que van a necesitar para escribir la narración de una enfermedad. Aquí hay algunos ejemplos. Ustedes deben añadir por lo menos 3 o 4 preguntas. **¡OJO!** Usen el pretérito y el imperfecto con cuidado.

1. ¿Fue una enfermedad grave o leve (*minor*)? ¿O era crónica?
2. ¿Cuándo ocurrió? ¿Cuántos años tenías?
3. ¿Cuáles eran los síntomas?
4. ¿ ?

A escribir

Ahora escriba la narración, usando la información que consiguió en **Antes de escribir.** O, si usted prefiere, puede escribir sobre la enfermedad de un amigo o un pariente. Hay más ayuda en Connect.

Para escribir bien

Considere estas opciones para su ensayo:

- Palabras y expresiones para marcar el tiempo y la secuencia de acciones: **ayer, anteayer, anoche, la semana pasada, un día, una vez**
- Otras expresiones para indicar cómo pasan las acciones: **de repente, frecuentemente, desgraciadamente...**
- Conectores de ideas: **pero, también, además, sin embargo, en contraste**
- Expresiones para cualificar una situación: **lo bueno / malo / importante**

En la comunidad

Entreviste a una persona hispana de su universidad o ciudad sobre el cuidado médico en su país de origen.

Preguntas posibles

- En su país de origen, ¿qué hace una persona cuando tiene una enfermedad que no es muy seria? ¿Va al médico? ¿Habla con el farmacéutico? ¿Va a alguna persona que cura con remedios naturales?
- ¿Qué alimentos se consideran muy sanos en su país? ¿Se usan algunos productos naturales? ¿Cuáles son? ¿Para qué sirven de remedio?
- ¿Cómo se dice *flu* en su país? ¿Y *cold*?

Producción audiovisual

Filme a una persona que habla de un remedio casero (*homemade*) que se usa en su familia. Puede ser algo serio o cómico.

Más ideas para el portafolio

- Incluya 5 consejos que usted considera fundamentales para estar bien físicamente.
- Dé un resumen de su historia favorita (de un libro o una película) cuando usted era pequeño/a.
- Si ha estado jugando (*you have been playing*) Practice Spanish: Study Abroad, en Quest 8 usted leyó la historia de los dos cadejos (animales fantásticos), una leyenda que trata del equilibrio (*deals with the balance*) entre el bien y el mal. ¿Conoce usted otras historias sobre la armonía entre el bien y el mal? Escriba un informe (*report*) que resuma la leyenda de los dos cadejos y compárela con leyendas, cuentos (*stories*) o creencias (*beliefs*) de su propia cultura o de otras culturas que usted conoce sobre el bien y el mal.

Sugerencia: You are now ready to play Quest 8 in **Practice Spanish: Study Abroad.**

EN RESUMEN En este capítulo

AFTER STUDYING THIS CHAPTER I CAN ...

☐ name many parts of the body and activities related to a healthy life (328)

☐ talk about illnesses and medical exams (330)

☐ use the preterite and imperfect together to talk about the past and tell stories (333–335)

☐ use **que, quien,** and **lo que** to avoid repetition (341–343)

☐ express the concept of "each other" with pronouns (344)

☐ recognize/describe at least 2–3 aspects of Venezuelan cultures

Gramática en breve

30. Using the <u>Preterite</u> and the <u>Imperfect</u>

Uses of the <u>Preterite</u>	Uses of the <u>Imperfect</u>
beginning/end of an action	habitual/repeated action
completed action	ongoing action
series of completed actions	background information
the action on the "stage"	the setting for the action

31. Relative Pronouns

que = refers to things and people

quien(es) = refers only to people

lo que = refers to a situation

32. Reciprocal Actions with Reflexive Pronouns

each other = **nos, os, se**

Vocabulario

Los verbos

abra<u>z</u>arse (<u>c</u>)	to embrace
besarse	to kiss each other
<u>d</u>arse la mano	to shake hands
enc<u>o</u>ntrarse (me enc<u>ue</u>ntro) (con)	to meet (*someone somewhere*)
qu<u>e</u>rerse	to love each other; to be fond of each other
saludarse	to greet each other

La salud y el bienestar

los anteojos	glasses
la caminadora	treadmill
los lentes	glasses
los lentes de contacto	contact lenses
el bienestar	well-being
la salud	health

Repaso: el deporte, llevar (*to wear*)

cuidar de	to take care of
cuidarse	to take care of oneself
dejar de + *inf.*	to stop (*doing something*)
d<u>o</u>ler (d<u>ue</u>le) (*like* **gustar**)	to hurt; to ache
enfermarse	to get sick
guardar cama	to stay in bed
<u>hacer</u>...	to do ...
ejercicios aeróbicos	aerobics
pilates / zumba	Pilates / Zumba
levantar pesas	to lift weights
llevar una vida sana/tranquila	to lead a healthy/calm life
molestar (*like* **gustar**)	to bother
<u>poner</u>(se)...	to get ...
una inyec<u>ci</u>ón	a shot
una vacuna (de)	a vaccination (against)
resfr<u>i</u>arse (me resfr<u>í</u>o)	to get/catch a cold
respirar	to breathe
sa<u>c</u>ar (<u>qu</u>) la lengua	to stick out one's tongue
<u>tener</u> dolor de	to have a pain/ache in
tomarle la temperatura	to take someone's temperature
toser	to cough

Repaso: caminar, correr, <u>dormir</u> (d<u>ue</u>rmo) (<u>u</u>), <u>hacer</u> ejercicio, pra<u>c</u>ticar (<u>qu</u>), <u>sentirse</u> (me s<u>i</u>ento) (<u>i</u>) bien

El cuerpo humano

la boca	mouth
el brazo	arm
la cabeza	head
el cerebro	brain
el corazón	heart
el cuello	neck
el dedo (de la mano)	finger
el dedo del pie	toe
el estómago	stomach
la garganta	throat
la lengua	tongue
la mano	hand

la muela	molar, back tooth
la nariz (*pl.* narices)	nose
el oído	inner ear
el ojo	eye
la oreja	(outer) ear
el pie	foot
la pierna	leg
los pulmones	lungs
la sangre	blood
el cuerpo humano	human body

Repaso: el diente

Las enfermedades

el chequeo	check-up
el consultorio	(medical) office
el dolor (de)	pain, ache (in)
la fiebre	fever
la gripe	flu
el jarabe	(cough) syrup
la pastilla	pill
la receta	prescription
el resfriado	cold (*illness*)
el síntoma	symptom
la tos	cough
el tratamiento	treatment
la enfermedad	illness, sickness

Cognados: el antibiótico, el/la COVID-19, la medicina, la temperatura, la visita

El personal médico

| el/la enfermero/a | nurse |
| el/la farmacéutico/a | pharmacist |

Cognado: el/la dentista, el/la paciente

Repaso: el/la médico/a

Otros sustantivos

| la cita | appointment; date |
| la vida | life |

Los adjetivos

demasiado/a/os/as	too much; too many
mareado/a	dizzy; nauseated
pasado/a	past, last
resfriado/a	congested, stuffed up
rutinario/a	routine
sano/a	healthy
suficiente	enough

Repaso: enfermo/a, todo/a, tranquilo/a

Palabras adicionales

anoche	last night
de repente	suddenly
desgraciadamente	unfortunately
dos veces	twice
eso quiere decir...	that means ...
frecuentemente	frequently
lo + *adjective*	
lo bueno	the good thing/news
lo malo	the bad thing/news
lo suficiente	enough
mal (*adv.*)	sick

Repaso: anteayer, ayer, de adolescente, de niño/a, enseguida lo que, mientras, que, quien(es), siempre, todos los días, una vez

Vocabulario personal

Use this space or a vocabulary notebook to write down other words and phrases you learn in this chapter.

12

¡Conectad@s!°

Connected!

En este capítulo

VOCABULARY

Housing and neighborhoods   358

Technology   361

GRAMMAR

More about telling people to do things   364

Another Spanish verb system   369

Another way to ask others to do things   375

COUNTRY OF FOCUS: COLOMBIA

Una de las varias placitas (*little plazas*) que hay en Cartagena, Colombia

Radius/SuperStock

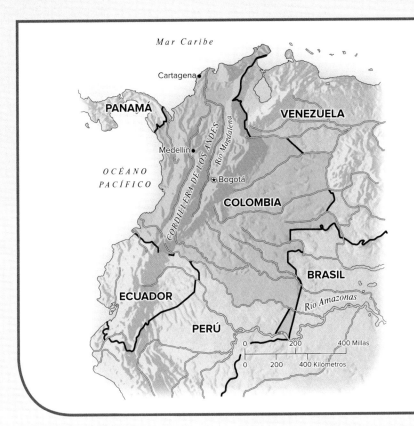

 COLOMBIA

51,3 (coma tres)
millones de habitantes

- La diversidad natural de Colombia es magnífica. Este país comprende[a] territorio caribeño, andino[b] y amazónico.

- Además, Colombia tiene muchísimos recursos naturales: petróleo, oro, platino y esmeraldas. Es uno de los principales productores y exportadores de café del mundo. También exporta flores.

[a]*includes*   [b]*Andean*

ENTREVISTA

These questions related to the chapter theme are answered here by a native speaker. You will be able to ask and answer them yourself with personal information in the **Entrevista** activity in the **Portafolio** section at the end of the chapter.

Ismael Pérez Mendizábal contesta las preguntas.

— **¿Dónde vive usted? ¿Vive en una zona bien comunicada[a] con el resto de la ciudad?**

— Mi carrera es Estudios Urbanos, en la Universidad Nacional de Colombia, en Bogotá, y vivo bastante[b] cerca de la Universidad. Vivo con mi familia en un barrio[c] que está muy bien comunicado, así que[d] puedo llegar a la universidad en bus.

— **¿Se mantiene usted[e] en contacto con sus parientes y amigos que no viven cerca? ¿Cómo lo hace?**

— Bueno, mis abuelos y la mayoría de mis tíos viven en Bogotá, así que nos vemos con frecuencia en las reuniones familiares. Pero ahora mi hermana está estudiando en España. Por eso nos comunicamos por *WhatsApp*.

— **Después de su computadora y su celular, ¿qué aparato electrónico considera usted más necesario en su vida diaria? ¿Por qué?**

— Pues me gusta mucho mi *Kindle*, porque me encanta leer y es más cómodo leer con el *Kindle* que con un libro tradicional.

[a]*connected*   [b]*rather*   [c]*neighborhood*   [d]*así... so*   [e]*¿Se... Do you stay*

Daniel Ernst/Getty Images

VOCABULARIO: PREPARACIÓN

You can hear the pronunciation of theme vocabulary words and phrases in the eBook.

¿Dónde vive usted?

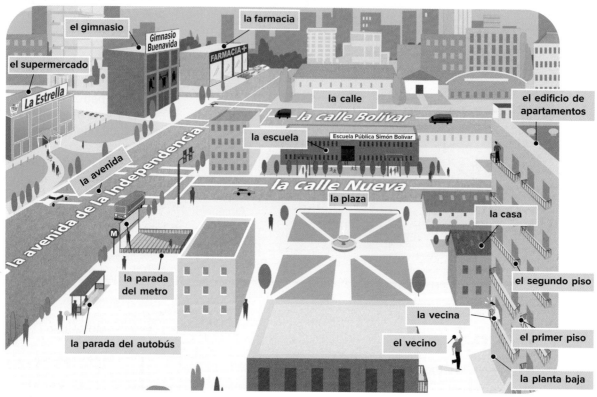

el gimnasio · la farmacia · el supermercado · la calle · el edificio de apartamentos · la calle Bolívar · la escuela · Escuela Pública Simón Bolívar · la avenida · la avenida de la Independencia · la calle Nueva · la plaza · la casa · la parada del metro · el segundo piso · la vecina · el vecino · el primer piso · la parada del autobús · la planta baja

La vivienda	Housing
el dueño / la dueña	owner; landlord, landlady
el inquilino / la inquilina	tenant; renter
el portero / la portera	building manager; doorman
el ascensor	elevator
el piso	floor (*of a building*)
el primer piso	first floor (*second story*)
el segundo piso	second floor (*third story*)
la planta baja	ground floor
la residencia de ancianos	nursing home
la vista (a, de)	view (of)

La zona	
las afueras	outskirts; suburbs
el barrio	neighborhood
la calle	street
el centro	downtown
la dirección	address
mudarse	to move (*residences*)

Los gastos	Expenses
alquilar	to rent
el alquiler	rent
la calefacción	heat
la electricidad	electricity
el gas	gas (*residential; not for cars*)

¡OJO!

The word **suburbio** is a false cognate; it means *slum*. To say you live in the suburbs, say **vivo en las afueras.**

Así se dice

el apartamento = el departamento (*Mex., Arg.*), el piso (*Sp.*)
el ascensor = el elevador

El barrio is the word most generally used to express *neighborhood* in Spanish, although it is often said by Hispanics with more affection than its English counterpart. To talk about **mi barrio** is to talk about a place to which one is emotionally linked, not just the area where one lives. Many other words are used regionally and can depend on the kind of neighborhood. **La colonia** and **el fraccionamiento** are used in Mexico. Other common terms are **el vecindario** and **la zona residencial.**

Comunicación

A. Definiciones. Defina las siguientes palabras en español, según el modelo.

MODELO: la residencia de estudiantes →
Es un lugar donde viven muchos estudiantes. Por lo general está situada en el campus universitario.

1. el inquilino
2. el centro
3. el alquiler
4. el portero
5. la vecina
6. la dueña
7. la dirección
8. las afueras
9. el barrio
10. el ascensor
11. la avenida
12. la residencia de ancianos
13. la planta baja
14. la vista
15. la electricidad

B. Buscamos un apartamento. Lea los siguientes avisos de venta (*sale ads*) de viviendas en Bogotá y conteste las preguntas. **¡OJO!** $ = el peso colombiano

ZONA NORTE

Casa bien ubicada,[a] cerca de la Calle 170. Buenas rutas y cerca de colegios,[b] centros comerciales y supermercados. Zona de alta valorización.[c] 130 m².[d] Parqueadero privado con acceso directo a casa. 3 niveles;[e] 4 habitaciones, 3 baños, sala-comedor, estudio y ático. $450.000.000
Tel.: 3005566177
E-mail: micasa@gmail.com

BARRIO TEUSAQUILLO

Apartamento de 2 habitaciones, 1 baño, cocina y sala-comedor. Tercer[f] piso en edificio con ascensor. Excelente ubicación[g] cerca de bancos, supermercados, centros médicos y parque.
$325.000.000
Tel.: 310448776
E-mail: micasa@gmail.com

BARRIO PRADERA NORTE-TORRE[h] DE MADRID

Dos habitaciones, dos baños, estudio, sala-comedor, pisos laminados, ascensor, garaje cubierto,[i] balcón, 100 m², 4°[j] piso. Adicionales: piscina, gimnasio, sauna, cancha de *squash*. $350.000.000.
Tel.: 316545650.
Email: micasa@gmail.com

[a]*situated, located* [b]*schools* [c]*alta.... high property values* [d]*metros cuadrados (square meters)*
[e]*levels* [f]*Third* [g]*location* [h]*Tower* [i]*covered* [j]*cuarto (fourth)*

1. ¿Qué tipo de vivienda se vende en cada anuncio?
2. ¿Cuántas habitaciones tiene cada vivienda?
3. ¿Cuál de las viviendas sería (*would be*) mejor para una familia con dos hijas adolescentes? ¿para una pareja de profesionales sin hijos y sin planes para tenerlos? ¿para una mujer profesional que ya tiene su primer trabajo, bien pagado (*well paying*)?

Algo sobre la ciudad de Medellín

Con una población de más de 4 millones de habitantes en el área metropolitana, Medellín es la capital del departamento[a] de Antioquia y la segunda ciudad más grande de Colombia. Está considerada como una de las mejores ciudades para vivir en Latinoamérica. No solo tiene vistas fabulosas de los Andes y un clima primaveral todo el año, sino que[b] es un importante centro de desarrollo[c] e innovación. Medellín también es una ciudad modelo en sostenibilidad y movilidad.[d]

En su país, ¿hay alguna ciudad comparable con Medellín por su clima, su interés como centro de innovación o como modelo de ciudad sostenible?

Medellín, Colombia

Karol Kozlowski/Alamy Stock Photo

[a]*región* [b]*sino... but also* [c]*development* [d]*mobility*

C. Mi situación de vivienda

Paso 1. Prepare cinco preguntas que usted puede hacerle sobre su vivienda actual (*current*) a una persona de la clase.

Paso 2. Ahora, en parejas, túrnense para entrevistarse sobre su vivienda actual, usando las preguntas del **Paso 1**. Luego hablen de dónde les gustaría vivir si el dinero se lo permitiera (*if you could financially*). Traten de (*Try to*) usar palabras y frases de los anuncios (**Comunicación B**).

MODELOS: ¿Cuántos pisos hay en la casa de tus padres?
¿Dónde te gustaría vivir, en el centro o en las afueras?

Paso 3. Díganle a la clase lo que ustedes tienen en común.

Textos de todos los días: Alquiler de vivienda

Alquilar una habitación es una experiencia muy común, especialmente para los estudiantes. En esta actividad, usted puede ver un anuncio típico de alquiler para una habitación en Bogotá. ¡Esta información le puede ser útil si decide estudiar por un tiempo en un país hispanohablante!

Objetivo: Crear un perfil personal para una página web especializada en alquiler de habitaciones.

Antes de empezar

- Primero, piense en su experiencia alquilando vivienda. ¿Alquiló alguna vez un apartamento, una casa o una habitación? ¿Tenía usted un apartamento o una casa y necesitaba encontrar a otras personas más para compartir el alquiler? ¿Qué cosas son importantes saber sobre un alquiler?
- Después, lea el anuncio de una empresa (*company*) que alquila viviendas para estudiantes. Tome nota de las opciones que mencionan y también de las (*those*) que no mencionan, ya que (*since*) pueden ser importantes para usted.
- Finalmente, mire el perfil de una persona que está buscando una habitación y úselo como modelo para crear el suyo (*your own*). Hay opciones de habitaciones para parejas también. ¡No es necesario ser realista para hacer esta actividad!

Se alquila

Habitaciones en apartamentos estudiantiles de 2, 3 y 4 habitaciones. Edificios cerca de Universidad de Los Andes (todos a menos de 15 minutos a pie). El alquiler incluye gas y electricidad. Todos los apartamentos cuentan con cocina, 1–2 baños, sala con mobiliario. Metro y bus a menos de 5 minutos.

Servicios

- 🛜 Internet/wifi
- 💨 secadora
- 🚻 baño compartido
- 🛋 amueblado
- 📷 lavadora
- 📺 TV por cable
- 👮 personal de seguridad

Nela

Presupuesto en COP:[a] 600.000.

○ Estudio   ○ Trabajo   ◉ Los dos

Busco: **en (zona):**

| habitación |
| apartamento |

| cerca de la Universidad de los Andes |

Necesito/Deseo:
(escribe hasta 5 cosas que buscas en el alquiler)

1. Habitación exterior
2. No amueblado
3. Transporte público cerca
4. Lavadora y secadora
5. Baño propio (no esencial)

[a]pesos colombianos

La tecnología

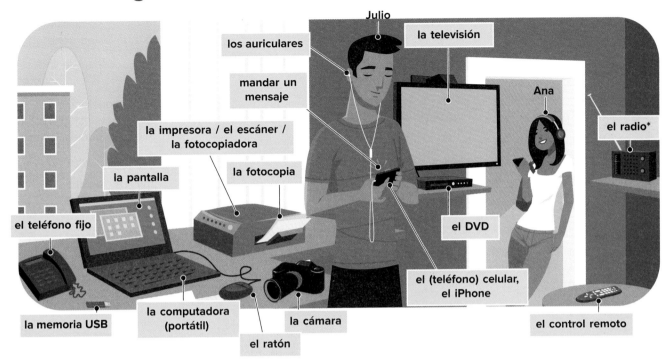

El equipo° electrónico °equipment

el archivo	(computer) file
el buzón de voz	voice mailbox
la carpeta	(computer) folder
la contraseña	password
el disco duro	hard drive
el espacio (de almacenamiento)	(storage) space
la pantalla (grande/plana)	(big/flat) screen (monitor)

Cognados: el android, la aplicación, el CD, el CD-ROM, el documento, el fax, el iPhone, la memoria, el módem, el video, el wifi

En internet (m.)

la arroba	@
el buscador	search engine
el correo electrónico	e-mail
la nube	cloud
la página web	web page
la red social	social network
el sitio web	website
el usuario / la usuaria	user

Cognados: el blog, el chateo, el e-mail, Facebook (m.), el Instagram, el TikTok, el tuit, Twitter (m.)

Los verbos

almacenar	to store; to save
apagar (gu)	to turn off (a machine)
bajar/descargar (gu)	to download
buscar (qu) en internet	to look up on the internet
cambiar (de canal [m.], de ropa...)	to change (channels, clothing ...)
conseguir (like seguir)	to get, obtain
copiar/hacer (foto)copia	to copy
encender (ie), poner	to turn on (a machine)
entrar/estar en internet	to go/be online
entrar/estar en Facebook	to go/be on Facebook
fallar	to "crash" (computer)
funcionar	to work, function; to run (machines)
grabar	to record; to tape
guardar	to keep; to save (documents)
imprimir	to print
mandar...	to send ...
un correo electrónico / e-mail	an email
un mensaje (de texto)	a (text) message
manejar	to operate (a machine)
navegar (gu) la red	to surf the internet
obtener (like tener)	to get, obtain
publicar (qu)	to post (as on Facebook); to publish
subir	to upload

Cognados: conectarse, hacer clic, instalar, tuitear

---

*El radio (masc.) refers to the object and la radio (fem.) refers to the medium.

Comunicación

A. Lo que tenemos y lo que necesitamos

Paso 1. Haga una lista de todas las cosas electrónicas que usted tiene.

Paso 2. Ahora, en grupos de tres o cuatro, hablen de las cosas que todos tienen. ¿Necesita usted algo que está en la lista de uno de sus compañeros?

Paso 3. Ahora usted y sus compañeros del **Paso 2** deben escoger los cinco aparatos electrónicos que ustedes consideran esenciales para los estudiantes de hoy. Luego compartan (*share*) su lista con la clase y expliquen sus decisiones.

B. Asociaciones. ¿Qué cosas asocia usted con los siguientes verbos?

1. mandar   **2.** fallar   **3.** conseguir   **4.** grabar   **5.** guardar   **6.** cambiar   **7.** imprimir   **8.** instalar

C. Definiciones

Paso 1. Dé la palabra definida. **¡OJO!** Puede haber (*There can be*) más de una respuesta en algunos casos.

1. Es un aparato que hace copias de un documento.
2. Es un aparato que sirve para hacer una copia electrónica de un documento.
3. Es lo que usamos para cambiar el programa de televisión sin levantarnos del sofá.
4. Este sistema recibe mensajes cuando no podemos (o no queremos) contestar el teléfono.
5. Es lo que usamos para escuchar música sin hacer ruido.
6. Esto se hace cuando hay en la tele una película que queremos ver pero que ahora mismo no podemos verla.
7. Es un sinónimo de guardar, como guardar un documento en el disco duro.

Paso 2. Ahora le toca a usted darles una o dos definiciones a sus compañeros de clase. Siga el modelo del **Paso 1.**

D. La tecnología y yo

Paso 1. Complete las siguientes oraciones para describir su relación con la tecnología.

1. No puedo imaginar la vida sin mi(s) _____ (aparato) porque...
2. Estoy conectado/a a internet _____ (¿con qué frecuencia?) porque...
3. Entro en internet sobre todo (*especially*) para...

Paso 2. Ahora, en parejas, comparen sus respuestas. ¿Son muy similares sus preferencias y hábitos con relación a la tecnología?

E. Actitudes sobre el uso del celular en los Estados Unidos

Paso 1. Mire la lista de usos en la tabla **Hábitos de uso...** e indique si usted entra dentro de los porcentajes de hábitos. Luego compare sus respuestas con las de otras dos personas de la clase. ¿Qué tienen en común entre ustedes? ¿y con los porcentajes a escala nacional?

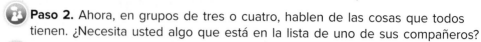

**Hábitos de uso del celular en los Estados Unidos
Porcentaje de personas que...**

se sienten incómodas[a] cuando se dejan[b] el celular en casa — 74 % (por ciento)
al despertarse,[c] miran su teléfono dentro de los primeros 10 minutos — 71 %
al recibir[d] una notificación, miran su teléfono dentro de los primeros 5 minutos — 70 %
usan su celular en el baño — 64 %
no han pasado[e] más de 24 horas sin su celular — 53 %
sienten ansiedad o pánico si la batería del teléfono baja del 20% — 48 %
se consideran «adictas» a sus teléfonos — 47 %
dicen que su celular es su posesión más valiosa[f] — 45 %
usan o miran su teléfono en una cita romántica — 43 %
usan o miran su teléfono mientras manejan[g] — 35 %

Source: Perrin, Andrew. June 28, 2017. "10 Facts about smartphone as the iPhone turns 10." Pew Research Center.

[a]*uneasy*   [b]*se... they leave*   [c]*al... upon waking up*   [d]*al... upon receiving*   [e]*no... haven't spent*   [f]*valuable*   [g]*they drive*

Paso 2. En parejas, indiquen cuáles de los usos y actitudes de la tabla **Los estudiantes y el uso...** son ciertos para ustedes. ¿Con cuáles de ellos están más/menos de acuerdo? ¿Por qué? Finalmente, comenten entre ustedes si creen que una universidad debe prohibir o restringir (*restrict*) algunos usos de los aparatos personales. Si creen que sí, ¿cómo se pueden implementar estas restricciones?

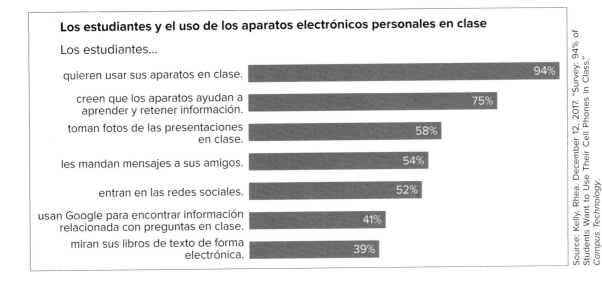

Los estudiantes y el uso de los aparatos electrónicos personales en clase

Los estudiantes...

quieren usar sus aparatos en clase.	94%
creen que los aparatos ayudan a aprender y retener información.	75%
toman fotos de las presentaciones en clase.	58%
les mandan mensajes a sus amigos.	54%
entran en las redes sociales.	52%
usan Google para encontrar información relacionada con preguntas en clase.	41%
miran sus libros de texto de forma electrónica.	39%

Source: Kelly, Rhea. December 12, 2017. "Survey: 94% of Students Want to Use Their Cell Phones in Class." *Campus Technology.*

Nota cultural: El español y la tecnología

El español ocupa el tercer[a] puesto entre las lenguas por número de internautas,[b] después del inglés y el chino, con casi el 8% de los usuarios en total (según datos de 2020). El crecimiento[c] en número de usuarios hispanohablantes ha sido[d] impresionante en la última década. Y el acceso y uso de internet sigue creciendo,[e] gracias a los teléfonos celulares inteligentes.

Como ocurre en inglés, la lengua española que aparece[f] en textos, redes sociales y otros sitios web es con frecuencia muy «oral» y poco pulida,[g] y los emoticonos se usan con frecuencia. Aquí hay algunas características y ejemplos del español de textos y redes sociales:

- muchas abreviaturas: **que = k, q; para = p; por = x; porque = pq; besos = bss; te = t**
- onomatopeyas: **jeje, jaja, uf**
- falta de signos de puntuación y acentos: **q tal?**
- abuso[h] de las mayúsculas y signos de interrogación y admiración: **COMO??? Bien!!!!**

Por otro lado,[i] el inglés es una fuente[j] interminable de vocabulario relacionado con la tecnología, tanto para el español como para todas las otras lenguas del mundo. La lista de vocabulario de **La tecnología** (en este

E	Significado	E	Significado
	Sonrisa		Guiño
	Carcajada		Inseguridad
	Tristeza		Ángel
	Llanto		Demonio
	Confusión		Corazón
	Sacar la lengua		Felicidad
	Susto		Beso

capítulo) pone en evidencia[k] esta situación. Algunos de estos términos luego encuentran una traducción directa al español, como **el disco duro** por *hard drive*, o terminan escribiéndose y pronunciándose en una manera que es normal para el español, como **hacer clic, cliquear** o **clicar** por *to click*.

 ¿Usa usted algunas convenciones específicas cuando escribe mensajes de texto o chateo? ¿Cuáles son?

[a]*third* [b]*internet users* [c]*growth* [d]*ha... has been* [e]*growing* [f]*appears* [g]*polished* [h]*overuse* [i]*Por... On the other hand* [j]*source* [k]*pone... illustrates*

GRAMÁTICA

♻ Repaso

In **Gramática 20 (Cap. 7)** you learned how to form **usted** and **ustedes** (formal) commands with the "opposite" vowel. Remember that the commands are based on the **yo** form of the present tense of irregular and stem-changing verbs, and that verbs that end in **-car, -gar,** and **-zar** have spelling changes in the command forms.

hablar → habl**e**	comer → com**an**	vivir → viv**a**
jugar → jue**guen**	poner → pong**a**	volver → vuelv**an**

Also remember that object pronouns (direct, indirect, reflexive) must follow and be attached to affirmative commands; they must precede negative commands: **Háblele usted. No le hable usted.**
Give the indicated command forms, affirmative and negative.

1. sentarse (usted)   **3.** llamarnos (usted)   **5.** escucharme (ustedes)
2. dárselo (usted)   **4.** acostarse (ustedes)   **6.** vestirse (ustedes)

You'll learn how to form informal commands in **Gramática 33.**

33 Influencing Others (Part 2) • Tú (Informal) Commands

Gramática en acción: Mandatos para situaciones sociales

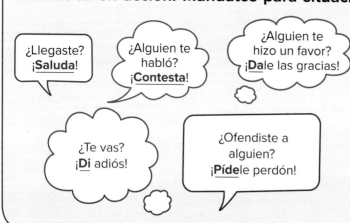

¿Llegaste? ¡**Salud**a!

¿Alguien te habló? ¡**Contest**a!

¿Alguien te hizo un favor? ¡**Da**le las gracias!

¿Te vas? ¡**Di** adiós!

¿Ofendiste a alguien? ¡**Píde**le perdón!

¿Y usted?

Pensando en la clase de español, ¿qué preguntas puede usted hacer para los siguientes mandatos, según el modelo de las imágenes?

1. ¡**Pregunt**a!
2. ¡**Estúdia**los!

In English, the command forms are the same regardless of whom you're giving them to: *Go ...* , *Put ...* , *Don't touch ...* In Spanish, however, the forms for formal **(usted, ustedes)** commands are different from those you use with a person whom you address as **tú.** And unlike **usted** and **ustedes** commands, whose form is the same whether affirmative or negative, the negative **tú** commands have different forms than the affirmative commands.

> *a command or imperative / un* **mandato** = a verb form used to tell someone to do something

---

Commands for social situations ■ *Did you arrive? Say hello!* ■ *Someone spoke to you? Answer!* ■ *Someone did you a favor? Say thanks to them!* ■ *Are you leaving? Say good-bye!* ■ *Did you offend someone? Ask them for forgiveness!*

Negative **tú** Commands / **Los mandatos informales negativos**

-ar → no + -**es**
-er/-ir → no + -**as**

-**ar** verbs		-**er**/-**ir** verbs	
no habl**es**	don't speak	no com**as**	don't eat
no bail**es**	don't dance	no escrib**as**	don't write
no to**ques**	don't play	no pid**as**	don't order
no jue**gues**	don't play	no sal**gas**	don't leave
no empie**ces**	don't start	no **vayas**	don't go

1. Formation of Negative Informal Commands

Negative **tú** commands are very similar to **usted/ustedes** commands. They use the "opposite" vowel but with the **-s** that is characteristic of **tú** forms.

No lo **guardes** en esa carpeta. No **imprimas** ese documento.
Don't save it in that folder. Don't print that document.

All of the irregularities that you have already learned for **usted/ustedes** commands apply to the negative **tú** commands.

- Stem-changing verbs show the stem change: **no cierres, no vuelvas, no sirvas.**
- Verbs that end in **-car, -gar,** and -**zar** have a spelling change: **no busques, no descargues, no almuerces.**
- Verbs with irregular **yo** forms show the irregularity in the command: **no pongas, no digas.**
- The same verbs that have irregular **usted/ustedes** commands have irregular negative **tú** commands, identical to the **usted/ustedes** form but with characteristic **-s** of **tú** forms.

dar → no de**s**
estar → no esté**s**
ir → no vaya**s**
saber → no sepa**s**
ser → no sea**s**

2. Position of Pronouns

As with negative **usted/ustedes** commands, object pronouns—direct, indirect, and reflexive—precede negative **tú** commands.

No lo mires.
Don't look at him.

No les escribas.
Don't write to them.

No te levantes.
Don't get up.

No se lo des.
Don't give it to them.

Affirmative **tú** Commands / **Los mandatos informales afirmativos**

-ar → -**a**
-er/-ir → -**e**

-**ar** verbs		-**er**/-**ir** verbs	
habl**a**	speak	com**e**	eat
toc**a**	play	escrib**e**	write
jueg**a**	play	pid**e**	order
empiez**a**	start	oy**e**	listen

1. Formation of Regular Informal Affirmative Commands

Most affirmative **tú** commands are identical to the third person singular (**usted, él, ella**) form of the present tense. All stem-changes appear (because they occur in that person in the present), but there are no spelling changes in verbs ending in **-car, -gar,** and **-zar.**

Descarga la aplicación, por favor.
Download the application, please.

Enciende la computadora.
Turn on the computer.

2. Irregular Informal Affirmative Commands

Some verbs have irregular affirmative **tú** command forms.

decir → <u>di</u>	salir → <u>sal</u>
hacer → <u>haz</u>	ser → <u>sé</u>
ir → <u>ve</u>	tener → <u>ten</u>
poner → <u>pon</u>	venir → <u>ven</u>

¡OJO!

Sé, the informal affirmative command of **ser,** has an accent mark to distinguish it from the pronoun **se.**

Sé puntual, pero **ten** cuidado.
Be there on time, but be careful.

¡OJO!

The affirmative **tú** commands for **ir** and **ver** are identical: **ve.** Context will clarify meaning. The command form of **ver** is rarely used.

¡Ve esa película!
See that movie!

Ve a casa ahora mismo.
Go home right now.

3. Position of Pronouns

As with affirmative **usted/ustedes** commands, object and reflexive pronouns follow affirmative **tú** commands and are attached to them. Accent marks are necessary except when a single pronoun is added to a one-syllable command.

One pronoun: **Lée**lo. **Levánta**te. **Di**me la verdad.
Two pronouns: **Dá**selo. **Regála**mela. **Dí**mela.

Summary of Informal Commands

Negative:	-ar → <u>-es</u>	-er/-ir → <u>-as</u>
Affirmative:	-ar → <u>-a</u>	-er/-ir → <u>-e</u>

Affirmative:	*command + pronoun(s)* (<u>1</u> word)
Negative:	**no** + *pronoun(s) + command* (<u>3</u> words)

Práctica y comunicación

A. Mandatos frecuentes

Paso 1. Autoprueba. Complete las siguientes oraciones con el mandato apropiado.

1. _____me qué quieres.
2. No _____ al parque sola.
3. No le _____ nada de la fiesta.
4. _____te un abrigo.
5. _____ a la fiesta.
6. No _____ eso en mi cama.

a. di
b. digas
c. pon
d. pongas
e. vayas
f. ve

Paso 2. Haga mandatos informales basados en las siguientes frases.

1. **buscar** la información en Google
2. **lavar** los platos
3. **ir** al gimnasio con más frecuencia
4. **imprimir** la tarea
5. **salir** con nosotros el viernes por la noche
6. no: **entrar** en esa página web
7. no: **hacer** eso
8. no: **encender** el celular
9. no: **decirle** esta información a nadie
10. no: **descargar** esa aplicación de internet

Paso 3. Ahora, en parejas, díganse cuáles son los mandatos de la lista que se oyen con frecuencia. También deben decirse quiénes se los dicen y en qué situaciones.

Prác. A, Paso 1: Answers: 1. a 2. e 3. b 4. c 5. f 6. d

B. Recuerdos de la niñez

Paso 1. Haga mandatos informales basados en las siguientes frases. ¿Oía usted estos mandatos cuando era niño/a? ¿Quién se los daba?

1. **limpiar** tu cuarto
2. **hacer** la tarea
3. **lavarse** las manos
4. **decirme** la verdad
5. **ser** bueno
6. **irse** a la cama
7. no: **cruzar** (*to cross*) la calle solo/a
8. no: **jugar** con mis cosas
9. no: **darles** tu comida a los otros niños
10. no: **decir** mentiras (*lies*)
11. no: **ponerse** esa camiseta sucia

Paso 2. Finalmente, en parejas, den otros mandatos negativos y afirmativos que ustedes oían con frecuencia en casa o en la escuela durante su niñez o adolescencia.

Nota comunicativa: Verbos derivados de *poner, tener* y *venir*

Many Spanish verbs are formed with a prefix (a syllable or syllables added to the beginning of a word) plus **poner, tener,** and **venir.** You already know one verb of this kind: **conseguir.** Can you infer the meaning of the following infinitives? **Componer** (*to compose; to form, make up*) is harder to guess, but the others should be obvious.

> **poner:** <u>com</u>poner, <u>pro</u>poner, <u>su</u>poner
>
> **tener:** <u>con</u>tener, <u>man</u>tener, <u>ob</u>tener
>
> **venir:** <u>inter</u>venir, <u>pre</u>venir

These verbs are conjugated just like the verbs on which they are based. The only difference is that they need an accent mark in the **tú** affirmative commands. Here are some of the forms of **componer.**

Present: **compongo, compones...**	Imperfect: **componía, componías...**
Preterite: **compuse, compusiste...**	Present participle: **componiendo**
Commands: **componga usted, compongan ustedes no compongas, compón**	

You will practice some of these verbs in **Práctica C.** Recognizing and using them will increase your Spanish vocabulary. Only **obtener** is listed in the end-of-chapter **Vocabulario** list.

C. Modo avión

Paso 1. ¿Estamos demasiado «conectad@s»? Compare lo que hacía y sentía la gente en el siglo XX con lo que pasa hoy día.

1. ¿Qué hacía la gente para obtener información sobre algo que no sabía? ¿Y ahora?
2. ¿Qué hacía la gente para mantenerse en contacto con los amigos, la familia, etcétera? ¿Y ahora?
3. ¿Cree usted que las personas del siglo XX se sentían culpables (*guilty*) por estar desconectadas durante las vacaciones? ¿Y ahora?

Mark Dierker/McGraw Hill

Paso 2. Ahora, en parejas, usen las siguientes ideas para dar consejos en forma de mandatos informales para vivir «en modo avión», por lo menos temporalmente (*temporarily*). Es decir (*That is*), den consejos sobre cómo usar la tecnología sin dejarse absorber por ella.

1. no **tener** el celular al lado de la almohada (*pillow*) toda la noche / **poner**lo lejos de la cama
2. no **mantener** el celular encendido (*on*) todo el tiempo / **desconectar** a veces
3. **proponer** actividades físicas para hacer con los amigos en lugar de mirar una pantalla / **hacer** ejercicio
4. **contener** las ganas de contestar todos los mensajes inmediatamente / **ser** paciente
5. **bajar** el volumen de las notificaciones para no molestar a los demás (*others*)

Paso 3. Finalmente, inventen un mandato importantísimo para todo el mundo con respecto al uso de tecnología en la vida diaria.

Algo sobre la cumbia

Kobby Dagan/Shutterstock

Un grupo folclórico de cumbia

La cumbia es un género[a] musical y un baile tradicional de la costa caribeña de Colombia y Panamá. Se cree que su origen fue una danza de cortejo[b] africana. La cumbia combina el ritmo y percusión de origen africano con instrumentos indígenas, como la gaita[c] colombiana, y europeos, como la guitarra. La cumbia es tan famosa como la salsa en algunos países de Sudamérica.

 ¿Qué géneros musicales de los Estados Unidos son populares fuera de[d] este país? ¿Son bailables? ¿Qué tipos de instrumentos se usan?

[a]*genre, type*   [b]*courtship*
[c]*woodwind instrument*   [d]*fuera... outside of*

 D.   Anuncios turísticos.

Paso 1. Los mandatos se usan con frecuencia en los anuncios, como este que nos invita a visitar Colombia. En parejas, inventen por lo menos ocho mandatos que podrían (*might*) ser útiles para un anuncio turístico sobre los Estados Unidos. ¡No repitan verbos, por favor!

Colombia te invita.
¡Ven y conócenos!

Digital Archive Japan/Alamy Stock Photo

Paso 2. Ahora lean la información sobre Colombia en esta página y en otras partes del capítulo. Luego escriban ocho mandatos informales (**tú**) para crear un anuncio turístico sobre Colombia. Usen una variedad de verbos.

E.   Mandatos y preguntas

Paso 1. Imagine que estas personas son sus amigos. Deles consejos en forma de mandatos informales.

1. Su amiga Mariana trabaja demasiado. Duerme poco y bebe muchísimo café. Jamás hace ejercicio. Siempre está mirando su iPhone.
2. Su primo Jorge vive solo en una casa grande en la mejor zona de la ciudad, con dos perros y dos gatos. Tiene demasiados gastos para su sueldo (*salary*). Antes, sus abuelos le mandaban dinero, pero ahora no pueden seguir mandándoselo.
3. Celia quiere salir a divertirse, especialmente los viernes por la noche. Pero su pareja está muy cansada los viernes después de la semana de trabajo.

 Paso 2. Ahora, en parejas, digan cómo se expresarían (*you would express yourselves*) en las siguientes situaciones. **¡OJO!** Consideren bien si es mejor usar la forma de **tú** o de **usted** en cada situación. Recuerden que no se debe usar mandatos en ciertas situaciones, incluso (*even*) con los buenos amigos y familiares.

1. A la profesora de español: usted no entendió lo que acaba de decir.
2. A un compañero de clase que quiere usar las respuestas de usted porque no hizo la tarea.
3. A una compañera de cuarto o de casa que nunca contribuye con nada para la comida... y hoy quiere tomarse la leche que usted tiene en el refrigerador.
4. A un señor en la calle: usted necesita saber dónde está la parada del autobús.
5. A un amigo en la mesa: usted quiere la sal.
6. A una persona joven en el campus: usted quiere saber dónde está el edificio X.
7. A una compañera de clase: usted quiere saber la hora.
8. A un profesor que no puede encontrar una aplicación en la computadora: usted le dice cómo hacerlo.

34 Expressing Subjective Actions or States • Present Subjunctive (Part 1): An Introduction

Gramática en acción: Manuela busca apartamento

—Por supuesto, **quiero que** el apartamento **esté** en un buen barrio.

—Claro, por eso **es muy importante que** <u>haya</u> una parada del autobús cerca.

—Sí, **¡espero que** mi sueldo <u>sea</u> suficiente para el alquiler y todos los gastos mensuales!

—¿El depósito? **Es probable que** mis padres me <u>den</u> el dinero para pagarlo.

Comprensión

Según lo que dice Manuela por teléfono, ¿es probable que...

1. ella **esté** hablando con su mejor amiga?
2. **tenga** un perro?
3. no **tenga** coche?
4. **viva** en una ciudad grande?
5. los padres de Manuela **estén** preocupados por la situación económica de su hija?

Present Subjunctive / El presente de subjuntivo

1. Indicative Mood

Except for **usted/ustedes** and negative **tú** commands, all the verb forms you have learned so far in *Puntos de partida* are part of the *indicative mood* (**el modo indicativo**). In both English and Spanish, the indicative is used to state facts and to ask questions; it objectively expresses what the speaker considers to be true.

El modo indicativo

Prefiero llegar temprano a casa.
I prefer getting home early.

Vienes a la fiesta, ¿verdad?
You're coming to the party, right?

2. Subjunctive Mood

Spanish has another verb system called the *subjunctive mood* (**el modo subjuntivo**). The subjunctive is used to express the attitude of the speaker with respect to what he/she says. These include things that the speaker

- wants to happen or wants others to do
- reacts to emotionally
- does not yet know to be true

To sum up:

- indicative = objective reality (speaker knows it)
- subjunctive = subjective or conceptual (that is, in the mind of the speaker)

El modo subjuntivo

Prefiero que <u>llegues</u> temprano a casa.
I prefer for you to be (that you be) home early.

Espero que <u>vengas</u> a la fiesta.
I hope (that) you're coming to the party.

Es probable que <u>vengas</u> a la fiesta, ¿no?
You're probably coming (It's probable that you will come) to the party, aren't you?

Manuela is looking for an apartment —*"Naturally, I want the apartment to be (lit., that the apartment be) in a good neighborhood." —"Of course, that's why it's really important for there to be (lit., that there be) a bus stop nearby." —"Yes, I hope (that) my salary will be enough for the rent and all the monthly expenses!" —"The deposit? It's probable that my parents will give me the money to pay for it."*

3. Simple vs. Complex Sentences

In English and in Spanish, sentences may be simple or complex.

- A *simple sentence* (**una oración simple**) has one conjugated verb.

- A *complex sentence* (**una oración compleja**) has two or more *clauses* (**las cláusulas**), each with a conjugated verb.

> ### ¡OJO!
> As you can see in the example sentences, in English the word *that* introduces the second clause, but it can be and is often omitted. The word **que** is never omitted in Spanish.

Oraciones simples

Vienes a la fiesta.
You are coming to the party.

Alicia **está** en casa.
Alicia is at home.

Oraciones complejas

Yo **sé** que **vienes** a la fiesta.
I know (that) you're coming to the party.

Miguel **piensa** que Alicia **está** en casa.
Miguel thinks (that) Alicia is at home.

4. Two Types of Clauses

In English and in Spanish, there are two types of clauses: main and subordinate.

- *Main clauses* (**Las cláusulas principales**) (under ①) express an idea that controls the subordinate clause. These are also called independent clauses.

- *Subordinate clauses* (**Las cláusulas subordinadas**) (under ②) contain an incomplete thought and cannot stand alone. They require a main clause to form a complete sentence. Because they depend on the main clause, they are also called dependent clauses.

> *a clause* / **una cláusula**
> = a group of words that contains a subject and a verb

> ### ¡OJO!
> In English, there are different ways to express Spanish sentences that contain the subjunctive, as you can see in the examples.

Oraciones complejas
El indicativo

①		②
Yo **sé**	**que**	esta impresora no **funciona**.
I know	*(that)*	*this printer doesn't work.*
Miguel **piensa**	**que**	Alicia **está** en casa.
Miguel thinks	*(that)*	*Alicia is at home.*

El subjuntivo

①		②
Quiero	**que**	**leas** mi blog.
I want	*(for)*	*you to read my blog.*
Miguel **espera**	**que**	Alicia **esté** en casa.
Miguel hopes	*(that)*	*Alicia is at home.*
Dudo	**que**	esta impresora **funcione**.
I doubt	*(that)*	*this printer works.*

5. Use of the Subjunctive in Subordinate Clauses

As you can see in the sentences in Point 4, when the subjects of the clauses in a complex sentence are different, the subjunctive is often used in the subordinate clause in Spanish.

①		②
first subject = **indicative**	**que**	second subject = **subjunctive**

6. Same Subject → Infinitive

As you already know, when there is no change of subject in the sentence, the infinitive often follows the conjugated verb and no conjunction is necessary. In this type of sentence, the infinitive is the direct object of the conjugated verb.

Quiero ir a la fiesta.
I want to go to the party.

Necesitan estudiar para el examen.
They need to study for the test.

Es necesario estudiar para los exámenes.
It's necessary to study for tests.

7. Common Uses of the Subjunctive

In Spanish, the subjunctive is commonly used in the subordinate clause:

- when the main clause verb expresses *influence*, *emotion*, or *doubt* or *denial*

AND

- when there is a different subject in the main and subordinate clauses.

You will practice all these uses of the subjunctive in this section, and learn more about them in **Gramática 38**, **39**, and **40**.

Influencia:	**Necesito** que mis padres me <u>**den**</u> más dinero.
Emoción:	**Espero** que mis padres me <u>**den**</u> más dinero.
Duda:	**Dudo** que mis padres me <u>**den**</u> más dinero.
Negación:	**No creo** que mis padres me <u>**den**</u> más dinero.

Forms of the Present Subjunctive / Las formas del presente de subjuntivo

The **usted/ustedes** and negative **tú** command forms that you have already learned are part of the subjunctive system.

Terminaciones del presente de subjuntivo
-ar: -<u>e</u>, -<u>e</u>s, -<u>e</u>, -<u>e</u>mos, -<u>é</u>is, -<u>e</u>n
-er/-ir: -<u>a</u>, -<u>a</u>s, -<u>a</u>, -<u>a</u>mos, -<u>á</u>is, -<u>a</u>n

	-ar verbs	-er verbs	-ir verbs	stem-changing verbs	irregular verbs
	hab<u>lar</u>: habl-	**com<u>er</u>: com-**	**escrib<u>ir</u>: escrib-**	<u>**volver: vuelv-**</u>	<u>**decir: dig-**</u>
Singular	hab<u>le</u> hab<u>le</u>s hab<u>le</u>	com<u>a</u> com<u>a</u>s com<u>a</u>	escrib<u>a</u> escrib<u>a</u>s escrib<u>a</u>	vuelv<u>a</u> vuelv<u>a</u>s vuelv<u>a</u>	dig<u>a</u> dig<u>a</u>s dig<u>a</u>
Plural	hab<u>le</u>mos hab<u>lé</u>is hab<u>le</u>n	com<u>a</u>mos com<u>á</u>is com<u>a</u>n	escrib<u>a</u>mos escrib<u>á</u>is escrib<u>a</u>n	volv<u>a</u>mos volv<u>á</u>is vuelv<u>a</u>n	dig<u>a</u>mos dig<u>á</u>is dig<u>a</u>n

1. Present Indicative *yo* Stem + Present Subjunctive Endings

The personal endings of the present subjunctive are formed with the "opposite" vowel. They are added to the first person singular (**yo**) of the present indicative, minus its **-o** ending: **habl-, com-, escrib-, vuelv-, dig-**, as shown in the preceding chart.

¡OJO!

present subjunctive stem = present indicative **yo** form minus **-o**

2. *-ar* and *-er* Stem-changing Verbs

These verbs follow the stem-changing pattern of the present indicative.

p<u>e</u>nsar (p<u>ie</u>nso):	p<u>ie</u>nse	pensemos
	p<u>ie</u>nses	penséis
	p<u>ie</u>nse	p<u>ie</u>nsen
p<u>o</u>der (p<u>ue</u>do):	p<u>ue</u>da	podamos
	p<u>ue</u>das	podáis
	p<u>ue</u>da	p<u>ue</u>dan

3. *-ir* Stem-changing Verbs

The present subjunctive of **-ir** stem-changing verbs has the same stem change as that of the present indicative when the stem vowel is stressed.

- pref<u>e</u>rir: e → <u>ie</u>
- p<u>e</u>dir: e → <u>i</u>
- d<u>o</u>rmir: o → <u>ue</u>

- **preferir (pref<u>ie</u>ro) (i)**

pref<u>ie</u>ra	pref<u>i</u>ramos
pref<u>ie</u>ras	pref<u>i</u>ráis
pref<u>ie</u>ra	pref<u>ie</u>ran

pref<u>i</u>riendo / pref<u>i</u>rió, pref<u>i</u>rieron

Remember that when infinitives appear in vocabulary lists, the stem changes are always indicated. All you have to do is remember where they occur.

(Continúa).

In addition, these verbs show a second stem change in the **nosotros** and **vosotros** forms. This change is highlighted in the verbs on the previous page and here.

- e → i
- o → u

This is *the same change* that happens in the present participle (**-ndo**) and in the third person singular and plural of the preterite of **-ir** stem-changing verbs, so you have already learned to make it.

- **pedir (pido) (i)**

pida	pidamos
pidas	pidáis
pida	pidan

pidiendo / pidió, pidieron

- **dormir (duermo) (u)**

duerma	durmamos
duermas	durmáis
duerma	duerman

durmiendo / durmió, durmieron

---

4. **Verbs Ending in *-car*, *-gar*, and *-zar***

These verbs have a spelling change in *all* persons of the present subjunctive to preserve the **c, g,** and **z** sounds. This is the same change that happens in the **usted/ustedes** commands, in the negative **tú** commands, and in the first person singular of the preterite of these verbs.

- **-car: c → qu**
- **-gar: g → gu**
- **-zar: z → c**

buscar (qu)		pagar (gu)		empezar (c)	
busque	busquemos	pague	paguemos	empiece	empecemos
busques	busquéis	pagues	paguéis	empieces	empecéis
busque	busquen	pague	paguen	empiece	empiecen
busque(n), no busques / busqué		pague(n), no pagues / pagué		empiece(n), no empieces / empecé	

---

5. **Verbs with Irregular *yo* Forms**

Since the present subjunctive stem is the **yo** form of the present indicative (minus **-o**), verbs with irregular **yo** forms in the present indicative show that irregularity in *all* persons of the present subjunctive.

conocer: conozca, conozcas, conozca, conozcamos, conozcáis, conozcan

decir:	**diga,...**	tener:	**tenga,...**
hacer:	**haga,...**	traer:	**traiga,...**
oír:	**oiga,...**	venir:	**venga,...**
poner:	**ponga,...**	ver:	**vea,...**
salir:	**salga,...**		

---

6. **Irregular Verbs**

A few verbs have irregular present subjunctive forms.

dar:	dé, des, dé, demos, deis, den
estar:	esté, estés, estés, estemos, estéis, estén
ir:	vaya, vayas, vaya, vayamos, vayáis, vayan
saber:	sepa, sepas, sepa, sepamos, sepáis, sepan
ser:	sea, seas, sea, seamos, seáis, sean

---

7. **Present Subjunctive of *haber: haya***

Remember that the infinitive form of **hay** is **haber**. The present subjunctive of **hay** is **haya**.

No creo que **haya** clases hoy.
I don't think there are any classes today.

Práctica y comunicación

A. El próximo semestre/trimestre

Paso 1. Autoprueba. Dé las formas indicadas del presente de subjuntivo de los siguientes verbos. ¡OJO! Hay algunos cambios ortográficos (*spelling changes*).

1. bajar: yo
2. subir: tú
3. conocer: nosotros
4. decir: ustedes
5. sacar: tú
6. entregar: ella
7. conseguir: yo
8. morir: ellos

Paso 2. Complete las siguientes oraciones con la forma apropiada de los infinitivos. En algunos casos el infinitivo es la forma apropiada, pero en otros casos es necesario usar el presente de subjuntivo. Si alguna oración es falsa para usted, use **no** antes del verbo principal (es decir, el verbo en el indicativo).

El próximo semestre/trimestre...

1. quiero _____ (tomar) otra clase de español.
2. mi padre/madre (esposo/a, hijo/a, amigo/a...) quiere que yo _____ (tomar) una clase de economía.
3. mi consejero/a recomienda que yo _____ (tomar) una clase de matemáticas.
4. recomiendo que todas las personas de esta clase _____ (tomar) otra clase de español.
5. deseo _____ (vivir) fuera del campus.
6. espero _____ (encontrar) un apartamento o una casa cerca del campus.
7. espero que mis padres/amigos _____ (ayudarme) con el alquiler.
8. deseo que mi mejor amigo/a _____ (vivir) conmigo fuera del campus.

Paso 3. Ahora, en parejas, entrevístense sobre las oraciones del **Paso 2** para ver si las oraciones son ciertas o falsas para ustedes. Luego díganle al resto de la clase algo que ustedes tienen en común.

MODELO: 2. E1: ¿Tu padre quiere que **tomes** una clase de economía el próximo trimestre?
E2: No, mi padre no quiere que **tome** una clase de economía. ¿Y tu padre?
E1: Mi padre tampoco. → Nuestros padres no quieren que **tomemos** una clase de economía el próximo trimestre.

B. En la clase de español.

Complete las oraciones de la columna de la izquierda con la cláusula más lógica de la columna de la derecha.

1. La profe quiere que sus estudiantes ___.
2. Y espera que ___.
3. Es necesario ___.
4. Yo espero que ___.
5. No creo que ___.

a. nadie en la clase pueda recordar todos los verbos.
b. sus estudiantes tomen otra clase de español.
c. hablen español mucho para practicar.
d. hacer la tarea todos los días.
e. la profe no nos dé demasiada tarea.

C. Consideraciones sobre el uso de la tecnología.

Haga oraciones completas conectando las dos frases. En algunos casos no es necesario hacer cambios, pero en otros casos es necesario añadir la palabra **que** y conjugar el segundo verbo en el presente de subjuntivo.

MODELOS: Para la mayoría de las personas es necesario / **tener** un celular para tener acceso al GPS → Para la mayoría de las personas es necesario **tener** un celular para tener acceso al GPS.

Yo prefiero / otra persona: **mirar** el GPS cuando yo manejo (*drive*) → Yo prefiero **que otra persona mire** el GPS cuando yo manejo.

1. Es necesario / todas las personas: **tener** acceso a internet hoy día
2. Todas las personas universitarias necesitan / **tener** una portátil
3. A los profesores les molesta / sus estudiantes: **mandar** mensajes en clase
4. Mucha gente quiere / **tener** cientos de amigos en Facebook
5. Otros no quieren / gente desconocida (*unknown*): **saber** de su vida por Facebook
6. Algunas personas no quieren / otra gente: **subir** fotos de ellas sin su permiso

Prác. A, Paso 1: Answers: 1. baje 2. subas 3. conozcamos 4. digan 5. saques 6. entregue 7. consiga 8. mueran

D. ¿Puede usted sustituir a su profesor(a) en el salón de clase? Demuéstrele a su profesor(a) que usted lo/la conoce bien, haciendo oraciones como las (*those*) que dice él/ella en clase. (Solo tiene que cambiar el infinitivo).

| quiero que
espero que
prohíbo que
dudo que
es necesario que
me alegro de (*I'm glad*) que
no creo que
recomiendo que | + | (nombre de un[a]
estudiante)
todos ustedes
nadie
alguien de la clase
yo | + | (no) | + | copiar en un examen
dormirse / entrar en
internet / estar en
Facebook en clase
estudiar
hacer la tarea
llegar a tiempo
saber el subjuntivo
sacar notas mejores
tener un blog
¿ ? |

Vocabulario útil

Es necesario / bueno /
  importante /
  esencial que... ⎫
Recomendamos que... ⎬ + *subjuntivo*
Sugerimos que... ⎭

E. Cómo dar una buena fiesta

Paso 1. Haga una lista de las cosas que hay que hacer para dar una fiesta exitosa (*successful*), en su opinión. Use infinitivos en su lista.

MODELOS: llamar a los amigos con anticipación (*ahead of time*), comprar...

Paso 2. En parejas, comparen sus listas del **Paso 1** y hagan una sola lista de por lo menos seis acciones.

Paso 3. Conviertan la lista en una serie de recomendaciones para dar una buena fiesta.

MODELO: Recomendamos que llamen a los amigos con anticipación.

Algo sobre el café

El café colombiano es famoso en todo el mundo y tiene su propia denominación de origen: Café de Colombia. El país ocupa el tercer[a] lugar entre los países productores de café del mundo y los Estados Unidos es el país que más consume café colombiano.

Sin duda, parte de la fama del café colombiano se debe a la exitosa campaña publicitaria[b] con la figura de Juan Valdez, un personaje[c] ficticio que representa a los campesinos[d] y cafeteros[e] colombianos desde[f] 1959.

¿Hay algún producto distintivo de este país? ¿Y de su estado?

[a]*third* [b]*exitosa... successful ad campaign* [c]*character* [d]*farm workers*
[e]*coffee producers* [f]*since*

Trabajadores en un cafetal (*coffee plantation*) colombiano

Chester Voyage/Alamy Stock Photo

Repaso

In **Gramática 35** and in the grammar sections of **Capítulo 13**, you will learn more about the three major uses of the subjunctive. Summarize what you have learned so far by completing the following sentences.

1. In Spanish, there are at least _____ clauses in a sentence that contains the subjunctive.
2. The subjunctive appears in the _____ clause.
3. The indicative appears in the _____ clause.
4. The word _____ must always appear.
5. The verb subjects in each clause are _____.

35 Expressing Desires and Requests • Use of the Subjunctive (Part 2): Influence

Gramática en acción: ¿Quién debe hacerlo?

Comprensión

Escoja la oración más apropiada para cada dibujo.

1. La profesora dice: _____
  a. No quiero usar el celular ahora.
  b. No quiero que <u>usen</u> el celular ahora.

2. La madre dice: _____
  a. Es necesario expresar el talento artístico.
  b. Es necesario que <u>exprese</u> su talento artístico.

3. El compañero de casa dice: _____
  a. ¡Quiero bajar el volumen!
  b. ¡Te pido que <u>bajes</u> el volumen!

---

1. Features of the Subjunctive

So far, as you know, you have learned to identify the subjunctive by the features listed here.

In addition, the subjunctive is associated with three concepts or conditions that "trigger" the use of it in the subordinate clause: influence, emotion, and doubt or denial.

- It is conjugated with the "opposite" vowel.
- It appears in a complex sentence, one that has at least two clauses and thus two conjugated verbs.
- It is used in the dependent clause when the subject of that clause is different from the subject of the main clause.
- It is preceded by **que.**

---

2. The Subjunctive after Verbs of Influence

①		②
INFLUENCE		
first subject = **indicative**	**que**	second subject = <u>**subjunctive**</u>

One trigger for the use of the subjunctive in the subordinate clause is the concept of *influence* (**la influencia**). The subject of the main clause *wants*, *prefers*, *insists*, and so on, that the subject of the subordinate clause do something, expressed by a verb in the subjunctive. The verb in the main clause is always in the indicative.

Influence

①		②
Yo **quiero**	**que**	tú <u>**pagues**</u> la cuenta.
I want		*you to pay the bill.*
La profesora **prefiere**	**que**	no <u>**lleguemos**</u> tarde.
The professor prefers	*that*	*we don't don't arrive late.*

3. Verbs of Influence

There are many verbs of influence, some very strong and direct, some very soft and polite. The verbs marked with * are new or are listed with a new meaning.

STRONG(ER)	SOFT(ER)
*insistir en	desear
*mandar (to order)	*esperar (to expect)
*permitir (to permit, allow)	pedir (pido) (i)
*prohibir (prohíbo)	preferir (prefiero) (i)
querer (quiero)	recomendar (recomiendo)
	sugerir (sugiero) (i)

4. Impersonal Expressions of Influence

An impersonal generalization (**es** + *adjective*) can also be the main clause that triggers the subjunctive. The subject of the impersonal expression is *it* (expressed by the verb **es**), and the subjunctive is used when there is another subject in the sentence.

Es necesario que
Es urgente que } Paco **estudie** español.
Es mejor que

¡OJO!

As you know, when there is no second subject, the infinitive follows verbs of influence and impersonal expressions of influence.

Quiero / Deseo / Prefiero estudiar español.
Es necesario / urgente / mejor / importante estudiar español.

5. Indicative in two-clause sentences

Not all sentences that have two clauses contain the subjunctive. You have been using two-clause sentences with two different subjects like the ones to the right for some time. What is lacking in these sentences is one of the three subjunctive "triggers."

Sé que la clase **es** a las ocho de la mañana.
Creo/Pienso que esa computadora vieja **va** a fallar pronto.

Summary of Influence

influence + **que** + change of subject → **subjunctive**

Práctica y comunicación

A. Opiniones sobre la tecnología

Paso 1. Autoprueba. Indique cuál(es) de los siguientes conceptos *no se* asocia(n) con el subjuntivo.

1. un infinitivo ☐
2. la influencia en la cláusula independiente ☐
3. dos sujetos ☐
4. dos cláusulas ☐
5. **que** para unir dos cláusulas ☐

Paso 2. Indique las oraciones que son ciertas para usted. Indique también las oraciones con cláusulas subordinadas que tienen subjuntivo.

	CIERTO PARA MÍ	SUBJUNTIVO
1. Muchos de mis profesores quieren que los estudiantes usemos la computadora en clase.	☐	☐
2. Algunos de mis profesores prefieren que no usemos la computadora en clase.	☐	☐
3. Todos mis profesores insisten en que no usemos el celular en clase.	☐	☐
4. Es mejor que haya una multa (*fine*) muy grande para las personas que mandan mensajes mientras conducen (*they drive*).	☐	☐
5. Es necesario que los padres y los maestros (*teachers*) prohíban a los menores el uso frecuente de los celulares.	☐	☐
6. Quiero eliminar varias aplicaciones de mi celular.	☐	☐

Paso 3. Ahora, en parejas, entrevístense sobre las ideas del **Paso 1.**

MODELO: **1. E1:** ¿Quieren muchos de tus profesores que los estudiantes usen la computadora en clase?

E2: Sí, muchos de mis profesores quieren eso. ¿Y tus profesores?

E1: También.

B. Gabriel García Márquez. Complete las siguientes oraciones sobre el escritor colombiano con el verbo apropiado.

1. Es importante que todo el mundo _____ (sabe / sepa / saber) quién es Gabriel García Márquez.

2. Todos los profesores de literatura quieren que sus estudiantes _____ (conocen / conozcan / conocer) la obra de este escritor.

3. Los profesores de español sugieren que todo el mundo _____ (lee / lea / leer) algo escrito (*written*) por García Márquez.

4. Mi amiga colombiana insiste en que yo _____ (busco / busque / buscar) un cuento de García Márquez en español.

5. Pero yo prefiero _____ (leo / lea / leer) algo traducido (*translated*) al inglés.

6. ¿Con qué novela de García Márquez me recomiendas que _____ (*yo:* empiezo / empiece / empezar)?

Algo sobre Gabriel García Márquez

REUTERS/Alamy Stock Photo

Gabriel García Márquez, o «Gabo», como lo llamaban, es sin duda[a] el escritor colombiano más famoso del mundo. Su obra[b] literaria fue una de las más influyentes del siglo XX. Empezó trabajando como periodista[c] y escribió cuentos,[d] novelas y ensayos;[e] luego, en 1982, recibió el Premio Nobel de Literatura. Su obra más famosa es *Cien años de soledad*, ejemplo de un estilo literario que se llama realismo mágico. La novela narra la historia de una familia a través de[f] varias generaciones.

> Gabriel García Márquez (1927–2014), un escritor (*writer*) colombiano leído (*read*) y admirado en todo el mundo

¿Puede nombrar usted a algunos escritores muy importantes de su país? ¿Cuál es su escritor favorito?

[a]*sin... without a doubt* [b]*body of work* [c]*journalist*
[d]*short stories* [e]*essays* [f]*a... throughout*

C. ¿Qué quiere usted?

Paso 1. En parejas, hablen de cómo desean afectar las acciones de otras personas.

MODELO: **E1:** ¿Qué quieres que haga tu padre?

E2: Quiero que mi padre me **compre** una computadora.

| insistir en
mandar
permitir
preferir
prohibir
querer
recomendar | + | padre/madre
amigos/as
hermano/a
profesor(a)
novio/a
esposo/a
compañero/a de cuarto
hijo/a, hijos
¿ ? | + | comprarme... (una televisión, rosas, ¿ ?)
visitarme... (mañana, el jueves, ¿ ?)
invitarme... (al cine, a cenar, ¿ ?)
(no) dar tarea... (hoy, mañana, ¿ ?)
ayudarme... (a hacer la tarea, ¿ ?)
salir con... (otra persona, ¿ ?)
llamarme... (el viernes, ¿ ?)
explicarme... (la gramática, ¿ ?)
¿ ? |

Paso 2. Ahora hablen de las cosas que otras personas quieren, prefieren, permiten, etcétera, que ustedes hagan.

MODELO: **E1:** ¿Qué quieren tus hijos que hagas?

E2: Quieren que yo compre una computadora nueva.

D. El programa de radio

Paso 1. *Te escucho* es un programa de radio que da consejos sobre todo tipo de problemas. Hoy son problemas relacionados con el uso y abuso de la tecnología. En parejas, imaginen que ustedes son los presentadores del programa. Lean lo que dicen los siguientes radioyentes (*listeners*) y preparen las respuestas que ustedes creen que los moderadores del programa deben darles.

1. **Habla Hortensia:** «Soy una chica de 20 años. Acabo de mudarme a esta ciudad y tengo pocos amigos aquí. Pero no me siento sola porque siempre estoy conectada a internet. Mi madre dice que no es normal que yo pase tantas horas en la computadora y que no salga con los amigos. ¿Qué piensan ustedes? ¿Qué me recomiendan?»

2. **Habla la Sra. Silva:** «Mi esposo es un hombre bueno y responsable. Pero la mayor parte del tiempo que pasa en casa, está en el estudio, en internet. Yo no comprendo por qué pasa tanto tiempo en eso. Estoy preocupada y también aburrida. ¿Qué me recomiendan que haga? ¿Qué le debo decir a mi esposo?»

> **Estrategia**
>
> Empiecen sus consejos con cláusulas como las siguientes.
>
> **Te/Le recomendamos/ sugerimos que...**
> **Es importante / urgente / necesario que...**
> **Dudamos que...**

3. **Habla Guillermo, un joven de 17 años:** «Mi hermano de 13 años está en Instagram, lo que es normal. Pero ayer descubrí que pone fotos de él y de toda la familia en internet. Yo no quiero que ponga fotos de nosotros, pero él dice que las fotos son suyas (*his*). Hay una foto horrible de mi madre. No quiero decírselo a mis padres porque tengo miedo de que le quiten el teléfono celular a mi hermano. Pero no sé qué otra cosa puedo hacer. ¿Cuáles son mis opciones? ¿Es mejor que no haga nada?»

Paso 2. Ahora piensen en un problema con la tecnología que sea similar a los del **Paso 1.** Descríbanlo por escrito (*in writing*). El resto de la clase les va a hacer sugerencias sobre cómo resolverlo.

E. Intercambios

Paso 1. Complete las siguientes oraciones lógicamente... ¡y con sinceridad!

1. Mis padres (hijos, abuelos,...) insisten en que (yo) _____.
2. Mi mejor amigo/a (esposo/a, novio/a,...) desea que (yo) _____.
3. Prefiero que mis amigos _____.
4. No quiero que mis amigos _____.
5. Es urgente que (yo) _____.
6. Es necesario que mi mejor amigo/a (esposo/a, novio/a,...) _____.

Paso 2. En parejas, entrevístense para saber cómo completaron las oraciones del **Paso 1.** Luego díganle a la clase algo que ustedes tienen en común.

MODELO: **1.** ¿En qué insisten tus padres?

F. Prevención de los peligros (*dangers*) de la tecnología

Paso 1. Todo el mundo sabe que las tecnologías de la información y la comunicación (TIC) presentan problemas para muchas personas, especialmente para los niños y adolescentes. Haga una lista de cinco recomendaciones básicas para los padres, siguiendo los modelos.

Considere las siguientes ideas:

- el uso de los aparatos en general
- el tiempo y los lugares de acceso
- el uso de los datos personales y las contraseñas
- el acceso a las redes sociales
- el uso de la cámara

MODELOS: Prohíban que sus hijos usen...
　　　　　Es necesario que su hijo / sus hijos limite(n)...

> **Vocabulario útil**
>
> desconectar　　　quitar *to take away*
> limitar　　　　　supervisar

CONTROL PARENTAL

VIDEO JUEGOS

PRIVACIDAD

REDES SOCIALES

WEBCAM

Paso 2. Ahora, en parejas, compartan (*share*) sus consejos. Luego díganle a la clase los cinco mejores consejos de ustedes.

✦ Todo junto

A. Lengua y cultura: La ciudad de Cartagena, Colombia

Paso 1. Completar. Complete the following passage with the correct forms of the words in parentheses, as suggested by context. When two possibilities are given, select the correct word. **¡OJO!** As you conjugate the verbs in this activity, put the infinitives preceded by I: in the imperfect. Other verbs will be present indicative, present subjunctive, or infinitive as determined by the context.

Mayra y Joaquín son dos colombianos que viven en mi ciudad. Los dos (ser / estar)¹ de Cartagena, una _____ (grande)² ciudad colombiana que (ser / estar)³ en el mar Caribe. De niña, Mayra _____ (I: vivir)⁴ en la parte más antigua (en la / de la)⁵ ciudad, el Centro Amurallado[a] colonial. La familia de Joaquín _____ (tener)⁶ un apartamento en Bocagrande, la zona (más / mejor)⁷ moderna de Cartagena. Sin embargo, los dos les hacen las _____ (mismo)⁸ recomendaciones a las personas (que / quienes)⁹ desean visitar la ciudad.

Unos edificios de apartamentos muy modernos en Bocagrande

Mayra y Joaquín (ser / estar)¹⁰ de acuerdo en que el Centro Amurallado tiene _____ (mucho)¹¹ cosas que ver. Por eso, los dos recomiendan (que / lo que)¹² los turistas en Cartagena _____ (dar)¹³ un paseo por ese centro histórico de la ciudad. También es necesario (que / —)¹⁴ vean y admiren las fortalezas y las murallas.[b] Además (ser / haber)¹⁵ playas muy chéveres en el Parque Natural Corales del Rosario y en la isla Barú.* Para cenar Mayra y Joaquín _____ (sugerir)¹⁶ que los turistas vayan a un restaurante en la Boquilla[†] y que _____ (pedir)¹⁷ mariscos. Luego deben _____ (ir)¹⁸ a un club a bailar cumbia.

[a]Centro... *Walled Center*   [b]fortalezas... *forts and walls*

Paso 2. Comprensión

1. ¿De qué ciudad son Mayra y Joaquín?
2. ¿Qué es lo que distingue la geografía de esta ciudad?
3. ¿En qué partes de la ciudad vivían Mayra y Joaquín de niños?
4. ¿Qué recomiendan Mayra y Joaquín que hagan los turistas que visitan Cartagena?

👆 Paso 3. En acción

 Ahora, en parejas, hagan una serie de recomendaciones para las personas que visitan su ciudad y su universidad.

MODELO: Les recomendamos que suban a la colina Foss porque desde allí hay una vista muy bonita de la universidad.

Vocabulario útil

Verbos/frases para recomendar	Ideas	Lugares	
pro**poner**	**comer** en	la **colina**	hill
recom**endar** (**ie**)	**dar** un paseo por	la **fuente**	fountain
sug**erir** (**ie**) (**i**)	**subir**/**bajar** por/a	el **puente**	bridge
es buena idea/interesante	**ir** a / **ver** / visitar	la **torre**	tower

---

*La isla Barú *is about ten minutes by motorboat from Cartagena. It has white sand beaches, crystal-clear water, and big coral reefs.*
†La Boquilla *is a fishing village outside of Cartagena; it has a long, secluded beach with restaurants and bars.*

B. Proyecto: Cómo mejorar la contaminación acústica

No hay duda (*doubt*) de que vivimos en un mundo con mucho ruido. Por eso, en parejas, van a crear unas reglas (*rules*) para mejorar (*improve*) la situación en algún lugar concreto.

Vocabulario útil

la ambulancia	
el claxon	(car) horn
el despertador	alarm clock
el megáfono	loudspeaker
el ronquido	snoring
la sirena	
el sonido	sound
el taladro (eléctrico)	(electric) drill
el timbre	ring (*on a phone, door,* and so on)
el volumen	volume

Paso 1. Preparación. Hagan dos listas: una de cosas que causan ruido y la otra de espacios o situaciones que son especialmente ruidosos (*noisy*). La ilustración les puede dar algunas ideas.

Paso 2. Desarrollo. (*Development.*) Ahora elijan uno de los espacios o situaciones que ustedes creen que pueden mejorar, pensando especialmente en la gente joven. Hagan una lista de recomendaciones o reglas sobre lo que se debe o no se debe hacer para reducir el nivel de ruido. Usen mandatos de **tú**.

Paso 3. Presentación. Finalmente, elijan un buen título para su lista y, si es posible, añadan una imagen. Luego impriman su lista y preséntenla a la clase.

Video: Salu2 «¡No sin mi celular!»

You can watch two segments of this chapter's video in the **Video: Salu2** section, found at the end of the eBook.

Telmex es una compañía mexicana de telecomunicaciones.

Klic Video Productions/McGraw Hill

Enfoque cultural: Espacios urbanos

Antes de leer

¿Conoce usted a sus vecinos? ¿Qué relación mantiene con ellos? ¿Hablan con frecuencia o solo se saludan?

En Colombia

Dos vecinos en una calle de Bogotá

Es común que los vecinos de un barrio colombiano desarrollen[a] una relación estrecha[b] con los otros vecinos y que hasta[c] organicen juntos fiestas y celebraciones en el barrio para fechas especiales. Es normal saber los nombres de muchos de los vecinos del barrio, no solo los[d] del edificio o de la calle donde uno vive. Con frecuencia, la gente habla de los amigos del barrio como un grupo específico, parecido[e] a los amigos del colegio,[f] de la universidad o del trabajo. En el barrio, es normal ver grupos de personas que charlan[g] juntas, en la plaza o en una esquina[h] o simplemente en la puerta de un edificio o tienda. Por eso el barrio es un lugar de intensa vida social, especialmente para las personas que no trabajan fuera de casa o para las personas mayores. Y, por supuesto,[i] para los niños.

[a]develop [b]close [c]even [d]those [e]similar [f]grade/high school [g]are chatting [h]corner [i]por... of course

Comprensión ¿Por qué es importante el barrio en la vida de una ciudad hispana?

En otros países hispanos

El edificio de la Alcaldía Municipal (*town hall*) en la Plaza de Bolívar, Bogotá

- **En todo el mundo hispanohablante** Lo común es que haya una plaza central, rodeada de[a] algunos de los edificios más importantes de la ciudad, como el ayuntamiento[b] o la catedral. Estas plazas centrales frecuentemente reciben el nombre de plaza Mayor o plaza de Armas. Había plazas de este tipo en España antes de la conquista de América. Los españoles llevaron el diseño[c] a sus nuevas ciudades americanas.

- **En México y la Argentina** Varias ciudades hispanas tienen metro, pero los[d] de México y la Argentina son notables. El[e] de Buenos Aires es el más antiguo del hemisferio sur. Su construcción comenzó en 1913. Pero el más impresionante es sin duda el metro de la Ciudad de México. Es el segundo metro en longitud[f] de Norteamérica y el mayor de Latinoamérica. Por el número de pasajeros, es el quinto[g] del mundo. Su sistema para nombrar las estaciones es muy colorido y eficiente. Usa palabras y dibujos, para que las personas analfabetas[h] también puedan interpretarlo.

[a]rodeada... *surrounded by* [b]*town hall* [c]*design* [d]*those* [e]*That* (i.e. el metro) [f]*length* [g]*fifth* [h]para... *so that people who can't read*

Comprensión ¿Por qué hay una plaza central en las ciudades latinoamericanas? ¿Cuál es el metro más antiguo de Latinoamérica? ¿Y el más impresionante?

En acción

Describe la plaza más importante o famosa de su ciudad. ¿Cómo se llama? ¿Por qué o de quién recibió ese nombre? ¿Qué edificios están allí?

Lectura

Antes de leer

Conteste las siguientes preguntas.

1. ¿En qué tipo de lugar vive usted ahora: en una ciudad grande o pequeña, o en una zona residencial o rural? ¿Y cómo era el lugar donde vivía de niño/a?
2. ¿De qué maneras influye en usted el lugar donde vive ahora (o vivía de niño/a) en cuanto a (*as far as*) las siguientes ideas?
   - sus preferencias en cuanto a la comida
   - la manera en que se viste
   - cómo pasa su tiempo libre
   - cómo se relaciona con otras personas
   - sus necesidades materiales
   - sus ideas políticas y sociales

Vocabulario para leer

el alma	soul
la espalda	back
la fila	row
la lágrima	teardrop
cuadrado/a	square
enfilado/a	lined up

Unos edificios de apartamentos

«Cuadrados y ángulos», de Alfonsina Storni

Casas enfiladas, casas enfiladas,
casas enfiladas.
Cuadrados, cuadrados, cuadrados.
Casas enfiladas.
5 Las gentes ya tienen el alma cuadrada,
ideas en fila
y ángulos en la espalda.
Yo misma he vertido[a] ayer una lágrima,
Dios mío, cuadrada.

[a]Yo... *I myself shed*

Comprensión

A. Elementos del poema. Identifique los siguientes aspectos del poema.

1. las palabras y frases que se repiten
2. los versos (*lines*) que describen las casas
3. el tipo de lugar que describe el poema
4. los versos que describen a las personas
5. los versos que se refieren a la poeta misma (*herself*)

B. Comentario. Conteste las siguientes preguntas para expresar su opinión como lector(a) (*reader*).

1. ¿Qué efecto tiene la repetición en este poema?
2. ¿Qué relación existe entre las personas y las casas?
3. ¿Qué tipo de persona es la poeta? ¿Qué efecto tiene en ella el ambiente que describe?
4. ¿Cree usted que la poeta se refiere solo a un lugar determinado? ¿O cree que se refiere a un problema más grande?
5. ¿Cree usted que la poeta podría (*could*) ser más feliz en un ambiente diferente? ¿En cuál?

Vocabulario útil

la arquitectura	
la monotonía	
el sentido	sense
sensible	sensitive

Proyecto: Un poema sobre un lugar

Paso 1. Piense en un lugar que no le gusta nada (o si prefiere, uno que le gusta mucho). Visualice ese lugar y haga una lista de algunos de los elementos de ese lugar. También describa la reacción emocional que puedan tener las personas cuando están en ese lugar y el efecto que ese lugar tiene en usted cuando está allí.

Paso 2. De las frases e ideas que anotó para el **Paso 1,** elija las más interesantes y escriba un poema como el (*that*) de Alfonsina Storni. Use la repetición de frases para ayudar a sus lectores a visualizar el lugar y a comprender cómo se sienten las personas cuando están allí.

Paso 3. En grupos, compartan sus poemas. ¿Son suficientemente descriptivos para que (*so that*) todos los miembros del grupo puedan visualizar los lugares y comprender los sentimientos que provocan en el autor / la autora del poema?

Textos orales

Un doctor habla de un proyecto tecnológico

Antes de escuchar

Empareje cada término médico con su definición.

1. _____ un componente necesario para el funcionamiento del cuerpo que es regulado (*regulated*) por la insulina
2. _____ un órgano del cuerpo humano
3. _____ una hormona que produce el páncreas

   a. la glucosa
   b. la insulina
   c. el páncreas

Comprensión

A. La diabetes. Empareje la información de las dos columnas.

1. _____ la característica de diabetes tipo 1
2. _____ el porcentaje de la población adulta mundial que va a sufrir de diabetes en el futuro
3. _____ el nombre común de la diabetes tipo 1
4. _____ el porcentaje de pacientes diabéticos que sufren de diabetes tipo 1
5. _____ el porcentaje de la población adulta mundial que sufre de diabetes en la actualidad

   a. casi el 7%
   b. casi el 8%
   c. el 10%
   d. la diabetes juvenil
   e. la ausencia total de insulina

James R Clarke/Alamy Stock Photo

Dos herramientas (*tools*) útiles en la lucha contra (*struggle against*) la diabetes: un monitor continuo de glucosa y una bomba (*pump*) de insulina

B. Más detalles. Conteste las siguientes preguntas.

1. ¿Dónde ocurre esta conversación? ¿Cómo se llama el programa?
2. ¿Qué es el páncreas artificial? ¿Qué tipo de personas lo necesitan?
3. ¿Existe ya esa máquina?
4. ¿Por qué es un gran proyecto?

 En acción

Nombre y describa un aparato médico que, en su opinión, es muy útil. Explique también cuál es su función principal.

PORTAFOLIO

🎤 Entrevista

Use de modelo las preguntas y respuestas de la sección **Entrevista** al principio de este capítulo para hablar de la zona donde usted vive y de los aparatos que usted usa diariamente para mantener sus relaciones sociales.

💻 Escritura

La educación universitaria: ¿presencial o a distancia?

Una clase presencial y una clase por internet

👥 Antes de escribir

¿Prefieren ustedes las clases presenciales o a distancia? Piensen en las opciones que existen hoy para obtener un título universitario: presencial (es decir, asistiendo a una universidad, según la manera tradicional) o a distancia, gracias a internet. ¿Cuál es el método más usado? ¿Qué ventajas y desventajas tiene cada opción? ¿Cuál fue la opción que ustedes eligieron (*chose*)? ¿Están contentos/as con su decisión? En parejas, hagan una lista de argumentos a favor y en contra de cada una de las dos opciones para obtener un título universitario: de forma presencial o a distancia. Deben incluir ejemplos específicos para apoyar (*support*) sus argumentos.

A escribir

Ahora use las ideas de **Antes de escribir** para comparar las dos opciones educativas. O, si lo prefiere, puede defender una de ellas. Hay más ayuda en Connect.

Para escribir bien

Considere estas opciones para su ensayo:

- Conectores para contrastar ideas: **sin embargo = no obstante, por eso / por un lado** (*on the one hand*), **por otro lado** (*on the other hand*)
- Conectores para transiciones: **en primer lugar, además, para terminar, en resumen**
- Frases para expresar información: **los expertos afirman** (*state*) **que...** + indicativo, **los estudios muestran** (*show*) **que...** + indicativo
- Generalizaciones: **es importante / necesario / mejor... que...** + subjuntivo

---

✿ En la comunidad

Entreviste a una persona hispana de su universidad o ciudad sobre su ciudad de origen y el barrio donde vivía en su país.

Preguntas posibles

- ¿Qué tipo de ciudad es? ¿Es grande o pequeña? ¿antigua o moderna?
- ¿Hay buenas vistas desde algún punto de la ciudad? ¿Hay un buen sistema de transporte público, como autobuses o metro?
- ¿Dónde vivía su familia? ¿En el centro o en las afueras? ¿en un barrio histórico o moderno? ¿en una casa individual o en un apartamento?
- ¿Cómo es (o era) la vida del barrio? Pida detalles.

◉ Producción audiovisual

Filme dos entrevistas con estudiantes o personal (*personnel*) de habla hispana en su universidad. Sus personas entrevistadas deben hablar de donde viven y de los usos que hacen de la tecnología. Use las preguntas de la **Entrevista** como modelo.

Más ideas para el portafolio

- Publique algo en español en su muro (*wall*) de Facebook. Luego saque una foto de su post e inclúyala en su portafolio, con una explicación de lo que escribió.
- Incluya un anuncio de celulares en español, de internet o de una revista o periódico. Explique lo que le gusta del anuncio y del producto o servicio mismo (*itself*) y también si el producto o servicio es comparable con lo que hay en este país.
- Si ha estado jugando (*you have been playing*) Practice Spanish: Study Abroad, en Quest 9 usted tuvo que decidir dónde quedarse cuando estaba de vacaciones en Colombia. Ahora haga un breve video dándoles consejos a los turistas que quieran visitar la ciudad donde usted vive. ¿Dónde deben quedarse? ¿en un hotel? ¿en una tienda de campaña? ¿en una pensión (*hostel*)? ¿con usted? Explique por qué. ¿Qué servicios (*amenities*) ofrece este lugar?

Sugerencia: You are now ready to play Quest 9 in **Practice Spanish: Study Abroad.**

EN RESUMEN En este capítulo

Gramática en breve

33. *Tú* Commands

Negative **tú** commands = "opposite" vowel

-ar → -es

-er/-ir → -as

Affirmative **tú** commands = **usted** form of the present indicative

-ar → -a

-er/-ir → -e

34. Present Subjunctive: An Introduction

Endings: "opposite" vowel

-ar: -e, -es, -e, -emos, -éis, -en

-er/-ir: -a, -as, -a, -amos, -áis, -an

Structure:

①   ②

first subject = **que** second subject =
indicative **subjunctive**

35. Uses of the Subjunctive: Influence

①   ②

INFLUENCE

first subject = **que** second subject =
indicative **subjunctive**

Vocabulario

Los verbos

alegrarse (de)	to be glad, happy (about)
dudar	to doubt
esperar	to hope
haber (*inf. of* hay)	(there is, there are)
insistir (en)	to insist (on)
mandar	to order
obtener (like tener)	to get, obtain
permitir	to permit, allow
prohibir (prohíbo)	to prohibit, forbid

Repaso: desear, esperar (*to expect*), pedir (pido) (i), preferir (prefiero) (i), querer (quiero), recomendar (recomiendo), sugerir (sugiero) (i)

La tecnología

el archivo	(computer) file
la arroba	@
los auriculares	earphones/headphones
el buscador	search engine
el buzón de voz	voice mailbox
el canal	channel
la carpeta	(computer) folder
la contraseña	password
el correo electrónico	e-mail
el disco duro	hard drive
el equipo (electrónico)	(electronic) equipment
el espacio (de almacenamiento)	(storage) space
la impresora	printer
la nube	cloud
la página web	web page
la pantalla (grande/plana)	(big/flat) screen (monitor)
el ratón	mouse
la red social	social network
el sitio web	website
el teléfono fijo	landline

Cognados: el android, la aplicación, el blog, la cámara, el CD, el CD-ROM, el chateo, el control remoto, el documento, el DVD, el e-mail, el escáner, el Instagram, Facebook (*m.*), el fax, la (foto)copia, la fotocopiadora, el internet, el iPhone, memoria, la la memoria USB, el módem, el radio, el TikTok, el tuit, Twitter (*m.*), el video, el wifi

Repaso: la computadora (portátil), la ropa, el (teléfono) celular, la tele(visión)

almacenar	to store; to save
apagar (gu)	to turn off (a machine)
bajar	to download
buscar (qu) en internet	to look up on the internet
cambiar (de)	to change
descargar (gu)	to download
encender (ie)	to turn on (a machine)
entrar/estar en Facebook / en internet	to go/be on Facebook / online
fallar	to "crash" (computer)
funcionar	to work, function; to run (machines)
grabar	to record; to tape
guardar	to keep; to save (documents)
imprimir	to print
manejar	to operate (a machine)
navegar (gu) la red	to surf the internet
obtener (like tener)	to get, obtain
publicar (qu)	to post (as on Facebook); to publish
subir	to upload

Cognados: conectarse, copiar, hacer clic, hacer (foto)copia, instalar, tuitear

Repaso: buscar (qu), conseguir (like seguir), entrar, estar, hacer, mandar un mensaje (de texto), poner (to turn on [a machine])

La vivienda

las afueras	outskirts; suburbs
el alquiler	rent
el ascensor	elevator
la avenida	avenue
el barrio	neighborhood
la calefacción	heat
la calle	street
el/la dueño/a	landlord, landlady
el edificio de apartamentos	apartment building
la farmacia	pharmacy
el gas	gas (residential; not for cars)
el gasto	expense
el gimnasio	gym
el/la inquilino/a	tenant; renter
la parada del autobús	bus stop
la parada del metro	subway stop
el piso	floor (of a building)
el primer piso	first floor (second story)
el segundo piso	second floor (third story)

la planta baja	ground floor
el/la portero/a	building manager; doorman
la residencia de ancianos	nursing home
el/la vecino/a	neighbor
la vista (a, de)	view (of)
la zona	zone; area
la vivienda	housing

Cognados: la electricidad, el supermercado

Repaso: el apartamento, el autobús, la casa, el centro, la dirección, el/la dueño/a (owner), la escuela, la plaza

alquilar	to rent
mudarse	to move (residences)

Repaso: vivir

Otros sustantivos

los/las demás	others
la mentira	lie
el/la usuario/a	user

Los adjetivos

actual	current
plano/a	flat

Repaso: electrónico/a, grande

Palabras adicionales

es importante que + subjunctive	it's important that
es mejor que + subjunctive	it's best that
es necesario que + subjunctive	it's necessary that
es urgente que + subjunctive	it's urgent that

Vocabulario personal

Use this space or a vocabulary notebook to write down other words and phrases you learn in this chapter.

13

El arte y la cultura

En este capítulo

VOCABULARY
The arts   390
Ranking things (*first, second ...*)   394

GRAMMAR
Expressing emotion with the subjunctive   395
Expressing doubt or denial with the subjunctive   400
A summary of subjunctive uses so far   404

COUNTRIES OF FOCUS: ECUADOR AND BOLIVIA

Cuadros en venta (*Paintings on sale*) de una artista ecuatoriana

Bernai Velarde

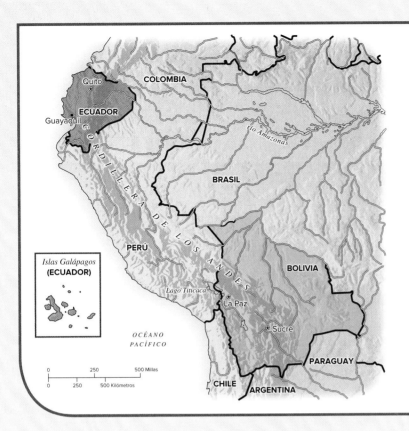

EL ECUADOR

18,2 (coma dos) millones de habitantes

- Las islas Galápagos, donde Darwin empezó a idear su teoría de la evolución, son territorio ecuatoriano.

- El Ecuador y Bolivia tienen una geografía impresionante, caracterizada por la cordillera de los Andes y la Amazonia.

- Los dos países tienen un alto porcentaje de población indígena y mestiza.

BOLIVIA

12 millones de habitantes

- Bolivia (como el Paraguay) no tiene litoral (costa) marítimo.

⟨🔊⟩ ENTREVISTA

These questions related to the chapter theme are answered here by a native speaker. You will be able to ask and answer them yourself with personal information in the **Entrevista** activity in the **Portafolio** section at the end of the chapter.

Ismael Pérez Mendizábal contesta las preguntas.

– **¿Le interesa el arte en general? ¿Qué tipo de expresión artística le interesa más? ¿Le fascina la pintura, la escultura, la arquitectura, la danza, el cine, el teatro o el diseño de moda**[a]**? ¿O prefiere alguna otra?**

– Bueno... la verdad es que depende. Me encanta el cine y también me interesa la literatura porque me gusta mucho leer. Y... pues, claro,[b] me gusta la música pop y para bailar. Pero las otras artes no me interesan tanto.

– **¿Hay museos en su ciudad? ¿De qué tipo?**

– Sí, claro. Hay museos muy buenos y de diferentes enfoques.[c] Por ejemplo, hay el Museo Nacional sobre la historia de Colombia. Y también está el Museo de Arte Moderno de Bogotá. Y el Museo del Oro, que tiene la mejor colección en todo el mundo de piezas metalúrgicas de la época precolombina. Y el Maloka, un museo interactivo de ciencias. ¡Es bien chévere[d]!

– **¿Hay artesanía típica de su región, como la cerámica o textiles o de otro tipo?**

– En Colombia hay mucha tradición de artesanías, ya desde[e] la época precolombina. Hay mucho trabajo textil por todo el país.

[a]diseño... *fashion design*   [b]*of course*   [c]*emphases*   [d]bien... *really cool*
[e]ya... *dating from*

Daniel Ernst/Getty Images

VOCABULARIO: PREPARACIÓN

You can hear the pronunciation of theme vocabulary words and phrases in the eBook.

Las artes

La expresión artística	Los/Las artistas	Los verbos		Las obras artísticas
la arquitectura	el arquitecto / la arquitecta	diseñar	to design	el edificio
el baile / la danza	el bailarín / la bailarina	bailar		el baile, el ballet, la danza
el cine / el teatro / la ópera	el actor / la actriz (*pl.* actrices) el director / la directora el dramaturgo / la dramaturga playwright	actuar (actúo) dirigir (dirijo)	to direct	la película, la obra de teatro, la ópera
el dibujo	el/la dibujante	dibujar	to draw	el dibujo
la escultura	el escultor / la escultora	esculpir	to sculpt	la escultura
la literatura	el autor / la autora el escritor / la escritora el/la novelista el/la poeta	escribir		la obra de teatro, la novela, el poema
la pintura	el pintor / la pintora	pintar		el cuadro, la pintura

¡OJO!

The word **arte** is both masculine and feminine. The masculine articles and adjectives are normally used with **arte** in the singular (**el arte abstracto**). The feminine articles are used in the plural (**las artes visuales**). Note that **las artes** often refers to "the arts" in general.

Más sobre las obras artísticas

las entradas	tickets (*to a performance, movie ...*)
el espectáculo	show
la fotografía	photography
el/la guía	guide
el guion	script
la imagen	image
el museo	museum
la obra (de arte)	work (of art)
la obra de teatro	play
la obra maestra	masterpiece
el papel	role
el siglo	century

Cognados: la comedia, el concierto, el drama, la escena, la música, el mural

Otros verbos

crear	to create
tejer	to weave

La tradición cultural

la artesanía	arts and crafts
la cerámica	pottery; ceramics
las ruinas	ruins
los tejidos	woven goods
folclórico/a	traditional

Así se dice

Various words are used to describe comedians: **el/la comediante, el/la humorista,** or **el cómico / la cómica.**

An alternative spelling of **folclórico/a** is **folklórico/a.**

Comunicación

A. Obras de arte

Paso 1. ¿Qué clase de arte representan las siguientes obras y qué son?

1. la catedral de una gran ciudad
2. las obras de Diego Rivera y Frida Kahlo
3. la Estatua de la Libertad
4. *El cascanueces* (*The Nutcracker*)
5. las obras de los directores Alfonso Cuarón y Guillermo del Toro
6. *La bohème* y *La traviata*
7. las pirámides aztecas y mayas
8. *Don Quijote* y *Hamlet*
9. *Las meninas*, de Diego Velázquez
10. «El cuervo (*The Raven*)», de Edgar Allan Poe
11. las imágenes de los actores en las revistas o en internet
12. las obras de Selena Gómez o de Lady Gaga

Paso 2. Ahora dé otros ejemplos de obras en cada una de las categorías artísticas que usted mencionó en el **Paso 1.**

B. ¿Qué hacen?

Paso 1. Haga oraciones completas, usando una palabra o frase de cada columna. **¡OJO!** Hay más de una posibilidad en algunos casos.

MODELO: La compositora compone música para una película.

el/la compositor(a) el/la artesano/a el actor / la actriz el/la director(a) el/la músico/a el bailarín / la bailarina el/la dramaturgo/a el/la pintor(a) el/la escritor(a) el/la arquitecto/a el/la poeta	+	bailar componer dirigir diseñar escribir esculpir hacer interpretar mirar pintar tocar trabajar	+	música, canciones, musicales novelas, poesía en el ballet cerámica edificios y casas papeles en la televisión guiones tejidos con actores obras de teatro cuadros instrumentos

(Continúa).

Paso 2. Ahora, con dos o tres compañeros, dé nombres de artistas en cada categoría. ¿Cuántos artistas hispanos pueden nombrar?

Nota comunicativa: Más sobre los gustos y preferencias

You already know a number of verbs for talking about what you like and don't like: **gustar, encantar, molestar.** As you know, these verbs are used with indirect object pronouns, and the verb always agrees with the thing or things liked or disliked, not with the person whose preferences are being described.

Here are some additional verbs that are used like **gustar.**

- **aburrir**   **Me aburre** el baile moderno.
  Modern dance is boring to me (bores me).
- **atraer**   A Juan **le atraen** las ruinas incas.
  Juan is drawn to (attracted by) Incan ruins.
- **fascinar**   **Nos fascinan** las artesanías indígenas.
  We're fascinated by (We love) indigenous handicrafts.

You can use some of these verbs in **Comunicación C.**

C. Actividades culturales

Paso 1. Complete las siguientes oraciones de manera que sean ciertas para usted.

Vocabulario útil

los conciertos de música clásica
el *country* / *hip hop* / jazz / el pop / el *rap* / el rock
los museos de arte moderno / de ciencias / de historia
la música de los años 90 (2000,...)
las obras de teatro
las películas extranjeras con subtítulos
los recitales de poesía en algún café

1. Me gusta mucho _____ (una actividad relacionada con el arte).
2. El arte que más me atrae como espectador(a) es _____.
3. (No) Tengo talento artístico para _____.
4. (No) Me gusta ir a mercados y ferias de artesanía. Allí (no) compro _____.
5. En la universidad, los espectáculos que más me atraen son _____.
6. En cuanto a (*As for*) música, prefiero _____. Mi canción / artista / cantante favorito/a es _____.

Paso 2. Ahora haga cinco preguntas sobre las oraciones que usted completó (*completed*) en el **Paso 1,** usando verbos de la **Nota comunicativa.**

MODELO: ¿Te gustan mucho las películas extranjeras con subtítulos?

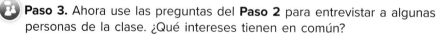 **Paso 3.** Ahora use las preguntas del **Paso 2** para entrevistar a algunas personas de la clase. ¿Qué intereses tienen en común?

Nota cultural: La arquitectura en el mundo hispano

La arquitectura de los países hispanohablantes refleja la variedad de herencias[a] estéticas a través de[b] los siglos: las[c] que ya estaban en el continente antes de la llegada de los españoles y las que estos[d] trajeron.

- **Los pueblos indígenas** Estos pueblos crearon obras arquitectónicas impresionantes en la época prehispánica. Los grandes imperios azteca, maya e inca, entre otros, construyeron edificios y ciudades que les fascinaron a los españoles. Algunos ejemplos: Machu Picchu, la ciudad sagrada[e] de los incas en el Perú, y los centros urbanos de Tikal en Guatemala (maya) y Teotihuacán en México (azteca).

La iglesia (*Church*) de San Francisco, del siglo XVII, en Quito, Ecuador

- **Los españoles** Los españoles trajeron a América los estilos artísticos europeos del momento y los aplicaron a las ciudades que inmediatamente empezaron a construir: edificios civiles y religiosos que compiten en belleza[f] con los edificios europeos. Ejemplos: la catedral de Quito (1567, el Ecuador) y la de la Ciudad de México (1571).

  Parte de la tradición estética de los españoles incluía el estilo que dejaron los musulmanes[g] durante los 800 años que ocuparon España (del siglo VIII al siglo XV). Un ejemplo de esa herencia es el uso de los azulejos,[h] muy común ahora en todo el mundo hispanohablante, para decorar las paredes y otras partes de los edificios.

- **Las ciudades modernas** En la actualidad,[i] la arquitectura sigue transformando ciudades a ambos[j] lados del Atlántico. La Ciudad de México, la ciudad de Panamá, Santiago de Chile, Buenos Aires y Madrid son algunos ejemplos más sobresalientes[k] de las grandes ciudades modernas, en donde los rascacielos[l] conviven[m] con edificios representativos de la larga historia de cada país. Los viejos edificios se renuevan[n] y se modifican para darles nuevos usos, de tal manera que[ñ] siguen siendo parte activa en la vida de cada ciudad.

¿Cuáles son los edificios o complejos arquitectónicos sobresalientes en su estado o ciudad?

[a]*heritages* [b]*a... across* [c]*those* [d]*they (the Spanish)* [e]*sacred* [f]*beauty* [g]*Muslims* [h]*tiles* [i]*En... Currently* [j]*both* [k]*outstanding* [l]*skyscrapers* [m]*coexist* [n]*se... are being renovated* [ñ]*de... so that*

D. *Ternura.* Después de leer **Algo sobre Oswaldo Guayasamín** y contemplar su obra, complete las siguientes ideas.

1. El cuadro *Ternura* muestra (*shows*)...
2. *Ternura* refleja (*reflects*)...
3. (No) Me gusta el cuadro *Ternura* porque...
4. Es importante que los artistas...
5. Creo que Guayasamín quiere que...

Algo sobre Oswaldo Guayasamín

El pintor y escultor Oswaldo Guayasamín (1919–1999) era un artista ecuatoriano mundialmente reconocido[a] y admirado. Era hijo de padre quechua y madre mestiza. Por eso su obra, que se considera expresionista, tiene toques[b] indigenistas. Sus pinturas y esculturas hablan del sufrimiento[c] y las injusticias que soportan[d] los seres[e] humanos.

Piense en una de las pinturas o esculturas que más le gusta. ¿Qué sentimientos refleja? ¿Por qué le gusta a usted esa obra?

[a]*mundialmente... recognized throughout the world* [b]*touches, elements* [c]*suffering* [d]*withstand, bear* [e]*beings*

Ternura (*Tenderness*), un cuadro de la serie «Mientras viva siempre te recuerdo», que Guayasamín dedicó a su madre y a todas las madres del mundo

Los ordinales

primer(o/a)	first	**sexto/a**	sixth
segundo/a	second	**séptimo/a**	seventh
tercer(o/a)	third	**octavo/a**	eighth
cuarto/a	fourth	**noveno/a**	ninth
quinto/a	fifth	**décimo/a**	tenth

- The masculine singular form of ordinals is often used to organize instructions or items in a list.

  Primero, den un paseo por el centro de Quito. **Segundo,** les recomiendo que visiten la casa de Guayasamín. **Tercero,** tomen el teleférico para ver una vista magnífica de la ciudad.

- When they accompany a noun, ordinals are adjectives and they must agree in number and gender. Ordinals usually precede the nouns: **el <u>cuarto</u> concierto, la <u>quinta</u> película, las <u>primeras</u> entradas, los <u>primeros</u> pasos.**

- When they precede masculine singular nouns, **primero** and **tercero** shorten to **primer** and **tercer: el <u>primer</u> día, el <u>tercer</u> mes.**

- As in English, ordinal numbers are sometimes abbreviated. The endings of the abbreviations show gender and number agreement: **el 1er grado, la 3ª persona, el 5° guion.** When agreement is not needed, as in instructions, ordinals are abbreviated as **1°, 2°, 3°,** and so on.

Comunicación

A. ¿Cultura, yo?

Paso 1. Veamos (*Let's see*) si usted tiene interés en la cultura o no. Ordene las siguientes actividades según sus preferencias y hábitos, empezando por **1°.**

_____ ir al cine a ver las últimas películas en inglés

_____ ver películas extranjeras dobladas (*dubbed*) o subtituladas

_____ visitar museos, preferentemente en visitas guiadas

_____ comprar o sacar de la biblioteca libros de ficción

_____ ver obras de teatro

_____ bailar en clubes y fiestas

_____ ver programas de la tele

_____ ir a conciertos de música clásica/*jazz*

_____ ir a conciertos de música pop / rock / *country*

_____ leer o escribir poesía

Paso 2. Ahora, en parejas, entrevístense sobre sus cinco actividades favoritas. Usen números ordinales.

MODELO: Mi actividad favorita es ir a ver películas extranjeras subtituladas. Mi **segunda** actividad favorita es...

B. Autorretrato (*Self-portrait*) de un(a) estudiante. Complete las oraciones.

1. Soy estudiante de _____ año.
2. Estoy en mi _____ semestre/trimestre de español.
3. Los lunes, mi primera clase es la (*that*) de _____, a la(s) _____ (hora). Mi segunda clase es la de _____, a la(s) _____.
4. Con frecuencia, soy la _____ persona en llegar a la clase de español.
5. Soy la _____ persona de mi familia que asiste a una universidad. Y soy la _____ persona de mi familia que asiste a *esta* universidad.

GRAMÁTICA

 Repaso

Review what you know about the present subjunctive by answering the following questions.

1. Is the subjunctive used in one- or two-clause sentences?
2. Is it used in the main (independent) or subordinate (dependent) clause?
3. Is it used before or after the word **que**?
4. When the subjunctive is used, is the subject the same in both clauses?
5. What verb form follows an impersonal expression when there is no change of subject?
6. Influence is one "cause" of the subjunctive. What are two more subjunctive "triggers"?

You will learn about those two subjunctive "triggers" in **Gramáticas 36** and **37**.

36 Expressing Feelings • Use of the Subjunctive (Part 3): Emotion

Gramática en acción: Diego y Lupe oyen tocar a los mariachis

DIEGO: Ay, ¡cómo me encanta esta música!

LUPE: **Me alegro de que <u>te guste</u>.**

DIEGO: Y **yo me alegro de que <u>estemos</u>** aquí. ¿Sabes el origen de la palabra **mariachi**?

LUPE: No... ¿Lo sabes tú?

DIEGO: Bueno, una de las teorías es que viene del siglo XIX, cuando los franceses ocuparon México. Ellos contrataban a grupos de músicos para tocar en las bodas. Y como los mexicanos no podían pronunciar bien la palabra francesa *mariage,* pues acabaron por decir **mariachi.** Y de allí viene el nombre de los grupos.

LUPE: ¡Qué fascinante! **Me sorprende que <u>sepas</u>** tanto de nuestra historia.

DIEGO: Pues, todo buen antropólogo debe saber un poco de historia también, ¿no?

Un grupo de mariachi

¿Y usted?

1. **¿Le sorprende que** la palabra mariachi **<u>venga</u>** del francés?
2. **¿Le sorprende que** tantas personas **<u>estudien</u>** español en su universidad?
3. **¿Se alegra de que <u>haya</u>** mucha información cultural en esta clase?

Diego and Lupe hear mariachis play DIEGO: *Oh, how I love this music!* LUPE: *I'm glad you like it.* DIEGO: *And I'm glad we're here. Do you know the origin of the word* **mariachi**? LUPE: *No ... Do you?* DIEGO: *Well, one of the theories is that it comes from the nineteenth century, when the French occupied Mexico. They used to hire groups of musicians to play at weddings. And since Mexicans couldn't correctly pronounce the French word* mariage, *they ended up saying* **mariachi.** *And that's where the name of the groups comes from.* LUPE: *How fascinating! I'm surprised (that) you know so much about our history.* DIEGO: *Well, all good anthropologists should also know a bit of history, shouldn't they?*

①	②
EMOTION	
first subject = **indicative** que	second subject = **subjunctive**

1. The Concept of Emotion

Another "trigger" for the use of the subjunctive in the subordinate clause is the concept of *emotion* (**la emoción**). The subject of the main clause *is glad, fears, hopes*, and so on, that the subject of the subordinate clause does something, expressed by a verb in the subjunctive. The verb in the main clause is always in the indicative.

Esperamos que usted **pueda** asistir.
We hope (that) you'll be able to come.

Temo que mi abuelo **esté** muy enfermo.
I'm afraid (that) my grandfather is very ill.

Es una lástima que no **den** conciertos.
It's a shame (that) they're not putting on any concerts.

2. Verbs of Emotion

Here are some verbs of emotion. The ones marked with * are new.

alegrarse de	to be happy about
esperar	to hope; to expect
*****lamentar**	to regret; to feel sorry
*****sentir (siento) (i)**	to regret; to feel sorry
*****temer**	to fear, be afraid
tener miedo (de)	to be afraid (of)

Temo que María **se caiga** mientras baila.
I'm afraid (that) María will fall while she's dancing.

3. Verbs of Emotion Like *gustar*

Gustar and similar verbs are frequently used to express emotion. If there is a change of subject in the subordinate clause, the subjunctive will be used. Only the verb marked with * is new. Notice that a subordinate clause is viewed as a singular subject, so **gusta** (not **gustan**) is used in the sentences.

encantar	molestar
fascinar	*****sorprender** to surprise
gustar	

Me (Te/Le...) encanta / fascina / gusta / molesta / sorprende que...
I'm (You're/He's ...) very glad / fascinated / pleased / annoyed / surprised that ...

¡OJO!

Remember that these verbs are used with indirect object pronouns in Spanish.

Me molesta que las entradas del museo **sean** tan caras.
It bothers me that museum entrance fees are so expensive.

Nos sorprende que este cantante **tenga** tanto éxito.
I'm surprised that this singer is so successful.

4. Impersonal Expressions of Emotion

When a new subject is introduced after a generalization of emotion, it is followed by the subjunctive in the subordinate clause. Here are some general expressions of emotion.

¡OJO!

As you know, when there is no second subject, the infinitive follows verbs of emotion and impersonal expressions of emotion:

Me alegro de / Siento / Tengo miedo de estar aquí. **Es absurdo / bueno / extraño estar** aquí.

es absurdo que...	it's absurd that ...
es extraño que...	it's strange that ...
¡qué extraño que... !	how strange that ... !
es increíble que...	it's incredible that ...
es mejor / bueno /	it's better / good /
malo que...	bad that ...
es normal que...	it's normal that ...
es terrible que...	it's terrible that ...
es una lástima que...	it's a shame that ...
¡qué lástima que... !	what a shame that ... !

Es terrible que la cantante **esté** enferma.
It's awful (that) the singer is ill.

¡Qué extraño que **haya** pocos turistas en las ruinas hoy!
How strange (that) there are so few tourists at the ruins today!

Práctica y comunicación

A. Opiniones sobre el cine

Summary of Emotion

emotion + **que** + change of subject → **subjunctive**

Paso 1. Autoprueba. Diga si en español se debe usar el subjuntivo o el infinitivo en la cláusula subordinada de las siguientes oraciones.

MODELO: I'm surprised you're here. → **subjuntivo**

1. I'm sorry you're angry.
2. I'm sorry to anger you.
3. We're happy to get this present.
4. We're afraid the guide will change the trip.
5. It's great they want to buy the sculpture.
6. I'm not thrilled about working with that director.
7. I'm thrilled they're visiting us.

Paso 2. Complete las siguientes oraciones incompletas con las cláusulas principales más apropiadas para expresar su opinión.

ORACIONES INCOMPLETAS

1. _____ que muchas películas sean violentas.
2. _____ que algunos actores ganen (*earn*) tanto dinero.
3. _____ que haya más representación de actores de otras razas.
4. _____ que no haya muchos papeles interesantes para mujeres de más de 50 años.
5. _____ que gasten millones de dólares en hacer películas mientras que hay gente que se muere de hambre.
6. _____ que _____ (nombre de un actor / una actriz) sea tan famoso/a.

CLÁUSULAS PRINCIPALES

a. Me molesta
b. Es increíble/ extraordinario
c. Es ridículo
d. Espero
e. Me sorprende
f. Es absurdo/ilógico

Paso 3. Ahora, en parejas, túrnense para entrevistarse sobre las ideas del **Paso 2.** Luego díganle al resto de la clase una opinión que tengan en común.

MODELO: **1. E1:** ¿Te molesta que muchas películas sean violentas?
E2: Sí, me molesta mucho. ¿Y a ti?
E2: A mí también. →
A los dos nos molesta que muchas películas sean violentas.

B. Comentarios sobre el arte

Paso 1. Complete las siguientes opiniones sobre esta pintura de Roberto Mamani Mamani. Use la forma apropiada de los verbos entre paréntesis.

1. Este pintor es famoso. Me sorprende que su pintura le _____ (gustar) a la gente. Temo que sus obras _____ (ser) demasiado extrañas para mí. Es una lástima que _____ (haber) tantas obras de arte que yo no comprendo.

Sin título, del pintor aymara Roberto Mamani Mamani (Bolivia, 1962 -)

Ana Nance/Redux Pictures

(Continúa).

2. ¡Me encanta esta pintura! ¡Qué lástima que _____ (haber) gente que no aprecia el arte. Me alegro de que esta pintura _____ (estar) en este libro, porque yo no conocía la obra de Mamani Mamani. Me sorprende que (él) no _____ (tener) más fama fuera de (*outside of*) Bolivia.

Paso 2. Ahora, en parejas, entrevístense sobre sus opiniones de esta pintura. Deben explicar lo que les gusta más y lo que les gusta menos.

Nota comunicativa: Cómo expresar los deseos con *ojalá*

Ojalá is one way to express *I hope* in Spanish. It comes from the Arabic meaning *if Allah wishes*, and it is similar to English *God willing* and Spanish **quiera Dios (si Dios quiere).**

As an expression of emotion, **ojalá** is followed by the present subjunctive. **Ojalá** is invariable in form and the use of **que** with it is optional.

Ojalá can also be used alone as an interjection in response to a question.

You will use **ojalá (que)** in **Práctica C.**

¡Ojalá (que) yo **gane** la lotería algún día!
I hope (that) I win the lottery someday!

¡Ojalá (que) **haya** paz en el mundo algún día!
I hope (that) there will be peace in the world some day!

Ojalá (que) no **pierdan** tu equipaje.
I hope (that) they don't lose your luggage.

—¿Te va a ayudar Julio a estudiar para el examen?
—**¡Ojalá!**

C. Una noche en la ópera. Dos amigos van a la ópera. Usando **ojalá,** diga lo que temen y lo que esperan.

MODELO: las entradas / no costar mucho →
      Ojalá (que) las entradas no **cuesten** mucho.

1. los escenarios: ser fantásticos
2. haber subtítulos en inglés
3. el director (*conductor*): estar preparado
4. los músicos: tocar bien
5. nuestros asientos: no estar lejos del escenario
6. (nosotros) llegar a tiempo

D. Situaciones

Paso 1. Las siguientes personas están pensando en otra persona o en algo que van a hacer. ¿Qué emociones sienten? ¿Qué temen? Conteste las preguntas según los dibujos.

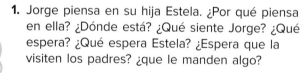

1.

1. Jorge piensa en su hija Estela. ¿Por qué piensa en ella? ¿Dónde está? ¿Qué siente Jorge? ¿Qué espera? ¿Qué espera Estela? ¿Espera que la visiten los padres? ¿que le manden algo?

2. ¿Dónde quiere pasar las vacaciones Mariana? ¿Espera que alguien la acompañe? ¿Dónde espera que estén juntas? ¿Qué teme Mariana? ¿Qué espera?

2.

 Paso 2. Ahora, en parejas, comparen sus respuestas del **Paso 1.** ¿Tuvieron los/las dos la misma impresión de los dibujos?

E. ¿Cómo es nuestra sociedad? Diga lo que usted opina de las siguientes declaraciones. Empiece sus opiniones con las **Expresiones** indicadas o con cualquier (*any*) otra.

MODELO: Los futbolistas profesionales ganan sueldos (*salaries*) fenomenales →
Es increíble que los futbolistas **ganen** sueldos fenomenales.

1. Muchas personas viven para trabajar. No saben descansar.
2. La nuestra (*Ours*) es una sociedad de consumidores.
3. Juzgamos (*We judge*) a los otros por las cosas materiales que tienen.
4. Las personas ricas tienen mucho prestigio en esta sociedad.
5. Las mujeres generalmente no ganan tanto dinero como los hombres por hacer igual trabajo.
6. Algunas obras de arte cuestan millones de dólares.
7. Para mucha gente joven, ver videos en YouTube es más atractivo que leer libros.
8. Hay discriminación contra la gente mayor en ciertas profesiones.

F. Esta universidad. Diga lo que usted opina de las siguientes declaraciones respecto a lo que ocurre en esta universidad. Use frases como: **Me gusta que...** , **Me molesta que...** , **Es terrible que...** , **Sé que...**

MODELO: Gastan mucho/poco dinero en construir nuevos edificios. →
Me molesta que gasten mucho dinero en construir nuevos edificios.

1. Se les da mucha/poca importancia a los deportes.
2. El precio de la matrícula es exagerado / muy bajo.
3. Se ofrecen muchos/pocos cursos en mi especialización.
4. Es necesario estudiar ciencias/lenguas para graduarse.
5. Hay muchos/pocos requisitos (*requirements*) para graduarse.
6. En general, hay mucha/poca gente en las clases.

Expresiones	
es bueno/ malo que	
es extraño/ increíble que	
es normal que	
es una lástima que	+ subjuntivo
lamento que	
me sorprende que	
creo que	
es obvio que	
es verdad que	+ indicativo
la realidad es que	
(yo) sé que	

Algo sobre la Amazonia y los Andes

Es sorprendente que el Ecuador y Bolivia, sin tener territorios adyacentes,[a] compartan[b] tantas características geográficas. Para empezar, los dos países tienen territorio en la Amazonia, una inmensa zona que se extiende por[c] un total de nueve naciones sudamericanas. Además, la cordillera de los Andes cruza Bolivia y el Ecuador y hace que sus capitales sean las capitales más altas del mundo. La Paz está a 12.000 pies (3.650 metros) sobre el nivel del mar. Sucre y Quito están a más de 9.000 pies (2.800 metros).

¿Cuáles son los factores geográficos más importantes de su país? ¿Y de su estado?

[a]*adjacent*   [b]*share*   [c]*through*

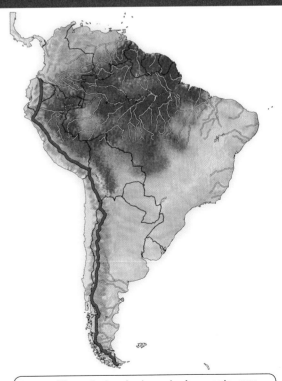

La cordillera de los Andes y la Amazonia, que dominan el mapa de Sudamérica

37 Expressing Uncertainty • Use of the Subjunctive (Part 4): Doubt and Denial

Gramática en acción: El traje tradicional de las bolivianas

Unas mujeres bolivianas con su ropa tradicional, en La Paz

¿Cuánto sabe usted de la ropa que llevan las indígenas bolivianas? ¿Cree que son ciertas o falsas las siguientes declaraciones? Las respuestas están al pie de la página.

1. **Es verdad que** los sombreros hongo son una parte del traje tradicional de las indígenas del altiplano boliviano.
2. **Es probable que** <u>sea</u> muy frecuente ver a bolivianas que llevan sombrero hongo.
3. **Dudo que** los pantalones <u>sean</u> parte del traje tradicional de las bolivianas del altiplano.
4. **No creo que** el uso de los sombreros hongo <u>sea</u> una tradición inca.
5. En Bolivia, **es obvio que** llevar sombrero es una buena protección contra el sol.

¿Y usted?

1. ¿Le gusta el traje tradicional de las mujeres bolivianas? ¿Cree que es hermoso (*beautiful*)? ¿práctico?
2. ¿Le sorprende que las bolivianas indígenas <u>lleven</u> sombrero?

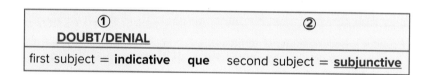

①		②
DOUBT/DENIAL		
first subject = **indicative**	que	second subject = <u>**subjunctive**</u>

1. The Concepts of Doubt and Denial

The concepts of *doubt* (**la duda**) and *denial* (**la negación**) are also "triggers" for the use of the subjunctive in the subordinate clause. The subject of the main clause *doubts, does not believe, denies,* and so on, that the subject of the subordinate clause does something, expressed by a verb in the subjunctive. The verb in the main clause is always in the indicative.

No creo que <u>sean</u> cuadros de Goya.
I don't believe (that) they're paintings by Goya.

Dudo que la actriz <u>pueda</u> terminar el ensayo.
I doubt (that) the main female actor can finish the rehearsal.

The traditional costume of Bolivian women How much do you know about the clothing that indigenous Bolivian women wear? Do you think that the following statements are true or false? The answers are at the bottom of the page. **1.** It's true that bowler hats are a part of the traditional costume of indigenous women of the Bolivian high plateau. **2.** It's likely that one frequently sees Bolivian women who are wearing bowler hats. **3.** I doubt that pants are part of the traditional costume of Bolivian women from the high plateau. **4.** I don't think that the use of bowler hats is an Incan tradition. **5.** In Bolivia, it's obvious that wearing a hat is good protection from the sun.

Respuestas: 1. cierto: Muchas indígenas bolivianas lo llevan. **2.** cierto: Bolivia tiene el porcentaje más alto de población indígena en toda América. Por eso es muy normal ver a mujeres que llevan ropa tradicional. **3.** cierto: La pollera, un tipo de falda con mucho vuelo (flare) y colores, es la ropa típica de las indígenas bolivianas. **4.** cierto: Es una tradición colonial (de la época de los españoles). **5.** cierto: La región del altiplano boliviano está tan elevada que la exposición a los rayos solares es un problema serio. Por eso, el sombrero es una protección ideal para la cara, y también protege a los habitantes del frío.

2. Verbs and Expressions of Doubt (versus Certainty)

Here are some verbs and expressions that imply doubt. They are followed by subjunctive in the subordinate clause if there is a change of subject. New verbs and expressions are marked with *.

*no <u>creer</u>	to disbelieve
dudar	to doubt
*no <u>estar</u> seguro/a de	to be uncertain of
no pensar (pienso)	to not think
*no es seguro que...	it's not certain / a sure thing that ...
*(no) es posible que...	it's (not) possible that ...
*(no) es probable	it's (not) probable
*es improbable que...	it's improbable that ...

> verb or expression of doubt → <u>subjunctive</u> in subordinate clause with different subject

Mis padres **dudan** que yo <u>pueda</u> conseguir una entrada ahora.
My parents doubt that I can get a ticket now.

No es seguro que Emma <u>toque</u> en el concierto.
It's not certain that Emma will play in the concert.

No creo que nadie <u>sepa</u> la verdad.
I don't think (that) anyone knows the truth.

In contrast, verbs and expressions of *certainty* (**la certeza**) and *belief* (**la creencia**) are followed by the indicative in the subordinate clause when there is another subject, because they express what the speaker knows to be the reality or to be true. They express affirmation.

creer	to believe
*estar seguro/a de	to be certain of
no dudar	to believe (not doubt)
pensar (pienso)	to think
*es cierto que	it's certain that
*es seguro que	it's certain / a sure thing that
*es verdad que	it's true that

> verb or expression of certainty → **indicative** in subordinate clause with different subject

Mis padres **creen / están seguros de** que puedo conseguir una entrada ahora.
My parents believe / are sure that I can get a ticket today.

Es verdad que Emma toca en el concierto.
It's certain that Emma plays in the concert.

Pienso que todo el mundo sabe la verdad.
I think everyone knows the truth.

¿Crees que es auténtica la pieza?
Do you think (that) the piece is authentic?
   (I think it's possible that it is.)

¿Crees que <u>sea</u> auténtico el cuadro?
Do you think (that) the painting is authentic?
   (I'm doubtful that it is.)

¡OJO!

When used in questions, these verbs may be followed by either the indicative or the subjunctive in the dependent clause, depending on the level of certainty implied.

3. Verbs and Expressions of Denial

These are always followed by the subjunctive in the dependent clause because they negate the reality or truth of what follows them. They express negation. Only **negar** is new.

*negar (niego) (gu)	to deny
es imposible que...	it's impossible that ...
no es verdad que...	it's not true that ...

> verb or expression of denial → <u>subjunctive</u> in subordinate clause with different subject

Niego / Es imposible / No es verdad que todo el mundo <u>sepa</u> la verdad.
I deny / It's impossible / It isn't true that everyone knows the truth.

4. Infinitive with no Change of Subject

All of these verbs and expressions are generally followed by the infinitive when there is no change of subject.

Creo / No creo saber la verdad.
Niego / Es imposible saber la verdad.

¡OJO!

An exception: it is very common for **creer, dudar,** and **pensar** to be followed by a conjugated verb, indicative or subjunctive, when there is no change of subject.

No creo / Dudo / No pienso que (yo) <u>sepa</u> la verdad.
Creo / Pienso / No dudo que (yo) <u>sé</u> la verdad.

Summary of Doubt and Denial

doubt/denial + **que** + change of subject ➔ <u>subjunctive</u>

Cláusulas Principales

(No) Creo/Dudo que...
(No) Es cierto que...
(No) Estoy seguro/a de que...
(No) Es posible/probable que...

Práctica y comunicación

A. Preferencias artísticas

Paso 1. Autoprueba. Indique las frases que expresan duda o negación.

_____ **1.** Dudamos que...   _____ **5.** No es posible que...
_____ **2.** Estoy segura de que...   _____ **6.** No creen que...
_____ **3.** Niega que...   _____ **7.** No es cierto que...
_____ **4.** Es cierto que...   _____ **8.** Pensamos que...

Paso 2. Exprese su opinión sobre las siguientes declaraciones. Empiece su opinión con una de las cláusulas principales de la lista y cambie el verbo de la cláusula subordinada al subjuntivo si es necesario.

MODELO: **1.** A la mayoría de la gente le gusta ir a los museos de arte. ➔
No creo que a la mayoría de la gente le **guste** ir a los museos de arte.

1. A la mayoría de la gente le gusta ir a los museos de arte.
2. Todos mis amigos prefieren el teatro al cine.
3. La arquitectura le fascina a muchísimas personas.
4. Me encanta regalar artesanía.
5. Voy a conciertos de música clásica con frecuencia.
6. *El cascanueces* (*The Nutcracker*) es el ballet más famoso del mundo.
7. La música es la expresión artística más popular entre la gente joven.
8. Un videoblog se puede considerar una forma de arte.

Paso 3. Ahora, en parejas, túrnense para hacerse preguntas sobre sus opiniones del **Paso 2.** Luego díganle a la clase una opinión que tengan en común.

MODELO: **E1:** No creo que a mucha gente le guste ir a los museos de arte. ¿Y tú?
E2: Yo tampoco. ➔ No creemos / Ninguno de nosotros dos cree que a mucha gente le guste ir a los museos de arte.

B. **Una vasija (*vessel*) en el museo.** Haga oraciones completas para expresar las especulaciones de dos antropólogos sobre una nueva pieza que está en el museo.

Habla el profesor Martín:

1. «creer / que / ser una vasija de la civilización inca»
2. «ser obvio / que / estar hecha de barro (*made of clay*)»
3. «ser posible / que / el diseño (*design*): representar algo en especial»
4. «¿creer / que / ser una pieza auténtica?»

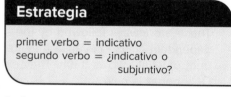

Estrategia

primer verbo = indicativo
segundo verbo = ¿indicativo o subjuntivo?

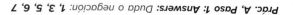

Andreas Wolochow/Shutterstock

Una vasija incaica

Habla la profesora Figueroa:

5. «no creer / que / ser una vasija inca»
6. «ser probable / que / ser una pieza auténtica de la civilización tiahuanacota»
7. «dudar / que / el diseño: simbolizar algo en especial»

C. En el mercado de artesanía de Otavalo, Ecuador. ¿Cómo pueden reaccionar las personas extranjeras que van a un mercado de artesanía como el (*that*) de Otavalo? Complete las oraciones, pensando en los precios de las cosas que por lo general les gustan a los turistas.

1. ¡Es fantástico (que)... !
2. No creo que los precios del mercado...
3. Dudo mucho que estos vendedores...
4. Estoy seguro/a de que...
5. No es muy probable que...
6. Creo que los otavaleños...

> **Vocabulario útil**
>
> **la figurita de cerámica** ceramic figurine
> **la muñeca** doll
> **el poncho**

Una turista y una vendedora en el mercado de Otavalo, Ecuador

Robertharding/Alamy Stock Photo

Nota comunicativa: Verbos que requieren preposiciones

You learned in earlier chapters that when two verbs occur in a series (one right after the other), the second verb is usually the infinitive.

Prefiero/Pienso <u>cenar</u> a las siete.   *I prefer/intend to eat at seven.*

Some Spanish verbs, however, require that a preposition or other word be placed before the second verb (still the infinitive). You have already used many of the Spanish verbs that have this feature. New vocabulary is indicated with*.

- The following verbs require the preposition **a** before an infinitive.

aprender a	empezar (emp<u>ie</u>zo) (<u>c</u>) a	invitar a	venir a
ayudar a	enseñar a	ir a	volver (v<u>ue</u>lvo) a

Mis padres me **enseñaron <u>a</u> bailar.**   *My parents taught me to dance.*

- These verbs or verb phrases require **de** before an infinitive.

acabar de	dejar de tener ganas de
*ac<u>o</u>rdarse (me ac<u>ue</u>rdo) de (*to remember*)	*tratar de (*to try to*)

Siempre **tratamos <u>de</u> llegar** puntualmente.   *We always try to arrive on time.*

- **Insistir** requires **en** before an infinitive.

Insisten <u>en</u> venir esta noche.   *They insist on coming over tonight.*

- Two verbs require **que** before an infinitive: *<u>**hay**</u> **que, tener que.**

Both of them express obligation, but only **tener que** can be conjugated in all persons. **Hay que** is invariable (like **hay**), but of course it can be used in other tenses and moods (**había**, **haya**).

Hay <u>que</u> ver el nuevo museo.   *You (One) must/should see the new museum.*

You will use these verbs in **Práctica D.**

D. En los próximos cinco años... En parejas, hagan oraciones para expresar lo que ustedes creen que les puede ocurrir en el futuro próximo (*near*). Hay que usar una palabra o frase de cada columna o terminar la oración con una idea propia (*of your own*). ¿Cuántas respuestas similares tienen ustedes?

Algo sobre las islas Galápagos

Una tortuga galápago, la especie de tortuga más grande del mundo

El archipiélago de las islas Galápagos está formado por unas 19 islas y más de 40 islotes.[a] Son territorio del Ecuador, país que las protege rigurosamente. Están a casi 600 millas (1.000 km) de la costa ecuatoriana, en el océano Pacífico. La isla más grande es Isabela. El nombre del archipiélago viene de las tortugas gigantes que son endémicas de estas islas. Además de[b] las tortugas galápagos, hay pingüinos, cormoranes, iguanas, leones marinos y otros animales. La variedad de especies endémicas de las Galápagos sirvió de base a la teoría de la evolución de Darwin.

 ¿Cuál es el archipiélago más grande de este país? ¿Por qué es conocido[c] o visitado?

[a]*islets* [b]*Además... Besides*
[c]*well-known*

¿INDICATIVO, SUBJUNTIVO O INFINITIVO?

(no) creo que...
(no) dudo que...
es (im)posible que...
(no) estoy seguro/a de que...
(no) es cierto que...
tengo que...

+

(yo) {
acordarse de
aprender a
dejar de
empezar a
ir a
tratar de
volver a
}

+

ser famoso/a
estar casado/a (*married*)
ganar la lotería
jugar a la lotería
pintar cuadros
fumar
tener hijos
terminar mis estudios
esculpir
¿ ?

38 Expressing Influence, Emotion, Doubt, and Denial • The Subjunctive (Part 5): A Summary

Gramática en acción: Las islas Galápagos

Lea **Algo sobre las islas Galápagos**. Luego complete las oraciones, eligiendo (*choosing*) con lógica un verbo principal.

La iguana terrestre de las islas Galápagos

Quiero (que)...
Espero (que)...
Es fascinante (que)...
} **+ subjuntivo / infinitivo**

Dicen que...
Sé que...
Es obvio que...
} **+ indicativo**

1. ...**haya** tantas especies endémicas.
2. ...las islas Galápagos están en el Pacífico.
3. ...es un lugar especial para los biólogos.
4. ...**estén** muy protegidas (*protected*).
5. ...el Ecuador las **siga** protegiendo.

¿Y usted?

¿Quiere ir a las Galápagos algún día? ¿Quiere visitar otros lugares del Ecuador?

①	②
INFLUENCE / EMOTION / **DOUBT OR DENIAL** }	que + <u>subjunctive</u> infinitive

①	②
INFORMATION / BELIEF / CERTAINTY }	que + **indicative** infinitive

This section will help you review what you have already learned about using the subjunctive and when to use the indicative or the infinitive instead.

1. The Subjunctive in Two-clause Sentences

Remember that, in Spanish, the subjunctive occurs primarily in the second clause of two-clause sentences, with a different subject in each clause. If there is no change of subject, an infinitive follows the first verb.

Quiero
 Es necesario } que **los estudiantes** <u>saquen</u> una buena nota.

I want
 It's necessary for } **the students** *to get a good grade.*

Quiero
 Es necesario } <u>sacar</u> una nota buena.

I want
 It's necessary } *to get a good grade.*

2. Subjunctive "Triggers": Influence, Emotion, Doubt or Denial

The main clause must also contain an expression of *influence, emotion,* or *doubt* or *denial* for the subjunctive to occur in the subordinate clause. If there is no such expression, the indicative is used.

The verb **decir** is a subjunctive "trigger" (first sentence to the right) when it conveys an order. When **decir** conveys information rather than influence (second sentence), it triggers the indicative.

Similarly, **creer** conveys certainty or belief (third sentence) but **no creer** conveys denial (fourth sentence). When **creer** affirms rather than denies information, it is followed by the indicative.

Dicen que <u>cante</u> Carlota.
 They say that Carlota should sing.

Dicen que Julio **canta** muy mal; por eso **quieren** que <u>cante</u> Carlota.
 They say that Julio sings very badly; that's why they want Carlota to sing.

Yo creo que Julio **canta** muy bien.
 I think that Julio sings very well.

No creo que Carlota <u>cante</u> mejor que él.
 I don't think that Carlota sings better than he (does).

> ## ¡OJO!
> Remember to look for the "triggers," not just for specific verbs. If you see the verbs **decir** or **creer** in the main clause, you must think about how they are used.

3. Influence + *indirect object pronoun*

Some expressions of influence are frequently used with indirect object pronouns. The indirect object pronoun in the main clause indicates the subject of the subordinate clause, as in the sample sentences: **Nos → (nosotros) vayamos.**

Nos dicen
 Nos piden
 Nos recomiendan } que <u>vayamos</u> al concierto.

They tell us to
 They ask us to
 They recommend that we } *go to the concert.*

4. Same Subject → Infinitive

Remember that verbs and expressions of influence, emotion, and doubt/denial are usually followed by an infinitive when there is no change of subject.

Es importante **practicar** todos los días.
 It's important to practice every day.

Esta noche pienso **estudiar** para el examen.
 Tonight I plan (intend) to study for the test.

5. Noun Clauses

The uses of the subjunctive that you have learned so far fall into the general category of the use of the subjunctive in *noun clauses* (**las cláusulas nominales**). The noun clause is the second (subordinate) clause in the sentence, the one that contains the subjunctive. It is called a noun clause because it functions like a noun in the sentence, usually as the direct object of the verb in the main clause.

In the first two pairs of example sentences, the subordinate clause is the direct object of the main verb, answering the question *what?*

He wants *what?* → that they stop playing
They hope *what?* → that there will be many spectators

However, when used with **gustar,** the subordinate clause is the subject (not the direct object).

What isn't pleasing? → that ticket prices are high

A subordinate clause is viewed as a singular subject in Spanish, so **gusta** (not **gustan**) is used in the sentence.

> **cláusula subordinada nominal = complemento directo**

—¿Qué quiere el director de la orquesta?
—Quiere **que los músicos dejen de tocar.**
"What does the orchestra director want?"
"He wants the musicians to stop playing."

—¿Qué esperan los músicos?
—Esperan **que haya muchos espectadores en el concierto.**
"What do the musicians want?"
"They hope (that) there will be many spectators at the concert."

> **cláusula subordinada nominal = sujeto**

—¿Qué no les gusta a los espectadores?
—No les gusta **que las entradas sean muy caras.**
"What don't the spectators like?"
"They don't like tickets to be (that ticket prices are) so expensive."

Summary of Subjunctive

influence, emotion, doubt/denial + **que** + change of subject → **subjunctive**

Práctica y comunicación

A. Lo que deseo

Paso 1. Autoprueba. ¿Qué necesitan las siguientes cláusulas principales en la cláusula subordinada: subjuntivo, indicativo o depende?

1. El director de cine quiere que los espectadores...
2. Los artistas esperan que la gente...
3. Ojalá que...
4. Mis profesores piensan que lo más importante...
5. Yo no creo que lo más importante...
6. Mi madre dice que...

Paso 2. Complete las frases de la Columna A con una idea de la Columna B. A veces hay que conjugar el verbo y a veces no.

COLUMNA A

1. Quiero que...
2. Espero...
3. Ojalá (que)...
4. Pienso...
5. No creo que...
6. Digo que...

COLUMNA B

a. graduarme de esta universidad en cuatro años
b. tener un buen trabajo después de graduarme
c. sacar (*to get*) una buena nota en esta clase
d. ganar dinero como artista algún día
e. mi profesor(a) de español: dar mucha tarea
f. hablar español con soltura (*fluently*) en el futuro
g. mis compañeros de clase: practicar el español durante el almuerzo.

Prác. A, Paso 1: Answers: 1. *subjuntivo* **2.** *subjuntivo* **3.** *subjuntivo* **4.** *indicativo* **5.** *subjuntivo* **6.** *depende*

406 ■ cuatrocientos seis

Capítulo 13 El arte y la cultura

Paso 3. Ahora, en parejas, túrnense para hacerse preguntas sobre las ideas del **Paso 2.** Luego díganle a la clase una idea que tengan en común.

MODELO: **E1:** ¿Quieres que tus compañeros de clase practiquen el español durante el almuerzo?
E2: Sí, quiero que lo practiquen durante el almuerzo. →
Queremos que nuestros compañeros de clase practiquen el español durante el almuerzo.

B. En el Museo del Prado. Explique con oraciones completas por qué es buena idea tener la ayuda de un(a) guía en un museo.

1. Quiero que el guía...
   a. enseñarme los cuadros más famosos de Velázquez
   b. explicarme algunos detalles de los cuadros
   c. saber mucho sobre la vida del pintor
2. Me sorprende que muchos cuadros de Velázquez...
   a. tener como tema la vida cotidiana (*everyday*)
   b. estar en otros museos fuera de (*outside of*) España
   c. ser de la familia real (*royal*) de Felipe IV
3. Es posible que el guía...
   a. recomendarme algunos libros sobre la vida y el arte del pintor
   b. preguntarle a un colega si sabe algo más sobre Velázquez
   c. no tener más tiempo para hablar conmigo

Las meninas, de Diego Velázquez (España, 1599–1660)

C. ¡Qué maravilla de robot! Imagine que usted tiene un robot último modelo que va a hacer todo lo que usted le diga, especialmente las cosas que usted odia o que son difíciles. ¿Qué le va a mandar al robot que haga? Haga oraciones completas.

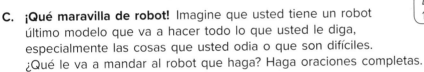

Le voy a decir que...
Le voy a mandar que...

+

lavarme la ropa
hacerme la tarea de español
poner la mesa
tomar notas en todas mis clases
pagar mis cuentas
apagar y encender mi computadora semanalmente (*once a week*)
¿ ?

D. El lugar ideal para vivir

Paso 1. Piense en el lugar ideal para vivir. ¿Es una casa o un apartamento? ¿Está en una ciudad grande o pequeña? ¿Qué actividades culturales ofrece la ciudad? Lea la siguiente lista de factores e indique los que son indispensables para usted, más otros dos que no estén en la lista.

☐ casa con jardín grande
☐ apartamento grande
☐ apartamento con vista
☐ buenos museos
☐ cerca de una universidad importante
☐ buena orquesta y teatros

☐ muchos cines
☐ cerca de un gran centro comercial
☐ parques
☐ zonas naturales cerca de usted
☐ ¿ ?
☐ ¿ ?

(Continúa).

Algo sobre el Lago Titicaca

Christophe Boisvieux/ Hemis/Alamy Stock Photo

[El Lago Titicaca]

El Perú y Bolivia comparten[a] el lago Titicaca, que se encuentra en los Andes centrales. Este lago es muy importante para Bolivia, ya que[b] el país no tiene salida al mar.[c] Está a 12.500 pies (3.800 metros) sobre el nivel del mar, lo que lo hace el lago navegable más alto del mundo. El lago Titicaca es el segundo lago más grande de Sudamérica, después del lago de Maracaibo.

 ¿Hay lagos navegables en este país? ¿Y lagos compartidos[d] con otro país?

[a]*share*   [b]*ya... since*
[c]*no... is landlocked*   [d]*shared*

 Paso 2. Ahora, en parejas, describan el lugar ideal para vivir para cada uno de ustedes. Usen las siguientes frases como modelo. ¿En cuántos detalles coincidieron los dos?

MODELOS: Deseo que mi casa/apartamento...
No quiero vivir en...
(No) Me importa (mucho) (que)...
Es importante que la casa / el apartamento...
(No) Es absolutamente necesario que...
Espero (que)...

Textos de todos los días: Un poema

¿Le gusta la poesía? ¿Y escribir poemas? En esta actividad tiene la oportunidad de crear un texto poético en español.

Objetivo: Escribir un poema en español sobre su vida diaria.

Antes de empezar

- Piense en lo que usted considera un texto poético: ¿Tiene que tener rima? ¿Tiene que usar un lenguaje muy complicado o puede usar primariamente expresiones de todos los días?

- Antes de empezar, es buena idea leer el poema de Gloria Fuertes, «Sale caro ser poeta», que está en la sección de **Lectura** de este capítulo. Es posible que ese poema le vaya a dar algunas ideas para su propio poema.

- Luego siga la estructura del poema que se da abajo (*below*). Tiene solo seis versos (*lines*) pero usted puede añadir todos los que quiera (*as many as you want*). También puede añadir más acciones o adjetivos.

No es fácil ser _____
                              (profesión)

Cada vez que[a] _____, me siento _____.
                    (acción)   (adjetivo)

Y todos los días, _____.
                    (1-2 acciones en 1ª persona)

_____ espera/desea que yo _____.
(Alguien)   (acción)

Es bueno / terrible /... _____.
Me importa / fascina / molesta (que) _____.
¡Ojalá _____ !

[a]*Cada... Every time that*

⚙ Todo junto

A. Lengua y cultura: En un museo, contemplando una obra de Fernando Botero

Paso 1. Completar. A guide and some visitors are discussing a work by Fernando Botero. Complete their conversation with the correct form of the words in parentheses, as suggested by context. When two possibilities are given in parentheses, select the correct word or phrase. Conjugate the verbs in the present indicative, the **ustedes** command form, the present subjunctive, or the preterite, or leave them in the infinitive, if appropriate.

GUÍA: Y ahora, vamos a ver una obra de Fernando Botero. _____ (Pasar)[1] ustedes por aquí, por favor. También les pido que _____ (permitir)[2] suficiente espacio para todos. Y bien, aquí estamos (delante / detrás)[3] de (este / esto)[4] cuadro _____ (de el / del)[5] pintor y escultor colombiano Fernando Botero. Mucha gente cree que Botero (estar / ser)[6] el artista (latinoamericano / latinoamericana)[7] más reconocido[a] del mundo. Un detalle curioso sobre Botero, que mucha gente no (conocer / saber)[8]: _____ (él: empezar)[9] su vida profesional como torero.[b] Pero pronto su familia _____ (descubrir)[10] que su vocación era la pintura. (Estar / Ser)[11] obvio que sus figuras no son una copia exacta de la realidad, ¿verdad?

VISITANTE 1: ¿(Por qué / Porque)[12] son gordas sus figuras?

GUÍA: Es el estilo muy personal de Botero de representar la realidad. También (le / se)[13] gusta hacer crítica social y política con humor. Pero a veces solo representa una escena cotidiana,[c] algo trágico o íntimo. Su estilo (le / se)[14] llama el boterismo. ¿(Le / Les)[15] gusta a ustedes?

VISITANTE 1: No (yo: conocer / saber)[16]... Me (gusta / gustan)[17] los colores y la escena, pero no me gusta que las figuras _____ (ser)[18] tan obesas. Me sorprende que Botero _____ (ser)[19] tan famoso internacionalmente.

VISITANTE 2: Pues (a mí / yo)[20] no me sorprende. Para mí, hay sensualidad y movimiento en esas figuras.

Pareja bailando, de Fernando Botero (Colombia, 1932-2023). Botero pintó varios cuadros sobre el mismo tema y con el mismo título.

[a]*well-known*   [b]*bullfighter*   [c]*everyday*

Paso 2. Comprensión. ¿Quién pudo decir lo siguiente: el guía, la visitante 1 o el visitante 2?

	EL GUÍA	VISITANTE 1	VISITANTE 2
1. «Prefiero las figuras más realistas».	☐	☐	☐
2. «Me encanta que estas figuras sean voluminosas y redondas (*round*)».	☐	☐	☐
3. «Es posible que Botero quiera mostrarnos la sensualidad del baile».	☐	☐	☐
4. «Quiero que todos me sigan ahora, por favor».	☐	☐	☐

Paso 3. En acción

Dé sus propias opiniones sobre el cuadro. Después compárelas a las opiniones de una persona de la clase. ¿Coinciden en algo?

Expresiones útiles

Me gusta / sorprende / molesta que...
Es interesante que...
Es obvio que...

En este proyecto, va a comentar una obra de arte visual que le gusta o que le interesa por alguna razón. Recuerde que hay muchas formas de expresión artística: la pintura, la escultura, la arquitectura…

Paso 1. Preparación. Elija a un(a) artista del mundo hispanohablante y una obra suya (*of his/hers*) en concreto. En este capítulo hay información sobre varios pintores hispanohablantes (Botero, Guayasamín, Mamani Mamani y Velázquez), pero es posible que usted conozca a otros. Aquí tiene algunos nombres adicionales (no todos son pintores).

José Clemente Orozco	Wilfredo Lam	Remedios Varo
June Beer	Antonio Gaudi	Alfredo Matta
Antonio Berni	Doris Salcedo	Frida Kahlo

Paso 2. Investigación. (*Research*.) Haga una investigación sobre el/la artista y la obra que usted escogió en el **Paso 1**. Asegúrese de (*Be sure to*) obtener la siguiente información básica: época; tipo de arte y estilo principal del/de la artista; título de la obra en español; año en que fue creada (pintada, esculpida, construida…). También debe buscar información sobre el significado (*meaning*) de la obra: ¿Qué representa? ¿Cree que contiene un mensaje (*message*)? También piense en por qué le gusta la obra.

Paso 3. Presentación. Combine la información de los **Pasos 1** y **2** para crear una presentación de aproximadamente dos minutos. Su objetivo es explicarles una obra a personas que probablemente no la conocen y no saben mucho de arte. Debe comunicar su interés en la obra y su visión personal de ella. Finalmente, haga su presentación en clase.

Estrategia

Before you present, consider what makes a presentation attractive and interesting:

- Good organization
- Interesting information and explanation, just the right amount of complexity and depth for your audience
- Comprehensibility, a function of appropriate vocabulary, correct grammar, and clear pronunciation

Video: Salu2 «Arte angelino°»   de Los Ángeles

You can watch two segments of this chapter's video in the **Video: Salu2** section, found at the end of the eBook.

La Ofrenda (*Offering*), un mural de Yrenia Cervantes, en Los Ángeles

Enfoque cultural: Las artes

Antes de leer

¿Cuáles son los museos más importantes de su ciudad, su estado o su país? ¿Los conoce? ¿Cuál es su favorito?

En el Ecuador y Bolivia

Erick Serrano/Shutterstock

La Casa de la Cultura Ecuatoriana, Quito, Ecuador

Tanto el Ecuador como Bolivia son países multiculturales, donde diferentes grupos étnicos contribuyen a las artes en general.

En el Ecuador, la institución encargada de apoyar y promover[a] la cultura es La Casa de la Cultura Ecuatoriana Benjamín Carrión (CCE), una red nacional de bibliotecas, cines, museos, teatros y publicaciones, con sede[b] en Quito. Su misión es la[c] de «[p]reservar, promover,[d] fomentar,[e] investigar y difundir[f] el arte, ciencia y patrimonio cultural ecuatoriano» para fortalecer[g] la identidad nacional del país.

En Bolivia, la editorial[h] Yerba Mala[i] Cartonera es una iniciativa a destacar.[j] Publican las obras de todo tipo de escritores locales, en libros impresos[k] en papel ordinario y con tapas[l] recicladas de las cajas de cartón que se botan[m] en los supermercados. Los autores de los libros publicados[n] ceden sus derechos,[o] por lo que[p] los libros pueden comprarse a precios económicos.

[a]encargada... *in charge of supporting and promoting* [b]*headquarters*
[c]*that* [d]*to promote* [e]*to encourage* [f]*to spread* [g]*strengthen*
[h]*publishing house* [i]Yerba... *Weeds* [j]*highlight* [k]*printed* [l]*covers*
[m]cajas... *cardboard boxes that are thrown away* [n]*published*
[o]ceden... *donate their copyrights* [p]por... *and because of that*

Comprensión ¿Qué institución está encargada de fomentar la cultura ecuatoriana? ¿Por qué son económicos los libros que publica?

En otros países hispanos

Philip Scalia/Alamy Stock Photo

El Museo del Barrio, Latino Cultural Center, Manhattan, Nueva York

- **En España** Uno de los museos de arte más importantes del mundo es el Museo del Prado, en Madrid. Allí se puede admirar las obras de Velázquez y Goya, entre otros muchos artistas españoles y europeos anteriores al siglo XX.
- **En México** El Museo Nacional de Antropología, en la Ciudad de México, es uno de los mejores del mundo en su género.[a] En este museo se puede admirar y apreciar la excelencia de la artesanía y arquitectura de los pueblos indígenas mesoamericanos.
- **En los Estados Unidos** En Nueva York está el Museo del Barrio, dedicado a la obra de artistas latinos, con énfasis en el arte puertorriqueño.

[a]*category, genre*

Comprensión ¿Cuáles son algunos de los museos famosos del mundo hispanohablante y en qué se especializan?

En acción

Haga una breve descripción de su museo favorito o del museo más importante de su ciudad o estado: cómo se llama, dónde está, en qué se especializa y por qué recomienda usted que se visite.

Gloria Fuertes
Poeta de guardia

Phatymak's Studio/Shutterstock

La portada (*cover*) del libro de Gloria Fuertes donde apareció este poema

Vocabulario para leer

el bostezo	yawn
el esclavo	enslaved person
la madrugada	dawn
el recital	reading
la sombra	shadow
acribillar	to harass
acudir (a)	to attend
espantar	to frighten
<u>salir</u> **caro**	to be expensive
suceder	to occur

Lectura

Antes de leer

1. ¿Qué hacen los poetas? ¿Dónde y cuándo escriben?
2. En su opinión, ¿es fácil o difícil ser poeta?
3. ¿Cree usted que, en general, los poetas tienen otro trabajo además del de (*besides that of*) escribir poemas?

«Sale caro ser poeta», de Gloria Fuertes

Sale caro, señores, ser poeta.
La gente va y se acuesta tan tranquila
—que después del trabajo da buen sueño—.[a]
Trabajo como esclavo llego a casa,
5 me siento ante[b] la mesa sin cocina,
me pongo a meditar[c] lo que sucede.
La duda me acribilla todo espanta;
comienzo a ser comida por las sombras
las horas se me pasan sin bostezo
10 el dormir se me asusta[d] se me huye[e]
—escribiendo me da la madrugada—.
Y luego los amigos me organizan recitales
a los que acudo y leo como tonta,
y la gente no sabe de esto nada.
15 Que me dejo la linfa[f] en lo que escribo
me caigo de la rama[g] de la rima
asalto las trincheras[h] de la angustia
me nombran su héroe los fantasmas,[i]
me cuesta[j] respirar cuando termino.
20 Sale caro señores ser poeta.

©Fundación Gloria Fuertes. Reprinted by permission.

[a]que... *after work one gets good and sleepy* [b]*at* [c]me... *I start to meditate* [d]se... *is frightened away* [e]se... (el dormir) *flees from me* [f]me... *I leave my lymph (i.e., my heart and soul)* [g]*branch* [h]asalto... *I assail the trenches* [i]me... *ghosts call me their hero* [j]me... *it's hard for me*

Comprensión

A. ¿Dónde lo dice? Conteste la pregunta y dé los números de los versos (*lines*) del poema donde aparece la siguiente información.

1. ¿Tiene más de un trabajo la poeta?
2. ¿Cuándo escribe su poesía?
3. ¿Pasa rápido el tiempo mientras escribe?
4. ¿Se siente tranquila cuando escribe?
5. ¿Tiene audiencia esta poeta?
6. ¿Entiende el público cuánto trabaja la poeta?
7. ¿Es fácil el trabajo de poeta, según dice la poeta misma (*herself*)?

B. Preguntas

1. ¿Qué cree usted que significa «esto» en «la gente no sabe de esto nada» (verso 14)?
2. ¿Por qué cree usted que después de escribir sus poemas le cuesta respirar (verso 19)?
3. Si la autora cree que «sale caro ser poeta», ¿por qué se dedica a escribir poesías? ¿Le parece a usted lógico?

Mucha gente tiene una noción idealizada de cómo es la vida y del trabajo de los artistas. Pero el trabajo artístico puede ser duro.

Paso 1. Elija una forma de expresión artística que le interesa (la arquitectura, el baile, el cine, etcétera). Considere y describa el proceso de creación y exposición (*exhibition*) de esa forma de arte.

Paso 2. Del proceso que describió en el **Paso 1,** ¿cuáles son—en su opinión—los pasos más difíciles? ¿Qué pasos cree usted que los artistas disfrutan *(enjoy)* más?

Paso 3: Busque en internet y lea una biografía breve de un(a) artista que trabaja con el tipo de arte que usted eligió. ¿Cómo corresponde esta biografía a las ideas que usted expresó en el **Paso 2**?

Textos orales

Una reseña° de la película *La vida de Susana Jiménez*

review

Antes de escuchar

¿Le gusta el cine? ¿Tiene un género (*genre*) preferido de películas: las (*those*) de acción, de artes marciales, de aventura, de ciencia ficción, de horror, de suspenso, de guerra (*war*), las comedias, los dramas, las musicales? En su opinión, ¿qué características necesita tener una película para que (*so that*) sea interesante y/o buena? ¿Lee usted en el periódico o en internet reseñas de las películas antes de verlas? ¿Las lee después de verlas? ¿O no las lee nunca?

Vocabulario para escuchar	
el punto de vista	point of view
trata de	deals with
inesperado/a	unexpected
el argumento	plot
la actuación	performance
cursi	in poor taste; trite
al elegir	when she chose
recrea	it recreates

Comprensión

A. ¿Cierto o falso? ¿Qué dicen los críticos de la película? Corrija las oraciones falsas.

	CIERTO	FALSO
1. El hombre piensa que es una película que se debe ver.	☐	☐
2. La mujer piensa que es una película recomendable.	☐	☐
3. Los dos críticos piensan que la actriz principal es buena.	☐	☐
4. Los críticos están de acuerdo: el guion es bueno.	☐	☐

B. Más detalles. Conteste las siguientes preguntas.

1. Según la mujer, ¿cuál es el problema principal de la película?

2. ¿Cuáles son algunos aspectos positivos de la película, según los críticos?

En acción

Haga una sinopsis de su película favorita, incluyendo una recomendación sobre el tipo de público que debe verla. Incluya el título en español, el año que salió (*it came out*) y los nombres del director / de la directora y de los actores principales.

PORTAFOLIO

Daniel Ernst/Getty Images

Entrevista

Use de modelo las preguntas y respuestas de la sección **Entrevista** al principio de este capítulo para hablar sobre las artes y las artesanías que a usted le interesan y el lugar donde se pueden ver en su ciudad.

Escritura

Un ensayo sobre la expresión artística en las escuelas

SuperStock/Age fotostock

Unos niños en una clase de arte, en el Ecuador

Antes de escribir

Paso 1. En parejas, piensen en los siguientes aspectos de la importancia del arte.

1. ¿Qué significa la palabra **arte**? ¿Cómo puede afectar el arte la vida de una persona?
2. ¿Cómo/Dónde se debe aprender las diversas formas de arte? ¿En la escuela o en el tiempo libre?
3. En general, ¿qué formas de arte se promueven (*are promoted*) y se enseñan en las escuelas públicas? ¿Creen que se enseñan de manera suficiente?

Paso 2. Luego, hagan una lista de argumentos a favor de la idea de apoyar (*supporting*) y enseñar las artes en las escuelas públicas y otra de argumentos en contra.

A escribir

Ahora use las ideas de **Antes de escribir** para escribir un ensayo a favor o en contra de la enseñanza de las artes en las escuelas públicas. Hay más ayuda en Connect.

En la comunidad

Entreviste a una persona hispana de su universidad o ciudad sobre el arte y la artesanía de su país de origen.

Preguntas posibles

- ¿Cuáles son los artistas más conocidos (*best known*) de su país? ¿A qué tipo de arte se dedican?
- ¿Qué tipo de artesanía se hace en su país? ¿y en su ciudad o región? ¿Tiene muestras (*examples*) de esta artesanía en su casa?
- ¿Hay muchas oportunidades de asistir a eventos culturales (por ejemplo, exposiciones en museos, conciertos, espectáculos de danza, teatro o cine) en su país? Por lo general, ¿son baratas o caras las entradas para los eventos culturales?
- ¿Cuáles son los eventos culturales que usted prefiere? ¿Asiste a ellos con frecuencia?

Producción audiovisual

Haga un fotomontaje con voz en off (*voice-over*) sobre la obra de un artista hispano / una artista hispana cuya (*whose*) obra le interesa mucho a usted.

Más ideas para el portafolio

- Incluya una imagen de una de sus obras de arte favoritas (de arquitectura, escultura, pintura, cine, música o lo que sea). Explique por qué le gusta y cómo la descubrió.
- Incluya la imagen de alguna obra artística que usted ya ha hecho (*have made*) recientemente o antes de llegar a la universidad. Explique si se siente orgulloso/a (*proud*) de ella y por qué. Dé detalles sobre la obra: cuándo y por qué la hizo, dónde está o quién la tiene ahora, etcétera.
  Si no tiene ninguna obra suya (*of your own*) que comentar, hable de una obra hecha (*made*) por un pariente u otra persona.
- Si ha estado jugando (*you have been playing*) Practice Spanish: Study Abroad, en Quest 10 usted aprendió sobre algunos remedios caseros (*home remedies*) tradicionales de Colombia. En parejas, escriban un diálogo en el cual (*which*) una persona trata de ayudar a su amigo enfermo recomendándole unos remedios caseros populares en su país. El amigo / La amiga debe reaccionar a las sugerencias, expresando su opinión. Ensayen (*Rehearse*) bien y luego presenten su diálogo a la clase.

Sugerencia: You are now ready to play Quest 10 in **Practice Spanish: Study Abroad.**

EN RESUMEN En este capítulo

AFTER STUDYING THIS CHAPTER I CAN ...

☐ talk about creative endeavors of all kinds (390–391)

☐ express the order of things (394)

☐ use the present subjunctive to express emotion (395–396)

☐ use the present subjunctive to express doubt and denial (400–402)

☐ use the indicative or the subjunctive in noun clauses (404–406)

☐ recognize/describe at least 2–3 aspects of Ecuadorian and Bolivian cultures

Gramática en breve

36. Uses of the Subjunctive: Emotion

①	②
EMOTION	
first subject = **indicative**	**que** second subject = **subjunctive**

37. Uses of the Subjunctive: Doubt and Denial

①	②
DOUBT AND DENIAL	
first subject = **indicative**	**que** second subject = **subjunctive**

38. The Subjunctive: A Summary

①	②
influence / emotion / doubt or denial	**que** **subjunctive**
information / certainty or belief	**que** **indicative**

Vocabulario

Los verbos

aburrir (*like* **gustar**)	to bore
acordarse (me acuerdo) (de)	to remember

atraer (*like* **traer**) (*like* **gustar**)	to draw, attract
fascinar (*like* **gustar**)	to fascinate
ganar	to earn (*income*)
lamentar	to regret; to feel sorry
negar (niego) (gu)	to deny
no creer	to disbelieve
sentir (siento) (i)	to regret; to feel sorry
sorprender (*like* **gustar**)	to surprise
temer	to fear, be afraid
tratar de + *inf.*	to try to (*do something*)

Repaso: alegrarse de, **creer**, dudar, encantar, esperar, gustar, molestar, **pensar**, **tener** miedo de

La expresión artística

el baile	dance
el cuadro	painting (*specific piece*)
la danza	dance
el dibujo	drawing
las entradas	tickets (*to a performance, movie ...*)
el escenario	stage; scenery
la escultura	sculpture
el espectáculo	show
la fotografía	photography
el guion	script
la imagen	image
la obra (de arte)	work (of art)
la obra de teatro	play
la obra maestra	masterpiece
el papel	role
la pintura	painting (*in general; specific piece*)

Cognados: la arquitectura, las artes (*pl.*), el ballet, la comedia, el drama, la escena, el mural, la música, el musical, la novela, la ópera, el poema

Repaso: el arte, la canción, el cine, el concierto, el edificio, la foto(grafía), la literatura, el museo, la película, el siglo, el teatro

actuar (actúo)	to act
componer (compongo) (*like* **poner**)	to compose
crear	to create
dibujar	to draw
dirigir (dirijo)	to direct
diseñar	to design

esculpir — to sculpt
tejer — to weave

Cognado: pintar

Repaso: bailar, cantar, escribir

Las personas

el actor, la actriz (*pl.* actrices)	actor
el bailarín, la bailarina	dancer
el/la cantante	singer
el/la compositor(a)	composer
el/la dibujante	drawer
el/la director(a)	director; conductor
el/la dramaturgo/a	playwright
el/la escritor(a)	writer
el/la escultor(a)	sculptor
el/la espectador(a)	spectator; *pl.* audience
el/la guía	guide
el/la músico/a	musician
la orquesta	orchestra
el/la pintor(a)	painter

Cognados: el/la arquitecto/a, el/la artista, el/la autor(a), el/la novelista, el/la poeta, el público

La tradición cultural

la artesanía	arts and crafts
la cerámica	pottery; ceramics
los tejidos	woven goods

Cognado: las ruinas

Los adjetivos

folclórico/a	traditional

Cognados: artístico/a, clásico/a, moderno/a

Los números ordinales

primer(o/a)	sexto/a
segundo/a	séptimo/a
tercer(o/a)	octavo/a
cuarto/a	noveno/a
quinto/a	décimo/a

Palabras adicionales

es... + indicative	it's ...
cierto que	certain that
seguro que	certain / a sure thing that
verdad que	true that
es... + subjunctive	it's ...
absurdo que...	absurd that ...
extraño que...	strange that ...
¡qué extraño que... !	how strange that ... !
(im)posible que...	(im)possible that ...
(im)probable que...	(un)likely, (im)probable that ...
increíble que...	incredible that ...
normal que...	normal that ...
terrible que...	terrible that ...
es una lástima que + subjunctive	it's a shame that
¡qué lástima que... !	what a shame that ... !
hay que + *inf.*	it is necessary to (*do something*)
no es... + subjunctive	it's not ...
(im)probable que...	(im)probable that ...
posible que...	possible that ...
seguro que...	certain / a sure thing that ...
verdad que...	true that ...
(no) <u>estar</u> seguro/a de	to be (un)certain of
ojalá (que)	I hope (that)

Repaso: es mejor / bueno / malo que, primero (*adv.*)

Vocabulario personal

Use this space or a vocabulary notebook to write down other words and phrases you learn in this chapter.

14

Las presiones° de la vida

Las... *Pressures*

En este capítulo

VOCABULARY
The life of a student   420
Bad luck and accidents   423

GRAMMAR
Telling how long something has been happening   427
Talking about unplanned and unexpected events   430
How to use **por** and **para**   434

COUNTRY OF FOCUS: PERU

La hora punta (*Rush hour*) en Lima, Perú

COLOMBIA

ECUADOR

Río Amazonas

BRASIL

CORDILLERA DE LOS ANDES

Lima ✶

•Cusco

PERÚ

Lago Titicaca

OCÉANO PACÍFICO

BOLIVIA

CHILE

0   250   500 Millas

0   250   500 Kilómetros

EL PERÚ

33,4 (coma cuatro) millones de habitantes

- El Perú es otro de los países andinos que tiene costa en el océano Pacífico y territorio amazónico. También tiene una zona desértica al sur.

- Lima, la capital del Perú, es una inmensa ciudad de más de 10 millones de habitantes. Es la quinta entre las ciudades más grandes de Latinoamérica y una de las treinta ciudades más grandes del mundo.

- El Perú es un país multiétnico: más del 25% de su población es amerindia, principalmente quechua, seguida por[a] un gran porcentaje de mestizos, después blancos y, finalmente, negros, asiáticos (de origen chino y japonés) y árabes.

[a]*seguida... followed by*

ENTREVISTA

These questions related to the chapter theme are answered here by a native speaker. You will be able to ask and answer them yourself with personal information in the **Entrevista** activity in the **Portafolio** section at the end of the chapter.

Ismael Pérez Mendizábal contesta las preguntas.

– **¿Cree usted que la vida de hoy día es motivo de muchas presiones? ¿Y la vida estudiantil?**

– No hay duda de que el ritmo[a] de la vida de hoy día es la causa de que suframos muchas presiones y mucho estrés, tanto si[b] estás trabajando o estudiando. A muchos jóvenes nos preocupa salir bien en la universidad porque es difícil conseguir un buen trabajo cuando terminas.

– **En su opinión, ¿tenemos hoy más presiones en la vida diaria que hace 50 años[c]? Explique su respuesta.**

– Yo diría[d] que tenemos más presiones hoy. En realidad no creo que la vida ahora sea más difícil que hace 50 años, pero sí creo que vivimos con más tensión día a día. Y también nos causan estrés las expectativas[e] que tenemos para nuestro futuro.

– **¿Qué hace usted para calmarse cuando se siente muy estresado/a?**

– Pues... hago lo normal, creo. Salgo con mis amigos para distraerme,[f] duermo una siesta si puedo. También trato de hacer deporte, como correr o levantar pesas, porque eso me hace sentirme mejor físicamente.

[a]*pace*   [b]*tanto... regardless of whether*   [c]*que... than 50 years ago*   [d]*would say*
[e]*expectations*   [f]*take my mind off things*

You can hear the pronunciation of theme vocabulary words and phrases in the eBook.

Las presiones° de la vida académica

Las... *Pressures*

- la agenda
- los informes
- la profesora Ortega
- las llaves
- Talía
- la tarjeta de identificación
- el calendario
- el examen
- Efraín
- la nota
- el despertador
- Lina
- Leo

Más causas de estrés°	*stress*
la agenda	personal calendar
la ansiedad	anxiety
el calendario	calendar (*of the year*)
el horario	schedule
el informe (oral/escrito)	(oral/written) report
el plazo	deadline
el programa (del curso)	(course) syllabus
la prueba	quiz; test
la tarea	homework
el trabajo	job, work; report, (piece of) work
acordarse (me acuerdo) (de)	to remember
corregir (corrijo) (i)*	to grade; to correct
devolver (like volver) (algo a alguien)	to return (something to someone)
entregar (gu)	to turn/hand in
estacionar	to park
estar	to be
(muy) estresado/a	(very) stressed
bajo muchas presiones	be under a lot of pressure
llegar (gu) a tiempo / tarde	to arrive on time / late
olvidar	to forget

sacar (qu) buenas/ malas notas	to get good/bad grades
ser	to be
(in)flexible	(in)flexible
estresante	stressful
sufrir (de)	to suffer (from)
tomar apuntes	to take notes (*academic*)

Más cortesía: Las disculpas°	Las... *Apologies*
disculparse / pedir (pido) (i) disculpas	to apologize
Disculpa. (*fam.*) Disculpe. (*form.*)	Pardon me. I'm sorry.
Fue mi culpa.	It was my fault.
Fue sin querer.	I didn't mean (to do) it.
Lo siento (mucho).	I'm (very) sorry.
Perdón.	Pardon me. I'm sorry.
aceptar (las) disculpas	to accept apologies
Está bien.	It's fine. It's O.K.
No hay problema.	No problem.
No se preocupe. (*form.*) No te preocupes. (*fam.*)	Don't worry. No worries.

---

*Note the present indicative conjugation of **corregir**: corrijo, corriges, corrige, corregimos, corregís, corrigen.

Así se dice

la nota = la calificación
el plazo = la fecha límite

estacionar = aparcar (*Sp.*), parquear (*Mex.*)

la tarjeta de identificación nacional = la cédula de ciudadanía (*Col.*), el documento
nacional de identidad (DNI) (*Arg., Per., Sp.*)

Comunicación

A. Asociaciones

Paso 1. ¿Qué palabras asocia usted con los siguientes verbos? Pueden ser
sustantivos o verbos, antónimos o sinónimos.

1. estacionar
2. corregir
3. acordarse
4. entregar

5. sacar
6. sufrir
7. pedir
8. llegar

Paso 2. ¿Qué palabras o situaciones asocia usted con los siguientes
sustantivos?

1. el calendario
2. el despertador
3. las notas
4. las pruebas
5. el plazo
6. el horario
7. los informes

8. las llaves
9. la tarjeta de identificación
10. las disculpas
11. las presiones
12. la inflexibilidad
13. los apuntes
14. el trabajo

B. Situaciones

Paso 1. En parejas, emparejen las preguntas o comentarios con las
respuestas apropiadas.

PREGUNTAS/COMENTARIOS

1. _____ —Disculpe. Anoche no me acordé de
poner el despertador.
2. _____ —No puedes estacionar el coche aquí
sin permiso.
3. _____ —¿Sacaste buena nota en la prueba?
4. _____ —¡Ay perdón! ¡Lo siento! No sabía que
había alguien.
5. _____ —Disculpe, profesor, pero aquí tiene mi
trabajo sobre la Unión Europea.
6. _____ —Disculpa, pero no puedo hablar
contigo ahora. Tengo que terminar el
programa de curso para el semestre
que viene y corregir todos estos
trabajos finales.

RESPUESTAS

a. —No te preocupes. Siento que tengas tanto
trabajo. Llámame cuando puedas.
b. —Lo siento mucho, señor agente. No vi la señal
de prohibido estacionar (*no parking sign*).
c. —Otra vez tarde. Esto afecta tu nota de
participación.
d. —¿Pero no se acordó de que el plazo era
ayer? Es la última vez que le acepto un
informe tarde.
e. —Muy buena, pero es una sorpresa. No tuve
tiempo para estudiar.
f. —¡Está bien! ¡No hay problema! Ya puede
entrar.

Paso 2. Ahora inventen un contexto para cada diálogo. ¿Dónde están las
personas que hablan? ¿En una oficina? ¿en clase? ¿Quiénes son?

MODELO: **1.** → Las personas que hablan están en la universidad.
La persona de la columna de la izquierda es un estudiante que
llega tarde a clase y la otra persona es un(a) profesor(a).

C. Presiones y diversiones

Paso 1. Cree una lista con las cinco causas mayores de estrés para usted este semestre/trimestre. Use los ordinales (**primero, segundo...**) para establecer un orden de mayor a menor.

Paso 2. Ahora cree otra lista de las cinco mejores cosas del semestre/trimestre, es decir (*that is*), las cosas que más le gustan o lo/la divierten. Recuerde usar los ordinales.

Paso 3. Finalmente, en parejas, comparen sus listas. ¿Tienen mucho o poco en común? ¿Piensan que las listas del resto de la clase van a ser muy diferentes o similares?

D. Sobre la vida y el éxito (*success*).
En parejas, lean las siguientes citas (*quotes*) sobre la vida, la educación y el éxito y contesten las preguntas.

«*El éxito se mide[a] en si usaste tu cabeza tanto como tu corazón, si fuiste generoso, si amaste[b] a los niños y a la naturaleza, si te preocupaste por los ancianos. Es acerca de tu bondad,[c] tu deseo de servir, tu capacidad de escuchar y tu valor sobre la conducta[d]*».

Carlos Slim Helú, hombre de negocios (*business*) mexicano

«*El destino es una mezcla[e] de la preparación y la suerte.[f]*»

Luis Miguel, cantante mexicano

«*Les digo con todo mi corazón, con toda mi vida. Yo no tengo talento natural. No soy un genio. Pero mis padres a pesar de[g] ser tan humildes[h] me dieron educación[i]*».

Edward James Olmos, actor mexicoamericano

[a]*se... is measured* [b]*you loved* [c]*acerca... about your kindness* [d]*valor... courage in the way you act* [e]*mix* [f]*luck* [g]*a... in spite of* [h]*poor* [i]*me... taught me to be courteous*

1. ¿Qué creen ustedes que es más importante para triunfar en la vida, tener talento natural o preparación?
2. ¿Creen que la educación que están recibiendo va a ayudarlos/las a encontrar un buen trabajo?
3. ¿Son importantes las buenas notas para conseguir un buen trabajo? ¿O creen que es suficiente obtener un título universitario, no importa con qué notas?
4. ¿Cómo creen ustedes que se debe medir (*measure*) el éxito individual en la vida?

¡Qué mala suerte!°

¡Qué... *What bad luck!*

SALA DE URGENCIAS

chocar (**qu**) con/contra

estar/ir distraído/a

caerse (me caigo)*

dolerle (duele) la cabeza

romperse† el brazo

lastimarse la pierna

la profesora Ortega   Enrique   Samuel   la madre de Samuel

Los accidentes

doler (duele) (*like* **gustar**)	to hurt, ache
equivocarse (qu) (de)	to make a mistake (about/with)
hacerse daño	to hurt oneself
hacerse daño en	to hurt one's (*body part*)
levantarse con el pie izquierdo	to get up on the wrong side of the bed
ocurrir, pasar	to happen
pegar (gu)	to hit, strike
pegar(se) (gu) con/contra	to run/bump into/against
tener buena/mala suerte	to have good/bad luck; to be (un)lucky

Las reacciones

distraído/a	absent-minded, distracted
torpe	clumsy
¡Qué + *adjective*!	How ... !
¡Qué distraído!	How absent-minded!
¡Qué torpe!	How clumsy!
¡Qué + *noun*!	What (a) ... !
¡Qué desastre!	What a mess! What a disaster!
¡Qué dolor!	It hurts! (*lit.*, What pain!)
¡Qué buena/mala suerte!	Such good/bad luck!

Más reacciones (opcional)

- Para expresar dolor, sorpresa o compasión

¡Ay!	Ouch! Oops!
¡Uy!	Oops! Oh!
¡No puede ser!	No way!
¡No me diga(s)!	No! No way!
¿Qué le vamos a hacer?	What can you do (about it)?
¡Cuánto lo siento!	I am so sorry!
¡Qué maravilla!	How wonderful!
¡Qué bonito / feo / bien!	
¡Qué horror!	
¡Qué pena/lástima (*shame*)!	
¡Qué terrible/triste!	

- Con referencia a la suerte

¡Buena suerte!	Good luck!
¡Que te/le vaya bien!	Hope it goes well!

Así se dice

chocar con/contra = darse con/contra
distraído/a = despistado/a
romperse = quebrarse

---

*Note that the first person singular of **caer** (to fall) is irregular: **caigo**. The present participle is **cayendo**.
†**Romper** means to break. It is generally used with **se**: **Se rompió la ventana.**

Comunicación

A. Accidentes y tropiezos (*mishaps*)

Paso 1. ¿Le pasaron a usted alguna de las siguientes cosas en los últimos meses? Modifique las oraciones, usando palabras afirmativas y negativas, para que sean (*so that they are*) verdaderas para usted.

MODELOS: **1.** Me caí por las escaleras (*stairs*) de _____. **Nunca** me caí por las escaleras de **mi casa.**

1. Me caí por las escaleras de _____.
2. No me acordé de hacer la tarea para la clase de _____.
3. Me equivoqué al contestar (*when I answered*) una pregunta en la clase de _____.
4. El despertador sonó, pero no me desperté.
5. Soy un poco torpe. Rompí sin querer _____ (algo) de _____ (alguien).
6. Choqué con un/una _____ y me hice daño en el/la _____ (parte del cuerpo).
7. Olvidé el plazo para entregar un informe de _____ (materia).
8. Olvidé devolverle el/la _____ (algo) a _____ (alguien).
9. Iba un poco distraído/a y me equivoqué de puerta en el edificio _____.

Paso 2. Ahora, usando las oraciones del **Paso 1** como guía, entrevístense sobre los accidentes que les han ocurrido (*have happened*) en la vida. También deben preguntarle a su compañero/a si le pasaron otros desastres.

MODELO: **1.** ¿Te caíste por las escaleras? ¿Te hiciste daño? ¿Qué (más) te pasó/ocurrió?

B. Un anuncio para un seguro.
La palabra **seguro** no solo significa *sure.* También quiere decir *insurance.* Lea este anuncio de un seguro de accidentes y conteste las preguntas.

1. ¿Por qué el anuncio de SegurVita dice «La vida te da sorpresas... »?
2. ¿Qué tipos de accidentes se ven en los dibujos?
3. ¿Tiene usted un seguro de accidentes?

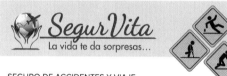

SEGURO DE ACCIDENTES Y VIAJE
Protégete y protege a las personas que dependen de ti.

Nota cultural: Megalópolis estresantes... y pueblitos relajantes

Tose/iStock/Getty Images

Un pueblo tranquilo en los Andes peruanos

Muchas capitales de los países hispanohablantes son hoy día inmensas megalópolis con muchos millones de habitantes. En algunas de estas ciudades llega a concentrarse[a] más del 25% de la población total del país, como es el caso de Buenos Aires (Argentina), Lima (Perú) y Santiago (Chile).

Obviamente, el estrés causado por la congestión del tráfico en estas ciudades es altísimo. Pero el exceso de tráfico conlleva[b] el problema de encontrar estacionamiento, lo que produce más estrés. Algunas de estas ciudades tienen un centro histórico muy antiguo[c] en el que[d] la circulación[e] y el estacionamiento son prácticamente imposibles. Y, por supuesto,[f] hay que recordar el problema de la contaminación.

Para compensar el estrés de la vida urbana, mucha gente que emigró a la ciudad en busca de[g] mejores oportunidades laborales mantiene su conexión con su pueblo, su pequeña ciudad de origen. Allí vuelven con frecuencia a ver a sus parientes, a la celebración de fiestas o simplemente a relajarse.[h]

Población de las mayores áreas metropolitanas hispanohablantes

Área metropolitana	habitantes (en millones)
Ciudad de México	22
Buenos Aires	15
Lima	11
Bogotá	11
Santiago	7
Madrid	7

¿Cuáles son las megalópolis de los Estados Unidos? ¿Cree usted que es estresante vivir en una? ¿Por qué?

[a]llega... *is concentrated* [b]*brings with it* [c]*old* [d]el... *which* [e]*driving* [f]por... *of course* [g]en... *in search of* [h]*relax*

C. ¿Qué le vamos a hacer? (*What can one do?*) Indique lo que puede pasar o algo que una persona puede hacer en cada una de las siguientes situaciones. También indique expresiones que se pueden decir en cada caso.

MODELO: Una estudiante choca contra el escritorio de un compañero de clase. ➔
Lo que puede pasar: La estudiante se hace daño en la pierna o el pie y se cae. Las cosas del escritorio de su compañero también se caen.
Se puede decir: ¡Ay! ¡Qué torpe soy! ¡Perdón! ¡Fue sin querer!

1. A alguien le duele mucho la cabeza.
2. Una persona que va distraída choca con otra en la cafetería.
3. Una persona torpe se cae mientras lleva la computadora en la mano.
4. Un compañero de clase se equivocó en muchas preguntas en el último examen.
5. Una amiga se hizo daño mientras jugaba a su deporte favorito.
6. Un amigo se levantó con el pie izquierdo.

Nota comunicativa: Más sobre los adverbios: *adjetivo* + *-mente*

You already know the most common Spanish adverbs: words like **bien/mal, mucho/poco, siempre/nunca...**

Adverbs that end in *-ly* in English usually end in **-mente** in Spanish. The suffix **-mente** is added to the feminine singular form of adjectives. Note that the accent mark on the stem word (if there is one) is retained.

ADJETIVO	ADVERBIO	INGLÉS
rápida	**rápidamente**	*rapidly*
fácil	**fácilmente**	*easily*
paciente	**pacientemente**	*patiently*

¡OJO!

Here are two frequently used adverbs whose meaning is not identical to the adjective from which they are derived.

solamente	only
últimamente	lately

You will use adverbs in **Práctica D.**

D. ¿Cómo lo hacen?

Paso 1. Explique cómo hace usted las siguientes acciones, usando un adverbio basado en los adjetivos de la lista de **Vocabulario útil.**

MODELO: estudiar para las clases ➔
Para mis clases, estudio **constantemente.**

(Continúa).

Vocabulario útil

constante	inmediato/a
diario/a	paciente
directo/a	puntual
elegante	rápido/a
fácil	torpe
frecuente	tranquilo/a

1. vestirse para una fiesta formal
2. esperar a los amigos que llegan tarde
3. estudiar para las clases
4. estar confundido/a en la clase de _____
5. hacer la tarea de español
6. llegar a la clase de español
7. escuchar música
8. bailar reguetón

 Paso 2. Ahora, en parejas, túrnense para entrevistarse sobre las acciones del **Paso 1.** Deben obtener información interesante y personal de su compañero/a.

MODELOS: estudiar para las clases → ¿Cómo estudias para tus clases en general? ¿Y para la clase de español?

Paso 3. Díganle a la clase por lo menos un detalle interesante de su compañero/a.

Algo sobre la marinera

Como casi todos los países hispanohablantes, el Perú también tiene su danza particular,[a] que es un símbolo nacional: la marinera. Es un baile originario de la costa (de ahí[b] su nombre), y se baila en pareja. Es un baile de cortejo,[c] en el que[d] típicamente el hombre trata de seducir a la mujer.

Hay varios tipos de marinera, según la región. Por ejemplo, la marinera limeña, es decir, de la ciudad de Lima, se baila con un pañuelo[e] en la mano. En la hermosa[f] ciudad colonial de Trujillo, hay un famoso concurso[g] anual de marineras.

¿Hay algún tipo de música o folclore en su país en que participen caballos u otros animales?

[a]*unique* [b]*de… that's where… comes from* [c]*courtship* [d]*el… which* [e]*handkerchief* [f]*beautiful* [g]*contest*

¡En esta marinera el hombre baila en un caballo!

James Strachan/GettyImages

GRAMÁTICA

39 Telling How Long and Expressing *Ago* • *Hace... que:* Another Use of **hacer**

Gramática en acción: Cusco, una ciudad histórica

Rodrigo Torres/Glow Images

La Plaza de Armas de la bella (*beautiful*) ciudad de Cusco, con vista de la Catedral

Cusco fue la capital del imperio de los incas. Luego, durante la dominación española, fue una importante ciudad colonial.

1. La ciudad de Cusco **continúa** habitada **desde hace** más de 3.000 años. Esto la hace la ciudad más antigua de Sudamérica.
2. **Hace** aproximadamente 500 años **que** los conquistadores españoles **llegaron** a Cusco por primera vez. La convirtieron en una ciudad importante de su imperio.

¿Y los Estados Unidos?

¿Cuánto tiempo **hace que...** ?
1. son un país independiente
2. tienen cincuenta estados
3. hubo elecciones presidenciales

has/have been (doing) for (period of time)	
• **hace** + *(period of time)* + **que** + *PRESENT* • *PRESENT* + **desde hace** + *(period of time)*	**Hace** un año **que estudio** español. **Estudio** español **desde hace** un año. *I've been studying Spanish for one year.*
did (period of time) ago	
• **hace** + *(period of time)* + **que** + *PRETERITE* • *PRETERITE* + **hace** + *(period of time)*	**Hace** un año **que empecé** a estudiar español. **Empecé** a estudiar español **hace** un año. *I started studying Spanish a (one) year ago.*

1. **Hace** + *time*

   In Spanish, a phrase with **hace** + *time* is used to express two perspectives on time.

   • With the *present* tense, the **hace** phrase tells how long something *has been happening*. English uses the present perfect progressive tense to express this: *has/have been verb + -ing for ...*

Hace dos semanas **que estoy** estresada con esta clase.
Estoy estresada con esta clase **desde hace** dos semanas.
I've been stressing out about this class for two weeks.

> **¡OJO!**
>
> Use **que** when the **hace** phrase comes before the verb, **desde hace** when it comes after.

(Continúa).

Cusco, a historic city *Cusco was the capital of the Inca Empire. Then, during the Spanish occupation, it was an important colonial city.*
1. The city of Cusco has been continually inhabited for more than 3,000 years. That makes it the oldest city in South America.
2. The Spanish conquistadors arrived in Cusco for the first time about 500 years ago. They made it into an important city in their empire.

- With the *preterite*, the **hace** phrase tells how long *ago* something *happened*.

  When the **hace** phrase comes before the verb, **que** is used with it.

Hace una semana **que entregué** el informe.
Entregué el informe **hace** una semana.
I handed in the report a week ago.

¡OJO!

In this context, the word **hace** is invariable with a present tense or a preterite tense verb.

Hace dos años **que vivo** en el Perú.
I've been living in Peru for two years.

Hace dos años **que fui** al Perú.
I went to Peru two years ago.

2. Questions with *hace*

The question **¿Cuánto tiempo hace que... ?** is used with both structures, with the present and the preterite. You can answer a question of this kind just by saying the time.

- + *present tense* = to ask how long something *has been happening*
- + *preterite tense* = to ask how long *ago* something *happened*

—**¿Cuánto tiempo hace que te duele** la cabeza?
—Varias horas.
"How long have you been having a headache?"
"(For) Several hours."

—**¿Cuánto tiempo hace que te caíste?**
—Tres días.
"How long ago did you fall down?"
"Three days ago."

Summary of Uses of *hace*

hace + *time* + que + *present* ⎫
present + desde hace + *time* ⎭ = *has/have been doing*

hace + *time* + que + *preterite* ⎫
preterite + hace + *time* ⎭ = *ago*

Práctica y comunicación

A. Información personal

Paso 1. Autoprueba. Empareje las oraciones con el equivalente apropiado.

a. *for x years*   b. *x years ago*

1. _____ Hace dos años que te conozco.
2. _____ Te conocí hace dos años.
3. _____ Hace tres años que tomé cálculo.
4. _____ Hace tres años que estudio español.

Paso 2. Complete las siguientes oraciones con información personal.

1. Hace _____ que mi familia vive en el estado / la ciudad de _____.
2. Hace _____ que yo vivo en este estado.
3. Hace _____ que empecé a estudiar en esta universidad.
4. Vi a mi mejor amigo/a hace _____.
5. Hace _____ que practico/hago _____ (deporte o pasatiempo).

Paso 3. Ahora, en parejas, túrnense para entrevistarse sobre las ideas del **Paso 2.** Luego díganle al resto de la clase algo que tengan en común.

MODELO: **1. E1:** ¿Dónde vive tu familia? ¿Cuánto tiempo hace que vive en ese estado?
E2: Mi familia vive en Nevada desde hace 10 años. ¿Y tu familia?
E1: Mi familia vive en Oklahoma. Vive allí desde hace 10 años también.

B. Situaciones: ¿De qué tiene ganas?

Paso 1. Lea las siguientes situaciones. Luego indique cuánto tiempo hace que existe la situación. Finalmente, explique qué tienen ganas de hacer las personas en cada circunstancia. Siga el modelo.

MODELO: Marina se levantó a las ocho de la mañana y es la una de la tarde. No tuvo tiempo de comer nada entre clase y clase. → **Hace** cinco horas **que** no come. **Tiene ganas de** comer.

Prác. A, Paso 1: Answers: 1. a 2. b 3. b 4. a

1. Manuela empezó a escribir un informe a las cinco de la tarde. Ahora son las ocho de la noche y todavía sigue escribiendo.

2. Usted y sus amigos llegaron a una fiesta a las nueve de la noche. Son las cuatro de la mañana y todavía están en la fiesta.

3. Gabi tiene el mismo coche que tenía en el tercer año de la escuela secundaria (2016).

4. Empezó a llover el miércoles. Hoy es domingo y sigue lloviendo.

Paso 2. Ahora prepare usted una situación similar a las (*those*) del **Paso 1** y dígasela a la clase. Sus compañeros le van a decir qué tienen ganas de hacer.

C. **Eventos históricos.** ¿Cuánto tiempo hace que pasaron los siguientes eventos? Haga oraciones completas con las palabras indicadas. Si es necesario, mire los años en que pasaron estos eventos.*

MODELO: la primera persona / llegar a la Luna →
> **Hace más de cincuenta años** que la primera persona **llegó** a la Luna.

1. Cristóbal Colón / llegar a América
2. la Segunda Guerra (*War*) Mundial / terminar
3. Michael Jackson / morir
4. el presidente actual / ser elegido (*to be elected*)
5. el profesor / la profesora de español / empezar a enseñar en esta universidad

D. **Intercambios**

Paso 1. Haga preguntas basadas en las siguientes ideas. **¡OJO!** Algunas requieren un verbo en el presente y otras un verbo en el pretérito.

MODELOS: **1.** vivir en esta ciudad →
> ¿Cuánto tiempo hace que **vives** en esta ciudad?

7. visitar a sus abuelos la última vez →
> ¿Cuánto tiempo hace que **visitaste** a tus abuelos la última vez?

1. vivir en esta ciudad
2. asistir a esta universidad
3. vivir en su apartamento / casa / residencia
4. estudiar español
5. escribir el último trabajo para una de sus clases
6. conocer a su mejor amigo/a
7. visitar a sus abuelos (a ¿ ?) la última vez
8. sacar una mala nota

Paso 2. Ahora use las preguntas del **Paso 1** para entrevistar a un compañero o una compañera de clase. Luego díganle a la clase un detalle interesante.

Repaso

You have learned a number of uses for the word **se.** Match each function of **se** with the appropriate sentence.

1. _____ Los niños tienen que bañar**se** ahora.
2. _____ Los amigos **se** quieren mucho.
3. _____ ¿El regalo? **Se** lo di a Ana ayer.
4. _____ Aquí **se** habla español.

a. to express *one* or *you*
b. to replace the indirect object pronoun **le** or **les** before **lo / la / los / las**
c. to express a reflexive action
d. to express a reciprocal action

In **Gramática 40** you will learn another use for the word **se.**

Prác. C: **Los años:** MODELO: 1969 **1.** 1492 **2.** 1945 **3.** 2009 **4.** ¿ ? **5.** ¿ ?

Algo sobre la herencia indígena peruana

Allik/Shutterstock

Jóvenes quechuas con ropa tradicional

El Perú tiene una gran diversidad étnica y racial. Y como en todos los países andinos,[a] tiene un alto porcentaje de población indígena (25% aproximadamente). Los pueblos[b] amerindios más numerosos son los quechuas y los aymaras, que también habitan en países vecinos (Bolivia, el Ecuador, Chile y la Argentina).

La riqueza[c] histórico-cultural peruana viene de sus pueblos originarios. Cuando los españoles llegaron en el siglo XVI (dieciséis), los incas dominaban un gran territorio sudamericano entre lo que hoy son Chile y el Ecuador. Pero los incas eran los herederos[d] culturales de varias civilizaciones que existieron antes, como los mochicas y los nazcas.

 ¿Hay una notable población de origen indígena en su estado?

[a]*Andean* [b]*peoples* [c]*richness* [d]*heirs*

40 Expressing Unplanned or Unexpected Events • Another Use of se

Gramática en acción: Un día terrible

1. A Diego **se le cayó** la taza de café.

2. A Antonio **se le olvidaron** los libros.

3. A Antonio y a Diego **se les olvidó** apagar las luces del coche.

¿Y usted?

¿También pasó un día terrible ayer? Para describir su día, indique si las siguientes oraciones son ciertas o falsas.

	CIERTO	FALSO		CIERTO	FALSO
1. **Se me perdió** algo.	☐	☐	**3.** **Se me cayeron** algunas cosas.	☐	☐
2. **Se me olvidó** hacer algo importante.	☐	☐	**4.** **Se me rompió** algo de valor (*value*).	☐	☐

El *se* accidental

A + Noun (A + Pronoun)	se	Indirect Object Pronoun	Verb	Subject
A Antonio	**se**	**le**	olvid**an**	las llaves muchas veces.
A Carmen y yo	**se**	**nos**	olvid**ó**	cerrar el coche con llave.
A los estudiantes	**se**	**les**	olvid**ó**	el examen.
(A mí)	**Se**	**me**	olvid**a**	entregar la tarea a veces.
(A ti)	**Se**	**te**	olvid**aba**	la tarea con frecuencia cuando eras pequeño.
(A nosotros)	**Se**	**nos**	olvid**aron**	los informes ayer.
(A ustedes / ellos / ellas)	**Se**	**les**	olvid**a**	estudiar los fines de semana.

1. Using *se* to Express Accidental Events

Unplanned or unexpected events (*I dropped ... , We lost ... , You forgot ...*) are frequently expressed in Spanish with **se** and a third person form of the verb. The event is viewed as happening *to* someone—the unwitting "victim" of the action. This structure is called the *accidental se* (**el *se* accidental**).

Se me cayó el papel.
I dropped the paper. (The paper slipped out of my hands. [I didn't drop it on purpose.])

Se te olvidó llamar a tu hija.
You forgot to call your daughter. (Calling your daughter slipped your mind.)

A mi hermano **se le olvidaron** las llaves.
My brother forgot the keys. (It slipped his mind to bring them.)

A terrible day 1. Diego dropped a cup of coffee. **2.** Antonio forgot his books. **3.** Antonio and Diego forgot to turn off the car headlights.

2. Agreement with the Subject

In these kinds of sentences, as with **gustar** and similar verbs, the subject of the sentence is the thing that is dropped, forgotten, and so on. The subject usually follows the verb.

- When the subject is singular, the verb will be singular, even if the "victim" is plural.
- When the subject is plural, the verb will be plural, even if the "victim" is singular.

> ## ¡OJO!
> Remember that an infinitive is a singular subject: **A los niños se les olvidó <u>llamar</u> a su madre.**

Se me ca<u>yó la computadora</u>.
My computer fell.

Se me ca<u>yeron los libros</u>.
My books fell.

Al niño **se le olvid<u>ó el cumpleaños</u>** de su madre.
The child forgot his mother's birthday.

A los niños **se les olvid<u>ó el cumpleaños</u>** de su madre.
The children forgot their mother's birthday.

A Antonio **se le perd<u>ieron los apuntes</u>.**
Antonio forgot his notes.

A Antonio y Diego **se les perd<u>ieron los apuntes</u>.**
Antonio and Diego forgot their notes.

3. Parts of the Sentence

- An accidental **se** sentence must have these elements:

(No)	Se	*IO pronoun*	verb	subject

Notice that **no** comes before **se**.

- When the "victim" is specifically named (with a noun or a person's name), the sentence will also have an **a** + *name/noun* phrase: **a Tomás / a los Sres. Pérez / al gato / a los niños.**

A + *name/noun*	(no)	se	*IO pronoun*	verb	subject

- The indirect object pronoun can be clarified or emphasized with an **a** + *pronoun* phrase: **a mí, a ti, a usted / él / ella, a nosotros, a vosotros, a ustedes / ellos / ellas.**

A + *pronoun*	(no)	se	*IO pronoun*	verb	subject

- The phrase **a** + *name / noun / pronoun* can appear at the beginning or the end of the **se** sentence.

Se <u>le</u> rompió el brazo.
He/She broke his/her arm.

No se <u>le</u> rompió el brazo.
He/She didn't break his/her arm.

<u>**A Ana**</u> / <u>**A la niña**</u> **se <u>le</u>** rompió el brazo.
Ana / The child broke her arm.

¡Y luego <u>**a ti**</u> **se <u>te</u>** cae el café! ¡Y luego **se <u>te</u>** cae el café <u>**a ti**</u>!
*And then **you** drop the coffee!*

<u>**A ella**</u> **se <u>le</u>** rompió el brazo.
She broke her arm.

<u>**A ella/Ana**</u> **se <u>le</u>** olvidó el informe.
Se le olvidó el informe <u>**a ella / a Ana**</u>.

¡<u>**A mí**</u> todo se <u>**me**</u> olvida!
¡**Se <u>me</u>** olvida todo <u>**a mí**</u>!

4. Verbs Frequently Used with *se*

Here are some verbs frequently used in this construction. The verbs marked with * are new.

*acabar	to finish; to run out of
<u>caer</u>	to fall; to drop
olvidar	to forget
perder (p**ie**rdo)	to lose
*quedar	to remain, be left
romper	to break

5. Accident Versus Intent

This structure is used to emphasize the accidental nature of an event. When the speaker wishes to emphasize *who* committed the act, or that the act was intentional, that person becomes the subject of the verb and the **se** structure is not used.

Se <u>me</u> rompió el plato.
The plate broke on me. (accidentally)

(Yo) Rompí el plato.
I broke the plate. (emphasizes either who broke the plate or the intentionality of the act)

Práctica y comunicación

A. ¿Algo deliberado o accidental?

Paso 1. Autoprueba. Empareje las oraciones de las dos columnas.

1. _____ No encuentro las llaves.
2. _____ Tu calculadora no funciona.
3. _____ Paco no entregó la tarea.
4. _____ Necesito comprar leche.

a. Se te rompió.
b. Se me acabó.
c. Se me perdieron.
d. Se le olvidó.

Paso 2. Indique si a usted le ocurrieron los siguientes accidentes o hizo las siguientes acciones.

1. ☐ Se me rompió algo de otra persona sin querer.
2. ☐ Rompí algo de alguien, con intención de hacerlo.
3. ☐ Se me cayó un plato de comida sin querer.
4. ☐ Tiré (*I threw*) comida a la basura porque no me gustaba.
5. ☐ Se me perdió algo de un ex novio / una ex novia.
6. ☐ Quemé (*I burned*) o rompí algo de un ex novio / una ex novia.

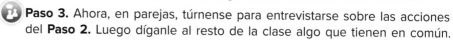 **Paso 3.** Ahora, en parejas, túrnense para entrevistarse sobre las acciones del **Paso 2.** Luego díganle al resto de la clase algo que tienen en común.

MODELO: **1. E1:** ¿Se te rompió algo de otra persona sin querer?
E2: Sí. ¿Y a ti se te rompió algo de otra persona sin querer?
E1: También. → A nosotros se nos rompieron cosas de otras personas sin querer.

B. ¡Qué distraída!

Paso 1. Hortensia es muy distraída y siempre se le olvida hacer muchas cosas importantes antes de salir de viaje. Empareje los olvidos (*lapses*) de Hortensia con las consecuencias.

OLVIDOS

1. _____ Se le olvida cerrar la puerta de su casa.
2. _____ Se le olvida pagar las cuentas.
3. _____ Se le olvida cancelar el correo (*mail*).
4. _____ Se le olvida pedirle permiso a su jefa (*boss*).
5. _____ Se le olvidan las gafas para leer.
6. _____ Se le olvida hacer reserva en un hotel.

CONSECUENCIAS

a. Va a perder el trabajo.
b. No va a poder leer los documentos de inmigración.
c. Le van a suspender el servicio de la electricidad y del gas... ¡y cancelar sus tarjetas de crédito!
d. Alguien le va a robar las cosas de valor (*value*).
e. No va a tener dónde pasar la noche.
f. Todos van a saber que no está en casa.

Paso 2. Ahora ponga las oraciones de las dos columnas en el pretérito, para narrar lo que le pasó a Hortensia cuando fue al Perú.

MODELO: **1.** Se le olvida cerrar la puerta de su casa. Alguien le va a robar las cosas de valor.
→ Se le **olvidó** cerrar la puerta de su casa. Por eso alguien le **robó** las cosas de valor.

C. Una mañana terrible. Complete la siguiente descripción de lo que le pasó a Pablo ayer. **¡OJO!** Use el **se** accidental.

Pablo tuvo una mañana terrible. Primero _____ (olvidar)¹ poner el despertador. Se levantó tarde y se vistió rápidamente. No cerró bien su maletín;ª por eso _____ (caer)² unos papeles importantes. Recogió los papeles y subió al coche, pero después de cinco minutos, _____ (acabar)³ la gasolina y se le paróᵇ el coche. Dejó el coche en la calle y decidió ir a pie. Llevaba el maletín en una mano y las llaves y un documento urgente en la otra. Desgraciadamente, en el caminoᶜ _____ (perder)⁴ el

ª*briefcase*   ᵇ*se... (the car) stopped on him*   ᶜ*en... on the way*

Prác. A, Paso 1: Answers: 1. c 2. a 3. d 4. b

documento. Cuando llegó a la oficina, buscó a su jefe[d] para entregarle el documento, pero no podía encontrarlo entre sus papeles. Cansado y enojado, cerró el maletín sin cuidado y _____ (romper)[5] los lentes.

[d]*boss*

 D. Unos dichos (*colloquial expressions*) hispanos. El **se** accidental se usa en muchos dichos en español. En parejas, traten de dar su equivalente en inglés. Luego emparejen los dichos con la situación apropiada.

DICHOS

a. Se le hace la boca agua.
b. Se le hacía tarde.
c. Se le cayó el alma (*soul*) a los pies.
d. Se le fue la lengua.
e. Se le acabó la paciencia.
f. Se le cae la baba (*drool*) por (algo o alguien).

SITUACIONES

1. La clase empezaba a las dos. Eran las dos menos veinte y Raúl todavía estaba en la ducha. A Raúl _____
2. Ramón le contó a María un secreto, pero María se lo dijo a Luisa. A María _____
3. La hija de Carmen es preciosa. A Carmen _____
4. Julio tiene muchísimas ganas de comer la comida de su madre. ¡Qué rica! Solo de pensarlo, a Julio _____
5. «¡Ya no más! (*Enough already!*)», gritó (*screamed*) la madre. «Vete a tu cuarto ahora mismo». A la madre _____
6. Una joven tuvo un grave accidente. A su padre _____

E. ¡Desastres por todas partes (*everywhere*)!

Paso 1. ¿Es usted una persona distraída o torpe? Indique las oraciones que describen lo que le pasa a usted. Cambie algunos de los detalles de las oraciones si es necesario. **¡OJO!** Se usa el presente para hablar de acciones típicas.

1. ☐ Con frecuencia se me caen las cosas (el celular, los platos,...).
2. ☐ Se me pierden constantemente las llaves (mi tarjeta de identificación de la universidad,...).
3. ☐ Siempre se me rompen los lentes (la pantalla del celular,...).
4. ☐ A veces se me queda la botella de agua (la portátil,...) en el salón de clase.
5. ☐ Se me olvida fácilmente mi horario (el nombre de alguien,...).

Paso 2. ¿Es usted igual ahora que cuando era más joven? Complete cada oración del **Paso 1** para describir cómo era de niño/a. **¡OJO!** Use el imperfecto.

MODELO: De niño/a, (no) se me **caían** los libros con frecuencia.

 Paso 3. Ahora compare sus respuestas con las (*those*) de un compañero o una compañera. ¿Quién es más distraído/a o torpe ahora? ¿Quién era así de niño/a?

F. Encuesta (*Poll*): Accidentes de la semana

Paso 1. Haga una lista de cinco accidentes o cosas que ocurren con frecuencia en la vida diaria y que a nosotros nos parecen desastres. Debe usar por lo menos tres verbos diferentes.

MODELO: perder las llaves de la casa o apartamento

 Paso 2. Ahora hágales cinco preguntas a cinco personas de la clase sobre los accidentes o desastres del **Paso 1**. Luego dígale a la clase cuál fue el accidente o desastre más común.

MODELO: perder las llaves de la casa o apartamento ➜
La semana pasada, ¿se te perdieron las llaves de la casa o apartamento?

Algo sobre el cajón

Xinhua/Alamy Stock Photo

Un grupo que toca el cajón peruano

Se calcula que más del 3.5% de la población peruana actual es afrodescendiente. Las primeras personas africanas llegaron con los conquistadores españoles a principios del[a] siglo XVI (dieciséis). Hasta el siglo XIX (diecinueve) llegaron al Perú (y a Latinoamérica) millones de personas que habían sido[b] capturadas en países del África subsahariana[c] y traídas[d] como personas esclavizadas.[e]

Los afroperuanos han contribuido[f] a la diversidad y riqueza[g] cultural del país. Una de sus aportaciones[h] mundialmente[i] conocida es el cajón, un instrumento musical de percusión similar a una caja,[j] que ha entrado[k] en la música de otros países, incluyendo el flamenco en España.

 ¿Qué instrumento musical considera usted más emblemático de su país? ¿En qué tipo de música se utiliza?

[a]*a... at the beginning of the* [b]*habían... had been* [c]*sub-Saharan* [d]*brought* [e]*enslaved* [f]*han... have contributed* [g]*richness* [h]*contributions* [i]*worldwide* [j]*box* [k]*ha... has entered*

Repaso

Review what you know about **por** and **para** by completing these sentences.

1. ¡Gracias **para/por** el regalo!
2. Esta comida es **para/por** ti.
3. ¿Trabajas **para/por** la noche?
4. Tomo cinco clases. **Para/Por** eso tengo mucha tarea.
5. **Para/Por** aprender, hay que estudiar.
6. Dame el plato, **para/por** favor.
7. ¡**Para/Por** fin llegamos!
8. El informe es **para/por** mañana.

You will learn more about using these prepositions in **Gramática 41**.

41 ¿Por o para? • A Summary of Their Uses

Gramática en acción: Ideas sobre la educación

A

B   ᵃUnidos... *United by*   ᵇ*secure*

Lea los anuncios sobre la educación. ¿Cuál de los dos anuncios expresa las siguientes ideas sobre la educación?

1. La educación nos conecta.
2. La educación no debe ser solo para algunas personas.
3. Un buen sistema educativo es muy importante para el futuro de todas las personas.
4. Hay niñas y niños que no tienen acceso a una buena educación.
5. Un buen sistema educativo es una tarea nacional.

¿Y usted?

Para usted, ¿qué otras cosas son de tod@s y para tod@s?

You have been using **por** and **para** since you started to study Spanish. Each preposition has some English equivalents that are unique to it, making it easy to decide between them in those cases. However, both **por** and **para** can mean *for*, depending on the context. You already know much of the information in this section.

Por

1. **Unique Meanings of *por***

   The preposition **por** has a number of English equivalents that are not expressed with *for* in English. **Para** can never express these meanings.

   - *by / by means of*

     El libro fue escrito **por** Mario Vargas Llosa.
     The book was written by Mario Vargas Llosa.

     Nos hablamos **por** teléfono mañana.
     We'll talk by (on the) phone tomorrow.

   - *through/along*

     Me gusta pasear **por** el parque y **por** la playa.
     I like to stroll through the park and along the beach.

   - *during/in* (time of day)

     Trabajo **por** la mañana.
     I work in the morning.

   - *because of / due to*

     Estoy nervioso **por** la entrevista.
     I'm nervous because of the interview.

2. **For = *Por***

   When it expresses *for*, **por** looks back at the *reason* or *cause* for something. To remember this, think of the interrogative **¿por qué?** = *why?* and the expressions **por eso...** (*that's why ... *) and **gracias por...** (*thanks for ... *).

   - *for = for the sake of, on behalf of*

     Lo hago **por** ti.
     I'm doing it for you (for your sake).

   - *for = in place of*

     No puedo tomar el examen **por** ti.
     I can't take the exam for you (in your place).

   - *for = in exchange for*

     Piden 1.000 dólares **por** el coche.
     They're asking $1,000 for the car.

     Gracias por todo.
     Thanks for everything.

   - *for = period of time* (often omitted)

     Vivieron allí (**por**) un año.
     They lived there for a year.

3. **Fixed Expressions with *por***

   Por is used in the expressions to the right, some of which (like **por eso** and **por si acaso**) express the *reason* or *cause* of something. The expressions marked with * are new.

*por Dios	for heaven's sake
*por ejemplo	for example
por eso	that's why
por favor	please
por fin	finally
por lo general	generally, in general
por lo menos	at least
*por primera/última vez	for the first/last time
*por si acaso	just in case
*¡por supuesto!	of course!
por teléfono	on the phone
*por todas partes	everywhere

Para

1. Unique Meaning of *para*: in order to

The English phrase *in order to* + infinitive is expressed by **para** (never by **por**).

- *in order to* + infinitive

Regresaron pronto **para** estudiar.
They returned soon (in order) to study.

Estudian **para** conseguir un buen trabajo.
They're studying (in order) to get a good job.

---

2. For = *Para*

When it expresses *for*, **para** looks ahead, toward the *goal, purpose,* or *destination* of something. To remember this, think of the interrogative **¿para qué?** = *for what purpose?*

- *for = destined for / to be given to*

Todo esto es **para** ti.
All this is for you.

Le di un libro **para** su hijo.
I gave her a book for her son.

- *for = by (deadline, specified future time)*

Para mañana, estudien *por* y *para*.
For tomorrow, study por *and* para.

La composición es **para** el lunes.
The composition is for Monday.

- *for = toward / in the direction of*

Salió **para** el Perú ayer.
She left for Peru yesterday.

- *for = to be used for, purpose*

El dinero es **para** la matrícula.
The money is for tuition.

Tengo que hacer un trabajo final **para** el curso de historia.
I have to do a final paper for the history course.

- *for = as compared with / in relation to others*

Para mí, el español es fácil.
For me, Spanish is easy.

Para (ser) **extranjera,** habla muy bien el inglés.
For (being) a foreigner, she speaks English very well.

- *for = in the employ of, in preparation for*

Trabajan **para** el gobierno.
They work for the government.

Estudio **para** (la carrera de) dentista.
I'm studying to be (for a career as) a dentist.

Práctica y comunicación

Summary of *por* and *para*

por: reason or cause
for; by / by means of, through / along, during / in, because of / due to

para: goal, purpose, or destination
for; in order to

A. ¿Por o para?

Paso 1. Autoprueba. ¿Con qué preposición asocia usted las siguientes frases?

1. _____ gracias
2. _____ una fecha en el futuro
3. _____ durante
4. _____ la persona que creó algo
5. _____ con el propósito (*purpose, goal*) de
6. _____ en lugar de otra persona
7. _____ a causa de
8. _____ a lo largo de (*along*)
9. _____ trabajar en una compañía
10. _____ pagar dinero
11. _____ en comparación con otros
12. _____ una carrera

Prác. A, Paso 1: Answers: 1. por **2.** para **3.** por **4.** por **5.** para **6.** por **7.** por **8.** por **9.** para **10.** por **11.** para **12.** para

Paso 2. Complete las siguientes oraciones con **por** o **para.**

1. ¿_____ qué organización o compañía trabaja tu padre/madre?
2. ¿Estudias mejor _____ la mañana o _____ la tarde?
3. ¿_____ qué calles pasas para llegar a esta clase?
4. ¿Cuánto pagaste _____ tu celular?
5. ¿_____ qué sirve hablar español en los Estados Unidos?
6. ¿_____ cuándo es la próxima tarea de español?
7. ¿_____ qué profesión estudias?
8. ¿Estás nervioso/a _____ el examen final en esta clase?

Paso 3. Ahora, en parejas, túrnense para hacer y contestar las preguntas del **Paso 2.** Luego díganle a la clase algo que tienen en común.

B. Situaciones

Paso 1. Complete las siguientes oraciones con **por** o **para.** Luego empareje las preguntas/situaciones con las respuestas apropiadas.

PREGUNTAS/SITUACIONES

1. _____ —¡Uf! Vengo de jugar un partido de basquetbol. ¡Jugamos _____ dos horas!
2. _____ —¿No vas a comer nada? _____ lo menos un sándwich.
3. _____ —¡Cuánto lo siento, don Javier! Sé que llegué tarde a la cita. Discúlpeme.
4. _____ —Es imposible que tome el examen hoy, _____ muchas razones.
5. _____ —¿No lo oíste? Juana acaba de tener un accidente horrible.
6. _____ —¡Pero, papá, quiero ir!
7. _____ —Ay, Mariana, ¿sabes que hubo un tornado? Murieron dos personas.

RESPUESTAS

a. —¡ _____ Dios! ¡Qué desgracia!
b. —Te digo que no, _____ última vez.
c. —No se preocupe. Lo importante es que _____ fin está aquí.
d. —¡ _____ Dios! ¿Qué pasó? ¿Está bien?
e. —No, gracias. No tengo mucha hambre y además tengo que irme enseguida.
f. —¿ _____ ejemplo? Dígame...
g. —Ah, _____ eso tienes tanto calor.

Paso 2. Ahora, en parejas, lean las preguntas/situaciones y respuestas. Luego inventen un breve contexto para cada diálogo. ¿Dónde están las personas que hablan? ¿Quiénes son? ¿Por qué dicen lo que dicen?

C. Una organización por la equidad

Paso 1. Lea la siguiente descripción de una ONG (organización no gubernamental) que promueve (*promotes*) la equidad en la educación. Luego explique por qué se usa **por** y **para** en cada contexto.

Paso 2. Ahora, en parejas, usen las siguientes ideas y el vocabulario del texto en el **Paso 1** para hablar de su participación en organizaciones o asociaciones. Hagan otras preguntas pertinentes para obtener información relevante.

Hablen de...

1. si son miembros de alguna asociación u ONG y qué causa defiende o promueve
2. por qué les interesa esa causa
3. qué tipo de personas la integran (*are members of it*)
4. cómo colaboran ustedes
5. dónde se puede encontrar más información sobre esa organización o asociación

ASOCIACIÓN POR LA EQUIDAD EDUCATIVA
por una educación justa e inclusiva

Para algunas personas el acceso a la educación es muy difícil. Por eso surgió[a] la Asociación por la Equidad Educativa, una ONG que está integrada[b] por estudiantes, educadores, personas expertas en educación, madres y padres que aspiran a que haya mayor igualdad de oportunidades educativas para todo el mundo, sin distinciones. Esta asociación trabaja para crear opciones educativas y promover[c] la coordinación de iniciativas diversas. AEE está presente en muchas escuelas y universidades por todo el país.

Para obtener más información, entra en www.equidadeducativa.com.

[a]*emerged* [b]*una... an NGO made up, consisting of* [c]*promote*

Algo sobre Mario Vargas Llosa

Mario Vargas Llosa (Arequipa, Perú, 1936–) es uno de los escritores e intelectuales de la lengua castellana[a] más famosos e influyentes de las últimas generaciones. Su reconocimiento[b] es mundial. Novelista y ensayista, Vargas Llosa ha recibido[c] numerosos premios,[d] entre ellos el Premio Nobel de Literatura. El tono de sus obras va de lo trágico a lo más cómico, pero sus obras más importantes se enfocan en el abuso del poder[e] en los gobiernos,[f] especialmente las dictaduras.

 ¿Puede usted nombrar a algunos escritores de su país que se consideran influyentes en todo el mundo?

[a]española [b]recognition [c]ha... has received
[d]awards, prizes [e]power [f]governments

Mario Vargas Llosa, Premio Nobel de Literatura en 2010

D. Más sobre Mario Vargas Llosa. Aprenda más sobre este importante escritor peruano completando las siguientes oraciones con la preposición apropiada, **para** o **por.**

1. Mario Vargas Llosa recibió el Premio Nobel _____ sus novelas.
2. Es obvio que _____ el año 2010 Vargas Llosa ya era famoso.
3. _____ este escritor, la estabilidad democrática de Latinoamérica es muy importante.
4. _____ ser escritor, Vargas Llosa es muy famoso _____ mucha gente.
5. _____ sus ensayos, podemos saber de sus preocupaciones políticas y sociales.
6. _____ muchos críticos y expertos, Vargas Llosa es uno de los mejores escritores de la lengua castellana de los últimos cincuenta años.

E. Entrevisten a su profesor(a). Háganle preguntas a su profesor(a) para saber la siguiente información.

1. la tarea para mañana y para la semana que viene
2. lo que hay que estudiar para el próximo examen
3. si para él/ella son interesantes o aburridas las ciencias
4. lo que piensa de la pronunciación de ustedes, para ser principiantes (*beginners*)
5. qué deben hacer ustedes para mejorar su pronunciación del español
6. cuánto tiempo deben ustedes dedicar todos los días a practicar el español

F. Preguntas con *por* y *para*

Paso 1. Complete las siguientes frases con **por** o **para.**

1. prepararse _____ una profesión
2. estar nervioso/a _____ algo
3. trabajar _____ una compañía
4. hablar _____ teléfono con frecuencia
5. tener algo que hacer _____ mañana
6. pasear _____ el campus
7. tener algo que comprar _____ su casa / apartamento / cuarto
8. la idea de pagar mil dólares _____ un abrigo
9. tener algo que hacer _____ alguien
10. la idea de vivir en un sitio _____ toda la vida

Paso 2. Ahora, en parejas, hagan y contesten preguntas, usando las frases del **Paso 1.**

MODELO: **1.** prepararse _____ una profesión →
¿Sabes para qué profesión estás preparándote?

438 ■ cuatrocientos treinta y ocho

Capítulo 14 Las presiones de la vida

Durante su experiencia académica, es muy probable que usted haya tenido que (*have had to*) mandar algún mensaje a sus profesores para pedir disculpas por no asistir a clase o para pedir una extensión para entregar un trabajo de clase. En esta actividad, va a practicar cómo escribir en español mensajes de ese tipo.

Objetivo: Escribirle un mensaje a un profesor / una profesora de español explicando por qué no pudo asistir a la última clase (por una enfermedad) y pidiéndole una extensión del plazo para entregar un trabajo o tarea de clase. También puede pedirle una cita para hacerle preguntas sobre la gramática que se explicó recientemente.

Antes de empezar: Piense en las formalidades típicas de este tipo de mensajes. Las siguientes ideas pueden ayudar con la estructura del mensaje.

- el saludo: Estimado/a^a Profesor(a) _____,
- la disculpa
- lo que pide/necesita
- información para convencer a su profesor(a)
- el cierre:^b Le doy las gracias de antemano^c por su atención y su ayuda.
- firma^d

^a*Dear* (formal) ^b*closing* ^c*de... beforehand* ^d*signature*

Enviar	De:	
	Para:	
	Asunto:	

Todo junto

A. Lengua y cultura: De turismo por el Perú

Paso 1. Completar. Complete the following passage with the correct form of the words in parentheses, as suggested by context. When two possibilities are given in parentheses, select the correct word. **¡OJO!** As you conjugate the verbs in this activity, use the **usted** command when you see *comm:* in front of the infinitive. For other verbs, you will decide whether to use the present indicative or subjunctive, the preterite or imperfect, or simply the infinitive. Context will indicate which forms to use.

¿Le interesa la historia? ¿Le (gusta / gustan)¹ los lugares espirituales? Entonces, _____ (*comm:* ir)² a Machu Picchu. (Son / Están)³ las ruinas de una antigua ciudad inca que (es / está)⁴ en (el / la)⁵ corazón de los Andes, cerca de Cusco. No es fácil (llegue / llegar)⁶ a ese lugar. (Por / Para)⁷ eso (se / la)⁸ llaman «la ciudad perdida^a de los incas». En el pasado, _____ (ser)⁹ a la vez^b lugar de refugio y de vacaciones de los reyes^c y nobles incas. Después de la llegada de los españoles, esta ciudad fue ignorada y estuvo oculta^d hasta que Hiram Bingham, un profesor y explorador estadounidense, la _____ (encontrar)¹⁰ en 1911.

_____ (Hacer)¹¹ un siglo que Machu Picchu es un sitio famoso y un atractivo destino turístico (por / para)¹² muchas personas de todas partes del mundo.

Pero Machu Picchu no (es / está)¹³ el único lugar interesante que se puede visitar en el Perú. Si visita (el / la)¹⁴ país con tiempo suficiente, le recomendamos que _____ (hacer)¹⁵ una excursión (por / para)¹⁶ la selva.^e Además, _____ (*comm:* pasar)¹⁷ unos días en las playas de Máncora y Cabo Blanco. Finalmente, ojalá ____ (*usted*: poder)¹⁸ visitar las ciudades de Lima y Trujillo. ¡Perú es un destino fabuloso!

Machu Picchu, la ciudad imperial de los incas durante el siglo XV (1400–1500)

David Madison/Photographer's Choice/Getty Images

^a*lost* ^b*a... at the same time* ^c*kings* ^d*hidden* ^e*jungle*

(Continúa).

Paso 2. Comprensión. Las siguientes oraciones son falsas. Corríjalas con información de la lectura.

1. El actual rey del Perú vive en Machu Picchu.
2. Es fácil llegar a Machu Picchu.
3. Hiram Bingham fue un explorador español.
4. Machu Picchu es el único sitio de interés turístico en el Perú.
5. Para los turistas, no es nada atractivo viajar al Perú.

 Paso 3. En acción

 Ahora, en parejas, piensen en algún lugar considerado sagrado o espiritual en su campus, ciudad, estado o país. ¿Quiénes lo consideran así (*that way*)? ¿Por qué? ¿Lo visita mucha gente? ¿De dónde son esos visitantes?

 B. Proyecto: Encuesta sobre la vida universitaria

 ¿Cómo es la vida de los estudiantes en su campus? ¿Lo pasan bien en general o sufren de mucho estrés por las presiones académicas o sociales?

ENCUESTA

Paso 1. Preparación. En parejas, elijan uno de los siguientes temas relacionados con la vida universitaria para encuestar a sus compañeros de clase:

- una semana típica
- un semestre o trimestre típico
- «accidentes» frecuentes
- las presiones que sufren los estudiantes

Piensen bien en el objetivo (u objetivos) de su encuesta. Por ejemplo, si el tema es la semana típica, la encuesta puede enfocarse en la cantidad y el tipo de trabajo que hacen los estudiantes durante una semana.

Preparen una serie de 3 a 5 preguntas específicas, que pueden tener una variedad de formatos. Para ser más útiles, las preguntas deben incluir una escala o pedir información personal.

MODELOS: —¿Te sientes estresado/a esta semana? Contesta con un número del 1 al 5. 1 significa nada o casi nada y 5 significa muchísimo.

—Ordena las siguientes cosas de mayor a menor según la ansiedad que te causan: los exámenes, la vida social...

Paso 2. Encuesta. Háganles sus preguntas a varios compañeros de clase. Antes de empezar a preguntar, deben tener un plan para apuntar (*write down*) las respuestas.

Paso 3. Análisis de datos. Con la información de la encuesta, preparen una breve presentación y análisis de los datos. Incluyan una valoración (*assessment*) del grupo sobre los datos.

Vocabulario útil

la importancia
la necesidad

demostrar   to show
(dem**ue**stro)

sug**e**rir (sug**ie**ro)   to suggest that;
(i) que +   to show that
indicativo

según
x veces al día / a la semana / al mes

Video: Salu2 «¡Ay, qué estrés!»

You can watch two segments of this chapter's video in the **Video: Salu2** section, found at the end of the eBook.

Klic Video Productions/McGraw Hill

Un profesor universitario que habla de las presiones que sufren sus estudiantes

Enfoque cultural: Preocupaciones y motivos de ansiedad

Antes de leer

¿Qué cuestiones (*topics*) sociales son motivo de ansiedad entre la gente de su ciudad, estado o país?

En el Perú

La zona metropolitana de Lima, con 11 millones de personas, la tercera más grande de Latinoamérica

Como ocurre en todos los países, hay múltiples cuestiones que les causan ansiedad a las personas del Perú. El tema de la educación es una de estas cuestiones. La educación pública requiere una mayor inversión[a] de dinero para que[b] el sistema sea más efectivo y sirva a todos. Además, se necesita que los maestros[c] tengan mejores salarios.

El tema de los salarios es otra de las serias preocupaciones de muchos peruanos. En el Perú existe la Remuneración Mínima Vital, que es el salario mínimo establecido[d] por la ley.[e] Es el salario que recibe gran parte de los trabajadores[f] peruanos, pero que para muchos de ellos no resulta suficiente para cubrir[g] sus gastos cotidianos.[h]

[a]*investment* [b]*para... so that* [c]*teachers* [d]*established* [e]*law* [f]*workers* [g]*cover* [h]*daily*

Comprensión ¿Qué cuestiones les causan ansiedad a las personas peruanas? ¿Qué es la Remuneración Mínima Vital?

✋ En acción

Haga una investigación (*research*) sobre un movimiento migratorio de hispanohablantes y luego haga una breve presentación al resto de la clase.

En otros países hispanos

Una manifestación de emigrantes venezolanos en Buenos Aires

- **La emigración** Los procesos migratorios son una constante del mundo hispano, ya que[a] todos los países han sufrido[b] condiciones políticas y económicas adversas que provocaron tales[c] procesos. Por otro lado, los países hispanos también han recibido[d] y siguen recibiendo inmigrantes de todo el mundo, especialmente personas que hablan español. Hay un ejemplo reciente en Colombia. Aunque numerosas personas de este país han emigrado[e] en los últimos 25 años para buscar mejores oportunidades económicas (especialmente en los Estados Unidos y España), alrededor de[f] dos millones de venezolanos han entrado[g] en Colombia en más o menos el mismo tiempo (a un ritmo impresionante[h] desde 2016). Otros países con historias de emigración e inmigración son la Argentina, México, el Perú y España.

- **En todo el mundo hispanohablante** Hay creencias[i] populares sobre acciones que traen mala suerte:
  - romper un espejo[j] (¡Esto significa siete años de mala suerte!)
  - pasar por debajo de una escalera[k]
  - derramar[l] sal (Hay un «antídoto»: tirar[m] un poco de la sal derramada por encima del hombro[n] izquierdo).
  - cruzarse con un gato negro en el camino[ñ]
  - los días martes 13

[a]*ya... since* [b]*han... have suffered* [c]*such* [d]*han... have received* [e]*han... have migrated* [f]*alrededor... approximately* [g]*han... have entered* [h]*a... at an impressive pace* [i]*beliefs* [j]*mirror* [k]*ladder* [l]*to spill* [m]*to throw* [n]*por... over the shoulder* [ñ]*path*

Comprensión ¿Qué causa los procesos migratorios en el mundo hispanohablante? ¿Qué países tienen historias de emigración e inmigración? ¿Cuáles son dos de las supersticiones de uso frecuente en el mundo hispano?

Lectura

Antes de leer

Uno de los temas del poema que usted va a leer es el contraste entre los animales vertebrados y los invertebrados. De los siguientes términos que aparecen en el poema, ¿cuáles asocia con los animales vertebrados, entre los que (*among which*) están los seres (*beings*) humanos?

articulaciones	célula	cráneo	esqueleto	frágil
huesos	humedad	piernas	pluricelulares	unicelulares

«Ciencias naturales», de Washington Cucurto

Hoy pasé la tarde enseñándole ciencias naturales a mi hijo.
Tiene una prueba el martes, el miércoles y el jueves.
Enseñar es rememorar[a] viejos temas de infancia.[b]
Aprendí que los seres vivos[c] están divididos en unicelulares
5   y pluricelulares, los que se ven[d] y los que se ven solo con microscopio.
Aprendí que los animales se dividen en dos grupos,
vertebrados e invertebrados.
Y tienen esqueleto, articulaciones, vértebras que pueden ser quebradas.[e]
Me enteré que los humanos somos muy frágiles.
10   Cualquier[f] accidente podría partirnos las[g] vértebras.
Mejores son los invertebrados como las lombrices,
los cascarudos, las medusas o las víboras.[h]
Pienso en mis huesos, mis células y toda la humedad
que hay dentro de mí. ¡Detesto la humedad!
15   ¡Y soy húmedo por naturaleza!
Mis piernas, mi cráneo, cuando subo al bondi[i] los veo débiles[j]
y frágiles y me lamento por ser como soy, tan[k] frágil.

[a]*to recall* [b]*childhood* [c]*seres... living beings* [d]*los... those that are seen* [e]*broken* [f]*Any*
[g]*podría... could break our* [h]*lombrices... worms, beetles, jellyfish, or snakes* [i]*bus* [j]*weak* [k]*so*

Source: Washington Cucurto, Ciencias naturales, in Tarambaneadas importantísimas. 2015. Edition: 1st, Page 16. Ediciones VOX. Reproduced with permission.

Vocabulario para leer

la articulación	joint
el cráneo	cranium
el esqueleto	skeleton
el hueso	bone
la humedad	moisture
el (animal) vertebrado	**que tiene huesos**
enterarse	to realize
lamentarse	to lament

Comprensión

A. Una prueba sobre las ciencias naturales. Elija la opción correcta para terminar cada idea. Si tiene alguna duda, busque la información en el poema.

1. Los seres vivos unicelulares se ven _____   **a.** con microscopio.   **b.** sin microscopio.
2. Los seres vivos vertebrados son _____   **a.** unicelulares.   **b.** pluricelulares.
3. Las medusas son animales _____   **a.** invertebrados.   **b.** pluricelulares.
4. Los vertebrados son _____   **a.** humedos.   **b.** secos (*dry*).
5. Los animales que tienen esqueleto son _____   **a.** invertebrados.   **b.** vertebrados.
6. Los animales vertebrados _____   **a.** somos frágiles.   **b.** no somos frágiles.

B. Interpretación. Conteste las siguientes preguntas sobre los temas del poema.

1. El poema está dividido en tres partes con diferentes temas. Identifíquelas.
2. En el poema se dice que los animales vertebrados tenemos «esqueleto, articulaciones, vértebras que pueden ser quebradas» (verso 8), pero no se explican los riesgos (*risks*) que enfrentan los animales invertebrados. ¿Por qué, en su opinión, no se mencionan en el poema los problemas de los invertebrados?
3. ¿Por qué dice el padre que «mejores son los invertebrados» (verso 11)? ¿Está usted de acuerdo con él?
4. Para el padre, rememorar la biología animal provoca una reacción de ansiedad y también asco (*disgust*). ¿Cómo se puede explicar esa reacción?

Proyecto: La biofilia, un antídoto al estrés de ser humano

En el poema «Ciencias naturales», el autor se preocupa por su fragilidad como ser humano. Ejercer (*Tapping into*) nuestra innata «biofilia» (pasión o amor hacia otros organismos vivos) puede ser un posible antídoto para el estrés que el autor siente. En este proyecto, usted va a explorar cómo el contacto con los animales y las plantas lo/la puede ayudar a reducir el estrés en su vida.

Paso 1. Haga una lista de dos tipos de seres vivos (aparte de los seres humanos) con los que usted se relaciona o se ha relacionado (*with which you interact or have interacted*) habitualmente. Pueden ser animales o plantas. Indique una cosa que usted hace/hizo por ellos y un efecto que el contacto con ellos tienen sobre usted.

 Paso 2. En parejas o grupos, compartan su lista del **Paso 1.** ¿Qué animales, acciones y sentimientos son los más compartidos?

 Paso 3. Después de compartir las respuestas más comunes de cada grupo, discutan las razones para esas coincidencias. ¿Por qué los seres humanos nos sentimos más compenetrados (*understood*) o atraídos por esos animales o plantas?

Textos orales

La depresión entre los adolescentes

Antes de escuchar

Piense en una persona que usted conoce bien o en una persona famosa que sufre o ha sufrido (*has suffered*) de depresión. ¿Cómo se siente o sentía? ¿Qué hizo para mejorarse?

Vocabulario para escuchar

la tristeza	sadness	deprimido/a	depressed
el estado de ánimo	mood	la desesperanza	hopelessness
el comportamiento	behavior	emocionar	to get (*someone*) excited about (*something*)
enfrentarse a	to face		
hacer frente a	to face up to	el peso	weight
el aprendizaje	learning	evitar	to avoid
el acoso	harassment; bullying	tratable	treatable

Comprensión

A. Hablando de la depresión. ¿Qué dice el Dr. Carvajal sobre la depresión? Las siguientes oraciones son falsas. Corríjalas.

1. Todo el mundo (*Everyone*) sufre de depresión.
2. La depresión tiene solo una causa.
3. Uno de los síntomas de la depresión es querer estar siempre con los amigos y la familia.
4. La depresión es una de las enfermedades menos tratables.

B. Más detalles. Conteste las siguientes preguntas.

1. ¿Cuáles son tres de las causas de la depresión?
2. ¿Cuáles son tres de los síntomas de la depresión?
3. Según el Dr. Carvajal, ¿qué es lo primero que se debe hacer cuando un joven está deprimido?

 En acción

Usando la información de **Textos orales** y otra información que usted sepa o encuentre, prepare un breve mensaje sobre la depresión orientado a los estudiantes de la escuela secundaria o de la universidad. Incluya los síntomas más típicos de la depresión y lo que se debe hacer para combatirla.

Daniel Ernst/Getty Images

Entrevista

Use de modelo las preguntas y respuestas de la sección **Entrevista** al principio de este capítulo para hablar de las presiones que usted sufre y lo que hace para reducir su nivel de estrés.

Escritura

Un ensayo sobre las presiones de la vida estudiantil

A lo largo de este capítulo ha habido (*there have been*) muchas oportunidades para hablar de las causas del estrés que sufren las personas. Ahora usted va a concentrarse en las presiones de los estudiantes de su universidad para escribir un artículo para el periódico universitario.

Antes de escribir

Llene (*Fill in*) la siguiente tabla con las presiones que usted cree que lo/la afectan más. Luego entreviste a dos personas de la clase para conocer sus opiniones.

Jamie Grill/JGI/Blend Images/Getty Images

¿Triste, estresada o deprimida?

Las presiones...	académicas	sociales	financieras	familiares
usted				
compañero/a 1				
compañero/a 2				

A escribir

Ahora, analice la información de **Antes de escribir,** saque algunas conclusiones y dé algunos consejos. ¿Cuáles son las presiones que más afectan a las personas universitarias? ¿Cómo se manifiestan los efectos de estas presiones? ¿Cómo se puede mitigar las presiones y sus efectos? Hay más ayuda en Connect.

Para escribir bien

Considere las siguientes opciones para su ensayo.

- Conectores: **para poner un ejemplo / por ejemplo, por eso, por lo general, por lo menos, por supuesto, por un lado / por otro lado**
- Adverbios: **(des)afortunadamente, generalmente, solamente, únicamente**
- Expresiones útiles para generalizar:

  es cierto / verdad que + *indicativo*

  es normal / una lástima / posible / probable / que + *subjuntivo*

  hay que + *infinitivo*

En la comunidad

Entreviste a una persona hispana de su universidad o ciudad sobre lo que más les causa estrés a él/ella y a otras personas de su comunidad.

Preguntas posibles

- ¿Cuáles son los problemas que más les preocupan a usted y a su familia o a sus amigos? ¿Hay alguno que les cause más estrés que los otros?
- Si vive en una ciudad grande, ¿son el tráfico y el estacionamiento problemas para usted?
- ¿Qué presiones tiene la gente joven de su familia o comunidad? ¿Les preocupa su acceso a la universidad? ¿Por qué?
- ¿Qué actividades hace usted para relajarse (*relax*)?
- ¿Es usted una persona torpe o distraída? ¿Se le olvida hacer unas cosas o pierde cosas con bastante frecuencia? ¿Tiene accidentes relacionados con el estrés?

Producción audiovisual

Filme dos entrevistas con personas de su universidad (estudiantes, profesores o personal universitario) que hablan del estrés que sufren y sus causas.

Más ideas para el portafolio

- Incluya la imagen de un lugar al que (*to which*) usted puede volar con su mente para escaparse temporalmente (*temporarily*) de la realidad. Diga dónde está y descríbalo. ¿Lo conoce en persona o solo es un lugar que desea visitar?
- Haga una lista de las cosas que usted asocia con la buena suerte en su vida. Si usted no es nada supersticioso/a, puede hablar de las palabras que usted asocia con tres momentos agradables de su vida. Piense en eventos importantes o familiares, en canciones o lugares especiales, etcétera.
- Si ha estado jugando (*you have been playing*) Practice Spanish: Study Abroad, en Quest 10 usted ayudó a su amigo cuando se cayó y se hizo daño en el brazo. Ahora imagine una situación parecida (*similar*) y escriba un guion entre un médico / una médica y un(a) paciente que tuvo otro tipo de accidente. ¿Qué pasó? ¿Cuáles son las heridas (*injuries*) del / de la paciente? ¿Qué consejos recibe? Interprete la situación en clase con un compañero o una compañera.

Sugerencia: You are now ready to play Quest 10 in **Practice Spanish: Study Abroad.**

EN RESUMEN En este capítulo

AFTER STUDYING THIS CHAPTER I CAN ...

☐ talk about the typical things that cause stress in life (420–421)

☐ talk about accidents (423)

☐ use **hace** + time to express how something has been happening or how long ago something happened (427–428)

☐ express some actions as unexpected or unintended events (430–431)

☐ use **por** and **para** accurately in more contexts (434–436)

☐ recognize/describe at least 2–3 aspects of Peruvian cultures

Gramática en breve

39. Hace + *time*

hace = has/have been doing

> **hace** + *time* + **que** + ***present***
> ***present*** + **desde hace** + *time*

hace = ago

> **hace** + *time* + **que** + ***preterite***
> ***preterite*** + **hace** + *time*

40. Accidental *se*

a + *noun* + **se** + *indirect object pronoun* + *verb* + *subject*

(**a** + *pronoun*) **se** + *indirect object pronoun* + *verb* + *subject*

41. ¿Por o para?

por = reason, cause

> by / by means of   through/along
> because of / due to   during/in (time of day)

> *for* = in exchange for, for the sake of / on behalf of, in place of, for (*period of time*)

para = goal, purpose, destination
> *in order to* + inf.

> *for* = destined for / to be given to, by (*future time*), toward / in the direction of, to be used for, as compared with / in relation to others, in the employ of, in preparation for

Vocabulario

Los verbos

acabar	to finish; to run out of
aceptar	to accept
quedar	to remain, be left

Repaso: olvidar, perder (pierdo), pedir (pido) (i)

Las presiones de la vida académica

la agenda	personal calendar
la ansiedad	anxiety
los apuntes	notes (*academic*)
el despertador	alarm clock
el estrés	stress
el horario	schedule
el informe (oral/escrito)	(oral/written) report
el plazo	deadline
la presión	pressure
el programa (del curso)	(course) syllabus
la prueba	quiz; test
la tarjeta de identificación	identification card, ID
el trabajo	report, (piece of) work

Cognados: el calendario, la causa

Repaso: el examen, la llave, la nota, la tarea, el trabajo (*job; work*), la vida

corregir (corrijo) (i)	to grade; to correct
devolver (like volver) (algo a alguien)	to return (something to someone)
estacionar	to park
estar bajo muchas presiones	to be under a lot of pressure
estar (muy) estresado/a	to be (very) stressed, under (a lot of) stress
sacar (qu)	to get (*grades*)
sufrir (de)	to suffer (from)

Repaso: acordarse (me acuerdo) (de), entregar (gu), llegar (gu) a tiempo / tarde, olvidar, ser, tomar

Las disculpas

Disculpa. (*fam.*)	Pardon me. I'm sorry.
Disculpe. (*form.*)	Pardon me. I'm sorry.
Fue mi culpa.	It was my fault.
Fue sin querer.	I didn't mean (to do) it.
Lo siento (mucho).	I'm (very) sorry.
aceptar (las) disculpas	to accept apologies

No hay problema. No problem.
No se preocupe. *(form.)* Don't worry.
No te preocupes. *(fam.)* No worries.

Repaso: la cortesía, está bien, perdón

Los accidentes

el desastre	disaster
la suerte	luck

Repaso: el dolor

caer (caigo)	to fall; to drop
caerse (me caigo)	to fall down
chocar (qu) con/contra	to run into, bump against
disculparse	to apologize
equivocarse (qu) (de)	to make a mistake (about/with)
estar/ir distraído/a	to be distracted
hacerse daño	to hurt oneself
hacerse daño en	to hurt one's (*body part*)
lastimarse	to hurt (*a body part*)
levantarse con el pie izquierdo	to get up on the wrong side of the bed
ocurrir	to happen
pedir (pido) (i) disculpas	to apologize
pegar (gu)	to hit, strike
pegarse (gu) con/contra	to run, bump into/against
romper(se)	to break
tener buena/mala suerte	to have good/bad luck; to be (un)lucky

Repaso: doler (duele), pasar

Los adjetivos

distraído/a	absentminded, distracted
escrito/a	written
estresado/a	stressed out, under stress
estresante	stressful
torpe	clumsy
universitario/a	(of the) university

Cognados: académico/a, (in)flexible, oral

Repaso: bueno/a, malo/a

Otros sustantivos

las escaleras	stairs
la luz (*pl.* **luces**)	light
la taza	cup

Palabras adicionales

bajo (*prep.*)	under
hace + *time* **+ preterite, preterite +** **hace +** *time*	ago
hace + *time* **+ que +** *present,* **Present +** **desde hace +** *time*	to have been (*doing something*) for (*time*)
-mente	-ly (*adverbial suffix*)
¿para qué?	for what purpose?
por	by
por Dios	for heaven's sake
por ejemplo	for example
por primera/última vez	for the first/last time
por si acaso	just in case
¡por supuesto!	of course!
por todas partes	everywhere
¡qué + *adj.***!**	how + *adj.*!
¡qué + *noun***!**	what (a) + *noun*!
solamente	only
últimamente	lately

Repaso: gracias por, para, por (because of; through; in; for), **por eso, por favor, por fin, por la mañana / tarde / noche, por lo general, por lo menos, por teléfono**

Vocabulario personal

Use this space or a vocabulary notebook to write down other words and phrases you learn in this chapter.

15

La naturaleza y el medio ambiente° La... *Nature and the environment*

En este capítulo

VOCABULARY
Urban versus natural environments   450
Cars and driving   454

GRAMMAR
A verb form used as an adjective   458
Expressing *I have done* (*said, written ...*)   462

COUNTRIES OF FOCUS: ARGENTINA AND URUGUAY

La Pampa, la inmensa pradera (*grassland*) que se extiende por varias provincias de la Argentina, el Uruguay y el Brasil

Paul Stead/Alamy Stock Photo

LA ARGENTINA

45,8 (coma ocho)
millones de habitantes

EL URUGUAY

3,5 (tres y medio)
millones de habitantes

- La Argentina y el Uruguay
son dos países del Cono
Sur, el triángulo de territorio
sudamericano que está
al sur del Trópico de
Capricornio.

- El Uruguay y la Argentina
están unidos por la historia
y la cultura. Las capitales de
estos países están en el
inmenso estuario del Río
de la Plata.

🔊 ENTREVISTA

These questions related to the chapter theme are answered here by a
native speaker. You will be able to ask and answer them yourself with
personal information in the **Entrevista** activity in the **Portafolio** section at
the end of the chapter.

Gabriela Romano Acosta contesta las preguntas.

– **¿Cómo llega usted al campus? ¿Necesita usted un coche para llegar a
la universidad o al trabajo?**

– Voy en colectivo[a] al trabajo. Trabajo en la Facultad de Farmacia y
Bioquímica de la Universidad de Buenos Aires, que está en la Ciudad
Universitaria. Es más práctico llegar en transporte público porque el
estacionamiento[b] es un problema.

– **¿Le gusta a usted estar en contacto con la naturaleza? ¿Qué
actividades hace cuando está al aire libre?**

– ¡Me encanta estar en contacto con la naturaleza! Mis abuelos tienen una
finca[c] cerca de la ciudad de Córdoba. Cuando los visito, paso mucho
tiempo al aire libre, haciendo tareas agrícolas[d] o simplemente
caminando y disfrutando del[e] aire limpio.

– **¿Hay mucha contaminación en el área donde usted vive? ¿Es la
contaminación un problema que le preocupa?**

– ¡Claro! En Buenos Aires hay problemas de contaminación porque
es una ciudad inmensa. Y sí, la contaminación me preocupa,
especialmente la calidad del aire que respiramos todos los días.

[a]autobús [b]parking [c]farm [d]agricultural [e]disfrutando... enjoying the

VOCABULARIO: PREPARACIÓN

You can hear the pronunciation of theme vocabulary words and phrases in the eBook.

¿Dónde prefiere usted vivir?

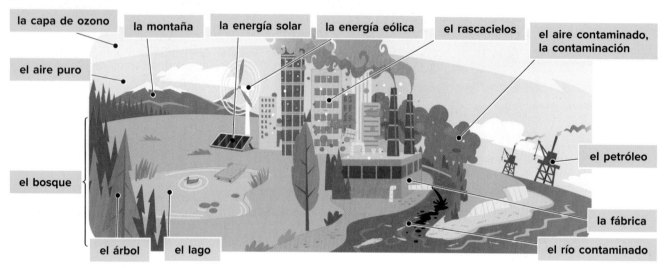

la capa de ozono
la montaña
la energía solar
la energía eólica
el rascacielos
el aire contaminado, la contaminación
el aire puro
el petróleo
el bosque
la fábrica
el árbol
el lago
el río contaminado

Los recursos naturales°	Los... *Natural resources*
la energía	energy
eólica	wind
renovable	renewable
el medio ambiente	environment
la naturaleza	nature
el reciclaje	recycling
la Tierra	Earth

Cognados: la energía eléctrica / nuclear / solar, el planeta

bello/a	beautiful
contaminado/a	contaminated, polluted
puro/a	pure

Los animales

la ballena	whale
el caballo	horse
la especie (en peligro de extinción)	(endangered) species
el gato	cat
el pájaro	bird
el perro	dog
el pez (*pl.* peces)	fish
el toro	bull
la vaca	cow

Cognados: el elefante, el gorila

doméstico/a	domesticated, tame
salvaje	wild

El desarrollo°	El... *Development*
el agricultor / la agricultora	farmer
la agricultura	farming, agriculture
el campesino / la campesina	farmer; field laborer
el campo	field; countryside
el delito	crime
la densidad de población	population density
la falta	lack; absence
la finca	farm; ranch
el gobierno	government
la población	population
el ritmo lento/ acelerado de la vida	slow/fast pace of life
el servicio	service
el transporte	transportation
público/a	public
acabar	to finish, run out (of); to use up completely
conservar	to save, conserve
construir*	to build
contaminar	to pollute
desarrollar	to develop
destruir (*like* construir)	to destroy
fabricar (qu)	to manufacture
proteger (protejo)	to protect
reciclar	to recycle

---

*Note the present indicative conjugation of __construir__: construyo, construyes, construye, construimos, construís, construyen.

Comunicación

A. ¿En la ciudad o en el campo?

Paso 1. ¿Con qué relaciona usted las siguientes ideas, con la ciudad o con el campo?

	LA CIUDAD	EL CAMPO
1. El aire es más puro; hay menos contaminación.	☐	☐
2. La naturaleza es más bella.	☐	☐
3. El ritmo de vida es más acelerado.	☐	☐
4. Hay más delitos.	☐	☐
5. Los servicios profesionales (financieros, legales...) son más accesibles.	☐	☐
6. Hay pocos medios de transporte públicos.	☐	☐
7. Hay menos densidad de población.	☐	☐
8. Hay falta de viviendas.	☐	☐

Paso 2. Ahora, en parejas, den dos ideas más que ustedes asocian con la ciudad y con el campo.

B. Definiciones. Defina las siguientes palabras en español.

MODELO: **9.** el agricultor → Es el dueño de una finca.

1. la fábrica
2. el campesino
3. la falta

4. la finca
5. la naturaleza
6. la población

7. el río
8. el rascacielos
9. el agricultor

Así se dice

la fábrica = la factoría
la finca = la granja, el rancho, la estancia

El árbol is also called **el palo** in Mexico, Central America, and the Caribbean. The names of at least two California cities contain the word **palo:** Palo Alto and Palos Verdes.

Nota cultural: Programas medioambientales

En muchos países del mundo es necesario equilibrar[a] la protección del medio ambiente con los objetivos del desarrollo económico. En muchos casos, la explotación de recursos naturales es la mayor fuente de ingresos[b] para la economía de un país. Los gobiernos latinoamericanos están conscientes de la necesidad de proteger el medio ambiente y de conservar los recursos naturales. Los siguientes son algunos de los muchos programas medioambientales que existen en los países hispanohablantes.

- En las grandes ciudades de varios países (Bolivia, Chile, Colombia, el Ecuador, Honduras y México, entre otros) se han establecido[c] programas de restricción vehicular, que tratan de regular la cantidad de tráfico en determinadas horas o días. Se basan en un sistema que limita el uso de un vehículo según su placa.[d] Además de[e] reducir el tráfico diario en la ciudad, estos programas pueden mejorar[f] la calidad del aire.

- En muchos países hispanohablantes (la Argentina, el Uruguay, España y México, entre otros) existen programas de reciclaje, basados en sistemas de separación de basura. Es decir que, según su clase, los materiales se depositan en contenedores[g] de colores diferentes: el papel y el cartón[h] en un contenedor; el vidrio,[i] el metal y el plástico en otro; y en algunos casos los desperdicios de materia orgánica,[j] en otro.

¿Qué programas medioambientales hay en su ciudad o estado?

[a]*to balance* [b]*fuente... source of income* [c]*se... have been established* [d]*license plate* [e]*Además... Besides* [f]*improve* [g]*containers, receptacles* [h]*cardboard* [i]*glass* [j]*los... organic waste matter*

C. ¿Cuánto saben ustedes de los animales?

Paso 1. En parejas, hagan listas en español de todos los animales que ustedes conocen en las siguientes categorías: **domésticos, salvajes, en peligro de extinción, insectos.** ¡OJO! Algunos animales pueden estar en más de una lista.

LOS ANIMALES: **el águila, el camello, el cocodrilo, el cóndor, la cucaracha, el delfín, el hipopótamo, el jaguar, la jirafa, el león, el mosquito, el orangután, la ostra, la rata, el rinoceronte, el tigre**

Paso 2. Ahora, hablen de cuáles son sus animales favoritos (domésticos y no domésticos). También compartan sus sentimientos sobre el peligro de extinción de muchas especies de animales debido a (*due to*) la crisis climática. ¿Les preocupa? ¿Qué se debe o puede hacer?

 D. Problemas medioambientales

Paso 1. En parejas, indiquen cuáles de los siguientes problemas y temas afectan a su ciudad, estado o país. Añadan por lo menos un tema que ustedes consideren importante.

AFECTA A...	MI CIUDAD	MI ESTADO	MI PAÍS
1. la contaminación del aire	☐	☐	☐
2. la destrucción de la capa de ozono	☐	☐	☐
3. la deforestación de los bosques	☐	☐	☐
4. el desarrollo de energías renovables	☐	☐	☐
5. la falta de transporte público adecuado	☐	☐	☐
6. el ritmo acelerado de la vida	☐	☐	☐
7. la falta de protección de los espacios naturales	☐	☐	☐
8. ¿ ?	☐	☐	☐

Paso 2. Ahora escojan dos de estos temas y explíquenle a la clase una de las causas del problema y una de las cosas que es necesario hacer para resolverlo.

 E. Opiniones. Con toda la clase, comenten las siguientes opiniones. Pueden usar las siguientes expresiones para aclarar (*clarify*) su posición con respecto a cada tema. ¡OJO! Todas las expresiones requieren el uso del subjuntivo.

1. La crisis climática es una exageración.
2. Podemos eliminar la crisis climática si todas las personas aplican en su vida la regla (*rule*) de las tres erres: Reducir, Reusar, Reciclar.
3. Se debe crear más parques urbanos, estatales y nacionales.
4. La protección del medio ambiente no debe impedir la explotación de los recursos naturales.
5. Para evitar la contaminación urbana, debemos limitar el uso de los coches a ciertos días de la semana.
6. El gobierno debe ponerles multas (*fines*) muy graves a las compañías e individuos que causan la contaminación.

> ### Vocabulario útil
>
> **Es Me/Nos parece** { necesario/esencial que... importantísimo que... absurdo que...
>
> **Me opongo / Nos oponemos a que...** I am / We are against ...
> **No creo/creemos que...**

Algo sobre el Río de la Plata

El Río de la Plata está formado por la confluencia de los ríos Paraná y Uruguay, que se unen al entrar en el océano Atlántico. En realidad,[a] hay un debate sobre si el Río de la Plata es un río o un estuario. En cualquier caso,[b] forma una frontera[c] natural entre el Uruguay y la Argentina, cuyas[d] capitales, Montevideo y Buenos Aires, respectivamente, están junto a estas aguas.

 ¿Hay algún accidente (*feature*) geográfico compartido (*shared*) entre su país y un país vecino?

[a]En... *In fact* [b]En... *In any case* [c]*border* [d]*whose*

Cristian Lazzari/Getty Images

Vista aérea de Buenos Aires y el Río de la Plata

F. Anuncios medioambientales

Paso 1. Lea los siguientes anuncios y conteste las preguntas.

ᵃheater

1. ¿Qué cosa sugieren los anuncios que ahorremos?
2. ¿Puede usted explicar el uso de la imagen de la bombilla (*light bulb*) en el anuncio de la izquierda?
3. ¿Qué significa en inglés «MAYOR AHORRO = MEJOR PLANETA»? ¿Con qué palabras juega el anuncio?
4. ¿Qué imagen predomina en el anuncio de Solesluz? ¿Por qué es apropiada esta imagen?

Paso 2. En grupos, hablen de lo que ustedes hacen personalmente para conservar los recursos naturales. Deben considerar las siguientes ideas y añadir otras. Luego díganle a la clase algunas de las ideas interesantes de su grupo.

1. reciclar
2. apagar/encender las luces
3. caminar en vez de manejar (*instead of driving*)
4. pasear en bicicleta
5. consumir lo que se produce localmente
6. usar menos papel

Algo sobre la Pampa

La palabra «pampa» viene del quechua y significa llanura.ᵃ Las pampas cubrenᵇ una inmensa región sudamericana: varias provincias del centro de la Argentina, casi todo el Uruguay y el extremo sur del Brasil.

    La región pampeana se divide en subregiones según el clima y la ubicación.ᶜ Pero en general es una zona dedicada a la explotaciónᵈ del ganadoᵉ y de la agricultura, especialmente de granos como la soja, el trigoᶠ y el maíz.

 ¿Qué zona de este país se dedica especialmente a la explotación del ganado y al cultivo de granos?

ᵃ*grassland* ᵇ*cover* ᶜ*location* ᵈ*development*
ᵉ*cattle* ᶠ*wheat*

la Pampa

La Pampa: un territorio multinacional

¿Sabe usted manejar°?

to drive

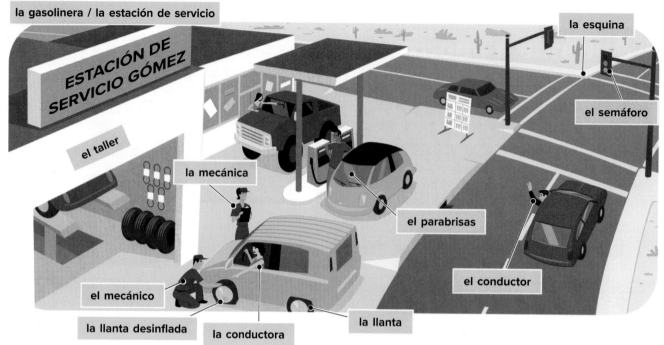

la gasolinera / la estación de servicio

ESTACIÓN DE SERVICIO GÓMEZ

el taller

la mecánica

el mecánico

la llanta desinflada

la conductora

la llanta

el parabrisas

el conductor

la esquina

el semáforo

la acera	sidewalk	arrancar (**qu**)	to start up (*a car*)
la autopista	freeway; interstate	arreglar	to fix, repair
la avenida	avenue	chocar (**qu**) con	to run into, collide (with)
la calle	street	estacionar	to park
la camioneta	(mini)van	gastar (mucha/	to use (a lot of / little gas)
la carretera	road; highway	poca gasolina)	
la circulación, el tránsito	traffic	llenar	to fill (up)
el coche/carro	(convertible, hybrid,	manejar, <u>conducir</u>	to drive
(descapotable,	all-terrain) car	(condu**zc**o)*	
híbrido, todoterreno)		obede**c**er (obede**zc**o)*	to obey
el estacionamiento	parking place/lot	parar	to stop
los frenos	brakes	revisar el aceite	to check the oil
la licencia de manejar	driver's license	to**c**ar (**qu**) la bocina	to honk the horn (*car*)
la moto(cicleta)	motorcycle		
el tanque	tank	**Cognado: reparar**	
el vehículo	vehicle		

**Cognados: el auto(móvil), la batería,
la bicicleta, la gasolina, el SUV, el tráfico**

Así se dice

el estacionamiento = el aparcamiento,
  el parking
la licencia de manejar = el carnet
  de conducir, el permiso de manejar
la llanta = el neumático, la rueda

arrancar = encender el motor
estacionar = aparcar (*Sp.*), parquear (*Col., Mex.*)

There are many ways to express *car* in Spanish. You already know **el coche. El carro**
is frequently used. **El automóvil,** or simply **el auto,** is perhaps the most generic word,
understood in all parts of the Spanish-speaking world.

---

*Like the verb **cono<u>c</u>er, condu<u>c</u>ir** and **obede<u>c</u>er** have a spelling change in the **yo** form of the present
indicative: **cono<u>zc</u>o, condu<u>zc</u>o, obede<u>zc</u>o.** This spelling change is also used in all forms of the
present subjunctive.

Comunicación

A. Definiciones

Paso 1. Empareje las definiciones con las palabras y frases.

DEFINICIONES

1. _____ Se pone en el tanque.
2. _____ Se llenan de aire.
3. _____ Lubrica el motor.
4. _____ Es necesaria para arrancar el motor.
5. _____ Es necesario cambiarla cuando no tiene aire suficiente.
6. _____ Se usan para parar el coche.
7. _____ El policía nos la pide cuando nos para en el coche.

PALABRAS Y FRASES

a. los frenos
b. la batería
c. una llanta desinflada
d. la gasolina
e. las llantas
f. el aceite
g. la licencia de manejar

Paso 2. Ahora, siguiendo el modelo de las definiciones del **Paso 1,** dé una definición de las siguientes palabras.

1. el semáforo
2. la circulación
3. estacionar
4. el conductor
5. la gasolinera
6. la autopista
7. la carretera
8. el taller

B. ¿Maneja usted responsablemente?

Paso 1. En parejas, túrnense para entrevistarse sobre sus hábitos cuando manejan. ¿Quién es más responsable?

MODELO: **1.** olvidar la licencia en casa cuando va a manejar →
    E1: ¿Olvidas alguna vez la licencia en casa cuando vas a manejar?
    E2: No, nunca. ¿Y tú?
    E1: Yo tampoco/casi nunca.

1. olvidar la licencia en casa cuando va a manejar
2. acelerar (*to speed up*) cuando ve un coche de la policía
3. tomar bebidas alcohólicas y después manejar
4. respetar el límite de velocidad o excederlo
5. estacionar el coche donde dice «Prohibido estacionar»
6. revisar el aceite y la batería
7. seguir a toda velocidad cuando no sabe llegar a su destino
8. adelantar (*to pass*) tres carros a la vez (*at the same time*)
9. mandar mensajes electrónicos mientras maneja
10. no parar cuando el semáforo está en rojo

Paso 2. Ahora, en parejas, hagan una lista de cinco recomendaciones importantes sobre lo que se debe o no se debe hacer cuando uno maneja. Pueden usar las ideas del **Paso 1.**

MODELOS: Es importante respetar el límite de velocidad.
    No exceda/excedas el límite de velocidad.

C. Intercambios. En parejas, compartan (*share*) sus opiniones sobre los siguientes temas relacionados con el uso de los carros en este país y en su universidad. Expliquen por qué tienen esas opiniones.

1. ¿Hay demasiados carros? ¿Se usan demasiado?
2. ¿Les preocupa el uso excesivo de los carros? ¿Qué se puede cambiar para reducir su uso?
3. ¿Hay buen acceso a su universidad usando el transporte público? ¿Es fácil el acceso al estacionamiento si uno llega en su propio carro?

D. En el centro de Montevideo

Paso 1. Complete las siguientes instrucciones sobre cómo llegar a varios sitios en Montevideo.

Centro de Montevideo

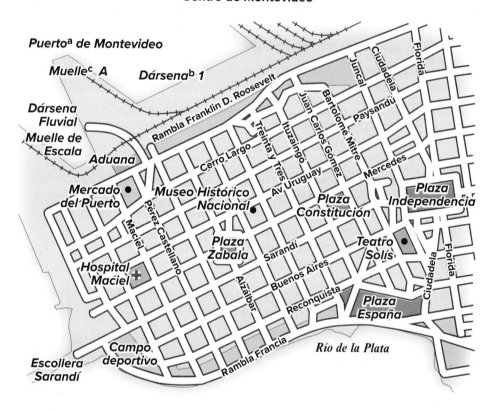

^aPort ^bDock ^cPier

1. **Del Museo Histórico Nacional al Mercado del Puerto:** Salga del Museo y vaya _____ (a la derecha / a la izquierda). _____ (Siga todo recto por / Doble en) la Avenida Uruguay hasta la calle Pérez Castellano. Allí doble _____ (a la derecha / a la izquierda) y _____ (siga/ doble) hasta la calle Cerro Largo. El Mercado está enfrente.
2. **Del Mercado del Puerto hasta la Plaza Zabala:** Saliendo del Mercado, tome la calle Pérez Castellano y _____ (doble / siga todo recto) hasta llegar a la calle Mercedes. Allí, doble _____ (a la derecha / a la izquierda) y siga hasta llegar a la Plaza.

Paso 2. Ahora dé usted las instrucciones sobre cómo llegar de la Plaza Zabala a la Plaza de la Constitución y de esa plaza a la Plaza España.

E. ¿Cómo se llega a... ?

Paso 1. En parejas, escriban o den verbalmente direcciones para ir desde su campus a los siguientes lugares. Usen mandatos con **tú**.

1. a un cine que está cerca del campus
2. al centro de la ciudad
3. a un centro comercial popular
4. a un restaurante bien conocido (*well-known*)

Paso 2. Ahora lean las direcciones del **Paso 1** a la clase pero sin dar el nombre del destino. La clase lo va a tratar de adivinar (*guess*).

Textos de todos los días: Direcciones en el GPS

Sin duda, los navegadores GPS están entre las aplicaciones y programas más utilizados. En esta actividad usted va a practicar cómo entender las instrucciones de GPS en español.

Objetivo: Buscar y entender las instrucciones de GPS en español, practicando con las instrucciones sobre cómo llegar al lugar donde usted (o su familia) vive desde su universidad.

Antes de empezar

- Cambie la lengua de su teléfono o portátil al español.
- Tenga en cuenta (*Keep in mind*) los siguientes detalles importantes sobre los navegadores GPS en el mundo hispanohablante: Usan mandatos informales y están programadas para dar las distancias en el sistema métrico decimal, es decir, metros y kilómetros, como opción predeterminada (*default*).
- ¿Qué cree que significan las siguientes frases en español?
  1. instrucciones sobre cómo llegar
  2. agregar destino
  3. dirígete al sur por la Av. de la Constitución
  4. gira a la izquierda en la C. Santiago
- Busque las direcciones para ir de la universidad a su casa y léalas. ¿Qué otras palabras son nuevas para usted? Si es necesario manejar para llegar al lugar donde usted vive, preste atención al vocabulario para *roads*, *exits* y otras palabras relevantes.

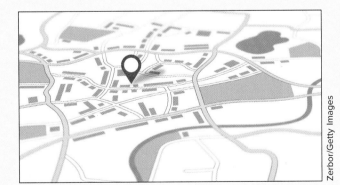

Zerbor/Getty Images

Answers: 1. directions 2. add (a) destination 3. head south on Constitution Avenue 4. turn left onto Santiago Street

GRAMÁTICA

As you know, the Spanish present participle, like its English equivalent, does not change according to the subject of a sentence.

Cecilia
Juan } está cant**ando**, beb**iendo**, durm**iendo**.

Give the English equivalent of the following:

cantar: cantando   **beber: bebiendo**   **dormir: durmiendo**

In both English and Spanish, there is another kind of participle: the past participle. Like the present participle, it does not change its form when used as a verb. But it can also be used as an adjective. A number of adjectives you learned to use with **estar** are actually past participles.

Here are some past participle adjectives. Can you explain how they are formed?

1. **-ar** verbs: **cansado/a, cerrado/a, encantado/a, pasado/a, resfriado/a**
2. **-er/-ir** verbs: **aburrido/a, divertido/a, querido/a**
3. irregular verbs: **abierto/a, escrito/a**

You will learn more about past participles and how they are used in **Gramática 42** and **43**.

42 *Más descripciones* • Past Participle Used as an Adjective

Gramática en acción: Algunos refranes y dichos en español

a. En boca **cerrada** no entran moscas.

b. Estar tan **aburrido** como una ostra.

c. Cuando está **abierto** el cajón, hasta el más **honrado** es ladrón.

Comprensión

Empareje estas oraciones con el refrán o dicho que explican.

1. _____ Es posible que una persona buena sienta la tentación de hacer algo malo si la oportunidad se le presenta.
2. _____ Hay que ser prudente. A veces es mejor no decir nada para evitar (*avoid*) problemas.
3. _____ Ejemplifican el aburrimiento (*boredom*) porque llevan una vida tranquila... siempre igual.

A few Spanish proverbs and sayings a. Into a closed mouth no flies enter. *b.* To be as bored as an oyster. *c.* When the drawer is open, even the most honest person is (can become) a thief.

The Past Participle / **El participio pasado**	
verbos en *-ar*	**verbos en** *-er/-ir*
habl**ar** → habl**ado** spoken	com**er** → com**ido** eaten viv**ir** → viv**ido** lived

the past participle / **el participio pasado** = the form of a verb used with *to have* in English to form the perfect tenses (*I have written, I had written ...*)

Forming the Past Participle / **Cómo se forma el participio pasado**

1. Regular Forms

The past participle of most English verbs ends in -*ed: to walk* → *walked, to close* → *closed*. Many, however, are irregular: *to sing* → *sung, to write* → *written*.

In Spanish, the *past participle* (**el participio pasado**) is formed by adding **-ado** to the stem of regular **-ar** verbs, and **-ido** to the stem of regular **-er** and **-ir** verbs.

An accent mark is used on the past participle of **-er/-ir** verbs with stems ending in **-a, -e,** or **-o.**

El participio pasado		
-ar	→	-**ado**
-er/-ir:	→	-**ido**

Pronunciation hint: **-d-** = [ð], like English *th*

caer	→ caído	oír	→ oído
creer	→ creído	(son)reír	→ (son)reído
leer	→ leído	traer	→ traído

2. Irregular Forms

Some Spanish verbs have irregular past participles. Only the verbs with * are new.

> ## ¡OJO!
> The past participle of most compound verbs (such as **descubrir**) that have an irregular root verb (in this case, **cubrir**) have the same irregularity in the past participle: **(des)cubierto.**

abrir:	**abierto**	morir:	**muerto**
*cubrir:	**cubierto**	poner:	**puesto**
(to cover)		*resolver:	**resuelto**
decir:	**dicho**	(to solve,	
*descubrir:	**descubierto**	resolve)	
(to discover)		romper:	**roto**
escribir:	**escrito**	ver:	**visto**
hacer:	**hecho**	volver:	**vuelto**

The Past Participle as an Adjective / **El participio pasado como adjetivo**

1. Used as an Adjective

In both English and Spanish, the past participle can be used as an adjective to modify a noun. Like other Spanish adjectives, the past participle must agree in number and gender with the noun modified.

Viven en **un<u>a</u> cas<u>a</u> construid<u>a</u>** en 1920.
They live in a house built in 1920.

El español es solo una de **l<u>as</u> lengu<u>as</u> hablad<u>as</u>** en los Estados Unidos.
Spanish is only one of the languages spoken in the United States.

2. With *estar*

The past participle is frequently used with **estar** to describe conditions that are the result of a previous action.

> ## ¡OJO!
> English past participles often have the same form as the past tense.
>
> > I **closed** the book.
> > The thief stood behind the **closed** door.
>
> The Spanish past participle is never identical in form or use to a past tense.

El lago **está <u>contaminado</u>.**
The lake is polluted.

Todos los peces **estaban <u>cubiertos</u>** de crudo.
All the fish were covered with crude oil.

Cerré la puerta. Ahora la puerta está **<u>cerrada</u>.**
*I **closed** the door. Now the door is **closed**.*

Resolvieron el problema. Ahora el problema está **<u>resuelto</u>.**
*They **solved** the problem. Now the problem is **solved**.*

Vocabulario útil

estar parado/a	to be standing up
estar sentado/a	to be sitting

Algo sobre el mate

Dave G. Houser/Getty Images

El mate, una tradición en la Argentina y el Uruguay

El mate es también conocido como la yerba[a] mate. Es un tipo de infusión[b] inmensamente popular en la Argentina y en el Uruguay. Se toma tradicionalmente en un recipiente[c] también llamado «mate», hecho de una calabaza,[d] y con una bombilla, que es una pajilla[e] de metal para sorber[f] la infusión. El mate con frecuencia se comparte entre familiares y amigos.

 En su opinión, ¿cuál es la bebida más popular de este país? ¿Cuál es la bebida que usted prefiere?

[a]small plant, grass   [b]herbal tea
[c]container   [d]gourd   [e]straw
[f]sucking up

Práctica y comunicación

A. En este momento

Paso 1. Autoprueba. Dé el infinitivo de los siguientes participios pasados.

1. estudiadas
2. leído
3. vistos
4. dicha
5. abiertas
6. bebido

Paso 2. Use uno de los participios entre paréntesis en la forma apropiada para describir las siguientes cosas y personas del salón de clase o del lugar donde usted está si no toma la clase de forma presencial (*in person*).

1. la puerta y las ventanas (cerrado / abierto)
2. mi portátil (cerrado / abierto)
3. las luces (apagado / encendido)
4. el proyector (apagado / encendido)
5. yo (sentado / parado)
6. el profesor / la profesora (sentado / parado)

Paso 3. Ahora, en parejas, den ejemplos de las siguientes ideas.

MODELOS: **1.** algo que puede estar cerrado o abierto →
Una puerta puede estar cerra**da** o abier**ta.**
Algo que puede estar cerra**do** o abier**to** es una puerta.

1. algo que puede estar cerrado o abierto y que no está en el salón de clase
2. un edificio del campus bien diseñado
3. algo contaminado
4. el transporte público más usado en su ciudad
5. algo deseado por muchos estudiantes
6. el mejor libro escrito en inglés
7. una cosa rota en su casa/cuarto

B. ¿Cuánto sabe de la Argentina y del Uruguay? Para saber más, complete las siguientes oraciones con el participio pasado de uno de los siguientes infinitivos.

VERBOS: **acelerar, celebrar, conquistar** (*to conquer*), **desarrollar, escribir, establecer** (*to establish*), **preferir, reconocer** (*to recognize*), **separar, traer**

1. La Argentina y el Uruguay son dos países muy _____.
2. Los dos países están _____ por el estuario del Río de la Plata.
3. El gaucho es una figura _____ como símbolo nacional.
4. En la Pampa, hay grandes fincas _____ en la época colonial.
5. El mate es la bebida _____ de los argentinos y uruguayos.
6. Los guaraníes son un pueblo indígena _____ por los españoles.
7. Muchos guaraníes murieron a causa de enfermedades _____ por los europeos.
8. «El Aleph» es un cuento _____ por el famoso escritor argentino Jorge Luis Borges.
9. El carnaval de Montevideo, _____ por cuarenta días, es una de las celebraciones más largas del mundo.
10. En Buenos Aires y Montevideo, el ritmo de vida es muy _____.

Prác. A, Paso 1: Answers: 1. estudiar 2. leer 3. ver 4. decir 5. abrir 6. beber

460 ■ cuatrocientos sesenta

Capítulo 15 La naturaleza y el medio ambiente

C. Comentarios sobre nuestro mundo. Complete cada párrafo con el participio pasado de los verbos de cada lista.

VERBOS: **desperdiciar** (*to waste*), **destruir, hacer, reciclar**

Todos los días, se bota[a] a la basura aproximadamente media libra[b] de papel por persona. Todo ese papel _____[1] constituye un gran número de árboles _____.[2] Esto es un buen motivo para convencer a las personas con quienes estudiamos o trabajamos de no imprimir papel innecesariamente. También debe recordarles que solo se puede completar el ciclo del reciclaje si se compran productos _____[3] con materiales _____.[4]

[a]se... *people throw*   [b]media... *half a pound*

VERBOS: **agotar** (*to exhaust*), **comprometer con** (*to commit to*), **convencer, limitar, preparar**

El petróleo como fuente[a] de energía no está _____[5] todavía,[b] pero su duración[c] es _____.[6] Desafortunadamente, todavía no estamos _____[7] para sustituirlo[d] completamente con otras energías renovables. El problema es que muy pocos países están verdaderamente[e] _____[8] con la reducción de emisiones de carbono y no están _____[9] de que es necesario que cambiemos la manera en que consumimos energía.

[a]*source*   [b]*yet*   [c]su... *the amount of time it will last*   [d]*replace it*   [e]*really*

D. ¡Ojo alerta! Las cocinas de los dibujos A y B se diferencian (*differ*) en por lo menos siete detalles. En parejas, encuéntrenlos todos. Si pueden, usen adjetivos que son participios pasados para describir los detalles.

A.

B.

Vocabulario útil	
el grifo	faucet
agitar	
cortar	
(des)ordenar	to (dis)organize

E. ¿Hecho o por hacer todavía (*yet to be done*)?

Paso 1. Haga oraciones completas que sean verdaderas para usted. Use un participio pasado como adjetivo, según el modelo. Si usted no tiene ninguna de estas cosas, diga **«No tengo... »**, según el modelo.

MODELOS: una tarea para la clase de _____ ➜
Mi tarea para la clase de inglés **ya** está escrita.
Mi tarea para la clase de inglés **no** está escrita **todavía**.
No tengo que hacer ninguna tarea escrita para ninguna clase.

1. un informe (oral/escrito) para la clase de _____
2. una presentación oral para la clase de _____
3. los problemas para la clase de matemáticas _____
4. ¿ ?

Vocabulario útil	
escribir	
investigar (**gu**)	to research
organizar (**c**)	
preparar	
resolver (**resuelvo**).	

Paso 2. Ahora, en parejas, comparen sus respuestas. Díganle a la clase algo que tienen en común.

43 ¿Qué has hecho? • Perfect Forms: Present Perfect Indicative and Present Perfect Subjunctive

Gramática en acción: Una llanta desinflada

¿Qué **ha pasado**? ¡Ay, no! ¡Una llanta desinflada! ¡Nunca **he cambiado** una llanta desinflada!

¿Y usted?

Diga si **ha hecho** lo siguiente alguna vez (*ever*).

1. ¿Le **ha cambiado** una llanta desinflada a un carro? (Le **he...** / **Nunca** le **he...**)
2. ¿Le **ha revisado** el aceite al coche?
3. ¿Le **ha reparado** otras cosas al coche?
4. **¿Ha tenido** un accidente automovilístico?
5. **¿Ha excedido** el límite de velocidad en la autopista?

Present Perfect Indicative / El presente perfecto de indicativo

haber + past participle (-ar → **-ado**, -er/-ir → **-ido**)			
he	I have		
has	you have		
ha	you have / he/she has	conserv**ado**	conserved
hemos	we have	proteg**ido**	protected
habéis	you have	constru**ido**	built
han	you/they have		

> **¡OJO!**
> Remember that some verbs have irregular past participles: **abierto, cubierto, dicho...**

1. Present Perfect Indicative

In English, to say *I have* (*written, spoken, ...*), you use a present tense form of *to have* plus the past participle. This compound tense is called the *present perfect*. The Spanish equivalent, **el presente perfecto,** is formed with present tense forms of **haber** plus the **-o** form of the past participle.

In general, the Spanish present perfect tense is used just like the English present perfect.

¿Has ido al zoo de San Diego?
Have you been to the San Diego zoo?

El accidente en la autopista nos **ha retrasado**.
The accident on the highway has delayed us.

¿Ya **has escrito** el ensayo?
Have you written the essay yet?

> **¡OJO!**
> **Haber** is the only verb that can be used with the past participle to form the Spanish present perfect, which is never formed with **tener**. However, **tener** *can* be conjugated in the present perfect, using **haber**, of course.

He tenido muchos problemas con el carro desde que tuve el accidente.
I have had many problems with the car since I had the accident.

A flat tire What has happened? Oh, no! A flat tire! I've never changed a flat tire!

2. Form and Placement

Here is how **el presente perfecto** is formed.

- The masculine singular form of the past participle is *always* used.

- **Haber** and the past participle are never separated and their order never changes.

- **No** and object pronouns always come before the form of **haber: no** first, then the pronouns.

> ### ¡OJO!
>
> Remember that **acabar** + **de** + *infinitive*—not the present perfect tense—is used to state that something *has just happened.*

Ella **ha cambiado** llantas varias veces.
She's changed tires several times.

¿Han cambiado ustedes una llanta alguna vez?
¿Ustedes **han cambiado** una llanta alguna vez?
Have you ever changed a tire?

Todavía **no he escrito** el ensayo.
I haven't written the essay yet.

—¿**Le han dado** el coche a su hija ya?
—No, **no se lo** han dado todavía.
"Have they given the car to their daughter already?" "No, they haven't given it to her yet."

Acabo de mandar el ensayo.
I've just sent the essay.

3. Present Perfect of *hay*

The present perfect form of **hay** is **ha habido.** It is invariable, and it expresses both *there has been* and *there have been.*

Ha habido mucha discusión sobre este tema.
There has been a lot of discussion about this topic.

Ha habido muchos accidentes en esta esquina.
There have been many accidents at this corner.

Present Perfect Subjunctive / El presente perfecto de subjuntivo

To express *I have written (spoken, …)* in a context that requires the subjunctive, use the present subjunctive forms of **haber** to form the *present perfect subjunctive* (**el presente perfecto de subjuntivo**).

The English equivalent of the Spanish present perfect subjunctive will vary according to the context, as shown in the examples. It can be either the simple past (*built, came, did*) or the present perfect (*have built, have come, have done*).

haya habl**ado**	**hayamos** viv**ido**
hayas com**ido**	**hayáis** abi**erto**
haya d**icho**	**hayan** ten**ido**

Es bueno que **haya cambiado** usted el aceite.
It's good (that) you changed (have changed) the oil.

Me alegro de que **hayas venido.**
I'm glad (that) you've come (you came).

Es posible que **haya habido** un grave problema ecológico.
It's possible (that) there was (has been) a serious ecological problem.

Práctica y comunicación

A. ¿Una vida interesante?

> **Paso 1. Autoprueba.** Dé la forma indicada de **haber.**
>
> INDICATIVO:
>
> **1.** yo _____
> **2.** tú _____
> **3.** nosotros _____
>
> SUBJUNTIVO:
>
> **4.** yo _____
> **5.** ella _____
> **6.** ellos _____
>
> Ahora dé el participio pasado de los siguientes verbos.
>
> **7.** arrancar _____
> **8.** conducir _____
> **9.** conservar _____
> **10.** construir _____
> **11.** obedecer _____
> **12.** proteger _____
> **13.** morir _____
> **14.** romper _____
> **15.** ver _____

Prác. A, Paso 1: Answers: 1. he **2.** has **3.** hemos **4.** haya **5.** haya **6.** hayan **7.** arrancado **8.** conducido **9.** conservado **10.** construido **11.** obedecido **12.** protegido **13.** muerto **14.** roto **15.** visto

(Continúa).

Paso 2. Diga si usted ha hecho alguna vez las siguientes cosas o no. Siga el modelo.

MODELO: **1.** hacer un viaje al extranjero →
   (No) He hecho un viaje al extranjero.

1. hacer un viaje al extranjero
2. montar en camello
3. comprar un auto nuevo
4. ocupar un cargo (*position*) político
5. tener una mascota
6. ver una película en español
7. escribir un poema
8. romperse el brazo o la pierna

Paso 3. Ahora, en parejas, hagan y contesten preguntas sobre las acciones del **Paso 2.** Luego díganle al resto de la clase una o dos acciones que tienen en común.

MODELO: **1.** hacer un viaje al extranjero →
   E1: ¿**Has hecho** un viaje al extranjero?
   E2: Sí, **he viajado** a México. ¿Y tú?
   E1: Yo también **he viajado** a México. →
      Los/Las dos **hemos viajado** a México.

B. **El auto de Carmina.** Carmina acaba de comprarse un auto usado. Describa lo que le ha pasado a Carmina, según el modelo.

MODELO: ir a la agencia de compra-venta →
   Ha ido a la agencia de compra-venta.

1. pedirle ayuda a un amigo
2. ver diferentes coches y compararlos
3. mirar uno baratísimo
4. revisarle las llantas
5. conducirlo para probarlo
6. pensarlo y regresar a la agencia
7. decidir comprarlo
8. comprarlo
9. volver a casa
10. llevar a sus amigas al cine en su coche

C. **¡No lo creo!**

Paso 1. Complete las siguientes oraciones con la forma apropiada del presente perfecto (indicativo o subjuntivo). Luego indique cuál de las oraciones de cada par expresa su opinión sobre sus compañeros de clase. Luego su profesor(a) va a hacerles preguntas a todos para saber cuál es la verdad en cada caso.

1. Creo que alguien en esta clase _____ las pirámides de Egipto. (ver) ☐
   Es dudoso que alguien _____ las pirámides de Egipto. (ver) ☐
2. Estoy seguro/a de que por lo menos uno de mis compañeros _____ una montaña alta. (escalar) ☐
   No creo que nadie _____ una montaña alta. (escalar) ☐
3. Creo que alguien _____ autostop en un viaje. (hacer) ☐
   Dudo que alguien _____ autostop en un viaje. (hacer) ☐
4. Creo que alguien _____ en paracaídas. (saltar) ☐
   Es improbable que alguien _____ en paracaídas. (saltar) ☐
5. Estoy seguro/a de que alguien _____ el metro en Nueva York. (tomar) ☐
   No creo que nadie _____ el metro neoyorquino. (tomar) ☐

Vocabulario útil	
el paracaídas	parachute
escalar	to climb
<u>hacer</u> autostop	to hitchhike
saltar	to jump

Paso 2. Ahora complete las siguientes ideas sobre las actividades de sus compañeros esta semana. **¡OJO!** Hay que usar el indicativo o el subjuntivo.

1. (No) Creo que todos _____ un examen. (tener)
2. (No) Estoy seguro/a de que todos mis compañeros _____ varios mensajes. (escribir)
3. (No) Dudo que muchos compañeros _____ más de 100 videos en YouTube. (ver)
4. Es probable que nadie _____ un hueso (*bone*). (romperse)
5. Es obvio que nadie _____. (morir)

Capítulo 15 La naturaleza y el medio ambiente

D. Opiniones sobre el medio ambiente

Paso 1. ¿Qué se ha hecho en los últimos años para proteger el medio ambiente? En parejas, hagan oraciones completas en el presente perfecto de indicativo. Sus oraciones pueden ser afirmativas o negativas, según su opinión.

MODELO: este país: **desarrollar** nuevas formas de energía renovable →
Este país (no) **ha desarrollado** nuevas formas de energía renovable.

1. este país: **desarrollar** la energía eólica/solar
2. la población de esta ciudad: **reciclar** el papel, el plástico y el vidrio (*glass*) con regularidad
3. los seres humanos (*humans*): **proteger** muchas especies de animales
4. varios países: **destruir** zonas naturales para construir más viviendas
5. el aire de esta ciudad: **contaminarse** más
6. este estado: **construir** muchas carreteras nuevas

Paso 2. Ahora añadan un comentario personal a sus oraciones del **Paso 1.** Puede ser una explicación (con el indicativo) o una reacción personal (con el subjuntivo).

MODELOS: Este país no ha desarrollado suficientemente sus fuentes de energía renovable **porque tenemos mucho petróleo.**
Es terrible que este país no **haya desarrollado** suficientemente sus fuentes de energía renovable todavía.

E. Entrevista: ¿Lo has hecho o no?

Paso 1. Indique si usted ha hecho o no las siguientes cosas, según el modelo. Añada una cosa interesante que usted ha hecho ya y otra que no ha hecho todavía, pero que quiere hacer.

MODELOS: **visitar** la Argentina o el Uruguay →
He visitado la Argentina una vez.
Nunca **he visitado** la Argentina, pero sí **he visitado** el Uruguay.

1. **bailar** el tango
2. **manejar** un Alfa Romeo
3. **escribir** un poema
4. **actuar** en una obra teatral
5. **conocer** a una persona famosa
6. **caerse** de una bicicleta/moto(cicleta)
7. ¿ ?
8. ¿ ?

Paso 2. Ahora, usando como base las actividades del **Paso 1,** complete las siguientes oraciones con referencia a sus compañeros de clase o a su profesor(a). **¡OJO!** Tiene que decidir si va a usar el indicativo o el subjuntivo en estas oraciones.

MODELO: Creo que... → Creo que **la profesora ha manejado** un Alfa Romeo.

1. Creo que...
2. Dudo que...
3. Es probable que...
4. Estoy seguro/a de que...
5. Ojalá que...

 Paso 3. Lea sus oraciones del **Paso 2** a la clase entera. La persona nombrada en la oración va a decir si la oración es cierta o falsa.

Algo sobre el tango

Buena Vista Images/The Image Bank/Getty Images

Una pareja que baila un tango en Buenos Aires

El tango es sin duda uno de los bailes hispanos más conocidos en todo el mundo. Es netamente[a] argentino y uruguayo, ya que[b] nació[c] en la zona del Río de la Plata, pero tiene origen africano.

Es un baile muy sensual que se baila en pareja. Con frecuencia la letra de los tangos es sentimental: habla de conflictos amorosos o de tristes recuerdos de los años pasados. El instrumento básico del tango, y el más tradicional, es el bandoneón, un tipo de acordeón.

 ¿Le gusta a usted bailar en pareja? ¿Qué baila? ¿algún baile latino?

[a]*distinctly* [b]ya... *since*
[c]*it originated*

Nota comunicativa: El pluscuamperfecto: *había* + *participio pasado*

Use the past participle with the imperfect forms of **haber (había, habías, había, habíamos, habíais, habían)** to talk about what you had—or had not—done before a given time in the past. This form, called the *past perfect* (**el pluscuamperfecto**), is used like its English equivalent.

Antes de graduarme de la escuela secundaria, no **había estudiado** español.	*Before graduating from high school, I hadn't studied Spanish.*
Antes de 2010, mi hermana menor no **había nacido**.	*Before 2010, my youngest sister hadn't been born yet.*
Para agosto de 2022 ya **habíamos obtenido** la licencia de manejar.	*By August 2022, we had already gotten our driver's license.*

You will use the past perfect in **Práctica F** and **G.**

Vocabulario útil

empez**ar** (emp**ie**zo) la universidad	
na**c**er (na**z**co)	to be born
recibir una multa	to get a fine
terminar la escuela secundaria	

F. Fechas importantes en su vida

Paso 1. ¿Qué había hecho o no había hecho usted para las siguientes fechas?

1. para julio de 2006
2. antes de enero de 2015
3. antes del verano de 2020
4. para la primavera de 2023
5. antes del verano pasado
6. para septiembre de este año

 Paso 2. Ahora, en parejas, comparen sus respuestas. ¿Tienen alguna fecha en común? Díganselo al resto de la clase.

G. Intercambios

Paso 1. En parejas, hagan y contesten preguntas basadas en las siguientes frases. Inventen por lo menos una pregunta original.

MODELO: ¿qué cosa? / no **haber** aprendido a hacer antes del año pasado →
 E1: ¿Qué cosa no **habías aprendido** a hacer antes del año pasado?
 E2: Pues... no **había aprendido** a nadar. Aprendí a nadar este año en la clase de natación.

1. ¿qué cosa? / no **haber** aprendido a hacer antes de este semestre/trimestre
2. ¿qué materia? / no **haber** estudiado antes de venir a esta universidad
3. ¿qué deporte? / (no) **haber** practicado mucho antes de cumplir 16 años
4. ¿qué libro clásico o importante? / no **haber** leído antes de venir a esta universidad
5. ¿qué decisión? / no **haber** tomado antes de cumplir 18 años
6. ¿a quién de las personas importantes en su vida? / no **haber** conocido antes de venir a la universidad
7. ¿ ?

Paso 2. Ahora díganle a la clase algo de su historia personal que ustedes tienen en común. Si no tienen nada en común, cada uno debe contarle a la clase algo interesante de la vida de su compañero/a.

Todo junto

A. Lengua y cultura: El Parque Nacional Los Glaciares

Paso 1. Completar. Complete the following paragraphs with the correct form of the words in parentheses, as suggested by context. When two possibilities are given, select the correct word. Form adverbs with **-mente,** as needed. **¡OJO!** *PP:* = present perfect (indicative or subjunctive) *P/I:* = preterite or imperfect. Other infinitives are either present subjunctive or must remain in the infinitive form.

El monte (*Mt.*) Fitz Roy, en la Patagonia

Algunos aspectos de la cultura y de la geografía de la Argentina son bien conocidos por todos. Seguro que ustedes _____ (*PP:* ver)[1] bailar el tango, porque es un baile que se _____ (*PP:* hacer)[2] muy popular _____ (reciente)[3] entre los bailes de salón.[a] Y casi todos (saben / conocen)[4] qué es la Pampa y quiénes (son / están)[5] los gauchos.

Pero es fácil _____ (olvidar)[6] que la Argentina es un país larguísimo que se extiende desde la selva[b] tropical en la frontera[c] con el Brasil hasta la Antártida. _____ (Por / Para)[7] eso el país tiene una increíble variedad climática y geográfica.

Si usted es aficionado/a al ecoturismo, (se / le)[8] aconsejamos que _____ (visitar)[9] el Parque Nacional Los Glaciares, en (el / la)[10] región de la Patagonia, al sur del país. El gobierno argentino _____ (*P/I:* crear)[11] el parque en 1937, y en 1982 la UNESCO (lo / la)[12] _____ (*P/I:* declarar)[13] Patrimonio Natural de la Humanidad. Allí, en las 600.000 hectáreas[d] del parque, los visitantes pueden explorar impresionantes glaciares. Es posible _____ (escalar)[14] montañas de hielo[e] con grandes precipicios, que es un desafío[f] aun[g] para los _____ (mejor)[15] escaladores.[h]

[a]*bailes... ballroom dances* [b]*jungle* [c]*border* [d]*hectares (1 hectare = 2.47 acres)* [e]*ice* [f]*challenge* [g]*even* [h]*climbers*

Paso 2. Comprensión. Conteste las siguientes preguntas.

1. ¿Qué aspectos de la cultura argentina son bien conocidos?
2. ¿Por qué hay gran variedad climática y geográfica en la Argentina?
3. ¿En qué región está el Parque Nacional Los Glaciares?
4. ¿Por qué es tan (*so*) bueno el Parque para el alpinismo (*mountain climbing*)?

Paso 3. En acción

En parejas, comparen la Argentina con los Estados Unidos (o con su país de origen) en cuanto a (*with regard to*) la diversidad geográfica y climática. ¿Son comparables? ¿Cómo y por qué? Den ejemplos específicos.

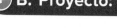
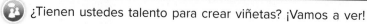 ¿Tienen ustedes talento para crear viñetas? ¡Vamos a ver!

ᵃ*Welcome* ᵇ*me… they sent me*

ᶜaunque… *although adults* ᵈhistorias… *scary stories*

Paso 1. Preparación. En parejas, estudien las dos viñetas en esta página. ¿En qué se enfocan? ¿Son cómicas? ¿críticas? ¿Conocen ustedes algunas viñetas similares? ¿Dónde las encuentran?

Paso 2. Investigación. Busquen dos viñetas en inglés sobre el medio ambiente o el tráfico y los conductores. Escriban el texto en español para cada una. O mejor aún (*even better*), creen sus propias viñetas. No se preocupen por el dibujo: si no son buenos dibujantes, simplemente describan la escena con palabras.

Paso 3. Presentación. Presenten sus viñetas a la clase.

Video: Salu2 «EcoSalu2»
You can watch two segments of this chapter's video in the **Video: Salu2** section, found at the end of the eBook.

Una casa con paneles solares

Klic Video Productions/McGraw Hill

Enfoque cultural: Diversidad y recursos naturales

Antes de leer

¿Qué ejemplos de belleza (*beauty*) natural hay en la zona donde usted vive?

En la Argentina y el Uruguay

Un bosque de ombúes

Tanto el Uruguay como la Argentina son países orgullosos[a] de la diversidad de su naturaleza. De norte a sur y de este a oeste, la Argentina tiene formidables atracciones naturales. Al norte, en la frontera con el Brasil y el Paraguay, están las cataratas[b] del Iguazú, una de las maravillas[c] del mundo natural. Al sur se encuentra el impresionante glaciar Perito Moreno. Al oeste, en la frontera con Chile, está el monte Aconcagua, de 6.962 metros (22.841 pies) de altura: es la montaña más alta de la cordillera[d] de los Andes y de todo el continente americano. En el centro, en un territorio compartido[e] con el Uruguay, se encuentra la Pampa, una interminable planicie[f] de tierras para el ganado[g] y el cultivo de granos. Al sur profundo, la Argentina continúa más allá del estrecho de Magallanes[h] hasta la Antártida.

Por su parte, el Uruguay contiene los Humedales de Santa Lucía y del Este. Son tierras cubiertas de agua que mantienen ecosistemas de gran valor[i] medioambiental y el mayor parque de ombúes[j] del mundo.

[a]*proud* [b]*waterfalls* [c]*wonders* [d]*mountain range* [e]*shared*
[f]*plain* [g]*cattle* [h]*Estrecho... Straight of Magellan* [i]*value*
[j]*large shade trees*

Comprensión ¿Qué atracción natural se destaca (*stands out*) al norte de la Argentina? ¿Por qué son interesantes los Humedales de Santa Lucía y del Este en el Uruguay?

En otros países hispanos

Una planta de energía termosolar en la región de Andalucía, España

- **En Costa Rica, Colombia, el Ecuador, México, el Perú y Venezuela** Estas naciones están entre los diecisiete países megadiversos identificados por el Centro de Monitoreo de Conservación Ambiental, un organismo[a] del Programa de las Naciones Unidas para el Medio Ambiente (el PNUMA). Los países megadiversos, en su mayoría tropicales, son países que tienen el mayor porcentaje de biodiversidad en el planeta.

- **En España** En la actualidad, es uno de los países líderes en almacenamiento[b] de energía y en la creación de energías renovables (eólica y solar), ya que[c] el país disfruta de[d] innumerables horas de sol y buenas zonas de viento.

[a]*agency* [b]*storage* [c]*ya... since* [d]*disfruta... enjoys*

Comprensión ¿Qué países hispanos se encuentran entre los más megadiversos del mundo? ¿En qué es líder España?

En acción

Haga una lista de los animales y plantas que son distintivos de su país. ¿Es un país megadiverso?

Lectura

Antes de leer

¿Qué medio(s) de transporte usa usted habitualmente? ¿Qué ventajas o desventajas tiene cada uno de esos medios para usted?

Vocabulario para leer

el alma	soul	**apresurar**	to speed up
el azul celeste	light sky blue	<u>**caer**</u> **en la**	to realize
la matrícula	car license plate	**cuenta (de)**	
el rey	king	**fijarse (en)**	to notice
la tartana	**un coche viejo**	**percatarse (de)**	to notice
	e inútil	**resplandecer**	to shine

«Azul Cielo», de Laura Busom Fuertes

Estaba diseñado para correr, acelerar y apresurar el movimiento. Su motor tenía alma de león, opinaban algunos, de rey de los coches deportivos.

Conducía arañando[a] el asfalto y llegaba siempre el primero. Le decían que había alcanzado la cima del éxito.[b] Pese a todo, a las piezas de su motor les faltaba algo.[c]

Parado a su lado, aquel día se fijó en él. Era una tartana. No sabía exactamente por qué, pero le despertó curiosidad.[d] Así pues,[e] decidió seguirlo.

Bramó con prolongados pasos[f] imitando a aquella matrícula de hace 20 años. Durante el camino, se percató de la bonita buganvilla que se desperezaba[g] al lado del semáforo. Y al levantar la vista,[h] el degradado azul celeste del cielo resplandeció. Entonces cayó en la cuenta de que jamás había tenido tiempo de mirar a su alrededor.[i]

Un coche viejo estacionado en la calle

[a]*clawing*   [b]*había... it had reached the height of success*   [c]*Pese... In spite of everything, something was missing from its motor.*
[d]*le... it awakened its curiosity*   [e]*Así... Therefore*   [f]*Bramó... It roared in long stretches*   [g]*buganvilla... bougainvillea bush that stretched out*
[h]*al... when it looked up*   [i]*a... around*

Source: Laura Busom Fuertes, Azul cielo. From: Sonidos de algodón. March 30, 2021, pp. 29–30. Platero Editorial S.L. Reprinted by permission.

Comprensión

A. Resumen del cuento. Conteste las siguientes preguntas sobre los dos personajes (*characters*) del cuento.

  1. ¿Quién y cómo es el protagonista?

  2. ¿Quién y cómo es el personaje secundario?

  3. ¿Dónde está el protagonista cuando ve al personaje secundario?

  4. ¿Qué decide hacer el protagonista para saber más del otro personaje?

  5. ¿En qué cayó en cuenta el protagonista, gracias al personaje secundario?

B. Interpretación. Las alegorías, como este cuento, tienen personajes y eventos que simbolizan otras cosas. También tienen moralejas, que son lecciones para los lectores. ¿Qué símbolos ve usted en el cuento? ¿Cuál es la moraleja?

⚙ Proyecto: Fijarse en el camino°

en... along the way

En este capítulo usted ha estudiado diferentes formas de transporte. En «Azul cielo» se ve cómo cierto medio de transporte puede permitirnos ver y apreciar o no el ambiente natural. En este proyecto usted va a pensar en los medios de transporte que usa, así como en los beneficios y desventajas de esos medios.

Paso 1: Escriba una lista de los lugares a los que (*which*) usted tiene que ir en una semana típica. Mencione también los medios de transporte que usa para cada recorrido (*trip*), incluyendo si va a pie.

Paso 2: Elija uno de los recorridos y escriba una descripción del medio de transporte que usa, o de lo que usted ve en el camino.

Paso 3: Lea las descripciones de otras personas de la clase. ¿Hay semejanzas?

🔊 Textos orales

Una campaña° para Greenpeace en la radio

campaign

Antes de escuchar

¿Qué problemas medioambientales le preocupan a usted? ¿Le preocupan más los problemas locales o los internacionales? ¿Es usted miembro/a de alguna organización dedicada a la protección del medio ambiente?

Comprensión

A. ¿Cierto o falso? Indique si las siguientes oraciones son ciertas o falsas. Corrija las falsas.

	CIERTO	FALSO
1. Greenpeace tiene una organización en la Argentina.	☐	☐
2. Greenpeace recibe dinero de varios gobiernos.	☐	☐
3. Greenpeace solo se preocupa por los problemas de la contaminación del aire y el agua.	☐	☐
4. Greenpeace solo busca miembros que contribuyan con dinero a la organización.	☐	☐

B. Más detalles. Conteste las siguientes preguntas.

1. ¿Cómo se llama el programa? ¿En qué tipo de estación de radio se presenta?
2. ¿Para qué tipo de oyentes (*listeners*) es este programa? ¿Por qué dice usted eso?
3. ¿Cómo trata de convencer el locutor (*host*) del programa a sus oyentes de que es importante hacerse miembro de Greenpeace?
4. ¿Cuáles son dos de los temas que preocupan a Greenpeace?

✋ En acción

Busque la página web de Greenpeace Argentina. Lea algunas de las noticias que reporta la organización allí y haga un resumen de tres de ellas para decírselo a la clase.

Vocabulario para escuchar

<u>hacer</u> campaña	to have a campaign
el partido político	political party
las pilas	batteries

dpa picture alliance/Alamy Stock Photo

Una protesta medioambientalista durante un evento del presidente argentino

¡OJO!

En la Argentina y el Uruguay, así como (*as well as*) en muchos países centroamericanos, se usa el pronombre personal **vos** en vez del (*instead of the*) pronombre **tú**. Los mandatos informales con **vos** tienen formas diferentes de los mandatos con **tú**. En el programa de radio, usted va a escuchar algunos de estos mandatos.

escuchá = escucha
pensá = piensa
unite = únete
hacete = hazte
ayudá = ayuda
andá = anda (*go*)
defendé = defiende

Daniel Ernst/Getty Images

🎤 Entrevista

Use de modelo las preguntas y respuestas de la sección **Entrevista** al principio de este capítulo para hablar de sus preocupaciones por el medio ambiente (si las tiene) y de su necesidad del coche o de su uso en su vida diaria.

💻 Escritura

Un ensayo sobre los efectos del cambio° climático   *change*

Como usted sabe, hay un debate internacional sobre el cambio climático y lo que las naciones deben hacer para cambiar esta situación. En este capítulo, va a escribir un ensayo en el que (*which*) defiende su postura (*position*) personal sobre el tema.

👥 Antes de escribir

En parejas, piensen en el tema del cambio climático. ¿Hay más de una postura con respecto al tema? Según algunos científicos, ¿cuáles son las causas del cambio climático? ¿Cuáles son sus efectos? ¿Qué opinan las personas que no están de acuerdo con la idea del cambio climático?

Hagan una lista de los cuatro o cinco efectos del cambio climático que, en su opinión, son más problemáticos. También hagan una lista de los argumentos de los defensores del cambio climático, y otra, de los que (*those who*) se oponen a este concepto.

Unmillonedeelefantes/Shutterstock

¿Van a sobrevivir (*survive*) el cambio climático los pingüinos?

A escribir

Ahora defina su postura personal y defiéndala en un su ensayo. Hay más ayuda en Connect.

Para escribir bien

Considere las siguientes opciones para su ensayo.

- Conectores de causa y efecto: **a causa de, puesto que** (*since*), **por consiguiente** (*therefore*), **como consecuencia/resultado (de)** (as a result)
- Verbos útiles: **causar, ocasionar, provocar, resultar en**
- Frases útiles para expresar hechos (*facts*) y datos (*data*): **estudios científicos / los expertos muestran/afirman que... + *indic.***

🕸️ En la comunidad

Entreviste a una persona hispana de su universidad o ciudad sobre cuestiones medioambientales relacionadas con su país de origen.

Preguntas posibles

- ¿Hay problemas de contaminación en su ciudad o país de origen? ¿Qué los causa?
- ¿Qué está haciendo el país para preservar los recursos naturales? ¿Y para disminuir la contaminación?
- ¿Ve un cambio en la actitud de las personas de su país o ciudad con relación a la conservación de los recursos naturales?
- ¿Hay programas de reciclaje? ¿Cree que son efectivos?

⏺️ Producción audiovisual

Filme un corto (*short segment*) o haga un fotomontaje en defensa de su propia posición sobre un tema de interés. Puede ser a favor o en contra de alguna medida (*measure*) o iniciativa. Puede entrevistar a algunos expertos, tomar datos de otras fuentes (*sources*) y usar su voz en off.

Más ideas para el portafolio

- Incluya una lista de las cosas que usted ha hecho en su vida de las que (*which*) se siente más orgulloso/a (*proud*) y otra lista de las cosas que no ha hecho todavía pero que desea hacer.
- Lo más... Incluya una lista de las cosas más raras o extraordinarias ¡o peores! que usted ha visto (hecho, comido...) en su vida.
- Si ha estado jugando Practice Spanish: Study Abroad, en Quest 9 usted aprendió sobre tres medios de transporte público en Colombia: el minibús, el autobús y el superbús. ¿Cuál es la diferencia entre ellos? ¿Ha tomado usted el autobús en un país hispanohablante o en el país donde usted vive? Escriba un párrafo sobre su experiencia. Si ha tomado el autobús en ambos (*both*) lugares, haga una comparación entre las dos experiencias.

Sugerencia: You are now ready to play Quest 9 in **Practice Spanish: Study Abroad.**

EN RESUMEN En este capítulo

AFTER STUDYING THIS CHAPTER I CAN ...

☐ talk about natural and urban environments (450–451)

☐ talk about cars and driving (454)

☐ describe with adjectives that are also past participles (458–459)

☐ use the present and past perfect to express what *has* and *had happened* (462–463, 466)

☐ recognize/describe at least 2–3 aspects of Argentine and Uruguayan cultures

Gramática en breve

42. Past Participle Used As Adjective

Regular Past Participles

-ar → -ado/a
-er/-ir → -ido/a

Irregular Past Participles

abierto/a, cubierto/a, descubierto/a, dicho/a, escrito/a, hecho/a, muerto/a, puesto/a, resuelto/a, roto/a, visto/a, vuelto/a

43. Present Perfect Indicative and Subjunctive

Present Perfect Indicative	**Present Perfect Subjunctive**
present indicative of **haber** + *past participle*	present subjunctive of **haber** + *past participle*

he	hemos	haya	hayamos
has	habéis	hayas	hayáis
ha	han	haya	hayan

Past Perfect Indicative

imperfect of **haber** + *past participle*

había	habíamos
habías	habíais
había	habían

Vocabulario

Los verbos

cubrir	to cover
descubrir (*like* cubrir)	to discover
evitar	to avoid
resolver (*like* **volver**)	to solve, resolve

Los recursos naturales

el bosque	forest
la energía (eólica, renovable)	(wind, renewable) energy
el lago	lake
el medio ambiente	environment
la naturaleza	nature
el reciclaje	recycling
el río	river
la Tierra	Earth
el recurso natural	natural resource

Cognados: el aire, la energía eléctrica / nuclear / solar, el petróleo, el planeta

Repaso: el árbol, la montaña

conservar	to save, conserve
construir	to build
contaminar	to pollute
desarrollar	to develop
destruir (*like* construir)	to destroy
fabricar (qu)	to manufacture
proteger (protejo)	to protect
reciclar	to recycle

Repaso: acabar

El desarrollo

el/la agricultor(a)	farmer
la agricultura	farming, agriculture
el/la campesino/a	farmer; field laborer
el campo	field; countryside
la capa de ozono	ozone layer
el delito	crime
la densidad de población	population density
la fábrica	factory
la falta	lack; absence
la finca	farm; ranch
el gobierno	government
la población	population
el rascacielos	skyscraper
el ritmo lento/ acelerado de la vida	slow/fast pace of life
el servicio	service
el desarrollo	development

Repaso: la contaminación, el transporte, la vida

Los animales

la ballena	whale
la especie (en peligro de extinción)	(endangered) species
el pez (*pl.* peces)	fish

| el toro | bull |
| la vaca | cow |

Cognados: el elefante, el gorila

Repaso: el caballo, el gato, el pájaro, el perro

Los vehículos

el carro / el coche (descapotable/híbrido/ todoterreno)	(convertible/hybrid/ all-terrain) car
la estación de servicio	gas station
los frenos	brakes
la gasolinera	gas station
la llanta (desinflada)	(flat) tire
el/la mecánico/a	mechanic
el parabrisas	windshield
el taller	(repair) shop
el tanque	tank
el vehículo	vehicle

Cognados: el auto(móvil), la batería, el carro, la gasolina, la moto(cicleta), el SUV

Repaso: el aceite, la bicicleta, la camioneta, el coche

arrancar (qu)	to start up (a car)
arreglar	to fix, repair
gastar	to use (gas)
llenar	to fill (up)
revisar	to check

Cognado: reparar

En la carretera

la acera	sidewalk
la autopista	freeway; interstate
la bocina	horn (car)
la circulación	traffic
el/la conductor(a)	driver
la esquina	(street) corner
el estacionamiento	parking place/lot
la licencia de manejar	driver's license
el límite de velocidad	speed limit
la policía	police force
el semáforo	traffic signal
el tránsito	traffic
la carretera	road; highway

Cognado: el tráfico

Repaso: la avenida, la calle

conducir	to drive
doblar	to turn
manejar	to drive
obedecer (obedezco)	to obey
parar	to stop
seguir (sigo) (i)	to keep on going
tocar (qu)	to honk

Repaso: chocar (qu) (con), estacionar

| ¿Cómo se llega a... ? | How do you get to ... ? |
| (todo) derecho/recto | straight ahead |

Repaso: a la derecha, a la izquierda, por (through)

Los adjetivos

acelerado/a	fast, accelerated
bello/a	beautiful
contaminado/a	contaminated, polluted
descapotable	convertible
doméstico/a	domesticated, tame
lento/a	slow
salvaje	wild
todoterreno (inv.)	all-terrain

Cognados: híbrido/a, natural, público/a, puro/a

Palabras adicionales

| alguna vez | ever |

Vocabulario personal

Use this space or a vocabulary notebook to write down other words and phrases you learn in this chapter.

16 La vida social y afectiva°

emotional

En este capítulo

VOCABULARY

Social relationships   478

The stages of life   481

GRAMMAR

How to describe things and people in more complex sentences   482

When one action depends on another   487

COUNTRY OF FOCUS: PARAGUAY

¡Viva el amor! (en Asunción, Paraguay)

Nora Pelaez/Visual Ideas/Getty Images

EL PARAGUAY

7,2 (coma dos) millones de habitantes

- El Paraguay es uno de los dos países sudamericanos que no tiene salida[a] al mar. (El otro es Bolivia).

- Los guaraníes son el pueblo indígena que habitaba en el territorio que hoy es el Paraguay, así como[b] en partes del noreste de la Argentina, el sureste de Bolivia y el suroeste del Brasil.

- El nombre «Paraguay» viene de la lengua guaraní. También es el nombre de uno de los grandes ríos que atraviesan[c] el país. El otro es el río Paraná.

[a]*access* [b]*así... as well as* [c]*cross*

🔊 ENTREVISTA

These questions related to the chapter theme are answered here by a native speaker. You will be able to ask and answer them yourself with personal information in the **Entrevista** activity in the **Portafolio** section at the end of the chapter.

Gabriela Romano Acosta contesta las preguntas.

— **¿Tiene usted pareja? ¿novio o novia? ¿esposo o esposa? ¿O sale con alguien?**

— Sí, tengo pareja. Bueno, es algo reciente. Empecé a salir con un chico de la universidad hace un mes más o menos. No es nada serio... por ahora. Pero está bien. Es lindo.[a]

— **En este momento, ¿cuál es la relación social más importante de su vida? ¿Es una relación romántica o una de amistad[b]? ¿O es su relación con su familia?**

— En este momento, mi familia y mis amigos de siempre son lo más importante. En el futuro, espero tener un compañero e hijos y que ellos sean lo más importante de mi vida. Pero, por ahora, es pronto para eso.

— **¿Cree usted en el amor a primera vista? ¿Y en el amor para toda la vida? En su opinión, ¿qué es necesario para que[c] haya una relación feliz y duradera[d] entre una pareja?**

— ¡Ay, no sé! Creo que uno puede enamorarse[e] a primera vista, pero no creo que eso sea suficiente para que el amor dure[f] para siempre. Es difícil que el amor dure toda la vida, ¿no? Pero es bonito pensar que puede ser. Y para eso es necesario que las dos personas de la pareja se comprendan y se apoyen[g] mutuamente.

[a]*Es... It's nice.* [b]*friendship* [c]*para... so that* [d]*lasting* [e]*fall in love* [f]*lasts*
[g]*se... support each other*

Daniel Ernst/Getty Images

You can hear the pronunciation
of theme vocabulary words
and phrases in the eBook.

VOCABULARIO: PREPARACIÓN

Las relaciones sentimentales

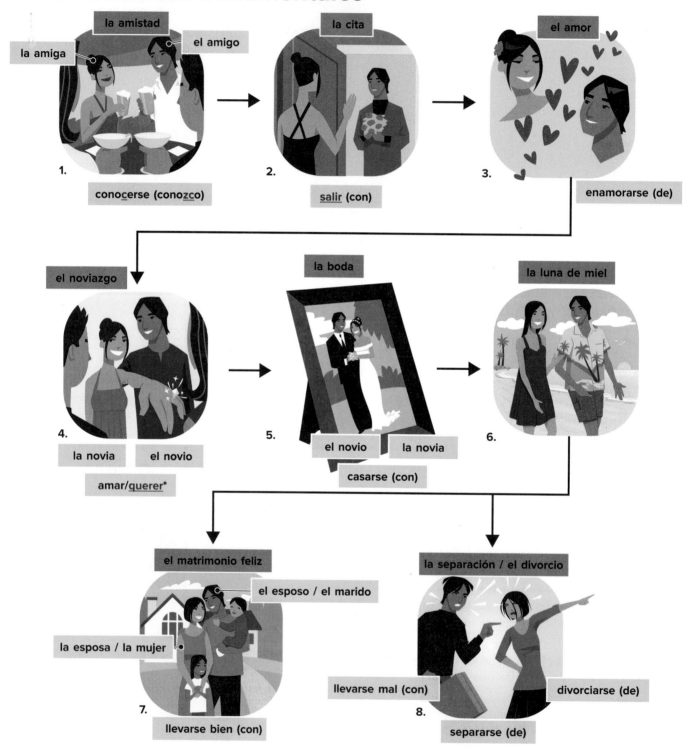

1. la amistad — la amiga — el amigo — **conocerse (conozco)**
2. la cita — **salir (con)**
3. el amor — **enamorarse (de)**
4. el noviazgo — la novia — el novio — **amar/querer***
5. la boda — el novio — la novia — **casarse (con)**
6. la luna de miel
7. el matrimonio feliz — el esposo / el marido — la esposa / la mujer — **llevarse bien (con)**
8. la separación / el divorcio — llevarse mal (con) — divorciarse (de) — separarse (de)

__Amar__ and __querer__ both mean to love, but __amar__ can imply more romantic passion in some dialects of Spanish.

Los estados civiles° y las relaciones románticas	Los... *Marital statuses*
el cariño	affection
el matrimonio	marriage; married couple
el noviazgo	engagement period
el novio / la novia	boyfriend/girlfriend; fiancé(e); groom/bride
la pareja	partner; significant other; couple
el viudo / la viuda	widower/widow
<u>**estar**</u>**...**	
casado/a (con)	married (to)
recién casado/a	a newlywed

divorciado/a (de)	divorced (from)
enamorado/a (de)	in love (with)
separado/a (de)	separated (from)
soltero/a	single
pelear(se) (con)	to fight (with)
romper (con)	to break up (with)
<u>**ser**</u> **cariñoso/a**	affectionate

Lugares para ceremonias

la iglesia	church
la mezquita	mosque
el templo	temple

Comunicación

A. ¡Usemos la lógica! Complete las siguientes oraciones lógicamente.

1. Mi abuelo es el _____ de mi abuela, es decir, está _____ con ella.
2. Muchos novios tienen un _____ bastante (*rather*) largo antes de la boda.
3. María y Julio tienen una _____ el viernes para comer en un restaurante. Luego van a bailar.
4. La _____ de Juan y Pati es el domingo a las dos de la tarde, en la iglesia de San Martín.
5. La _____ entre exesposos es imposible. No pueden ser amigos.
6. ¡El _____ es ciego (*blind*)!
7. Para algunas personas, el _____ es un concepto anticuado. Prefieren vivir juntos, sin casarse.
8. Algunas personas no tienen el dinero para una _____ después de la boda.

> ### Así se dice
>
> la boda = el casamiento, el matrimonio
> el matrimonio homosexual = el matrimonio gay
> la unión civil = la pareja de hecho

Nota cultural: Expresiones familiares de cariño

En el mundo hispano se usan muchas palabras y frases para referirse a las personas queridas y para expresar cariño. Estas pueden ser diferentes en cada país. Las siguientes palabras son de uso común, aunque[a] algunas no se usan en todos los países.

- Entre personas unidas romántica o familiarmente: **mi amor, amorcito/a, mi vida, cielo,**[b] **corazón, querido/a, cariño, gordo/a, viejo/a, flaco/a,**[c] **negro/a**
- De hijos a padres: **viejo/a, mis viejos** (la Argentina, el Uruguay)
- Para referirse a una pareja con quien no se está casado: **mi compañero/a**
- De padres a los padrinos de sus hijos y viceversa: **la comadre / el compadre**

La gente joven siempre tiene su propia jerga[d] en cada país, pero no siempre son palabras que se usan para dirigirse[e] a las personas mayores.

- **cuate:** una palabra del náhuatl, la lengua de los aztecas (México, Centroamérica, Bolivia)
- **pana:** significa **compañero/a** (Venezuela, Colombia, la República Dominicana y otros países)
- **compa:** derivado de **compañero**
- **negro/a:** se usa entre amigos en varios países
- **tío/a** (España)
- **buey** (México)

En un bautizo en una iglesia católica, los padrinos (*godparents*) sujetan (*hold*) al bebé. (Ciudad de México)

Frans Lemmens/Alamy Stock Photo

Como se nota en la lista anterior,[f] una de las grandes diferencias entre el español y el inglés es el hecho de usar[g] como palabras cariñosas adjetivos que describen características físicas: **gordo/a, flaco/a, negro/a, viejo/a.** Estos adjetivos se aplican indistintamente[h] a cualquier[i] persona, es decir, no es necesario que la persona sea gorda o delgada, blanca o negra, joven o vieja.

¿Con qué palabras se dirige usted a sus amigos? ¿y a las personas que ama?

[a]*although* [b]*heaven* [c]*skinny one* [d]*slang* [e]*address* [f]*preceding* [g]*el... using* [h]*indiscriminately* [i]*any*

B. Preguntas impertinentes

Paso 1. Use las siguientes palabras para hacer preguntas muy personales. Las preguntas pueden ser sobre el presente o el pasado.

MODELOS: ¿**Has roto** alguna vez con un novio / una novia?
¿De quién **estás enamorado/a** ahora mismo?

1. romper con
2. salir con
3. una cita
4. estar enamorado/a

5. amar
6. la luna de miel
7. llevarse mal con
8. estar divorciado/a

Paso 2. Ahora, en parejas, hagan y contesten las preguntas del **Paso 1.** Si creen que alguna pregunta es demasiado personal, pueden contestar cortésmente: «**Prefiero no contestar esa pregunta**». También pueden contestar sin cortesía: «**¿Y a ti qué te importa?**»

Paso 3. Díganle a la clase las cosas que ustedes tienen en común.

Nota comunicativa: El uso del infinitivo como sustantivo

Amar es volar

y **traspasar** barreras[a]

[a]traspasar... *crossing boundaries*

Oleksii Telnov/Alamy Stock Photo

In English, the present participle (the verb form that ends in *-ing*) is commonly used as a noun, often as the subject or object of a sentence. In Spanish, the infinitive is the verb form that is used as a noun, rather than the present participle (**-ando/-iendo**).

Amar es **perdonar.**
Loving is forgiving. (To love is to forgive.)

Hablar con calma es mejor que **pelear.**
Talking calmly is better than arguing.

If the infinitive is used with a pronoun, the pronoun is attached to the end of the infinitive.

Casarse no es un ideal para todas las personas.
Getting married is not right for everyone.

Conocerte es lo mejor que me ha pasado.
Meeting you was the best thing that ever happened to me.

You will use infinitives in this way in **Práctica C.**

Vocabulario útil

asistir a la universidad
llevarse bien con todos

C. Opiniones

Paso 1. Complete las siguientes oraciones para expresar su opinión sobre varios temas. Use infinitivos cuando pueda y la palabra **no** cuando sea necesario.

1. Amar es _____.
2. Divorciarse debe ser / es _____.
3. Tener un noviazgo largo es mejor que _____.
4. Es ideal pasar la luna de miel en _____ (lugar).
5. _____ es lo mejor que me ha pasado en esta universidad.
6. _____ es lo mejor que me ha pasado en la vida.
7. _____ debe ser un ideal para todas las personas.

Paso 2. Ahora, en grupos de tres o cuatro personas, comparen las oraciones que crearon en el **Paso 1.** Elijan las mejores respuestas para decírselas a la clase.

Las etapas° de la vida

Las... *Stages*

la infancia / la niñez	la adolescencia	la juventud	la madurez	la vejez

la muerte	death
na**c**er (na**zc**o)	to be born
cre**c**er (cre**zc**o)	to grow
m**o**rir (m**ue**ro) (**u**)	to die

Comunicación

A. Etapas de la vida

Paso 1. Relacione las siguientes palabras y frases con las distintas etapas de la vida de una persona. **¡OJO!** Hay más de una relación posible en algunos casos.

1. el amor   **3.** los juguetes (*toys*)   **5.** los hijos en la universidad   **7.** la universidad
2. los nietos   **4.** no poder comer sin ayuda   **6.** los granos (*pimples*)   **8.** la boda

Paso 2. Ahora dé una definición o descripción de las siguientes etapas de la vida. Pueden ser descripciones serias o divertidas.

MODELOS: La infancia es cuando una persona tiene menos de dos años.
            La infancia es la etapa de la vida en que solo te importa comer, dormir y jugar.

1. la niñez   **2.** la adolescencia   **3.** la madurez   **4.** la vejez

B. Etapas de su vida

Paso 1. Describa lo que usted hacía, hace o piensa hacer, y sus sentimientos, en cada etapa de su vida.

MODELOS: mi niñez → **Vivía** en Oklahoma. **Tuve** una niñez feliz. Siempre...

1. mi niñez   **3.** mi juventud   **5.** mi vejez
2. mi adolescencia   **4.** mi madurez

 Paso 2. Ahora, en parejas o en grupos, comparen sus descripciones. Luego díganle a la clase lo que ustedes tienen en común.

Estrategia

Para hablar de cada etapa de la vida, es apropiado usar diferentes tiempos verbales. Ejemplos:
- **el pasado:** el pretérito, el imperfecto, el presente perfecto
- **la época actual:** el presente, el presente progresivo
- **el futuro:** ir + a + *infinitive*

Algo sobre el Gran Chaco

El Gran Chaco es una inmensa altiplanicie[a] aluvial[b] formada por los ríos Paraguay y Pilcomayo. Ocupa gran parte del Paraguay, además de[c] parte de Bolivia, la Argentina y el Brasil. Su nombre, que viene del quechua, significa «tierra de caza».[d] Es una región poco poblada. Sin embargo, fue el lugar elegido por emigrantes del Canadá, Alemania y la Unión Soviética que llegaron al Paraguay en la décadas de 1920 y 1930 para fundar varias colonias menonitas.

¿Hay en este país alguna región transnacional, es decir, que va más allá de las fronteras nacionales?

[a]*high plateau*   [b]*alluvial, formed by river deposits*   [c]*además... in addition to*   [d]*hunting*

GRAMÁTICA

 Repaso

Before studying **Gramática 44,** review the indefinite and negative words that you learned in **Gramática 19 (Cap. 7)**. Remember that **alguien** and **nadie** take the personal **a** when they are used as direct objects.

> Busco **a alguien** de la familia.   *I'm looking for someone from the family.*
> **No** veo **a nadie** en el salón de baile. *I don't see anyone in the dance hall.*

Give the opposite of the following words.

1. nada   **2.** algunos   **3.** alguien

44 ¿Hay alguien que... ? ¿Hay un lugar donde... ? • The Subjunctive (Part 6): The Subjunctive After Nonexistent and Indefinite Antecedents

Gramática en acción: Los buenos padres

Maskot/Image Source

- Un buen padre, así como una buena madre, es **alguien que quiere** a sus hijos de manera incondicional, **se preocupa** por su formación y les **enseña** a ser personas útiles en la vida.
- Todos los niños y niñas **necesitan una familia que** los **quiera** incondicionalmente, los **eduque** y los **cuide.**

¿Y usted?

Complete las siguientes oraciones.

1. No hay nadie que me **quiera** más que mi(s) _____.

2. Mi madre/padre es la persona que me enseñó a _____.

3. La persona que se preocupa más por mí en la actualidad es mi _____.

---

the antecedent / el **antecedente** = a word or phrase modified by an adjective clause

	①		②
indicative: definite/existing antecedent		que/donde	indicative

	①		②
indicative: **in**definite/**non**existent antecedent		que/donde	subjunctive

---

Good parents ■ *A good father, just like a good mother, is someone who loves his/her children unconditionally, worries about their education, and teaches them to live useful lives (i.e., be useful in life).* ■ *All children need a family that loves them unconditionally, educates them, and takes care of them.*

1. Adjective Clauses and Antecedents

As you know, noun clauses function like nouns in a sentence. Adjective clauses function like adjectives: they modify/describe a noun or a pronoun. In the sentences here, the nouns *car* and *house* (*for sale*) are modified by dependent adjective clauses. The noun that is modified is called the *antecedent* (**el antecedente**) of the dependent clause.

I have a <u>car</u> **that gets good gas mileage.**
Is there a <u>house for sale</u> **that is closer to the city**?

2. Indicative with Existing Antecedents

The indicative is used in the adjective clause when it refers to or modifies something that the speaker knows exists.

| DEFINITE/EXISTING ANTECEDENT: INDICATIVE |

Vi un coche que me **gusta** y que no **es** caro.
I saw a car (that) I like and that's not expensive.

Hay algo aquí que **quiero** ver.
There's something here that I want to see.

Estoy buscando un libro que **estaba** aquí.
I'm looking for a book that was here.

3. Subjunctive with <u>Non</u>existent and <u>In</u>definite Antecedents

Sometimes the antecedent of an adjective clause is something that does not exist from the point of view of the speaker, or something whose existence is indefinite, uncertain, or just not yet identified. In these cases, the subjunctive must be used in the adjective (dependent) clause in Spanish.

| <u>IN</u>DEFINITE/<u>NON</u>EXISTENT ANTECEDENT: <u>SUBJUNCTIVE</u> |

No hay nadie aquí que **hable** guaraní.
There is no one here who speaks Guaraní.

Busco a alguien que **hable** guaraní.
I'm looking for someone who speaks Guaraní.
  (*That person may exist, but I don't know for sure.*)

No conozco a nadie que **hable** guaraní.
I don't know anyone who speaks Guaraní.

Necesito un coche que no **gaste** mucha gasolina.
I need a car that doesn't use much gas. (*The car may exist, but I haven't identified it yet.*)

4. Questions Versus Answers with Adjective Clauses

The *subjunctive* is used in the dependent clause in a question about something that the speaker does not know exists for certain. However, the indicative or the subjunctive may be used in the answer, depending on whether the person who answers the question is sure of the existence of the antecedent or not.

| QUESTION: <u>SUBJUNCTIVE</u> |

—¿**Hay algo** aquí que te **guste**?
"Is there anything here that you like?"

| DEFINITE ANTECEDENT: INDICATIVE |

—Sí, **hay varios bolsos** que me **gustan.**
"Yes, there are several purses that I like."

| <u>NEGATIVE</u> ANTECEDENT: <u>SUBJUNCTIVE</u> |

—No, **no hay nada** aquí que me **guste.**
"No, there's nothing here that I like."

5. Adjective Clauses That Describe a Place

When the adjective clause describes a place, the word **donde** can also be used to introduce it. If the place exists, the indicative is used in the dependent clause (first example). If the place is indefinite or nonexistent, the subjunctive is used (second example).

| <u>IN</u>DEFINITE/<u>NON</u>EXISTENT ANTECEDENT: <u>SUBJUNCTIVE</u> |

Este es el hotel donde tuvimos nuestra luna de miel.
This is the hotel where we had our honeymoon.

Buscamos un lugar donde <u>podamos</u> celebrar el banquete de boda.
We are looking for a place where we can celebrate the wedding banquet.

6. Use of the Personal *a*

Remember that the personal **a** is used only before specific persons or animals. It is not used before unknown or nonspecific persons.

¡OJO!

The personal **a** is always used before **alguien** and **nadie** when they are direct objects.

UNKNOWN PERSON: SUBJUNCTIVE

Busco un estudiante que <u>sepa</u> francés.
I'm looking for a student who knows French.
  (*I don't know of any.*)

KNOWN PERSON: INDICATIVE

Busco <u>al</u> estudiante que sabe francés.
I'm looking for the student who knows French.
  (*I know there's one in our office.*)

DIRECT OBJECT

¿Conoces a <u>alguien</u> que sepa francés?
Do you know someone who speaks French?

NOT DIRECT OBJECT

No hay <u>nadie</u> aquí que sepa francés.
There's no one here who speaks French.

Summary of Nonexistent and Indefinite Antecedents

existing, definite → indicative
nonexistent, indefinite → <u>subjunctive</u>

Práctica y comunicación

A. Hablando de la gente que conocemos

Paso 1. Autoprueba. Indique cuáles de las siguientes oraciones expresan antecedentes indefinidos o inexistentes.

1. A friend is looking for a counselor who speaks Spanish.
2. I have a friend who is a marriage counselor.
3. I don't know of a good counselor who has an office downtown.
4. I'm looking for the counselor who helped us the last time.

Paso 2. Indique las oraciones que sean verdaderas para usted y cambie las otras para que (*so that*) sean verdaderas.

MODELO: **1.** Conozco a alguien que va a casarse este año. →
No conozco a **nadie** que **vaya** a casarse este año.

	CIERTO	FALSO
1. Conozco a alguien que va a casarse este año.	☐	☐
2. Tengo un amigo íntimo / una amiga íntima (*close friend*) que está casado/a.	☐	☐
3. Conozco a alguien que está recién casado.	☐	☐
4. Tengo un pariente cercano (*close*) que se está divorciando.	☐	☐
5. Tengo un buen amigo que es viudo.	☐	☐
6. Conozco a una estudiante de mi año que está en su viaje de luna de miel.	☐	☐
7. No conozco a nadie que haya roto con su novio/a este año.	☐	☐
8. Sé de alguien que sale con una persona famosa.	☐	☐

Paso 3. Ahora, en parejas, entrevístense sobre las oraciones del **Paso 2.** Luego díganle a la clase la coincidencia que ustedes consideren más curiosa.

MODELO: **1.** Conozco a alguien que va a casarse este año →
E1: ¿Conoces a alguien que vaya a casarse este año?
E2: No, no conozco a nadie que vaya a casarse este año.

Prác. A, Paso 1: Answers: 1, 3

B. Hablando de bodas

Paso 1. Complete las siguientes oraciones según lo que se ve en el dibujo.

1. Hay un hombre que _____ (está / esté) sacando una foto.
2. Hay una persona que _____ (está / esté) llorando.
3. Hay un hombre que _____ (está / esté) sonriendo.
4. Hay dos niñas que se _____ (están / estén) peleando.
5. No hay nadie que _____ (está / esté) cantando.
6. ¿Hay alguien que _____ (está / esté) tirando (*throwing*) arroz?

Paso 2. Ahora piense en una boda ideal. Complete las oraciones conjugando los verbos en el indicativo o el subjuntivo, según el caso, y dé los detalles necesarios.

Para mí, en una boda ideal...

1. (no) hay muchas personas que _____ (asistir).
2. (no) hay una ceremonia que _____ (ser) civil / formal / religiosa.
3. hay gente / no hay nadie que _____ (llorar) por la emoción.
4. (no) hay una persona que _____ (estar) contratada (*hired*) para organizar el evento.
5. (no) hay un gran banquete donde también se _____ (poder) bailar.
6. hay algunas personas / no hay nadie que no _____ (divertirse).
7. ¿ ?

C. Una encuesta (*poll*).

¿Qué sabe usted de las personas que están en su clase de español? Pregúnteles si saben hacer lo siguiente o a quién le ocurre lo siguiente. Deben levantar la mano solo los que puedan contestar afirmativamente. Luego la persona que hizo la pregunta debe hacer un comentario apropiado. Siga el modelo.

MODELOS: hablar otra lengua →
En esta clase, ¿hay alguien que **hable** bien más de dos lenguas?
(*Nadie levanta la mano*). No hay nadie que **hable** bien más de dos lenguas.
(*Alguien levanta la mano*). Hay una (dos) persona(s) que **habla(n)** bien más de dos lenguas.

1. hablar bien más de dos lenguas
2. saber tocar un instrumento musical
3. ser vegetariano/a
4. querer estudiar en el extranjero
5. cumplir años este mes / en agosto...
6. tomar cinco clases
7. estar casado/a
8. ¿ ?

D. Intercambios

Paso 1. Complete las siguientes declaraciones de acuerdo con su vida real y sus deseos.

1. Tengo un amigo / una amiga que...
2. No conozco a nadie que...
3. Este verano quiero tener un trabajo que...
4. En las próximas vacaciones no quiero hacer nada que...
5. Busco una pareja que...
6. En este mundo, no hay nada que sea más importante que...
7. Este semestre/trimestre tengo cursos que...
8. El próximo semestre/trimestre quiero tomar cursos que...

Paso 2. Ahora, en parejas, hagan y contesten preguntas basadas en las declaraciones del **Paso 1.** Luego díganle a la clase las coincidencias o diferencias más interesantes que ustedes tienen.

Algo sobre la represa° de Itaipú

dam

La represa de Itaipú es una obra de ingeniería impresionante. Es la central[a] hidroeléctrica que genera la segunda mayor cantidad de electricidad en el mundo. Es el resultado de un proyecto binacional entre el Paraguay y el Brasil que explota el río Paraná, la frontera[b] natural entre los dos países. La represa, que se abrió en 1984, provee[c] casi toda la energía que necesita el Paraguay y un cuarto de la energía que consume el Brasil.

 ¿Cuáles son algunas de las obras de ingeniería más importantes de los Estados Unidos? ¿Hay alguna que esté en su estado?

La represa de Itaipú, entre el Paraguay y el Brasil

Mike Goldwater/Alamy Stock Photo

[a]*power station*   [b]*border*   [c]*provides*

Textos de todos los días: Anuncio para compartir° un apartamento o casa

share

En las grandes ciudades y ciudades universitarias hay mucha gente que comparte apartamento. En esta actividad, usted va a crear un perfil (*profile*) personal en una página web de búsqueda (*search*) de apartamentos para compartir y de personas para compartirlos.

Objetivo: Escribir un breve texto que sirva como anuncio para buscar personas con quienes compartir una vivienda. El texto debe dar un mínimo de información sobre usted, así como del (*as well as about the*) número y tipo de personas que espera encontrar.

Antes de empezar

- Piense en cuánta información personal es necesario dar en un portal de este tipo.
- Lea los textos de ejemplo. Preste atención al uso de las formas de los verbos: las formas de **tú** (y no de **usted**) son las más apropiadas en este contexto.
- Decida si quiere vivir con personas de un sexo determinado o si no tiene preferencia. Los portales de alquiler de vivienda tienen categorías para el número y género de las personas que busca (además del precio, ubicación, etcétera). Pero es buena idea que su texto muestre cómo se identifica usted y si espera compartir la vivienda con personas de un género en particular o si esto no le importa. Los siguientes textos son ejemplos de búsquedas no específicas.

> **¡Hola! Me llamo Emi, tengo 22 años y estudio Comunicación Audiovisual. Busco 2–3 compis[a] para alquilar un piso[b] cerca de la universidad. Me gusta estudiar en casa y pasar tiempo con los amigos. Soy ordenada y limpia. Me gustaría compartir el apartamento con estudiantes que tengan un estilo de vida similar y compatible. ¡Si te interesa, contáctame!**

> **Buscamos compi estudiante para compartir un piso en el centro, de septiembre a junio.**
> **Alguien que sea buena gente y sepa convivir.[c] ¡Llama!**

[a]*short for* compañero/a   [b]*apartamento*   [c]*to coexist, get along*

45 *Lo hago para que tú...* • The Subjunctive (Part 7): The Subjunctive After Conjunctions of Purpose and Contingency

Gramática en acción: Relaciones familiares y sociales

A.   **B.**   **C.**

¿A qué dibujo corresponde cada una de las siguientes oraciones? ¿Quién las dice?

1. _____ «Aquí tienes la tarjeta de crédito, pero úsala solo **en caso de que** <u>haya</u> una emergencia, ¿eh?» (¿el abuelo o la nieta?)

2. _____ «Deja ya de jugar. No te permito que juegues **antes de que** <u>termines</u> la tarea. ¿Me entiendes?» (¿la madre o el hijo?)

3. _____ «Quiero casarme contigo **para que** <u>estemos</u> siempre juntos y no <u>salgas</u> más con Raúl». (¿Marco o Ariadna?)

¿Y a usted?

¿Alguien...

1. le ha dado dinero para que usted **<u>pague</u>** la matrícula de la universidad?

2. le ha ofrecido un trabajo fabuloso antes de que usted **<u>se gradúe</u>**?

3. le ha dicho que quiere casarse con usted con tal de que (*provided that*) usted lo/la **<u>ame</u>**?

---

①		②
indicative	conjunction of contingency or purpose	**<u>subjunctive</u>**

> *a conjunction /* **una conjunción** = a word or phrase that connects other words, phrases, or clauses

1. Conjunctions of Purpose and Contingency

The conjunctions in the chart express *purpose* (**el propósito**) or *contingency* (**la contingencia**), that is, when one action depends on another = *I'll do X unless Y occurs*. The dependent clauses introduced by them function as adverbs in the sentence.

When there is a change of subject, the Spanish subjunctive is *always* used in the dependent clause introduced by these conjunctions.

Las conjunciones de propósito y contingencia	
a menos que	unless
antes (de) que	before
con tal (de) que	provided (that), as long as
en caso de que	in case
para que	so that, in order that
sin que	without; unless

(Continúa).

Family and social relationships To which drawing does each of the following sentences correspond? Who is saying them? **1.** *"Here's the credit card, but use it only in case there's an emergency, OK?"* **2.** *"Stop playing right now. I don't allow you to play before you finish your homework. Do you understand me?"* **3.** *"I want to marry you so that we can always be together and (so that) you don't go out with Raúl again."*

Note in the examples:
- Each conjunction contains the word **que,** which is obligatory in Spanish but optional in some cases in English.
- There is a change of subject in the dependent clause (the one introduced by the conjunction).

Yo voy **con tal (de) que** ellos <u>**vengan**</u> conmigo.
I'm going, provided (that) they go with me.

En caso de que <u>**llegue**</u> Juan, dile que ya salí.
In case Juan arrives, tell him (that) I already left.

No voy a la fiesta **sin que** tú <u>**vengas**</u> conmigo.
I won't go to the party unless you go with me.

2. Order of the Clauses

An adverbial clause that expresses purpose and contingency may precede or follow the main clause, separated by a comma, just as in English. Here are the sentences from Point 1 with the adverbial clause in a different position.

Con tal (de) que ellos <u>**vengan**</u> conmigo, yo voy.
Dile a Juan que ya salí, **en caso de que** <u>**llegue**</u>.
Sin que tú <u>**vengas**</u> conmigo a la fiesta, yo no voy.

3. Same Subject = *preposition + infinitive*

When there is no change of subject, a *preposition + infinitive* phrase is often used to express purpose or contingency, rather than a *conjunction + subjunctive*. Only **a menos que** does not have a prepositional equivalent.

> PREPOSITIONS: **antes de, con tal de, en caso de, para, sin** + infinitive
> CONJUNCTIONS: **antes (de)** <u>que</u>**, con tal (de)** <u>que</u>**, en caso de** <u>que</u>**, para** <u>que</u>**, sin** <u>que</u> + subjunctive

Estoy aquí **para aprender.** (subject = **yo**)
Estoy aquí **para que** ustedes <u>**aprendan.**</u>
   (subjects = **yo, ustedes**)

Coma usted algo **antes de salir.** (subject = **usted**)
Coma usted algo **antes de que** <u>**salgamos.**</u>
   (subjects = **usted, nosotros**)

Podemos salir **con tal de tener** tiempo.
   (subject = **nosotros**)
Podemos salir **con tal de que** <u>**tengas**</u> tiempo.
   (subjects = **nosotros, tú**)

Es difícil salir con los amigos **sin gastar** dinero.
   (subject = **impersonal**)
Es difícil salir con los amigos **sin que** <u>**gastemos**</u> dinero.
   (subjects = **impersonal, nosotros**)

Summary of Conjunctions of Purpose and Contingency

a menos que, antes (de) que, con tal (de) que, en caso de que, para que, sin que + change of subject → <u>**subjunctive**</u>

Práctica y comunicación

A. ¿Buenos amigos y buenas parejas?

> **Paso 1. Autoprueba.** Empareje las conjunciones con su significado en inglés.
>
> 1. _____ para que
> 2. _____ antes (de) que
> 3. _____ con tal (de) que
> 4. _____ a menos que
> 5. _____ en caso de que
> 6. _____ sin que
>
> a. *without; unless*
> b. *unless*
> c. *before*
> d. *provided (that), as long as*
> e. *in case*
> f. *so that, in order that*

Paso 2. Complete las siguientes oraciones con la conjunción o preposición apropiada en cada caso. ¡OJO! Algunas oraciones necesitan **que** y otras no.

1. Les hago favores a mis amigos _____ que sea posible.
2. Trato de escuchar y comprender a mis amigos _____ juzgarlos (*judging them*).
3. Llevo a mis amigos a casa cuando beben demasiado _____ no conduzcan.
4. Nunca les miento a mis amigos, _____ que sea necesario para su beneficio.
5. _____ tener problemas personales, busco el apoyo de mis mejores amigos.
6. Nunca les doy consejos a mis amigos _____ me los pidan.

Paso 3. Ahora, en parejas, túrnense para entrevistarse sobre las ideas del **Paso 2.** Luego díganle a la clase algo que tienen en común o en que son radicalmente diferentes.

MODELO: **1. E1:** ¿Les haces favores a tus amigos con tal de que sea posible?
E2: Sí. ¿Y tú?
E1: Yo también. ➜ Les hacemos favores a nuestros amigos con tal de que sea posible.

B. Un fin de semana romántico

Paso 1. Un matrimonio está planeando hacer una escapada (*getaway*) de fin de semana para esquiar. Combine las siguientes ideas para explicar sus planes.

MODELO: Quieren pasar tres días esquiando _____ (con tal de / con tal de que) su hija no se enferme. ➜
Quieren pasar tres días esquiando **con tal de que** su hija no se enferm**e.**

1. Desean ir sin su hija _____ (para / para que) poder celebrar su aniversario de boda de una manera especial.
2. Van a pasar el fin de semana esquiando _____ (con tal de / con tal de que) los abuelos puedan quedarse con la niña.
3. No pueden ir _____ (sin / sin que) los abuelos se queden con la niña.
4. El plan es salir temprano el sábado _____ (menos / a menos que) estén muy cansados el viernes por la noche.
5. Es importante que lleguen a la estación de esquí _____ (antes de / antes de que) empiece a nevar.
6. Llevan cadena (*chains*) para las llantas _____ (en caso de / en caso de que) haya mucha nieve en las montañas.
7. Piensan regresar el lunes _____ (antes de / antes de que) sea de noche.

Paso 2. Diga si las siguientes oraciones son ciertas o falsas o si no se menciona la información, según el **Paso 1.**

	CIERTO	FALSO	NO SE MENCIONA
1. Los esposos acaban de casarse.	☐	☐	☐
2. Casi siempre salen de vacaciones con su hija.	☐	☐	☐
3. Los dos se preocupan mucho por su hija.	☐	☐	☐
4. Piensan que va a ser muy fácil llegar a la estación de esquí y regresar a casa.	☐	☐	☐

C. Relaciones sociales. Hay relaciones sociales de muchos tipos en las que (*which*) unas personas dependen de otras. Complete las siguientes oraciones con el presente de subjuntivo para describir algunas de ellas.

1. A algunos abuelos les gusta mimar (*to spoil*) a sus nietos con tal de que los padres... _____ (permitirlo).
2. Los padres esperan que los padrinos (*godparents*) cuiden a sus hijos en caso de que ellos... _____ (morirse).
3. Los buenos amigos siempre saben lo que necesitamos antes de que... _____ (decírselo).
4. Los amigos paraguayos se reúnen afuera para tomar el tereré con tal de que... _____ (hacer) buen tiempo.
5. Los estudiantes no estudian sin que los profesores... _____ (darles) tarea.
6. Las parejas se llevan bien a menos que... _____ (haber) entre ellos una gran diferencia de opiniones.
7. Los padres trabajan para que sus hijos... _____ (tener) lo que necesitan.

Nota comunicativa: *¿Para qué? / para (que)...* and *¿por qué? / porque...*

These words are all close in meaning, but they are used for different purposes. Their use is similar to the use of their English equivalents.

¿Para qué?	What for? For what purpose?	**¿Por qué?**	Why? For what reason?
para que (*conj.*)	so that	**porque...**	because ...
para (*prep.*)	(in order) to		

Compare the use of these words in the following sentences.

—¿**Para qué** necesitas ahora la lista de invitados a la boda?

— **Para** confirmar el número de invitados que van a asistir. Y **para que** el dueño del restaurante sepa exactamente cuántos invitados van a venir.

—¿**Por qué** estás tan nervioso?

—¡**Porque** me caso en una semana!

You will use these words and phrases in **Práctica D**.

D. Razones para hacer las cosas que hacemos

Paso 1. Empareje las frases de las dos columnas para hacer oraciones completas.

1. _____ Las universidades tienen cursos que son requisitos para...
2. _____ Los profesores corrigen tareas para...
3. _____ Estudiamos español para...
4. _____ Trabajamos en parejas en clase para...
5. _____ Los profesores organizan actividades en grupo en clase para que...

a. los estudiantes tengan más oportunidad de hablar español.
b. poder comunicarnos con mucha más gente.
c. que los estudiantes tengan un conocimiento amplio (*broad knowledge*) del mundo.
d. darles a los estudiantes más ayuda.
e. hablar más en clase.

> **¡OJO!**
>
> **¿Por qué... ?** / **Porque...**
> → *indicative*
> **para...** + *infinitive*
> **para que...** → *subjunctive*

Paso 2. Ahora, en parejas, den explicaciones sobre la razón de las siguientes situaciones.

1. Estudiamos en la universidad para (que) / porque...
2. Asistir a la universidad cuesta mucho dinero para (que) / porque...
3. Los profesores les dan tarea a los estudiantes para (que) / porque...
4. Los estudiantes quieren sacar buenas notas para (que) / porque...

E. Intercambios

Paso 1. Complete las siguientes oraciones usando una conjunción de contingencia y propósito o una preposición: **a menos que, antes de (que), con tal de (que), en caso de (que), para (que), sin (que).**

MODELO: **1.** Voy a graduarme de esta universidad... → Voy a graduarme de esta universidad en dos años **a menos que saque malas notas en varias clases.**

1. Voy a graduarme de esta universidad...
2. (No) Voy a casarme con mi novio/a actual... (Mi hijo/a [no] va a casarse con su novio/a actual...)
3. Espero tener un buen trabajo en dos o tres años...
4. Deseo tener hijos/nietos...
5. Voy a quedarme en este estado...

Paso 2. Ahora, en parejas o grupos, comparen sus oraciones. Luego díganle a la clase cuáles de sus ideas son muy similares o muy diferentes.

⚙ Todo junto

Algo sobre la cultura guaraní

El Paraguay es un modelo de conservación e integración de la herencia ancestral. Más del 80% de la población es bilingüe en guaraní y español, las dos lenguas oficiales del país. La población paraguaya es una de las más homogéneas de Latinoamérica, debido a que[a] es inmensamente mestiza,[b] de ascendencia guaraní y española.

El pueblo guaraní se asentó[c] varios siglos antes de la llegada de los españoles en lo que hoy es el Paraguay (y regiones adyacentes en la Argentina, Bolivia y el Brasil).

🗿❓ **¿Cuáles son los grupos étnicos o raciales más numerosos en su ciudad o estado? ¿Hay muchas personas bilingües?**

[a]*debido... due to the fact that*   [b]*racially mixed*   [c]*se... settled*

La moneda (*currency*) oficial del Paraguay es el guaraní. Su símbolo es el ₲.

A. Lengua y cultura: ¿Cómo se divierten los jóvenes hispanos?

Paso 1. Completar. Complete the following description of the favorite pastimes of Hispanic youths. Give the correct form of the words in parentheses, as suggested by context. When two possibilities are given in parentheses, select the correct word. **¡OJO!** Context will help you choose what to do with the infinitives. If verbs don't remain in the infinitive form, these are your choices.

**INDICATIVO: el presente, el presente perfecto,
el pretérito, el imperfecto**
SUBJUNTIVO: el presente, el presente perfecto

Asunción, Paraguay

¿**S**abía usted que hay muchas palabras diferentes en español para referirse a las personas jóvenes? (Para / Por)[1] ejemplo, en el Paraguay se dice chicas y chicos, en Chile, gallas y gallos, patojas y patojos en Guatemala, y peladas y pelados en Colombia. Pero los _____ (joven)[2] hispanohablantes, como los[a] de todo el mundo, tienen (mucho / mucha)[3] en común. (Para / Por)[4] empezar, (se / les)[5] encanta la música. (Para / Por)[6] eso, no es extraño que _____ (ellos: ir)[7] a las discotecas para _____ (bailar)[8] hasta el amanecer.[b] Y por supuesto, a muchos también (le / les)[9] _____ (encantar)[10] los eventos deportivos.

En las últimas décadas el concepto del centro comercial se _____ (desarrollar)[11] en las ciudades hispanas. Como en este país, (a menos / con tal de)[12] que _____ (haber)[13] tiendas de moda juvenil y electrónica, así como[c] restaurantes económicos, _____ (este)[14] centros atraen[d] (a / —)[15] los jóvenes. También puede haber[e] cines y hasta[f] supermercados en los centros comerciales. Por todo esto, los centros comerciales pueden sustituir a las plazas y parques tradicionales como lugares donde la gente joven _____ (ir)[16] a pasear y pasar el tiempo.

---

[a]*those*   [b]*dawn*   [c]*así... as well as*   [d]*attract*   [e]*puede... there can be*   [f]*even*

(Continúa).

Paso 2. Comprensión. Conteste las siguientes preguntas.

1. Según la información en los párrafos, ¿cuáles son algunas de las semejanzas en la forma de divertirse entre los jóvenes hispanos y norteamericanos?
2. ¿Qué palabras se usan para expresar «muchachas y muchachos» en varios países hispanos?
3. ¿Qué lugares tradicionales pueden sustituir a los centros comerciales?

 Paso 3. En acción

 En su cultura, ¿cuáles son los pasatiempos típicos de las personas según su edad? En parejas, den por lo menos una opinión sobre cada grupo.

1. los adolescentes, hasta los 16 o 17 años
2. los jóvenes entre 18 y 30 años
3. los adultos entre 30 y 60 años
4. las personas mayores
5. las reuniones familiares, con personas de diferentes generaciones

---

B. Proyecto: Frases famosas

En todos los idiomas hay muchas frases cortas y memorables que ofrecen una regla (*guidance*) para la vida. Algunas son atribuibles (es decir [*that is*], se sabe quién las creó) y otras son refranes y proverbios populares. En este proyecto van a crear algunas frases en español sobre las relaciones sentimentales y el ciclo de vida.

Paso 1. Pensar. En parejas, para empezar, piensen en tres o cuatro frases de este tipo que ustedes conozcan del inglés y tradúzcanlas al español. Recuerden que el infinitivo es la forma del verbo que se usa en español como un nombre (*noun*), como en el aforismo (*saying*) «**ver para creer**» *("seeing is believing")*.

Paso 2. Desarrollar. Ahora creen cuatro o cinco frases sobre las etapas de la vida y sobre las relaciones afectivas (*emotional*).

Paso 3. Compartir. (*Share.*) Entre todos los miembros de la clase, elijan las cuatro mejores frases. ¿Creen que se puede hacer tarjetas de felicitaciones (*greeting cards*) con ellas?

Szefei/Shutterstock

Ver para creer

Video: Salu2 «Cosas del amor»

You can watch two segments of this chapter's video in the **Video: Salu2** section, found at the end of the eBook.

Klic Video Productions/McGraw Hill

Laura entrevista a una pareja.

Enfoque cultural: Relaciones románticas

Antes de leer

Hay relaciones sentimentales de muchos tipos. ¿Qué expresiones usa usted en inglés para referirse a los diferentes tipos de relaciones entre parejas?

En el Paraguay

Dos jóvenes parejas paraguayas en motocicletas

En el Paraguay, como en casi todo el mundo hispanohablante, el concepto de noviazgo es un poco diferente del de[a] este país. «Tener novio/a» o «estar de novio/a» indica que una relación es seria y formal, con miras al[b] futuro. Novio y novia, además, son los términos que se aplican a las personas que se casan durante la ceremonia de la boda. Como el noviazgo ya señala un compromiso,[c] no es tan frecuente usar la palabra prometido/a[d] para referirse a los novios que van a casarse.

Cuando las relaciones entre dos personas son informales, se dice que andan[e] o salen juntos, o simplemente que la persona tiene un amigo o amiga. Con frecuencia se usa la palabra «pareja» para referirse a una persona que convive[f] con otra sin casarse. Por ejemplo, se dice: «Te presento a mi pareja».

[a]del... *from that of* [b]con... *(one that is) looking ahead to the* [c]señala... *indicates a commitment* [d]*fiancé/fiancée* [e]lit., *are walking* [f]*cohabits*

Comprensión ¿En qué es diferente el concepto de novio/a del (*from that*) de *boyfriend/girlfriend*? ¿Qué palabra se usa para referirse a las personas que conviven en una relación amorosa sin estar casadas?

En otros países hispanos

Una pareja de hombres casados, en la Argentina

- **En todo el mundo hispanohablante** Es muy común ver demostraciones de afecto entre una pareja en parques, plazas y calles, lo cual[a] a veces resulta chocante[b] a algunas personas de otras culturas. Pero es necesario recordar que la mayoría de los jóvenes vive con su familia y no tiene muchas oportunidades de intimidad.[c]

- **En varios países hispanos** El matrimonio entre personas del mismo sexo es una realidad legal en varios países hispanohablantes (el año de aprobación de la ley aparece entre paréntesis).

  España (2005)
  Argentina (2010)
  Uruguay (2013)
  Colombia (2016)
  Ecuador (2019)
  Costa Rica (2020)
  Chile (2021)
  Cuba (2022)
  México (2022)

[a]lo... *which* [b]*distasteful* [c]*privacy*

Comprensión ¿Por qué es normal que los jóvenes demuestren su cariño en público? ¿En cuántos países hispanohablantes pueden casarse legalmente las personas del mismo sexo?

 **En acción**

En parejas, hagan una lista de los cinco lugares de la ciudad donde está su universidad para que unos turistas extranjeros tengan una cita romántica mientras visitan el estado.

Lectura

Antes de leer

¿Cuáles son algunas de las ventajas de conocer a la gente por internet? ¿Tiene esto sus desventajas también? ¿Cuáles son?

«Amor cibernauta», de Diego Muñoz Valenzuela

Se conocieron por la red. Él era tartamudo[a] y tenía un rostro de neandertal: cabeza enorme, frente abultada,[b] ojos separados, redondos[c] y rojos, dientes de conejo[d] que sobresalían[e]
5 de una boca enorme y abierta, cuerpo endeble[f] y barriga[g] prominente. Ella estaba inválida del cuello hacia abajo[h] y dictaba los mensajes al computador con una voz hermosa, pausada[i] y clara que no parecía
10 tener nada que ver[j] con ella; tenía el cuerpo de una muñeca maltratada.[k] Fue un amor a primer intercambio de mensajes: hablaron de la armonía del universo y de los sufrimientos terrestres, de la necesidad del imperio[l] de la

Una conexión virtual

 Ievgen Chabanov/Alamy Stock Photo

15 belleza y de los abyectos afanes[m] de los mercaderes de la guerra,[n] de la abrumadora[ñ] generosidad del espíritu humano que contradice la miseria[o] de unos pocos. Leían incrédulos[p] las réplicas donde encontraban una mirada equivalente del mundo, no igual, similar aunque[q] enriquecida[r] por historias y percepciones diferentes. Durante meses evitaron hablar de sí mismos,[s] menos aún de[t] la posibilidad de encontrarse en un sitio real y no virtual. Un día él le envió[u] la foto digitalizada de un galán. Ella
20 le retribuyó con la imagen de una bailarina. Él le escribió encendidos[v] versos de amor que ella leyó embelesada.[w] Ella le envió canciones con su propia voz, él lloró de emoción al escuchar esa música maravillosa. Él le narraba con gracia[x] su agitada vida social, burlándose agudamente[y] de los mediocres. Ella le enviaba descripciones pormenorizadas[z] de sus giras[aa] por el mundo con compañías famosas. Ninguno de los dos jamás propuso[bb] encontrarse en el mundo real. Fue un amor verdadero, no virtual,
25 como los que suelen acontecernos[cc] en ese lugar que llamamos realidad.

[a]*a stutterer* [b]frente... *a bulging forehead* [c]*round* [d]*dientes... bucktoothed* [e]*protruded* [f]*rickety* [g]*belly* [h]inválida... *paralyzed from the neck down* [i]*slow* [j]no... *didn't seem to have anything in common* [k]una... *a beat-up doll* [l]*reign* [m]*ambitions* [n]los... *the merchants of war* [ñ]*overwhelming* [o]*stinginess* [p]*sin creer* [q]*although* [r]*enriched* [s]evitaron... *they avoided talking about themselves* [t]menos... *even less about* [u]*mandó* [v]*passionate* [w]*entranced* [x]con... *gracefully* [y]burlándose... *pointedly making fun* [z]*detailed* [aa]*tours* [bb]*proposed* [cc]los... *those that tend to happen to us*

Source: Diego Muñoz Valenzuela, Amor cibernauta. Used with permission.

Comprensión

A. Un resumen del cuento. Seleccione la opción apropiada, según el cuento.

1. El hombre del cuento es (muy feo / muy guapo).
2. La mujer (tiene / no tiene) una discapacidad (*disability*) física.
3. Primero, los dos mandan mensajes sobre (temas románticos / la vida y el mundo).
4. Por su intercambio de mensajes, sienten (mucha / poca) armonía entre sí (*between them*).
5. Cuando por fin se comunican detalles sobre su apariencia y su vida, envían información (falsa / verdadera).
6. Los dos (eventualmente / nunca) se conocen en persona.

B. ¿Qué piensa usted? Conteste las siguientes preguntas.

1. ¿Por qué cree usted que se dijeron mentiras sobre sí mismos? ¿Era eso necesario?
2. La pareja de cibernautas del cuento se mintió muchas veces. Sin embargo, a pesar de (*in spite of*) las mentiras, ¿cree usted que había algo verdadero en sus mensajes?
3. ¿Por qué el hombre y la mujer del cuento no tienen nombres?

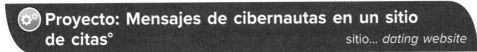

Proyecto: Mensajes de cibernautas en un sitio de citas°

sitio... *dating website*

Para este proyecto, va a crear un perfil (*profile*) ficticio para un sitio de citas por internet y va a contestar al perfil de una persona de su interés.

Paso 1. Invente un personaje (como un avatar) y escriba su perfil. Debe incluir lo siguiente por lo menos: nombre, género (*gender*), profesión, intereses, cualidades personales, aficiones y cualquier (*any*) otro detalle importante.

Paso 2. Lea los perfiles de las demás personas de la clase y elija uno que sea especialmente interesante para usted. Asumiendo la personalidad del personaje que usted ha inventado, escríbale un mensaje. En el mensaje, descríbase a sí mismo/a, explique por qué le interesa esa persona y hágale unas preguntas. Mándele su mensaje.

Paso 3. Lea el mensaje que recibe y contéstelo.

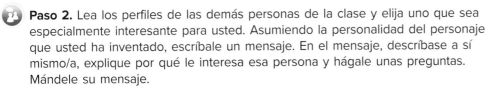

Textos orales

Un anuncio para Naranjas, un sitio web para encontrar pareja

Antes de escuchar

¿Cómo se puede encontrar a la pareja ideal? Según su experiencia, ¿es difícil conocer a personas que podrían (*could*) ser su pareja? ¿Qué es necesario o fundamental para que haya una buena relación entre una pareja?

Vocabulario para escuchar

la media naranja	better half
el éxito	success
el cuestionario	questionnaire
los pilares	pillars, bases
cualquier	any
los terapeutas	therapists
los investigadores	researchers
los compatibles	**las personas compatibles**
comprobado/a	demonstrated
lograr	to achieve
duradero/a	long-lasting
los valores	values
la afinidad	compatibility
elegir (elijo)	to select
inscríbete gratis	register for free
el perfil	profile
la soledad	loneliness

Comprensión

A. La información correcta. Las siguientes oraciones son falsas. Corríjalas.

1. El cuestionario de Naranjas se hace con papel y lápiz.
2. El éxito de este sitio está basado en las reuniones con los terapeutas.
3. La afinidad de valores e intereses no es importante para una buena relación entre dos personas.
4. Es necesario pagar para inscribirse.

B. Más detalles. Conteste las siguientes preguntas.

1. ¿Qué ventajas ofrece Naranjas sobre otros sitios?
2. ¿Por qué es importante el cuestionario de Naranjas?
3. ¿Qué ofrece gratis Naranjas?
4. ¿Cuál es la oferta para los nuevos miembros?
5. ¿Por qué cree usted que este sitio se llama Naranjas?

👆 En acción

Escriba un perfil de usted misma/o para un sitio web que empareja (*matches*) personas. No tiene que ser para una relación romántica. También puede ser para encontrar compañeros de casa o de cuarto. Aquí hay unas sugerencias.

- Busco _____ (compañero/a, pareja,...) para _____ (compartir [*to share*] casa / cuarto / la vida...)
- Soy _____ (un hombre / una mujer / una persona) de _____ años que... (varias características)
- Me gustan las personas que...
- No me gusta la gente que...
- En general, me llevo bien con todo el mundo, a menos que/con tal de que...

🎙 Entrevista

Use de modelo las preguntas y respuestas de la sección **Entrevista** al principio de este capítulo para hablar de sus relaciones personales y sus creencias (*beliefs*) sobre el amor.

Daniel Ernst/Getty Images

💻 Escritura

Consejos sentimentales

En este capítulo usted va a escribir una columna de consejos sobre las relaciones personales. Para empezar, decida si quiere escribir sobre relaciones románticas o amistosas (*friendly*).

Sollina Images/Blend Images

Una relación de más de cuarenta años

👥 Antes de escribir

En parejas, hablen de las cualidades más importantes para mantener una buena amistad o una relación amorosa. Hablen también de los problemas más comunes con que se enfrentan (*are faced*) los amigos o las parejas.

A escribir

Ahora use las ideas de **Antes de escribir** para desarrollar su ensayo. Hay más ayuda en Connect.

Para escribir bien

Considere las siguientes opciones para su ensayo.

- Conjunciones [+ inf. / subj.]: **a menos que, antes (de) que, con tal (de) que, en caso (de) que, para (que), sin (que)**
- Conjunciones para explicar [+ ind.]: **porque, ya que (*since*), puesto que (*given that*)**
- Expresiones útiles para generalizar: **no hay nadie que** + *subj.* / **la experiencia nos enseña/muestra que** + *indic.*, **todo el mundo sabe que** + *indic.*, **no hace falta (*it isn't necessary*) saber mucho para** + *inf.*

🔄 En la comunidad

Entreviste a una persona hispana de su universidad o ciudad sobre las relaciones afectivas en su país.

Preguntas posibles

- ¿Qué palabras cariñosas se usan con más frecuencia entre padres e hijos en su país de origen? ¿Y entre esposos o novios? ¿Y entre amigos?
- ¿Cómo se celebra una boda típica en su país?
- ¿Cuál es el porcentaje de divorcios? ¿Es más alto que el (*that*) de este país o más bajo? Comparado con lo que era hace veinte o treinta años, ¿ha cambiado recientemente?

◯ Producción audiovisual

Filme una entrevista que usted le hace con una pareja en la que (*which*) hablen de cuándo y cómo se conocieron y cuánto tiempo hace que están juntos.

Sugerencia: You are now ready to play Quest 11 in **Practice Spanish: Study Abroad.**

Más ideas para el portafolio

- Incluya la foto de alguien con quien tiene una relación especial. Explique lo que esta persona representa para usted y dé otros detalles: las cualidades que usted admira de esta persona, cómo se conocieron, qué les gusta hacer juntos, etcétera.
- Escriba un párrafo sobre una pareja especial en su vida (sus padres, sus abuelos, unos amigos...). Describa la relación entre ellos: su historia, cómo han influido en la vida de usted, por qué son muy importantes para usted. Si es posible, incluya una foto de la pareja.
- Si ha estado jugando Practice Spanish: Study Abroad, en Quest 11 usted aprendió que fue la poesía de Pablo Neruda que inspiró a doña Jiménez a escribir. Busque y lea el poema «Oh Tierra, espérame» de Neruda y después haga un breve análisis literario. ¿De qué se trata (*is about*) el poema? ¿Cómo describe el poema la relación entre el ser humano y la naturaleza? Escriba su propio poema que contenga sus ideas y sus sentimientos sobre el medio ambiente.

EN RESUMEN En este capítulo

AFTER STUDYING THIS CHAPTER I CAN ...

- ☐ talk about relationships (478–479)
- ☐ talk about the stages of one's life (481)
- ☐ use the indicative or subjunctive after antecedents to describe things and people in complex sentences (482–484)
- ☐ express contingency and purpose in complex sentences using the subjunctive (487–488)
- ☐ recognize/describe at least 2–3 aspects of Paraguayan cultures

Gramática en breve

44. The Subjunctive After Nonexistent and Indefinite Antecedents

①		②
definite/existing antecedent	**que**	**indicative**

Hay alguien/algo que...

①		②
indefinite/ **non**existent antecedent	**que**	**subjunctive**

No hay nadie/nada que...
¿Hay alguien/algo que... ?

45. The Subjunctive After Conjunctions of Purpose and Contingency

①		②
indicative	conjunction of purpose or contingency	**subjunctive**

Conjunctions: **a menos que, antes (de) que, con tal (de) que, en caso de que, para que, sin que**

Vocabulario

Los estados civiles y las relaciones sentimentales

amar	to love
casarse (con)	to marry
conocerse (conozco)	to meet
enamorarse (de)	to fall in love (with)
llevarse bien/mal (con)	to get along well/poorly (with)
querer	to love
romper (con)	to break up (with)

Cognados: divorciarse (de), separarse (de)

Repaso: pelear (se) (con), salir (con)

la amistad	friendship
el amor	love
la boda	wedding (ceremony)
el cariño	affection
la luna de miel	honeymoon
el matrimonio	marriage; married couple
la novia	fiancée; bride
el noviazgo	engagement period
el novio	fiancé; groom
el/la viudo/a	widower/widow
el estado civil	marital status

Cognados: el divorcio, la separación

Repaso: el/la amigo/a, la cita, el/la esposo/a, el marido, la mujer (*wife*), el/la novio/a (*boy/girlfriend*), la pareja

estar	to be
casado/a (con)	married (to)
recién casado/a	newlywed
enamorado/a (de)	in love (with)
soltero/a	single

Cognados: divorciado/a (de), romántico/a, separado/a (de)

Repaso: cariñoso/a, feliz (*pl.* felices)

Lugares para ceremonias

la iglesia	church
la mezquita	mosque
el templo	temple

Las etapas de la vida

la infancia	infancy; childhood
la juventud	youth
la madurez	middle age
la muerte	death
la niñez	infancy; childhood
la vejez	old age
la etapa	stage, phase

Cognado: la adolescencia

Repaso: la vida

crecer (crezco)	to grow
nacer (nazco)	to be born

Repaso: morir (muero) (u)

Las conjunciones

a menos que	unless
antes (de) que	before
con tal (de) que	provided (that), as long as
en caso de que	in case
para que	so that, in order that
sin que	without; unless

Las preposiciones

con tal de	provided
en caso de	in case

Repaso: antes de, para, sin

Palabras adicionales

bastante	rather, sufficiently; enough

Repaso: para, ¿para qué... ?, ¿por qué?, porque

Vocabulario personal

Use this space or a vocabulary notebook to write down other words and phrases you learn in this chapter.

17

¿Trabajar para vivir o vivir para trabajar?

En este capítulo

VOCABULARY

Professions and careers   502

The working world   504

Money matters   505

GRAMMAR

Talking about the future   509

Talking about the future in another way   515

COUNTRY OF FOCUS: CHILE

Durante la cosecha (*harvest*) de uvas chardonnay, en Chile

John Warburton–Lee Photography/Alamy Stock Photo

CHILE

19,2 (coma dos) millones de habitantes

- Chile es un país muy largo y angosto[a] que tiene casi todos los tipos de climas, con excepción del tropical. Se extiende desde el desierto de Atacama, el lugar más seco[b] del mundo, hasta la Antártida.

- La minería, especialmente del cobre,[c] representa una gran parte del producto nacional bruto[d] de Chile.

- Los vinos chilenos, producidos en la zona central del país, están entre los mejores del mundo. De hecho,[e] Chile ocupa un lugar entre los mayores exportadores de vino a los Estados Unidos.

[a]*narrow* [b]más... *driest* [c]*copper*
[d]producto... *gross national income*
[e]De... *In fact*

🔊 ENTREVISTA

These questions related to the chapter theme are answered here by a native speaker. You will be able to ask and answer them yourself with personal information in the **Entrevista** activity in the **Portafolio** section at the end of the chapter.

Gabriela Acosta Romano contesta las preguntas.

— **En este momento de su vida, ¿trabaja usted y estudia o solo estudia?**

— Estoy trabajando como asistente de laboratorio desde que[a] terminé la carrera de química el año pasado. Pero el curso[b] próximo voy a empezar una maestría.[c]

— **Si ha trabajado, ¿cómo ha sido su experiencia laboral? ¿Qué trabajos ha tenido?**

— Aparte de[d] trabajar en el laboratorio, he sido tutora de niños y, antes, en el verano trabajaba en la finca de mis abuelos haciendo labores agrícolas[e] o empacando[f] las verduras para la venta.[g]

— **¿Qué condiciones y beneficios laborales considera usted importantes? ¿Un seguro[h] de salud? ¿un horario flexible? ¿muchos días de vacaciones al año? ¿la posibilidad de viajar o trabajar desde la casa?**

— Supongo[i] que las normales: un buen horario, un mes de vacaciones pagadas, seguro de salud... El trabajo de laboratorio no se puede hacer en casa. Pero sí es posible tener flexibilidad de horario.

[a]desde... *since* [b]año académico [c]*master's (degree)* [d]Aparte... *Besides*
[e]labores... *agricultural work, chores* [f]*packing* [g]*sale* [h]*insurance* [i]*I suppose*

Daniel Ernst/Getty Images

VOCABULARIO: PREPARACIÓN

You can hear the pronunciation of theme vocabulary words and phrases in the eBook.

Las profesiones y ocupaciones

el maestro (la maestra) (de escuela)

la médica (el médico)

el plomero (la plomera)

la cocinera (el cocinero)

el peluquero (la peluquera)

la soldado (el soldado)

el abogado / la abogada	lawyer	el/la periodista	journalist
el amo/ama de casa	housekeeper	el sicólogo / la sicóloga	psychologist
el/la asistente de vuelo	flight attendant	el/la siquiatra	psychiatrist
el bibliotecario / la bibliotecaria	librarian	el técnico / la técnica	technician
el cajero / la cajera	(check-out) cashier; (bank) teller	el trabajador social / la trabajadora social	social worker
el camarero / la camarera	waiter/waitress	el traductor / la traductora	translator
el consejero / la consejera	counselor	el vendedor / la vendedora	salesperson
el contador / la contadora	accountant		
el dependiente / la dependienta	clerk		
el enfermero / la enfermera	nurse		
el hombre / la mujer de negocios	businessperson		
el ingeniero / la ingeniera	engineer		
el obrero / la obrera	worker, laborer		

Cognados: el/la analista de sistemas, el/la artista, el/la astronauta, el/la dentista, el diseñador gráfico / la diseñadora gráfica, el/la electricista, el/la electricista, el fotógrafo / la fotógrafa, el mecánico / la mecánica, el/la militar, el profesor / la profesora, el programador / la programadora, el secretario / la secretaria, el veterinario / la veterinaria

¡OJO!

If the vocabulary needed to describe your (intended) career is not listed here, look it up in a dictionary or ask your instructor.

Comunicación

A. ¿A quién necesitamos si... ?

Paso 1. ¿A quién se debe llamar o con quién se debe consultar en estas situaciones? **¡OJO!** Hay más de una respuesta posible en algunos casos.

1. La tubería del agua (*plumbing*) de la cocina no funciona bien.
2. Tenemos un accidente automovilístico. El conductor del otro coche dice que fue nuestra culpa.
3. La vida profesional nos crea problemas emocionales.
4. Un nuevo restaurante necesita a alguien que prepare la comida.
5. La lavadora no funciona.
6. Sabemos muchos detalles de un escándalo político y queremos divulgarlos.

 Paso 2. Ahora, en parejas, inventen situaciones como las (*those*) del **Paso 1.** Luego léanlas a otros estudiantes para que ellos digan a quién deben consultar.

 B. Tipos de trabajo. ¿Con qué profesiones u ocupaciones asocian ustedes las siguientes características laborales? Digan también si conocen a alguien que haga cada uno de estos tipos de trabajo. Consulten la lista de profesiones y oficios y usen el **Vocabulario útil.**

1. creativo/rutinario
2. muchos/pocos años de preparación o experiencia
3. buen salario / salario regular
4. mucha/poca responsabilidad
5. mucho/poco prestigio
6. mucha flexibilidad / horas fijas (*fixed*) (como «de nueve a cinco»)
7. trabajo en equipo / trabajo individual
8. peligroso (*dangerous*) / seguro (*safe*)
9. solo para hombres o solo para mujeres en el pasado / todavía solo para hombres/mujeres

Así se dice

el/la contador(a) = el/la contable (*Sp.*)
el/la periodista = el/la reportero/a
el/la plomero/a = el/la fontanero/a (*Sp.*)

Vocabulario útil

actor/actriz	pintor(a)
arquitecto/a	poeta
camarero/a	policía
cantinero/a	político/a
bartender	presidente/a
carpintero/a	pastor(a)
chófer	rabino/a
detective	sacerdote
imán	priest
niñero/a	senador(a)

Nota cultural: Nuevas tendencias del español para evitar el sexismo lingüístico

Con el incremento de posiciones y cargos[a] ocupados por mujeres en todos los ámbitos[b] profesionales y de poder,[c] el debate por eliminar el sexismo en la lengua española se ha intensificado.

- Se evita usar exclusivamente la forma masculina para designar a grupos de personas de los dos sexos.
- Se usan palabras que incluyen a personas de los dos sexos, como las siguientes:

  el estudiantado[d] = estudiantes (hombres y mujeres)
  el profesorado[e] = profesores y profesoras
  la infancia = niños y niñas
  la tercera edad, las personas mayores = ancianos y ancianas

- En muchos ambientes laborales, se evita dar el tratamiento de «señorita» a todas las mujeres y se prefiere el[f] de «señora», para no hacer distinción entre las mujeres solteras y las casadas, al igual que[g] esta distinción no se hace entre los hombres.
- La aplicación de la forma femenina a algunos cargos importantes, títulos y profesiones se ha estabilizado a medida que[h] las mujeres han conquistado estos puestos: jefa,[i] médica, ministra, presidenta.
- Para integrar en una sola[j] palabra las formas masculina y femenina, se han empezado a usar terminaciones inclusivas, como e, x, o @ (el símbolo de la arroba).

Michelle Bachelet, presidenta de Chile dos veces (2006–2010 y 2014–2018) y anteriormente (*formerly*) Ministra de Salud y Ministra de Defensa

Por ejemplo: lxs / les / l@s jóvenes = los jóvenes y las jóvenes. La limitación de esta forma es que es solo un recurso gráfico.[k]

Aunque queda mucho por hacer[l] para eliminar el sexismo en la lengua española, se han dado grandes pasos en todos los países y a todos los niveles.

 ¿Conoce usted algún ejemplo de sexismo en su lengua materna?

[a]*posts* [b]*arenas* [c]*power* [d]*student body, the students* [e]*faculty, the professors* [f]*that* [g]*al... just as* [h]*a... as* [i]*boss* [j]*single*

[k]*un... a graphic solution* [l]*Aunque... Although much remains to be done*

C. ¿Qué preparación se necesita para ser... ? En parejas, piensen en las carreras (*majors*) y materias específicas que se deben o se pueden estudiar para prepararse para cada profesión de la siguiente lista.

MODELO: profesor(a) de una lengua extranjera → Debe estudiar por lo menos dos lenguas extranjeras o la lingüística. Es necesario que hable una de las lenguas perfectamente. También debe estudiar literatura, historia y geografía.

1. traductor(a) en la ONU (Organización de las Naciones Unidas)
2. reportero deportivo / reportera deportiva en la televisión
3. contador(a) para un grupo de abogados
4. periodista para una revista de ecología
5. trabajador(a) social, especializado/a en los problemas de las personas ancianas
6. maestro/a de primaria, especializado/a en la educación bilingüe

El mundo laboral

hacer/tener una entrevista
la Sra. Alonso
la entrevistadora (el entrevistador)
el Sr. Cardozo
el currículum (vítae)
el entrevistado (la entrevistada)

el/la aspirante	job candidate; applicant
el empleo/trabajo	job; position
bien/mal pagado	well-/poorly paying
de tiempo completo/ parcial	full-/part-time
la empresa	corporation; business
el gerente / la gerente	manager
el jefe / la jefa	boss
el puesto	job; position
el salario	pay, wages (*often per hour*)
la solicitud	job application (*form*)
el sueldo	salary
conseguir (*like* <u>seguir</u>) un empleo	to get a job
despedir (*like* <u>pedir</u>)	to let (*someone*) go; to fire (*someone*) (*from a job*)
gradu<u>a</u>rse (me grad<u>ú</u>o) (de)	to graduate (from)
jubilarse	to retire (*from a job*)
llenar (un formulario)	to fill out (a form)
renunciar (a)	to resign (from)
solicitar	to apply for (*a job*)

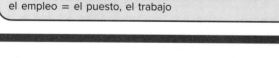

Así se dice

el empleo = el puesto, el trabajo

Comunicación

A. Definiciones. Defina las siguientes palabras y frases en español.

MODELO: la empresa → una compañía grande, como IBM o Ford

1. el currículum
2. renunciar
3. la aspirante
4. el gerente
5. el sueldo
6. llenar una solicitud

B. Pasos para conseguir un empleo

Paso 1. En parejas, hagan una lista de las acciones que típicamente se hacen durante el proceso de buscar empleo.

MODELO: **1.** antes de la entrevista de trabajo →
Se miran los avisos clasificados para encontrar puestos interesantes.

1. antes de la entrevista de trabajo
2. al principio (*at the beginning*) de la entrevista
3. durante la entrevista
4. después de la entrevista

Paso 2. Ahora, en parejas, narren lo que hicieron para conseguir su empleo actual o el último empleo que han tenido. Si alguno/a de ustedes no tiene trabajo, esa persona debe narrar lo que va a hacer para conseguirlo.

MODELO: Necesitaba un trabajo de tiempo parcial en la universidad. Por eso fui al centro de orientación profesional de la universidad...

C. Preguntas para una entrevista

Paso 1. En parejas, escriban una lista de cinco de las preguntas que pueden hacer los entrevistadores en el proceso de seleccionar candidatos para una variedad de trabajos. **¡OJO!** Usen **tú** o **usted** en sus preguntas de manera consecuente (*consistent*). No hagan preguntas sobre la identidad racial, preferencias sexuales, edad, religión y afiliación política de los candidatos.

Paso 2. Ahora, en parejas, hagan una lista de las cosas que los candidatos deben saber bien antes de aceptar una oferta (*offer*) de trabajo.

Una cuestión de dinero

la cuenta	account; bill
el interés	interest
el préstamo	loan
el presupuesto	budget
el recibo	receipt
ahorrar	to save (*money*)
cobrar	to cash (*a check*); to charge (*someone for an item or service*)
depositar	to deposit
ganar	to earn
gastar	to spend (*money*)
pagar (**gu**) a plazos / con cheque / en efectivo	to pay in installments / by check / in cash
prestar	to lend
sacar (**gu**)	to withdraw, take out

el cajero automático

BANCO POPULAR

la factura / la cuenta

TELÉFONO

el banco

la moneda

el billete

el cheque

BANCO POPULAR

el efectivo

la tarjeta bancaria / la tarjeta de crédito/débito

Comunicación

A. El mes pasado. Piense en sus finanzas personales del mes pasado. ¿Fue un mes típico? ¿Tuvo dificultades al final del mes o todo le salió bien?

Paso 1. Indique las respuestas apropiadas, según su experiencia.

	SÍ	NO
1. Hice un presupuesto al principio del mes.	☐	☐
2. Deposité más dinero en el banco del que (*than what*) saqué.	☐	☐
3. Saqué dinero del cajero automático más de tres veces.	☐	☐
4. Pagué todas mis cuentas a tiempo.	☐	☐
5. Les pedí un préstamo a mis padres.	☐	☐
6. Almorcé en casa para ahorrar un poco.	☐	☐
7. Gasté mucho dinero en divertirme.	☐	☐
8. Le presté dinero a un amigo.	☐	☐
9. Usé la tarjeta de crédito solo un par de veces.	☐	☐
10. No gasté dinero en café de Starbucks.	☐	☐

Paso 2. Pensando todavía en sus respuestas, diga tres cosas que usted debe hacer para mejorar su situación económica.

MODELO: Debo hacer un presupuesto mensual (*monthly*).

B. Diálogos

Paso 1. Empareje las preguntas de la izquierda con las respuestas de la derecha.

1. _____ ¿Cómo prefiere usted pagar?

2. _____ ¿Hay algún problema con la cuenta?

3. _____ ¿Me muestra una identificación, por favor? Necesito verla para que usted pueda cobrar su cheque.

4. _____ ¿Va a depositar este cheque o prefiere cobrarlo?

5. _____ ¿Le pongo el recibo en la bolsa (*bag*)?

a. Deposítelo, por favor.

b. No, mejor me lo da a mí.

c. Voy a pagar en efectivo.

d. Sí, señora. Usted me cobró demasiado por el postre.

e. Aquí la tiene.

Paso 2. Ahora, en parejas, inventen un contexto posible para cada diálogo. ¿Dónde están las personas que hablan? ¿En un banco? ¿en una tienda? ¿Qué hacen? ¿Quiénes son? ¿Clientes? ¿cajeros? ¿dependientes?

C. Situaciones. En parejas, describan lo que pasa en los siguientes dibujos. Usen estas preguntas como guía.

- ¿Quiénes son estas personas?
- ¿Dónde están?
- ¿Cómo van a pagar?
- ¿Qué van a hacer después de pagar?

1.

2.

Un cajero automático del Banco Santander. ¿Hay uno donde usted vive?

Formatoriginal/Alamy Stock Photo

Nota comunicativa: Más pronombres posesivos

You have been using Spanish possessive adjectives (**mi[s], tu[s]...**) for some time. As you know, they come before the noun (**mi maleta, su padre...**). There is another set of possessives, the *stressed possessives* (**las formas tónicas de los posesivos**) that come after the noun. The noun is always preceded by a definite or indefinite article.

Es **un** amigo <u>mío</u>.	*He's a friend of mine.*

Stressed possessives are often used in Spanish to contrast one thing with another.

Esta es **la** cuenta <u>mía</u> y esa es **la** <u>suya</u>.	*This is my bill and that's (that one is) yours (his, hers, yours).*

As you can see in the preceding example (**la suya**) and in the following one, stressed possessives can also be used without the noun. Sometimes the article is omitted.*

—¿De quién es este libro?	*"Whose book is this?"*
—Es <u>mío</u>.	*"It's mine."*

> **¡OJO!**
>
> The **nosotros/as** and **vosotros/as** forms are identical to the possessives you already know.

Here are the forms of the stressed possessives.

mí<u>o</u>/<u>a</u>(s)	my, (of) mine	**nuestr<u>o</u>/<u>a</u>(s)**	our, (of) yours
tuy<u>o</u>/<u>a</u>(s)	your, (of) yours	**vuestr<u>o</u>/<u>a</u>(s)**	your, (of) yours
suy<u>o</u>/<u>a</u>(s)	your, (of) yours, his, of (his), her, (of) hers	**suy<u>o</u>/<u>a</u>(s)**	your, (of) yours their, (of) theirs

You will use stressed possessives in **Comunicación D** and **E.**

D. Comparaciones. Compare los siguientes aspectos de su vida con lo que pasa en general.

1. Las clases de esta universidad son _____ (fáciles / regulares / difíciles). Creo que las mías...
2. Las clases aquí son _____ (grandes / pequeñas). Pienso que la nuestra...
3. En esta ciudad, los alquileres son _____ (altos / regulares). Creo que...
4. La familia es _____ (un apoyo [*support*] / una molestia) cuando uno tiene problemas. En general...
5. Muchas ciudades modernas _____ (tienen / no tienen) serios problemas con la contaminación. ...
6. Las finanzas son _____ (fáciles / difíciles) de manejar. ...

E. Información personal

Paso 1. En parejas, túrnense para hacer y contestar preguntas, usando posesivos en sus respuestas según el modelo.

MODELO: **1.** Mi banco es... → Mi banco es University Bank. **¿Y el tuyo?**

1. Mi banco es...
2. Mis facturas mensuales (*monthly*) para los gastos de vivienda (no) son muy altas.
3. Hoy (no) tengo mucho dinero en mi cuenta corriente (*checking account*).
4. Mi celular es un...
5. Mi consejero académico / consejera académica es...
6. Un amigo mío / Una amiga mía juega en un equipo de...

Paso 2. Ahora díganle a la clase una cosa interesante sobre su compañero/a.

See Appendix 3 (More About Stressed Possessives) for more information about using the stressed possessive forms.

Textos de todos los días: Un curriculum (vitae)

Es muy probable que usted ya haya escrito un currículum para un trabajo. En esta actividad va a escribir uno en español.

Objetivo: Crear un currículum en español siguiendo el modelo. ¡No tiene que ser realista! Puede imaginar que escribe su currículum para encontrar empleo después de graduarse de la universidad o puede inventar completamente el perfil (*profile*).

Antes de empezar

- Tenga en cuenta (*Keep in mind*) que, en español y en inglés, hay una diversidad de formatos que se puede usar en un currículum, pero las categorías respecto a la información por lo general son similares.
- Use un diccionario online para encontrar el vocabulario que no sepa (su profesor/profesora puede aconsejarle uno que sea bueno).
- Sea consistente con las listas: empiece con el mismo tipo de palabras (infinitivos o nombres, con más frecuencia).

Marta Giráldez Rebollo

INFORMACIÓN

Dirección: Calle Gorbea, 88 – Santiago, 832000, Región Metropolitana, Chile

Teléfono:
+56 9 4444-4444

Correo electrónico:
mgr2025@gmail.com

Linkedin:
linkedin.com/marta.giraldez.rebollo

Aptitudes informáticas

Excel	Java
Teams	Word
Zoom	WordPress

Perfil

Busco oportunidad laboral en un ambiente[a] dinámico que me permita seguir aprendiendo y desarrollándome en el campo de la comunicación audiovisual. Soy emprendedora y cumplidora;[b] excelente trabajadora en equipo.

Estudios

2023   Licenciatura en Comunicación Audiovisual
Universidad Nacional de Chile

Experiencia laboral

2022 – presente   Tutora de inglés y para estudiantes de escuela media y superior
- Clases individuales y en grupo, en persona y por Zoom

marzo-agosto/2023   Práctica profesional durante la licenciatura en Imagina, S.A., empresa especializada en grabación[c] de imágenes y videos de archivo
Tareas en las que asistí:
- grabar • categorizar y archivar grabaciones
- pedir permisos • tomar y archivar notas de reuniones[d] creativas

2023 – presente   Voluntaria en Biblioarte, ONG que realiza talleres[e] de arte para adolescentes en bibliotecas
- talleres mensuales de fotografía y grabación audiovisual

Lenguas

Español: hablar, leer y escribir   Nivel: nativo
Inglés: hablar, leer y escribir   Nivel: avanzado
Francés: hablar, leer y escribir   Nivel: intermedio

Otras habilidades

- capacidad organizativa
- experiencia con atención al cliente
- técnicas de contabilidad[f]
- licencia de manejar

[a]*environment*   [b]*emprendedora... enterprising and reliable*   [c]*recording*   [d]*meetings*   [e]*workshops*   [f]*accounting*

GRAMÁTICA

♻ **Repaso**

Before studying the future tense in **Gramática 46,** review **Gramática 3 (Cap. 2)** and **Gramática 11 (Cap. 4),** where you learned ways of expressing future actions. Then indicate which of the following sentences can be used to express a future action.

1. ☐ Trabajé hasta las dos.   **4.** ☐ Trabajaba a las dos.
2. ☐ Trabajo a las dos.   **5.** ☐ Estoy trabajando.
3. ☐ Voy a trabajar a las dos.   **6.** ☐ He trabajado a las dos.

46 Talking About the Future • Future Verb Forms

Gramática en acción: ¿Cómo **será** su futuro?

- **Seré** rica y famosa porque **escribiré** un blog que **tendrá** millones de seguidores.
- Todo el mundo en Middletown me **conocerá.**
- **Viajaré** mucho con mi mejor amiga y con mi familia.
- **Viviré** en Nueva York, Londres y París.

¿Y usted?

1. ¿**Será** usted rico/a y famoso/a algún día? ([No] **Seré**...)
2. ¿Dónde **vivirá** en 10 años?
3. ¿**Viajará** mucho?

So far, you have been expressing future actions in Spanish mostly with the present tense or with **ir + a +** *infinitive*. But Spanish also has a future tense, like English (*I will … , you will …*). In Spanish the *future* (**el futuro**) is used to express strong intentions and dreams.

Future of Regular Verbs / **El futuro de los verbos regulares**					
hablar		**comer**		**vivir**	
hablar**é**	hablar**emos**	comer**é**	comer**emos**	vivir**é**	vivir**emos**
hablar**ás**	hablar**éis**	comer**ás**	comer**éis**	vivir**ás**	vivir**éis**
hablar**á**	hablar**án**	comer**á**	comer**án**	vivir**á**	vivir**án**

What will your future be like? ■ *I'll be rich and famous because I'll write a blog that will have millions of followers.* ■ *Everyone in Middletown will know me.* ■ *I'll travel a lot with my best friend and with my family.* ■ *I'll live in New York, London, and Paris.*

1. Future Tense Endings

In English the *future* (**el futuro**) is a compound tense, formed with the auxiliary (helping) verbs *will* or *shall*: *I **will** speak, you **shall** do what I say*, and so on. The Spanish future is a simple verb form (only one word). It is formed by adding the identical set of future endings to **-ar, -er,** and **-ir** infinitives. No auxiliary verbs are needed.

Las terminaciones del futuro		
infinitivo +	-é	⎰ -emos
	-ás	⎱ -éis
	-á	-án

2. Irregular Future Forms

Here are the most common Spanish verbs that are irregular in the future. The future endings are attached to their irregular stems.

decir: diré, dirás, dirá, diremos, diréis, dirán

decir:	dir-	
hacer:	har-	
poder:	podr-	-é
poner:	pondr-	-ás
querer:	querr-	-á
saber:	sabr-	-emos
salir:	saldr-	-éis
tener:	tendr-	-án
venir:	vendr-	

3. The future of *hay → habrá (haber)*

As in the present and past (indicative and subjunctive), one word, **habrá,** meaning *there will be,* is used for singular and plural.

Habrá quince nuevos **empleados** el próximo mes.
There will be 15 new employees next month.

Habrá una gran **demanda** para profesionales en el campo de la salud.
There will be a great demand for professionals in the medical field.

4. The Future Perfect Tense

Spanish also has a *future perfect* tense (**el futuro perfecto**) that is used to express what *will have occurred* by a certain time in the future. The future perfect is formed with all the persons of **haber,** like all the other perfect tenses, followed by the past participle of the verb.

You will not practice this tense in ***Puntos de partida***, but you can find a more detailed presentation of it in **Appendix 4 (Additional Perfect Tenses).**

habré	
habrás	
habrá	+ participio pasado =
habremos	**sido / terminado / trabajado...**
habrán	

En cuatro años nos **habremos graduado** de la universidad.
In four years we will have graduated from college.

Habré terminado el currículum para las 3. Entonces podemos salir.
I will have finished the resumé by 3. Then we can go out.

5. Using the Future Tense

The Spanish future tense is mostly used to express serious goals and projects farther into the future, as when expressing dreams and aspirations. You saw this in **Gramática en acción.**

Remember that you have already been using other tenses to express actions that refer to the near future.

- the simple present indicative
- **ir** + **a** + infinitive
- the simple present subjunctive

Trabajaré mucho y **me haré** rico.
I'll work very hard, and I'll get rich.

La empresa **contratará** cien nuevos empleados.
The company will hire a hundred new employees.

Nos vemos mañana a las ocho.
We'll see each other tomorrow at 8:00.

Voy a llevar una chaqueta para la entrevista.
I will wear (am going to wear) a jacket to the interview.

No creo que ella **consiga** ese puesto.
I don't think (that) she'll get that job.

6. Expressing Willingness

When the English *will* refers not to future time, but to the *willingness* of someone to do something, Spanish does not use the future but rather the verbs **querer** or **poder**, or simply the present tense of any verb. In this context, **querer** has almost the force of a command.

¿Quieres/Puedes cerrar la puerta, por favor?
Will/Could you please close the door?

¿Cierras la puerta, por favor?
Can you close the door, please?

Práctica y comunicación

A. Predicciones para el futuro

Paso 1. Autoprueba. Dé la forma apropiada del futuro de los siguientes verbos.

1. yo: vivir
2. ella: decir
3. ellos: salir
4. ustedes: venir
5. nosotros: comer
6. tú: querer

Summary of the future

Infinitive + **-é, -ás, -á, -emos, -éis, -án**

Paso 2. Haga oraciones sobre cómo será su vida en los próximos 10–15 años, usando el tiempo futuro y las siguientes frases. Añada detalles y use la palabra **no** cuando sea necesaria.

MODELO: **1.** ser _____ (profesión) ➜
     (No) **Seré** profesor universitario / profesora universitaria.

1. ser _____ (profesión)
2. conseguir una maestría (*masters*) o un doctorado (*Ph.D.*) en _____
3. vivir en un país hispanohablante
4. trabajar para una empresa internacional

5. tener _____ (número) hijos.
6. participar activamente en la política
7. estar jubilado/a
8. ¿ ?

Paso 3. Ahora, en parejas, entrevístense sobre las ideas del **Paso 2.** Luego díganle a la clase algo que tienen en común o en lo que son muy diferentes.

MODELO: **1.** ser _____ (profesión) ➜
     E1: ¿**Serás** profesora universitaria?
     E2: No, **seré** analista de sistemas.
     E2: Pues yo sí **seré** profesor universitario.

B. ¿Qué harán?
Explique lo que harán las siguientes personas en su trabajo futuro. Luego, para cada grupo, diga qué profesión se describe.

MODELO: yo / darles consejos a los estudiantes ➜
     Les **daré** consejos a los estudiantes.

1. yo
- hablar bien el español
- pasar mucho tiempo en la biblioteca
- escribir artículos sobre la literatura latinoamericana
- enseñar clases en español

2. tú
- trabajar en una oficina y en la corte
- ganar mucho dinero
- tener muchos clientes
- cobrar por muchas horas de trabajo

3. Felipe
- ver a muchos pacientes
- resolver muchos problemas mentales
- leer a Freud y a Jung
- hacerle un sicoanálisis a un paciente

4. Susana y Juanjo
- pasar mucho tiempo sentados
- usar el teclado (*keyboard*) constantemente
- inventar nuevos programas
- mandarles mensajes electrónicos a todos los amigos

Algo sobre «Gracias a la vida»

Violeta Parra, en concierto

La canción «Gracias a la vida» es famosa en todo el mundo hispanohablante. Fue compuesta por la cantautora y folclorista chilena Violeta Parra (1917–1967). Es un himno[a] a la vida que habla de las cosas importantes y cotidianas[b] que muchas veces olvidamos. Muchos cantantes de todo el mundo han cantado esta canción, incluyendo a la folclorista estadounidense Joan Baez y, más recientemente, Michael Bublé.

 Aparte del[c] himno nacional, ¿hay alguna canción que usted considere un símbolo de su país? ¿Cuál es?

[a]*hymn, anthem*   [b]*daily*
[c]*Aparte... Besides the*

Prác. A, Paso 1: Answers: 1. *viviré* **2.** *dirá* **3.** *saldrán* **4.** *vendrán* **5.** *comeremos* **6.** *querrás*

C. Este mes

Paso 1. Describa lo que usted hará o no hará este mes en cuanto a (*as far as*) sus finanzas.

MODELO: **1.** (no) gastar más/menos este mes ➜ (No) **Gastaré** menos este mes.

1. (no) gastar más/menos este mes
2. (no) pagar a tiempo todas mis cuentas
3. (no) hacer un presupuesto y / pero (no) seguirlo
4. (no) depositar mucho / poco dinero en mi cuenta
5. (no) cobrar un cheque de mi empleo
6. (no) seguir usando mis tarjetas de crédito
7. (no) pedirles dinero a mis amigos / padres / hijos
8. (no) buscar un trabajo de tiempo completo / parcial

 Paso 2. Ahora, en parejas, comparen sus respuestas. Díganle a la clase si ustedes son responsables en cuanto a asuntos (*matters*) de dinero, siguiendo los modelos. También díganle a la clase las cosas que tienen en común.

MODELOS: Dylan y yo somos muy responsables con nuestro dinero porque...
Dylan es muy responsable con su dinero, pero yo tengo que aprender a ser más responsable con el mío porque...

D. El horóscopo

Paso 1. ¿Creen ustedes en la astrología? Es posible que no, pero eso no importa para esta actividad. En parejas, hagan una lista de los temas y verbos que con frecuencia aparecen en los horóscopos.

Paso 2. Ahora escojan dos signos del Zodíaco y escriban predicciones para los próximos siete días basadas en cada uno de esos dos signos. ¡Sean creativos y demuestren su sentido del humor!

MODELO: Miércoles: Conocerás a una persona muy interesante en una clase o en una fiesta.

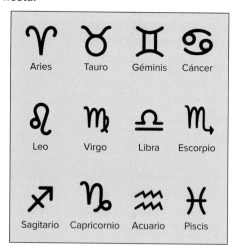

Paso 3. Finalmente, lean a la clase las predicciones para los signos que escogieron. ¿Cuáles son las reacciones de sus compañeros de clase ante (*to*) sus predicciones?

E. El mundo del año 2200

Paso 1. ¿Cómo será el mundo del futuro? En parejas, hagan una lista de cosas que ustedes creen que van a ser diferentes para el año 2200 (por ejemplo: el transporte, la comida, la vivienda). Piensen también en temas globales (por ejemplo: la política, los problemas que presenta la capa de ozono). Consulten la lista de **Vocabulario útil** en la próxima página y usen un diccionario si es necesario.

Algo sobre los Andes

Los majestuosos Andes, que cruzan todo Chile de norte a sur

Marianna Ianovska/ Shutterstock

La cordillera[a] de los Andes recorre[b] Chile, el país más largo del mundo, de norte a sur. Los Andes forman la frontera natural entre Chile y sus países vecinos Bolivia y la Argentina. Chile, además, es un país angosto,[c] lo que hace que los Andes sean muy visibles por gran parte del territorio.

En su opinión, ¿cuál es el accidente[d] geográfico más determinante y emblemático de su país? ¿Y de su estado?

[a]*mountain range*   [b]*runs along*   [c]*narrow*   [d]*feature*

Vocabulario útil

la colonización	el transbordador espacial space shuttle
el espacio	la vida artificial
la estación espacial	
los OVNIs (Objetos Voladores	diseñar
No Identificados)	eliminar
la pobreza poverty	intergaláctico/a
el robot	interplanetario/a
el satélite	sintético/a

Paso 2. En base a su lista, hagan una serie de predicciones para el futuro.

MODELO: La gente **comerá** (**Comeremos**) comidas sintéticas.

Nota comunicativa: Cómo expresar probabilidad con el futuro

Estela, en el aeropuerto

Cecilia, en la carretera

—¿Dónde **estará** Cecilia? ¿Qué le **pasará**?

"I wonder where Cecilia is." ("Where can Cecilia be?") "I wonder what's up with her." ("What can be wrong?")

—**Estará** en un atasco.

"She's probably (must be) in a traffic jam." ("I bet she's in a traffic jam.")

In Spanish, the future can also be used to express probability or conjecture about what is happening now. This use of the future is called the *future of probability* (**el futuro de probabilidad**). Note in the preceding examples that the English cues for expressing probability (*probably, I bet, must be, I wonder, Where can ... ?*, and so on) are not directly expressed in Spanish. Their sense is conveyed in Spanish simply by the use of the future form of the verb.

You will use the future of probability in **Práctica F.**

Algo sobre la Isla de Pascua°

Easter

La Isla de Pascua, llamada Rapa Nui en la lengua indígena rapanui, es una isla chilena que está en el Pacífico. De hecho,ᵃ es la isla más aislada de las islas polinésicas y esto ha permitido que la cultura del pueblo rapanui haya mantenido características únicas. La Isla de Pascua tiene una población de aproximadamente 8.600 habitantes y es hoy día un centro turístico importante. Su mayor atracción sin duda son los misteriosos moáis, inmensas estatuas de piedra cuyoᵇ significado no se comprende todavía.

En su opinión, ¿cuál es el lugar más misterioso o espiritual de su país? ¿Lo ha visitado usted?

ᵃDe... *In fact*   ᵇ*whose*

Los moáis, la imagen más famosa de la Isla de Pascua

F. Predicciones. ¿Quiénes serán las personas en las siguientes fotos? ¿Qué estarán haciendo? ¿Dónde estarán? En parejas, usen lo que saben de Chile e inventen todos los detalles que puedan.

Vocabulario útil

la bodega	wine cellar
la cata de vino	wine tasting
la Isla de Pascua	Easter Island
el moái	*monolithic statue on Easter Island*
el pueblo rapanui	people of Easter Island
la viña	vineyard
pr<u>o</u>bar (pr<u>ue</u>bo)	to taste

1.

2.

♻ Repaso

In **Gramática 45 (Cap. 16),** you learned about a series of adverbial conjunctions that always require the use of the subjunctive in the dependent clause. There are six such conjunctions. Complete the following phrases to name them all.

1. a _____ que = *unless*

2. _____ (de) que = *before*

3. con _____ (_____) que = *provided that, as long as*

4. en _____ de que = *in case*

5. _____ que = *so that*

6. _____ que = *without; unless*

You will learn more about using one of these conjunctions and about others like it in **Gramática 47**.

47 Expressing Future or Pending Actions • The Subjunctive (Part 8): The Subjunctive and Indicative After Conjunctions of Time

Gramática en acción: Planes para el futuro

1. Después de graduarme, tendré que buscar trabajo. **Tan pronto como <u>tenga</u>** trabajo, ganaré mucho dinero y pagaré los préstamos de la universidad.

2. En cuanto <u>me jubile</u>, jugaré al golf por lo menos tres veces por semana. ¡Pero desgraciadamente quedan quince años **hasta que <u>pueda</u>** jubilarme!

3. Cuando trabajaba, siempre estaba cansado. Ahora me siento mejor que nunca. ¡Y voy a jugar al golf **hasta que <u>tenga</u>** 100 años!

¿Y usted?

1. ¿Buscará trabajo justo **después de** graduarse o piensa seguir estudiando?
2. ¿Cuál es una cosa que *no* puede hacer ahora pero que quiere hacer **cuando <u>tenga</u>** un trabajo después de graduarse?
3. Cuando <u>tenga</u> un trabajo, ¿estará más cansado/a que ahora?

①		②
FUTURE/PENDING ACTION: **present/future indicative command**	adverbial conjunction of time +	<u>**subjunctive**</u>

①		②
HABITUAL/COMPLETED ACTION: **present/past indicative**	adverbial conjunction of time +	**indicative**

1. Adverbial Conjunctions of Time

Future events are often expressed in Spanish in two-clause sentences in which the dependent clause is introduced by a conjunction of time. The most common ones are listed at the right.

Las conjunciones de tiempo			
antes (de) que	before	**en cuanto**	as soon as
cuando	when	**hasta que**	until
después (de) que	after	**tan pronto como**	as soon as

Plans for the future ***1.*** *After I graduate, I'll have to look for a job. As soon as I have a job, I'll earn lots of money, and I'll pay off my university loans.* ***2.*** *As soon as I retire, I'll play golf at least three times a week. But unfortunately it'll be fifteen more years until I can retire!* ***3.*** *When I was still working, I was always tired. Now I feel better than ever. And I'm going to play golf until I'm 100 (years old)!*

2. Use of the Indicative After Time Conjunctions

The indicative is used when the dependent clause introduced by a time conjunction describes a habitual action (present or past) or a completed event in the past.

> ### ¡OJO!
> Clauses that start with a time conjunction can appear before or after the main clause. If they appear before, they are usually followed by a comma.

MAIN CLAUSE: HABITUAL ACTIONS → INDICATIVE

Siempre pago las cuentas **en cuanto recibo** mi cheque.
I always pay bills as soon as I get my check.

Tan pronto como recibía mi cheque, lo depositaba en el banco.
As soon as I got my check, I would (used to) deposit it in the bank.

MAIN CLAUSE: COMPLETED PAST ACTION → INDICATIVE

El mes pasado pagué las cuentas **en cuanto recibí** mi cheque.
Last month I paid my bills as soon as I got my check.

Cuando recibí el cheque, lo deposité.
When I got the check, I deposited it.

3. Use of the Subjunctive After Time Conjunctions

The subjunctive is used when the dependent clause introduced by a time conjunction describes an event that has not happened yet. This happens even when there is no change of subject in the dependent clause, as in the examples.

> ### ¡OJO!
> When the present subjunctive is used in this way to express pending future actions, the *main-clause* verb is in the present indicative or future, or is a command.

MAIN CLAUSE: PRESENT/FUTURE INDICATIVE OR COMMAND → SUBJUNCTIVE

Debo depositar el dinero **tan pronto como** lo <u>reciba</u>.
I should deposit the money as soon as I get it.

Pagaré las cuentas **en cuanto** <u>reciba</u> mi cheque.
I'll pay the bills as soon as I get my check.

Pague usted las cuentas **en cuanto** las <u>reciba</u>.
Pay bills as soon as you get them.

Note that the use of the subjunctive after clauses that begin with **Cuando...** is very frequent in Spanish.

Cuando <u>sea</u> grande/mayor...
When I'm older ...

Cuando <u>tenga</u> tiempo...
When I have the time ...

4. *Antes (de) que* + subjunctive

As you know, the subjunctive is always used after the time conjunction **antes (de) que**. You can review this usage in **Gramática 45 (Cap. 16)**.

No puedo comprar nada **antes de que** me <u>paguen</u>.
I can't buy anything until they pay me.

Antes de que <u>lleguen</u> los candidatos, los entrevistadores deben leer las solicitudes y los currículum de cada uno.
Before candidates arrive, interviewers should read the applications and resumés of each one.

5. Preposition + infinitive

When there is no change of subject, the prepositions **antes de, después de,** and **hasta** are often used instead of the conjunctions **antes (de) que, después (de) que,** and **hasta que.**

¡Claro que no puedo depositar el dinero **antes de** <u>recibir</u> el cheque!
Of course I can't deposit the money before receiving the check!

Después de <u>tener</u> la entrevista, me sentí muy tranquila.
After having the interview, I felt very calm.

Summary of Time Conjunctions

	FUTURE/PENDING
antes de que	<u>subjunctive</u>
all other conjunctions of time	<u>subjunctive</u>
	HABITUAL/PAST
antes de que	<u>subjunctive</u>
all other conjunctions of time	indicative

Práctica y comunicación

A. ¿Futuro o presente?

Paso 1. Autoprueba. Indique cuáles de las siguientes oraciones indican una acción futura, que debe ser expresada con el subjuntivo en español.

	ACCIÓN FUTURA
1. I'll call <u>as soon as I get home</u>.	☐
2. We always interview applicants <u>after we check their references</u>.	☐
3. Some people apply for graduate school <u>as soon as they enter their senior year</u>.	☐
4. They won't deposit the check <u>until you sign it</u>.	☐

Prác. A, Paso 1: Answers 1, 4

Paso 2. Indique si las siguientes oraciones expresan una acción habitual (**H**) o futura (**F**). Luego complételas con la forma apropiada del indicativo o del subjuntivo e indique las (*those*) que son verdaderas (**V**) para usted.

			H	F	V
1.	Generalmente hago ejercicio cuando _____ (salir) de clase.		☐	☐	☐
2.	Mañana voy a hacer ejercicio cuando _____ (salir) de clase.		☐	☐	☐
3.	Necesito actualizar (*to update*) mi currículum tan pronto como _____ (tener) tiempo.		☐	☐	☐
4.	Generalmente actualizo el currículum cuando el año académico _____ (terminar).		☐	☐	☐
5.	No voy a buscar empleo hasta que _____ (graduarse).		☐	☐	☐
6.	Voy a buscar empleo antes de _____ (graduarse).		☐	☐	☐
7.	En cuanto _____ (*yo*: tener) un rato libre esta semana, voy a ir al centro de orientación profesional.		☐	☐	☐

Paso 3. Ahora, en parejas, entrevístense sobre las oraciones del **Paso 2.**

MODELO: **1. E1:** ¿Haces ejercicio cuando sales de clase generalmente?
E2: Sí, generalmente los lunes, miércoles y viernes. ¿Y tú?
E1: Yo prefiero hacer ejercicio por la mañana temprano.

B. Decisiones económicas

Paso 1. Lea las siguientes oraciones sobre Rigoberto e indique si se trata de (*each is about*) una acción habitual (**H**) o de una acción futura (**F**). Luego escoja la frase que complete mejor cada oración.

H F
☐ ☐   **1.** _____ Rigoberto va a comprarse un auto en cuanto...
     a. ahorre suficiente dinero.   **b.** ahorra suficiente dinero.

☐ ☐   **2.** _____ Siempre usa su tarjeta de crédito cuando...
     a. no tenga dinero en efectivo.   **b.** no tiene dinero en efectivo.

☐ ☐   **3.** _____ Pagará su préstamo estudiantil tan pronto como...
     a. consiga un trabajo.   **b.** consigue un trabajo.

☐ ☐   **4.** _____ No puede pagar sus cuentas este mes hasta que...
     a. su hermano le devuelva el dinero que le prestó.
     b. su hermano le devuelve el dinero que le prestó.

Paso 2. Ahora diga cómo maneja usted sus propios asuntos económicos. Indique si la oración describe una acción habitual (**H**) o una acción futura (**F**).

H F
☐ ☐   **1.** En cuanto tenga más dinero, voy a comprarme _____.
☐ ☐   **2.** Cuando no tengo dinero en efectivo, siempre uso _____.
☐ ☐   **3.** Tan pronto como consiga un trabajo, voy a _____.
☐ ☐   **4.** Este mes, voy a _____ antes de que se me olvide.
☐ ☐   **5.** En cuanto _____, empezaré a buscar trabajo.

> **Estrategia**
>
> Use un sustantivo en las oraciones 1 y 2. Use un infinitivo en las oraciones 3 y 4. En la oración 5, debe usar el subjuntivo.

C. Cosas de la vida. Las siguientes oraciones describen algunos aspectos de la vida de Mariana. Complételas con la forma apropiada de los infinitivos.

1. Hace cuatro años, cuando Mariana _____ (graduarse) de la escuela secundaria, sus padres _____ (darle) una computadora. El año que viene, cuando _____ (graduarse) de la universidad, _____ (darle) un carro.

2. Cuando _____ (ser) niña, Mariana _____ (querer) ser actriz. Cuando _____ (tener) 18 años, _____ (decidir) ser enfermera. Cuando _____ (terminar) su carrera este año, _____ (poder) encontrar un buen empleo.

3. Antes Mariana siempre _____ (pagar) sus cuentas con cheque. Ahora las _____ (pagar) por internet en cuanto le _____ (*ellos*: depositar) el sueldo en su cuenta.

4. Mariana _____ (tener) que comprar un regalo para la boda de unos amigos. No puede comprarlo hasta que su hermana le _____ (devolver) el dinero que Mariana le _____ (prestar).

Algo sobre el pueblo mapuche

Los mapuches son un pueblo originario de lo que hoy es Chile y parte de la Argentina. Forman el grupo indígena numéricamente más importante de Chile (hay aproximadamente 1,7 [uno coma siete] millones de mapuches en el país). Se calcula que han estado en el territorio chileno desde el año 500 a. e. c.[a] o antes. Como casi todos los pueblos indígenas de las Américas, los mapuches reivindican[b] territorios y más reconocimiento[c] por parte del[d] gobierno, a fin de mejorar[e] la situación socioeconómica de muchos de ellos y proteger su cultura.

Un grupo de mapuches con su bandera (*flag*)

Martín Bernetti/AFP/Getty Images

 ¿Cree usted que las reivindicaciones de los mapuches son diferentes o similares a las[f] de algunos pueblos indígenas de los Estados Unidos?

[a]*before Common Era* [b]*claim* [c]*recognition* [d]*por... from the* [e]*a... in order to improve* [f]*those*

D. Los planes de David

Paso 1. David va a graduarse en sociología de la Universidad de Chile, en Santiago. Describa sus planes, haciendo oraciones completas con las siguientes frases y usando las conjunciones de tiempo en **negrilla**.

MODELO: querer tener un buen empleo / **tan pronto como** / graduarse →
David **querrá** tener un buen empleo tan pronto como **se gradúe**.

1. estar buscando un empleo / **antes de** / graduarse
2. independizarse de sus padres / **en cuanto** / ser posible
3. **cuando** / ahorrar dinero, / poder viajar a la Patagonia con su novia
4. **después de** / trabajar por un tiempo, / estudiar para obtener un doctorado
5. estudiar el mapudungún, la lengua de los mapuches, / **hasta que** / poder hablarlo bien
6. pero / **antes de que** / todo esto ser realidad, / necesitar estudiar mucho

Paso 2. Ahora use las ideas apropiadas del **Paso 1** para hablar de sus propios planes para el futuro. Haga los cambios necesarios.

MODELO: querer tener un buen empleo / **tan pronto como** / graduarse →
Querré tener un buen empleo tan pronto como **me gradúe**.

 E. Descripciones. En parejas, completen la oración que acompaña cada escena. Luego completen las oraciones con información personal.

1. Esta noche, Pablo va a estudiar hasta que...

¿Y ustedes?
• Esta noche, voy a estudiar hasta que...
• Siempre estudio hasta que...
• Anoche estudié hasta que...

2. Los Sres. Castro van a cenar tan pronto como...

¿Y ustedes?
• Esta noche, voy a cenar tan pronto como...
• Generalmente ceno cuando / antes de (que)...
• Anoche cené tan pronto como / después de (que)...

F. Intercambios

Paso 1. Invente preguntas que a usted le gustaría hacerles a sus compañeros de clase sobre el futuro en general y sobre el futuro de ellos en particular.

MODELO: ¿Cuántos años tendrás... ? / cuando / jubilarse →
¿Cuántos años tendrás cuando **te jubiles**?

¿Cómo será tu vida... ? ¿Dónde vivirás... ? ¿Qué harás... ? ¿Cuántos años tendrás... ?	**+** cuando **+**	la humanidad: colonizar otros planetas los científicos: descubrir una cura para casi todos los casos de cáncer las mujeres: tener igualdad de oportunidades, de verdad haber paz en todas partes del mundo ¿ ? graduarse tener suficiente dinero para casarse / tener hijos / ¿ ? jubilarse ¿ ?

Paso 2. En parejas, entrevístense usando las preguntas que crearon en el **Paso 1.** Luego díganle a la clase algo interesante de su conversación.

¿Qué quieres ser cuando seas grande?

Quiero ser feliz.

MODELO: **E1:** ¿Cuántos años tendrás cuando te jubiles?

      E2: Probablemente tendré más de 65 años cuando me jubile. Voy a ser maestro y creo que no voy a ganar mucho dinero. Por eso no voy a poder jubilarme antes.

Todo junto

A. Lengua y cultura: Trabajos para estudiantes universitarios

Paso 1. Completar. Complete the following paragraphs with the correct form of the words in parentheses, as suggested by context. When two possibilities are given in parentheses, select the correct word. *P / I:* will show you when to use the preterite or the imperfect. Conjugate all other infinitives in the future, present indicative, or subjunctive, or leave them in the infinitive form.

La necesidad de dinero es un problema para muchos estudiantes en todas partes del mundo. En la mayoría de los países hispanohablantes, es común que los estudiantes _____ (vivir)[1] con sus familias, (por qué / porque)[2] la mayoría estudian en (el / la)[3] universidad más cercana.[a]

Sin embargo, muchos estudiantes no buscan trabajo de tiempo completo hasta que _____ (*ellos:* terminar)[4] sus estudios universitarios. Y, así como en este país, hay estudiantes que _____ (conseguir)[5] trabajo de tiempo parcial antes de (terminar / terminen)[6] la escuela secundaria. A continuación[b] se puede leer las experiencias laborales de algunos estudiantes durante la época universitaria.

    Una joven paraguaya: «Desde los 16 años, _____ (*yo:* trabajar)[7] en una oficina. Así puedo (cobrar / pagar)[8] la matrícula en la universidad y mi ropa y gastos personales y también _____ (*yo:* poder)[9] colaborar un poquito con la economía familiar».

    Un joven chileno: «Cuando _____ (*P / I: yo:* ser / estar)[10] estudiante universitario, _____ (*P / I:* trabajar)[11] como fotógrafo. _____ (*P / I: Yo:* Sacar)[12] fotos en bodas, bautizos y primeras comuniones. Era un _____ (bueno)[13] trabajo (por / para)[14] un estudiante, porque _____ (*P / I: yo:* tener)[15] (de / que)[16] trabajar los fines de semana pero casi nunca los días de clase».

    Una estudiante uruguaya de la escuela secundaria: «Tan pronto como las clases _____ (terminar)[17] este verano, _____ (*yo:* empezar)[18] a trabajar en la tienda de mi tía y _____ (ganar)[19] un poco de dinero. No quiero que mis padres _____ (tener)[20] que pagarlo todo cuando yo _____ (ser / estar)[21] en la universidad».

Jon Arnold Images Ltd/Alamy Stock Photo

Universidad de Chile, en Santiago

(Continúa).

[a]*más... nearest*   [b]*A... In what follows*

Paso 2. Comprensión. Conteste las siguientes preguntas.

1. ¿Qué necesidad comparten los estudiantes de todo el mundo?
2. ¿Es caro o barato el sistema universitario de los países hispanos?
3. ¿Dónde vive la mayoría de los estudiantes hispanos?
4. ¿Qué trabajos se describen en estos párrafos?

 **Paso 3. En acción**

Ahora, en parejas, hablen de los trabajos que tienen los estudiantes universitarios en este país mientras estudian. ¿Cuáles son los más comunes? Hablen también de sus propios trabajos si es que trabajan.

B. Proyecto: Mucho más que un título

Todos los trabajos implican mucho más que un solo tipo de actividad o aptitud. En este proyecto, van a usar su conocimiento y creatividad para crear un perfil (*profile*), serio o cómico, sobre algunas profesiones y ocupaciones.

Hacemos trabajos de lingüística y traducción.

Actuamos y hacemos mímica.

Facilitamos y animamos.

Dibujamos y diseñamos.

Nos importa el medio ambiente y la justicia social.

Hacemos todo esto y mucho más.

¡Enseñamos lenguas!

Paso 1. Preparación. En parejas, elijan una o dos ocupaciones profesionales. Consideren no solo los trabajos tradicionales (médico/a, enfermero/a, abogado/a...), sino (*but*) también los que han surgido (*those that have emerged*) en los últimos veinte años. Después de decidir en cuál de las profesiones se van a enfocar, hagan una lista de todo lo que saben de ellas: ¿Qué actividades realizan (*achieve*) esos profesionales? ¿Qué aptitudes deben tener? ¿Qué deben saber? ¿Tienen que tener algún estilo de vida determinado?

Paso 2. Creación. Ahora hagan un perfil creativo de esas profesiones. Antes de empezar, elijan el objetivo para crearlo. Algunas posibilidades:

- la facultad de una universidad que promueve (*is promoting*) una carrera para atraer estudiantes
- un organismo del gobierno que considera necesario que en el país haya más especialistas en ese campo
- un artículo para una revista sobre profesiones antiguas y nuevas
- una viñeta (*cartoon*) cómica

Luego adapten la información de su lista a un formato adecuado para su proyecto.

MODELOS: maestros/maestras y profesores/profesoras de lenguas →

Son personas que estudian una o varias lenguas. Saben interpretarlas, traducirlas y analizar la cultura de los lugares en donde se hablan. También saben enseñárselas a otras personas.

Hazte profesor(a) de español si quieres ayudar a otras personas para que puedan comunicarse con más de 500 millones de personas en 20 países.

Recuerden ser consecuentes (*consistent*) con el formato y elegir un estilo en particular (serio, cómico o irónico).

Paso 3. Competición. Compartan su perfil con toda la clase. De todos los perfiles de la clase, ¿cuáles les parece que son los mejores? ¿Por qué?

Video: Salu2 «Los hispanos que admiramos»

You can watch two segments of this chapter's video in the **Video: Salu2** section, found at the end of the eBook.

Una doctora que habla sobre su trabajo

Enfoque cultural:
El mundo laboral

Antes de leer

¿Cree usted que hay muchas personas preocupadas por la seguridad de su empleo hoy día? ¿Por qué existe esta preocupación?

En Chile

Vista de Antofagasta, capital de la región minera (*mining*) del norte de Chile

Como ocurrió en prácticamente todos los países del mundo, la pandemia provocada por el COVID-19 causó graves problemas en la situación económica y laboral en Chile. Antes del comienzo de la pandemia, la economía chilena se consideraba la más fuerte de Latinomérica. Incluso[a] en 2021 tuvo un crecimiento impresionante[b] (11,7%). Pero para 2022, la OCDE (Organización para la Cooperación y el Desarrollo Económicos) preveía[c] una recesión económica para el país en 2023. Debido a[d] la pandemia, muchas personas perdieron su empleo y para 2022 el país no había conseguido volver a los niveles de empleo prepandémicos. Esta situación ha afectado más a mujeres que a hombres. Y como es normal en todo el mundo, la brecha salarial[e] sigue siendo un problema que afecta negativamente a las chilenas.

[a]*Even* [b]crecimiento... *impressive growth* [c]*predicted*
[d]Debido... *Due to* [e]brecha... *salary gap*

Comprensión ¿Qué afectó negativamente la economía de Chile? ¿Qué problema respecto a la desigualdad (*inequality*) es evidente en Chile, como en todos los países?

MUNDO HISPANO

En otros países hispanos

El sistema de salud español, parte del Ministerio de Empleo y Seguridad Social

- **En algunos países hispanohablantes** La Real Academia Española de la Lengua define la palabra «trabajólico/a» como «Que trabaja afanosa[a] y compulsivamente». Curiosamente, la Real Academia identifica este adjetivo como una expresión chilena. En general, el hecho[b] de trabajar mucho o en exceso, de ser una persona trabajólica o creer que trabajar mucho es una buena cualidad, son contrarios a la manera de pensar de los hispanos. Para la mayoría de estos, hay que trabajar para vivir, pero nunca al revés.[c]

- **En España** En este país, como en muchos otros países europeos, los trabajadores disfrutan de[d] buenos beneficios laborales que están establecidos por la ley.[e] Por ejemplo, un mes de vacaciones al año es el mínimo legal. Otro ejemplo es la licencia[f] por maternidad o paternidad, que la ley garantiza[g] con cuatro meses, además de[h] otros beneficios asociados. Además, España tiene un sistema nacional de salud que cubre prácticamente a toda la población.

[a]*eagerly* [b]*act* [c]al... *the other way around* [d]disfrutan... tienen
[e]*law* [f]*leave* [g]*guarantees* [h]además... *in addition to*

Comprensión ¿Qué significa «trabajólico/a»? ¿Cuáles son dos de los beneficios laborales que existen en España?

 En acción

Haga una lista de todos los beneficios laborales que usted pueda imaginar. Luego, indique los (*those*) que considera más importantes. ¿Cree usted que hay algún beneficio laboral que deba ser protegido por la ley (*law*)? ¿Cuál es? Explique por qué debe protegerse.

Lectura

Antes de leer

Conteste las siguientes preguntas.

1. Mire el cuadro del pintor chileno Roberto Matta en esta página y también busque otros cuadros suyos en internet. ¿Le gustan? Explique por qué.
2. Piense en la creación de un cuadro. ¿Qué cree usted que el/la artista hace primero?

Detalle de *Los poderes* (powers) *del desorden*, de Roberto Matta (1911–2002)

Vocabulario para leer

el/la asistente	attendee
las autoridades	authorities
la exposición	exhibition
la inauguración	opening
el maestro /	master
la maestra	(artist)
la muestra	**exposición**
cumplir una	to keep a
promesa	promise
prometer	to promise
vanagloriarse	to boast
ansioso/a	anxious

Roberto Matta = un famoso pintor abstracto chileno

«La oportunidad de Salomón Bobadilla», de Tito Matamala

El amigo Salomón Bobadilla me lo había prometido desde hacía muchos años.[a] Siempre esperó su oportunidad, y un día la oportunidad llegó, cuando la universidad pudo vanagloriarse de traer a su Casa del Arte una exposición retrospectiva de Roberto Matta. Y a
5 Roberto Matta en persona para la inauguración.

—Es mi oportunidad, repitió Salomón Bobadilla, ansioso. No me pregunten cómo se consiguió una chaqueta y una corbata, y menos podré[b] explicar cómo Salomón Bobadilla pudo infiltrarse entre los
10 exclusivos asistentes al cóctel con que se abría la muestra artística.

Allí, en medio de[c] autoridades civiles y militares, Salomón Bobadilla se acercó furtivamente[d] al maestro. Y cuando al fin estuvo a un metro de distancia, como si fuese un invitado de largo abolengo[e] le preguntó:
15 —Don Roberto, ¿cuándo va a pasar sus pinturas en limpio[f]? Eso tenía[g] Salomón Bobadilla: siempre cumplía sus promesas.

[a]desde... *many years ago* [b]menos... *even less will I be able* [c]en... *in the midst of* [d]se... *stealthily approached* [e]como... *as if he were an important guest* [f]pasar... *create the final version of your paintings* [g]Eso... *That's one thing you can really say about*

Source: Hispanic Fiesta. Reprinted by permission.

Comprensión

A. La exposición. ¿Qué podemos inferir (*infer*) de este microcuento?

	CIERTO	FALSO
1. Bobadilla esperó mucho tiempo para tener la ocasión de conocer al pintor.	☐	☐
2. La exposición de Matta en la Casa del Arte fue un evento importante para la universidad.	☐	☐
3. Muchas personas importantes de la sociedad asistieron a la inauguración.	☐	☐
4. Bobadilla asiste a inauguraciones de arte exclusivas con frecuencia.	☐	☐
5. Bobadilla no se vistió apropiadamente para la inauguración.	☐	☐
6. Matta no pudo asistir a la inauguración de su exposición.	☐	☐
7. Bobadilla decidió no hablar con Matta.	☐	☐

B. Su opinión

1. ¿Cree usted que a Bobadilla le gusta el arte de Matta?
2. ¿Piensa que la pregunta de Bobadilla era apropiada? ¿seria?
3. ¿Cómo cree usted que el pintor reaccionó a la pregunta de Bobadilla?

Proyecto: La recreación de una obra de arte

Paso 1. Elija un cuadro de Roberto Matta o uno de otro pintor hispano que le guste mucho. Llévelo a la clase—impreso (*printed*) en una hoja de papel o como versión digital en su computadora—pero no se lo enseñe a nadie.

Paso 2. En parejas, siéntense espalda contra espalda (*back to back*) para no verse. Uno de ustedes va a mirar y describir su cuadro detalladamente (*in great detail*), mientras que el otro va a escuchar y tratar de recrearlo en una hoja de papel.

Paso 3. Finalmente, comparen el cuadro original con la reproducción. ¿Son similares? ¿Qué diferencias hay? Repitan el proceso, cambiando de papeles (*roles*) y cuadros.

Vocabulario útil

abajo	down, down below
arriba	up, up top
en el fondo	in the background

Textos orales

Mundo laboral

Antes de escuchar

¿Qué debe o puede hacer una persona para prepararse para una entrevista de trabajo? ¿Es normal que alguien se ponga nervioso cuando sabe que tiene una entrevista?

Vocabulario para escuchar

la petición	request	**averigüe**	find out
cualquier	any	**asegúrese**	be sure
la formación	education, training	**la cartera**	portfolio; folder
la carrera	career	**hacer falta**	to need
acerca de	about	**el agradecimiento**	thanks

Comprensión

A. Sugerencias específicas. Haga por lo menos una sugerencia para cada momento del proceso de una entrevista laboral.

1. varios días antes de la entrevista
2. el día antes de la entrevista
3. el mismo día, antes de la entrevista
4. durante la entrevista
5. después de la entrevista

B. El programa de radio. Conteste las siguientes preguntas.

1. ¿Por qué se repite la programación de la semana anterior?
2. Según el programa, ¿cuál es la mejor manera de reducir el estrés de una entrevista?
3. ¿Dónde se puede encontrar el texto del programa?

Aspirantes esperando una entrevista de trabajo

Sturti/E+/Getty Images

En acción

Haga una lista de las cosas que usted hizo antes de su última entrevista de trabajo. ¿Sentía que estaba bien preparado/a para la entrevista? ¿Cómo se sintió al final de la entrevista?

Daniel Ernst/Getty Images

🎤 Entrevista

Use de modelo las preguntas y respuestas de la sección **Entrevista** al principio de este capítulo para hablar de su experiencia laboral y de las condiciones de trabajo que usted tiene ahora o desea tener en el futuro.

💻 Escritura

Un trabajo ideal

En este capítulo usted va a describir un trabajo que, en su opinión, es ideal.

👥 Antes de escribir

En parejas, piensen en las características que debe tener un trabajo ideal. Incluyan muchos aspectos diferentes: el tipo de trabajo/profesión, el sueldo, el horario, el lugar de trabajo, etcétera. Describan el impacto que este empleo puede tener en la comunidad y en la sociedad. Hablen también de la persona ideal para ocupar ese puesto. Es posible que no estén de acuerdo en varias cosas, pero esta conversación los ayudará a planear su ensayo.

Adam Hester/Blend Images

Haciendo un proyecto en una oficina

A escribir

Ahora use las ideas de **Antes de escribir** para escribir su ensayo. Hay más ayuda en Connect.

Para escribir bien

Considere las siguientes opciones para su ensayo.

- Palabras para poner en orden: **al principio, después, primero, segundo, tercero, además**

- Conectores: **por eso, por un lado / por otro lado, sin embargo / no obstante**

- Frases para expresar una opinión personal: **en mi opinión, para mí**

- Estructura para describir cosas ideales o que no existen concretamente: **que** + *subj.* (ejemplo: un trabajo **que sea...**)

✿ En la comunidad

Entreviste a una persona hispana de su universidad o ciudad sobre algunos temas laborales.

Preguntas posibles

- ¿A qué se dedica? (¿Cuál es su trabajo?) ¿Cuánto tiempo hace que se dedica a eso? ¿Le gusta su trabajo? ¿Por qué?
- ¿Vino a este país por razones de trabajo?
- ¿Cómo es la situación laboral en su país de origen?
- ¿Qué piensa de la situación laboral en este país hoy día? ¿Cree que es mejor que cuando llegó a este país o peor?

◻ Producción audiovisual

Filme 2–3 entrevistas en las que (*which*) los entrevistados hablen de las personas que más admiran y expliquen por qué.

Más ideas para el portafolio

- Incluya un aviso clasificado de un trabajo que le interese aunque (*even if*) esté en inglés. Puede traducirlo si quiere. Debe explicar por qué le interesa ese trabajo.
- Escriba un párrafo sobre una persona que tiene una profesión que usted admira. Describa el trabajo que hace y explique por qué usted admira a esa persona.
- Si ha estado jugando Practice Spanish: Study Abroad, en Quest 11 usted aprendió que la catleya es la flor nacional colombiana. Busque en internet la planta o el animal nacional de otro país hispanohablante y haga un afiche (*poster*) con una foto y su propia descripción. ¿Por qué cree usted que escogieron esta planta o animal como representante del país?

Sugerencia: You are now ready to play Quest 11 in **Practice Spanish: Study Abroad.**

EN RESUMEN En este capítulo

AFTER STUDYING THIS CHAPTER I CAN ...

- ☐ name many professions (502)
- ☐ talk about finding and having a job (504)
- ☐ talk about money and finances (505)
- ☐ express future plans using the future (509–511)
- ☐ express probability using the future (513)
- ☐ use time conjunctions to talk about actions in the past, present, and future (515–516)
- ☐ recognize/describe at least 2–3 aspects of Chilean cultures

Gramática en breve

46. The Future

Infinitive + **-é, -ás, -á, -emos, -éis, -án**

Irregular forms: **dir-, habr-, har-, podr-, pondr-, querr-, sabr-, saldr-, tendr-, vendr-** + *future endings*

47. The Subjunctive After Conjunctions of Time

	Future/ Pending	Habitual/ Past
most conjunctions of time	<u>subjunctive</u>	indicative
antes (de) que	<u>subjunctive</u>	<u>subjunctive</u>

Conjunctions: **antes (de) que, cuando, después (de) que, en cuanto, hasta que, tan pronto como**

Vocabulario

Las profesiones y ocupaciones

el/la abogado/a	lawyer
el amo/ama de casa	housekeeper
el/la cajero/a	(check-out) cashier; (bank) teller
el/la cocinero/a	cook; chef
el/la contador(a)	accountant
el hombre / la mujer de negocios	businessperson
el/la ingeniero/a	engineer
el/la maestro/a (de escuela)	schoolteacher
el/la obrero/a	worker, laborer

el/la peluquero/a	hairstylist
el/la periodista	journalist
el/la plomero/a	plumber
el/la sicólogo/a	psychologist
el/la siquiatra	psychiatrist
el/la soldado	soldier
el/la técnico/a	technician
el/la trabajador(a) social	social worker
el/la traductor(a)	translator
el/la vendedor(a)	salesperson

Cognados: el/la analista de sistemas, el/la astronauta, el/la diseñador(a) gráfico/a, el/la electricista, el/la fotógrafo/a, el/la militar, el/la programador(a), el/la veterinario/a

Repaso: el/la artista, el/la asistente de vuelo, el/la bibliotecario/a, el/la camarero/a, el/la consejero/a, el/la dentista, el/la dependiente/a, el/la enfermero/a, el/la mecánico/a, el/la médico/a, el/la profesor(a), el/la secretario/a

El mundo laboral

el/la aspirante	job candidate; applicant
el currículum (vitae)	resumé
el empleo	job; position
bien/mal pagado	well-/poorly paid
de tiempo completo / parcial	full time / part-time
la empresa	corporation; business
la entrevista	interview
el/la entrevistado/a	interviewee
el/la entrevistador(a)	interviewer
el formulario	form (*to fill out*)
el/la gerente	manager
el/la jefe/a	boss
el puesto	job; position
el salario	pay, wages (*often per hour*)
la solicitud	job application (*form*)
el sueldo	salary

Repaso: el mundo, el trabajo

despedir (*like* <u>pedir</u>)	to let (*someone*) go; to fire (*someone*) (*from a job*)
graduarse (me gradúo) (de)	to graduate (from)
<u>hacer</u> una entrevista	to conduct an interview
jubilarse	to retire (*from a job*)
llenar	to fill out (*a form*)
renunciar (a)	to resign (from)
solicitar	to apply for (*a job*)
<u>tener</u> una entrevista	to have an interview

Repaso: conseguir (*like* <u>seguir</u>)

Una cuestión de dinero

ahorrar	to save (*money*)
cobrar	to cash (*a check*); to charge (*someone for an item or service*)
sa<u>c</u>ar (<u>qu</u>)	to withdraw, take out

Cognados: depositar

Repaso: ganar, gastar, pa<u>g</u>ar (<u>gu</u>), prestar

el banco	bank
el billete	bill (*money*)
el cajero automático	automatic teller machine (ATM)
el cheque	check
la cuenta	account
el efectivo	cash
la factura	bill
el interés	interest
la moneda	coin
el préstamo	loan
el presupuesto	budget
el recibo	receipt
la tarjeta bancaria / la tarjeta de débito	credit/debit card

Repaso: la cuenta (*bill*), el dinero, la tarjeta de crédito

a plazos	in installments
con cheque	by check
en efectivo	in cash

Los adjetivos

laboral	work, work-related

Las formas posesivas

mío/a(s)	mine, of mine
tuyo/a(s)	yours, of yours (*fam. sing.*)
suyo/a(s)	your, of yours (*form., sing./pl.*); his, of his; hers, of hers; their, of theirs
nuestro/a(s)	ours, of ours
vuestro/a(s)	yours, of yours (*fam. pl.*)

Las conjunciones de tiempo

después (de) que	after
en cuanto	as soon as
hasta que	until
tan pronto como	as soon as

Repaso: antes (de) que, cuando

Palabras adicionales

al principio de	at the beginning of

Vocabulario personal

Use this space or a vocabulary notebook to write down other words and phrases you learn in this chapter.

18

La actualidad

En este capítulo

VOCABULARY
What's in the news   530
Governments and related topics   532
GRAMMAR
Using the subjunctive in the past   536
Talking about what you *would* do   543
COUNTRY OF FOCUS: SPAIN

Manifestación (*Demonstration*) en la Puerta del Sol, Madrid

Pablo Blazquez Dominguez/Getty Images

ESPAÑA

47,4 (coma cuatro) millones de habitantes

- España es un país donde muchas culturas se han encontrado a través de su milenaria[a] historia. Los fenicios, griegos, romanos y árabes son solo algunos de los más influyentes.

- El nombre del país viene de *Hispania,* el nombre en latín que los romanos le dieron al territorio español cuando era una provincia de su imperio.

- España es un país diverso en geografía, clima y culturas. De hecho,[b] existen otras lenguas oficiales junto al[c] español, como el catalán, el gallego y el vasco.

[a]*a... throughout its thousand-year* [b]*De... In fact*
[c]*junto... besides*

ENTREVISTA

These questions related to the chapter theme are answered here by a native speaker. You will be able to ask and answer them yourself with personal information in the **Entrevista** activity in the **Portafolio** section at the end of the chapter.

Javier Aguirre Pereira contesta las preguntas.

— **¿Es importante para usted estar al día[a] en cuanto a[b] lo que pasa en el mundo?**

— Sí, para mí es importante estar al día sobre lo que pasa en mi país y en el mundo. Y también en mi ciudad, claro.

— **¿Qué medios de comunicación usa principalmente para mantenerse informado? ¿La radio y la televisión? ¿la prensa[c]? ¿internet?**

— Me mantengo informado sobre la actualidad de diferentes maneras. Normalmente, escucho las noticias en el coche camino a[d] la oficina o de vuelta[e] a casa. Pero también leo el periódico en internet. Y en casa vemos el telediario[f] a la hora de cenar.

— **¿Votó en las últimas elecciones? ¿Cree que es importante votar?**

— ¡Por supuesto que sí![g] He votado en todas las elecciones desde que soy mayor de edad.[h] No siempre me gustan los candidatos, la verdad. Pero creo que votar es una responsabilidad en una democracia, no solo un derecho.[i]

[a]*al... up to date* [b]*en... as far as* [c]*press* [d]*camino... on the way to* [e]*de... on the way back* [f]*tv news program* [g]*¡Por... Of course!* [h]*mayor... old enough to vote* [i]*right*

VOCABULARIO: PREPARACIÓN

You can hear the pronunciation of theme vocabulary words and phrases in the eBook.

Las noticias

la huelga
la reportera
el canal de televisión

la manifestación
la estación de radio
el reportero

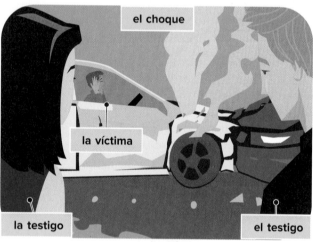

el choque
la víctima
la testigo
el testigo

la crisis climática
el incendio
la bombera
el bombero

Los acontecimientos°	Los... *Events, Happenings*
el asesinato	assassination
asesinar	to assassinate
matar	to kill
el desastre (natural)	(natural) disaster
la esperanza	hope, wish
mantener (*like* **tener**)	to maintain; to keep
la guerra	war
la huelga	strike (*labor*)
la lucha	fight; struggle
luchar	to fight
el medio de comunicación	medium of communication (*pl.* mass media)
la muerte	death
la paz (*pl.* **paces**)	peace

el periódico	newspaper
la prensa	(print) press; news media
la revista	magazine

Cognados: el ataque (terrorista), el blog, la bomba, la erupción, la radio (*medium*), la televisión, el terrorismo, el/la terrorista

El noticiero°	El... *Newscast*
comunicar(se) (**qu**) (con)	to communicate (with)
enterarse (de)	to find out; to learn (about)
estar al día	to be up to date
ofrecer (ofrezco)	to offer

Cognado: informar

Comunicación

Así se dice

el acontecimiento = el evento,
  el hecho, el suceso
estar al día = estar al tanto,
  estar al corriente
la huelga = el paro

A. En tertulia. La tertulia es la tradición hispana de reunirse regularmente con un grupo de amigos/colegas para hablar de las noticias del día y otros temas interesantes de la actualidad y comentarlos.

Paso 1. ¿De qué tipo de noticias le interesaría más a usted (*would most interest you*) hablar en una tertulia?

1. ☐ las noticias sobre la política internacional
2. ☐ las noticias sobre la política nacional
3. ☐ las noticias locales de su ciudad o estado
4. ☐ las noticias sobre desastres o tragedias
5. ☐ las noticias de interés humano
6. ☐ las noticias de deportes
7. ☐ las noticias financieras o de negocios
8. ☐ las noticias sobre el arte y la cultura
9. ☐ ¿ ?

Paso 2. Ahora, en grupos de cinco o seis, comparen sus respuestas. ¿Hay temas que les interesen a casi todos los estudiantes de su grupo? ¿Hay temas que no le interesen a nadie?

Paso 3. Con toda la clase, hagan una lista de los medios de comunicación que se usan hoy en día. Luego, pónganlos en orden de popularidad en el mundo de hoy, empezando por el más popular.

B. ¿Quién sabe más? En grupos de tres o cuatro, den un ejemplo actual o histórico de las siguientes cosas o personas.

MODELO: **1.** un reportero → Jorge Ramos Ávalo

1. un reportero / una reportera
2. un asesinato
3. una huelga o una lucha
4. una guerra
5. un desastre natural
6. otro tipo de desastre (por ejemplo, un accidente)
7. un ataque terrorista
8. un canal de televisión o estación de radio

C. Definiciones

Paso 1. Dé las palabras definidas.

1. un programa que nos informa diariamente de lo que pasa en el mundo
2. una muerte violenta causada intencionadamente
3. un medio de comunicación que presenta la información por escrito
4. la persona que investiga y presenta una noticia
5. una persona que emplea la violencia para causar pánico
6. cuando los obreros dejan de trabajar para protestar por su situación laboral o por su salario
7. una persona que está presente cuando ocurre algo y lo ve todo

Paso 2. Ahora, en parejas, definan las siguientes palabras en español.

1. la guerra
2. la muerte
3. el terrorismo
4. ofrecer
5. luchar
6. estar al día

Paso 3. Lean a la clase las definiciones que crearon en el **Paso 2** para que sus compañeros adivinen (*guess*) la palabra definida.

D. Ustedes y los medios de comunicación. En parejas, expresen y justifiquen su opinión sobre las siguientes ideas.

1. El éxito (*success*) de los programas de telerrealidad demuestra que al público no le interesan realmente los problemas actuales del mundo.
2. La prensa de los países democráticos es con frecuencia irresponsable y parcial.
3. Ver la televisión o YouTube es una pérdida (*waste*) de tiempo.
4. Hay demasiado sexo y violencia en las películas y los programas de televisión.
5. Internet es una fuente (*source*) de información tan buena como los otros medios de comunicación.

El gobierno y la responsabilidad cívica

Las personas

el ciudadano /	citizen
la ciudadana	
los/las demás	(the) others
el rey / la reina	king/queen

Cognados: el dictador / la dictadora, el/la representante al congreso, el senador / la senadora

Los conceptos

el deber	responsibility; obligation
el derecho	right
la (des)igualdad	(in)equality
la dictadura	dictatorship
la discriminación	discrimination
la ley	law
el partido (político)	(political) party

la política	politics; policy
el servicio militar	military service

Las acciones

durar	to last
ganar	to win
obedecer (obedezco)	to obey
perder (pierdo)	to lose
postularse (para un cargo /	to run (for a position /
como candidato/a)	as a candidate)
votar	to vote

Así se dice

postularse para (un cargo político) = presentarse a

Comunicación

A. ¿Quién sabe más de política?

Paso 1. ¿Cuánto sabe usted de política? Dé un ejemplo de las siguientes categorías.

1. un país con un rey o una reina
2. un país que tenga o haya tenido una dictadura
3. un dictador o una dictadora
4. un cargo político que dure dos / cuatro / seis años
5. el mes típico para votar en este país
6. un político o una política muy conocido/a hoy en día
7. un partido político de este país
8. un derecho esencial de todos los ciudadanos de este país
9. una causa de la desigualdad social o política

 Paso 2. En parejas, comparen sus respuestas del **Paso 1.** Luego díganle a la clase cuál de ustedes pudo dar ejemplos en más categorías y qué respuestas tienen en común.

Nota cultural: El panorama social y político en el mundo hispano

Aquí hay algunos datos de interés sobre los países de habla española.

- **La mayoría de edad**[a] En el mundo hispano en general se llega a la mayoría de edad a los 18 años, que es la edad en que la ley permite consumir bebidas alcohólicas y obtener el permiso de manejar. También es la edad para votar, aunque[b] en cuatro países se puede votar a partir de[c] los 16 años (la Argentina, Cuba, el Ecuador y Nicaragua).

- **El servicio militar** Hoy día el servicio militar es voluntario en España y la Argentina y obligatorio en la mayoría de los otros países. Sin embargo, «obligatorio» no significa que todo el mundo lo haga o que todo el mundo lo haga de manera igual.

- **Las mujeres en el ejército** Las mujeres pueden ser militares en la Argentina, Chile, Colombia, España y México.

- **Las mujeres en la política** A pesar de[d] la fama del machismo que existe en la cultura hispana y aunque no hay igualdad en la representación de cargos del gobierno, las mujeres han llegado a ser presidentas en varios países (la Argentina, Chile, Costa Rica, Nicaragua, Panamá y el Perú) y también vicepresidentas y primeras ministras, incluso ministras de Defensa aun[e] siendo civiles (en Chile y en España). Además, hay numerosas juezas[f] y mujeres que ocupan otros cargos políticos de importancia.

Sonia Sotomayor, primera jueza hispana de la Corte Suprema de los Estados Unidos

Steven Petteway, Collection of the Supreme Court of the United States

 ¿En cuáles de estos datos hay grandes similitudes (*similarities*) entre su país y los países hispanohablantes?

[a]mayoría... *legal age*   [b]*although*   [c]a... *starting at*   [d]A... *In spite of*   [e]*even*   [f]*judges*

ZUMA Press, Inc./Alamy Stock Photo

Los reyes de España, Felipe VI y Letizia

Vocabulario útil

Aunque... Although ...
De hecho,... In fact ...
En mi opinión,...
Por un lado,... On the one hand ...
Por otro lado,... On the other hand ...
Sin embargo,...

B. El gobierno de España. Complete el siguiente párrafo sobre España con las palabras de la lista.

ciudadano	los demás	rey
ejército	monarquía	servicio militar
gobierno	políticos	vota
igualdad	reina	

España es un país democrático, con principios de _____¹ muy similares a los principios que existen en países con democracias bien establecidas, como los Estados Unidos y el Canadá. Sin embargo, una diferencia es el tipo de _____². En España existe una _____³ parlamentaria, lo que significa que hay un _____⁴ y una _____⁵. Los reyes son figuras representativas, sin poder ejecutivo. Nadie _____⁶ por el rey, pero sí se vota para elegir al presidente y todos _____⁷ cargos _____⁸. España tiene un _____⁹ voluntario; es decir, que no hay _____¹⁰ obligatorio para ningún _____¹¹.

C. ¿Qué opina usted? En parejas, den su opinión sobre las siguientes ideas. Las palabras y expresiones del **Vocabulario útil** los ayudarán a expresar bien sus opiniones.

1. En este país, se permite que consumamos demasiado petróleo (energía, carne, azúcar).
2. Votar es un deber, no un privilegio.
3. En este país, la igualdad de todos no es una realidad todavía.
4. Es posible que una dictadura sea una buena alternativa a la democracia en algunos casos.
5. El personal a cargo (*in charge*) de los servicios básicos de un país (por ejemplo, del agua) no debe tener derecho a declararse en huelga.

Algo sobre la diversidad lingüística de España

España, por su larga y complicada historia, tiene regiones con marcadas diferencias unas de otras, incluyendo diferencias lingüísticas. No solo hay dialectos sino[a] también lenguas diferentes. El español, también llamado castellano tanto en España como en algunos países latinoamericanos, es la lengua mayoritaria; se habla por todo el país. Pero hay otras lenguas que se hablan y son cooficiales en sus regiones. El catalán se habla en Cataluña (donde también hay otra lengua oficial, el aranés) y tiene variantes oficiales en Valencia y las islas Baleares. El gallego se habla en Galicia, la región al noroeste de la península que hace frontera[b] con Portugal. Y también tiene numerosos hablantes el vasco o euskera, que se habla en el País Vasco (con regiones en España y Francia). Es interesante notar que el español, el catalán y el gallego son lenguas romances, es decir, derivadas del latín. En contraste, el vasco no lo es y es muy diferente de los otros idiomas de la península ibérica. En la tabla, se comparan tres palabras comunes en las cuatro lenguas.

español o castellano	catalán	gallego	vasco
hola	hola	ola	kaixo
adiós	adéu	adeus	agur
gracias	gràcies	grazas	eskerrik asko

Mapa lingüístico de España que muestra dónde se hablan las lenguas cooficiales con más hablantes

 ¿Cree usted que hay diferencias lingüísticas muy marcadas en los Estados Unidos? Si las hay, ¿puede explicar a qué se deben?

[a]*but* [b]*border*

Textos de todos los días: Secciones de un periódico

Probablemente usted se entera de las noticias de forma electrónica. ¿Las recibe automáticamente o entra en un periódico de su preferencia? En este capítulo va a aprender los nombres de las secciones típicas de un periódico en español.

Objetivo: Leer un periódico digital en español para identificar seis de las secciones más relevantes y tomar nota de los titulares (*headlines*) de una noticia en cada categoría.

Antes de empezar

- Piense en las categorías que hay en un periódico nacional de su país y en cómo se encuentran en la versión digital. ¿Dónde se puede encontrar la barra de menú para seleccionarlas?

- ¿Qué se ve cuando se entra en el sitio del periódico que usted más lee en inglés? (Esto es como la portada [*front cover*] de un periódico tradicional). ¿Son todas las noticias sobre el mismo tema?

- Entre en la página de un periódico digital en español. Aquí hay una lista de algunos de los diarios más leídos en el mundo hispanohablante pero hay muchas otras opciones.

Clarín, Argentina (clarin.com)

El País, España (elpais.com)

El Tiempo, Colombia (eltiempo.com)

La República, Perú (larepublica.pe)

La Tercera, Chile (latercera.com)

Milenio, México (milenio.com)

	Sección	Titular
1.	Internacional	
2.	Opinión	
3.	...	

GRAMÁTICA

 Repaso

The forms of the past subjunctive, which you will learn in **Gramática 48,** are based on the third person plural of the preterite. Here is a brief review of that preterite form.

- regular **-ar** verbs: **-ar → -aron**
- regular **-er/-ir** verbs: **-er/-ir → -ieron**
- **-ir** stem-changing verbs: **e → i, o → u** in the stem: **p**i**dieron, d**u**rmieron**
- verbs whose stem ends in a vowel (**leer, construir,** and so on): **-ieron → -yeron: le**y**eron, constru**y**eron**
- irregular preterite stems: **quisieron, hicieron, dijeron,** and so on
- four totally irregular verbs: **ser/ir → fueron, dar → dieron, ver → vieron**

Give the third person plural of the preterite for these infinitives.

1. hablar	**5.** perder	**9.** estar	**13.** traer	**17.** decir
2. comer	**6.** dormir	**10.** tener	**14.** dar	**18.** creer
3. vivir	**7.** reír	**11.** destruir	**15.** saber	**19.** ir
4. jugar	**8.** leer	**12.** mantener	**16.** vestirse	**20.** poder

48 *Queríamos que todo el mundo votara* • The Subjunctive (Part 9): The Past Subjunctive

Gramática en acción: Las últimas elecciones

Indique las condiciones que eran verdaderas para usted sobre las últimas elecciones en su país o estado.

En las últimas elecciones...

1. ☐ yo no tenía edad para votar.
2. ☐ yo tenía edad para votar, pero no voté.
3. ☐ para mí era importante que **votara** mucha gente.
4. ☐ yo dudaba que **ganara** uno de los candidatos que yo apoyaba, ¡pero sí ganó!
5. ☐ no se postuló ningún candidato que me **convenciera** o me **entusiasmara** de verdad.
6. ☐ en mi estado no hubo clases para los niños, para que las escuelas primarias **sirvieran** de centros electorales.

VOTAR ES TU DERECHO Y TU DEBER.

¡No faltes[a]!

Lisa S./Shutterstock

[a]¡No... *Show up!*

Although Spanish has two simple indicative past tenses (preterite and imperfect), it has only one simple subjunctive past tense, the *past subjunctive* (**el imperfecto de subjuntivo**). Generally speaking, this tense is used in the same situations as the present subjunctive but to talk about past events. The exact English equivalent depends on the context in which it is used.

Past Subjunctive of Regular Verbs / **El imperfecto de subjuntivo de los verbos regulares**					
hablar: habla~~ron~~		**comer: comie~~ron~~**		**vivir: vivie~~ron~~**	
habla**ra**	habl**á**ramos	comie**ra**	comi**é**ramos	vivie**ra**	vivi**é**ramos
habla**ras**	hablar**ais**	comie**ras**	comier**ais**	vivie**ras**	vivier**ais**
habla**ra**	habla**ran**	comie**ra**	comie**ran**	vivie**ra**	vivie**ran**

The last elections *Indicate the conditions that were true for you about the last elections in your country or state. In the last elections ...* **1.** *I wasn't old enough to vote.* **2.** *I was old enough to vote, but I didn't vote.* **3.** *it was important to me that many people voted.* **4.** *I doubted that one of the candidates that I supported would win, but he did win!* **5.** *there was no candidate (lit. no candidate ran) who won me over or about whom I got really enthusiastic.* **6.** *in my state there were no classes for children, so that elementary schools could serve as polling places.*

Forms of the Past Subjunctive / **Las formas del imperfecto de subjuntivo**

1. Past Subjunctive Endings

As you can see in the chart on the previous page, the past subjunctive endings are identical for **-ar, -er,** and **-ir** verbs. Those endings are added to the past subjunctive stem: the third person plural of the preterite minus **-on.** For this reason, the forms of the past subjunctive reflect all of the irregularities of the third person preterite (points 2–4, below).

An alternate form of the past subjunctive ends in **-se: hablase, hablases, hablase, hablásemos, hablaseis, hablasen.** This form will not be practiced in *Puntos de partida.*

Las terminaciones del imperfecto de subjuntivo			
verbos en -ar		**verbos en -er / -ir**	
-ara	-áramos	-iera	-iéramos
-aras	-arais	-ieras	-ierais
-ara	-aran	-iera	-ieran

---

2. The Past Subjunctive of Stem-changing Verbs

• **-ar** and **-er** verbs: no change

> empezar: empezar~~on~~ ➔ **empezara, empezaras,...**
> volver: volvier~~on~~ ➔ **volviera, volvieras,...**

• **-ir** verbs: All persons of the past subjunctive have the vowel change of the third person plural of the preterite.

> Remember that the stem change for the third person preterite of -**ir** verbs is shown in parentheses in vocabulary lists. It is this change that occurs in *all* persons of the past subjunctive.

pedir (pido) (i): pidier~~on~~ ➔

pidiera	pidiéramos
pidieras	pidierais
pidiera	pidieran

dormir (duermo) (u): durmier~~on~~ ➔

durmiera	durmiéramos
durmieras	durmierais
durmiera	durmieran

---

3. The Past Subjunctive of Verbs with Spelling Changes

All persons of the past subjunctive reflect the change from **i** to **y** between two vowels.

Other preterite spelling changes (**c ➔ qu, g ➔ gu, z ➔ c**) do not occur in the past subjunctive because those changes do not appear in the third person plural of the preterite: **bus<u>c</u>aron, pa<u>g</u>aron, empe<u>z</u>aron.**

> **i ➔ y** (caer, construir, creer, destruir, leer, oír)

creer: creyer~~on~~ ➔

creyera	creyéramos
creyeras	creyerais
creyera	creyeran

---

4. The Past Subjunctive of Verbs with Irregular Preterites

The same formula (endings are added to the third person plural of the preterite) applies to all irregular verbs.

dar: dier~~on~~ ➔

diera	diéramos
dieras	dierais
diera	dieran

dar:	dier~~on~~ ➔ **diera,...**	querer:	quisier~~on~~ ➔ **quisiera,...**
decir:	dijer~~on~~ ➔ **dijera,...**	**saber:**	supier~~on~~ ➔ **supiera,...**
estar:	estuvier~~on~~ ➔ **estuviera,...**	**ser:**	fuer~~on~~ ➔ **fuera,...**
hacer:	hicier~~on~~ ➔ **hiciera,...**	**tener:**	tuvier~~on~~ ➔ **tuviera,...**
ir:	fuer~~on~~ ➔ **fuera,...**	**traer:**	trajer~~on~~ ➔ **trajera...**
poder:	pudier~~on~~ ➔ **pudiera,...**	**venir:**	vinier~~on~~ ➔ **viniera,...**
poner:	pusier~~on~~ ➔ **pusiera,...**		

5. The Imperfect Subjunctive of *hay* → *hubiera (haber)*

As in the present/past (indicative and subjunctive) and future, one word, **hubiera**, expresses *there was/were* or *there would be*. It is used for singular and plural.

Nadie esperaba que **hubiera** un huracán en abril.
No one expected (that) there would be a hurricane in April.

Dudo que **hubiera más de cien personas** en la protesta.
I doubt (that) there were more than 100 people in the protest.

6. The Past Perfect Subjunctive

Spanish also has a *past perfect subjunctive* (**el pluscuamperfecto de subjuntivo**), used in contexts in which both the pluperfect and the subjunctive are needed. The past perfect subjunctive is formed with all the persons of **haber**, like all the other perfect tenses, followed by the past participle of the verb.

You will not practice this tense in *Puntos de partida*, but you can find a more detailed presentation of it in Appendix 4 (Additional Perfect Tenses).

hubiera		
hubieras		
hubiera	**+**	participio pasado =
hubiéramos		**hablado / comido / escrito...**
hubierais		
hubieran		

Yo dudaba que **hubieran asistido** más de cien personas a la protesta.
I doubted that more than 100 people had attended the protest.

La policía buscaba a alguien que **hubiera sido** testigo del accidente.
The police were looking for someone who would have been a witness to the accident.

Uses of the Past Subjunctive / Los usos del imperfecto de subjuntivo

1. Expressing Past Events

The past subjunctive usually has the same uses as the present subjunctive, but for talking about the past. Compare the pairs of sentences here. The first sentence in each pair is in the present tense, the second in the past.

El presidente **quiere** que los ciudadanos **se enteren** de la tragedia inmediatamente.
The president wants the citizens to find out about the tragedy immediately.
El presidente **quería** que los ciudadanos **se enteraran** de la tragedia inmediatamente.
The president wanted the citizens to find out about the tragedy immediately.

Siento que mis padres no **puedan** estar allí esta noche.
I'm sorry (that) my parents can't be there tonight.
Sentí que mis padres no **pudieran** estar allí anoche.
I was sorry (that) my parents couldn't be there last night.

Dudamos que esos países **mantengan** la paz.
We doubt (that) those countries will keep the peace.
Dudábamos que esos países **mantuvieran** la paz.
We doubted (that) those countries would keep the peace.

2. Subjunctive "Triggers"
Remember that the subjunctive is used after:

(1) expressions of influence, emotion, and doubt/denial

(2) nonexistent and indefinite antecedents

(3) conjunctions of contingency and purpose, as well as those of time

(1) **Era necesario** que **nos enteráramos** de todo.
It was necessary for us to learn about everything.
(1) **Temí** que no **pudieran** ir a Granada.
I was afraid (that) they couldn't go to Granada.
(1) **No creía** que **hubiera** tiempo para hacerlo.
I didn't think (that) there was time to do it.
(2) **No había nadie** que **pudiera** resolverlo.
There wasn't anyone who could (might have been able to) solve it.
(3) Los padres **trabajaron** mucho **para que** sus hijos **asistieran** a la universidad.
The parents worked hard so that their children could (might) go to the university.
(3) Anoche, **íbamos** a salir **en cuanto llegara** Felipe.
Last night, we were going to leave as soon as Felipe arrived.

3. Past Subjunctive of *querer* to Express Requests

The past subjunctive of the verb **querer** is often used to make a request sound more polite.

Quisiéramos hablar con usted enseguida.
We would like to speak with you immediately.
Quisiera un café, por favor.
I would like a cup of coffee, please.

Práctica y comunicación

A. Cuando era adolescente

> **Paso 1. Autoprueba.** Dé la forma del pasado de subjuntivo de los siguientes verbos.
>
> | | | | |
> |---|---|---|---|
> | **1.** quise | **3.** salí | **5.** estuve | **7.** pedí |
> | **2.** tuve | **4.** supe | **6.** traje | **8.** leí |

Summary of the Imperfect Subjunctive

Third person plural of the preterite minus **-on** + **-a, -as, -a, -amos, -ais, -an**

Paso 2. Complete las oraciones con el pasado de subjuntivo para que sean verdaderas para usted cuando usted tenía más o menos 13 años.

(No) Era obligatorio que yo...

1. _____ (ir) a un servicio religioso _____ (en la iglesia / la mezquita / el templo...)
2. _____ (sacar) buenas notas para poder recibir el estipendio (*allowance*) semanal
3. _____ (poner) la mesa con frecuencia
4. _____ (leer) casi todos los días
5. _____ (mantener) mi cuarto ordenado

Mis padres no querían que... / A mis padres no les importaba que...

6. _____ (*yo:* tener) novio o novia
7. _____ (*yo:* estar) solo/a en casa
8. _____ (*yo:* mirar) la tele o cualquier (*any*) pantalla por más de dos horas al día
9. _____ (*yo:* comer) demasiada comida rápida
10. mis amigos _____ (venir) a casa cuando ellos no estaban

Paso 3. Ahora, en parejas, entrevístense sobre las ideas del **Paso 2.** Luego díganle a la clase algo que tenían en común o que era muy diferente para cada uno de ustedes.

MODELO: **1. E1:** Cuando tenías 13 años, ¿era necesario que fueras a un servicio religioso?
E2: No, para mí no era necesario. ¿Y para ti?
E1: Para mí tampoco. / Para mí sí.

B. Noticias

Paso 1. Empareje cada idea de la **Columna A** con una de la **Columna B.** Luego conjugue el verbo de la **Columna B** en el presente de subjuntivo para formar una oración completa y lógica.

COLUMNA A

1. _____ El Presidente pide que la Guardia Nacional...
2. _____ El Congreso ha votado una nueva ley para que...
3. _____ La policía va de puerta en puerta buscando a alguien que...
4. _____ La Ministra de Defensa dice que espera que...
5. _____ La Corte Suprema proclama que no es legal que...
6. _____ Los bomberos van a rescatar (*rescue*) a la víctima antes de que...

COLUMNA B

a. _____ (saber) algo del crimen
b. _____ (colapsar) el edificio
c. _____ (haber) más ayuda económica para los estudiantes
d. _____ (ir) al lugar del desastre natural
e. los sospechosos _____ (estar) detenidos sin pruebas (*proof*)
f. la intervención militar _____ (ser) corta

Paso 2. Ahora ponga las oraciones del **Paso 1** en el pasado, usando el pretérito del verbo principal y haciendo otros cambios necesarios.

MODELO: Para no ir a la huelga, los obreros exigen que la compañía les dé un aumento de sueldo. → Para no ir a la huelga, los obreros **exigieron** que la compañía les **diera** un aumento de sueldo.

Una sesión en el Congreso español

Evrim Aydin/Anadolu Agency/Getty Images

Prác. A, Paso 1: Answers: 1. quisiera 2. tuviera 3. saliera 4. supiera 5. estuviera 6. trajera 7. pidiera 8. leyera

Gramática

quinientos treinta y nueve ■ **539**

C. Acontecimientos históricos

Vocabulario útil

los colonos ingleses en los
   Estados Unidos / Australia
los cuáqueros Quakers
los españoles y los
   portugueses
grupos de Asia / de África /
   del Medio Oriente
los irlandeses

Paso 1. Complete las siguientes oraciones con la forma correcta del imperfecto de subjuntivo de uno de los verbos de la lista. Si puede, nombre un grupo al que puede referirse cada oración.

   haber   poder   practicar   seguir   tener

   1. Las leyes de su país de origen no permitían que este grupo _____ libremente su religión.
   2. Estas personas esperaban que _____ oro y plata en América.
   3. El rey no quería que estos criminales _____ viviendo en su país.
   4. Estos inmigrantes buscaban un país donde _____ tener paz y prosperidad.
   5. Este grupo buscaba un país donde sus miembros no _____ que pasar hambre.

Paso 2. Ahora exprese algunos acontecimientos de la historia de los Estados Unidos, haciendo oraciones completas con los siguientes elementos.
¡OJO! El verbo en la primera cláusula debe estar en el pasado.

   1. Inglaterra: _____ (desear) / que / los colonos: _____ (conseguir) más tierras en Norteamérica
   2. los indígenas americanos: _____ (temer) / que / los colonos: _____ (quitarles) sus tierras
   3. el rey de Inglaterra: _____ (querer) / que / los colonos: _____ (pagar) impuestos (*taxes*)
   4. los estadounidenses: _____ (ir) a la guerra / para que / México: _____ (darles) parte de su territorio
   5. a los estados del sur: no _____ (gustarles) / que / los estados del norte: _____ (controlar) las leyes
   6. los abolicionistas: _____ (desear) / que / todas las personas del país: _____ (tener) los mismos derechos

Paso 3. Ahora, en parejas, contesten la siguiente pregunta: ¿Qué buscaban los primeros inmigrantes que llegaron a lo que es hoy los Estados Unidos?

   Buscaban un lugar donde...

Vocabulario útil

haber abundantes recursos naturales
haber menos restricciones / más libertad política y personal
poder practicar su religión
tener que pagar menos impuestos (*taxes*)

D. Hace más de cien años. Combine ideas de las dos columnas para describir cómo era la vida a finales del siglo XIX y principios del siglo XX.

COLUMNA A
Las leyes prohibían que...
Los padres esperaban que sus hijas...
Las mujeres tenían que aceptar esposos que...
Los hombres buscaban esposas que...
No había muchas personas que...

COLUMNA B
casarse jóvenes
tener muchos hijos
personas de razas diferentes: casarse
personas de origen africano: ser candidatos políticos
las mujeres: votar
tomar todas las decisiones
aceptar sus decisiones
poder imaginar ¿ ? (un derecho o una situación actual)

E. Una encuesta (*poll*)

Paso 1. Haga cinco oraciones completas con elementos de cada columna. Trate de no repetir muchos elementos.

MODELO: Cuando yo era niña, mi hermana mayor no permitía que yo jugara con sus videojuegos.

cuando yo era niño/a cuando yo era adolescente (13 o 14 años) cuando yo estaba en el último año de la escuela secundaria	**+**	(yo) mi madre/padre mis padres mi mejor amigo/a mi hermano/a mis hermanos (no) era necesario/imposible ¿ ?	**+**	tener miedo de (que)... (no) querer (que)... necesitar un trabajo para (que)... prohibir que... (no) permitir que... (no) gustar (que)... ¿ ?

Paso 2. Ahora convierta sus oraciones del **Paso 1** en preguntas generales sobre los temas que usted escogió. Use las preguntas para encuestar (*poll*) a cinco compañeros de clase para ver si tuvieron experiencias similares.

MODELO: Cuando eras niño, ¿te permitían tus hermanos que jugaras con sus videojuegos?

Paso 3. Dígale a la clase por lo menos dos detalles interesantes de su encuesta.

F. Con mucha cortesía

Paso 1. Lea el dibujo y conteste las preguntas.

1. ¿Dónde está el niño?
2. ¿Qué hora será?
3. ¿Qué problema tiene el niño?
4. ¿Cómo demuestra (*shows*) el niño que es muy cortés y considerado?
5. ¿Por qué usa el niño tanta cortesía?

No te preocupes, mamá; no me pasa nada. Solo quisiera saber si podría volver otra vez[a] más tarde, en caso de que tuviera sed o me pasara algo.

[a]podría... *I could come back again*

Paso 2. Ahora, en parejas, digan cómo pedirían (*you would ask for*) lo que necesitan en las siguientes situaciones.

1. Usted quiere el número de teléfono de una persona que acaba de conocer. Habla con un amigo de él/ella.
2. Ustedes quieren saber cuándo es el examen final en esta clase y qué va a incluir.
3. Usted necesita una extensión del plazo para la tarea de este capítulo.
4. Usted necesita una carta de recomendación del profesor / de la profesora.
5. Usted ha llamado a un amigo a las diez de la noche para invitarlo a salir, pero él ya estaba dormido y usted lo ha despertado.
6. Usted llega a casa muy enfermo/a, con tos y fiebre. Debe guardar cama. Pero la persona con quien vive le ha preparado una fiesta sorpresa de cumpleaños. Todos sus amigos lo/la saludan cuando entra.

G. ¡Ojalá!

Paso 1. Complete las siguientes oraciones lógicamente.

1. Ojalá que (yo) tuviera…
2. Ojalá que (yo) pudiera…
3. Ojalá inventaran una máquina que…
4. Ojalá solucionaran el problema de…
5. Ojalá que en esta universidad fuera posible…

Paso 2. ¿Qué dirían (*would say*) estas personas en las siguientes situaciones?

1. el presidente / la presidenta de un país en guerra
2. un político / una política, durante una campaña electoral muy disputada
3. una persona que está muy enferma
4. un niño que quiere un juguete (*toy*) de último modelo muy caro (¡piense en lo que usted deseaba de niño/a!)
5. un(a) estudiante que tiene que pedir un préstamo para pagar la matrícula

---

Algo sobre el flamenco

El flamenco no es la música típica de todas las regiones españolas, pero es sin duda la música que más se asocia con España a nivel internacional. Tiene su origen en Andalucía, la región más al sur, y lleva la marca indeleble del pueblo gitano.[a]

El flamenco es un género musical de gran diversidad que va desde canciones muy lentas y tristes a muy animadas y alegres. Los cantantes de flamenco se llaman cantaores y el instrumento tradicional es la guitarra acompañada de las palmas.[b] Los bailaores, que son los bailarines de flamenco, también hacen música con el taconeo[c] de sus zapatos.

¿Hay algún género musical en este país que incluya instrumentos musicales, canciones y bailes al mismo tiempo?

Un espectáculo de flamenco, con una bailaora, un cantaor y otros músicos

Image Professionals GmbH/ Alamy Stock Photo

[a]*Romani*   [b]*acompañada... accompanied by clapping*   [c]*stamping*

Repaso

In **Gramática 49** you will learn the forms and uses of the conditional. You have already learned one conditional form: **me gustaría (Capítulo 8).** Review what you know by giving the English equivalent of the following sentence.

Hoy **me gustaría** ir al museo.

Knowing the future, which you studied in **Gramática 46 (Capítulo 17),** will help you learn the conditional. Can you provide the correct future forms of the following verbs?

1. (yo) viajar
2. (ellos) beber
3. (tú) ir

4. (usted) venir
5. (nosotros) hacer
6. (ella) poner

49 Expressing What You Would Do • Conditional Verb Forms

Gramática en acción: Un mundo utópico

En un mundo ideal...

- **habría** paz en todos los países.
- no **tendríamos** una crisis climática.
- todas las personas **vivirían** con los mismos derechos y oportunidades.
- nadie **cometería** ningún acto criminal.
- ningún niño **sufriría** de hambre ni de enfermedades.

¿Y usted?

¿Cómo **sería** un mundo ideal si usted pudiera cambiarlo? ¿Qué otras características **añadiría** usted?

En mi mundo ideal,

1. (no) **habría** _____.
2. todo el mundo **podría** _____.
3. nadie **tendría** _____.
4. yo **sería** _____ (profesión/adjetivo)

The phrase **me gustaría** expresses what you *would like* to (do, say, and so on). The verb **gustaría** is a conditional form. You will learn to form the *conditional* (**el condicional**) of all verbs in this section.

Conditional of Regular Verbs / **El condicional de los verbos regulares**		
hablar	**comer**	**vivir**
hablar<u>ía</u> hablar<u>íamos</u>	comer<u>ía</u> comer<u>íamos</u>	vivir<u>ía</u> vivir<u>íamos</u>
hablar<u>ías</u> hablar<u>íais</u>	comer<u>ías</u> comer<u>íais</u>	vivir<u>ías</u> vivir<u>íais</u>
hablar<u>ía</u> hablar<u>ían</u>	comer<u>ía</u> comer<u>ían</u>	vivir<u>ía</u> vivir<u>ían</u>

A perfect world *In an ideal world ...* ■ *there would be peace in all countries.* ■ *we wouldn't have a climate crisis.* ■ *everyone would live with the same rights and opportunities.* ■ *no one would engage in any criminal acts.* ■ *no child would be hungry or sick.*

1. Conditional Endings

In English the conditional, like the future, is a compound tense, formed with the auxiliary (helping) verb *would: I* **would** *speak, you* **would** *do,* and so on.

The Spanish *conditional* (**el condicional**), like the future, is a simple verb form (only one word). It is formed by adding the identical set of conditional endings to **-ar, -er,** and **-ir** infinitives. No auxiliary verb is needed.

Las terminaciones del condicional		
infinitivo +	-ía	-íamos
	-ías	-íais
	-ía	-ían

2. Irregular Conditional Forms

Verbs that form the future on an irregular stem use the same stem to form the conditional.

decir: diría, dirías, diría, diríamos, diríais, dirían

decir:	dir-	
hacer:	har-	
poder:	podr-	-ía
poner:	pondr-	-ías
querer:	querr-	-ía
saber:	sabr-	-íamos
salir:	saldr-	-íais
tener:	tendr-	-ían
venir:	vendr-	

3. The Conditional of *hay → habría (haber)*

As in the present/past (indicative and subjunctive) and future, one word, **habría,** expresses *there would be.* It is used for singular and plural.

No **habría** **más de 10 personas** en la sala.
There wouldn't be more than 10 people in the room.

Los trabajadores anunciaron que **habría** una huelga.
The workers announced that there would be a strike.

4. The Conditional Perfect Tense

Spanish also has a *conditional perfect* tense (**el condicional perfecto**) that is used to express what *would have occurred* at a certain time. The conditional perfect is formed with all the persons of **haber,** like all the other perfect tenses, followed by the past participle of the verb.

You will not practice this tense in *Puntos de partida,* but you can find a more detailed presentation of it in Appendix 4 (Additional Perfect Tenses).

habría		
habrías		
habría	+	participio pasado =
habríamos		**hablado / comido / escrito...**
habríais		
habrían		

Con mejor publicidad, más personas **habrían asistido** al evento.
With better publicity, more people would have attended the event.
Con más bomberos, se **habría podido** apagar el incendio antes.
With more firefighters, the fire could have been extinguished earlier.

5. Uses of the Conditional

Most uses of the Spanish conditional are the same as those of the conditional in English.

- to express what you *would* do in a particular situation or given a particular set of circumstances

—Manuel, **¿hablarías** español en Portugal?
—No, **hablaría** portugués.
"Manuel, would you speak Spanish in Portugal?"
"No, I would speak Portuguese."

—**¿Irías** a la playa en las islas Canarias?
—Sí, claro. Me **gustaría** nadar allí.
"Would you go to the beach in the Canary Islands?"
"Yes, of course. I would like to swim there."

- to report what someone said that he/she/they *was/were going to do*, that is, to express the future from the point of view of the past

MANUEL: —Iré a Madrid en enero. → Manuel dijo que **iría** a Madrid en enero.
MANUEL: *"I'll go to Madrid in January."* → *Manuel said that **he would go** to Madrid in January.*
ANITA Y CARLOS: —Iremos a la manifestación esta noche. → Anita y Carlos dijeron que **irían** a la manifestación esta noche.
ANITA AND CARLOS: *"We'll go to the demonstration tonight."* → *Anita and Carlos said that **they would go** to the demonstration tonight.*

6. Another Way to Express *would*

Remember that *would = used to* (a habitual action) is expressed with the imperfect tense in Spanish.

Manuel **iba** a España todos los veranos.
Manuel would (used to) go to Spain every summer.

Práctica y comunicación

Summary of the Conditional

Infinitive + **-ía, -ías, -ía, -íamos, -íais, -ían**

A. ¿Qué haría usted en España?

Paso 1. Autoprueba. Complete las siguientes formas del condicional.

1. salir: sal____ía
2. hacer: ha____íamos
3. querer: que____ías
4. decir: d____ían
5. tener: ten____ía
6. poder: po____ía

Paso 2. Para describir un posible viaje a España, complete las siguientes oraciones con la forma apropiada del condicional y la información indicada.

1. _____ (Ir) a España con _____.
2. _____ (Viajar) en _____ (mes o estación) porque _____.
3. _____ (Hablar) español todo el tiempo para _____.
4. _____ (Comer) _____ (plato[s], comidas).
5. _____ (Ver) un espectáculo de _____.
6. _____ (Querer) _____ (infinitivo) durante el viaje.
7. _____ (Gustar) conocer a _____ durante mi visita.
8. No _____ (poder) volver a casa sin _____ (infinitivo).

 Paso 3. Ahora, en parejas, entrevístense sobre las oraciones del **Paso 1.** Luego añadan a la lista dos cosas más que harían en su viaje y díganselas a la clase.

MODELO: **1. E1:** ¿Con quién irías a España?
E2: Iría con mi hermana mayor, porque habla español y juntas nos divertimos mucho. ¿Y tú?

Algo sobre las tapas

Las tapas son pequeños platos de comida que se toman como aperitivos o en lugar del almuerzo o la cena. Es una distintiva manera española no solo de comer sino[a] de socializar en los muchos bares que existen en cualquier[b] ciudad del país. Las tapas son siempre comida salada[c] (nunca postres). Pueden ser platos fríos o calientes, simples o complicados. El concepto de las tapas ha alcanzado[d] ahora cierta popularidad en los Estados Unidos y en otros países.

En su opinión, ¿cuál es una de las comidas o tipo de comida más distintivamente estadounidense?

[a]*but also*   [b]*any*   [c]*con sal*   [d]*achieved*

Algunas de las tapas típicas españolas: calamares (*squid*) fritos, camarones, sardinas, aceitunas (*olives*) y mejillones (*mussels*)

Jenny Cundy/Image Source

B. **¿Es posible escapar?**

Paso 1. Cuente la siguiente fantasía de una pareja, dando la forma condicional de los verbos.

Necesitamos escapar de todo esto... Pensamos que _____ (deber)[1] ir al Caribe... No _____ (trabajar)[2]... _____ (Poder)[3] nadar todos los días... _____ (Tomar)[4] el sol en la playa... _____ (Beber)[5] el agua de un coco... _____ (Ver)[6] bellos lugares naturales... El viaje _____ (ser)[7] ideal...

Pero... , tarde o temprano, _____ (tener)[8] que volver a lo de siempre... a los rascacielos de la ciudad... al tráfico... al medio ambiente contaminado... al trabajo... _____ (Poder)[9] usar tarjetas de crédito, como dice el anuncio —pero ¡_____ (tener)[10] que pagar después!

Paso 2. Comprensión. ¿Cierto, falso o no lo dice? Corrija las oraciones falsas.

	CIERTO	FALSO	NO LO DICE.
1. Esta pareja trabaja en una ciudad grande.	☐	☐	☐
2. No les interesan los deportes acuáticos.	☐	☐	☐
3. Pueden pagar este viaje de sueños en efectivo.	☐	☐	☐
4. Quisieran hacer el viaje con sus padres.	☐	☐	☐

C. **¿Qué dijo?**

Paso 1. Repita lo que dijeron las siguientes personas.

MODELO: María: —Llegaré el lunes por la noche. →
María **dijo que llegaría** el lunes por la noche.

1. Tomás: —Estaré en el café a las dos.
2. Marta y Clara: —Vamos a hacer una fiesta este sábado.
3. La profesora de español: —Salgo para Madrid pronto.
4. Los padres: —Nos vemos en casa.
5. Usted: —No podré ir al cine con ustedes.
6. Yo: —No tener tiempo para ir de compras.

Paso 2. Ahora, en parejas, digan lo que dijeron algunas personas o noticieros recientemente, usando un elemento de cada columna.

MODELO: el pronóstico del tiempo →
El pronóstico del tiempo **dijo que** este fin de semana **haría** buen tiempo.

COLUMNA A	COLUMNA B
el pronóstico del tiempo	haber un examen el día _____
el profesor / la profesora	hacer buen/mal tiempo _____ (día / el fin de semana)
de español	(no) haber un examen final
otro profesor / otra	(no) venir a visitarme pronto
profesora	ser necesario escribir un ensayo sobre _____
su padre/madre	querer estudiar juntos para un examen
su mejor amigo/a	¿ ?

Nota comunicativa: Cláusulas con *si*

To express hypothetical situations, Spanish uses sentences with **si** (*if*) clauses, just like English.*

if CLAUSE	RESULT
si + *past subjunctive*	*conditional*
Si yo **pudiera,**	**iría** a España de vacaciones.
If I could,	*I would go to Spain on vacation.*
Si yo **fuera** tú,	no **haría** eso.
If I were you,	*I wouldn't do that.*

You are already familiar with **si** clauses with the present indicative. They present actions that are habitual in the present or likely to happen.

Si ahorro suficiente dinero, **iré** de vacaciones a España.
If I save enough money, I'll go to Spain on vacation.

You will create **si**-clause sentences in **Práctica D** through **H**.

¡OJO!

The present subjunctive is never used after **si**.

---

*These contrary-to-fact situations express speculations about the present and the future. The perfect forms of the conditional and the past subjunctive are used to speculate about the past; that is, what would have happened if a particular event had occurred: Si **hubiera tenido** el dinero, **habría hecho** el viaje. (If **I had had** the money, **I would have made** the trip.) You will find a more detailed presentation of this structure in Appendix 4 (Additional Perfect Tenses).

Capítulo 18 La actualidad

D. Si usted fuera...

Paso 1. Conteste las preguntas según sus preferencias.

Si usted fuera...

1. una puerta, ¿estaría cerrada, abierta o entreabierta (*half open*)?
2. científico/a, ¿qué investigaría (*would you do research on*)?
3. inmensamente rico/a, ¿dónde tendría una casa?
4. un libro, ¿sería un libro de texto, un libro de historia, un libro de poemas o una novela?
5. un animal, ¿cuál sería?
6. un personaje (*character*) de ficción, ¿cuál le gustaría ser?

Paso 2. Ahora, en parejas, túrnense para comparar sus oraciones del **Paso 1.** Luego díganle a la clase lo que ustedes tienen en común.

E. Situaciones

Paso 1. Empareje los siguientes dibujos con las descripciones. Luego complete las descripciones, conjugando los verbos y añadiendo los detalles necesarios.

a.　　　　　　　b.　　　　　　　c.　　　　　　　d.

_____ **1.** Miriam _____ (ir) en coche al trabajo como siempre si su coche no _____ (tener) un serio problema con los frenos. Si su padre _____ (vivir) cerca, _____ (poder) arreglarlo él, pero (él)...

_____ **2.** Si el avión no _____ (ser) tan pequeño, la Sra. Blanco no _____ (tener) tanto miedo. _____ (Preferir) ir en coche, pero es un caso de emergencia: su hijo...

_____ **3.** Si Mariana _____ (tener) suficiente dinero, ahora mismo _____ (comprar) ese traje pantalón. _____ (Ser) ideal para... (un evento o una situación)

_____ **4.** Si la compañera de casa de Julia _____ (poder) llevarla al trabajo, Julia _____ (seguir) durmiendo hasta las ocho por lo menos. Y Julia no _____ (estar) tan cansada si...

Paso 2. Ahora imagine una solución para cada situación. Use el futuro para expresar lo que pasará. ¡Sea imaginativo/a!

MODELO: **3.** Mariana le pedirá dinero a... Esta persona no se lo dará / se lo dará como regalo de cumpleaños.

F. ¿En qué circunstancias lógicas... ? En parejas, hagan y contesten preguntas sobre los siguientes temas.

MODELO: comprar un coche nuevo →
E1: ¿En qué circunstancias **comprarías** un coche nuevo?
E2: **Compraría** un coche nuevo **si tuviera** más dinero.

1. dejar de estudiar en esta universidad
2. emigrar a otro país
3. estudiar otro idioma
4. no obedecer a tus padres / a tu jefe/a
5. luchar por su país
6. ser candidato/a para presidente/a
7. no decirle la verdad a un amigo / una amiga

 G. ¿Qué haría si... ?

Paso 1. En parejas, inventen soluciones para los siguientes dilemas.

1. Si su mejor amigo/a le pidiera 500 dólares para algo muy urgente.
2. Si su compañera/o de apartamento usara su champú sin pedir permiso.
3. Si usted encontrara 100 dólares en un salón de clase.
4. Si de pronto tuviera un millón de dólares hoy.

Paso 2. Ahora inventen una situación bien difícil de resolver que la clase tiene que solucionar. ¡Sean imaginativos!

 H. Si el mundo fuera diferente... ¿Qué ocurriría si el mundo fuera diferente? En parejas, hablen de las siguientes circunstancias.

MODELO: Si yo fuera la única (*only*) persona en el mundo... →
• **tendría** que aprender a hacer muchas cosas.
• **sería** la persona más importante —y más ignorante— del mundo.

1. Si yo pudiera tener solamente un amigo o amiga, _____.
2. Si yo tuviera que pasar un año en una isla desierta, _____.
3. Si yo fuera _____ (otra persona), _____.
4. Si el presidente / la presidenta fuera _____, _____.
5. Si yo vlvlera en (nombre de país), _____.

Algo sobre Don Quijote de la Mancha

El ingenioso hidalgo[a] *Don Quijote de la Mancha*,[b] de Miguel de Cervantes, es una de las obras cumbres[c] de la literatura mundial. Se considera la primera novela moderna y es el libro más editado y traducido del mundo, después de la Biblia.

La novela cuenta la historia de don Quijote, un señor mayor que se vuelve loco[d] y decide hacerse[e] caballero andante[f] como los[g] de las novelas que le encanta leer. Por eso toma un escudero,[h] Sancho Panza, que en realidad es solo un campesino local. Sancho intenta disuadir a su señor de meterse en líos.[i] Juntos pasarán por una larga serie de aventuras que revelan la naturaleza humana. Don Quijote es un símbolo del espíritu humano que siempre lucha por algo noble, aunque[j] sean causas perdidas, mientras que Sancho Panza es símbolo de lealtad.[k]

 ¿Qué figura de la literatura de este país es icónica? ¿Qué representa?

[a]*nobleman* [b]*region in the center of Spain* [c]*obras... masterpieces* [d]*se... goes mad* [e]*to become* [f]*caballero... a knight errant* [g]*those* [h]*squire* [i]*de... from getting himself into trouble* [j]*even if* [k]*loyalty*

Pixtal/age fotostock

Hay estatuas de don Quijote de la Mancha y Sancho Panza por todo el país. Estas están en la Plaza de España, en Madrid.

Todo junto

A. Lengua y cultura: Maneras de practicar el español fuera de clase

Paso 1. Completar. Complete the following paragraphs with the correct form of the words in parentheses, as suggested by context. When two possibilities are given, select the correct word. **¡OJO!** As you conjugate verbs, decide whether to use the subjunctive (present, present perfect, or past) or the indicative (present, present perfect, future, preterite, or imperfect). For items flagged with *comm.*, use a command. Start out in the present.

Una joven mira una serie en español.

Claro está que usted habla español en clase. También es probable que lo _____ (hablar)[1] con su profesor(a) cuando lo/la _____ (ver)[2] en el campus de la universidad. Pero (por / para)[3] hablar español con soltura,[a] usted tiene que practicar más.

«¡Ojalá que _____ (*yo:* poder)[4] practicar español fuera de clase!» ¿_____ (*pres. perf.:* Decir)[5] usted eso alguna vez? Pues hay muchas maneras de hacerlo. Por ejemplo, los compañeros de una misma clase de español siempre pueden hablar español cuando _____ (verse)[6] para no _____ (perder)[7] _____ (ninguno)[8] oportunidad de practicar.

Otra idea es _____ (mirar)[9] una telenovela[b] o (un / una)[10] programa de noticias en español. También puede escuchar la radio cuando _____ (manejar)[11]. Lo importante es dedicar un rato[c] a escuchar español auténtico con frecuencia. Muchas personas _____ (sentirse)[12] muy frustradas con estas actividades _____ (por qué/porque)[13] no pueden comprenderlo todo. Pero _____ (haber)[14] que recordar que no es necesario entender cada una de las palabras que se oyen. Para los estudiantes principiantes,[d] es suficiente identificar (el / la)[15] tema y _____ (alguno)[16] palabras y expresiones. Si usted _____ (escuchar)[17] español habitualmente en los medios de comunicación, _____ (aprender)[18] mucho... y rápidamente.

Otra actividad útil es leer el periódico o una revista de actualidad en español. _____ (*comm., Usted:* Buscar)[19] un sitio en internet. (Por / Para)[20] ejemplo, muchos gobiernos tienen páginas relacionadas con el turismo.

Finalmente, _____ (*comm., usted:* recordar)[21] su propia comunidad. Es muy posible que usted _____ (vivir)[22] en una ciudad o estado que tiene una comunidad hispana. Le sugerimos que _____ (*usted:* visitar)[23] tiendas o supermercados hispanos para que _____ (*usted:* ver)[24] las cosas que se venden allí. ¡Leer la lista de los ingrediente de cualquier[e] producto es un ejercicio de lectura!

[a]con... *fluently*   [b]*soap opera*   [c]*un... a bit of time*   [d]*beginning*   [e]*any*

Paso 2. Comprensión. Conteste las siguientes preguntas.

1. Además de (*Besides*) hablar español en clase, ¿qué cosas puede usted hacer para practicar el idioma fuera de (*outside of*) la clase?
2. ¿Es buena o mala la idea de mirar la televisión en español? ¿Qué tipos de programas se recomienda ver?
3. ¿Es necesario que un estudiante entienda cada una de las palabras de lo que oye en los medios de comunicación?
4. ¿Qué tipos de lecturas puede usted conseguir en español para practicar más?

Paso 3. En acción

Ahora, en parejas, hablen sobre su futuro con respecto al español. Las siguientes preguntas les darán algunas ideas para su conversación.

1. ¿Van a tomar otra clase de español el próximo semestre/trimestre? ¿Por qué sí o por qué no?

2. ¿Piensan estudiar en un país hispanohablante? ¿En dónde? ¿Cuándo?

3. ¿Creen que en el futuro usarán el español en su trabajo? ¿Por qué?

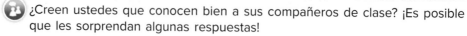

B. Proyecto: Una encuesta (*poll*) sobre decisiones personales

¿Creen ustedes que conocen bien a sus compañeros de clase? ¡Es posible que les sorprendan algunas respuestas!

ImageFlow/Shutterstock

¿Qué preguntas les quiere usted hacer a las personas de su clase?

Paso 1. Preparación. En parejas, preparen cuatro preguntas que presenten dilemas personales. Piensen en temas importantes en la vida, como la familia, los estudios, el trabajo, el medio ambiente y las relaciones sociales. Usen el condicional para indicar la cualidad hipotética de sus preguntas. También pueden usar oraciones hipotéticas con **si**.

MODELOS: ¿**Podrías** pasar más de una semana sin mirar el celular?

Si **tuvieras** la opción de irte a otra universidad, ¿**te irías**?

Vocabulario útil

poder vivir sin la televisión / la computadora / el celular
presentarse como candidato político / candidata política
   a nivel estatal
prestar (*to do*) **servicio militar**
tener más de dos hijos / adoptar hijos
vivir permanentemente en este estado / esta ciudad

Paso 2. Encuesta. Ahora entrevisten a todas las personas que puedan de la clase. Recuerden apuntar (*to take down notes*) de las respuestas.

Paso 3. Información. Finalmente, preparen una breve presentación con los resultados de su encuesta. Añadan un comentario personal a cada una de las respuestas que van a presentar.

MODELO: (No) Nos sorprendió que la mayoría de la clase pensara que no podría pasar más de una semana sin mirar el celular.

Video: Salu2 «¡Noticias!»

You can watch two segments of this chapter's video in the **Video: Salu2** section, found at the end of the eBook.

Klic Video Productions/ McGraw Hill

Una joven mexicana que habla sobre las noticias que le interesan

Enfoque cultural: Sociedad, historia y economía

Antes de leer

¿Cuáles pueden ser las ventajas y desventajas cuando hay una gran diversidad étnica, lingüística y/o cultural en un país?

En España

Roman Babakin/Shutterstock

Edificio del Parlamento de Andalucía, una de las regiones autónomas, con las banderas de Andalucía, España y la Unión Europea (de izquierda a derecha)

España es un país de una gran diversidad geográfica y cultural. En el país conviven[a] regiones con identidades bien definidas a lo largo de[b] una historia milenaria.[c] Estas diferencias incluyen hasta lenguas diferentes.

Con la Constitución de 1978, España reconoce[d] esta diversidad, constituyéndose[e] como un estado de regiones autónomas: diecisiete regiones que funcionan de manera descentralizada, no muy diferente del sistema federativo estadounidense.

La diversidad de España es una fuente[f] de innumerables tensiones lingüísticas, políticas, presupuestarias,[g] etcétera. Pero también es motivo de orgullo[h] general, porque con un territorio un poco más pequeño que el tamaño[i] de Texas, España es un país de intensos contrastes.

[a]coexist [b]a... throughout [c]of thousands of years [d]recognizes [e]organizing itself [f]source [g]budgetary [h]pride [i]size

Comprensión ¿Cómo está dividida España administrativamente? ¿Qué tipo de tensiones causan las diferentes identidades regionales que existen en España?

En todo el mundo hispano

Aberu.Go/Shutterstock

El Monumento a la Independencia, más conocido como el Ángel, en el Paseo de la Reforma, en la Ciudad de México

- **En muchos países americanos hispanohablantes** El año 2010 marcó el principio de una década en la que[a] muchos países celebraron el bicentenario de su independencia de España. El proceso de independencia y la formación de las nuevas naciones independientes comenzó a principios del siglo XIX y duró más de una década. Para 1898, solo Cuba y Puerto Rico eran todavía colonias españolas. En ese año, tuvo lugar la Guerra hispano-estadounidense, por la cual[b] los Estados Unidos obtuvieron Cuba y Puerto Rico como colonias. Cuba se independizaría en 1902.
- **En la Argentina, el Paraguay y el Uruguay** Junto con el Brasil, estos países firmaron un tratado[c] para formar el Mercado Común del Sur, o MERCOSUR. Es un acuerdo[d] que fomenta[e] la libre circulación de productos y servicios. En la actualidad MERCOSUR tiene más países asociados: Bolivia, Chile, Colombia, el Ecuador, el Perú, Guyana y Surinam.

[a]la... which [b]por... because of which [c]firmaron... signed a treaty [d]agreement [e]encourages

Comprensión ¿Cuántos siglos hace que son independientes muchas naciones latinoamericanas? ¿Qué es MERCOSUR?

En acción

En parejas, decidan cuáles son los grandes íconos humanos de su país. Pueden ser personajes (*characters*) de ficción, como don Quijote y Sancho, o personajes reales e históricos.

Lectura

Antes de leer

Usted va a leer unos artículos de la Constitución española que vienen de la sección de «Derechos y libertades». Empiece leyendo solamente los títulos de los artículos 14, 15 y 16 y trate de predecir (*predict*) algunos de los derechos y libertades permitidos por esta Constitución. En su opinión, ¿hay alguno de los tres artículos en particular que sea más importante, o cree usted que los tres tienen la misma importancia? Explique su respuesta.

Vocabulario para leer

la confesión	faith	**la pena**	punishment
la creencia	belief	**la pena de muerte**	death penalty
el culto	worship	**el trato**	treatment
el individuo	individual		
el nacimiento	birth	**declarar**	to testify

Constitución española, Capítulo segundo. Derechos y libertades

Artículo 14. Igualdad ante la ley

Los españoles son iguales ante la ley, sin que pueda prevalecer discriminación alguna por razón[a] de nacimiento, raza, sexo, religión, opinión o cualquier[b] otra condición o circunstancia personal o social.

SECCIÓN 1ª. De los derechos fundamentales y de las libertades públicas

Artículo 15. Derecho a la vida

Todos tienen derecho a la vida y a la integridad física y moral, sin que, en ningún caso, puedan ser sometidos a[c] tortura ni a penas o tratos inhumanos o degradantes. Queda abolida[d] la pena de muerte, salvo lo que puedan disponer[e] las leyes penales[f] militares para tiempos de guerra.

Artículo 16. Libertad ideológica y religiosa

1. Se garantiza la libertad ideológica, religiosa y de culto de los individuos y las comunidades sin más limitación, en sus manifestaciones, que la necesaria para el mantenimiento[g] del orden público protegido por la ley.
2. Nadie podrá ser obligado a declarar sobre su ideología, religión o creencias.
3. Ninguna confesión tendrá carácter estatal. Los poderes públicos tendrán en cuenta[h] las creencias religiosas de la sociedad española y mantendrán las consiguientes relaciones de cooperación con la Iglesia Católica y las demás confesiones.

[a]sin... *without the possibility of any discrimination on the grounds* [b]*any* [c]sometidos... *subjected to* [d]Queda... *Is abolished* [e]salvo... *except as stipulated by* [f]*criminal* [g]el... *maintaining* [h]tendrán... *will take into account*

Source: Spanish Constitution (1978), www.lamoncloa.gob.es.

Comprensión

A. Los derechos y libertades en España. Según los Artículos 14, 15 y 16 de la Constitución española, ¿son ciertas o falsas las siguientes afirmaciones? Indique el artículo al que corresponda (*matches*) cada afirmación y corrija las afirmaciones falsas.

	CIERTO	FALSO
1. En España, las mujeres tienen más libertad que los hombres.	☐	☐
2. Excepto en situaciones de guerra, el gobierno no puede torturar a ningún individuo.	☐	☐
3. El gobierno puede obligar a sus ciudadanos a expresar sus ideas políticas o religiosas.	☐	☐
4. En España, las cárceles (*jails*) no tienen el derecho de tratar a los prisioneros de forma inhumana.	☐	☐
5. En España existe la pena de muerte en tiempos de paz.	☐	☐
6. España se establece como un país católico.	☐	☐

B. Pensando como abogado/a constitucional. Imagine que usted es abogado/a y que tiene clientes en las siguientes situaciones. ¿Qué artículos de la Constitución española puede usted citar para ayudarlos? **¡OJO!** Recuerde que a veces es necesario que los abogados y jueces (*judges*) interpreten artículos de la Constitución, ya que (*since*) ninguna constitución contempla todas las posibles situaciones.

1. Su cliente cree que sufre discriminación por pertenecer (*belonging*) a una religión minoritaria.

2. Su cliente está en la cárcel (*jail*) y dice que los otros presos (*prisoners*) abusan de él.

3. Su cliente una persona transgénero y es víctima de discriminación en el trabajo.

Proyecto: Una comparación entre los derechos y libertades de dos constituciones

Para este proyecto, ustedes van a hacer una comparación entre algunos artículos de la Constitución española y los artículos correspondientes de la constitución de otro país hispanohablante. Van a determinar, en su opinión, en cuál de los dos países los artículos con respecto a la protección de los derechos y libertades son más claros.

Paso 1. En parejas, elijan la constitución de otro país hispanohablante y busquen las secciones que correspondan a los artículos 14, 15 y 16 de la Constitución española. ¿Qué semejanzas y diferencias hay entre ellas?

Paso 2. Busquen en internet la Constitución española entera y lean en ella otro artículo sobre los derechos y libertades. Luego busquen la sección correspondiente en la constitución del otro país. De nuevo (*Once again*), identifiquen las semejanzas y diferencias.

Paso 3. Preparen una breve presentación sobre las semejanzas y diferencias entre las dos constituciones. Después de escuchar todas las presentaciones, determinen entre todos si hay algunos países que le garanticen más derechos y libertades al individuo.

◀)) Textos orales

Una breve historia de España

Antes de escuchar

¿Qué sabe usted de la historia de España? Seguro que sabe que tuvo un gran imperio, pero ¿sabía que en ese país hubo una guerra civil, como en los Estados Unidos? ¿Cómo cree que es el país en la actualidad, pobre o rico? ¿moderno o tradicional?

lovelypeace/123RF

El acueducto de Segovia, construido por los romanos

Vocabulario para escuchar

autóctono/a	indígena	**tras**	after
la huella	trace; mark	**listo/a**	ready
la caída	fall	**pasar de ser**	to go from being
el imperio	empire	**creciente**	growing
a lo largo de	throughout	**milenario/a**	thousand-year
el reino	kingdom	**acoger**	to welcome

Estrategia

- Para indicar los siglos en español, se usan los números romanos. Por ejemplo, el siglo XV = el siglo quince (*1400s*).
- a. e. c. = antes de la era común (antes de Cristo) / e. c. = era común (después de Cristo)

Comprensión

A. Una breve historia. Lea primero la **Estrategia**. Luego escriba el siglo al que corresponden los eventos.

1. Los griegos, fenicios y otros pueblos se establecieron en la península ibérica antes del siglo _____ e. c.
2. Los romanos dominaron la península ibérica desde el siglo _____ hasta el siglo _____.
3. La conquista árabe de España ocurrió en el siglo _____.
4. Los árabes fueron expulsados de la península ibérica en el siglo _____.
5. El país que hoy se conoce como España comenzó en el siglo _____.
6. El final del gran imperio español ocurrió en el siglo _____.
7. España tuvo una guerra civil en el siglo _____.

B. La España de hoy. ¿Cómo es España hoy? Use palabras de la conferencia y sus propias palabras para describir la España de hoy.

1. el gobierno
2. la economía
3. la población

En acción

Compare lo que estaba pasando en España con lo que estaba pasando en su país al mismo tiempo (*at the same time*) en cuatro momentos del pasado.

Por ejemplo: En el siglo VIII ocurrió la conquista árabe de la península ibérica, pero no hubo ninguna conquista importante en Norteamérica.

PORTAFOLIO

🎙 Entrevista

Use de modelo las preguntas y respuestas de la sección **Entrevista** al principio de este capítulo para decir si es importante para usted estar al día con lo que pasa en el mundo y qué hace para enterarse de las noticias.

Eric Audras/Getty Images

💻 Escritura

Un ensayo sobre la mayoría de edad°

mayoría... *legal age*

¿Cuál es su opinión sobre la mayoría de edad? ¿Está de acuerdo con la idea de que haya una edad mínima para tener derecho a ciertas actividades? ¿Coincide su opinión con la (*that*) de muchos de sus compañeros?

VectorPic/Shutterstock

👥 Antes de escribir

En parejas, hagan una lista de los puntos que uno debe considerar para escribir un ensayo sobre el tema de la mayoría de edad. Luego preparen una serie de preguntas basadas en esas consideraciones y úsenlas para encuestar (*interview*) a cinco de sus compañeros.

A escribir

Después de hacer su encuesta, use las respuestas para escribir el ensayo. Hay más ayuda en Connect.

Para escribir bien

Considere las siguientes opciones para su ensayo.

- Conectores para contrastar ideas: **por un lado / por otro lado, sin embargo / no obstante**
- Conectores para organizar: **en primer/segundo lugar, además, por otra parte**
- Expresiones útiles para presentar información:

  mi encuesta demuestra que + *indic.*

  las personas que encuesté prefieren que + *subj.*

🌐 En la comunidad

Entreviste a una persona hispana de su universidad o ciudad sobre el gobierno de su país de origen y sobre sus preferencias políticas.

Preguntas posibles

- ¿Qué tipo de gobierno hay en su país? ¿Ha habido algún cambio grande en la estructura del gobierno en los últimos años? ¿Y en las últimas décadas?
- ¿Quién es el presidente o la presidenta del país? ¿Hay un congreso y un senado?
- ¿Cuáles son los partidos políticos más importantes? Si hay más de dos partidos, ¿se forman coaliciones de partidos para gobernar?
- ¿Estaba afiliado/a a algún partido en su país? ¿Votó alguna vez? ¿En qué elecciones?

▶ Producción audiovisual

Filme una entrevista que le hace a una persona que trabaja de voluntario/a en alguna organización local o de la universidad.

Más ideas para el portafolio

- Haga una lista de las cosas que usted haría durante un viaje ideal a un país hispanohablante en las próximas vacaciones.
- Si usted pudiera, ¿qué cosas cambiaría en el mundo? Haga una lista de cinco o seis cosas que usted haría. Puede ser una lista seria o cómica.
- Si ha estado jugando Practice Spanish: Study Abroad, en Quest 12 usted participó en una actividad que usó varios dichos y refranes de países hispanohablantes. Investigue otros refranes en español y trate de interpretarlos. Después, compárelos con refranes de su cultura de origen. ¿Hay semejanzas y correspondencias entre los refranes de diferentes culturas, o nota usted diferencias? ¿Qué importancia cultural tienen los refranes en general? Presente algunos refranes en clase y pídales a sus compañeros que den sus interpretaciones.

Sugerencia: You are now ready to play Quest 12 in **Practice Spanish: Study Abroad.**

AFTER STUDYING THIS CHAPTER I CAN ...

☐ talk about current events (530)

☐ talk about government and civic responsibilities (532)

☐ express situations in the past that require the subjunctive (536–538)

☐ talk about hypothetical events using the conditional (543–545)

☐ recognize/describe at least 2–3 aspects of Spanish culture

Gramática en breve

48. The Past Subjunctive

Third person plural preterite minus **-on** + **-a, -as, -a, -amos, -ais, -an**

49. The Conditional

Infinitive + **-ía, -ías, -ía, -íamos, -íais, -ían**

Irregular forms: **dir-, habr-, har-, podr-, pondr-, querr-, sabr-, saldr-, tendr-, vendr-** + *conditional endings*

Vocabulario

Las noticias

el acontecimiento	event, happening
el asesinato	assassination
el/la bombero/a	firefighter
el choque	collision, crash
la esperanza	hope, wish
la estación de radio	radio station
la guerra	war
la huelga	strike (*labor*)
el incendio	fire
la lucha	fight; struggle
la manifestación	demonstration; march
el medio de comunicación	medium of communication (*pl.* mass media)
el noticiero	newscast
la paz (*pl.* paces)	peace
la prensa	(print) press; news media
el/la testigo	witness

Cognados: el ataque (terrorista), la bomba, la crisis climática, la erupción, la radio (*medium*), **el/la reportero/a, el terrorismo, el/la terrorista, la víctima**

Repaso: el blog, el canal (de televisión), el desastre, la muerte, las noticias, el periódico, la revista, la televisión

asesinar	to assassinate
comunicarse (**qu**) (con)	to communicate (with)
enterarse (de)	to find out; to learn (about)
estar al día	to be up to date
interesar (*like* gustar)	to be of interest
luchar	to fight
mantener (*like* tener)	to maintain; to keep
matar	to kill

Cognado: informar

Repaso: ofrecer (ofrezco)

El gobierno y la responsabilidad cívica

el cargo	(political) office
el centro	center (*political*)
el/la ciudadano/a	citizen
el deber	responsibility; obligation
el derecho	right
la (des)igualdad	(in)equality
la dictadura	dictatorship
el ejército	army
la ley	law
el partido	political party
la política	politics; policy
el/la político/a	politician
el rey / la reina	king/queen
el servicio militar	military service

Cognados: el/la candidato/a, el concepto, la discriminación, el/la representante al congreso, el/la senador(a), el/la dictador(a)

Repaso: los/las demás, la derecha, el gobierno, la izquierda, el/la soldado

durar	to last
postularse (para un cargo / como candidato/a)	to run (for a position / as a candidate)

Cognado: votar

Repaso: ganar, obedecer (obedezco), perder (pierdo)

Los adjetivos

Cognados: cívico/a, climático/a, político/a

Repaso: natural

Vocabulario personal

Use this space or a vocabulary notebook to write down other words and phrases you learn in this chapter.

El español en el resto del mundo

A lo largo de[a] dieciocho capítulos, se ha presentado en *Puntos de partida* el inmenso y variado mundo hispanohablante, desde[b] los Estados Unidos hasta el Cono Sur en las Américas y, dentro de Europa, en España.

Pero el español es una lengua importante en otros países también. En África, sobrevive[c] bien arraigado[d] en la Guinea Ecuatorial, así como[e] en las ciudades norteafricanas de Ceuta y Melilla, que son territorio español. En Oceanía,* en las islas Filipinas, la lengua española es parte de su herencia[f] colonial, aunque[g] ya no es una lengua oficial en ese país. Y también hay que mencionar el Canadá, país donde hay una creciente[h] inmigración hispanohablante.

[a]*A... Throughout* [b]*from* [c]*it survives* [d]*established* [e]*así... as well as* [f]*heritage* [g]*although* [h]*growing*

*The term **Oceanía** refers to the islands of the tropical Pacific Ocean, including Polynesia, Australia, and New Zealand, as well as the Philippines and other island groups.*

 ## GUINEA ECUATORIAL

Guinea Ecuatorial es uno de los países más pequeños de África, pero también es uno de los más prósperos, debido a los yacimientos[a] de petróleo que se encuentran en su territorio. Fue colonia española desde[b] 1778 hasta 1968, y desde 1844 el español es una de sus lenguas oficiales, además del[c] francés y el portugués.

Aunque[d] tradicionalmente el país no se considera un país hispano, la realidad es que la mayoría de la población habla español, especialmente en la capital, Malabo. El español es también la lengua de varios escritores ecuatoguineanos, que se están abriendo camino[e] en el mundo literario hispanohablante.

La influencia de España en Guinea Ecuatorial, así como[f] pasó en los países americanos de habla española, fue mucho más allá[g] de lo lingüístico. Es evidente en la religión (ya que[h] en el país existe una inmensa mayoría católica), en el sistema de apellidos que se usa (dos apellidos: primero el[i] del padre y luego el de la madre) y hasta[j] en la comida (entre otros platos, las empanadas).

[a]*debido... due to the deposits* [b]*from* [c]*además... in addition to* [d]*Although* [e]*que... who are making a name for themselves* [f]*así... as* [g]*más... beyond* [h]*ya... since* [i]*that* [j]*even*

Malabo, la capital de la Guinea Ecuatorial

LAS ISLAS FILIPINAS

Las islas Filipinas son un archipiélago formado por más de 7.000 islas en el océano Pacífico. Fueron territorio español por más de 300 años. El fin de la colonización española ocurrió en 1898, cuando España cedió[a] el control de las Filipinas a los Estados Unidos, como consecuencia de la guerra hispanoamericana. Aunque[b] el español era la primera lengua oficial del país, el uso del español disminuyó[c] con la ocupación estadounidense y se perdió en la gran mayoría de la población. Sin embargo, los nombres y apellidos de muchos filipinos, así como[d] los nombres de muchos lugares y cosas de uso cotidiano,[e] son españoles, testimonio de la gran influencia de la lengua española en el país.

La Universidad de Santo Tomás, fundada por los frailes dominicanos (*Dominican friars*) en 1611

La herencia de España ha quedado reflejada[f] también en la cocina filipina, en la que[g] se combinan las influencias española, china y del sudeste asiático. En las islas Filipinas se preparan muchos platos que mantienen el nombre en español y que son adaptaciones de recetas españolas tradicionales, como la paella, el cocido,[h] el lechón asado[i] y la torta, similar a la españolísima tortilla de patatas, por solo nombrar algunos.

[a]*gave up* [b]*Although* [c]*declined* [d]*así... just like* [e]*everyday* [f]*ha... can still be seen reflected*
[g]*la... which* [h]*stew* [i]*lechón... roasted suckling pig*

Cartel (*Poster*) para la *Hispanic Fiesta* de 2010

 # EL CANADÁ

Se estima que en el Canadá viven hoy más de un millón de hispanohablantes, cuya mayoría[a] se concentra en la zona de las ciudades de Toronto y Montreal. También hay comunidades hispanas importantes en el oeste del país, porque a finales[b] del siglo XIX hubo una ola[c] inmigratoria de argentinos y chilenos a la provincia de Alberta.

Los hispanocanadienses disfrutan de[d] acceso a numerosos medios de comunicación en español. Además, hay en el Canadá varios festivales y eventos que conmemoran la presencia hispana en el país. Uno de los más importantes es la Hispanic Fiesta, que se celebra anualmente en el mes de agosto en Toronto. Allí se encuentra comida de todas partes del mundo hispanohablante, se puede escuchar música andina y mexicana, entre otras formas musicales, y ver demostraciones de tango, flamenco y otros bailes.

[a]*cuya... the majority of whom* [b]*a... at the end* [c]*wave* [d]*disfrutan... enjoy*

Comprensión

1. ¿En qué continentes y regiones del mundo se habla español como lengua oficial?
2. ¿En qué países tiene el español una presencia actual o histórica muy importante, aunque (*although*) no es la lengua oficial?
3. ¿Qué colonia española se independizó de España en el siglo XX?
4. En general, ¿en qué se nota la influencia española en Guinea Ecuatorial, las Filipinas y el Canadá?

ADJECTIVE A word that describes a noun or pronoun.

una casa **grande**
a **big** house

Ana es **inteligente.** Ella es **inteligente.**
*Ana is **smart**. She is **smart**.*

Demonstrative adjective An adjective that points out a particular noun.

este chico, **esos** libros, **aquellas** personas
***this** boy, **those** books, **those** people (over there)*

Interrogative adjective An adjective used to form questions.

¿Qué cuaderno?
***Which** notebook?*

¿Cuáles son los carteles que buscas?
***Which ones** are the posters (that) you're looking for?*

Possessive adjective (unstressed) An adjective that indicates possession or a special relationship.

sus coches
***their** cars*

mi hermana
***my** sister*

Possessive adjective (stressed) An adjective that more emphatically describes possession.*

Es **una** amiga **mía.**
*She's **my** friend. / She's a friend **of mine**.*

Es **un** coche **suyo.**
*It's **her** car. / It's a car **of hers**.*

ADVERB A word that describes an adjective, a verb, or another adverb.

Roberto es **muy** alto.
*Roberto is **very** tall.*

María escribe **bien.**
*María writes **well**.*

Van **demasiado rápido.**
*They are going **too** quickly.*

ARTICLE A determiner that sets off a noun.

el/un libro
***the/a** book*

Definite article An article that indicates a specific noun.

el país
***the** country*

la silla
***the** chair*

las mujeres
***the** women*

Indefinite article An article that indicates an unspecified noun.

un chico
***a** boy*

una ciudad
***a** city*

unas zanahorias
*(**some**) carrots*

---

*See Appendix 3 on page A–7 for a more detailed explanation.

CLAUSE A construction that contains a subject and a verb.

Main (Independent) clause A clause that can stand on its own because it expresses a complete thought.

Busco una muchacha.
I'm looking for a girl.

Si yo fuera rica, **me compraría una casa.**
*If I were rich, **I would buy a house.***

Subordinate (Dependent) clause A clause that cannot stand on its own because it does not express a complete thought.

Busco a la muchacha **que juega al tenis.**
*I'm looking for the girl **who plays tennis.***

Si yo fuera rica, me compraría una casa.
***If I were rich,** I would buy a house.*

COMPARATIVE The form of adjectives and adverbs used to compare two nouns or actions.

Luis es <u>menos</u> hablador <u>que</u> Julián.
*Luis is **less talkative than** Julián.*

Luis corre <u>más</u> rápido <u>que</u> Julián.
*Luis runs **faster than** Julián.*

CONJUGATION The different forms of a verb for a particular tense or mood. A present indicative conjugation:

(yo) habl<u>o</u>	(nosotros/as) habl<u>amos</u>
(tú) habl<u>as</u>	(vosotros/as) habl<u>áis</u>
(usted) habl<u>a</u>	(ustedes) habl<u>an</u>
(él/ella) habl<u>a</u>	(ellos/as) habl<u>an</u>

I speak	*we speak*
you (fam. sing.) speak	*you (fam. pl.) speak*
you (form. sing.) speak	*you (pl.) speak*
he/she speaks	*they speak*

CONJUNCTION An expression that connects words, phrases, or clauses.

Cristóbal **y** Diana
*Cristóbal **and** Diana*

Hace frío, **pero** hace buen tiempo.
*It's cold, **but** it's nice out.*

DIRECT OBJECT The noun or pronoun that receives the action of a verb.

Veo **la caja.**
*I see **the box.***

<u>La</u> veo.
*I see **it.***

GENDER A grammatical category of words. In Spanish, there are two genders: masculine and feminine.

	MASCULINE	FEMININE
ARTICLES AND NOUNS:	**el** disco compacto	**la** cinta
PRONOUNS:	**él**	**ella**
ADJECTIVES:	bonit<u>o</u>, list<u>o</u>	bonit<u>a</u>, list<u>a</u>
PAST PARTICIPLES:	El informe está **escrit<u>o</u>.**	La composición está **escrit<u>a</u>.**

IMPERATIVE See Mood.

IMPERFECT (*IMPERFECTO*) In Spanish, a verb tense that expresses a past action with no specific beginning or ending.

Nadábamos con frecuencia.
*We **used to swim** often.*

IMPERSONAL CONSTRUCTION One that contains a third person singular verb but no specific subject in Spanish. The subject of English impersonal constructions is generally *it*.

Es importante que...
It is important that ...

Es necesario que...
It is necessary that ...

INDICATIVE *See* Mood.

INDIRECT OBJECT The noun or pronoun that indicates *for who(m)* or *to who(m)* an action is performed. In Spanish, the indirect object pronoun is usually included, even when the indirect object is explicitly stated as a noun.

Marcos <u>le</u> da el suéter **a Raquel.** / Marcos <u>le</u> da el suéter.
*Marcos gives the sweater **to Raquel.** / Marcos gives **her** the sweater.*

INFINITIVE The form of a verb introduced in English by *to: to play, to sell, to come.* In Spanish dictionaries, the infinitive form of the verb appears as the main entry.

Luisa va a **comprar** un periódico.
*Luisa is going **to buy** a newspaper.*

MOOD A set of categories for verbs indicating the attitude of the speaker toward what he or she is saying.

Imperative mood A verb form expressing a command.

¡**Ten** cuidado!
***Be** careful!*

Indicative mood A verb form denoting actions or states considered facts.

Voy a la biblioteca.
***I'm going** to the library.*

Subjunctive mood A verb form, uncommon in English, used in Spanish primarily in subordinate clauses after expressions of desire, emotion, or doubt. Spanish constructions with the subjunctive have many possible English equivalents.

Quiero que **vayas** inmediatamente.
*I want you **to go** immediately.*

NOUN A word that denotes a person, place, thing, or idea. Proper nouns are capitalized names.

abogado, ciudad, periódico, libertad, Luisa
lawyer, city, newspaper, freedom, Luisa

NUMBER

Cardinal number A number that expresses an amount.

una silla, **tres** estudiantes
one chair, three students

Ordinal number A number that indicates position in a series.

la **primera** silla, el **tercer** estudiante
*the **first** chair, the **third** student*

PAST PARTICIPLE The form of a verb used in compound tenses (*see* Perfect Tenses). Used with forms of *to have* or *to be* in English and with **ser, estar,** or **haber** in Spanish.

comido, terminado, perdido
eaten, finished, lost

PERFECT TENSES Compound tenses that combine the auxiliary verb **haber** with a past participle.

Present perfect indicative This form uses a present indicative form of **haber**. The use of the Spanish present perfect generally parallels that of the English present perfect.

No **he viajado** nunca a México.
I've never traveled to Mexico.

Past perfect indicative This form uses **haber** in the imperfect tense to talk about something that had or had not been done before a given time in the past.

Antes de 2020, **no había estudiado** español.
Before 2020, I hadn't studied Spanish.

Present perfect subjunctive This form uses the present subjunctive of **haber** to express a present perfect action when the subjunctive is required.

¡Ojalá que Marisa **haya llegado** a su destino!
*I hope (that) Marisa **has arrived** at her destination!*

PERSON The form of a pronoun or verb that indicates the person involved in an action.

	SINGULAR	PLURAL
FIRST PERSON:	*I* / **yo**	*we* / **nosotros/as**
SECOND PERSON:	*you* / **tú, usted**	*you* / **vosotros/as, ustedes**
THIRD PERSON:	*he, she* / **él, ella**	*they* / **ellos, ellas**

PREPOSITION A word or phrase that specifies the relationship of one word (usually a noun or pronoun) to another. The relationship is usually spatial or temporal.

a la escuela
to school

cerca de la biblioteca
near the library

con él
with him

antes de la medianoche
before midnight

PRESENT PARTICIPLE The verb form that ends in *-ing* in English. Used with forms of *to be* in English and with **estar** in Spanish to form the progressive.

hablando, comiendo, pidiendo
speaking, eating, asking

PRETERITE (*PRETÉRITO*) In Spanish, a verb tense that expresses a past action with a specific beginning and ending.

Salí para Roma el jueves.
I left for Rome on Thursday.

PROGRESSIVE The verb that expresses continuing or developing action.

Julio **está durmiendo** ahora.
*Julio **is sleeping** now.*

Anita **estaba comiendo** cuando sonó el teléfono.
*Anita **was eating** when the phone rang.*

PRONOUN A word that refers to a person (I, you) or that is used in place of one or more nouns.

¿Ana? **Ella** no está aquí.
*Ana? **She** isn't here.*

Demonstrative pronoun A pronoun that singles out a particular person, place, thing, or idea.

Aquí están dos libros. **Este** es interesante, pero **ese** es aburrido.
*Here are two books. **This one** is interesting, but **that one** is boring.*

Interrogative pronoun A pronoun used to ask a question.

¿**Quién** es él?
***Who** is he?*

¿**Qué** prefieres?
***What** do you prefer?*

Object pronoun A pronoun that replaces a direct object noun or an indirect object noun. Both direct and indirect object pronouns can be used together in the same sentence.

However, when they appear before **lo, la, los,** or **las,** the pronouns **le** or **les** change to **se.**

Si **me** llamas más tarde, **te** doy el número de teléfono de David.
*If you call **me** later, I'll give **you** David's phone number.*

Veo a **Alejandro. Lo** veo.
*I see **Alejandro**. I see **him.***

Le doy el libro <u>a Juana</u>.
*I give the book **to Juana**.*

<u>**Se**</u> **lo** doy (a ella).
*I give **it** to **her**.*

Reflexive pronoun A pronoun that represents the same person as the subject of the verb.

Me miro en el espejo.
*I look at **myself** in the mirror.*

Relative pronoun A pronoun that introduces a dependent clause and denotes a noun already mentioned.

El hombre con **quien** hablaba era mi vecino.
*The man with **whom** I was talking was my neighbor.*

Aquí está el bolígrafo **que** buscas.
*Here is the pen (**that**) you're looking for.*

Subject pronoun A pronoun representing the person, place, thing, or idea performing the action of a verb.

Lucas y Julia juegan al tenis. → **Ellos** juegan al tenis.
Lucas and Julia play tennis. → ***They** play tennis.*

SUBJECT The word(s) denoting the person, place, thing, or idea performing an action or existing in a state.

Sara trabaja aquí.
***Sara** works here.*

¡**Buenos Aires** es una ciudad magnífica!
***Buenos Aires** is a great city!*

Mis **libros** y mi **computadora** están allí.
*My **books** and my **computer** are over there.*

SUBJUNCTIVE *See* Mood.

SUPERLATIVE The form of an adjective or adverb that expresses an extreme. In English, the superlative is marked by *most, least,* or *-est.*

Escogí <u>**el**</u> vestido <u>**más**</u> caro.
*I chose **the most expensive** dress.*

Ana es **la** persona <u>**menos**</u> **habladora** que conozco.
*Ana is **the least talkative person** I know.*

TENSE The form of a verb indicating time: present, past, or future.

Raúl **era, es** y siempre **será** mi mejor amigo.
*Raúl **was, is,** and always **will be** my best friend.*

VERB A word that reports an action or state.

Maribel **llegó.**
*Maribel **arrived.***

La niña **estaba** cansada.
*The child **was** tired.*

Auxiliary verb A verb in conjunction with a participle to convey distinctions of tense and mood. In Spanish, one auxiliary verb is **haber.**

Han viajado por todas partes del mundo.
*They **have** traveled everywhere in the world.*

Reflexive verb A verb whose subject and object are the same.

Juan **se corta** la cara cuando **se afeita.**
*Juan **cuts himself** when he **shaves** (**himself**).*

APPENDIX 2

Using Adjectives as Nouns

Nominalization means using an adjective as a noun. In Spanish, adjectives can be nominalized in a number of ways, all of which involve dropping the noun that accompanies the adjective, then using the adjective in combination with an article or other word. One kind of adjective, the demonstrative, can simply be used alone. In most cases, these usages parallel those of English, although the English equivalent may be phrased differently from the Spanish.

Article + Adjective

Simply omit the noun from an *article + noun + adjective* phrase.

el **libro** azul → **el azul** (*the blue one*)
la **hermana** casada → **la casada**
   (*the married one*)
el **señor** mexicano → **el mexicano**
   (*the Mexican [man]*)
los **pantalones** baratos → **los baratos**
   (*the inexpensive ones*)

You can also drop the first noun in an *article + noun + de + noun* phrase.

la **casa** de Julio → **la de Julio** (*Julio's*)
los **coches** del Sr. Martínez → **los del Sr. Martínez**
   (*Mr. Martínez's*)

In both cases, the construction is used to refer to a noun that has already been mentioned. The English equivalent uses *one* or *ones,* or a possessive without the noun.

— ¿Necesitas el **libro** grande?
— No. Necesito **el pequeño.**
"Do you need the big book?"
"No. I need the small one."

— ¿Usamos el **coche** de Ernesto?
— No. Usemos **el de Ana.**
"Shall we use Ernesto's car?"
"No. Let's use Ana's."

Note that in the preceding examples the noun is mentioned in the first part of the exchange (**libro, coche**) but not in the response or rejoinder.

Note also that a demonstrative can be used to nominalize an adjective: **este rojo** (*this red one*), **esos azules** (*those blue ones*).

Lo + Adjective

As seen in **Capítulo 11, lo** combines with the masculine singular form of an adjective to describe general qualities or characteristics. The English equivalent is expressed with words like *part* or *thing.*

lo mejor   *the best thing (part), what's best*
lo mismo   *the same thing*
lo cómico   *the funny thing (part), what's funny*

Article + Stressed Possessive Adjective

The stressed possessive adjectives—but not the unstressed possessives—can be used as possessive pronouns: **la maleta suya → la suya.** The article and the possessive form agree in gender and number with the noun to which they refer.

Este es mi **banco.** ¿Dónde está **el suyo**?
This is my bank. Where is yours?

Sus **bebidas** están preparadas; **las nuestras,** no.
Their drinks are ready; ours aren't.

No es la **maleta** de Juan; es **la mía.**
It isn't Juan's suitcase; it's mine.

Note that the definite article is frequently omitted after forms of **ser:**

¿Esa maleta? Es suya.
That suitcase? It's his / hers / yours / theirs.

Demonstrative Pronouns

The demonstrative adjective can be used alone, without a noun. An accent mark can be added to the demonstrative pronoun (**éste, ése, aquél**) to distinguish it from the demonstrative adjectives if context does not make meaning clear.

Necesito este diccionario y **ese (ése).**
I need this dictionary and that one.

Estas señoras y **aquellas (aquéllas)** son las
   hermanas de Sara, ¿no?
*These women and those (over there) are Sara's
   sisters, aren't they?*

It is acceptable in modern Spanish, according to the **Real Academia Española,** to omit the accent on demonstrative pronouns when context makes the meaning clear and no ambiguity is possible.

APPENDIX 3

More About Stressed Possessives

When in English you would emphasize the possessive with your voice or with *of mine* (*of yours, of his*, and so on), you will use the *stressed possessives* (**las formas tónicas de los posesivos**) in Spanish. As the term implies, they are more emphatic than the *unstressed forms* (**las formas átonas de los posesivos**).

The stressed forms follow the noun, and the noun *must* be preceded by a definite or indefinite article or by a demonstrative adjective. The stressed forms agree with the noun modified in number and gender. In the following examples, boldface italic type in the English translations indicates voice stress.

Es **su** perro.	*It's her dog.*

But:

Es **un** perro **suyo**.	*It's **her** dog (i.e., not ours). It's a dog of hers.*
El perro **suyo** se llama King.	***Her** dog is named King.*
Ese perro **suyo** es bravo.	*That dog of **hers** is fierce.*

Es **su** maleta.	*It's **his** suitcase.*

But:

Es **una** maleta **suya**.	*It's **his** suitcase.*
La maleta **suya** está perdida.	***His** suitcase (i.e., not ours) is lost.*
Esa maleta **suya** está perdida.	*That suitcase of his is lost.*

The stressed possessives are often used as nouns. See **Appendix 2: Using Adjectives as Nouns.**

APPENDIX 4

Additional Perfect Forms (Indicative and Subjunctive)

As you know, some indicative verb tenses have corresponding perfect forms in the indicative and subjunctive moods. Here is the present tense system.

el presente: yo hablo, como, pongo
el presente perfecto: yo he hablado, comido, puesto
el presente perfecto de subjuntivo: (que) yo haya hablado, comido, puesto

Other indicative forms that you have learned also have corresponding perfect indicative and subjunctive forms. Here are the most important ones, along with examples of their use. In each case, the tense or mood is formed with the appropriate form of **haber.**

El pluscuamperfecto de subjuntivo

yo:	hubiera hablado, comido, vivido...
tú:	hubieras hablado, comido, vivido...
usted/él/ella:	hubiera hablado, comido, vivido...
nosotros:	hubiéramos hablado, comido, vivido...
vosotros:	hubierais hablado, comido, vivido...
ustedes/ellos/ellas:	hubieran hablado, comido, vivido...

These forms correspond to **el pluscuamperfecto de indicativo** (*past perfect indicative*) (**Capítulo 15**). The **pluscuamperfecto de subjuntivo** is most frequently used in **si** clause sentences, along with the conditional perfect. See examples in *Si* **Clauses: Sentences About the Past.**

El futuro perfecto

yo:	habré hablado, comido, vivido...
tú:	habrás hablado, comido, vivido...
usted/él/ella:	habrá hablado, comido, vivido...
nosotros:	habremos hablado, comido, vivido...
vosotros:	habréis hablado, comido, vivido...
ustedes/ellos/ellas:	habrán hablado, comido, vivido...

These forms correspond to **el futuro** (**Capítulo 17**) and are most frequently used to tell what *will have already happened* at some point in the future. (In contrast, the future is used to tell what *will happen.*)

Mañana **hablaré** con Miguel.
I'll speak with Miguel tomorrow.

Para las tres, ya **habré hablado** con Miguel.
By 3:00, I'll already have spoken with Miguel.

El año que viene **visitaremos** a los nietos.
We'll visit our grandchildren next year.

Para las Navidades, ya **habremos visitado** a los nietos.
We'll already have visited our grandchildren by Christmas.

El condicional perfecto

yo:	habría hablado, comido, vivido...
tú:	habrías hablado, comido, vivido...
usted/él/ella:	habría hablado, comido, vivido...
nosotros:	habríamos hablado, comido, vivido...
vosotros:	habríais hablado, comido, vivido...
ustedes/ellos/ellas:	habrían hablado, comido, vivido...

These forms correspond to **el condicional** (**Capítulo 18**). They are frequently used to tell what *would have happened* at some point in the past. (In contrast, the conditional tells what one *would do.*)

Yo **hablaría** con Miguel.
I would speak with Miguel (if I were you, at some point in the future).

Yo **habría hablado** con Miguel.
I would have spoken with Miguel (if I had been you, at some point in the past).

Si Clause: Sentences About the Past

You have learned (**Capítulo 18**) to use the past subjunctive and conditional to speculate about the present in **si** clause sentences: what *would happen* if a particular event *were* (or *were not*) to occur.

Si **tuviera** tiempo, **aprendería** francés.
If I had the time, I would learn French.

The perfect forms of the past subjunctive and the conditional are used to speculate about the past: what *would have happened* if a particular event *had* (or *had not*) occurred.

En la escuela superior, si **hubiera tenido** tiempo, **habría aprendido** francés.
In high school, if I had had the time, I would have learned French.

A. Regular Verbs: Simple Tenses

Infinitive Present Participle Past Participle	INDICATIVE					SUBJUNCTIVE		IMPERATIVE
	Present	Imperfect	Preterite	Future	Conditional	Present	Imperfect	
hablar hablando hablado	hablo hablas habla hablamos habláis hablan	hablaba hablabas hablaba hablábamos hablabais hablaban	hablé hablaste habló hablamos hablasteis hablaron	hablaré hablarás hablará hablaremos hablaréis hablarán	hablaría hablarías hablaría hablaríamos hablaríais hablarían	hable hables hable hablemos habléis hablen	hablara hablaras hablara habláramos hablarais hablaran	habla tú, no hables hable usted hablemos hablad, no habléis hablen
comer comiendo comido	como comes come comemos coméis comen	comía comías comía comíamos comíais comían	comí comiste comió comimos comisteis comieron	comeré comerás comerá comeremos comeréis comerán	comería comerías comería comeríamos comeríais comerían	coma comas coma comamos comáis coman	comiera comieras comiera comiéramos comierais comieran	come tú, no comas coma usted comamos comed, no comáis coman
vivir viviendo vivido	vivo vives vive vivimos vivís viven	vivía vivías vivía vivíamos vivíais vivían	viví viviste vivió vivimos vivisteis vivieron	viviré vivirás vivirá viviremos viviréis vivirán	viviría vivirías viviría viviríamos viviríais vivirían	viva vivas viva vivamos viváis vivan	viviera vivieras viviera viviéramos vivierais vivieran	vive tú, no vivas viva usted vivamos vivid, no viváis vivan

B. Regular Verbs: Perfect Tenses

INDICATIVE														SUBJUNCTIVE				

INDICATIVE

Present Perfect		Past Perfect		Preterite Perfect		Future Perfect		Conditional Perfect	
he		había		hube		habré		habría	
has	hablado	habías	hablado	hubiste	hablado	habrás	hablado	habrías	hablado
ha	comido	había	comido	hubo	comido	habrá	comido	habría	comido
hemos	vivido	habíamos	vivido	hubimos	vivido	habremos	vivido	habríamos	vivido
habéis		habíais		hubisteis		habréis		habríais	
han		habían		hubieron		habrán		habrían	

SUBJUNCTIVE

Present Perfect		Past Perfect	
haya		hubiera	
hayas	hablado	hubieras	hablado
haya	comido	hubiera	comido
hayamos	vivido	hubiéramos	vivido
hayáis		hubierais	
hayan		hubieran	

C. Irregular Verbs

Infinitive Present Participle Past Participle	INDICATIVE					SUBJUNCTIVE		IMPERATIVE
	Present	Imperfect	Preterite	Future	Conditional	Present	Imperfect	
andar	ando	andaba	anduve	andaré	andaría	ande	anduviera	
andando	andas	andabas	anduviste	andarás	andarías	andes	anduvieras	anda tú, no andes
andado	anda	andaba	anduvo	andará	andaría	ande	anduviera	ande usted
	andamos	andábamos	anduvimos	andaremos	andaríamos	andemos	anduviéramos	andemos
	andáis	andabais	anduvisteis	andaréis	andaríais	andéis	anduvierais	andad, no andéis
	andan	andaban	anduvieron	andarán	andarían	anden	anduvieran	anden
caber	quepo	cabía	cupe	cabré	cabría	quepa	cupiera	
cabiendo	cabes	cabías	cupiste	cabrás	cabrías	quepas	cupieras	cabe tú, no quepas
cabido	cabe	cabía	cupo	cabrá	cabría	quepa	cupiera	quepa usted
	cabemos	cabíamos	cupimos	cabremos	cabríamos	quepamos	cupiéramos	quepamos
	cabéis	cabíais	cupisteis	cabréis	cabríais	quepáis	cupierais	cabed, no quepáis
	caben	cabían	cupieron	cabrán	cabrían	quepan	cupieran	quepan

C. Irregular Verbs (continued)

Infinitive Present Participle Past Participle	INDICATIVE						SUBJUNCTIVE		IMPERATIVE
	Present	Imperfect	Preterite	Future	Conditional		Present	Imperfect	
caer cayendo caído	caigo caes cae caemos caéis caen	caía caías caía caíamos caíais caían	caí caíste cayó caímos caísteis cayeron	caeré caerás caerá caeremos caeréis caerán	caería caerías caería caeríamos caeríais caerían		caiga caigas caiga caigamos caigáis caigan	cayera cayeras cayera cayéramos cayerais cayeran	cae tú, no caigas caiga usted caigamos caed, no caigáis caigan
creer creyendo creído	creo crees cree creemos creéis creen	creía creías creía creíamos creíais creían	creí creíste creyó creímos creísteis creyeron	creeré creerás creerá creeremos creeréis creerán	creería creerías creería creeríamos creeríais creerían		crea creas crea creamos creáis crean	creyera creyeras creyera creyéramos creyerais creyeran	cree tú, no creas crea usted creamos creed, no creáis crean
dar dando dado	doy das da damos dais dan	daba dabas daba dábamos dabais daban	di diste dio dimos disteis dieron	daré darás dará daremos daréis darán	daría darías daría daríamos daríais darían		dé des dé demos deis den	diera dieras diera diéramos dierais dieran	da tú, no des dé usted demos dad, no deis den
decir diciendo dicho	digo dices dice decimos decís dicen	decía decías decía decíamos decíais decían	dije dijiste dijo dijimos dijisteis dijeron	diré dirás dirá diremos diréis dirán	diría dirías diría diríamos diríais dirían		diga digas diga digamos digáis digan	dijera dijeras dijera dijéramos dijerais dijeran	di tú, no digas diga usted digamos decid, no digáis digan

C. Irregular Verbs (continued)

Infinitive Present Participle Past Participle	INDICATIVE					SUBJUNCTIVE		IMPERATIVE
	Present	Imperfect	Preterite	Future	Conditional	Present	Imperfect	
estar estando estado	estoy estás está estamos estáis están	estaba estabas estaba estábamos estabais estaban	estuve estuviste estuvo estuvimos estuvisteis estuvieron	estaré estarás estará estaremos estaréis estarán	estaría estarías estaría estaríamos estaríais estarían	esté estés esté estemos estéis estén	estuviera estuvieras estuviera estuviéramos estuvierais estuviera	está tú, no estés esté usted estemos estad, no estéis estén
haber habiendo habido	he has ha hemos habéis han	había habías había habíamos habíais habían	hube hubiste hubo hubimos hubisteis hubieron	habré habrás habrá habremos habréis habrán	habría habrías habría habríamos habríais habrían	haya hayas haya hayamos hayáis hayan	hubiera hubieras hubiera hubiéramos hubierais hubieran	
hacer haciendo hecho	hago haces hace hacemos hacéis hacen	hacía hacías hacía hacíamos hacíais hacían	hice hiciste hizo hicimos hicisteis hicieron	haré harás hará haremos haréis harán	haría harías haría haríamos haríais harían	haga hagas haga hagamos hagáis hagan	hiciera hicieras hiciera hiciéramos hicierais hicieran	haz tú, no hagas haga usted hagamos haced, no hagáis hagan
ir yendo ido	voy vas va vamos vais van	iba ibas iba íbamos ibais iban	fui fuiste fue fuimos fuisteis fueron	iré irás irá iremos iréis irán	iría irías iría iríamos iríais irían	vaya vayas vaya vayamos vayáis vayan	fuera fueras fuera fuéramos fuerais fueran	ve tú, no vayas vaya usted vayamos id, no vayáis vayan

C. Irregular Verbs (continued)

Infinitive / Present Participle / Past Participle	INDICATIVE						SUBJUNCTIVE		IMPERATIVE
	Present	Imperfect	Preterite	Future	Conditional		Present	Imperfect	
oír / oyendo / oído	oigo	oía	oí	oiré	oiría		oiga	oyera	
	oyes	oías	oíste	oirás	oirías		oigas	oyeras	oye tú, no oigas
	oye	oía	oyó	oirá	oiría		oiga	oyera	oiga usted
	oímos	oíamos	oímos	oiremos	oiríamos		oigamos	oyéramos	oigamos
	oís	oíais	oísteis	oiréis	oiríais		oigáis	oyerais	oíd, no oigáis
	oyen	oían	oyeron	oirán	oirían		oigan	oyeran	oigan
poder / pudiendo / podido	puedo	podía	pude	podré	podría		pueda	pudiera	
	puedes	podías	pudiste	podrás	podrías		puedas	pudieras	
	puede	podía	pudo	podrá	podría		pueda	pudiera	
	podemos	podíamos	pudimos	podremos	podríamos		podamos	pudiéramos	
	podéis	podíais	pudisteis	podréis	podríais		podáis	pudierais	
	pueden	podían	pudieron	podrán	podrían		puedan	pudieran	
poner / poniendo / puesto	pongo	ponía	puse	pondré	pondría		ponga	pusiera	
	pones	ponías	pusiste	pondrás	pondrías		pongas	pusieras	pon tú, no pongas
	pone	ponía	puso	pondrá	pondría		ponga	pusiera	ponga usted
	ponemos	poníamos	pusimos	pondremos	pondríamos		pongamos	pusiéramos	pongamos
	ponéis	poníais	pusisteis	pondréis	pondríais		pongáis	pusierais	poned, no pongáis
	ponen	ponían	pusieron	pondrán	pondrían		pongan	pusieran	pongan
querer / queriendo / querido	quiero	quería	quise	querré	querría		quiera	quisiera	
	quieres	querías	quisiste	querrás	querrías		quieras	quisieras	quiere tú, no quieras
	quiere	quería	quiso	querrá	querría		quiera	quisiera	quiera usted
	queremos	queríamos	quisimos	querremos	querríamos		queramos	quisiéramos	queramos
	queréis	queríais	quisisteis	querréis	querríais		queráis	quisierais	quered, no queráis
	quieren	querían	quisieron	querrán	querrían		quieran	quisieran	quieran

C. Irregular Verbs (continued)

Infinitive / Present Participle / Past Participle	INDICATIVE						SUBJUNCTIVE		IMPERATIVE
	Present	Imperfect	Preterite	Future	Conditional		Present	Imperfect	

saber
sabiendo
sabido
	sé
	sabes
	sabe
	sabemos
	sabéis
	saben
		sabía
		sabías
		sabía
		sabíamos
		sabíais
		sabían
			supe
			supiste
			supo
			supimos
			supisteis
			supieron
				sabré
				sabrás
				sabrá
				sabremos
				sabréis
				sabrán
					sabría
					sabrías
					sabría
					sabríamos
					sabríais
					sabrían
							sepa
							sepas
							sepa
							sepamos
							sepáis
							sepan
								supiera
								supieras
								supiera
								supiéramos
								supierais
								supieran
									sabe tú, no
									  sepas
									sepa usted
									sepamos
									sabed, no
									  sepáis
									sepan

salir
saliendo
salido
	salgo
	sales
	sale
	salimos
	salís
	salen
		salía
		salías
		salía
		salíamos
		salíais
		salían
			salí
			saliste
			salió
			salimos
			salisteis
			salieron
				saldré
				saldrás
				saldrá
				saldremos
				saldréis
				saldrán
					saldría
					saldrías
					saldría
					saldríamos
					saldríais
					saldrían
							salga
							salgas
							salga
							salgamos
							salgáis
							salgan
								saliera
								salieras
								saliera
								saliéramos
								salierais
								salieran
									sal tú, no
									  salgas
									salga usted
									salgamos
									salid, no
									  salgáis
									salgan

ser siendo sido	soy eres es somos sois son	era eras era éramos erais eran	fui fuiste fue fuimos fuisteis fueron	seré serás será seremos seréis serán	sería serías sería seríamos seríais serían		sea seas sea seamos seáis sean	fuera fueras fuera fuéramos fuerais fueran	sé tú, no seas sea usted seamos sed, no seáis sean

tener
teniendo
tenido
	tengo
	tienes
	tiene
	tenemos
	tenéis
	tienen
		tenía
		tenías
		tenía
		teníamos
		teníais
		tenían
			tuve
			tuviste
			tuvo
			tuvimos
			tuvisteis
			tuvieron
				tendré
				tendrás
				tendrá
				tendremos
				tendréis
				tendrán
					tendría
					tendrías
					tendría
					tendríamos
					tendríais
					tendrían
							tenga
							tengas
							tenga
							tengamos
							tengáis
							tengan
								tuviera
								tuvieras
								tuviera
								tuviéramos
								tuvierais
								tuvieran
									ten tú, no
									  tengas
									tenga usted
									tengamos
									tened, no
									  tengáis
									tengan

C. Irregular Verbs (continued)

Infinitive / Present Participle / Past Participle	INDICATIVE						SUBJUNCTIVE		IMPERATIVE
	Present	Imperfect	Preterite	Future	Conditional		Present	Imperfect	
traer / trayendo / traído	traigo	traía	traje	traeré	traería		traiga	trajera	trae tú, no traigas
	traes	traías	trajiste	traerás	traerías		traigas	trajeras	traiga usted
	trae	traía	trajo	traerá	traería		traiga	trajera	traigamos
	traemos	traíamos	trajimos	traeremos	traeríamos		traigamos	trajéramos	traed, no traigáis
	traéis	traíais	trajisteis	traeréis	traeríais		traigáis	trajerais	traigan
	traen	traían	trajeron	traerán	traerían		traigan	trajeran	
venir / viniendo / venido	vengo	venía	vine	vendré	vendría		venga	viniera	ven tú, no vengas
	vienes	venías	viniste	vendrás	vendrías		vengas	vinieras	venga usted
	viene	venía	vino	vendrá	vendría		venga	viniera	vengamos
	venimos	veníamos	vinimos	vendremos	vendríamos		vengamos	viniéramos	venid, no vengáis
	venís	veníais	vinisteis	vendréis	vendríais		vengáis	vinierais	vengan
	vienen	venían	vinieron	vendrán	vendrían		vengan	vinieran	
ver / viendo / visto	veo	veía	vi	veré	vería		vea	viera	ve tú, no veas
	ves	veías	viste	verás	verías		veas	vieras	vea usted
	ve	veía	vio	verá	vería		vea	viera	veamos
	vemos	veíamos	vimos	veremos	veríamos		veamos	viéramos	ved, no veáis
	veis	veíais	visteis	veréis	veríais		veáis	vierais	vean
	ven	veían	vieron	verán	verían		vean	vieran	

D. Stem-Changing and Spelling Change Verbs

Infinitive Present Participle Past Participle	INDICATIVE					SUBJUNCTIVE		IMPERATIVE
	Present	Imperfect	Preterite	Future	Conditional	Present	Imperfect	
pensar (pienso) pensando pensado	pienso piensas piensa pensamos pensáis piensan	pensaba pensabas pensaba pensábamos pensabais pensaban	pensé pensaste pensó pensamos pensasteis pensaron	pensaré pensarás pensará pensaremos pensaréis pensarán	pensaría pensarías pensaría pensaríamos pensaríais pensarían	piense pienses piense pensemos penséis piensen	pensara pensaras pensara pensáramos pensarais pensaran	piensa tú, no pienses piense usted pensemos pensad, no penséis piensen
volver (vuelvo) volviendo vuelto	vuelvo vuelves vuelve volvemos volvéis vuelven	volvía volvías volvía volvíamos volvíais volvían	volví volviste volvió volvimos volvisteis volvieron	volveré volverás volverá volveremos volveréis volverán	volvería volverías volvería volveríamos volveríais volverían	vuelva vuelvas vuelva volvamos volváis vuelvan	volviera volvieras volviera volviéramos volvierais volvieran	vuelve tú, no vuelvas vuelva usted volvamos volved, no volváis vuelvan
dormir (duermo) (u) durmiendo dormido	duermo duermes duerme dormimos dormís duermen	dormía dormías dormía dormíamos dormíais dormían	dormí dormiste durmió dormimos dormisteis durmieron	dormiré dormirás dormirá dormiremos dormiréis dormirán	dormiría dormirías dormiría dormiríamos dormiríais dormirían	duerma duermas duerma durmamos durmáis duerman	durmiera durmieras durmiera durmiéramos durmierais durmieran	duerme tú, no duermas duerma usted durmamos dormid, no durmáis duerman
sentir (siento) (i) sintiendo sentido	siento sientes siente sentimos sentís sienten	sentía sentías sentía sentíamos sentíais sentían	sentí sentiste sintió sentimos sentisteis sintieron	sentiré sentirás sentirá sentiremos sentiréis sentirán	sentiría sentirías sentiría sentiríamos sentiríais sentirían	sienta sientas sienta sintamos sintáis sientan	sintiera sintieras sintiera sintiéramos sintierais sintieran	siente tú, no sientas sienta usted sintamos sentid, no sintáis sientan
pedir (pido) (i) pidiendo pedido	pido pides pide pedimos pedís piden	pedía pedías pedía pedíamos pedíais pedían	pedí pediste pidió pedimos pedisteis pidieron	pediré pedirás pedirá pediremos pediréis pedirán	pediría pedirías pediría pediríamos pediríais pedirían	pida pidas pida pidamos pidáis pidan	pidiera pidieras pidiera pidiéramos pidierais pidieran	pide tú, no pidas pida usted pidamos pedid, no pidáis pidan

D. Stem-Changing and Spelling Change Verbs (continued)

Infinitive / Present Participle / Past Participle	INDICATIVE					SUBJUNCTIVE		IMPERATIVE
	Present	Imperfect	Preterite	Future	Conditional	Present	Imperfect	
reír (río) (i) / riendo / reído	río	reía	reí	reiré	reiría	ría	riera	ríe tú, no rías
	ríes	reías	reíste	reirás	reirías	rías	rieras	ría usted
	ríe	reía	rio	reirá	reiría	ría	riera	riamos
	reímos	reíamos	reímos	reiremos	reiríamos	riamos	riéramos	reíd, no riáis
	reís	reíais	reísteis	reiréis	reiríais	riáis	rierais	rían
	ríen	reían	rieron	reirán	reirían	rían	rieran	
seguir (sigo) (i) / siguiendo / seguido	sigo	seguía	seguí	seguiré	seguiría	siga	siguiera	sigue tú, no sigas
	sigues	seguías	seguiste	seguirás	seguirías	sigas	siguieras	siga usted
	sigue	seguía	siguió	seguirá	seguiría	siga	siguiera	sigamos
	seguimos	seguíamos	seguimos	seguiremos	seguiríamos	sigamos	siguiéramos	seguid, no sigáis
	seguís	seguíais	seguisteis	seguiréis	seguiríais	sigáis	siguierais	sigan
	siguen	seguían	siguieron	seguirán	seguirían	sigan	siguieran	
construir (construyo) / construyendo / construido	construyo	construía	construí	construiré	construiría	construya	construyera	construye tú, no construyas
	construyes	construías	construiste	construirás	construirías	construyas	construyeras	construya usted
	construye	construía	construyó	construirá	construiría	construya	construyera	construyamos
	construimos	construíamos	construimos	construiremos	construiríamos	construyamos	construyéramos	construid, no construyáis
	construís	construíais	construisteis	construiréis	construiríais	construyáis	construyerais	construyan
	construyen	construían	construyeron	construirán	construirían	construyan	construyeran	
conducir (conduzco) / conduciendo / conducido	conduzco	conducía	conduje	conduciré	conduciría	conduzca	condujera	conduce tú, no conduzcas
	conduces	conducías	condujiste	conducirás	conducirías	conduzcas	condujeras	conduzca usted
	conduce	conducía	condujo	conducirá	conduciría	conduzca	condujera	conduzcamos
	conducimos	conducíamos	condujimos	conduciremos	conduciríamos	conduzcamos	condujéramos	conducid, no conduzcáis
	conducís	conducíais	condujisteis	conduciréis	conduciríais	conduzcáis	condujerais	conduzcan
	conducen	conducían	condujeron	conducirán	conducirían	conduzcan	condujeran	

VOCABULARIES

This **Spanish-English Vocabulary** contains all the words that appear in the text, with the following exceptions: (1) most close or identical cognates that do not appear in the chapter vocabulary lists; (2) most conjugated verb forms; (3) diminutives ending in **-ito/a;** (4) absolute superlatives in **-ísimo/a;** (5) most adverbs ending in **-mente,** and (6) words listed or glossed in the **Vocabulario del segmento** and **Fragmento del guion** features of the **Salu2** sections. Active vocabulary is indicated by the number of the chapter in which a word or given meaning is first listed (**1 = Capítulo 1**); vocabulary that is glossed in the text is not considered to be active vocabulary and is not numbered. Only meanings that are used in the text are given. The **English-Spanish Vocabulary** is based on the chapter lists of active vocabulary.

The gender of nouns is indicated, except for masculine nouns ending in **-o** and feminine nouns ending in **-a.** Because **ch** and **ll** are no longer considered separate letters, words beginning with **ch** and **ll** are found as they would be found in English. The letter **ñ** follows the letter **n: añadir** follows **anuncio,** for example.

Irregular verbs found in the verb charts of Appendix 5 are set in red and underlined: <u>andar</u>. No changes are indicated for them in these vocabularies. Verbs with stem changes or spelling changes in the *present tense* show the **yo** form of the present tense in parentheses with the stem-vowel or spelling changes indicated in text in red and underlined: **s<u>e</u>ntarse (me s<u>ie</u>nto); cono<u>c</u>er (cono<u>zc</u>o); esco<u>g</u>er (esco<u>j</u>o); act<u>u</u>ar (act<u>ú</u>o).** Verbs with stem changes in the third person *preterite* and the *present participle* show the stem vowel in red and underlined (<u>i</u> or <u>u</u>) in parentheses after the present tense **yo** form: **pr<u>e</u>ferir (pref<u>ie</u>ro) (<u>i</u>); m<u>o</u>rirse (me m<u>ue</u>ro) (<u>u</u>).** Verbs with any other spelling changes in the first person *preterite* or *present subjunctive* show the change in parentheses: **bus<u>c</u>ar (<u>qu</u>); pa<u>g</u>ar (<u>gu</u>); emp<u>e</u>zar (emp<u>ie</u>zo) (<u>c</u>); averig<u>u</u>ar (<u>ü</u>).**

The following abbreviations are used:

adj.	adjective	*interj.*	interjection
adv.	adverb	*inv.*	invariable form
Arg.	Argentina	*L.A.*	Latin America
C.A.	Central America	*m.*	masculine
Carib.	Caribbean	*Mex.*	Mexico
Col.	Colombia	*n.*	noun
conj.	conjunction	*obj. (of prep.)*	object (of a preposition)
def. art.	definite article	*pl.*	plural
d.o.	direct object	*poss.*	possessive
f.	feminine	*p.p.*	past participle
fam.	familiar	*prep.*	preposition
form.	formal	*pron.*	pronoun
gram.	grammatical term	*refl. pron.*	reflexive pronoun
Guat.	Guatemala	*s.*	singular
ind. art.	indefinite article	*sl.*	slang
inf.	infinitive	*Sp.*	Spain
i.o.	indirect object	*sub. pron.*	subject pronoun

Spanish-English Vocabulary

A

a to; at (*with time*) (1); **a base de** based on; **a causa de** because of; **a continuación** following; **a este respecto** in this regard; **a la derecha de** to the right of (6); **a la izquierda de** to the left of (6); **a la moda** in fashion, in a stylish way; **a la(s)...** at ... (*time of day*) (1); **a menos que** unless (16); **a partir de** beyond (4); **a pesar de** in spite of; **a plazos** in installments (17); **¿a qué hora... ?** at what time ... ? (1); **a solas** alone; **a tiempo** on time (8); **a través de** across, through; throughout; **¿a usted le gusta... ?** do you (*form. s.*) like ... ? (1); **a veces** sometimes, at times (3); **a ver** let's see

abacería grocery store

abajo below; underneath

abandonar to abandon

aba<u>rc</u>ar (<u>qu</u>) to cover (*a topic*)

abarrotes *m. pl.* groceries

abecedario alphabet

abierto/a (*p.p. of* **abrir**) open (6)

abogado/a lawyer (17)

abo<u>g</u>ar (<u>gu</u>) to advocate

abolengo lineage

abolicionista *m., f.* abolitionist

aborto abortion

abra<u>z</u>ar(se) (<u>c</u>) to embrace (11)

abrazo hug, embrace

abreviatura abbreviation

abrigo coat (4)

abril *m.* April (6)

abrir (*pp.* **abierto**) to open (3)

abrumador(a) overwhelming

absoluto/a absolute

abstenerse (*like* <u>tener</u>) to refrain

absurdo/a absurd; **es absurdo que** + *subjunctive* it's absurd that (13)

abuelo/a grandfather/grandmother (3); *m. pl.* grandparents (3)

abundante abundant

aburrido/a bored (6); **<u>ser</u> aburrido/a** to be boring (10)

aburrimiento boredom

aburrir (*like* **gustar**) to bore (13); **aburrirse** to get bored (10)

abuso abuse

abyecto/a wretched

acá here

acabar to finish (14); to run out of (14); **acabar de** + *inf.* to have just (*done something*) (7)

academia academy

académico/a *adj.* academic (14); **año académico** school year; **vida académica** academic life (14)

acampar to camp; **tienda de acampar** tent

acaso: por si acaso just in case (14)

acatar to obey

acceso access

accesorio accessory

accidente *m.* accident (14)

acción *f.* action; **Día** (*m.*) **de (Acción de) Gracias** Thanksgiving (9)

aceite (*m.*) **(de oliva)** (olive) oil (7)

acelerado/a fast, accelerated (15); **ritmo acelerado de la vida** fast pace of life (15)

acelerar to accelerate; to speed up

acento accent; **acento diacrítico** diacritical mark; **acento ortográfico** accent mark

acentuación *f.* accent mark

acentuado/a accentuated

aceptable acceptable

aceptar to accept (14); **aceptar (las) disculpas** to accept apologies (14)

acera sidewalk (15)

acerca de *prep.* about, concerning, regarding

acer<u>c</u>arse (<u>qu</u>) (a) to come near to

ace<u>r</u>tar (ac<u>ie</u>rto) to guess correctly

ácido acid

acompañar to accompany

acondicionado/a: aire (*m.*) **acondicionado** air conditioning

aconsejable advisable

aconsejar to advise

acontecer to occur

acontecimiento event, happening (18)

ac<u>o</u>rdarse (me ac<u>ue</u>rdo) (de) to remember (13)

acordeón *m.* accordion

acoso harassment, bullying

ac<u>o</u>starse (me ac<u>ue</u>sto) to go to bed (5)

acostumbrarse (a) to become accustomed (to); to get used (to)

acribillar to bombard

acrílico/a acrylic

actitud *f.* attitude

actividad *f.* activity

activo/a active

acto act

actor *m.* actor (13)

actriz *f.* (*pl.* **actrices**) actor (13)

actuación *f.* performance

actual *adj.* current, present-day (12)

actualidad: en la actualidad currently, right now (10)

actuali<u>z</u>ar (<u>c</u>) to update

act<u>u</u>ar (act<u>ú</u>o) to act (13)

acuario aquarium

Acuario Aquarius

acuático/a aquatic

acudir (a) to go (to)

acueducto aqueduct

acuerdo agreement; **(no) <u>estar</u> de acuerdo** to (dis)agree (3)

acumular to accumulate

adaptación *f.* adaptation

adaptarse (a) to adapt (to)

adecuado/a appropriate

adelante forward

adelga<u>z</u>ar (<u>c</u>) to lose weight

además *adv.* besides (3); **además de** *prep.* besides

adentro inside

adicción *f.* addiction

adicional additional (1)

adiós good-bye (1)

adivinar to guess (9)

adjetivo *gram.* adjective (3); **adjetivo de nacionalidad** adjective of nationality (3); **adjetivo posesivo** possessive adjective (3)

administración *f.* administration; **administración de empresas** business administration (2)

administrar to administer; to manage; to run

admiración *f.* admiration

admirar to admire

admitir to admit

adolescencia adolescence (16)

adolescente *m., f.* adolescent, teenager; **de adolescente** as an adolescent (10)

¿adónde? where (to)? (4)

adoptar to adopt

adoquinado/a cobblestoned

adorar to adore

adquirir to acquire

adquisitivo/a: poder (*m.*) **adquisitivo** purchasing power

aduana customs (*at a border*) (8); **pasar por la aduana** to go/pass through customs (8)

adulto/a adult

adverbio *gram.* adverb

adverso/a adverse

advertencia warning

adyacente adjacent

aéreo/a aerial

aeróbico/a: <u>hacer</u> ejercicios aeróbicos to do aerobics (11)

aerolínea airline

aeropuerto airport (8)

afán *m.* effort

afanoso/a laborious, hard

afectación *f.* affectation

afectar to affect

afectivo/a: estado afectivo emotional state (9)

afecto affection

afeitarse to shave (5)

afición *f.* hobby (10)

aficionado/a fan (10); <u>ser</u> **aficionado/a (a)** to be a fan (of) (10)

afiliación *f.* affiliation

afiliado/a (a) affiliated (with)

afín related

afinidad *f.* compatibility

afirmación *f.* statement

afirmar to affirm

afirmativo/a affirmative

afluente affluent

afortunado/a fortunate, lucky

africano/a *n., adj.* African

afroamerindo/a *n., adj.* Afro-Amerindian

afroantillano/a Afro-Antillian

afroperuano/a Afro-Peruvian

afuera *adv.* outdoors (6)

afueras *f. pl.* outskirts (12); suburbs (12)

agencia agency; **agencia de compra-venta (de coches)** used car dealership; **agencia de viajes** travel agency

agenda personal calendar (14)

agente *m., f.* agent (8); **agente de viajes** travel agent

ágil agile

agitar to agitate

agnóstico/a agnostic

agobiado/a overwhelmed

agosto August (6)

agotar to empty; to drain

agradable agreeable, pleasant

agradar (*like* **gustar**) to please

agradecimiento *n.* thanks

agregar (gu) to add

agresivo/a aggressive

agrícola *adj. m., f.* agricultural

agricultor(a) farmer (15)

agricultura farming, agriculture (15)

agrio/a bitter

agroturismo agritourism

agroturista *m., f.* agritourist

agroturístico/a *adj.* of rural tourism

agrupar to group

agua *f.* (*but* **el agua**) **(mineral)** (mineral) water (7); **botella de agua** water bottle (2)

aguacate *m.* avocado (7)

aguar (ü) to dilute; water down

agudo/a sharp

águila *f.* (*but* **el águila**) eagle

agujero hole

ahí there

ahijado/a godson/goddaughter

ahora now (2); **ahora mismo** right now (6)

ahorrar to save (*money*) (17)

ahorro savings; **cuenta de ahorros** savings account

aimara *n.* Aymara

airado/a angry; annoyed

aire *m.* air (15); **aire acondicionado** air conditioning; **al aire libre** outdoors (10)

ajedrez *m.* chess; **jugar (juego) (gu) al ajedrez** to play chess (10)

ajo garlic

al (*contraction of* **a** + **el**) to the (4); **al** + *inf.* while (*doing something*); **al aire libre** outdoors (10); **al alcance** within reach; **al instante** right away; **al lado de** alongside of (6); **al menos** at least; **al principio de** at the beginning of (17)

alameda tree-lined avenue

alberca swimming pool (*Mex.*)

álbum *m.* album

alcance: al alcance within reach

alcanzar (c) to reach; to achieve

alce *m.* elk; moose

alcohol *m.* alcohol

alcohólico/a alcoholic; **bebida alcohólica** alcoholic beverage

alegrarse (de) to be glad, happy (about) (12)

alegre happy (6)

alemán *m.* German (*language*) (2)

alemán, alemana *n., adj.* German (3)

Alemania Germany

alergia allergy

alérgico/a allergic

alerta: ojo alerta eagle eye

alfabeto alphabet

alfombra rug (5)

algo something, anything (7)

algodón *m.* cotton (4); **de algodón** *adj.* (made of) cotton (4)

alguien someone, anyone (7)

algún (alguna/os/as) some, any (7); **alguna vez** once; ever (15)

alimentación *f.* diet

alimenticio/a of eating

alimento food

aliviar to alleviate

allá (way) over there (4)

allí there (4)

alma *m.* soul

almacén *m.* department store (4)

almacenamiento: espacio de almacenamiento storage space (12)

almacenar to store (12); to save (12)

almohada pillow

almorzar (almuerzo) (c) to have lunch (5)

almuerzo lunch (7)

¿aló? hello? (*telephone greeting*)

alojarse to lodge

alpinismo mountain climbing; **practicar (qu) el alpinismo** to mountain climb

alquilar *v.* to rent (12)

alquiler *n. m.* rent (12)

alrededor (de) around

alternar to take turns

alternativa *n.* alternative

alternativo/a *adj.* alternative

altiplanicie *f.* high plateau

altiplano high plateau

altitud *f.* height; altitude

alto/a tall (3); **de alta costura** high fashion; **de alto riesgo** high risk

altura altitude

alucinante incredible

alumno/a student

aluvial alluvial

amabilidad *f.* kindness

amable kind (3); nice (3)

amanecer *m.* dawn

amar to love (16)

amarillo/a yellow (4)

amasijo dough; mixture

Amazonas *m. s.* Amazon (River)

amazónico/a *adj.* Amazonian; **Selva Amazónica** Amazon Jungle

ambiental environmental

ambiente *m.* atmosphere; environment; **medio ambiente** environment (15)

ambigüedad *f.* ambiguity

ámbito area

ambos/as both

ambulante *adj.* traveling

América: América Latina Latin America; **Estados** (*m. pl.*) **Unidos de América** United States of America

americano/a American; **fútbol** (*m.*) **americano** football

amerindo/a *n., adj.* Amerindian

amigo/a friend (2)

amistad *f.* friendship (16)

amo/a (*but* **el ama**) **de casa** housekeeper (17)

amoníaco ammonia

amor *m.* love (16)

amoroso/a loving

ampliar (amplío) to widen

amplio/a wide; large; spacious

amueblado/a furnished

amueblar to furnish

amuleto charm; amulet

amurallado/a walled

analfabetismo *n.* illiteracy

analfabeto/a illiterate

análisis *m. inv.* analysis

analista *m., f.* analyst; **analista de sistemas** systems analyst (17)

analizar (c) to analyze

ananá *m.* pineapple
anaranjado/a orange (4)
ancho/a wide
anciano/a *n.* old person; *adj.* old; ancient; **residencia de ancianos** nursing home (12)
Andalucía Andalusia
andaluz(a) *n., adj.* Andalusian
andante: caballero andante knight-errant
andar to walk; **andar en bicicleta** to ride a bicycle (10); **cinta de andar** treadmill
andino/a Andean
android *m.* android (12)
anécdota anecdote
anémico/a anemic
anfibio amphibian
anfitrión, anfitriona host (*of an event*) (9)
ángel *m.* angel
angelino/a *adj.* from Los Angeles; *n.* person from Los Angeles
angloparlante *adj.* English-speaking
anglosajón, anglosajona Anglo Saxon
angosto/a narrow
ángulo angle
angustia anguish
anillo ring
ánima *f.* (*but* **el ánima**) soul
animado/a lively; animated; **dibujos** (*m. pl.*) **animados** cartoons
animal *m.* animal (15); **animal de peluche** stuffed animal; **animal doméstico** pet
animar(se) to cheer up; **animarse a** to get up the courage to (*do something*)
ánimo: estado de ánimo state of mind
aniversario anniversary
anoche *adv.* last night (11)
anónimo/a anonymous
ansiedad *f.* anxiety (14)
ansioso/a anxious
antártico/a *adj.* Antarctic
Antártida Antarctica
ante *prep.* before; in front of
anteayer *adv.* the day before yesterday (5)
antecedente *m. gram.* antecedent
anteojos *m. pl.* glasses (11)
antepenúltimo/a third from the end
anterior previous, preceding
antes *adv.* before; **antes de** *prep.* before (5); **antes de Cristo (a.C.)** before Christ (B.C.); **antes (de) que** *conj.* before (16)
antibiótico antibiotic (11)
anticipar to anticipate
anticipo advance
anticuado/a antiquated
antídoto antidote

antiguo/a old; ancient; former
antillano/a *adj.* of/from the Antilles
Antillas (*f. pl.*) **Mayores** Greater Antilles
antipático/a unpleasant, unlikeable (*people*) (3)
antojo appetizer
antónimo antonym
antropología anthropology
antropólogo/a anthropologist
anual annual
anualmente annually
anunciar to announce (8)
anuncio announcement; advertisement
añadir to add
año year (6); **año académico** school year; **año bisiesto** leap year; **el año entrante** next year; **Año Nuevo** New Year; **el año pasado** last year; **el año que viene** next year; **cumplir años** to have a birthday (9); **fin** (*m.*) **de año** end of the year (9); **tener... años** to be ... years old (3)
apagar (gu) to turn off (*a machine*) (12)
apagón *m.* blackout
aparato appliance (10); **aparato doméstico** home appliance (10)
aparcamiento parking place; parking lot
aparcar (qu) to park
aparecer (aparezco) to appear
apariencia appearance
apartamento apartment (2); **edificio de apartamentos** apartment building (12)
aparte also
apellido surname
apenas barely
aperitivo appetizer
apetecer (apetezco) (*like* **gustar**) to appeal to
apetito appetite
apio celery
aplicación *f.* app (12)
aplicar (qu) to apply
aportar to contribute
apóstol *m., f.* apostle
apoyar to support
apoyo support; help
apreciar to appreciate
aprender to learn (3); **aprender a** + *inf.* to learn how to (*do something*) (3)
aprendizaje *m.* learning
apropiado/a appropriate
aproximadamente approximately
aproximado/a approximate
aptitud *f.* aptitude
apuntar to write down; **apuntarse** to enroll; to add one's name to the list
apuntes *m. pl.* notes (*academic*) (14)
aquel, aquella *adj.* that ([way] over there) (4); *pron.* that one ([way] over there)

aquello (*neuter pron.*) that ([way] over there) (4)
aquellos/as *adj.* those ([way] over there) (4) *pron.* those ones ([way] over there)
aquí here (2)
árabe *m.* Arabic (*language*); *n., adj. m., f.* Arab
Arabia Saudita Saudi Arabia
arábico/a *adj.* Arabic
arado *n.* plow
araña spider
árbol *m.* tree (9); **árbol genealógico** family tree
arcángel *m.* archangel
archipiélago archipelago
archivo (computer) file (12)
arco arch
ardilla squirrel
área *f.* (*but* **el área**) area, region
arena sand
arepa *patty made of cornmeal and flour and stuffed with different foods*
aretes *m. pl.* earrings (4)
argentino/a *n., adj.* Argentine
argumento argument; plot
árido/a arid, dry
aristocrático/a aristocratic
arma *f.* (*but* **el arma**) weapon
armado/a: fuerzas (*f. pl.*) **armadas** armed forces
armar un bochinche to throw a (loud) party
armario armoire, free-standing closet (5)
armonía harmony
arpa *f.* (*but* **el arpa**) harp
arqueológico/a archaeological
arquitecto/a architect (13)
arquitectónico/a architectural
arquitectura architecture (13)
arraigado/a deeply rooted
arrancar (qu) to start up (*a car*) (15)
arreglar to fix, repair (15)
arrepentido/a sorry; repentant
arriba (de) *prep.* above
arroba @ (12)
arrodillarse to kneel
arrogancia arrogance
arrogante arrogant
arroz *m.* (*pl.* **arroces**) rice (7)
arruinar to ruin
arte *m.* art (2); **artes** *f. pl.* the arts (13); **bellas artes** fine arts; **obra de arte** work of art (13)
arteria artery
arterial: presión (*f.*) **arterial** blood pressure
artesanía arts and crafts (13)
artesano/a artisan
Ártico *adj.* Arctic

artículo article; **artículo (in)definido** *gram.* (in)definite article

artista *m., f.* artist (13)

artístico/a artistic (13); **expresión** (*f.*) **artística** artistic expression (13)

arvejas *f. pl.* green peas (7)

asado/a roast(ed) (7); grilled (7); **lechón** (*m.*) **asado** roast suckling pig; **pollo asado** roast chicken (7)

asaltar to rob

asamblea assembly

ascendencia ancestry, descent

ascensor *m.* elevator (12)

asco: ¡qué asco! yuck!

asegurar to assure; **asegurarse (de que)** to make certain (that)

asentamiento settlement

asentarse (me asiento) to settle

asesinar to assassinate (18)

asesinato assassination (18); murder

asesino *m., f.* murderer

así thus; so; **así como** as well as; **así que** therefore, consequently, so

asiático/a *adj.* Asian

asiento seat (8)

asignar to assign

asimismo additionally

asistencia sanitaria health care

asistente (*m., f.*) **de vuelo** flight attendant (8)

asistir (a) to attend, go to (*a class, function*) (3)

asma *m.* asthma

asociación *f.* association

asociado/a associated; **estado libre asociado** commonwealth

asociar to associate

aspecto aspect

aspiradora vacuum cleaner (10); **pasar la aspiradora** to vacuum (10)

aspirante *m., f.* job candidate; applicant (17)

aspirar to vacuum

aspirina aspirin

astronauta *m., f.* astronaut (17)

asumir to assume

asunto matter

asustar to scare

atacar (qu) to attack

ataque (*m.*) **(terrorista)** (terrorist) attack (18)

atar to tie

Atenas Athens

atención *f.* attention; **poner atención** to pay attention

atender (atiendo) to look after

atenerse (*like* **tener**) to deal with

ateo/a atheist

ático attic

Atlántico Atlantic

atleta *m., f.* athlete (10)

atmosférico/a atmospheric

átomo atom

atracción *f.* attraction

atractivo/a attractive

atraer (*like* **traer**) (*like* **gustar**) to draw, to attract (13)

atrás *adv.* back, backward; behind; **de atrás** backwards

atrasado/a (*with* **estar**) late (8)

atravesar (atravieso) to go through

atributo attribute

atún *m.* tuna (7)

audaz (*pl.* **audaces**) bold, daring

audiencia audience

auditivo/a aural

aula *f.* (*but* **el aula**) classroom

aumentar to increase

aumento raise

aun *adv.* even

aún *adv.* still, yet

aunque although

auriculares *m. pl.* headphones (12)

auscultar to listen (*with a stethoscope*)

ausencia absence

ausente absent

austeridad *f.* austerity

australiano/a *n., adj.* Australian

auténtico/a authentic

autobiográfico/a autobiographical

autobús *m.* bus (8); **estación** (*f.*) **de autobuses** bus station (8); **ir en autobús** to go/travel by bus (8); **parada del autobús** bus stop (12)

autóctono/a indigenous

autoestima self-esteem

automático/a automatic; **cajero automático** automatic teller machine (ATM) (17)

auto(móvil) *m.* auto(mobile) (15)

automovilístico/a *adj.* automobile

automutilación *f.* self-mutilation

autonomía autonomy; region

autónomo/a autonomous

autopista freeway, interstate (15)

autoprueba self-test

autor(a) author (13)

autoridad *f.* authority

autorizado/a authorized

autorretrato self-portrait

autostop: hacer autostop to hitchhike

autosuficiencia self-sufficiency

autosuficiente self-sufficient

auxiliar to help; to assist

avance *m.* preview

avanzado/a advanced

ave *f.* (*but* **el ave**) bird

avenida avenue (12)

aventura adventure

aventurero/a adventurous

aventurismo adventure tourism

aventurista *m., f.* adventure tourist

avergonzado/a embarrassed (9)

averiguar (ü) to find out

avión *m.* airplane (8); **ir en avión** to go/travel by plane (8); **volar (vuelo) en avión** to fly (8); to go by plane (8)

avisar to warn

aviso warning

¡ay! *interj.* ah!; ouch!

ayer yesterday (5); **ayer fue (miércoles...)** yesterday was (Wednesday ...) (5)

ayuda help (7)

ayudante *m., f.* assistant

ayudar to help (7); **ayudar a** + *inf.* to help to (*do something*) (7)

ayuntamiento local government

azteca *n., adj. m., f.* Aztec

azúcar *m.* sugar (7)

azul blue (4)

azulejo tile

B

baba saliva; **se le cae la baba por** he/she is drooling over

bacán: ¡qué bacán! fantastic!

bahía bay

bailable danceable

bailaor(a) flamenco dancer

bailar to dance (2)

bailarín, bailarina dancer (13)

baile *m.* dance (13)

bajada ebb; dip

bajar to lower; to download (12); **bajarse (de)** to get down (from) (8); to get off (of) (*a vehicle*) (8)

bajareque *n.* mud wall

bajo *prep.* under (14); **estar bajo muchas presiones** to be under a lot of pressure (14)

bajo/a short (*in height*) (3); low

balcón *m.* balcony

ballena whale (15)

ballet *m.* ballet (13)

baloncesto basketball

banana banana (7)

banano banana tree

bancario/a: tarjeta bancaria debit card (17)

banco bank (17)

banda band

bandeja tray

bandera flag

bandoneón *m.* large concertina

bañarse to take a bath, bathe (5)

bañera bathtub (5)

baño bathroom (5); **traje** (*m.*) **de baño** swimsuit (4)

bar *m.* bar; **ir a un bar** to go to a bar (10)

barato/a inexpensive (4)

barba beard

barbacoa barbecue (7)

barcelonés, barcelonesa of Barcelona (*Sp.*)

barco boat, ship (8); **ir en barco** to go/ travel by boat, ship (8)

barra bar

barrer (el piso) to sweep (the floor) (10)

barriga belly

barrio neighborhood (12)

barro mud

basarse en to base one's ideas/ opinions on

base *f.* base; **a base de** based on; **base de datos** data base; **con base en** based on

básico/a basic

basquetbol *m.* basketball (10)

bastante rather, sufficiently; enough (16)

bastar to be enough

basura trash (10); **sacar (qu) la basura** to take out the trash (10)

bata robe

batalla battle

batería battery (15)

bautizo baptism

bebé *m., f.* baby

beber to drink (3)

bebida drink (5); **bebida alcohólica** alcoholic beverage

beca scholarship

béisbol *m.* baseball (10)

beisbolista *m., f.* baseball player

Bélgica Belgium

belleza beauty

bello/a beautiful (15); **bellas artes** (*f. pl.*) fine arts

bendecir (*like* **decir**) to bless; **que Dios te bendiga** God bless you

bendito/a blessed

beneficio benefit

besar to kiss; **besarse** to kiss each other (11)

beso kiss

bestia beast

Biblia Bible

biblioteca library (2)

bibliotecario/a librarian (2)

bicentenario bicentennial

bicho insect

bici *f.* bike

bicicleta bicycle (10); **andar en bicicleta** to ride a bicycle (10)

bien *adv.* well (1); **caerle bien a alguien** to make a good impression on someone; **empleo bien pagado** well-paid job/position (17); **está bien** it's fine, OK (6); **estar bien** to be well; to be comfortable (*temperature*) (6); **llevarse bien (con)** to get along well (with) (16); **muy bien** fine, very well (1); **pasarlo bien** to have a good time (9); **portarse bien** to behave (9); **salir bien** to come/turn out well (5); to do well (5)

bienes raíces *m. pl.* real estate

bienestar *m.* well-being (11)

bienvenida *n.* welcome

bienvenido/a *adj.* welcome

bife *m.* beef

bilingüe bilingual

billete *m.* bill (*money*) (17); ticket (*Sp.*) (8); **billete de ida** one-way ticket (8); **billete de ida y vuelta** round-trip ticket (8); **billete electrónico** e-ticket (8)

binacional binational

biodiversidad *f.* biodiversity

biografía biography

biología biology

bioluminiscencia bioluminescence

bioquímica biochemistry

bisabuelo/a great-grandfather/ great-grandmother

bisiesto/a: año bisiesto leap year

bisonte *m.* bison

bistec *m.* steak (7)

blanco/a white (4); **pizarrón** (*m.*) **blanco** whiteboard (2); **vino blanco** white wine (7)

blando/a soft

blog *m.* blog (12)

bloqueador (*m.*) **solar** sunscreen (8)

bloqueo de llamadas call blocker

bluejeans *m. pl.* jeans

blusa blouse (4)

boca mouth (11)

bocadillo sandwich (*Sp.*)

bochinche: armar un bochinche to throw a (loud) party

bocina horn (*car*) (15)

boda wedding (*ceremony*) (16)

bodega grocery store (*Carib.*)

bogotano/a *adj.* from Bogotá, Colombia

bola ball

bolero love song

boleto ticket (*L.A.*) (8); **boleto de ida** one-way ticket (8); **boleto de ida y vuelta** round-trip ticket; **boleto electrónico** e-ticket (8)

bolígrafo pen (2)

bolívar *m. Venezuelan currency unit*

boliviano/a *n., adj.* Bolivian

bolso purse (4)

bomba bomb (18)

bombardeo bombing

bombero/a firefighter (18)

bombilla light bulb

bombo legüero *Argentine drum*

bonanza boom (*economic*)

bongó bongo

bonito/a pretty (*people and things*) (3)

boricua *n., adj.* Puerto Rican

Borinquen *indigenous name of Puerto Rico*

borinqueño/a *adj.* Puerto Rican

borrador *m.* draft (of a document)

borrasca storm

bosque *m.* forest (15); **bosque tropical lluvioso** tropical rain forest

bostezo yawn

botanas *f. pl.* (*Mex.*) appetizers (9)

botanía botany

botánico/a botanical

botar to throw out

botas *f. pl.* boots (4)

botella (de agua) (water) bottle (2)

botón *m.* button

boxeador(a) boxer

brasileño/a *n., adj.* Brazilian

brazo arm (11)

brecha gap; **brecha digital** digital gap; **brecha salarial** wage gap

Bretaña: Gran Bretaña Great Britain

breve brief

británico/a British

bronce *m.* bronze

broncear to tan

bruja witch

brujo wizard; warlock

bruto/a: producto nacional bruto gross national product

bucear to scuba dive; to snorkel

budismo Buddhism

budista *n., adj. m., f.* Buddhist

buen, bueno/a good (3); **¡buen provecho!** bon appetit! (7); enjoy your meal!; **buenas noches** good night (1); **buenas tardes** good afternoon (1); **buenos días** good morning (1); **hace (muy) buen tiempo** it's (very) good weather (6); it's (very) nice out (6); **lo bueno** the good news/thing (11); **muy buenas** good afternoon/evening (1); **tener buena suerte** to have good luck (14); to be lucky (14)

buey *sl.* dude (*Mex.*)

bufanda scarf

burlarse de to make fun of

buscador *m.* search engine (12)

buscar (qu) to look for (2); **buscar en internet** to look up on the internet (12)

búsqueda search

buzón (*m.*) **de voz** voice mailbox (12)

C

caballero andante knight-errant

caballo horse (10); **montar a caballo** to ride a horse (10)

caber to fit (*into an area*)

cabeza head (11); **dolor** (*m.*) **de cabeza** headache

cabina cabin (*on a ship*) (8)

cacerola casserole dish

cacique, cacica chief

cada *inv.* each, every (5); **cada vez más** increasingly; **cada vez mayor** greater and greater

cadena chain

caer to fall (14); to drop (14); **caer en** to fall on (*day of the week*); **caerle bien/mal a alguien** to make a good/bad impression on someone; **caerse** to fall down (14); **se le cae la baba por** he/she is drooling over

café *m.* coffee (2); *adj.* **(de) color café** brown (4)

cafeína caffeine

cafetal *m.* coffee plantation

cafetera coffeemaker (10)

cafetería cafeteria (2)

cafetero/a coffee plantation worker

caída fall (*from a height*)

caimán *m.* alligator

caja box

cajero/a (check-out) cashier; (bank) teller (17); **cajero automático** automatic teller machine (ATM) (17)

cajón *m.* drawer

calabaza pumpkin; squash

calabozo prison cell

calamar *m.* squid

calcetines *m. pl.* socks (4)

calculadora calculator (2)

calcular to calculate

cálculo calculus

calefacción *f.* heat (12)

calendario calendar (14)

calentador(a) *adj.* warming

calentar (caliento) to warm

calidad *f.* quality (*excellence*)

cálido/a hot

caliente hot (*in temperature, not taste*) (7)

calificación *f.* grade

caligrafía calligraphy; handwriting

callar to silence

calle *f.* street (12)

callejero/a *adj.* (of the) street

calma calm

calmarse to calm down

calor *m.* heat; **hace (mucho) calor** to be (very) hot (6); **tener (mucho) calor** to be (very) warm, hot (6)

caloría calorie

caluroso/a hot

cama bed (5); **guardar cama** to stay in bed (11); **hacer la cama** to make the bed (10); **tender (tiendo) la cama** to make the bed

cámara camera (12)

camarero/a waiter/waitress (7)

camarones *m. pl.* shrimp (7)

cambiar (de) to change (12)

cambio change; **cambio climático** climate change

camélidos *m. pl.* Camelidae (*ruminant mammal*)

camello camel

caminadora treadmill (11)

caminar to walk (10)

caminata: dar una caminata to hike (10); to go for a hike (10)

caminero/a: furia caminera road rage

camino road; path

camión *m.* truck

camioneta (mini) van (8)

camisa shirt (4)

camiseta T-shirt (4)

campamento campsite

campaña campaign; **tienda (de campaña)** tent (8)

campeón, campeona champion

campeonato championship

campesino/a farmer; field laborer (15)

camping *m.* campground (8); **hacer camping** to go camping (8)

campo field (15); countryside (15)

Canadá Canada; **Día (*m.*) del Canadá** Canada Day

canadiense *n., adj. m., f.* Canadian

canal *m.* channel (12)

canario canary

cancelar to cancel

cáncer *m.* cancer

cancha field; court (*tennis*)

canción *f.* song (7)

candidato/a candidate (18); **postularse como candidato/a** to run as a candidate (18)

cansado/a tired (6)

cansancio fatigue

cantante *m., f.* singer (13)

cantaor(a) flamenco singer

cantar to sing (2)

cantautor(a) singer, songwriter

cantidad *f.* quantity

cantinero/a bartender

caña sugar cane

cañonazo cannon shot

capa layer (15); **capa de ozono** ozone layer (15)

capacidad *f.* capacity

capaz (*pl.* capaces) able

Caperucita Roja Little Red Ridinghood

capilla chapel

capital *f.* capital city (6)

capitán, capitana captain

capítulo chapter

Capricornio Capricorn

cara face

caracola large shell

característica *n.* characteristic

característico/a *adj.* characteristic

caracterizar (c) to characterize

caramañola *torpedo-shaped meat pie of Colombia and Panama*

cárcel *f.* jail

cardinal: punto cardinal cardinal point (6)

cardiólogo/a cardiologist

carga load; **carga de trabajo** workload

cargo (political) office (18); **postularse para un cargo** to run for a position (18)

Caribe *m.* Caribbean; **mar (*m.*) Caribe** Caribbean Sea

caribeño/a Caribbean

caricatura caricature

cariño affection (16)

cariñoso/a affectionate (6)

carnaval *m.* carnival

carne *f.* meat (7)

carnet (*m.*) de identificación / de identidad identification card

carnicería butcher's shop

caro/a expensive (4)

carpa tent

carpeta (computer) folder (12)

carpintero/a carpenter

carrera career

carreta cart, wagon

carretera highway (15)

carretilla wheelbarrow

carril *m.* lane

carro (descapotable) (convertible) car (15)

carta letter (3); card; **jugar (juego) (gu) a las cartas** to play cards (10)

cartera wallet (4); handbag (4)

cartón *m.* cardboard

casa house, home (3); **amo/a (*but el ama*) de casa** housekeeper (17); **casa natal** house where someone was born; **en casa** at home (2); **limpiar la casa** to clean (the) house (10); **regresar a casa** to go home (2)

casabe *m.* tortilla-type bread made of cassava

casado/a married; **estar casado/a (con)** to be married (to) (16); **recién casado/a (con)** newlywed (to) (16)

casarse (con) to marry (16)

cascanueces *m. inv.* nutcracker

caserío hamlet; farmhouse

casero/a home-made

casi *adv.* almost (3); **casi nunca** almost never (3)

caso case; **en caso de** *prep.* in case (16); **en caso de que** *conj.* in case (16)

castaño/a brown (chestnut-colored)

castañuelas *f. pl.* castinets

castellano Spanish (language)

castigar (gu) to punish

cata (de vino) (wine) tasting

catalán *m.* Catalan (*language*); **catalán, catalana** *adj.* Catalan

catálogo catalogue

Cataluña Catalonia

catarata waterfall

catarro cold (*health condition*)

catedral *f.* cathedral

categoría category

catolicismo Catholicism
católico/a n., adj. Catholic
catorce fourteen (1)
caucásico/a Caucasian
causa cause (14); **a causa de** because of
causar to cause
cava cellar
cazador(a) hunter
ca**z**ar (**c**) to hunt
CD m. CD (compact disc) (12)
CD-ROM m. CD-ROM (12)
cebolla onion (7)
cédula identity card
celda cell (*prison*)
celebración f. celebration
celebrar to celebrate (6)
celíaco/a gluten intolerant
celos m. pl. jealousy
celta n., adj. m., f. Celtic
celular: (teléfono) celular m. cell
    phone (2)
cementerio cemetery
cena dinner, supper (7)
cenar to have (eat) dinner, supper (7)
Cenicienta Cinderella
centavo cent
centígrado Celsius
céntrico/a central
centro center (*political*) (18); downtown
    (4); **centro comercial** shopping
    mall (4)
Centroamérica Central America
centroamericano/a Central American
cepillarse los dientes to brush one's
    teeth (5)
cerámica pottery (13); ceramics (13)
cerca adv. near, nearby, close; **cerca de**
    prep. close to (6)
cercano/a adj. close, near
cerdo pork (7); **chuleta de cerdo** pork
    chop (7)
cereal m. cereal (7)
cerebro brain (11)
ceremonia ceremony (16)
cero zero (1)
cerrado/a closed (6)
c**e**rrar (c**ie**rro) to close (5); **cerrarse** to
    close; to finish
cerro hill
certeza certainty
cerveza beer (7)
césped m. lawn; grass
cesto basket
ceviche m. *raw fish dish*
champán m. champagne (9)
champiñones m. pl. mushrooms (7)
chanclas f. pl. flip-flops (4)
chaqueta jacket (4)
charango *stringed instrument*
charco puddle
charlar to chat
chatear to chat

chateo n. chat (12)
chauchas f. pl. green beans (*Arg.*)
cheque m. check (17); **con cheque** by
    check (17)
chequeo check-up (11)
chévere sl. cool
chibcha n., adj. m., f. indigenous
    people of the Colombian Andes
chicha *natural fruit soft drink*
chicle m. gum
chico/a guy/girl (4)
chileno/a n., adj. Chilean
chino Chinese (*language*)
chino/a n., adj. Chinese
chisme m. gossip
chiste m. joke (8)
chocante shocking
cho**c**ar (**qu**) con/contra to run into,
    bump against (14)
chocolate m. chocolate
chofer m., f. driver
choque m. collision, crash (18)
chuleta (de cerdo) (pork) chop (7)
churro *strip of fried dough*
cibernauta adj. of the internet; n. / m., f.
    internet user
ciclismo bicycling (10)
ciclo cycle
ciclón m. cyclone
ciego/a blind
cien one hundred (3)
ciencia science (2); **ciencia ficción**
    science fiction; **ciencias** (f. pl.)
    naturales natural sciences (2);
    ciencias (f. pl.) **políticas** political
    science (2); **ciencias** (f. pl.) **sociales**
    social sciences (2)
científico/a scientist
ciento one hundred (4); **ciento dos** one
    hundred two (4); **ciento noventa y**
    nueve one hundred ninety-nine (4);
    ciento uno/a one hundred one (4)
cierto/a true (13); **es cierto que** +
    indicative it's certain that (13)
ciervo deer; stag
cifra figure, number
cigarrillo cigarette
cinco five (1)
cincuenta fifty (3)
cine m. s. movies (5); movie theater (5)
cineasta m., f. filmmaker
cinematográfico/a adj. movie, film
cinta: cinta de <u>andar</u>/correr treadmill;
    cinta rodante treadmill
cinturón m. belt (4)
circulación f. traffic (15)
circular to circulate
círculo circle
circunstancia circumstance
cirugía surgery
cisne m. swan
cita appointment (11); date (11)

citar to cite, quote
ciudad f. city (3)
ciudadano/a citizen (18)
cívico/a civic (18); **responsabilidad** (f.)
    cívica civic duty (18)
civil civil (16); **estado civil** marital
    status (16); **guerra civil** civil war
civilización f. civilization
clarifi**c**ar (**qu**) to clarify
claro/a clear
clase f. class (*of students*) (2); class,
    course (*academic*) (2); **compañero/a**
    (de clase) classmate (2); <u>dar</u> **clases**
    to teach class; **salón** (m.) **de clase**
    classroom (2)
clásico/a classic(al) (13)
clasifi**c**ar (**qu**) to classify
cláusula gram. clause
clave f. n., adj. inv. key
clic: <u>hacer</u> **clic** to click (12)
cli**c**ar (**qu**) to click
cliente/a client (2)
clima m. climate (6)
climático/a adj. climate (18); **cambio**
    climático climate change; **crisis** (f.)
    climática climate crisis (18)
clínica clinic
cliquear to click
clóset m. closet
club club (10); <u>ir</u> **a un club** to go to
    a club (10)
coalición f. coalition
cobrar to cash (*a check*) (17); to charge
    (*someone for an item or service*) (17)
cobre m. copper
coche m. car (3); **agencia de**
    compra-venta (de coches) used
    car dealership; **coche descapotable**
    convertible (car) (15)
cochera garage; carport
cochinilla cochineal
cocido/a adj. cooked
cocina kitchen (5); cuisine (7)
cocinar to cook (7)
cocinero/a cook (17); chef (17)
coco coconut
cocodrilo crocodile
cóctel m. cocktail party
codiciado/a coveted
código code
codirector(a) codirector
codo elbow
coexistir to coexist
co**g**er (co**j**o) to take (*things*) (*Sp.*)
cognado gram. cognate
coherente coherent
cohesión f. cohesion
coincidencia coincidence
coincidir to coincide
cola line (*of people*) (8); <u>hacer</u> **cola** to
    stand in line (8)
colaborar to collaborate

colección *f.* collection
coleccionar to collect
colectivo bus
colega *m., f.* colleague
colegio school
colérico/a furious
colesterol *m.* cholesterol
coletilla tag (*as in* tag question)
colgar (cuelgo) (gu) to post (*on the internet*)
colina hill
collar *m.* necklace
colmado small grocery store (*Carib.*)
colocar (qu) to place
colombiano/a Colombian
colonia colony
colonización *f.* colonization
colonizador(a) colonist
colonizar (c) to colonize
colono/a settler
coloquial colloquial
color *m.* color (4); *adj.* **(de) color café** brown (4)
colorado/a red-colored
colorido/a colorful
columna column
comadre *f.* godmother
combatir to combat
combinación *f.* combination
combinar to combine
comedia comedy (13)
comediante *m., f.* comedian
comedor *m.* dining room (5)
comentar to talk about
comentario comment
comentarista *m., f.* commentator
comenzar (comienzo) (c) to begin; **comenzar a** + *inf.* to begin to (*do something*)
comer to eat (3); **comerse** to eat up
comercial: centro comercial shopping mall (4)
comercio business, commerce; **libre comercio** free trade
comestibles *m. pl.* groceries, foodstuff (7)
cometa *m.* comet
cometer to commit
cómico/a funny; **tira cómica** comic strip
comida food (7); meal (7); **comida rápida** fast food
comienzo beginning
comillas *f. pl.* quotation marks
como like; as; **así como** as well as; **tan... como** as ... as (6); **tanto como** as much as (6); **tanto/a(os/as)... como** as much/many ... as (6)
¿cómo? how?; what? (1); **¿cómo es usted?** what are you (*form. s.*) like? (1); **¿cómo está?** how are you (*form. s.*)? (1); **¿cómo estás?** how are you (*fam. s.*)? (1); **¿cómo se llama usted?** what is your (*form. s.*) name? (1); **¿cómo se**

llega a... ? how do you get to ... ? (15); **¿cómo te llamas?** what is your (*fam. s.*) name? (1)
cómoda bureau (5); dresser (5)
comodidad *f.* convenience
cómodo/a comfortable (4)
compacto/a: disco compacto (**CD** *m.*) compact disc (CD) (12)
compadre *m.* godfather
compañero/a companion; friend; **compañero/a (de clase)** classmate (2); **compañero/a de cuarto** roommate (2)
compañía company
comparación *f.* comparison (6)
comparar to compare
comparativo/a comparative
compartir to share
compasión *f.* compassion
compensar to make up for
competencia competition
competente competent
competición *f.* competition
competitivo/a competitive
complejo/a complex
complemento accessory (4)
complemento (in)directo *gram.* (in)direct object
completar to complete
completo/a complete
complicación *f.* complication
componer (*like* **poner**) to compose (13)
comportamiento behavior
composición *f.* composition
compositor(a) composer (13)
compostero composter
compra-venta: agencia de compra-venta (de coches) used car dealership
comprador(a) buyer
comprar to buy (2); **comprar por internet** to buy online (4)
compras: de compras shopping (4); **ir de compras** to go shopping (4)
comprender to understand (3)
comprensible understandable
comprensión *f.* understanding; comprehension
comprensivo/a *adj.* understanding
comprobar (compruebo) to prove
comprometido/a committed
compuesto/a composed; compound (*gram.*)
compulsivo/a compulsive
computación *f.* computer science (2)
computadora (portátil) (laptop) computer (2)
común common
comunicación *f.* communication; *pl.* **comunicaciones** (*subject*) (2); **medio de comunicación** medium of communication (18)

comunicarse (qu) (con) to communicate (with) (18)
comunicativo/a communicative
comunidad *f.* community
comunión *f.* communion
comunitario/a *adj.* community
con with (2); **chocar (qu) con** to run into, bump against (14); **comunicarse (qu) (con)** to communicate (with) (18); **con base en** based on; **con cheque** by check (17); **con cuidado** carefully; **con frecuencia** frequently (2); **con permiso** excuse me (1); **¿con qué frecuencia... ?** how often ... ? (3); **con respecto a** regarding; **con tal de** *prep.* provided (16); **con tal (de) que** *conj.* provided (that), as long as (16); **darse con** to run into; **pegarse (gu) con** to run/bump into (14)
conceder to concede
concentración *f.* concentration
concentrar to concentrate
concepto concept (18)
conciencia conscience
concienciación *f. n.* conscious-raising
concierto concert (10); **ir a un concierto** to go to a concert (10)
conciso/a concise
conclusión *f.* conclusion
concordancia *gram.* agreement
concreto: en concreto in particular
concursante *m., f.* contestant
concurso contest
condenado/a condemned
condición *f.* condition
condicional *gram.* conditional
cóndor *m.* condor
conducción *f.* driving
conducir to drive (15)
conductor(a) driver (15)
conectar to connect; **conectarse** to connect (12)
conector *m.* connector
conejo/a rabbit
conexión *f.* connection
conferencia lecture
confesional confessional
confianza confidence
confiar (confío) to trust
configurar to configure
confirmar to confirm
conflicto conflict
confluencia *n.* coming-together
confundido/a confused
congelado/a frozen (6); very cold (6)
congelador *m.* freezer (10)
congestión *f.* congestion
congresista *m., f.* member of congress
congreso congress; **representante** (*m., f.*) **al congreso** congressional representative (18)

conjugación *f. gram.* conjugation

conjugar (gu) *gram.* to conjugate

conjunción *f. gram.* conjunction (16); **conjunción de tiempo** conjunction of time (17)

conjunto group

conllevar to involve

conmemorar to commemorate

conmigo with me (6)

Cono Sur Southern Cone

conocer (conozco) to know (*a person*) (7); be acquainted, familiar with (*a place*) (7); to meet (*a person*) (7); **conocerse** to meet (16)

conocimiento knowledge

conquista conquest

conquistador(a) conqueror

consciente conscious, aware

consecuencia consequence

consecutivo/a consecutive

conseguir (*like* **seguir)** to get (9); to obtain (9); **conseguir + inf.** to succeed in (*doing something*) (9)

consejero/a advisor (2)

consejo (piece of) advice (7)

conservación *f.* conservation

conservacionista conservationist

conservador(a) conservative

conservar to save; to conserve (15)

consideración *f.* consideration

considerar to consider

consigo with himself, herself, themselves

consiguiente: por consiguiente as a result

consistencia consistency

consistir (en) to consist (of)

constante constant

constar (de) to consist of

constatar to confirm

constipado/a: estar constipado/a to have a cold

constitución *f.* constitution

constituir (*like* **construir)** to constitute

construcción *f.* construction

construir to build (15)

consuelo consolation

consulta consultation

consultar to consult

consultorio (medical) office (11); consultation

consumidor(a) consumer

consumir to consume

consumo consumption

contabilidad *f.* accounting

contable *m., f.* accountant (*Sp.*)

contacto contact; **lentes** (*m. pl.*) **de contacto** contact lenses (11); **mantenerse (***like* **tener) en contacto** to stay in touch

contador(a) accountant (17)

contaminación *f.* pollution (6); **hay (mucha) contaminación** there's (lots of) pollution (6)

contaminado/a contaminated, polluted (15)

contaminar to pollute (15)

contar (cuento) to tell (8); to narrate (8)

contemplación *f.* contemplation

contemplar to contemplate

contemporáneo/a contemporary

contenedor *m.* container

contener (*like* **tener)** to contain

contenido contents

contento/a content, happy (6)

contestar to answer (7)

contexto context

contigo with you (*fam.*) (6)

continente *m.* continent

contingencia contingency

continuación: a continuación following

continuar (continúo) to continue (6)

contra against; **chocar (qu)/pegarse (gu) contra** to run into; to bump against (14); **darse contra** to run into

contrabajo double bass (*musical instrument*)

contradecir (*like* **decir)** to contradict

contraer (*like* **traer)** to contract

contrario contrary

contrarrestar to resist

contraseña password (12)

contrastar to contrast

contraste *m.* contrast

contrastivo/a contrasting

contribución *f.* contribution

contribuir (*like* **construir)** to contribute

control *m.* control (8); **control de seguridad** security (check) (8); **control remoto** remote control (12); **pasar por el control de seguridad** to go/pass through security (check) (8)

controlador(a) controller

controlar to control

convencer (convenzo) to convince

convención *f.* convention; system

conversación *f.* conversation

conversar to converse

convertir (convierto) (i) to convert

convivencia cohabitation; living together

convivir to live together

coordinar to coordinate

copa (wine) glass

Copa del Mundo World Cup (*soccer*); **Copa Mundial** World Cup (*soccer*)

copia copy; **hacer copia** to copy

copiar to copy (12)

copioso/a copious

coquí *m. small frog of Puerto Rico*

corazón *m.* heart (11)

corbata tie (4)

cordillera mountain range

coreano/a *n., adj.* Korean

cormorán cormorant (*aquatic bird*)

coro chorus

corona crown

corporación *f.* corporation

correcto/a correct

corregir (corrijo) (i) to correct (14); to grade (14)

correo mail; **correo electrónico** e-mail (12)

correr to run (10); **cinta de correr** treadmill

correspondencia correspondence

corresponder (a) to correspond (to)

correspondiente *m., f.* correspondent; *adj.* corresponding

corrido *Mexican folk song*

corriente: cuenta corriente checking account; **estar al corriente** to be up to date

cortar to cut

cortejo courting

cortés *m., f.* polite

cortesía courtesy; **expresión** (*f.*) **de cortesía** courteous expression (1)

cortijo country house

cortina curtain

corto *n.* short segment (*film*)

corto/a short (*in length*) (3); **pantalones** (*m. pl.*) **cortos** shorts (4)

cosa thing (5)

cosecha harvest; crop

cosechar to harvest

cosmético/a cosmetic

cosmopolita *m., f.* cosmopolitan

cosmovisión *f.* world view

costa coast

costar (cuesto) to cost; **¿cuánto cuesta(n)?** how much does it (do they) cost? (4)

costarricense *n., adj. m., f.* Costa Rican

costero/a coastal

costo cost

costoso/a expensive

costumbre *f.* custom

costura: de alta costura high fashion

cotidiano/a daily

country *m.* country music

COVID-19 *m., f.* COVID-19 (11)

creación *f.* creation

crear to create (13)

creatividad *f.* creativity

creativo/a creative

crecer (crezco) to grow (16)

crecimiento *n.* rise, growth

credencial *f.* identity card

crédito credit; **tarjeta de crédito** credit card (7)

creencia belief

creer (en) to think (3); to believe (in) (3); **no creer** to not think/believe (13)

creíble believable

crema cream

cremoso/a creamy

creyente *m., f.* believer

criado/a servant

criatura child

crimen *m. (pl.* **crímenes)** crime

criollo/a *n., adj.* creole

crisis climática climate crisis (18)

cristal *m.* glass

cristianismo Christianity

cristiano/a *n., adj.* Christian

Cristo Christ; **antes de Cristo (a.C.)** before Christ (B.C.); **después de Cristo (a.D.)** Anno Domini (A.D.)

crítica criticism

criticar (qu) to criticize

crítico/a critic

crónica chronicle

crónico/a chronic

cronológico/a chronological

croqueta croquette

crucero cruise (ship) (8)

crudo/a raw

cruz *f. (pl.* **cruces)** cross; **Día (*m.*) de la Cruz** Day of the Cross

cruzar (c) to cross; **cruzarse con** to cross paths with

cuaderno notebook (2)

cuadrado *n.* square

cuadrado/a *adj.* square

cuadro painting (*specific piece*) (13); **de cuadros** plaid (4)

cuajar to fit in

cual: el/la cual, lo cual, los/las cuales which

¿cuál(es)? what? (2); which? (2); **¿cuál es la fecha de hoy?** what's today's date? (6); **¿cuál es tu onda?** what's your style?

cualidad *f.* quality (*characteristic*)

cualquier *adj. inv.* any

cuando when

¿cuándo? when? (2)

cuanto: en cuanto as soon as (17); **en cuanto a** regarding

¿cuánto? how much? (2); **¿cuánto cuesta(n)?** how much does it (do they) cost? (4); **¿cuánto tiempo hace que... ?** how long ago (*did something happen*)? / for how long (*has something been happening*)?

¿cuántos/as? how many? (2)

cuáquero/a *n.* Quaker

cuarenta forty (3)

Cuaresma Lent

cuartel *m.* barracks

cuarto room (2); one-fourth; quarter (*of an hour*); **compañero/a de cuarto**

roommate (2); **menos cuarto** a quarter to (*hour*) (1); **y cuarto** a quarter (fifteen minutes) after (*the hour*) (1)

cuarto/a *adj.* fourth (13)

cuate *sl. m., f.* buddy, pal

Cuatro de Julio Independence Day (9)

cuatro four (1)

cuatrocientos/as four hundred (4)

cubano/a *n., adj.* Cuban

cubanoamericano/a *n., adj.* Cuban American

cubierto/a (*p.p. of* **cubrir**) covered

cubiertos *m. pl.* cutlery

cubrir (*p.p.* **cubierto**) to cover (15)

cucaracha cockroach

cuchara spoon

cucharada spoonful

cuchillo knife

cuello neck (11)

cuenta check, bill (7); **cargar (gu) a una cuenta** to charge to an account (17); **cuenta corriente** checking account

cuento story

cuerda string

cuero leather (4); **de cuero** leather (4)

cuerpo (humano) (human) body (11)

cuervo crow

cuestión *f.* question (*issue*); matter (17)

cuestionable questionable

cuestionario questionnaire

cuidado care; *interj.* careful!; **con cuidado** carefully; **tener cuidado** to be careful

cuidar a to care for; **cuidar de** to take care of (11); **cuidarse** to take care of oneself (11)

culebra snake

culinario/a culinary

culminar to culminate

culpa fault; **tener la culpa** to be at fault; **fue mi culpa** it was my fault (14)

cultivar to cultivate

cultivo cultivation

culto cult; **rendir (rindo) (i) culto** to worship

cultrún *m.* ceremonial Mapuche drum

cultura culture

cultural cultural (13); **tradición** (*f.*) **cultural** cultural tradition (13)

cumbia *Colombian folk dance now popular throughout Latin America*

cumbre *f.* summit

cumpleaños *m. inv.* birthday (6); **pastel** (*m.*) **de cumpleaños** birthday cake (9)

cumplir to fulfill; **cumplir años** to have a birthday (9)

cuñado/a brother-in-law, sister-in-law

cupo quota; capacity (*space*)

cupón *m.* coupon

cura cure

curación *f.* cure

curar to cure

curativo/a curing, curative

curioso/a curious

currículum (vitae) *m.* résumé (17)

cursi in poor taste; trite

curso course; **programa** (*m.*) **del curso** course syllabus (14)

cuyo/a whose

D

dama lady

danza dance (13)

daño: hacerse daño to hurt oneself (14); **hacerse daño en** to hurt one's (*body part*) (14)

dar to give (8); **dar clases** to teach class; **dar un paseo** to take a walk (10); **dar una caminata** to hike; to go for a hike (10); **darle una fiesta (a alguien)** to give (someone) a party (9); to have a party (for someone) (9); **darse con/contra** to run into; **darse la mano** to shake hands (11)

darwinista *m., f.* Darwinian

datar de to date back to

datos *m. pl.* data; **base** (*f.*) **de datos** data base

de of (1); from (1); **de adolescente** *adj.* adolescent (10); **de algodón** *m.* (made of) cotton (4); **de alta costura** high fashion; **de alto riesgo** high risk; **de atrás** backwards; **de compras** shopping (4); **de cuadros** plaid (4); **de cuero** leather (4); **¿de dónde eres (tú)?** where are you (*fam. s.*) from? (1); **¿de dónde es (usted)?** where are you (*form. s.*) from? (1); **de estatura mediana** of medium height; **de exposición** expository; **de forma presencial** in person; **de la mañana** in the morning, A.M. (1); **de la noche** in the evening, P.M. (1); **de la tarde** in the afternoon, P.M. (1); **de lana** wool (4); **de lunares** polka-dot (4); **de manera que** so that, in such a way that; **de modo que** in such a way that; **de nada** you're welcome (1); **de niño/a** as a child (10); **de oro** gold (4); **de plata** silver (4); **¿de quién?** whose? (3); **de rayas** striped (4); **de remate** hopeless(ly); **de repente** suddenly (11); **de seda** silk (4); **de todo** everything (4); **de todo tipo** of all kinds; **de vacaciones** on vacation (8); **¿de veras?** really?; **de viaje** on a trip, traveling (8); **es de...** it is made of ... (4); **estar de vacaciones** to be on vacation (8)

debajo de below (6)

debate *m.* debate

debatir to debate

deber *n. m.* responsibility (18); obligation (18)

deber *v.* + *inf.* should, must, ought to (*do something*) (3)

debido/a a due to; because of

débito debit (17); **tarjeta de débito** debit card (17)

década decade

decadencia decadence

decente decent

decidir to decide

décimo/a tenth (13)

decimotercer(o/a) thirteenth

decir to say (8); to tell (8); **eso quiere decir...** that means ... (11)

decisión *f.* decision

declaración *f.* statement

declarar to state

decoración *f.* decoration

decorar to decorate

decorativo/a decorative

dedicarse (qu) (a) to dedicate oneself (to)

dedo (de la mano) finger (11); **dedo del pie** toe (11)

deducir (*like* **conducir**) to deduce

defender (defiendo) to defend

defensa defense

defensor(a) defender

deficiencia deficiency

deficiente deficient

definición *f.* definition

definido: artículo definido *gram.* definite article

definir to define

degustar to taste

dejar to leave; to let, allow; to quit (17); **dejar de** + *inf.* to stop (*doing something*) (11)

del (*contraction of* **de** + **el**) of the; from the (3)

delante de in front of (6)

delegación *f.* delegation

delfín *m.* dolphin

delgado/a thin, slender (3)

deliberado/a deliberate

delicia delicacy

delicioso/a delicious

delito crime (15)

demanda demand

demás: los/las demás the rest, others (12)

demasiado *adv.* too (9)

demasiado/a *adj.* too much (9); **demasiados/as** too many (9)

democracia democracy

demócrata *m., f.* democrat

democrático/a democratic

demonio demon, devil

demora delay (8)

demostración *f.* demonstration

demostrar (demuestro) to demonstrate

demostrativo/a *gram.* demonstrative (4)

denominación *f.* denomination

densidad *f.* density (15)

dentista *m., f.* dentist (11)

dentro *adv.* inside; **dentro de** *prep.* inside; within; in (*time*)

departamento department

dependencia dependence

depender (de) to depend (on)

dependiente/a clerk (2)

deporte *m.* sport (10); **practicar (qu) un deporte** to play a sport

deportista *m., f.* athlete

deportivo/a *adj.* sporting, sports (10); sports-loving (10)

depositar to deposit (17)

depósito deposit

depresión *f.* depression

deprimido/a depressed

derecha *n.* right side (6); **a la derecha de** to the right of (6)

derecho *n.* right (18); **(todo) derecho** straight ahead (15)

derivación *f.* branch, offshoot

derivarse (de) to derive (from)

derramar to spill

desacuerdo disagreement

desafío challenge

desagradable disagreeable

desahogarse (gu) to let off steam; to vent

desamor *m.* lack of affection

desaparecer (desaparezco) to disappear

desarrollar to develop (15)

desarrollo development (15)

desastre *m.* disaster (14)

desastroso/a disastrous

desayunar to have (eat) breakfast (7)

desayuno breakfast (7)

descansar to rest (5)

descanso rest

descapotable: coche/carro descapotable convertible (car) (15)

descargar (gu) to download (12)

descendiente *m., f.* descendent

descentralizado/a decentralized

descifrar to decipher; to figure out

desconectar to unplug; to disconnect

desconocido/a unknown

descontento/a unhappy

descortés *m., f.* rude, impolite

describir (*p.p.* **descrito**) to describe

descripción *f.* description

descriptivo/a descriptive

descrito/a (*p.p. of* **describir**) described

descubierto/a (*p.p. of* **descubrir**) discovered

descubrimiento discovery

descubrir (*p.p.* **descubierto**) to discover (15)

desde *prep.* from; since

desear to want (2)

desempleo unemployment

deseo wish

desequilibrio imbalance

desértico/a *adj.* desert

desesperanza desperation

desfile *m.* parade

desgracia misfortune; disgrace

desgraciadamente unfortunately (11)

deshumanización *f.* dehumanization

desierto desert

designación *f.* designation

designar to appoint; to designate

desigualdad *f.* inequality (18)

desilusión *f.* disillusion

desinflado/a: llanta desinflada flat tire (15)

desocupado/a empty; available

desordenado/a messy (6)

desorganizado/a unorganized

despacio *adv.* slowly

despedida farewell

despedir (*like* **pedir**) to let (*someone*) go (17); to fire (*someone*) (*from a job*) (17); **despedirse (de)** to say good-bye (to) (9)

despejado/a clear (*sky*)

desperdiciar to waste

desperdicio waste

despertador *m.* alarm clock (14)

despertarse (me despierto) to wake up (5)

despierto/a (*p.p. of* **despertar**) awake

despistado/a absent-minded; forgetful

después *adv.* then, later next (5); **después de** *prep.* after (5); **después de Cristo (a.D.)** Anno Domini (A.D.); **después (de) que** *conj.* after (17)

destacar (qu) to emphasize; **destacarse** to stand out

destino destination (8); destiny

destrucción *f.* destruction

destruir (*like* **construir**) to destroy (15)

desventaja disadvantage

detalle *m.* detail (9)

detective *m., f.* detective

detenerse (*like* **tener**) to stop

determinación *f.* determination

determinado/a specific

determinante decisive

determinar to determine

detestar to detest

detrás de behind (6)

deuda debt

devolver (*like* **volver**) to return (*something to someone*) (14)

devoto/a devout

día *m.* day (2); **buenos días** good morning (1); **Día de (Acción de) Gracias** Thanksgiving (9); **Día de la**

Cruz Day of the Cross; **Día de la Madre** Mother's Day; **Día de los Difuntos** Day of the Dead; **Día de los Muertos** Day of the Dead; **Día de los Pueblos Indígenas** Columbus Day (9); **Día de los Reyes Magos** Day of the Magi (Three Kings) (9); **Día de San Patricio** St. Patrick's Day; **Día de San Valentín** St. Valentine's Day; **Día del Padre** Father's Day; **día festivo** holiday (9); **Día Internacional de la No Violencia Contra la Mujer** International Day for the Elimination of Violence against Women; **días** (*m. pl.*) **de la semana** days of the week (5); **estar al día** to be up to date (18); **¿qué día es hoy?** what day is today? (5); **todos los días** every day (2)

diabetes (*f. inv.*) **(juvenil)** (childhood) diabetes

diabético/a diabetic

diablo devil

diacrítico/a: acento diacrítico diacritical mark

diagnosticar (qu) to diagnose

diágrafo group of letters that represent a single sound

dialecto dialect

diálogo dialogue

diamante *m.* diamond

diariamente daily

diario/a daily (5)

dibujante *m., f.* drawer (*person*) (13)

dibujar to draw (13)

dibujo drawing (13); **dibujos** (*m. pl.*) **animados** cartoons

diccionario dictionary (2)

dicho saying

diciembre *m.* December (6)

dictador(a) dictator (18)

dictadura dictatorship (18)

dictar to dictate

diecinueve nineteen (1)

dieciocho eighteen (1)

dieciséis sixteen (1)

diecisiete seventeen (1)

diente *m.* tooth (5); **cepillarse los dientes** to brush one's teeth (5)

dieta diet (7); **estar a dieta** to be on a diet (7)

dietético/a *adj.* diet

diez ten (1)

diferencia difference; **a diferencia de** unlike

diferenciado/a differentiated

diferente different

difícil hard, difficult (6)

dificultad *f.* difficulty

difundir to disseminate

difunto/a dead; **Día** (*m.*) **de los Difuntos** Day of the Dead

digestión *f.* digestion

digital digital; **brecha digital** digital gap

dígito digit

dignidad *f.* dignity

dilema *m.* dilemma

diligente diligent

dimensión *f.* dimension

diminutivo *n. gram.* diminutive

Dinamarca Denmark

dinero money (2)

dinoflagelado *type of marine plankton*

dios *m. s.* god; **Dios** God; **por Dios** for heaven's sake (14)

diosa goddess

diptongo *gram.* diphthong

dirección *f.* address (7)

directo/a direct; **complemento directo** *gram.* direct object

director(a) director (13); conductor (13)

directorio directory

dirigir (dirijo) to direct (13)

discapacidad *f.* disability

discapacitado/a disabled

disco disc; **disco duro** hard drive (12)

discoteca discotheque; **ir a una discoteca** to go to a disco (10)

discriminación *f.* discrimination (18)

disculpa apology (14); excuse; **pedir (pido) (i) disculpas** to apologize (14)

disculpar to excuse, pardon; **disculpa, pardon me** (*fam. s.*) (14); I'm sorry (*fam. s.*) (14); **disculpe, pardon me** (*form. s.*) (14); I'm sorry (*form. s.*) (14)

disculparse to apologize (14)

discurso speech

discusión *f.* argument; discussion

discutir con (alguien) por/sobre (algo) to argue with (someone) about (something) (9)

diseñador(a) (gráfico/a) (graphic) designer (17)

diseñar to design (13)

diseño design

disfraz *m.* (*pl.* **disfraces**) costume, disguise

disfrutar (de) to enjoy

disminuir (*like* **construir**) to diminish

disparar to shoot

dispensario clinic

disponible available

disposición *f.* disposition

dispositivo device

dispuesto/a ready; prepared (*to do something*)

disputarse to compete for

distancia distance

distante distant

distinción *f.* distinction

distintivo/a distinctive

distinto/a different

distracción *f.* distraction

distraer (*like* **traer**) to distract

distraído/a absentminded (14); distracted (14); **estar/ir distraído/a** to be distracted (14)

distribuido/a distributed

distrito district

disuadir to dissuade

diversidad *f.* diversity

diversión *f.* fun activity (10)

diverso/a diverse

divertido/a fun (10); **ser divertido/a** to be fun (10)

divertirse (me divierto) (i) to have a good time; to enjoy oneself (5)

dividirse to be divided

divorciado/a (de) divorced (from) (16)

divorciarse (de) to get divorced (from) (16)

divorcio divorce (16)

divulgar (gu) to divulge

doblar to turn (15)

doble *m.* double

doce twelve (1)

dócil docile

doctor(a) doctor

doctorado doctorate

documento document

dólar *m.* dollar (4)

doler (duele) (*like* **gustar**) to hurt (11); to ache (11)

dolor (*m.*) **(de)** pain, ache (in) (11); **dolor de cabeza** headache; **tener dolor de** to have a pain/ache in (11)

doméstico/a domestic, related to the home (10); domesticated, tame (15); **animal** (*m.*) **doméstico** pet; **aparato doméstico** home appliance (10); **tarea doméstica** household chore (10)

domicilio home

dominación *f.* domination

dominar to control; to dominate

domingo Sunday (5)

dominicano/a *n., adj.* Dominican

dominio control

don *m.* title of respect used with a man's first name

donar to donate

donde where

¿dónde? where? (1); **¿de dónde eres (tú)?** where are you (*fam. s.*) from? (1); **¿de dónde es usted?** where are you (*form. s.*) from? (1)

doña title of respect used with a woman's first name

dormir (duermo) (u) to sleep (5); **dormir la siesta** to take a nap (5); **dormirse** to fall asleep (5)

dormitorio bedroom

dos two (1); **dos veces** twice (11)

doscientos/as two hundred (4)

drama *m.* drama (13)
dramático/a dramatic
dramatizar (c) to dramatize
dramaturgo/a playwright (13)
droga drug
dromedario dromedary
ducha *n.* shower
ducharse to take a shower (5)
duda *n.* doubt
dudar to doubt (12)
dudoso/a doubtful
duelo duel
dueño/a landlord, landlady (12); owner (7)
dulce *adj.* sweet
dulces *n. m. pl.* sweets (7); candy (7)
duración *f.* duration
duradero/a lasting
durante during (5)
durar to last (18)
duro/a hard (12); **disco duro** hard drive (12)
DVD *m.* DVD (12)

E

e and (*before words beginning with the sound* **i**-) (3)
echar to throw out
ecocasa ecological house
ecología ecology
ecológico/a ecological
ecologista *m., f.* ecologist
economía economy; *s.* economics (2)
económico/a economical
economista *m., f.* economist
ecoturismo ecotourism
ccoturista *m., f.* ecotourist
ecoturístico/a *adj.* ecotourist
ecuador *m.* equator
ecuatoguineano/a of or from Equatorial Guinea
ecuatoriano/a Ecuadoran
edad *f.* age
edificio building (2); **edificio de apartamentos** apartment building (12)
editar to edit
editorial *f.* publishing house
educación *f.* education
educador(a) educator
educarse (qu) to be educated
educativo/a educational
efectivo cash (17); **en efectivo** in cash (17)
efectivo/a effective
efecto effect
efectuar (efectúo) to carry out, execute
eficiencia efficiency
eficiente efficient
Egipto Egypt
egoísmo selfishness
egoísta *m., f.* selfish

ejecutivo/a *n., adj.* executive
ejemplar exemplary
ejemplificar (qu) to exemplify
ejemplo example (14); **por ejemplo** for example (14)
ejercer (ejerzo) to apply, exercise
ejercicio exercise (5); **hacer ejercicio** to exercise (5); **hacer ejercicios aeróbicos** to do aerobics (11)
ejército army (18)
el *def. art. m. s.* the; **el cual** which; **el lunes (martes...)** on Monday (Tuesday ...) (5); **el primero de** the first of (*month*) (6); **el próximo (martes...)** next (Tuesday ...) (5)
él *sub. pron.* he (2)
elaboración *f.* elaboration
elección *f.* choice; *pl.* election
electricidad *f.* electricity (12)
electricista *m., f.* electrician (17)
eléctrico/a electrical (15); **energía eléctrica** electrical energy (15)
electrónica electronic equipment
electrónico/a electronic (8); **billete** (*m.*) (*Sp.*) / **boleto** (*L.A.*) **electrónico** e-ticket (8); **equipo electrónico** electronic equipment (12)
elefante *m.* elephant (15)
elegante elegant
elegir (elijo) (i) to select; to elect
elemento element
elevado/a high
elevador *m.* elevator
elevarse to rise
eliminar to eliminate
ella *sub. pron.* she (2)
ello: por ello therefore
ellos/as *sub. pron.* they (2); *obj.* (*of prep.*) them
e-mail *m.* e-mail (12)
embarazada pregnant
embargo: sin embargo nevertheless (6)
embarque: puerta de embarque boarding gate (8); **tarjeta de embarque** boarding pass (8)
emberá Embera person
emblema *m.* emblem
emblemático/a emblematic
embotellamiento traffic jam
embutido sausage
emergencia emergency
emigración *f.* emigration
emigrante *m., f.* emigrant
emigrar to emigrate
emisario/a emissary
emitir to emit
emoción *f.* emotion (9)
emocionado/a excited
emocional emotional
emocionante exciting
emocionarse to get excited
emoticono emoticon

empacar (qu) to pack
empanada *turnover pie or pastry*
emparedado sandwich
emparejar to match
empezar (empiezo) (c) to begin, start (5); **empezar a** + *inf.* to begin to (*do something*) (5)
empleado/a employee
empleador(a) employer
emplear to use; to employ
empleo job, position (17); **empleo bien/mal pagado** well-/poorly paid job/position (17); **empleo de tiempo completo/parcial** full-/part-time position (17)
empresa corporation (17); business (17); **administración** (*f.*) **de empresas** business administration (2)
empresario/a businessman/woman
en in (1); on (1); at (*a place*) (1); **en casa** at home (2); **en caso de** *prep.* in case (16); **en caso de que** *conj.* in case (16); **en cuanto** as soon as (17); **en efectivo** in cash (17); **en la actualidad** currently, right now (10); **en negrilla** boldface; **en onda** in style; **en punto** on the dot (*time*) (1); **en rebaja** on sale; **en resumen** in summary; **en vez de** instead of
enamorado/a (de) in love (with) (16)
enamorarse (de) to fall in love (with) (16)
enano/a dwarf
encantado/a pleased to meet you (1); enchanted
encantar (*like* **gustar**) to like very much (8); to love (8)
encanto charm
encapuchado/a hooded
encarcelado/a incarcerated
encargado/a in charge
encender (enciendo) to turn on (*a machine*) (12); to light
encerado blackboard
encima de on top of (6)
encomendarse (me encomiendo) a to commend yourself to
encontrar (encuentro) to find (9); **encontrarse (con)** to meet (*someone somewhere*) (11)
encuentro encounter
encuesta survey
encuestar to survey
endeble unstable
endémico/a endemic
enemigo enemy
energía energy (15); **energía eléctrica** electrical energy (15); **energía eólica** wind energy (15); **energía nuclear** nuclear energy (15); **energía renovable** renewable energy (15); **energía solar** solar energy (15)

enérgico/a energetic

enero January (6)

enfado anger

énfasis *m. inv.* emphasis

enfático/a emphatic

enfatizar (c) to emphasize

enfermarse to get sick (11)

enfermedad *f.* illness, sickness (11)

enfermero/a nurse (11)

enfermo/a sick (6)

enfilado/a in a line

enfocar (qu) to focus

enfoque *m.* focus

enfrentar(se) (a) to face

enfrente de *prep.* in front of; across from; facing

englobar to encompass

engordar to gain weight; to fatten

enhorabuena congratulations

enojado/a angry (9); upset (9)

enojarse con (alguien) por (algo) to get angry with (someone) about (something) (9)

enorme enormous

enriquecer (enriquezco) to enrich

ensalada salad (7)

ensayar to test

ensayista *m., f.* essayist

ensayo essay

enseñanza teaching

enseñar to teach (2); **enseñar a** + *inf.* to teach to (*do something*)

enseguida immediately (5)

ensuciarse to get dirty

entender (entiendo) to understand (5)

enterarse (de) to find out (18); to learn (about) (18)

entero/a entire

enterrado/a buried

entidad *f.* entity

entonces then (8); in that case (8)

entrada entrance; ticket (*to a performance, movie ...*) (12)

entrante: el año entrante next year

entrañable moving, touching

entrar to enter (12); **entrar en internet** to go on the internet (12); **entrar en Facebook** to go onto Facebook (12)

entre *prep.* between (6); among (6)

entregar (gu) to hand in (8)

entrenador(a) coach (10)

entrenamiento training

entrenar(se) to practice (10); to train (10)

entresemana during the week

entrevista interview (17)

entrevistado/a interviewee (17)

entrevistador(a) interviewer (17)

entrevistar to interview

entusiasmar to enthuse

envase *m.* container

envenenar to poison

enviar (envío) to send

envidia envy

envuelto/a covered

eólico/a: energía eólica wind energy (15)

episodio chapter

epitafio epitaph

época era, time (*period*)

equilibrar to balance

equilibrio balance

equipaje *m.* baggage, luggage (8); **facturar el equipaje** to check baggage (8)

equipar to equip

equipo team (10); equipment (12); **equipo electrónico** electronic equipment (12)

equivalente *m.* equivalent

equivaler (*like* **salir**) to equal

equivocarse (qu) (de) to make a mistake (about/with) (14)

eructar to burp, belch

erupción *f.* eruption (18)

escala stop (8); **hacer escala** to make a stop (8)

escalador(a) climber

escalar to climb

escalera staircase; *pl.* stairs (14); ladder

escándalo scandal

escanear to scan

escáner *m.* scanner (12)

escaparate *m.* store (display) window

escapar(se) (de) to escape (from)

escaso/a scarce

escena scene (13)

escenario stage (13); scenery (13)

esclavitud *f.* slavery

esclavo/a slave

esclusa lock (*of a canal*)

escoba broom

escoger (escojo) to choose; to select

escolar *adj.* school

Escorpión *m.* Scorpio

escribir (*p.p.* **escrito**) to write (3)

escrito/a (*p.p. of* **escribir**) written (14); **informe** (*m.*) **escrito** written report (14)

escritor(a) writer (13)

escritorio desk (2)

escuálido/a scrawny

escuchar to listen (to) (2)

escuela school (10); **escuela primaria** elementary school; **escuela secundaria** high school; **maestro/a de escuela** schoolteacher (17)

esculpir to sculpt

escultor(a) sculptor (13)

escultura sculpture (13)

ese/a *adj.* that (4)

esencia essence

esencial essential

esfuerzo effort

eso (*neuter pron.*) that (4); **eso quiere decir...** that means ... (11); **por eso** for that reason (3)

esos/as *adj.* those (4)

espacial *adj.* space; **nave** (*f.*) **espacial** spaceship; **transbordador** (*m.*) **espacial** space shuttle

espacio space (10); **espacio de almacenamiento** storage space (12)

espacioso/a spacious

espalda back

espantapájaros *m. inv.* scarecrow

espantar to scare

español *m.* Spanish (*language*) (2)

español(a) *n.* Spaniard; *adj.* Spanish (3)

espárragos *m. pl.* asparagus (7)

especial special

especialidad *f.* specialty

especialización *f.* major (*academic*); specialization

especializarse (c) (en) to major (in)

especie *f.* species (15); **especie en peligro de extinción** endangered species (15)

especificar (qu) to specify

específico/a specific

espectacular spectacular

espectáculo show (13)

espectador(a) spectator (13); *pl.* audience (13)

especulación *f.* speculation

espejo mirror

espera wait; **llamada de espera** call-waiting; **sala de espera** waiting room (8)

esperanza hope, wish (18)

esperar to wait (for) (7); to expect (7); to hope (12)

espeso/a thick

espinaca spinach

espíritu *m.* spirit

espiritual spiritual

esplendor *m.* splendor

esposado/a handcuffed

esposo/a husband/wife (3)

esqueleto skeleton

esquema *m.* outline

esquí *m.* skiing (10)

esquiador(a) skier

esquiar (esquío) to ski (10)

esquina (street) corner (15)

esta noche tonight (6)

estabilidad *f.* stability

estable stable

establecer (establezco) to establish

estación *f.* station (8); season (6); **estación de autobuses** bus station (8); **estación de radio** radio station (18); **estación de servicio** gas station (15); **estación de trenes** train station (8)

estacionamiento parking place/lot (15)

estacionar to park (14)
estadio stadium
estadística *s.* statistics
estadístico/a statistical
estado state (3); **estado afectivo** emotional state; **estado** legal status (16) **estado de ánimo** state of mind; **estado libre asociado** commonwealth; **Estados** (*m. pl.*) **Unidos de América** United States of America
estadounidense *n., adj.* U.S. (3)
estancia stay (*in a hotel*)
estante *m.* bookshelf (5)
estar to be (2); **¿cómo está?** how are you (*form. s.*)? (1); **¿cómo estás?** how are you (*fam. s.*)? (1); **está bien** it's fine, OK (6); **está de moda** it's trendy (hot) (4); **está (muy) nublado** it's (very) cloudy, overcast (6); **estar a dieta** to be on a diet (7); **estar al corriente** to be up to date; **estar al día** to be up to date (18); **estar bajo muchas presiones** to be under a lot of pressure (14); **estar bien** to be comfortable (*temperature*) (6); **estar casado/a (con)** to be married (to) (16); **estar de vacaciones** to be on vacation (8); **estar distraído/a** to be distracted (14); **estar (muy) estresado/a** to be (very) stressed, under (a lot of) stress (14); **(no) estar de acuerdo** to (dis)agree (3); **(no) estar seguro/a de** to be (un)certain of (13)
estatal *adj.* state, of the government
estatua statue
estatura height; **de estatura mediana** of medium height
este *m.* east (6)
este/a *adj.* this (3)
estéreo stereo
estereotípico/a stereotypical
estereotipo stereotype
estético/a aesthetic
estilizado/a slender
estilo style
estimar to estimate
estipendio stipend
estipular to stipulate
estirar to stretch
esto (*neuter pron.*) this (3)
estómago stomach (11)
estornudo sneeze
estos/as *adj.* these (3)
estrategia strategy
estrecho *n.* straight; **Estrecho de Magallanes** Strait of Magellan
estrella star
estrépito crashing
estrés *m. inv.* stress (14)
estresado/a stressed out, under stress (14); **estar (muy) estresado/a**

to be (very) stressed, under (a lot of) stress (14)
estresante stressful (14)
estresar to cause stress
estricto/a strict
estrofa verse (*poem*)
estructura structure
estructurar to structure
estuario estuary
estudiantado student body
estudiante *m., f.* student (2)
estudiantil *adj.* (of) student(s)
estudiar to study (2)
estudio office (*in a home*) (5); studio (*television*); *pl.* studies (*education*)
estudioso/a studious
estufa stove (5)
estupendo/a stupendous
etapa stage, phase (16); **etapa de la vida** life stage (16)
etcétera etcetera
eterno/a eternal
ético/a ethical
etnia ethnicity
étnico/a ethnic
etnolingüístico/a ethnolinguistic
Europa Europe
europeo/a *n., adj.* European
euskera *m.* Basque (*language*)
evaluación *f.* evaluation
evangélico/a *n., adj.* evangelical
evangelismo evangelism
evento event
evidencia evidence
evidente evident
evitar to avoid (15)
evolución *f.* evolution
exacto/a exact
exagerado/a exaggerated
examen *m.* exam, test (4)
examinar to examine
exceder to exceed
excelencia excellence
excelente excellent
excepción *f.* exception
excepcional exceptional
excepto except
excesivo/a excessive
exceso excess
exclamar to exclaim
excluir (*like* **construir**) to exclude
exclusivo/a exclusive
excursión *f.* excursion
excusa excuse
exigente demanding
exigir (exijo) to demand
exiliarse to go into exile
existencia existence
existir to exist
éxito success; **tener éxito** to be successful

exitoso/a successful
exótico/a exotic
expandir to expand
expectativa expectation
expedición *f.* expedition
experiencia experience
experto/a expert
explicación *f.* explanation
explicar (qu) to explain (8)
exploración *f.* exploration
explorador(a) explorer
explotación *f.* exploitation
explotar to exploit
exponer (*like* **poner**) (*p.p.* **expuesto**) to display; to propose
exportador(a) exporter
exportar to export
exposición *f.* exposition; **de exposición** expository
expresar to express
expresión *f.* expression (1); **expresión artística** artistic expression (13); **expresión de cortesía** courteous expression (1)
expresionista expressionist
expresivo/a expressive
expulsar to expel
expulsión *f.* expulsion
exquisito/a exquisite
extender (extiendo) to extend
extensión *f.* extension
externo/a external
extinción *f.* extinction (15); **especie** (*f.*) **en peligro de extinción** endangered species (15)
extinguirse (me extingo) to become extinct
extracto extract
extranjero/a *n.* foreigner (2); *adj.* foreign; **ir al extranjero** to go abroad (8); **lengua extranjera** foreign language (2)
extrañar to miss
extraño/a strange; **es extraño que** + *subjunctive* it's strange that (13); **¡qué extraño que... +** *subjunctive*! how strange that ... ! (13)
extraordinario/a extraordinary
extravagante extravagant
extremo/a extreme
extrovertido/a extrovert(ed)

F

fábrica factory (15)
fabricar (qu) to manufacture (15)
fábula fable
fabuloso/a fabulous
Facebook *m.* Facebook (12); **entrar en Facebook** to go into Facebook (12)
fácil easy (6)

facilidad *f.* ease
facilitar to facilitate
factor *m.* factor
factura bill (17)
facturar el equipaje to check baggage (8)
facultad *f.* department (*university*)
falda skirt (4)
fallar to crash (*computer*) (12)
falso/a false
falta lack (15); absence (15)
faltar (a) to be absent (from) (9); to not attend (9)
fama fame
familia family (3)
familiar *adj.* (of the) family
famoso/a famous
fantasía fantasy
fantasma *m.* ghost
fantástico/a fantastic
farmacéutico/a pharmacist (11)
farmacia pharmacy (12)
faro lighthouse
fascinante fascinating
fascinar (*like* **gustar**) to fascinate (13)
fastidioso/a tedious
fatal *sl.* bad, awful
fatalista *m., f.* fatalist
fauna animal species
fauno faun
favor *m.* favor; **a favor de** in favor of; **por favor** please (1)
favorito/a favorite
fax *m.* FAX (12)
fe *f.* faith
febrero February (6)
fecha date (*calendar*) (6); **¿cuál es la fecha de hoy?** what's today's date? (6); **fecha límite** deadline; **¿qué fecha es hoy?** what's today's date? (6)
federación *f.* federation
federativo/a federative
felicidades *f. pl.* congratulations
felicitaciones *f. pl.* congratulations (9)
felicitar to congratulate
feliz (*pl.* **felices**) happy (9)
femenino/a feminine
fenicio/a Phoenician
fénix *m.* phoenix
fenomenal phenomenal
fenómeno phenomenon
feo/a ugly (3)
feria fair
feriado/a: día (*m.*) **feriado** holiday
fertilidad *f.* fertility
festejar to celebrate
festividad *f.* festival
festivo/a festive, celebratory (9); **día** (*m.*) **festivo** holiday (9)
ficción *f.* fiction; **ciencia ficción** science fiction
ficticio/a fictitious

fiebre *f.* fever (11); **tener fiebre** to have a fever
fiel faithful (3)
fiesta party (2); **darle / hacerle una fiesta (a alguien)** to give (someone) a party (9); to have a party (for someone) (9); **fiesta patronal** party dedicated to a patron saint
fiestero/a happy; fond of parties
figura figure
fijarse (en) to notice
fijo/a set, fixed; **teléfono fijo** landline (12)
fila line
Filadelfia Philadelphia
filantrópico/a philanthropic
Filipinas *f. pl.* Philippines
filipino/a *n., adj.* Philippine
filmar to film; to record
filosofía philosophy (2)
filosófico/a philosophical
fin *m.* end (9); **a fines de** at the end of; **fin de año** end of the year (9); **fin de semana** weekend (2); **por fin** finally (5); **sin fines de lucro** non-profit
final *m.* end
finalmente finally (5)
financiar to finance
financiero/a financial
finanzas *f. pl.* finances
finca farm (15)
Finlandia Finland
fino/a fine
firmar to sign
física physics (2)
físico/a physical
flaco/a skinny
flamenco *music and dance form of southern Spain*
flan *m.* (baked) custard (7)
flauta flute
flexibilidad *f.* flexibility
flexible flexible (14)
flor *f.* flower (8)
flora plant species
flota fleet
folclore folklore
folclórico/a traditional (13)
folclorista *m., f.* folklorist
folklórico/a traditional
fomentar to encourage; to promote
fondo background; fund; bottom
fontanero/a plumber (*Sp.*)
forma form (4); shape; way; **de forma presencial** in person
formación *f.* formation; education, training
formar to form
formato format
formidable tremendous
fórmula formula
formulario form (*to fill out*) (17)

fortalecer (**fortalezco**) to strengthen
fortaleza fort
fosforescente phosphorescent
fotocopia photocopy (12)
fotocopiadora copy machine (12)
fotocopiar to photocopy
foto(grafía) *f.* photo(graph) (8); **sacar** (**qu**) **fotos** to take photos (8)
fotografía photography (13)
fotógrafo/a photographer (17)
fotomontaje *m.* photo montage
fragmentado/a fragmented
fragmento fragment; excerpt
francés *m.* French (*language*) (2)
francés, francesa *n.* French person; *adj.* French
Francia France
franja stripe, band; border, fringe
frase *f.* phrase; sentence
fraternidad *f.* fraternity
frecuencia frequency (2); **con frecuencia** frequently (2); **¿con qué frecuencia... ?** how often ... ? (3)
frecuente frequent
frecuentemente frequently (11)
frenos *m. pl.* brakes (15)
frente a facing; **hacer frente a** to face up to
fresa strawberry
fresco/a fresh (7)
fresco: hace fresco it's cool (weather) (6)
frigorífico refrigerator
frijoles *m. pl.* beans (7)
frío: hace (mucho) frío it's (very) cold (*weather*) (6); **tener (mucho) frío** to be (very) cold (6)
frío/a *adj.* cold (6)
frito/a fried (7); **papa frita** French fried potato (7)
frituras *f. pl.* fried food
frontera border
frotar to rub
frustración *f.* frustration
frustrado/a frustrated
fruta fruit (7); **jugo de fruta** fruit juice (7)
frutería fruit store, stand
frutilla strawberry
fruto fruit
fuego fire
fuente *f.* source; fountain; serving dish
fuera *adv.* outside
fuerza force; **fuerzas** (*f. pl.*) **armadas** armed forces
fumador(a) smoker (8); **sala de fumadores** smoking area (8)
fumar to smoke (8); **sala de fumar** smoking area (8)
funcionamiento *n.* functioning, working
funcionar to work (12); to function (12); to run (*machines*) (12)

fundación *f.* foundation
fundador(a) founder
fundar to found
furia rage; **furia al volante** road rage; **furia caminera** road rage
furioso/a furious, angry (6)
fútbol *m.* soccer (10); **fútbol americano** football (10)
futbolista *m., f.* soccer player
futuro *n.* future
futuro/a *adj.* future

G

gabinete *m.* cabinet
gafas *f. pl.* glasses (4); **gafas de sol** sunglasses (4)
gaita *Colombian indigenous flute*
galán *m.* handsome man
gallego Galician (*language*)
galleta cookie (7)
gallo/a rooster, hen; **Misa del Gallo** Midnight Mass
galope *m. traditional dance of Paraguay*
galopera *traditional dance of Paraguay*
gambas *f. pl.* shrimp (*Sp.*)
ganador(a) winner
ganancia earning
ganar to win (10); to earn (*income*) (13)
ganas: tener ganas de + *inf.* to feel like (*doing something*) (4)
gandules *m. pl.* pigeon peas
ganga bargain (4)
garaje *m.* garage (5)
garantizar (c) to guarantee
garbanzos *m. pl.* chickpeas (7)
garganta throat (11)
garifunas *m. pl.* Black Caribs (*descendents of Carib indigenous people and African slaves in Honduras*)
gas *m.* gas (*residential, not for cars*) (12)
gaseosa soft drink
gasolina gasoline (15)
gasolinera gas station (15)
gastar to spend (*money*) (9); to use (*gas*) (15)
gasto expense (12)
gastronómico/a gastronomic
gato cat (3)
gaucho *Argentine cowboy*
gazpacho *cold tomato soup of southern Spain*
gemelo/a twin
genealógico/a: árbol (*m.*) **genealógico** family tree
generación *f.* generation
general general; **en general** in general; **por lo general** generally (5)
generar to generate; to create
genérico/a generic

género genre; gender
generosidad *f.* generosity
generoso/a generous
gente *f. s.* people (8)
genuinamente genuinely
geografía geography
geográfico/a geographic
geología geology
geométrico/a geometric
gerente *m., f.* manager (17)
gerundio *gram.* gerund
gigante *adj.* giant
gimnasio gym(nasium) (12)
ginecólogo/a gynecologist
gira tour
gitano/a *n., adj.* Romani
globalización *f.* globalization
gobernador(a) governor
gobierno government (15)
gol *m.* goal (*soccer*)
golf *m.* golf (10)
golfo gulf
golpe *m.* blow; **golpe de estado** coup d'état
gordo/a fat (3)
gorila *m.* gorilla (15)
gorra baseball cap (4)
gótico/a Gothic
grabadora (tape) recorder/player
grabar to record (12); to tape (12)
gracia grace
gracias thank you (1); **Día** (*m.*) **de (Acción de) Gracias** Thanksgiving (9); **gracias por** + *noun/inf.* thanks for (9); **muchas gracias** thank you very much (1)
grado grade, year (*in school*); degree (*temperature*)
graduarse (me gradúo) (de) to graduate (from) (17)
gráfico/a graphic (17); **diseñador(a) gráfico/a** graphic (17)
grafiti *m.* graffiti
gramática grammar
gramo gram
gran, grande large, big; great (3); **Gran Bretaña** Great Britain; **pantalla grande** big screen (monitor) (12)
granero barn
granizo hail
granja farm
grano grain
grasa fat
gratis *inv.* free (of charge)
gratuito/a free (of charge)
grave serious
Grecia Greece
griego/a *n., adj.* Greek
grifo faucet
gripa flu (*Mex.*)
gripe *f.* flu (11)
gris gray (4)
gritar to shout

grito shout; cry
grueso/a thick
grupo group; band
guagua bus (*Carib.*)
guaguanco *subgenre of rumba*
guampa *cup made from a hollowed bull's horn used to drink* mate; *cup used to drink* **tereré**
guanábana soursop (*tropical fruit*)
guancasco *traditional dance of the Lenca of Honduras*
guante *m.* glove
guapo/a handsome, good-looking (*people*) (3)
guaraní *m. indigenous language of South America*
guardacostas *m. inv.* Coast Guard
guardar to keep (12); to save (*documents*) (12); **guardar cama** to stay in bed (11); **guardar un puesto** to save a place (*in line*) (8)
guatemalteco/a *n., adj.* Guatemalan
gubernamental governmental
guerra war (18); **guerra civil** civil war
guerrero/a warrior
guía *m., f.* guide (13)
guiado/a guided
guion *m.* script (13)
güiro *Latin American musical instrument*
guitarra guitar
guitarrista *m., f.* guitarist
gustar to be pleasing (8); **¿a usted le gusta... ?** do you (*form. s.*) like ... ? (1); **me gustaría (mucho)...** I would (really) like ... (8); **(no,) no me gusta...** (no,) I don't like ... (1); **(sí,) me gusta...** (yes), I like ... (1); **¿te gusta... ?** do you (*fam. s.*) like ... ? (1)
gusto like, preference; **gustos** *pl.* likes (1); **mucho gusto** nice to meet you (1)

H

haber (*inf. of* **hay**) (there is, there are) (12)
habichuelas *f. pl.* beans
habilidad *f.* ability
habitación *f.* bedroom (5)
habitante *m., f.* inhabitant
habitar to inhabit
hábito habit
hablante *m., f.* speaker
hablar to speak; to talk (2); **hablar con soltura** to speak fluently; **hablar por teléfono** to talk on the phone (2)
hacer to do; to make (5); **hace** + *time* + **que** + *present* to have been (*doing something*) for (*time*) (14); **hace** + *time* + **que** + *preterite* ago (14);

present + desde hace + time to have been (*doing something*) for (*time*) (14); *preterite* + **hace** + *time* ago (14); **hace (muy) buen/mal tiempo** it's (very) good/bad weather (6); **hace (mucho) calor** it's (very) hot (weather) (6); **hace (mucho) fresco** it's cool (very) (weather) (6); **hace (mucho) frío** it's (very) cold (*weather*); **hace (mucho) sol** it's (very) sunny (6); **hace (mucho) viento** it's (very) windy (6); **hacer autostop** to hitchhike; **hacer *camping*** to go camping (8); **hacer clic** to click (12); **hacer cola** to stand in line (8); **hacer ejercicio** to exercise (5); **hacer ejercicios aeróbicos** to do aerobics (11); **hacer (el) yoga** to do yoga (10); **hacer escala** to make a stop (8); **hacer frente a** to face up to; **hacer la cama** to make the bed (10); **hacer la(s) maleta(s)** to pack one's suitcase(s) (8); **hacer parada** to make a stop (8); **hacer Pilates** to do Pilates (11); **hacer planes (*m.*) para** + *inf.* to make plans to (*do something*) (10); **hacer reserva** to make a reservation; **hacer un pícnic** to have a picnic (10); **hacer un viaje** to take a trip (5); **hacer una juerga** to throw a party; **hacer una pregunta** to ask a question (5); **hacer zumba** to do Zumba (11); **hacerle una fiesta (a alguien)** to give (someone) a party (9); to have a party (for someone) (9); **hacerse daño** to hurt oneself (14); **hacerse daño en** to hurt one's (*body part*) (14); **¿qué tiempo hace?** what's the weather like? (6)

hacia *prep.* towards

hada *f.* (*but* **el hada**) fairy

hallaca *Venezuelan meat pastry*

hamaca hammock

hambre *f.* hunger (7); **pasar hambre** to go hungry; tener (mucha) hambre to be (very) hungry (7)

hamburguesa hamburger (7)

harina flour

hasta *adv.* until; even; *prep.* until; **hasta luego** see you later (1); **hasta mañana** see you tomorrow (1); **hasta pronto** see you soon; **hasta que** *conj.* until (17)

hay there is/are (1); **¿hay?** is there / are there? (1); **hay que** + *inf.* it is necessary to (*do something*) (13); **no hay** there is/are not (1); **no hay de qué** you're welcome (1); **no hay problema** no problem (14)

hebreo Hebrew (*language*)

hecho/a (*p.p. of* hacer) made

hectárea *land measure equal to 2.5 acres*

helado ice cream (7)

heliconia *flowering tropical plant*

hemisferio hemisphere

herbolario/a herbalist

heredar to inherit

herencia inheritance

hermanastro/a stepbrother, stepsister

hermano/a brother/sister (3); *m. pl.* siblings (3)

hermoso/a beautiful

héroe *m.* hero

heroína heroine

hervir (hiervo) (i) to boil

híbrido/a hybrid (15)

hidalgo nobleman

hidroeléctrico/a hydroelectric

hielo ice

hierba grass

hígado liver

hijastro/a stepson, stepdaughter

hijo/a son/daughter (3); *m. pl.* children (3)

himno hymn; **himno nacional** national anthem

hipopótamo hippopotamus

hispánico/a Hispanic

hispano/a Hispanic (3)

Hispanoamérica Hispanic America

hispanoamericano/a *adj.* Hispanic American

hispanohablante *adj. m., f.* Spanish-speaking

historia history (2); story (8)

historiador(a) historian

histórico/a historical

hockey *m.* hockey (10)

hogar *m.* home (5)

hoja leaf

hola hi (1); hello (1)

Holanda Holland

hombre *m.* man (2); **hombre de negocios** businessman (17)

homeópata *m., f.* homeopath

homeopático/a homeopathic

homogeneidad *f.* homogeneity

homogéneo/a homogenous

hondureño/a *n., adj.* Honduran

honesto/a honest

hongo mushroom; toadstool; fungus; **sombrero hongo** bowler hat, derby

honor *m.* honor

honrado/a honest; honorable

hora hour; time (1); **¿a qué hora... ?** at what time ... ? (1); **es hora de...** it's time to ... ; **hora punta** peak hour **¿qué hora es?** what time is it? (1)

horario schedule (14)

horchata *Mexican drink made from rice*

hormona hormone

horno oven; **horno de microondas** microwave oven (10)

horóscopo horoscope

horror *m.* horror

hospital *m.* hospital

hospitalario/a hospitable

hospitalidad *f.* hospitality

hospitalización *f.* hospitalization

hotel *m.* hotel

hoy today (1); **¿cuál es la fecha de hoy?** what's today's date? (6); **¿qué día es hoy?** what day is today? (5); **¿qué fecha es hoy?** what's today's date? (6)

huelga strike (*labor*) (18)

huella mark; (finger)print

huerto orchard

hueso bone

huésped *m., f.* guest

huevo egg (7)

huipil *m. traditional Mayan blouse*

huir (*like* construir) to flee

humanidad *f.* humanity; *pl.* humanities (2)

humanista *n., adj.* humanist

humanitario/a humanitarian

humanizar (c) to make more human

humano/a human (11); **cuerpo humano** human body (11); **ser (*m.*) humano** human being

humedad *f.* humidity

húmedo/a humid

humilde humble

humorístico/a humorous

huracán *m.* hurricane

I

ibérico/a *adj.* Iberian

íbero/a *n.* Iberian

icónico/a iconic

ícono icon

ida: billete (*m.*) (*Sp.*) / boleto (*L.A.*) de ida one-way ticket (8); **billete (*m.*) (*Sp.*) / boleto (*L.A.*) de ida y vuelta** round-trip ticket (8)

idealista *m., f.* idealistic

idear to think up; to conceive (*idea*)

idéntico/a identical

identidad *f.* identity; **carnet (*m.*) de identidad** identification card

identificación *f.* identification (14); **carnet (*m.*) de identificación** identification card; **tarjeta de identificación** identification card, ID (14)

identificar(se) (qu) to identify (oneself)

idioma *m.* language

idiomático/a idiomatic

ídolo idol

iglesia church (16)

ignorante ignorant

ignorar to ignore

igual same; equal

igualdad *f.* equality (18)

igualitario/a egalitarian

igualmente likewise (1); same here (1)
ilimitado/a unlimited
ilógico/a illogical
iluminar to light up
ilusorio/a false
ilustrar to illustrate
ilustrativo/a illustrative
imagen *f.* image (13)
imaginación *f.* imagination
imaginar(se) to imagine
imaginativo/a imaginative
imitar to imitate
impaciente impatient
impacto impact
impedimento impediment
impedir (*like* **pedir**) to impede
imperfecto *gram.* imperfect
imperio empire
impermeable *n. m.* raincoat (4); *adj.* impermeable
impertinente impertinent
implementar to implement
implicar (qu) to imply
imponer (*like* **poner**) to impose
importancia importance
importante important (12); **es importante que** + *subjunctive* it's important that (12)
importar (*like* **gustar**) to matter; to be important
imposible impossible (13); **es imposible que** + *subjunctive* it's impossible that (13); **no es imposible que** + *subjunctive* it's not impossible (13)
impresión *f.* impression
impresionante impressive
impresionar to impress
impreso/a printed
impresora printer (12)
imprimir to print (12)
improbable unlikely (13); **es improbable que** + *subjunctive* it's unlikely, improbable that (13); **no es improbable que** + *subjunctive* it's not improbable that (13)
improvisar to improvise
impuesto tax
impulsivo/a impulsive
inalámbrico/a wireless
inauguración *f.* inauguration
inca *n. m., f.* Inca; *adj. m., f.* Incan
incaico/a *adj.* Inca
incapacidad *f.* inability
incendio fire (18)
incidente *m.* incident
incienso incense
inclinación *f.* inclination
inclinarse to lean
incluir (*like* **construir**) to include
incómodo/a uncomfortable
incompleto/a incomplete
inconcebible inconceivable

inconveniencia inconvenience
inconveniente *n. m; adj.* inconvenient
incorporar to incorporate; to include
incorrecto/a incorrect
incrédulo/a incredulous
increíble incredible (13); **es increíble que** + *subjunctive* it's incredible that (13)
incrementar to increase
incremento increment
indefinido/a indefinite; **artículo indefinido** *gram.* indefinite article; **palabra indefinida y negativa** *gram.* indefinite and negative word (7)
indeleble indelible
independencia independence
independiente independent
independizarse (c) to become independent
indescriptible indescribable
indicación *f.* instruction; direction
indicar (qu) to indicate
indicativo *gram.* indicative
índice *m.* index
Índico Indian (Ocean)
indiferente indifferent
indígena *n. m., f.* indigenous person; *adj. m., f.* indigenous
indigenista *m., f.* pertaining to indigenous topics and themes
indio/a *n., adj.* Indian
indirecto/a indirect; **complemento indirecto** *gram.* indirect object
indiscreto/a indiscreet
indispensable indispensible, essential
indistinto/a indistinct
individualidad *f.* individuality
individuo *n.* individual
individuo/a *adj.* individual
industria industry
inesperado/a unexpected
inexistente nonexistent
infancia infancy (16); childhood (16)
infantil *adj.* child, children's
infatigable tireless
infección *f.* infection
inferir (infiero) (i) to infer
infiltrarse to infiltrate
infinitivo *gram.* infinitive
inflexible inflexible (14)
inflexibilidad *f.* inflexibility
influencia influence
influir (*like* **construir**) to influence
influyente influential
infografía computer graphic
información *f.* information
informar to inform (18)
informática computer science
informativo/a informative
informe (*m.*) **(oral/escrito)** (oral/written) report (14)
infraestructura infrastructure

infrecuente infrequent
infusión *f.* infusion
ingeniería engineering
ingeniero/a engineer (17)
ingenioso/a ingenious
Inglaterra England
inglés *m.* English (*language*) (2)
inglés, inglesa *n., adj.* English (3)
ingrediente *m.* ingredient
ingresar to deposit (*in an account*)
ingreso income
inicial *f.* initial (*letter*)
iniciar to start
iniciativa initiative
inicio beginning
injusticia injustice
injusto/a unfair
inmediato/a immediate
inmenso/a immense
inmerso/a immersed
inmigración *f.* immigration
inmigrante *n., m., f.* immigrant
inmobiliario/a *adj.* real estate; property
inmóvil unmoving
innecesario/a unnecessary
innumerable countless
inocente innocent
inolvidable unforgettable
inquilino/a tenant (12); renter (12)
inscribir(se) (*p.p.* **inscrito**) **(en)** to sign up; to register (for)
inscripción *f.* inscription
inscrito/a (*p.p. of* **inscribir**) registered
insecto insect
insistir (en) to insist (on) (12)
insoportable unbearable
inspiración *f.* inspiration
instalación *f.* facility
instalar to install (12)
instantáneo/a instantaneous
instante: al instante right away
institución *f.* institution
instituto institute
instrucciones *f. pl.* instructions
instructor(a) instructor
instrumento instrument
insulina insulin
insulto insult
integración *f.* integration
integrarse to integrate oneself
intelectual intellectual
inteligencia intelligence
inteligente intelligent (3)
intención *f.* intention
intencionadamente intentionally
intensidad *f.* intensity
intensificar (qu) to intensify
intenso/a intense
intentar to attempt (to)
interacción *f.* interaction
interactivo/a interactive
intercambiar to exchange

intercambio exchange

interés *m.* interest (17)

interesante interesting

interesar (*like* **gustar**) to interest (*someone*) (18)

intergaláctico/a intergalactic

interior interior; inner (4); **ropa interior** underwear (4)

intermedio/a intermediate

interminable endless

internacional international; **Día** (*m.*) **Internacional de la No Violencia Contra la Mujer** International Day for the Elimination of Violence against Women

internauta *m., f.* internet user

internet *m.* internet (12); **buscar** (**qu**) **en internet** to look up on the internet (12); **entrar en internet** to go on the internet (12)

interno/a internal

interplanetario/a interplanetary

interpretación *f.* interpretation

interpretar to interpret

interrogación (*f.*): **signo de interrogación** question mark

interrogativo/a *gram.* interrogative (1)

interrumpir to interrupt

interrupción *f.* interruption

intervención *f.* intervention

intimidad *f.* intimacy

íntimo/a intimate; close

intolerancia intolerance

intranquilidad *f.* restlessness

introducción *f.* introduction

introducir (*like* **conducir**) to introduce

inundación *f.* flood

inútil useless

invadido/a invaded

inválido/a disabled

invasión *f.* invasion

invasor(a) *adj.* invading

inventar to invent

inversión *f.* investment

invertir (invierto) (i) to invest

investigación *f.* investigation; research

investigador(a) researcher

investigar (**gu**) to investigate; to research

invierno winter (6)

invitación *f.* invitation

invitado/a guest (9)

invitar to invite (7)

invocar (**qu**) to invoke

inyección *f.* injection (11); **poner(se) una inyección** to get a shot (11)

iPhone *m.* iPhone (12)

ir to go (4); **ir a** + *inf.* to be going to (*do something*) (4); **ir a un bar** to go to a bar (10); **ir a un club** to go to a club (10); **ir a un concierto** to go to a concert (10); **ir a un museo** to go to a museum

(10); **ir a una discoteca** to go to a disco (10); **ir al extranjero** to go abroad (8); **ir al teatro** to go to the theater (10); **ir de compras** to go shopping (4); **ir de safari** to go on a safari; **ir de vacaciones a...** to go on vacation to/in ... (8); **ir distraído/a** to be distracted (14); **ir en...** to go/travel by ... (8); **ir en autobús** to go/travel by bus (8); **ir en avión** to go/travel by plane (8); **ir en barco** to go/travel by boat, ship (8); **ir en tren** to go/travel by train (8); **irse** to leave; **vamos** let's go (4)

ira al manejar road rage

iraní (*pl.* **iraníes**) *n., adj.* Iranian

iraquí (*pl.* **iraquíes**) *n., adj.* Iraqi

iridiscencia iridescence

Irlanda Ireland

irlandés, irlandesa *n., adj.* Irish

ironía irony

irónico/a ironic

irresponsable irresponsible

-ísimo/a *adj., adv.* very very (9)

isla island (6)

Islandia Iceland

islote *m.* islet

israelí (*pl.* **israelíes**) *n., adj.* Israeli

Italia Italy

italiano Italian (*language*) (2)

italiano/a *n., adj.* Italian

itinerario itinerary

-ito/a *diminuitive suffix* (10)

izquierda *n.* left-hand side (6); **a la izquierda de** to the left of (6)

izquierdo/a *adj.* left (14); **levantarse con el pie izquierdo** to get up on the wrong side of the bed (14)

J

jaguar *m.* jaguar

jamaica hibiscus

jamás never (7)

jamón *m.* ham (7)

Janucá Hanukkah (9)

Japón *m.* Japan

japonés *m.* Japanese (*language*)

japonés, japonesa *n., adj.* Japanese

jarabe *m.* (cough) syrup (11)

jardín *m.* garden (5)

jarra jar

jazz *m.* jazz

jeans *m. pl.* blue jeans (4)

jefe/a boss (17)

jerarquía hierarchy

jersey *m.* sweater; pullover

jirafa giraffe

jornada de tiempo parcial part-time job

joropo *folkloric music of Venezuela*

joven *n. m., f.* (*pl.* **jóvenes**) youth; *adj.* young (3); **de joven** as a youth

joyería jewelry

jubilarse to retire (17)

judaísmo Judaism

juego game; **Juegos** (*m. pl.*) **Olímpicos** Olympic Games

juerga party; **hacer una juerga** to have/throw a party

jueves *m. inv.* Thursday (5)

jugador(a) player (10)

jugar (juego) (gu) (a, al) to play (*a game, sport*) (5); **jugar a las cartas / a los videojuegos / al ajedrez** to play cards/videogames/chess (10)

jugo (de fruta) (fruit) juice (7)

juguete *m.* toy

julio July (6)

junio June (6)

junto a *prep.* near

juntos/as together (8)

jurar to swear (*oath*)

justicia justice

justificación *f.* justification

justificar (**qu**) to justify

justo/a fair

juvenil *adj.* youth; youthful; **diabetes** (*f.*) **juvenil** childhood diabetes

juventud *f.* youth (16)

juzgar (**gu**) to judge

K

kaki: color (*m.*) **kaki** khaki

kilo(gramo) kilo(gram)

kilómetro kilometer

L

la *def. art. f. s.* the; *d.o. f. s.* you (*form.*); her, it; **a la(s)...** at ... (*time of day*) (1); **la cual** which

labor *f.* work, job

laboral *adj.* work, work-related (17)

laboratorio laboratory

lácteo/a *adj.* dairy

lado side; **al lado de** alongside of (6); **por otro lado** on the other hand; **por un lado** on one hand

ladrar to bark

ladrón, ladrona thief

lagarto lizard

lago lake (15)

lágrima tear

lamentar to regret (13); to feel sorry (13)

laminado/a laminated

lámpara lamp (5)

lana wool (4); **de lana** wool (4)

langosta lobster (7)

lapicero pen

lápiz *m.* (*pl.* **lápices**) pencil (2)

largo/a long (3)

las *def. art. pl.* the; *d.o. f. pl.* you (*form. pl.*); **a la(s)...** at ... (*time of day*) (1); **las cuales** which

lasaña lasagne

lástima shame; **es una lástima que** + *subjunctive* it's a shame that (13); **¡qué lástima que... ** + *subjunctive*! what a shame that ... ! (13)

lastimarse to hurt (*a body part*) (14)

lata can

latín *m.* Latin (*language*)

latino/a *adj.* Latin; **América Latina** Latin America

Latinoamérica Latin America

latinoamericano/a *n., adj.* Latin American

lavabo (bathroom) sink (5)

lavadora washing machine (10)

lavandería laundry

lavaplatos *m. inv.* dishwasher (10)

lavar to wash (10); **lavarse** to wash (oneself)

le *indir. obj. pron.* to/for him/her; to/for you (*s. form.*); to/for it; **¿(a usted) le gusta... ?** do you (*form. s.*) like ... ? (1)

lealtad *f.* loyalty

lección *f.* lesson

leche *f.* milk (7)

lechón (*m.*) **asado** roast suckling pig

lechuga lettuce (7)

lector(a) reader

lectura reading

leer (*like* **creer**) to read (3)

legislación *f.* legislation

legumbre *f.* legume

lejos *adv.* far; **lejos de** *prep.* far from (6)

lema *m.* motto

lempira *currency of Honduras*

lengua language (2); tongue (11); **lenguas extranjeras** (*f. pl.*) foreign languages (2); **sacar** (**qu**) **la lengua** to stick out one's tongue (11)

lentes *m. pl.* glasses (11); **lentes de contacto** contact lenses (11)

lentillas *f. pl.* contact lenses (*Sp.*)

lento/a slow (15); **ritmo lento de la vida** slow pace of life (15)

león *m.* lion; **león marino** sea lion

leopardo leopard

letra letter (*of the alphabet*); lyrics (*of a song*) (7)

levantar to raise; to lift (11); **levantar pesas** to lift weights (11); **levantarse** to get up (out of bed) (5); to stand up (5); **levantarse con el pie izquierdo** to get up on the wrong side of the bed (14)

leve *adj.* light

ley *f.* law (18)

leyenda legend

libanés, libanesa Lebanese

liberar(se) to free (oneself)

libertad *f.* freedom, liberty

libertador(a) liberator

libra pound (*measurement*)

libre free, unoccupied (10); **al aire** (*m.*) **libre** outdoors (10); **estado libre asociado** commonwealth; **libre comercio** free trade; **tiempo libre** free time (10)

librería bookstore (2)

libro (de texto) (text) book (2)

licencia license (15); **licencia de manejar** driver's license (15)

licor *m.* liqueur

licuar (licúo) to liquefy

líder *m., f.* leader

liga league

ligero/a light, not heavy (7)

lima lime

limeño/a *adj.* from Lima, Peru

limitación *f.* limitation

limitar to limit

límite *m.* limit; **fecha límite** deadline; **límite de velocidad** speed limit (15)

limón *m.* lemon

limonada lemonade

limonero lemon tree

limosina limousine

limpiar (la casa) to clean (the) house (10)

limpieza cleanliness

limpio/a clean (6)

lindo/a pretty

línea line

lingüístico/a linguistic

linterna flashlight

lío problem; trouble; **meterse en líos** to get into trouble

liquidación *f.* liquidation

líquido liquid

Lisboa Lisbon

lista list

listo/a smart (3); clever (3); **estar listo/a** to be ready

literario/a literary

literatura literature (2)

litoral *m.* coast

llamada call; **bloqueo de llamadas** call blocker

llamar to call (7); **¿cómo se llama usted?** what is your (*form. s.*) name? (1); **¿cómo te llamas?** what is your (*fam. s.*) name? (1); **llamarse** to be called (5); **me llamo...** my name is ... (1)

llanero *Venezuelan cowboy*

llanero/a of or pertaining to the plains

llano *n.* plain

llanta (desinflada) (flat) tire (15)

llanura *n.* plain

llave *f.* key (5)

llegada arrival (8)

llegar (**gu**) to arrive (3); **¿cómo se llega a... ?** how do you get to ... ? (15); **llegar a ser** to become

llenar to fill (*a car*) (15); to fill out (*a form*) (17)

lleno/a full

llevar to wear (4); to carry (4); to take (4); **llevar una vida sana/tranquila** to lead a healthy/calm life (11); **llevarse bien/mal (con)** to get along well/ poorly (with) (16)

llorar to cry (9)

llover (llueve) to rain (6); **llueve** (it's raining) (6)

lluvia rain (6)

lluvioso/a *adj.* rainy; of rain; **bosque** (*m.*) **tropical lluvioso** tropical rain forest

lo *d.o. m. s.* you (*form.*); him; it; **lo bueno** the good news/thing (11); **lo cual** which; **lo malo** the bad news/ thing (11); **lo que** what, that which (5); **lo siento (mucho)** I'm (very) sorry (14); **lo suficiente** enough (11); **por lo general** generally (5); **por lo menos** at least (9); **por lo regular** in general

lobo/a wolf

localidad *f.* ticket to a movie

localización *f.* location

loco/a crazy (6)

locutor(a) commentator

lógico/a logical

logotipo logo

lograr to achieve

logro achievement

Londres London

longitud *f.* longitude

los *def. art. m. pl.* the; *d.o. m. pl.* you (*form. pl.*) them; **los cuales** which; **los lunes (los martes...)** on Mondays (Tuesdays ...) (5)

lotería lottery

lubricar (**qu**) to lubricate

lucha fight (18); struggle (18)

luchar to fight (18)

lucro: sin fines de lucro non-profit

luego then, later next (5); **hasta luego** see you later (1)

lugar *m.* place (2)

lujo luxury

lujoso/a luxurious

luminiscente luminescent

luminoso/a lit up

luna moon; **luna de miel** honeymoon (16)

lunares: de lunares polka-dot (4)

lunes *m. inv.* Monday (5); **el lunes** on Monday (5); **los lunes** on Mondays (5); **el lunes que viene** next Monday (5)

Luxemburgo Luxembourg
luz *f.* (*pl.* **luces**) light (14)

M

madera wood
madrastra stepmother
madre *f.* mother (3); **Día** (*m.*) **de la Madre** Mother's Day
madrileño/a of or pertaining to Madrid
madrina godmother
madrugada dawn
madurez *f.* middle age (16)
maduro/a mature
maestría master's degree
maestro/a (de escuela) schoolteacher (17); *adj.* master; **obra maestra** masterpiece (13)
Magallanes: Estrecho de Magallanes Strait of Magellan
mágico/a *adj.* magic
magnífico/a magnificent
mago wizard
mahones *m. pl.* jeans
maíz *m.* (*pl.* **maíces**) corn
mal *adv.* poorly (2); **caerle mal a alguien** to make a bad impression on someone; **empleo mal pagado** poorly paid job/position (17); **llevarse mal (con)** to get along poorly (with) (16); **pasarlo mal** to have a bad time (9); **portarse mal** to misbehave (9); **salir mal** to come/turn out poorly (5); to do poorly (5)
mal, malo/a *adj.* bad (3); **hace (muy) mal tiempo** it's (very) bad weather (6); **lo malo** the bad news/thing (11); **tener mala suerte** to have bad luck (14); to be unlucky (14)
maleducado/a spoiled
malestar *m.* discomfort
maleta suitcase (8); **hacer la(s) maleta(s)** to pack one's suitcase(s) (8)
malatero/a porter (8)
malvado/a evil
mamá mother, mom (3)
mami *f.* mom, mommy
mamífero mammal
mancha stain
mandar to send (2); to order (12); **mandar un mensaje (de texto)** to (send a) text (2)
mandarín *m.* Mandarin (*language*)
mandato command (7)
manejar to drive; to operate (a *machine*) (12); **ira al manejar** road rage; **licencia de manejar** driver's license (15)
manera way, manner; **de manera que** so that, in such a way that
manga sleeve

manifestación *f.* demonstration (18); march (18)
maniquí *m.* mannequin
mano *f.* hand (11); **darse la mano** to shake hands (11)
mansión *f.* mansion
mantener (*like* **tener**) to maintain (18); to keep (18); **mantenerse en contacto** to stay in touch
mantequilla butter (7)
manzana apple (7); (city) block
mañana tomorrow (1); **de la mañana** in the morning, A.M. (1); **hasta mañana** see you tomorrow (1); **pasado mañana** the day after tomorrow (5); **por la mañana** in the morning (2)
mapa *m.* map (2)
mapudungún *m. language of the Mapuche people*
maquillarse to put on makeup (5)
máquina machine
mar *m.* sea (8); **mar Caribe** Caribbean Sea
maracuyá *m.* passion fruit
maratón *m.* marathon
maravilla wonder, marvel
maravillar to delight
maravilloso/a marvelous
marca brand; label
marcar (**qu**) to mark
marcial martial
mareado/a dizzy (11); nauseated (11)
marido husband (3)
marihuana marijuana
marinera *folkloric dance of coastal Peru*
marino/a marine; **león** (*m.*) **marino** sea lion
mariscos *m. pl.* shellfish (7)
marítimo/a maritime; sea, marine
marketing *m.* marketing
marrón *adj. m., f.* brown
martes *m. inv.* Tuesday (5); **los martes** on Tuesdays (5)
Maruecos Morocco
marzo March (6)
más more (2); **cada vez más** increasingly; **más de** + *number* more than + *number* (6); **más... que** more (-er) ... than (6)
masa mass; dough
máscara mask
mascota pet (3)
masculino/a masculine
masivo/a massive
masticar (**qu**) to chew
matar to kill (18)
mate *m. traditional drink of Argentina*
matemáticas *f. pl.* math (2)
materia subject area (2)
material *m.* material (4)
materialidad *f.* material aspect; outward appearance

materialista *m., f.* materialistic
maternidad *f.* maternity
materno/a maternal
matinal *adj.* morning
matriarcado matriarchy
matriarcal matriarchal
matrícula tuition (2)
matricularse to enroll; to register
matrimonio marriage (16); married couple (16)
máximo/a maximum
maya *n., adj. m., f.* Mayan
mayo May (6)
mayor older (6); oldest; greater; greatest; **mayor(es) que** older than (6); **Antillas** (*f. pl.*) **Mayores** Greater Antilles; **cada vez mayor** greater and greater
mayoría majority
mayoritariamente primarily
mayoritario/a *adj.* majority
mayúscula capital (letter), uppercase
me *d.o.* me; *i.o.* to/for me; *refl. pron.* myself; **me gustaría (mucho)...** I would (really) like ... (8); **me llamo...** my name is ... (1); **(no,) no me gusta...** (no,) I don't like ... (1); **(sí,) me gusta...** (yes,) I like ... (1)
mecánico/a mechanic (15)
mecanización *f.* mechanization
mecanografía typing
medalla medal
mediano/a: de estatura mediana of medium height
medianoche *f.* midnight (6)
mediante *prep.* by, with
medias *f. pl.* stockings (4)
medicamento medicine
medicina medicine (11)
médico/a (medical) doctor (3)
medio *n.* medium; means; *pl.* mass media (18); **medio ambiente** environment (15); **medio de comunicación** medium of communication (18); **medio de transporte** means of transportation (8)
medio/a *adj.* half; middle; average; **media naranja** better half; **y media** half past (*the hour*) (1)
medioambiental environmental
medioambiente *m.* environment
mediodía *m.* noon (6)
medir (**mido**) (**i**) to measure
meditar to meditate
megadiverso/a megadiverse
megalópolis *f. inv.* super-city
mejor better (6); best (6); **es mejor que** + *subjunctive* it's better that (12); **mejor(es) que** better than (6); best (6)
mejora improvement
mejorar(se) to improve; to get better

mellizo/a fraternal twin
melódico/a melodious
memoria memory (12); **memoria USB** pen drive (12)
mencionar to mention
menonito/a *adj.* Mennonite
menor younger (6); youngest; less; least; **menor(es) que** younger than (6)
menorá menorah
menos less; least; minus; **a menos que** *conj.* unless (16); **al menos** at least; **menos cuarto** a quarter to (*hour*) (1); **menos de** + *number* fewer than + *number* (6); **menos quince** fifteen minutes till (*hour*) (1); **por lo menos** at least (9)
mensaje *m.* message; **mandar un mensaje (de texto)** to (send a) text (2)
mensual monthly
mente *f.* mind
-mente -ly (*averbial suffix*) (14)
mentir (miento) (i) to lie
mentira lie (12)
menú *m.* menu (7)
menudo: a menudo *adv.* often
mercadeo marketing
mercader *m., f.* merchant
mercado market(place) (4)
mercadotecnia marketing
merecer (merezco) to deserve
merendar (meriendo) to snack (7)
merengue *m. dance from the Dominican Republic*
merienda snack (7)
mes *m.* month (6)
mesa table (2); **poner la mesa** to set the table (10), **quitar la mesa** to clear the table (10)
meseta plateau
mesita end table (5)
mesoamericano/a *n., adj.* Meso-American
mestizaje *m.* mixing of races
meta goal
metáfora metaphor
metal *m.* metal
metálico/a metallic
metalúrgico/a metallurgical
meteorológico/a meteorological
meter to put (into); to place; **meterse en líos** to get into trouble
método method
metro subway; **parada del metro** subway stop (12)
metrópoli *f.* metropolis
metropolitano/a urban
mexicano/a Mexican (3)
mexicoamericano/a Mexican American
mezcla mix
mezclar to mix
mezclilla denim

mezquita mosque (16)
mí *obj. of prep.* me (6)
mi(s) *poss. adj.* my (3)
microbio microbe
microcuento very short story
microondas (*f. pl.*): **horno de microondas** microwave oven (10)
microorganismo microorganism
miedo fear (4); **tener miedo (de)** to be afraid (of) (4)
miel *f.* honey; **luna de miel** honeymoon (16)
miembro/a member
mientras while (10)
miércoles *m. inv.* Wednesday (5); **ayer fue miércoles...** yesterday was Wednesday ... (5)
mil (one) thousand (4)
milagro miracle
milenario/a thousand-year
mililitro milliliter
militar *n. m., f.* soldier; (17) *adj.* military; **servicio militar** military service (18)
milla mile
millón one million (4)
millonario/a millionaire
mimar to spoil; to pamper
mineral: agua *f.* (*but* **el agua**) **(mineral)** (mineral) water (7)
minidiálogo minidialogue
mínimo minimum
ministerio ministry
ministro/a minister
minoría minority
minuto minute
mío/a(s) *poss. adj.* my; *poss. pron.* mine, (of) mine (17)
mirada look
mirar to look at (3); to watch (3); **mirar la tele(visión)** to watch television (3)
misa mass; **Misa del Gallo** midnight mass
miseria misery
misil *n.m.* missile
misión *f.* mission
mismo/a same (6); **ahora mismo** right now (6)
misterio mystery
misterioso/a mysterious
mitad *f.* half
mixto/a mixed
moái *m. statue on Easter Island, Chile*
mochila backpack (2)
moda fashion; style; **a la moda** in fashion, in a stylish way; **es de última moda** it's trendy (hot) (4); **está de moda** it's trendy (hot) (4)
modales *m. pl.* manners
modelar to model
modelo model, example
módem *m.* modem (12)
moderación *f.* moderation

modernidad *f.* modernity
modernismo modernism
modernista *m., f.* modernist
moderno/a modern (13)
modificar (qu) to modify
modismo idiom
modista dressmaker
modo way, matter; mode; *gram.* mood; **de modo que** in such a way that
mole *m. Mexican sauce*
molestar (*like* **gustar**) to bother (11)
molestia *n.* bother
molesto/a annoyed (6)
molino: rueda de molino treadmill
momento moment
momia mummy
monarquía monarchy
monasterio monastery
moneda coin (17); currency
monedero coin purse
monitor *m.* monitor
monitorizar (c) to monitor
mono monkey
monolingüe *adj.* monolingual
monoparental *adj.* single-parent
monopatín *m.* skateboard
monotonía monotony
monótono/a monotonous
monovolumen *m.* minivan
monstruo monster
montaje *m.* montage
montaña mountain (8)
montañoso/a mountainous
montar to ride; **montar a caballo** to ride a horse (10)
montón (*m.*): **un montón** a lot
montuno *traditional hat of Panama*
monumento monument
morado/a purple (4)
morales *f. pl.* morals
morderse (me muerdo) to bite
moreno/a brunet(te) (3)
morir(se) ([me] muero) (u) (*p.p.* **muerto**) to die (9)
moro/a *n.* Moor; *adj.* Moorish
mosaico mosaic
mosca fly
mostrador *m.* counter (8)
mostrar (muestro) to show (8)
motivación *f.* motivation
motivo motive
moto(cicleta) *f.* motorcycle (15)
motor *m.* motor
mover (muevo) to move
móvil mobile
movimiento movement
muchacho/a young boy/girl
muchísimo an awful lot (8)
mucho *adv.* much (2); a lot (2); **lo siento mucho** I'm very sorry (14); **me gustaría mucho...** I would really like ... (8)

mucho/a a lot (of) (3); *pl.* many (3); <u>estar</u> **bajo muchas presiones** to be under a lot of pressure (14); **hace (mucho) calor** it's (very) hot (6); **hace (mucho) fresco** it's (very) cool (6); **hace (mucho) frío** it's (very) cold (6); **hace (mucho) sol** it's (very) sunny (6); **hace (mucho) viento** it's (very) windy (6); **hay (mucha) contaminación** there's (lots of) pollution (6); **muchas gracias** thank you very much (1); **(mucho) gusto** nice to meet you (1); <u>tener</u> **(mucha) hambre** to be (very) hungry (7); <u>tener</u> **(mucha) sed** to be (very) thirsty (7); <u>tener</u> **(mucho) calor** to be (very) warm, hot (6); <u>tener</u> **(mucho) frío** to be (very) cold (6)

mudanza *n.* move

mudarse to move (*residence*) (12)

mueble *m.* piece of furniture (5)

muela molar, back tooth (11)

muerte *f.* death (16)

muerto/a (*p.p. of* **morir** [**muero**] [**u**]) dead; **Día** (*m.*) **de los Muertos** Day of the Dead

mujer *f.* woman (2); wife (3); **Día** (*m.*) **Internacional de la No Violencia Contra la Mujer** International Day for the Elimination of Violence against Women; **mujer de negocios** businesswoman (17); **mujer soldado** female soldier (17)

mula mule

mulato/a mulatto

multa fine

multilingüe multilingual

multinacional multinational

múltiple multiple

multiplicarse (qu) to multiply; to grow in number

multirracial multiracial

mundial *adj.* world; **Copa Mundial** World Cup

mundo world (3); **Copa del Mundo** World Cup (soccer)

municipio municipality

muñeca doll

mural *m.* mural (13)

muralismo muralism

muralista *m., f.* muralist

muralla city wall

murciélago bat (*animal*)

muro wall

músculo muscle

museo museum (10); **ir a un museo** to go to a museum (10)

música music (13)

musical musical (13)

músico *m., f.* musician (13)

musulmán, musulmana Muslim

mutuo/a mutual

muy very (1); **muy bien** fine, very well (1); **muy buenas** good afternoon/evening (1)

N

nacer (nazco) to be born (16)

nacimiento birth

nación *f.* nation; **Organización** (*f.*) **de Naciones Unidas (ONU)** United Nations (U.N.)

nacional national; **himno nacional** national anthem; **producto nacional bruto** gross national product

nacionalidad *f.* nationality; **adjetivo de nacionalidad** adjective of nationality (3)

nada nothing, not anything (7); **de nada** you're welcome (1); **para nada** at all (8)

nadar to swim (8)

nadie no one, nobody, not anybody (7)

náhuatl *m.* Nahuatl (*language of the Aztecs*)

nana *fam.* grandma

naranja *n.* orange (7); **media naranja** better half

nariz *f.* (*pl.* **narices**) nose (11)

narración *f.* narration

narrador(a) narrator

narrar to narrate

natación *f.* swimming (10)

natal: casa natal house where someone was born

nativo/a native

natural natural; **ciencias** (*f. pl.*) **naturales** natural sciences (2); **recurso natural** natural resource (15)

naturaleza nature (15)

naturópata *m., f.* naturopath

náufrago shipwreck

nave (*f.*) **espacial** spaceship

navegable navigable

navegación *f.* navigation

navegar (gu) to navigate (12); **navegar la red** to surf the internet

Navidad *f.* Christmas (9)

navideño/a *adj.* Christmas

neblina mist; fog

necesario/a necessary (3)

necesidad *f.* need, necessity

necesitar to need (2)

negación *f.* negation

negar (niego) (gu) to deny (13)

negativo/a negative; **palabra indefinida y negativa** *gram.* indefinite and negative word (7)

negociar to negotiate

negocio business; **hombre** (*m.*) **de negocios** businessman (17);

mujer (*f.*) **de negocios** businesswoman (17)

negrilla: en negrilla boldface

negro/a black (4)

neoyorquino/a *adj.* of or pertaining to New York

nerviosismo nervousness

nervioso/a nervous (6)

neumático tire (*automobile*)

neutralizar (c) to neutralize

neutro/a neutral

nevar (nieva) to snow (6); **nieva** it's snowing (6)

nevera refrigerator

ni neither; nor; **ni... ni** neither ... nor

nicaragüense *n., adj. m., f.* Nicaraguan

niebla fog

nieto/a grandson/granddaughter (3)

nieve *f.* snow (6)

ningún, ninguna no, not any (7)

niñero/a baby-sitter (10)

niñez *f.* infancy (16); childhood (16)

niño/a small child (3); boy/girl (3); **de niño/a** as a child (10)

nivel *m.* level

no no (1); **no creer** + *subjunctive* to not think/believe (13); **no es seguro/(im) posible, (im)probable** it's not certain / a sure thing/(im)possible, (im)probable (13); **no estar de acuerdo** to disagree (3); **no estar seguro/a de** to not be sure of (13); **no hay** there is/are not (1); **no hay de qué** you're welcome (1); **no hay problema** no problem (14); **no obstante** however; **no tener razón** to be wrong (4); **ya no** no longer

¿no? right, don't they (you...)? (4)

noche *f.* night; **buenas noches** goodnight (1); **de la noche** in the evening, P.M. (1); **esta noche** tonight (6); **por la noche** at night, in the evening (2)

Nochebuena Christmas Eve (9)

Nochevieja New Year's Eve (9)

nombrar to name

nombre *m.* name (7)

nopal *m.* cactus

noreste *m.* northeast

norma rule; norm

normal normal; **es normal que** + *subjunctive* it's normal that (13)

normalidad *f.* normality

noroeste *m.* northwest

norte *m.* north (6)

Norteamérica North America

norteamericano/a North American

nos *d. o. pron.* us; *i. o. pron.* to/for us; *refl. pron.* ourselves; **nos vemos** see you around (1)

nosotros/as *subj. pron.* we (2); *obj.* (*of prep.*) us

nota grade (*academic*) (5); note
notar to note; to notice
noticias *f. pl.* news (5)
noticiero newscast (18)
notificación *f.* notification
novecientos/as nine hundred (4)
novela novel (13)
novelista *m., f.* novelist (13)
noveno/a ninth (13)
noventa ninety (3)
noviazgo engagement period (16)
noviembre *m.* November (6)
novio/a boyfriend/girlfriend (6); fiancé(e) (16); groom/bride (16)
nube *f.* cloud (12)
nublado/a cloudy (6); **está (muy) nublado** it's (very) cloudy, overcast (6)
nuclear: energía nuclear nuclear energy (15)
nuestro/a(s) *poss. adj.* our (3); *poss. pron.* ours, of ours (17)
nueve nine (1)
nuevo/a new (3); **Año Nuevo** New Year; **Nueva York** New York
numérico/a numerical
número number (1); **número ordinal** ordinal number (13)
numeroso/a numerous
nunca never (3); **casi nunca** almost never (3)
nupcial nuptial; **votos** (*m. pl.*) **nupciales** wedding vows
nutritivo/a nutritious

O

o or (1)
obedecer (obedezco) to obey (15)
obispo bishop
objetivo *n.* objective
objeto object (2)
obligación *f.* obligation
obligado/a customary
obligatorio/a obligatory
obra work; **obra de arte** work of art (13); **obra de teatro** play (13); **obra maestra** masterpiece (13); **obra teatral** play
obrero/a worker, laborer (17)
observación *f.* observation
observar to observe
obstáculo obstacle
obstante: no obstante however
obtener (*like* **tener**) to get, obtain (12)
obvio/a obvious
ocasión *f.* occasion
ocasionar to cause
océano ocean (8); **océano Pacífico** Pacific Ocean
ochenta eighty (3)
ocho eight (1)
ochocientos/as eight hundred (4)

octavo/a eighth (13)
octubre *m.* October (6)
oculista *m., f.* ophthalmologist
oculto/a hidden
ocupación *f.* occupation (17)
ocupado/a busy (6)
ocupar to hold; to occupy
ocurrir to occur (14)
odiar to hate (8)
oeste *m.* west (6)
ofensivo/a offensive
off: voz en off voice-over
oficial official
oficina office (2)
ofrecer (ofrezco) to offer (8)
ofrenda *n.* offering
oído inner ear (11)
oír to hear (5); to listen to (*music, the radio*) (5)
ojalá (que) I hope (that) (13)
ojo eye (11); **¡ojo!** *interj.* watch out!; **ojo alerta** eagle eye
olímpico/a: Juegos (*m. pl.*) **Olímpicos** Olympic Games
oliva: aceite (*m.*) **de oliva** olive oil (7)
olor *m.* odor
olvidar to forget (9)
omnipresente omnipresent
once eleven (1)
onda wave; **¿cuál es tu onda?** what's your style?; **en onda** in style; **¿qué onda?** what's new/happening?
onomatopeya onomatopoeia
onomatopéyico/a onomatopoeic
ONU *f.* **(Organización** [*f.*] **de Naciones Unidas)** U.N. (United Nations)
opción *f.* option
opcional optional
ópera opera (13)
operación *f.* operation
opinar to think; to have/express an opinion
opinión *f.* opinion
oponerse (a) (*like* **poner**) to oppose
oportunidad *f.* opportunity
optar (por) to opt (for)
optimista *m., f.* optimist; *adj.* optimistic
opuesto/a opposite
oración *f. gram.* sentence (2)
oral oral (14); **informe** (*m.*) **oral** oral report (14)
órale *interj. sl.* wow
orangután *m.* orangutan
órbita orbit
orden *m.* order
ordenado/a neat (6)
ordenador *m.* computer (*Sp.*)
ordenar to put in order
ordinal: número ordinal ordinal number (13)
ordinario/a ordinary
oreja (outer) ear (11)

orgánico/a organic
organismo organism
organización *f.* organization
organizar (c) to organize
órgano organ
orgullo pride
orgulloso/a proud
orientación *f.* orientation
oriental eastern
origen *m.* origin
originario/a native
originarse de to come from
oriundo/a native
oro gold (4); **de oro** gold (4)
orquesta orchestra (13)
orquídea orchid
ortografía spelling
ortográfico/a: acento ortográfico accent mark
oscuridad *f.* darkness
oso/a bear
ostra oyster
otavaleno/a resident of Otavalo (Ecuador)
otoño fall, autumn (6)
otorgar (gu) to grant
otro/a other, another (3); **otra vez** again; **por otro lado** on the other hand
oveja sheep
ozono: capa de ozono ozone layer (15)

P

paciencia patience
paciente *n. m., f.* patient (11); *adj.* patient
pacífico/a pacific; **océano Pacífico** Pacific Ocean
padrastro stepfather
padre *m.* father (3); *m. pl.* parents (3); **Día** (*m.*) **del Padre** Father's Day
padrino godfather
paella *Spanish dish made with rice, shellfish, and often chicken, and flavored with saffron*
pagado/a: empleo bien/mal pagado well-/poorly paid job/position (17)
pagar (gu) to pay (for) (2)
página page; **página web** webpage (12)
país *m.* country (3)
pájaro bird (3)
Pakistán Pakistan
pakistaní *m., f.* (*pl.* **pakistaníes**) Pakistani
palabra word (1); **palabra indefinida y negativa** *gram.* indefinite and negative word (7)
palacio palace
palestino/a Palestinian
palma palm tree
palmera palm tree
palo stick
palomitas *f. pl.* popcorn

pampa plain (*geography, Arg.*)
pan *m.* bread (7); **pan tostado** toast (7)
panadería bakery
panameño/a *n., adj.* Panamanian
páncreas *m. inv.* pancreas
pandemia pandemic
pandilla gang
pánel (*m.*) **solar** solar panel
panhispano/a Pan-Hispanic
pánico panic
panorama *m.* panorama
pantalla (grande/plana) (big/flat) screen (monitor) (12)
pantalones *m. pl.* pants (4); **pantalones cortos** shorts (4)
pañuelo handkerchief
papa (frita) (French fried) potato (7)
papá *m.* father, dad (3)
papel *m.* paper (2); role (13)
papi *m.* dad, daddy
par *m.* pair
para (intended) for; in order to (3); **para** + *inf.* (*do something*) (3); **para nada** at all (8); **¿para qué?** for what purpose? (14); **para que** so that, in order that (16)
parabrisas *m. inv.* windshield (15)
paracaídas *m. inv.* parachute
paracaidismo skydiving
parada stop (8); **hacer parada** to make a stop (8); **parada del autobús** bus stop (12); **parada del metro** subway stop (12)
paraguayo/a *n., adj.* Paraguayan
parar to stop (15)
parcial partial (14); **empleo de tiempo parcial** part-time job/position (17)
pardo/a brown
parecer (parezco) (*like* **gustar**) to seem; **parecerse (a)** to resemble
pared *f.* wall (5)
pareja partner (3); significant other (3); couple (3)
paréntesis *m. inv.* parentheses
pariente *m.* relative (3)
parlamentario/a parliamentary
parque *m.* park
parqueadero parking lot
parquear to park
párrafo paragraph
parranda Christmas party (Cuba)
parrilla grill
parte *f.* part (5); **por todas partes** everywhere (14)
participación *f.* participation
participante *m., f.* participant
participar to participate
particular particular; unique; **en particular** particularly
partida: punto de partida starting point
partido game, match (10); political party (18)

partir: a partir de beyond (4)
pasado/a past, last (11); **el año pasado** last year; **pasado mañana** the day after tomorrow (5)
pasaje *m.* fare, price (*of a transportation ticket*) (8)
pasajero/a passenger (8)
pasaporte *m.* passport (8)
pasar to spend (*time*) (6); to happen (6); **pasar hambre** to go hungry; **pasar la aspiradora** to vacuum (10); **pasar las vacaciones en...** to spend one's vacation in ... (8); **pasar por el control de seguridad** to go/pass through security (check) (8); **pasar por la aduana** to go/pass through customs (8); **pasar tiempo** to spend time (6); **pasarlo bien/mal** to have a good/bad time (9)
pasatiempo pastime (10)
Pascua Easter (9)
Pascua judía Hanukkah (9)
pasear to take a walk, stroll; to go for a ride
paseo walk, stroll (10); **dar un paseo** to take a walk (10)
pasillo aisle (8)
pasión *f.* passion
paso step
pastel *m.* cake (7); pie (7); **pastel de cumpleaños** birthday cake (9)
pastilla pill (11)
pastor(a) minister
pata leg (*of an animal*)
patata potato
paternidad *f.* paternity
paterno/a paternal
patinaje *m.* skating (10)
patinar to skate (10)
patio patio (5); yard (5)
patojo/a *sl.* young man/woman (Guat.)
patriarcal patriarchal
Patricio: Día (*m.*) **de San Patricio** St. Patrick's Day (9)
patrimonio patrimony
patriota *m., f.* patriot
patriótico/a patriotic
patronal: fiesta patronal *party dedicated to patron saint*
pavo turkey (7)
paz *f.* (*pl.* **paces**) peace (18)
peca freckle
pecho chest
pedazo piece
pedir (pido) (i) to ask for (5); to order (5); **pedir disculpas** to apologize (14)
pegar (gu) to hit, strike (14); **pegarse con/contra** to run, bump into/ against (14)
peinarse to comb/brush one's hair (5)
Pekín Peking

pelado/a *sl.* young man/woman (Col.)
pelear to fight (10)
pelícano pelican
película movie (5)
peligro danger (15); **especie** (*f.*) **en peligro de extinción** endangered species (15)
peligroso/a dangerous
pelo hair; **teñirse (me tiño) (i) el pelo** to dye one's hair; **tomarle el pelo** to pull someone's leg
pelota ball (10)
pelotero/a baseball player
peluche: animal (*m.*) **de peluche** stuffed animal
peluquero/a hairstylist (17)
pena pity
pendiente *m.* earring (Sp.)
península peninsula
pensar (pienso) (de/en) to think (about) (5); **pensar** + *inf.* to intend, plan to (*do something*) (5); **pensar que** to think that (5)
penúltimo/a next to last
peor worse (6); **peor(es) que** worse than (6)
pepino cucumber (7)
pequeño/a small (3)
percatarse to realize
percepción *f.* perception
percibir to perceive
percusión *f.* percussion
perder (pierdo) to lose; to miss (*an event*) (5)
perdón excuse me (1)
perdonar to forgive
perdurable lasting
peregrinación *f.* pilgrimage
perezoso/a lazy (3)
perfección *f.* perfection
perfecto/a perfect
pérfido/a treacherous
perfil *m.* profile
perforación *f.* drilling (*well*)
perfume *m.* perfume
periódico newspaper (3)
periodismo journalism
periodista *m., f.* journalist (17)
período period (*of time*)
permanecer (permanezco) to remain, stay
permanente permanent
permiso permission; permit; **(con) permiso** excuse me (1); **permiso de manejar** driving permit
permitir to permit, allow (12)
pero but (1)
perro dog (3)
persecución *f.* persecution
perseguir (*like* **seguir**) to chase; to pursue
persona person (2)

personaje *m.* character (*book, movie*)

personal (*m.*) **médico** medical personnel (11)

personal *adj.* personal; **pronombre** (*m.*) **personal** *gram.* personal pronoun (2)

personalidad *f.* personality

perspectiva perspective

persuasivo/a persuasive

pertenecer (**pertenezco**) **a** to belong to

perturbar to perturb, bother

peruano/a *n., adj.* Peruvian

pesado/a boring (10); heavy

pesar to weigh; **a pesar de** in spite of

pesas (*f. pl.*): **levantar pesas** to lift weights (11)

pescadería fish market

pescado fish (*cooked*) (7)

pescar (**qu**) to fish

pesimista *m., f.* pessimistic

peso weight

pestaña eyelash

petición *f.* request

petróleo petroleum, oil (15)

petrolero/a *adj.* oil; petroleum

pez *m.* (*pl.* **peces**) fish (*live*) (15)

picante hot, spicy (7)

picar (**qu**) to bite; to sting

pícnic: **hacer un pícnic** to have a picnic (10)

pico peak

pie *m.* foot (11); **dedo del pie** toe (11); **levantarse con el pie izquierdo** to get up on the wrong side of the bed (14)

piedra stone

piel *f.* skin

pierna leg (11)

pieza piece

pila battery; **ponerse las pilas** to get one's act together; to energize oneself

pilar *m.* pillar

Pilates: **hacer Pilates** to do Pilates (11)

píldora pill

piloto *m., f.* pilot (8)

pimienta pepper (*condiment*) (7)

pingüino penguin

pino pine (tree)

pinola *m.* typical Nicaragua drink

pintar to paint (13)

pintor(a) painter (13)

pintura painting (*in general; specific piece*) (12)

piña pineapple

pirámide *f.* pyramid

piraña piranha

Pirineos *m. pl.* Pyrenees

piscina swimming pool (5)

Piscis *m.* Pisces

pisco *alcoholic beverage of Peru and Chile*

piso floor (*of a building*) (12); floor (*of a room*); **barrer el piso** to sweep the floor (10); **primer piso** first floor

(second story) (12); **segundo piso** second floor (third story) (12)

pizarra chalkboard

pizarrón *m.* (**blanco**) (white)board (2)

placa license plate

placer *m.* pleasure

plan *m.* plan (10); **hacer planes para** + *inf.* to make plans to (*do something*) (10)

planchar to iron (10)

planeación *f.* planning

planear to plan

planeta *m.* planet (15)

planetario/a planetary

plano map (*of a city*); blueprint

plano/a flat (12); **pantalla plana** flat screen (monitor) (12)

planta plant

planta baja ground floor (12)

plantación *f.* plantation

plástico plastic

plata *n.* silver (4); **de plata** *adj.* silver (4)

plátano plantain

platino platinum

plato dish (*food prepared in a particular way*) 7; course (7); plate (5); **plato principal** main course (7)

playa beach (6)

plaza plaza, square (4)

plazo deadline (14); **a plazos** in installments (17)

pleno/a complete; full

plomero/a plumber (17)

pluma pen

plurinacional multinational

población *f.* population (15)

pobre poor (3)

pobreza poverty

poco (a) little (2); few (4); **un poco (de)** a little bit (of) (2)

poder *v.* to be able, can (4)

poder *n. m.* power; **poder adquisitivo** purchasing power

poderoso/a powerful

poema *m.* poem (13)

poesía poetry

poeta *m., f.* poeta (13)

poético/a poetic

polaco/a Polish

policía police force (15)

polinésico/a Polynesian

política politics (18); policy (18)

político/a *n.* politician (18); *adj.* political; **ciencias** (*f. pl.*) **políticas** political science (2)

pollera *indigenous skirt of the Andes*

pollo chicken (7); **pollo asado** roast chicken (7); **pollo frito** fried chicken

polvo dust

poner to put (5); to place (5); to turn on (*an appliance*) (5); **poner atención** to pay attention; **poner la mesa** to set

the table (10); **poner(se) una inyección** to get a shot (11); **ponerse** to put on (*an article of clothing*) (5); **ponerse una vacuna** (**de**) to get a vaccination (against) (11) **ponerse** + *adj./adv.* to become, get + *adj./adv.* (9); **ponerse las pilas** to get one's act together; to energize oneself; **ponerse rojo/a** to blush (9)

popularidad *f.* popularity

por about (6); because of (6); through (8); for (8); by (14); **gracias por** + *noun/inf.* thanks for (9); **por consiguiente** as a result; **por Dios** for heaven's sake (14); **por ejemplo** for example (14); **por ello** therefore; **por eso** for that reason (3); **por favor** please (1); **por fin** finally (5); **por la mañana** in the morning (2); **por la noche** at night, in the evening (2); **por la tarde** in the afternoon (2); **por lo general** generally (5); **por lo menos** at least (9); **por lo regular** in general; **por otro lado** on the other hand; **por primera/última vez** for the first/last time (14); **por si acaso** just in case (14); **¡por supuesto!** of course! (14); **por todas partes** everywhere (14); **por un lado** on one hand

porcentaje *m.* percentage

porción *f.* portion, part

pormenorizado/a detailed

poro pore

porotos *m. pl.* beans

¿por qué? why? (3)

porque because (3)

portafolio portfolio

portarse bien/mal to (mis)behave (9)

portátil portable (2); **computadora portátil** laptop (computer) (2); **ordenador** (*m.*) **portátil** (*Sp.*) laptop (computer)

portero/a building manager (12); doorman (12)

portón *m.* front door; gate

portugués *m.* Portuguese (*language*)

portugués, portuguesa *n., adj.* Portuguese

posar to pose

posesión *f.* possession

posesivo/a possessive (17); **adjetivo posesivo** *gram.* possessive adjective (3)

posibilidad *f.* possibility

posible possible (3); **es posible que** + *subjunctive* it's possible that (13); **no es posible que** + *subjunctive* it's not possible that (13)

posición *f.* position

positivo/a positive

posponer (*like* **poner**) to postpone

postal: tarjeta postal postcard (8)

posterior later, subsequent

postre *m.* dessert (7)
postularse to run (18); **postularse como candidato/a** to run as a candidate (18); **postularse para un cargo** to run for a position (18)
postura posture
potencia power
potencial *m.* potential; *adj.* potential
práctica practice
practicar (qu) to practice (2); **practicar el alpinismo** to mountain climb; **practicar un deporte** to play a sport
práctico/a practical
pradera meadow
preadolescencia preadolescence
precedente *m.* precedent
preceder to precede
precio price (4)
precioso/a precious
precipicio precipice
precipitado/a hasty
precisamente precisely
precolombino/a pre-Columbian
predicción *f.* prediction
predominante predominant
predominar to predominate
preescolar *adj.* preschool
preferencia preference (1)
preferir (prefiero) (i) to prefer (4)
pregunta question (5); **hacer una pregunta** to ask a question (5)
preguntar to ask (*a question*) (8)
prehispánico/a pre-Hispanic (*before the arrival of the Spanish*)
prehistórico/a prehistoric
premio prize
prenda article of clothing
prender to fasten
prensa (print) press (18); news media (18)
prensado/a pressed
preocupación *f.* worry
preocupado/a worried (6)
preocupar(se) to worry; **no se preocupe** (*form. s.*) don't worry; **no te preocupes** (*fam. s.*) don't worry
preparación *f.* preparation
preparar to prepare (7); **prepararse** to prepare oneself; to get ready
preparatoria (prepa) pre-university study
preposición *f. gram.* preposition (5)
prescribir to prescribe
preseleccionado/a pre-selected
presencia presence
presencial: de forma presencial in person
presentación *f.* presentation
presentador(a) presenter; (television) anchor
presentar to introduce; to present
presente *m.* present (*time*); *gram.* present tense; *adj.* present

preservar to preserve
presidencia presidency
presidencial presidential
presidente/a president
presión *f.* pressure (14); **estar bajo muchas presiones** to be under a lot of pressure (14)
preso/a prisoner
préstamo loan (17)
prestar to lend (8)
prestigioso/a prestigious
presupuestario/a budgetary
presupuesto budget (17)
pretérito *gram.* preterite
preuniversitario/a pre-university
prevenir (*like* **venir**) to warn
primario/a primary; first; elementary; **escuela primaria** elementary school
primavera spring (6)
primero *adv.* first (5)
primer(o/a) first (5); **el primero de** the first of (*month*) (6); **por primera vez** for the first time (14); **primer piso** first floor (second story) (12)
primo/a cousin (3); *m. pl.* cousins (3)
princesa princess
principal main; **plato principal** main course (7)
príncipe *m.* prince
principiante *m., f.* beginner; novice
principio beginning; **al principio de** at the beginning of (17)
priorizar (c) to prioritize
prisa: tener prisa to be in a hurry (4)
privacidad *f.* privacy
privado/a private
privilegio privilege
probabilidad *f.* probability
probable probable (13); **es probable que** + *subjunctive* it's likely, probable that (13); **no es probable que** + *subjunctive* it's not probable that (13)
probar (pruebo) to try, taste
problema *m.* problem; **no hay problema** no problem (14)
problemático/a problematic
procedimiento procedure
procesión *f.* procession
proceso process
proclamar to proclaim
procurar to procure
producción *f.* production
producir (*like* **conducir**) to produce
productivo/a productive
producto product; **producto nacional bruto** gross national product
productor(a) producer
profesión *f.* profession (17)
profesional *n. m., f.* professional, person with a profession; *adj.* professional
profesionista *n. m., f.* professional, person with a profession

profesor(a) professor (1)
profesorado faculty
profundidad *f.* depth
profundo/a deep
programa *m.* program; **programa (del curso)** (course) syllabus (14)
programación *f.* programming
programador(a) programmer (17)
progresivo/a progressive
progreso progress
prohibir (prohíbo) to prohibit, forbid (12)
proliferación *f.* proliferation
promedio average
promesa promise
prometer to promise (8)
prominente prominent
promover (promuevo) to promote
pronombre *m. gram.* pronoun (2); **pronombre personal** *gram.* personal pronoun (2); **pronombre relativo** *gram.* relative pronoun
pronosticar (qu) to forecast
pronóstico forecast
pronto *adv.* soon; **hasta pronto** see you soon; **tan pronto como** *conj.* as soon as (17)
pronunciación *f.* pronunciation
pronunciar to pronounce
propiedad *f.* property; characteristic
propio/a own, one's own (4)
proponer (*like* **poner**) to propose
proporción *f.* proportion
proporcionar to provide
propósito purpose
prórroga extension
protagonista *m., f.* protagonist
protección *f.* protection
protector(a) protective
proteger (protejo) to protect (15)
proteína protein
protestante *n., adj. m., f.* Protestant
protestantismo Protestantism
protestar to protest
provecho: ¡buen provecho! bon appetit! (7); enjoy your meal! (7)
proveedor(a) provider
proveer (*like* **creer**) to provide
proverbio proverb
providencia providence
provincia province
provocar (qu) to cause
próximo/a next (5); **el próximo (martes...)** next (Tuesday ...) (5); **la próxima semana** next week (5)
proyección *f.* projection
proyecto project
prudente prudent
prueba quiz (14); test (14); proof
publicación *f.* publication
publicar (qu) to post (*as on Facebook*) (12); to publish (12)

publicidad *f.* publicity
publicitario/a *adj.* advertising
público *n.* audience (13)
público/a *adj.* public (15); **transporte** (*m.*) **público** public transportation
pueblo town
puente *m.* bridge
puerco pig
puerta door (2); **puerta de embarque** boarding gate (8)
puerto port (8)
puertorriqueño/a *n., adj.* Puerto Rican
pues *conj.* well
puesto job; position; place (*in line*) (8)
pulgada inch
pulido/a polished
pulmones *m. pl.* lungs (11)
pulpería grocery store (*C.A.*)
pulpo octopus
punto point; **a punto de** + *inf.* about to + *inf.;* **en punto** on the dot (*time*) (1); **hora punta** peak hour; **punto cardinal** cardinal point (6); **punto de partida** starting point; **punto de vista** point of view
puntuación *f.* punctuation
pupusa *thick stuffed corn tortilla*
puro cigar
puro/a pure (15)
púrpura *n.* purple
purpúreo/a *adj.* purple

Q

que that, which (3); who (3); **así que** therefore, consequently, so; **hasta que** *conj.* until (17); **que Dios te bendiga** God bless you; **ya que** since
¿qué? what? which? (1); **¿a qué hora... ?** at what time ... ? (1); **¿con qué frecuencia... ?** how often ... ? (3); **¿por qué?** why? (3)
¡qué... ! what ... !; **¡qué** + *adj.***!** how + *adj.*! (14); **¡qué** + *noun***!** what (a) + *noun* (14); **¡qué bacán!** fantastic!
quebrarse (me quiebro) to break
quedar to remain, be left (14); **quedarse** to stay, remain (*in a place*) (6)
quejarse (de) to complain (about) (8)
quemada *n.* burn
quemar to burn
querer to want (4); to love (16); **eso quiere decir...** that means ... (11); **fue sin querer** I didn't mean (to do) it (14); **quererse** to love each other (11); to be fond of each other (11)
querido/a dear (6)
queso cheese (7)
quetzal *currency of Guatemala*
quien who; whom

¿quién(es)? who? whom? (1); **¿de quién?** whose? (3)
química chemistry (2)
quince fifteen (1); **menos quince** fifteen minutes until (*hour*) (1); **y quince** fifteen minutes after (*the hour*) (1)
quinceañera young woman's fifteenth birthday party (9); young woman who is turning fifteen
quinientos/as five hundred (4)
quinto/a fifth (13)
quiropráctico/a chiropractor
quitar to remove; **quitar la mesa** to clear the table (10); **quitarse** to take off (*an article of clothing*) (5)
quizás *adv.* perhaps

R

rabia rutera road rage
ración *f.* portion
radiante bright, shining, radiant
radical *m. gram.* root
radio *m.* radio (*apparatus*) (12); *f.* radio (*medium*) (18); **estación** (*f.*) **de radio** radio station (18)
radioyente *m., f.* radio listener; *m. pl.* radio audience
raíz *f.* (*pl.* **raíces**) root
rama branch
rana frog
ranchera *traditional music of Mexico*
rancho ranch
rap *m.* rap music
rapanui *n. m., f. indigenous person of Easter Island*
rápido *adv.* quickly
rápido/a fast; **comida rápida** fast food
rápidos *m. pl.* rapids
raqueta racket
raro/a rare; strange
rascacielos *m. inv.* skyscraper (15)
rata rat
rato while, short time
ratón *m.* mouse (12)
raya: de rayas striped (4)
rayar to scratch
raza race (*ethnic*)
razón *f.* reason; **no tener razón** to be wrong (4); **tener razón** to be right (4)
reacción *f.* reaction
reaccionar to react
real royal; real
realidad *f.* reality
realismo realism
realista *m., f.* realistic
realizar (c) to achieve; to attain
rebaja sale, reduction (4); *pl.* sales, reductions (4); **en rebaja** on sale
rebanada slice

rebasar to pass (*a vehicle*)
rebelde *n. m., f.* rebel; *adj.* rebellious
rebelión *f.* rebellion
recado message
recámara bedroom
recepción *f.* reception
recepcionista *m., f.* receptionist
receptor *m.* receiver; recipient
receta recipe (7); prescription (11)
recetar to prescribe
recibir to receive (3)
recibo receipt (17)
reciclaje *m.* recycling (15)
reciclar to recycle (15)
recién recently (16); **recién casado/a** newlywed (16)
reciente recent
recipiente *m.* container
recíproco/a reciprocal
recitar to recite
recomendable recommendable
recomendación *f.* recommendation
recomendar (recomiendo) to recommend (8)
reconocer (*like* **conocer**) to recognize
reconocimiento recognition
reconquista reconquest
reconstituido/a remarried; hybrid (*of a family*)
reconstituir (*like* **construir**) to reconstitute; to reconstruct
recordar (recuerdo) to remember (9)
recrear to recreate
recreo recess
recto/a straight; **(todo) recto** straight ahead (15)
rector(a) university president
recuerdo memory
recuperación *f.* recuperation
recuperador(a) recuperative
recuperar to recuperate
recurso resource (15); **recurso natural** natural resource (15)
red *f.* network; internet; **navegar (gu) la red** to surf the internet; **red social** social network (12)
redacción *f.* editing
redactar to write; to edit
reducción *f.* reduction
reducir (*like* **conducir**) to reduce
reemplazar (c) to replace
referencia reference
referirse (me refiero) (i) (a) to refer (to)
refinado/a refined
reflejar to reflect
reflexivo/a reflexive (5); **verbo reflexivo** *gram.* reflexive verb (5)
reforma change
refrán *m.* saying, proverb
refresco soft drink (7)
refrigerador *m.* refrigerator (10)

refrigeradora refrigerator
refugio refuge
regalar to give (*as a gift*) (8)
regalo present, gift (3)
regatear to bargain
regateo bartering
reggae *m.* reggae
régimen *m.* regime
región *f.* region
regir (rijo) (i) to govern
registración *f.* registration
registrar to register
registro register; record
regla rule
regresar to return (*to a place*) (2);
   regresar a casa to go home (2)
regulador(a) regulator
regular *adj.* so-so (1); **por lo regular** in
   general; *v.* to regulate
regularidad *f.* regularity
reina queen (18)
reinar to reign
reino kingdom
reírse (de) to laugh (about) (9)
reiterar to reiterate
reivindicación *f.* vindication
reivindicar (qu) to reclaim
reja bar (*of prison*)
relación *f.* relation; relationship;
   relación sentimental emotional
   relationship (16)
relacionar to relate
relajado/a relaxed
relajante relaxing
relajarse to relax
relámpago lightning
relativo/a: pronombre (*m.*) **relativo**
   gram. relative pronoun
relevante relevant
religión *f.* religion
religioso/a religious
relleno/a filled
reloj *m.* watch (4)
remarcar (qu) to remark
remate: de remate hopeless(ly)
remedio remedy
remodelado/a remodeled
remoto/a: control (*m.*) **remoto** remote
   control (12)
remuneración *f.* remuneration
renovable renewable (15); **energía**
   renovable renewable energy (15)
renovar (renuevo) to renew
rentar to rent (*Mex.*)
renunciar (a) to resign (from) (17)
reparar to repair (15)
repasar to review
repaso review
repeler to repel
repente: de repente suddenly (11)
repetición *f.* repetition

repetir (repito) (i) to repeat
repetitivo/a repetitive
reportaje *m.* report (*on a news show*)
reportar to report
reportero/a reporter (18)
represa dam
representación *f.* representation
representante *n. m., f.* representative;
   representante al congreso
   congressional representative (18)
representar to represent
representativo/a *adj.* representative
república republic
republicano/a republican
requerir (requiero) (i) to require
requisito requirement
rescatar to rescue
reseña review (*book, movie*)
reserva reserve; reservation (*Sp.*);
   hacer reserva to make a reservation
resfriado *n.* cold (*illness*) (11)
resfriado/a *adj.* congested, stuffed
   up (11)
resfriarse (me resfrío) to catch/get a
   cold (11)
residencia dormitory (2); **residencia de**
   ancianos nursing home (12)
residente *m., f.* resident
residuos *m. pl.* waste
resistente resistant; strong
resistir to resist
resolver (resuelvo) (*p.p.* **resuelto**) to
   solve (15); to resolve (15)
respectivo/a respective
respecto: a este respecto in this
   regard; **(con) respecto a** regarding
respetar to respect
respeto respect
respiración *f.* breathing
respirar to breathe (11)
responder to respond
responsabilidad *f.* responsibility (18);
   responsabilidad cívica civic
   duty (18)
responsable responsible
respuesta answer (6)
restablecimiento re-establishment;
   restoration
restaurante *m.* restaurant (7)
resto rest, remainder
restricción *f.* restriction
resuelto/a (*p.p. of* **resolver**) resolved
resultado result
resumen *m.* summary; **en resumen** in
   summary
resumir to summarize
resurrección *f.* resurrection
retribuir (*like* **contribuir**) to reward
retrospectivo/a retrospective
retumbar to resound
reunión *f.* meeting

reunirse (me reúno) (con) to get
   together (with) (9)
revelar to reveal
revés: al revés backwards
revisar to check (15)
revista magazine (3)
revolucionario/a revolutionary
revolver (*like* **volver**) to stir
rey *m.* king (18)
rezar (c) to pray
Ricitos de Oro Goldilocks
rico/a rich (3); tasty, savory; rich
   (*in calories*) (7)
ridículo/a ridiculous
riesgo risk; **de alto riesgo** high risk
rígido/a rigid
rima rhyme
rimar to rhyme
rincón *m.* corner
rinoceronte *m.* rhinoceros
riñón *m.* kidney
río river (15)
rioplatense *adj., m., f.* of or from the
   Río de la Plata area
riqueza richness
risa laughter
ritmo rhythm; **ritmo lento / acelerado**
   de la vida slow / fast pace of life (15)
rito rite; ritual
robar to rob; to steal
robo theft; robbery
rodante: cinta rodante treadmill
rodeado/a (de) surrounded (by)
rodear to go around
rojo/a red (4); **ponerse rojo/a** to
   blush (9)
Roma Rome
romano/a Roman
romántico/a romantic (16)
romper(se) (*p.p.* **roto**) to break (14);
   romper (con) to break up (with) (16)
ron *m.* rum
ropa clothing (4); **ropa interior**
   underwear (4)
ropero wardrobe
rosa rose; **rosa té** tea rose
rosado/a pink (4)
rosario rosary
rostro face
roto/a (*p.p. of* **romper**) broken
rotulador *m.* felt-tipped pen
rubio/a blond(e) (3)
rueda wheel, tire; **rueda de molino**
   treadmill
ruido noise (5)
ruidoso/a noisy
ruina ruin (13)
ruso Russian (*language*)
ruso/a *n., adj.* Russian
ruta route
rutero/a: rabia rutera road rage

rutina routine (5)
rutinario/a *adj.* routine (11)

S

sábado Saturday (5)
saber (sé) to know (*facts, information*) (7); **saber** + *inf.* to know how to (*do something*) (7)
sabiduría wisdom
sabio/a wise
sabor *m.* flavor
sabroso/a tasty
sacar (qu) to get (*grades*) (14); to withdraw, take out (17); **sacar dinero** to withdraw money; **sacar fotos / fotografías** to take photos (8); **sacar la basura** to take out the trash (10); **sacar la lengua** to stick out one's tongue (11)
sacerdote *m.* priest
safari: ir de safari to go on a safari
Sagitario Sagittarius
sagrado/a sacred
sal *f.* salt (7)
sala living room (5); **sala de espera** waiting room (8); **sala de fumadores/ de fumar** smoking area (8); **sala de urgencias** emergency room
salarial: brecha salarial wage gap
salario pay, wages (*often per hour*) (17)
salchicha sausage (7); hot dog (7)
salida departure (8)
salir (de) to leave (*a place*) (5); **salir bien/mal** to come/turn out well/ poorly (5); to do well/poorly (5); **salir (con)** to go out (with) (5); **salir de vacaciones** to leave on vacation (8); **salir (para)** to leave (for) (*a place*) (5)
salmón *m.* salmon (7)
salón (*m.*) **de clase** classroom (2)
salsa sauce (7); salsa (*music*)
salsero/a *adj.* salsa (*music*)
saltar to jump
salud *f.* health (11)
saludable healthy
saludarse to greet each other (11)
saludo greeting (1)
salvadoreño/a *n., adj.* Salvadoran
salvaje wild (15)
salvar to save
san, santo/a *n.* saint; **Día** (*m.*) **de San Patricio** St. Patrick's Day (9); **Día** (*m.*) **de San Valentín** St. Valentine's Day
sanador(a) healer
sancocho *stew made with meat, cassava, and plantains*
sandalias *f. pl.* sandals (4)
sandía watermelon
sándwich *m.* sandwich (7)
sangre *f.* blood (11)
sangriento/a bloody

sanitario/a health; **asistencia sanitaria** health care
sano/a healthy (11); **llevar una vida sana** to lead a healthy life (11)
santo saint
santo/a holy
santuario sanctuary
sarcástico/a sarcastic
sartén *f.* skillet
satélite *m.* satellite
satírico/a satirical
satisfacción *f.* satisfaction
satisfactorio/a satisfactory
satisfecho/a satisfied
Saudito/a: Arabia Saudita Saudi Arabia
sazonar to season
secadora clothes dryer (10)
secar(se) (qu) to dry (oneself)
sección *f.* section
seco/a dry
secretario/a secretary (2)
secreto *n.* secret
secreto/a *adj.* secret
secuencia sequence
secundario/a secondary; **escuela secundaria** high school
sed *f.* thirst (7); **tener (mucha) sed** to be (very) thirsty (7)
seda silk (4); **de seda** *adj.* silk (4)
sedentario/a sedentary
seducir (*like* **conducir**) to seduce
segmento segment
seguidor(a) follower
seguimiento following
seguir (sigo) (i) to continue (6); to keep on going (15)
según according to (3)
segundo/a second (13); **segundo piso** second floor (third story) (12)
seguridad *f.* security; safety; **control** (*m.*) **de seguridad** security (check) (8); **pasar por el control de seguridad** to go/pass through security (check) (8)
seguro *n.* insurance
seguro/a *adj.* sure, certain (6); **es seguro que** + *indicative* it's certain/a sure thing that (13); **no es seguro que** + *subjunctive* it's not sure that (13); **no estar seguro/a de** to not be sure of (13)
seis six (1)
seiscientos/as six hundred (4)
selección *f.* selection; choice
seleccionador(a) *adj.* selection
seleccionar to select; to choose
selva jungle; **Selva Amazónica** Amazon Jungle
selvático/a *adj.* jungle
semáforo traffic signal (15)

semana week; **días** (*m. pl.*) **de la semana** days of the week (5); **fin** (*m.*) **de semana** weekend (2); **la próxima semana** next week (5); **la semana que viene** next week (5); **una vez a la semana** once a week (3)
semanal *m., f.* weekly
sembrar (siembro) to sow, plant
semejante similar
semejanza similarity
semestre *m.* semester
semi-cerrado/a semiclosed
semilla seed
senado senate
senador(a) senator (18)
sencillo/a simple
senda path
senderismo *n.* hiking
sendero path
sensación *f.* sensation
sensibilidad *f.* sensitivity
sensible sensitive
sentarse (me siento) to sit down (5)
sentido sense
sentimental: relación (*f.*) **sentimental** emotional relationship (16)
sentimiento feeling, emotion
sentir (siento) (i) to regret (13); to feel sorry (13); **lo siento (mucho)** I'm (very) sorry (14); **sentirse** + *adj./adv.* to feel + *adj./adv.* (9)
señalar to note; to point out
señor (Sr.) *m.* man; Mr.; sir (1)
señora (Sra.) woman; Mrs.; ma'am (1)
señorita (Srta.) young woman; Miss; Ms. (1)
separación *f.* separation (16)
separado/a (de) separated (from) (16)
separarse (de) to separate (from) (16)
septiembre *m.* September (6)
séptimo/a seventh (13)
ser to be (1); **ayer fue (miércoles...)** yesterday was (Wednesday ...) (5); **¿cómo es usted?** what are you (*form. s.*) like? (1); **¿de dónde eres (tú)?** where are you (*fam. s.*) from? (1); **¿de dónde es (usted)?** where are you (*form. s.*) from? (1); **de última moda** it's trendy (hot) (4); **eres** you are (1); **es** he/ she is, you (*form. s.*) are (1); **es absurdo que** + *subjunctive* it's absurd that (13); **es cierto que** + *indicative* it's certain that (13); **es de...** it is made of ... (4); **es extraño que** + *subjunctive* it's strange that (13); **es importante que** + *subjunctive* it's important that (12); **es (im)posible que** + *subjunctive* it's (im)possible that (13); **es (im)probable que** + *subjunctive* it's (un)likely, (im)probable that (13); **es increíble que** + *subjunctive* it's

incredible that (13); **es la una** it's one o'clock (1); **es mejor** it's better (12); **es necesario** it's necessary (12); **es normal que** + *subjunctive* it's normal that (13); **es seguro que** + *indicative* it's certain / a sure thing that (13); **es terrible que** + *subjunctive* it's terrible that (13); **es una lástima que** + *subjunctive* it's a shame that (13); **es urgente** *que* + *subj.* it's urgent that (12); **es verdad que** + *indicative* it's true that (13); **fue sin querer** I didn't mean (to do) it (14); **llegar (gu) a ser** to become; **no es (im)probable que** + *subjunctive* it's not (im)probable that (13); **no es posible que** + *subjunctive* it's not possible that (13); **no es seguro que** + *subj.* it is not certain / a sure thing that (13); **pasar de ser** to go from being; **¿qué hora es?** what time is it? (1); **ser aburrido/a** to be boring (10); **ser aficionado/a (a)** to be a fan (of) (10); **ser divertido/a** to be fun (10); **ser en** + *place* to take place in/at (*a place*) (9); **son las...** it's ... o'clock (1); **soy** I am (1) **(yo) soy de...** I am from ... (1)

ser (*m.*) **humano** human being
serie *f.* series
serio/a serious
serpiente *f.* snake
servicio service (15); **estación** (*f.*) **de servicio** gas station (15); **servicio militar** military service (18)
servilleta napkin
servir (sirvo) (i) to serve (5); **servir para** to be used for (5)
sesenta sixty (3)
sesión *f.* session
setecientos/as seven hundred (4)
setenta seventy (3)
sevillano/a of or pertaining to Seville
sexismo sexism
sexo sex
sexto/a sixth (13)
si if (4); **por si acaso** just in case (14)
sí yes (1); **sí, me gusta...** yes, I like ... (1)
sicología psychology (2)
sicólogo/a psychologist (17)
siempre always (3)
sierra mountain
siesta nap; **dormir (duermo) (u) la siesta** to take a nap (5)
siete seven (1)
siglo century (10)
significado meaning
significar (qu) to mean
significativo/a significant
signo sign
siguiente following (5)
sílaba syllable
silencio silence

silla chair (2)
sillón *m.* armchair (5)
simbólico/a symbolic
simbolizar (c) to symbolize
símbolo symbol
similaridad *f.* similarity
similitud *f.* similarity
simpático/a nice, likeable (*people*) (3)
sin without (5); **fue sin querer** I didn't mean (to do) it (14); **sin duda** without a doubt; **sin embargo** nevertheless (6); **sin que** *conj.* without; unless (16)
sinagoga synagogue
sinceridad *f.* sincerity
sincero/a sincere
sino but (rather); **sino que** *conj.* but (rather)
sinónimo synonym
sintético/a synthetic
síntoma *m.* symptom (11)
siquiatra *m., f.* psychiatrist (17)
sísmico/a seismic
sismorresistente earthquake resistant
sistema *m.* system (17); **analista** (*m., f.*) **de sistemas** systems analyst (17)
sistemático/a systematic
sitio place, location (12); **sitio web** website (12)
situación *f.* situation
situado/a situated
situarse (me sitúo) to situate oneself; to be placed (*in time*)
snowboard *m.* snowboarding
soberano/a sovereign
sobre *prep.* about (4); on; on top of; over
sobremesa after-dinner conversation
sobrenatural *adj.* supernatural
sobresaliente outstanding
sobresalir (*like* **salir**) to stand out
sobreviviente *adj., m., f.* surviving
sobrevivir to survive
sobrino/a nephew/niece (3)
social social (2); **ciencias** (*f. pl.*) **sociales** social sciences (2); **red** (*f.*) **social** social network (12); **trabajador(a) social** social worker (17)
socialismo socialism
socialista *n., adj. m., f.* socialist
socializar (c) to socialize
sociedad *f.* society
socioeconómico/a socioeconomic
sociología sociology (2)
sodio sodium
sofá *m.* couch (5)
soja soybean
sol *m.* sun (6); **gafas** (*f. pl.*) **de sol** sunglasses (4); **hace (mucho) sol** it's (very) sunny (6); **tomar el sol** to sunbathe (8)

solamente only (14)
solar solar (8); **bloqueador** (*m.*) **solar** sunscreen (8); **energía solar** solar energy (15); **pánel** (*m.*) **solar** solar panel
solas: a solas alone
soldado *m., f.* soldier
soleado/a sunny
soledad *f.* solitud
soler (suelo) to tend to
solicitante *m., f.* applicant
solicitar to apply for (*a job*) (17)
solicitud *f.* job application (*form*) (17)
sólido/a solid
solitario/a solitary, lonely
solo *adv.* only (2)
solo/a *adj.* alone (5)
soltero/a: **estar soltero/a** to be single, not married (16)
soltura: hablar con soltura to speak fluently
solución *f.* solution
sombra shadow; shade
sombrero hat (4); **sombrero hongo** bowler hat, derby
sonar (sueno) to ring (10); to sound (10)
sonido sound
sonreír (*like* **reír**) to smile (9)
sopa soup (7)
soportar to bear
sor *f.* sister (*religious*)
sorber to absorb
sorprendente surprising
sorprender (*like* **gustar**) to surprise (13)
sorpresa surprise
sospechoso/a suspicious
sostenible sustainable
sostenido/a held
su(s) *poss. adj.* his, her, its, your (*form. s.*); their, your (*form. pl.*) (3)
suave mild, smooth, soft
subir (a) to go up; to get on (*a vehicle*) (8); to upload (12)
subjuntivo *gram.* subjunctive
subordinado/a: cláusula subordinada *gram.* subordinate clause
subregión *f.* subregion
substituir (*like* **construir**) to substitute
subtítulo subtitle
suburbio suburb
suceder to occur; to happen
suceso happening
sucesor(a) successor
sucio/a dirty (6)
sudadera sweatshirt (4)
Sudamérica South America
sudamericano/a South American
Suecia Sweden
sueco/a Swedish
suegro/a father-in-law, mother-in-law
sueldo salary (17)
suelo floor (*of a room*)

sueño dream; <u>**tener**</u> **sueño** to be sleepy (4)

suerte *f.* luck (14); <u>**tener**</u> **buena/mala suerte** to have good/bad luck (14); to be (un)lucky (14)

suéter *m.* sweater (4)

suficiente enough (11); **lo suficiente** enough (11)

sufijo *gram.* suffix

sufrimiento suffering

sufrir (de) to suffer (from) (14)

sugerencia suggestion

sugerir (sugiero) (i) to suggest (9)

suicidio suicide

suizo/a Swiss

sujeto *gram.* subject

sumo/a supreme

superar to overtake

superhombre *m.* superman

superlativo *gram.* superlative

supermercado supermarket (12)

superstición *f.* superstition

supersticioso/a superstitious

supervisor(a) supervisor

suplemento supplement

suponer (*like* <u>**poner**</u>) to suppose

supremo/a supreme

supuesto: ¡por supuesto! of course! (14)

sur *m.* south (6)

sureste *m.* southeast

surfear to surf (10)

suroeste *m.* southwest

surrealismo surrealism

surrealista *adj. m., f.* surrealist

suscripción *f.* subscription

suspender to suspend

suspenso suspense

sustantivo *gram.* noun (2)

sustrato essence

sutil subtle

SUV *m.* SUV (15)

suyo/a(s) *poss. adj.* your (*form. s., pl.*) (17); his, her, its, their (17); *poss. pron.* (of) your, yours (*form. s., pl.*) (17); (of) his, her, its, their (17); (of) theirs (17)

T

tabaco tobacco

tabla table; chart

tableta tablet

tabú *f.* taboo

tacón *m.* heel

taconeo heel tap

tailandés, tailandesa Thai

Tailandia Thailand

taíno/a *pre-Hispanic culture of the Caribbean*

tal such, such a; **con tal de** *prep.* provided (16); **con tal (de) que** *conj.* provided (that), as long as (16); **¿qué tal?** how are you? (1); **tal como** just as; **tal vez** perhaps

taladro drill

talento talent

talla size

taller *m.* (repair) shop (15)

tamal *m.* tamale

tamalada *get-together to make and eat tamales*

tamaño size

también also (1)

tambor *m.* drum

tambora African drum

tampoco neither, not either (7)

tan *adv.* so; as; **tan... como** as ... as (6); **tan pronto como** as soon as (17)

tanque *m.* tank (15)

tanto/a *adj.* as much, so much; such (a); *pl.* so many; as many; **tanto como** as much as (6); **tanto/a(os/as)... como** as much/many ... as (6)

tapa lid

tapar to cover

tapas *f. pl.* appetizers (9)

tapir *m.* tapir

taquigrafía shorthand

tardar to be long / take (a long) time

tarde *adv.* late (2)

tarde *f.* afternoon (1); **buenas tardes** good afternoon (1); **de la tarde** in the afternoon, P.M. (1); **por la tarde** in the afternoon (2)

tarea homework (3); **tarea doméstica** household chore (10)

tarjeta card (8); **tarjeta bancaria / de débito** debit card (17); **tarjeta de crédito** credit card (7); **tarjeta de embarque** boarding pass (8); **tarjeta de identidad** identification card; **tarjeta de identificación** identification card, ID (14); **tarjeta postal** postcard (8)

tarta cake

tartamudo/a stutterer

tata *m. fam.* grandpa

tatuaje *m.* tattoo

taza cup (14)

te *dir. obj. pron.* you (*s. fam.*); *indir. obj. pron.* to/for you (*s. fam.*); *refl. pron.* yourself (*s. fam.*); **¿te gusta... ?** do you (*fam. s.*) like ... ? (1)

té *m.* tea (7); **rosa té** tea rose

teatral theatrical; **obra teatral** play

teatro theater; <u>**ir**</u> **al teatro** to go to the theater (10); **obra de teatro** play (13)

techo roof

teclado keyboard

técnico/a technician (17)

tecnología technology (12)

tecnológico/a technological

teja tile

tejedor(a) weaver

tejer to weave (13)

tejido weaving; *pl.* woven goods (13); textiles

tela cloth

tele *f.* T.V.

telediario news program

telefonear to phone

telefonía telephone systems

telefónico/a *adj.* telephone

teléfono (celular) (cell) phone (2); **hablar por teléfono** to talk on the phone (2); **teléfono fijo** landline (12)

telegrama *m.* telegram

telenovela soap opera

telespectador(a) television viewer

televidente *m., f.* television viewer

tele(visión) (*f.*) television (3); **mirar la tele(visión)** to watch television (3)

televisor *m.* television set

tema *m.* theme, topic

temblar (tiemblo) to tremble

temblor *m.* trembling

temer to fear, be afraid (13)

temperatura temperature (11); **tomarle la temperatura** to take someone's temperature (11)

templo temple (16)

temporada season (*hunting, fashion, etc.*)

temporal temporary

temprano *adv.* early (2)

tendencia tendency

tender (tiendo): tender la cama to make the bed

tenedor *m.* fork

<u>**tener**</u> to have (4); **no tener razón** to be wrong (4); **tener... años** to be ... years old (3); **tener buena/mala suerte** to have good/bad luck (14); to be (un)lucky (14); **tener cuidado** to be careful; **tener dolor de** to have a pain/ache in (11); **tener éxito** to be successful; **tener fiebre** to have a fever; **tener ganas de** + *inf.* to feel like (*doing something*) (4); **tener la culpa** to be at fault; **tener miedo (de)** to be afraid (of) (4); **tener (mucha) hambre** to be (very) hungry (7); **tener (mucha) sed** to be (very) thirsty (7); **tener (mucho) calor** to be (very) warm, hot (6); **tener (mucho) frío** to be (very) cold (6); **tener prisa** to be in a hurry (4); **tener que** + *inf.* to have to (*do something*) (4); **tener razón** to be right (4); **tener sueño** to be sleepy (4)

tenis *m. inv.* tennis (10); *pl.* tennis shoes (4)

tensión *f.* tension; **tensión arterial** blood pressure

tentación *f.* temptation

tentempié *m.* snack

teñirse (me tiño) (i) el pelo to dye one's hair
teoría theory
terapeuta *m., f.* therapist
terapia therapy
tercer(o/a) third (13)
tereré *m. traditional Paraguayan drink*
terminación *f. gram.* ending
terminal *m.* station, terminal
terminar to finish
término term
termómetro thermometer
ternura tenderness
terraza terrace
terremoto earthquake
terreno piece of land
terrestre *adj.* earth
terrible terrible (13); **es terrible que** + *subjunctive* it's terrible that (13)
territorio territory
terrorismo terrorism (18)
terrorista *m., f.* terrorist (18); **ataque** (*m.*) **terrorista** (terrorist) attack (18)
tertulia get-together
tesis *f. inv.* thesis
testigo *m., f.* witness (18)
testimonio testimony
texteo text (message)
textil *adj.* textile
texto text; **libro de texto** textbook (2); **mandar un mensaje (de texto)** to (send a) text (2)
ti (*obj. of prep.*) you (*fam.*) (6)
tibetano/a Tibetan
tiempo weather (6); time (6); *gram.* tense; **a tiempo** on time (8); **conjunción** (*f.*) **de tiempo** conjunction of time (17); **empleo de tiempo completo/parcial** full-/part-time job/ position (17); **hace (muy) buen/mal tiempo** it's (very) good/bad weather (6); **jornada de tiempo parcial** part-time job; **¿qué tiempo hace?** what's the weather like? (6); **tiempo libre** free time (10)
tienda shop, store (4); **tienda de acampar** tent; **tienda (de campaña)** tent (8)
tierra land
Tierra Earth (15)
tigre *m.* tiger
tihuanaco/a Tiwanakan (*of or pertaining to the pre-Columbian Tiwanaku civilization of Bolivia*)
tilma poncho; shawl
timbre *m.* doorbell
tímido/a shy
tina bathtub
tinieblas *f. pl.* darkness
tinto/a: vino tinto red wine (7)
tío/a uncle/aunt (3); *m. pl.* aunts and uncles (3)

típico/a typical
tipo type, kind; **de todo tipo** of all kinds
tira cómica comic strip
tirar to throw
tiritar to shiver
títere *m.* puppet
título title
toalla towel (5)
toallero towel rack
tocar (qu) to touch; to play (*a musical instrument*) (2); to honk (15); **tocarle a uno** to be someone's turn (10)
todavía still (6); yet
todo *n.* everything; **de todo** everything (4); **de todo tipo** of all kinds
todo/a *adj.* all (3); every (3); **por todas partes** everywhere (14); **todo derecho/recto** straight ahead (15); **todos los días** every day (2)
todoterreno *inv.* all-terrain (15)
tolerante tolerant
tomar to take (2); to drink (2); **tomar el sol** to sunbathe (8); **tomar unas vacaciones** to take a vacation (8); **tomarle el pelo** to pull (someone's) leg; **tomarle la temperatura** to take someone's temperature (11)
tomate *m.* tomato (7)
tono tone
tonto/a silly, foolish (3)
toque *f.* touch
torno: en torno a around
toro bull (15)
torpe clumsy (14)
torre *f.* tower
torta sandwich (*Mex.*)
tortilla potato omelet (*Sp.*); *thin unleavened cornmeal or flour pancake* (*Mex.*)
tortuga turtle
tos *f.* cough (11)
tosco/a rustic; crude
toser to cough (11)
tostado/a toasted (7); **pan** (*m.*) **tostado** toast (7)
tostadora toaster (10)
tostones *m. pl. crispy fried plantain slices*
totalidad *f.* totality
trabajador(a) *adj.* hardworking (3)
trabajador(a) *n.* worker (17); **trabajador(a) social** social worker (17)
trabajar to work (2)
trabajo work (10); job (10); report, (piece of) work (14); **carga de trabajo** workload
trabajólico/a workaholic
trabalenguas *m. inv.* tongue twister
tractor *m.* tractor

tradición *f.* tradition (13); **tradición cultural** cultural tradition (13)
tradicional traditional
traducción *f.* translation
traducir (*like* **conducir**) to translate
traductor(a) translator (17)
traer to bring (5)
tráfico traffic (15)
tragedia tragedy
trágico/a tragic
traje *m.* suit (4); **traje de baño** swimsuit (4)
trámite *m.* step; procedure
tranquilo/a calm (9); **llevar una vida tranquila** to lead a calm life (11)
transatlántico *n.* ocean liner
transbordador (*m.*) **espacial** space shuttle
transformar to transform
transición *f.* transition
tránsito traffic (15)
transmitir to pass on; to transmit
transnacional international
transporte *m.* transportation (8); **medio de transporte** means of transportation (8); **transporte público** public transportation
tras *prep.* after
trasero/a back, rear
trasladarse to move
trastienda back room (*of a store*)
tratable treatable
tratado treaty
tratamiento treatment (11)
tratar de + *inf.* to try to (*do something*) (13); **tratar de** + *noun* to deal with + *noun*
través: a través de across; through; throughout
travieso/a mischievous
trayectoria trajectory; path
trébol *m.* clover
trece thirteen (1)
treinta thirty (1); **y treinta** thirty minutes past (*the hour*) (1)
tren *m.* train (8); **estación** (*f.*) **de trenes** train station (8); **ir en tren** to go/travel by train (8)
tres three (1)
trescientos/as three hundred (4)
triángulo triangle
tribu *f.* tribe
tributo tribute
trigo wheat
trilogía trilogy
trimestre *m.* trimester
triste sad (6)
tristeza sadness
triunfar to triumph
trofeo trophy
trompeta trumpet

tropical tropical; **bosque** (*m.*) **tropical lluvioso** tropical rain forest

trópico *n. s.* tropics

tropiezo mistake

trotadora treadmill

trozo piece

trucha trout

trueno thunder

tú *subj. pron.* you (*fam. s.*) (2); *obj.* (*of prep.*) you (*fam. s*); **¿de dónde eres (tú)?** where are you (*fam. s.*) from? (1); **¿y tú?** and you (*fam. s.*)? (1)

tu(s) your (*fam. s.*) (3)

tuit *m.* tweet (12)

tuitear to tweet (12)

tumba tomb

tuna cactus fruit

turismo tourism

turista *n. m., f.* tourist

turístico/a *adj.* tourist

turnarse to take turns

turno shift (*on a job*)

turrón *m. type of candy traditionally eaten at Christmas*

tutor(a) tutor

tuyo/a(s) *poss. adj.* your (*fam. s.*); *poss. pron.* yours, of yours (*fam. s.*) (17)

Twitter *m.* Twitter (12)

U

u or (*before words beginning with the sound* **o-**) (3)

ubicar (qu) to locate

ucraniano/a Ukranian

¡uf! *interj.* oof!; whew!

últimamente lately (14)

último/a last, final (14); latest (4); **es de última moda** it's trendy (hot) (4); **por última vez** for the last time (14)

ultramoderno/a ultramodern

un, uno/a one (1); *ind. art.* a, an; **un millón (de)** one million (4); **un poco (de)** a little bit (of) (2); **una vez a la semana** once a week (3)

unánime unanimous

único/a *adj.* only; unique

unidad *f.* unity

unido/a united; **Estados** (*m. pl.*) **Unidos de América** United States of America; **Naciones** (*f. pl.*) **Unidas** United Nations; **Organización** (*f.*) **de Naciones Unidas (ONU)** United Nations (U.N.)

unificar (qu) to unify

unión *f.* union

unir to join (together); to unite; **unirse a** to join (*a cause, organization*)

universidad *f.* university (2)

universitario/a *adj.* (of the) university (14)

universo universe

urbanístico/a *adj.* of or pertaining to urban development

urbano/a urban

urgencias: sala de urgencias emergency room

urgente urgent (12); **es urgente que** + *subjunctive* it's urgent that (12)

uruguayo/a *n., adj.* Uruguayan

usar to wear (4); to use (4)

USB: memoria USB pen drive (12)

uso use

usted (Ud., Vd.) *sub. pron.* you (*form. s.*) (2); *obj.* (*of prep.*) you (*form. s.*); **¿a usted le gusta... ?** do you (*form. s.*) like ... ? (1); **¿cómo es usted?** what are you (*form. s.*) like? (1); **¿cómo se llama usted?** what is your (*form. s.*) name? (1); **¿de dónde es usted?** where are you (*form. s.*) from? (1); **¿y usted?** and you (*form. s.*)? (1)

ustedes (Uds., Vds.) *sub. pron.* you (*form. pl.*); *obj.* (*of prep.*) you (*form pl.*)

usuario/a user (12)

útil useful

utilidad *f.* utility

utilizar (c) to use; to utilize

uva grape

¡uy! *interj.* oh!; ah!

V

vaca cow (15)

vacaciones *f. pl.* vacation (8); **de vacaciones** on vacation (8); **estar de vacaciones** to be on vacation (8); **ir de vacaciones a...** to go on vacation to/in ... (8); **pasar las vacaciones en...** to spend one's vacation in ... (8); **salir de vacaciones** to leave on vacation (8); **tomar unas vacaciones** to take a vacation (8)

vacuna vaccine (11); **poner(se) una vacuna (de)** to get a shot (against) (11)

vacunación *f.* vaccination

vacunarse to get a shot

vainilla vanilla

valenciano/a Valencian

Valentín: Día (*m.*) **de San Valentín** St. Valentine's Day

valiente courageous

valioso/a valuable

valle *m.* valley

vallenato *Colombian folk music*

valor *m.* value

valorar to value

valorización *f.* appreciation

vals *m. inv.* waltz

vampiro vampire

vanagloriarse to brag

vandalismo vandalism

vapor *m.* mist

vaquero/a cowboy/cowgirl

variación *f.* variation

variante variant

variar (varío) to vary

variedad *f.* variety

varios/as several

vasco/a *n., adj.* Basque

vasija earthenware pot; vessel

vaso (drinking) glass

vasto/a vast

vecindario neighborhood

vecino/a neighbor (12)

vegano/a *n., adj.* vegan

vegetariano/a *n., adj.* vegetarian

vehículo vehicle (15)

veinte twenty (1)

veinticinco twenty-five (1)

veinticuatro twenty-four (1)

veintidós twenty-two (1)

veintinueve twenty-nine (1)

veintiocho twenty-eight (1)

veintiséis twenty-six (1)

veintisiete twenty-seven (1)

veintitrés twenty-three (1)

veintiún, veintiuno/a twenty-one (1)

vejez *f.* old age (16)

vela candle (9)

velocidad *f.* speed (15); **límite** (*m.*) **de velocidad** speed limit (15)

vena vein

vendedor(a) salesperson (17)

vender to sell (3)

Venecia Venice

venerar to revere; to venerate

venezolano/a *n., adj.* Venezuelan

venir to come (4); **el año que viene** next year; **el lunes que viene** next Monday (5); **la semana que viene** next week (5)

venta sale

ventaja advantage

ventana window (2)

ventanilla small window (*on a plane*) (8)

ver to see (5); **a ver** let's see; **nos vemos** see you around (1)

verano summer (6)

veras: ¿de veras? really

verbo *gram.* verb (2); **verbo reflexivo** *gram.* reflexive verb (5)

verdad *f.* truth; **es verdad que** it's true that (13)

¿verdad? right, don't they (you...)? (4)

verdadero/a true; real

verde green (4)

verduras *f. pl.* vegetables (7)

vergonzoso/a shameful

vergüenza embarrassment

verificar (qu) to verify

versión *f.* version

verso verse; line of a poem

verter (vierto) (i) to spill; to shed (*a tear*)

vestido dress (4)

vestir (visto) (i) to dress; **vestirse** to get dressed (5)

veterano/a *n.* veteran

veterinario/a veterinarian (17)

vez *f.* (*pl.* **veces**) time (3); **a veces** sometimes, at times (3); **alguna vez** once; ever (15); **cada vez más** increasingly; **cada vez mayor** greater and greater; **dos veces** twice (11); **en vez de** instead of; **otra vez** again; **por primera/última vez** for the first/last time (14); **tal vez** perhaps; **una vez** once (3); **una vez a la semana** once a week (3)

viajar to travel (8)

viaje *m.* trip (5); **agencia de viajes** travel agency; **agente de viajes** travel agent; **de viaje** on a trip, traveling (8); **hacer un viaje** to take a trip (5)

viajero/a traveler

vial *adj.* road

vicepresidente/a vice president

víctima victim (18)

victoria victory

vicuña vicuna (llama)

vida life (11); **vida académica** academic life (14); **llevar una vida sana/tranquila** to lead a healthy/calm life (11); **ritmo lento / acelerado de la vida** slow / fast pace of life (15)

video video (12)

videocasetera video cassette recorder

videojuego videogame; **jugar (juego) (gu) a los videojuegos** to play videogames (10)

videollamada video call

videoturismo videotourism

vidrio glass

viejo/a old (3)

viento wind (6); **hace (mucho) viento** it's (very) windy (6)

viernes *m. inv.* Friday (5)

vietnamita *n., adj. m., f.* Vietnamese

vikingo/a Viking

vinagre *m.* vinegar

vino (blanco, tinto) (white, red) wine (7)

violación *f.* violation

violencia violence; **Día** (*m.*) **Internacional de la No Violencia**

Contra la Mujer International Day for the Elimination of Violence against Women

violento/a violent

violín *m.* violin

Virgen *f.* Virgin (Mary)

virreinato viceroyalty

virus *m. inv.* virus

visión *f.* vision

visita visit (11)

visitante *m., f.* visitor

visitar to visit (10)

víspera eve

vista view (12); **punto de vista** point of view

viudo/a widower/widow (16)

vivienda housing (12)

vivir to live (3)

vivo/a lively; bright (*of colors*)

vocabulario vocabulary

vocal *f.* vowel

voga: en voga in vogue

volante *m.* steering wheel; **furia al volante** road rage

volar (vuelo) to fly; **volar en avión** to fly (8); to go by plane (8)

volcán *m.* volcano

volcánico/a volcanic

voleibol *m.* volleyball (10)

voltear to turn (over)

volumen *m.* volume

voluntario/a volunteer

volver to return (*to a place*) (5); **volver a** + *inf.* to (*do something*) again (5)

vos *subj. pron.* you (*fam. s. C.A., S.A.*)

vosotros/as *sub. pron.* you (*fam. pl. Sp.*) (2); *obj.* (*of prep.*) you (*fam. pl. Sp.*)

votación *f.* vote; voting

votante *m., f.* voter

votar to vote (18)

votos (*m. pl.*) **nupciales** wedding vows

voz *f.* (*pl.* **voces**) voice (12); **buzón** *m.* **de voz** voice mailbox (12); **voz en off** voice over

vudú *m.* voodoo

vuelo flight (8); **asistente** (*m., f.*) **de vuelo** flight attendant (8)

vuelta: billete *m.* (*Sp.*) / **boleto** (*L.A.*) **de ida y vuelta** round-trip ticket (8)

vuelto/a (*p.p. of* **volver**) returned

vuestro/a(s) your (*fam. pl. Sp.*) (3); *poss. pron.* your, of yours (*fam. pl. Sp.*) (17)

W

web: página web webpage (12); **sitio web** website (12)

wifi *m.* wifi (12)

Y

y and (1); **y cuarto** a quarter (fifteen minutes) after (*the hour*) (1); **y media** half past (*the hour*) (1); **y quince** fifteen minutes after (*the hour*) (1); **y treinta** thirty minutes past (*the hour*) (1) **¿y tú?** and you (*fam. s.*)? (1); **¿y usted?** and you (*form. s.*)? (1)

ya already (9); **ya no** no longer; **ya que** since

yacimiento deposit (*mineral*)

yerba herb

yerno son-in-law

yo *sub. pron.* I (2); **yo soy de...** I am from ... (1)

yoga *m.* yoga; **hacer (el) yoga** to do yoga (10)

yogur *m.* yogurt (7)

yuca cassava, manioc; **¡qué yuca!** how difficult!

Z

zalamería flattery

zampoña *South American panpipe*

zanahoria carrot (7)

zancudo mosquito

zapatería shoe store

zapato shoe (4); *pl.* shoes (4)

zarzuela *traditional Spanish operetta*

zócalo central plaza (*Mex.*)

Zodíaco Zodiac

zona zone (12); area (12)

zoología zoology

zumba: hacer zumba to do Zumba (11)

zumo juice (*Sp.*)

VOCABULARIES

English-Spanish Vocabulary

A

@ **arroba** (12)

A.M. **de la mañana** (1)

able: to be able **poder** (4)

about **por** (6); **sobre** (4)

abroad: to go abroad **ir al extranjero** (8)

absence **falta** (15)

absent: to be absent (from) **faltar (a)** (9)

absentminded **distraído/a** (14)

absurd: it's absurd that **es absurdo que** + *subjunctive* (13)

academic **académico/a** (14); academic life **vida académica** (14)

accelerated **acelerado/a** (15); **ritmo acelerado de la vida** fast pace of life (15)

accept **aceptar** (14)

accessory **complemento** (4)

accident **accidente** *m.* (14)

according to **según** (3)

account **cuenta** (17)

accountant **contador(a)** (17)

ache *n.* (in) **dolor (de)** (11); *v.* **doler (duele)** (*like* gustar) (11); to have an ache in **tener dolor de** (11)

acquainted: to be acquainted with **conocer (conozco)** (7)

act *v.* **actuar (actúo)** (13)

activity: fun activity **diversión** *f.* (10)

actor **actor** *m.* (13); **actriz** *f.* (*pl.* **actrices**)

additional **adicional** (1)

address **dirección** *f.* (7)

adjective *gram.* **adjetivo** (3); adjective of nationality **adjetivo de nacionalidad** (3); possessive adjective **adjetivo posesivo** (3)

administration: business administration **administración** (*f.*) **de empresas** (2)

adolescence **adolescencia** (16)

adolescent: as an adolescent **de adolescente** (10)

advice (piece of) **consejo** (7)

advisor **consejero/a** (2)

aerobics: to do aerobics **hacer ejercicios aeróbicos** (11)

affection **cariño** (16)

affectionate **cariñoso/a** (6)

afraid: to be afraid (of) **tener miedo (de)** (4), **temer** (13)

after *prep.* **después de** (5); *conj.* **después (de) que** (17)

afternoon: good afternoon **buenas tardes** (1); **muy buenas** (1); in the afternoon **de la tarde** (1), **por la tarde** (2)

afterward **luego** (5); afterwards **después** (5)

agent **agente** *m., f.* (8)

ago **hace** + *time* + **que** + *preterite* (14); *preterite* + **hace** + *time* (14)

agree **estar de acuerdo** (3)

agriculture **agricultura** (15)

ahead: straight ahead **(todo) derecho** (15), **todo recto** (15)

air **aire** *m.* (15)

airplane **avión** *m.* (8)

airport **aeropuerto** (8)

aisle **pasillo** (8)

alarm clock **despertador** *m.* (14)

all **todo/a** (3)

all-terrain **todoterreno** *inv.* (15)

allow **permitir** (12)

almost **casi** *inv.* (3); almost never **casi nunca** (3)

alone **solo/a** (5)

alongside of **al lado de** (6)

already **ya** (9)

also **también** (1)

always **siempre** (3)

am: I am **soy** (1); I am from **soy de** (1)

America: of the United States of America *n., adj.* **estadounidense** (3)

among *prep.* **entre** (6)

analyst: systems analyst **analista** (*m., f.*) **de sistemas** (17)

and **y** (1); **e** (*before words beginning with the sound* i-) (3); and you? **¿y tú?** (*fam. s.*) (1), **¿y usted?** (*form. s.*) (1)

android **android** *m.* (12)

angry **enojado/a** (9); **furioso/a** (6); to get angry with (someone) about (something) **enojarse con (alguien) por (algo)** (9)

animal **animal** *m.* (15)

announce **anunciar** (8)

annoyed **molesto/a** (6)

another **otro/a** (3)

answer *n.* **respuesta** (6); *v.* to answer **contestar** (7)

antibiotic **antibiótico** (11)

anxiety **ansiedad** *f.* (14)

any **algún (alguna/os/as)** (7); not any **ningún (ninguna)** (7)

anybody: not anybody **nadie** (7)

anyone **alguien** (7)

anything **algo** (7); not anything **nada** (7)

apartment **apartamento** (2); apartment building **edificio de apartamentos** (12)

apologize **disculparse** (11); **pedir (i) disculpas** (14)

apology **disculpa** (14)

app **aplicación** *f.* (12)

appetizers **botanas** *f. pl.* (*Mex.*) (9); **tapas** *f. pl.* (9)

apple **manzana** (7)

appliance: home appliance **aparato doméstico** (10)

applicant **aspirante** *m., f.* (17)

application (*form*) **solicitud** *f.* (17)

apply for (*a job*) **solicitar** (17)

appointment **cita** (11)

April **abril** *m.* (6)

architect **arquitecto/a** (13)

architecture **arquitectura** (13)

are: you (*fam. s.*) are **eres** (1); you (*form. s.*) are **es** (1)

area **zona** (12); smoking area **sala de fumadores/de fumar** (8)

argue with (someone) about (something) **discutir con (alguien) por/sobre (algo)** (9)

arm **brazo** (11)

armchair **sillón** *m.* (5)

armoire **armario** (5)

army **ejército** (18)

arrival **llegada** (8)

arrive **llegar (gu)** (3)

art **arte** *m.* (2); arts and crafts **artesanía** (13); the arts **artes** *f. pl.* (13); work of art **obra de arte** (13)

artist **artista** *m., f.* (13)

artistic **artístico/a** (13); artistic expression **expresión** (*f.*) **artística** (13)

as: as ... as **tan... como** (6); as a child **de niño/a** (10); as a youth **de adolescente** (10); as long as *conj.* **con tal (de) que** (16); as much as **tanto como** (6); as much/many ... as **tanto/a(os/as)... como** (6); as soon as **en cuanto** (17), **tan pronto como** (17)

ask (a question) **hacer una pregunta** (5), **preguntar** (8); to ask for **pedir** (5)

asleep: to fall asleep **dormir(se) ([me] duermo) (u)** (5)

asparagus **espárragos** *m. pl.* (7)

assassinate **asesinar** (18)

assassination **asesinato** (18)

astronaut **astronauta** *m., f.* (17)

at **en** (1); at ... (*time of day*) **a la(s)...** (1); at all **(para) nada** (8); at home **en casa** (2); at least **por lo menos** (9); at the beginning of **al principio de** (17); at times **a veces** (3); at what time ... ? **¿a qué hora... ?** (1)

athlete **atleta** *m., f.* (10)

attack **ataque** *m.* (18); terrorist attack **ataque terrorista** (18)

attend (*class, function*) **asistir (a)** (3); to not attend **faltar (a)** (9)

attendant: flight attendant **asistente** (*m., f.*) **de vuelo** (8)

attract **atraer** (*like* <u>traer</u>) (*like* **gustar**) (13)

audience **espectadores** *m. pl.* (13); **público** (13)

August **agosto** (6)

aunt **tía** (3); aunts and uncles **tíos** *m. pl.* (3)

author **autor(a)** (13)

automatic teller machine (ATM) **cajero automático** (17)

auto(mobile) **auto(móvil)** *m.* (15)

autumn **otoño** (6)

avenue **avenida** (12)

avocado **aguacate** *m.* (7)

avoid **evitar** (15)

awful: an awful lot **muchísimo** (8)

B

babysitter **niñero/a** (10)

back tooth **muela** (11)

backpack **mochila** (2)

bad **mal, malo/a** (3); (very) bad (weather) out **(muy) mal tiempo** (6); the bad news/thing **lo malo** (11); to have a bad time **pasarlo mal** (9); to have bad luck **tener mala suerte** (14)

badly: to come/turn out badly **<u>salir</u> mal** (5)

baggage **equipaje** *m.* (8); to check baggage **facturar el equipaje** (8)

baked custard **flan** *m.* (7)

ball **pelota** (10)

ballet **ballet** *m.* (13)

banana **banana** (7)

bank **banco** (17)

bar: to go to a bar **ir a un bar** (10)

barbecue **barbacoa** (7)

bargain *n.* **ganga** (4)

baseball **béisbol** *m.* (10); baseball cap **gorra** (4)

basketball **basquetbol** *m.* (10)

bath: to take a bath **bañarse** (5)

bathe **bañarse** (5)

bathroom **baño** (5); bathroom sink **lavabo** (5)

bathtub **bañera** (5)

battery **batería** (15)

be **estar** (2); **ser** (1), (3); to be ... years old **tener... años** (3); to be a fan (of) **ser aficionado/a (a)** (10); to be able **poder** (4); to be absent (from) **faltar (a)** (9); to be afraid **temer** (13); to be afraid (of) **tener miedo (de)** (4); to be boring **ser aburrido/a** (10); to be born **na<u>c</u>er (na<u>zc</u>o)** (16); to be certain of **estar seguro/a de** (13); to be (very) cold **tener (mucho) frío** (6); to be comfortable (*temperature*) **estar bien** (6); to be distracted **ir distraído/a** (14); to be fond of each other **quererse** (11); to be fun **ser divertido/a** (10); to be happy (about) **alegrarse (de)** (12); to be (very) hungry **tener (mucha) hambre** (7); to be in a hurry **tener prisa** (4); to be left **quedar** (14); to be lucky **tener buena suerte** (14); to be married (to) **estar casado/a (con)** (16); to be on a diet **estar a dieta** (7); to be on vacation **estar de vacaciones** (8); to be right **tener razón** (4); to be single **estar soltero/a** (16); to be sleepy **tener sueño** (4); to be (very) stressed, under (a lot of) stress **estar (muy) estresado/a** (14); to be (very) thirsty **tener (mucha) sed** (7); to be under a lot of pressure **estar bajo muchas presiones** (14); to be uncertain of **no estar seguro/a de** (13); to be unlucky **tener mala suerte** (14); to be up to date **estar al día** (18); to be used for **s<u>e</u>rvir (s<u>i</u>rvo) (i) para** (5); to be (very) warm, hot **tener (mucho) calor** (6); to be wrong **no tener razón** (4)

beach **playa** (6)

beans **frijoles** *m. pl.* (7)

beautiful **bello/a** (15)

because **porque** (3); because of **por** (6)

become + *adj./adv.* **<u>pone</u>rse + *adj./ adv.*** (9)

bed **cama** (5); to get out of bed **levantarse** (5); to get up on the wrong side of the bed **levantarse con el pie izquierdo** (14); to go to bed **ac<u>o</u>starse (me ac<u>u</u>esto)** (5); to make the bed **<u>hacer</u> la cama** (10); to stay in bed **guardar cama** (11)

bedroom **habitación** *f.* (5)

beer **cerveza** (7)

before *prep.* **antes de** (5); *conj.* **antes (de) que** (16)

begin **emp<u>e</u>zar (emp<u>ie</u>zo) (<u>c</u>)** (5); to begin to (*do something*) **empezar a + *inf.*** (5)

beginning: at the beginning of **al principio de** (17)

behave **portarse bien** (9)

behind *prep.* **detrás de** (6)

believe (in) **<u>creer</u> (en)** (3); to not believe **no creer** (13)

below *prep.* **debajo de** (6)

belt **cinturón** *m.* (4)

besides **además** (2)

best **mejor** (6); better than **mejor(es) que** (6)

better **mejor** (6)

between *prep.* **entre** (6)

beyond **a partir de** (4)

bicycle **bicicleta** (10) to ride a bicycle **andar en bicicleta** (10)

bicycling **ciclismo** (10)

big **gran, grande** (3); big screen (monitor) **pantalla grande** (12)

bill (*restaurant*) **cuenta** (7); **factura** (17); (*money*) **billete** *m.* (17)

bird **pájaro** (3)

birthday **cumpleaños** *m. inv.* (6); birthday cake **pastel** (*m.*) **de cumpleaños** (9); to have a birthday **cumplir años** (9)

black **negro/a** (4)

blog **blog** *m.* (12)

blond(e) **rubio/a** (3)

blood **sangre** *f.* (11)

blouse **blusa** (4)

blue **azul** (4)

blue jeans **jeans** *m. pl.* (4)

blush *v.* **<u>pone</u>rse rojo/a** (9)

board **pizarrón** *m.* (2)

boarding: boarding gate **puerta de embarque** (8); boarding pass **tarjeta de embarque** (8)

boat **barco** (8); to go/travel by boat **ir en barco** (8)

body: human body **cuerpo humano** (11)

bomb **bomba** (18)

bon appetit! **¡buen provecho!** (7)

book **libro** (2)

bookshelf **estante** *m.* (5)

bookstore **librería** (2)

boots **botas** *f. pl.* (4)

bore **aburrir** (*like* **gustar**) (13)

bored **aburrido/a** (6); to get bored **aburrirse** (10)

boring **pesado/a** (10); to be boring **ser aburrido/a** (10)

born: to be born **na<u>c</u>er (na<u>zc</u>o)** (16)

bother **molestar** (*like* **gustar**) (11)

bottle **botella** (2)

boy **niño** (3); **chico** (4)

boyfriend **novio** (6)

brain **cerebro** (11)

brakes **frenos** *m. pl.* (15)

bread **pan** *m.* (7)

break **romper(se)** (14); to break up (with) **romper (con)** (16)

breakfast **desayuno** (7); to have (eat) breakfast **desayunar** (7)

breathe **respirar** (11)

bride **novia** (16)

bring **traer** (5)
brother **hermano** (3)
brown **(de) color café** (4)
brunet(te) **moreno/a** (3)
brush one's hair **peinarse** (5); to brush
one's teeth **cepillarse los dientes** (5)
budget **presupuesto** (17)
build **construir** (15)
building **edificio** (2); apartment building
edificio de apartamentos (12);
building manager **portero/a** (12)
bull **toro** (15)
bump against **chocar (qu) con/contra**
(14); **pegarse (gu) con/contra** (14)
bureau **cómoda** (5)
bus **autobús** m. (8); bus station
estación (f.) **de autobuses** (8);
bus stop **parada del autobús** (12);
to go/travel by bus **ir en autobús** (8)
business **empresa** (17); business
administration **administración** (f.) **de
empresas** (2)
businessman **hombre** (m.) **de
negocios** (17)
businesswoman **mujer** (f.) **de
negocios** (17)
busy **ocupado/a** (6)
but **pero** (1)
butter **mantequilla** (7)
buy **comprar** (2); **comprar por internet**
to buy online (4)
by **por** (14); by check **con cheque** (17)

C

cabin (on a ship) **cabina** (8)
cafeteria **cafetería** (2)
cake **pastel** m. (7); birthday cake **pastel
de cumpleaños** (9)
calculator **calculadora** (2)
calendar **calendario** (14); personal
calendar **agenda** (14)
call **llamar** (7); to be called **llamarse** (5)
calm **tranquilo/a** (9); to lead a calm life
llevar una vida tranquila (11)
camera **cámara** (12)
campground *camping* m. (8)
camping: to go camping **hacer
*camping*** (8)
can (be able) **poder** (4)
candidate (for a job) **aspirante** m., f. (17);
(political) **candidato/a** (18); to run
as a candidate **postularse como
candidato/a** (18)
candle **vela** (9)
candy **dulces** m. pl. (7)
cap (baseball) **gorra** (4)
capital city **capital** f. (6)
car **coche** m. (3); **carro** (15); convertible
car **coche/carro descapotable** (15)
card: (post)card **tarjeta (postal)** (8);
credit card **tarjeta de crédito** (7);

debit card **tarjeta bancaria** (17),
tarjeta de débito (17); identification
card **tarjeta de identificación** (14); to
play cards **jugar (juego) (gu) a las
cartas** (10)
cardinal point **punto cardinal** (6)
care: to take care of **cuidar de** (11); to
take care of oneself **cuidarse** (11)
carrot **zanahoria** (7)
carry **llevar** (4)
case: in case *prep.* **en caso de** (16); in
that case *adv.* **entonces** (8); *conj.* **en
caso de que** (16); just in case **por si
acaso** (14)
cash (a check) **cobrar** (17); n. **efectivo** (17);
in cash **en efectivo** (17)
cashier (check-out) **cajero/a** (17)
cat **gato** (3)
catch a cold **resfriarse (me resfrío)** (11)
cause **causa** (14)
CD **CD** m. (12)
CD-ROM **CD-ROM** m. (12)
celebrate **celebrar** (6)
celebratory **festivo/a** (9)
cell phone **teléfono celular** (2)
center (political) **centro** (18)
century **siglo** (10)
ceramics **cerámica** s. (13)
cereal **cereal** m. (7)
ceremony **ceremonia** (16)
certain **seguro/a** (6); it's certain that **es
cierto que** + *indicative* (13); **estar
seguro/a de** to be certain of (13)
chair **silla** (2)
champagne **champán** m. (9)
change **cambiar (de)** (12)
channel **canal** m. (12)
charge (someone for an item or
service) **cobrar** (17)
chat n. **chateo** (12)
check (bank) **cheque** m. (17);
(restaurant) **cuenta** (7); by check **con
cheque** (17); v. **revisar** (15); to check
baggage **facturar el equipaje** (8)
check-up **chequeo** (11)
cheese **queso** (7)
chef **cocinero/a** (17)
chemistry **química** (2)
chess: to play chess **jugar (juego) (gu)
al ajedrez** (10)
chicken **pollo** (7); roast chicken **pollo
asado** (7)
chickpeas **garbanzos** m. pl. (7)
child: as a child **de niño/a** (10); small
child **niño/a** (3)
childhood **infancia** (16); **niñez** f. (16)
children **hijos** m. pl. (3)
chop: (pork) chop **chuleta (de cerdo)** (7)
chore: household chore **tarea
doméstica** (10)
Christmas **Navidad** (9)
Christmas Eve **Nochebuena** (9)

church **iglesia** (16)
citizen **ciudadano/a** (18)
city **ciudad** f. (3)
civic duty **responsabilidad** (f.) **cívica** (18)
class (of students) **clase** f. (2);
(academic) **clase** (2)
classic(al) **clásico/a** (13)
classmate **compañero/a (de clase)** (2)
classroom **salón** (m.) **de clase** (2)
clean adj. **limpio/a** (6); to clean (house)
limpiar (la casa) (10)
clear the table **quitar la mesa** (10)
clerk **dependiente/a** (2)
clever **listo/a** (3)
click v. **hacer clic** (m.) (12)
client **cliente/a** (2)
climate adj. **climático/a** (18)
climate **clima** n. m. (6); climate crisis
crisis (f.) **climática** (18)
clock: alarm clock **despertador** m. (14)
close **cerrar (cierro)** (5)
close to prep. **cerca de** (6)
closed **cerrado/a** (6)
closet (free-standing) **armario** (5)
clothes dryer **secadora** (10)
clothing **ropa** (4)
cloud **nube** f. (12)
cloudy: it's (very) cloudy **está (muy)
nublado** (6)
club: to go to a club **ir a un club** (10)
clumsy **torpe** (14)
coach **entrenador(a)** (10)
coat **abrigo** (4)
coffee **café** m. (2)
coffeemaker **cafetera** (10)
cognate **cognado** (2)
coin **moneda** (17)
cold (illness) **resfriado** n. (11); it's (very)
cold (weather) **hace (mucho) frío** (6);
to be (very) cold **tener (mucho)
frío** (6); to catch/get a cold **resfriarse
(me resfrío)** (11); very cold
congelado/a (6)
collision **choque** m. (18)
color **color** m. (4)
Columbus Day **Día** (m.) **de los Pueblos
Indígenas** (9)
comb one's hair **peinarse** (5)
come **venir** (4); to come out badly **salir
mal** (5); to come out well **salir bien** (5)
comedy **comedia** (13)
comfortable **cómodo/a** (4); to be
comfortable (temperature) **estar
bien** (6)
coming (time) **que viene** (5)
command **mandato** (7)
communicate (with) **comunicarse (qu)
(con)** (18)
communication (subject) **comunicaciones** f. pl. (2); medium of communication **medio de comunicación** (18)
comparison **comparación** f. (6)

complain (about) **quejarse (de)** (8)

compose **componer** (*like* <u>poner</u>) (13)

composer **compositor(a)** (13)

computer **computadora** (2); computer file **archivo** (12); computer folder **carpeta** (12); computer science **computación** *f.* (2); laptop (computer) **computadora portátil** (2)

concept **concepto** (18)

concert **concierto** (10); to go to a concert **ir a un concierto** (10)

conductor **director(a)** (13)

congested (*with a cold*) *adj.* **resfriado/a** (11)

congratulations! **¡felicitaciones!** (9)

congressional representative **representante** (*m., f.*) **al congreso** (18)

conjunction *gram.* **conjunción** *f.* (16); conjunction of time **conjunción de tiempo** (17)

connect **conectarse** (12)

conserve **conservar** (15)

contact lenses **lentes** (*m. pl.*) **de contacto** (11)

contaminated **contaminado/a** (15)

content *adj.* **contento/a** (6)

continue **continuar (continúo)** (6); **seguir (sigo) (i)** (6)

control: remote control **control** (*m.*) **remoto** (12)

convertible car **coche/carro descapotable** (12)

cook *v.* **cocinar** (7); *n.* **cocinero/a** (17)

cookie **galleta** (7)

cool: it's (very) cool (weather) **hace (mucho) fresco** (6)

copy *n.*: copy machine **fotocopiadora** (12); *v.* **copiar** (12); <u>hacer</u> **(foto)copia** (12)

corner (*street*) **esquina** (15)

corporation **empresa** (17)

correct *v.* **corr<u>eg</u>ir (corri<u>j</u>o) (i)** (14)

cost: how much does it (do they) cost? **¿cuánto cuesta(n)?** (4)

cotton *n.* **algodón** *m.* (4); **de algodón** *adj.* (4)

couch **sofá** *m.* (5)

cough *n.* **tos** *f.* (11); cough syrup **jarabe** *m.* (11); *v.* **toser** (11)

counter **mostrador** *m.* (8)

country **país** *m.* (3)

countryside **campo** (15)

couple **pareja**; (3); married couple **matrimonio** (16)

course (*academic*) **clase** *f.* (2); (*of a meal*) **plato** (7); course syllabus **programa** (*m.*) **del curso** (14); main course **plato principal** (7); of course! **¡por supuesto!** (14)

courteous expression **expresión** (*f.*) **de cortesía** (1)

courtesy **cortesía** (1)

cousin **primo/a** (3); *m. pl.* **primos** (3)

cover **cubrir** (*p.p.* **cubierto**) (15)

COVID-19 *m., f.* **COVID-19** (11)

cow **vaca** (15)

craft: arts and crafts **artesanía** (13)

crash *n.* **choque** *m.* (18); *v.* (*computer*) **fallar** (12)

crazy **loco/a** (6)

create **crear** (13)

credit card **tarjeta de crédito** (7)

crime **delito** (15)

crisis: climate crisis **crisis** (*f.*) **climática** (18)

cruise (ship) **crucero** (8)

cry **llorar** (9)

cucumber **pepino** (7)

cuisine **cocina** (7)

cultural **cultural** (13); cultural tradition **tradición** (*f.*) **cultural** (13)

cup **taza** (14)

current *adj.* **actual** (12)

currently **en la actualidad** (10)

custard: baked custard **flan** *m.* (7)

customs (*at a border*) **aduana** (8); to go/pass through customs **pasar por la aduana** (8)

D

dad **papá** *m.* (3)

daily **diario/a** (5)

dance *n.* **baile** *m.* (13); **danza** (13); *v.* **bailar** (2)

dancer **bailarín, bailarina** (13)

date **cita** (11); (*calendar*) **fecha** (6); to be up to date **estar al día** (18); what's today's date? **¿cuál es la fecha de hoy?** (6), **¿qué fecha es hoy?** (6)

daughter **hija** (3)

day **día** *m.* (2); day after tomorrow **pasado mañana** (5); days of the week **días** (*m. pl.*) **de la semana** (5); every day **todos los días** (2); the day before yesterday **anteayer** (5); what day is today? **¿qué día es hoy?** (5)

Day of the Magi (Three Kings) **Día** (*m.*) **de los Reyes Magos** (9)

deadline **plazo** (14)

dear **querido/a** (6)

death **muerte** *f.* (16)

debit card **tarjeta bancaria, tarjeta de débito** (17)

December **diciembre** *m.* (6)

delay **demora** (8)

demonstration **manifestación** *f.* (18)

demonstrative *gram.* **demostrativo/a** (4)

density **densidad** *f.* (15)

dentist **dentista** *m., f.* (11)

deny **n<u>eg</u>ar (ni<u>eg</u>o) (<u>gu</u>)** (13)

department store **almacén** *m.* (4)

departure **salida** (8)

deposit **depositar** (17)

design **diseñar** (13)

designer: graphic designer **diseñador(a) gráfico/a** (17)

desk **escritorio** (2)

dessert **postre** *m.* (7)

destination **destino** (8)

destroy **destruir** (*like* <u>construir</u>) (15)

detail **detalle** *m.* (9)

develop **desarrollar** (15)

development **desarrollo** (15)

dictator **dictador(a)** (18)

dictatorship **dictadura** (18)

dictionary **diccionario** (2)

die **m<u>o</u>rir(se) ([me] m<u>ue</u>ro) (<u>u</u>)** (9)

diet: to be on a diet **estar a dieta** (7)

difficult **difícil** (6)

dining room **comedor** *m.* (5)

dinner **cena** (7); to have (eat) dinner **cenar** (7)

direct **diri<u>g</u>ir (diri<u>j</u>o)** (13)

director **director(a)** (13)

dirty **sucio/a** (6)

disagree **no <u>estar</u> de acuerdo** (3)

disaster **desastre** *m.* (14)

disc: compact disc (CD) **disco compacto (CD** *m.*) (12)

disco: to go to a disco **ir a una discoteca** (10)

discover **descubrir** (*p.p.* **descubierto**) (15)

discrimination **discriminación** *f.* (18)

dish (*food prepared in a particular way*) **plato** (7)

dishwasher **lavaplatos** *m. inv.* (10)

distracted **distraído/a** (14); to be distracted **ir distraído/a** (14)

divorce *n.* **divorcio** (16); *v.* **divorciarse (de)** (16)

divorced (from) **divorciado/a (de)** (16)

dizzy **mareado/a** (11)

do <u>hacer</u> (5); do you like … ? **¿a usted le gusta… ?** (*form. s.*) (1); to do aerobics **<u>hacer</u> ejercicios** (*m. pl.*) **aeróbicos** (11); to (*do something*) again **volver a** + *inf.* (5); to do Pilates **<u>hacer</u> pilates** (11); to do poorly **salir mal** (5); to do well **salir bien** (5); to do yoga **<u>hacer</u> (el) yoga** (10); to do Zumba **<u>hacer</u> zumba** (11)

doctor (*medical*) **médico/a** (3)

document **documento** (12)

dog **perro** (3)

dollar **dólar** *m.* (4)

domestic, related to the home **doméstico/a** (10)

domesticated **doméstico/a** (15)

don't they (you …)? **¿no?** (4), **¿verdad?** (4)

door **puerta** (2)

doorman **portero/a** (12)

dormitory **residencia** (2)

dot: on the dot (*time*) **en punto** (1)

doubt **dudar** (12)

download **bajar** (12); **descar<u>g</u>ar (<u>gu</u>)** (12)

downtown **centro** (4)

drama **drama** *m.* (13)

draw **dibujar** (13); (*attract*) **atraer** (*like* <u>traer</u>) (*like* **gustar**) (13)

drawer (*person*) **dibujante** *m., f.* (13)

drawing **dibujo** (13)

dress **vestido** (4)

dressed: to get dressed **v<u>e</u>stirse (me v<u>i</u>sto) (<u>i</u>)** (5)

dresser **cómoda** (5)

drink *n.* **bebida** (5); soft drink **refresco** (7); *v.* **beber** (3); **tomar** (2)

drive *n.:* hard drive **disco duro** (12); *v.* **manejar** (12); <u>conduc</u>ir (condu<u>zc</u>o) (15)

driver **conductor(a)** (15); driver's license **licencia de manejar** (15)

drop <u>caer</u> (14)

dryer: clothes dryer **secadora** (10)

during **durante** (5)

duty: civic duty **responsabilidad** (*f.*) **cívica** (18)

DVD **DVD** *m.* (12)

E

e-mail **e-mail** *m.* (12); **correo electrónico** (12)

e-ticket **billete** (*m.*) (*Sp.*) / **boleto** (*L.A.*) **electrónico** (8)

each **cada** *inv.* (5)

ear **oreja** (11); inner ear **oído** (11)

early *adv.* **temprano** (2)

earn (*income*) **ganar** (13)

earphones **auriculares** *m. pl.* (12)

earrings **aretes** *m. pl.* (4)

Earth **Tierra** (15)

east **este** *m.* (6)

Easter **Pascua** (9)

easy **fácil** (6)

eat **comer** (3); to eat breakfast **desayunar** (7); to eat dinner, supper **cenar** (7); to eat lunch **alm<u>o</u>rzar (<u>ue</u>) (<u>c</u>)** (5)

economics **economía** (2)

egg **huevo** (7)

eight **ocho** (1)

eight hundred **ochocientos/as** (4)

eighteen **dieciocho** (1)

eighth **octavo/a** (13)

eighty **ochenta** (3)

either: not either **tampoco** (7)

electrical **eléctrico/a** (15); electrical energy **energía eléctrica** (15)

electrician **electricista** *m., f.* (17)

electricity **electricidad** *f.* (12)

electronic equipment **equipo electrónico** (12)

elephant **elefante** *m.* (15)

elevator **ascensor** *m.* (12)

eleven **once** (1)

embarrassed **avergonzado/a** (9)

embrace **abra<u>z</u>arse (<u>c</u>)** (11)

emotion **emoción** *f.* (9)

emotional relationship **relación** (*f.*) **sentimental** (16)

end of the year **fin** (*m.*) **de año** (9)

end table **mesita** (5)

endangered species **especie** (*f.*) **en peligro de extinción** (15)

energy **energía** (15); electrical energy **energía eléctrica** (15); nuclear energy **energía nuclear** (15); renewable energy **energía renovable** (15); solar energy **energía solar** (15); wind energy **energía eólica** (15)

engagement period **noviazgo** (16)

engineer **ingeniero/a** (17)

English (*language*) **inglés** *n. m.* (2); *n., adj.* **inglés, inglesa** (3)

enjoy oneself **div<u>e</u>rtirse (me div<u>i</u>erto) (<u>i</u>)** (5)

enough **bastante** (16), **suficiente** (11); **lo suficiente** (11)

environment **medio ambiente** (15)

equality **igualdad** *f.* (18)

equipment **equipo** (12); electronic equipment **equipo electrónico** (12)

eruption **erupción** *f.* (18)

evening: good evening **buenas noches** (1); **muy buenas** (1); in the evening **de la noche** (1); **por la noche** (2)

event **acontecimiento** (18)

ever **alguna vez** (15)

every **cada** *inv.* (5); **todo/a** (3); every day **todos los días** (2)

everything **de todo** (4)

everywhere **por todas partes** (14)

exam **examen** *m.* (4)

example: for example **por ejemplo** (14)

excuse me **(con) permiso** (1), **perdón** (1)

exercise *n.* **ejercicio** (5); *v.* <u>hacer</u> **ejercicio** (5)

expect **esperar** (7)

expense **gasto** (12)

expensive **caro/a** (4)

explain **expli<u>c</u>ar (<u>qu</u>)** (8)

expression (*phrase*) **expresión** *f.* (1); artistic expression **expresión artística** (13)

extinction **extinción** *f.* (15)

eye **ojo** (11)

F

Facebook **Facebook** *m.* (12); to go into Facebook **entrar en Facebook** (12)

factory **fábrica** (15)

faithful **fiel** (3)

fall (*season*) *n.* **otoño** (6); *v.* <u>caer</u> (14); to fall asleep **d<u>o</u>rmir(se) ([me] d<u>u</u>ermo) (<u>u</u>)** (5); to fall down <u>caer</u>se (14); to fall in love (with) **enamorarse (de)** (16)

familiar: to be familiar with **cono<u>c</u>er (cono<u>zc</u>o)** (7)

family **familia** (3)

fan: to be a fan (of) <u>ser</u> **aficionado/a (a)** (10)

far from **lejos de** (6)

fare **pasaje** *m.* (8)

farm **finca** (15)

farmer **agricultor(a)** (15), **campesino/a** (15)

farming **agricultura** (15)

fascinate **fascinar** (*like* **gustar**) (13)

fast **acelerado/a** (15)

fat **gordo/a** (3)

father **padre** *m.* (3), **papá** *m.* (3)

fault: it was my fault **fue mi culpa** (14)

FAX **fax** *m.* (12)

fear *n.* **miedo** (4); *v.* **temer** (13)

February **febrero** (6)

feel **sentir (s<u>i</u>ento) (<u>i</u>)** (13); feel + *adj./adv.* **sentirse (me s<u>i</u>ento) (i)** + *adj./adv.* (9); to feel like (*doing something*) <u>tener</u> **ganas de** + *inf.* (4); to feel sorry **lamentar** (13)

female housekeeper **ama** (*f.*) (*but* **el ama**) **de casa** (17)

female soldier **mujer** (*f.*) **soldado** (17)

festive **festivo/a** (9)

fever **fiebre** *f.* (11)

few **poco/a** (4)

fiancé **novio** (16)

fiancée **novia** (16)

field **campo** (15); field laborer **campesino** (15)

fifteen **quince** (1); fifteen minutes until (*hour*) **menos cuarto/quince** (1); young woman's fifteenth birthday party **quinceañera** (9)

fifth **quinto/a** (13)

fifty **cincuenta** (3)

fight *n.* **lucha** (18); *v.* **luchar** (18), **pelear** (10)

file (*computer*) **archivo** (12)

fill (*a car*) **llenar** (15); to fill out (*a form*) **llenar** (17)

final **último/a** (4)

finally **por fin** (5), **finalmente** (5)

find **enc<u>o</u>ntrar (enc<u>ue</u>ntro)** (9); to find out (about) **enterarse (de)** (18)

fine **muy bien** (1); it's fine **está bien** (6)

finger **dedo (de la mano)** (11)

finish **acabar** (14)

fire *n.* **incendio** (18)

fire (*someone*) (*from a job*) **despedir** (*like* <u>pedir</u>) (17)

firefighter **bombero/a** (18)

first *adv.* **primero** (5); first *adj.* **primero/a** (5); first floor (second story) **primer piso** (12); for the first time **por primera vez** (14); the first of (*month*) **el primero de** (6)

fish (*cooked*) **pescado** (7); (*live*) **pez** *m.* (*pl.* **peces**) (15)

five **cinco** (1)

five hundred **quinientos/as** (4)

fix **arreglar** (15)

flat: **plano/a** (12); flat screen (*monitor*) **pantalla plana** (12); flat tire **llanta desinflada** (15)

flexible **flexible** (14)

flight **vuelo** (8); flight attendant **asistente** (*m., f.*) **de vuelo** (8)

flip-flops **chanclas** *f. pl.* (4)

floor (*of a building*) **piso** (12); first/ second floor (second/third story) **primer/segundo piso** (12); ground floor **planta baja** (12); to sweep the floor **barrer el piso** (10)

flower **flor** *f.* (8)

flu **gripe** *f.* (11)

fly *v.* **v<u>o</u>lar (v<u>ue</u>lo) en avión** (8)

folder (*computer*) **carpeta** (12)

following *adj.* **siguiente** (5)

fond: to be fond of each other **qu<u>e</u>rerse** (11)

food **comida** (7)

foodstuff **comestibles** *m. pl.* (7)

foolish **tonto/a** (3)

foot **pie** *m.* (11)

football **fútbol** (*m.*) **americano** (10)

for **para** (3); **por** (8); for example **por ejemplo** (14); for heaven's sake **por Dios** (14); for that reason **por eso** (3); for what purpose? **¿para qué... ?** (14)

forbid **proh<u>i</u>bir (proh<u>í</u>bo)** (12)

foreign **extranjero/a** (2); foreign language **lengua extranjera** (2)

foreigner **extranjero/a** (2)

forest **bosque** *m.* (15)

forget **olvidar** (9)

form **forma** (4); (*to fill out*) **formulario** (17)

forty **cuarenta** (3)

four **cuatro** (1)

four hundred **cuatrocientos/as** (4)

fourteen **catorce** (1)

fourth *adj.* **cuarto/a** (13)

free (*unoccupied*) **libre** (10); **tiempo libre** (10)

freeway **autopista** (15)

freezer **congelador** *m.* (10)

French (*language*) **francés** *m.* (2); French fried potato **papa frita** (7)

frequently **con frecuencia** (2); **frecuentemente** (11)

fresh **fresco/a** (7)

Friday **viernes** *m. inv.* (5)

fried **frito/a** (7); French fried potato **papa frita** (7)

friend **amigo/a** (2)

friendship **amistad** *f.* (16)

from **de** (1); from the **del** (3); I am from ... **(yo) soy de...** (1); where are you from?

¿de dónde eres (tú)? (*fam. s.*) (1); **¿de dónde es usted?** (*form. s.*) (1)

front: in front of **delante de** (6)

frozen **congelado/a** (6)

fruit **fruta** (7); fruit juice **jugo de fruta** (7)

full-time job **empleo de tiempo completo** (17)

fun: fun activity **diversión** *f.* (10); to be fun **ser divertido/a** (10)

function **funcionar** (12)

furious **furioso/a** (6)

furniture (*piece*) **mueble** *m.* (5)

G

game **partido** (10)

garage **garaje** *m.* (5)

garden **jardín** *m.* (5)

gas (*residential, not for cars*) **gas** *m.* (12)

gas station **estación** (*f.*) **de servicio** (15), **gasolinera** (15)

gasoline **gasolina** (15)

gate: boarding gate **puerta de embarque** (8)

generally **por lo general** (5)

German (*language*) **alemán** *m.* (2); *n., adj.* **alemán, alemana** (3)

get **obtener** (*like* **t<u>e</u>ner**) (12); get + *adj./ adv.* **p<u>o</u>nerse** + *adj./adv.* (9); how do you get to ... ? **¿cómo se llega a... ?** (15); to get **conseguir** (*like* **seguir**) (9); to get (*grades*) **sa<u>c</u>ar (<u>qu</u>)** (14); to get a cold **resfr<u>i</u>arse (me resfr<u>í</u>o)** (11); to get a shot **p<u>o</u>ner(se) una inyección** (11); to get a shot (against) **p<u>o</u>ner(se) una vacuna** (de) (11); to get along poorly (with) **llevarse mal (con)** (16); to get along well (with) **llevarse bien (con)** (16); to get angry (with) **eno-jarse (con)** (9); to get bored **aburrirse** (10); to get down (from) **bajarse (de)** (8); to get dressed **v<u>e</u>stirse (me v<u>i</u>sto) (<u>i</u>)** (5); to get off (of) (*a vehicle*) **ba-jarse (de)** (8); to get on (*a vehicle*) **subir (a)** (8); to get sick **enfermarse** (11); to get together (with) **re<u>u</u>nirse (me re<u>ú</u>no) (con)** (9); to get up (out of bed) **levantarse** (5); to get up on the wrong side of the bed **levantarse con el pie izquierdo** (14)

gift **regalo** (3)

girl **chica** (4); **niña** (3)

girlfriend **novia** (6)

give **dar** (8); to give (*as a gift*) **regalar** (8); to give (someone) a party **darle/ hacerle una fiesta (a alguien)** (9)

glad: to be glad about **alegrarse de** (12)

glasses **anteojos** *m. pl.* (11), **lentes** *m. pl.* (11)

go **ir** (4); let's go **vamos** (4); to be going to (*do something*) **ir a** + *inf.* (4); to go

abroad **ir al extranjero** (8); to go by boat/ship **ir en barco** (8); to go by bus **ir en autobús** (8); to go by plane **ir/v<u>o</u>lar (v<u>ue</u>lo) en avión** (8); to go by train **ir en tren** (8); to go camping **hacer** *camping* (8); to go for a hike **dar una caminata** (10); to go home **regresar a casa** (2); to go on the internet **entrar en internet** (12); to go on vacation to/in ... **ir de vacaciones a...** (8); to go onto Facebook **entrar en Facebook** (12); to go out (with) **salir (con)** (5); to go shopping **ir de compras** (4); to go through customs **pasar por la aduana** (8); to go through security (check) **pasar por el control de seguridad** (8); to go to (*a class, function*) **asistir (a)** (3); to go to a bar **ir a un bar** (10); to go to a club **ir a un club** (10); to go to a concert **ir a un concierto** (10); to go to a disco **ir a una discoteca** (10); to go to a museum **ir a un museo** (10); to go to bed **ac<u>o</u>starse (me ac<u>ue</u>sto)** (5); to go to the theater **ir al teatro** (10); to go up **subir (a)** (8)

gold *n.* **oro** (4); *adj.* **de oro** (4)

golf **golf** *m.* (10)

good **buen, bueno/a** (3); good afternoon **buenas tardes** (1); good afternoon/evening **muy buenas** (1); good morning **buenos días** (1); good night **buenas noches** (1); the good news/thing **lo bueno** (11); it's (very) good weather **hace (muy) buen tiempo** (6); to have a good time **pasarlo bien** (9), **div<u>e</u>rtirse (me div<u>ie</u>rto) (i)** (5); to have good luck **tener buena suerte** (14)

good-bye **adiós** (1); to say good-bye (to) **despedir(se)** (*like* **p<u>e</u>dir**) (de) (9)

good-looking (*people*) **guapo/a** (3)

goods: woven goods **tejidos** *m. pl.* (13)

gorilla **gorila** *m.* (15)

government **gobierno** (15)

grade (*academic*) **nota** (5); *v.* **corr<u>e</u>gir (corr<u>i</u>jo) (i)** (14)

graduate (from) **grad<u>u</u>arse (me grad<u>ú</u>o) (de)**

granddaughter **nieta** (3)

grandfather **abuelo** (3)

grandmother **abuela** (3)

grandparents **abuelos** *m. pl.* (3)

grandson **nieto** (3)

graphic designer **diseñador(a) gráfico/a** (17)

gray **gris** (4)

great **gran, grande** (3)

green **verde** (4)

green peas **arvejas** *f. pl.* (7)

greet each other **saludarse** (11)

greeting **saludo** (1)

grilled **asado/a** (7)
groceries **comestibles** *m. pl.* (7)
groom **novio** (16)
ground floor **planta baja** (12)
grow **crecer (crezco)** (16)
guess **adivinar** (9)
guest **invitado/a** (9)
guide **guía** *m., f.* (13)
guy **chico** (4)
gym **gimnasio** (12)

H

hair: to brush one's hair **peinarse** (5)
hairstylist **peluquero/a** (17)
half past (*the hour*) **y media** (1)
ham **jamón** *m.* (7)
hamburger **hamburguesa** (7)
hand **mano** *f.* (11); to shake hands **darse la mano** (11)
hand in **entregar (gu)** (8)
handbag **cartera** (4)
handsome (*people*) **guapo/a** (3)
Hanukkah *f.* **Janucá** (9)
happen **pasar** (6); **ocurrir** (14)
happening **acontecimiento** (18)
happy *adj.* **alegre** (6), **contento/a** (6); **feliz** (*pl.* **felices**) (9); *v.* to be happy (about) **alegrarse (de)** (12)
hard **difícil** (6)
hard drive **disco duro** (12)
hardworking **trabajador(a)** (3)
hat **sombrero** (4)
hate **odiar** (8)
have **tener** (4); (*auxilliary verb*) **haber** (12); to have a bad time **pasarlo mal** (9); to have a birthday **cumplir años** (9); to have a good time **divertirse (me divierto) (i)** (5), **pasarlo bien** (9); to have a pain/ache in **tener dolor de** (11); to have a party (for someone) **darle / hacerle una fiesta (a alguien)** (9); to have a picnic **hacer un pícnic** (10); to have a snack **merendar (meriendo)** (7); to have bad luck **tener mala suerte** (14); to have been (*doing something*) for (*time*) **hace** + *time* + **que** + *present* (14), *present* + **desde hace** + *time* (14); to have breakfast **desayunar** (7); to have dinner, supper **cenar** (7); to have good luck **tener buena suerte** (14); to have just (*done something*) **acabar de** + *inf.* (7); to have lunch **almorzar (almuerzo) (c)** (5); to have to (*do something*) **tener que** + *inf.* (4)
he *sub. pron.* **él** (2); he is **es** (1)
head **cabeza** (11)
headphones **auriculares** *m., pl.* (12)
health **salud** *f.* (11)
healthy **sano/a** (11); to lead a healthy life **llevar una vida sana** (11)

hear **oír** (5)
heart **corazón** *m.* (11)
heat **calefacción** *f.* (12)
heaven: for heaven's sake **por Dios** (14)
heavy: not heavy **ligero/a** (7)
hello **hola** (1)
help *n.* **ayuda** (7); *v.* **ayudar** (7); to help to (*do something*) **ayudar a** + *inf.* (7)
her *poss. adj.* **su(s)** (3); her, (of) hers *poss. adj., poss. pron.* **suyo/a(s)** (17)
here **aquí** (2)
hi **hola** (1)
highway **carretera** (15)
hike: to hike, go for a hike **dar una caminata** (10)
his *poss. adj.* **su(s)** (3); his, of his *poss. adj., poss. pron.* **suyo/a(s)** (17)
Hispanic **hispano/a** (3)
history **historia** (2)
hit **pegar (gu)** (14)
hobby **afición** *f.* (10)
hockey **hockey** *m.* (10)
holiday **día** (*m.*) **festivo** (9)
home *n.* **casa** (3); **hogar** *m.* (5); at home **en casa** (2); nursing home **residencia de ancianos** (12); to go home **regresar a casa** (2); *adj.* (*related to the home*) **doméstico/a** (10)
home appliance **aparato doméstico** (10)
homework **tarea** (3)
honeymoon **luna de miel** (16)
honk **tocar (qu)** (15)
hope *n.* **esperanza** (18); I hope (that) **ojalá (que)** (13); *v.* to hope **esperar** (12)
horn (*car*) **bocina** (15)
horse: to ride a horse **montar a caballo** (10)
host (*of an event*) **anfitrión, anfitriona** (9)
hot (*spicy*) **picante** (7); (*in temperature, not taste*) **caliente** (7); it's (very) hot (weather) **hace (mucho) calor** (6); it's hot (trendy) **está de moda** (4); **es de última moda** (4); to be (very) hot **tener (mucho) calor** (6)
hot dog **salchicha** (7)
house **casa** (3)
household chore **tarea doméstica** (10)
housekeeper: female housekeeper **ama** (*f.*) (*but* **el ama**) **de casa** (17); male housekeeper **amo de casa** (17)
housing **vivienda** (12)
how + *adj.*! **¡qué** + *adj.*!** (14); how strange that ... ! **¡qué extraño que... !** (13)
how? **¿cómo?** (1); how are you ? **¿cómo está(s)?** (1), **¿qué tal?** (1); how do you get to ... ? **¿cómo se llega a... ?** (15); how many? **¿cuántos/as?** (2); how

much? **¿cuánto?** (2); how much does it (do they) cost? **¿cuánto cuesta(n)?** (4); how often ... ? **¿con qué frecuencia... ?** (3)
human **humano/a** (11); human body **cuerpo humano** (11)
humanities **humanidades** *f. pl.* (2)
hungry: to be (very) hungry **tener (mucha) hambre** (7)
hurry: to be in a hurry **tener prisa** (4)
hurt **doler (duele)** (*like gustar*) (11); to hurt oneself **hacerse daño** (14); to hurt (*a body part*) **lastimarse** (14); to hurt one's (*body part*) **hacerse daño en** (14)
husband **esposo** (3), **marido** (3)
hybrid **híbrido/a** (15)

I

I *sub. pron.* **yo** (2); I am **soy** (1); I am from ... **(yo) soy de...** (1); I didn't mean (to do it) **fue sin querer** (14); I hope (that) **ojalá (que)** (13); I would (really) like ... **me gustaría (mucho)...** (8); **(no,) no me gusta...** (no,) I don't like ... (1); **(sí,) me gusta...** (yes,) I like ... (1); I'm sorry/pardon me **disculpa,** (*fam. s.*) (14); **disculpe,** (*form. s.*) (14); I'm (very) sorry **lo siento (mucho)** (14)
ice cream **helado** (7)
ID **tarjeta de identificación** (14)
identification card **tarjeta de identificación** (14)
if **si** (4)
illness **enfermedad** *f.* (11)
image **imagen** *f.* (13)
immediately **enseguida** (5)
important: it's important that **es importante que** + *subjunctive* (12)
impossible **imposible** (13); it's impossible that **es imposible que** + *subjunctive* (13); it's not impossible **no es imposible que** + *subjunctive* (13)
improbable **improbable** (13); it's improbable that **es improbable que** + *subjunctive* (13); it's not improbable **no es improbable que** + *subjunctive* (13)
in **en** (1); in case **en caso de (que)** (16); in that case *adv.* **entonces** (8); in cash **en efectivo** (17); in front of **delante de** (6); in love (with) **enamorado/a (de)** (16); in order that **para que** (16); in order to (*do something*) **para** + *inf.* (3); in the afternoon **de la tarde** (1); in the evening **de la noche** (1); in the morning **de la mañana** (1); in the morning/afternoon/evening **por la mañana/tarde/noche** (2)

incredible **increíble** (13); it's incredible that **es increíble que** + *subjunctive* (13)

indefinite and negative word *gram.* **palabra indefinida y negativa** (7)

inequality **desigualdad** *f.* (18)

inexpensive **barato/a** (4)

infancy **infancia** (16), **niñez** *f.* (16)

inflexible **inflexible** (14)

inform **informar** (18)

injection **inyección** *f.* (11)

inner ear **oído** (11)

insist (on) **insistir (en)** (12)

install **instalar** (12)

installments: in installments **a plazos** (17)

intelligent **inteligente** (3)

intend to (*do something*) **pensar (pienso)** + *inf.* (5)

intended for **para** (3)

interest *n.* **interés** *m.* (17); *v.* to interest (*someone*) **interesar** (*like* **gustar**) (18)

internet **internet** *m.* (12); **red** (*f.*) (12); to go on the internet **entrar en internet** (12); to look up on the internet **buscar (qu) en internet** (12); to surf the internet; **navegar (gu) la red** (12)

interrogative *gram.* **interrogativo/a** (2); interrogative word **palabra interrogativa** (2)

interstate **autopista** (15)

interview **entrevista** (17)

interviewee **entrevistado/a** (17)

interviewer **entrevistador(a)** (17)

invite **invitar** (7)

iPhone **iPhone** *m.* (12)

iron *v.* **planchar** (10)

island **isla** (6)

issue **cuestión** *f.* (17)

it is … (*time*) **es la…** (1), **son las…** (1)

it's: it's absurd that **es absurdo que** + *subjunctive* (13); it's certain that **es cierto que** + *indicative* (13); it's certain / a sure thing that **es seguro que** + *indicative* (13); it's (im)possible that **es (im)posible que** + *subjunctive* (13); it's (im)probable that **es (im)probable que** + *subjunctive* (13); it's normal that **es normal que** + *subjunctive* (13); it's not certain / a sure thing that **no es seguro que** + *subjunctive* (13); it's not (im)probable that **no es (im)probable que** + *subjunctive* (13); it's not possible that **no es posible que** + *subjunctive* (13); it's strange that **es extraño que** + *subjunctive* (13); it's terrible that **es terrible que** + *subjunctive* (13); it's true that **es verdad que** + *indicative* (13); **no es (im)probable que** + *subjunctive* it's not (im) probable that (13); **no es posible que** + *subjunctive* it's not possible that (13);

¡**qué extraño que… !** how strange that … ! (13); ¡**qué lástima que… !** what a shame that … ! (13)

Italian (*language*) **italiano** (2)

its *poss. adj.* **su(s)** (3); (of) its *poss. adj., poss. pron.* **suyo/a(s)** (17)

J

jacket **chaqueta** (4)

January **enero** (6)

jeans *jeans* *m. pl.* (4)

job **empleo** (17), **trabajo** (10); full-/part-time job **empleo de tiempo completo/parcial** (17), job application (*form*) **solicitud** *f.* (17); part-time job **empleo de tiempo parcial** (17); poorly paid job **empleo mal pagado** (17); well-paid job **empleo bien pagado** (17)

joke **chiste** *m.* (8)

journalist **periodista** *m., f.* (17)

juice **jugo** (7); fruit juice **jugo de fruta** (7)

July **julio** (6)

June **junio** (6)

just in case **por si acaso** (14)

K

keep **guardar** (12); **mantener** (*like* **tener**) (18); to keep on going **seguir (sigo) (i)** (15)

key **llave** *f.* (5)

kill **matar** (18)

kind **amable** (3)

king **rey** *m.* (18)

kiss: to kiss each other **besarse** (11)

kitchen **cocina** (5)

know (*a person*) **conocer (conozco)** (7); (*facts*) **saber** (7); to know how to (*do something*) **saber** + *inf.* (7)

L

laborer **obrero/a** (17); field laborer **campesino/a** (15)

lack **falta** (15)

lake **lago** (15)

lamp **lámpara** (5)

landlady **dueña** (12)

landline **teléfono fijo** (12)

landlord **dueño** (12)

language **lengua** (2); foreign language **lengua extranjera** (2)

laptop (computer) **computadora portátil** (2)

large **gran, grande** (3)

last *adj.* **pasado/a** (11); **último/a** (4); for the last time **por última vez** (14); last night *adv.* **anoche** (11); *v.* to last **durar** (18)

late *adj.* **atrasado/a** (8); *adv.* **tarde** (2)

lately **últimamente** (14)

later **después** (5); **luego** (5); see you later **hasta luego** (1)

latest (*new*) **ultimo/a** (4)

laugh **reírse (de)** (9)

law **ley** *f.* (18)

lawyer **abogado/a** (17)

layer: ozone layer **capa de ozono** (15)

lazy **perezoso/a** (3)

lead a calm/healthy life **llevar una vida tranquila/sana** (11)

learn **aprender** (3); to learn (about) **enterarse (de)** (18); to learn how to (*do something*) **aprender a** + *inf.* (3)

least: at least **por lo menos** (9)

leather *n.* **cuero** (4); *adj.* **de cuero** (4)

leave (*a place*) **salir (de)** (5); to leave for (*a place*) **salir para** (5); to leave on vacation **salir de vacaciones** (8)

left: to the left of **a la izquierda de** (6); to be left **quedar** (*like* **gustar**) (14)

leg **pierna** (11)

lend **prestar** (8)

lenses: contact lenses **lentes** (*m. pl.*) **de contacto** (11)

less than **menos que** (6); less … than **menos… que** (6); less than + *number* **menos de** + *number* (6)

let (*someone*) go **despedir** (*like* **pedir**) (17)

let's go **vamos** (4)

letter **carta** (3)

lettuce **lechuga** (7)

librarian **bibliotecario/a** (2)

library **biblioteca** (2)

license: driver's license **licencia de manejar** (15)

lie **mentira** (12)

life **vida** (11); academic life **vida académica** (14); slow / fast pace of life **ritmo lento / acelerado de la vida** (15)

lift weights **levantar pesas** (11)

light *n.* **luz** *f.* (*pl.* **luces**) (14); *adj.* light (*not heavy*) **ligero/a** (7)

like *n.* **gusto** (1); do you like … ? ¿**te gusta… ?** (*fam. s.*) (1); ¿**a usted le gusta… ?** (*form. s.*) (1); I would (really) like … **me gustaría (mucho)…** (8); (no,) I don't like … **(no,) no me gusta** (1); to like **gustar** (8); to like very much **encantar** (*like* **gustar**) (8); what are you like? ¿**cómo es usted?** (*form. s.*) (1); yes, I like … **sí, me gusta…** (1)

likeable (*people*) **simpático/a** (3)

likely: it's likely that **es probable que** + *subjunctive* (13)

likewise **igualmente** (1)

limit: speed limit **límite** (*m.*) **de velocidad** (15)

line (*of people*) **cola** (8); to stand in line **hacer cola** (8) listen to (*music, the radio*) **oír** (5); to listen (to) **escuchar** (2)

literature **literatura** (2)

little *adv.* (a) little **poco** (2); (adjective suffix) **-ito/a** (10); a little bit (of) **un poco (de)** (2); *adj.* **poco/a** (4)

live **vivir** (3)

living room **sala** (5)

loan **préstamo** (17)

lobster **langosta** (7)

long **largo/a** (3)

look at **mirar** (3); to look for **buscar (qu)** (2); to look up on the internet **buscar (qu) en internet** (12)

lose **perder (pierdo)** (5)

lot: a lot *adv.* **mucho** (2); a lot *adj.* (of) **mucho/a** (3); an awful lot **muchísimo** (8); to be under (a lot of) stress **estar (muy) estresado/a** (14)

love *n.* **amor** *m.* (16); *adj.* in love (with) **enamorado/a (de)** (16); *v.* **amar** (16); **querer** (16); **encantar** (*like* **gustar**) (8); to fall in love (with) **enamorarse (de)** (16); to love each other **quererse** (11)

luck: to have bad/good luck **tener mala/buena suerte** (14)

lucky: to be lucky **tener buena suerte** (14)

luggage **equipaje** *m.* (8)

lunch *n.* **almuerzo** (7); to have lunch **almorzar (almuerzo) (c)** (5)

lungs **pulmones** *m. pl.* (11)

-ly (*adverbial suffix*) **-mente** (14)

lyrics (*of a song*) **letra** (7)

M

ma'am **señora (Sra.)** (1)

machine: automatic teller machine (ATM) **cajero automático** (17)

made: it is made of ... **es de...** (4)

magazine **revista** (3)

mailbox: voice mailbox **buzón** (*m.*) **de voz** (12)

main course **plato principal** (7)

maintain **mantener** (*like* **tener**) (18)

make **hacer** (5); to make a mistake (about) **equivocarse (qu) (de)** (14); to make plans to (*do something*) **hacer planes** (*m.*) **para** + *inf.* (10); to make a stop **hacer escala/parada** (8); to make the bed **hacer la cama** (10)

makeup: to put on makeup **maquillarse** (5)

male housekeeper **amo de casa** (17)

mall: shopping mall **centro comercial** (4)

man **hombre** *m.* (2); business man **hombre de negocios** (17)

manager **gerente** *m., f.* (17); building manager **portero/a** (12)

manufacture **fabricar (qu)** (15)

many **muchos/as** (3); as many ... as **tanto/a(os/as) ... como** (6); how many? **¿cuántos/as?** (2)

map **mapa** *m.* (2)

march **manifestación** *f.* (18)

March **marzo** (6)

market(place) **mercado** (4)

marriage **matrimonio** (16)

married: to be married (to) **estar casado/a (con)** (16); **estar recién casado/a** recently married (16)

marry **casarse (con)** (16)

mass media **medios** *m. pl.* (18)

masterpiece **obra maestra** (13)

match (*game*) **partido** (10)

material **material** *m.* (4)

math **matemáticas** *f. pl.* (2)

matter **cuestión** *f.* (17)

May **mayo** (6)

me *obj. of prep.* **mí** (6); with me **conmigo** (6)

meal **comida** (7)

mean: I didn't mean (to do) it **fue sin querer** (14); that means ... **eso quiere decir...** (11)

means of transportation **medio de transporte** (8)

meat **carne** *f.* (7)

mechanic **mecánico/a** (15)

medical **médico/a** (11); medical office **consultorio** (11); medical personnel **personal** (*m.*) **médico** (11)

medicine **medicina** (11)

medium of communication **medio de comunicación** (18)

meet (*a person*) **conocer (conozco)** (7); **conocerse (conozco)** (16); nice to meet you **mucho gusto** (1); to meet (*someone somewhere*) **encontrarse (me encuentro) (con)** (11)

memory **memoria** (12)

menu **menú** *m.* (7)

messy **desordenado/a** (6)

Mexican **mexicano/a** (3)

microwave oven **horno de microondas** (10)

middle age **madurez** *f.* (16)

midnight **medianoche** *f.* (6)

military *adj.* **militar** (18); military service **servicio militar** (18)

milk **leche** *f.* (7)

million: one million **un millón (de)** (4)

mine, (of) mine *poss. adj., poss. pron.* **mío/a(s)** (17)

mineral water **agua** (*f.,* but **el agua**) **mineral** (7)

minivan **camioneta** (8)

minute: fifteen minutes until (*hour*) **menos quince** (1); thirty minutes past (*the hour*) **y treinta** (1)

misbehave **portarse mal** (9)

miss (*an event*) **perder (pierdo)** (5)

Miss **señorita (Srta.)** (1)

mistake: to make a mistake (about) **equivocarse (qu) (de)** (14)

modem **módem** *m.* (12)

modern **moderno/a** (13)

molar **muela** (11)

mom **mamá** (3)

Monday **lunes** *m. inv.* (5); next Monday **el lunes que viene** (5); on Monday **el lunes** (5); on Mondays **los lunes** (5)

money **dinero** (2)

monitor **pantalla** (12); big screen monitor **pantalla grande** (12); flat screen monitor **pantalla plana** (12)

month **mes** *m.* (6)

moped **moto(cicleta)** *f.* (15)

more **más** (2); more than **más que** (6); more ... than **más... que** (6); more than + *number* **más de** + *number* (6)

morning: good morning **buenos días** (1); in the morning **por la mañana** (2); **de la mañana** (1)

mosque **mezquita** (16)

mother **madre** *f.* (3); **mamá** (3)

motorcycle **moto(cicleta)** *f.* (15)

mountain **montaña** (8)

mouse **ratón** *m.* (12)

mouth **boca** (11)

move (*residence*) **mudarse** (12)

movie **película** (5); movie theater **cine** *m.* (5); movies **cine** *m. s.* (5)

Mr. **señor (Sr.)** *m.* (1)

Mrs. **señora (Sra.)** (1)

Ms. **señorita (Srta.)** (1)

much **mucho** (2); as much ... as **tanto/a(os/as)... como** (6); as much as **tanto como** (6); how much? **¿cuánto?** (2); how much does it (do they) cost? **¿cuánto cuesta(n)?** (4)

mural **mural** *m.* (13)

museum **museo** (13); to go to a museum **ir a un museo** (10)

mushrooms **champiñones** *m. pl.* (7)

music **música** (13)

musical **musical** *n. m.* (13)

musician **músico/a** (13)

must (*do something*) **deber** + *inf.* (3)

my *poss. adj.* **mi(s)** (3); *poss. adj., poss. pron.* **mío/a(s)** (17)

N

name **nombre** *m.* (7); my name is ... **me llamo...** (1); what is your name? **¿cómo se llama usted?** (*form. s.*) (1), **¿cómo te llamas?** (*fam. s.*) (1)

nap: to take a nap **dormir (duermo) (u) la siesta** (5)

narrate **contar (cuento)** (8)

nationality **nacionalidad** *f.* (3); adjective of nationality **adjetivo de nacionalidad** (3) natural **natural** (15); natural resource **recurso natural** (15); natural sciences **ciencias** (*f. pl.*) **naturales** (2)

nature **naturaleza** (15)

nauseated **mareado/a** (11)

navigate **navegar** (**gu**) (12)

neat **ordenado/a** (6)

necessary **necesario/a** (3); it is necessary to (*do something*) **hay que** + *inf.* (13)

neck **cuello** (11)

need *v.* **necesitar** (2)

negative: indefinite and negative word *gram.* **palabra indefinida y negativa** (7)

neighbor **vecino/a** (12)

neighborhood **barrio** (12)

neither **tampoco** (7)

nephew **sobrino** (3)

nervous **nervioso/a** (6)

network: social network **red** (*f.*) **social** (12)

never **jamás** (7), **nunca** (3); almost never **casi nunca** (3)

nevertheless **sin embargo** (6)

new **nuevo/a** (3)

New Year's Eve **Nochevieja** (9)

newlywed **recién casado/a** (16)

news **noticias** *f. pl.* (5); news media **prensa** (18); the bad news **lo malo** (11); the good news **lo bueno** (11)

newscast **noticiero** (18)

newspaper **periódico** (3)

next *adv.* **luego** (5); **después** (5); *adj.* **próximo/a** (5); next (Tuesday …) **el próximo (martes…)** (5); next Monday **el lunes** (*m.*) **que viene** (5); next week **la próxima semana** (5), **la semana que viene** (5)

nice (*people*) **amable** (3), **simpático/a** (3); nice to meet you **mucho gusto** (1); it's (very) nice out **hace (muy) buen tiempo** (6)

niece **sobrina** (3)

night: at night **de la noche** (1), **por la noche** (2); last night *adv.* **anoche** (11)

nine **nueve** (1)

nine hundred **novecientos/as** (4)

nineteen **diecinueve** (1)

ninety **noventa** (3)

ninth **noveno/a** (13)

no **no** (1); **ningún (ninguna)** (7); no, I don't like … **(no,) no me gusta** (1); no problem **no hay problema** (14)

no one **nadie** (7)

nobody **nadie** (7)

noise **ruido** (5)

noon **mediodía** *m.* (6)

normal **normal** (13); it's normal that **es normal que** + *subjunctive* (13)

north **norte** *m.* (6)

nose **nariz** *f.* (*pl.* **narices**) (11)

not any **ningún (ninguna)** (7)

not married **soltero/a** (16)

notebook **cuaderno** (2)

notes (*academic*) **apuntes** *m. pl.* (14)

nothing **nada** (7)

noun *gram.* **sustantivo** (2)

novel **novela** (13)

novelist **novelista** *m., f.* (13)

November **noviembre** *m.* (6)

now **ahora** (2); right now **ahora mismo** (6)

nuclear energy **energía nuclear** (15)

number **número** (1); ordinal number *gram.* **número ordinal** (13)

nurse **enfermero/a** (11)

nursing home **residencia de ancianos** (12)

O

o'clock: it's … o'clock **es la… , son las…** (1)

obey **obedecer (obedezco)** (15)

object **objeto** (2)

obligation **deber** *m.* (18)

obtain **obtener** (*like* **tener**) (12); **conseguir** (*like* **seguir**) (9)

occupation **ocupación** (17)

ocean **océano** (8)

October **octubre** *m.* (6)

of **de** (1); of course! **¡por supuesto!** (14); of the **del** (3)

off: to turn off **apagar** (**gu**) (12)

offer **ofrecer (ofrezco)** (8)

office **oficina** (2); (*in a home*) **estudio** (5); (*medical*) **consultorio** (11); (*political*) **cargo** (18)

often: how often … ? **¿con qué frecuencia… ?** (3)

oil (*cooking*) **aceite** *m.* (7); (*fuel*) **petróleo** (15)

OK: it's OK **está bien** (6)

old **viejo/a** (3); old age **vejez** *f.* (16)

older (than) **mayor(es) (que)** (6)

olive oil **aceite** (*m.*) **de oliva** (7)

on **en** (1); on a trip **de viaje** (8); on Monday **el lunes** (5); on the dot (*time*) **en punto** (1); on time **a tiempo** (8); on top of **encima de** (6); on Tuesdays **los martes** (5); on vacation **de vacaciones** (8)

once a week **una vez a la semana** (3)

one **uno** (1); it's one o'clock **es la una** (1)

one hundred **cien** (3); (*used with 101–199*) **ciento** (4)

one hundred ninety-nine **ciento noventa y nueve** (4)

one hundred one **ciento uno/a** (4)

one hundred two **ciento dos** (4)

one million **un millón (de** + *noun*) (4)

one thousand **mil** (4)

one-way ticket **billete** *m.* (*Sp.*) / **boleto** (*L.A.*) **de ida** (8)

onion **cebolla** (7)

online: to buy online **comprar en internet** (4)

only *adv.* **solo** (2); **solamente** (14)

open *v.* **abrir** (*p.p.* **abierto**) (3); *adj.* **abierto/a** (6)

opera **ópera** (13)

operate (*a machine*) **manejar** (12)

opinion: to have an opinion about/that **pensar** (**pienso**) **de/that** (5)

or **o** (1); **u** (*before words beginning with the sound* **o-**) (3)

oral **oral** (14); oral report **informe** (*m.*) **oral** (14)

orange *n.* **naranja** (7); *adj.* **anaranjado/a** (4)

orchestra **orquesta** (13)

order **mandar** (12); (*in a restaurant*) **pedir** (**pido**) (**i**) (5); in order to (*do something*) **para** + *inf.* (3); in order that **para que** (16)

ordinal number *gram.* **número ordinal** (13)

other **otro/a** (3); others **los/las demás** (12); significant other **pareja** (3)

ought to (*do something*) **deber** + *inf.* (3)

our *poss. adj.* **nuestro/a(s)** (3); our, of ours *poss. adj., poss. pron.* **nuestro/a(s)** (17)

outdoors *adv.* **afuera** (6); **al aire libre** (10)

outer ear **oreja** (11)

outskirts **afueras** *f. pl.* (12)

oven: microwave oven **horno de microondas** (10)

overcast: it's (very) overcast **está (muy) nublado** (6)

own, one's own **propio/a** (4)

owner **dueño/a** (7)

ozone layer **capa de ozono** (15)

P

p.m. **de la noche** (1); **de la tarde** (1)

pace: slow / fast of life **lento / acelerado ritmo de la vida** (15)

pack one's suitcase(s) **hacer la(s) maleta(s)** (8)

page: webpage **página web** (12)

paid: well/poorly paid job/position **empleo bien/mal pagado** (17)

pain (in) **dolor** *m.* (**de**) (11); to have a pain in **tener dolor de** (11)

paint **pintar** (13)

painter **pintor(a)** (13)

painting (*in general; specific piece*) **pintura** (13); (*specific piece*) **cuadro** (13) pants **pantalones** *m. pl.* (4)

paper **papel** *m.* (2)

pardon me **con permiso** (1); **disculpa**, (*fam. s.*) (14); **disculpe**, (*form. s.*) (14)

parents **padres** *m. pl.* (3)

park (*a vehicle*) **estacionar** (14)

parking lot/place **estacionamiento** (15)

part **parte** *f.* (5)

part-time job/position **empleo de tiempo parcial** (17)

partner **pareja** (3)

party **fiesta** (2); political party **partido** (18); to give (someone) a party <u>dar</u>le/<u>hacer</u>le una fiesta (a alguien) (9); to have a party (for someone) <u>dar</u>le/<u>hacer</u>le una fiesta (a alguien) (9)

pass *n.*: boarding pass **tarjeta de embarque** (8)

pass *v.*: pass through customs **pasar por la aduana** (8); to pass through security (check) **pasar por el control de seguridad** (8)

passenger **pasajero/a** (8)

passport **pasaporte** *m.* (8)

password **contraseña** (12)

past **pasado/a** (11)

pastime **pasatiempo** (10)

patient **paciente** *n. m., f.* (11)

patio **patio** (5)

pay *n.* (*often per hour*) **salario** (17); *v.* to pay (for) <u>pag</u>ar (<u>gu</u>) (2)

pea: green peas **arvejas** *f. pl.* (7)

peace **paz** *f.* (*pl.* **paces**) (18)

pen **bolígrafo** (2); pen drive **memoria USB** (12)

pencil **lápiz** *m.* (*pl.* **lápices**) (2)

people **gente** *f. s.* (8)

pepper (*condiment*) **pimienta** (7)

permit **permitir** (12)

person **persona** (2)

personal: personal calendar **agenda** (14); personal pronoun *gram.* **pronombre** (*m.*) **personal** (2)

personnel: medical personnel **personal** (*m.*) **médico** (11)

pet **mascota** (3)

petroleum **petróleo** (15)

pharmacist **farmacéutico/a** (11)

pharmacy **farmacia** (12)

phase **etapa** (16)

philosophy **filosofía** (2)

phone **teléfono** (2); cell phone **teléfono celular** (2); to talk on the phone **hablar por teléfono** (2)

photocopier **fotocopiadora** (12)

photocopy **fotocopia** (12)

photo(graph) **foto(grafía)** (8); to take photos sa<u>c</u>ar (<u>qu</u>) fotos/fotografías (8)

photographer **fotógrafo/a** (17)

photography **fotografía** (13)

physics **física** (2)

picnic: to have a picnic <u>hacer</u> un **pícnic** (10)

pie **pastel** *m.* (7)

piece: piece of advice **consejo** (7); piece of furniture **mueble** *m.* (5)

Pilates: to do Pilates <u>hacer</u> **Pilates** (11)

pill **pastilla** (11)

pilot **piloto** *m., f.* (8)

pink **rosado/a** (4)

place *n.* **lugar** *m.* (2); (*in line*) **puesto** (8); parking place **estacionamiento** (15); *v.* <u>poner</u> (5); to take place in/at (*a place*) <u>ser</u> en + *place* (9)

plaid **de cuadros** (4)

plan **plan** *m.* (10); to plan to (*do something*) <u>pensar</u> (pi<u>e</u>nso) + *inf.* (5); to make plans to (*do something*) <u>hacer</u> planes para + *inf.* (10)

plane **avión** *m.* (8); to fly; to go/travel by plane v<u>o</u>lar (v<u>ue</u>lo) en avión (8); <u>ir</u> en avión (8)

planet **planeta** *m.* (15)

plate **plato** (5)

play (*dramatic*) *n.* **drama** *m.* (13), **obra de teatro** (13); (*a game, sport*) *v.* <u>jugar</u> (j<u>ue</u>go) (<u>gu</u>) (a, al) (5); (*a musical instrument*) to<u>c</u>ar (<u>qu</u>) (2); to play cards <u>jugar</u> (j<u>ue</u>go) (<u>gu</u>) a las cartas (10); to play chess <u>jugar</u> (j<u>ue</u>go) (<u>gu</u>) al ajedrez (10); to play videogames <u>jugar</u> (j<u>ue</u>go) (<u>gu</u>) a los videojuegos (10)

player **jugador(a)** (10)

playwright **dramaturgo/a** (13)

plaza **plaza** (4)

pleasantry **expresión** (*f.*) **de cortesía** (1)

please **por favor** (1)

pleased to meet you **encantado/a** (1), **mucho gusto** (1)

pleasing: to be pleasing **gustar** (8)

plumber **plomero/a** (17)

poem **poema** *m.* (13)

poet **poeta** *m., f.* (13)

point: cardinal point **punto cardinal** (6)

police force **policía** (15)

policy **política** (18)

political: political office **cargo** (18); political party **partido** (18); political science **ciencias** (*f. pl.*) **políticas** (2)

politician **político/a** (18)

politics **política** *s.* (18)

polka-dot **de lunares** (4)

pollute **contaminar** (15)

polluted **contaminado/a** (15)

pollution: there's (lots of) pollution **hay (mucha) contaminación** *f.* (6)

pool **piscina** (5)

poor **pobre** (3); poorly paid job/position **empleo mal pagado** (17); to do/turn out poorly <u>salir</u> **mal** (5)

poorly *adv.* **mal** (2); to get along poorly (with) **llevarse mal (con)** (16)

population **población** *f.* (15)

pork chop **chuleta de cerdo** (7)

port **puerto** (8)

porter **maletero/a** (8)

position **empleo** (17); full-time / part-time position **empleo de tiempo completo / parcial** (17); poorly paid position **empleo mal pagado** (17); to run for a position **postularse para un cargo** (18); well-paid position **empleo bien pagado** (17)

possessive **posesivo/a** (17); possessive adjective *gram.* **adjetivo posesivo** (3)

possible **posible** (3); it's not possible **no es posible que** + *subjunctive* (13); it's possible that **es posible que** + *subjunctive* (13)

post (*as on Facebook*) **publi<u>c</u>ar** (<u>qu</u>) (12)

postcard **tarjeta postal** (8)

potato **papa** (7); French fried potato **papa frita** (7)

pottery **cerámica** (13)

practice (*play*) **practi<u>c</u>ar** (<u>qu</u>) (2); (*train*) **entrenar(se)** (10)

prefer **pref<u>e</u>rir** (pref<u>ie</u>ro) (i) (4)

preference **preferencia** (1)

prepare **preparar** (7)

preposition *gram.* **preposición** *f.* (5)

prescription **receta** (11)

present **regalo** (3)

press (*print*) **prensa** (18)

pressure **presión** *f.* (14); to be under a lot of pressure **estar** bajo muchas presiones (14)

pretty (*people and things*) **bonito/a** (3)

price (*of a transportation ticket*) **pasaje** *m.* (8); price **precio** (4)

print **imprimir** (12)

printer **impresora** (12)

probable **probable** (13); it's not probable **no es probable que** + *subjunctive* (13); it's probable that **es probable que** + *subjunctive* (13)

problem: no problem **no hay problema** (14)

profession **profesión** *f.* (17)

professor **profesor(a)** (1)

programmer **programador(a)** (17)

prohibit **proh<u>i</u>bir** (proh<u>í</u>bo) (12)

promise **prometer** (8)

pronoun: personal pronoun *gram.* **pronombre** (*m.*) **personal** (2)

protect **prote<u>g</u>er** (prot<u>e</u>jo) (15)

provided *prep.* **con tal de** (16); provided (that) *conj.* **con tal (de) que** (16)

psychiatrist **siquiatra** *m., f.* (17)

psychologist **sicólogo/a** (17)

psychology **sicología** (2)

public *n.* **público** (13); *adj.* **público/a** (15)

publish **public_ar** (**qu**) (12)
pure **puro/a** (15)
purple **morado/a** (4)
purpose: for what purpose? **¿para qué?** (14)
purse **bolso** (4)
put **poner** (5); to put on (*an article of clothing*) **poner**se (5); to put on makeup **maquillarse** (5)

Q

quarter: a quarter (fifteen minutes) after (*the hour*) **y cuarto/quince** (1); a quarter to (*hour*) **menos cuarto/quince** (1)
queen **reina** (18)
question **pregunta** (5); to ask a question **hacer una pregunta** (5), **preguntar** (8)
quit **dejar** (17)
quiz **prueba** (14)

R

radio (*apparatus*) **radio** *m.* (12); radio station **estación** (*f.*) **de radio** (18)
rain *n.* **lluvia** (6); *v.* **llover** (**llueve**) (6); it rains, it's raining **llueve** (6)
raincoat **impermeable** *m.* (4)
rather **bastante** (16)
read **leer** (*like* **creer**) (3)
really: I would really like … **me gustaría mucho…** (8)
reason: for that reason **por eso** (3)
receipt **recibo** (17)
receive **recibir** (3)
recently married **recién casado/a** (16)
recipe **receta** (7)
recommend **recomendar** (**recomiendo**) (8)
record **grabar** (12)
recycle **reciclar** (15)
recycling **reciclaje** *m.* (15)
red **rojo/a** (4); red wine **vino tinto** (7)
reduction **rebajas** *f. pl.* (4)
reflexive verb *gram.* **verbo reflexivo** (5)
refrigerator **refrigerador** *m.* (10)
regret **lamentar** (13), **sentir** (**siento**) (**i**) (13)
relationship: emotional relationship **relación** (*f.*) **sentimental** (16)
relative **pariente** *m.* (3)
remain (*in a place*) **quedarse** (6); to remain; to be left **quedar** (14)
remember **acordarse** (**me acuerdo**) (**de**) (13); **recordar** (**recuerdo**) (9)
remote control **control** (*m.*) **remoto** (12)
renewable **renovable** (15); renewable energy **energía renovable** (15)

rent *n.* **alquiler** *m.* (12); *v.* to rent **alquilar** (12)
renter **inquilino/a** (12)
repair **arreglar** (15), **reparar** (15); repair shop **taller** *m.* (15)
report **informe** *m.* (14), **trabajo** (14); oral report **informe oral** (14); written report **informe escrito** (14)
reporter **reportero/a** (18)
representative: congressional representative **representante** (*m., f.*) **al congreso** (18)
resign (from) **renunciar (a)** (17)
resolve **resolver** (**resuelvo**) (15)
resource: natural resource **recurso natural** (15)
responsibility **deber** *m.* (18), **responsabilidad** *f.* (18)
rest **descansar** (5)
restaurant **restaurante** *m.* (7)
résumé **currículum** (**vitae**) *m.* (17)
retire (*from a job*) **jubilarse** (17)
return (*something to someone*) **devolver** (*like* **volver**) (14); (*to a place*) **regresar** (2), **volver** (**vuelvo**) (5); to return home **regresar a casa** (2)
review **repaso** (2)
rice **arroz** *m.* (*pl.* **arroces**) (7)
rich (*wealthy*) **rico/a** (3); (*in calories*) **rico/a** (7)
ride: to ride a bicycle **andar en bicicleta** (10); to ride a horse **montar a caballo** (10)
right (*legal*) **derecho** (18); right now **ahora mismo** (6); right now (*currently*) **en la actualidad** (10); to be right **tener razón** (4); to the right of **a la derecha de** (6)
right? **¿no?** (4); **¿verdad?** (4)
ring **sonar** (**suena**) (10)
river **río** (15)
roast(ed) **asado/a** (7); roast chicken **pollo asado** (7)
role (*in a play, an event*) **papel** *m.* (13)
romantic **romántico/a** (16)
room **cuarto** (2); waiting room **sala de espera** (8)
roommate **compañero/a de cuarto** (2)
round-trip ticket **billete** *m.* (*Sp.*) / **boleto** (*L.A.*) **de ida y vuelta** (8)
routine *n.* **rutina** (5); *adj.* **rutinario/a** (11)
rug **alfombra** (5)
ruin **ruina** (13)
run **correr** (10); (*machines*) **funcionar** (12); to run out of **acabar** (14); to run as a candidate **postularse como candidato/a** (18); to run for a position **postularse para un cargo** (18); to run into **chocar** (**qu**) **contra/con** (14); **pegarse** (**gu**) **con/contra** (14)

S

sad **triste** (6)
sake: for heaven's sake **por Dios** (14)
salad **ensalada** (7)
salary **sueldo** (17)
sales **rebajas** *f. pl.* (4)
salesperson **vendedor(a)** (17)
salmon **salmón** *m.* (7)
salt **sal** *f.* (7)
same **mismo/a** (6); same here (likewise) **igualmente** (1)
sandals **sandalias** *f. pl.* (4)
sandwich **sándwich** *m.* (7)
Saturday **sábado** (5)
sauce **salsa** (7)
sausage **salchicha** (7)
save **conservar** (15); to save a place in line **guardar un puesto** (8); (*documents*) **almacenar** (12), **guardar** (12); (*money*) **ahorrar** (17)
savory **rico/a** (7)
say **decir** (8); to say good-bye (to) **despedirse** (*like* **pedir**) (**de**) (9)
scanner **escáner** *m.* (12)
scene **escena** (13)
scenery **escenario** (13)
schedule **horario** (14)
school **escuela** (10)
schoolteacher **maestro/a de escuela** (17)
science **ciencia** (2); computer science **computación** *f.* (2); natural sciences **ciencias** (*f. pl.*) **naturales** (2); political science **ciencias** (*f. pl.*) **políticas** (2); social sciences **ciencias** (*f. pl.*) **sociales** (2)
screen **pantalla** (12); big screen (monitor) **pantalla grande** (12); flat screen (monitor) **pantalla plana** (12)
script **guion** *m.* (13)
sculpt **esculpir** (13)
sculptor **escultor(a)** (13)
sculpture **escultura** (13)
sea **mar** *m.* (8)
search engine **buscador** *m.* (12)
season (*of the year*) **estación** *f.* (6)
seat **asiento** (8)
second **segundo/a** (13); second floor (third story) **segundo piso** (12)
secretary **secretario/a** (2)
security (check) **control** (*m.*) **de seguridad** (8); to go/pass through security (check) **pasar por el control de seguridad** (8)
see **ver** (5); see you around **nos vemos** (1); see you later **hasta luego** (1); see you tomorrow **hasta mañana** (1)
sell **vender** (3)
senator **senador(a)** (18)
send a text **mandar un mensaje (de texto)** (2)
sentence *gram.* **oración** *f.* (2)

separate (from) **separarse (de)** (16)
separated from **separado/a (de)** (16)
separation **separación** f. (16)
September **septiembre** m. (6)
serve s<u>e</u>rvir (s<u>i</u>rvo) (<u>i</u>) (5)
service **servicio** (15); military service
   servicio militar (18)
set the table <u>poner</u> la mesa (10)
seven **siete** (1)
seven hundred **setecientos/as** (4)
seventeen **diecisiete** (1)
seventh **séptimo/a** (13)
seventy **setenta** (3)
shake hands <u>darse</u> la mano (11)
shame **lástima** (13); it's a shame that **es
   una lástima que** + subjunctive (13);
   what a shame that ... ! **¡qué lástima
   que... + subjunctive!** (13)
shave **afeitarse** (5)
she sub. pron. **ella** (2); she is **es** (1)
shellfish **mariscos** m. pl. (7)
ship **barco** (8); cruise ship **crucero** (8);
   to go/travel by ship <u>ir</u> en barco (8)
shirt **camisa** (4)
shoes **zapatos** m. pl. (4)
shop **tienda** (4); repair shop **taller** m. (15)
shopping **de compras** (4); shopping
   mall **centro comercial** (4); to go
   shopping <u>ir</u> de compras (4)
short (in height) **bajo/a** (3); (in length)
   corto/a (3)
shorts **pantalones** (m. pl.) **cortos** (4)
shot: to get a shot **poner(se)
   una inyección** (11); to get a
   shot (against) **poner(se) una
   vacuna (de)** (11)
should (do something) **deber** + inf. (3)
show n. **espectáculo** (13); v. m<u>o</u>strar
   (m<u>ue</u>stro) (8)
shower: to take a shower **ducharse** (5)
shrimp **camarones** m., pl. (7)
siblings **hermanos** m. pl. (3)
sick **enfermo/a** (6); to get/become sick
   enfermarse (11)
sickness **enfermedad** f. (11)
sidewalk **acera** (15)
signal: traffic signal **semáforo** (15)
significant other **pareja** (3)
silk n. **seda** (4); adj. **de seda** (4)
silly **tonto/a** (3)
silver n. **plata** (4); adj. **de plata** (4)
sing **cantar** (2)
singer **cantante** m., f. (13)
single: to be single **estar soltero/a** (16)
sink: bathroom sink **lavabo** (5)
sir **señor (Sr.)** m. (1)
sister **hermana** (3)
sit down s<u>e</u>ntarse (me si<u>e</u>nto) (5)
six **seis** (1)
six hundred **seiscientos/as** (4)
sixteen **dieciséis** (1)
sixth **sexto/a** (13)

sixty **sesenta** (3)
skate v. **patinar** (10)
skating **patinaje** m. (10)
ski esqu<u>i</u>ar (esqu<u>í</u>o) (10)
skiing **esquí** m. (10)
skirt **falda** (4)
skyscraper **rascacielos** m. inv. (15)
sleep d<u>o</u>rmir (d<u>ue</u>rmo) (<u>u</u>) (5)
sleepy: to be sleepy **tener sueño** (4)
slender **delgado/a** (3)
slow **lento/a** (15); slow pace of life **ritmo
   lento de la vida** (15)
small **pequeño/a** (3); (adjective suffix)
   -ito/a (10); small child **niño/a** (3)
smart **listo/a** (3)
smile **sonreír** (like r<u>e</u>ír) (9)
smoke **fumar** (8)
smoking area **sala de fumadores / de
   fumar** (8)
snack **merienda** (7); to have a snack
   mer<u>e</u>ndar (meri<u>e</u>ndo) (7)
snow n. **nieve** f. (6); v. n<u>e</u>var (ni<u>e</u>va) (6);
   it snows, it's snowing **nieva** (6)
so that **para que** (16)
so-so **regular** (1)
soccer **fútbol** m. (10)
social: social network **red** (f.) **social** (12);
   social sciences **ciencias** (f. pl.)
   sociales (2); social worker
   trabajador(a) social (17)
sociology **sociología** (2)
socks **calcetines** m. pl. (4)
soft drink **refresco** (7)
solar energy **energía solar** (15)
soldier **militar** m., f. (17); **soldado** m., f. (17)
solve res<u>o</u>lver (res<u>ue</u>lvo) (15)
some **algún (alguna/os/as)** (7)
someone **alguien** (7)
something **algo** (7)
son **hijo** (3)
song **canción** f. (7)
soon: as soon as **en cuanto** (17), **tan
   pronto como** (17)
sorry: to feel sorry **lamentar** (13), <u>sentir</u>
   (s<u>ie</u>nto) (<u>i</u>) (13); I'm (very) sorry **lo
   siento (mucho)** (14)
sound s<u>o</u>nar (su<u>e</u>na) (10)
soup **sopa** (7)
south **sur** m. (6)
space: storage space **espacio de
   almacenamiento** (12)
Spanish (language) **español** m. (2);
   n., adj. **español, española** (3)
spare (free) time
speak **hablar** (2)
species **especie** f. (15); endangered
   species **especie en peligro de
   extinción** (15)
spectator **espectador(a)** (13)
speed **velocidad** f. (15); speed limit
   límite (m.) **de velocidad** (15)

spend (money) **gastar** (9); (time) **pasar**
   (6); to spend one's vacation in ...
   pasar las vacaciones en... (8); to
   spend time **pasar tiempo** (6)
spicy **picante** (7)
sport **deporte** m. (10)
sporting adj. **deportivo/a** (10)
sports adj., sports-loving
   adj. **deportivo/a** (10)
spring (season) **primavera** (6)
square **plaza** (4)
stage **escenario** (13); (phase) **etapa** (16);
   life stage **etapa de la vida** (16)
stairs **escaleras** f. pl. (14)
stand: stand up **levantarse** (5); to stand
   in line <u>hacer</u> cola (8)
start emp<u>e</u>zar (emp<u>ie</u>zo) (<u>c</u>) (5); to start
   up (a car) arran<u>c</u>ar (<u>qu</u>) (15)
state **estado** (3)
station **estación** f. (8); bus station
   estación de autobuses (8); gas
   station **estación de servicio** (15);
   radio station **estación de radio** (18);
   train station **estación de
   trenes** (8)
status: legal status **estado civil** (16)
stay **quedarse** (6); to stay in bed
   guardar cama (11)
steak **bistec** m. (7)
stick out one's tongue sa<u>c</u>ar (<u>qu</u>) la
   lengua (11)
still **todavía** (6)
stockings **medias** f. pl. (4)
stomach **estómago** (11)
stop n. **escala** (in a trip) (8); bus stop
   parada del autobús (12); subway
   stop **parada del metro** (12); to make
   a stop <u>hacer</u> escala/parada (8); to
   stop **parar** (15); to stop (doing
   something) **dejar de** + inf. (11)
storage (space) **(espacio de)
   almacenamiento** (12)
store n. **tienda** (4) department store
   almacén m. (4); v. (computer)
   almacenar (12)
story **historia** (8)
stove **estufa** (5)
straight ahead **(todo) derecho** (15),
   todo recto (15)
strange: how strange that ... ! **¡qué
   extraño que... + subjunctive!** (13);
   it's strange that **es extraño que** +
   subjunctive (13)
street **calle** f. (12)
street corner **esquina** (15)
stress **estrés** m. (14); to be under (a lot
   of) stress <u>estar</u> (muy) estresado/a
   (14); under stress, stressed out
   estresado/a (14)
stressed: to be (very) stressed <u>estar</u>
   (muy) estresado/a (14)
stressful **estresante** (14)

strike (*labor*) *n.* **huelga** (18); *v.* **pe**g**ar** (**gu**) (14)

striped **de rayas** (4)

struggle **lucha** (18)

student **estudiante** *m., f.* (2)

study **estudiar** (2)

stuffed up (*with a cold*) *adj.* **resfriado/a** (11)

subject area **materia** (2)

suburbs **afueras** *f. pl.* (12)

subway stop **parada del metro** (12)

succeed in (*doing something*) **conseguir** (*like* **seguir**) + *inf.* (9)

suddenly **de repente** (11)

suffer **sufrir (de)** (14)

sufficiently **bastante** (16)

sugar **azúcar** *m.* (7)

suggest **su**g**erir (su**g**iero) (i)** (9)

suit **traje** *m.* (4)

suitcase **maleta** (8); to pack one's suitcase(s) **hacer la(s) maleta(s)** (8)

summer **verano** (6)

sunbathe **tomar el sol** (8)

Sunday **domingo** (5)

sunglasses **gafas** (*f. pl.*) **de sol** (4)

sunny: it's (very) sunny **hace (mucho) sol** (6)

sunscreen **bloqueador** (*m.*) **solar** (8)

supermarket **supermercado** (12)

supper **cena** (7); to have (eat) supper **cenar** (7)

sure **seguro/a** (6); it's a sure thing that **es seguro que** + *indicative* (13); it's not sure **no es seguro que** + *subjunctive* (13)

surf **surfear** (10)

surprise **sorprender** (*like* **gustar**) (13)

SUV **SUV** *m.* (15)

sweater **suéter** *m.* (4)

sweatshirt **sudadera** (4)

sweep (the floor) **barrer (el piso)** (10)

sweets **dulces** *m. pl.* (7)

swim **nadar** (8)

swimming **natación** *f.* (10); swimming pool **piscina** (5)

swimsuit **traje** (*m.*) **de baño** (4)

syllabus **programa** (*m.*) **del curso** (14)

symptom **síntoma** *m.* (11)

syrup: cough syrup **jarabe** *m.* (11)

systems analyst **analista** (*m., f.*) **de sistemas** (17)

T

T-shirt **camiseta** (4)

table **mesa** (2); to clear the table **quitar la mesa** (10); to set the table **poner la mesa** (10)

take **tomar** (2); **llevar** (4); to take a bath **bañarse** (5); to take a nap **d**o**rmir (d**u**ermo) (u) la siesta** (5); to take a

shower **ducharse** (5); to take a trip **hacer un viaje** (5); to take a vacation **tomar unas vacaciones** (8); to take a walk **dar un paseo** (10); to take care of **cuidar de** (11); to take care of oneself **cuidarse** (11); to take off (*an article of clothing*) **quitarse** (5); to take out **sa**c**ar** (**qu**) (17); to take out the trash **sa**c**ar** (**qu**) **la basura** (10); to take photos **sa**c**ar** (**qu**) **fotos/ fotografías** (8); to take place at/in (*a place*) **ser en** + *place* (9); to take someone's temperature **tomarle la temperatura** (11)

talk **hablar** (2); to talk on the phone **hablar por teléfono** (2)

tall **alto/a** (3)

tame **domesticado/a** (15)

tank **tanque** *m.* (15)

tape **grabar** (12)

tasty **rico/a** (7)

tea **té** *m.* (7)

teach **enseñar** (2)

teacher: school teacher **maestro/a de escuela** (17)

team **equipo** (10)

technician **técnico/a** (17)

technology **la tecnología** (12)

teeth: to brush one's teeth **cepillarse los dientes** (5)

television **tele(visión)** *f.* (3); to watch television **mirar la tele(visión)** (3)

tell **c**o**ntar (c**u**ento)** (8); **decir** (8)

teller (bank) **cajero/a** (17); automatic teller machine (ATM) **cajero automático** (17)

temperature **temperatura** (11); to take someone's temperature **tomarle la temperatura** (11)

temple **templo** (16)

ten **diez** (1)

tenant **inquilino/a** (12)

tennis **tenis** *m.* (10)

tennis shoes **tenis** *m. pl.* (4)

tent **tienda (de campaña)** (8)

tenth **décimo/a** (13)

terrible **terrible** (13); it's terrible that **es terrible que** + *subjunctive* (13)

terrorism **terrorismo** (18)

terrorist **terrorista** *m., f.* (18); terrorist attack **ataque** (*m.*) **terrorista** (18)

test **examen** *m.* (4); **prueba** (14)

text (*electronic*) **mensaje** *m.* (2); to (send a) text **mandar un mensaje (de texto)** (2)

textbook **libro de texto** (2)

than: better than **mejor(es) que** (6); less ... than **menos... que** (6); less than + *number* **menos de** + *number* (6); more ... **más... que** (6); more than + *number* **más de** + *number* (6); older than **mayor(es) que** (6); worse

than **peor(es) que** (6); younger than **menor(es) que** (6)

thank you (very much) **(muchas) gracias** (1); thanks for **gracias por** + *inf./ noun* (9)

Thanksgiving **Día** (*m.*) **de (Acción de) Gracias** (9)

that *conj.* **que** (3); that *adj., pron.* **ese/a** (4); *neuter pron.* **eso** (4); that ([way] over there) *adj., pron.* **aquel, aquella** (4); that ([way] over there) *neuter pron.* **aquello** (4); that means ... **eso quiere decir...** (11); that which **lo que** (5)

theater **teatro** (10); to go to the theater **ir al teatro** (10)

their *poss. adj.* **su(s)** (3); (of) theirs *poss. adj., poss pron.* **suyo/a(s)** (17)

them *obj.* (*of prep.*) **ellos/as** (2)

then **luego** (5); **después** (5); **entonces** (8)

there **allí** (4)

there: (way) over there **allá** (4)

there is/are **hay** (1); is there / are there? **¿hay?** (1); there is/are not **no hay** (1); infinitive form of **hay haber** (12)

these *adj., pron.* **estos/as** (3)

they *sub. pron.* **ellos/as** (2)

thin **delgado/a** (3)

thing **cosa** (5); the bad thing **lo malo** (11); the good thing **lo bueno** (11)

think **creer** (3); to not think **no creer** (13); to think (about) **p**e**nsar (p**i**enso) (de/ en)** (5); to think that **p**e**nsar (p**i**enso) que** (5)

third **tercer(o/a)** (13)

thirsty: to be (very) thirsty **tener (mucha) sed** (7)

thirteen **trece** (1)

thirty **treinta** (1); thirty minutes past (*the hour*) **y treinta** (1)

this *adj., pron.* **este/a** (3); *neuter pron.* **esto** (3)

those *adj., pron.* **esos/as** (4); those ([way] over there) *adj., pron.* **aquellos/as** (4)

three **tres** (1)

three hundred **trescientos/as** (4)

Three Kings Day **Día** (*m.*) **de los Reyes Magos** (9)

throat **garganta** (11)

through **por** (8)

Thursday **jueves** *m. inv.* (5)

ticket **billete** *m.* (*Sp.*) / **boleto** (*L.A.*) (8); one-way ticket **billete/bolleto de ida** (8); round-trip ticket **billete/boleto de ida y vuelta** (8); (*to a performance, movie* ...) **entrada** (12)

tie **corbata** (4)

time **tiempo** (6); at what time ... ? **¿a qué hora... ?** (1); at times **a veces** (3); conjunction of time **conjunción** (*f.*) **de tiempo** (17); for the first/last time **por primera/última vez** (14); **tiempo libre**

(10); on time **a tiempo** (8); to have a bad time **pasarlo mal** (9); to have a good time **divertirse (me divierto) (i)** (5), **pasarlo bien** (9); to spend time **pasar tiempo** 6); what time is it? **¿qué hora es?** (1)

tire **llanta** (15); flat tire **llanta desinflada** (15)

tired **cansado/a** (6)

to **a** (1); to the **al** (4); to the left of **a la izquiera de** (6); to the right of **a la derecha de** (6)

toast **pan tostado** (7)

toasted **tostado/a** (7)

toaster **tostadora** (10)

today **hoy** (1); what day is today? **¿qué día es hoy?** (5); what's today's date? **¿cuál es la fecha de hoy?** (6), **¿qué fecha es hoy?** (6)

toe **dedo del pie** (11)

together **juntos/as** (8); to get together (with) **reunirse (me reúno) (con)** (9)

tomato **tomate** m. (7)

tomorrow **mañana** (1); see you tomorrow **hasta mañana** (1); the day after tomorrow **pasado mañana** (5)

tongue **lengua** (11); to stick out one's tongue **sacar (qu) la lengua** (11)

tonight **esta noche** (6)

too (much) **demasiado** adv. (9); adj. too much **demasiado/a**; too many **demasiados/as**

tooth **diente** m. (5); back tooth **muela** (11); to brush one's teeth **cepillarse los dientes** (5)

top: on top of **encima de** (6)

towel **toalla** (5)

tradition: cultural tradition **tradición** (f.) **cultural** (13)

traditional **folclórico/a** (13)

traffic **circulación** f. (15), **tráfico** (15), **tránsito** (15); traffic signal **semáforo** (15)

train **tren** m. (8); to go/travel by train **ir en tren** (8); to train **entrenar(se)** (10); train station **estación** (f.) **de trenes** (8)

translator **traductor(a)** (17)

transportation: means of transportation **medio de transporte** (8)

trash **basura** (10); to take out the trash **sacar (qu) la basura** (10)

travel **viajar** (8); to travel by boat/ship **ir en barco** (8); to travel by bus **ir en autobús** (8); to travel by plane **ir en avión** (8)

traveling **de viaje** (8)

treadmill **caminadora** (11)

treatment **tratamiento** (11)

tree **árbol** m. (9)

trendy: it's trendy **está de moda** (4), **es de última moda** (4)

trip **viaje** m. (5); on a trip **de viaje** (8); to take a trip **hacer un viaje** (5)

true: it's true that **es verdad que** + indicative (13)

try to (do something) **tratar de** + inf. (13)

Tuesday **martes** m. inv. (5); on Tuesdays **los martes** (5)

tuition **matrícula** (2)

tuna **atún** m. (7)

turkey **pavo** (7)

turn **doblar** (15); to be someone's turn **tocarle (qu) a uno** (10); to turn on (a machine) **encender (enciendo)** (12); to turn off (machine) **apagar (gu)** (12); to turn on (appliance) **poner** (10); to turn out badly **salir mal** (5); to turn out well **salir bien** (5)

tweet n. **tuit** m. (12); v. **twitear** (12)

twelve **doce** (1)

twenty **veinte** (1)

twenty-eight **veintiocho** (1)

twenty-five **veinticinco** (1)

twenty-four **veinticuatro** (1)

twenty-nine **veintinueve** (1)

twenty-one **veintiuno** (1)

twenty-seven **veintisiete** (1)

twenty-six **veintiséis** (1)

twenty-three **veintitrés** (1)

twenty-two **veintidós** (1)

twice **dos veces** (11)

Twitter **Twitter** m. (12)

two **dos** (1)

two hundred **doscientos/as** (4)

U

ugly **feo/a** (3)

uncertain: to be uncertain of **no estar seguro/a de** (13)

uncle **tío** (3); aunts and uncles **tíos** m. pl. (3)

under stress **estresado/a** (14); to be under a lot of stress **estar (muy) estresado/a** (14); to be under a lot of pressure **estar bajo muchas presiones** (14)

understand **comprender** (3); **entender (entiendo)** (5)

underwear **ropa interior** (4)

unfortunately **desgraciadamente** (11)

United States: of the United States of America n., adj. **estadounidense** (3)

university n. **universidad** f. (2); adj. **universitario/a** (14)

unless conj. **a menos que** (16); **sin que** (16)

unlikeable (people) **antipático/a** (3)

unlikely: it's unlikely that **es improbable que** + subjunctive (13)

unlucky: to be unlucky **tener mala suerte** (14)

unoccupied **libre** (10)

unpleasant (people) **antipático/a** (3)

until prep. **hasta** (1); conj. **hasta que** (17)

up: to be up to date **estar al día** (18)

upload v. **subir** (12)

upset **enojado/a** (9)

urgent **urgente** (12); it's urgent (that) **es urgente que** (12)

use **usar** (4); (gas) **gastar** (15); to be used for **servir (sirvo) (i) para** (5)

user **usuario/a** (12)

V

vacation: on vacation **de vacaciones** (8); to be on vacation **estar de vacaciones** (8); to go on vacation to/ in … **ir de vacaciones a…** (8); to leave on vacation **salir de vacaciones** (8); to spend one's vacation in … **pasar las vacaciones en…** (8); to take a vacation **tomar unas vacaciones** (8)

vacuum cleaner **aspiradora** (10); to vacuum **pasar la aspiradora** (10)

van **camioneta** (8)

vegetables **verduras** f. pl. (7)

vehicle **vehículo** (15)

verb gram. **verbo** (2); reflexive verb gram. **verbo reflexivo** (5)

very adv. **muy** (1); very much **muchísimo**; very very **-ísimo** (9); very well **muy bien** (1); to be (very) stressed **estar (muy) estresado/a** (14)

veterinarian **veterinario/a** (17)

victim **víctima** (18)

video **video** (12); videogame **videojuego** (10); to play videogames **jugar (juego) (gu) a los videojuegos** (10)

view **vista** (12)

visit **visita** (11)

voice mailbox **buzón** (m.) **de voz** (12)

volleyball **voleibol** m. (10)

vote **votar** (18)

W

wages (often per hour) **salario** (17)

wait (for) **esperar** (7)

waiter/waitress **camarero/a** (7)

waiting room **sala de espera** (8)

wake up **despertarse (me despierto)** (5)

walk **caminar** (10); to take a walk **dar un paseo** (10)

wall **pared** f. (5)

wallet **cartera** (4)

want **desear** (2); **querer** (4)

war **guerra** (18)

was **fue** (5)

wash **lavar** (10)

washing machine **lavadora** (10)

watch *n.* **reloj** *m.* (4); *v.* **mirar** (3); to watch (*a program, movie*) **ver** (5); to watch television **mirar la tele(visión)** (3)

water **agua** *f.* (*but* **el agua**) (7); mineral water **agua mineral** (7)

water bottle **botella de agua** (2)

way over there **allá** (4)

we *sub. pron.* **nosotros/as** (2)

wear **llevar** (4); **usar** (4)

weather **tiempo** (6); what's the weather like? **¿qué tiempo hace?** (6); it's (very) good/bad weather **hace (muy) buen/mal tiempo** (6)

weave **tejer** (13)

webpage **página web** (12)

website **sitio web** (12)

wed: newly wed **recién casado/a** (16)

wedding (*ceremony*) **boda** (16)

Wednesday **miércoles** *m. inv.* (5)

week **semana** (5); days of the week **días** (*m. pl.*) **de la semana** (5); next week **la próxima semana** (5), **la semana que viene** (5); once a week **una vez a la semana** (3)

weekend **fin** (*m.*) **de semana** (2)

weight: to lift weights **levantar pesas** (11)

welcome: you're welcome **de nada** (1), **no hay de qué** (1)

well **bien** (1); to get along well (with) **llevarse bien (con)** (16); very well **muy bien** (1); to come/turn out well **salir bien** (5); to do well **salir bien** (5)

well-being **bienestar** *m.* (11)

well-paid job/position **empleo bien pagado** (17)

west **oeste** *m.* (6)

whale **ballena** (15)

what (that which) **lo que** (5)

what? **¿cómo?** (1); **¿cuál?** (2); **¿qué?** (1); at what time? **¿a qué hora... ?** (1); for what purpose? **¿para qué... ?** (14); what (a) + *noun*! **¡qué** + *noun*! (14); what a shame that ... ! **¡qué lástima que... + *subjunctive*!** (13); what are you like? **¿cómo es usted?** (*form. s.*) (1); what day is today? **¿qué día es hoy?** (5); what is your name? **¿cómo se llama usted?** (*form. s.*) (1); **¿cómo te llamas?** (*fam. s.*) (1); what time is it? **¿qué hora es?** (1); what's the weather like? **¿qué tiempo hace?** (6); what's

today's date? **¿cuál es la fecha de hoy?** (6), **¿qué fecha es hoy?** (6)

when? **¿cuándo?** (2)

where? **¿dónde?** (1); where (to)? **¿adónde?** (4); where are you from? **¿de dónde eres (tú)?** (*fam. s.*) (1), **¿de dónde es usted?** (*form. s.*) (1)

which *conj.* **que** (3)

which? **¿cuál?** (2)

while **mientras** (10)

white **blanco/a** (4); white wine **vino blanco** (7)

whiteboard **pizarrón** (*m.*) **blanco** (2)

who *rel. pron.* **que** (3)

who? **¿quién?** (1)

whose? **¿de quién?** (3)

why? **¿por qué?** (3)

widow **viuda** (16)

widower **viudo** (16)

wife **esposa** (3), **mujer** *f.* (3)

wifi **wifi** *m.* (12)

wild **salvaje** (15)

win **ganar** (10)

wind **viento** (6); wind energy **energía eólica** (15)

window **ventana** (2); small window (*on a plane*) **ventanilla** (8)

windshield **parabrisas** *m. inv.* (15)

windy: it's (very) windy **hace (mucho) viento** (6)

wine (white, red) **vino (blanco, tinto)** (7)

winter **invierno** (6)

wish **esperanza** (18)

with **con** (2); with me **conmigo** (6); with you (*fam. s.*) **contigo** (6)

withdraw (*from an account*) **sacar (qu)** (17)

without *prep.* **sin** (5); *conj.* **sin que** (16)

witness **testigo** *m., f.* (18)

woman **mujer** *f.* (2); business woman **mujer de negocios** (17)

wool *n.* **lana** (4); *adj.* **de lana** (4)

word **palabra** (1); indefinite and negative word *gram.* **palabra indefinida y negativa** (7); interrogative word **palabra interrogativa** (2)

work (*labor*) *n.;* **trabajo** (10); (*piece of*) **trabajo** (14); work of art **obra de arte** (13); *v.* to work (*function*) **funcionar** (12); to work (*at a job*) **trabajar** (2); *adj.* **laboral** (17)

worker **obrero/a** (17); social worker **trabajador(a) social** (17)

world **mundo** (3)

worried **preocupado/a** (6)

worry: don't worry **no se preocupe** (*form. s.*) (14); **no te preocupes** (*fam. s.*) (14)

worse **peor** (6); worse than **peor(es) que** (6)

woven goods **tejidos** *m. pl.* (13)

write **escribir** (*p.p.* **escrito**) (3)

writer **escritor(a)** (13)

written **escrito/a** (*p.p. of* **escribir**) (14); written report **informe** (*m.*) **escrito** (14)

wrong: to be wrong **no tener razón** (4); to get up on the wrong side of the bed **levantarse con el pie izquierdo** (14)

Y

yard **patio** (5)

year **año** (6); (*in school*) **grado** (10); end of the year **fin** (*m.*) **de año** (9); to be ... years old **tener... años** (3)

yellow **amarillo/a** (4)

yes **sí** (1)

yesterday **ayer** (5); yesterday was ... **ayer fue...** (5); the day before yesterday *adv.* **anteayer** (5)

yet **todavía** (6)

yoga: to do yoga **hacer (el) yoga** (10)

yogurt **yogur** *m.* (7)

you *sub. pron.* **tú** (*fam. s.*) (2); **usted (Ud.)** (*form. s.*) (2); **vosotros/as** (*fam. pl.*) (*Sp.*) (2); **ustedes (Uds.)** (*form. pl.*) (2); *obj. of prep.* **ti** (*fam. s.*) (6); **usted** (*form. s.*); **ustedes** (*Uds.*) (*form. pl.*) (6); and you? **¿y tú?** (*fam. s.*) (1); **¿y usted?** (*form. s.*) (1); how are you? **¿cómo está(s)?** (1), **¿qué tal?** (1); with you (*fam. s.*) **contigo** (6); you are (*fam. s.*) **eres** (1), (*form. s.*) **es** (1)

young **joven** (3); young woman **señorita (Srta.)** (1)

younger (than) **menor (que)** (6)

your *poss. adj.* **tu(s)** (*fam. s.*) (3); **su(s)** (*form. s., pl.*) (3); **vuestro/a(s)** (*fam. pl.*) (*Sp.*) (3); your, (of) yours *poss. adj., poss. pron.* **tuyo/a(s)** (*fam. s.*) (17); **suyo/a(s)** (*form. s., pl.*) (17); **vuestro/a(s)** (*fam. pl.*) (*Sp.*) (17)

you're welcome **de nada** (1), **no hay de qué** (1)

youth **juventud** *f.* (16)

Z

zero **cero** (1)

zumba: to do Zumba **hacer zumba** (11)

zone **zona** (12)

INDEX

In this index, cultural notes, authors of the literature presentations (**Lectura**), and vocabulary topic groups are listed by individual topic as well as under those headings.

A

a, 210, 214
  + **el**, 123
  + **ir** + **a** + infinitive versus, 123
  personal, 210, 214
  + pronouns objects of prepositions, 287
  with **gustar**, 251
  with some stem-changing verbs, 149
acabar de + infinitive, 218, 234
  present perfect versus, 463
academic life (*vocabulary*), 420
academic subjects (*vocabulary*), 32
accent marks, 72
  informal (irregular) commands, 366
  interrogative words, 5, 83
  preterite, 256
  pronoun as object of preposition, 174
  stress and, 72, 112–113
  when to drop, 74
accidental events, 430–431
accidents (*vocabulary*), 423
adjective clauses, 484
  questions versus answers with, 484
  that describe a place, 484
adjectives. *See also* Appendix 1
  adverbs compared, 121
  agreement, 74, 76
  articles +. *See* Appendix 2
  common (list), 75
  definition, 73
  demonstrative, 75, 114–115. *See also* Appendix 2
  descriptive (*vocabulary*), 71, 75
  emphatic form (**-ísimo/a(os/as)**), 277
  gender agreement, 74
  lo and, 332
  names of languages, 74
  number agreement, 74
  of nationality, 74, 77
  of quality, 75
  of quantity, 75
  past participles used as, 458–459
  plural, 74
  position of, 75
  singular, 74
  stressed possessive, 507. *See also* Appendix 3
  superlative, forms of, 276, 315
  unstressed possessive, 84–85
  with **estar**, 183–184
  with **por**, 185
  with **ser**, 73, 183–184
adverbial conjunctions of time, 515–516
¿adónde?, 312
adverbs. *See also* Appendix 1
  agreement (invariable), 121
  compared with adjectives, 121
  definition, 115, 121
  emphatic form (**-ísimo**), 277
  sequence of events, 156
affection, expressions of, 479. *See also* diminutives
age, expressing, 69
ago (with **hace**), 427–428

B

bañarse, 154
béisbol, 302
bien, 192

agreement
  definition, 74
  of adjectives, 74, 76
  of adverbs, 121
  possessive adjectives, 85
al, 123
algo, 220
Algo sobre. *See* culture
alguien, 220
algún, alguno/a, 220–221
alphabet, Spanish, 8
Amazon and Andes regions, 399, 512
americano/a and **estadounidense**, 50
animals (*vocabulary*), 450
antecedents, 482–484
  indicative with existing, 483
antes (de) que + subjunctive, 516
appliances (*vocabulary*), 303
aprender + **a** + infinitive, 89
aquel and **ese**, 115
aquél. *See* Appendix 2
-ar verbs, 44–46. *See also* Appendix 5
  conditional tense, 543–544
  formal command forms, 223
  future tense, 509
  imperfect tense, 307
  important, 45
  informal command forms, 365
  past subjunctive, 537
  present progressive, 178
  present subjunctive, 371
  present tense, 44–46
  preterite, 255
  stem-changing preterite, 283
architecture in the Hispanic world, 393
Argentina, 24, 189, 199, 263, 302, 320, 381, 449, 452, 453, 460, 465, 467, 469, 471, 481, 518, 551
art in the Hispanic world, 411
articles. *See also* Appendix 1
  definite, 38–39, 173. *See also* Appendix 1; Appendix 2
  definition, 38
  indefinite, 38–39
  plural forms, 41
  singular forms, 38–39, 41
  with nouns, 38–39
artists
  Botero, Fernando, 409
  De la Loza, Ernesto, 53
  Guayasamín, Oswaldo, 393
  Guillermo, Erwin, 107
  Kahlo, Frida, 83
  Mamani Mamani, Roberto, 397
  Matta, Roberto, 523
  Rivera, Diego, 113
  Velázquez, Diego, 408
arts and artists (*vocabulary*), 390–391

biodiversity and natural resources, 467, 469
Blades, Rubén, 210
body, parts of (*vocabulary*), 423
Bolívar, Simón, 338
Bolivia, 275, 389, 399, 400, 403, 408, 411, 481
buen(o/a), 75, 192
buscar, 45
Busom Fuertes, Laura, 470

C

caer (*irregular*). *See* Appendix 5
Canada, 558, 559
capitalization
  days of the week, 139
  names of languages, 74
  nationalities, 74, 77
cardinal directions, 175
cardinal numbers, 14
  dates, 173
Caribbean region, 306, 318
Carnaval, 270, 273, 292
cars and driving (*vocabulary*), 454
celebrations and holidays (*vocabulary*), 272–273
Central America, 141, 158, 175
Chile, 24, 197, 198, 501, 511, 512, 514, 518, 521
cien(to), 68, 110
clauses. *See also* Appendix 1
  definition, 370
  independent, 370
  main, 370
  subordinate, 370
climate, atmospheric conditions, 174, 197, 199
clothing
  colors, 107
  in the Hispanic world, 105, 109
  Latin American traditional, 127, 400
  sizes, 109
clothing (*vocabulary*), 104–105
coffee, 374
cognates, 9
Colombia, 222, 292, 338, 357, 359, 368, 374, 377, 379, 381, 409, 469
colors (*vocabulary*), 107
comer
  conditional tense, 543
  future tense, 509
  imperfect tense, 307
  past subjunctive, 536
  present tense, 44, 88
commands
  definition, 224, 364
  formal, with **usted** and **ustedes**, 223–225
  indirect object pronouns with, 245
  informal, with **tú**, 364–366
  oír, for attention, 143
  position of pronouns, 225
common illnesses (*vocabulary*), 330
communication strategies
  acabar + **de** + infinitive, 218
  adjective + **-mente**, 425

adjective + **por**, 185
adverbs, 425
age, expressing, 69
being emphatic with **-ísimo**, 277
cognates, 9
days of the week, expressing, 139
diminutives, 317
estar, expressions with, 49
explaining your reasons, 83
expressing frequency, 92
expressing future probability, 513
expressing hopes/wishes with **ojalá**, 398
expressing impossible wishes with
  ojalá, 542
expressing likes and dislikes, 253, 392
food-related phrases, 207
gender and number, 14
giving directions, 456
infinitive used as noun, 480
interrogative words, 34
lo + adjective, 332
mucho and **poco**, 121
nationalities, 77
obligation, expressing, 305
other uses of **se**, 242
part of the day, expressing, 48
past progressive (**-ndo**), 309
polite expressions, 6
present progressive (**-ndo**), 181
sequence expressions, 156
si clauses, 546
stressed possessives, 507
tag questions, 106
tener, expressions with, 171
time of day, expressing, 18
verbs derived from **poner**, **tener**, and
  venir, 367
verbs that require prepositions, 403
words and expressions associated with
  preterite and imperfect, 336
¿cómo?, 312
comparisons, 189–192
  comparatives defined, 189, *See also*
    Appendix 1
  of adjectives, 190, 191
  of adverbs, 190, 191
  of equality, 190, 191
  of inequality, 190
  of nouns, 190, 191
  of quantity, 190
  of verbs, 190, 191
conditional perfect, *See* Appendix 4;
  Appendix 5
conditional tense, 543–545. *See also*
  Appendix 5
  irregular verbs, 544
conducir. *See* Appendix 5
conjugation, 45. *See also* Appendix 1
conjunctions. *See also* Appendix 1
  defined, 487
  of purpose and contingency, 487–488
  of time, 515–516
conocer (*irregular*), **saber** versus, 210, 280
conocer, uses of the verb (*vocabulary*), 210
construir. *See* Appendix 5
continuar, 181
contractions
  al, 123
  del, 80, 123
Costa Rica, 169, 179, 185, 186, 189, 197, 469
Cruz, Celia, 289
Cruz, Sor Juana Inés de la, 78
¿cuál?, 312–313
  versus **¿qué?**, 34, 312–313
¿cuándo?, 312
¿cuánto tiempo hace que...?, 428
¿cuántos/as?, 67, 312

Cuba, 271, 273, 274, 281, 285, 286, 289,
  292, 551
Cucurto, Washington, 442
culture
  affection, expressions of, 479
  Amazon and Andes regions, 399, 512
  americano/a and **estadounidense**, 50
  architecture in the Hispanic world, 393
  Argentina, 24, 189, 199, 263, 302, 320,
    381, 449, 452, 453, 460, 465, 467, 469,
    471, 481, 518, 551
  arts in the Hispanic world, 53, 83, 107, 411
  béisbol, 302
  biodiversity and natural resources, 467, 469
  Bolivia, 275, 389, 399, 400, 403, 408,
    411, 481
  Canada, 558, 559
  Caribbean region, 306, 318
  Carnaval, 270, 273, 292
  Central American coastline, 141
  Chile, 24, 197, 198, 501, 511, 512, 514, 518, 521
  climate, 174, 197, 199
  clothing in the Hispanic world, 105, 109, 127
  clothing, traditional, 127, 400
  coffee, 374
  Colombia, 222, 292, 338, 357, 359, 368,
    374, 377, 379, 381, 409, 469
  Costa Rica, 169, 179, 185, 186, 189, 197, 469
  Cruz, Celia, 289
  Cruz, Sor Juana Inés de la, 78
  Cuba, 271, 273, 274, 281, 285, 286, 289,
    292, 551
  Dominican Republic, 23, 237, 243, 248,
    250, 254, 257, 260–261, 263, 306
  Ecuador, 23, 222, 389, 393, 399, 403,
    404, 411, 469
  El Salvador, 121, 135, 141, 147, 159, 161
  emoticons, 363
  environmental programs, 451
  Equatorial Guinea, 558
  families, 93, 95–96
  food and meals in the Hispanic world, 90,
    91, 209, 227, 229, 230, 248, 281, 332,
    337, 489, 545
  fútbol, 302
  geography of the Spanish-speaking world,
    23–24
  greetings in the Hispanic world, 5
  Guatemala, 103, 107, 113, 121, 125, 127, 292
  hand-written numbers, 14
  health care and well-being, 331, 349
  Hispanic last names, 68
  Hispanic presence in U.S. universities, 56
  holidays in the Hispanic world, 273, 275,
    290–291, 292–293
  Honduras, 103, 113, 121, 125, 127
  houses and cities in the Hispanic world,
    138, 158–159, 161, 381, 393
  indigenous peoples, 78, 103, 113, 121, 127,
    158, 222, 306, 393, 429, 491, 514, 518
  Kahlo, Frida, 83
  large cities of Hispanic countries, 424
  leisure time, 320
  linguistic sexism, avoiding, 503
  mate, 460, 489
  MERCOSUR, 551
  merienda, 207
  Mexico, 24, 65, 69, 75, 78, 83, 90, 93, 96,
    121, 290–291, 381, 393, 411, 469
  murals and urban art, 53
  music and dance, 210, 254, 289, 318, 368,
    426, 433, 465, 511, 542
  Nicaragua, 135, 138, 146, 147, 158, 161
  numbers, 14
  origins of U.S. Hispanic population, 12
  Pampa, 453, 469
  Panama, 205, 212, 217, 222, 227, 229, 368

Paraguay, 469, 477, 481, 486, 489, 491,
  493, 551
passtimes, 320
Peru, 24, 174, 241, 393, 408, 419, 424,
  426, 429, 433, 439, 441, 469
Philippines, 559
plazas, 381
proverbs, 458
Puerto Rico, 299, 304, 305, 306, 311, 318,
  320, 323, 551
recycling, 451
romantic relationships, 493
seasons, 195
shopping in the Hispanic world, 125,
  127–128, 243, 403
soccer. *See* **fútbol**
society, history and economy in the
  Hispanic world, 533, 551, 552
sources of stress in the Hispanic world, 441
Spain, 24, 46, 95, 197, 263, 275, 302, 349, 381,
  393, 411, 469, 521, 529, 534, 542, 548,
  551, 554
Spain's linguistic diversity, 534
Spanish in U.S. universities, 54
Spanish-speaking world, 3, 12–13, 558–559
sports in the Hispanic world, 302
subways, 381
technology and Spanish, 363
tourism in the Hispanic world, 241,
  263, 264
United States, 31, 50, 53, 54, 56, 229,
  263, 411
universities in the Hispanic world, 31, 32
Uruguay, 449, 452, 453, 456, 460, 465,
  469, 471
Venezuela, 302, 327, 332, 338, 341, 346,
  349, 469
working world, 521

D

daily routines, 153–154, 180
dar (*irregular*), 246, *See also* Appendix 5
  preterite, 257
dates, 111, 173
days of the week (*vocabulary*), 138
days of the week, expressing, 20, 139
de
  + **el**, 80, 123
  comparison, with number, 190
  with **salir**, 143
deber + infinitive, 89, 305
decimals, 109
decir (*irregular*), 247. *See also* Appendix 5
  preterite, 280
¿de dónde?, 312
definite articles
  days of the week, 138–139
  definition, 38
  forms of, 38–39
  when talking about a person, 34
  with dates, 173
  with personal titles, 49
  with superlatives, 316
del, 80, 123
De la Loza, Ernesto, 53
demonstrative adjectives, 75
  agreement, 115
  definition, 114
  forms and uses, 114–115
demonstrative pronouns, 115. *See also*
  Appendix 2
  agreement, 115
  neuter, 115
¿de quién?, 312
describing yourself (*vocabulary*), 10
descriptions, expressing with **ser**, 80
descriptive adjectives (*vocabulary*), 71

destination, expressing with **ser**, 81
diminutives, 317
diphthongs, 36, 112
direct object pronouns, 215
    placement, 215
    with indirect object pronouns, 286–287
direct objects, definition, 214. *See also*
    Appendix 1
directions, expressions to give, 456
doctor's office, at the (*vocabulary*), 330
doler, 330
Dolz, Gregori, 128
Dominican Republic, 23, 237, 243, 248, 250,
    254, 257, 260–261, 263, 306
¿dónde?, 312
dormir, 283. *See also* Appendix 5
double negative, 220
double object pronouns, 287–288

E

e to **ei**, 148–149
e to **i**, 148–149
each other, 344
Ecuador, 23, 222, 389, 393, 399, 403, 404,
    411, 469
    Islas Galápagos, 404
El Salvador, 121, 135, 141, 147, 159, 161
el, 38–39, 173
emojis, 363
emotion
    subjunctive uses, 396, 405
    verbs of, 396
emotions and feelings (*vocabulary*), 276–277
emphatic, being, 277
environment, urban versus natural
    (*vocabulary*), 450
Equatorial Guinea, 558
-er verbs. *See also* Appendix 5
    conditional tense, 543–544
    formal command forms, 224
    future tense, 509–510
    imperfect, 307
    informal command forms, 365–366
    past subjunctive, 537
    present progressive, 178
    present subjunctive, 371–372
    present tense, 88–89
    preterite, 255
    stem-changing preterite, 283
escuchar, 45
    versus **oír**, 143
ese and **aquel**, 115
ése. *See* Appendix 2
estar (*irregular*).
    + past progressive (**-ndo**), 309
    + present progressive (**-ndo**), 177–178
estar (*irregular*). *See also* Appendix 5
    past participle with, 459
    present tense, 49
    preterite, 279
    ser versus, 183–184
    summary of uses, 183
    with adjectives, 183–184
este, ese, 115
este, esto, 75
ése. *See* Appendix 2

F

family and relatives (*vocabulary*), 66–67
feminine nouns, 38
food and meals (*vocabulary*), 206–207
food and meals in the Hispanic world, 209,
    227, 229, 248, 281, 332, 337, 489, 545
    guacamole recipe, 223
    merienda, 207, 337
    recipe for tortilla lasagna, 230
food-related phrases, 207

formal commands, with **usted** and **ustedes**,
    223–225
    dar and **decir**, 246
    position of pronoun, 225
frequency expressions, 92
Fuertes, Gloria, 412
furniture (*vocabulary*), 136
fútbol, 16, 302
future
    ir + **a** + infinitive, 124
    uses, 510–511, 513
    ways of expressing, 510
future of probability, 513
future or pending actions, 515–516
future perfect tense, 510. *See also*
    Appendix 4; Appendix 5
future tense, 509–511. *See also* Appendix 5
    of irregular verbs, 510

G

García Márquez, Gabriel, 377
gender. *See also* Appendix 1
    colors, 107
    of adjectives, 74
    of adverbs, 121
    of nouns, 14, 37–38
    of pronouns, 43–44
    professions and trades, 502–503
generalizations (impersonal expressions), 80.
    See also impersonal expressions
    use of **se** with, 242
    with **ser**, 80, 183
geography of the Hispanic world, 23–24
gerundios, 177–178
government and civic duties (*vocabulary*), 532
grammatical terms. *See* Appendix 1
gran(de), 75
greetings and courtesy (*vocabulary*), 4–5
greetings in the Hispanic world, 5
    formal and informal, 5
Guatemala, 103, 107, 113, 121, 125, 127, 292
    Popol Vuh, 113
gustar, 16
    uses, 250–251
    verbs like, 330, 392
    verbs of emotion like, 396
    with noun clauses as subject, 406
gustaría, 251

H

haber. *See also* Appendix 5
    conditional tense, 544
    conjugation, 462
    future perfect tense, 510
    future tense, 510
    imperfect form, 466
    past (imperfect) subjunctive tense, 538
    past perfect tense, 466
    present perfect subjunctive, 463
    present perfect tense, 462–463
    present subjunctive forms, 372, 463
    present tense (**hay**), 15
hablar. *See also* Appendix 5
    conditional tense, 543
    conjugation in present tense, 45
    future tense, 509
    imperfect tense, 307
    past subjunctive, 536
    present tense, 45
hace + time period + **que**, 427–428
hace + time, 427–428
hacer, (*irregular*), 142. *See also* Appendix 5
    idioms, 144
    present tense, 143–144
    preterite, 257
    with weather expressions, 170

hay que, 403
hay, 15
    conditional form, 544
    imperfect, 307
    indefinite article with, 39
    present perfect, 463
    present subjunctive, 372
    preterite, 280
health and wellness (*vocabulary*), 328
health care and well-being in the Hispanic
    world, 331, 349
Hispanic last names, 68
Hispanic presence in U.S. universities, 56
holidays in the Hispanic world, 273, 275,
    290–291, 292–293
Honduras, 103, 113, 121, 125, 127
    Popol Vuh, 113
horoscope signs, 174
house, parts of (*vocabulary*), 136
household chores (*vocabulary*), 303
houses and cities in the Hispanic world, 138,
    158–159, 161, 381, 393
housing and neighborhoods (*vocabulary*),
    358–359
hypothetical situations, 546

I

idioms
    defined, 119
    with **hacer**, 143
    with **tener**, 69, 119, 171, 207, 308
imperative. *See also* Appendix 5;
    commands definition, 224
imperfect indicative. *See also* Appendix 1;
    Appendix 5
    expressing habitual actions, 545
    forms of, 307–308
    irregular, 308
    preterite versus, 307, 308, 333–335
    regular, 307
    summary of uses, 308
    uses, 308
    words and expressions associated
        with, 336
imperfect subjunctive tense. *See* past
    subjunctive
impersonal expressions. *See also* Appendix 1;
    generalizations (impersonal expressions)
    lists of, 396
    of emotion, 396
    of influence, 376
    se with, 242
    with **ser**, 80, 183
Inca culture, 439
indefinite and negative words, 219–220
indefinite antecedents, 482–484
indefinite articles, 38–39
    definition, 38
indicative. *See also* Appendix 4; Appendix 5;
    imperfect indicative; present indicative
    in two-clause sentences, 376
    indicative mood, 369
    subjunctive versus, 369, 396, 401, 402,
        405, 483–484, 515–516
indigenous peoples, 78, 103, 113, 121, 127, 158,
    222, 306, 393, 403, 429, 491, 514, 518
indirect object pronouns, 244–246
    defined, 244
    placement, 245
    verbs of emotion with, 396
    verbs of influence with, 405
    with direct object pronouns, 287–288
    with **gustar**, 251
indirect objects
    definition, 244. *See also* Appendix 1
    verbs often used with, 246

infinitive. *See also* Appendix 1
  deber followed by, 89
  definition, 16, 44
  direct object pronouns with, 215
  used as noun or pronoun, 480
  with conjugated verb, 45
  with **ir a**, 140
informal commands
  vos commands, 471
  with **tú**, 364–366
information questions, 51
interrogative words, 34
  accent marks, 5, 83, 113
  definition, 33
  expressing *what?*, 34
  in information questions, 51
  + **ir**, 123
  personal **a** use with, 214
  relative pronouns versus, 343
  summary of, 312–313
  uses of, 312–313
inversion, 51
ir (*irregular*), 308. *See also* Appendix 5
  conjugation, 123
  forms and uses, 123
  preterite, 257
ir + **a** + infinitive, 124, 141
-ir verbs. *See also* Appendix 5
  conditional tense, 543–544
  formal command forms, 224
  future tense, 509–510
  imperfect tense, 307
  informal command forms, 365–366
  past subjunctive, 537
  present progressive, 178
  present subjunctive, 371–372
  present tense, 88–89
  preterite, 255
  stem-changing preterite, 284
irregular verbs. *See also* Appendix 5
  conditional, 544
  future tense, 510
  imperfect tense, 308
  participles, 178, 179, 458, 459
  past subjunctive tense, 537
  preterite, 257, 279–280, 283–284
  subjunctive forms, 372
-ísimo/a, 277

J

jamás, 219
jugar, 149

L

la, 38–39
languages, gender and number, 74
large cities in Hispanic countries, 424
last names, Hispanic, 68
le(s), 244–245
le, becomes **se**, 288
Lecturas (*readings*)
  «Algo más que ropa», de Gregori Dolz, 128
  «Amor cibernauta», de Diego Muñoz Valenzuela, 494
  «Azul Cielo», de Laura Busom Fuertes, 470
  «Ciencias naturales», de Washington Cucurto, 442
  Constitución española, Capítulo segundo. Derechos y libertades, 552
  «Cuadrados y ángulos», de Alfonsina Storni, 382
  El español en el resto del mundo, 558
  I *love* viajes, 264
  Infografía: La familia en México, 96
  «La oportunidad de Salomón Bobadilla», de Tito Matamala, 522

  La sicología de los colores en la decoración interior, 162
  Prepara a tu familia para la temporada de lluvias, 198
  «Prescripción», de Daisy Zamora, 350
  «Sale caro ser poeta», de Gloria Fuertes, 412
  Un anuncio de Inglés USA, 57
  Una declaración de propósitos: 12 propósitos para el Año Nuevo, 293
  Una receta: Lasaña de tortillas, 230
  Volver a conectar, 321
leisure time activities (*vocabulary*), 300–301
leisure time in the Hispanic world, 320
likes and dislikes (*vocabulary*), 16
likes and dislikes, expressing, 253, 392
  gustar, 16, 250–251, 253
lo que, 342
lo. *See also* Appendix 2
  + adjective, 332
  as direct object pronoun, 215
lo/la/los/las, 215
Luis Miguel, 422

M

mal(o/a), 75, 192
maps
  Amazon and Andes regions, 399
  Argentina, 199, 449, 453
  Bolivia, 389
  Caribbean region, 306
  Central American countries and capitals, 176
  Chile, 501
  Colombia, 357
  Costa Rica, 169
  Cuba, 271
  Dominican Republic, 237, 262
  Ecuador, 389
  El Salvador, 135
  Guatemala, 103
  Honduras, 103
  linguistic map, 534
  Mexico, 65
  Montevideo, 456
  Nicaragua, 135
  Panama, 205
  Paraguay, 477, 481
  Peru, 419
  Puerto Rico, 299
  South American countries and capitals, 176
  Spain, 529, 534
  Spanish-speaking world, 3, 13
  United States, 29
  Uruguay, 449, 453, 456
  Venezuela, 327
  weather in Southern Cone, 199
Martí, José, 285
más (...) que, 190
Matamala, Tito, 522
Matta, Roberto, 522
mayor, 192, 316
mejor, 192, 316
menor, 192, 316
menos (...) que, 190
-mente, 425
Mexico, 24, 65, 69, 75, 78, 83, 90, 93, 96, 121, 290–291, 381, 393, 411, 469
mi, mis, 85
mientras, 308
mirar vs. **ver**, 144
molestar, 330
money matters (*vocabulary*), 505
months and seasons of the year (*vocabulary*), 173
mood of verbs, 369. *See also* Appendix 1
mucho, 121

Muñoz Valenzuela, Diego, 494
murals and urban art, 53
music
  Argentina, 465
  Chile, 511
  Colombia, 368
  Cuba, 289
  Dominican Republic, 254
  Panama, 210, 368
  Peru, 426, 433
  Puerto Rico, 318
  Spain, 542
  Uruguay, 465
muy, 121

N

nada, 220
nadie, 218, 220
nationalities, 74, 77. *See also* adjectives, of nationality
nations, names of, 81
negation
  commands, 225
  double negative, 220
  indefinite and negative words, 219–220
  verbs and, 46
negative sentences, 46
negative **tú** commands, 365
neuter demonstrative, 75, 115
news (*vocabulary*), 530
Nicaragua, 135, 138, 146, 147, 158, 161
ningún, ninguno/a, 220, 221
no, 46
nominalization. *See* Appendix 2
Notas comunicativas. *See* communication strategies
Notas culturales. *See* culture
noun clauses, 406
nouns. *See also* Appendix 1
  + adjectives. *See also* Appendix 2
  + articles, 38–39
  definition, 14
  gender of, 14, 37–39
  plural, 41
  singular, 38–39
numbers (*vocabulary*), 0 to 30, 14; 31 to 100, 68; 100 on, 110
numbers. *See also* Appendix 1
  in dates, 173
  ordinal, 394
nunca, 219

O

o to **ue**, 148–149
object
  direct object pronouns, 215
  double object pronouns, 287–288
  indirect object pronouns, 244–246
  pronouns objects of prepositions, 288
obligation, expressing, 305
oír. *See also* Appendix 5
  present tense (*irregular*), 142–143
ojalá (que), 398, 542
Olmos, Edward James, 422
ordinal numbers (*vocabulary*), 394
origins, expressing with **ser**, 80
otro/a, 75

P

pagar, 45
Panama, 205, 212, 217, 222, 227, 229, 368
  Panama Canal, 212
para
  + infinitive, 83, 106
  por versus, 435–436
  ser with, 81, 183

Paraguay, 469, 477, 481, 486, 489, 491, 493, 551
¿para qué? /para (que)... and **¿por qué?** /
    porque..., 490
Parra, Violeta, 511
parts of the body (*vocabulary*), 328
past participle. *See also* Appendix 1;
    Appendix 5
    forms of, 459
    used as adjective, 458–459
    with **había** (past perfect), 466
past perfect tense, 466
past progressive (**-ndo**), 309
past subjunctive, 536–539. *See also*
    Appendix 5
    of irregular verbs, 537
    uses, 538–539
    with **ojalá (que)**, 542
pastimes, 320
pedir. *See also* Appendix 5
    present tense, 148–149
    preterite, 284
pensar. *See also* Appendix 5
    present tense, 148
    uses of, 149
peor, 192, 316
perfect tenses, 462–463. *See also*
    Appendix 1; Appendix 4; Appendix 5
performing arts (*vocabulary*), 390–391
person. *See* Appendix 1
personal **a**, 209, 214
    specific persons or animals, 484
    with **alguien** and **nadie**, 484
personal endings, 45
personal pronouns, 43–44, 89
Peru, 24, 174, 241, 393, 408, 419, 424, 426,
    429, 433, 439, 441, 469
    Machu Picchu, 393
pets (*vocabulary*), 66
Philippines, 559
plural
    accent mark use, 112
    of adjectives, 74
    of adverbs, 121
    of nouns, 41
pluscuamperfecto de subjuntivo. *See*
    Appendix 4
pluscuamperfecto. *See* past perfect tense
poco, 121
poder (*irregular*), 118–119. *See also*
    Appendix 5
poner (*irregular*), 142–143. *See also*
    Appendix 5
    verbs derived from, 367
por, 48, 435
    adjectives with, 185
    in fixed expressions, 435
    para versus, 435–436
porque, 83
possession
    unstressed possessive adjectives, 85
    with **ser** and **de**, 80
possessive adjectives. *See also* Appendix 3
    definition, 85
    unstressed, 85
possessive pronouns, 507
    stressed, 507
preferir, 118–119
prepositions, 140–141. *See also* Appendix 1
    defined, 140
    + infinitive, 516
    of location, 175
    verbs requiring, 403
    with time of day, 48
present indicative, 44–46. *See also*
    Appendix 5
    English equivalents, 89, 148
    expressing actions, 142–143

expressing future meaning, 148
    of **-ar** verbs, 44–46
    of **-er** and **-ir** verbs, 88–89
    present progressive and simple present
      compared, 178, 187
    stem-changing verbs, 148–149
present participle, 178, 458. *See also*
    Appendix 1; Appendix 5
    direct object pronouns with, 215
    with verbs other than **estar**, 181
present perfect subjunctive, 463
present perfect tense, 462–463. *See also*
    Appendix 4; Appendix 5
present progressive, 177–178
    reflexive pronouns with, 178, 181
present subjunctive, 369–372. *See also*
    Appendix 5
    after conjunctions of purpose and
      contingency, 487–488
    after nonexisting and indefinite
      antecedents, 482–484
    feelings and emotion, 396
    forms, 371–372
    future or pending actions, 515–516
    indicative compared, 369, 482, 484
    influence, emotion, doubt, and denial, 405
    subjective actions or states, 369–372
    uncertainty, 400–402
    uses, 371, 375–376
    with verbs of influence, 375–376, 405
preterite. *See also* Appendix 1; Appendix 5
    imperfect versus, 307, 308, 333–335
    of irregular verbs, 257, 279–280, 283–284
    of regular verbs, 255–256
    of stem-changing verbs, 256, 283–284
    verbs that change in meaning, 280, 335
    words and expressions associated with, 336
primer(o), 173
professions and careers (*vocabulary*),
    502–503
progressive forms, 177–178
    past progressive, 309
    present progressive, 178
    verbs other than **estar**, 181
pronouns. *See also* Appendix 1
    as objects of prepositions, 175
    definition, 43
    demonstrative, 115. *See also* Appendix 2
    direct object, 215
    double object, 287–288
    indirect object, 244–246
    position in informal commands, 365, 366
    position with negative commands, 225
    possessive, 507
    reflexive, 153–155, 344
    relative, 342–343
    subject, 43–44, 89
    with affirmative commands, 225
pronunciation, 7
    diphthongs, 36, 112
    linking, 36
    rising or falling intonation, 51
    schwa, 7
    stress and written accent marks, 72, 112–113
    vowels, 7
    y, 7
proverbs, 458
Puerto Rico, 299, 304, 305, 306, 311, 318,
    320, 323, 551
punctuation
    comma and period uses, 109
    inverted question mark in tag questions, 106

Q

que, 342–343
    with subjunctive, 370, 375

¿qué?
    ¿cuál? versus, 34, 312
querer (*irregular*), 118–119. *See also* Appendix 5
    past subjunctive to express requests, 538
    preterite changes in meaning, 280
questions. *See also* interrogative words
    information, 51
    inversion in, 51
    rising or falling intonation, 51
    with **hace**, 428
    yes/no, 51–52
¿quién(es)?, 312, 342–343

R

radical changing verbs. *See* stem-
    changing verbs
reciprocal actions, 344–345
reflexive pronouns, 153–155. *See also*
    Appendix 1
    placement, 154–155
    reciprocal actions, 344–345
    with present progressive, 178, 181
reír, 276. *See also* Appendix 5
relative pronouns, 342–343. *See also*
    Appendix 1
    definition, 342
romantic relationships (*vocabulary*), 478–479

S

saber (*irregular*). *See also* Appendix 5
    conocer versus, 210, 280
    preterite changes in meaning, 280
saber, uses of the verb (*vocabulary*), 210
salir. *See also* Appendix 5
    present tense, 142–143
schwa, 7
se, 242
    for accidental or unplanned events, 430–431
    le becomes **se** (pronouns), 288
    reflexive use, 154–155
    verbs frequently used with, 431
seasons of the year (*vocabulary*), 173
seasons of the year, hemispheric
    differences, 195
seguir. *See* Appendix 5
self/selves, 153–155
sentences, simple versus complex, 370
sentir. *See* Appendix 5
sequence
    of verbs, 46
    putting events in, 156
ser, 10, 79–81, 308. *See also* Appendix 5
    + adjectives, 73, 183–184
    + **de**, 183
    estar versus, 183–184
    forms, 79
    possession, 80
    preterite, 257
    summary of uses, 80–81, 183
    to tell time, 308
shopping (*vocabulary*), 104–105
shopping in the Hispanic world, 125,
    127–128, 243, 403
shortened forms
    buen, 75
    gran, 75
    mal, 75
    primer, 394
    tercer, 394
si clauses, 546. *See also* Appendix 4
siempre, 219
simple tense, defined, 255
simple versus complex sentences, 370
Slim Helú, Carlos, 422
soccer. *See* **fútbol**
softened requests, 376, 539. *See also*
    gustaría; past subjunctive

sonreír, 276, 284
Sotomayor, Sonia, 533
South America, 176
Southern Cone, 449
Spain, 24, 46, 95, 197, 263, 275, 302, 349, 381, 393, 411, 469, 521, 529, 534, 542, 551, 554
Spanish
  alphabet, 8
  in the U.S. and the world, 3, 12–13
  in U.S. universities, 54
  spelling changes. See also Appendix 5
    in formal commands, 224
    in informal commands, 365
    in present participle, 178
    in preterite, 256, 279–280, 283–284
    in stem-changing verbs, 118–119, 148–149
    in superlative, 277, 316
    past subjunctive, 537
sports (vocabulary), 300
sports in the Hispanic world, 302
stages of life (vocabulary), 481
stem, 45
stem-changing verbs, 118–119, 148–149.
    See also Appendix 5
  commands, 224
  in preterite, 256
  in preterite (irregular verbs), 283–284
  lists of, 149, 284
  past subjunctive, 537
  present participle of -ir verbs, 178
  present subjunctive, 371
Storni, Alfonsina, 382
stress and written accent marks, 72, 112–113.
    See also pronunciation
stressed possessive pronouns, 507.
    See also Appendix 3
su(s), 85
subject pronouns, 10
  gender, 43–44
  plural, 43–44
  singular, 43–44
  use and omission of, 10, 44, 51–52, 89
subjects
  definition, 43. See also Appendix 1
  in questions and answers, 51
subjunctive, 369. See also Appendix 1; Appendix 5
  after conjunctions of purpose and contingency, 487–488
  after nonexisting and indefinite antecedents, 482–484
  concepts that "trigger," 375, 396, 400–402, 405, 538
  definition, 369
  doubt and denial, 400–402, 405
  expressing emotion, 396, 405
  expressing uncertainty, 400–402, 405
  features of, 375
  forms, 371–372
  future or pending actions, 515–516
  indicative versus, 369, 483–484, 515–516
  influence, 375–376, 405
  past subjunctive, 536–539
  present perfect, 463
  present, 369–372
  uses, 371, 396, 405
superlative, 315–316. See also Appendix 1
  irregular, 316
  -ísimo/a, 277
syllables, 112–113
  stress on, 72

T

tag phrases, 106
también, 219
tampoco, 219
tan (...) como, 190, 191

tanto/a (...) como, 190, 191
technology (vocabulary), 361
technology and Spanish, 363
tener (irregular), 66, 118–119. See also Appendix 5
  expressions with, 69, 119, 171, 207, 308
  uses, 69
  verbs derived from, 367
tener ganas de + infinitive, 119
tener que + infinitive, 119, 305
  uses, 403
tense, 46. See also Appendix 1
  definition, 44
text messages, 363
Textos de todos los días, 35, 70, 109, 152, 172, 223, 249, 278, 314, 340, 360, 408, 439, 457, 486, 508, 535
ti, 175
time conjunctions, 515–516
time expressions, 139
  for parts of the day, 48
time, telling (vocabulary), 18
titles, 5, 34, 40, 49
tocar + indirect object, 305
tourism in the Hispanic world, 241, 263, 264
traer (irregular), See also Appendix 5
  present tense, 142, 144
  preterite, 280
traveling (vocabulary), 238–239
tú, 43–44
  commands, 364–366
  usted versus, 44
  vos versus, 471

U

United States, 30, 50, 53, 54, 56, 229, 263, 411
  abbreviations in Spanish, 50
  Hispanic population in, 12
  technology and the, 362
universities in the Hispanic world, 32
university, at the (vocabulary), 30–31
uno/a, 68
Uruguay, 449, 452, 453, 456, 460, 465, 469, 471
  MERCOSUR and, 551
usted, ustedes, 43–44
  tú versus, 44

V

vacations (vocabulary), 240
Vargas Llosa, Mario, 438
Venezuela, 302, 327, 341, 346, 349, 469
  Lake Maracaibo, 346
venir (irregular), 118–119. See also Appendix 5
  verbs derived from, 367
ver, 308. See also Appendix 5
  present tense, 142, 144
verbs. See also commands; comparison; indicative; subjunctive mood
  conditional tense, 543
  definition, 10. See also Appendix 1
  future tense, 509
  imperfect tense, 307
  nonreflexive use of, 155
  of influence, 376
  past subjunctive, 536
  present tense, 44, 88
  requiring prepositions, 403
  used in sequence, 46
Virgin of Guadalupe, 290–291
vivir. See also Appendix 5
Vocabulario: Preparación. See vocabulary
vocabulary
  academic life, 420
  academic subjects, 32
  accidents, 423

animals, 450
appliances, 303
arts and artists, 390–391
body, parts of, 423
cars and driving, 454
celebrations and holidays, 272–273
clothing, 104–105
colors, 107
common illnesses, 330
conocer, uses of the verb, 210
days of the week, 138
describing yourself, 10
descriptive adjectives, 71
doctor's office, at the, 330
emotions and feelings, 276–277
environment, urban versus natural, 450
family and relatives, 66–67
foods and meals, 206–207
furniture, 136
government and civic duties, 532
greetings and courtesy, 4–5
health and wellness, 328
house, parts of, 136
household chores, 303
housing and neighborhoods, 358–359
leisure time activities, 300–301
likes and dislikes, 16
money matters, 505
months and seasons of the year, 173
news, 530
numbers, 0–30, 14; 31–100, 68; from 100 on, 110
ordinal numbers, 394
parts of the body, 328
performing arts, 390–391
pets, 66
professions and careers, 502–503
romantic relationships, 478–479
saber, uses of the verb, 210
seasons of the year, 173
shopping, 104–105
sports, 300
stages of life, 481
technology, 361
time, telling, 18
traveling, 238–239
university, at the, 30–31
vacations, 240
weather, 170
working world, 504
volver. See also Appendix 5
  present tense, 148, 149
vos, 185, 471
vosotros/as, 43–44
vowels, 7
  pronunciation, 7
  stress and, 72
vuestro/a/os/as, 85

W

weather (vocabulary), 170
willingness, expressing, 511
with other verbs, 178
working world (vocabulary), 504
would, 543–545
written accents. See accent marks

Y

y
  in numbers, 68
  pronunciation of, 7
years, expressing, 172
yes/no questions, 51–52

Z

Zamora, Daisy, 350

MANDATOS° Y FRASES COMUNES EN EL SALÓN DE CLASE

Commands

Los estudiantes

Practice saying these sentences aloud. Then try to give the Spanish as you look at the English equivalents.

Tengo una pregunta.	*I have a question.*
¿Cómo se dice *page* en español?	*How do you say "page" in Spanish?*
Otra vez, por favor. No entiendo.	*(Say that) Again, please. I don't understand.*
¿Cómo?	*What (did you say)?*
Un momento, por favor.	*Just a minute, please.*
(Sí,) Cómo no.	*(Yes,) Of course.*
No sé (la respuesta).	*I don't know (the answer).*

Los profesores

After you read these Spanish sentences, cover the English equivalents and say what each expression means.

¿Hay preguntas?	*Are there any questions?*
¿Qué opina/cree usted?	*What do you think?*
Escuchen.	*Listen.*
Repitan.	*Repeat.*
Lean (en voz alta).	*Read (aloud).*
Escriban/Completen (la siguiente oración).	*Write/Complete (the next sentence).*
Contesten en español.	*Answer in Spanish.*
Preparen (el ejercicio) para mañana.	*Prepare (the exercise) for tomorrow.*
Abran el libro en la página _____.	*Open your book to page _____.*
Cierren el cuaderno.	*Close your notebook.*
Saquen (una hoja).	*Take out (a sheet of paper).*
Levanten la mano si...	*Raise your hand if ...*
Vayan al pizarrón.	*Go to the board.*
Pregúntele a otra persona de la clase...	*Ask another person in the class ...*
Dele _____ a _____.	*Give _____ to _____.*
En parejas...	*In pairs ...*
Busque una persona para trabajar en pareja.	*Look for a partner.*
Hagan la actividad en parejas / tríos / grupos de cuatro.	*Do the activity in pairs / threes / groups of four.*
Formen grupos de cinco estudiantes.	*Get into groups of five students.*

SELECTED VERB FORMS

Regular Verbs | Simple Tenses and Present Perfect (Indicative)

	PRESENT	PRETERITE	IMPERFECT	PRESENT PERFECT
hablar	hablo	hablé	hablaba	he hablado
comer	como	comí	comía	he comido
vivir	vivo	viví	vivía	he vivido

Common Irregular Verbs | Present and Preterite (Indicative)

caer	caigo	caí	**poner**	pongo	puse
dar	doy	di	**querer**	quiero	quise
decir	digo	dije	**saber**	sé	supe
estar	estoy	estuve	**ser**	soy	fui
hacer	hago	hice	**tener**	tengo	tuve
ir	voy	fui	**traer**	traigo	traje
oír	oigo	oí	**venir**	vengo	vine
poder	puedo	pude	**ver**	veo	vi

Irregular Verbs | Imperfect (Indicative)

ir	iba	**ser**	era	**ver**	veía

Regular Verbs | Simple Tenses and Present Perfect (Subjunctive)

	PRESENT	IMPERFECT	PRESENT PERFECT
hablar	hable	hablara	haya hablado
comer	coma	comiera	haya comido
vivir	viva	viviera	haya vivido

Regular and Irregular Verbs | Future and Conditional

hablar	hablaré	hablaría
comer	comeré	comería
vivir	viviré	viviría

decir	diré	diría	**querer**	querré	querría
hacer	haré	haría	**saber**	sabré	sabría
poder	podré	podría	**tener**	tendré	tendría
poner	pondré	pondría	**venir**	vendré	vendría

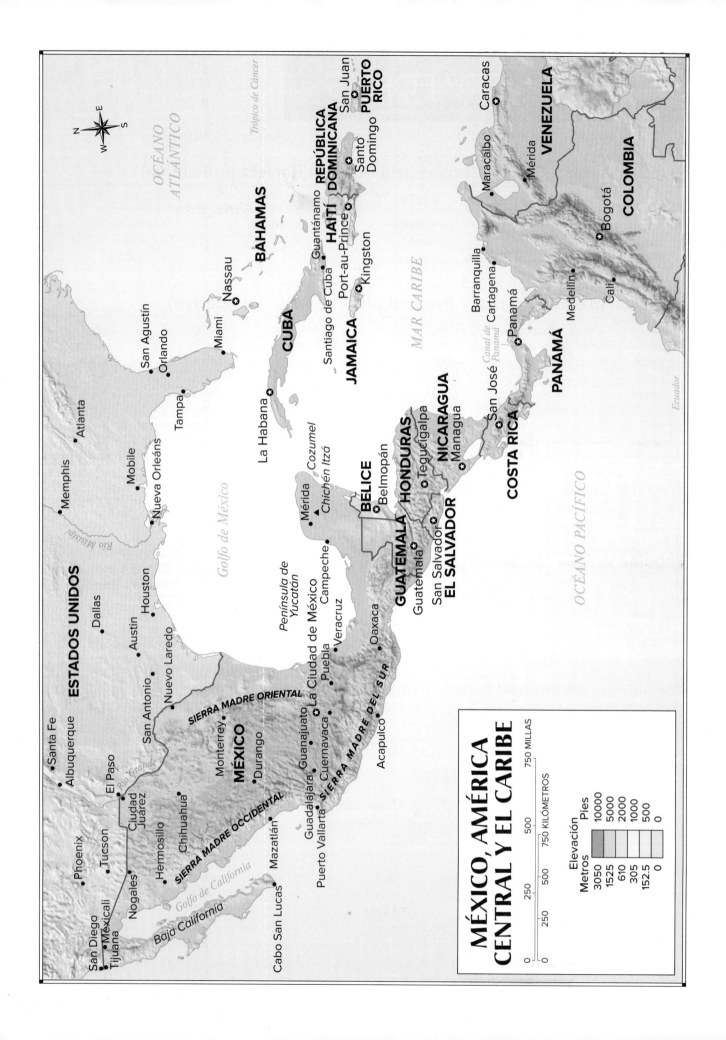

MÉXICO, AMÉRICA CENTRAL Y EL CARIBE

OCÉANO ATLÁNTICO

Trópico de Cáncer

ESTADOS UNIDOS

Santa Fe
Albuquerque
Phoenix
Tucson
San Diego
Tijuana
Mexicali
Nogales
El Paso
Ciudad Juárez
Chihuahua
Hermosillo
Memphis
Atlanta
Mobile
Nueva Orleáns
Dallas
Austin
San Antonio
Nuevo Laredo
Houston
Río Grande
Monterrey
Durango
Mazatlán
Cabo San Lucas
Baja California
Golfo de California

SIERRA MADRE OCCIDENTAL
SIERRA MADRE ORIENTAL
SIERRA MADRE DEL SUR

MÉXICO

Río Misisipi

San Agustín
Orlando
Tampa
Miami
Nassau

BAHAMAS

Golfo de México

Península de Yucatán

Mérida
Cozumel
Chichén Itzá
Campeche
Veracruz
La Ciudad de México
Puebla
Cuernavaca
Guanajuato
Guadalajara
Puerto Vallarta
Acapulco
Oaxaca

CUBA

La Habana
Santiago de Cuba
Guantánamo

BELICE
Belmopán

GUATEMALA
Guatemala

HONDURAS
Tegucigalpa

EL SALVADOR
San Salvador

NICARAGUA
Managua

COSTA RICA
San José

JAMAICA
Kingston

HAITÍ
Port-au-Prince

REPÚBLICA DOMINICANA
Santo Domingo

PUERTO RICO
San Juan

MAR CARIBE

Barranquilla
Cartagena
Panamá
Canal de Panamá

PANAMÁ
Panamá

COLOMBIA
Bogotá
Medellín
Cali

VENEZUELA
Caracas
Maracaibo
Mérida

OCÉANO PACÍFICO

Ecuador

N E S W

Elevación

Metros	Pies
3050	10000
1525	5000
610	2000
305	1000
152.5	500
0	0

0 250 500 750 KILÓMETROS
0 250 500 750 MILLAS

NICARAGUA

COSTA RICA

PANAMÁ

MAR CARIBE

Barranquilla
Maracaibo
Caracas
Rio Orinoco

VENEZUELA

Medellín
Bogotá
Cali

COLOMBIA

Quito
ECUADOR

Guayaquil

OCÉANO ATLÁNTICO

Georgetown
Paramaribo
GUYANA
Cayenne
GUAYANA FRANCESA

SURINAM

Ecuador

Manaus
Río Amazonas
Belém

CORDILLERA DE LOS ANDES

PERÚ

BRASIL

Recife

OCÉANO PACÍFICO

Lima
Machu Picchu
Cuzco

Lago Titicaca

Arequipa

BOLIVIA
La Paz

Sucre

Brasília

OCÉANO PACÍFICO

Isla Pinta
Isla Marchena
Isla San Salvador
Isla Santa Cruz
Isla Isabela
Isla San Cristóbal
Puerto Baquerizo Moreno

ISLAS GALÁPAGOS
(ECUADOR)

0   100 MILLAS
0   100 KILÓMETROS

Antofagasta

PARAGUAY

Asunción

São Paulo
Puerto Iguazú

Río de Janeiro

Trópico de Capricornio

CHILE

Río Paraná

0   8 MILLAS
0   8 KILÓMETROS

Valparaíso

Cabo Cummings
Hanga Roa
Mataveri
Cabo Sur

OCÉANO PACÍFICO

ISLA DE PASCUA
(CHILE)

Córdoba

Rosario

Santiago

ARGENTINA

Concepción

Buenos Aires

URUGUAY
Montevideo

Río de la Plata

OCÉANO ATLÁNTICO

Bahía Blanca

AMÉRICA DEL SUR

0   250   500   750 MILLAS
0   250   500   750 KILÓMETROS

San Carlos de Bariloche

OCÉANO PACÍFICO

Elevación

Metros	Pies
3050	10000
1525	5000
610	2000
305	1000
152.5	500
0	0

Punta Arenas

Estrecho de Magallanes

Islas Malvinas

Tierra del Fuego

Cabo de Hornos

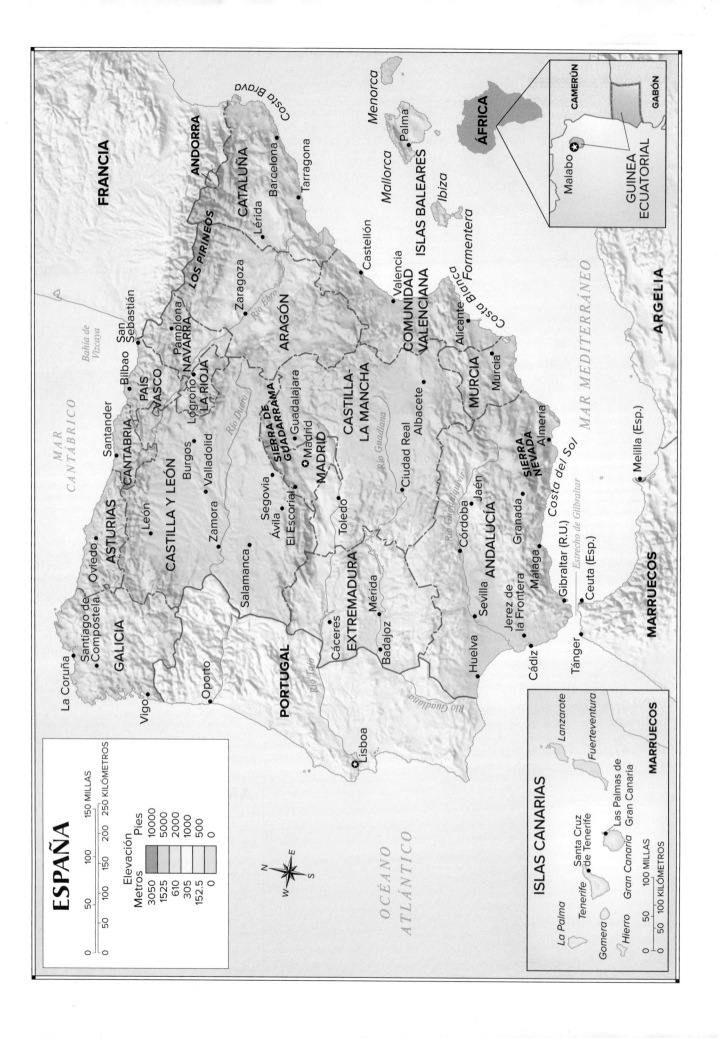

ESPAÑA

Elevación

Metros	Pies
3050	10000
1525	5000
610	2000
305	1000
152.5	500
0	0

150 MILLAS
250 KILÓMETROS

N E S W

OCÉANO ATLÁNTICO

MAR CANTÁBRICO

Bahía de Vizcaya

FRANCIA

ANDORRA

Costa Brava

LOS PIRINEOS

CATALUÑA

Menorca

Mallorca

ISLAS BALEARES

Ibiza

Formentera

MAR MEDITERRÁNEO

Palma

GALICIA

La Coruña

Santiago de Compostela

Vigo

Oporto

PORTUGAL

Lisboa

Río Tajo

ASTURIAS

Oviedo

Santander

CANTABRIA

PAÍS VASCO

Bilbao

San Sebastián

Pamplona

NAVARRA

LA RIOJA

Logroño

ARAGÓN

Zaragoza

Río Ebro

Lérida

Barcelona

Tarragona

Castellón

Valencia

COMUNIDAD VALENCIANA

Costa Blanca

Alicante

MURCIA

Murcia

CASTILLA Y LEÓN

León

Zamora

Valladolid

Burgos

Salamanca

Río Duero

SIERRA DE GUADARRAMA

Segovia

Ávila

El Escorial

MADRID

Madrid

Guadalajara

CASTILLA-LA MANCHA

Toledo

Ciudad Real

Albacete

Río Guadiana

EXTREMADURA

Cáceres

Mérida

Badajoz

Río Guadiana

ANDALUCÍA

Río Guadalquivir

Huelva

Sevilla

Córdoba

Jaén

Granada

SIERRA NEVADA

Almería

Costa del Sol

Málaga

Jerez de la Frontera

Cádiz

Gibraltar (R.U.)

Estrecho de Gibraltar

Ceuta (Esp.)

Tánger

Melilla (Esp.)

MARRUECOS

ARGELIA

ÁFRICA

CAMERÚN

GABÓN

GUINEA ECUATORIAL

Malabo

100 MILLAS

100 KILÓMETROS

ISLAS CANARIAS

La Palma

Tenerife

Gomera

Hierro

Gran Canaria

Santa Cruz de Tenerife

Las Palmas de Gran Canaria

Lanzarote

Fuerteventura

MARRUECOS